Dear West Customer:

West Academic Publishing has changed the look of its American Casebook Series®.

In keeping with our efforts to promote sustainability, we have replaced our former covers with book covers that are more environmentally friendly. Our casebooks will now be covered in a 100% renewable natural fiber. In addition, we have migrated to an ink supplier that favors vegetable-based materials, such as soy.

Using soy inks and natural fibers to print our textbooks reduces VOC emissions. Moreover, our primary paper supplier is certified by the Forest Stewardship Council, which is testament to our commitment to conservation and responsible business management.

The new cover design has migrated from the long-standing brown cover to a contemporary charcoal fabric cover with silver-stamped lettering and black accents. Please know that inside the cover, our books continue to provide the same trusted content that you've come to expect from West.

We've retained the ample margins that you have told us you appreciate in our texts while moving to a new, larger font, improving readability. We hope that you will find these books a pleasing addition to your bookshelf.

Another visible change is that you will no longer see the brand name Thomson West on our print products. With the recent merger of Thomson and Reuters, I am pleased to announce that books published under the West Academic Publishing imprint will once again display the West brand.

It will likely be several years before all of our casebooks are published with the new cover and interior design. We ask for your patience as the new covers are rolled out on new and revised books knowing that behind both the new and old covers, you will find the finest in legal education materials for teaching and learning.

Thank you for your continued patronage of the West brand, which is both rooted in history and forward looking towards future innovations in legal education. We invite you to be a part of our next evolution.

Best regards,

Louis H. Higgins
Editor in Chief, West Academic Publishing

WHITE COLLAR CRIME
LAW AND PRACTICE

Third Edition

■ ■ ■

By
Jerold H. Israel
Alene and Allan F. Smith Professor of Law Emeritus,
University of Michigan Law School
Ed Rood Eminent Scholar Emeritus,
University of Florida, Levin College of Law

Ellen S. Podgor
Professor of Law
Stetson University College of Law

Paul D. Borman
Judge, United States District Court for the
Eastern District of Michigan

Peter J. Henning
Professor of Law
Wayne State University Law School

AMERICAN CASEBOOK SERIES®

WEST®
A Thomson Reuters business

Mat #40658819

COPYRIGHT © 1996 WEST PUBLISHING CO.
© West, a Thomson business, 2003
© 2009 Thomson Reuters
    610 Opperman Drive
    St. Paul, MN 55123
    1–800–313–9378
Printed in the United States of America

ISBN: 978–0–314–18504–4

Dedicated To:

Florence & Harry Israel

Joel R. Podgor

Sarah & Tom Borman

Karen M. Henning

Preface

This course grew out of materials originally prepared for a seminar jointly taught by Paul Borman and Jerry Israel at the University of Michigan Law School. The objective of that seminar was to take a narrow slice of criminal justice practice - the investigation and prosecution of white collar crime in the federal system - and apply to it what is commonly described as a "transactional" analysis. We wanted the students to appreciate how the practice was impacted by the interaction of legal doctrines that traditionally were taught in a wide range of separate law school courses. In the field of white collar crime, they would see how the legal transactions involved in a single case often required consideration of substantive criminal law, criminal procedure, administrative procedure, corporate law, evidence, civil procedure, sentencing law, and even highly specialized regulatory law. We also wanted students to appreciate the influence of administrative policies (in particular, the Department of Justice's internal guidelines) and the influence of the basic "culture" of white collar criminal practice.

Since these materials are designed for a course on White Collar Crime, they are more comprehensive than the Michigan seminar materials, but in large part, the basic objectives remain the same. Accordingly, we utilize a combination of traditional materials (cases and statutes) and not-so-traditional materials (e.g., newspaper articles, forms, and practice manuals). We have sought to keep to a minimum our own shaping of the discussion of these materials. Our "Notes and Questions" contain many more notes than questions, and most of the questions are designed simply to suggest the relevance of additional material.

The conversion of the original Michigan seminar materials into a full fledged set of course materials came about with the addition of Ellen S. Podgor to this project, who added several chapters and filled in gaps in others. In writing the Second Edition we were fortunate to have Peter Henning joining us to add new materials and reshape some of the older material. Now in the Third Edition we again offer a statutory and document supplement that accompanies this casebook.

Notwithstanding the editorial efforts of all of us, we are sure that there are flaws here and there, and hope that the reader will call them to our attention so that they can be corrected in future editions.

Far too many people assisted us in this venture to list them all. The product was enhanced by discussions with many colleagues. We would like to thank, in particular, Nancy King of Vanderbilt Law School, who used an earlier version of those materials and pointed us in the direction of some needed cuts and additions. We also thank Eli Lederman of Tel Aviv University Faculty of Law, who provided a much needed encouragement in initially bringing about this project. We also appreciated the response of faculty, such as Lance Cole, and students who used portions of these materials in courses we taught at the University of Alabama, University of Florida, Georgia State University, the University of Michigan, Kansas University, Stetson University, and Wayne State University.

We also thank Olive Hyman, Diane M. Oeste, Shannon Mullins, Louise Petren, Sue Stinson, and Janice Strawn. We would also like to thank research assistants Jonathan M. Adelman, Rebecca Guinn, Robert J. Kiser, Wendy N. Kurtzer, and Sean McIlhinney and Librarians Rhea Ballard-Thrower and Joe Morris who assisted with the First Edition of this book.

Professors Podgor and Henning and Judge Borman add a special thank you to Professor Jerold H. Israel for his wonderful suggestions throughout this project. He has been a teacher to all in the process of writing and editing a casebook.

J.H.I.
E.S.P.
P.D.B.
P.J.H.

May, 2009

Acknowledgments

Excerpts from the following books and articles appear with the kind permission of the copyright holders.[a]

The American College of Trial Lawyers Report and Proposal on Section 5K1.1 of the United States Sentencing Guidelines, 38 Am. Crim. L. Rev. 1503 (2001). Copyright © 2001 by the Georgetown University Law Center. Reprinted by permission.

Baxter, Andrew T., Federal Discretion in the Prosecution of Local Political Corruption, 10 Pepperdine L. Rev. 321 (1983). Reprinted from Pepperdine Law Review, Volume 10, Number 2, 1983. Copyright © 1983 by the Pepperdine University School of Law. Reprinted by permission.

Beale, Sara Sun, Bryson, William C., Felman, James E., Elston, Michael J., Grand Jury Law and Practice (2d ed.) §§ 5.11; 6.21; 9.21; 9.31 (1997). Copyright © 1997 West Group. Reprinted with permission.

Henry J. Bemporad, An Introduction to Federal Sentencing (11th Ed. 2009). Reprinted with permission.

Bradley, Craig M., Foreward: Mail Fraud After McNally and Carpenter: The Essence of Fraud, 79 J. of Crim. L. & Crim. 573 (1988). Reprinted by special permission of Northwestern University School of Law, Journal of Criminal Law and Criminology, Vol. 79, Issue 3, pp. 573, 586-89, 592, 593, 595, 602-603, (1989).

Brickey, Kathleen F., Criminal Mischief: The Federalization of American Criminal Law, 46 Hastings L. J. 1135, 1172 (1995). Copyright © 1995 by the University of California, Hastings College of Law. Reprinted by permission of University of California, Hastings College of Law and Kathleen F. Brickey.

Bucy, Pamela H., Corporate Ethos: A Standard for Imposing Corporate Criminal Liability, 75 Minn. L. Rev. 1099 (1991). Copyright © 1991 by the University of Minnesota Law School. Reprinted by permission.

---

[a]Case citations in the text, the footnotes of judicial opinions, and in the writings of commentators have been omitted without so specifying. Footnotes in judicial opinions and articles are also omitted without specifying. Numbered footnotes are from the original source; lettered footnotes are written by the authors of this casebook. Asterisks and brackets are used to designate omissions from the original materials.

Coffee, John C., Jr., From Tort to Crime: Some Reflections on the Criminalization of Fiduciary Breaches and the Problematic Line Between Law and Ethics, 19 Amer. Crim. L. Rev. 117 (1981). Copyright © 1981 American Bar Association. Reprinted by permission.

Coffee, John C., Jr., "Corporate Criminal Responsibility," Excerpted with permission of Macmillan Library Reference USA, a Division of Simon & Shuster, from Encyclopedia of Crime and Justice, Sanford H. Kadish, Editor in Chief, Vol. 1, pp. 253-264. Copyright © 1983 by The Free Press.

Coffee, John C., Jr., Hush!: The Criminal Status of Confidential Information After McNally and Carpenter and the Enduring Problem of Overcriminalization, 26 Amer. Crim. L. Rev. 121 (1988). Copyright © 1988 by John C. Coffee, Jr. Reprinted by permission.

Cole, Lance, The Fifth Amendment and Compelled Production of Personal Documents After United States v. Hubbell: New Protection for Private Papers?, 29 Am. J. Crim. L. 123 (2002). Copyright © 2002 by the University of Texas School of Law and Lance Cole. Reprinted by permission.

Cole, Lance, Revoking Our Privileges: Federal Law Enforcement's Multi-Front Assault on The Attorney-Client Privilege (and Why It Is Misguided), 48 Vil. L. Rev. 469 (2003). Copyright © 2003 by Villanova University and Lance Cole. Reprinted by permission.

The Criminal Justice Newsletter, Volume 19, No. 6 at 4-5 (March 15, 1988). Copyright © 1988 by Pace Publications. Reprinted by permission.

Curriden, Mark, Selective Prosecution: Are Black Officials Investigative Targets, 78 A.B.A. J. 54 (Feb. 1992). Copyright © 1992. Printed in the U.S.A. American Bar Association. Reprinted by permission of the ABA Journal.

Daly, Kathleen, Gender and Varieties of White-Collar Crime, 27 Crim. 769 (1989). Copyright © 1989 by the American Society of Criminology. Reprinted by permission of American Society of Criminology and Kathleen Daly.

Deputy Attorney General Testifies on Fight Against White Collar Crime, 38 Crim.L. Rep. 2486 (1986). Reprinted with permission from Criminal Law Reporter, Vol. 38, p. 2485 (March 26, 1986). Copyright © 1986 by The Bureau of National Affairs, Inc. (800-372-1033).

Edelhertz, Herbert, The Nature, Impact, and Prosecution of White-Collar Crime (1970). Project funded by a grant from the National Institute of Justice. Reprinted by permission.

Excerpts: Regulators and Lawyers, 14 Nat. L.J., April 13, 1992, at 10. Copyright © 1992 by The Association of the Bar of the City of New York. Reprinted with permission.

FBI's White Collar Crime Program, Expanding Rapidly, 8 Corp. Crime Rep. 4 (October 17, 1994). Copyright © 1994 by the American Communications and Publishing Company, Inc. Reprinted by permission.

Fee Forfeiture - Federal Preemption, 9 Crim. Prac. Manual 120 (1995). Copyright © 1995. Reprinted with permission of Pike and Fischer.

Friedenthal, Jack; Kane, Mary Kay; Miller, Arthur R., Civil Procedure 387 (2d ed. 1993). Reprinted from Civil Procedure, Jack Friedenthal, Mary Kay Kane, Arthur Miller, 2d ed., Copyright © 1993, with permission of the West Publishing Corporation.

Garrett, Brandon L., Corporate Confessions, 30 CARDOZO L. REV. 917 (2009). Copyright © 2009. Reprinted by permission.

Geis, Gilbert, White-Collar Crime - What is It?, From White-Collar Crime Reconsidered edited by Kip Schlegel and David Weisburd. Copyright © 1992 by Kip Schlegel and David Weisburd. Reprinted with the permission of Northeastern University Press.

Genego, William J., The New Adversary, 54 Brooklyn L.Rev. 781 (1988). Copyright © 1988 by the Brooklyn Law Review. Reprinted by permission.

Gershman, Bennett L., The New Prosecutors, 53 U. Pitt. L. Rev. 393 (1993). Copyright © 1993 University of Pittsburgh Law Review. Reprinted by permission of University of Pittsburgh Law Review and Bennett Gersham.

Goldsmith, Michael, RICO and Enterprise Liability: A Response to Gerald E. Lynch, 88 Col. L. Rev. 774 (1988). This article originally appeared at 88 Columbia Law Review 774 (1988). Reprinted by permission of the Columbia Law Review and Michael Goldsmith.

Gorelick, Jamie, Litman, Harry, Keynote Address, Prosecutorial Discretion and the Federalization Debate, 46 Hastings L. J. 978 (1995). Copyright © 1995 by the University of California, Hastings College of Law. Reprinted by permission.

Green, Stuart P., Lying, Misleading, and Falsely Denying: How Moral Concepts Inform the Law of Perjury, Fraud, and False Statements, 53 Hastings L.J. 157 (2001). Copyright © 2001 by University of California, Hastings College of the Law and Stuart Green. Reprinted from HASTINGS LAW JOURNAL, Volume 53, Number 1, November 2001, 157-212, by permission.

Gruner, Richard, Towards an Organizational Jurisprudence: Transforming Corporate Criminal Law Through Federal Sentencing Reform, 36 Arizona L. Rev. 407 (1994). Copyright © 1994 by the Arizona Board of Regents. Reprinted by permission.

Maus, Donna M., Comment, License Procurement and the Federal Mail Fraud Statute, 58 U. Chi. L. Rev. 1125 (1991). Copyright © 1991 by the University of Chicago Law Review. Reprinted by permission.

Model Penal Code, Section 2.07. Copyright by the American Law Institute. Reprinted with the permission of The American Law Institute.

Model Rules of Professional Conduct, Rules 1.13, 3.8, and 4.2. Copyright © 2002 American Bar Association. All rights reserved. Reprinted by permission of the American Bar Association.

Mokhiber, Russell, Voices: Viewpoint; Don't Hinder Pollution Police, The New York Times, October 15, 1995, § 3, at 11, col. 4. Copyright © 1995 by The New York Times Company. Reprinted by permission.

Mosteller, Robert P., Simplifying Subpoena Law: Taking the Fifth Amendment Seriously, 73 Va. L. Rev. 1 (1987). Copyright © 1987 by the Virginia Law Review Association and Robert P. Mosteller. Reprinted by permission.

Mulroy, Thomas R. & Munoz, Eric J., The Internal Corporate Investigation, 1 DePaul Bus. & Com. L.J. 49 (2002). Copyright © 2002 by DePaul Business & Commercial Law Journal, Thomas R. Mulroy, and Eric J. Munoz. Reprinted by permission.

Palm, Craig W., RICO Forfeiture and the Eighth Amendment: When Is Everything Too Much? 53, U. Pitt. L. Rev. 1, 37 (1991). Copyright © 1991 by the University of Pittsburgh School of Law. Reprinted by permission of University of Pittsburgh Law Review and Craig Palm.

Raab, Selwyn, New York Investigators Searched Tons of Records, The New York Times, March 6, 1986, at Y16. Copyright © 1986 by The New York Times Company. Reprinted by permission.

Richman, Daniel C., Cooperating Clients, 56 Ohio St. L.J. 69 (1995). Copyright © 1995 by The Ohio State University. Reprinted by permission.

Shabecoff, Philip, Federal Statutes Cited in Indictment of Exxon, The New York Times, Mar. 1, 1990, A14. Copyright © 1990 by The New York Times Company. Reprinted by permission.

Shapiro, Susan, Thinking About White-Collar Crime: Matters of Conceptualization and Research (1980). Copyright © 1980 by Susan Shapiro. Reprinted by permission.

Simons, Michael A., Vicarious Snitching: Crime, Cooperation, and "Good Corporate Citizenship," 76 St. John's L. Rev. 979 (2002). Copyright © 2002 by the St. John's Law Review Association and Michael A. Simons. Reprinted by permission.

Spaulding, Karla R., "Hit Them Where It Hurts": RICO Criminal Forfeitures and White-Collar Crime, 80 J. of Crim. L. and Criminology 197 (1989). Copyright © (1989) by Karla R. Spaulding. Reprinted by permission.

Sutherland, Edwin H., White Collar Crime: The Uncut Version (1983). Copyright © 1983 by the Yale University Press. Reprinted by permission.

Tarlow, Barry, RICO: The New Darling of the Prosecutor's Nursery, 49 Fordham L. Rev. 165 (1980). Copyright © 1980 by the Fordham University Law Review. Reprinted by permission.

Underwood, Richard H., Perjury! The Charges and the Defenses, 36 Duq. L. Rev. 715 (1998). Copyright © 1998 by Duquesne University and Richard H. Underwood. Reprinted by permission.

Wheeler, Stanton; Weisbund, David; Warning, Elin, White-Collar Crime and Criminals, 25 Amer. Crim. L. Rev. 351 (1988). Reprinted with the permission of the publisher, © (1988) and Georgetown University.

Whether Salomon Could Survive Criminal Charges Not a Factor in Settlement Discussions, SEC Enforcement Chief Says, Corporate Crime Reporter, Volume 6, May 25, 1992 page 1, cont. on page 3. Copyright © 1992 by the American Communications and Publishing Company, Inc. Reprinted by permission.

Whitley, Joe D., White-Collar Crime: A Real Priority, Legal Times page 19, cont. page 22, September 27, 1993. Reprinted with permission of the Legal Times. Copyright © 1993.

Whitley, Joe D., Garber, Marc N., McCarty, Mark A., and Henry, Steven D., The Case for Reevaluating DOJ Policies on Prosecuting White Collar Crime, Washington Legal Foundation, Working Paper Series No. 108, May 2002. Copyright © 2002 by Washington Legal Foundation, Joe D. Whitley, Marc N. Garber,Mark A. McCarty, and Steven D. Henry. Reprinted by permission.

Winter, Ralph K., Paying Lawyers, Empowering Prosecutors, and Protecting Managers: Raising the Cost of Capital in America, 42 Duke L. J. 945 (1993). Copyright © 1993 by the Duke University School of Law. Reprinted by permission.

Wizard of ID, Cartoon, August 13, 1979. Copyright © 1979. Reprinted by permission of Johnny Hart and Creators Syndicate, Inc.

Zabel, Richard B. & Benjamin, James J., "Queen for a Day" or "Courtesan for a Day": The Sixth Amendment Limits to Proffer Agreements, 15 White-Collar Crime Rep. 1 (Oct. 2001). Copyright © 2001 by the Andrews Publications, Richard B. Zabel, and James J. Benjamin. Reprinted by permission.

Summary of Contents

Table of Contents

PART TWO
WHITE COLLAR OFFENSES

PART THREE
PROCEDURAL ISSUES

PART FOUR
PUNISHMENT

Table of Cases

Principal cases are in bold type. Cases cited or discussed in the text are in roman type. References are to the pages where the case appears in the text. References to principal cases are not repeated within the principal case.

Table of Statutes, Standards, and Court Rules

References are to the pages where statutes, standards, or court rules appear in the text. References, however, within principal cases are cited to the first time that they appear within the principal case and are not repeated throughout the principal case.

SECURITIES EXCHANGE ACT

SECURITIES EXCHANGE COMMISSION RULES

UNITED STATES ATTORNEYS MANUAL (U.S.A.M.)

UNITED STATES CODE ANNOTATED (U.S.C.A.)

WEST VIRGINIA CODE

WHITE COLLAR CRIME

LAW AND PRACTICE

Third Edition

*

CHAPTER ONE
INTRODUCTION

---

* * * An examination of the various definitions of "white-collar crime" and their actual usage in the literature yields fundamental inconsistencies and incompatibilities. It is unclear whether the term characterizes acts or actors, types of offenses or types of offenders; or whether it refers to the social location of deviant behavior, the social role or social status of the actor, the *modus operandi* of the behavior, or the social relationship of victim and offender. There are frequent disputes over whether the phenomenon is necessarily "white collar," and even more serious disagreement over whether the behavior is criminal. * * *

These fundamental confusions result from the fact that "white collar crime" has always been a catch-all category for social theorists, policy analysts, and law enforcement officials. It has referred to that group of offenders (wealthy, respectable persons, corporations, etc.) for whom traditional explanations of criminal behavior are not appropriate or to that group of offenses to which the criminal justice system responds differently—if at all. The category—white collar crime— generally has been used to demonstrate the incompleteness of our knowledge, the inadequacy of our theory, or the injustice of our social control responses. * * *

Susan Shapiro, THINKING ABOUT WHITE-COLLAR CRIME: MATTERS OF CONCEPTUALIZATION AND RESEARCH 1 (1980).

Edwin Sutherland, a sociologist, coined the term "white collar crime" in a speech given to the American Sociological Society in 1939. In the years following this lecture, the nonlegal origins of this term evolved with varying sociological perspectives. The adaptation of this term by the legal community has resulted in ambiguity as to what is encompassed within the term "white collar crime" and what impact the term should play in grading offenses, lawyer specialization, and prosecutorial priorities.

In examining the various definitions of "white collar crime," consider the following two questions: (1) Is there a useful categorization of something called "white collar crime" (a category that could be employed, for example,

1

in establishing a special investigative or prosecutorial unit, in a defense counsel's designation of his or her special area of expertise, or in assessing appropriate levels of punishment for different groupings of crime), and (2) if so, what characteristics would be useful in establishing a white collar category for the particular purpose?

A. DEFINITIONS OF CRIMINOLOGISTS AND SOCIOLOGISTS

1. Social Status, Occupation, and Organization

In his speech to the American Sociological Society, Edwin Sutherland concentrated on "crime in relation to business." He criticized those who claimed that crime was "concentrated in the lower classes." The thesis of his speech was that the explanation of crime as being "closely correlated with poverty or with the psychopathic and sociopathic conditions associated with poverty" was "misleading and incorrect." He claimed that "conventional explanations [were] invalid principally because they [were] derived from biased samples." He focused in his talk on a "neglected" area of crime, that being "the criminal behavior of business and professional men." *Reprinted in* Edwin H. Sutherland, *White-Collar Criminality*, 5 AM. SOC. REV. 1 (1940).

In his later book, Sutherland defined "white-collar crime" in terms of social status and occupation. He stated:

> * * * This concept is not intended to be definitive, but merely to call attention to crimes which are not ordinarily included within the scope of criminology. White collar crime may be defined approximately as a crime committed by a person of respectability and high social status in the course of his occupation. * * * (emphasis added).

Edwin H. Sutherland, WHITE COLLAR CRIME: THE UNCUT VERSION 7 (1983). For a summary of white-collar crime theory as it developed from Sutherland's work, see James William Coleman, *The Theory of White-Collar Crime: From Sutherland to the 1990s*, WHITE-COLLAR CRIME RECONSIDERED 53 (KIP SCHLEGEL & DAVID WEISBURD, EDS.) (1992); see also David T. Johnson & Richard A. Leo, *The Yale White-Collar Crime Project: A Review and Critique*, LAW AND SOCIAL INQUIRY 63 (1993) (review of varying definitions of white collar crime).

NOTES AND QUESTIONS

1. *Social Status.* Does a definition of "white collar crime" premised upon the class or social status of the individual provide a biased methodology for examining criminal behavior? Consider the following questions raised by Susan Shapiro, supra at 3:

* * * Does one want to definitionally discriminate, for example, between medicaid fraud by doctors and that engaged in by patients; between the business executive who does not disclose perks in his tax return and the waitress who fails to disclose tips on her return? Does one take a single illegal activity reflecting the conspiracy of assorted individuals and label the activities of the wealthier participants white collar crime and those of the less wealthy traditional crime? * * *

2. *Occupation*. What limitations result from Sutherland's prerequisite that the crime occur in the *course of one's occupation*? Does this requirement focus on the use of occupation as an aspect of the offense or on the position of the particular actor? "Is the motorist who pays a bribe to a traffic policeman or meter maid a traditional criminal and the bribe recipient a white collar criminal?" Susan Shapiro, supra at 6. Does it draw an artificial distinction even as to the character of the offense? Consider the following comments by Susan Shapiro, supra at 17:

> Similarly, the behavior of individuals may not differ in kind when they move from non-business to business contexts. * * * Individuals both in and out of business often assert their eligibility for particular benefits, and do so by misrepresenting their status. The employee pads his or her expense account or falsifies the number of hours worked; the individual lies on his or her tax return, application for welfare, food stamps, or insurance compensation. * * *

3. *Organization*. Although Sutherland spoke in terms of social status and occupation, "his book was devoted * * * to the crimes of organizations, not of persons: seventy large corporations and fifteen public utilities. * * * Those following Sutherland sometimes focused on persons of high status, sometimes on occupation, and sometimes on corporate bodies." Stanton Wheeler, *White-Collar Crime: History of an Idea*, 4 ENCYCLOPEDIA OF CRIME AND JUSTICE 1652, 1653 (1983). Does concentrating on the organization provide a more comprehensive definition of white collar crime? Consider the following excerpt from Susan Shapiro, supra at 11, on adding an organizational component to the definition of white collar crime:

> It includes business and non-business settings. Violations that pertain to government, non-profit organizations, associations, educational institutions, religious groups, and the like, would be included in this definition. Futhermore, the stipulation does not require that the violation be made by an organization or occur in an organizational role—only that organizations be involved in the violative activity. Thus, the case of the insurance company that defrauds consumers by promising non-existent benefits reflects white collar illegality. So too does the case of the policy holder who defrauds the insurance company by submitting false claims for benefit. * * *

Perhaps the only events commonly thought of as white collar crimes that would be excluded by this standard are abuses that occur in face-to-face interactions between individuals—very simply con games, "consumer" type frauds in the sale of personal property or illicit goods or services. * * *

What problems arise in employing a definition that focuses on the organization? Consider the following excerpt from Susan Shapiro, supra at 16-17:

> In order to determine whether illicit behavior is organizational, then, one must possess considerable information about organizational norms, organizational socialization, and the extent of knowledge about the behavior across the organizational leadership hierarchy. * * * But this is the very problem. The boundaries of organizational norms are incredibly unclear. * * *

> More troubling is the fact that the categories sometimes differentiate identical behavior. For example, both individuals and organizations engage in tax violations or in misrepresentations in the application for credit and insurance or the qualification for benefits and services, and presumably for the same reasons.

2. Behavior Characteristics

Eventually, there was a shift from concentrating on the offender to focusing on the offense in defining white collar crime. A chief proponent of this approach was Herbert Edelhertz, former chief of the Fraud Section-Criminal Division of the Department of Justice, who defined "white-collar crime" as "an illegal act or series of illegal acts committed by nonphysical means and by concealment or guile, to obtain money or property, to avoid the payment or loss of money or property, or to obtain business or personal advantage." See Herbert Edelhertz, THE NATURE, IMPACT AND PROSECUTION OF WHITE-COLLAR CRIME 3, 12 (1970). He noted:

> In any white-collar crime, we will find the following elements:
>
> (a) Intent to commit a wrongful act or to achieve a purpose inconsistent with law or public policy.
>
> (b) Disguise of purpose or intent.
>
> (c) Reliance by perpetrator on ignorance or carelessness of victim.
>
> (d) Acquiescence by victim in what he believes to be the true nature and content of the transaction.
>
> (e) Concealment of crime by—
>
>   (1) Preventing the victim from realizing that he has been victimized, or

(2) Relying on the fact that only a small percentage of victims will react to what has happened, and making provisions for restitution to or other handling of the disgruntled victim, or

(3) Creation of a deceptive paper, organizational, or transactional facade to disguise the true nature of what has occurred.

As with other definitions of white-collar crime, the approach taken by Edelhertz also met with criticism. Consider the following excerpt from Gilbert Geis, *White-Collar Crime—What Is It?*, WHITE-COLLAR CRIME RECONSIDERED 31, 39 (Kip Schlegel & David Weisburd, eds.) (1992):

> Criticism of the Edelhertz position predictably came from sociologists who regretted his slighting of the idea of abuse of power as the key aspect of white-collar offenses and his expansive extension of the term to such a variegated range of behaviors. They were puzzled by the excision of violence from the realm of white-collar crime, noting that crimes such as unnecessary surgical operations, the manufacture of unsafe automobiles, and the failure to label poisonous substances at the workplace could be regarded as white-collar crimes with a strong component of violence. * * * Later, the American Bar Association would adopt the term "economic offense" for behaviors within the white-collar crime realm set forth by Edelhertz, and would modify the term "nonviolent" with the footnoted observation that this referred to "the means by which crime is committed" even though "the harm to society can frequently be described as violent."

Professor Stuart P. Green in his book LYING, CHEATING, AND STEALING (2006) notes the disagreement in how to define the term "white-collar crime." He concludes that "in the absence of any viable alternative, and in light of its powerful cultural resonances—the term 'white-collar crime' is worth preserving, provided that certain features are understood, and various caveats observed." He states that "[w]e would do better to think of the term 'white-collar crime' as referring to a set of offenses connected by a series of what philosophers call 'family resemblances,' rather than as susceptible to definition through a precise set of necessary and sufficient conditions." Id. at 18.

B. LAW ENFORCEMENT DEFINITIONS

Department of Justice, Attorney General's Report (1983)

White collar crimes are illegal acts that use deceit and concealment—rather than the application or threat of physical force or violence—to obtain money, property, or service; to avoid the payment or loss of money; or to secure a business or personal advantage. White-collar criminals occupy positions of responsibility and trust in government, industry, the professions, and civic organizations.

Bureau of Justice Statistics, U.S. Department of Justice, Dictionary of Criminal Justice Data Terminology 215 (2d Ed. 1981)

White-collar crime: Definition. Nonviolent crime for financial gain committed by means of deception by persons whose occupational status is entrepreneurial, professional or semi-professional and utilizing their special occupational skills and opportunities; also, nonviolent crime for financial gain utilizing deception and committed by anyone having special technical and professional knowledge of business and government, irrespective of the person's occupation.

Annotation.   * * * The term reflects a traditional classification of occupations into white-collar: those utilizing technical knowledge and skills in the manipulation of numbers and concepts, and blue-collar: those utilizing skill in the manipulation of objects. It originally referred to nonviolent crime committed by persons in the upper socio-economic class in their occupational roles, and defined a social class of interest to social scientists. In current criminal justice usage of the term, the focus of the meaning has shifted to the nature of the crime instead of the persons or occupations. The categorization of "white-collar" crime as crime having a particular modus operandi (committed in a manner that utilizes deception and special knowledge of business practices and committed in a particular kind of economic environment) is of use in coordinating the resources of the appropriate agencies for purposes of investigation and prosecution.

Federal Bureau of Investigation (Cynthia Barnett, The Measurement of White Collar Crime Using Uniform Crime Reporting (UCR) Data) (2002)

* * * The Federal Bureau of Investigation has opted to approach white collar crime in terms of the offense. The Bureau has defined white-collar crime as "... those illegal acts which are characterized by deceit, concealment, or violation of trust and which are not dependent upon the application or threat of physical force or violence. Individuals and organizations commit these acts to obtain money, property, or services; to avoid the payment or loss of money or services; or to secure personal or business advantage." Some experts have criticized defining white-collar in terms or type of offense because this definition emphasizes the nature of the acts rather than the background of the offender. Within the FBI definition, there is no mention of the type of occupation or the socioeconomic position of the "white-collar" offender. * * *

NOTES AND QUESTIONS

1. *Prosecutorial Selection/Enforcement Priorities.* How does the definition adopted by the Department of Justice (DOJ) impact on the prosecutorial selection of cases? Does the definition given to white collar crime impact the enforcement priorities, resources provided to these priorities, and statistical reporting of cases in this area? See *FBI'S White Collar Crime Program Expanding Rapidly*, 8 CORP. CRIME REP. 4 (Oct. 17, 1994) ("The [FBI] spokesperson could not answer why there is not a public FBI generated database for corporate and white-collar crime that mirrors the FBI's annual Crime in the United States report on street crime.").

2. *Gender Considerations.* Does a definition that focuses on the offense, as opposed to the offender, fail to account for gender distinctions in white-collar crime? Consider the following excerpt from Kathleen Daly, *Gender and Varieties of White-Collar Crime*, 27 CRIM. 769, 770-771, 789-791 (1989):

> The disagreement in defining white-collar crime revolves around whether characteristics of the offense or the offender should be primary. An offense-related approach focuses on how a crime is committed, while an offender-related approach focuses on a particular group of people—those in high-status or "respected" occupations or in positions of power. If one takes an offender-related approach, a Medicaid fraud is considered a white-collar crime if it is carried out by a doctor or nursing home owner, but not if it is carried out by a clerical worker or poor person. If one uses an offense-related approach, that distinction is not important.

> The different definitions affect how scholars conceptualize gender and white-collar crime. * * * The offense-based approach suggests a rising tide of "new" female white-collar criminals; the offender-based approach suggests that white-collar crime is a male-only domain. * * *

> In this group of white-collar offenders, some men are "big fish," but most are "little fish" and do not comport with images of highly placed or powerful white-collar criminals. Men's white-collar crimes were both petty and major, but almost all the women's were petty. Although half or more of the employed men were managerial or professional workers, most employed women were clerical workers. * * *

> Finally, in building theories of white-collar crime, scholars should be cognizant of the points of gender difference found in this study. * * * Men's white-collar crime, though more frequent than women's and exacting more social injury or harm, should not be used as the "norm" from which women's white-collar crime is thought to deviate.

Women's illegalities should be explored on their own terms. The multiple influences of gender, class, and race relations, both within and outside work organizations and occupations, should also be investigated. These relations not only generate many varieties of white-collar crime, they also undoubtedly play a role in who is caught and prosecuted for white-collar crime.

Compare Ellen S. Podgor, *Corporate and White Collar Crime: Simplifying The Ambiguous*, 31 AM. CRIM. L. REV. 391, 393-394 (1994) (rejects a definition that encompasses gender, class, or race of a person and suggests "[a]n approach that looks to the activity involved and classifies that activity based upon its attributes as opposed to the socio-economic status of the individuals who engage in the acts.[20]"). According to the National Incident-Based Reporting System (NIBRS) data for 1997 through 1999:

> * * * white collar offenders are, on average, in their late-twenties to early-thirties, which is only slightly older than most other offenders captured in NIBRS. The majority of white-collar crime offenders are white-males, except for those who committed embezzlement. However, in comparison to offenders committing property crimes, there is a higher proportion of females committing these white-collar offenses.

Cynthia Barnett, *The Measurement of White-Collar Crime Using Uniform Crime Reporting (UCR) Data*, NIBRS Publications Series 5 (2002).

3. *Quantifying White Collar Crime.* In an attempt to quantify the amount of white collar crime, the FBI issued a report using offense categories as the basis for determining the level of white collar crime using Uniform Crime Reporting Data. The report designated the following offenses as white collar crimes: "fraud, bribery, counterfeiting/forgery, embezzlement (all of which are Group A offenses), and bad checks (a Group B offense)." The report found:

> In 1997 through 1999, white-collar crime accounted for approximately 3.8 percent of the incidents reported to the FBI. The majority of those offenses are frauds and counterfeiting/forgery. Additionally, the Group B offense of *bad checks* accounted for approximately 4 percent of the arrests during 1997-1999.

Cynthia Barnett, *The Measurement of White-Collar Crime Using Uniform Crime Reporting (UCR) Data*, NIBRS Publications Series 2 (2002). Recent data can be found on TRAC Reports, Inc., with tracking in a variety of

---

[20] These factors, however, may warrant consideration in sentencing an individual. See generally Myrna Raeder, Gender and Sentencing: Single Moms, Battered Women, and Other Sex-Based Anomalies in the Gender-Free World of the Federal Sentencing Guidelines, 20 PEPP. L. REV. 905 (1993).See also Laura Mansnerus, *Sometimes, the Punishment Fits the Gender*, N.Y.Times, Nov. 16, 1997, at Sec. 4, p. 1.

categories of white collar crime. For example, reports are now issued on criminal mortgage fraud cases. See http://trac.syr.edu/tracreports/crim/200/.

4. *Specific White Collar Offenses.* Even though a specific crime may be thought of as white collar crime, the conduct may fall into the category of both white collar and street crime depending upon the specific conduct involved in crime. For example, one can use a computer to commit both a white collar or non-white collar offense. According to a recent FBI Report, supra Note 3, "[o]f the offense committed using computer equipment, 42 percent are white-collar offenses. The largest proportion of those offense are larceny-thefts." Id. at 4.

C. THE WHITE COLLAR CRIMINAL LAWYER

By Permission of Johnny L. Hart FLP and Creators Syndicate, Inc.

NOTES

1. *White Collar Crime/Street Crime.* Professor Kenneth Mann, in Defending White Collar Crime (1985), describes several characteristics of white collar defense practice that distinguish it from criminal defense in "street crime" cases. He notes that defense attorneys handling street crime typically come onto the scene after the police have investigated the offense and arrested counsel's client. Accordingly, the defense attorney "usually assumes when he takes the case that the government has sufficient evidence to convict his client," and focuses his energy on achieving a satisfactory plea-bargain. The white collar crime defense attorney, in contrast, enters the picture substantially before the government has completed its investigation and sometimes before the investigation has even started. The "white-collar defense attorney does not assume that the government has the evidence to convict his client" but assumes instead that, even if "his client is guilty, he may be able to keep the government from knowing this or from concluding that it has a strong enough case to prove it." Counsel's first line of defense accordingly is "information control," which "entails keeping documents away from and preventing clients and witnesses from talking to government investigators, prosecutors, and judges."

Information control, Professor Mann notes, is practiced in two different ways. First, counsel "oppose their [government] adversaries in quasi-judicial and court settings," challenging subpoenas and seeking to suppress evidence already obtained by the government. Second, counsel uses a strategy that "focuses on the potential sources of inculpatory information," and seeks to ensure that such sources will not make that information available to the government apart from its use of the legal process. Success here depends on a variety of factors, including: (1) the influence that the client has over the information sources; (2) how broadly damaging evidence and information is dispersed among third-party sources (the greater the number of sources, the more likely that the government will locate and gain the cooperation of at least one); and (3) whether the crime is one that, in effect, manufactures and exposes its own sources of incriminating evidence, or is one that is reflected only in evidence that remains hidden in particular artifacts and persons not readily distinguishable from all others that relate to the client.[a]

White collar defense attorneys also are said to have a "distinctive role," separating them from the attorney handling street crime, in their presentation of "substantive defenses" (i.e., a defense claiming that the client has not violated the law). "Rather than waiting until trial or until the immediate pretrial period when plea negotiations usually take place, these defense attorneys [have] an opportunity to make a substantive defense before a charge is made," as white collar cases "typically [present a] series of institutionalized settings for conducting precharge adversarial proceedings on questions of substantive criminal responsibility." Defense counsel in white collar cases also have a further advantage in this regard because of the character of the substantive offense. White collar offenses are more likely to have ambiguity in their definition (although that is hardly true of all white collar offenses), and "ambiguity of definition leads to increased substantive legal arguments about the scope of prohibited behavior."

Client resources also tend to shape the practice of the defense attorney handling a white collar case. "In contrast to the attorney handling street

---

[a] "Certain crimes create sources of information—witnesses and artifacts—which are exposed as potential evidence of sources of evidence. One example is the victim of crime who knows that he has been victimized * * *. Other crimes do not expose information as evidence to the same extent. * * * [The] crimes do not alert the victim * * *. The artifacts used for the commission of [the] crimes are not readily identifiable as evidence, for instance, individual documents in a complex filing system. And witnesses * * *are not readily exposed because the location of the occurrence of the crime is not apparent, as in a bankruptcy of a multistate company. * * * When inculpatory information is embedded in normal social life, that is, when it is not easily identifiable as potential evidence, there is a higher probability that the government will not identify it. Thus even where the client has no influence over the source and the information is concentrated in one third-party source (not dispersed)—conditions that work against the success of an information control defense—the defense attorney may conclude that he can rely on the government not discovering the information because it is embedded." Mann, supra at 233-34.

crime, his time is not a scarce resource, and each case is individually cultivated with great care. * * * The defense attorney employs his own investigators, who are experts in accounting and finance, as well as a staff of legal researchers." Of equal significance, client resources are often accompanied by client sophistication that leads the client to call upon the lawyer at an early stage, which will enable the lawyer to employ strategies that would not be available if the government was farther along in its investigation.

2. *Prosecutorial Practices.* Margaret Cronin Fisk, *White Collar Boom*, 14 Nat. L.J., No. 13, Dec, 2, 1991, reports that prosecutors are seeking to offset what they see as potential adversarial advantages of the white collar defense bar. In particular, they are coming to treat suspected white collar offenders in much the same manner as persons suspected of committing other crimes. For example, they are making more frequent use of arrest and search authority rather than utilizing alternatives (summons and subpoena) that are less disruptive to the individual. The end result, it is noted, is "more pressure on the lawyers who defend accused white-collar offenders." Consider also William J. Genego, *The New Adversary*, 54 BROOK. L. REV. 781, 782-84 (1988):

> In recent years federal prosecutors have adopted practices which respond to the special investigative and prosecutorial needs associated with drug and white collar offenses. Many of these practices directly affect criminal defense attorneys and, in turn, the representation received by criminal defendants. Examples of third party enforcement practices utilized by the government include grand jury and trial subpoenas directed to defense counsel, summonses from the Internal Revenue Service (IRS), forfeiture of attorneys' fees, law office searches, tapping of attorneys' telephones, use of undisclosed informants at defense meetings, and efforts to disqualify attorneys. Criminal defense lawyers have been the subject of criminal investigations and prosecutions in which it is alleged that they participated in or supported criminal activity in their professional capacities. While many of the practices were previously available to prosecutors, they were used infrequently. Recently, however, prosecutors have begun to increase the use of such practices. In addition, the government has sought and obtained legislation and judicial decisions which enable prosecutors to affect the manner in which defense attorneys investigate and prepare cases and which, in turn, affect defense attorneys' willingness to represent certain defendants. The legislative changes mandate special fee reporting requirements, and in some cases limit attorneys' ability to obtain fees for their services.

> A heated debate has emerged in the legal community over claims that federal prosecutors regularly engage in aggressive practices hostile to criminal defense attorneys with the purpose of restricting defendants' right to counsel. Criminal defense attorneys charge that federal prosecutors employ these third party enforcement practices not to fulfill legitimate prosecutorial needs, but to discourage zealous representation by defense attorneys and to prevent particular

attorneys from representing specific clients. For example, defense attorneys claim that prosecutors direct grand jury subpoenas and IRS summonses to attorneys to seek information about past or present clients, even though the information is available from other sources. Such practices place the attorney in the position of providing information which can be used against the client, thus creating a potential conflict and possibly preventing the attorney from further representation of the client. The defense bar maintains that these practices are part of a general prosecutorial program which targets vigorous and successful attorneys for government harassment. Defense attorneys also charge that prosecutors are using these practices in a calculated effort to affect the representation received by criminal defendants.

Government attorneys respond that the challenged practices are used only for legitimate investigatory and prosecutorial reasons; that the peculiar needs and demands of white collar and drug offense prosecutions, as well as the role that lawyers occasionally play in the perpetration of such crimes, warrant and require such practices. Prosecutors deny that they target criminal defense lawyers or attempt to interfere with defendants' constitutional rights to representation. Further, prosecutors insist that such practices are not widespread but are used selectively in appropriate circumstances. Commentators reach different conclusions as to the constitutionality of these practices. * * *[b]

---

[b] For a discussion of government practices against criminal defense attorneys, see Chapter 16.

CHAPTER TWO
THE FEDERAL ROLE

A. LIMITS OF THE FEDERAL CRIMINAL JUSTICE SYSTEM

The Numbers. In many fields in which both federal and state governments have the authority to legislate, the federal law has come to dominate. It is the primary source of regulation and the vast majority of all litigation deals with that law. A similar dominance is not found in the field of criminal law. Here the vast majority of all prosecutions are brought under state law in state courts, and the applicable process is governed, apart from federal constitutional law, by the law of the particular state. Indeed, measured by the number of prosecutions alone, the federal criminal justice system is just another player among the fifty-two criminal justice systems found in this country (i.e., the fifty state systems, the District of Columbia, and the federal system) and far less significant than a good many of the state systems.

Congressional Policy. The Supreme Court has noted on numerous occasions that "the States under our federal system have the principal responsibility for defining and prosecuting crimes." At one time it was thought that the federal constitutional structure prevented the federal government from assuming any such responsibility for itself, for that structure was seen as allowing federal legislation to reach only a narrow slice of all criminal activity. Today, however, that structure generally is considered to impose only a fairly modest restriction upon the reach of federal criminal law. While it places on federal legislative authority limitations that do not apply to the states, the key to the limited reach of current federal substantive law is the refusal of Congress to exercise that legislative authority to its fullest extent and the role of the Supreme Court in limiting federal jurisdiction.

Unlike the states, which have an inherent power to legislate in the interest of the general welfare (i.e., a general "police power"), federal legislative authority is limited to the enumerated powers granted to Congress in the United States Constitution. Thus, while the state may reach in its criminal code all behavior within its jurisdiction that threatens the health, safety, welfare or morals of the public, Congress can criminalize behavior only where doing so is "necessary and proper" to the implementation of one of the powers specifically given to it by the Constitution. The offense must relate to an operational function (e.g., to operate a postal system or coin money) or to a regulatory authority (e.g., to "regulate commerce . . . among the several states") that the Constitution specifically confers upon the federal government. Over the years, however, the Supreme Court has adopted an exceptionally broad interpretation of what may be necessary and proper in the exercise of these enumerated powers and has allowed Congress considerable leeway in reaching what might be viewed as "local" activities, particularly under the commerce clause. Thus, Congress presumably could make it a federal offense to engage in various "local" activities currently punished under state law, such as robberies committed with a firearm (typically shipped in interstate commerce). Of course, even the flexible commerce clause authority has its limits. Congressional authority could not readily be stretched to reach many other commonplace local crimes (e.g., assaults or petty thefts) which are punished by the states.

Congress over the years has extended federal legislative authority into more and more areas traditionally viewed as the primary responsibility of the states. To some extent, that tendency has also been reflected in the field of criminal law, but as compared to fields such as labor relations and environmental protection, here the congressional movement toward nationalization has been much more restrained. Initially, the federal criminal code was limited basically to prohibiting acts directly injurious to the federal government itself. It was not until after the Civil War that the nation was launched upon a course of employing the federal criminal law to protect private individuals from invasions of their rights by other private individuals—a traditional function of state criminal law. That first step was confined to civil rights legislation, but shortly thereafter Congress turned to other sources of federal legislative authority as the springboard for a steady growth in what came to be known as "federal auxiliary criminal jurisdiction." These were offenses, primarily relying on the commerce power, reaching activities as to which there was no special federal interest or federal responsibility, with the offense designed primarily to supplement state laws that also encompassed the same basic criminality. Those early auxiliary offenses included the mail fraud statute enacted in 1872 and the Dyer Act enacted in 1919 (prohibiting interstate transportation of stolen vehicles). The enactment of such offenses was commonly a response to a particular problem of the moment, as Congress failed to develop a general blueprint as to what types of basic criminal prohibitions should be "nationalized" through their inclusion in the federal criminal code. Thus, *a cause celebre*, the Lindberg kidnapping, led to a federal statute reaching most kidnappings; the progressive era focus upon major social problems produced anti-vice provisions like the Mann Act (prohibiting transporting a woman across state lines for illicit purposes); and the threat of "gangsterism" contributed to the adoption of a series of federal offenses relating to dealings in firearms, robbery of federally insured banks, and racketeering extortion.

The one common justification offered for all such legislation was that the social problem presented was serious and that state law enforcement lacked the capacity (or willingness) to answer it. In the latter half of this century, the nationalization movement gained considerable impetus through a wholesale expansion of federal auxiliary offenses. As a result, the federal criminal code today substantially overlaps with many strands of state criminal law. It reaches the vast bulk of narcotics offenses, almost all offenses involving the use of fraud to obtain property, and a much smaller but still significant and ever growing slice of various "street crimes" (e.g., carjackings, drug related crimes, drive-by shootings, and gang violence).

The Supreme Court has occasionally restricted the expansion of federal statutes into areas that are exclusive to state law. In **United States v. Lopez**, 514 U.S. 549 (1995), the Court held that the Gun-Free School Zones Act exceeded Congress' Commerce Clause authority in that it involved intrastate activity that was not involved in commerce and was not an economic activity. Chief Justice Rehnquist, writing for the majority, stated:

> Consistent with this structure, we have identified three broad categories of activity that Congress may regulate under its commerce power. * * * First, Congress may regulate the use of the channels of interstate commerce. Second, Congress is empowered to regulate and protect the instrumentalities of interstate commerce, or persons or things in interstate commerce, even though the threat may come only from intrastate activities. * * * Finally, Congress' commerce authority includes the power to regulate those activities having a substantial relation to interstate commerce, i.e., those activities that substantially affect interstate commerce.

> Within this final category, admittedly, our case law has not been clear whether an activity must "affect" or "substantially affect" interstate commerce in order to be within Congress' power to regulate it under the Commerce Clause.* * * We conclude, consistent with the great weight of our case law, that the proper test requires an analysis of whether the regulated activity "substantially affects" interstate commerce.

In **United States v. Morrison**, 529 U.S. 598 (2000), the Court held that "like [the] Gun-Free School Zones Act at issue in *Lopez,* § 13981 [provision of the Violence Against Women Act of 1994] contains no jurisdictional element establishing that the federal cause of action is in pursuance of Congress' power to regulate interstate commerce." The Court stated:

> We accordingly reject the argument that Congress may regulate noneconomic, violent criminal conduct based solely on that conduct's aggregate effect on interstate commerce. The Constitution requires a distinction between what is truly national and what is truly local. * * * In recognizing this fact we preserve one of the few principles that has been consistent since the Clause was adopted. The regulation and punishment of intrastate violence that is not directed at the instrumentalities, channels, or goods involved in interstate commerce has always been the province of the States.

Id. 617-18.

Though Congress has continuously expanded the federal code to include more and more offenses that substantially overlap with state offenses, it also has continuously noted its adherence to the view that the states must carry the primary responsibility for protecting the public against criminal activity. Thus, the Omnibus Crime Control and Safe Streets Act of 1968, while including a series of federal firearms provisions that supplemented state criminal prohibitions, also provided substantial federal financial assistance to state enforcement agencies and set forth in support of that aid the following congressional finding: "Congress finds further that crime is essentially a local problem that must be dealt with by State and local governments if it is to be controlled effectively."

Congressional recognition of the primacy of the states' role is reflected only in part by Congress' refusal to extend the federal criminal code to fully encompass all harmful acts subject to federal legislative authority (which would provide an even greater overlap with state law than currently exists). The major impact of that policy, however, is found in Congress' refusal to expand the federal law enforcement apparatus commensurate with the expanded reach of the federal criminal law. The four basic components of the federal system are: a substantial number of agencies (F.B.I., Homeland Security) that may have personnel with arrest and investigative authority, the offices of the United States Attorneys and the Criminal Division of the Department of Justice, the federal courts, and the United States Bureau of Prisons.[a]

Congressional expansion can be seen in some areas, with the passage of legislation such as the Patriot Act and the Sarbanes-Oxley Act of 2002. Although the number of criminal prosecutions in federal district courts rose significantly in the last twenty-five years, state dockets also increased, and the ratio of state-federal prosecutions has not been significantly altered.

---

[a] To view the structural organization of the Department of Justice see <http://www.usdoj. gov/dojorg.htm>.

NOTES AND QUESTIONS

1. *Federal Crimes.* Should federal criminal jurisdiction be limited to specific categories of crime and "only in instances in which state court prosecution is not appropriate or where federal interests are paramount"? Commenting on such a proposed plan of the Committee on Long Range Planning of the Federal Judicial Conference, Deputy Attorney General Jamie Gorelick and Deputy Assistant Attorney General Harry Litman stated:

> * * * First, we believe that Congress should not be foreclosed from enacting legislation in areas that are also appropriate for state regulation; rather, where there are aspects of a criminal law problem that states cannot adequately address, and where the federal government would be positioned to make a qualitative difference, it is appropriate for Congress to act. Once Congress has acted, the federalization issue becomes a question of prosecutorial discretion. It falls to the Department, in cooperation with state and local counterparts, to target for prosecution only those few cases in which federal prosecution is the most effective way to bring criminal justice resources to bear on our nation's law enforcement problems.
> * * *

Jamie Gorelick & Harry Litman, Keynote Address, *Prosecutorial Discretion and the Federalization Debate*, 46 HASTINGS L.J. 967, 978 (1995). See also G. Robert Blakey, *Federal Criminal Law: The Need, Not for Revised Constitutional Theory or New Congressional Statutes, But the Exercise of Responsible Prosecutive Discretion*, 46 HASTINGS L. J. 1175 (1995).

2. *Overfederalization.* An American Bar Association Task Force that studied the federalization of criminal law, documented the increase in federal cases and federal crimes. The Preface to the Report states that "[a]lthough it may be impossible to determine exactly how many federal crimes could be prosecuted today, it is clear that of all federal crimes enacted since 1865, over forty percent have been created since 1970." Preface, *Report of the Task Force on the Federalization of Criminal Law*, ABA Criminal Justice Section 2 (1998). Are the concerns about increased federalization being "overstated"? For a discussion of the "myths" of the federalization debate see Rory K. Little, *Myths and Principles of Federalization*, 46 HASTINGS L.J. 1029 (1995).

B. FEDERAL PRIORITIES

Should white collar crime be a Justice Department priority? Consider the following excerpt from Joe D. Whitley, *White Collar-Crime: A Real Priority*, Legal Times, Sept. 27, 1993, at 19, cont. on 22.

Increased demand on federal prosecutors also comes from the expanding list of agencies referring matters for criminal prosecution. Although federal prosecutors receive a substantial percentage of their white-collar crime cases from such well-known agencies as the Federal Bureau of Investigation, the Internal Revenue Service, and Secret Service, numerous other agencies now investigate and refer such cases. As a result of the Inspectors General Act, virtually every federal agency has an inspector general whose mission is to ferret out fraud, waste, and abuse in their respective agencies' programs. Federal prosecutors also receive referrals in white-collar crime cases from the Defense Criminal Investigative Service and individual branches of the military. There are also criminal investigators who investigate willful regulatory criminal violations at the Department of Agriculture, the Environmental Protection Agency, the Food and Drug Administration, the Fish and Wildlife Service, among others.

Government agencies that do not have criminal investigators are encouraged to coordinate with U.S. attorneys' offices on potential white-collar criminal matters.   Accordingly, bank regulatory agencies like the Federal Reserve, the Federal Deposit Insurance Corp., the Office of Thrift Supervision, the Office of the Comptroller of the Currency, and the Resolution Trust Corp. are part of bank-fraud working groups around the country that meet periodically to discuss cases with federal prosecutors. Likewise, the Office of the U.S. Bankruptcy Trustee and the Securities Exchange Commission coordinate with, and refer cases, to U.S. attorneys.

Furthermore, states regulators and investigators now look almost exclusively to the federal government for prosecution of criminal activities involving state programs that receive federal funds. These state regulators and investigators refer these cases to federal prosecutors because they are confronted with an unwillingness or inability on the part of many state and local prosecutors to devote significant resources to white-collar crime. * * *

Finally, federal prosecutors now do not simply prosecute but, as a result of laws passed in the 1980s, have responsibilities for such matters as asset forfeiture, fine collection, restitution, and notification to victims and witnesses * * *

With respect to white-collar crime, the federal government has a unique role to play, with only a minimum of overlap with state prosecutors. The reality is that cases of criminal tax violations, fraud, and corruption in such federal programs as health care, multi-victim interstate consumer frauds, large-scale interstate business frauds, including insurance frauds, securities fraud, environmental crime, corruption by public officials, civil-rights prosecutions and money laundering, would go unprosecuted in most states if they were not handled by federal prosecutors. Even assuming that state district attorneys had the financial resources to tackle these cases, they would be severely hindered by lack of applicable statutes and the complications of securing witnesses and other evidence in other states and foreign countries. * * *

NOTES AND QUESTIONS

1. ***Drugs, Violent Crimes, & Immigration Offenses.*** The three fastest growing areas of the federal docket have been drug offenses, immigration offenses, and firearms offenses. WAYNE R. LAFAVE, JEROLD H. ISRAEL, NANCY J. KING, & ORIN S. KERR, CRIMINAL PROCEDURE 3D § 1.2(d)(2007) at 71. The Department of Justice has stressed the prosecution of drug offenses over the last few decades. Violent crimes received national attention in the late 1990s, with some arguing that this area should become a top priority of the Department of Justice. See, e.g., Senator Arlen Specter (former Philadelphia D.A.) and Paul Michel (former Associate Deputy Atty. Gen.), *The Need For A New Federalism In Criminal Justice*, July 1982, Annals of the AAPSS. This increased federal emphasis on violent crimes was met with criticism by those who believed that the prosecution of white collar offenses would suffer. "[S]ome defense lawyers fear that the Justice Department, responding to political perceptions rather than reality, is shrinking its white-collar caseload and trumpeting a $30-billion crime bill with little to say on office-suite crime." Benjamin Wittes, *Defense Bar Sees Dip in White-Collar Crime Cases*, 17 Legal Times, Oct. 24, 1994, at 2. The DOJ, however, continued to see white collar crime as a growing area of concentration, although one in which priorities must be drawn to accommodate limited resources. Consider the following excerpt from *FBI'S White Collar Crime Program Expanding Rapidly*, 8 Corp. Crime Rep. 4 (Oct. 17, 1994):

> The Federal Bureau of Investigation's (FBI) white collar crime program has been expanding rapidly in recent years, with the program consuming 27 percent of the FBI's Direct Agent Workyears in FY 1993, federal officials said last week. The number of white-collar crime cases the FBI investigates has been increasing steadily over the years, with the FBI reporting 4,596 convictions and pre-trial diversions and $1 billion in fines imposed in FY 1993. The FBI's white-collar crime program covers a broad range of activities which include financial institution fraud, government fraud, including health care fraud and environmental crimes, public corruption and economic crimes. An FBI spokesperson told Corporate Crime Reporter that "because limited resources make it impossible for the FBI to address all white-collar cases that come to our attention, we are constantly analyzing trends and evaluating priorities to ensure maximum efficiency."

2. ***Terrorism.*** The tragic events of September 11th had a profound effect on the priorities of the Justice Department. On November 8, 2001, Attorney

General Ashcroft and Deputy Attorney General Thompson announced a "reorganization and mobilization" of the Department of Justice. The following is an excerpt from Attorney General Ashcroft's speech:

> * * * The attacks of September 11th have redefined the mission of the Department of Justice. Defending our nation and defending the citizens of America against terrorist attacks is now our first and overriding priority. To fulfill this mission, we are devoting all the resources necessary to eliminate terrorist networks, to prevent terrorist attacks, and to bring to justice those who kill Americans in the name of murderous ideologies.

Following September 11, 2001 the FBI shifted "nearly one-third of all agents in criminal programs, to terrorism and intelligence duties." Eric Lichtblau, David Johnston & Ron Nixon, *F.B.I. Struggles to Handle Financial Fraud Cases*, N.Y.Times, Oct. 19, 2008, at A1.

3. *Corporate Criminality.* Did white collar crime become a top priority as a result of a "general social movement" in which people are "concerned about white-collar crime, and more specifically, about corporate criminality?" Is this a reflection of "a shift in cultural values about corporate misbehavior, and, at the same time, a strong commitment to equal justice as the ideological underpinnings of the legal order"? Francis T. Cullen, William J. Maakestad & Gray Cavender, CORPORATE CRIME UNDER ATTACK 27 (1987); see also Stephen Labaton, *Downturn and Shift in Population Feed Boom in White-Collar Crime,* The N.Y. Times, June 2, 2002, at A1 ("The bursting of the stock market bubble, combined with the changing face of the American Population, has led to a surge in business fraud and corruption prosecutions and investigations."). Consider the following excerpt from Ralph K. Winter, *Paying Lawyers, Empowering Prosecutors, and Protecting Managers: Raising the Cost of Capital in America,* 42 DUKE L.J. 945, 953 (1993):

> One can no longer teach or practice in the area of corporate or securities law without being attentive to the possible exposure of the corporation or its managers to criminal liability. This liability has become important for a number of reasons, including: new attitudes on the part of prosecutors, the substantial penalties that now may be levied on corporations under the Federal Sentencing Guidelines, the extraordinary breadth the federal courts accord the definition of fraud in the mail and wire fraud statutes, and the use of forfeiture as an adjunct to criminal RICO and money laundering prosecutions.

Perhaps the most significant impact on corporate criminal prosecution came in the wake of the Enron debacle. On September 27, 2002, Attorney General John Ashcroft stated the following at a Corporate Fraud/Responsibility Conference:

* * * The past months have revealed a series of allegations of deception, fraud and malfeasance among a few individuals in whom we have placed our trust, and who have in turn assumed a fiduciary obligation to us. These are allegations of criminal conduct spanning years and, as their numbers have mounted, they have eroded confidence in the integrity of U.S. markets. Some investors both at home and overseas have done what was previously unthinkable: questioned the security, stability, and honesty of American markets.

The malignancy of corporate corruption threatens more than the future of a few companies - it destroys workers' incomes, decimates families' savings and casts a shadow on the health, integrity and good name of American business itself. The success of the free market depends on a marketplace of integrity - a marketplace that operates on information of integrity. Reliable, truthful information is the unseen force that drives the economy. * * *

Under the leadership of our Corporate Fraud Task Force, created earlier this summer by President Bush and headed by Deputy Attorney General Larry Thompson, the Department of Justice is taking a tough, new, cooperative approach to the real time enforcement of our corporate fraud statutes. The result is a lengthening list of both individuals and corporations that have become the targets of Department of Justice investigations and prosecutions * * *

http://www.usdoj.gov/ag/speeches/2002/092702agremarkscorporatefraudco nference.htm. See also Chapter 3.

4. *Financial Fraud.* In assessing the first one-hundred days of the Obama Administration, Attorney General Holder discussed as one of his policy initiatives, "targeting financial fraud." A Department of Justice Progress Report stated that:

the Department has devoted significant attention to preventing, investigating, and prosecuting mortgage fraud. The Federal Bureau of Investigation is currently investigating more than 2,100 mortgage fraud cases, up almost 400 percent from five years ago. The Bureau also has more than doubled the number of agents investigating mortgage scams, has created a National Mortgage Fraud Team at headquarters in Washington, and is working hand-in-hand with our partners at other agencies. The Department also has brought indictments and obtained convictions against perpetrators of rescue schemes in the past months. In one case, the Department recently indicted 24 individuals for alleged activity related to an extensive mortgage fraud scheme based in San Diego, which involved 220 properties with a total sales price of more than $100 million dollars.

Progress Report, Department of Justice, available at http://www.usdoj.gov/ag/progress-report.htm#fraud (April 2009).

C. FEDERAL INFLUENCE AND LOCAL CORRUPTION

In the early 1970's, federal prosecutors began to target local political corruption as a major federal law enforcement priority. Federal prosecutors believed that "corrupt schemes at the state and local level . . . [were] at least as corrosive of the governmental process as corruption at the federal level." They determined that vigorous federal enforcement efforts were "required to fill a vacuum created by the inability or unwillingness of state and local law enforcement agencies to deal adequately with the task of ferreting out corruption."

Faced with an inadequate statutory basis for prosecuting corrupt local officials, federal enforcement officials began to apply four federal statutes which traditionally had been applied to other forms of criminal activity: the Hobbs Act, the Mail Fraud Act, the Travel Act, and most significantly, the Racketeer Influenced and Corrupt Organizations Act (RICO). The interpretations of the general language of the four statutes advanced by federal prosecutors have been described by many Justice Department officials as "creative" and by others as inconsistent with the legislative intent. Nonetheless, the federal courts generally validated the application of these statutes to local corruption. Encouraged by continuing judicial acquiescence, federal prosecutors dramatically escalated their efforts to police local corruption in the following decade. * * *

Assuming that Congress *had* clearly granted federal jurisdiction over local corruption, there are admittedly instances in which a substantial federal interest in the exercise of that jurisdiction does exist. However, federal discretion under RICO and the other federal statutes is so broad that prosecutions which fail to serve a substantial federal interest can and do result.

If state and local corruption causes the breakdown of local law enforcement, the case for federal intervention is strong. Corruption in enforcement of state laws often encourages offenses that are also federal crimes. * * *

Federal prosecutions of corrupt local officials who are not involved in law enforcement are often justified by the argument that local enforcement officials are unwilling to prosecute such defendants themselves. When local officials request federal intervention or when there is evidence of systematic or improper failure to prosecute

at the local level, federal intervention is, * * * perhaps justified.
* * *

Federal prosecution of local offenses such as political corruption is justified in cases where local enforcement officials are incapable of successfully prosecuting serious offenses. For example, federal intervention may be necessary to police complex multistate criminal ventures that involve corruption of state and local government units. It is inefficient and impractical for local authorities to investigate multistate crime because they are limited to prosecution of the local aspects of the criminal activity. Moreover, the states lack the legal mechanisms possessed by federal officials to bring scattered defendants to a single trial and compel the appearance of distant witnesses. Finally, it seems inequitable to saddle one jurisdiction with the entire cost of investigation and prosecution of criminal conduct that transcends that jurisdiction.

Federal exercise of criminal jurisdiction in political corruption cases may also be appropriate when organized crime is involved, since the adverse social consequences of allowing such activity to escape enforcement are substantial. "Corruption of public officials is one of the standard techniques of organized crime." A study by the Senate indicated that attorneys general in many states lack the authority to prosecute, successfully, complex organized crime activities.

Efficient prosecution of local corruption frequently requires the use of highly specialized investigatory techniques which the Federal Bureau of Investigation and United States Attorneys (USA's) are better equipped to employ. * * * However, "if efficiency were the sole criterion for federal participation, many traditional state functions might be usurped by a more efficient federal bureaucracy. . . . Federalism, rather than efficient administration, is the issue." Given a "state's special interest in policing its own political process," a federal interest greater than relative efficiency seems necessary to justify federal intervention. * * *

Prosecution may serve a substantial federal interest when the applicable state or local charges are less serious than the applicable federal charges. If the federal offense covering particular conduct is more grave than the relevant state offense, local prosecution will not vindicate those federal interests that Congress contemplated in enacting the provision.

A sufficient federal interest in intervention may also exist where the jurisdictional base is closely related to the offense involved. For example, an offense which substantially threatens the integrity of the United States mails or imposes a direct burden on interstate commerce would seem appropriate for federal prosecution. A substantial federal interest in the prosecution of local political corruption may also arise from resulting interference with federal programs or the improper use of federal funds.

There are many examples, however, of federal prosecutions lacking any of the federal interests discussed above. The increasing occurrence of federal prosecutions of local corruption, when there is no substantial federal interest, indicates that prosecutorial discretion is too broad and that its exercise is inconsistent with constitutional notions of federalism. * * *

Andrew T. Baxter, *Federal Discretion in the Prosecution of Local Political Corruption,* 10 PEPPERDINE L. REV. 321 (1983).

NOTES AND QUESTIONS

1. *Federal/State Prosecution of Corruption.* Should federal prosecutors take a backseat to local prosecutors in the prosecution of local corruption? Should priority be granted to the prosecutor who initiated the investigation? Should the controlling considerations be expertise and resources? What happens when there is a conflict between the federal and local prosecutor? Who has the authority to take the lead, and who resolves the conflict? See Arnold H. Lubasch, *Lindenhauer Pleads Not Guilty as Officials Debate Subpoena,* The New York Times, Mar. 1, 1986, at A29 (describing a conflict between then federal prosecutor Rudolph W. Guiliani and Robert M. Morgenthau. the Manhattan District Attorney).

2. *Federalism Challenges.* In **Sabri v. United States,** 541 U.S. 600 (2004), the Supreme Court rejected a federalism challenge to § 666, a federal anti-corruption statute that targets, among others, officials of state and local governments. The defendant was a real estate developer who offered bribes to a member of the Board of Commissioners of the Minneapolis Community Development Agency. He was charged with a violation of § 666(a)(2). Sabri argued that the statute is facially unconstitutional because it does not require a nexus between the local corruption and the federal funds received by the organization or agency, and therefore violated the limitations imposed by federalism on congressional power to punish local crimes. The Court upheld the constitutionality of § 666, stating:

We can readily dispose of th[e] position that, to qualify as a valid exercise of Article I power, the statute must require proof of connection with federal money as an element of the offense. We simply do not presume the unconstitutionality of federal criminal statutes lacking explicit provision of a jurisdictional hook, and there is no occasion even to consider the need for such a requirement where there is no reason to suspect that enforcement of a criminal statute would extend beyond a legitimate interest cognizable under Article I, § 8.

Congress has authority under the Spending Clause to appropriate federal monies to promote the general welfare, Art. I, § 8, cl. 1, and it has corresponding authority under the Necessary and Proper Clause, Art. I, § 8, cl. 18, to see to it that taxpayer dollars appropriated under that power are in fact spent for the general welfare, and not frittered away in graft or on projects undermined when funds are siphoned off or corrupt public officers are derelict about demanding value for dollars. See generally M'Culloch v. Maryland, 4 Wheat. 316, (1819) (establishing review for means-ends rationality under the Necessary and Proper Clause). Congress does not have to sit by and accept the risk of operations thwarted by local and state improbity. See, e.g., M'Culloch, (power to " 'establish post-offices and post- roads' " entails authority to "punish those who steal letters"). Section 666(a)(2) addresses the problem at the sources of bribes, by rational means, to safeguard the integrity of the state, local, and tribal recipients of federal dollars.

It is true, just as Sabri says, that not every bribe or kickback offered or paid to agents of governments covered by § 666(b) will be traceably skimmed from specific federal payments, or show up in the guise of a quid pro quo for some dereliction in spending a federal grant. But this possibility portends no enforcement beyond the scope of federal interest, for the reason that corruption does not have to be that limited to affect the federal interest. Money is fungible, bribed officials are untrustworthy stewards of federal funds, and corrupt contractors do not deliver dollar-for-dollar value. Liquidity is not a financial term for nothing; money can be drained off here because a federal grant is pouring in there. And officials are not any the less threatening to the objects behind federal spending just because they may accept general retainers. See Westfall v. United States, 274 U.S. 256 (1927) (majority opinion by Holmes, J.) (upholding federal law criminalizing fraud on a state bank member of federal system, even where federal funds not directly implicated). It is certainly enough that the statutes condition the offense on a threshold amount of federal dollars defining the federal interest, such as that provided here, and on a bribe that goes well beyond liquor and cigars.

3. *Prosecutorial Guidelines.* Would guidelines assist in resolving potential state-federal conflicts? The United States Attorneys' Manual provides that prosecution should be declined when "1. No substantial federal interest would be served by prosecution; 2. The person is subject to effective prosecution in another jurisdiction; or 3. There exists an adequate non-criminal alternative to prosecution." U.S.A.M. § 9-27.220. The Manual further notes that:

A. In determining whether prosecution should be declined because the person is subject to effective prosecution in another jurisdiction, the attorney for the government should weigh all relevant considerations, including:

1. The strength of the other jurisdiction's interest in prosecution;

2. The other jurisdiction's ability and willingness to prosecute effectively; and

3. The probable sentence or other consequences if the person is convicted in the other jurisdiction.

U.S.A.M. § 9-27.240. See also Charles F. C. Ruff, *Federal Prosecution of Local Corruption: A Case Study in the Making of Law Enforcement Policy*, 65 GEO. L.J. 1171 (1977). Professor Sara Sun Beale states that "[g]enerally, the decision to bring charges in federal rather than state court is made on an ad hoc basis. The United States Attorney's Manual (the Manual) does contain some general standards for the exercise of prosecutorial discretion, but they are written so broadly that they provide little guidance." Sara Sun Beale, *Too Many and Yet Too Few: New Principles to Define the Proper Limits for Federal Criminal Jurisdiction*, 46 HASTINGS L.J. 979, 999 (1995).

4. ***Benefits of State/Federal Prosecution.*** Are there beneficial aspects to having both state and federal prosecutors pursue the same alleged local or state corruption? "Many Federal and local prosecutors maintain that competition between their offices is healthy and prevents possible cover-ups and oversights." Selwyn Raab, *Why Federal Attorneys Are the Gang-Busters Nowadays*, The New York Times, Mar. 8, 1987, at D6.

5. ***Dual Sovereignty Rule.*** Neither the double jeopardy bar of the federal constitution nor its due process requirement preclude federal and state entities from both prosecuting the same defendant for the same criminal conduct. "In the case of *United States v. Lanza*, [260 U.S. 377 (1922)], the Supreme Court promulgated what is customarily referred to as the 'dual sovereignty' doctrine: 'an act denounced as a crime by both national and state sovereignties is an offense against the peace and dignity of both and may be punished by each.' That the dual sovereignty doctrine allows a federal prosecution notwithstanding a prior state prosecution for the same conduct was thereafter affirmed in *Abbate v. United States*, [359 U.S. 187 (1959)]." WAYNE R. LaFAVE, JEROLD H. ISRAEL, & NANCY J. KING, ORIN S. KERR, CRIMINAL PROCEDURE, § 25.5 (a) (3d Ed. 2007). The Department of Justice, however, has a policy on dual prosecution and successive federal prosecution that:

* * * precludes the initiation or continuation of a federal prosecution, following a prior state or federal prosecution based on substantially the same act(s) or transaction(s), unless:

1. The following three substantive prerequisites are satisfied:

a. the matter must involve a substantial federal interest;

b. the prior prosecution must have left that interest demonstrably unvindicated; and

    c.   applying the same test applicable to all federal prosecutions, the government must believe that the defendant(s)' conduct constitutes a federal offense, and that the admissible evidence probably will be sufficient to obtain and sustain a conviction by an unbiased trier of fact; and

  2.   The following procedural prerequisite is satisfied: the prosecution must be approved by the appropriate Assistant Attorney General.

U.S.A.M. § 9-2.142. This policy is known as the *Petite* policy, based on its recognition by the Supreme Court in Petite v. United States, 361 U.S. 529 (1960). The most prominent federal authorizations of criminal prosecutions following state prosecutions have come in civil rights cases. See Symposium, *The Rodney King Trials: Civil Rights Prosecutions and Double Jeopardy*, 41 U.C.L.A. L. Rev. 509-720 (1994).

6. *Political or Racial Motivations.* Will the federal emphasis on prosecution of local corruption invariably open the door to discriminatory decision-making (or at least allegations of discriminatory decision-making)? Consider the following excerpts from Mark Curriden, *Selective Prosecution: Are Black Officials Investigative Targets*, 78 A.B.A. J. 54 (Feb. 1992):

> Kansas City, Mo., Mayor Emanuel Cleaver admits he is paranoid. The rookie chief executive of one of the largest cities in the Midwest fears that he will be investigated by the federal government.
>
> "I've done nothing wrong," Cleaver asserts. "But from what I've heard and seen, that really doesn't matter. Some of my colleagues say I can expect to be investigated at least once during my term in office, even if there is no probable cause. It appears that selective prosecution is the order of the day at the Department of Justice."
>
> Mayor Cleaver, who is black, is no radical. Nor does he subscribe to the conspiracy theory that envisions a secret plot master-minded by members of the Justice Department, the Federal Bureau of Investigation and the Internal Revenue Service against elected and appointed black officials in the United States. But he is concerned about the possibility, suggested by extensive anecdotal evidence, that black officials are subject to selective investigation and prosecution. * * * Mayor Cleaver is not alone in his thinking. A growing number of politicians, lawyers and researchers say selective prosecution exists, although their explanations for its causes vary widely.
>
> Some, like New York City attorney William Kunstler, who has represented political radicals throughout his career, believe that there is an organized effort to destroy the country's black leadership,

which even includes the use of an alleged FBI "hit squad" that travels across the country setting up black officials just to disgrace their race. "The proof that these guys exist is impossible to come up with," acknowledges Kunstler, "but the pure number of black officials being investigated tells me there's a conspiracy and a belief at [the Justice Department] that blacks are not qualified to be in positions of leadership." Others, like Kenneth O'Reilly, a political science professor at the University of Alaska, maintain that there are a few renegade prosecutors and agents remaining from the days of J. Edgar Hoover, the late FBI director. * * *

A more mainstream view is that the issue intertwines politics and race. According to this view, black officials, who by and large are Democrats, find themselves on the receiving end of a very political criminal justice system controlled, at least at the federal level, by prosecutors and investigators with largely Republican backgrounds. As Democratic officials who happen to be black, they find themselves likely targets for investigation.

"Whatever the case," says Julius Chambers, director of the NAACP's Legal Defense Fund in New York City, "it appears that black leaders are being investigated more frequently than their white counterparts simply because of their race, and that's not fair, and it's certainly not constitutional." Officials at the Justice Department and the FBI deny engaging in selective prosecutions, but otherwise refused to comment on the issue to the ABA Journal. * * *

A 1990 study by the National Council of Churches shows that more than 14 percent of the public corruption cases over the past five years targeted black officials, who make up less than two percent of the country's elected officials. In the South, where three percent of all elected officials are black, the study found that 40 percent of public corruption cases were pursued against blacks. More than half of the 24 members of the Congressional Black Caucus report being targeted for investigation or subjected to harassment by federal investigators. Since 1980, 21 black elected officials have been prosecuted in Alabama alone. Of those, 16 were found not guilty, two pleaded guilty, and three were convicted. Though less than one-half of one percent of the federal judiciary is black, three of the five U.S. District Court judges indicted in the past decade were black. * * *

In 1990, 77 percent of black respondents to a poll conducted by the New York Times said they believed that 'the government deliberately singles out and investigates black elected and appointed officials in order to discredit them in a way it doesn't do with white officials. "Thirty-four percent of the whites responding also believed that such selective prosecution 'could be going on."

D. *FEDERAL INFLUENCE IN INTERNATIONAL PROSECUTIONS*

UNITED STATES v. CASTLE
925 F.2d 831 (5th Cir. 1991)

PER CURIAM: In this case, we are called upon to consider the Foreign Corrupt Practices Act of 1977 (hereinafter "FCPA"), 15 U.S.C. §§ 78dd-1, 78dd-2, and determine whether "foreign officials," who are excluded from prosecution under the FCPA itself, may nevertheless be prosecuted under the general conspiracy statute, 18 U.S.C. § 371, for conspiring to violate the FCPA.

We hold that foreign officials may not be prosecuted under 18 U.S.C. § 371 for conspiring to violate the FCPA. The scope of our holding, as well as the rationale that undergirds it, is fully set out in Judge Sanders's memorandum opinion of June 4, 1990, 741 F.Supp. 116, which we adopt and attach as an appendix hereto.   * * *

APPENDIX

*   *   * Defendants Castle and Lowry have moved to dismiss the indictment against them on the grounds that as Canadian officials, they cannot be convicted of the offense charged against them. The two other defendants, Blondek and Tull, are U.S. private citizens, and they do not challenge their indictment on this ground. * * *

The indictment charges all four defendants with conspiring to bribe foreign officials in violation of the FCPA. Blondek and Tull were employees of Eagle Bus Company, a U.S. concern as defined in the FCPA. According to the indictment, they paid a $50,000 bribe to Defendants Castle and Lowry to ensure that their bid to provide buses to the Saskatchewan provincial government would be accepted.

There is no question that the payment of the bribe by Defendants Blondek and Tull is illegal under the FCPA, and that they may be prosecuted for conspiring to violate the Act. Nor is it disputed that Defendants Castle and Lowry could not be charged with violating the FCPA itself, since the Act does not criminalize the receipt of a bribe by a foreign official. The issue here is whether the Government may prosecute Castle and Lowry under the general conspiracy statute, 18 U.S.C. § 371, for conspiring to violate the FCPA. Put more simply, the question is whether foreign officials, whom the Government concedes it cannot prosecute under the FCPA itself, may be prosecuted under the general conspiracy statute for conspiring to violate the Act.   * * *

The principle enunciated by the Supreme Court in *Gebardi* [v. United States, 287 U.S. 112 (1932)], squarely applies to the case before this Court.

Congress intended in both the FCPA and the Mann Act to deter and punish certain activities which necessarily involved the agreement of at least two people, but Congress chose in both statutes to punish only one party to the agreement. In *Gebardi* the Supreme Court refused to disregard Congress' intention to exempt one party by allowing the Executive to prosecute that party under the general conspiracy statute for precisely the same conduct. Congress made the same choice in drafting the FCPA, and by the same analysis, this Court may not allow the Executive to override the Congressional intent not to prosecute foreign officials for their participation in the prohibited acts.

* * * [T]he exclusive focus [of Congress in passing the FCPA] was on the U.S. companies and the effects of their conduct within and on the United States.

First, Congress was concerned about the domestic effects of such payments. In the early 1970's, the Watergate affair and resulting investigations revealed that the payment of bribes to foreign officials was a widespread practice among U.S. companies. In the House Report accompanying an earlier version of the Act, it was noted that more than 400 companies had admitted making such payments, distributing well over 300 million dollars in corporate funds to foreign officials. Such massive payments had many negative domestic effects, not the least of which was the distortion of, and resulting lack of confidence in, the free market system within the United States.

> The payment of bribes to influence the acts or decision of foreign officials . . . is unethical. It is counter to the moral expectations and values of the American public. But not only is it unethical, it is bad business as well. It erodes public confidence in the integrity of the free market system . . . . In short, it rewards corruption instead of efficiency and puts pressure on ethical enterprises to lower their standards or risk losing business.

The House Committee further noted that many of the payments were made not to compete with foreign companies, but rather to gain an edge over a competitor in the United States.

Congress' second motivation was the effect of such payments by U.S. companies on the United States' foreign relations. The legislative history repeatedly cited the negative effects the revelations of such bribes had wrought upon friendly foreign governments and officials. Yet the drafters acknowledged, and the final law reflects this, that some payments that would be unethical or even illegal within the United States might not be perceived similarly in foreign countries, and those payments should not be criminalized. For example, grease payments, those payments made "to assure or to speed the proper performance of a foreign official's duties," are not illegal under the Act since they were often a part of the custom of doing business in foreign countries. Additionally, the Act was later amended to permit an affirmative defense on the grounds that the payment was legal in the country in which it was made. 15 U.S.C. § 78dd-2(c)(1). These exclusions reinforce the proposition that Congress had absolutely no intention of prosecuting the foreign officials involved, but was concerned solely with regulating the conduct of U.S. entities and citizens.[1]

[The government argued that a statement in a House Report showed congressional intent to allow conspiracy prosecutions of foreign officials.] * * *

This language [in the House Report] does not refute the overwhelming evidence of a Congressional intent to exempt foreign officials from prosecution for receiving bribes, especially since Congress knew it had the power to reach foreign officials in many cases, and yet declined to exercise that power. (United States has power to reach conduct of noncitizens under international law). Congress' awareness of the extent of its own power reveals the fallacy in the Government's position that only those classes of persons deemed by Congress to need protection are exempted from prosecution under the conspiracy statute. The question is not whether Congress could have included foreign officials within the Act's proscriptions, but rather whether Congress intended to do so, or more specifically, whether Congress intended the general conspiracy statute, passed many years before the FCPA, to reach foreign officials.

The drafters of the statute knew that they could, consistently with international law, reach foreign officials in certain circumstances. But they were equally well aware of, and actively considered, the "inherent jurisdictional, enforcement, and diplomatic difficulties" raised by the application of the bill to non-citizens of the United States. In the conference report, the conferees indicated that the bill would reach as far as possible, and listed all the persons or entities who could be prosecuted. The list includes virtually every person or entity involved, including foreign nationals who participated in the payment of the bribe when the U.S. courts had jurisdiction over them. But foreign officials were not included.

---

[1] Congress considered, and rejected, the idea that a demand for a payment by a foreign official would be a valid defense to a criminal prosecution under the Act, because

> at some point the U.S. company would make a conscious decision whether or not to pay a bribe. That the payment may have been first proposed by the recipient rather than the U.S. company does not alter the corrupt purpose on the part of the person paying the bribe.

The very fact that Congress considered this issue underscores Congress' exclusive focus on the U.S. companies in making the payment. If the drafters were concerned that a demand by a foreign official might be considered a defense to a prosecution, they clearly were expecting that only the payors of the bribes, and not the foreign officials demanding and/or receiving the bribes, would be prosecuted.

It is important to remember that Congress intended that these persons would be covered by the Act itself, without resort to the conspiracy statute. Yet the very individuals whose participation was required in every case--the foreign officials accepting the bribe--were excluded from prosecution for the substantive offense. Given that Congress included virtually every possible person connected to the payments except foreign officials, it is only logical to conclude that Congress affirmatively chose to exempt this small class of persons from prosecution.

Most likely Congress made this choice because U.S. businesses were perceived to be the aggressors, and the efforts expended in resolving the diplomatic, jurisdictional, and enforcement difficulties that would arise upon the prosecution of foreign officials was not worth the minimal deterrent value of such prosecutions. Further minimizing the deterrent value of a U.S. prosecution was the fact that many foreign nations already prohibited the receipt of a bribe by an official. * * * In fact, whenever a nation permitted such payments, Congress allowed them as well. *See* 15 U.S.C. § 78dd-2(c)(1).

Based upon the language of the statute and the legislative history, this Court finds in the FCPA what the Supreme Court in *Gebardi* found in the Mann Act: an affirmative legislative policy to leave unpunished a well-defined group of persons who were necessary parties to the acts constituting a violation of the substantive law. The Government has presented no reason why the prosecution of Defendants Castle and Lowry should go forward in the face of the congressional intent not to prosecute foreign officials. If anything, the facts of this case support Congress' decision to forego such prosecutions since foreign nations could and should prosecute their own officials for accepting bribes. * * *

NOTES AND QUESTIONS

1. *International Bribery.* At the time of the *Castle* case, the United States was the only country with a Foreign Corrupt Practices Act. The International Anti-Bribery and Fair Competition Act of 1998, signed into law on November 18, 1998, serves to strengthen the prohibitions on international bribery. See also *Effort to Implement OECD Anti-Corruption Convention Continues*, 16 INT. ENFORCEMENT RPTR. 763 (2000); *Foreign Corrupt Practice Act-DOJ Brochure*, <http://www/usdoj.gov/criminal/fraud/fcpa/ dojdocb. htm>.

2. *Coordinated Enforcement Actions.* Siemens Aktiengesellschaft (Siemens AG), a German corporation, and three of its subsidiaries plead guilty to violations of the Foreign Corrupt Practices Act (FCPA), and "Siemens AG agreed to pay a $448.5 million fine; and Siemens Argentina, Bangladesh, and Venezuela each agreed to pay a $500,000 fine, for a combined total criminal fine of $450 million." "Siemens AG also reached a settlement of a related civil complaint filed by the Securities and Exchange Commission (SEC), charging Siemens AG with violating the FCPA's anti-bribery, books and records, and internal controls provisions in connection

with many of its international operations including those discussed in the criminal charges. Siemens AG agreed to pay $350 million in disgorgement of profits relating to those violations. "Also at this same time, "Siemens AG agreed to a disposition resolving an ongoing investigation by the Munich Public Prosecutor's Office of Siemens AG's operating groups other than the Telecommunications group. The charges were based on corporate failure to supervise its officers and employees, and in connection with those charges Siemens AG agreed to pay €395 million or approximately $569 million, including a €250,000 corporate fine and €394.75 million in disgorgement of profits.'" The coordinated efforts of U.S. and German law enforcement authorities in this case set the standard for multi-national cooperation in the fight against corrupt business practices,' said U.S. Attorney for the District of Columbia Jeffrey A. Taylor." DOJ Press Release, December 15, 2008, available at http://www.usdoj.gov/opa/pr/2008/December/08-crm-1105.html.

3. *Scope of FCPA.* In addition to limiting who can be charged with a violation of the Foreign Corrupt Practices Act, the statute also limits the conduct subject to prosecution and it offers exceptions to accommodate necessary business practices in foreign countries. Consider the following case:

UNITED STATES v. KAY
359 F.3d 738 (5th Cir. 2004)

Judge Weiner:

In 2001, a grand jury charged Kay with violating the FCPA and subsequently returned the indictment, which charges both Kay and Murphy with 12 counts of FCPA violations. * * * The indictment * * * spells out in detail how Kay and Murphy allegedly orchestrated the bribing of Haitian customs officials to accept false bills of lading and other documentation that intentionally understated by one-third the quantity of rice shipped to Haiti, thereby significantly reducing ARI's customs duties and sales taxes. * * *

Because an offense under the FCPA requires that the alleged bribery be committed for the purpose of inducing foreign officials to commit unlawful acts, the results of which will assist in obtaining or retaining business in their country, the questions before us in this appeal are (1) whether bribes to obtain illegal but favorable tax and customs treatment can ever come within the scope of the statute, and (2) if so, whether, in combination, there are minimally sufficient facts alleged in the indictment to inform the defendants regarding the nexus between, on the one hand, Haitian taxes avoided through bribery, and, on the other hand, assistance in getting or keeping some business or business opportunity in Haiti. * * *

None contend that the FCPA criminalizes every payment to a foreign official: It criminalizes only those payments that are intended to (1) influence a foreign official to act or make a decision in his official capacity, or (2) induce such an official to perform or refrain from performing some act in violation of his duty, or (3) secure some wrongful advantage to the payor. And even then, the FCPA criminalizes these kinds of payments only if the result they are intended to produce–their quid pro quo–will assist (or is intended to assist) the payor in efforts to get or keep some business for or with "any person." Thus, the first question of statutory interpretation presented in this appeal is whether payments made to foreign officials to obtain unlawfully reduced customs duties or sales tax liabilities can ever fall within the scope of the FCPA, i.e., whether the illicit payments made to obtain a reduction of revenue liabilities can ever constitute the kind of bribery that is proscribed by the FCPA. The district court answered this question in the negative * * *

The principal thrust of the defendants' argument is that the business nexus element, i.e., the "assist . . . in obtaining or retaining business" element, narrowly limits the statute's applicability to those payments that are intended to obtain a foreign official's approval of a bid for a new government contract or the renewal of an existing government contract. In contrast, the government insists that, in addition to payments to officials that lead directly to getting or renewing business contracts, the statute covers payments that indirectly advance ("assist") the payor's goal of obtaining or retaining foreign business with or for some person. The government reasons that paying reduced customs duties and sales taxes on imports, as is purported to have occurred in this case, is the type of "improper advantage" that always will assist in obtaining or retaining business in a foreign country, and thus is always covered by the FCPA. * * *

Congress enacted the FCPA in 1977, in response to recently discovered but widespread bribery of foreign officials by United States business interests. Congress resolved to interdict such bribery, not just because it is morally and economically suspect, but also because it was causing foreign policy problems for the United States. In particular, these concerns arose from revelations that United States defense contractors and oil companies had made large payments to high government officials in Japan, the Netherlands, and Italy. Congress also discovered that more than 400 corporations had made questionable or illegal payments in excess of $300 million to foreign officials for a wide range of favorable actions on behalf of the companies.

In deciding to criminalize this type of commercial bribery, the House and Senate each proposed similarly far-reaching, but non-identical, legislation. In its bill, the House intended "broadly [to] prohibit[ ] transactions that are corruptly intended to induce the recipient to use his or her influence to affect any act or decision of a foreign official . . . ." Thus, the House bill contained no limiting "business nexus" element. Reflecting a somewhat narrower purpose, the Senate expressed its desire to ban payments made for the purpose of inducing foreign officials to act "so as to direct business to any person, maintain an established business opportunity with any person, divert any business opportunity from any person or influence the enactment or promulgation of legislation or regulations of that government or instrumentality."

At conference, compromise language "clarified the scope of the prohibition by requiring that the purpose of the payment must be to influence any act or decision of a foreign official ... so as to assist an issuer in obtaining, retaining or directing business to any person." In the end, then, Congress adopted the Senate's proposal to prohibit only those payments designed to induce a foreign official to act in a way that is intended to facilitate ("assist") in obtaining or retaining of business.

Congress expressly emphasized that it did not intend to prohibit "so-called grease or facilitating payments," such as "payments for expediting shipments through customs or placing a transatlantic telephone call, securing required permits, or obtaining adequate police protection, transactions which may involve even the proper performance of duties." Instead of making an express textual exception for these types of non-covered payments, the respective committees of the two chambers sought to distinguish permissible grease payments from prohibited bribery by only prohibiting payments that induce an official to act "corruptly," i.e., actions requiring him "to misuse his official position" and his discretionary authority, not those "essentially ministerial" actions that "merely move a particular matter toward an eventual act or decision or which do not involve any discretionary action."

In short, Congress sought to prohibit the type of bribery that (1) prompts officials to misuse their discretionary authority and (2) disrupts market efficiency and United States foreign relations, at the same time recognizing that smaller payments intended to expedite ministerial actions should remain outside of the scope of the statute. The Conference Report explanation, on which the district court relied to find a narrow statutory scope, truly offers little insight into the FCPA's precise scope, however; it merely parrots the statutory language itself by stating that the purpose of a payment must be to induce official action "so as to assist an issuer in obtaining, retaining or directing business to any person."

To divine the categories of bribery Congress did and did not intend to prohibit, we must look to the Senate's proposal, because the final statutory language was drawn from it, and from the SEC Report on which the Senate's legislative proposal was based. In distinguishing among the types of illegal payments that United States entities were making at the time, the SEC Report identified four principal categories: (1) payments "made in an effort to procure special and unjustified favors or advantages in the enactment or administration of the tax or other laws" of a foreign country; (2) payments "made with the intent to assist the company in obtaining or retaining government contracts"; (3) payments "to persuade low-level government officials to perform functions or services which they are obliged to perform as part of their governmental responsibilities, but which they may refuse or delay unless compensated" ("grease"), and (4) political contributions. The SEC thus exhibited concern about a wide range of questionable payments (explicitly including the kind at issue here) that were resulting in millions of dollars being recorded falsely in corporate books and records.

As noted, the Senate Report explained that the statute should apply to payments intended "to direct business to any person, maintain an established business opportunity with any person, divert any business opportunity from any person or influence the enactment or promulgation of legislation or regulations of that government or instrumentality." * * * It is clear, however, that even though the Senate was particularly concerned with bribery intended to secure new business, it was also mindful of bribes that influence legislative or regulatory actions, and those that maintain established business opportunities, a category of economic activity separate from, and much more capacious than, simply "directing business" to someone.

The statute's ultimate language of "obtaining or retaining" mirrors identical language in the SEC Report. But, whereas the SEC Report highlights payments that go toward "obtaining or retaining government contracts," the FCPA, incorporating the Senate Report's language, prohibits payments that assist in obtaining or retaining business, not just government contracts. Had the Senate and ultimately Congress wanted to carry over the exact, narrower scope of the SEC Report, they would have adopted the same language. We surmise that, in using the word "business" when it easily could have used the phraseology of SEC Report, Congress intended for the statute to apply to bribes beyond the narrow band of payments sufficient only to "obtain or retain government contracts." The Senate's express intention that the statute apply to corrupt payments that maintain business opportunities also supports this conclusion.

For purposes of deciding the instant appeal, the question nevertheless remains whether the Senate, and concomitantly Congress, intended this broader statutory scope to encompass the administration of tax, customs, and other laws and regulations affecting the revenue of foreign states. To reach this conclusion, we must ask whether Congress's remaining expressed desire to prohibit bribery aimed at getting assistance in retaining business or maintaining business opportunities was sufficiently broad to include bribes meant to affect the administration of revenue laws. When we do so, we conclude that the legislative intent was so broad. Congress was obviously distraught not only about high profile bribes to high-ranking foreign officials, but also by the pervasiveness of foreign bribery by United States businesses and businessmen. Congress thus made the decision to clamp down on bribes intended to prompt foreign officials to misuse their discretionary authority for the benefit of a domestic entity's business in that country. This observation is not diminished by Congress's understanding and accepting that relatively small facilitating payments were, at the time, among the accepted costs of doing business in many foreign countries. * * *

After the FCPA's enactment, United States business entities and executives experienced difficulty in discerning a clear line between prohibited bribes and permissible facilitating payments. As a result, Congress amended the FCPA in 1988, expressly to clarify its original intent in enacting the statute. Both houses insisted that their proposed amendments only clarified ambiguities "without changing the basic intent or effectiveness of the law."

In this effort to crystallize the scope of the FCPA's prohibitions on bribery, Congress chose to identify carefully two types of payments that are not proscribed by the statute. It expressly excepted payments made to procure "routine governmental action" (again, the grease exception), and it incorporated an affirmative defense for payments that are legal in the country in which they are offered or that constitute bona fide expenditures directly relating to promotion of products or services, or to the execution or performance of a contract with a foreign government or agency.

We agree with the position of the government that these 1988 amendments illustrate an intention by Congress to identify very limited exceptions to the kinds of bribes to which the FCPA does not apply. A brief review of the types of routine governmental actions enumerated by Congress shows how limited Congress wanted to make the grease exceptions. Routine governmental action, for instance, includes "obtaining permits, licenses, or other official documents to qualify a person to do business in a foreign country," and "scheduling inspections associated with contract performance or inspections related to transit of goods across country." Therefore, routine governmental action does not include the issuance of every official document or every inspection, but only (1) documentation that qualifies a party to do business and (2) scheduling an inspection—very narrow categories of largely non-discretionary, ministerial activities performed by mid- or low-level foreign functionaries. In contrast, the FCPA uses broad, general language in prohibiting payments to procure assistance for the payor in obtaining or retaining business, instead of employing similarly detailed language, such as applying the statute only to payments that attempt to secure or renew particular government contracts. Indeed, Congress had the opportunity to adopt narrower language in 1977 from the SEC Report, but chose not to do so. * * *

As we have demonstrated, the 1977 and 1988 legislative history already make clear that the business nexus requirement is not to be interpreted unduly narrowly. We therefore agree with the government that there really was no need for Congress to add "or other improper advantage" to the requirement. In fact, such an amendment might have inadvertently swept grease payments into the statutory ambit—or at least created new confusion as to whether these types of payments were prohibited—even though this category of payments was excluded by Congress in 1977 and remained excluded in 1988; and even though Congress showed no intention of adding this category when adopting its 1998 amendments. That the Convention, which the Senate ratified without reservation and Congress implemented, would also appear to prohibit the types of payments at issue in this case only bolsters our conclusion that the kind of conduct allegedly engaged in by defendants can be violative of the statute.

Given the foregoing analysis of the statute's legislative history, we cannot hold as a matter of law that Congress meant to limit the FCPA's applicability to cover only bribes that lead directly to the award or renewal of contracts. Instead, we hold that Congress intended for the FCPA to apply broadly to payments intended to assist the payor, either directly or indirectly, in obtaining or retaining business for some person, and that bribes paid to foreign tax officials to secure illegally reduced customs and tax liability constitute a type of payment that can fall within this broad coverage. * * *

NOTE

Should the United States use federal statutes to prosecute conduct occurring outside its boundaries? In some cases the federal statute is enacted with the purpose of reaching extraterritorial activities. For example, in the case of the Foreign Corrupt Practices Act, Congress wrote the statute with a clear intent that the statute have an international application. This is also true with respect to export control legislation.

Some statutes have a specific extraterritorial provision to indicate the extraterritorial application. For example, 18 U.S.C. § 1621, a perjury statute, provides that "[t]his section is applicable whether the statement or subscription is made within or without the United States." Although the statute itself has a national focus, it is clear that Congress intended for either the specific provision or the entire statute to be used both for acts occurring within its borders and for acts occurring extraterritorially.

In deciding whether a statute should have an extraterritorial application, courts examine the issue from a national perspective and/or an international perspective. When approaching the issue nationally, courts are trying to discern whether Congress intended for the statute to have an international application. When approaching the question internationally, courts are looking to see if under international law the United States has jurisdiction.

In international law there are five principles commonly used to determine whether a criminal statute should have extraterritorial application. These five general principles are:

(1) territorial, wherein jurisdiction is based on the place where the offense is committed; (2) national, wherein jurisdiction is based on the nationality or national character of the offender; (3) protective, wherein jurisdiction is based on whether the national interest is injured; (4) universal, which amounts to physical custody of the offender; and (5) passive personality, wherein jurisdiction is based on the nationality or national character of the victim.

Chua Han Mow v. United States, 730 F.2d 1308 (9th Cir. 1984). See also *Harvard Research in International Law, Jurisdiction With Respect to Crime*, 28 AM. J. INT'L. 437 (1935). Consider the First Circuit's resolution of extraterritoriality with regard to an antitrust prosecution:

UNITED STATES v. NIPPON PAPER INDUSTRIES CO., LTD.
109 F.3d 1 (1st Cir. 1997)

SELYA, Circuit Judge.

This case raises an important, hitherto unanswered question. In it, the United States attempts to convict a foreign corporation under the Sherman Act, a federal antitrust statute, alleging that price-fixing activities which took place entirely in Japan are prosecutable because they were intended to have, and did in fact have, substantial effects in this country. The district court, declaring that a criminal antitrust prosecution could not be based on wholly extraterritorial conduct, dismissed the indictment. * * * We reverse. * * *

In 1995, a federal grand jury handed up an indictment naming as a defendant Nippon Paper Industries Co., Ltd. (NPI), a Japanese manufacturer of facsimile paper. The indictment alleges that in 1990 NPI and certain unnamed coconspirators held a number of meetings in Japan which culminated in an agreement to fix the price of thermal fax paper throughout North America. NPI and other manufacturers who were privy to the scheme purportedly accomplished their objective by selling the paper in Japan to unaffiliated trading houses on condition that the latter charge specified (inflated) prices for the paper when they resold it in North America. The trading houses then shipped and sold the paper to their subsidiaries in the United States who in turn sold it to American consumers at swollen prices. The indictment further relates that, in 1990 alone, NPI sold thermal fax paper worth approximately $6,100,000 for eventual import into the United States; and that in order to ensure the success of the venture, NPI monitored the paper trail and confirmed that the prices charged to end users were those that it had arranged. These activities, the indictment posits, had a substantial adverse effect on commerce in the United States and unreasonably restrained trade in violation of Section One of the Sherman Act, 15 U.S.C. § 1 (1994).

NPI moved to dismiss because, inter alia, if the conduct attributed to NPI occurred at all, it took place entirely in Japan, and, thus, the indictment failed to limn an offense under Section One of the Sherman Act. The government opposed this initiative on two grounds. First, it claimed that the law deserved a less grudging reading and that, properly read, Section One of the Sherman Act applied criminally to wholly foreign conduct as long as that conduct produced substantial and intended effects within the United States. Second, it claimed that the indictment, too, deserved a less grudging reading and that, properly read, the bill alleged a vertical conspiracy in restraint of trade that involved overt acts by certain coconspirators within the United States. Accepting a restrictive reading of both the statute and the indictment, the district court dismissed the case. ***

Our law has long presumed that "legislation of Congress, unless a contrary intent appears, is meant to apply only within the territorial jurisdiction of the United States." EEOC v. Arabian American Oil Co., 499 U.S. 244, 248, S.Ct. 1227, 1230, 113 L.Ed.2d 274 (1991). In this context, the Supreme Court has charged inquiring courts with determining whether Congress has clearly expressed an affirmative desire to apply particular laws to conduct that occurs beyond the borders of the United States.

The earliest Supreme Court case which undertook a comparable task in respect to Section One of the Sherman Act determined that the presumption against extraterritoriality had not been overcome. In American Banana Co. v. United Fruit Co., 213 U.S. 347, 29 S.Ct. 511, 53 L.Ed. 826 (1909), the Court considered the application of the Sherman Act in a civil action concerning conduct which occurred entirely in Central America and which had no discernible effect on imports to the United States. Starting with what Justice Holmes termed "the general and almost universal rule" holding "that the character of an act as lawful or unlawful must be determined wholly by the law of the country where the act is done," and the ancillary proposition that, in cases of doubt, a statute should be "confined in its operation and effect to the territorial limits over which the lawmaker has general and legitimate power," the Court held that the defendant's actions abroad were not proscribed by the Sherman Act.

Our jurisprudence is precedent-based, but it is not static. By 1945, a different court saw a very similar problem in a somewhat softer light. In United States v. Aluminum Co. of Am., 148 F.2d 416 (2d Cir.1945) (Alcoa), the Second Circuit, sitting as a court of last resort, mulled a civil action brought under Section One against a Canadian corporation for acts committed entirely abroad which, the government averred, had produced substantial anticompetitive effects within the United States. The Alcoa court read American Banana narrowly; that case, Judge Learned Hand wrote, stood only for the principle that "[w]e should not impute to Congress an intent to punish all whom its courts can catch, for conduct which has no consequences within the United States." But a sovereign ordinarily can impose liability for conduct outside its borders that produces consequences within them, and while considerations of comity argue against applying Section One to situations in which no effect within the United States has been shown--the American Banana scenario--the statute, properly interpreted, does proscribe extraterritorial acts which were "intended to affect imports [to the United States] and did affect them." On the facts of Alcoa, therefore, the presumption against extraterritoriality had been overcome, and the Sherman Act had been violated.

Any perceived tension between American Banana and Alcoa was eased by the Supreme Court's most recent exploration of the Sherman Act's extraterritorial reach. In Hartford Fire Ins. Co. v. California, 509 U.S. 764, 113 S.Ct. 2891, 125 L.Ed.2d 612 (1993), the Justices endorsed Alcoa 's core holding, permitting civil antitrust claims under Section One to go forward despite the fact that the actions which allegedly violated Section One occurred entirely on British soil. While noting American Banana's initial disagreement with this proposition, the Hartford Fire Court deemed it "well established by now that the Sherman Act applies to foreign conduct that was meant to produce and did in fact produce some substantial effect in the United States." The conduct alleged, a London-based conspiracy to alter the American insurance market, met that benchmark.

To sum up, the case law now conclusively establishes that civil antitrust actions predicated on wholly foreign conduct which has an intended and substantial effect in the United States come within Section One's jurisdictional reach. * * *

Were this a civil case, our journey would be complete. But here the United States essays a criminal prosecution for solely extraterritorial conduct rather than a civil action. This is largely uncharted terrain; we are aware of no authority directly on point, and the parties have cited none.

Be that as it may, one datum sticks out like a sore thumb: in both criminal and civil cases, the claim that Section One applies extraterritorially is based on the same language in the same section of the same statute: "Every contract, combination in the form of trust or otherwise, or conspiracy, in restraint of trade or commerce among the several States, or with foreign nations, is declared to be illegal." 15 U.S.C. § 1. Words may sometimes be chameleons, possessing different shades of meaning in different contexts, but common sense suggests that courts should interpret the same language in the same section of the same statute uniformly, regardless of whether the impetus for interpretation is criminal or civil. * * *

NPI and its amicus, the Government of Japan, urge that special reasons exist for measuring Section One's reach differently in a criminal context. We have reviewed their exhortations and found them hollow. We discuss the five most promising theses below. The rest do not require comment.

1. *Lack of Precedent.* NPI and its amicus make much of the fact that this appears to be the first criminal case in which the United States endeavors to extend Section One to wholly foreign conduct. We are not impressed. There is a first time for everything, and the absence of earlier criminal actions is probably more a demonstration of the increasingly global nature of our economy than proof that Section One cannot cover wholly foreign conduct in the criminal milieu.

Moreover, this argument overstates the lack of precedent. There is, for example, solid authority for applying a state's criminal statute to conduct occurring entirely outside the state's borders. * * *

2. *Difference in Strength of Presumption.* The lower court and NPI both cite United States v. Bowman, 260 U.S. 94, 43 S.Ct. 39, 67 L.Ed. 149 (1922), for the proposition that the presumption against extraterritoriality operates with greater force in the criminal arena than in civil litigation. This misreads the opinion. To be sure, the *Bowman* Court, dealing with a charged conspiracy to defraud, warned that if the criminal law "is to be extended to

include those [crimes] committed outside of the strict territorial jurisdiction, it is natural for Congress to say so in the statute, and failure to do so will negative the purpose of Congress in this regard." But this pronouncement merely restated the presumption against extraterritoriality previously established in civil cases like *American Banana*. The *Bowman* Court nowhere suggested that a different, more resilient presumption arises in criminal cases. * * *

3. *The Restatement.* NPI and the district court, both sing the praises of the Restatement (Third) of Foreign Relations Law (1987), claiming that it supports a distinction between civil and criminal cases on the issue of extraterritoriality. The passage to which they pin their hopes states:

> [I]n the case of regulatory statutes that may give rise to both civil and criminal liability, such as the United States antitrust and securities laws, the presence of substantial foreign elements will ordinarily weigh against application of criminal law. In such cases, legislative intent to subject conduct outside the state's territory to its criminal law should be found only on the basis of express statement or clear implication.

Id. at § 403 cmt. f. We believe that this statement merely reaffirms the classic presumption against extraterritoriality--no more, no less. After all, nothing in the text of the Restatement proper contradicts the government's interpretation of Section One. * * * What is more, other comments indicate that a country's decision to prosecute wholly foreign conduct is discretionary. * * *

4. *The Rule of Lenity.* The next arrow which NPI yanks from its quiver is the rule of lenity. The rule itself is venerable; it provides that, in the course of interpreting statutes in criminal cases, a reviewing court should resolve ambiguities affecting a statute's scope in the defendant's favor. * * * But the rule of lenity is inapposite unless a statutory ambiguity looms, and a statute is not ambiguous for this purpose simply because some courts or commentators have questioned its proper interpretation. * * * Put bluntly, the rule of lenity cannot be used to create ambiguity when the meaning of a law, even if not readily apparent, is, upon inquiry, reasonably clear. * * * In view of the fact that the Supreme Court deems it "well established" that Section One of the Sherman Act applies to wholly foreign conduct, *Hartford Fire*, we effectively are foreclosed from trying to tease an ambiguity out of Section One relative to its extraterritorial application. Accordingly, the rule of lenity plays no part in the instant case.

5. *Comity.* International comity is a doctrine that counsels voluntary forbearance when a sovereign which has a legitimate claim to jurisdiction concludes that a second sovereign also has a legitimate claim to jurisdiction under principles of international law. * * * Comity is more an aspiration than a fixed rule, more a matter of grace than a matter of obligation. * * *

In this case the defendant's comity-based argument is even more attenuated. The conduct with which NPI is charged is illegal under both Japanese and American laws, thereby alleviating any founded concern about NPI being whipsawed between separate sovereigns. And, moreover, to the extent that comity is informed by general principles of reasonableness, see Restatement (Third) of Foreign Relations Law § 403, the indictment lodged against NPI is well within the pale. In it, the government charges that the defendant orchestrated a conspiracy with the object of rigging prices in the United States. If the government can prove these charges, we see no tenable reason why principles of comity should shield NPI from prosecution. We live in an age of international commerce, where decisions reached in one corner of the world can reverberate around the globe in less time than it takes to tell the tale. Thus, a ruling in NPI's favor would create perverse incentives for those who would use nefarious means to influence markets in the United States, rewarding them for erecting as many territorial firewalls as possible between cause and effect.

We need go no further. *Hartford Fire* definitively establishes that Section One of the Sherman Act applies to wholly foreign conduct which has an intended and substantial effect in the United States. We are bound to accept that holding. Under settled principles of statutory construction, we also are bound to apply it by interpreting Section One the same way in a criminal case. The combined force of these commitments requires that we accept the government's cardinal argument, reverse the order of the district court, reinstate the indictment, and remand for further proceedings. * * * Reversed and remanded.

LYNCH, Circuit Judge (concurring).

* * * While courts, including this one, speak of determining congressional intent when interpreting statutes, the meaning of the antitrust laws has emerged through the relationship among all three branches of government. In this criminal case, it is our responsibility to ensure that the executive's interpretation of the Sherman Act does not conflict with other legal principles, including principles of international law.

That question requires examination beyond the language of Section One of the Sherman Act. It is, of course, generally true that, as a principle of statutory interpretation, the same language should be read the same way in all contexts to which the language applies. But this is not invariably true. New content is sometimes ascribed to statutory terms depending upon context. * * * Where Congress intends that our laws conform with international law, and where international law suggests that criminal enforcement and civil enforcement be viewed differently, it is at least conceivable that different content could be ascribed to the same language depending on whether the context is civil or criminal. * * *

NOTES AND QUESTIONS

1. *Using Civil Law for Extraterritoriality.* Considering the different standards of proof applicable to civil and criminal matters, should a substantive holding in a civil case be authority for a criminal action? Do criminal and civil matters use the same standard of causation? Does the fact that the statute involves antitrust, a business crime that crosses into both civil and criminal actions, provide a basis for using civil law cases as authority? The United States is not the only country scrutinizing price-fixing. See Stephen Labaton, *The World Gets Tough on Price Fixers*, N.Y.Times, June 3, 2001, at Sec.3. ("Taking the lead from the United States, governments in Europe and Asia are beginning to take price-fixing more seriously.").

2. *Extraterritoriality and the Revenue Rule.* In **Pasquantino v. United States**, 544 U.S. 349 (2005), the Court considered an extraterritorial application of the wire fraud statute, and whether the revenue rule precludes a prosecution of a scheme involving the smuggling of "large quantities of liquor into Canada from the United States." "[T]he Pasquantinos, while in New York, ordered liquor over the telephone from discount package stores in Maryland." They employed individuals "to drive the liquor over the Canadian border, without paying the required excise taxes.""Uncontested evidence at trial showed that Canadian taxes then due on alcohol purchased in the United States and transported to Canada were approximately double the liquor's purchase price." Justice Thomas writing the opinion for the majority stated:

> * * * We granted certiorari to resolve a conflict in the Courts of Appeals over whether a scheme to defraud a foreign government of tax revenue violates the wire fraud statute. * * *
>
> Neither the antismuggling statute, 18 U.S.C. § 546, nor U.S. tax treaties convince us that petitioners' scheme falls outside the terms of the wire fraud statute. Unlike the treaties and the antismuggling statute, the wire fraud statute punishes fraudulent use of domestic wires, whether or not such conduct constitutes smuggling, occurs aboard a vessel, or evades foreign taxes. Petitioners would be equally liable if they had used interstate wires to defraud Canada not of taxes due, but of money from the Canadian treasury. * * *
>
> [T]his prosecution poses little risk of causing the principal evil against which the revenue rule was traditionally thought to guard: judicial evaluation of the policy-laden enactments of other sovereigns. See, e.g., Moore v. Mitchell, 30 F.2d 600 (2d Cir. 1929) (L.Hand, J., concurring). As Judge Hand put it, allowing courts to enforce another country's revenue laws was thought to be a delicate inquiry

> when it concerns the relations between the foreign state
> and its own citizens .... To pass upon the provisions for
> the public order of another state is, or at any rate should
> be, beyond the powers of a court; it involves the
> relations between the states themselves, with which
> courts are incompetent to deal, and which are intrusted
> to other authorities.

The present prosecution creates little risk of causing international friction through judicial evaluation of the policies of foreign sovereigns. This action was brought by the Executive to enforce a statute passed by Congress. In our system of government, the Executive is "the sole organ of the federal government in the field of international relations," United States v. Curtiss-Wright Export Corp., 299 U.S. 304 (1936), and has ample authority and competence to manage "the relations between the foreign state and its own citizens" and to avoid "embarass[ing] its neighbor[s]," *Moore* (L.Hand, J., concurring). True, a prosecution like this one requires a court to recognize foreign law to determine whether the defendant violated U.S. law. But we may assume that by electing to bring this prosecution, the Executive has assessed this prosecution's impact on this Nation's relationship with Canada, and concluded that it poses little danger of causing international friction. We know of no common-law court that has applied the revenue rule to bar an action accompanied by such a safeguard, and neither petitioners nor the dissent directs us to any. The greater danger, in fact, would lie in our judging this prosecution barred based on the foreign policy concerns animating the revenue rule, concerns that we have "neither aptitude, facilities nor responsibility" to evaluate.

More broadly, petitioners argue that the revenue rule avoids giving domestic effect to politically sensitive and controversial policy decisions embodied in foreign revenue laws, regardless of whether courts need pass judgment on such laws. This worries us little here. The present prosecution, if authorized by the wire fraud statute, embodies the policy choice of the two political branches of our Government — Congress and the Executive — to free the interstate wires from fraudulent use, irrespective of the object of the fraud. Such a reading of the wire fraud statute gives effect to that considered policy choice. It therefore poses no risk of advancing the policies of Canada illegitimately.

Still a final revenue rule rationale petitioners urge is the concern that courts lack the competence to examine the validity of unfamiliar foreign tax schemes. Foreign law, of course, posed no unmanageable complexity in this case. The District Court had before it uncontroverted testimony of a Government witness that petitioners' scheme aimed at violating Canadian tax law.

Nevertheless, Federal Rule of Criminal Procedure 26.1 addresses petitioners' concern by setting forth a procedure for interpreting foreign law that improves on those available at common law. Specifically, it permits a court, in deciding issues of foreign law, to consider "any relevant material or source — including testimony — without regard to the Federal Rules of Evidence." By contrast, common-law procedures for dealing with foreign law — those available to the courts that formulated the revenue rule--were more cumbersome. Rule 26.1 gives federal courts sufficient means to resolve the incidental foreign law issues they may encounter in wire fraud prosecutions.

Finally, our interpretation of the wire fraud statute does not give it "extraterritorial effect." Petitioners used U.S. interstate wires to execute a scheme to defraud a foreign sovereign of tax revenue. * * * It may seem an odd use of the Federal Government's resources to prosecute a U.S. citizen for smuggling cheap liquor into Canada. But the broad language of the wire fraud statute authorizes it to do so and no canon of statutory construction permits us to read the statute more narrowly. * * *

Justice Ginsburg, in her dissent, advocated that the wire fraud statute should not extend to schemes to evade foreign tax and customs laws. She stated in part:

* * * Today's novel decision is all the more troubling for its failure to take account of Canada's primary interest in the matter at stake. United States citizens who have committed criminal violations of Canadian tax law can be extradited to stand trial in Canada. Canadian courts are best positioned to decide "whether, and to what extent, the defendants have defrauded the governments of Canada and Ontario out of tax revenues owed pursuant to their own, sovereign, excise laws."

* * * Expansively interpreting the text of the wire fraud statute, which prohibits "any scheme or artifice to defraud, or for obtaining money or property by means of . . . fraudulent pretenses," the Court today upholds the Government's deployment of § 1343 essentially to enforce foreign tax law. * * * Construing § 1343 to encompass violations of foreign revenue laws, the Court ignores the absence of anything signaling Congress' intent to give the statute such an extraordinary extraterritorial effect. "It is a longstanding principle of American law," *Aramco*, that Congress, in most of its legislative endeavors, "is primarily concerned with domestic conditions."

Section 1343, which contains no reference to foreign law as an element of the domestic crime of wire fraud, contrasts with federal criminal statutes that chart the courts' course in this regard. See, e.g., 18 U.S.C. § 1956(c)(1) (defendant must know that transaction involved the proceeds of activity "that constitutes a felony under State, Federal, or foreign law"); 16 U.S.C. § 3372(a)(2)(A) (banning importation of wildlife that has been "taken, possessed, transported, or sold in violation of any . . . foreign law"). These statutes indicate that Congress, which has the sole authority to determine the extraterritorial reach of domestic laws, is fully capable of conveying its policy choice to the Executive and the courts. I would not assume from legislative silence that Congress left the matter to Executive discretion.

The presumption against extraterritoriality, which guides courts in the absence of congressional direction, provides ample cause to conclude that § 1343 does not extend to the instant scheme. Moreover, as to foreign customs and tax laws, there is scant room for doubt about Congress' general perspective: Congress has actively indicated, through both domestic legislation and treaties, that it intends "strictly [to] limit the parameters of any assistance given" to foreign nations. * * *

Complementing the principle that courts ordinarily should await congressional instruction before giving our laws extraterritorial thrust, the common-law revenue rule holds that one nation generally does not enforce another's tax laws. The Government argues, and the Court accepts, that domestic wire fraud prosecutions premised on violations of foreign tax law do not implicate the revenue rule because the court, while it must "recognize foreign [revenue] law to determine whether the defendant violated U.S. law," need only "enforce" foreign law "in an attenuated sense." As discussed above, however, the defendants' conduct arguably fell within the scope of § 1343 only because of their purpose to evade Canadian customs and tax laws; shorn of that purpose, no other aspect of their conduct was criminal in this country. It seems to me unavoidably obvious, therefore, that this prosecution directly implicates the revenue rule. It is equally plain that Congress did not endeavor, by enacting § 1343, to displace that rule. * * *

3. *Foreign Commerce.* In **United States v. Tarkoff**, 242 F.3d 991 (11th Cir. 2001), the court considered "whether a defendant may be convicted for conspiring to violate and violating the money laundering statute, 18 U.S.C. § 1956(h) and (a)(1)(B)(i), where the indictment charged and the government proved that the two monetary transactions at issue occurred wholly outside the United States." On appeal, Michael Tarkoff, a criminal defense attorney, contended that "that he was entitled to [a] judgment of acquittal because the transactions in which he took part occurred wholly outside the United States, and therefore did not affect interstate or foreign commerce, which is a necessary component of an element of the money laundering statute under which he was convicted." In affirming the conviction, Circuit Judge Kravitch writes:

Tarkoff's convictions are based on his participation in two transactions: (1) the wire transfer of $400,000 from Curacao to Fernandez's bank account in Israel, and (2) the transfer of $50,000 of those funds to Tarkoff's Israeli bank account. * * * Because the evidence is sufficient to prove that Tarkoff correctly believed that the funds involved in the Israeli transactions were the proceeds of Arnaiz's Medicare fraud, and that Tarkoff participated in conducting the transactions knowing that they were designed in whole or in part to conceal or disguise the nature, location, source, ownership, or control of the proceeds of the Medicare fraud, we address only the first element of a section 1956(a)(1)(B)(i) offense-that is, whether the Israeli transactions satisfy the statutory definition of 'financial transaction.'

The statute defines "financial transaction" as "(A) a transaction which in any way or degree affects interstate or foreign commerce (i) involving the movement of funds by wire or other means or (ii) involving one or more monetary instruments ..., or (B) a transaction involving the use of a financial institution which is engaged in, or the activities of which affect, interstate or foreign commerce in any way or degree." 18 U.S.C. § 1956(c)(4). Tarkoff argues that because the two transactions with the Israeli bank occurred wholly outside the United States, they were not "financial transactions" under 18 U.S.C. § 1956(c)(4). In support of this proposition, Tarkoff relies primarily on United States v. Kramer, 73 F.3d 1067 (11th Cir.1996), in which this Court reversed a money laundering conviction under 18 U.S.C. § 1956(a)(2)(B)(i) because the defendant participated only in a transfer of money from Switzerland to Luxembourg, and not a transfer of money to or from the United States, as required to violate section 1956(a)(2)(B)(i). * * * *Kramer* does not control in this case, however, because Tarkoff was convicted under a different subsection of the money laundering statute (§ 1956(a)(1)(B)(i)) than the one at issue in *Kramer*. The difference between the two subsections is that violation of the subsection at issue in *Kramer* specifically requires a transfer of funds to or from the United States, whereas a violation of the subsection under which Tarkoff was convicted can occur so long as the defendant was involved in a "financial transaction."

There are two ways to establish that a defendant conducted a "financial transaction" under 18 U.S.C. § 1956(a)(1)(B)(i). To satisfy its burden, the government had to prove either (1) that Tarkoff participated in a transaction that *in any way or degree* affected interstate or foreign commerce and involved the transfer of funds or the use of one or more monetary instruments, that Tarkoff participated in a transaction that involved the use of a financial institution that was engaged in, or the activities of which affected, interstate or foreign commerce *in any way or degree.*

The government argues that it proved Tarkoff participated in a 'financial transaction' as defined in section 1956(c)(4)(A) by virtue of the evidence that Tarkoff and Fernandez, two U.S. citizens, traveled from the United States to Israel to transact business with a bank there, and that the Israeli bank transactions required telephone communication between Israel and Miami, and between Miami and Curacao, to arrange for the funds transfer from Curacao to Israel. We agree that these facts support a finding that Tarkoff participated in a "financial transaction" as that term is defined in 18 U.S.C. § 1956(c)(4)(A) because the international travel and communication required to execute the wire transactions affected foreign commerce "in any way or degree." The evidence also supports a finding that Tarkoff participated in a "financial transaction" as that term is defined in 18 U.S.C. § 1956(c)(4)(B) because the transactions involved the use of the Israeli bank-a financial institution which, by communicating with parties in the United States and providing banking services to United States citizens, was a "financial institution that was engaged in, or the activities of which affected, foreign commerce in any way or degree." * * *

Because Tarkoff knowingly participated in a financial transaction designed in whole or in part to conceal or disguise the nature, the location, the source, the ownership, or the control of the proceeds of specified unlawful activity, we affirm his conviction for violating and conspiring to violate 18 U.S.C. § 1956(a)(1)(B)(i).

CHAPTER THREE
CORPORATE AND INDIVIDUAL RESPONSIBILITY

A. CORPORATE LIABILITY

1. Introduction

NEW YORK CENTRAL & HUDSON RIVER RAILROAD COMPANY
v. UNITED STATES
212 U.S. 481, 29 S.Ct. 304, 53 L.Ed. 613 (1909)

Justice DAY delivered the opinion of the Court.

* * * The principal attack in this court is upon the constitutional validity of certain features of the Elkins act. That act, among other things, provides:

> (1) That anything done or omitted to be done by a corporation common carrier subject to the act to regulate commerce, and the acts amendatory thereof, which, if done or omitted to be done by any director or officer thereof, or any receiver, trustee, lessee, agent, or person acting for or employed by such corporation, would constitute a misdemeanor under said acts, or under this act, shall also be held to be a misdemeanor committed by such corporation; and, upon conviction thereof, it shall be subject to like penalties as are prescribed in said acts, or by this act, with reference to such persons, except as such penalties are herein changed.   * * *

> In construing and enforcing the provisions of this section, the act, omission, or failure of any officer, agent, or other person acting for or employed by any common carrier, acting within the scope of his employment, shall, in every case, be also deemed to be the act, omission, or failure of such carrier, as well as that of the person.

It is contended that these provisions of the law are unconstitutional because Congress has no authority to impute to a corporation the commission of criminal offenses, or to subject a corporation to a criminal prosecution by reason of the things charged. The argument is that to thus punish the corporation is in reality to punish the innocent stockholders, and to deprive them of their property without opportunity to be heard, consequently without due process of law. And it is further contended that these provisions of the statute deprive the corporation of the presumption of innocence,—a presumption which is part of due process in criminal prosecutions. It is urged that, as there is no authority shown by the board of directors or the stockholders for the criminal acts of the agents of the company, in contracting for and giving rebates, they could not be lawfully charged against the corporation. As no action of the board of directors could legally authorize a crime, and as, indeed, the stockholders could not do so, the arguments come to this: that, owing to the nature and character of its organization and the extent of its power and authority, a corporation cannot commit a crime of the nature charged in this case.

Some of the earlier writers on common law held the law to be that a corporation could not commit a crime. It is said to have been held by Lord Chief Justice Holt that "a corporation is not indictable, although the particular members of it are." In Blackstone's Commentaries, we find it stated: "A corporation cannot commit treason, or felony, or other crime in its corporate capacity, though its members may, in their distinct individual capacities." The modern authority, universally, so far as we know, is the other way. In considering the subject, Bishop's New Criminal Law, § 417, devotes a chapter to the capacity of corporations to commit crime, and states the law to be: "Since a corporation acts by its officers and agents, their purposes, motives, and intent are just as much those of the corporation as are the things done. If, for example, the invisible, intangible essence or air which we term a corporation can level mountains, fill up valleys, lay down iron tracks, and run railroad cars on them, it can intend to do it, and can act therein as well viciously as virtuously." Without citing the state cases holding the same view, we may note Telegram Newspaper Co. v. Commonwealth, 172 Mass. 294, 52 N.E. 445, in which it was held that a corporation was subject to punishment for criminal contempt; and the court, speaking by Mr. Chief Justice Field, said: "We think that a corporation may be liable criminally for certain offenses of which a specific intent may be a necessary element. There is no more difficulty in imputing to a corporation a specific intent in criminal proceedings than in civil. A corporation cannot be arrested and imprisoned in either civil or criminal proceedings, but its property may be taken either as compensation for a private wrong or as punishment for a public wrong."
* * *

It is now well established that, in actions for tort, the corporation may be held responsible for damages for the acts of its agent within the scope of his employment. * * * And this is the rule when the act is done by the agent in the course of his employment, although done wantonly or recklessly or against the express orders of the principal. In such cases the liability is not imputed because the principal actually participates in the malice or fraud, but because the act is done for the benefit of the principal, while the agent is acting within the scope of his employment in the business of the principal, and justice requires that the latter shall be held responsible for damages to the individual who has suffered by such conduct.

A corporation is held responsible for acts not within the agent's corporate powers strictly construed, but which the agent has assumed to perform for the corporation when employing the corporate powers actually authorized, and in such cases there need be no written authority under seal or vote of the corporation in order to constitute the agency or to authorize the act.

In this case we are to consider the criminal responsibility of a corporation for an act done while an authorized agent of the company is exercising the authority conferred upon him. It was admitted by the defendant at the trial that, at the time mentioned in the indictment, the general freight traffic manager and the assistant freight traffic manager were authorized to establish rates at which freight should be carried over the line of the New York Central & Hudson River Company, and were authorized to unite with other companies in the establishing, filing, and publishing of through rates, including the through rate or rates between New York and Detroit referred to in the indictment. Thus, the subject-matter of making and fixing rates was within the scope of the authority and employment of the agents of the company, whose acts in this connection are sought to be charged upon the company. Thus clothed with authority, the agents were bound to respect the regulation of interstate commerce enacted by Congress, requiring the filing and publication of rates and punishing departures therefrom. Applying the principle governing civil liability, we go only a step farther in holding that the act of the agent, while exercising the authority delegated to him to make rates for transportation, may be controlled, in the interest of public policy, by imputing his act to his employer and imposing penalties upon the corporation for which he is acting in the premises.

It is true that there are some crimes which, in their nature, cannot be committed by corporations. But there is a large class of offenses, of which rebating under the Federal statutes is one, wherein the crime consists in purposely doing the things prohibited by statute. In that class of crimes we see no good reason why corporations may not be held responsible for and charged with the knowledge and purposes of their agents, acting within the authority conferred upon them. If it were not so, many offenses might go unpunished and acts be committed in violation of law where, as in the present case, the statute requires all persons, corporate or private, to refrain from certain practices, forbidden in the interest of public policy.   * * *

We see no valid objection in law, and every reason in public policy, why the corporation, which profits by the transaction, and can only act through its agents and officers, shall be held punishable by fine because of the knowledge and intent of its agents to whom it has intrusted authority to act in the subject-matter of making and fixing rates of transportation, and whose knowledge and purposes may well be attributed to the corporation for which the agents act. While the law should have regard to the rights of all, and to those of corporations no less than to those of individuals, it cannot shut its eyes to the fact that the great majority of business transactions in modern times are conducted through these bodies, and particularly that interstate commerce is almost entirely in their hands, and to give them immunity from all punishment because of the old and exploded doctrine that a corporation cannot commit a crime would virtually take away the only means of effectually controlling the subject-matter and correcting the abuses aimed at.

There can be no question of the power of Congress to regulate interstate commerce, to prevent favoritism, and to secure equal rights to all engaged in interstate trade. It would be a distinct step backward to hold that Congress cannot control those who are conducting this interstate commerce by holding them responsible for the intent and purposes of the agents to whom they have delegated the power to act in the premises.   * * *

NOTES AND QUESTIONS

1. *Development of Corporate Criminal Liability.*   At common law, corporations were not subject to criminal liability. "[I]t had no mind, and thus was incapable of the criminal intent then required for all crimes; it had no body, and thus could not be imprisoned." WAYNE R. LAFAVE & AUSTIN W. SCOTT, JR., CRIMINAL LAW 2D ED. 257 (1986). The development of corporate criminal liability initially occurred in regulatory offenses involving acts of omission.   This extension was consistent with the arguments that a corporation could not form intent and could not be imprisoned. Since these offenses involved strict liability crimes, requiring no *mens rea*, and assessed a penalty of merely a fine, a corporation could legitimately be subject to criminal liability.   Ellen S. Podgor, *Corporate and White Collar Crime: Simplifying the Ambiguous*, 31 AM. CRIM. L. REV. 391, 394 (1994). To what extent does *New York Central* extend corporate criminal liability beyond the strict liability realm?

2. *Corporate Sentencing.* At the time of *New York Central,* a finding of corporate criminal liability meant that fines could be imposed against the corporation. Today the consequences to the corporation include a range of sanctions beyond those imposed at the time of *New York Central.* The Organizational Sentencing Guidelines increase fines and also provide for sanctions such as restitution and court-ordered compliance programs. Consideration is given to organizational culpability. [Chapter 17, pt. E].

3. *Pros/Cons of Corporate Criminal Liability.* As a matter of legislative policy, does it make sense to have corporate criminal liability?   Does corporate criminal liability in fact impose punishment on innocent shareholders, as argued in *New York Central?* Will the real effect of corporate criminal liability be to punish the consumer by increasing the cost of products in the market? Does competition within the market balance these concerns? See FRANCIS T. CULLEN, WILLIAM J. MAAKESTAD, GRAY CAVENDER, CORPORATE CRIME UNDER ATTACK: THE FORD PINTO CASE AND BEYOND 352-53 (1987) (rejects the argument that corporate criminal fines will just result in increased prices to consumers). See also Jennifer Arlen, *Rewarding Whistleblowers: The Costs and Benefits of an Incentive-Based Compliance Strategy, in* CORPORATE DECISION-MAKING IN CANADA (Ronald Daniels &

RANDALL MORCK EDS., 1995); Jennifer Arlen, *The Potentially Perverse Effects of Corporate Criminal Liability,* 23 J. OF LEGAL STUD. 833 (1994).

4. *Deterrence.* Does the imposition of corporate criminal liability truly serve as a deterrent of future criminality? "Corporations are largely undeterrable; fines are ineffective, and only the imprisonment of guilty individuals achieves real deterrence." John S. Coffee, Jr., *Corporate Criminal Responsibility,* 1 ENCYCLOPEDIA OF CRIME AND JUSTICE 257 (1983). Could deterrence be better accomplished by using civil remedies? See Eliezer Lederman, *Criminal Law, Perpetrator and Corporation: Rethinking a Complex Triangle,* 76 J. CRIM. L. & CRIMINOLOGY 285, 315-16 (1985); V.S. Khanna, *Corporate Criminal Liability: What Purpose Does It Serve?,* 109 HARV. L. REV. 1477 (1996). Consider the following from Joe D. Whitley, Marc N. Garber, Mark A. McCarty, and Steven D. Henry, *The Case for Reevaluating DOJ Policies on Prosecuting White Collar Crime,* Washington Legal Foundation, Working Paper Series No. 108, May 2002, at 14-15:

> In the case of a corporate conviction, a wide variety of individuals are punished, including the corporation's shareholders and its innocent employees. Such shareholders and innocent employees will have had no involvement in the wrongful conduct and may not have benefitted from it. As a result, no just retribution is dispensed when they are punished along with the truly culpable parties. Moreover, because these individuals most likely lacked the ability to prevent the wrongful conduct, punishing such individuals does not provide any deterrent effect on other, similarly situated shareholders and innocent employees who may, likewise, be unable to stop wrongful conduct in their own organization.

5. *Government Position on Corporate Criminal Liability.* On July 25, 2002, in a speech to the Citizens' Crime Commission in New York, Deputy Attorney General Larry D. Thompson, who also served as Chair of the Corporate Fraud Task Force, ad interagency group, stated:

> Although it should be done sparingly, we should never hesitate to prosecute corporations themselves when the circumstances warrant it. * * * [T]he reasons why I believe that it is imperative to continue to prosecute business organizations where appropriate:

> First, corporations are economic and cultural facts in our society. Employees act on the corporation's behalf and take on the corporation's identity. Large corporations, develop their own methods and culture that guide employees' thoughts and actions. That culture is a web of attitudes and practices that tends to replicate and perpetuate itself beyond the tenure of any individual manager. That culture may instill respect for the law or breed contempt and malfeasance. The organization itself must be held accountable for the culture and the conduct it promotes. Without this tool, the public would have no adequate deterrent to corporate

criminal conduct because the culture that condoned, or at least acquiesced in, that behavior would be beyond the criminal law's power to correct. Only by clearly preserving the possibility of prosecuting the corporation itself can we ensure systemic reform.

Second, the corporations that are prosecuted have generally transgressed before and proven themselves immune to civil persuasion. The Justice Department has long recognized the principle that an employee's criminal wrongdoing does not mean that the employing organization should automatically be charged with a crime, especially where it would not serve a substantial federal interest to prosecute and adequate non-criminal alternatives exist. In reality, the corporations that are criminally prosecuted - that is, for which the enforcement authorities choose to subject their case to the criminal standard of proof beyond a reasonable doubt - are ones in which the company has flagrantly crossed the line in one or more ways that demonstrate that the guilty mind of individual actors was borne out of the guilty culture of the organization itself.

Third, civil regulatory regimes may do a good job sorting out the normal range of problems in an industry, but it takes criminal sanctions to deal with extreme cases of serious or repeated wrongdoing. Traditional civil remedies have proven ineffective against recidivist companies that are the primary targets of criminal prosecution. Civil sanctions simply do not have the power of criminal penalties to concentrate the corporate mind and change corporate culture. Large business organizations, particularly public companies that are already regulated in myriad ways, sometimes have the disappointing tendency to view civil sanctions as merely the "cost of doing business" - a cost that can be passed on to customers and shareholders without lingering effect in the management suite and the board room. Civil sanctions are particularly impotent in combating crimes against society at large, such as regulatory reporting violations or obstruction of justice, that may undermine the legal system, but do not create easily quantifiable harm. The severe potential collateral consequences to a corporation resulting from a criminal conviction is sometime the best and most effective way to punish a corporation.

Without corporate criminal liability, there would be no effective deterrent to a corporate culture that -- expressly or tacitly -- condones criminal conduct. * * *

6. *Good Faith Defense.*   Should a corporation that acts in good faith be entitled to a defense when a rogue employee within the corporation fails to abide by a corporate compliance program that has been properly administered? A good faith defense is offered to companies in civil actions when facing respondeat superior in tort. See Burlington Industries v. Ellerth, 524 U.S. 742 (1998)(providing an affirmative defense for corporations

in sexual harassment cases). Amici, in the case of **United States v. Ionia Management S.A.,** 555 F.3d 303 (2d Cir. 2009), suggested that the court consider such an affirmative defense, but the Second Circuit stated that "regardless of asserted new Supreme Court cases in other areas of the law," there was no precedent for an affirmative defense for corporate criminal liability. The court stated that "a corporate compliance program may be relevant to whether an employee was acting in the scope of his employment, but it is not a separate element." See Andrew Weissmann & David Newman, *Rethinking Criminal Corporate Liability,* 82 IND. L.J. 411 (2007). Good faith may be considered by the court in imposing a sentence on the corporation. See Chapter 17.

2. "For the Benefit"

STANDARD OIL COMPANY OF TEXAS v. UNITED STATES
307 F.2d 120 (5th Cir. 1962)

BROWN, Circuit Judge.

This appeal by two corporate defendants [Standard and Pasotex], from fines imposed on judgments of conviction under the Connally Hot Oil Act, raises this basic question. May a corporate employer be held liable for a crime committed by employees who, although ostensibly acting in the performance of their duties, were really cooperating with a third person in the accomplishment of a criminal purpose for the benefit of that third person, and whose acts not only did not benefit the employer, but in some instances, at least, result in a theft of its property? * * *

* * * Standard's interest [here] was limited to that of a purchaser having a statutory duty of buying oil tendered to it by Thompson and other producers in the field.

* * * Thompson has nine wells. Some were capable of producing their daily allowable under rules of the Texas Railroad Commission. Some of them could not. But under the Texas Conservation Laws and Regulations, the underage from one lease may not be made up from other commonly owned leases which have a capacity in excess of their assigned allowables. Oil swapped in this fashion is most certainly hot oil under the Connally Act which, forbidding "the transportation in interstate commerce * * * of contraband oil * * *," 15 U.S.C.A. § 715b, defines this as "petroleum which, * * * was produced * * * or withdrawn * * * in excess of the amounts permitted to be produced * * * or withdrawn * * * under the laws of a State * * *," 15 U.S.C.A. § 715a(1).

Over a period of approximately twelve months, Morgan (or Hart as his relief) issued false run tickets covering oil supposedly received at Pumping Station No. 2 from or produced by specified Thompson wells. Some of these purported to show that the oil actually received (and receipted for) was produced by a given well rather than the one from which it was known by Morgan (or Hart) to have come. But in numerous other instances, a false run ticket was used showing receipt of Thompson oil which had never been produced or received at all. For rendering this vital and knowing participation in these two schemes which benefited Thompson, these two Pasotex [Standard's wholly owner subsidiary] employees were paid or received substantial sums in cash or merchandise from Thompson.

In those instances where, though receipted for, no oil was actually received at Pumping Station No. 2, a new problem came up. Oil received at Station No. 2 moved to Station No. 1 where Purcell was in charge. But since Station No. 2 had less oil than it had receipted for, the shortage continued at Station No. 1 when No. 2 "moved" all of its oil to No. 1. This was an actual shortage of oil in contrast to mere swapping of oil among leases. This shortage had to be made up or the whole scheme would collapse.

* * * As operator of Segment 1 of SACROC, [Standard] operated all of the wells * * *. It therefore had control over the movement of the oil from the leases. More than that, by reason of the unitizing agreement Standard was an owner of a substantial undivided interest (approximately 19%) in all such oil. Purcell, aware of the continuing shortages from Station No. 2, gave instructions to pumpers to increase production from Segment 1 sufficient to make up the shortage. This amounted to 6,000 or so barrels every month for a considerable period. Records, of course, had to be falsified so that this "excess" oil moving through Station No. 1 to make up Station No. 2 "shortages" would be concealed. Standard had still another role. It was the purchaser of the oil. Since this make-up of Station No. 2 shortage was the only way Standard was getting oil ostensibly purchased earlier by it from Thompson at Station No. 2, Standard was, in effect, paying Thompson for oil which belonged to Standard (and the other Unit co-owners).

How Standard or Pasotex may be held criminally liable for "knowingly violating" the statute by transportation of oil " * * * produced * * * in excess of the amounts permitted to be produced * * * under the laws of (the) state" of Texas when all of such oil came into the custody of each corporation solely as a result of a deliberate purpose by unfaithful employees to cheat or steal is the legal question for our determination. Adding irony to what some might regard as amazement is the fact that the very first moment knowledge of this activity came to light, Pasotex, after preliminary verification of its suspicions, reported the matter immediately to the Texas Railroad Commission. Thereafter followed this prosecution.

We start with the proposition that what is involved is statutory construction. We may assume that Congress can subject corporations to criminal accountability for acts of this kind committed by unfaithful servants. But the question is whether any such purpose was intended with regard to the Connally Hot Oil Act.

Since the record is absolutely barren of even the most remote whisper of suspicion that this was the case of corporations winking at dereliction by energetic, zealous employees, the Government stresses, for both a legal and psychological purpose, the contention that the two corporations received some benefit. But as we point out later, no benefit was either intended or obtained.

We have some difficulty in understanding the contentions which the Government makes in its effort to support the District Court's finding of guilt which, in turn, was based almost wholly on the idea that what these unfaithful agents were doing was their usual function for the corporation. * * *

As this statute prescribes a mental state as an element of the crime, usual principles must be applied in order to impute to the lifeless legal entity the requisite knowledge. So far as this case is concerned, we do not have to deal with the difficult and troublesome problem of determining whether the "knowledge" required is merely of the actions which constitute the crime as is true of some offenses, or whether it requires the so called "evil intent," that is a consciousness that the actions taken violate a known law. We may assume that the standard is the less exacting one and is satisfied if the evidence shows beyond a reasonable doubt that the acts were done "* * * deliberately and with knowledge * * *" and were "* * * not * * * merely careless or negligent or inadvertent. * * *" Browder v. United States, 312 U.S. 335, 341(1941).

The corporations can be found guilty, therefore, only if the evidence shows that each, acting through its human agents, deliberately did these acts, that is, with the corporation "knowing" that they were being done for it. Inquiry along this line brings us face-to-face with the everyday problem of imputing knowledge to a corporation.

* * * [T]he Court, in recognizing that Congress has the power to "personify the company" and thereby charge a partnership entity with criminal liability, spelled out that it was "through the doctrine of respondeat superior" that "corporations and other * * * impersonal entities can be guilty of 'knowing' or 'willful' violations of regulatory statutes * * *." United States v. A. & P. Trucking Co., 358 U.S. 121 (1958). And again the rationale is couched in the familiar concepts of civil tort law of (1) a purpose to benefit the corporation and (2) an act by an agent in line of his duties. "The treasury of the business may not with impunity obtain the fruits of violations which are committed knowingly by agents of the entity in the scope of their employment."

Of course the defendants do not contend, nor could they, that criminal accountability and actual benefit are equated. There have been many cases, and there may well be others in the future, in which the corporation is criminally liable even though no benefit has been received in fact. But while benefit is not essential in terms of result, the purpose to benefit the corporation is decisive in terms of equating the agent's action with that of the corporation. For it is an elementary principle of agency that "an act of a servant is not within the scope of employment if it is done with no intention to perform it as a part of or incident to a service on account of which he is employed." Restatement of the Law of Agency (2d) § 235.

It is for this reason that the simple "function" test applied by the District Court—while obviously a factor of relevance—is alone insufficient upon which to rest convictions here. Thus the taking in or paying out of money by a bank teller, while certainly one of his regular functions, would hardly cast the corporation for criminal liability if in such "handling" the faithless employee was pocketing the funds as an embezzler or handing them over to a confederate under some ruse.   * * *

On the facts of this record, only the most hypercritical, artificial view would find any benefit intended by the actions of Morgan, Hart or Purcell. * * * Standard's oil was either stolen from it or it was, through these faithless agents, compelled to pay twice for oil supposedly purchased by it from Thompson. While the matter is not a spectacular theft as to Pasotex, it is equally positive that no benefit was conferred, nor, as the critical thing, was one intended by the actions taken at Pumping Station No. 2 by Hart and Morgan. * * * As ostensible employees of Pasotex, they were each in the secret pay of Thompson for the purpose of assisting him in violating Texas (and hence federal) law through the movement and sale of oil produced in violation of applicable Texas statutes and regulations. Their purpose was to aid Thompson in his criminal enterprise. Of course it could not succeed for Thompson unless, through these false run tickets, the oil could be channeled into legitimate commercial transportation facilities. Without Pasotex and its pipeline transportation, and without Standard's purchase of such "hot" or non-existent oil, Thompson could not succeed. But Hart and Morgan were doing their usual tasks in handling run tickets not to advance or further the interest of Pasotex. This was done to further the criminal enterprise of which they were an indispensable part.

Hart and Morgan and Purcell each knew what he did and what he was doing. But to say that acts done by servants actuated by such evil and specifically unlawful motives were the acts of the very corporations thus sought to be cheated or implicated in practices known to be in serious violation of law and, moreover, to impute not only accountability but "knowledge" of such acts to the corporations, would be to disregard every accepted notion of respondeat superior. For these corporations to be found guilty of violating the Connally Hot Oil Act we may assume that it is not necessary to prove that through imputation each corporation consciously knew that the acts being done were in violation of the law. But to subject these corporations to criminal accountability it was necessary on accepted principles of imputation for each to know that these acts of Morgan, Hart and Purcell were being done. Under a statute requiring that there be "a specific wrongful intent," and the "presence of culpable intent as a necessary element of the offense * * *," the corporation does not acquire that knowledge or possess the requisite "state of mind essential for responsibility," through the activities of unfaithful servants whose conduct was undertaken to advance the interests of parties other than their corporate employer.   * * *

As to all counts, therefore, the judgments of conviction as to the corporate defendants must be reversed and rendered in favor of the appellants.

UNITED STATES v. HILTON HOTELS CORP.
467 F.2d 1000 (9th Cir. 1972)

BROWNING, Circuit Judge.

This is an appeal from a conviction under an indictment charging a violation of section 1 of the Sherman Act, 15 U.S.C. § 1.

Operators of hotels, restaurants, hotel and restaurant supply companies, and other businesses in Portland, Oregon, organized an association to attract conventions to their city. To finance the association, members were asked to make contributions in predetermined amounts. Companies selling supplies to hotels were asked to contribute an amount equal to one per cent of their sales to hotel members. To aid collections, hotel members, including appellant, agreed to give preferential treatment to suppliers who paid their assessments, and to curtail purchases from those who did not.

I

The jury was instructed that such an agreement by the hotel members, if proven, would be a per se violation of the Sherman Act. [The court rejected a challenge to that charge.] * * *

II

Appellant's president testified that it would be contrary to the policy of the corporation for the manager of one of its hotels to condition purchases upon payment of a contribution to a local association by the supplier. The manager of appellant's Portland hotel and his assistant testified that it was the hotel's policy to purchase supplies solely on the basis of price, quality, and service. They also testified that on two occasions they told the hotel's purchasing agent that he was to take no part in the boycott. The purchasing agent confirmed the receipt of these instructions, but admitted that, despite them, he had threatened a supplier with loss of the hotel's business unless the supplier paid the association assessment. He testified that he violated his instructions because of anger and personal pique toward the individual representing the supplier.

Based upon this testimony, appellant requested certain instructions bearing upon the criminal liability of a corporation for the unauthorized acts of its agents. These requests were rejected by the trial court. The court instructed the jury that a corporation is liable for the acts and statements of its agents "within the scope of their employment," defined to mean "in the corporation's behalf in performance of the agent's general line of work," including "not only that which has been authorized by the corporation, but also that which outsiders could reasonably assume the agent would have authority to do." The court added:

> "A corporation is responsible for acts and statements of its agents, done or made within the scope of their employment, even though their conduct may be contrary to their actual instructions or contrary to the corporation's stated policies."

Appellant objects only to the court's concluding statement.   * * * The breadth and critical character of the public interests protected by the Sherman Act, and the gravity of the threat to those interests that led to the enactment of the statute, support a construction holding business organizations accountable, as a general rule, for violations of the Act by their employees in the course of their businesses. In enacting the Sherman Act, "Congress was passing drastic legislation to remedy a threatening danger to the public welfare. . . ." United Mine Workers v. Coronado Coal Co., 259 U.S. 344 (1922). The statute "was designed to be a comprehensive charter of economic liberty aimed at preserving free and unfettered competition as the rule of trade. It rests on the premise that the unrestrained interaction of competitive forces will yield the best allocation of our economic resources, the lowest prices, the highest quality and the greatest material progress, while at the same time providing an environment conducive to the preservation of our democratic political and social institutions." Northern Pacific Ry. v. United States.

With such important public interests at stake, it is reasonable to assume that Congress intended to impose liability upon business entities for the acts of those to whom they choose to delegate the conduct of their affairs, thus stimulating a maximum effort by owners and managers to assure adherence by such agents to the requirements of the Act.   * * *

Because of the nature of Sherman Act offenses and the context in which they normally occur, the factors that militate against allowing a corporation to disown the criminal acts of its agents apply with special force to Sherman Act violations.

Sherman Act violations are commercial offenses. They are usually motivated by a desire to enhance profits. They commonly involve large, complex, and highly decentralized corporate business enterprises, and intricate business processes, practices, and arrangements. More often than not they also involve basic policy decisions, and must be implemented over an extended period of time.

Complex business structures, characterized by decentralization and delegation of authority, commonly adopted by corporations for business purposes, make it difficult to identify the particular corporate agents responsible for Sherman Act violations. At the same time, it is generally true that high management officials, for whose conduct the corporate directors and stockholders are the most clearly responsible, are likely to have participated in the policy decisions underlying Sherman Act violations, or at least to have become aware of them.

Violations of the Sherman Act are a likely consequence of the pressure to maximize profits that is commonly imposed by corporate owners upon managing agents and, in turn, upon lesser employees. In the face of that pressure, generalized directions to obey the Sherman Act, with the probable effect of foregoing profits, are the least likely to be taken seriously. And if a violation of the Sherman Act occurs, the corporation, and not the individual agents, will have realized the profits from the illegal activity.

In sum, identification of the particular agents responsible for a Sherman Act violation is especially difficult, and their conviction and punishment is peculiarly ineffective as a deterrent. At the same time, conviction and punishment of the business entity itself is likely to be both appropriate and effective.

For these reasons we conclude that as a general rule a corporation is liable under the Sherman Act for the acts of its agents in the scope of their employment, even though contrary to general corporate policy and express instructions to the agent.

Thus the general policy statements of appellant's president were no defense. Nor was it enough that appellant's manager told the purchasing agent that he was not to participate in the boycott. The purchasing agent was authorized to buy all of appellant's supplies. Purchases were made on the basis of specifications, but the purchasing agent exercised complete authority as to source. He was in a unique position to add the corporation's buying power to the force of the boycott. Appellant could not gain exculpation by issuing general instructions without undertaking to enforce those instructions by means commensurate with the obvious risks.   * * *

Affirmed.

NOTES AND QUESTIONS

1. *Statutory Basis for Corporate Liability.* To what extent is the imposition of corporate criminal liability contingent upon the statute the defendant is alleged to have violated? (E.g., Connolly Act, Sherman Act.) How does the statute's *mens rea*, or lack thereof, impact a finding of corporate criminal liability? Consider also Sea Horse Ranch v. Superior Court, 30 Cal.

Rptr. 2d 681 (Ct. App. 1994) (court considers, in the context of a probable cause determination, whether a president of a corporation and the corporation can be held criminally liable for involuntary manslaughter).

2. *Determining "For the Benefit"*. Should the benefit incurred to the corporation be used only to determine whether an agency relationship exists, or should it also serve as a basis for imposing criminal liability? Should a commercial focus of a statute be conclusive for finding that an agent's acts benefit the corporation? Can market supply and demand play a factor in determining whether acts of an agent are for the benefit of the corporation?

3. *Jury Unanimity*. What happens when the jury concurs that actors on behalf of the corporation violated the law, but the jury does not concur on the same actors? Are the acts of different officers separate "violations" or do they supply different "means"? In United States v. Andersen [p. 339], the jury asked whether it was necessary for them to agree on the individual employee who violated the law that served as the basis for a charge of obstruction of justice. The judge ruled that it was not necessary for the jurors to agree on which Andersen employee "had the intent to commit the crime," as they all agreed that someone from the a corporation intended to obstruct justice by impeding the investigation. See Kurt Eichenwald, *Judges Ruling on Andersen Hurts Defense,* June 15, 2002, at C1. But see Richardson v. United States, 526 U.S. 813, 815 (1999) (finding that "a jury in a federal criminal case brought under § 848 must unanimously agree not only that the defendant committed some 'continuing series of violations' but also that the defendant committed each of the individual 'violations' necessary to make up that continuing series.").

3. Restricting Corporate Criminal Liability

Corporate criminal liability has continually been the subject of criticism. The focus of much of this criticism has been on the disadvantages inherent in using a *respondeat superior* and vicarious liability approach in criminal law. It has been claimed that:

1. Vicarious liability is appropriate only as a principle of tort law since its justification lies in its allocation of the loss to the party more able to bear it (or at least more deserving of the burden), but it is unrelated to the purposes of retribution, deterrence, prevention, and rehabilitation that underlie the criminal law.

2. Vicarious liability is unjust because its burden falls on the innocent rather than the guilty—that is, the penalty is borne by stockholders and others having an interest in the corporation, rather than by the guilty individual.

3. Vicarious liability results in a disparity between businesses conducted in the corporate form and those run as a proprietorship, since the individual proprietor will not be criminally liable for independent acts of his employees.

4. Vicarious liability for the corporation may in the future open the door to expanded vicarious criminal liability for individuals as well.

John C. Coffee, Jr., *Corporate Criminal Responsibility,* 1 ENCYCLOPEDIA OF CRIME AND JUSTICE 257 (1983).

MODEL PENAL CODE

Section 2.07. Liability of Corporations, Unincorporated Associations and Persons Acting, or Under a Duty to Act, in Their Behalf.

(1) A corporation may be convicted of the commission of an offense if:

(a) the offense is a violation or the offense is defined by a statute other than the Code in which a legislative purpose to impose liability on corporations plainly appears and the conduct is performed by an agent of the corporation acting in behalf of the corporation within the scope of his office or employment, except that if the law defining the offense designates the agents for whose conduct the corporation is accountable, such provisions shall apply; or

(b) the offense consists of an omission to discharge a specific duty of affirmative performance imposed on corporations by law; or

(c) the commission of the offense was authorized, requested, commanded, performed or recklessly tolerated by the board of directors or by a high managerial agent acting in behalf of the corporation within the scope of his office or employment.

(2) When absolute liability is imposed for the commission of an offense, a legislative purpose to impose liability on a corporation shall be assumed, unless the contrary plainly appears.

* * *

(4) As used in this Section:

* * *

(c) "high managerial agent" means an officer of a corporation * * *, or any other agent of a corporation * * * having duties of such responsibility that his conduct may fairly be assumed to represent the policy of the corporation * * * .

(5) In any prosecution of a corporation * * * for the commission of an offense included within the terms of Subsection (1)(a) or Subsection (3)(a) of this Section, other than an offense for which absolute liability has been imposed, it shall be a defense if the defendant proves by a preponderance of evidence that the high managerial agent having supervisory responsibility over the subject matter of the offense employed due diligence to prevent its commission. This paragraph shall not apply if it is plainly inconsistent with the legislative purpose in defining the particular offense.

* * *

NOTES AND QUESTIONS

1. *Federal/Model Penal Code Distinction.* Federal courts and many state courts use the common law *respondeat superior* approach in assessing whether to impute the acts of an agent to the corporation for the purposes of criminal liability. These courts examine whether the agent acted within the scope of their employment and whether it was on behalf of the corporation. In contrast, the Model Penal Code focuses on whether the individual who committed the act was a "high managerial agent." Does the requirement of a "high managerial agent" unduly restrict corporate criminal liability? How difficult is it to discern whether an agent is a "high managerial agent?"

2. *Deficiencies of Model Penal Code Approach.* Do the acts of a high managerial agent truly have a connection with the blameworthiness of the corporation? See Brent Fisse, *Reconstructing Corporate Criminal Law: Deterrence, Retribution, Fault, and Sanctions*, 56 S. CAL. L. REV. 1141, 1186 (1983). In rejecting a Model Penal Code approach for imposing corporate criminal liability, the court in **Commonwealth v. Beneficial Finance Co.**, 275 N.E. 2d 33, 83 (Mass. 1971), stated:

> * * * [T]he title or position of an individual in a corporation should not be conclusively determinative in ascribing criminal responsibility. In a large corporation, with many numerous and distinct departments, a high ranking corporate officer or agent may have no authority or involvement in a particular sphere of corporate activity, whereas a lower ranking corporate executive might have much broader power in dealing with a matter peculiarly within the scope of his authority. Employees who are in the lower echelon of the corporate hierarchy often exercise more responsibility in the everyday operations of the corporation than the directors or officers. Assuredly, the title or office that the person holds may be considered, but it should not be the decisive criterion upon which to predicate corporate responsibility.

There has also been scholarly criticism of the Model Penal Code approach. See Michael E. Tigar, *Corporations' Liability for Criminal Acts*, National L.J., Vol. 8, No. 27, March 17, 1986, p. 15, cont. on p. 17.

3. *Corporate Dissolution.* Does criminal liability survive a corporate dissolution? See Melrose Distillers, Inc. v. United States, 359 U.S. 271 (1959) (Supreme Court permitted a criminal action against a corporation that had dissolved); see also United States v. Alamo Bank of Texas, 880 F.2d 828 (5th Cir. 1989). Does criminal liability transfer to successor corporations? See H. Lowell Brown, *Successor Corporate Criminal Liability: The Emerging Federal Common Law,* 49 ARK. L. REV. 469 (1996).

4. *Procedural Considerations.* The creation of corporate criminal liability does not have a bearing on the privilege against self-incrimination [p. 424], as the corporation has none. Thus corporate criminal liability does not expand the procedural protections with respect to investigations. Lawyer-client privileges and Fourth Amendment rights exist [p. 727], whether there is corporate liability or not.

4. Collective Knowledge

UNITED STATES v. BANK OF NEW ENGLAND
821 F.2d 844 (1st Cir. 1987)

BOWNES, Circuit Judge.

The Bank of New England appeals a jury verdict convicting it of thirty-one violations of the Currency Transaction Reporting Act (the Act). Department of Treasury regulations promulgated under the Act require banks to file Currency Transaction Reports (CTRs) within fifteen days of customer currency transactions exceeding $10,000. 31 C.F.R. § 103.22 (1986). The Act imposes felony liability when a bank willfully fails to file such reports "as part of a pattern of illegal activity involving transactions of more than $100,000 in a twelve-month period . . . ." 31 U.S.C. § 5322(b).

I. THE ISSUES

The Bank was found guilty of having failed to file CTRs on cash withdrawals made by James McDonough. It is undisputed that on thirty-one separate occasions between May 1983 and July 1984, McDonough withdrew from the Prudential Branch of the Bank more than $10,000 in cash by using multiple checks—each one individually under $10,000—presented simultaneously to a single bank teller. The Bank contends that such conduct did not trigger the Act's reporting requirements. * * * The Bank also argues that the trial judge's instructions on willfulness were fatally flawed, and that, in any event, the evidence did not suffice to show that it willfully failed to file CTRs on McDonough's transactions. * * *

The Bank had been named in a federal grand jury indictment which was returned on October 15, 1985. Count One of the indictment alleged that between May 1983 and May 1985, James McDonough, the Bank, and Carol Orlandella and Patricia Murphy—both of whom were former head tellers with the Bank's Prudential Branch—unlawfully conspired to conceal from the IRS thirty-six of McDonough's currency transactions. The trial court directed a verdict of acquittal on this count. Defendants Murphy and Orlandella were found not guilty of charges that they individually aided and abetted the failure to file CTRs on McDonough's transactions.

The bulk of the indictment alleged that the Bank, as principal, and McDonough, as an aider and abettor, willfully failed to file CTRs on thirty-six occasions between May 1983 and July 1984. Five counts were dismissed because, on those occasions, McDonough received cashier's checks from the Bank, rather than currency. McDonough was acquitted of all charges against him. The Bank was found guilty on the thirty-one remaining counts. We affirm.

II. THE REPORTABILITY OF McDONOUGH'S TRANSACTIONS

* * * On thirty-one occasions, James McDonough visited the same branch of the same bank at one time in a single day. He presented between two and four checks totalling more than $10,000 to one bank teller and received from the teller a single sum of cash in excess of $10,000. Since the regulations define transaction in currency to mean "the physical transfer of currency from one person to another," we hold that the Bank had adequate warning that a single, lump-sum transfer of cash exceeding $10,000 was reportable, regardless of the number of checks the customer uses to obtain the money.   * * *

IV. WILLFULNESS OF THE BANK'S CONDUCT

A. The Trial Court's Instruction on Willfulness

Criminal liability under 31 U.S.C. § 5322 only attaches when a financial institution "willfully" violates the CTR filing requirement. A finding of willfulness under the Reporting Act must be supported by "proof of the defendant's knowledge of the reporting requirements and his specific intent to commit the crime." Willfulness can rarely be proven by direct evidence, since it is a state of mind; it is usually established by drawing reasonable inferences from the available facts.

The Bank contends that the trial court's instructions on knowledge and specific intent effectively relieved the government of its responsibility to prove that the Bank acted willfully. The trial judge began her instructions on this element by outlining generally the concepts of knowledge and willfulness:

Knowingly simply means voluntarily and intentionally. It's designed to exclude a failure that is done by mistake or accident, or for some other innocent reason. Willfully means voluntarily, intentionally, and with a specific intent to disregard, to disobey the law, with a bad purpose to violate the law.

The trial judge properly instructed the jury that it could infer knowledge if a defendant consciously avoided learning about the reporting requirements. The court then focused on the kind of proof that would establish the Bank's knowledge of its filing obligations. The judge instructed that the knowledge of individual employees acting within the scope of their employment is imputed to the Bank. She told the jury that "if any employee knew that multiple checks would require the filing of reports, the bank knew it, provided the employee knew it within the scope of his employment, ..."

The trial judge then focused on the issue of "collective knowledge":

In addition, however, you have to look at the bank as an institution. As such, its knowledge is the sum of the knowledge of all of the employees. That is, the bank's knowledge is the totality of what all of the employees know within the scope of their employment. So, if Employee A knows one facet of the currency reporting requirement, B knows another facet of it, and C a third facet of it, the bank knows them all. So if you find that an employee within the scope of his employment knew that CTRs had to be filed, even if multiple checks are used, the bank is deemed to know it. The bank is also deemed to know it if each of several employees knew a part of that requirement and the sum of what the separate employees knew amounted to knowledge that such a requirement existed.

After discussing the two modes of establishing knowledge—via either knowledge of one of its individual employees or the aggregate knowledge of all its employees—the trial judge turned to the issue of specific intent:

There is a similar double business with respect to the concept of willfulness with respect to the bank. In deciding whether the bank acted willfully, again you have to look first at the conduct of all employees and officers, and, second, at what the bank did or did not do as an institution. The bank is deemed to have acted willfully if one of its employees in the scope of his employment acted willfully. So, if you find that an employee willfully failed to do what was necessary to file these reports, then that is deemed to be the act of the bank, and the bank is deemed to have willfully failed to file.
* * *

Alternatively, the bank as an institution has certain responsibilities; as an organization, it has certain responsibilities. And you will have to determine whether the bank as an organization consciously avoided learning about and observing CTR requirements. The

Government to prove the bank guilty on this theory, has to show that its failure to file was the result of some flagrant organizational indifference. In this connection, you should look at the evidence as to the bank's effort, if any, to inform its employees of the law; its effort to check on their compliance; its response to various bits of information that it got in August and September of '84 and February of '85; its policies, and how it carried out its stated policies.   * * *

If you find that the Government has proven with respect to any transaction either that an employee within the scope of his employment willfully failed to file a required report or that the bank was flagrantly indifferent to its obligations, then you may find that the bank has willfully failed to file the required reports.

The Bank contends that the trial court's instructions regarding knowledge were defective because they eliminated the requirement that it be proven that the Bank violated a known legal duty. It avers that the knowledge instruction invited the jury to convict the Bank for negligently maintaining a poor communications network that prevented the consolidation of the information held by its various employees. The Bank argues that it is error to find that a corporation possesses a particular item of knowledge if one part of the corporation has half the information making up the item, and another part of the entity has the other half.

A collective knowledge instruction is entirely appropriate in the context of corporate criminal liability. The acts of a corporation are, after all, simply the acts of all of its employees operating within the scope of their employment. The law on corporate criminal liability reflects this. Similarly, the knowledge obtained by corporate employees acting within the scope of their employment is imputed to the corporation. * * *   Corporations compartmentalize knowledge, subdividing the elements of specific duties and operations into smaller components. The aggregate of those components constitutes the corporation's knowledge of a particular operation. It is irrelevant whether employees administering one component of an operation know the specific activities of employees administering another aspect of the operation * * *: ["]Rather the corporation is considered to have acquired the collective knowledge of its employees and is held responsible for their failure to act accordingly.["] United States v. T.I.M.E.-D.C., Inc., 381 F.Supp. at 738. Since the Bank had the compartmentalized structure common to all large corporations, the court's collective knowledge instruction was not only proper but necessary.

Nor do we find any defects in the trial court's instructions on specific intent. The court told the jury that the concept of willfulness entails a voluntary, intentional, and bad purpose to disobey the law. Her instructions on this element, when viewed as a whole, directed the jury not to convict for accidental, mistaken or inadvertent acts or omissions. It is urged that the court erroneously charged that willfulness could be found via flagrant indifference by the Bank toward its reporting obligations. With respect to federal regulatory statutes, the Supreme Court has endorsed defining willfulness, in both civil and criminal contexts, as "a disregard for the governing statute and an indifference to its requirements." Trans World Airlines, Inc. v. Thurston, 469 U.S. 111, 127 & n. 20 (1985). Accordingly, we find no error in the court's instruction on willfulness.

B. Evidence of Willfulness

The Bank asserts that the evidence did not suffice to show that it had willfully failed to comply with the Act's reporting requirements. We review the evidence in the light most favorable to the government.

* * * [T]he language of the Treasury regulations itself gave notice that cash withdrawals over $10,000 were reportable, regardless of the number of checks used. Primary responsibility for CTR compliance in the Bank's branch offices was assigned to head tellers and branch managers. Head tellers Orlandella and Murphy, who knew of the nature of McDonough's transactions, also knew of the CTR filing obligations imposed by the Bank. The jury heard testimony from former bank teller Simona Wong, who stated that she knew McDonough's transactions were reportable, and that the source of her knowledge was head teller Murphy.

Even if some Bank personnel mistakenly regarded McDonough as engaging in multiple transactions, there was convincing evidence that the Bank knew that his withdrawals were reportable. An internal memo sent * * * to all branch managers and head tellers stated that "'[r]eportable transactions are expanded to include multiple transactions which aggregate more than $10,000 in any *one day*.' This includes deposits or withdrawals by a customer to or from more than one account." (Emphasis in original.) The Prudential Branch Manual instructed that if Bank personnel know that a customer has engaged in multiple transactions totalling $10,000 or more, then such transactions should be regarded as a single transaction. In addition, since 1980, the instructions on the back of CTR forms have directed that reports be filed on multiple transactions which aggregate to over $10,000. Finally, a Bank auditor discussed with Orlandella and Murphy, the Bank's obligation to report a customer's multiple transactions in a single day which amount to more than $10,000. We do not suggest that these evidentiary items in themselves legally bound the Bank to report McDonough's transactions; it is the language of the regulations that impose such a duty. This evidence, however, proved that the Bank had ample knowledge that transactions like McDonough's came within the purview of the Act.

Regarding the Bank's specific intent to violate the reporting obligation, Simona Wong testified that head teller Patricia Murphy knew that McDonough's transactions were reportable, but, on one occasion, deliberately chose not to file a CTR on him because he was "a good customer." In addition, the jury heard testimony that bank employees regarded McDonough's transactions as unusual, speculated that he was a bookie, and suspected that he was structuring his transactions to avoid the Act's reporting requirements. An internal Bank memo, written after an investigation of the McDonough transactions, concluded that a "person managing the branch would have to have known that something strange was going on." Given the suspicions aroused by McDonough's banking practices and the abundance of information indicating that his transactions were reportable, the jury could have concluded that the failure by Bank personnel to, at least, inquire about the reportability of McDonough's transactions constituted flagrant indifference to the obligations imposed by the Act.

We hold that the evidence was sufficient for a finding of willfulness. * * * Affirmed.

NOTES AND QUESTIONS

1. *Collective Knowledge.* Does holding a corporation liable based upon the "collective knowledge" of its employees add a new dimension to corporate criminal liability? Is "it better than designating a corporate officer as the 'Vice President in Charge of Going to Jail' or allowing wrongdoers to go unpunished"? Martin J. Weinstein & Patricia Bennett Ball, *Criminal Law's Greatest Mystery Thriller: Corporate Guilt Through Collective Knowledge*, 29 N. Eng. L. Rev. 65 (1994). How does this case impact information systems within corporations? Is this decision a recognition of the availability to corporations of technological advancements?

2. *"Corporate Ethos."* Professor Pamela H. Bucy, in her article *Corporate Ethos: A Standard for Imposing Corporate Criminal Liability*, 75 Minn. L. Rev. 1095, 1099 (1991), "proposes a standard of corporate criminal liability that uses a new conceptual paradigm for identifying and proving corporate intent." She states:

> * * * [E]ach corporate entity has a distinct and identifiable personality or "ethos." The government can convict a corporation under this standard only if it proves that the corporate ethos encouraged agents of the corporation to commit the criminal act. Central to this approach is the assumption that organizations possess an identity that is independent of specific individuals who control or work for the organization. This corporate identity, or "ethos," results from the dynamic of many individuals working together toward corporate goals. The living cell provides an apt analogy: Just as a living cell has an identity separate from the activities of its constituent molecules, a corporation has an identity separate from its individual agents.

3. *Corporate Self-Identity.* A new model of corporate criminal liability has been developing in legal literature. This new model, premised upon "self-identity," "resembles the theory of corporate organs." Eli Lederman, *Models*

for Imposing Corporate Criminal Liability: From Adaptation and Imitation Toward Aggregation and the Search for Self-Identity, 4 BUFF. CRIM. L. REV. 641, 678 (2000). "The chief assumption underlying the self-identity model of corporations is that a large organization is not only a collection of people who shape it and activate it, but also a set of attributes and positions, which influence, constrain, and at times even define the modes of thinking and behavior of the people who populate it..." Id. at 686.

5.   Government Responses to Corporate Misconduct

In the past few years, the government has proceeded against several major corporations with civil or criminal charges, although few actually proceed to trial. Many companies enter into deferred and non-prosecution agreements with the government. A variety of different terms and conditions can be found in these agreements. Some terms within these agreements, such as the non-payment of employees attorney fees [p. 777] and the waiver of attorney-client privilege, have been extremely controversial. Other less controversial terms include agreements to comply with the law and institute an effective compliance program. Consider the following different approaches taken by the government:

a. Faro Technologies. Faro Technologies entered into a non-prosecution agreement with the government and agreed to pay a $1.1 million dollar criminal fine "in connection with corrupt payments to Chinese government officials in violation of the Foreign Corrupt Practices Act (FCPA)." The Department of Justice Press Release (available at http://www.usdoj.gov/opa/pr/2008/ June/08-crm-505.html) states:

> In recognition of Faro's voluntary disclosure and thorough review of the improper payments, its cooperation with the Department's investigation, the company's implementation of and commitment to implement in the future enhanced compliance policies and procedures, and the company's agreement to engage an independent corporate monitor, the Department has agreed to enter into a non-prosecution agreement with a term of two years. If Faro abides by the terms of that agreement, the Department will not prosecute Faro for the conduct admitted in the statement of facts.

In a related matter, Faro agreed to the entry of a cease and desist order with the Securities and Exchange Commission and "to pay approximately $1.85 million in disgorgement and prejudgment interest in connection" with conduct similar to what was alleged by the Department of Justice.

b. UBS. UBS AG, Switzerland's largest bank entered into a deferred prosecution agreement on "charges of conspiring to defraud the United States by impeding the Internal revenue Service (IRS)." The DOJ Press Release announcing the agreement states that the company "agreed to immediately provide the United States government with the identities of, and account information for, certain United States customers of UBS's cross-border business." They also "agreed to expeditiously exit the business of providing banking services to United States clients with undeclared accounts," and they agreed to pay $780 million in fines, penalties, interest and restitution." See Press Release, *UBS Enters into Deferred Prosecution Agreement*, available at http://www.usdoj.gov/opa/pr/2009/ February/09-tax-136.html.

c. Archer Daniels.   Archer Daniels-Midland agreed to plead guilty to "conspiring with competitors to fix the prices of two agricultural products and pay $100 million in fines." "The settlement's most burdensome aspect for company employees may well be the cooperation agreement." "Archer Daniels will be required to dismiss employees [who have been granted immunity], who still fail to cooperate." Kurt Eichenwald, *Archer Daniels Agrees to Big Fine for Price Fixing*, N.Y. Times, Oct. 15, 1996, at A1; see also *Justice Department Hits ADM With $100 Million Criminal Fine. Shareholders, Victims Cry Foul*, 10 Corp. Crime Rep., No. 40, Oct. 21, 1996; Marilyn Geewax, *Punish White-Collar Criminals, Not Stockholders*, Atl. J./Const., Oct. 20, 1996, at H3; KURT EICHEHWALD, THE INFORMANT (2000); United States v. Andreas, 216 F.3d 645 (7th Cir. 2000).

d. Andersen. The government charged Arthur Andersen LLP, the auditor for Enron Corp., with obstruction of justice (18 U.S.C. § 1512(b)) for the alleged destruction of documents related to the Enron investigation. Anderson pled not guilty and proceeded to trial. After ten days of deliberation, the jury reached a verdict of guilty. The court sentenced Andersen to five years probation and a fine of $500,000. See Thereas M. Church, *Arthur Andersen Receives Probation, Fine*, Aberdeen Am. News, Oct. 17, 2002, at 7 (2002 WL 101098535) ("Probation seems like a hollow threat for a firm that shuttered its audit practice and closed offices across the country after its conviction in June."). A consequence of conviction can be exclusion as an auditor under SEC rules. Many clients left the partnership following indictment, but not all. See Ken Y. Chen & Jian Zhou, *Audit Committee, Board Characteristics and Auditor Switch Decisions by Andersen's Clients*, forthcoming *Contemporary Accounting Research*, available at http://papers.ssrn.com/sol3/papers.cfm? abstract_id=980938 (examining auditor switch decisions "where the auditor's reputation is clearly tarnished). Although the Supreme Court reversed the conviction, the partnership did not survive.

NOTES AND QUESTIONS

1. *Rationale for Different Approaches.* Do the different approaches taken by the government in Faro, UBS, Archer Daniels, and Andersen produce different results? Which, if any, is most likely to deter future corporate criminal conduct? Should the government have the discretion to chose a different approach for different types of conduct?

2. *Corporate Dilemma.* Are corporations placed in the position of having to accept a deferred prosecution agreement, and does the type of industry make

a difference in this decision? Is the stigma to the company more significant than the criminal penalty? In deciding on liability under a plea agreement, should the United States Attorney take into account potential civil liability that may accrue to the corporation as a result of the corporation pleading guilty or that collateral consequences may be more severe for certain companies?

3. *Corporation Versus Individual.* Does the prosecution of both the corporation and the individual increase the likelihood of a plea by one of these parties in return for their testimony against the other? What are the potential ramifications of pitting the corporation and the individuals working within the corporation against each other? See Ellen S. Podgor, Essay, *White Collar Cooperators: The Government in Employer-Employee Relationships,* 23 CARDOZO L. REV. 795 (2002). [See Chapter 15, pt. 3 & 4; Chapter 16].

4. *Government Policy.* The Department of Justice provides policy as to when it is appropriate to charge a corporation, although the policy has fluctuated under different Attorney Generals' administration. What does the government consider in deciding whether to prosecute a corporation? The Department of Justice Guidelines provide some general and specific guidance. Some of these guidelines are considered below:

9 - 28.200 - General Considerations of Corporate Liability

A.   General Principle: Corporations should not be treated leniently because of their artificial nature nor should they be subject to harsher treatment. Vigorous enforcement of the criminal laws against corporate wrongdoers, where appropriate, results in great benefits for law enforcement and the public, particularly in the area of white collar crime. Indicting corporations for wrongdoing enables the government to address and be a force for positive change of corporate culture, and a force to prevent, discover, and punish serious crimes. * * *

9 - 28.300 - Factors to Be Considered

A.   General Principle: Generally, prosecutors should apply the same factors in determining whether to charge a corporation as they do with respect to individuals.* * * Thus, the prosecutor should weigh all of the factors normally considered in the sound exercise of prosecutorial judgment: the sufficiency of the evidence, the likelihood of success at trial, the probable deterrent, rehabilitative, and other consequences of conviction, and the adequacy of non-criminal approaches. However, due to the nature of the corporate "person," some additional factors are present. In conducting an investigation, determining whether to bring charges, and negotiating plea or other agreements, prosecutors should consider the following factors in reaching a decision as to the proper treatment of a corporate target:

1. The nature and seriousness of the offense, including the risk of harm to the public, and applicable policies and priorities, if any, governing the prosecution of corporations for particular categories of crime * * *

2. The pervasiveness of wrongdoing within the corporation, including the complicity in, or the condoning of, the wrongdoing by corporate management * * *

3. The corporation's history of similar conduct, including prior criminal, civil, and regulatory enforcement actions against it * * *

4. The corporation's timely and voluntary disclosure of wrongdoing and its willingness to cooperate in the investigation of its agents, * * *

5. The existence and effectiveness of the corporation's existing compliance program * * *

6. The corporation's remedial actions, including any efforts to implement an effective corporate compliance program or to improve an existing one, to replace responsible management, to discipline or terminate wrongdoers, to pay restitution, and to cooperate with the relevant government agencies * * *

7. Collateral consequences, including whether there is disproportionate harm to shareholders, pension holders, employees, and others not proven personally culpable, as well as impact on the public arising from the prosecution * * *

8. The adequacy of the prosecution of individuals responsible for the corporation's malfeasance; and

9. The adequacy of remedies such as civil or regulatory enforcement actions * * *

9-28.400 - Special Policy Concerns

A.   General Principle: The nature and seriousness of the crime, including the risk of harm to the public from the criminal conduct, are obviously primary factors in determining whether to charge a corporation.   In addition, corporate conduct, particularly that of national and multi-national corporations, necessarily intersects with federal economic, tax, and criminal law enforcement policies. In applying these principles, prosecutors must consider the practices and policies of the appropriate Division of the Department, and must comply with those policies to the extent required.   * * *

9-28.500 - Pervasiveness of Wrongdoing Within the Corporation

A.   General Principle: A corporation can only act through natural persons, and it is therefore held responsible for the acts of such persons fairly attributable to it. Charging a corporation for even minor misconduct may be appropriate where the wrongdoing was pervasive and was undertaken by a large number of employees or by all the employees in a particular role within the corporation, or was condoned by upper management. On the other hand, it may not be appropriate to impose liability upon a corporation, particularly one with a robust compliance program in place, under a strict *respondeat superior* theory for the single isolated act of a rogue employee. There is, of course, a wide spectrum between these two extremes, and a prosecutor should exercise sound discretion in evaluating the pervasiveness of wrongdoing within a corporation. * * *

9-28.600 - The Corporation's Past History

A. General Principle: Prosecutors may consider a corporation's history of similar conduct, including prior criminal, civil, and regulatory enforcement actions against it, in determining whether to bring criminal charges and how best to resolve cases. * * *

9-29.700 - Cooperation and Voluntary Disclosure

A. General Principle: In determining whether to charge a corporation and how to resolve corporate cases, the corporation's timely and voluntary disclosure of wrongdoing and its cooperation with the government's investigation may be relevant factors. In gauging the extent of the corporation's cooperation, the prosecutor may consider among other things, whether the corporation made a voluntary and timely disclosure, and the corporation's willingness to provide relevant information and evidence and identify relevant actors within and outside the corporation, including senior executives. * * *

See also chapters 15 & 16. The guidelines also discuss other factors such as the attorney-client privilege (9-28.710), cooperation (9-28.720), obstructing the investigation (9-28-730), offering cooperation - no entitlement to immunity (9-28.740), corporate compliance programs (9-28.800), and plea agreements with corporations (9-28.1300). See Statutory and Documentary Supplement.

B. INDIVIDUAL RESPONSIBILITY

UNITED STATES v. PARK
421 U.S. 658, 95 S.Ct. 1903, 44 L.Ed.2d 489 (1975)

Chief Justice BURGER delivered the opinion of the Court.

We granted certiorari to consider whether the jury instructions in the prosecution of a corporate officer under § 301(k) of the Federal Food, Drug, and Cosmetic Act, 52 Stat. 1042, as amended, 21 U.S.C. § 331(k), were appropriate under United States v. Dotterweich, 320 U.S. 277 (1943).

Acme Markets, Inc., is a national retail food chain with approximately 36,000 employees, 874 retail outlets, 12 general warehouses, and four special warehouses.   Its headquarters, including the office of the president, respondent Park, who is chief executive officer of the corporation, are located in Philadelphia, Pa. In a five-count information filed in the United States District Court for the District of Maryland, the Government charged Acme and respondent with violations of the Federal Food, Drug and Cosmetic Act. Each count of the information alleged that the defendants had received food that had been shipped in interstate commerce and that, while the food was being held for sale in Acme's Baltimore warehouse following shipment in interstate commerce, they caused it to be held in a building accessible to rodents and to be exposed to contamination by rodents.   These acts were alleged to have resulted in the food's being adulterated within the meaning of 21 U.S.C. §§ 342(a)(3) and (4), in violation of 21 U.S.C. § 331(k).

Acme pleaded guilty to each count of the information. Respondent pleaded not guilty. The evidence at trial demonstrated that in April 1970 the Food and Drug Administration (FDA) advised respondent by letter of insanitary conditions in Acme's Philadelphia warehouse. In 1971 the FDA found that similar conditions existed in the firm's Baltimore warehouse. An FDA consumer safety officer testified concerning evidence of rodent infestation and other insanitary conditions discovered during a 12-day inspection of the Baltimore warehouse in November and December 1971.   He also related that a second inspection of the warehouse had been conducted in March 1972. On that occasion the inspectors found that there had been improvement in the sanitary conditions, but that "there was still evidence of rodent activity in the building and in the warehouses and we found some rodent-contaminated lots of food items."

The Government also presented testimony by the Chief of Compliance of the FDA's Baltimore office, who informed respondent by letter of the conditions at the Baltimore warehouse after the first inspection.   There was testimony by Acme's Baltimore division vice president, who had responded to the letter on behalf of Acme and respondent and who described the steps taken to remedy the insanitary conditions discovered by both inspections. The Government's final witness, Acme's vice president for legal affairs and assistant secretary, identified respondent as the president and chief executive officer of the company and read a bylaw prescribing the duties of the chief executive officer.   He testified that respondent functioned by delegating "normal operating duties," including sanitation, but that he retained "certain things, which are the big, broad, principles of the operation of the company," and had "the responsibility of seeing that they all work together."

At the close of the Government's case in chief, respondent moved for a judgment of acquittal on the ground that "the evidence in chief has shown that Mr. Park is not personally concerned in this Food and Drug violation." The trial judge denied the motion, stating that *Dotterweich* [p. 76] was controlling.

Respondent was the only defense witness. He testified that, although all of Acme's employees were in a sense under his general direction, the company had an "organizational structure for responsibilities for certain functions" according to which different phases of its operation were "assigned to individuals who, in turn, have staff and departments under them." He identified those individuals responsible for sanitation, and related that upon receipt of the January 1972 FDA letter, he had conferred with the vice president for legal affairs, who informed him that the Baltimore division vice president "was investigating the situation immediately and would be taking corrective action and would be preparing a summary of the corrective action to reply to the letter." Respondent stated that he did not "believe there was anything (he) could have done more constructively than what (he) found was being done."

On cross-examination, respondent conceded that providing sanitary conditions for food offered for sale to the public was something that he was "responsible for in the entire operation of the company," and he stated that it was one of many phases of the company that he assigned to "dependable subordinates." Respondent was asked about and, over the objections of his counsel, admitted receiving, the April 1970 letter addressed to him from the FDA regarding insanitary conditions at Acme's Philadelphia warehouse. He acknowledged that, with the exception of the division vice president, the same individuals had responsibility for sanitation in both Baltimore and Philadelphia. Finally, in response to questions concerning the Philadelphia and Baltimore incidents, respondent admitted that the Baltimore problem indicated the system for handling sanitation "wasn't working perfectly" and that as Acme's chief executive officer he was responsible for "any result which occurs in our company."

At the close of the evidence, respondent's renewed motion for a judgment of acquittal was denied. The relevant portion of the trial judge's instructions to the jury challenged by respondent is set out in the margin.[9] Respondent's

---

[9] "In order to find the Defendant guilty on any count of the Information, you must find beyond a reasonable doubt on each count . . . " * * *

Thirdly, that John R. Park held a position of authority in the operation of the business of Acme Markets, Incorporated.

"However, you need not concern yourselves with the first two elements of the case. The main issue for your determination is only with the third element, whether the Defendant held a position of authority and responsibility in the business of Acme Markets. * * *

"The statute makes individuals, as well as corporations, liable for violations. An individual is liable if it is clear, beyond a reasonable doubt, that the elements of the adulteration of the food as to travel in interstate commerce are present. As I have instructed you in this case, they are, and that the individual had a responsible relation to the situation, even though he may not have participated personally.

counsel objected to the instructions on the ground that they failed fairly to reflect our decision in *Dotterweich,* and to define "responsible relationship." The trial judge overruled the objection. The jury found respondent guilty on all counts of the information, and he was subsequently sentenced to pay a fine of $50 on each count.

The Court of Appeals reversed the conviction and remanded for a new trial. That court viewed the Government as arguing "that the conviction may be predicated solely upon a showing that . . . (respondent) was the President of the offending corporation," and it stated that as "a general proposition, some act of commission or omission is an essential element of every crime." 499 F.2d 839, 841 (CA4 1974). * * *

We granted certiorari because of an apparent conflict among the Courts of Appeals with respect to the standard of liability of corporate officers under the Federal Food, Drug, and Cosmetic Act as construed in *Dotterweich,* and because of the importance of the question to the Government's enforcement program. We reverse.

I

The question presented by the Government's petition for certiorari in *Dotterweich,* and the focus of this Court's opinion, was whether "the manager of a corporation, as well as the corporation itself, may be prosecuted under the Federal Food, Drug, and Cosmetic Act of 1938 for the introduction of misbranded and adulterated articles into interstate commerce." * * *

In reversing the judgment of the Court of Appeals and reinstating Dotterweich's conviction, this Court looked to the purposes of the Act and noted that they "touch phases of the lives and health of the people which, in the circumstances of modern industrialism, are largely beyond self-protection." It observed that the Act is of "a now familiar type" which "dispenses with the conventional requirement for criminal conduct—awareness of some wrongdoing. In the interest of the larger good it puts the burden of acting at hazard upon a person otherwise innocent but standing in responsible relation to a public danger."

Central to the Court's conclusion that individuals other than proprietors are subject to the criminal provisions of the Act was the reality that "the only way in which a corporation can act is through the individuals who act on its

---

"The individual is or could be liable under the statute, even if he did not consciously do wrong. However, the fact that the Defendant is pres(id)ent and is a chief executive officer of the Acme Markets does not require a finding of guilt. Though, he need not have personally participated in the situation, he must have had a responsible relationship to the issue. The issue is, in this case, whether the Defendant, John R. Park, by virtue of his position in the company, had a position of authority and responsibility in the situation out of which these charges arose."

behalf."

* * *   In this context, the Court concluded, those doctrines dictated that the offense was committed "by all who . . . have . . . a responsible share in the furtherance of the transaction which the statute outlaws."

The Court recognized that, because the Act dispenses with the need to prove "consciousness of wrongdoing," it may result in hardship even as applied to those who share "responsibility in the business process resulting in" a violation. It regarded as "too treacherous" an attempt "to define or even to indicate by way of illustration the class of employees which stands in such a responsible relation." The question of responsibility, the Court said, depends "on the evidence produced at the trial and its submission—assuming the evidence warrants it—to the jury under appropriate guidance." The Court added: "In such matters the good sense of prosecutors, the wise guidance of trial judges, and the ultimate judgment of juries must be trusted."

II

The rule that corporate employees who have "a responsible share in the furtherance of the transaction which the statute outlaws" are subject to the criminal provisions of the Act was not formulated in a vacuum. Cf. Morissette v. United States, 342 U.S. 246 (1952). Cases under the Federal Food and Drugs Act of 1906 reflected the view both that knowledge or intent were not required to be proved in prosecutions under its criminal provisions, and that responsible corporate agents could be subjected to the liability thereby imposed. Moreover, the principle had been recognized that a corporate agent, through whose act, default, or omission the corporation committed a crime, was himself guilty individually of that crime. The principle had been applied whether or not the crime required "consciousness of wrongdoing," and it had been applied not only to those corporate agents who themselves committed the criminal act, but also to those who by virtue of their managerial positions or other similar relation to the actor could be deemed responsible for its commission.

In the latter class of cases, the liability of managerial officers did not depend on their knowledge of, or personal participation in, the act made criminal by the statute. Rather, where the statute under which they were prosecuted dispensed with "consciousness of wrongdoing," an omission or failure to act was deemed a sufficient basis for a responsible corporate agent's liability. It was enough in such cases that, by virtue of the relationship he bore to the corporation, the agent had the power to prevent the act complained of.
* * *

Thus *Dotterweich* and the cases which have followed reveal that in providing sanctions which reach and touch the individuals who execute the corporate mission—and this is by no means necessarily confined to a single corporate agent or employee—the Act imposes not only a positive duty to seek out and remedy violations when they occur but also, and primarily, a duty to implement measures that will insure that violations will not occur. The requirements of foresight and vigilance imposed on responsible corporate agents are beyond question demanding, and perhaps onerous, but they are no more stringent than the public has a right to expect of those who voluntarily assume positions of authority in business enterprises whose services and products affect the health and well-being of the public that supports them.

The Act does not, as we observed in *Dotterweich,* make criminal liability turn on "awareness of some wrongdoing" or "conscious fraud." The duty imposed by Congress on responsible corporate agents is, we emphasize, one that requires the highest standard of foresight and vigilance, but the Act, in its criminal aspect, does not require that which is objectively impossible. The theory upon which responsible corporate agents are held criminally accountable for "causing" violations of the Act permits a claim that a defendant was "powerless" to prevent or correct the violation to "be raised defensively at a trial on the merits." United States v. Wiesenfeld Warehouse Co., 376 U.S. 86, 91 (1964). If such a claim is made, the defendant has the burden of coming forward with evidence, but this does not alter the Government's ultimate burden of proving beyond a reasonable doubt the defendant's guilt, including his power, in light of the duty imposed by the Act, to prevent or correct the prohibited condition. Congress has seen fit to enforce the accountability of responsible corporate agents dealing with products which may affect the health of consumers by penal sanctions cast in rigorous terms, and the obligation of the courts is to give them effect so long as they do not violate the Constitution.

III

We cannot agree with the Court of Appeals that it was incumbent upon the District Court to instruct the jury that the Government had the burden of establishing "wrongful action" in the sense in which the Court of Appeals used that phrase. The concept of a "responsible relationship" to, or a "responsible share" in, a violation of the Act indeed imports some measure of blameworthiness; but it is equally clear that the Government establishes a prima facie case when it introduces evidence sufficient to warrant a finding by the trier of the facts that the defendant had, by reason of his position in the corporation, responsibility and authority either to prevent in the first instance, or promptly to correct, the violation complained of, and that he failed to do so. * * *

Reading the entire charge satisfies us that the jury's attention was adequately focused on the issue of respondent's authority with respect to the conditions that formed the basis of the alleged violations. Viewed as a whole, the charge did not permit the jury to find guilt solely on the basis of respondent's position in the corporation; rather, it fairly advised the jury that to find guilt it must find respondent "had a responsible relation to the situation," and "by virtue of his position . . . had authority and responsibility" to deal with the situation. * * *

* * * Finally, we note that there was no request for an instruction that the Government was required to prove beyond a reasonable doubt that respondent was not without the power or capacity to affect the conditions which founded the charges in the information. In light of the evidence adduced at trial, we find no basis to conclude that the failure of the trial court to give such an instruction *sua sponte* was plain error or a defect affecting substantial rights.

IV

Our conclusion that the Court of Appeals erred in its reading of the jury charge suggests as well our disagreement with that court concerning the admissibility of evidence demonstrating that respondent was advised by the FDA in 1970 of insanitary conditions in Acme's Philadelphia warehouse. We are satisfied that the Act imposes the highest standard of care and permits conviction of responsible corporate officials who, in light of this standard of care, have the power to prevent or correct violations of its provisions. Implicit in the Court's admonition that "the ultimate judgment of juries must be trusted," however, is the realization that they may demand more than corporate bylaws to find culpability.

Respondent testified in his defense that he had employed a system in which he relied upon his subordinates, and that he was ultimately responsible for this system. He testified further that he had found these subordinates to be "dependable" and had "great confidence" in them. By this and other testimony respondent evidently sought to persuade the jury that, as the president of a large corporation, he had no choice but to delegate duties to those in whom he reposed confidence, that he had no reason to suspect his subordinates were failing to insure compliance with the Act, and that, once violations were unearthed, acting through those subordinates he did everything possible to correct them.

Although we need not decide whether this testimony would have entitled respondent to an instruction as to his lack of power, had he requested it,[19] the testimony clearly created the "need" for rebuttal evidence. That evidence was not offered to show that respondent had a propensity to commit criminal acts. * * * [I]ts purpose was to demonstrate that respondent was on notice that he could not rely on his system of delegation to subordinates to prevent or correct insanitary conditions at Acme's warehouses, and that he must have been aware of the deficiencies of this system before the Baltimore violations were discovered. The evidence was therefore relevant since it served to rebut respondent's defense that he had justifiably relied upon subordinates to handle sanitation matters. * * *

---

[19] Assuming, *arguendo,* that it would be objectively impossible for a senior corporate agent to control fully day-to-day conditions in 874 retail outlets, it does not follow that such a corporate agent could not prevent or remedy promptly violations of elementary sanitary conditions in 16 regional warehouses.

Reversed.

Mr. Justice STEWART, with whom Mr. Justice MARSHALL and Mr. Justice POWELL join, dissenting.

Although agreeing with much of what is said in the Court's opinion, I dissent from the opinion and judgment, because the jury instructions in this case were not consistent with the law as the Court expounds it.

As I understand the Court's opinion, it holds that in order to sustain a conviction under § 301(k) of the Food, Drug, and Cosmetic Act the prosecution must at least show that by reason of an individual's corporate position and responsibilities, he had a duty to use care to maintain the physical integrity of the corporation's food products. A jury may then draw the inference that when the food is found to be in such condition as to violate the statute's prohibitions, that condition as "caused" by a breach of the standard of care imposed upon the responsible official. This is the language of negligence, and I agree with it.

To affirm this conviction, however, the Court must approve the instructions given to the members of the jury who were entrusted with determining whether the respondent was innocent or guilty. Those instructions did not conform to the standards that the Court itself sets out today.

The trial judge instructed the jury to find Park guilty if it found beyond a reasonable doubt that Park "had a responsible relation to the situation . . . The issue is, in this case, whether the Defendant, John R. Park, by virtue of his position in the company, had a position of authority and responsibility in the situation out of which these charges arose." Requiring, as it did, a verdict of guilty upon a finding of "responsibility," this instruction standing alone could have been construed as a direction to convict if the jury found Park "responsible" for the condition in the sense that his position as chief executive officer gave him formal responsibility within the structure of the corporation. But the trial judge went on specifically to caution the jury not to attach such a meaning to his instruction, saying that "the fact that the Defendant is pres(id)ent and is a chief executive officer of the Acme Markets does not require a finding of guilt." "Responsibility" as used by the trial judge therefore had whatever meaning the jury in its unguided discretion chose to give it.

The instructions, therefore, expressed nothing more than a tautology. They told the jury: "You must find the defendant guilty if you find that he is to be held accountable for this adulterated food." In other words: "You must find the defendant guilty if you conclude that he is guilty." The trial judge recognized the infirmities in these instructions, but he reluctantly concluded that he was required to give such a charge under United States v. Dotterweich, which, he thought, in declining to define "responsible relation"

had declined to specify the minimum standard of liability for criminal guilt.
* * *

But before a person can be convicted of a criminal violation of this Act, a jury must find—and must be clearly instructed that it must find—evidence beyond a reasonable doubt that he engaged in wrongful conduct amounting at least to common-law negligence. There were no such instructions, and clearly, therefore, no such finding in this case.   * * *

NOTES AND QUESTIONS

1. *Indemnification of Corporate Officers.* Why is Park appealing a $250 fine all the way to the Supreme Court? Does society truly consider individuals such as Park to be criminals? What ramifications does this decision have on corporate officers? Should the corporation or the corporate executive pay the legal fees and fines assessed? See Pamela H. Bucy, *Indemnification of Corporate Executives Who Have Been Convicted of Crimes: An Assessment and Proposal*, 24 IND. L. REV. 279 (1991); see also United States v. Stein [p. 777], and note 2 at p. 792 (discussing attorney fees). Do directors and officers' insurance policies serve legitimate goals? See Note, *Liability Insurance for Corporate Executives*, 80 HARV. L. REV. 648 (1967). Do these policies mitigate the impact of decisions such as *Park*? See Bennett L. Ross, Note, *Protecting Corporate Directors and Officers: Insurance and Other Alternatives*, 40 VAND. L. REV. 775 (1987).

2. *Responsible Share.* Is the "responsible share" doctrine closer to a negligence or strict liability theory? Does the insertion of the concept of "powerlessness" in *Park* move it further from strict liability and closer to requiring some culpability? See Norman Abrams, *Criminal Liability of Corporate Officers for Strict Liability Offenses - A Comment on Dotterweich and Park*, 28 U.C.L.A. L. REV. 463 (1981); Kathleen F. Brickey, *Criminal Liability of Corporate Officers for Strict Liability Offenses - Another View*, 35 Vand. L. Rev. 1337 (1982). [For discussion of the "responsible corporate officer" in environmental cases and statutes, see chapter 7].

3. *Powerlessness of Corporate Officer.* When is a defendant entitled to an instruction on "objective impossibility" or lack of "power or capacity?" Is this defense available "to anyone, organization or individual, offering to prove inability to prevent or correct in [a] timely fashion a violation despite maintenance of the highest standard of foresight and vigilance?" Or is this defense "available only to the corporate officer and not the corporation itself, and appl[ied] only when the officer was in fact powerless to prevent or correct the violation, even by suspending the corporation's food warehousing activity if necessary." United States v. Y. Hata, 535 F.2d 508, 511 (9th Cir. 1976).

4. *Recent Prosecutions of Corporate Executives.* In 2002, President George W. Bush created the Corporate Fraud Task Force. In a 2008 report of the

Task Force, it stated that DOJ had "obtained nearly 1,300 corporate fraud convictions." This number included "convictions of more than 200 chief executives and corporate presidents, more than 120 corporate vice presidents, and more than 50 chief financial officers." See Report to the President, Corporate Fraud Task Force (2008). Some of the recent high-level executives convicted include Jeffrey Skilling – the former CEO of Enron; Bernard Ebbers - former CEO of Worldcom; John Rigas – former CEO of Adelphia Communications Corporation. In many cases the sentences given to the executives have been higher than those previously seen in white collar cases (e.g., Bernard Ebbers - 25 years). See Sentencing [p. 834]. In some of these cases, the courts have included jury instructions of willful blindness, when the executive claimed that he or she was unaware of the criminality occurring within the corporation.

5. *Compliance Programs-Obligations of Corporate Officers.* Do corporate directors have an obligation to adopt compliance programs that meet the standards of the Organizational Sentencing Guidelines [Chapter 17]? In **In re Caremark International Inc. Derivative Litigation**, 698 A.2d 959, 970 (Ct. Chancery Del. 1996) the court stated, "a director's obligation includes a duty to attempt in good faith to assure that a corporate information and reporting system, which the board concludes is adequate, exists, and that failure to do so under some circumstances may, in theory at least, render a director liable for losses caused by non-compliance with applicable legal standards." In **McCall v. Scott**, 239 F.3d 808 (6th Cir. 2001), the court after referring to the *Caremark* decision, stated that, "[u]nconsidered inaction can be the basis for director liability because, even though most corporate decisions are not subject to director attention, ordinary business decisions of officers and employees deeper in the corporation can significantly injure the corporation and make it subject to criminal sanctions." Amended 250 F.3d 997 (6th Cir. 2001). In **Stone v. Ritter**, 911 A.2d 362 (Del. 2006), the Delaware Supreme Court held:

> We hold that *Caremark* articulates the necessary conditions predicate for director oversight liability: (a) the directors utterly failed to implement any reporting or information system or controls; or (b) having implemented such a system or controls, consciously failed to monitor or oversee its operations thus disabling themselves from being informed of risks or problems requiring their attention. In either case, imposition of liability requires a showing that the directors knew that they were not discharging their fiduciary obligations. Where directors fail to act in the face of a known duty to act, thereby demonstrating a conscious disregard for their responsibilities, they breach their duty of loyalty by failing to discharge that fiduciary obligation in good faith

6. *Verdict Consistency (Individual/Corporation).* Is there any requirement for consistency between a verdict against a corporation and a verdict against an individual defendant who is an employee of the corporation acting on behalf of the corporation? In *Dotterwich*, the corporation was

acquitted while the individual was convicted. The Court held that "[w]hether the jury's verdict was a result of carelessness or compromise or a belief that the responsible individual should suffer the penalty instead of merely increasing, as it were, the cost of running the business of the corporation, is immaterial." In **United States v. Hughes Aircraft Co., Inc.,** 20 F.3d 974 (9th Cir. 1994) the court considered this issue stating:

> * * * Hughes contracted with the United States to manufacture microelectronic circuits, known as "hybrids," which are used as components in weapons defense systems. The contracts required Hughes to perform a series of tests on each hybrid. As the hybrids made their way through the testing process, they were accompanied by paperwork indicating what tests had been performed, the results of those tests, and the identity of the operator of the testing equipment.
>
> Hughes's former employee, Donald LaRue ("LaRue"), was a supervisor responsible for ensuring the accuracy of the hybrid testing process. LaRue arranged for the paperwork to indicate falsely that all tests had been performed and that each hybrid had passed each test. When LaRue's subordinates called his actions to the attention of LaRue's supervisors, the supervisors did nothing about it. Instead, they responded that LaRue's decisions were his own and were not to be questioned by his subordinates.
>
> Hughes and LaRue were charged with one count of conspiracy to defraud and make false statements to the United States in violation of 18 U.S.C. § 371, and two counts of making false statements in furtherance of that conspiracy in violation of 18 U.S.C. § 1001. LaRue was acquitted on all counts. Hughes was convicted of the conspiracy charge, but acquitted of the other two charges. Hughes appeals from both its conviction and fine of $3.5 million.
>
> * * * Hughes first argues that it must be acquitted as a matter of law because the same jury that convicted Hughes acquitted its "indispensable co- conspirator," LaRue, of the identical charges on identical evidence. Hughes bases its argument on three Supreme Court cases from the 1930's and 1940's, arguing that they provide an exception to the general rule that inconsistency of jury verdicts is not a ground for reversal. See Dunn v. United States, 284 U.S. 390, 393, 52 S.Ct. 189, 190, 76 L.Ed. 356 (1932); United States v. Powell, 469 U.S. 57, 64-65, 105 S.Ct. 471, 476, 83 L.Ed.2d 461 (1984). According to Hughes, the post-Dunn Supreme Court cases indicate that the inconsistent verdict rule applies only to situations involving inconsistencies in multiple verdicts against a single defendant, not inconsistencies in multiple verdicts against multiple defendants. Controlling Ninth Circuit precedent precludes us from adopting such a rule. * * * The Supreme Court's decision in *Powell* supports this extension of the application of the *Dunn* rule insulating inconsistent

jury verdicts from appellate review. "[T]he Government's inability to invoke review, the general reluctance to inquire into the workings of the jury, and the possible exercise of lenity--suggest that the best course to take is simply to insulate jury verdicts from review on [inconsistency] ground." * * * Contrary to Hughes's contentions, this Circuit has not recognized a post-*Powell* exception to the *Dunn* rule. Accordingly, the conviction of one co-conspirator is valid even when all the other co-conspirators are acquitted. * * *

Hughes next argues that it is entitled to a judgment of acquittal because the evidence against it and LaRue was identical, yet one was convicted while the other was acquitted. This argument is predicated on the assumption that LaRue was the sole employee for whose actions Hughes could be found vicariously guilty and that the evidence against each of the two defendants was necessarily identical. However, some of the evidence of conspiracy was offered against Hughes alone. Moreover, as this evidence indicates, the jury could have found Hughes guilty based on the actions or omissions of its supervisors and employees other than LaRue. As Hughes's assumption that the facts against both defendants were identical is erroneous, and no other facts support its argument, we reject this contention.

Hughes's third argument is that the plain language of 18 U.S.C. § 371, which states that if "two or more persons conspire ... each" may be punished, prevents its conviction because it is legally impossible for a party to conspire with itself. Hughes argues that, because it is vicariously liable for each of its employees, a conspiracy between employees would necessitate a finding that Hughes conspired with itself. We reject this creative construction. The statutory language does not exclude criminal liability for a corporation simply because its employees are the actual conspirators. To rule otherwise would effectively insulate all corporations from liability for conspiracies involving only employees acting on behalf of that corporation. We hold that a corporation may be liable under § 371 for conspiracies entered into by its agents and employees. * * *

Hughes also contends that we should extend the reach of the intracorporate conspiracy doctrine in antitrust law, which holds that a conspiracy requires "an agreement among two or more persons or distinct business entities." * * * While this doctrine has been extended by some circuits to civil rights cases, * * * other circuits have declined to do so, * * * and we have reserved the issue.

However, this doctrine has never been applied to criminal cases. As the First Circuit noted, "There is a world of difference between invoking the fiction of corporate personality to subject a corporation to civil liability for acts of its agents and invoking it to shield a corporation or its agents from criminal liability where its agents acted on its behalf." * * * Every other circuit to address the issue has come to the same conclusion. * * *

Hughes argues that public policy requires us to apply the intracorporate conspiracy doctrine to criminal cases. However, a stronger public policy mandates a contrary result. Simply because no other corporation or individual is involved, or there is no joining of previously divergent goals, does not mean there is no conspiracy. If we applied the intracorporate conspiracy doctrine to this case, no corporation acting on its own behalf by and through its employees could be found guilty of conspiracy. This result is illogical. * * * We decline to extend the intracorporate conspiracy doctrine to criminal activity. * * *

Wharton's Rule prevents a conspiracy conviction when an underlying substantive offense requires more than one actor, such as adultery or dueling, and in which "the immediate consequences of the crime rest on the parties themselves rather than on society." Iannelli v. United States, 420 U.S. 770, 782-83, 95 S.Ct. 1284, 1293, 43 L.Ed.2d 616 (1975). Here we have a conspiracy to defraud the government, a violation of 18 U.S.C. § 1001.

Hughes argues that a corporation could only violate 18 U.S.C. § 1001 through the efforts of at least two of its employees due to the supervisory and reporting structure of a corporation. Of course, that is not true: a corporation could be liable under § 1001 for false statements to the government by just one of its employees. A conspiracy arises when more than one of its employees agree to defraud the government.

Moreover, the consequences of government fraud certainly do not rest on the parties themselves rather than society. Government fraud has an adverse effect on the government treasury, the quality of government projects, and in cases such as this one, the safety of individuals utilizing the government goods purchased. * * * This argument is rejected.* * * Because we find no merit to any of Hughes's arguments on this point, we affirm the conviction. * * *AFFIRMED.

CHAPTER FOUR
PRINCIPLES OF STATUTORY
INTERPRETATION

Certain situations do not readily demonstrate that a crime has occurred. One cannot make a reliable presumption that the elements of a crime are present, as one can when a bank manager finds a vault broken open. In situations of ambiguity, determining whether a crime occurred requires careful examination of fact and law. Many suspected cases of fraud— tax and securities fraud, for instance—leave open basic questions about whether criminal intent was formed by the so-called perpetrator. In the extreme, this phenomenon is exemplified by the potential client who thinks that he has committed a crime—say, he failed to report certain income—but the attorney can demonstrate that it was quite reasonable for the client to believe that an exemption or offset permitted the client's not reporting that income. There are at least two characteristics in potential criminal situations that create ambiguity. First, unclarity about the facts creates ambiguity. When the evidence to prove a crime is dispersed among many sources, the government's access to a limited number of sources may create suspicion but leave doubt. Second, and even where all the facts are known to the government, statutory definitions create ambiguity at their margins about what behavior is criminal and what is not. Certain kinds of statutes create more ambiguity than others. Attorneys interviewed said that white-collar crimes typically are defined in language creating a broad margin of ambiguity.

KENNETH MANN, DEFENDING WHITE-COLLAR CRIME 114-15 (1985).

A. THE MENS REA ELEMENT

RATZLAF v. UNITED STATES
510 U.S. 137, 114 S.Ct. 655, 126 L.Ed.2d 615 (1994)

Justice GINSBURG delivered the opinion of the Court.

Federal law requires banks and other financial institutions to file reports with the Secretary of the Treasury whenever they are involved in a cash transaction that exceeds $10,000. 31 U.S.C. § 5313; 31 CFR § 103.22(a) (1993). It is illegal to "structure" transactions—i.e., to break up a single transaction above the reporting threshold into two or more separate transactions—for the purpose of evading a financial institution's reporting requirement.   31 U.S.C. § 5324.   "A person willfully violating" this antistructuring provision is subject to criminal penalties. § 5322. This case presents a question on which Courts of Appeals have divided: Does a defendant's purpose to circumvent a bank's reporting obligation suffice to sustain a conviction for "willfully violating" the antistructuring provision? We hold that the "willfulness" requirement mandates something more. To establish that a defendant "willfully violat[ed]" the antistructuring law, the Government must prove that the defendant acted with knowledge that his conduct was unlawful.

I.

On the evening of October 20, 1988, defendant-petitioner Waldemar Ratzlaf ran up a debt of $160,000 playing blackjack at the High Sierra Casino in Reno, Nevada. The casino gave him one week to pay. On the due date, Ratzlaf returned to the casino with cash of $100,000 in hand. A casino official informed Ratzlaf that all transactions involving more than $10,000 in cash had to be reported to state and federal authorities. The official added that the casino could accept a cashier's check for the full amount due without triggering any reporting requirement.   The casino helpfully placed a limousine at Ratzlaf's disposal, and assigned an employee to accompany him to banks in the vicinity. Informed that banks, too, are required to report cash transactions in excess of $10,000, Ratzlaf purchased cashier's checks, each for less than $10,000 and each from a different bank. He delivered these checks to the High Sierra Casino.

Based on this endeavor, Ratzlaf was charged with "structuring transactions" to evade the banks' obligation to report cash transactions exceeding $10,000; this conduct, the indictment alleged, violated 31 U.S.C. §§ 5322(a) and 5324(3).   The trial judge instructed the jury that the Government had to prove defendant's knowledge of the banks' reporting obligation and his attempt to evade that obligation, but did not have to prove defendant knew the structuring was unlawful. Ratzlaf was convicted, fined, and sentenced to prison.[2]

Ratzlaf maintained on appeal that he could not be convicted of "willfully violating" the antistructuring law solely on the basis of his knowledge that a financial institution must report currency transactions in excess of $10,000 and his intention to avoid such reporting. To gain a conviction for "willful" conduct, he asserted, the Government must prove he was aware of the illegality of the "structuring" in which he engaged. The Ninth Circuit upheld the trial court's construction of the legislation and affirmed Ratzlaf's conviction. We granted certiorari, and now conclude that, to give effect to the statutory "willfulness" specification, the Government had to prove Ratzlaf

---

[2] Ratzlaf's wife and the casino employee who escorted Ratzlaf to area banks were codefendants. For convenience, we refer only to Waldemar Ratzlaf in this opinion.

knew the structuring he undertook was unlawful. We therefore reverse the judgment of the Court of Appeals.

II

* * * Congress enacted the Currency and Foreign Transactions Reporting Act (Bank Secrecy Act) in 1970, in response to increasing use of banks and other institutions as financial intermediaries by persons engaged in criminal activity. The Act imposes a variety of reporting requirements on individuals and institutions regarding foreign and domestic financial transactions. The reporting requirement relevant here, § 5313(a), applies to domestic financial transactions. Section 5313(a) reads:

> "When a domestic financial institution is involved in a transaction for the payment, receipt, or transfer of United States coins or currency (or other monetary instruments the Secretary of the Treasury prescribes), in an amount, denomination, or amount and denomination, or under circumstances the Secretary prescribes by regulation, the institution and any other participant in the transaction the Secretary may prescribe shall file a report on the transaction at the time and in the way the Secretary prescribes ..."[3]

To deter circumvention of this reporting requirement, Congress enacted an antistructuring provision, 31 U.S.C. § 5324, as part of the Money Laundering Control Act of 1986,[4] Section 5324, which Ratzlaf is charged with "willfully violating," reads:

> "No person shall for the purpose of evading the reporting requirements of section 5313(a) with respect to such transaction—
> * * *
>
> "(3) structure or assist in structuring, or attempt to structure or assist in structuring, any transaction with one or more domestic financial institutions."[6]

---

[3] By regulation, the Secretary ordered reporting of "transaction[s] in currency of more than $10,000." 31 CFR § 103.22(a) (1993). Although the Secretary could have imposed a report-filing requirement on "any . . . participant in the transaction," 31 U.S.C. § 5313(a), the Secretary chose to require reporting by the financial institution but not by the customer. 31 CFR § 103.22(a) (1993).

[4] Other portions of this Act make "money laundering" itself a crime. See 18 U.S.C. § 1956(a)(2)(B) (prohibiting various transactions involving the "proceeds of some form of unlawful activity"). The Government does not assert that Ratzlaf obtained the cash used in any of the transactions relevant here in other than a lawful manner.

[6] Regarding enforcement of § 5324, the Secretary considered, but did not promulgate, a regulation requiring banks to inform currency transaction customers of the section's proscription. * * *

The criminal enforcement provision at issue, 31 U.S.C. § 5322(a), sets out penalties for "[a] person willfully violating," *inter alia*, the antistructuring provision. Section 5322(a) reads:

> "A person willfully violating this subchapter [31 U.S.C. § 5311 et seq.] or a regulation prescribed under this subchapter (except section 5315 of this title or a regulation prescribed under section 5315) shall be fined not more than $250,000, or imprisoned for not more than five years, or both."

* * * Section 5324 forbids structuring transactions with a "purpose of evading the reporting requirements of section 5313(a)." Ratzlaf admits that he structured cash transactions, and that he did so with knowledge of, and a purpose to avoid, the banks' duty to report currency transactions in excess of $10,000. The statutory formulation (§ 5322) under which Ratzlaf was prosecuted, however, calls for proof of "willful[ness]" on the actor's part. The trial judge in Ratzlaf's case, with the Ninth Circuit's approbation, treated § 5322(a)'s "willfulness" requirement essentially as surplusage—as words of no consequence. Judges should hesitate so to treat statutory terms in any setting, and resistance should be heightened when the words describe an element of a criminal offense. * * *

"Willful," this Court has recognized, is a "word of many meanings," and "its construction [is] often ... influenced by its context." Spies v. United States, 317 U.S. 492, 497 (1943). Accordingly, we view §§ 5322(a) and 5324(3) mindful of the complex of provisions in which they are embedded. In this light, we count it significant that § 5322(a)'s omnibus "willfulness" requirement, when applied to other provisions in the same subchapter, consistently has been read by the Courts of Appeals to require both "knowledge of the reporting requirement" and a "specific intent to commit the crime," i.e., "a purpose to disobey the law." * * *

Notable in this regard are 31 U.S.C. § 5314, concerning records and reports on monetary transactions with foreign financial agencies, and § 5316, concerning declaration of the transportation of more than $10,000 into, or out of, the United States. Decisions involving these provisions describe a "willful" actor as one who violates "a known legal duty."[10] * * *

The United States urges, however, that § 5324 violators, by their very conduct, exhibit a purpose to do wrong, which suffices to show "willfulness" * * *. " '[S]tructuring is not the kind of activity that an ordinary person would engage in innocently,' " the United States asserts. It is therefore "reasonable," the Government concludes, "to hold a structurer responsible for

---

[10] "[S]pecific intent to commit the crime[s]" described in 31 U.S.C. §§ 5313, 5314, and 5316 might be negated by, e.g., proof that defendant relied in good faith on advice of counsel. See United States v. Eisenstein [p. 100].

evading the reporting requirements without the need to prove specific knowledge that such evasion is unlawful."

Undoubtedly there are bad men who attempt to elude official reporting requirements in order to hide from Government inspectors such criminal activity as laundering drug money or tax evasion. But currency structuring is not inevitably nefarious. Consider, for example, the small business operator who knows that reports filed under 31 U.S.C. § 5313(a) are available to the Internal Revenue Service. To reduce the risk of an IRS audit, she brings $9,500 in cash to the bank twice each week, in lieu of transporting over $10,000 once each week. That person, if the United States is right, has committed a criminal offense, because she structured cash transactions "for the specific purpose of depriving the Government of the information that Section 5313(a) is designed to obtain." Nor is a person who structures a currency transaction invariably motivated by a desire to keep the Government in the dark. But under the Government's construction an individual would commit a felony against the United States by making cash deposits in small doses, fearful that the bank's reports would increase the likelihood of burglary, or in an endeavor to keep a former spouse unaware of his wealth.

Courts have noted "many occasions" on which persons, without violating any law, may structure transactions "in order to avoid the impact of some regulation or tax." This Court, over a century ago, supplied an illustration:

"The Stamp Act of 1862 imposed a duty of two cents upon a bank-check, when drawn for an amount not less than 20 dollars. A careful individual, having the amount of twenty dollars to pay, pays the same by handing to his creditor two checks of ten dollars each. He thus draws checks in payment of his debt to the amount of twenty dollars, and yet pays no stamp duty. . . . While his operations deprive the government of the duties it might reasonably expect to receive, it is not perceived that the practice is open to the charge of fraud. He resorts to devices to avoid the payment of duties, but they are not illegal. He has the legal right to split up his evidences of payment, and thus to avoid the tax." United States v. Isham, 84 U.S. (17 Wall.) 496, 506 (1873).

In current days, as an *amicus* noted, countless taxpayers each year give a gift of $10,000 on December 31 and an identical gift the next day, thereby legitimately avoiding the taxable gifts reporting required by 26 U.S.C. § 2503(b).

In light of these examples, we are unpersuaded by the argument that structuring is so obviously "evil" or inherently "bad" that the "willfulness" requirement is satisfied irrespective of the defendant's knowledge of the illegality of structuring. Had Congress wished to dispense with the requirement, it could have furnished the appropriate instruction.[16]

* * * In § 5322, Congress subjected to criminal penalties only those "willfully violating" § 5324, signaling its intent to require for conviction proof that the defendant knew not only of the bank's duty to report cash transactions in excess of $10,000, but also of his duty not to avoid triggering such a report. There are, we recognize, contrary indications in the statute's legislative history.[17] But we do not resort to legislative history to cloud a

---

[16] Congress did provide for civil forfeiture without any "willfulness" requirement in the Money Laundering Control Act of 1986. See 18 U.S.C. § 981(a) (subjecting to forfeiture "[a]ny property, real or personal, involved in a transaction . . . in violation of section 5313(a) or 5324(a) of title 31 . . ."); see also 31 U.S.C. § 5317(a) (subjecting to forfeiture any "monetary instrument . . . being transported [when] a report on the instrument under section 5316 of this title has not been filed or contains a material omission or misstatement").

[17] The United States points to one of the Senate Reports accompanying the Money Laundering Control Act of 1986, which stated that "a person who converts $18,000 in currency to cashier's checks by purchasing two $9,000 cashier's checks at two different banks or on two different days with the specific intent that the participating bank or banks not be required to file Currency Transaction Reports for those transactions, would be subject to potential civil and criminal liability." S.Rep. No. 99-433, p. 22 (1986). The same Report also indicated that § 5324 "would codify [United States v.] Tobon-Builes [706 F.2d 1092 (11th Cir. 1983)] and like cases [by] expressly subject[ing] to potential liability a person who causes or attempts to cause a financial institution to fail to file a required report or who causes a financial institution to file a required report that contains material omissions or misstatements of fact." S.Rep. No. 99-433, at 22.

But the legislative history cited by the United States is hardly crystalline. The reference to Tobon-Builes is illustrative. In that case, the defendant was charged under 18 U.S.C. § 1001, the False Statements Act, with "conceal[ing] . . . the existence, source, and transfer of approximately $185,200 in cash by purchasing approximately twenty-one cashier's checks in amounts less than $10,000 [and] using a variety of names, including false names . . . ." The defendant's "main contention," rejected by the Eleventh Circuit, was that he "could not have violated the concealment prohibition of § 1001 because he was under no legal duty to report any of his cash transactions." No "ignorance of the law" defense was asserted. Congress may indeed have "codified" that decision in § 5324 by "expressly subject[ing] to potential liability a person who causes or attempts to cause a financial institution to fail to file a required report or who causes a financial institution to file a required report that contains material omissions or misstatements of fact," but it appears that Congress did so in the first and second subsections of § 5324, which track the Senate Report language almost verbatim. See 31 U.S.C. § 5324(1) (no person shall "cause or attempt to cause a domestic financial institution to fail to file a report required under section 5313(a)"); 31 U.S.C. § 5324(2) (no person shall "cause or attempt to cause a domestic financial institution to file a report required under section 5313(a) that contains a material omission or misstatement of fact"). Indeed, the Senate Report stated that "[i]n addition " to codifying Tobon-Builes § 5324 would also "create the offense of structuring a transaction to evade the reporting requirements." The

statutory text that is clear. Moreover, were we to find § 5322(a)'s "willfulness" requirement ambiguous as applied to § 5324, we would resolve any doubt in favor of the defendant. Hughey v. United States, 495 U.S. 411, 422 (1990) (lenity principles "demand resolution of ambiguities in criminal statutes in favor of the defendant") * * *.

We do not dishonor the venerable principle that ignorance of the law generally is no defense to a criminal charge. See Cheek v. United States, [p. 104]. In particular contexts, however, Congress may decree otherwise. That, we hold, is what Congress has done with respect to 31 U.S.C. § 5322(a) and the provisions it controls. To convict Ratzlaf of the crime with which he was charged, violation of 31 U.S.C. §§ 5322(a) and 5324(3), the jury had to find he knew the structuring in which he engaged was unlawful.[19] Because the jury was not properly instructed in this regard, we reverse the judgment of the Ninth Circuit and remand this case for further proceedings consistent with this opinion.

Justice BLACKMUN, with whom THE CHIEF JUSTICE, Justice O'CONNOR, and Justice THOMAS join, dissenting.

* * * A jury found beyond a reasonable doubt that Ratzlaf knew of the financial institutions' duty to report cash transactions in excess of $10,000 and that he structured transactions for the specific purpose of evading the reporting requirements.

The Court today, however, concludes that these findings are insufficient for a conviction under 31 U.S.C. §§ 5322(a) and 5324(3), because a defendant also must have known that the structuring in which he engaged was illegal. Because this conclusion lacks support in the text of the statute, conflicts in my view with basic principles governing the interpretation of criminal statutes, and is squarely undermined by the evidence of congressional intent, I dissent.

I

"The general rule that ignorance of the law or a mistake of law is no defense to criminal prosecution is deeply rooted in the American legal

---

relevance of *Tobon-Builes* to the proper construction of § 5324(3), the subsection under which Ratzlaf was convicted, is not evident.

[19] The dissent asserts that our holding "largely nullifies the effect" of § 5324 by "mak[ing] prosecution for structuring difficult or impossible in most cases." Even under the dissent's reading of the statute, proof that the defendant knew of the bank's duty to report is required for conviction; we fail to see why proof that the defendant knew of his duty to refrain from structuring is so qualitatively different that it renders prosecution "impossible." A jury may, of course, find the requisite knowledge on defendant's part by drawing reasonable inferences from the evidence of defendant's conduct, see Spies v. United States, 317 U.S. 492, 499-500 (1943) * * *.

system." Cheek v. United States. The Court has applied this common-law rule "in numerous cases construing criminal statutes."

Thus, the term "willfully" in criminal law generally "refers to consciousness of the act but not to consciousness that the act is unlawful." * * *

* * * The offense of structuring * * * requires (1) knowledge of a financial institution's reporting requirements, and (2) the structuring of a transaction for the purpose of evading those requirements. These elements define a violation that is "willful" as that term is commonly interpreted. The majority's additional requirement that an actor have actual knowledge that structuring is prohibited strays from the statutory text, as well as from our precedents interpreting criminal statutes generally and "willfulness" in particular.

The Court reasons that the interpretation of the Court of Appeals for the Ninth Circuit, and that of nine other circuits, renders § 5322(a)'s willfulness requirement superfluous. This argument ignores the generality of § 5322(a), which sets a single standard—willfulness—for the subchapter's various reporting provisions. Some of those provisions do not themselves define willful conduct, so the willfulness element cannot be deemed surplusage. Moreover, the fact that § 5322(a) requires willfulness for criminal liability to be imposed does not mean that each of the underlying offenses to which it applies must involve something less than willfulness. Thus, the fact that § 5324 does describe a "willful" offense, since it already requires "the purpose of evading the reporting requirements," provides no basis for imposing an artificially heightened scienter requirement.

* * * The Court next concludes that its interpretation of "willfully" is warranted because structuring is not inherently "nefarious." It is true that the Court, on occasion, has imposed a knowledge-of-illegality requirement upon criminal statutes to ensure that the defendant acted with a wrongful purpose. [citing Liparota v. United States, p. 107]. I cannot agree, however, that the imposition of such a requirement is necessary here. First, the conduct at issue—splitting up transactions involving tens of thousands of dollars in cash for the specific purpose of circumventing a bank's reporting duty—is hardly the sort of innocuous activity involved in cases such as *Liparota*, in which the defendant had been convicted of fraud for purchasing food stamps for less than their face value. Further, an individual convicted of structuring is, by definition, aware that cash transactions are regulated, and he cannot seriously argue that he lacked notice of the law's intrusion into the particular sphere of activity. By requiring knowledge of a bank's reporting requirements as well as a "purpose of evading" those requirements, the antistructuring provision targets those who knowingly act to deprive the Government of information to which it is entitled. In my view, that is not so plainly innocent a purpose as to justify reading into the statute the additional element of knowledge of illegality. In any event, Congress has determined that purposefully structuring transactions is not innocent conduct.

In interpreting federal criminal tax statutes, this Court has defined the term "willfully" as requiring the "voluntary, intentional violation of a known legal duty." Cheek v. United States. Our rule in the tax area, however, is an "exception to the traditional rule," applied "largely due to the complexity of the tax laws." The rule is inapplicable here, where, far from being complex, the provisions involved are perhaps among the simplest in the United States Code.

II

Although I believe the statutory language is clear in light of our precedents, the legislative history confirms that Congress intended to require knowledge of (and a purpose to evade) the reporting requirements but not specific knowledge of the illegality of structuring.[9]

Before 1986, the reporting requirements included no provision explicitly prohibiting the structuring of transactions to evade the reporting requirements. The Government attempted to combat purposeful evasion of the reporting requirements through 18 U.S.C. § 1001, which applies to anyone who "knowingly and willfully falsifies, conceals or covers up by any trick, scheme, or device a material fact" within the jurisdiction of a federal agency, and 18 U.S.C. § 2(b), which applies to anyone who "willfully causes an act to be done which if directly performed by him or another would be an offense" under federal law. Some Courts of Appeals upheld application of those criminal statutes where a report would have been filed but for the defendant's purposeful structuring. As the leading case explained, a defendant's willfulness was established if he "knew about the currency reporting requirements and . . . purposely sought to prevent the financial institutions from filing required reports . . . by structuring his transactions as multiple smaller transactions under $10,000." *Tobon-Builes.*

Other courts rejected imposition of criminal liability for structuring under §§ 1001 and 2(b), concluding either that the law did not impose a duty not to structure or that criminal liability was confined to limited forms of structuring. See, e.g., United States v. Varbel, 780 F.2d 758 (9th Cir. 1986); United States v. Denmark, 779 F.2d 1559 (11th Cir. 1986); United States v. Anzalone, 766 F.2d 676 (1st Cir. 1985).

Congress enacted the antistructuring provision in 1986 "to fill a loophole in the Bank Secrecy Act caused by" the latter three decisions, which "refused to apply the sanctions of [the Act] to transactions 'structured' to evade the act's $10,000 cash reporting requirement." As explained by the Report of the Senate Judiciary Committee: "[The antistructuring provision] would codify

---

[9] Because the statutory language unambiguously imposes no requirement of knowledge of the illegality of structuring, I would not apply the rule of lenity. Moreover, I am not persuaded that that rule should be applied to defeat a congressional purpose that is as clear as that evidenced here. See *Liparota*, 471 U.S., at 427.

Tobon-Builes and like cases and would negate the effect of *Anzalone, Varbel* and *Denemark.* * * * " Congress' stated purpose to "codify *Tobon-Builes*" reveals its intent to incorporate *Tobon-Builes'* standard for a willful violation, which required knowledge of the reporting requirements and a purpose to evade them. Nothing in *Tobon-Builes* suggests that knowledge of the illegality of one's conduct is required.[10]

The Senate Report proceeds to explain the intent required under the antistructuring provision:

> "For example, a person who converts $18,000 in currency to cashier's checks by purchasing two $9,000 cashier's checks at two different banks or on two different days *with the specific intent that the participating bank or banks not be required to file Currency Transaction Reports for those transactions,* would be subject to potential civil and criminal liability. A person conducting the same transactions for any other reasons or a person splitting up an amount of currency that would not be reportable if the full amount were involved in a single transaction (for example, splitting $2,000 in currency into four transactions of $500 each), would not be subject to liability under the proposed amendment." (Emphasis added.)

The Committee's specification of the requisite intent as only the intent to prevent a bank from filing reports confirms that Congress did not contemplate a departure from the general rule that knowledge of illegality is not an essential element of a criminal offense.

---

[10] Contrary to the majority's suggestion, Congress did sanction *Tobon-Builes'* scienter standard. In that case, which Congress intended to "codify," the Eleventh Circuit clearly addressed the level of knowledge required for a willful violation. Moreover, Congress was aware of the standard that the court had adopted, explicitly characterizing *Tobon-Builes* as imposing criminal liability upon individuals who structure transactions "to evade the reporting requirements." The majority misreads the Senate Report as stating that § 5324 creates the structuring offense " '[i]n addition' to codifying *Tobon-Builes*." The phrase "in addition" plainly refers to the previous sentence in the Report, which states that § 5324 "would expressly subject to potential liability a person who causes or attempts to cause a financial institution to fail to file a required report or who causes a financial institution to file a required report that contains material omissions or misstatements of fact." The "codification" of *Tobon-Builes* encompasses both sentences, and thus all three subsections of the original § 5324. * * * Even more direct evidence of Congress's intent to incorporate the *Tobon- Builes* scienter standard is found in the response to a question from Senator D'Amato, the Senate sponsor of the antistructuring provision. He asked Deputy Assistant Attorney General Knapp and Assistant United States Attorney Sun: "Assuming that [the antistructuring] provision had been on the books, could you have demonstrated a willful violation in the *Anzalone, Varbel* and *Denemark* cases?" The written response stated: "Assuming that the terms of [the antistructuring provision] were in effect at the time of the conduct described in *Anzalone, Varbel,* and *Denemark,* the result would, or should have been markedly different." * * *

A recent amendment to § 5324 further supports the interpretation of the court below. In 1992, Congress enacted the Annunzio-Wylie Anti-Money Laundering Act, creating a parallel antistructuring provision for the reporting requirements under 31 U.S.C. § 5316, which governs international monetary transportation. Like the provision at issue here, the new provision prohibits structuring "for the purpose of evading the reporting requirements" (in that case, the requirements of § 5316). At the time Congress amended the statute, every court of appeals to consider the issue had held that a willful violation of the antistructuring provision requires knowledge of the bank's reporting requirements and an intent to evade them; none had held that knowledge of the illegality of structuring was required. * * *

* * * [T]he majority's interpretation of § 5324 as a practical matter largely nullifies the effect of that provision. In codifying the currency transaction reporting requirements in 1970, "Congress recognized the importance of reports of large and unusual currency transactions in ferreting out criminal activity." California Bankers Assn. v. Shultz, 416 U.S. 21, 38 (1974). Congress enacted the antistructuring law to close what it perceived as a major loophole in the federal reporting scheme due to easy circumvention. Because requiring proof of actual knowledge of illegality will make prosecution for structuring difficult or impossible in most cases, the Court's decision reopens the loophole that Congress tried to close. * * *

NOTES AND QUESTIONS

1. **Legislative Response.** Shortly after the Supreme Court's ruling in *Ratzlaf*, Congress, as part of the Riegle Community Development and Regulatory Improvement Act of 1994, modified § 5324. The statute now provides that, "[w]hoever violates this section shall be fined in accordance with title 18, United States Code, imprisoned not more than five years, or both." A House report states that it was Congress' intent to overrule the *Ratzlaf* decision by this amendment. This section "restores the clear Congressional intent that a defendant need only have the intent to evade the reporting requirment as the sufficient *mens rea* for the offense." See 1994 U.S.C.C.A.N. 1977. Although Congress modified § 5324, other statutes that use the original terminology have been faced with *Ratzlaf* type challenges. See, e.g., Hanlester Network v. Shalala, 51 F.3d 1390 (9th Cir. 1995) (applying *Ratzlaf* in interpreting the terms "knowingly and willfully" in a Medicare/Medicaid anti-kickback statute).

2. **Wilfulness in Tax Statutes.** In light of *Ratzlaf*, what should be the *mens rea* of 26 U.S.C.A. ' 6050I, which requires trades or businesses receiving more than $10,000 in cash to report the transaction to the Treasury on Form 8300? See United States v. Rogers, 18 F.3d 265 (4th Cir. 1994) (prosecution under ' 6050I(f), which prohibits various actions taken "for the purpose of evading the return requirements of this section," and ' 7203, which provides criminal penalty for a "willful violation" of that provision, remanded for new trial

where trial court's instruction, contrary to *Ratzlaf*, stated that "[w]illful means no more than the Defendant charged with the duty knows what he is doing"). [For discussion of the application of ' 6050I to attorneys, see Chapter 16]

3. *Ignorance of the Law.* In Lambert v. California, 355 U.S. 225 (1957), the majority reaffirmed the rule that "ignorance of the law will not excuse." The Court, however, excused the defendant's conduct finding a violation of due process when a felony registration ordinance was applied to an individual who had no knowledge of her duty to register. Justice Frankfurter, in his dissent in Lambert v. California, stated that "I feel confident that the present decision will turn out to be an isolated deviation from the strong current of precedents C a derelict on the waters of the law." Does the common law principle that "ignorance of the law will not excuse" remain intact after the *Ratzlaf* decision?

4. *Good Faith Reliance on Counsel. Ratzlaf,* in footnote 10, suggests that"specific intent to commit the crime * * * might be negated by "good faith reliance on the advice of counsel. To what extent should a defendant's reliance on the advice of counsel negate specific intent? See United States v. Eisenstein, 731 F.2d 1540, 1543-44 (11th Cir. 1984). Consider this issue in the context of United States v. Cheek, 3 F.3d 1057 (7th Cir. 1993). Defendant, a commercial airline pilot, was convicted of willfully attempting to evade payment of income taxes and willfully failing to file income tax returns. He failed to file returns after 1979 and increased his withholding allowances on his W-2 form to 60 allowances. In **Cheek v. United States**, 498 U.S. 192 (1991), the Supreme Court overturned his initial conviction, finding that the trial court's jury instruction improperly limited Cheek's claim that he truly believed that the tax code did not treat wages as income. The Court noted that the tax laws had long been held to reflect a congressional purpose of creating an exception to the general principle that ignorance of the law is no excuse. In this area of the law, Congress has required a "willful" violation of tax laws, which has been read to require a "specific intent to violate the law." Accordingly, a good faith belief that one is not violating the law negates willfulness. The Court held that it was error for the trial court to insist that this was only so if the good faith belief was objectively reasonable.

On retrial, Cheek argued that a good faith belief was established here because of his reliance upon the advice of counsel. The trial court refused an instruction on advice of counsel. Affirming Cheek's conviction, the Seventh Circuit noted:

> In order to establish an advice of counsel defense, a defendant must establish that:
>
> > (1) before taking action, (2) he in good faith sought the advice of an attorney whom he considered competent, (3) for the

purpose of securing advice of the lawfulness of his possible future conduct, (4) and made a full and accurate report to his attorney of all material facts which the defendant knew, (5) and acted strictly in accordance with the advice of his attorney who had been given a full report.

A crucial element of this defense is that "defendant secured the advice on the lawfulness of his *possible future conduct*."

Cheek testified that he received the advice of at least three different attorneys on the status of the tax laws, but we are not satisfied that he sought or received advice on "possible future conduct." He did not seek any advice until after 1980, when he first failed to file proper tax returns. Furthermore, Cheek had been told by the IRS, American Airlines personnel and by at least one court that his contentions were without merit prior to his discussions with counsel. Reduced to its essence, the record indicates that Cheek merely continued a course of illegal conduct begun prior to contacting counsel. * * *

Nowhere does Mr. Cheek contend either that he made a full and accurate report as to his tax status to any attorney or that he "acted strictly in accordance with the advice of his attorney." * * * None of these attorneys advised him not to file tax returns. To the contrary, each advised him that he might be criminally prosecuted if he failed to file. Accordingly, on the basis of the evidence presented, the district court did not err in refusing to give a jury instruction on the advice of counsel defense.

5. ***Reading in a Mens Rea Element.*** When is it appropriate for the Court to read a *mens rea* requirement into the statute? **United States v. United States Gypsum Company**, 438 U.S. 422 (1978), involved an appeal from convictions for alleged violations of the Sherman Act. The Act prohibits combinations "in restraint of trade," and the government argued that if the effect of the exchange of pricing information among the defendants was "to raise, fix, maintain, and stabilize prices," that was sufficient to establish liability, as the statute prohibited such action "if it has either the purpose or the effect of stabilizing prices." The defense argued that liability did not exist absent a culpable *mens rea*. Thus, the issue was presented as to "whether intent is an element of a criminal antitrust offense." Chief Justice Burger, writing for the court, stated:

We start with the familiar proposition that "[t]he existence of a mens rea is the rule of, rather than the exception to, the principles of Anglo-American criminal jurisprudence." Dennis v. United States, 341 U.S. 494, 500 (1951). * * *

This Court, in keeping with the common-law tradition and with the general injunction that "ambiguity concerning the ambit of criminal statutes should be resolved in favor of lenity," Rewis v. United States, 401 U.S. 808, 812 (1971), has on a number of occasions read a state-of-mind component into an offense even when the statutory definition did not in terms so provide. Indeed, the holding in *Morissette* [*v. United States*, 342 U.S. 246 (1952)] can be fairly read as establishing, at least with regard to crimes having their origin in the common law, an interpretative presumption that *mens rea* is required. "[M]ere omission . . . of intent [in the statute] will not be construed as eliminating that element from the crimes denounced"; instead Congress will be presumed to have legislated against the background of our traditional legal concepts which render intent a critical factor, and "absence of contrary direction [will] be taken as satisfaction with widely accepted definitions, not as a departure from them."

While strict-liability offenses are not unknown to the criminal law and do not invariably offend constitutional requirements, the limited circumstances in which Congress has created and this Court has recognized such offenses attest to their generally disfavored status. Certainly far more than the simple omission of the appropriate phrase from the statutory definition is necessary to justify dispensing with an intent requirement. In the context of the Sherman Act, this generally inhospitable attitude to non-*mens rea* offenses is reinforced by an array of considerations arguing against treating antitrust violations as strict-liability crimes.

6. *Level of Mens Rea In Antitrust Cases.* Having determined that intent was a necessary element of a criminal antitrust violation, the Court in *Gypsum* next examined what level of *mens rea* would be appropriate:

* * * [T]he language of the Act provides minimal assistance in determining what standard of intent is appropriate, and the sparse legislative history of the criminal provisions is similarly unhelpful. We must therefore turn to more general sources and traditional understandings of the nature of the element of intent in the criminal law. * * *

The ALI Model Penal Code is one source of guidance upon which the Court has relied to illuminate questions of this type. Recognizing that "mens rea is not a unitary concept," the Code enumerates four possible levels of intent—purpose, knowledge, recklessness, and negligence. In dealing with the kinds of business decisions upon which the antitrust laws focus, the concepts of recklessness and negligence have no place. Our question instead is whether a criminal violation of the antitrust laws requires, in addition to proof of anticompetitive effects, a demonstration that the disputed conduct was undertaken with the "conscious object" of producing such effects, or whether it is sufficient that the conduct is shown to have been undertaken with knowledge that the proscribed effects would most likely follow. While the difference between these formulations is a narrow one, we conclude that action undertaken with knowledge of its probable consequences and having the requisite anticompetitive effects can be a sufficient predicate for a finding of criminal liability under the antitrust laws.

Several considerations fortify this conclusion. The element of intent in the criminal law has traditionally been viewed as a bifurcated concept embracing either the specific requirement of purpose or the more general one of knowledge or awareness. * * * Generally this limited distinction between knowledge and purpose has not been considered important since "there is good reason for imposing liability whether the defendant desired or merely knew of the practical certainty of the results." In either circumstance, the defendants are consciously behaving in a way the law prohibits, and such conduct is a fitting object of criminal punishment.

Nothing in our analysis of the Sherman Act persuades us that this general understanding of intent should not be applied to criminal antitrust violations such as charged here. The business behavior which is likely to give rise to criminal antitrust charges is conscious behavior normally undertaken only after a full consideration of the desired results and a weighing of the costs, benefits, and risks. A requirement of proof not only of this knowledge of likely effects, but also of a conscious desire to bring them to fruition or to violate the law would seem, particularly in such a context, both unnecessarily cumulative and unduly burdensome. Where carefully planned and calculated conduct is being scrutinized in the context of a criminal prosecution, the perpetrator's knowledge of the anticipated consequences is a sufficient predicate for a finding of criminal intent.

7. *Level of Mens Rea in Other Criminal Statutes.* During the same Term in which *Ratzlaf* was decided, the Court also struggled with the required *mens rea* of two other federal statutes. **Posters 'N' Things Ltd. v. United States**, 511 U.S. 513 (1994), involved a prosecution under the Mail Order Drug Paraphernalia Control Act. That Act makes it unlawful "to make use of the services of the Postal Service or other interstate conveyance as part of a scheme to sell drug paraphernalia." It identifies two categories of drug paraphernalia: items "primarily intended . . . for use" with controlled substances and items "designed for use" with such substances. Justice Blackmun's opinion for the Court concluded that Congress intended to establish "objective standards" for determining what constitutes drug paraphernalia. An item falls within that classification if it is "designed specially" for use with controlled substances (having "no other use besides contrived ones—such as the use of a bong as a flower vase"). Whether an item falls within that classification under the "primarily intended" category

requires reference to still other objective factors, also specified in the statutes (e.g., advertising, instructions accompanying the items sold, expert testimony concerning common use, existence and scope of legitimate uses in the community). Thus, whether or not an item was drug paraphernalia did not depend upon whether the seller intended that it be used with drugs.

The Court concluded, however, that the statute did have a mens rea requirement as to the seller. Justice Blackmun reasoned:

> As in * * * *United States Gypsum*, we conclude that a defendant must act knowingly in order to be liable under § 857. Requiring that a seller of drug paraphernalia act with the 'purpose' that the items be used with illegal drugs would be inappropriate. The purpose of a seller of drug paraphernalia is to sell his product; the seller is indifferent as to whether that product ultimately is used in connection with illegal drugs, or otherwise. If § 857 required a purpose that the items be used with illegal drugs, individuals could avoid liability for selling bongs and cocaine freebase kits simply by establishing that they lacked the 'conscious object' that the items be used with illegal drugs.

> Further, we do not think that the knowledge standard in this context requires knowledge on the defendant's part that a particular customer actually will use an item of drug paraphernalia with illegal drugs. It is sufficient that the defendant be aware that customers in general are likely to use the merchandise with drugs. Therefore, the Government must establish that the defendant knew that the items at issue are likely to be used with illegal drugs. Cf. United States Gypsum (knowledge of "probable consequences" sufficient for conviction). * * *

> Finally, although the Government must establish that the defendant knew that the items at issue are likely to be used with illegal drugs, it need not prove specific knowledge that the items are "drug paraphernalia" within the meaning of the statute. * * *

United States v. Staples, 511 U.S. 600 (1994), was decided on the same day as *Posters 'N' Things*. Petitioner Staples was charged with possessing an unregistered machinegun in violation of § 5861(d) after officers searching his home seized a semiautomatic rifle, i.e., a weapon that normally fires only one shot with each trigger pull, but apparently had been modified for fully automatic firing. The National Firearms Act criminalizes possession of an unregistered *"firearm,"* 26 U.S.C.A. § 5861(d), which includes a "machinegun," defined as a weapon that automatically fires more than one shot with a single pull of the trigger, § 5845(b). At trial, Staples testified that the rifle had never fired automatically while he possessed it and that he had been ignorant of any automatic firing capability. He was convicted after the District Court rejected his proposed jury instruction under which, to establish a § 5861(d) violation, the Government would have been required to prove beyond a reasonable doubt that Staples knew that the gun would fire automatically. The Court of Appeals affirmed, concluding that the Government need not prove a defendant's knowledge of a weapon's physical properties to obtain a conviction under § 5861(d).

In an opinion by Justice Thomas, the Supreme Court majority reversed, holding that to obtain a § 5861(d) conviction, the Government should have been required to prove beyond a reasonable doubt that Staples knew his rifle had the characteristics that brought it within the statutory definition of a machinegun. This was not a "public welfare" or "regulatory" offense.[a] In cases involving public welfare offenses, the Court has inferred from silence a congressional intent to dispense with conventional *mens rea* requirements in statutes that regulate potentially harmful or injurious items. Guns, however, do not fall within the category of dangerous devices as developed in public welfare offense cases. The Court reasoned that had Congress intended to make outlaws of such citizens, it would have spoken more clearly to that effect. Moreover, the potentially harsh penalty attached to violation of § 5861(d)—up to 10 years' imprisonment —confirmed this reading of the Act.

Justice Stevens, joined by Justice Blackmun, dissented. They argued that, "[t]he Court has substituted its views of sound policy for the judgment Congress made." The dissent stated that "the text of the statute does provide 'explicit guidance' in this case." "An examination of § 5861(d) in light of our precedent dictates that the crime of possession of an unregistered machinegun is in a category of offenses described as 'public welfare' crimes." The dissent argued that "[t]he history and interpretation of the National Firearms Act supports the conclusion that Congress did not intend to require knowledge of all the facts that constitute the offense of possession of an unregistered weapon."

In **Bryan v. United States**, 524 U.S. 184 (1998), the Supreme Court held the "willfulness requirement of § 924(a)(1)(D), [an amendment added as part of the Firearms Owners' Protection Act], does not carve out an exception to the traditional rule that ignorance of the law is no excuse; knowledge that the conduct is unlawful" is sufficient without also knowing of the actual federal licensing requirement for dealing in firearms. In distinguishing *Ratzlaf* the Court stated:

> Both the tax cases and *Ratzlaf* involved highly technical statutes that presented the danger of ensnaring individuals engaged in apparently innocent conduct. As a result, we held that these statutes "carv[e] out an exception to the traditional rule" that ignorance of the law is no excuse and require that the defendant have knowledge of the law. The danger of convicting individuals engaged in apparently innocent activity that motivated our decisions

---

[a] See Chapter 7 for a discussion of regulatory offenses.

in the tax cases and *Ratzlaf* is not present here because the jury found that this petitioner knew that his conduct was unlawful.

Id. at 1947. See also United States v. Pitrone, 115 F.3d 1 (1st Cir. 1997) (Migratory Bird Treaty Act does not require willfulness.); United States v. Georgopoulos, 149 F.3d 169 (2nd Cir. 1998) (willfulness element of 29 U.S.C. § 186, prohibiting union officials from accepting payments from employers, "requires only a finding of general intent.").

B. AMBIGUITY IN OTHER ELEMENTS

DOWLING v. UNITED STATES
473 U.S. 207, 105 S.Ct. 3127, 87 L.Ed.2d 152 (1985)

Justice BLACKMUN delivered the opinion of the Court.

The National Stolen Property Act provides for the imposition of criminal penalties upon any person who "transports in interstate or foreign commerce any goods, wares, merchandise, securities or money, of the value of $5,000 or more, knowing the same to have been stolen, converted or taken by fraud." 18 U.S.C. § 2314. In this case, we must determine whether the statute reaches the interstate transportation of "bootleg" phonorecords, "stolen, converted or taken by fraud" only in the sense that they were manufactured and distributed without the consent of the copyright owners of the musical compositions performed on the records.

I

After a bench trial in the United States District Court for the Central District of California conducted largely on the basis of a stipulated record, petitioner Paul Edmond Dowling was convicted of one count of conspiracy to transport stolen property in interstate commerce, in violation of 18 U.S.C. § 371; eight counts of interstate transportation of stolen property, in violation of 18 U.S.C. § 2314; nine counts of copyright infringement, in violation of 17 U.S.C. § 506(a); and three counts of mail fraud, in violation of 18 U.S.C. § 1341. The offenses stemmed from an extensive bootleg record operation involving the manufacture and distribution by mail of recordings of vocal performances by Elvis Presley.[2] The evidence demonstrated that sometime

---

[2] A "bootleg" phonorecord is one which contains an unauthorized copy of a commercially unreleased performance. As in this case, the bootleg material may come from various sources. For example, fans may record concert performances, motion picture soundtracks, or television appearances. Outsiders may obtain copies of "outtakes," those portions of the tapes recorded in the studio but not included in the "master," that is, the final edited version slated for release after transcription to phonorecords or commercial tapes. Or bootleggers may gain possession of an "acetate," which is a phonorecord cut with a stylus rather than stamped, capable of

around 1976, Dowling, to that time an avid collector of Presley recordings, began in conjunction with codefendant William Samuel Theaker to manufacture phonorecords of unreleased Presley recordings. They used material from a variety of sources, including studio outtakes, acetates, soundtracks from Presley motion pictures, and tapes of Presley concerts and television appearances. Until early 1980, Dowling and Theaker had the records manufactured at a record-pressing company in Burbank, Cal. When that company later refused to take their orders, they sought out other record-pressing companies in Los Angeles and, through codefendant Richard Minor, in Miami, Fla. The bootleg entrepreneurs never obtained authorization from or paid royalties to the owners of the copyrights in the musical compositions. * * *

The eight § 2314 counts on which Dowling was convicted arose out of six shipments of bootleg phonorecords from Los Angeles to Baltimore and two shipments from Los Angeles to Miami. The evidence established that each shipment included thousands of albums, that each album contained performances of copyrighted musical compositions for the use of which no licenses had been obtained nor royalties paid, and that the value of each shipment attributable to copyrighted material exceeded the statutory minimum.   * * *

We granted certiorari to resolve an apparent conflict among the Circuits concerning the application of the statute [§ 2314] to interstate shipments of bootleg and pirated sound recordings and motion pictures whose unauthorized distribution infringed valid copyrights.

II

Federal crimes, of course, "are solely creatures of statute." Liparota v. United States, 471 U.S. 419, 424 (1985), citing United States v. Hudson, 7 Cranch 32, 3 L.Ed. 259 (1812). Accordingly, when assessing the reach of a federal criminal statute, we must pay close heed to language, legislative history, and purpose in order strictly to determine the scope of the conduct the enactment forbids. Due respect for the prerogatives of Congress in defining federal crimes prompts restraint in this area, where we typically find a "narrow interpretation" appropriate. Chief Justice Marshall early observed:

"The rule that penal laws are to be construed strictly, is perhaps not much less old than construction itself. It is founded on the tenderness of the law for the rights of individuals; and on the plain principle that the power of punishment is vested in the legislative,

---

being played only a few times before wearing out, and utilized to assess how a performance will likely sound on a phonorecord. Though the terms frequently are used interchangeably, a "bootleg" record is not the same as a "pirated" one, the latter being an unauthorized copy of a performance already commercially released.

not in the judicial department. It is the legislature, not the Court, which is to define a crime, and ordain its punishment." United States v. Wiltberger, 5 Wheat. 76, 95, 5 L.Ed. 37 (1820).

Thus, the Court has stressed repeatedly that " ' "when choice has to be made between two readings of what conduct Congress has made a crime, it is appropriate, before we choose the harsher alternative, to require that Congress should have spoken in language that is clear and definite." ' " Williams v. United States, 458 U.S., at 290, quoting United States v. Bass, 404 U.S. 336, 347 (1971), which in turn quotes United States v. Universal C.I.T. Credit Corp., 344 U.S. 218, 221-222 (1952).   * * *

Applying that prudent rule of construction here, we examine at the outset the statutory language. Section 2314 requires, first, that the defendant have transported "goods, wares, [or] merchandise" in interstate or foreign commerce; second, that those goods have a value of "$5,000 or more"; and, third, that the defendant "kno[w] the same to have been stolen, converted or taken by fraud." Dowling does not contest that he caused the shipment of goods in interstate commerce, or that the shipments had sufficient value to meet the monetary requirement. He argues, instead, that the goods shipped were not "stolen, converted or taken by fraud." In response, the Government does not suggest that Dowling wrongfully came by the phonorecords actually shipped or the physical materials from which they were made; nor does it contend that the objects that Dowling caused to be shipped, the bootleg phonorecords, were "the same" as the copyrights in the musical compositions that he infringed by unauthorized distribution of Presley performances of those compositions. The Government argues, however, that the shipments come within the reach of § 2314 because the phonorecords physically embodied performances of musical compositions that Dowling had no legal right to distribute. According to the Government, the unauthorized use of the musical compositions rendered the phonorecords "stolen, converted or taken by fraud" within the meaning of the statute.[7] We must determine, therefore, whether phonorecords that include the performance of copyrighted musical compositions for the use of which no authorization has been sought nor royalties paid are consequently "stolen,

---

[7] The Government argues in the alternative that even if the unauthorized use of copyrighted musical compositions does not alone render the phonorecords contained in these shipments "stolen, converted or taken by fraud," the record contains evidence amply establishing that the bootleggers obtained the source material through illicit means. The Government points to testimony, for example, that the custodians of the tapes containing the outtakes which found their way onto Dowling's records neither authorized their release nor permitted access to them by unauthorized persons. * * * [W]e decline to consider this alternative basis for upholding Dowling's convictions. The § 2314 counts in the indictment were founded exclusively on the allegations that the shipped phonorecords, which contained "Elvis Presley performances of copyrighted musical compositions," were "stolen, converted and taken by fraud, in that they were manufactured without the consent of the copyright proprietors." * * *

converted or taken by fraud" for purposes of § 2314. We conclude that they are not.

The courts interpreting § 2314 have never required, of course, that the items stolen and transported remain in entirely unaltered form. See, e.g., United States v. Moore, 571 F.2d 154, 158 (3d Cir. 1978) (counterfeit printed Ticketron tickets "the same" as stolen blanks from which they were printed). Nor does it matter that the item owes a major portion of its value to an intangible component. See, e.g., United States v. Seagraves, 265 F.2d 876 (3d Cir. 1959) (geophysical maps identifying possible oil deposits); United States v. Greenwald, 479 F.2d 320 (6th Cir. 1973) (documents bearing secret chemical formulae). But these cases and others prosecuted under § 2314 have always involved physical "goods, wares, [or] merchandise" that have themselves been "stolen, converted or taken by fraud." This basic element comports with the common-sense meaning of the statutory language: by requiring that the "goods, wares, [or] merchandise" be "the same" as those "stolen, converted or taken by fraud," the provision seems clearly to contemplate a physical identity between the items unlawfully obtained and those eventually transported, and hence some prior physical taking of the subject goods.

In contrast, the Government's theory here would make theft, conversion, or fraud equivalent to wrongful appropriation of statutorily protected rights in copyright. The copyright owner, however, holds no ordinary chattel. A copyright, like other intellectual property, comprises a series of carefully defined and carefully delimited interests to which the law affords correspondingly exact protections. * * * [T]he property rights of a copyright holder have a character distinct from the possessory interest of the owner of simple "goods, wares, [or] merchandise," for the copyright holder's dominion is subjected to precisely defined limits.

It follows that interference with copyright does not easily equate with theft, conversion, or fraud. The Copyright Act even employs a separate term of art to define one who misappropriates a copyright: " 'Anyone who violates any of the exclusive rights of the copyright owner,' that is, anyone who trespasses into his exclusive domain by using or authorizing the use of the copyrighted work in one of the five ways set forth in the statute, 'is an infringer of the copyright.' [17 U.S.C.] § 501(a)." There is no dispute in this case that Dowling's unauthorized inclusion on his bootleg albums of performances of copyrighted compositions constituted infringement of those copyrights. It is less clear, however, that the taking that occurs when an infringer arrogates the use of another's protected work comfortably fits the terms associated with physical removal employed by § 2314. * * * While one may colloquially like infringement with some general notion of wrongful appropriation, infringement plainly implicates a more complex set of property interests than does run-of-the-mill theft, conversion, or fraud. As a result, it fits but awkwardly with the language Congress chose—"stolen, converted or taken by fraud"—to describe the sorts of goods whose interstate shipment §

2314 makes criminal. "And, when interpreting a criminal statute that does not explicitly reach the conduct in question, we are reluctant to base an expansive reading on inferences drawn from subjective and variable 'understandings.' " Williams v. United States, 458 U.S., at 286.   * * *

In light of the ill-fitting language, we turn to consider whether the history and purpose of § 2314 evince a plain congressional intention to reach interstate shipments of goods infringing copyrights. Our examination of the background of the provision makes more acute our reluctance to read § 2314 to encompass merchandise whose contraband character derives from copyright infringement.

Congress enacted § 2314 as an extension of the National Motor Vehicle Theft Act, currently codified at 18 U.S.C. § 2312. Passed in 1919, the earlier Act was an attempt to supplement the efforts of the States to combat automobile thefts. Particularly in areas close to state lines, state law enforcement authorities were seriously hampered by car thieves' ability to transport stolen vehicles beyond the jurisdiction in which the theft occurred. Legislating pursuant to its commerce power, Congress made unlawful the interstate transportation of stolen vehicles, thereby filling in the enforcement gap by "strik[ing] down State lines which serve as barriers to protect [these interstate criminals] from justice." 58 Cong.Rec. 5476 (1919) (statement of Rep. Newton).

Congress acted to fill an identical enforcement gap when in 1934 it "extend [ed] the provisions of the National Motor Vehicle Theft Act to other stolen property" by means of the National Stolen Property Act. Again, Congress acted under its commerce power to assist the States' efforts to foil the "roving criminal," whose movement across state lines stymied local law enforcement officials. As with its progenitor, Congress responded in the National Stolen Property Act to "the need for federal action" in an area that normally would have been left to state law.

No such need for supplemental federal action has ever existed, however, with respect to copyright infringement, for the obvious reason that Congress always has had the bestowed authority to legislate directly in this area. Article I, § 8, cl. 8, of the Constitution provides that Congress shall have the power "To promote the Progress of Science and useful Arts, by securing for limited Times to Authors and Inventors the exclusive Right to their respective Writings and Discoveries." By virtue of the explicit constitutional grant, Congress has the unquestioned authority to penalize directly the distribution of goods that infringe copyright, whether or not those goods affect interstate commerce. Given that power, it is implausible to suppose that Congress intended to combat the problem of copyright infringement by the circuitous route hypothesized by the Government. * * * In sum, the premise of § 2314—the need to fill with federal action an enforcement chasm created by limited state jurisdiction—simply does not apply to the conduct the Government seeks to reach here.   * * *

The history of copyright infringement provisions affords additional reason to hesitate before extending § 2314 to cover the interstate shipments in this case. Not only has Congress chiefly relied on an array of civil remedies to provide copyright holders protection against infringement, see 17 U.S.C. §§ 502-505, but in exercising its power to render criminal certain forms of copyright infringement, it has acted with exceeding caution. * * *

* * * [T]he history of the criminal infringement provisions of the Copyright Act reveals a good deal of care on Congress' part before subjecting copyright infringement to serious criminal penalties. First, Congress hesitated long before imposing felony sanctions on copyright infringers. Second, when it did so, it carefully chose those areas of infringement that required severe response—specifically, sound recordings and motion pictures—and studiously graded penalties even in those areas of heightened concern. This step-by-step, carefully considered approach is consistent with Congress' traditional sensitivity to the special concerns implicated by the copyright laws.

In stark contrast, the Government's theory of this case presupposes a congressional decision to bring the felony provisions of § 2314, which make available the comparatively light fine of not more than $10,000 but the relatively harsh term of imprisonment of up to 10 years, to bear on the distribution of a sufficient quantity of any infringing goods simply because of the presence here of a factor—interstate transportation—not otherwise though relevant to copyright law. The Government thereby presumes congressional adoption of an indirect but blunderbuss solution to a problem treated with precision when considered directly. To the contrary, the discrepancy between the two approaches convinces us that Congress had no intention to reach copyright infringement when it enacted § 2314. * * *

The broad consequences of the Government's theory, both in the field of copyright and in kindred fields of intellectual property law, provide a final and dispositive factor against reading § 2314 in the manner suggested. ***

* * * [T]he field of copyright does not cabin the Government's theory, which would as easily encompass the law of patents and other forms of intellectual property. * * * [I]ts view of the statute would readily permit its application to interstate shipments of patent-infringing goods. Despite its undoubted power to do so, however, Congress has not provided criminal penalties for distribution of goods infringing valid patents. Thus, the rationale supporting application of the statute under the circumstances of this case would equally justify its use in wide expanses of the law which Congress has evidenced no intention to enter by way of criminal sanction. This factor militates strongly against the reading proffered by the Government. Cf. Williams v. United States, 458 U.S., at 287.

III

No more than other legislation do criminal statutes take on straitjackets upon enactment. In sanctioning the use of § 2314 in the manner urged by the Government here, the Courts of Appeals understandably have sought to utilize an existing and readily available tool to combat the increasingly serious problem of bootlegging, piracy, and copyright infringement. Nevertheless, the deliberation with which Congress over the last decade has addressed the problem of copyright infringement for profit, as well as the precision with which it has chosen to apply criminal penalties in this area, demonstrates anew the wisdom of leaving it to the legislature to define crime and prescribe penalties.[21] Here, the language of § 2314 does not "plainly and unmistakably" cover petitioner Dowling's conduct, United States v. Lacher, 134 U.S. 624, 628 (1890); the purpose of the provision to fill gaps in state law enforcement does not couch the problem under attack; and the rationale employed to apply the statute to petitioner's conduct would support its extension to significant bodies of law that Congress gave no indication it intended to touch. In sum, Congress has not spoken with the requisite clarity. Invoking the "time-honored interpretive guideline" that "ambiguity concerning the ambit of criminal statutes should be resolved in favor of lenity,' " Liparota v. United States, 471 U.S., at 427, quoting Rewis v. United States, 401 U.S. 808, 812 (1971), we reverse the judgment of the Court of Appeals.

Justice POWELL, with whom The Chief Justice and Justice WHITE join, dissenting.

The Court holds today that 18 U.S.C. § 2314 does not apply to this case because the rights of a copyright holder are "different" from the rights of owners of other kinds of property. The Court does not explain, however, how the differences it identifies are relevant either under the language of § 2314 or in terms of the purposes of the statute. Because I believe that the language of § 2314 fairly covers the interstate transportation of goods containing unauthorized use of copyrighted material, I dissent.

---

[21] Indeed, in opposing the petition for a writ of certiorari in this case, the Government acknowledged that it no longer needs § 2314 to prosecute and punish serious copyright infringement. Adverting to the most recent congressional copyright action, it advised the Court: "[A]pplication of Section 2314 . . . to the sort of conduct involved in this case is of considerably diminished significance since passage, subsequent to the offenses involved in this case, of the Piracy and Counterfeiting Amendments Act of 1982, (17 U.S.C. 506(a) and 18 U.S.C. 2318, 2319). The new statute provides for felony treatment for most serious cases of copyright infringement involving sound recordings and audiovisual materials and trafficking in counterfeit labels, while prior law provided only for misdemeanor treatment for first offenses under the copyright statutes. * * * These observations suggest the conclusion we have reached—that § 2314 was not in the first place the proper means by which to counter the spread of copyright infringement in sound recordings and motion pictures.

Section 2314 provides for criminal penalties against any person who "transports in interstate or foreign commerce any goods, wares, merchandise, securities or money, of the value of $5,000 or more, knowing the same to have been stolen, converted or taken by fraud." There is no dispute that the items Dowling transported in interstate commerce—bootleg Elvis Presley records—are goods, wares, or merchandise. Nor is there a dispute that the records contained copyrighted Elvis Presley performances that Dowling had no right to reproduce and distribute. The only issue here is whether the unauthorized use of a copyright may be "equate[d] with theft, conversion, or fraud" for purposes of § 2314. Virtually every court that has considered the question has concluded that § 2314 is broad enough to cover activities such as Dowling's. * * *

The Court focuses on the fact that "[t]he copyright owner . . . holds no ordinary chattel." The Court quite correctly notes that a copyright is "comprise[d] . . . of carefully defined and carefully delimited interests," and that the copyright owner does not enjoy " 'complete control over all possible uses of his work,' ". But among the rights a copyright owner enjoys is the right to publish, copy, and distribute the copyrighted work. Indeed, these rights define virtually the entire scope of an owner's rights in intangible property such as a copyright. Interference with these rights may be "different" from the physical removal of tangible objects, but it is not clear why this difference matters under the terms of § 2314. The statute makes no distinction between tangible and intangible property. The basic goal of the National Stolen Property Act, thwarting the interstate transportation of misappropriated goods, is not served by the judicial imposition of this distinction. Although the rights of copyright owners in their property may be more limited than those of owners of other kinds of property, they are surely "just as deserving of protection . . . ."

The Court concedes that § 2314 has never been interpreted to require that the goods, wares, or merchandise stolen and transported in violation of the statute remain in unaltered form. It likewise recognizes that the statute is applicable even when the misappropriated item "owes a major portion of its value to an intangible component." The difficulty the Court finds with the application of § 2314 here is in finding a theft, conversion, or fraudulent taking, in light of the intangible nature of a copyright. But this difficulty, it seems to me, has more to do with its views on the relative evil of copyright infringement versus other kinds of thievery, than it does with interpretation of the statutory language.   * * *

NOTES AND QUESTIONS

1. *Ambiguity.* To what extent does the Court employ the methodology used in *Ratzlaf* to interpret this statute? Ambiguity in statutes can in part be attributed to the legislators having to write laws in substantive areas that are constantly developing. In Fischer v. United States, 529 U.S. 667 (2000), the Supreme Court provided an interpretation of the word "benefits" and

found health care providers under the Medicare program as receiving "benefits"within the meaning of this statute. See also United States v. Giles, 213 F.3d 1247 (10th Cir. 2000) (trafficking in goods is found not to be the same as trafficking in labels for the purposes of a criminal trademark infringement statute).

2. *Trade Secrets.* Can conspiracy to violate the National Stolen Property Act be used to prosecute a theft of trade secrets? Would the "goods" stolen be the books and records or the "trade secrets?" See Harry First, *Protecting Soft Property Through the Criminal Law: The Emerging View From the United States,* 2 NIHON U. COMP. L. 1 (1985). To criminalize theft of trade secrets, Congress eventually passed the Economic Espionage Act (EEA). In **United States v. Hsu**, 155 F.3d 189. 194-97 (3rd Cir. 1998), the court summarized parts of the Act stating:

> * * * The EEA became law in October 1996 against a backdrop of increasing threats to corporate security and a rising tide of international and domestic economic espionage. The end of the Cold War sent government spies scurrying to the private sector to perform illicit work for businesses and corporations, and by 1996, studies revealed that nearly $24 billion of corporate intellectual property was being stolen each year. * * *

> The problem was augmented by the absence of any comprehensive federal remedy targeting the theft of trade secrets, compelling prosecutors to shoehorn economic espionage crimes into statutes directed at other offenses.

> For example, the government often sought convictions under the National Stolen Property Act ("NSPA"), 18 U.S.C. § 2314, or the mail and wire fraud statutes, 18 U.S.C. §§ 1341 and 1343. However, the NSPA "was drafted at a time when computers, biotechnology, and copy machines did not even exist," and industrial espionage often occurred without the use of mail or wire. Consequently, it soon became clear to legislators and commentators alike that a new federal strategy was needed to combat the increasing prevalence of espionage in corporate America. Congress recognized "the importance of developing a systematic approach to the problem of economic espionage," and stressed that "[o]nly by adopting a national scheme to protect U.S. proprietary economic information can we hope to maintain our industrial and economic edge and thus safeguard our national security." The House and Senate thus passed the Economic Espionage Act, and the President signed the bill into law on October 11, 1996. * * *

> The EEA consists of nine sections which protect proprietary information from misappropriation. * * * The EEA criminalizes two principal categories of corporate espionage, including "Economic espionage" as defined by 18 U.S.C. § 1831, and the "Theft of trade

secrets" as defined by § 1832. The former provision punishes those who knowingly misappropriate, or attempt or conspire to misappropriate, trade secrets with the intent or knowledge that their offense will benefit a foreign government, foreign instrumentality, or foreign agent. The legislative history indicates that ' 1831 is designed to apply only when there is "evidence of foreign government sponsored or coordinated intelligence activity." By contrast, § 1832, the section under which the defendants are charged, is a general criminal trade secrets provision. It applies to anyone who knowingly engages in the theft of trade secrets, or an attempt or conspiracy to do so, "with intent to convert a trade secret, that is related to or included in a product that is produced for or placed in interstate or foreign commerce, to the economic benefit of anyone other than the owner thereof, and intending or knowing that the offense will, injure any owner of that trade secret." Section 1832(a) makes clear that attempt and conspiracy are distinct offenses, and it lists them separately from those acts that constitute completed crimes under the statute.

Section 1832 also contains at least three additional limitations not found in ' 1831. First, a defendant charged under ' 1832 must intend to convert a trade secret "to the economic benefit of anyone other than the owner thereof," including the defendant himself. This "economic benefit" requirement differs from ' 1831, which states merely that the offense "benefit," in any manner, a foreign government, instrumentality, or agent. Therefore, prosecutions under ' 1832 uniquely require that the defendant intend to confer an economic benefit on the defendant or another person or entity. Second, ' 1832 states that the defendant must intend or know that the offense will injure an owner of the trade secret, a restriction not found in ' 1831. The legislative history indicates that this requires "that the actor knew or was aware to a practical certainty that his conduct would cause such a result." Finally, unlike ' 1831, ' 1832 also requires that the trade secret be "related to or included in a product that is produced for or placed in interstate or foreign commerce."

* * * The EEA defines a "trade secret" to expressly extend protection to the misappropriation of intangible information for the first time under federal law. 18 U.S.C. ' 1839(3) provides that a "trade secret" means:

all forms and types of financial, business, scientific, technical, economic, or engineering information, including patterns, plans, compilations, program devices, formulas, designs, prototypes, methods, techniques, processes, procedures, programs, or codes, whether tangible or intangible, and whether or how stored, compiled, or memorialized physically, electronically, graphically, photographically, or in writing if--

(A) the owner thereof has taken reasonable measures to keep such information secret; and

(B) the information derives independent economic value, actual or potential, from not being generally known to, and not being readily ascertainable through proper means by, the public.

The EEA's definition of a "trade secret" is similar to that found in a number of state civil statutes and the Uniform Trade Secrets Act ("UTSA"), a model ordinance which permits civil actions for the misappropriation of trade secrets. There are, though, several critical differences which serve to broaden the EEA's scope. First, and most importantly, the EEA protects a wider variety of technological and intangible information than current civil laws. Trade secrets are no longer restricted to formulas, patterns, and compilations, but now include programs and codes, "whether tangible or intangible, and whether or how stored." Second, the EEA alters the relevant party from whom proprietary information must be kept confidential. Under the UTSA, information classified as a "trade secret" cannot be generally known by businesspersons or competitors of the trade secret owner. The EEA, however, indicates that a trade secret must not be generally known to, or readily ascertainable by, the general public, rather than simply those who can obtain economic value from the secret's disclosure or use. Finally, the EEA contains a definition crafted to reach only illicit behavior. Although legislators eliminated language providing that general knowledge, skills, and experience are not "trade secrets," it is clear that Congress did not intend the definition of a trade secret to be so broad as to prohibit lawful competition such as the use of general skills or parallel development of a similar product. * * *

* * * The EEA also contains a provision designed to preserve the confidentiality of trade secrets during criminal prosecutions. 18 U.S.C. § 1835 states that a court:

shall enter such orders and take such other action as may be necessary and appropriate to preserve the confidentiality of trade secrets, consistent with the requirements of the Federal Rules of Criminal and Civil Procedure, the Federal Rules of Evidence, and all other applicable laws. An interlocutory appeal by the United States shall lie from a decision or order of a district court authorizing or directing the disclosure of any trade secret.

This section does not, of course, abrogate existing constitutional and statutory protections for criminal defendants. It does, however, represent a clear indication from Congress that trade secrets are to be protected to the fullest extent during EEA litigation. Moreover, it further encourages enforcement actions by protecting owners who might otherwise "be reluctant to cooperate in prosecutions for fear of further exposing their trade secrets to public view, thus further devaluing or even destroying their worth." Therefore, as with the definition of trade secrets, the confidentiality provision aims to strike a balance between the protection of proprietary information and the unique considerations inherent in criminal prosecutions. * * *

See also United States v. Martin, 228 F.3d 1 (1st Cir. 2000) (finding sufficient evidence to sustain conviction for conspiracy to steal trade secrets under the Economic Espionage Act).

3. **Supreme Court Interpretation.** Do some justices on the Supreme Court treat white collar cases differently than cases concerning street crimes? Professor J. Kelly Strader states that "[t]he justices' voting in white collar criminal cases [ ] often appears to be philosophically at odds with their overall criminal justice philosophies, a conclusion" he refers to as the "white collar paradox." J. Kelly Strader, *The Judicial Politics of White Collar Crime,* 50 HASTINGS L.J. 1199 (1999).

C. GOING BEYOND THE STATUTE?

McCORMICK v. UNITED STATES
500 U.S. 257, 111 S.Ct. 1807, 114 L.Ed.2d 307 (1991)

Justice WHITE delivered the opinion of the Court.

This case requires us to consider whether the Court of Appeals properly affirmed the conviction of petitioner, an elected public official, for extorting property under color of official right in violation of the Hobbs Act, 18 U.S.C. § 1951. We also must address the affirmance of petitioner's conviction for filing a false income tax return.

I

Petitioner Robert L. McCormick was a member of the West Virginia House of Delegates in 1984. He represented a district that had long suffered from a shortage of medical doctors. For several years, West Virginia had allowed foreign medical school graduates to practice under temporary permits while studying for the state licensing exams. Under this program, some doctors were allowed to practice under temporary permits for years even though they repeatedly failed the state exams. McCormick was a leading advocate and supporter of this program.

In the early 1980's, following a move in the House of Delegates to end the temporary permit program, several of the temporarily licensed doctors formed an organization to press their interests in Charleston. The organization hired a lobbyist, John Vandergrift, who in 1984 worked for legislation that would extend the expiration date of the temporary permit program. McCormick sponsored the House version of the proposed legislation and a bill was passed extending the program for another year. Shortly thereafter, Vandergrift and McCormick discussed the possibility of introducing legislation during the 1985 session that would grant the doctors a permanent medical license by virtue of their years of experience. McCormick agreed to sponsor such legislation.

During his 1984 reelection campaign, McCormick informed Vandergrift that his campaign was expensive, that he had paid considerable sums out of his own pocket, and that he had not heard anything from the foreign doctors. Vandergrift told McCormick that he would contact the doctors and see what he could do. Vandergrift contacted one of the foreign doctors and later received from the doctors $1,200 in cash. Vandergrift delivered an envelope containing nine $100 bills to McCormick. Later the same day, a second delivery of $2,000 in cash was made to McCormick. During the fall of 1984, McCormick received two more cash payments from the doctors. McCormick did not list any of these payments as campaign contributions[1] nor did he report the money as income on his 1984 federal income tax return. And although the doctors' organization kept detailed books of its expenditures, the cash payments were not listed as campaign contributions. Rather, the entries for the payments were accompanied only by initials or other codes signifying that the money was for McCormick.

In the spring of 1985, McCormick sponsored legislation permitting experienced doctors to be permanently licensed without passing the state licensing exams. McCormick spoke at length in favor of the bill during floor debate and the bill ultimately was enacted into law. Two weeks after the legislation was enacted, McCormick received another cash payment from the foreign doctors.

Following an investigation, a federal grand jury returned an indictment charging McCormick with five counts of violating the Hobbs Act,[2] by extorting payments under color of official right, and with one count of filing a false income tax return in violation of 26 U.S.C. § 7206(1), by failing to report as

---

[1] West Virginia law prohibits cash contributions in excess of $50 per person. W. Va. Code § 3-8-5d (1990).

[2] The Hobbs Act, 18 U.S.C. § 1951, provides in relevant part as follows:

"(a) Whoever in any way or degree obstructs, delays, or affects commerce . . . by robbery or extortion . . . in violation of this section shall be fined not more than $10,000 or imprisoned not more than twenty years, or both.

"(b) As used in this section— * * *

"(2) The term 'extortion' means the obtaining of property from another, with his consent, induced by wrongful use of actual or threatened force, violence, or fear, or under color of official right."

income the cash payments he received from the foreign doctors. At the close of a 6-day trial, the jury was instructed that to establish a Hobbs Act violation the Government had to prove that McCormick induced a cash payment and that he did so knowingly and willfully by extortion. * * *

The next day the jury informed the court that it "would like to hear the instructions again with particular emphasis on the definition of extortion under the color of official right and on the law as regards the portion of moneys received that does not have to be reported as income." The court then reread most of the extortion instructions to the jury, but reordered some of the paragraphs and made the following significant addition:

> "Extortion under color of official right means the obtaining of money by a public official when the money obtained was not lawfully due and owing to him or to his office. Of course, extortion does not occur where one who is a public official receives a legitimate gift or a voluntary political contribution even though the political contribution may have been made in cash in violation of local law. Voluntary is that which is freely given without expectation of benefit."

It is also worth noting that with respect to political contributions, the last two paragraphs of the supplemental instructions on the extortion counts were as follows:

> "It would not be illegal, in and of itself, for Mr. McCormick to solicit or accept political contributions from foreign doctors who would benefit from this legislation.

> "In order to find Mr. McCormick guilty of extortion, you must be convinced beyond a reasonable doubt that the payment alleged in a given count of the indictment was made by or on behalf of the doctors with the expectation that such payment would influence Mr. McCormick's official conduct, and with knowledge on the part of Mr. McCormick that they were paid to him with that expectation by virtue of the office he held."

The jury convicted McCormick of the first Hobbs Act count (charging him with receiving the initial $900 cash payment) and the income tax violation but could not reach verdicts on the remaining four Hobbs Act counts. The District Court declared a mistrial on those four counts.

The Court of Appeals affirmed, observing that nonelected officials may be convicted under the Hobbs Act without proof that they have granted or agreed to grant some benefit or advantage in exchange for money paid to them and that elected officials should be held to the same standard when they receive money other than "legitimate" campaign contributions. * * *

* * * Because of disagreement in the Courts of Appeals regarding the meaning of the phrase "under color of official right" as it is used in the Hobbs Act,[5] we granted certiorari. We reverse and remand for further proceedings.

II

McCormick's challenge to the judgment below affirming his conviction is limited to the Court of Appeals' rejection of his claim that the payments made to him by or on behalf of the doctors were campaign contributions, the receipt of which did not violate the Hobbs Act. Except for a belated claim not properly before us,[6] McCormick does not challenge any rulings of the courts below with respect to the application of the Hobbs Act to payments made to nonelected officials or to payments made to elected officials that are properly determined not to be campaign contributions. Hence, we do not consider how the "under color of official right" phrase is to be interpreted and applied in

---

[5] Until the early 1970's, extortion prosecutions under the Hobbs Act rested on allegations that the consent of the transferor of property had been "induced by wrongful use of actual or threatened force, violence, or fear—"; public officials had not been prosecuted under the "color of official right" phrase standing alone. Beginning with the conviction involved in United States v. Kenny, 462 F.2d 1205 (3rd Cir. 1972), however, the federal courts accepted the Government's submission that because of the disjunctive language of § 1951(b)(2), allegations of force, violence or fear were not necessary. Only proof of the obtaining of property under claims of official right was necessary. Furthermore, every Court of Appeals to have construed the phrase held that it did not require a showing that the public official "induced" the payor's consent by some affirmative act such as a demand or solicitation. Although there was some difference in the language of these holdings, the "color of official right" element required no more than proof of the payee's acceptance knowing that the payment was made for the purpose of influencing his official actions. In 1984, however, the Court of Appeals for the Second Circuit, en banc, held that some affirmative act of inducement by the official had to be shown to prove the Government's case. United States v. O'Grady, 742 F.2d 682 (1984). In 1988, the Ninth Circuit, en banc, agreed with the Second Circuit, overruling a prior decision expressing the majority rule. United States v. Aguon, 851 F.2d 1158 (1988). Other courts have been unimpressed with the view expressed in O'Grady and Aguon.

The conflict on this issue is clear, but this case is not the ocasion to resolve it. * * *

[6] In briefing the merits in this Court, McCormick has argued that the Hobbs Act was never intended to apply to corruption involving local officials and that in any event an official has not acted under color of official right unless he falsely represents that by virtue of his office he has a legal right to the money or property he receives. These arguments were not presented to the courts below. They are not expressly among the questions presented in the petition for certiorari and are only arguably subsumed by the questions presented. Nor in view of the language of the Hobbs Act and the many cases approving the conviction of local officials under the Act can it be said that plain error occurred in the lower courts for failure to recognize that the Act was inapplicable to the extortion charges brought against McCormick. * * * [The Court also rejected the false pretenses argument.]

those contexts. In two respects, however, we agree with McCormick that the Court of Appeals erred. * * *

First, we are quite sure that the Court of Appeals affirmed the conviction on legal and factual grounds that were never submitted to the jury. Although McCormick challenged the adequacy of the jury instructions to distinguish between campaign contributions and payments that are illegal under the Hobbs Act, the Court of Appeals' opinion did not examine or mention the instructions given by the trial court. The court neither dealt with McCormick's submission that the instructions were too confusing to give adequate guidance to the jury, nor, more specifically, with the argument that although the jury was instructed that voluntary campaign contributions were not vulnerable under the Hobbs Act, the word "voluntary" as used "in several places during the course of these instructions," was defined as "that which is freely given without expectation of benefit." Neither did the Court of Appeals note that the jury was not instructed in accordance with the court's holding that the difference between legitimate and illegitimate campaign contributions was to be determined by the intention of the parties after considering specified factors.[7] Instead, the Court of Appeals, after announcing a rule of law for determining when payments are made under color of official right, went on to find sufficient evidence in the record to support findings that McCormick was extorting money from the doctors for his continued support of the 1985 legislation, and further that the parties never intended any of the payments to be a campaign contribution.

It goes without saying that matters of intent are for the jury to consider. Cheek v. United States [p. 100]. It is also plain that each of the seven factors that the Court of Appeals thought should be considered in determining the parties' intent present an issue of historical fact. Thus even assuming the Court of Appeals was correct on the law, the conviction should not have been affirmed on that basis but should have been set aside and a new trial ordered. * * *

We agree with the Court of Appeals that in a case like this it is proper to inquire whether payments made to an elected official are in fact campaign contributions, and we agree that the intention of the parties is a relevant consideration in pursuing this inquiry. But we cannot accept the Court of

---

[7] "Some of the circumstances that should be considered in making this determination include, but are not limited to, (1) whether the money was recorded by the payor as a campaign contribution, (2) whether the money was recorded and reported by the official as a campaign contribution, (3) whether the payment was in cash, (4) whether it was delivered to the official personally or to his campaign, (5) whether the official acted in his official capacity at or near the time of the payment for the benefit of the payor or supported legislation that would benefit the payor, (6) whether the official had supported similar legislation before the time of the payment, and (7) whether the official had directly or indirectly solicited the payor individually for the payment."

Appeals' approach to distinguishing between legal and illegal campaign contributions. * * *

* * * Serving constituents and supporting legislation that will benefit the district and individuals and groups therein is the everyday business of a legislator. It is also true that campaigns must be run and financed. Money is constantly being solicited on behalf of candidates, who run on platforms and who claim support on the basis of their views and what they intend to do or have done. Whatever ethical considerations and appearances may indicate, to hold that legislators commit the federal crime of extortion when they act for the benefit of constituents or support legislation furthering the interests of some of their constituents, shortly before or after campaign contributions are solicited and received from those beneficiaries, is an unrealistic assessment of what Congress could have meant by making it a crime to obtain property from another, with his consent, "under color of official right." To hold otherwise would open to prosecution not only conduct that has long been thought to be well within the law but also conduct that in a very real sense is unavoidable so long as election campaigns are financed by private contributions or expenditures, as they have been from the beginning of the Nation. It would require statutory language more explicit than the Hobbs Act contains to justify a contrary conclusion.

This is not to say that it is impossible for an elected official to commit extortion in the course of financing an election campaign. Political contributions are of course vulnerable if induced by the use of force, violence, or fear. The receipt of such contributions is also vulnerable under the Act as having been taken under color of official right, but only if the payments are made in return for an explicit promise or undertaking by the official to perform or not to perform an official act. In such situations the official asserts that his official conduct will be controlled by the terms of the promise or undertaking. This is the receipt of money by an elected official under color of official right within the meaning of the Hobbs Act.   * * *

The United States agrees that if the payments to McCormick were campaign contributions, proof of a *quid pro quo* would be essential for an extortion conviction, and quotes the instruction given on this subject in 9 Department of Justice Manual § 9-85A.306: "campaign contributions will not be authorized as the subject of a Hobbs Act prosecution unless they can be proven to have been given in return for the performance of or abstaining from an official act; otherwise any campaign contribution might constitute a violation."

We thus disagree with the Court of Appeals' holding in this case that a quid pro quo is not necessary for conviction under the Hobbs Act when an official receives a campaign contribution.[10] By the same token, we hold, as McCormick urges, that the District Court's instruction to the same effect was error.[11]   * * *

Justice SCALIA, concurring.

I agree with the Court's conclusion and, given the assumption on which this case was briefed and argued, with the reasons the Court assigns. If the prohibition of the Hobbs Act, 18 U.S.C. § 1951, against receipt of money "under color of official right" includes receipt of money from a private source for the performance of official duties, that ambiguously described crime assuredly need not, and for the reasons the Court discusses should not, be interpreted to cover campaign contributions with anticipation of favorable future action, as opposed to campaign contributions in exchange for an explicit promise of favorable future action.

I find it unusual and unsettling, however, to make such a distinction without any hint of a justification in the statutory text: § 1951 contains not even a colorable allusion to campaign contributions or *quid pro quos*. I find it doubly unsettling because there is another interpretation of § 1951, contrary to the one that has been the assumption of argument here, that would render the distinction unnecessary. While I do not feel justified in adopting that interpretation without briefing and argument, neither do I feel comfortable giving tacit approval to the assumption that contradicts it. I write, therefore, a few words concerning the text of this statute, and the history that has produced the unexamined assumption underlying our opinion.

[Justice Scalia here discussed the position later taken in the *Evans* dissent, p. 134]

Justice STEVENS, with whom Justice BLACKMUN and Justice O'CONNOR join, dissenting.   * * *

As I understand its opinion, the Court would agree that these facts would constitute a violation of the Hobbs Act if the understanding that the money was a personal payment rather than a campaign contribution had been explicit rather than implicit and if the understanding that, in response to the payment, petitioner would endeavor to provide the payers with the specific benefit they sought had also been explicit rather than implicit. In my opinion there is no statutory requirement that illegal agreements, threats, or

---

[10] As noted previously, McCormick's sole contention in this case is that the payments made to him were campaign contributions. Therefore, we do not decide whether a *quid pro quo* requirement exists in other contexts, such as when an elected official receives gifts, meals, travel expenses, or other items of value.

[11] In so holding, we do not resolve the conflict mentioned * * * with respect to the necessity of proving inducement.

promises be in writing, or in any particular form. Subtle extortion is just as wrongful—and probably much more common—than the kind of express understanding that the Court's opinion seems to require.

Nevertheless, to prove a violation of the Hobbs Act, I agree with the Court that it is essential that the payment in question be contingent on a mutual understanding that the motivation for the payment is the payer's desire to avoid a specific threatened harm or to obtain a promised benefit that the defendant has the apparent power to deliver, either through the use of force or the use of public office. In this sense, the crime does require a "*quid pro quo*." * * *

* * * [T]he crime of extortion was complete when petitioner accepted the cash pursuant to an understanding that he would not carry out his earlier threat to withhold official action and instead would go forward with his contingent promise to take favorable action on behalf of the unlicensed physicians. What he did thereafter might have evidentiary significance, but could neither undo a completed crime or complete an uncommitted offense. When petitioner took the money, he was either guilty or not guilty. For that reason, proof of a subsequent *quid pro quo*—his actual support of the legislation—was not necessary for the Government's case. And conversely, evidence that petitioner would have supported the legislation anyway is not a defense to the already completed crime. The thug who extorts protection money cannot defend on the ground that his threat was only a bluff because he would not have smashed the shopkeeper's windows even if the extortion had been unsuccessful. It was in this sense that the District Court correctly advised the jury that the Government did not have to prove the delivery of a postpayment *quid pro quo,* * * *.

* * * Given that the District Court's instructions to the jury largely tracked the instructions requested by petitioner at trial, I can see no legitimate reason for this Court now to find these instructions inadequate. Because I am convinced that the petitioner was fairly tried and convicted by a properly instructed jury, I would affirm the judgment of the Court of Appeals. Of course, an affirmance of the Court of Appeals' judgment would not mean that we necessarily affirm the Court of Appeals' opinion. It is sufficient that an affirmance of McCormick's conviction rest on the legal and factual theories actually presented to the jury, whether or not these theories were the ones relied upon by the Court of Appeals.   I respectfully dissent.

EVANS v. UNITED STATES
504 U.S. 255, 112 S.Ct. 1881, 119 L.Ed.2d 57 (1992)

Justice STEVENS delivered the opinion of the Court.

We granted certiorari, to resolve a conflict in the Circuits over the question whether an affirmative act of inducement by a public official, such as a demand, is an element of the offense of extortion "under color of official right" prohibited by the Hobbs Act, 18 U.S.C. § 1951. We agree with the Court of Appeals for the Eleventh Circuit that it is not, and therefore affirm the judgment of the court below.

I

Petitioner was an elected member of the Board of Commissioners of DeKalb County, Georgia. During the period between March 1985 and October 1986, as part of an effort by the Federal Bureau of Investigation (FBI) to investigate allegations of public corruption in the Atlanta area, particularly in the area of rezonings of property, an FBI agent posing as a real estate developer talked on the telephone and met with petitioner on a number of occasions. Virtually all, if not all, of those conversations were initiated by the agent and most were recorded on tape or video. In those conversations, the agent sought petitioner's assistance in an effort to rezone a 25-acre tract of land for high-density residential use. On July 25, 1986, the agent handed petitioner cash totaling $7,000 and a check, payable to petitioner's campaign, for $1,000. Petitioner reported the check, but not the cash, on his state campaign-financing disclosure form; he also did not report the $7,000 on his 1986 federal income tax return. Viewing the evidence in the light most favorable to the Government, as we must in light of the verdict, we assume that the jury found that petitioner accepted the cash knowing that it was intended to ensure that he would vote in favor of the rezoning application and that he would try to persuade his fellow commissioners to do likewise. Thus, although petitioner did not initiate the transaction, his acceptance of the bribe constituted an implicit promise to use his official position to serve the interests of the bribe-giver.

In a two-count indictment, petitioner was charged with extortion in violation of 18 U.S.C. § 1951 and with failure to report income in violation of 26 U.S.C. § 7206(1). He was convicted by a jury on both counts. * * *

In affirming petitioner's conviction, the Court of Appeals noted that the [trial court's] instruction did not require the jury to find that petitioner had demanded or requested the money, or that he had conditioned the performance of any official act upon its receipt. The Court of Appeals held, however, that "passive acceptance of a benefit by a public official *is* sufficient to form the basis of a Hobbs Act violation if the official knows that he is being offered the payment in exchange for a specific requested exercise of his official power. The official need not take any specific action to induce the offering of the benefit." (emphasis in original).

This statement of the law by the Court of Appeals for the Eleventh Circuit is consistent with holdings in eight other Circuits. Two Circuits, however, have held that an affirmative act of inducement by the public official is required to support a conviction of extortion under color of official right. United States v. O'Grady, 742 F.2d 682, 687 (2d Cir. 1984) (en banc) ("Although receipt of benefits by a public official is a necessary element of the crime, there must also be proof that the public official did something, under color of his public office, to cause the giving of benefits"); United States v. Aguon, 851 F.2d 1158, 1166 (9th Cir. 1988) (en banc) ("We find ourselves in accord with the Second Circuit's conclusion that inducement is an element required for conviction under the Hobbs Act"). Because the majority view is consistent with the common-law definition of extortion, which we believe Congress intended to adopt, we endorse that position.

II

It is a familiar "maxim that a statutory term is generally presumed to have its common-law meaning." Taylor v. United States, 495 U.S. 575, 592 (1990). As we have explained, "where Congress borrows terms of art in which are accumulated the legal tradition and meaning of centuries of practice, it presumably knows and adopts the cluster of ideas that were attached to each borrowed word in the body of learning from which it was taken and the meaning its use will convey to the judicial mind unless otherwise instructed. In such case, absence of contrary direction may be taken as satisfaction with widely accepted definitions, not as a departure from them." Morissette v. United States, 342 U.S. 246, 263 (1952).

At common law, extortion was an offense committed by a public official who took "by colour of his office"[4] money that was not due to him for the performance of his official duties.[5] A demand, or request, by the public official was not an element of the offense. Extortion by the public official was the rough equivalent of what we would now describe as "taking a bribe." It is clear that petitioner committed that offense. The question is whether the federal statute, insofar as it applies to official extortion, has narrowed the common-law definition.

---

[4] Blackstone described extortion as "an abuse of public justice, which consists in an officer's unlawfully taking, *by colour of his office,* from any man, any money or thing of value, that is not due to him, or more than is due, or before it is due." 4 W. Blackstone, Commentaries (emphasis added). He used the phrase "by colour of his office," rather than the phrase "under color of official right," which appears in the Hobbs Act. Petitioner does not argue that there is any difference in the phrases. Hawkins' definition of extortion is probably the source for the official right language used in the Hobbs Act. See Lindgren, The Elusive Distinction Between Bribery and Extortion: From the Common Law to the Hobbs Act, 35 UCLA L.Rev. 815, 864 (1988) (hereinafter Lindgren). Hawkins defined extortion as follows:

"[I]t is said, That extortion in a large sense signifies any oppression under colour of right; but that in a strict sense, it signifies the taking of money by any officer, by colour of his office, either where none at all is due, or not so much is due, or where it is not yet due." 1 W. Hawkins, Pleas of the Crown 316 (6th ed. 1787).

[5] See Lindgren 882-889. The dissent says that we assume that "common law extortion encompassed any taking by a public official of something of value that he was not 'due.'" That statement, of course, is incorrect because, as stated in the text above, the payment must be "for the performance of his official duties."

Congress has unquestionably expanded the common-law definition of extortion to include acts by private individuals pursuant to which property is obtained by means of force, fear, or threats. It did so by implication in the Travel Act, 18 U.S.C. § 1952, and expressly in the Hobbs Act. * * *

* * * Although the present statutory text is much broader than the common-law definition of extortion because it encompasses conduct by a private individual as well as conduct by a public official, the portion of the statute that refers to official misconduct continues to mirror the common-law definition. There is nothing in either the statutory text or the legislative history that could fairly be described as a "contrary direction," from Congress to narrow the scope of the offense.

The legislative history is sparse and unilluminating with respect to the offense of extortion. There is a reference to the fact that the terms "robbery and extortion" had been construed many times by the courts and to the fact that the definitions of those terms were "based on the New York law." In view of the fact that the New York statute applied to a public officer "who asks, or receives, or agrees to receive" unauthorized compensation, N.Y.Penal Code § 557 (1881), the reference to New York law is consistent with an intent to apply the common-law definition. The language of the New York statute quoted above makes clear that extortion could be committed by one who merely received an unauthorized payment. This was the statute that was in force in New York when the Hobbs Act was enacted.

The two courts that have disagreed with the decision to apply the common-law definition have interpreted the word "induced" as requiring a wrongful use of official power that "begins with the public official, not with the gratuitous actions of another." United States v. O'Grady; see United States v. Aguon (" 'inducement' can be in the overt form of a 'demand,' or in a more subtle form such as 'custom' or 'expectation' "). If we had no common-law history to guide our interpretation of the statutory text, that reading would be plausible. For two reasons, however, we are convinced that it is incorrect.

First, we think the word "induced" is a part of the definition of the offense by the private individual, but not the offense by the public official. In the case of the private individual, the victim's consent must be "induced by wrongful use of actual or threatened force, violence or fear." In the case of the public official, however, there is no such requirement. The statute merely requires of the public official that he obtain "property from another, with his consent, . . . under color of official right." The use of the word "or" before "under color of official right" supports this reading.[15]

---

[15] This meaning would, of course, have been completely clear if Congress had inserted the word "either" before its description of the private offense because the word "or" already precedes the description of the public offense. The definition would then read: "The term 'extortion' means the obtaining of property from another, with

Second, even if the statute were parsed so that the word "induced" applied to the public officeholder, we do not believe the word "induced" necessarily indicates that the transaction must be initiated by the recipient of the bribe. Many of the cases applying the majority rule have concluded that the wrongful acceptance of a bribe establishes all the inducement that the statute requires. They conclude that the coercive element is provided by the public office itself. And even the two courts that have adopted an inducement requirement for extortion under color of official right do not require proof that the inducement took the form of a threat or demand.

Petitioner argues that the jury charge with respect to extortion, allowed the jury to convict him on the basis of the "passive acceptance of a contribution."[18] He contends that the instruction did not require the jury to find "an element of duress such as a demand," and it did not properly describe the *quid pro quo* requirement for conviction if the jury found that the payment was a campaign contribution.

We reject petitioner's criticism of the instruction, and conclude that it satisfies the *quid pro quo* requirement of *McCormick,* [p. 117], because the offense is completed at the time when the public official receives a payment in return for his agreement to perform specific official acts; fulfillment of the *quid pro quo* is not an element of the offense. We also reject petitioner's contention that an affirmative step is an element of the offense of extortion "under color of official right" and need be included in the instruction. As we explained above, our construction of the statute is informed by the common-law tradition from which the term of art was drawn and understood. We hold today that the Government need only show that a public official has obtained a payment to which he was not entitled, knowing that the payment was made in return for official acts.[20]

---

his consent, *either* induced by wrongful use of actual or threatened force, violence, or fear, or under color of official right."

[18] Petitioner also makes the point that "[t]he evidence at trial against [petitioner] is more conducive to a charge of bribery than one of extortion." Although the evidence in this case may have supported a charge of bribery, it is not a defense to a charge of extortion under color of official right that the defendant could also have been convicted of bribery. * * * We agree with the Seventh Circuit in United States v. Braasch, 505 F.2d 139, 151, n. 7 (1974), that " 'the modern trend of the federal courts is to hold that bribery and extortion as used in the Hobbs Act are not mutually exclusive.'"

[20] The dissent states that we have "simply made up," the requirement that the payment must be given in return for official acts. On the contrary, that requirement is derived from the statutory language "under color of official right," which has a well-recognized common-law heritage that distinguished between payments for private services and payments for public services. See, for example, Collier v. State, 55 Ala. 125 (1877), which the dissent describes as a "typical case."

Our conclusion is buttressed by the fact that so many other courts that have considered the issue over the last 20 years have interpreted the statute in the same way. Moreover, given the number of appellate court decisions, together with the fact that many of them have involved prosecutions of important officials well known in the political community, it is obvious that Congress is aware of the prevailing view that common-law extortion is proscribed by the Hobbs Act. The silence of the body that is empowered to give us a "contrary direction" if it does not want the common-law rule to survive is consistent with an application of the normal presumption identified in *Taylor* and *Morissette*.

III

An argument not raised by petitioner is now advanced by the dissent. It contends that common-law extortion was limited to wrongful takings under a false pretense of official right. It is perfectly clear, however, that although extortion accomplished by fraud was a well- recognized type of extortion, there were other types as well. As the court explained in Commonwealth v. Wilson, 30 Pa.Super. 26 (1906), an extortion case involving a payment by a would-be brothel owner to a police captain to ensure the opening of her house:

> "The form of extortion most commonly dealt with in the decisions is the corrupt taking by a person in office of a fee for services which should be rendered gratuitously; or when compensation is permissible, of a larger fee than the law justifies, or a fee not yet due; but this is not a complete definition of the offense, by which I mean that it does not include every form of common-law extortion."
> * * *

The dissent's theory notwithstanding, not one of the cases it cites holds that the public official is innocent unless he has deceived the payor by representing that the payment was proper. Indeed, none makes any reference to the state of mind of the payor, and none states that a "false pretense" is an element of the offense. Instead, those cases merely support the proposition that the services for which the fee is paid must be official and that the official must not be entitled to the fee that he collected—both elements of the offense that are clearly satisfied in this case. The complete absence of support for the dissent's thesis presumably explains why it was not advanced by petitioner in the District Court or the Court of Appeals, is not recognized by any Court of Appeals, and is not advanced in any scholarly commentary.

The judgment is affirmed.   * * *

Justice O'CONNOR, concurring in part and concurring in the judgment.
I join Parts I and II of the Court's opinion, because in my view they correctly answer the question on which the Court granted certiorari—whether or not an act of inducement is an element of the offense of extortion under color of official right. The issue raised by the dissent and

discussed in Part III of the Court's opinion is not fairly included in this question, see our Rule 14.1(a), and sound prudential reasons suggest that the Court should not address it. * * *

Justice KENNEDY, concurring in part and concurring in the judgment.

The Court gives a summary of its decision in these words: "We hold today that the Government need only show that a public official has obtained a payment to which he was not entitled, knowing that the payment was made in return for official acts." In my view the dissent is correct to conclude that this language requires a *quid pro quo* as an element of the Government's case in a prosecution under 18 U.S.C. § 1951, and the Court's opinion can be interpreted in a way that is consistent with this rule. Although the Court appears to accept the requirement of a *quid pro quo* as an alternative rationale, in my view this element of the offense is essential to a determination of those acts which are criminal and those which are not in a case in which the official does not pretend that he is entitled by law to the property in question. Here the prosecution did establish a *quid pro quo* that embodied the necessary elements of a statutory violation. I join part III of the Court's opinion and concur in the judgment affirming the conviction. I write this separate opinion to explain my analysis and understanding of the statute.

With regard to the question whether the word "induced" in the statutory definition of extortion applies to the phrase "under color of official right," 18 U.S.C. § 1951(b)(2), I find myself in substantial agreement with the dissent. Scrutiny of the placement of commas will not, in the final analysis, yield a convincing answer, and we are left with two quite plausible interpretations. Under these circumstances, I agree with the dissent that the rule of lenity requires that we avoid the harsher one. We must take as our starting point the assumption that the portion of the statute at issue here defines extortion as "the obtaining of property from another, with his consent, induced . . . under color of official right."

I agree with the Court, on the other hand, that the word "induced" does not "necessarily indicat[e] that the transaction must be *initiated* by the" public official. (emphasis in original). Something beyond the mere acceptance of property from another is required, however, or else the word "induced" would be superfluous. That something, I submit, is the *quid pro quo*. The ability of the official to use or refrain from using authority is the "color of official right" which can be invoked in a corrupt way to induce payment of money or to otherwise obtain property. The inducement generates a quid pro quo, under color of official right, that the statute prohibits. The term "under color of" is used, as I think both the Court and the dissent agree, to sweep within the statute those corrupt exercises of authority that the law forbids but that nevertheless cause damage because the exercise is by a governmental official.

The requirement of a *quid pro quo* means that without pretense of any entitlement to the payment, a public official violates § 1951 if he intends the payor to believe that absent payment the official is likely to abuse his office and his trust to the detriment and injury of the prospective payor or to give the prospective payor less favorable treatment if the *quid pro quo* is not satisfied. The official and the payor need not state the *quid pro quo* in express terms, for otherwise the law's effect could be frustrated by knowing winks and nods. The inducement from the official is criminal if it is express or if it is implied from his words and actions, so long as he intends it to be so and the payor so interprets it.

* * * [I] agree with the Court, that the *quid pro quo* requirement is not simply made up, as the dissent asserts. Instead, this essential element of the offense is derived from the statutory requirement that the official receive payment under color of official right, as well as the inducement requirement. And there are additional principles of construction which justify this interpretation. First is the principle that statutes are to be construed so that they are constitutional. * * *

Moreover, the mechanism which controls and limits the scope of official right extortion is a familiar one: a state of mind requirement. See Morissette v. United States, 342 U.S. 246 (1952) (refusing to impute to Congress the intent to create a strict liability crime despite the absence of any explicit mens rea requirement in the statute). Hence, even if the *quid pro quo* requirement did not have firm roots in the statutory language, it would constitute no abuse of judicial power for us to find it by implication.   * * *

The requirement of a *quid pro quo* in a § 1951 prosecution such as the one before us, in which it is alleged that money was given to the public official in the form of a campaign contribution, was established by our decision last term in McCormick v. United States, [p. 117]. Readers of today's opinion should have little difficulty in understanding that the rationale underlying the Court's holding applies not only in campaign contribution cases, but all § 1951 prosecutions. That is as it should be, for, given a corrupt motive, the *quid pro quo,* as I have said, is the essence of the offense.

Because I agree that the jury instruction in this case complied with the quid pro quo requirement, I concur in the judgment of the Court.

Justice THOMAS, with whom THE CHIEF JUSTICE and Justice SCALIA join, dissenting.

* * * The "under color of office" element of extortion, however, had a definite and well-established meaning at common law. "At common law it was essential that the money or property be obtained under color of office, *that is, under the pretense that the officer was entitled thereto by virtue of his office.* The money or thing received must have been claimed or accepted in right of office, and the person paying must have yielded to official authority." 3 R. Anderson, Wharton's Criminal Law and Procedure § 1393, pp. 790-791

(1957) (emphasis added). Thus, although the Court purports to define official extortion under the Hobbs Act by reference to the common law, its definition bears scant resemblance to the common-law crime Congress presumably codified in 1946. * * *

* * * *Regardless* of whether extortion contains an "inducement" requirement, bribery and extortion are different crimes. An official who solicits or takes a bribe does *not* do so "under color of office"; i.e., under any pretense of official entitlement. "The distinction between bribery and extortion seems to be that the former offense consists in offering a present or receiving one, the latter in *demanding* a fee or present *by color of office."* State v. Pritchard, 107 N.C. 921, 929 (1890) (emphasis added). Where extortion is at issue, the public official is the sole wrongdoer; because he acts "under color of office," the law regards the payor as an innocent victim and not an accomplice. With bribery, in contrast, the payor knows the recipient official is not entitled to the payment; he, as well as official, may be punished for the offense. Congress is well aware of the distinction between the crimes; it has always treated them separately. * * * By stretching the bounds of extortion to make it encompass bribery, the Court today blurs the traditional distinction between the crimes.   * * *

Perhaps because the common-law crime—as the Court defines it—is so expansive, the Court, at the very end of its opinion, appends a qualification: "We hold today that the Government need only show that a public official has obtained a payment to which he was not entitled, *knowing that the payment was made in return for official acts."* (emphasis added). This *quid pro quo* require-ment is simply made up. The Court does not suggest that it has any basis in the common law or the language of the Hobbs Act, and I have found no treatise or dictionary that refers to any such requirement in defining "extortion." * * * Its only conceivable source, in fact, is our opinion last Term in McCormick v. United States, [p. 117]. * * *

Because the common-law history of extortion was neither properly briefed nor argued in *McCormick,* the *quid pro quo* limitation imposed there represented a reasonable first step in the right direction. Now that we squarely consider that history, however, it is apparent that that limitation was in fact overly modest: at common law, McCormick was innocent of extortion not because he failed to offer a *quid pro quo* in return for campaign contributions, but because he did not take the contributions under color of official right. Today's extension of *McCormick's* reasonable (but textually and historically artificial) *quid pro quo* limitation to all cases of official extortion is both unexplained and inexplicable—except insofar as it may serve to rescue the Court's definition of extortion from substantial overbreadth.

* * * [A]ccording to the Court, the statute should read: " 'The term "extortion" means the obtaining of property from another, with his consent, *either* [1] induced by wrongful use of actual or threatened force, violence, or fear, or [2] under color of official right.' " That is, I concede, a *conceivable* con-struction of the words. But it is—at the very least—forced, for it sets up an

unnatural and ungrammatical parallel between the *verb* "induced" and the *preposition* "under."

The more natural construction is that the verb "induced" applies to *both* types of extortion described in the statute. Thus, the unstated "either" belongs *after* "induced": "The term 'extortion' means the obtaining of property from another, with his consent, induced *either* [1] by wrongful use of actual or threatened force, violence, or fear, or [2] under color of official right." This construction comports with correct grammar and standard usage by setting up a parallel between two prepositional phrases, the first beginning with "by"; the second with "under."

Our duty in construing this criminal statute, then, is clear: "The Court has often stated that when there are two rational readings of a criminal statute, one harsher than the other, we are to choose the harsher only when Congress has spoken in clear and definite language." Because the Court's expansive interpretation of the statute is not the only plausible one, the rule of lenity compels adoption of the narrower interpretation. * * * Given the text of the statute and the rule of lenity, I believe that inducement is an element of official extortion under the Hobbs Act.

Perhaps sensing the weakness of its position, the Court suggests an alternative interpretation: even if the statute *does* set forth an "inducement" requirement for official extortion, that requirement is always satisfied, because "the coercive element is provided by the public office itself." I disagree. A particular public official, to be sure, may wield his power in such a way as to coerce unlawful payments, even in the absence of any explicit demand or threat. But it ignores reality to assert that *every* public official, in *every* context, automatically exerts coercive influence on others by virtue of his office. If the Chairman of General Motors meets with a local court clerk, for example, whatever implicit coercive pressures exist will surely not emanate from the clerk. * * *

The Court's construction of the Hobbs Act is repugnant not only to the basic tenets of criminal justice reflected in the rule of lenity, but also to basic tenets of federalism. Over the past 20 years, the Hobbs Act has served as the engine for a stunning expansion of federal criminal jurisdiction into a field traditionally policed by state and local laws—acts of public corruption by state and local officials. See generally Ruff, Federal Prosecution of Local Corruption: A Case Study in the Making of Law Enforcement Policy, 65 Geo.L.J. 1171 (1977). * * * [C]oncerns of federalism require us to give a *narrow* construction to federal legislation in such sensitive areas unless Congress' contrary intent is "unmistakably clear in the language of the statute." Gregory v. Ashcroft, 111 S.Ct. 2395, 2401 (1991). * * * Similarly, in McNally v. United States, [p. 147]—a case closely analogous to this one—we rejected the Government's contention that the federal mail fraud statute, 18 U.S.C. § 1341, protected the citizenry's "intangible right" to good government, and hence could be applied to all instances of state and local corruption. * * *

I have no doubt that today's opinion is motivated by noble aims. Political corruption at any level of government is a serious evil, and, from a policy perspective, perhaps one well suited for federal law enforcement. But federal judges are not free to devise new crimes to meet the occasion. Chief Justice Marshall's warning is as timely today as ever: "It would be dangerous, indeed, to carry the principle that a case which is within the reason or mischief of a statute, is within its provisions, so far as to punish a crime not enumerated in the statute, because it is of equal atrocity, or of kindred character, with those which are enumerated." United States v. Wiltberger, 5 Wheat. 76, 96, 5 L.Ed. 37 (1820). * * *

NOTES AND QUESTIONS

1. *Interpreting Statutes.* How has the Court in *McCormick* and *Evans* dealt with the ambiguity in the statute? Has the Court, as a result of an inartfully drawn statute, created new doctrine that cannot be found in the statutory language? Is it necessary for courts to use federal statutes as "stopgap devices" [C.J. Burger, *Maze*, p. 145] until Congress can create particularized legislation "to deal directly with the evil?" For a discussion of the rule of lenity, see Dan. M. Kahan, *Lenity and Federal Common Law Crimes*, 1994 SUP. CT. REV. 345 (1994).

2. *Bribery/Extortion.* Can all acts of simple bribery by a public official be presented as extortion? Has the court "blurred" the distinction between bribery and extortion? See *Evans* (Thomas, dissenting), [p. 126]; James Lindgren, *The Theory, History, and Practice of the Bribery-Extortion Distinction*, 141 U. PA. L. REV. 1695 (1993).

3. *Quid Pro Quo.* After *Evans*, how explicit does the *quid pro quo* have to be? For a discussion of the varying views taken by lower courts, see Peter D. Hardy, Note, *The Emerging Role of the Quid Pro Quo Requirements in Public Corruption Prosecutions Under the Hobbs Act*, 28 MICH. J. L. REFORM 409, 436-41 (1995) ("[L]ower courts have grappled with whether officials must engage in explicit bribery to be convicted under the Hobbs Act, and, if so, just how explicit an 'explicit bribe must be.' Some courts have found that the existence of an explicitness requirement depends upon whether the payments at issue are campaign contributions.").

4. *Campaign Contributions.* Should the holdings in *McCormick* and *Evans* be limited to cases involving campaign contributions? In **United States v. Giles**, 246 F.3d 966, 972 (7th Cir. 2001), the court stated:

> We are not convinced that *Evans* clearly settles the question. And we recognize a policy concern which might justify distinguishing campaign contributions from other payments. After all, campaign contributions often are made with the hope that the recipient, if elected, will further interests with which the contributor agrees;

there is nothing illegal about such contributions. To distinguish legal from illegal campaign contributions, it makes sense to require the government to prove that a particular contribution was made in exchange for an explicit promise or undertaking by the official. Other payments to officials are not clothed with the same degree of respectability as ordinary campaign contributions. For that reason, perhaps it should be easier to prove that those payments are in violation of the law.

However, it is our view that this policy concern is outweighed by language in *Evans*, which, although not entirely clear, can easily be read to lend support to an inference that the quid pro quo requirement applies in all extortion prosecutions under the Hobbs Act--not to mention that four of the Justices read the language to include the requirement. We therefore join the circuits that require a quid pro quo showing in all cases. That said, we also agree with the Ninth Circuit in Tucker that the government need not show an explicit agreement, but only that the payment was made in return for official acts--that the public official understood that as a result of the payment he was expected to exercise particular kinds of influence on behalf of the payor.

5. ***Beyond Campaign Contributions.*** Should *Evans* and *McCormick* be extended to include an elected official's receipt of "gifts, meals, travel, expenses, or other items of value?" Consider this issue in the context of **United States v. Blandford**, 33 F.3d 685 (6th Cir. 1994):

Following a jury trial, defendant was convicted of (1) extortion, in violation of the Hobbs Act, 18 U.S.C. § 1951; (2) racketeering, in violation of the federal RICO statute, 18 U.S.C. § 1962(c); and (3) making false statements to federal investigators, in violation of 18 U.S.C. § 1001. On appeal, defendant challenges these convictions as well as his sentence. For the following reasons, we affirm.   * * *

This case arises out of an FBI investigation into public corruption in Kentucky.   The investigation, dubbed "Operation BOPTROT," focused on certain members of the Kentucky General Assembly who were suspected of extorting cash payments in exchange for assurances that they would take a particular stance on legislation pertaining to the horse racing industry. Initiated in September 1990, Operation BOPTROT ultimately ensnared several public officials, including Donald J. Blandford, Speaker of Kentucky's House of Representatives. * * *

On appeal, Blandford mounts several challenges to his Hobbs Act conviction. Title 18 U.S.C. § 1951, [p. 118] * * *.

First, Blandford takes issue with the district court's jury instructions pertaining to Counts 1 and 2 of his indictment. The instructions were in error, he complains, because they did not require the jury to find that he had entered into an explicit agreement (or *quid pro quo*) with Riverside Downs to oppose breed-to-breed legislation. Blandford also argues for the reversal of his extortion conviction on the ground that the evidence against him was insufficient to support the jury's verdict.

* * * Exactly what effect *Evans* had on *McCormick* is not altogether clear. The federal circuit courts that have considered the matter assume that the former establishes a modified or relaxed *quid pro quo* standard to be applied in non-campaign contribution cases. Under this view, the comparatively strict standard of *McCormick* still would govern when the alleged Hobbs Act violation arises out of the receipt of campaign contributions by a public official. See United States v. Martinez, 14 F.3d 543, 553 (11th Cir.1994); United States v. Taylor, 993 F.2d 382, 385 (4th Cir.1993); United States v. Garcia, 992 F.2d 409, 414 (2d Cir.1993). * * * [T]hese circuits have concluded that *Evans,* aside from addressing the question of inducement, also resolved an additional question ex-pressly left unanswered by the *McCormick* Court—"whether a *quid pro quo* re-quirement exists in other contexts, such as when an elected official receives gifts, meals, travel expenses, or other items of value."

We read *Evans* somewhat differently. *Evans,* we believe, merely clarified (1) that no affirmative step towards the performance of the public official's promise need be taken (i.e., fulfillment of the *quid pro quo* is not an element of the offense) and (2) that the *quid pro quo* of *McCormick* is satisfied by something short of a formalized and thoroughly articulated contractual arrangement (i.e., merely knowing the payment was made in return for official acts is enough). It was important for the Court to provide the former clarification because of a factual discrepancy between the two cases; in *McCormick,* unlike *Evans,* the defendant actually had performed his promise before his arrest. And in the case of the latter clarification, the Court gave content to what the *McCormick quid pro quo* entails. * * * *Evans* provided a gloss on the *McCormick* Court's use of the word "explicit" to qualify its quid pro quo require-ment. Explicit, as explained in *Evans,* speaks not to the form of the agreement between the payor and payee, but to the degree to which the payor and payee were aware of its terms, regardless of whether those terms were articulated. Put simply, Evans instructed that by "explicit" *McCormick* did not mean "express."

To the extent *Evans* charted entirely new waters, it did so not to differentiate campaign contribution cases from non-campaign contribution cases, but only to consider the issue on which certiorari was granted, the issue of inducement. Our reading of *Evans*—as limited to the campaign contribution context—is bolstered by the fact that the case, after all, involved campaign contributions. Moreover, the majority did not purport to extend its holding beyond the immediate context, nor did the issues before the Court require it to do so. See United States v. McDade, 827 F.Supp. 1153, 1171 n. 8 (E.D.Pa.1993) (refusing to apply *McCormick's quid pro quo* requirement in non-campaign contribution case); but see *Evans,* [p. 123] ("Readers of today's opinion should have little difficulty in understanding that the rationale underlying the Court's holding applies not only in campaign contribution cases, but all § 1951 prosecutions.") (Kennedy, J., concurring); id. at [p. 129] (suggesting that the Court extended *McCormick 's quid pro quo* requirement to all cases of official extortion) (Thomas, J., dissenting).

Pursuant to our interpretation of *Evans,* we cannot be certain whether the Supreme Court would have courts apply a different standard when a public official's acceptance of payments that are concededly not campaign contributions forms the basis for that official's extortion charge.   Indeed, a strong argument could be advanced for treating campaign contribution cases and non-campaign contribution cases disparately.   Campaign contributions, as the *McCormick* Court noted, enjoy what might be labeled a presumption of legitimacy. Although legitimate campaign contributions, not unlike Hobbs Act extortion payments, are given with the hope, and perhaps expectation, that the payment will make the official more likely to support the payor's interests, we punish neither the giving nor the taking presumably because we have decided that the alternative of financing campaigns with public funds is even less attractive than the current arrangement. Conversely, if any presumption is to be accorded to payments that occur outside of the campaign contribution context, the presumption would be the antithesis of the one described above. Stated another way, where, as in this case, a public official's primary justification for receiving, with relative impunity, cash payments from private sources, i.e., our present campaign financing system, is not available, that public official is left with few other means of rationalizing his actions.

That *Evans* and *McCormick* involved a public official's receipt of campaign contributions does not mean that they are inapposite for our present purposes. For instance, one thing that we do know from *Evans* is that a Hobbs Act conviction for extortion under color of official right will be sustained in campaign contribution cases when the government establishes the existence of a *quid pro quo,* as set forth in *McCormick* and informed by *Evans.* From this proposition, it follows a fortiori that in non-campaign contribution cases, which are perhaps less, but clearly not more, difficult to prove from the government's standpoint, the same showing of a *quid pro quo* also would suffice. * * * [The court examined the evidence before the jury and concluded that there was "sufficient evidence from which a reasonable juror could conclude that Blandford accepted a bribe," finding "not only that the motivation underlying the payments (i.e., the desire to buy or influence Blandford's vote) was corrupt, but also that Blandford understood he was being paid for his ability to act in this motivation."]

NELSON, Circuit Judge, concurring.

* * * In the case at bar, the defendant tendered a proposed jury instruction stating, among other things, that "[a]s used in these instructions 'wrongfully obtaining property from another . . . under color of official right' means that Mr. Blandford knowingly and deliberately agreed to accept property from Mr. McBee or others . . . in return for Mr. Blandford's promise to perform or not perform *specific* official acts or actions regarding proposed breed to breed legislation." (Emphasis supplied.) The instructions ultimately given by the district court omitted the word "specific." I believe it would have been preferable to include that term.   * * *[a]

6. *Gifts Under the Gratuities Statute.* How does the receipt of gifts by public officials differ in the context of the gratuities statute? Consider the issue in the context of the following case:

UNITED STATES v. SUN-DIAMOND GROWERS OF CALIFORNIA
526 U.S. 398, 119 S.Ct. 1402, 143 L.Ed.2d 576 (1999)

Justice SCALIA delivered the opinion of the Court.

Talmudic sages believed that judges who accepted bribes would be punished by eventually losing all knowledge of the divine law. The Federal Government, dealing with many public officials who are not judges, and with at least some judges for whom this sanction holds no terror, has constructed a framework of human laws and regulations defining various sorts of impermissible gifts, and punishing those who give or receive them with administrative sanctions, fines, and incarceration. One element of that framework is 18 U.S.C. § 201(c)(1)(A), the "illegal gratuity statute," which prohibits giving "anything of value" to a present, past, or future public official "for or because of any official act performed or to be performed by such public official." In this case, we consider whether conviction under the illegal gratuity statute requires any showing beyond the fact that a gratuity was given because of the recipient's official position.

---

[a] Dissent omitted.

Respondent is a trade association that engaged in marketing and lobbying activities on behalf of its member cooperatives, which were owned by approximately 5,000 individual growers of raisins, figs, walnuts, prunes, and hazelnuts. Petitioner United States is represented by Independent Counsel Donald Smaltz, who, as a consequence of his investigation of former Secretary of Agriculture Michael Espy, charged respondent with, inter alia, making illegal gifts to Espy in violation of § 201(c)(1)(A). That statute provides, in relevant part, that anyone who

"otherwise than as provided by law for the proper discharge of official duty ... directly or indirectly gives, offers, or promises anything of value to any public official, former public official, or person selected to be a public official, for or because of any official act performed or to be performed by such public official, former public official, or person selected to be a public official ... shall be fined under this title or imprisoned for not more than two years, or both."

Count One of the indictment charged Sun-Diamond with giving Espy approximately $5,900 in illegal gratuities: tickets to the 1993 U.S. Open Tennis Tournament (worth $2,295), luggage ($2,427), meals ($665), and a framed print and crystal bowl ($524). The indictment alluded to two matters in which respondent had an interest in favorable treatment from the Secretary at the time it bestowed the gratuities. First, respondent's member cooperatives participated in the Market Promotion Plan (MPP), a grant program administered by the Department of Agriculture to promote the sale of U.S. farm commodities in foreign countries. The cooperatives belonged to trade organizations, such as the California Prune Board and the Raisin Administrative Committee, which submitted overseas marketing plans for their respective commodities. If their plans were approved by the Secretary of Agriculture, the trade organizations received funds to be used in defraying the foreign marketing expenses of their constituents. Each of respondent's member cooperatives was the largest member of its respective trade organization, and each received significant MPP funding. Respondent was understandably concerned, then, when Congress in 1993 instructed the Secretary to promulgate regulations giving small-sized entities preference in obtaining MPP funds. If the Secretary did not deem respondent's member cooperatives to be small-sized entities, there was a good chance they would no longer receive MPP grants.   Thus, respondent had an interest in persuading the Secretary to adopt a regulatory definition of "small-sized entity" that would include its member cooperatives.

Second, respondent had an interest in the Federal Government's regulation of methyl bromide, a low-cost pesticide used by many individual growers in respondent's member cooperatives. In 1992, the Environmental Protection Agency announced plans to promulgate a rule to phase out the use of methyl bromide in the United States. The indictment alleged that respondent sought the Department of Agriculture's assistance in persuading EPA to abandon its proposed rule altogether, or at least to mitigate its impact. In the latter event, respondent wanted the Department to fund research efforts to develop reliable alternatives to methyl bromide.

Although describing these two matters before the Secretary in which respondent had an interest, the indictment did not allege a specific connection between either of them--or between any other action of the Secretary--and the gratuities conferred. The District Court denied respondent's motion to dismiss Count One because of this omission. The court stated:

> "[T]o sustain a charge under the gratuity statute, it is not necessary for the indictment to allege a direct nexus between the value conferred to Secretary Espy by Sun-Diamond and an official act performed or to be performed by Secretary Espy. It is sufficient for the indictment to allege that Sun- Diamond provided things of value to Secretary Espy because of his position."

At trial, the District Court instructed the jury along these same lines. It read § 201(c)(1)(A) to the jury twice (along with the definition of "official act" from § 201(a)(3)), but then placed an expansive gloss on that statutory language, saying, among other things, that "[i]t is sufficient if Sun-Diamond provided Espy with unauthorized compensation simply because he held public office," and that "[t]he government need not prove that the alleged gratuity was linked to a specific or identifiable official act or any act at all." The jury convicted respondent on, inter alia, Count One (the only subject of this appeal), and the District Court sentenced respondent on this count to pay a fine of $400,000. * * *

The Court of Appeals reversed the conviction on Count One and remanded for a new trial, stating:

> "Given that the 'for or because of any official act' language in ' 201(c)(1)(A) means what it says, the jury instructions invited the jury to convict on materially less evidence than the statute demands--evidence of gifts driven simply by Espy's official position."

In rejecting respondent's attack on the indictment, however, the court stated that the Government need not show that a gratuity was given "for or because of" any particular act or acts: "That an official has an abundance of relevant matters on his plate should not insulate him or his benefactors from the gratuity statute--as long as the jury is required to find the requisite intent to reward past favorable acts or to make future ones more likely." We granted certiorari.

Initially, it will be helpful to place § 201(c)(1)(A) within the context of the statutory scheme. Subsection (a) of § 201 sets forth definitions applicable to the section--including a definition of "official act," § 201(a)(3). Subsections (b) and (c) then set forth, respectively, two separate crimes--or two pairs of crimes, if one counts the giving and receiving of unlawful gifts as separate crimes--with two different sets of elements and authorized punishments. The first crime, described in § 201(b)(1) as to the giver, and § 201(b)(2) as to the recipient, is bribery, which requires a showing that something of value was corruptly given, offered, or promised to a public official (as to the giver) or corruptly demanded, sought, received, accepted, or agreed to be received or accepted by a public official (as to the recipient) with intent, inter alia, "to influence any official act" (giver) or in return for "being influenced in the performance of any official act" (recipient). The second crime, defined in § 201(c)(1)(A) as to the giver, and § 201(c)(1)(B) as to the recipient, is illegal gratuity, which requires a showing that something of value was given, offered, or promised to a public official (as to the giver), or demanded, sought, received, accepted, or agreed to be received or accepted by a public official (as to the recipient), "for or because of any official act performed or to be performed by such public official."

The distinguishing feature of each crime is its intent element. Bribery requires intent "to influence" an official act or "to be influenced" in an official act, while illegal gratuity requires only that the gratuity be given or accepted "for or because of" an official act. In other words, for bribery there must be a quid pro quo--a specific intent to give or receive something of value in exchange for an official act. An illegal gratuity, on the other hand, may constitute merely a reward for some future act that the public official will take (and may already have determined to take), or for a past act that he has already taken. The punishments prescribed for the two offenses reflect their relative seriousness: Bribery may be punished by up to 15 years' imprisonment, a fine of $250,000 ($500,000 for organizations) or triple the value of the bribe, whichever is greater, and disqualification from holding government office. See 18 U.S.C. §§ 201(b) and 3571. Violation of the illegal gratuity statute, on the other hand, may be punished by up to two years' imprisonment and a fine of $250,000 ($500,000 for organizations).

The District Court's instructions in this case, in differentiating between a bribe and an illegal gratuity, correctly noted that only a bribe requires proof of a quid pro quo. The point in controversy here is that the instructions went on to suggest that § 201(c)(1)(A), unlike the bribery statute, did not require any connection between respondent's intent and a specific official act. It would be satisfied, according to the instructions, merely by a showing that respondent gave Secretary Espy a gratuity because of his official position--perhaps, for example, to build a reservoir of goodwill that might ultimately affect one or more of a multitude of unspecified acts, now and in the future. The United States, represented by the Independent Counsel, and the Solicitor General as amicus curiae, contend that this instruction was correct. The Independent Counsel asserts that "section 201(c)(1)(A) reaches any effort to buy favor or generalized goodwill from an official who either has been, is, or may at some unknown, unspecified later time, be in a position to act favorably to the giver's interests." The Solicitor General contends that § 201(c)(1)(A) requires only a showing that a "gift was motivated, at least in part, by the recipient's capacity to exercise governmental power or influence in the donor's favor" without necessarily showing that it was connected to a particular official act.

In our view, this interpretation does not fit comfortably with the statutory text, which prohibits only gratuities given or received "for or because of any official act performed or to be performed". It seems to us that this means "for or because of some particular official act of whatever identity"--just as the question "Do you like any composer?" normally means "Do you like some particular composer?" It is linguistically possible, of course, for the phrase to mean "for or because of official acts in general, without specification as to which one"--just as the question "Do you like any composer?" could mean "Do you like all composers, no matter what their names or music?" But the former seems to us the more natural meaning, especially given the complex structure of the provision before us here. Why go through the trouble of requiring that the gift be made "for or because of any official act performed or to be performed by such public official," and then defining "official act" (in § 201(a)(3)) to mean "any decision or action on any question, matter, cause, suit, proceeding or controversy, which may at any time be pending, or which may by law be brought before any public official, in such official's official capacity," when, if the Government's interpretation were correct, it would have sufficed to say "for or because of such official's ability to favor the donor in executing the functions of his office"? The insistence upon an "official act," carefully defined, seems pregnant with the requirement that some particular official act be identified and proved.

Besides thinking that this is the more natural meaning of § 201(c)(1)(A), we are inclined to believe it correct because of the peculiar results that the Government's alternative reading would produce. It would criminalize, for example, token gifts to the President based on his official position and not linked to any identifiable act--such as the replica jerseys given by championship sports teams each year during ceremonial White House visits, see, e.g., Gail Gibson, Masters of the Game, Lexington Herald- Leader, Nov. 10, 1998, p. A1. Similarly, it would criminalize a high school principal's gift of a school baseball cap to the Secretary of Education, by reason of his office, on the occasion of the latter's visit to the school. That these examples are not fanciful is demonstrated by the fact that counsel for the United States maintained at oral argument that a group of farmers would violate § 201(c)(1)(A) by providing a complimentary lunch for the Secretary of Agriculture in conjunction with his speech to the farmers concerning various matters of USDA policy--so long as the Secretary had before him, or had in prospect, matters affecting the farmers. Of course the Secretary of Agriculture always has before him or in prospect matters that affect farmers, just as the President always has before him or in prospect matters that affect college and professional sports, and the Secretary of Education matters that affect high schools.

It might be said in reply to this that the more narrow interpretation of the statute can also produce some peculiar results. In fact, in the above-given examples, the gifts could easily be regarded as having been conferred, not only because of the official's position as President or Secretary, but also (and perhaps principally) "for or because of" the official acts of receiving the sports teams at the White House, visiting the high school, and speaking to the farmers about USDA policy, respectively. The answer to this objection is that those actions--while they are assuredly "official acts" in some sense--are not "official acts" within the meaning of the statute, which, as we have noted, defines "official act" to mean "any decision or action on any question, matter, cause, suit, proceeding or controversy, which may at any time be pending, or which may by law be brought before any public official, in such official's official capacity, or in such official's place of trust or profit." Thus, when the violation is linked to a particular "official act," it is possible to eliminate the absurdities through the definition of that term.   When, however, no particular "official act" need be identified, and the giving of gifts by reason of the recipient's mere tenure in office constitutes a violation, nothing but the Government's discretion prevents the foregoing examples from being prosecuted. * * *

Our refusal to read § 201(c)(1)(A) as a prohibition of gifts given by reason of the donee's office is supported by the fact that when Congress has wanted to adopt such a broadly prophylactic criminal prohibition upon gift giving, it has done so in a more precise and more administrable fashion. For example, another provision of Chapter 11 of Title 18, the chapter entitled "Bribery, Graft, and Conflicts of Interest," criminalizes the giving or receiving of any "supplementation" of an Executive official's salary, without regard to the purpose of the payment.   Other provisions of the same chapter make it a crime for a bank employee to give a bank examiner, and for a bank examiner to receive from a bank employee, "any loan or gratuity," again without regard to the purpose for which it is given.   A provision of the Labor Management Relations Act makes it a felony for an employer to give to a union representative, and for a union representative to receive from an employer, anything of value. With clearly framed and easily administrable provisions such as these on the books imposing gift-giving and gift-receiving prohibitions specifically based upon the holding of office, it seems to us most implausible that Congress intended the language of the gratuity statute--"for or because of any official act performed or to be performed"--to pertain to the office rather than (as the language more naturally suggests) to particular official acts. * * *

We hold that, in order to establish a violation of 18 U.S.C. § 201(c)(1)(A), the Government must prove a link between a thing of value conferred upon a public official and a specific "official act" for or because of which it was given. We affirm the judgment of the Court of Appeals, which remanded the case to the District Court for a new trial on Count One. Our decision today casts doubt upon the lower courts' resolution of respondent's challenge to the sufficiency of the indictment on Count One--an issue on which certiorari was neither sought nor granted.   We leave it to the District Court to determine whether that issue should be reopened on remand. * * * It is so ordered.

NOTES AND QUESTIONS

1. *Aftermath.* On December 2, 1998 a federal jury found former Agriculture Secretary Mike Espy not guilty of the thirty counts brought against him as a result of an investigation conducted by an Independent Counsel. Following this acquittal, Archibald R. Schaffer III, Tyson Foods' Director of Media, Public and Governmental Affairs, filed a motion for a new trial premised on the "newly-found and arguably exculpatory testimony of former Secretary of the Department of Agriculture, Alphonso Michael Espy, which had become available following Espy's own acquittal in a related prosecution." "On December 22, 2000, then-President Clinton granted a full and unconditional pardon to Schaffer." See United States v. Schaffer, 240 F.3d 35 (D.C. Cir. 2001).

2. *Reading Exceptions Into the Statute.* In United States v. Singleton, 165 F.3d 1297 (10th Cir.), cert. denied 527 U.S. 1024 (1999), an en banc court vacated a panel decision which had "reversed a conviction on the ground the prosecuting attorney violated 18 U.S.C. § 201(c)(2) when he offered leniency to a co-defendant in exchange for truthful testimony." The en banc court found that "18 U.S.C. § 201(c)(2) does not apply to the United States or an Assistant United States Attorney functioning within the official scope of the office."

CHAPTER FIVE
MAIL AND WIRE FRAUD

A. INTRODUCTION

The crime of mail fraud emanates from an 1872 recodification of the Postal Act. At its inception, the crux of the offense was on the misuse of the postal system by way of a counterfeit scheme. The emphasis of the offense has now shifted to the "scheme to defraud" element of the statute. A mail fraud prosecution requires the government to prove 1) a scheme devised or intending to defraud or for obtaining money or property by fraudulent means; and 2) use or causing the use of the mails (or private courier) in furtherance of the fraudulent scheme. Materiality is essential to proving mail fraud.

The mail fraud statute's enormous breadth allows federal prosecutors to use this offense to combat many different types of fraudulent conduct. Jed Rakoff called mail fraud the prosecutor's "Stradivarius" or "Colt 45." Jed S. Rakoff, *The Federal Mail Fraud Statute* (pt. 1), 18 DUQ. L. REV. 771, 784 (1980). Chief Justice Burger termed it the "stopgap" provision. United States v. Maze, below. Professor Ellen S. Podgor maintains that it is the prosecutor's "Uzi." Ellen S. Podgor, *Mail Fraud: Opening Letters,* 43 S.C. L. REV. 223, 224 (1992). Judge Ralph K. Winter notes that "[w]ith regard to the statutory weapons available to prosecutors, they rank by analogy with hydrogen bombs on stealth aircraft. Foremost among them are the various federal fraud statutes—in particular, the mail and wire fraud statutes * * *." Ralph K. Winter, *Paying Lawyers, Empowering Prosecutors and Protecting Managers: the Cost of Capital in America,* 42 DUKE L.J. 945, 954 (1993). The statute is used by prosecutors to criminalize fraudulent conduct that might not be covered in other legislation. See Peter Henning, *Maybe It Should Just Be Called Federal Fraud: The Changing Nature of the Mail Fraud Statute,* 36 B.C. L. REV. 435 (1995).

B. SCHEME TO DEFRAUD

In **United States v. Maze**, 414 U.S. 395 (1974), the United States Supreme Court rejected the use of the mail fraud statute where the mailing in furtherance of the scheme to defraud was premised on an alleged use of a stolen credit card and the subsequent mailing to collect on the bills. The Court rejected the government's argument that these collection mailings were necessary to the scheme's success. Dissenting, Chief Justice Burger, joined by Justice White, stated:

* * * Section 1341 of Title 18 U.S.C. has traditionally been used against fraudulent activity as a first line of defense. When a "new" fraud develops—as constantly happens—the mail fraud statute becomes a stopgap device to deal on a temporary basis with the new phenomenon, until particularized legislation can be developed and passed to deal directly with the evil. "Prior to the passage of the 1933 (Securities) Act, most criminal prosecutions for fraudulent securities transactions were brought under the Federal Mail Fraud Statute." * * * Loan sharks were brought to justice by means of 18 U.S.C. § 1341, * * * before Congress, in 1968, recognized the interstate character of loansharking and the need to provide federal protection against this organized crime activity, and enacted 18 U.S.C. § 891 et seq., outlawing extortionate extensions of credit. Although inadequate to protect the buying and investing public fully, the mail fraud statute stood in the breach against frauds connected with the burgeoning sale of undeveloped real estate, until Congress could examine the problems of the land sales industry and pass into law the Interstate Land Sales Full Disclosure Act, 82 Stat. 590, 15 U.S.C. § 1701 et seq. * * * Similarly, the mail fraud statute was used to stop credit card fraud, before Congress moved to provide particular protection by passing 15 U.S.C. § 1644.

The mail fraud statute continues to remain an important tool in prosecuting frauds in those areas where legislation has been passed more directly addressing the fraudulent conduct. Mail fraud counts fill pages of securities fraud indictments even today. * * * Despite the prevasive Government regulation of the drug industry, postal fraud statutes still play an important role in controlling the solicitation of mail-order purchases by drug distributors based upon fraudulent misrepresentations. * * *

The criminal mail fraud statute must remain strong to be able to cope with the new varieties of fraud that the ever-inventive American "con artist" is sure to develop. Abuses in franchising and the growing scandals from pyramid sales schemes are but some of the threats to the financial security of our citizenry that the Federal Government must be ever alert to combat. * * *

NOTES AND QUESTIONS

1. *Schemes to Defraud.* Courts have found that the "scheme to defraud" element of this statute encompasses an endless array of frauds. See, e.g., Carpenter v. United States, 484 U.S. 19 (1987) (securities fraud); United States v. Serlin, 538 F.2d 737 (7th Cir. 1976) (franchise fraud); United States v. Cavalier, 17 F.3d 90 (5th Cir. 1994) (insurance fraud); United States v. Edwards, 458 F.2d 875 (5th Cir. 1972) ("divorce mill" fraud); United States

v. Hayes, 231 F.3d 663 (9th Cir. 2000) (scheme to sell grades for classes that foreign students did not attend).

   2. *Limitations.* Are there any limits as to what fraudulent conduct can be prosecuted under the mail fraud statute? In Fasulo v. United States, 272 U.S. 620, 625 (1926), the Supreme Court found that a "use of the mails for the purpose of obtaining money by means of threats of murder or bodily harm" was not a scheme to defraud for the purposes of mail fraud.

   3. *Tax Fraud/Mail Fraud.* Can the mailing of a fraudulent tax return be charged as mail fraud? Compare the majority view as expressed in United States v. Miller, 545 F.2d 1204, 1216 (9th Cir. 1976) (mail fraud can be a cumulative and alternative charge to tax fraud) with the minority view expressed in United States v. Henderson, 386 F. Supp. 1048 (S.D.N.Y. 1974) (mail fraud improper for alleged income tax evasion due to existence of "particularized legislation"). The Department of Justice has issued a guideline instructing prosecutors that only in "exceptional circumstances" will tax fraud be approved for a mail fraud prosecution. U.S.A.M. § 6-4.211(1) (1990).

   4. *Particularized Legislation.* Once Congress provides the particularized legislation to combat the new fraud, can prosecutors still use the mail fraud statute? Compare the majority view expressed in United States v. Simon, 510 F. Supp. 232 (E.D. Pa. 1981) (permitted mail fraud despite the enactment of a specific Medicaid fraud statute) with the minority view expressed in United States v. Gallant, 570 F. Supp. 303, 310 (S.D. N.Y. 1983) (mail fraud improper where particularized legislation existed within the Copyright Act), but see United States v. Dowling, 739 F.2d 1445, 1450 (9th Cir. 1984), reversed on other grounds, [p. 106]. Particularized legislation was recently passed to address health care fraud. See 18 U.S.C. § 1347 (1996) (new health care fraud statute has penalties of up to 10 years imprisonment, 20 years if the violation results in serious bodily injury, and any term of years or life if the violation results in death). Congress also recently passed the Identity Theft and Assumption Deterrence Act of 1998.

McNALLY v. UNITED STATES
483 U.S. 350, 107 S.Ct. 2875, 97 L.Ed.2d 292 (1987)

Justice WHITE delivered the opinion of the Court.

   This action involves the prosecution of petitioner Gray, a former public official of the Commonwealth of Kentucky, and petitioner McNally, a private individual, for alleged violation of the federal mail fraud statute, 18 U.S.C. § 1341. The prosecution's principal theory of the case, which was accepted by the courts below, was that petitioners' participation in a self-dealing patronage scheme defrauded the citizens and government of Kentucky of certain "intangible rights," such as the right to have the Commonwealth's affairs conducted honestly. We must consider whether the jury charge permitted a conviction for conduct not within the scope of the mail fraud statute.

We accept for the sake of argument the Government's view of the evidence, as follows. Petitioners and a third individual, Howard P. "Sonny" Hunt, were politically active in the Democratic Party in the Commonwealth of Kentucky during the 1970's. After Democrat Julian Carroll was elected Governor of Kentucky in 1974, Hunt was made chairman of the state Democratic Party and given *de facto* control over selecting the insurance agencies from which the Commonwealth would purchase its policies. In 1975, the Wombwell Insurance Company of Lexington, Kentucky (Wombwell), which since 1971 had acted as the Commonwealth's agent for securing a workmen's compensation policy, agreed with Hunt that in exchange for a continued agency relationship it would share any resulting commissions in excess of $50,000 a year with other insurance agencies specified by him. The commissions in question were paid to Wombwell by the large insurance companies from which it secured coverage for the Commonwealth.

From 1975 to 1979, Wombwell funneled $851,000 in commissions to 21 separate insurance agencies designated by Hunt. Among the recipients of these payments was Seton Investments, Inc. (Seton), a company controlled by Hunt and petitioner Gray and nominally owned and operated by petitioner McNally.

Gray served as Secretary of Public Protection and Regulation from 1976 to 1978 and also as Secretary of the Governor's Cabinet from 1977 to 1979. Prior to his 1976 appointment, he and Hunt established Seton for the sole purpose of sharing in the commissions distributed by Wombwell. Wombwell paid some $200,000 to Seton between 1975 and 1979, and the money was used to benefit Gray and Hunt. Pursuant to Hunt's direction, Wombwell also made excess commission payments to the Snodgrass Insurance Agency, which in turn gave the money to McNally.

On account of the foregoing activities, Hunt was charged with and pleaded guilty to mail and tax fraud and was sentenced to three years' imprisonment. Petitioners were charged with one count of conspiracy and seven counts of mail fraud, six of which were dismissed before trial.[2] The remaining mail fraud count was based on the mailing of a commission check to Wombwell by the insurance company from which it had secured coverage for the State. This count alleged that petitioners had devised a scheme (1) to

---

[2] The six counts dismissed were based on the mailing of Seton's tax returns. The Court of Appeals held that mailings required by law cannot be made the basis for liability under § 1341 unless the documents are themselves false, see Parr v. United States, 363 U.S. 370 (1960), and that the six counts were properly dismissed since the indictment did not allege that Seton's tax returns were false. The Government has not sought review of this holding.

defraud the citizens and government of Kentucky of their right to have the Commonwealth's affairs conducted honestly, and (2) to obtain, directly and indirectly, money and other things of value by means of false pretenses and the concealment of material facts. * * *

After informing the jury of the charges in the indictment, the District Court instructed that the scheme to defraud the citizens of Kentucky and to obtain money by false pretenses and concealment could be made out by either of two sets of findings: (1) that Hunt had *de facto* control over the award of the workmen's compensation insurance contract to Wombwell from 1975 to 1979; that he directed payments of commissions from this contract to Seton, an entity in which he had an ownership interest, without disclosing that interest to persons in state government whose actions or deliberations could have been affected by the disclosure; and that petitioners, or either of them, aided and abetted Hunt in that scheme; or (2) that Gray, in either of his appointed positions, had supervisory authority regarding the Commonwealth's workmen's compensation insurance at a time when Seton received commissions; that Gray had an ownership interest in Seton and did not disclose that interest to persons in state government whose actions or deliberations could have been affected by that disclosure; and that McNally aided and abetted Gray (the latter finding going only to McNally's guilt).

The jury convicted petitioners on both the mail fraud and conspiracy counts, and the Court of Appeals affirmed the convictions. In affirming the substantive mail fraud conviction, the court relied on a line of decisions from the Courts of Appeals holding that the mail fraud statute proscribes schemes to defraud citizens of their intangible rights to honest and impartial government. * * *

We granted certiorari, and now reverse.

The mail fraud statute clearly protects property rights, but does not refer to the intangible right of the citizenry to good government. As first enacted in 1872, as part of a recodification of the postal laws, the statute contained a general proscription against using the mails to initiate correspondence in furtherance of "any scheme or artifice to defraud." The sponsor of the recodification stated, in apparent reference to the antifraud provision, that measures were needed "to prevent the frauds which are mostly gotten up in the large cities . . . by thieves, forgers, and rapscallions generally, for the purpose of deceiving and fleecing the innocent people in the country." Insofar as the sparse legislative history reveals anything, it indicates that the original impetus behind the mail fraud statute was to protect the people from schemes to deprive them of their money or property.

Durland v. United States, 161 U.S. 306 (1896), the first case in which this Court construed the meaning of the phrase "any scheme or artifice to defraud," held that the phrase is to be interpreted broadly insofar as property rights are concerned, but did not indicate that the statute had a more extensive reach. The Court rejected the argument that "the statute reaches only such cases as, at common law, would come within the definition of 'false pretences,' in order to make out which there must be a misrepresentation as to some existing fact and not a mere promise as to the future." Instead, it construed the statute to "includ[e] everything designed to defraud by representations as to the past or present, or suggestions and promises as to the future." Accordingly, the defendant's use of the mails to sell bonds which he did not intend to honor was within the statute. The Court explained that "[i]t was with the purpose of protecting the public against all such intentional efforts to despoil, and to prevent the post office from being used to carry them into effect, that this statute was passed . . . ."

Congress codified the holding of *Durland* in 1909, and in doing so gave further indication that the statute's purpose is protecting property rights. The amendment added the words "or for obtaining money or property by means of false or fraudulent pretenses, representations, or promises" after the original phrase "any scheme or artifice to defraud." Act of Mar. 4, 1909, ch. 321, § 215, 35 Stat. 1130. The new language is based on the statement in *Durland* that the statute reaches "everything designed to defraud by representations as to the past or present, or suggestions and promises as to the future." However, instead of the phrase "everything designed to defraud" Congress used the words "[any scheme or artifice] for obtaining money or property."

After 1909, therefore, the mail fraud statute criminalized schemes or artifices "to defraud" or "for obtaining money or property by means of false or fraudulent pretenses, representation, or promises . . . ." Because the two phrases identifying the proscribed schemes appear in the disjunctive, it is arguable that they are to be construed independently and that the money-or-property requirement of the latter phrase does not limit schemes to defraud to those aimed at causing deprivation of money or property. This is the approach that has been taken by each of the Courts of Appeals that has addressed the issue: schemes to defraud include those designed to deprive individuals, the people, or the government of intangible rights, such as the right to have public officials perform their duties honestly. As the Court long ago stated, however, the words "to defraud" commonly refer "to wronging one in his property rights by dishonest methods or schemes," and "usually signify the deprivation of something of value by trick, deceit, chicane or overreaching." Hammerschmidt v. United States, 265 U.S. 182, 188 (1924).[8]

---

[8] *Hammerschmidt* concerned the scope of the predecessor of 18 U.S.C. § 371, which makes criminal any conspiracy "to defraud the United States, or any agency thereof in any manner or for any purpose." Hammerschmidt indicates, in regard to that statute, that while "[t]o conspire to defraud the United States means primarily to cheat the Government out of property or money, . . . it also means to interfere with or obstruct one of its lawful governmental functions by deceit, craft or trickery, or at least by means that are dishonest." 265 U.S., at 188. Other cases have held that § 371 reaches conspiracies other than those directed at property interests. However, we believe that this broad construction of § 371 is based on a consideration not applicable to the mail fraud statute. * * *

The codification of the holding in *Durland* in 1909 does not indicate that Congress was departing from this common understanding. As we see it, adding the second phrase simply made it unmistakable that the statute reached false promises and misrepresentations as to the future as well as other frauds involving money or property.

We believe that Congress' intent in passing the mail fraud statute was to prevent the use of the mails in furtherance of such schemes. The Court has often stated that when there are two rational readings of a criminal statute, one harsher than the other, we are to choose the harsher only when Congress has spoken in clear and definite language. United States v. Bass, 404 U.S. 336, 347 (1971); United States v. Universal C.I.T. Credit Corp., 344 U.S. 218, 221-222 (1952). See also Rewis v. United States, 401 U.S. 808, 812 (1971). As the Court said in a mail fraud case years ago: "There are no constructive offenses; and before one can be punished, it must be shown that his case is plainly within the statute." Fasulo v. United States, 272 U.S. 620, 629 (1926). Rather than construe the statute in a manner that leaves its outer boundaries ambiguous and involves the Federal Government in setting standards of disclosure and good government for local and state officials, we read § 1341 as limited in scope to the protection of property rights. If Congress desires to go further, it must speak more clearly than it has.

For purposes of this action, we assume that Hunt, as well as Gray, was a state officer. The issue is thus whether a state officer violates the mail fraud statute if he chooses an insurance agent to provide insurance for the State but specifies that the agent must share its commissions with other named insurance agencies, in one of which the officer has an ownership interest and hence profits when his agency receives part of the commissions. We note that as the action comes to us, there was no charge and the jury was not required to find that the Commonwealth itself was defrauded of any money or property. It was not charged that in the absence of the alleged scheme the Commonwealth would have paid a lower premium or secured better insurance. Hunt and Gray received part of the commissions but those commissions were not the Commonwealth's money. Nor was the jury charged that to convict it must find that the Commonwealth was deprived of control over how its money was spent. Indeed, the premium for insurance would have been paid to some agency, and what Hunt and Gray did was to assert control that the Commonwealth might not otherwise have made over the commissions paid by the insurance company to its agent. Although the Government now relies in part on the assertion that petitioners obtained property by means of false representations to Wombwell, there was nothing in the jury charge that required such a finding. We hold, therefore, that the

---

Section 371 is a statute aimed at protecting the Federal Government alone; however, the mail fraud statute, as we have indicated, had its origin in the desire to protect individual property rights, and any benefit which the Government derives from the statute must be limited to the Government's interests as property holder.

jury instruction on the substantive mail fraud count permitted a conviction for conduct not within the reach of § 1341.

The Government concedes that if petitioners' substantive mail fraud convictions are reversed their conspiracy convictions should also be reversed.

The judgment of the Court of Appeals is reversed, and the case is remanded for proceedings consistent with this opinion.

It is so ordered.

Justice STEVENS, with whom Justice O'CONNOR joins as to Parts I, II, and III, dissenting.

* * * The same question of statutory construction has arisen in a variety of contexts over the past few decades. In the public sector, judges, State Governors, chairmen of state political parties, state cabinet officers, city aldermen, Congressmen and many other state and federal officials have been convicted of defrauding citizens of their right to the honest services of their governmental officials. In most of these cases, the officials have secretly made governmental decisions with the objective of benefitting themselves or promoting their own interests, instead of fulfilling their legal commitment to provide the citizens of the State or local government with their loyal service and honest government. Similarly, many elected officials and their campaign workers have been convicted of mail fraud when they have used the mails to falsify votes, thus defrauding the citizenry of its right to an honest election. In the private sector, purchasing agents, brokers, union leaders, and others with clear fiduciary duties to their employers or unions have been found guilty of defrauding their employers or unions by accepting kickbacks or selling confidential information. In other cases, defendants have been found guilty of using the mails to defraud individuals of their rights to privacy and other nonmonetary rights.[4] All of these cases have something in common—they involved what the Court now refers to as "intangible rights." They also share something else in common. The many federal courts that have confronted the question whether these sorts of schemes constitute a "scheme or artifice to defraud" have uniformly and consistently read the statute in the same, sensible way. They have realized that nothing in the words "any scheme or artifice to defraud," or in the purpose of the statute, justifies limiting its application to schemes intended to deprive victims of money or property.

---

[4] See e.g. United States v. Condolon, 600 F.2d 7 (4th Cir. 1979) (wire fraud conviction related to bogus talent agency designed to seduce women); United States v. Louderman, 576 F.2d 1383 (9th Cir.) (scheme to fraudulently obtain confidential personal information); see also United States v. Castor, 558 F.2d 379, 393 (7th Cir. 1977) (fraudulent information on application for liquor license).

I

The mail fraud statute sets forth three separate prohibitions. It prohibits the use of the United States mails for the purpose of executing "[1] *any* scheme or artifice to defraud, [2] *or* for obtaining money or property by means of false or fraudulent pretenses, representations, or promises, [3] *or* to sell, dispose of, loan, exchange, alter, give away, distribute, supply, or furnish or procure for unlawful use any counterfeit or spurious coin, obligation, security, or other article, or anything represented to be or intimated or held out to be such counterfeit or spurious article . . . ." 18 U.S.C. § 1341 (emphasis and brackets added).

As the language makes clear, each of these restrictions is independent. One can violate the second clause—obtaining money or property by false pretenses—even though one does not violate the third clause—counterfeiting. Similarly, one can violate the first clause—devising a scheme or artifice to defraud—without violating the counterfeiting provision. Until today it was also obvious that one could violate the first clause by devising a scheme or artifice to defraud, even though one did not violate the second clause by seeking to obtain money or property from his victim through false pretenses. *Cf.* Streep v. United States, 160 U.S. 128, 132-133 (1895). Every court to consider the matter had so held. Yet, today, the Court, for all practical purposes, rejects this longstanding construction of the statute by imposing a requirement that a scheme or artifice to defraud does not violate the statute unless its purpose is to defraud someone of money or property. I am at a loss to understand the source or justification for this holding. Certainly no canon of statutory construction requires us to ignore the plain language of the provision.

In considering the scope of the mail fraud statute it is essential to remember Congress' purpose in enacting it. Congress sought to protect the integrity of the United States mails by not allowing them to be used as "instruments of crime." United States v. Brewer, 528 F.2d 492, 498 (CA4 1975). * * * "The focus of the statute is upon the misuse of the Postal Service, not the regulation of state affairs, and Congress clearly has the authority to regulate such misuse of the mails. See Badders v. United States, 240 U.S. 391 (1916)." United States v. States, 488 F.2d 761, 767 (CA8 1973). Once this purpose is considered, it becomes clear that the construction the Court adopts today is senseless. Can it be that Congress sought to purge the mails of schemes to defraud citizens of money but was willing to tolerate schemes to defraud citizens of their right to an honest government, or to unbiased public officials? Is it at all rational to assume that Congress wanted to ensure that the mails not be used for petty crimes, but did not prohibit election fraud accomplished through mailing fictitious ballots?   Given Congress' "broad purpose," I "find it difficult to believe, absent some indication in the statute itself or the legislative history, that Congress would have undercut sharply that purpose by hobbling federal prosecutors in their effort to combat" use of the mails for fraudulent schemes. McElroy v. United States, 455 U.S. 642, 655 (1982).   * * *

II

* * * [T]he construction the courts have consistently given the statute is consistent with the common understanding of the term "fraud," and Congress' intent in enacting the statute. It is also consistent with the manner in which the term has been interpreted in an analogous federal statute; the way the term was interpreted at the time of this statute's enactment; and the statute's scant legislative history. There is no reason, therefore, to upset the settled, sensible construction that the federal courts have consistently endorsed.

The term "defraud" is not unique to § 1341. Another federal statute, 18 U.S.C. § 371, uses the identical term in prohibiting conspiracies to "defraud the United States," and the construction we have given to that statute should be virtually dispositive here. In Haas v. Henkel, 216 U.S. 462 (1910), the Court, dealing with the predecessor to § 371, rejected the argument that there could be no conspiracy to defraud in the absence of contemplated monetary or property loss. "The statute is broad enough in its terms to include any conspiracy for the purpose of impairing, obstructing or defeating the lawful function of any department of Government." Again, in Hammerschmidt v. United States, the Court described the scope of the statute as prohibiting not only conspiracies to "cheat the Government out of property or money, but it also means to interfere with or obstruct one of its lawful governmental functions by deceit, craft or trickery, or at least by means that are dishonest." It is thus clear that a conspiracy to defraud the United States does not require any evidence that the Government has suffered any property or pecuniary loss. * * *

There is no basis for concluding that the term "defraud" means something different in § 1341 (first enacted in 1872) than what it means in § 371 (first enacted in 1867). Although § 371 includes the words "in any manner or for any purpose," those words only modify the underlying act—fraud, and if that term does not include nonproperty interests then our longstanding interpretation of § 371 is unjustified. In any event, § 1341 itself includes the expansive phrase "any scheme or artifice to defraud."

The Court nonetheless suggests that interpreting the two statutes differently can be justified because § 371 applies exclusively to frauds against the United States, while § 1341 benefits private individuals. This argument is wide of the mark. The purpose of § 1341 is to protect the integrity of the United States Postal Service, and, as I have explained, it is ludicrous to think that a Congress intent on preserving the integrity of the Postal Service would have used the term "defraud" in a narrow sense so as to allow mailings whose purpose was merely to defraud citizens of rights other than money or property. There is, therefore, no reason to believe that Congress used the term "defraud" in a more limited way in § 1341 than it did in § 371. The Court is correct in pointing out that Congress intended to go beyond any common-law meaning of the word "defraud" in enacting § 371. But we have also rejected the argument that the common-law meaning of the term

"defraud" confines the scope of § 1341. See Durland v. United States.
* * *

III

To support its crabbed construction of the Act, the Court makes a straightforward but unpersuasive argument. Since there is no explicit, unambiguous evidence that Congress actually contemplated "intangible rights" when it enacted the mail fraud statute in 1872, the Court explains, any ambiguity in the meaning of the criminal statute should be resolved in favor of lenity. The doctrine of lenity is, of course, sound, for the citizen is entitled to fair notice of what sort of conduct may give rise to punishment. But the Court's reliance on that doctrine in this case is misplaced * * * .

IV

* * * In the long run, it is not clear how grave the ramifications of today's decision will be. Congress can, of course, negate it by amending the statute. Even without congressional action, prosecutions of corrupt officials who use the mails to further their schemes may continue since it will frequently be possible to prove some loss of money or property. But many other types of fraudulent use of the mail will now be immune from prosecution. The possibilities that the decision's impact will be mitigated do not moderate my conviction that the Court has made a serious mistake. Nor do they erase my lingering questions about why a Court that has not been particularly receptive to the rights of criminal defendants in recent years has acted so dramatically to protect the elite class of powerful individuals who will benefit from this decision.

I respectfully dissent.

NOTES AND QUESTIONS

1. *McNally's Reach.* Would the result of this case be different if the government had alleged a deprivation of money or property in the indictment and if the jury had been instructed on the necessity of the government proving a loss of money or property? Is *McNally* an extremely limited decision?

2. *Retroactivity.* Many of the convictions based upon intangible rights required reversal as a result of *McNally.* See Craig M. Bradley, *Foreward: Mail Fraud After* McNally *and* Carpenter: *The Essence of Fraud,* 79 J. CRIM. L. & CRIMINOLOGY 573 (1988); Peter M. Oxman, Note, *The Federal Mail Fraud Statute After* McNally v. United States, *107 S.Ct. 2875 (1987): The Remains of the Intangible Rights Doctrine and Its Proposed Congressional Restoration,* 25 AM. CRIM. L. REV. 743 (1988). Courts have not ruled consistently in deciding whether a *writ of coram nobis* should be granted for

defendants who are no longer in custody. See Deborah Sprenger, Annotation, *Effect Upon Prior Convictions of* McNally v. United States *Rule that Mail Fraud Statute* (18 U.S.C.A. § 1341) *Is Directed Solely at Deprivation of Property Rights,* 97 A.L.R. Fed. 797 (1990). "Most courts * * * determined that *McNally* is retroactive, thus affording persons who were convicted before *McNally* opportunities to collaterally attack their convictions. In addition, a number of mail fraud cases were pending direct appeal at the time *McNally* was decided, forcing the court of appeals to decide whether 'improper intangible rights instructions so polluted the jury's deliberations as to render the conviction invalid . . . .' In reviewing the outcome of such appeals and collateral attacks, one judge has noted that some courts have 'stretched to find more ingenious theories of property loss which purportedly satisfy *McNally* and affirmed on the basis of these theories even though they were not put before the jury.' These efforts to 'salvage' pre-*McNally* convictions have been described as 'commendable' for 'treating technicality with sophistication in the interest of substantial justice.'" Donna M. Maus, Comment, *License Procurement and the Federal Mail Fraud Statute,* 58 U. Chi. L. Rev. 1125, 1131-32 (1991).

3. *Kickback Schemes/Faithful Services.* Following *McNally,* the government, relying on Justice Stevens' dissent, argued that kickback schemes deprived the employer "of the salary and benefits paid to the employee in reliance on his faithful services free from conflict of interest." United States v. Johns, 688 F. Supp. 1017 (E.D. Pa. 1988). This position has been accepted by some courts and rejected by others.

4. *Kickback Schemes/Right to Information.* Another argument advanced by the government in kickback cases was that the employer suffered a loss because, had it known of the supplier's willingness to pay kickbacks, it might have used this information to drive a harder bargain. Ancillary to the employer's property right to control expenditures was its right to know any material information that might affect its control of expenditures. Here, too, there was a mixed response from the lower courts. One court viewed as a critical distinction whether the employee had the capacity to influence only the selection of the supplier (as in *McNally*) or also the amount paid to the supplier. See United States v. Perholtz, 842 F.2d 343 (D.C. Cir. 1988).

5. *Kickback Schemes/Constructive Trust.* Still another theory advanced by the government was the "constructive trust" or "fiduciary accountability" theory suggested by Justice Stevens, that the profits derived from the abuse of a fiduciary relationship (the kickbacks) belonged to the principal, not the corrupt agent. Here again, the lower courts divided. See United States v. Miller, 997 F.2d 1010, 1019-1020 (2d Cir. 1993) (rejecting constructive trust theory in a case involving apartments and the profits generated by their resale). One court suggested a variation of this theory—the employee could be liable for attempting to conceal his receipt of bribes and thereby hampering a civil action by the state to recoup the money he received. United States v. Holzer, 840 F.2d 1343, 1346-48 (7th Cir. 1988).

6. *Creative Property Rights.* Describing some of the above cases and others, one commentator noted: "[C]reative property rights began appearing in post-*McNally* mail fraud indictments; many of these have been recognized as property rights 'the right to control spending of [one's] own funds,' 'the right to pay for services alone, not services plus kickbacks,' 'information relevant to [one's] economic welfare concerning the existence of [a] kickback scheme,' and the 'economic value of ... knowledge that [a] contractor would sell for less.'" See, e.g., United States v. Shyres, 898 F.2d 647 (8th Cir. 1990); United States v. Little, 889 F.2d 1367 (1989). Are these theories needed by the prosecution after the congressional "overruling" of *McNally*, discussed infra p.172.

7. *Wording of the Indictment.* In alleging property rights, how important is the wording of the indictment. For example, will "an alleged scheme to defraud the Educational Testing Service, Inc. ('ETS'), by using imposters to take the Test of English as a Foreign Language ("TOEFL") on behalf of other students, constitutes a deprivation of property within the meaning of the mail-fraud statute? See United States v. Alkaabi, 223 F. Supp.2d 583 (D. N.J. 2002) (finding that the indictment did not allege a scheme to deprive the testing service of property); United States v. Alsugair, 256 F. Supp.2d 306 (D.N.J. 2003) (finding that a "superseding indictment adequately alleges that Alsugair obtained property from ETS.").

8. *Conspiracy to Defraud.* Justice Stevens argues in his dissent that "defraud" as used in § 1341 should be interpreted in the same way that the term has been interpreted in 18 U.S.C.A. § 371. (Conspiracy to Defraud the United States). 18 U.S.C.A. § 371 provides:

> If two or more persons conspire either to commit any offense against the United States, or to defraud the United States, or any agency thereof in any manner or for any purpose, and one or more of such persons do any act to effect the object of the conspiracy, each shall be fined under this title or imprisoned not more than five years, or both.

> If, however, the offense, the commission of which is the object of the conspiracy, is a misdemeanor only, the punishment for such conspiracy shall not exceed the maximum punishment provided for such misdemeanor.

This general conspiracy statute criminalizes both conspiracies to commit any offense against the United States as well as conspiracies to defraud the United States or its agencies. In referring to conspiracies to defraud the United States, the Department of Justice Manual notes that "[t]he general purpose of the statute is to protect governmental functions from frustration and distortion through deceptive practices. * * * Those activities which courts have held defraud the United States 'touch' the government in at least one of three ways: 1) They cheat the government out of money or property; 2) They interfere or obstruct legitimate Government activity; 3) They make wrongful use of a governmental instrumentality. United States v. Hay, 527 F.2d 990, 997-98 (10th Cir. 1975)." U.S.A.M. 9-42.300. See also Abraham S. Goldstein, *Conspiracy to Defraud the United States*, 68 YALE L.J. 405 (1959).

C. WHAT CONSTITUTES "PROPERTY"?

1. Intangible Property

CARPENTER v. UNITED STATES
484 U.S. 19, 108 S.Ct. 316, 98 L.Ed.2d 272 (1987)

Justice WHITE delivered the opinion of the Court.

Petitioners Kenneth Felis and R. Foster Winans were convicted of violating § 10(b) of the Securities Exchange Act of 1934, 48 Stat. 891, 15 U.S.C. § 78j(b),[1] and Rule 10b-5, 17 CFR § 240.10b-5 (1987).[2] They were also found guilty of violating the federal mail and wire fraud statutes, 18 U.S.C. §§ 1341, 1343, and were convicted for conspiracy under 18 U.S.C. § 371. Petitioner David Carpenter, Winans' roommate, was convicted for aiding and abetting. With a minor exception, the Court of Appeals for the Second Circuit affirmed; we granted certiorari.

I

In 1981, Winans became a reporter for the Wall Street Journal (the Journal) and in the summer of 1982 became one of the two writers of a daily column, "Heard on the Street." That column discussed selected stocks or groups of stocks, giving positive and negative information about those stocks and taking "a point of view with respect to investment in the stocks that it

---

[1] Section 10(b) provides: "It shall be unlawful for any person, directly or indirectly, by the use of any means or instrumentality of interstate commerce or of the mails, or of any facility of any national securities exchange—   * * *

"(b) To use or employ, in connection with the purchase or sale of any security registered on a national securities exchange or any security not so registered, any manipulative or deceptive device or contrivance in contravention of such rules and regulations as the [Securities and Exchange] Commission may prescribe as necessary or appropriate in the public interest or for the protection of investors."

[2] Rule 10b-5 provides: "It shall be unlawful for any person, directly or indirectly, by the use of any means or instrumentality of interstate commerce, or of the mails or of any national securities exchange, "(a) To employ any device, scheme, or artifice to defraud, "(b) To make any untrue statement of a material fact or to omit to state a material fact necessary in order to make the statements made, in the light of the circumstances under which they were made, not misleading, or "(c) To engage in any act, practice, or course of business which operates or would operate as a fraud or deceit upon any person, "in connection with the purchase or sale of any security."

reviews." Winans regularly interviewed corporate executives to put together interesting perspectives on the stocks that would be highlighted in upcoming columns, but, at least for the columns at issue here, none contained corporate inside information or any "hold for release" information. Because of the "Heard" column's perceived quality and integrity, it had the potential of affecting the price of the stocks which it examined. The District Court concluded on the basis of testimony presented at trial that the "Heard" column "does have an impact on the market, difficult though it may be to quantify in any particular case."

The official policy and practice at the Journal was that prior to publication, the contents of the column were the Journal's confidential information. Despite the rule, with which Winans was familiar, he entered into a scheme in October 1983 with Peter Brant and petitioner Felis, both connected with the Kidder Peabody brokerage firm in New York City, to give them advance information as to the timing and contents of the "Heard" column. This permitted Brant and Felis and another conspirator, David Clark, a client of Brant, to buy or sell based on the probable impact of the column on the market. Profits were to be shared. The conspirators agreed that the scheme would not affect the journalistic purity of the "Heard" column, and the District Court did not find that the contents of any of the articles were altered to further the profit potential of petitioners' stock-trading scheme. Over a 4-month period, the brokers made prepublication trades on the basis of information given them by Winans about the contents of some 27 "Heard" columns. The net profits from these trades were about $690,000.

In November 1983, correlations between the "Heard" articles and trading in the Clark and Felis accounts were noted at Kidder Peabody and inquiries began. Brant and Felis denied knowing anyone at the Journal and took steps to conceal the trades. Later, the Securities and Exchange Commission began an investigation. Questions were met by denials both by the brokers at Kidder Peabody and by Winans at the Journal. As the investigation progressed, the conspirators quarreled, and on March 29, 1984, Winans and Carpenter went to the SEC and revealed the entire scheme. This indictment and a bench trial followed. Brant, who had pleaded guilty under a plea agreement, was a witness for the Government.   * * *

The Court is evenly divided with respect to the convictions under the securities laws and for that reason affirms the judgment below on those counts. For the reasons that follow, we also affirm the judgment with respect to the mail and wire fraud convictions.

II

Petitioners assert that their activities were not a scheme to defraud the Journal within the meaning of the mail and wire fraud statutes;[6] and that in any event, they did not obtain any "money or property" from the Journal, which is a necessary element of the crime under our decision last Term in McNally v. United States. We are unpersuaded by either submission and address the latter first.

We held in *McNally* that the mail fraud statute does not reach "schemes to defraud citizens of their intangible rights to honest and impartial government," and that the statute is "limited in scope to the protection of property rights." Petitioners argue that the Journal's interest in prepublication confidentiality for the "Heard" columns is no more than an intangible consideration outside the reach of § 1341; nor does that law, it is urged, protect against mere injury to reputation. This is not a case like *McNally*, however. The Journal, as Winans' employer, was defrauded of much more than its contractual right to his honest and faithful service, an interest too ethereal in itself to fall within the protection of the mail fraud statute, which "had its origin in the desire to protect individual property rights." Here, the object of the scheme was to take the Journal's confidential business information—the publication schedule and contents of the "Heard" column—and its intangible nature does not make it any less "property" protected by the mail and wire fraud statutes. *McNally* did not limit the scope of § 1341 to tangible as distinguished from intangible property rights.

Both courts below expressly referred to the Journal's interest in the confidentiality of the contents and timing of the "Heard" column as a property right, and we agree with that conclusion. Confidential business information has long been recognized as property. See Ruckelshaus v. Monsanto Co., 467 U.S. 986, 1001-1004 (1984); Dirks v. SEC, 463 U.S. 646, 653, n. 10 (1983); Board of Trade of Chicago v. Christie Grain & Stock Co., 198 U.S. 236, 250-251 (1905); cf. 5 U.S.C. § 552(b)(4). "Confidential information acquired or compiled by a corporation in the course and conduct of its business is a species of property to which the corporation has the exclusive right and benefit, and which a court of equity will protect through the injunctive process or other appropriate remedy." 3 W. Fletcher, Cyclopedia of Law of Private Corporations § 857.1, p. 260 (rev. ed. 1986) (footnote omitted). The Journal had a property right in keeping confidential and making exclusive use, prior to publication, of the schedule and contents of the "Heard" column. Christie Grain, supra. As the Court has observed before: "[N]ews matter, however little susceptible of ownership or dominion in the absolute sense, is stock in trade, to be gathered at the cost of enterprise, organization, skill, labor, and money, and to be distributed and sold to those who will pay money

---

[6] The mail and wire fraud statutes share the same language in relevant part, and accordingly we apply the same analysis to both sets of offenses here.

for it, as for any other merchandise." International News Service v. Associated Press, 248 U.S. 215, 236 (1918).

Petitioners' arguments that they did not interfere with the Journal's use of the information or did not publicize it and deprive the Journal of the first public use of it miss the point. The confidential information was generated from the business, and the business had a right to decide how to use it prior to disclosing it to the public. Petitioners cannot successfully contend based on *Associated Press* that a scheme to defraud requires a monetary loss, such as giving the information to a competitor; it is sufficient that the Journal has been deprived of its right to exclusive use of the information, for exclusivity is an important aspect of confidential business information and most private property for that matter.

We cannot accept petitioners' further argument that Winans' conduct in revealing prepublication information was no more than a violation of workplace rules and did not amount to fraudulent activity that is proscribed by the mail fraud statute. Sections 1341 and 1343 reach any scheme to deprive another of money or property by means of false or fraudulent pretenses, representations, or promises. As we observed last Term in *McNally*, the words "to defraud" in the mail fraud statute have the "common understanding" of " 'wronging one in his property rights by dishonest methods or schemes,' and 'usually signify the deprivation of something of value by trick, deceit, chicane or overreaching.' " 483 U.S., at 358 (quoting Hammerschmidt v. United States). The concept of "fraud" includes the act of embezzlement, which is " 'the fraudulent appropriation to one's own use of the money or goods entrusted to one's care by another.' " Grin v. Shine, 187 U.S. 181, 189 (1902).

The District Court found that Winans' undertaking at the Journal was not to reveal prepublication information about his column, a promise that became a sham when in violation of his duty he passed along to his co-conspirators confidential information belonging to the Journal, pursuant to an ongoing scheme to share profits from trading in anticipation of the "Heard" column's impact on the stock market. * * * As the New York courts have recognized: "It is well established, as a general proposition, that a person who acquires special knowledge or information by virtue of a confidential or fiduciary relationship with another is not free to exploit that knowledge or information for his own personal benefit but must account to his principal for any profits derived therefrom." Diamond v. Oreamuno, 24 N.Y.2d 494, 497, 301 N.Y.S.2d 78, 80, 248 N.E.2d 910, 912 (1969); see also Restatement (Second) of Agency §§ 388, Comment c, 396(c) (1958).

We have little trouble in holding that the conspiracy here to trade on the Journal's confidential information is not outside the reach of the mail and wire fraud statutes, provided the other elements of the offenses are satisfied. The Journal's business information that it intended to be kept confidential was its property; the declaration to that effect in the employee manual merely removed any doubts on that score and made the finding of specific intent to defraud that much easier. Winans continued in the employ of the Journal, appropriating its confidential business information for his own use, all the while pretending to perform his duty of safeguarding it. In fact, he told his editors twice about leaks of confidential information not related to the stock-trading scheme, demonstrating both his knowledge that the Journal viewed information concerning the "Heard" column as confidential and his deceit as he played the role of a loyal employee. Furthermore, the District Court's conclusion that each of the petitioners acted with the required specific intent to defraud is strongly supported by the evidence.

Lastly, we reject the submission that using the wires and the mail to print and send the Journal to its customers did not satisfy the requirement that those mediums be used to execute the scheme at issue. The courts below were quite right in observing that circulation of the "Heard" column was not only anticipated but an essential part of the scheme. Had the column not been made available to Journal customers, there would have been no effect on stock prices and no likelihood of profiting from the information leaked by Winans.   * * *

Affirmed.

NOTES AND QUESTIONS

1. *Securities Fraud.* The Court was equally divided and therefore affirmed the securities fraud convictions. The lower court had accepted a misappropriation theory as the basis for finding a breach of section 10(b) and Rule 10b-5. See United States v. Carpenter, 791 F.2d 1024 (2d Cir. 1987). In *United States v. O'Hagan*, 561 U.S. 642 (1997), the Supreme Court endorsed the use of the misappropriation theory. The Court held that the "the misappropriation theory outlaws trading on the basis of nonpublic information by a corporate 'outsider' in breach of a duty owed not to a trading party, but to the source of the information. The misappropriation theory is thus designed to protec[t] the integrity of the securities markets against abuses by 'outsiders' to a corporation who have access to confidential information that will affect th[e] corporation's security price when revealed, but who owe no fiduciary or other duty to that corporation's shareholders." See also Jennifer H. Arlen & William J. Carney, *Vicarious Liability for Fraud on Securities Markets: Theory and Evidence*, 1992 U. OF ILL. L. REV. 691 (1992).

2. *Conspiracy to Commit Insider Trading.* When one adds a charge of conspiracy to commit insider trading, proof of the conspiracy is required. This can require an agreement to pass on the insider information. In *United States v. McDermott*, 245 F.3d 133, 138 (2d Cir. 2001), a Second Circuit court stated "[w]e decline to hold as a matter of law that a cheating heart must foresee a cheating heart."

COMMENTS ON CARPENTER

Excerpts from John C. Coffee, Jr., *Hush!: The Criminal Status of Confidential Information After* McNally *and* Carpenter *and the Enduring Problem of Overcriminalization*, 26 Am. Crim. L. Rev. 121 (1988).

> In *Carpenter*, the Court took two important doctrinal steps. First, it recognized that there can be intangible forms of property, of which a victim may be defrauded. This seems an obvious conclusion, as one can imagine many valuable forms of intangible property: for example, patents, copyrights, contract rights, etc. Second, it found that one form of intangible property, confidential business information, is embezzled whenever an employee reveals it to others so as to deprive the employer of exclusive possession.

> In contrast to this remarkable first step, the second step is extraordinary, because it eliminates any need for a showing of actual or intended economic injury to the employer. * * *

> The *Carpenter* decision is also a marked departure from prior law in its casual assertion that depriving the owner of exclusive possession of information amounts to an embezzlement. The history of embezzlement and the law of theft is long and tortuous, but one historical fact is clear beyond serious argument: intangibles could not be stolen or embezzled. * * *

Excerpts from Craig M. Bradley, *Foreward: Mail Fraud After* McNally *and* Carpenter: *The Essence of Fraud*, 79 J. Crim. L. & Criminology 573 (1988).

> * * * [I]t is not clear how the Journal was deprived of "property" here. As the case was originally tried by the government, the fraudulent behavior was the failure to disclose the breach and the harm to the victim was the loss of the Journal's intangible right to the honest and faithful services of its employee. After *McNally*, the government filed a supplemental brief urging that the fraudulent behavior was the embezzlement of confidential information and the harm was the loss of the exclusive use of that information. The Court adopted this latter theory, endeavoring to conform to the 'property' limitation of *McNally*.

> By holding that "the concept of fraud includes the act of embezzlement" the Court ignored the very history of fraud that it had relied on in *McNally*. On the contrary, the crime of fraud had always been understood by both Congress and the Supreme Court as proscribing only the fraud of false pretenses, rather than any crime that involved "fraudulent" behavior, which crimes included larceny, embezzlement, forgery, and larceny by trick as well as false pretenses. According to the Court's holding in *Carpenter*, any

employee who helps himself to money or property which his or her employer has entrusted to him or her is now guilty of the federal offense of wire or mail fraud if only the mails or wires are used or caused to be used in some way. The Congress that enacted this statute would surely have been surprised at this declaration.

But while it was an overstatement by the Court to suggest that any embezzlement is a "fraud," it is fair to say that Winans' acts constituted "fraud," whether they are characterized as "embezzlement" or "false pretenses." [Professor Bradley had previously noted that there had been a "breach of fiduciary duty not to disclose confidential information, and a further duty to disclose such breaches to his employer," that created a potential for harm to the employer, and "this had long been recognized as satisfying the 'deceit' element of fraud."] The difficulty arises because neither of these traditional crimes were defined in terms of intangible property.

* * * Contrary to *Carpenter*, the legislative history as well as the general understanding of "fraud" at the time of the enactment of the mail fraud statute suggests that "fraud" was limited to money or tangible property, * * *.

[O]nce it is recognized that the term "defraud" implied a deprivation of tangible property, the fact, as the Court observed in *Carpenter*, that "confidential business information has long been recognized as property" in other contexts is irrelevant. Whether or not confidential information had long been regarded as "property," it and other intangibles, such as a business' reputation, had not long been recognized, and certainly were not recognized in 1872 and 1909, as covered by a statute prohibiting "fraud."

The Court put itself in a box in *McNally* from which it could only escape, in *Carpenter*, by a gross distortion of the historical evidence on which *McNally* had been based. A far better approach would have been to have recognized the problem in *McNally* as being the lack of an identifiable victim who suffered economic harm, rather than holding that a traditional view of "property" was an essential element of fraud. Then, in *Carpenter*, it could have noted the presence of a specific victim and a potential economic loss to that victim as satisfying the *McNally* requirement. In response to the argument that "fraud" traditionally required a deprivation of tangible property, the Court in *Carpenter*, not constrained by a contrary reliance on history in *McNally*, could simply have agreed with this point but held, forthrightly, that, in this information age much that is intangible is just as valuable as tangible property. The key question is not what kind of property was involved but whether there was an economic loss to an identifiable victim as well as an unjust gain to the defendant. As will be argued, while this is not precisely what the Court said, this line of reasoning is the only way to explain what it did in *McNally* and Carpenter. * * *

McNally and *Carpenter,* read together, require an economic gain to the defendant and loss to the victim (or the prospect of same) but do not require that this gain and loss be of "property" as that term had been understood by Congress. * * *

2. Licenses

CLEVELAND v. UNITED STATES
531 U.S. 12, 121 S.Ct. 365, 148 L.Ed.2d 221 (2000)

Justice GINSBURG delivered the opinion of the Court.

This case presents the question whether the federal mail fraud statute, 18 U.S.C. § 1341, reaches false statements made in an application for a state license. Section 1341 proscribes use of the mails in furtherance of "any scheme or artifice to defraud, or for obtaining money or property by means of false or fraudulent pretenses, representations, or promises." Petitioner Carl W. Cleveland and others were prosecuted under this federal measure for making false statements in applying to the Louisiana State Police for permission to operate video poker machines. We conclude that permits or licenses of this order do not qualify as "property" within § 1341's compass. It does not suffice, we clarify, that the object of the fraud may become property in the recipient's hands; for purposes of the mail fraud statute, the thing obtained must be property in the hands of the victim. State and municipal licenses in general, and Louisiana's video poker licenses in particular, we hold, do not rank as "property," for purposes of § 1341, in the hands of the official licensor. * * *

Louisiana law allows certain businesses to operate video poker machines. La.Rev.Stat. Ann. §§ 27:301 to 27:324 (West Supp.2000). The State itself, however, does not run such machinery. The law requires prospective owners of video poker machines to apply for a license from the State. § 27:306. The licenses are not transferable, § 27:311(G), and must be renewed annually, La. Admin.Code, tit. 42, § 2405(B)(3) (2000). To qualify for a license, an applicant must meet suitability requirements designed to ensure that licensees have good character and fiscal integrity. La.Rev.Stat. Ann. § 27:310 (West Supp.2000).

In 1992, Fred Goodson and his family formed a limited partnership, Truck Stop Gaming, Ltd. (TSG), in order to participate in the video poker business at their truck stop in Slidell, Louisiana. Cleveland, a New Orleans lawyer, assisted Goodson in preparing TSG's application for a video poker license. The application required TSG to identify its partners and to submit personal financial statements for all partners. It also required TSG to affirm that the listed partners were the sole beneficial owners of the business and that no partner held an interest in the partnership merely as an agent or nominee, or intended to transfer the interest in the future.

TSG's application identified Goodson's adult children, Alex and Maria, as the sole beneficial owners of the partnership. It also showed that Goodson and Cleveland's law firm had loaned Alex and Maria all initial capital for the partnership and that Goodson was TSG's general manager. In May 1992, the State approved the application and issued a license. TSG successfully renewed the license in 1993, 1994, and 1995 pursuant to La. Admin. Code, tit. 42, § 2405(B)(3) (2000). Each renewal application identified no ownership interests other than those of Alex and Maria.

In 1996, the FBI discovered evidence that Cleveland and Goodson had participated in a scheme to bribe state legislators to vote in a manner favorable to the video poker industry. The Government charged Cleveland and Goodson with multiple counts of money laundering under 18 U.S.C. § 1957, as well as racketeering and conspiracy under § 1962. Among the predicate acts supporting these charges were four counts of mail fraud under § 1341. The indictment alleged that Cleveland and Goodson had violated § 1341 by fraudulently concealing that they were the true owners of TSG in the initial license application and three renewal applications mailed to the State. They concealed their ownership interests, according to the Government, because they had tax and financial problems that could have undermined their suitability to receive a video poker license. * * *

Before trial, Cleveland moved to dismiss the mail fraud counts on the ground that the alleged fraud did not deprive the State of "property" under § 1341. The District Court denied the motion, concluding that "licenses constitute property even before they are issued." 951 F.Supp. 1249, 1261 (E.D.La.1997). A jury found Cleveland guilty on two counts of mail fraud (based on the 1994 and 1995 license renewals) and on money laundering, racketeering, and conspiracy counts predicated on the mail fraud. The District Court sentenced Cleveland to 121 months in prison.

On appeal, Cleveland again argued that Louisiana had no property interest in video poker licenses, relying on several Court of Appeals decisions holding that the government does not relinquish "property" for purposes of § 1341 when it issues a permit or license. See United States v. Shotts, 145 F.3d 1289, 1296 (C.A.11 1998) (license to operate a bail bonds business); United States v. Schwartz, 924 F.2d 410, 418 (C.A.2 1991) (arms export license); United States v. Granberry, 908 F.2d 278, 280 (C.A.8 1990) (school bus operator's permit); Toulabi v. United States, 875 F.2d 122, 125 (C.A.7 1989) (chauffeur's license); United States v. Dadanian, 856 F.2d 1391, 1392 (C.A.9 1988) (gambling license); United States v. Murphy, 836 F.2d 248, 254 (C.A.6 1988) (license to conduct charitable bingo games).

The Court of Appeals for the Fifth Circuit nevertheless affirmed Cleveland's conviction and sentence, United States v. Bankston, 182 F.3d

296, 309 (1999), considering itself bound by its holding in United States v. Salvatore, 110 F.3d 1131, 1138 (1997), that Louisiana video poker licenses constitute "property" in the hands of the State. Two other Circuits have concluded that the issuing authority has a property interest in unissued licenses under § 1341. United States v. Bucuvalas, 970 F.2d 937, 945 (C.A.1 1992) (entertainment and liquor license); United States v. Martinez, 905 F.2d 709, 715 (C.A.3 1990) (medical license).

We granted certiorari to resolve the conflict among the Courts of Appeals, 529 U.S. 1017, 120 S.Ct. 1416, 146 L.Ed.2d 309 (2000), and now reverse the Fifth Circuit's judgment. * * *

In McNally v. United States, [p. 147], this Court held that the federal mail fraud statute is "limited in scope to the protection of property rights." *McNally* reversed the mail fraud convictions of two individuals charged with participating in "a self-dealing patronage scheme" that defrauded Kentucky citizens of "the right to have the Commonwealth's affairs conducted honestly." At the time *McNally* was decided, federal prosecutors had been using § 1341 to attack various forms of corruption that deprived victims of "intangible rights" unrelated to money or property. Reviewing the history of § 1341, we concluded that "the original impetus behind the mail fraud statute was to protect the people from schemes to deprive them of their money or property." * * *

Soon after *McNally,* in Carpenter v. United States, 484 U.S. 19, 25, 108 S.Ct. 316, 98 L.Ed.2d 275 (1987), we again stated that § 1341 protects property rights only. *Carpenter* upheld convictions under § 1341 and the federal wire fraud statute, 18 U.S.C. § 1343, of defendants who had defrauded the Wall Street Journal of confidential business information. Citing decisions of this Court as well as a corporate law treatise, we observed that "[c]onfidential business information has long been recognized as property."

The following year, Congress amended the law specifically to cover one of the "intangible rights" that lower courts had protected under § 1341 prior to *McNally:* "the intangible right of honest services." Anti-Drug Abuse Act of 1988, § 7603(a), 18 U.S.C. § 1346. Significantly, Congress covered only the intangible right of honest services even though federal courts, relying on *McNally,* had dismissed, for want of monetary loss to any victim, prosecutions under § 1341 for diverse forms of public corruption, including licensing fraud.

In this case, there is no assertion that Louisiana's video poker licensing scheme implicates the intangible right of honest services. The question presented is whether, for purposes of the federal mail fraud statute, a government regulator parts with "property" when it issues a license. For the reasons we now set out, we hold that § 1341 does not reach fraud in obtaining a state or municipal license of the kind here involved, for such a license is not "property" in the government regulator's hands. Again, as we said in

McNally, "[i]f Congress desires to go further, it must speak more clearly than it has."

To begin with, we think it beyond genuine dispute that whatever interests Louisiana might be said to have in its video poker licenses, the State's core concern is *regulatory.* Louisiana recognizes the importance of "public confidence and trust that gaming activities ... are conducted honestly and are free from criminal and corruptive elements." * * * The video poker licensing statute accordingly asserts the State's "legitimate interest in providing strict regulation of all persons, practices, associations, and activities related to the operation of ... establishments licensed to offer video draw poker devices." The statute assigns the Office of State Police, a part of the Department of Public Safety and Corrections, the responsibility to promulgate rules and regulations concerning the licensing process. It also authorizes the State Police to deny, condition, suspend, or revoke licenses, to levy fines of up to $1,000 per violation of any rule, and to inspect all premises where video poker devices are offered for play. In addition, the statute defines criminal penalties for unauthorized use of video poker devices, and prescribes detailed suitability requirements for licensees.

In short, the statute establishes a typical regulatory program. It licenses, subject to certain conditions, engagement in pursuits that private actors may not undertake without official authorization. In this regard, it resembles other licensing schemes long characterized by this Court as exercises of state police powers. * * *

Acknowledging Louisiana's regulatory interests, the Government offers two reasons why the State also has a property interest in its video poker licenses. First, the State receives a substantial sum of money in exchange for each license and continues to receive payments from the licensee as long as the license remains in effect. Second, the State has significant control over the issuance, renewal, suspension, and revocation of licenses.

Without doubt, Louisiana has a substantial economic stake in the video poker industry. The State collects an upfront "processing fee" for each new license application, * * * a separate "processing fee" for each renewal application, * * * an "annual fee" from each device owner, * * * an additional "device operation" fee, * * * and, most importantly, a fixed percentage of net revenue from each video poker device. It is hardly evident, however, why these tolls should make video poker licenses "property" in the hands of the State. The State receives the lion's share of its expected revenue not while the licenses remain in its own hands, but only *after* they have been issued to licensees. Licenses pre-issuance do not generate an ongoing stream of revenue. At most, they entitle the State to collect a processing fee from applicants for new licenses. Were an entitlement of this order sufficient to establish a state property right, one could scarcely avoid the conclusion that States have property rights in any license or permit requiring an upfront fee, including drivers' licenses, medical licenses, and fishing and hunting licenses.

Such licenses, as the Government itself concedes, are "purely regulatory." * * *

Tellingly, as to the character of Louisiana's stake in its video poker licenses, the Government nowhere alleges that Cleveland defrauded the State of any money to which the State was entitled by law.   Indeed, there is no dispute that TSG paid the State of Louisiana its proper share of revenue, which totaled more than $1.2 million, between 1993 and 1995. If Cleveland defrauded the State of "property," the nature of that property cannot be economic.

Addressing this concern, the Government argues that Cleveland frustrated the State's right to control the issuance, renewal, and revocation of video poker licenses under La.Rev.Stat. Ann. §§ 27:306, 27:308 (West Supp.2000). The Fifth Circuit has characterized the protected interest as "Louisiana's right to choose the persons to whom it issues video poker licenses." * * * But far from composing an interest that "has long been recognized as property," these intangible rights of allocation, exclusion, and control amount to no more and no less than Louisiana's sovereign power to regulate.   Notably, the Government overlooks the fact that these rights include the distinctively sovereign authority to impose criminal penalties for violations of the licensing scheme, La.Rev.Stat. Ann. § 27:309 (West Supp.2000), including making false statements in a license application, § 27:309(A).   Even when tied to an expected stream of revenue, the State's right of control does not create a property interest any more than a law licensing liquor sales in a State that levies a sales tax on liquor.   Such regulations are paradigmatic exercises of the States' traditional police powers. * * *

We reject the Government's theories of property rights not simply because they stray from traditional concepts of property.   We resist the Government's reading of § 1341 as well because it invites us to approve a sweeping expansion of federal criminal jurisdiction in the absence of a clear statement by Congress.   Equating issuance of licenses or permits with deprivation of property would subject to federal mail fraud prosecution a wide range of conduct traditionally regulated by state and local authorities. We note in this regard that Louisiana's video poker statute typically and unambiguously imposes criminal penalties for making false statements on license applications. * * * Moreover, to the extent that the word "property" is ambiguous as placed in § 1341, we have instructed that "ambiguity concerning the ambit of criminal statutes should be resolved in favor of lenity." Rewis v. United States, 401 U.S. 808, 812, 91 S.Ct. 1056, 28 L.Ed.2d 493 (1971). This interpretive guide is especially appropriate in construing § 1341 because, as this case demonstrates, mail fraud is a predicate offense under RICO, 18 U.S.C. § 1961(1) (1994 ed., Supp. IV), and the money laundering statute, § 1956(c)(7)(A).   In deciding what is "property" under § 1341, we think "it is appropriate, before we choose the harsher alternative, to require that Congress should have spoken in language that is clear and definite." * * *

Although we do not here question that video poker licensees may have property interests in their licenses, we nevertheless disagree with the Government's reading of § 1341. In *McNally*, we recognized that "[b]ecause the two phrases identifying the proscribed schemes appear in the disjunctive, it is arguable that they are to be construed independently." But we rejected that construction of the statute, instead concluding that the second phrase simply modifies the first by "ma[king] it unmistakable that the statute reached false promises and misrepresentations as to the future as well as other frauds involving money or property." Indeed, directly contradicting the Government's view, we said that "the mail fraud statute ... had its origin in the desire to protect individual property rights, and any benefit which the Government derives from the statute must be limited to *the Government's interests as property holder*." * * * For reasons already stated, * * * we decline to attribute to § 1341 a purpose so encompassing where Congress has not made such a design clear.

We conclude that § 1341 requires the object of the fraud to be "property" in the victim's hands and that a Louisiana video poker license in the State's hands is not "property" under § 1341. Absent clear statement by Congress, we will not read the mail fraud statute to place under federal superintendence a vast array of conduct traditionally policed by the States. Our holding means that Cleveland's § 1341 conviction must be vacated. Accordingly, the judgment of the United States Court of Appeals for the Fifth Circuit is reversed, and the case is remanded for further proceedings consistent with this opinion. * * *

D. INTANGIBLE RIGHT TO HONEST SERVICES

CONGRESSIONAL OVERRULING OF *MCNALLY*

As part of the Anti-Drug Abuse Act of 1988, Congress enacted 18 U.S.C.A. § 1346 which provides:

> For the purposes of this chapter, the term "scheme or artifice to defraud" includes a scheme or artifice to deprive another of the intangible right of honest services.

UNITED STATES v. SKILLING
554 F.3d 529 (5th Cir. 2009)

PRADO, Circuit Judge.

A jury convicted former Enron Corporation CEO Jeffrey K. Skilling ("Skilling") for conspiracy, securities fraud, making false representations to auditors, and insider trading. Skilling argues that the government prosecuted him using an invalid legal theory, that the district court used erroneous jury instructions, that the jury was biased, that prosecutors engaged in unconstitutional misconduct, and that his sentence is improper. We affirm the convictions, vacate the sentence, and remand for resentencing. * * *

Skilling's rise at Enron began when he founded Enron's Wholesale business in 1990. In 1997, he became Enron's President and Chief Operating Officer and joined the Board of Directors. In February 2001, he became Enron's CEO, and on August 14, 2001, Skilling resigned from Enron.

About four months after Skilling's departure, Enron crashed into sudden bankruptcy. An initial investiga-tion uncovered an elaborate conspiracy to deceive investors about the state of Enron's fiscal health. That conspiracy allegedly included overstating the company's financial situation for more than two years in an attempt to ensure that Enron's short-run stock price remained artificially high. With Congress looking on, the President appointed a team of investigators, the Enron Task Force. The investigation led to criminal charges against Skilling and many others.

According to the government, the conspiracy, led by Skilling and Ken Lay ("Lay"), Enron's CEO until Skilling took over (and again after his abrupt exit), worked to manipulate Enron's earnings to satisfy Wall Street's expectations. Other top Enron officials were key players in the unlawful scheme, including Richard Causey ("Causey"), the Chief Accounting Officer ("CAO"); Andrew Fastow ("Fastow"), the Chief Financial Officer ("CFO"); and Ben Glisan ("Glisan"), the Treasurer.

A. Conspiracy and Securities Fraud

Several of Skilling's convictions stem from allegations of conspiracy and securities fraud. The government presented evidence that Skilling engaged in fraud in several of Enron's business endeavors. As an international, multi-billion dollar enterprise, Enron had elaborate financial dealings. At the time of its bankruptcy, the company was comprised of four major businesses: Wholesale, which bought and sold energy; Transportation and Distribution, which owned energy networks; Retail, or Enron Energy Services ("EES"), which sold energy to end-users; and Broadband, or Enron Broadband Services ("EBS"), which bought and sold bandwidth capacity. The government alleged that Skilling took specific fraudulent actions with respect to Wholesale, EES, and EBS.

Wholesale, the most profitable division, accounted for nearly 90% of Enron's revenue. The government presented evidence to show that the conspirators lied about the nature of Wholesale, calling it a "logistics company," even though it was a much more economically volatile "trading company." Construing Wholesale as a "logistics company" had important ramifications for how investors valued the division. In fact, Skilling reportedly told Ken Rice ("Rice"), EBS's CEO, that if investors perceived Enron as a trading company, its stock would "get whacked." The alleged artifice also included masking the losses of Enron's other struggling subdivisions by shifting the losses to Wholesale. That made the struggling divisions appear financially sound and thus encouraged additional investment.

EES was a retail undertaking that Enron created to sell natural gas to customers in deregulated markets. Although Enron had high expectations for EES's profitability after its initial start-up period, EES did not meet these expectations. As of the fall of 2000, various utilities in California owed Enron substantial fees, which Enron had already booked as profits under its "mark-to-market accounting."The utilities, however, were suffering heavy financial losses and stopped paying these fees. Under general accounting rules, Enron should have recorded a loss of hundreds of millions of dollars based on the failure of the utilities to pay the fees, but Skilling and his co-conspirators tried to hide the harm by transferring the losses to Wholesale so that EES would continue to show promise, at least on paper.

The government claims that Skilling hid EES's other problems as well. For example, in early 2001, EES employees allegedly realized that Enron was not properly valuing EES's contracts and that, again because of Enron's use of mark-to-market accounting, Enron would need to record a loss of many millions of dollars. Skilling allegedly told David Delainey, who was in charge of EES, to "bleed the contract issues over time" instead of recognizing the loss all at once.

Skilling again concealed EES's losses within Wholesale in late March 2001, after the California Public Utilities Commission decided to add a surcharge to electricity. Enron lost hundreds of millions of dollars as a result of this surcharge because, under its contracts, it could not pass the extra fees on to its customers. After Skilling was consulted and signed off, Enron shifted the EES losses to Wholesale by transfering EES's risk-management books to Wholesale. Business at EES did not improve, and by August 2001, when Skilling left Enron, EES had lost over $700 million in that year alone. Enron failed to account for these losses properly, making EES appear to be in better financial shape than it really was.

EBS was Enron's attempt to enter the telecommunications industry. Enron invested more than $1 billion in EBS, but lost money every quarter as EBS struggled to meet earnings targets. The government claims that in 2000, EBS managed to reach its earnings targets, but only by means of transactions afield from its core business (such as selling and monetizing corporate assets). Skilling allegedly hid from investors EBS's failure to meet earnings targets through core business activities.

The government claims that Skilling knew EBS was struggling, at least based on its record of performance, but that he wanted to announce to the investing public that EBS was doing well and would do even better in 2001. Although EBS's executives said it was impossible, Skilling set EBS's earnings targets for 2001 to be a loss of only $65 million. EBS's personnel initially thought a loss estimate of nearly $500 million was more realistic, and, even with the best circumstances, they projected losses of at least $110 million. Rice, EBS's CEO, warned Skilling that the earnings targets for EBS were wrong, but Skilling apparently would not change them. Skilling told Rice that certain international assets were not producing sufficiently and that "we really need to hang in there for a year or two until EES and EBS could pick up the slack," because Enron "didn't need any more bad news."

In 2001, EBS was projected to lose $35 million in the first quarter, but Rice quickly realized that losses would actually be around $150 million. Skilling allegedly found out but would not budge on earnings targets, instead authorizing EBS to fire employees and engage in more non-core business to boost revenues. It worked for the first quarter, although Rice likened the monetizations to "one more hit of crack cocaine on these earnings."EBS faired a little better in the second quarter of 2001, reporting losses of approximately $100 million. Given that EBS continued to lose money, however, Enron decided to merge EBS into Wholesale. Ultimately, Enron lost the entire $1 billion that it had initially invested in EBS.

B. False Representations About Enron's Finances

Many of the allegations of fraud also stem from Skilling's representations to investors about the financial standing of Wholesale, EES, and EBS. Skilling, as a high ranking corporate officer, held conference calls with investors to update them on the company's progress. The government claims that Skilling misled investors during these calls. For example, on January 22, 2001, Enron released its earnings report for the previous quarter, and Skilling told investors that "the situation in California [regarding the utilities] had little impact on fourth quarter results. Let me repeat that. For Enron, the situation in California had little impact on fourth quarter results."Skilling also stated that "nothing can happen in California that would jeopardize" earnings targets.

However, when he made these statements, Skilling allegedly knew that the California utilities likely could not pay the fees that Enron was expecting and that Enron might have to write off a loss of hundreds of millions of dollars. He also listened silently as Mark Koenig ("Koenig"), Enron's Director of Investor Relations, assured investors that non-core business revenues were a "fairly small" amount of EBS's earnings, which the government alleges was not actually the case.

Three days later, Skilling spoke at Enron's annual analysts conference, claiming that EES and EBS, like Enron's other major businesses, had "sustainable high earnings power." Skilling argues that this statement was merely harmless puffery. At the conference, he also reasserted that Wholesale was "not a trading business. We are a logistics company."

On March 23, 2001, Enron held a special conference call with analysts. Enron's stock price had been declining, and investors began surmising that EBS was having financial difficulties. Skilling comforted investors, saying that EBS was "having a great quarter" and that Enron was "highly confident" that EES would meet its earning target. According to the government, however, Skilling knew both divisions were in extreme financial turmoil.

On April 17, 2001, Skilling hosted another conference call in which he explained the transfer of EES's risk-management books to Wholesale by saying that there was "such capacity in our wholesale business that were – we just weren't taking advantage of that in managing our portfolio at the retail side. And this retail portfolio has gotten so big so fast that we needed to get the best-the best hands working on risk management there." In fact, the government claims that Skilling used the transfer to hide losses. Skilling also said that the "first quarter results were great" at EES, even though they were down substantially, and he again praised EBS, explaining that there was a "very strong development of the marketplace in the commoditization of bandwidth" and "we're feeling very good about the development of this business."Skilling was silent again while Rice and Koenig understated EBS's non-core revenues.

On July 17, 2001, Skilling told investors that EES "had an outstanding second quarter" and was "firmly on track to achieve" its earnings targets. That quarter alone, EES lost hundreds of millions of dollars. Skilling reiterated that the EES reorganization was based on a concern for management efficiency, while the government contends that the only purpose of the EES reorganization was to hide EES's losses.

C. Manipulating Enron's Reserves

Skilling also allegedly committed fraud when he manipulated Enron's reserves to hit specific earnings targets in the fourth quarter of 1999, the second quarter of 2000, and the fourth quarter of 2000. Stock analysts made various projections regarding the earnings that Enron would announce each quarter, and the average of these estimates was known as the "consensus estimate." The government claims that Skilling was particularly committed to hitting or beating the consensus estimate. In January 2000, the consensus estimate for the fourth quarter of 1999 was earnings of 30¢ per share, which Enron could meet based on its earnings for that quarter. The day before the company was to announce its earnings, however, Koenig brought Skilling unwelcome news: the consensus estimate had jumped a penny per share. Skilling purportedly decided to announce earnings high enough to reach the estimate, even though the increase was not merited by any change in Enron's underlying financial portrait.

Skilling allegedly took a similar unwarranted action at the end of the second quarter of 2000. At that time, the consensus estimate was 32¢ per share. A draft earnings report showed that Enron was going to announce earnings that met the estimate. Skilling, however, wanted to beat the consensus estimate by reporting 34¢ per share. To do that, he allegedly told Wholesale to increase its earnings by $7 million, and then by an additional $7 million. Wholesale acquiesced both times, reopening its books and adding

$14 million from a reserve account that it had set aside to cover potential liabilities. The government claims that Enron did not have a business reason for using its reserves to increase Wholesale's earnings, instead doing so solely to exceed analysts' expectations.

The government contends that Skilling improperly used the reserve accounts again later that year. Wholesale's business was very profitable during the second half of 2000, and by late December it had placed over $850 million in reserves. The decision to put that money away was not based on feared future liabilities; instead, Wholesale set that money aside specifically to use in the event of an unfavorable consensus estimate. At the end of the fourth quarter, Skilling ordered that Enron recall some of that money to guarantee that Enron could announce a specific level of earnings.

D. Third-Party Entities LJM and LJM2

Another avenue of Skilling's alleged fraud came from his use of pseudo third-party entity LJM (and later LJM2) to improperly hedge its investments, doing so through four "secret" oral side deals. Fastow, Enron's CFO, proposed to Skilling and Causey that they create an entity to help Enron more easily meet market expectations. The impetus for creating LJM was the $200 million that Enron had received from an investment in a company called Rhythms Net. Enron wanted to book that money, but it was possible that the value of the investment would drop, meaning that the asset's expected value would have to be reduced. By transferring the asset to a pseudo third-party, however, Enron could hedge its investment without needing to pay market rates for this hedging service. The government claims that LJM became that pseudo third-party. Enron contributed $234 million of its own shares in seed money to form LJM. Fastow, who was LJM's general partner, contributed $1 million, and outside investors contributed $15 million.

Enron encountered a potential problem, however, with using LJM to hedge its investments. Fastow faced a conflict of interest, because he was both Enron's CFO and LJM's general partner. Before Enron could sign a deal with LJM, Enron's code of conduct required the Office of the Chairman, which consisted of Skilling and Lay, to waive the conflict rules, and Enron would have to disclose this waiver in its Securities and Exchange Commission ("SEC") filings. The Office of the Chairman granted the waiver, but allegedly not without first creating controversy within Enron's senior leadership.

After forming LJM to hedge the Rhythms Net investment, Enron's first deal with LJM involved an interest in a Brazilian power plant, known as Cuiaba, that Enron sold to LJM in 1999. Enron was concerned that its South American unit would not meet its earnings targets, so it decided to sell its interest in Cuiaba to obtain additional revenue. Initially, Enron tried to find a third party to buy the interest in Cuiaba, but was unsuccessful. Skilling, the government claims, then called Fastow and tried to sell Enron's interest in Cuiaba to LJM. Fastow at first was not interested; not only was the asset a bad investment, there was no time for due diligence. Skilling allegedly replied, "Don't worry. I'll make sure that you're all right on the project. You won't lose any money."That oral understanding did not appear in the deal write-up, and the accountants treated it as a real sale, even though, based on the alleged oral understanding between Skilling and Fastow, it was not a legitimate sale.

Enron eventually bought back the Cuiaba interest, paying full value (notwithstanding depreciation) plus 13%. Allegedly to camouflage the deal by avoiding round numbers, LJM received an extra $42,000 above the 13%. To allay further scrutiny, before Enron bought back the interest, Fastow apparently "sold" his interest in LJM to Michael Kopper ("Kopper"), a former Enron executive. That way, Enron did not need to describe the Cuiaba buyback as a transaction with a related party. For this to work, however, Skilling needed to honor his secret oral promise to Fastow that LJM would not lose money on the deal, despite Kopper becoming LJM's chief; the government claims that Skilling orally confirmed that he would do so.

The second allegedly fraudulent secret side deal between Enron and LJM involved the sale of Nigerian barges. The government claims that in the waning days of 1999, LJM warehoused assets for Enron, allowing Enron to claim earnings during 1999 while it arranged for permanent buyers after the end of the year. With respect to the Nigerian barges deal, in late 1999, Enron sought to sell its interest in a group of barges anchored off the coast of Nigeria to meet an earnings target at the end of the quarter. Most investors were nervous about putting money into Nigeria, so Enron could not find a buyer.

Skilling allegedly called Fastow into his office and asked for LJM to buy the barges, again saying he would "make sure" that LJM would not lose money. Fastow initially was reluctant, because he was trying to raise money for LJM and did not want to scare off investors. However, he told Skilling that LJM would purchase the Nigerian barges if Enron could not find another investor within six months.

Fastow, on behalf of Enron, then arranged for Merrill Lynch to buy the Nigerian barges from Enron. Although Merrill Lynch did not really want to purchase the barges, Fastow purportedly made an oral "guarantee" – although he likely did not use that word – that Merrill Lynch would have to hold the barges for only six months in return for a risk-free profit. Because Merrill Lynch's investment was not at risk, the government alleges that Enron improperly treated the transaction as a sale and should not have recorded any earnings from the deal. At the end of the six months, Enron still could not find another buyer, so LJM purchased the interest from Merrill Lynch, apparently without even negotiating over price. Causey allegedly assured LJM that it would earn a guaranteed return on the deal, meaning that there was no transfer of risk to LJM. In sum, the government asserts that the sale of the Nigerian barges was not a true sale and that Enron improperly recognized earnings from the deal.

The third secret oral side deal involved the "Raptors," which were special purpose entities ("SPE") that would hedge assets for Enron, meaning that if the assets decreased in value, a Raptor would cover the difference – at least on paper. The government asserts that for Enron to validly hedge an asset, a third party must own at least three percent of the SPE's equity, and that equity must be at risk. The government alleges that LJM acted as that "third party" even though it was not really a separate entity, agreeing to provide the equity that would be at risk.

The government contends that to fund the Raptors, LJM contributed $30 million and Enron spent $400 million of its own stock. Apparently, Fastow was at first against mixing LJM with the Raptors, but the government argues that Skilling convinced him through a "secret" side deal, whereby after funding the Raptors, LJM would recoup its $30 million and would receive an additional $11 million. To do this, Enron agreed to pay $41 million to the Raptors to purchase a "put"[7] on the stock Enron had contributed to the Raptors. The Raptors then transferred that $41 million to LJM. In return, the Raptors had to pay Enron if the price of the stock Enron used to capitalize the Raptors fell below a certain level. LJM thus had nothing at risk; if the hedged assets dropped in value, the hedging Raptor, not LJM, was liable for the loss, and LJM recouped the capital it initially invested in the Raptors, along with an additional $11 million.

To make this transaction work, however, Enron's accountants had to sign off. Arthur Andersen, Enron's external auditor, approved the $41 million payment to LJM once it was described as a return "on" capital to LJM and not a return "of" capital. The auditors allegedly were not told that LJM and Enron did not haggle over the value of the hedged assets or that LJM was not actually a true third party. The government terms this entire deal – both Enron's "put" and LJM's return promise to allow Enron to hedge an asset at any value – the "quid pro quo."

The Raptors were also involved in other transactions. For example, in 2000, Enron hedged EBS's investment in Avici, an internet company, into one of the Raptors. That asset, at its highest value, was worth around $160 million, but the value was decreasing. Enron allegedly hedged the Avici interest with a Raptor at its highest value. The asset plummeted in value over the next few months, but because of the allegedly fraudulent hedge, Enron did not record the loss. Under the government's theory, Skilling knew all about the deceit and even told Fastow to "[k]eep it up." The alleged fraud continued throughout 2000. In fact, by the end of 2000, another one of the Raptors lost more than $100 million because of similar hedging. In total, Enron's use of the Raptors allegedly kept nearly $500 million in losses off of Enron's books in 2000.

---

[7]A "put" is an option contract that gives the holder the right to sell certain stock to the writer of the option at a specified price up to a specified date.

The fourth "secret" side deal the government presented was "Global Galactic." Global Galactic was not actually a single deal but instead was the name that Fastow gave to the three-page handwritten list of his undocumented side deals with Enron. Fastow claimed that he created the list to keep track of the various deals and to ensure that he was on the same page as Enron's management on the substance of these deals. Skilling asserts that he had no connection to the deals on this list. * * *

II. Trial and Sentence

According to the government, Skilling's conduct constitutes multiple instances of criminal activity. In July 2004, a grand jury returned a superseding indictment charging Skilling, Lay, and Causey with various counts of conspiracy, securities fraud, wire fraud, and insider trading. The indictment charged Skilling with one count of conspiracy to commit securities and wire fraud, fourteen counts of securities fraud, four counts of wire fraud, six counts of making false representa-tions to auditors, and ten counts of insider trading. Several weeks before trial began, Causey pleaded guilty to one count of securities fraud, and the government dropped four counts against Skilling that involved Causey. Skilling and Lay went to trial, and, at the close of its case, the government eliminated four additional counts.

At trial, Skilling argued that he did not break any laws, that he was loyal to Enron, and that he consistently relied on competent legal and accounting advice; he characterized any falsehoods in his statements to analysts as immaterial in content and context. He also challenged the veracity of the government's witnesses, such as Fastow and Glisan. For example, Skilling claimed that Fastow's testimony regarding Skilling and Fastow's alleged shared understanding about Cuiaba and the Nigerian barges – "bear hugs," in Fastow's words – did not reflect what Skilling said but merely consisted of Fastow's misinterpretations. Skilling also questioned the validity of the so-called Global Galactic list.

In May 2006, the jury found Skilling guilty of nineteen counts: one count of conspiracy, twelve counts of securities fraud, five counts of making false statements, and one count of insider trading; the jury acquitted Skilling of nine counts of insider trading. The jury convicted Lay of every count against him.[9] The district court sentenced Skilling to 292 months' imprisonment, three years' supervised release, and $45 million in restitution.

III. Honest-Services Fraud Allegation

On appeal, Skilling argues that we must reverse all of his convictions because the government used an invalid theory of "honest-services fraud" to convict him. The jury convicted Skilling of one count of conspiracy. The

---

[9] On July 5, 2006, Lay died, causing the court to vacate his conviction and dismiss his indictment.

indictment and the government's theory allowed for three objects of the conspiracy: to commit (1) securities fraud, (2) wire fraud to deprive Enron and its shareholders of money and property, and (3) wire fraud to deprive Enron and its shareholders of the honest services owed by its employees. Because the jury returned a general verdict, we cannot know on which of the three objects it relied.

In Yates v. United States, 354 U.S. 297 (1957), the Supreme Court held that where a jury returns a general verdict of guilt that might rest on multiple legal theories, at least one insufficient in law and the others sufficient, the verdict must be set aside. In such a situation, we cannot trust the jury to have chosen the legally sufficient theory and to have ignored the insufficient one, because "[j]urors are not generally equipped to determine whether a particular theory of conviction submitted to them is contrary to law." Griffin v. United States, 502 U.S. 46 (1991). * * *

Likewise, if any of the three objects of Skilling's conspiracy offers a legally insufficient theory, we must set aside his conviction to avoid the possibility that the verdict rests on the insufficient theory. Skilling avers that the honest-services fraud object of the conspiracy count is legally insufficient, mandating the reversal of the conspiracy conviction. He claims that this would also taint the convictions that rely upon the conspiracy count. * * *

The honest-services statute provides that "the term 'scheme or artifice to defraud' includes a scheme or artifice to deprive another of the intangible right of honest services."18 U.S.C. § 1346. That is, the statute defines the "scheme or artifice to defraud" language found in the substantive mail and wire fraud statutes, 18 U.S.C. §§ 1341 and 1343, respectively, to include the substantive crime of depriving another of one's honest services. Thus, wherever mail or wire fraud is an object of a conspiracy, there are two possible objects that can be charged: use of the mails or wires to deprive another of (1) property or money or (2) honest services. See 18 U.S.C. §§ 1341, 1343. * * *

In United States v. Gray, 96 F.3d 769 (5th Cir.1996), we considered the honest-services statute in the context of a private employer and employees. A jury convicted three assistant basketball coaches at Baylor University ("Baylor") of conspiracy to commit mail and wire fraud by depriving Baylor of its honest services through a scheme to obtain credits and scholarships for players in violation of National Collegiate Athletic Association ("NCAA") rules. The coaches argued that honest-services fraud "improperly criminalize[d] mere deceit," because the coaches had broken no law, only a private association's rules, and "they lacked the requisite intent to either harm the victims or to obtain personal benefit . . . . Essentially, [the coaches] argue[d] that their scheme was not intended to harm Baylor but rather to help Baylor by ensuring a successful basketball team." We rejected the argument and noted that a breach of fiduciary duty of honesty or loyalty involving a violation of the duty to disclose could only result in criminal mail fraud where the information withheld from the employer was material and that, where the employer was in the private sector, information should be deemed material if the employee had reason to believe the information would lead a reasonable employer to change its business conduct.

We concluded that the information the coaches withheld, namely that they were cheating, was material; had Baylor been aware of their actions, it undoubtedly would have changed its business conduct by recruiting players who satisfied NCAA requirements. In light of our conclusions, the coaches' conspiracy to violate NCAA rules was a federal crime; that their intent was to help rather than harm the university was of no consequence.

In United States v. Brown, 459 F.3d 509 (5th Cir.2006), we again addressed honest-services fraud and refined our jurisprudence. The defendants arranged for the Nigerian barges deal we described above, whereby Enron "sold" three energy-producing barges to Merrill Lynch. The "purchase" allowed Enron to book, as earnings, the money it received from Merrill Lynch, thereby helping Enron meet its earnings targets. In return, Enron assured Merrill Lynch a fixed rate of return on the investment – a flat fee – and promised that Enron or a third party would repurchase the barges within six months. Such an agreement, however, would have rendered the deal a loan from Merrill Lynch to Enron, because Merrill Lynch had no equity at stake. As a loan, the transaction could have no positive impact on Enron's earnings, meaning that it was fraudulent for Enron to book any earnings from the deal.

After surveying our prior honest-services jurisprudence, we reversed the defendants' convictions, concluding that their conduct did not fall within the bounds of the honest-services statute. In particular, we held that

> where an employer intentionally aligns the interests of the employee with a specified corporate goal, where the employee perceives his pursuit of that goal as mutually benefiting him and his employer, and where the employee's conduct is consistent with that perception of the mutual interest, such conduct is beyond the reach of the honest-services theory of fraud as it has hitherto been applied.

Importantly, we expounded upon our understanding of honest-services fraud by providing a crucial distinction from the facts in *Gray*:

> *Gray* is distinguishable both factually and legally. *Gray* is dissimilar to this case in part because the opinion recognizes nothing akin to Enron's corporate incentive policy coupled with senior executive support for the deal (the deal was sanctioned by Fastow, Enron's Chief Financial Officer), which together created an understanding that Enron had a corporate interest in, and was a willing beneficiary

of, the scheme. The opinion in *Gray* presents only the coaches' own belief that their scheme benefited the university; no one or any authority outside the cadre of coaches encouraged, approved, or even knew of the wrongdoing.

Given the gloss this passage places on *Gray*, we can distill the holding in *Brown* to be the following: when an employer (1) creates a particular goal, (2) aligns the employees' interests with the employer's interest in achieving that goal, and (3) has higher-level management sanction improper conduct to reach the goal, then lower-level employees following their boss's direction are not liable for honest-services fraud. Thus, we reversed the convictions of the employees in *Brown* because they were acting both in the corporate interest and at the direction of their employer. In essence, *Brown* created an exception for honest-services fraud where an employer not only aligns its interests with the interests of its employees but also sanctions the fraudulent conduct, i.e., where the corporate decisionmakers, who supervised the employees being prosecuted, specifically authorized the activity.

Skilling does not contest that he owed Enron a fiduciary duty. Instead, he contends that his conduct did not breach that duty, because his fraud was in the corporate interest and therefore was not self-dealing. In particular, Skilling asserts that he did not engage in his conduct in secret. Skilling further latches onto our discussion in *Brown* regarding corporate interest and contends that his actions were not fraudulent because he acted in pursuit of Enron's goals of achieving a higher stock price.

If this were the correct reading of *Brown*, that decision would be in irreconcilable conflict with *Gray*, which binds us, as the basketball coaches in *Gray* acted pursuant to their employer's interest of having a win-ning basketball team. * * *

Skilling misconstrues our holding in *Brown*, however, because he fails to recognize the manner in which the court in *Brown* explicitly distinguished *Gray*. As we noted above, *Gray* and *Brown* present different facts; in *Gray*, the basketball coaches acted on their own volition, without any direction from their supervisors, while in *Brown*, a lower-level Enron employee acted at the direction of Fastow, who as a decisionmaker had the authority to tell his employee that Enron sanctioned the particular fraud in question. The difference is that in *Brown*, the employee undertook the specific fraud in question at the direction of the employer, while this did not occur in *Gray*. In essence, because the Enron decisionmaker in *Brown* sanctioned the specific fraudulent conduct of its employee, the employee (and the other conspirators) did not deprive Enron of its honest services. Thus, for example, had the basketball coaches in *Gray* showed that the President of Baylor University or other decisionmakers specifically directed their fraudulent conduct, then they would not have been liable for honest-services fraud.

Applying this rule, Skilling's convictions must stand. First, Enron created a goal of meeting certain earnings projections. Second, Enron aligned its interests with Skilling's personal interests, e.g., through his compensation structure, leading Skilling to undertake fraudulent means to achieve the goal. Third – and fatally to Skilling's argument – no one at Enron sanctioned Skilling's improper conduct. That is, Skilling does not allege that the Board of Directors or any other decisionmaker specifically directed the improper means that he undertook to achieve his goals. Of course, a senior executive cannot wear his "executive" hat to sanction a fraudulent scheme and then wear his "employee" hat to perpetuate that fraud. Therefore, it is not a matter of Skilling setting the corporation's policy himself. Instead, the question is whether anyone who supervised Skilling specifically directed his actions – such as how Fastow sanctioned the scheme in *Brown*. Skilling never alleged that he engaged in his conduct at the explicit direction of anyone, and therefore he cannot avail himself of the exception from *Brown*.

That the Board of Directors approved several of the fraudulent transactions is of no moment. Tacitly approving a sale is not the same as having senior executives direct their lower-level employees to engage in fraudulent conduct. Skilling reads a requirement of secrecy into the holding in *Brown*, asserting that it is not honest-services fraud if the employer knows of the fraud in question. This argument is unavailing, for two reasons. First, a requirement of secrecy (or lack thereof) does not appear in *Brown*. Second, it makes no difference that the Board of Directors knew of Skilling's conduct if Enron (through the Board or its senior executives) did not actually direct Skilling to undertake the fraudulent means to achieve his goals.

The elements of honest-services wire fraud applicable here are (1) a material breach of a fiduciary duty imposed under state law, including duties defined by the employer-employee relationship, (2) that results in a detriment to the employer. *Brown* sheds light on the employer-employee relationship by creating an exception for when the employer specifically directs the fraudulent conduct. Further, it is a sufficient detriment for an employee, contrary to his duty of honesty, to withhold material information, i.e., information that he had reason to believe would lead a reasonable employer to change its conduct. Accordingly, the jury was entitled to convict Skilling of conspiracy to commit honest-services wire fraud on these elements. Thus, although we do not know on which alleged object of the conspiracy the jury based its verdict, there is no risk that Skilling was convicted of conspiracy based on a legally insufficient theory, and the jury was entitled to convict on any or all of the three objects. * * *

NOTES AND QUESTIONS

1. *Vagueness.* How does one define honest services? In **United States v. Gray**, 96 F.3d 769 (5th Cir. 1996) "[t]he indictment charged members of the men's basketball coaching staff at Baylor University, and others, with executing a fraudulent scheme to establish academic eligibility for five transfer students to play basketball at Baylor during the 1993-94 academic year." Specifically Gray and Thomas, "assistant mens' basketball coaches in

1993" argued "that § 1346 is unconstitutionally vague as it applied to them." The Fifth Circuit rejected defendant's arguments, holding that § 1346 was not unconstitutionally vague as applied to the defendants.

2. *Limiting 1346.* Although § 1346 has not been found to be vague, many courts have limited its application. Consider some of these decisions as expressed by Justice Scalia, writing a dissent to a denial of certiorari in **Sorich v. United States**, 129 S.Ct. 1308 (2009):

> In McNally v. United States, [p. 147], this Court held that while "[t]he mail fraud statute clearly protects property rights, ... [it] does not refer to the intangible right of the citizenry to good government." * * * That holding invalidated the theory that official corruption and misconduct, by depriving citizens of their "intangible right" to the honest and impartial services of government, constituted fraud. Although all of the Federal Courts of Appeals had accepted the theory, * * * we declined to "construe the statute in a manner that leaves its outer boundaries ambiguous and involves the Federal Government in setting standards of disclosure and good government for local and state officials." * * * "If Congress desires to go further," we said, "it must speak more clearly than it has." Congress spoke shortly thereafter. "For the purposes of this chapter, the term 'scheme or artifice to defraud' includes a scheme or artifice to deprive another of the intangible right of honest services." * * * Whether that terse amendment qualifies as speaking "more clearly" or in any way lessens the vagueness and federalism concerns that produced this Court's decision in *McNally* is another matter.
>
> Though it consists of only 28 words, the statute has been invoked to impose criminal penalties upon a staggeringly broad swath of behavior, including misconduct not only by public officials and employees but also by private employees and corporate fiduciaries. Courts have upheld convictions of a local housing official who failed to disclose a conflict of interest, United States v. Hasner, 340 F.3d 1261, 1271 (C.A.11 2003) (per curiam); a businessman who attempted to pay a state legislator to exercise "informal and behind-the-scenes influence on legislation," United States v. Potter, 463 F.3d 9, 18 (C.A.1 2006); students who schemed with their professors to turn in plagiarized work, United States v. Frost, 125 F.3d 346, 369 (C.A.6 1997); lawyers who made side-payments to insurance adjusters in exchange for the expedited processing of their clients' pending claims, United States v. Rybicki, 354 F.3d 124, 142 (C.A.2 2003) (en banc); and, in the decision we are asked to review here, city employees who engaged in political-patronage hiring for local civil-service jobs, 523 F.3d 702, 705 (C.A.7 2008).
>
> If the "honest services" theory-broadly stated, that officeholders and employees owe a duty to act only in the best interests of their constituents and employers-is taken seriously and carried to its

logical conclusion, presumably the statute also renders criminal a state legislator's decision to vote for a bill because he expects it will curry favor with a small minority essential to his reelection; a mayor's attempt to use the prestige of his office to obtain a restaurant table without a reservation; a public employee's recommendation of his incompetent friend for a public contract; and any self-dealing by a corporate officer. Indeed, it would seemingly cover a salaried employee's phoning in sick to go to a ball game. In many cases, moreover, the maximum penalty for violating this statute will be added to the maximum penalty for violating 18 U.S.C. § 666, a federal bribery statute, since violation of the latter requires the additional factor of the employer's receipt of federal funds, while violation of the "honest services" provision requires use of mail or wire services, §§ 1341, 1343. Quite a potent federal prosecutorial tool.

To avoid some of these extreme results, the Courts of Appeals have spent two decades attempting to cabin the breadth of § 1346 through a variety of limiting principles. No consensus has emerged. The Fifth Circuit has held that the statute criminalizes only a deprivation of services that is unlawful under state law, United States v. Brumley, 116 F.3d 728, 735 (1997) (en banc), but other courts have not agreed, see United States v. Martin, 195 F.3d 961, 966 (C.A.7 1999) (Brumley "is contrary to the law in this circuit ... and in the other circuits to have addressed the question"). The Seventh Circuit has construed the statute to prohibit only the abuse of position "for private gain,"United States v. Bloom, 149 F.3d 649, 655 (1998), but other Circuits maintain that gain is not an element of the crime at all, e.g., United States v. Panarella, 277 F.3d 678, 692 (C.A.3 2002). Courts have expressed frustration at the lack of any "simple formula specific enough to give clear cut answers to borderline problems." United States v. Urciuoli, 513 F.3d 290, 300 (C.A.1 2008).

It is practically gospel in the lower courts that the statute "does not encompass every instance of official misconduct," United States v. Sawyer, 85 F.3d 713, 725 (C.A.1 1996). The Tenth Circuit has confidently proclaimed that the statute is "not violated by every breach of contract, breach of duty, conflict of interest, or misstatement made in the course of dealing," United States v. Welch, 327 F.3d 1081, 1107 (C.A.10 2003). But why that is so, and what principle it is that separates the criminal breaches, conflicts and misstatements from the obnoxious but lawful ones, remains entirely unspecified. Without some coherent limiting principle to define what "the intangible right of honest services" is, whence it derives, and how it is violated, this expansive phrase invites abuse by headline-grabbing prosecutors in pursuit of local officials, state legislators, and corporate CEOs who engage in any manner of unappealing or ethically questionable conduct.

In the background of the interpretive venture remain the two concerns voiced by this Court in *McNally*. First, the prospect of federal prosecutors' (or federal courts') creating ethics codes and setting disclosure requirements for local and state officials. Is it the role of the Federal Government to define the fiduciary duties that a town alderman or school board trustee owes to his constituents? * * * Second and relatedly, this Court has long recognized the "basic principle that a criminal statute must give fair warning of the conduct that it makes a crime." * * * There is a serious argument that § 1346 is nothing more than an invitation for federal courts to develop a common-law crime of unethical conduct. But "the notion of a common-law crime is utterly anathema today," * * * and for good reason. It is simply not fair to prosecute someone for a crime that has not been defined until the judicial decision that sends him to jail. "How can the public be expected to know what the statute means when the judges and prosecutors themselves do not know, or must make it up as they go along?" *Rybicki, supra,* at 160 (Jacobs, J., dissenting).

The present case in which certiorari is sought implicates two of the limiting principles that the Courts of Appeals have debated-whether the crime of deprivation of "honest services" requires a predicate violation of state law, and whether it requires the defendant's acquisition of some sort of private gain. The jury was instructed that petitioners, who were employed by the city of Chicago, were obliged, "[a]s part of the honest services they owed the City and the people of the City of Chicago," to abide by a laundry list of "laws, decrees, and policies," including a 1983 civil consent decree entered into by the city which barred patronage hiring for some city jobs. * * * The Seventh Circuit approved the instruction, again rejecting the Fifth Circuit's violation-of-state-law principle. "It may well be," the court said, "that merely by virtue of being public officials the defendants inherently owed the public a fiduciary duty to discharge their offices in the public's best interest."* * * And though petitioners received no direct personal benefit from the patronage they doled out on behalf of their political masters, the Seventh Circuit found it sufficient that the patronage *appointees*-who were not charged in the scheme-accrued private gain. * * *

Finally, in addition to presenting two of the principal devices the Courts of Appeals have used in an effort to limit § 1346, the case also squarely presents the issue of its constitutionality. The Court of Appeals rebuffed petitioners' argument that if § 1346 really criminalizes all conduct that is not "in the public's best interest" and that benefits *someone,* it is void for vagueness. * * * In light of the conflicts among the Circuits; the longstanding confusion over the scope of the statute; and the serious due process and federalism interests affected by the expansion of criminal liability that this case exemplifies, I would grant the petition for certiorari and squarely confront both the meaning and the constitutionality of § 1346. Indeed, it seems to me quite irresponsible to let the current chaos prevail.

3. *Private Sector Frauds.* In **United States v. DeVegter**, 198 F.3d 1324, 1328-29 (11th Cir. 1999) the court stated:

> This case involves the alleged commission of honest services fraud by private sector defendants, not a defrauding of the public of the honest governmental services of a public official. * * * The meaning of the "intangible right of honest services" has different implications, however, when applied to public official malfeasance and private sector misconduct. Public officials inherently owe a fiduciary duty to the public to make governmental decisions in the public's best interest. * * * "If the official instead secretly makes his decision based on his own personal interests--as when an official accepts a bribe or personally benefits from an undisclosed conflict of interest--the official has defrauded the public of his honest services." * * * Illicit personal gain by a government official deprives the public of its intangible right to the honest services of the official.

> On the other hand, such a strict duty of loyalty ordinarily is not part of private sector relationships.   Most private sector interactions do not involve duties of, or rights to, the "honest services" of either party. Relationships may be accompanied by obligations of good faith and fair dealing, even in arms-length transactions. These and similar duties are quite unlike, however, the duty of loyalty and fidelity to purpose required of public officials. For example, "[e]mployee loyalty is not an end in itself, it is a means to obtain and preserve pecuniary benefits for the employer. An employee's undisclosed conflict of interest does not by itself necessarily pose the threat of economic harm to the employer." A public official's undisclosed conflict of interest, in contrast, does by itself harm the constituents' interest in the end for which the official serves--honest government in the public's best interest. The "intangible right of honest services" must be given an analogous interpretation in the private sector.   Therefore, for a private sector defendant to have violated the victim's right to honest services, it is not enough to prove the defendant's breach of loyalty alone. Rather, as is always true in a breach of loyalty by a public official, the breach of loyalty by a private sector defendant must in each case contravene--by inherently harming--the purpose of the parties' relationship.

> Other Circuits have established a well-reasoned standard for determining whether private sector misconduct rises to the level of violating the victim's right to "honest services" under § 1346. "The

prosecution must prove that the employee intended to breach a fiduciary duty, and that the employee foresaw or reasonably should have foreseen that his employer might suffer an economic harm as a result of the breach." * * * The nature and interpretation of the duty owed is a question of federal law.

4. *Private Political Officials.* Do private officials owe the same fiduciary duty that is owed by public officials? In United States v. Margiotta, 688 F.2d 108 (2d Cir. 1982) the Second Circuit sustained a conviction of a county chair who used his "power to construct a contracts-for-payments scheme." Taking the position of Judge Winter, the author of a dissenting opinion in *Margiotta*, the Third Circuit recently stated that "[t]he prosecution of a private party official is, [ ], a horse of a different color." In United States v. Murphy, 323 F.3d 102 (3rd Cir. 2003) the court stated, "[w]e agree with Judge Winter that *Margiotta* fails to provide any logical rationale for treating private party officials in the same manner as public officials since such a loose interpretation of the mail fraud statute creates 'a catch-all political crime which has no use but misuse.'"

5. *Breach of Fiduciary Duty.* When does a breach of a fiduciary duty rise to the level of being criminal as mail fraud. Consider the following excerpt from John C. Coffee, Jr., *Some Reflections on the Criminalization of Fiduciary Breaches and the Problematic Line Between Law and Ethics*, 19 AM. CRIM. L. REV. 117 (1981), concerning the case of **United States v. Bronston**, 658 F.2d 920 (2d Cir. 1981):

> *Bronston* is clearly the most publicized recent case imposing criminal liability for private fiduciary breach; in part, this is because the defendant was a New York state senator and a partner in a respected New York law firm. But its greater significance lies in its articulation of a theory that reaches all who are members of the legal profession. * * *
>
> Is there any intermediate position before every breach by a fiduciary becomes a potential criminal prosecution at the option of the federal prosecutor? The facts of *Bronston* illustrate one potential compromise which neither denies that a fiduciary breach can amount to a criminal violation nor makes every ethical shortcoming a felony offense. Assume for the moment that Bronston has done nothing more than breach his fiduciary duty for personal pecuniary gain. Classically, this might seem sufficient to support criminal liability since, on these assumed facts, the conduct consisted of more than a naked fiduciary breach standing alone, but had the motive of personal profit. So simplified, the *Bronston* fact pattern as a paradigm has two critical elements: (1) a fiduciary breach, and (2) a self-seeking motive. What more could be required? Scrutinized carefully, previous mail fraud convictions based on a fiduciary breach and a pecuniary gain to the defendant

or loss to the victim; rather, the former must in some manner cause the latter.

Consider also the following excerpt from the response of Craig M. Bradley, *Foreward: Mail Fraud After* McNally *and* Carpenter: *The Essence of Fraud,* 79 J. CRIM. L. & CRIMINOLOGY 573 (1988):

> * * * In summary, the best way to reconcile *McNally, Carpenter* and the history of fraud (to the somewhat limited extent that they are reconcilable) is to conclude that mail fraud includes, in addition to the requisite mailings, a scheme in which the defendant, through knowingly deceitful behavior, intends an economic gain and is at least negligent as to economic harm to the victim. The "deceitful behavior" can include a breach of fiduciary duty. Thus, Winans committed fraud the first time he disclosed confidential information, with the requisite intent as to gain and loss.

> Consider how this formulation applies to a particular, controversial case, United States v. Bronston. In *Bronston* the defendant, a partner in a law firm, secretly worked for Client B, while his firm was representing Client A, both of which clients were competing for a city contract. However, Bronston did not use his fiduciary position to harm Client A. Bronston was convicted of defrauding Client A.

> Contrary to Professor Coffee, I have no difficulty with the *Bronston* case. Bronston knowingly breached his fiduciary duty to Client A, intended to gain from that breach and could reasonably foresee that the breach would cause harm to Client A. That is, he intended that, through his efforts, Client B should get the contract rather than Client A. The fact that he did not use his position to gain extra advantage, as Winans did, does not deny that the breach caused, or could have caused the harm. Accordingly, under the reading of *Carpenter* and *McNally* advanced in this Article, Bronston committed fraud.

6. ***Disagreements Among the Circuits.*** Although all circuits have found section 1346 constitutional, many issues continue to remain unresolved. In **United States v. Rybicki**, 354 F.3d 125 (2d Cir. 2003), the Second Circuit en banc affirmed the convictions of two personal injury attorneys who were convicted for their role in a scheme to expedite insurance claims. Although the court affirmed the convictions, a dissent examined some of the circuit splits on issues involving mail fraud case under section 1346:

> * * * Although a number of circuits have upheld section 1346 against a claim of facial vagueness, there is now wide disagreement among the circuits as to the elements of the "honest services" offense. These opinions, taken together, refute rather than support

the idea that section 1346 has any settled or ascertainable meaning or that the offense it describes has known contours:

- What mens rea must be proved by the government? The majority follows Second Circuit precedent in holding that an intent to cause economic harm is not required–a defendant need only have intended to deprive another of the "intangible right of honest services." However, in the Seventh Circuit, an intent to achieve personal gain is an element of the offense. See United States v. Bloom, 149 F.3d 649 (7th Cir. 1998). But see United States v. Welch, 327 F.3d 1081 (10th Cir. 2003) (holding that the text and structure of the mail fraud statutes do not support "adding an element" to "honest services" fraud requiring that defendant seek to obtain a personal benefit). The Eight Circuit describes the mens rea element as "caus[ing] or intend[ing] to cause actual harm or injury, and in most business contexts, that means financial or economic harm." See United States v. Pennington, 168 F.3d 1060 (8th Cir. 1999). One circuit has held that, to secure an honest services conviction, "[t]he prosecution must prove that the employee intended to breach a fiduciary duty." *Frost*. Other circuits merely require a showing of "fraudulent intent." See United States v. Cochran, 109 F.3d 660 (10th Cir.1997); United States v. Jain, 93 F.3d 436 (8th Cir.1996).

- Must the defendant have caused actual tangible harm? Compare *Jain* ("When there is no tangible harm to the victim of a private scheme, it is hard to discern what intangible 'rights' have been violated."), with *Frost* ("[A] defendant accused of scheming to deprive another of honest services does not have to intend to inflict an economic harm upon the victim."). Some circuits have required that the misrepresentation be material, i.e., that the employee have reason to believe that the information would lead a reasonable employer to change its business conduct. Other circuits only require a showing that it was reasonably foreseeable for the victim to suffer economic harm. We adopted this last requirement in the *Rybicki* panel opinion, and now abandon it.

- What is the duty that must be breached to violate section 1346? The majority holds that it is the duty owed by an employee to an employer, or by "a person in a relationship that gives rise to a duty of loyalty comparable to that owed by employees to employers" (whatever that means). Some circuits only allow prosecutions for breach of an employee's duty to an employer. Other circuits require the breach of a fiduciary duty.

- Is the source of that duty state or federal law? The majority does not say, and other circuits are split. Compare *Frost*

("Federal law governs the existence of fiduciary duty under the mail fraud statute." (emphasis added)), with *Brumley* ("We have held that services under § 1346 are those an employee must provide the employer under state law."

• Did section 1346 revive pre-McNally case law; if so must each circuit look to its own governing precedent or to some set of rules distilled from the whole body of pre-McNally cases? * * *

In sum, the circuits are fractured on the basic issues: (1) the requisite mens rea to commit the crime, (2) whether the defendant must cause actual tangible harm, (3) the duty that must be breached, (4) the source of that duty, and (5) which body of law informs us of the statute's meaning. This lack of coherence has created "a truly extraordinary statute, in which the substantive force of the statute varie[s] in each judicial circuit." *Brumley* (Jolly, J., dissenting). * * *

E. INTENT

UNITED STATES v. D'AMATO
39 F.3d 1249 (2d Cir. 1994)

WINTER, Circuit Judge.

* * * [Armand P.] D'Amato was convicted of seven counts of mail fraud in violation of 18 U.S.C. § 1341 and sentenced principally to a term of five months imprisonment, two years of supervised release including five months of home detention, and payment of $7,500 restitution. D'Amato's conviction arises from services he provided to the Unisys Corporation ("Unisys"). The government claimed at trial that D'Amato was hired by a "rogue" Unisys employee, Charles Gardner, and that D'Amato, with Gardner's aid, defrauded Unisys in two ways. First, the government maintained that D'Amato committed mail fraud by structuring his billings to conceal from those in control of corporate funds the nature of his relationship with Unisys and the fact that his actual services involved lobbying his brother, a United States Senator and member of the Senate Appropriations Committee. We will style this theory the "right to control theory." The government maintained, second, that D'Amato committed mail fraud by contracting with Unisys to provide written reports on Senate proceedings while never intending to provide those reports. We will style this theory the "false pretenses theory."

Because the evidence of criminal intent was insufficient on either theory, we reverse the judgment of conviction and order the indictment dismissed. * * *

D'Amato, an attorney, started a law partnership with Jeffrey Forchelli in 1976.　By 1988, the two were practicing as partners of D'Amato, Forchelli, Libert, Schwartz, Mineo & Carlino ("D'Amato Forchelli"), a firm of roughly twenty lawyers based in Mineola, New York.　D'Amato's brother, Alfonse D'Amato, was a United States Senator from the State of New York throughout the period of relevant events.　Senator D'Amato was a member of the Senate Appropriations Committee, the Senate committee charged with oversight of defense procurement programs.

Unisys, a Fortune 100 company, maintained a Surveillance and Fire Control Systems Division ("S & FCS") in Great Neck, New York.　This division manufactured radar missile control systems that were sold to the United States government.　Charles Gardner served as a Unisys vice president in charge of marketing for S & FCS from the early 1980's until March 1988.　Throughout the pertinent period, Gardner bribed Navy officials, made illegal campaign contributions to Congressmen, and personally profited through kickbacks.　The government has stipulated, however, that none of these illegal activities involved D'Amato or Senator D'Amato, and there was no evidence that D'Amato was aware of any of Gardner's illegal activities. * * *

In fall 1987, Unisys began an internal investigation of alleged unethical behavior by Unisys employees.　The investigation was headed by Lawrence Cresce, * * * In November 1987, Cresce questioned Gardner about his activities.　Gardner acknowledged that the reports mentioned in the purchase orders "just weren't worth the money," and that the "reports were window dressing, and simply paper so that the consultants can get paid." * * * Cresce eventually prepared a report dated May 1988 that concluded that Gardner had, among other activities, used D'Amato Forchelli to gain access to Senator D'Amato. * * *

In connection with the sentencing, the district court found that D'Amato spent approximately 100 hours performing lobbying services for Unisys. The court further found that D'Amato travelled three times to Washington, D.C., at least in part on behalf of Unisys.　In addition, D'Amato met with Unisys employee Lynch around ten times in his office, where Lynch briefed D'Amato on Unisys's programs and needs.　D'Amato also helped cause two letters by Senator D'Amato and one by Congressman Norman Lent to be sent to Navy and Commerce Department officials concerning defense contracts. * * *

The mail fraud statute criminalizes use of the mails in furtherance of a "scheme or artifice to defraud, or for obtaining money or property by means of false or fraudulent pretenses . . . ." 18 U.S.C. § 1341.　Therefore, an essential element of any mail fraud prosecution is proof of a "scheme or artifice to defraud." Id.; see also United States v. Starr, 816 F.2d 94, 98 (2d Cir.1987).　Essential to a scheme to defraud is fraudulent intent. Durland v. United States, [p. 151]. ("The significant fact is the intent and purpose."); Starr, 816 F.2d at 98 (fraudulent intent "critical" to a scheme to defraud);

United States v. Regent Office Supply Co., 421 F.2d 1174, 1180 (2d Cir.1970) (same).

The scheme to defraud need not have been successful or complete. Therefore, the victims of the scheme need not have been injured. United States v. Andreadis, 366 F.2d 423, 431-32 (2d Cir.1966). However, the government must show "that some actual harm or injury was contemplated by the schemer."

Because the defendant must intend to harm the fraud's victims, "[m]isrepresentations amounting only to a deceit are insufficient to maintain a mail or wire fraud prosecution. Instead, the deceit must be coupled with a contemplated harm to the victim." In many cases, this requirement poses no additional obstacle for the government. Actors are presumed to intend the natural and probable consequences of their actions. So when the "necessary result" of the actor's scheme is to injure others, fraudulent intent may be inferred from the scheme itself. Where the scheme does not cause injury to the alleged victim as its necessary result, the government must produce evidence independent of the alleged scheme to show the defendant's fraudulent intent.

1. The Right to Control Theory

a) The Elements.

We first address the right to control theory. That "theory is predicated on a showing that some person or entity has been deprived of potentially valuable economic information." *Wallach,* 935 F.2d at 462-63. Thus, "the withholding or inaccurate reporting of information that could impact on economic decisions can provide the basis for a mail fraud prosecution." A person charged with mail fraud under the right to control theory must intend to injure the person or entity misled—here Unisys, its management, and/or its shareholders—and the person or entity must thus be a specific target of the inaccurate or concealed information. Mail fraud cannot be charged against a corporate agent who in good faith believes that his or her (otherwise legal) misleading or inaccurate conduct is in the corporation's best interests.

Where no rule otherwise provides, persons acting on behalf of a corporation may well find it necessary to disguise or conceal certain matters in the interests of that corporation. For example, failure to disclose the nature of a service provided or the identity of the entity performing such a service may minimize the risk of disclosure of information that would enable competitors to learn of a corporation's future activities or plans. Mining companies may thus conceal the hiring of geologists and the site of their work. Such measures may be necessary also to protect company assets. A company may thus disguise the hiring of forensic accountants in order to avoid giving warning to an undetected embezzler. The preservation of a positive public relations image is a proper corporate goal and may be pursued by a policy of concealment. Such a policy may be necessary also to prevent insider trading. Firms planning a takeover may thus wish to conceal relationships with law firms, accountants, or banks until required to disclose under the Williams Act. 15 U.S.C. §§ 78m(d),(e) & 78n(d)-(f) (1988).

The critical elements are: (i) whether corporate management has made an otherwise lawful decision that concealment or a failure to disclose is in the corporation's best interests and (ii) whether management acted in good faith in making, and did not personally profit from, the decision. As we noted in *Wallach,* the principle that directors and officers may act on behalf of a corporation does not extend to acts of self-enrichment. However, a good faith, unconflicted decision may not be second-guessed by the government or by the courts. See *Miller,* 507 F.2d at 762 ("The sound business judgment rule . . . expresses the unanimous decision of American courts to eschew intervention in corporate decision-making if the judgment of directors and officers i[s] uninfluenced by personal considerations and is exercised in good faith.").

In the instant matter, of course, the defendant is not someone in corporate management but a person hired to perform services for the corporation. Such a person cannot be found to intend to harm a corporation or its shareholders through otherwise lawful misleading conduct if he or she follows the instructions of an appropriate corporate agent who appears to be unconflicted and acting in good faith. So far as the duty of a party contracting to provide ordinary business or professional services to the corporation is concerned, therefore, that party may rely upon instructions from a corporate agent with apparent authority and no ostensible conflict of interest to determine the contracting party's obligations and appropriate billing practices.

Additional considerations apply to a claim that shareholders have been deprived of their right to control. Unlike management, shareholders have no right to manage the business. Nevertheless, they do have property rights of which they may not be fraudulently deprived by "the withholding or inaccurate reporting of information that could impact on economic decisions."   * * *

The otherwise lawful "withholding or inaccurate reporting of information" must thus relate to: (i) information available to shareholders as provided by the state of incorporation's laws providing access to corporate books and records, see *Wallach,* 935 F.2d at 463 (maintenance of accurate books and records is of "central importance" to preservation of shareholders' property interest); (ii) information that, if withheld or inaccurate would result in rendering information that is public materially misleading, see id. (right to public information, required to be disclosed by law, is important component of shareholders' property rights), and (iii) information that would materially aid shareholders in enforcing management's fiduciary obligations under state law, see id. ("complete information" enables a stockholder to take "steps" to prevent corporate actions of which he or she disapproves). Where a third party acting upon instructions from a corporate agent is charged with depriving shareholders of their right to control, the government must prove that the third party knew that the concealment would involve (i), (ii), or (iii).

b) Sufficiency of the Evidence.

The government's claim that D'Amato intended to injure Unisys by depriving its management or its shareholders of their right to control was not based on legally sufficient evidence. The jury could have found that D'Amato knew that his services on behalf of Unisys were disguised. However, the government concedes that the payments to D'Amato for the purpose of gaining "access" to his brother were not illegal. From D'Amato's point of view, if such access resulted in political support from the Senator that helped Unisys's sales, Unisys and its shareholders would benefit. Also from D'Amato's point of view, it was evident that Unisys might desire to keep its source of access to the Senator confidential because the means of access could easily become controversial and self-defeating if disclosed. D'Amato thus could have intended to deprive Unisys management (or shareholders) of "valuable" information that "could impact" on economic decisions only if (i) Gardner had no authority to instruct D'Amato to disguise his services in billing Unisys and D'Amato knew it, (ii) the payments to D'Amato were otherwise unlawful and D'Amato knew it, or (iii) Gardner was personally profiting from the concealed arrangement with D'Amato and D'Amato knew it. None of these conditions has been met in the instant matter.   * * *

Our conclusion is in no way inconsistent with *Wallach.* In *Wallach,* false bills were submitted in order to perpetuate, in conjunction with Wedtech officers, securities fraud on Wedtech shareholders. Two of the defendants, London and Chinn, submitted false invoices in order to disguise the fact that they had been paid for assisting in a stock parking scheme. The third defendant, Wallach, performed lobbying services for Wedtech yet submitted bills that attributed his services to assistance with a public offering and various capital acquisitions. Wallach's misstatements enabled Wedtech to capitalize the cost of his services rather than to expense them in the current accounting period. This artificially inflated Wedtech's current earnings and caused misleading reports, which were available to shareholders, to be filed with the Securities and Exchange Commission. There was evidence, moreover, that Wallach was aware of, and was to share in, the diversion of Wedtech funds to London and Chinn. He was thus not an innocent provider of services to Wedtech unaware of the effect of his actions.

2. The False Pretenses Theory

The false pretenses theory, simply stated, is a claim that D'Amato represented to Unisys that he would prepare reports in exchange for the fees he received, and took the money but prepared no reports. The government's false pretenses theory thus rests on the allegation that D'Amato did not perform the services that he contracted to perform for Unisys and for which he was paid.

* * * The government's theory was and is that D'Amato was paid for lobbying his Senator brother, concededly lawful conduct. There is no evidence that he did not perform such services. It is inconceivable on this record that Unisys could survive a motion for summary judgment in a civil suit to recover fees from D'Amato based on a false pretenses theory, even under the lower burden of proof applicable to civil cases.

Finally, the government argues that D'Amato's services were not worth what Unisys paid for them. This argument is seriously misguided. The mail fraud statute does not criminalize the charging of an allegedly excessive fee, where, as here, a corporate agent with at least apparent authority to do so agreed to the fee, received no personal benefit from the fee, and was not deceived by the payee. Retainer agreements that keep providers of services available are commonplace, and sometimes those services are not needed. We decline the government's invitation to infer fraudulent intent on the part of an attorney who accepts a retainer arrangement and is subsequently not called upon to perform services that the government or trier of fact deems worth the fee paid. Moreover, the government offered no evidence that access to the Senator was not worth the fees paid.

We vacate the conviction, and order dismissal of the indictment.

NOTES AND QUESTIONS

1. *Political Prosecution?.* Prior to the second circuit's ruling, the propriety of the D'Amato prosecution was hotly debated in the New York and national press. See, e.g., Richard W. Painter, The Wall Street Journal, May 4, 1994, at A15 (questioning whether the decision to prosecute was related to "the fact that Mr. D'Amato's brother is a U.S. senator").

2. *Attorney Billing.* Can the mailing of a bill by a lawyer to a client ever be the basis for a mail fraud prosecution? Would a misleading bill constitute mail fraud? In **United States v. Myerson**, 18 F.3d 153, 156 (2d Cir. 1994), Myerson was convicted and sentenced to 60 months imprisonment after being charged with "defrauding six clients and his own law firm while he was a partner at the New York law firm he founded * * *. This fraud was based on Myerson's submitting a legal fee that overbilled his clients by millions of dollars and by his fraudulent claims that personal charges were legitimate business expenses."

F. MATERIALITY

NEDER v. UNITED STATES
527 U.S. 1, 119 S.Ct. 1827, 144 L.Ed.2d 35 (1999)

CHIEF JUSTICE REHNQUIST delivered the opinion of the Court.

* * * In the mid-1980's, petitioner Ellis E. Neder, Jr., an attorney and real estate developer in Jacksonville, Florida, engaged in a number of real estate transactions financed by fraudulently obtained bank loans. Between 1984 and 1986, Neder purchased 12 parcels of land using shell corporations set up by his attorneys and then immediately resold the land at much higher prices to limited partnerships that he controlled. Using inflated appraisals, Neder secured bank loans that typically amounted to 70 to 75% of the inflated resale price of the land. In so doing, he concealed from lenders that he controlled the shell corporations, that he had purchased the land at prices substantially lower than the inflated resale prices, and that the limited partnerships had not made substantial down payments as represented. In several cases, Neder agreed to sign affidavits falsely stating that he had no relationship to the shell corporations and that he was not sharing in the profits from the inflated land sales. By keeping for himself the amount by which the loan proceeds exceeded the original purchase price of the land, Neder was able to obtain more than $7 million. He failed to report nearly all of this money on his personal income- tax returns. He eventually defaulted on the loans.

Neder also engaged in a number of schemes involving land development fraud. In 1985, he obtained a $4,150,000 construction loan to build condominiums on a project known as Cedar Creek. To obtain the loan, he falsely represented to the lender that he had satisfied a condition of the loan by making advance sales of 20 condominium units. In fact, he had been unable to meet the condition, so he secured additional buyers by making their down payments himself. He then had the down payments transferred back to him from the escrow accounts into which they had been placed. Neder later defaulted on the loan without repaying any of the principal. He employed a similar scheme to obtain a second construction loan of $5,400,000, and unsuccessfully attempted to obtain an additional loan in the same manner.

Neder also obtained a consolidated $14 million land acquisition and development loan for a project known as Reddie Point. Pursuant to the loan, Neder could request funds for work actually performed on the project. Between September 1987 and March 1988, he submitted numerous requests based on false invoices, the lender approved the requests, and he obtained almost $3 million unrelated to any work actually performed.

Neder was indicted on, among other things, 9 counts of mail fraud, in violation of 18 U.S.C. § 1341; 9 counts of wire fraud, in violation of § 1343;

12 counts of bank fraud, in violation of § 1344; and 2 counts of filing a false income tax return, in violation of 26 U.S.C. § 7206(1). The fraud counts charged Neder with devising and executing various schemes to defraud lenders in connection with the land acquisition and development loans, totaling over $40 million. The tax counts charged Neder with filing false statements of income on his tax returns. According to the Government, Neder failed to report more than $1 million in income for 1985 and more than $4 million in income for 1986, both amounts reflecting profits Neder obtained from the fraudulent real estate loans.

In accordance with then-extant Circuit precedent and over Neder's objection, the District Court instructed the jury that, to convict on the tax offenses, it "need not consider" the materiality of any false statements "even though that language is used in the indictment." The question of materiality, the court instructed, "is not a question for the jury to decide." The court gave a similar instruction on bank fraud, and subsequently found, outside the presence of the jury, that the evidence established the materiality of all the false statements at issue. In instructing the jury on mail fraud and wire fraud, the District Court did not include materiality as an element of either offense. Neder again objected to the instruction. The jury convicted Neder of the fraud and tax offenses, and he was sentenced to 147 months' imprisonment, 5 years' supervised release, and $25 million in restitution.

The Court of Appeals for the Eleventh Circuit affirmed the conviction. It held that the District Court erred under our intervening decision in United States v. Gaudin, 515 U.S. 506, 115 S.Ct. 2310, 132 L.Ed.2d 444 (1995), in failing to submit the materiality element of the tax offense to the jury. It concluded, however, that the error was subject to harmless-error analysis and, further, that the error was harmless because "materiality was not in dispute," and thus the error " 'did not contribute to the verdict obtained,' " * * *. The Court of Appeals also held that materiality is not an element of the mail fraud, wire fraud, and bank fraud statutes, and thus the District Court did not err in failing to submit the question of materiality to the jury.

We granted certiorari, to resolve a conflict in the Courts of Appeals on two questions: (1) whether, and under what circumstances, the omission of an element from the judge's charge to the jury can be harmless error, and (2) whether materiality is an element of the federal mail fraud, wire fraud, and bank fraud statutes.

[The Court found the failure to submit materiality as an issue for the jury on the tax charges was harmless error.]

* * * We also granted certiorari in this case to decide whether materiality is an element of a "scheme or artifice to defraud" under the federal mail fraud (18 U.S.C. § 1341), wire fraud (§ 1343), and bank fraud (§ 1344) statutes. The Court of Appeals concluded that the failure to submit

materiality to the jury was not error because the fraud statutes do not require that a "scheme to defraud" employ material falsehoods. We disagree.

Under the framework set forth in United States v. Wells, 519 U.S. 482, 117 S.Ct. 921, 137 L.Ed.2d 107 (1997), we first look to the text of the statutes at issue to discern whether they require a showing of materiality. In this case, we need not dwell long on the text because, as the parties agree, none of the fraud statutes defines the phrase "scheme or artifice to defraud," or even mentions materiality. Although the mail fraud and wire fraud statutes contain different jurisdictional elements (§ 1341 requires use of the mails while § 1343 requires use of interstate wire facilities), they both prohibit, in pertinent part, "any scheme or artifice to defraud" or to obtain money or property "by means of false or fraudulent pretenses, representations, or promises." The bank fraud statute, which was modeled on the mail and wire fraud statutes, similarly prohibits any "scheme or artifice to defraud a financial institution" or to obtain any property of a financial institution "by false or fraudulent pretenses, representations, or promises." Thus, based solely on a "natural reading of the full text," materiality would not be an element of the fraud statutes.

That does not end our inquiry, however, because in interpreting statutory language there is a necessary second step. It is a well-established rule of construction that " '[w]here Congress uses terms that have accumulated settled meaning under ... the common law, a court must infer, unless the statute otherwise dictates, that Congress means to incorporate the established meaning of these terms.' " * * * Neder contends that "defraud" is just such a term, and that Congress implicitly incorporated its common-law meaning, including its requirement of materiality, into the statutes at issue.

The Government does not dispute that both at the time of the mail fraud statute's original enactment in 1872, and later when Congress enacted the wire fraud and bank fraud statutes, actionable "fraud" had a well-settled meaning at common law. Nor does it dispute that the well-settled meaning of "fraud" required a misrepresentation or concealment of material fact. Indeed, as the sources we are aware of demonstrate, the common law could not have conceived of "fraud" without proof of materiality. * * * Thus, under the rule that Congress intends to incorporate the well-settled meaning of the common-law terms it uses, we cannot infer from the absence of an express reference to materiality that Congress intended to drop that element from the fraud statutes. On the contrary, we must presume that Congress intended to incorporate materiality " 'unless the statute otherwise dictates.' "

The Government attempts to rebut this presumption by arguing that the term "defraud" would bear its common-law meaning only if the fraud statutes "indicated that Congress had codified the crime of false pretenses or one of the common-law torts sounding in fraud." Instead, the Government argues, Congress chose to unmoor the mail fraud statute from its common-law analogs by punishing, not the completed fraud, but rather any person "having devised or intending to devise a scheme or artifice to defraud." Read in this light, the Government contends, there is no basis to infer that Congress intended to limit criminal liability to conduct that would constitute "fraud" at common law, and in particular, to material misrepresentations or omissions. Rather, criminal liability would exist so long as the defendant intended to deceive the victim, even if the particular means chosen turn out to be immaterial, i.e., incapable of influencing the intended victim.

The Government relies heavily on Durland v. United States, 161 U.S. 306, 16 S.Ct. 508, 40 L.Ed. 709 (1896), our first decision construing the mail fraud statute, to support its argument that the fraud statutes sweep more broadly than common-law fraud. But Durland was different from this case. * * * Although Durland held that the mail fraud statute reaches conduct that would not have constituted "false pretenses" at common law, it did not hold, as the Government argues, that the statute encompasses more than common-law fraud.

In one sense, the Government is correct that the fraud statutes did not incorporate all the elements of common-law fraud. The common-law requirements of "justifiable reliance" and "damages," for example, plainly have no place in the federal fraud statutes. * * * By prohibiting the "scheme to defraud," rather than the completed fraud, the elements of reliance and damage would clearly be inconsistent with the statutes Congress enacted. But while the language of the fraud statutes is incompatible with these requirements, the Government has failed to show that this language is inconsistent with a materiality requirement.

Accordingly, we hold that materiality of falsehood is an element of the federal mail fraud, wire fraud, and bank fraud statutes. Consistent with our normal practice where the court below has not yet passed on the harmlessness of any error, we remand this case to the Court of Appeals for it to consider in the first instance whether the jury- instruction error was harmless. * * *

The judgment of the Court of Appeals respecting the tax fraud counts is affirmed. The judgment of the Court of Appeals on the remaining counts is reversed, and the case is remanded for further proceedings consistent with this opinion. * * *

JUSTICE STEVENS, concurring in part and concurring in the judgment.

[Disagreeing "with the Court's analysis of the harmless-error issue" in another part of its opinion.]

* * * The Court's conclusion that materiality is an element of the offenses defined in 18 U.S.C. §§ 1341, 1343, and 1344 is obviously correct.

In my dissent in United States v. Wells, 519 U.S. 482, 510, 117 S.Ct. 921, 137 L.Ed.2d 107 (1997), I pointed out that the vast majority of judges who had confronted the question had placed the same construction on the federal statute criminalizing false statements to federally insured banks, 18 U.S.C. § 1014. I repeat this point to remind the Congress that an amendment to § 1014 would both harmonize these sections and avoid the potential injustice created by the Court's decision in Wells.

JUSTICE SCALIA, with whom JUSTICE SOUTER and JUSTICE GINSBURG join, concurring in part and dissenting in part.

* * * I dissent from the judgment of the Court, because I believe that depriving a criminal defendant of the right to have the jury determine his guilt of the crime charged--which necessarily means his commission of every element of the crime charged--can never be harmless. * * *

NOTE

On remand the Eleventh Circuit Court of Appeals found that "the failure to instruct on materiality was harmless error." United States v. Neder, 197 F.3d 1122 (1999).

G. MAILING

The government must prove a mailing by the defendant or that the mailing was caused to be mailed by the defendant. Circumstantial evidence of office custom and procedure have been used to prove a mailing. See United States v. Flaxman, 495 F.2d 344, 349 (7th Cir. 1974). " [R]eliance upon inferences drawn from evidence of standard business practice without specific reference to the mailing in question is insufficient." United States v. Burks, 867 F.2d 795, 797 (3rd Cir. 1989).

Section 1341 was amended as part of the Violent Crime Control and Law Enforcement Act of 1994, inserting the language, "or deposits or causes to be deposited any matter or thing whatever to be sent or delivered by any private or commercial interstate carrier." Violent Crime Control and Law Enforcement Act of 1994 § 250006. Mailings using Federal Express or UPS may now be subject to prosecution under the mail fraud statute. Who is a private interstate carrier? Is this new provision using Congress' postal powers, the Commerce Clause, or both? See Ellen S. Podgor, *Mail Fraud: Limiting the Limitless*, 18 Champion 4 (Dec. 1994); see also Peter J. Henning, *Maybe It Should Just Be Called Federal Fraud: The Changing Nature of the Mail Fraud Statute*, 36 BOSTON COL. L. REV. 435 (1995).

H. IN FURTHERANCE

SCHMUCK v. UNITED STATES
489 U.S. 705, 109 S.Ct. 1443, 103 L.Ed.2d 734 (1989)

Justice BLACKMUN delivered the opinion of the Court.

I

In August 1983, petitioner Wayne T. Schmuck, a used-car distributor, was indicted in the United States District Court for the Western District of Wisconsin on 12 counts of mail fraud, in violation of 18 U.S.C. §§ 1341 and 1342.

The alleged fraud was a common and straightforward one. Schmuck purchased used cars, rolled back their odometers, and then sold the automobiles to Wisconsin retail dealers for prices artificially inflated because of the low- mileage readings. These unwitting car dealers, relying on the altered odometer figures, then resold the cars to customers, who in turn paid prices reflecting Schmuck's fraud. To complete the resale of each automobile, the dealer who purchased it from Schmuck would submit a title-application form to the Wisconsin Department of Transportation on behalf of his retail customer. The receipt of a Wisconsin title was a prerequisite for completing the resale; without it, the dealer could not transfer title to the customer and the customer could not obtain Wisconsin tags. The submission of the title- application form supplied the mailing element of each of the alleged mail frauds.

Before trial, Schmuck moved to dismiss the indictment on the ground that the mailings at issue—the submissions of the title-application forms by the automobile dealers—were not in furtherance of the fraudulent scheme and, thus, did not satisfy the mailing element of the crime of mail fraud. Schmuck also moved under Federal Rule of Criminal Procedure 31(c)[1] for a jury instruction on the then misdemeanor offense of tampering with an odometer, 15 U.S.C. §§ 1984 and 1990c(a) (1982 ed.).[2] The District Court denied both motions. After trial, the jury returned guilty verdicts on all 12 counts.

A divided panel of the United States Court of Appeals for the Seventh Circuit reversed and remanded the case for a new trial. Although the panel rejected Schmuck's claim that he was entitled to a judgment of acquittal because the mailings were not made in furtherance of his scheme, it ruled

---

[1] Rule 31(c) provides in relevant part: "The defendant may be found guilty of an offense necessarily included in the offense charged."

[2] In 1986, Congress made odometer tampering a felony. Pub.L. 99-579, § 3(b), 100 Stat. 3311, 15 U.S.C. § 1990c(a) (1982 ed., Supp. V).

that under Rule 31(c) the District Court should have instructed the jury on the lesser offense of odometer tampering. The panel applied the so- called "inherent relationship" test for determining what constitutes a lesser included offense for the purpose of Rule 31(c). * * *

We granted certiorari to define further the scope of the mail fraud statute and to resolve a conflict among the Circuits over which test to apply in determining what constitutes a lesser included offense for the purposes of Rule 31(c).

II

"The federal mail fraud statute does not purport to reach all frauds, but only those limited instances in which the use of the mails is a part of the execution of the fraud, leaving all other cases to be dealt with by appropriate state law." Kann v. United States, 323 U.S. 88, 95 (1944). To be part of the execution of the fraud, however, the use of the mails need not be an essential element of the scheme. Pereira v. United States, 347 U.S. 1, 8 (1954). It is sufficient for the mailing to be "incident to an essential part of the scheme," ibid., or "a step in [the] plot," Badders v. United States, 240 U.S. 391, 394 (1916).

Schmuck, relying principally on this Court's decisions in *Kann,* supra, Parr v. United States, 363 U.S. 370 (1960), and United States v. Maze, 414 U.S. 395 (1974), argues that mail fraud can be predicated only on a mailing that affirmatively assists the perpetrator in carrying out his fraudulent scheme. The mailing element of the offense, he contends, cannot be satisfied by a mailing, such as those at issue here, that is routine and innocent in and of itself, and that, far from furthering the execution of the fraud, occurs after the fraud has come to fruition, is merely tangentially related to the fraud, and is counterproductive in that it creates a "paper trail" from which the fraud may be discovered. We disagree both with this characterization of the mailings in the present case and with this description of the applicable law.

We begin by considering the scope of Schmuck's fraudulent scheme. Schmuck was charged with devising and executing a scheme to defraud Wisconsin retail automobile customers who based their decisions to purchase certain automobiles at least in part on the low-mileage readings provided by the tampered odometers. This was a fairly large-scale operation. Evidence at trial indicated that Schmuck had employed a man known only as "Fred" to turn back the odometers on about 150 different cars. Schmuck then marketed these cars to a number of dealers, several of whom he dealt with on a consistent basis over a period of about 15 years. Indeed, of the 12 automobiles that are the subject of the counts of the indictment, 5 were sold to "P and A Sales," and 4 to "Southside Auto." Thus, Schmuck's was not a "one-shot" operation in which he sold a single car to an isolated dealer. His was an ongoing fraudulent venture. A rational jury could have concluded that the success of Schmuck's venture depended upon his continued harmonious relations with, and good reputation among, retail dealers, which in turn required the smooth flow of cars from the dealers to their Wisconsin customers.

Under these circumstances, we believe that a rational jury could have found that the title-registration mailings were part of the execution of the fraudulent scheme, a scheme which did not reach fruition until the retail dealers resold the cars and effected transfers of title. Schmuck's scheme would have come to an abrupt halt if the dealers either had lost faith in Schmuck or had not been able to resell the cars obtained from him. These resales and Schmuck's relationships with the retail dealers naturally depended on the successful passage of title among the various parties. Thus, although the registration-form mailings may not have contributed directly to the duping of either the retail dealers or the customers, they were necessary to the passage of title, which in turn was essential to the perpetuation of Schmuck's scheme. As noted earlier, a mailing that is "incident to an essential part of the scheme," satisfies the mailing element of the mail fraud offense. The mailings here fit this description. * * *

Once the full flavor of Schmuck's scheme is appreciated, the critical distinctions between this case and the three cases in which this Court has delimited the reach of the mail fraud statute—*Kann, Parr,* and *Maze*—are readily apparent. The defendants in *Kann* were corporate officers and directors accused of setting up a dummy corporation through which to divert profits into their own pockets. As part of this fraudulent scheme, the defendants caused the corporation to issue two checks payable to them. The defendants cashed these checks at local banks, which then mailed the checks to the drawee banks for collection. This Court held that the mailing of the cashed checks to the drawee banks could not supply the mailing element of the mail fraud charges. The defendants' fraudulent scheme had reached fruition. "It was immaterial to them, or to any consummation of the scheme, how the bank which paid or credited the check would collect from the drawee bank."

In *Parr,* several defendants were charged, inter alia, with having fraudulently obtained gasoline and a variety of other products and services through the unauthorized use of a credit card issued to the school district which employed them. The mailing element of the mail fraud charges in Parr was purportedly satisfied when the oil company which issued the credit card mailed invoices to the school district for payment, and when the district mailed payment in the form of a check. Relying on *Kann,* this Court held that these mailings were not in execution of the scheme as required by the statute because it was immaterial to the defendants how the oil company went about collecting its payment.[7]

Later, in *Maze,* the defendant allegedly stole his roommate's credit card, headed south on a winter jaunt, and obtained food and lodging at motels along the route by placing the charges on the stolen card. The mailing element of the mail fraud charge was supplied by the fact that the defendant knew that each motel proprietor would mail an invoice to the bank that had issued the credit card, which in turn would mail a bill to the card owner for payment. The Court found that these mailings could not support mail fraud charges because the defendant's scheme had reached fruition when he checked out of each motel. The success of his scheme in no way depended on the mailings; they merely determined which of his victims would ultimately bear the loss. 414 U.S., at 402.

The title-registration mailings at issue here served a function different from the mailings in *Kann, Parr,* and *Maze.* The intrabank mailings in *Kann* and the credit card invoice mailings in *Parr* and *Maze* involved little more than post-fraud accounting among the potential victims of the various schemes, and the long-term success of the fraud did not turn on which of the potential victims bore the ultimate loss. Here, in contrast, a jury rationally could have found that Schmuck by no means was indifferent to the fact of who bore the loss. The mailing of the title-registration forms was an essential step in the successful passage of title to the retail purchasers. Moreover, a failure of this passage of title would have jeopardized Schmuck's relationship of trust and goodwill with the retail dealers upon whose unwitting cooperation his scheme depended. Schmuck's reliance on our prior cases limiting the reach of the mail fraud statute is simply misplaced.

To the extent that Schmuck would draw from these previous cases a general rule that routine mailings that are innocent in themselves cannot supply the mailing element of the mail fraud offense, he misapprehends this Court's precedents. In *Parr* the Court specifically acknowledged that "innocent" mailings—ones that contain no false information—may supply the mailing element. In other cases, the Court has found the elements of mail fraud to be satisfied where the mailings have been routine. See, e.g., Carpenter v. United States, [p.158].

---

[7] *Parr* also involved a second fraudulent scheme through which the defendant school board members misappropriated school district tax revenues. The Government argued that the mailing element of the mail fraud charges was supplied by the mailing of tax statements, checks, and receipts. This Court held, however, that in the absence of any evidence that the tax levy was increased as part of the fraud, the mailing element of the offense could not be supplied by mailings "made or caused to be made under the imperative command of duty imposed by state law." 363 U.S., at 391. No such legal duty is at issue here. * * *

We also reject Schmuck's contention that mailings that someday may contribute to the uncovering of a fraudulent scheme cannot supply the mailing element of the mail fraud offense. The relevant question at all times is whether the mailing is part of the execution of the scheme as conceived by the perpetrator at the time, regardless of whether the mailing later, through hindsight, may prove to have been counterproductive and return to haunt the perpetrator of the fraud. The mail fraud statute includes no guarantee that the use of the mails for the purpose of executing a fraudulent scheme will be risk free. Those who use the mails to defraud proceed at their peril.

For these reasons, we agree with the Court of Appeals that the mailings in this case satisfy the mailing element of the mail fraud offenses.   * * *

V

We conclude that Schmuck's conviction was consistent with the statutory definition of mail fraud and that he was not entitled to a lesser included offense instruction on odometer tampering. The judgment of the Court of Appeals, accordingly, is affirmed. It is so ordered.

Justice SCALIA, with whom Justice BRENNAN, Justice MARSHALL, and Justice O'CONNOR join, dissenting.

* * * The purpose of the mail fraud statute is "to prevent the post office from being used to carry [fraudulent schemes] into effect." Durland v. United States, [p. 149]; Parr v. United States. The law does not establish a general federal remedy against fraudulent conduct, with use of the mails as the jurisdictional hook, but reaches only "those limited instances in which the use of the mails is a part of the execution of the fraud, leaving all other cases to be dealt with by appropriate state law." In other words, it is mail fraud, not mail and fraud, that incurs liability. This federal statute is not violated by a fraudulent scheme in which, at some point, a mailing happens to occur—nor even by one in which a mailing predictably and necessarily occurs. The mailing must be in furtherance of the fraud.   * * *

What Justice Frankfurter observed almost three decades ago remains true: "The adequate degree of relationship between a mailing which occurs during the life of a scheme and the scheme is . . . not a matter susceptible of geometric determination." Parr v. United States, (dissenting opinion). All the more reason to adhere as closely as possible to past cases. I think we have not done that today, and thus create problems for tomorrow.

NOTES AND QUESTIONS

1. *Limitations to "In Furtherance".* Prior to *Schmuck* the cases reflected four types of limitations to a mailing being "in furtherance" of a scheme to

defraud. See Ellen S. Podgor, *Mail Fraud: Opening Letters,* 43 S.C. L.Rev. 223, 242-254 (1992).

a. Mailings that conflicted with the scheme to defraud, that aided in detection, or that were diametrically opposed to the defendant acting with an evil mens rea, were not in furtherance of the scheme to defraud. See United States v. Maze, [p. 202].

b. Mailings that were part of an imperative duty to the state were not considered to be in furtherance of the scheme to defraud. See Parr v. United States, [p.202].

c. Mailing that were prior to the commencement of the scheme to defraud were not in furtherance of the scheme. See United States v. Beall, 126 F. Supp. 363 (N. Cal. 1954).

d. Mailings after fruition of the scheme to defraud were not considered to be in furtherance of the scheme. See Kann v. United States, [p. 202]; Parr v. United States, [p. 202]; United States v. Maze, [p. 202].

Do these legal limitations to "in furtherance" exist after *Schmuck?*

2. *Non-Misleading Compelled Mailings.* In **United States v. Lake**, 372 F.3d 1247 (10th Cir. 2007), the court held that "[m]ost circuits to address the issue have interpreted *Parr* to hold that "mailings of documents which are required by law to be mailed, and which are not themselves false and fraudulent, cannot be regarded as mailed for the purpose of executing a fraudulent scheme."

3. *Lulling.* Prior to *Schmuck* there were two Supreme Court cases that allowed mail fraud charges that were after the scheme to defraud. These cases involved mailings that were used to "lull" the victims into the defendant's scheme. See United States v. Sampson, 371 U.S. 75 (1962); United States v. Lane, 474 U.S. 438 (1986). Why did the Supreme Court ignore the cases of *Lane* and *Sampson* in deciding the *Schmuck* case?

I. WIRE FRAUD AND OTHER FRAUDS

UNITED STATES v. BRYANT
766 F.2d 370 (8th Cir. 1985)

ARNOLD, Circuit Judge.

Henry Paul Bryant and Melissa Dalton appeal their convictions on three counts of mail fraud and two counts of wire fraud involving a scheme to bribe Emeric Martin, then Director of the Cervantes Convention Center in

St. Louis, for favorable treatment of their convention-booking business, known as Showboard. * * *

II

Dalton and Bryant argue that their convictions under 18 U.S.C. § 1343 (1982) for wire fraud must be vacated because the government has failed to prove that they knew or could reasonably foresee that the telegrams were being sent interstate. Both of the telegrams at issue were sent from Kansas City, Missouri, to Bridgeton, Missouri, but were routed through Middletown, Virginia.[4]

In response, the United States contends that there is no requirement under § 1343 that the accused know or foresee that the telegram is being sent interstate. The legislative history of § 1343 sheds no light on this question, but we agree with the government that the words of the statute, the general purpose of interstate requirements, and the decisions of other courts support the conclusion that the accused need not know or foresee that the communication was interstate.

We start with the language of Section 1343. It reads as follows:

Whoever, having devised or intending to devise any scheme or artifice to defraud, or for obtaining money or property by means of false or fraudulent pretenses, representations, or promises, transmits or causes to be transmitted by means of wire, radio, or television communication in interstate or foreign commerce, any writings, signs, signals, pictures, or sounds for the purpose of executing such scheme or artifice, shall be fined not more than $1,000 or imprisoned not more than five years, or both.

Certainly the statute requires that defendant be a party to some kind of scheme to defraud, a requirement that includes a high degree of scienter and moral culpability. It also requires that the defendant intend that a communication by wire be sent in furtherance of the scheme, or at least that the use of wire communication be reasonably foreseeable. But the words themselves, read literally, require only that the wire communication be interstate, not that defendants know that it is to be interstate. The literal meaning of the statute should control, unless it is contrary to the manifest purpose of Congress or inconsistent with binding case law.

Section 1343 was intended to proscribe the use of certain interstate communication media to perpetrate or facilitate a fraudulent scheme. The

---

[4] Appellants do not dispute that these communications are "interstate" within the terms of § 1343. Their argument is that they did not know that Western Union would route the telegrams in question through another State.

requirement of an interstate nexus arises from constitutional limitations on congressional power over intrastate activities under the Commerce Clause. Its inclusion in criminal and civil statutes is most often solely for the purpose of conferring federal jurisdiction rather than of defining substantive elements of an offense. * * * Here, likewise, the requirement seems clearly to be only jurisdictional. The interstate nature of the communication does not make the fraud more culpable. Thus, whether or not a defendant knows or can foresee that a communication is interstate, the offense is still every bit as grave in the moral sense. * * *

The government, however, admits that there is an exception to the general rule that knowledge or foreseeability of the interstate character of the communication is not required under § 1343. The government must show that the accused knew or could have foreseen that a communication in furtherance of a fraudulent scheme was interstate, if the conduct giving rise to the scheme would not be a violation of state law and was not itself morally wrongful. See United States v. Feola, 420 U.S. 671, 685 (1975). In other words, if what happened was not a violation of state law or wrongful in nature, but is a violation of federal law, an innocent defendant could be ensnared in a federal prosecution if, unknown to him, the communication is in fact interstate. [The court rejected appellants' argument that their conduct was "lawful under state law and morally blameless."] * * * The convictions of the appellants are affirmed.

NOTES AND QUESTIONS

1. *Wire Fraud.* Congress added the wire fraud statute (18 U.S.C.A. § 1343) in 1952. Wire fraud operates parallel to the mail fraud statute with the differing element being the method used in the transmission. Wire fraud requires the transmission to be "by means of wire, radio, or television communication." According to *Bryrant* the accused may not be required to have knowledge of the jurisdiction element of this offense. There may, however, be a venue requirement imposed on the government, limiting venue only where there is a direct of causal connection to the misuse of wires." United States v. Pace, 301 F.3d 1034 (9th Cir. 2002).

2. *Other "Scheme to Defraud" Statutes .* In addition to mail and wire fraud, Congress has added other fraud statutes that require a similar "scheme to defraud" as an element of the offense. See, e.g., bankruptcy fraud (18 U.S.C. § 157); health care fraud (18 U.S.C. § 1347); bank fraud (18 U.S.C. § 1344); travel fraud (18 U.S.C. § 2314). Many of the cases emanating from these statutes use the precedent found in mail and wire fraud cases. See Ellen S. Podgor, *Criminal Fraud,* 48 Am. U. L.Rev. 729 (1999). As with many white collar crime cases, the intent of the accused is often an issue. For example,   **United States v. Gellene,** 182 F.3d 578 (7th Cir. 1999), affirmed convictions, stating:

John G. Gellene, a partner at the law firm of Milbank Tweed Hadley & McCloy ("Milbank") in New York, represented the Bucyrus-Erie Company ("Bucyrus") in its Chapter 11 bankruptcy. Mr. Gellene filed in the bankruptcy court a sworn declaration that was to include all of his firm's connections to the debtor, creditors, and any other parties in interest. The declaration failed to list the senior secured creditor and related parties. Mr. Gellene was charged with two counts of knowingly and fraudulently making a false material declaration in the Bucyrus bankruptcy case, in violation of 18 U.S.C. § 152, and one count of using a document while under oath, knowing that it contained a false material declaration, in violation of 18 U.S.C. § 1623. Although Mr. Gellene admitted that he had used bad judgment in concluding that the representations did not need to be disclosed, he asserted that he had no fraudulent intent. After a six-day trial, on March 3, 1998, the jury returned guilty verdicts against Mr. Gellene on all three counts. Mr. Gellene was sentenced to 15 months of imprisonment on each count, to run concurrently, and was fined $15,000. * * *

Mr. Gellene submits that the court's definition of "fraudulent" as "with intent to deceive" is erroneous. In his view, the statute requires that the statement be made not simply with the intent to deceive but with the intent to defraud. He further claims that, because the government misapprehended the statutory requirement, it failed to present evidence that he made his declarations with an intent to defraud because it believed it needed to prove merely an intent to deceive. He submits that the distinction between the two terms is significant: To deceive is to cause to believe the false or to mislead; to defraud is to deprive of some right, interest or property by deceit. Therefore, under § 152 of the Bankruptcy Code, he contends, the defendant must have a specific intent to alter or to impact the distribution of a debtor's assets and not merely to impact the integrity of the legal system, as the government argued. * * *

We cannot accept Mr. Gellene's narrowly circumscribed definition of "intent to defraud" or "fraudulently." Mr. Gellene would limit exclusively the statute's scope to false statements that deprive the debtor of his property or the bankruptcy estate of its assets. In our view, such a parsimonious interpretation was not intended by Congress. * * *

We agree that § 152 requires that materiality be an element of the crime of bankruptcy fraud and, indeed, we have incorporated such a requirement in our analysis of § 152 fraud. * * * The statute is therefore construed to require that the false oath be in relation to some material matter. * * *

Materiality in this context does not require harm to or adverse reliance by a creditor, nor does it require a realization of a gain by the defendant. Rather, it requires that the false oath or account relate to some significant aspect of the bankruptcy case or proceeding in which it was given, or that it pertain to the discovery of assets or to the debtor's financial transactions. Just what is significant is difficult to say for the general case: failing to disclose ownership of a ream of paper in a multi-million dollar bankruptcy is probably not material, but in many cases a false social security number or a false prior address may be.

Statements given by individuals in order to secure a particular adjudication carry their own reliable index of materiality; the person giving the statement believed it sufficiently important--and hence, material--to the goal of obtaining the desired action.

Collier on Bankruptcy, ¶ 7.02[2][a][iv] at 7-46 to 7-47. We conclude that the materiality element does not require proof of the potential impact on the disposition of assets. * * *

3. *Specific Fraud Statutes.* In some instances, Congress has provided a fraud statute that is not premised upon a "scheme to defraud," but is premised on specific types of fraudulent conduct. For example, the marriage fraud statute does not require proof of a "scheme or artifice to defraud." See 8 U.S.C. § 1325(c). Likewise, the computer fraud statute limits the possible schemes to defraud by listing specific activities that can be subject to prosecution. See 18 U.S.C. § 1030. But this specificity may not be needed when the government pursues conduct that falls outside the boundaries of both the general (wire fraud) and specific (computer fraud) statute. Consider the application of the computer fraud statute and wire fraud statute in the following case:

UNITED STATES v. CZUBINSKI
106 F.3d 1069 (1st Cir. 1997)

TORRUELLA, Chief Judge.

Defendant-appellant Richard Czubinski ("Czubinski") appeals his jury conviction on nine counts of wire fraud, 18 U.S.C. §§ 1343, 1346, and four counts of computer fraud, 18 U.S.C. § 1030(a)(4). * * *

For all periods relevant to the acts giving rise to his conviction, the defendant Czubinski was employed as a Contact Representative in the Boston office of the Taxpayer Services Division of the Internal Revenue Service ("IRS"). To perform his official duties, which mainly involved answering questions from taxpayers regarding their returns, Czubinski routinely accessed information from one of the IRS's computer systems known as the Integrated Data Retrieval System ("IDRS"). Using a valid password given to Contact Representatives, certain search codes, and taxpayer social security numbers, Czubinski was able to retrieve, to his terminal screen in Boston, income tax return information regarding virtually any taxpayer--information that is permanently stored in the IDRS "master file" located in Martinsburg, West Virginia. In the period of Czubinski's employ, IRS rules plainly stated that employees with passwords and access codes were not permitted to access files on IDRS outside of the course of their official duties.

In 1992, Czubinski carried out numerous unauthorized searches of IDRS files. He knowingly disregarded IRS rules by looking at confidential information obtained by performing computer searches that were outside of the scope of his duties as a Contact Representative, including, but not limited to, the searches listed in the indictment. Audit trails performed by internal IRS auditors establish that Czubinski frequently made unauthorized accesses on IDRS in 1992. For example, Czubinski accessed information regarding: the tax returns of two individuals involved in the David Duke presidential campaign; the joint tax return of an assistant district attorney (who had been prosecuting Czubinski's father on an unrelated felony offense) and his wife; the tax return of Boston City Counselor Jim Kelly's Campaign Committee (Kelly had defeated Czubinski in the previous election for the Counselor seat for District 2); the tax return of one of his brothers' instructors; the joint tax return of a Boston Housing Authority police officer, who was involved in a community organization with one of Czubinski's brothers, and the officer's wife; and the tax return of a woman Czubinski had dated a few times. Czubinski also accessed the files of various other social acquaintances by performing unauthorized searches.

Nothing in the record indicates that Czubinski did anything more than knowingly disregard IRS rules by observing the confidential information he accessed. No evidence suggests, nor does the government contend, that Czubinski disclosed the confidential information he accessed to any third parties. The government's only evidence demonstrating any intent to use the confidential information for nefarious ends was the trial testimony of William A. Murray, an acquaintance of Czubinski who briefly participated in Czubinski's local Invisible Knights of the Ku Klux Klan ("KKK") chapter and worked with him on the David Duke campaign. Murray testified that Czubinski had once stated at a social gathering in "early 1992" that "he intended to use some of that information to build dossiers on people" involved in "the white supremacist movement." There is, however, no evidence that Czubinski created dossiers, took steps toward making dossiers (such as by printing out or recording the information he browsed), or shared any of the information he accessed in the years following the single comment to Murray. No other witness testified to having any knowledge of Czubinski's alleged intent to create "dossiers" on KKK members.

The record shows that Czubinski did not perform any unauthorized searches after 1992. He continued to be employed as a Contact Representative until June 1995, when a grand jury returned an indictment against him on ten counts of federal wire fraud under 18 U.S.C. §§ 1343, 1346, and four counts of federal interest computer fraud under 18 U.S.C. § 1030(a)(4).

The portion of the indictment alleging wire fraud states that Czubinski defrauded the IRS of confidential property and defrauded the IRS and the public of his honest services by using his valid password to acquire confidential taxpayer information as part of a scheme to: 1) build "dossiers" on associates in the KKK; 2) seek information regarding an assistant district attorney who was then prosecuting Czubinski's father on an unrelated criminal charge; and 3) perform opposition research by inspecting the records of a political opponent in the race for a Boston City Councilor seat. The wire fraud indictment, therefore, articulated particular personal ends to which the unauthorized access to confidential information through interstate wires was allegedly a means. * * *

* * * To support a conviction for wire fraud, the government must prove two elements beyond a reasonable doubt: (1) the defendant's knowing and willing participation in a scheme or artifice to defraud with the specific intent to defraud, and (2) the use of interstate wire communications in furtherance of the scheme. * * *   The government pursued two theories of wire fraud in this prosecution: first, that Czubinski defrauded the IRS of its property, under section 1343, by acquiring confidential information for certain intended personal uses; second, that he defrauded the IRS and the public of their intangible right to his honest services, under sections 1343 and 1346.   We consider the evidence with regard to each theory, in turn.

* * * The government correctly notes that confidential information may constitute intangible "property" and that its unauthorized dissemination or other use may deprive the owner of its property rights. See Carpenter v. United States [p. 158] Where such deprivation is effected through dishonest or deceitful means, a "scheme to defraud," within the meaning of the wire fraud statute, is shown.   Thus, a necessary step toward satisfying the "scheme to defraud" element in this context is showing that the defendant intended to "deprive" another of their protected right.

The government, however, provides no case in support of its contention here that merely accessing confidential information, without doing, or clearly intending to do, more, is tantamount to a deprivation of IRS property under the wire fraud statute. In *Carpenter*, for example, the confidential information regarding the contents of a newspaper column was converted to the defendants's use to their substantial benefit. * * * We do not think that Czubinski's unauthorized browsing, even if done with the intent to deceive the IRS into thinking he was performing only authorized searches, constitutes a "deprivation" within the meaning of the federal fraud statutes.

Binding precedents, and good sense, support the conclusion that to "deprive" a person of their intangible property interest in confidential information under section 1343, either some articulable harm must befall the holder of the information as a result of the defendant's activities, or some gainful use must be intended by the person accessing the information, whether or not this use is profitable in the economic sense. Here, neither the taking of the IRS' right to "exclusive use" of the confidential information, nor Czubinski's gain from access to the information, can be shown absent evidence of his "use" of the information. Accordingly, without evidence that Czubinski used or intended to use the taxpayer information (beyond mere browsing), an intent to deprive cannot be proven, and, a fortiori, a scheme to defraud is not shown. * * *

The fatal flaw in the government's case is that it has not shown beyond a reasonable doubt that Czubinski intended to carry out a scheme to deprive the IRS of its property interest in confidential information. Had there been sufficient proof that Czubinski intended either to create dossiers for the sake of advancing personal causes or to disseminate confidential information to third parties, then his actions in searching files could arguably be said to be a step in furtherance of a scheme to deprive the IRS of its property interest in confidential information. The government's case regarding Czubinski's intent to make any use of the information he browsed rests on the testimony of one witness at trial who stated that Czubinski once remarked at a social gathering that he intended to build dossiers on potential KKK informants. We must assume, on this appeal, that Czubinski did indeed make such a comment. Nevertheless, the fact that during the months following this remark-- that is, during the period in which Czubinski made his unauthorized searches-- he did not create dossiers (there was no evidence that he created dossiers either during or after the period of his unauthorized searches); given the fact that he did not even take steps toward creating dossiers, such as recording or printing out the information; given the fact that no other person testifying as to Czubinski's involvement in white supremacist organizations had any knowledge of Czubinski's alleged intent to create dossiers or use confidential information; and given the fact that not a single piece of evidence suggests that Czubinski ever shared taxpayer information with others, no rational jury could have found beyond a reasonable doubt that, when Czubinski was browsing taxpayer files, he was doing so in furtherance of a scheme to use the information he browsed for private purposes, be they nefarious or otherwise. In addition, there was no evidence that Czubinski disclosed, or used to his advantage, any information regarding political opponents or regarding the person prosecuting his father.

Mere browsing of the records of people about whom one might have a particular interest, although reprehensible, is not enough to sustain a wire fraud conviction on a "deprivation of intangible property" theory. Curiosity on the part of an IRS officer may lead to dismissal, but curiosity alone will not sustain a finding of participation in a felonious criminal scheme to deprive the IRS of its property. * * *

[The court then discussed 18 U.S.C. § 1346]

* * * First, this case falls outside of the core of honest services fraud precedents. Czubinski was not bribed or otherwise influenced in any public decisionmaking capacity. Nor did he embezzle funds. He did not receive, nor can it be found that he intended to receive, any tangible benefit. His official duty was to respond to informational requests from taxpayers regarding their returns, a relatively straightforward task that simply does not raise the specter of secretive, self-interested action, as does a discretionary, decision-making role. * * *

Second, we believe that the cautionary language of *Sawyer* is particularly appropriate here, given the evidence amassed by the defendant at trial indicating that during his span of employment at IRS, he received no indication from his employer that this workplace violation--the performance of unauthorized searches--would be punishable by anything more than dismissal. "To allow every transgression of state governmental obligations to amount to mail fraud would effectively turn every such violation into a federal felony; this cannot be countenanced." Here, the threat is one of transforming governmental workplace violations into felonies. We find no evidence that Congress intended to create what amounts to a draconian personnel regulation. We hesitate to imply such an unusual result in the absence of the clearest legislative mandate.

These general considerations, although serious, are not conclusive: they raise doubts as to the propriety of this conviction that can be outweighed by sufficient evidence of a scheme to defraud. The third principle identified in Sawyer, instructing us as to the basic requirements of a scheme to defraud in this context, settles any remaining doubts. The conclusive consideration is that the government simply did not prove that Czubinski deprived, or intended to deprive, the public or his employer of their right to his honest services. Although he clearly committed wrongdoing in searching confidential information, there is no suggestion that he failed to carry out his official tasks adequately, or intended to do so.

The government alleges that, in addition to defrauding the public of his honest services, Czubinski has defrauded the IRS as well. The IRS is a public entity, rendering this contention sufficiently answered by our holding above that Czubinski did not defraud the public of his honest services. Even if the IRS were a private employer, however, the pre-*McNally* honest services convictions involving private fraud victims indicate that there must be a breach of a fiduciary duty to an employer that involves self-dealing of an order significantly more serious than the misconduct at issue here. * * * Once again, the government has failed to prove that Czubinski intended to use the IRS files he browsed for any private purposes, and hence his actions, however reprehensible, do not rise to the level of a scheme to defraud his employer of his honest services. * * *

* * * For the same reasons we deemed the trial evidence could not support a finding that Czubinski deprived the IRS of its property, see discussion of wire fraud under section 1343 supra, we find that Czubinski

has not obtained valuable information in furtherance of a fraudulent scheme for the purposes of section 1030(a)(4).   * * *

We add a cautionary note. The broad language of the mail and wire fraud statutes are both their blessing and their curse. They can address new forms of serious crime that fail to fall within more specific legislation. * * * On the other hand, they might be used to prosecute kinds of behavior that, albeit offensive to the morals or aesthetics of federal prosecutors, cannot reasonably be expected by the instigators to form the basis of a federal felony. The case at bar falls within the latter category. Also discomforting is the prosecution's insistence, before trial, on the admission of inflammatory evidence regarding the defendant's membership in white supremacist groups purportedly as a means to prove a scheme to defraud, when, on appeal, it argues that unauthorized access in itself is a sufficient ground for conviction on all counts. Finally, we caution that the wire fraud statute must not serve as a vehicle for prosecuting only those citizens whose views run against the tide, no matter how incorrect or uncivilized such views are.

For the reasons stated in this opinion, we hold the district court's denial of defendant's motion for judgment of acquittal on counts 1, 2, and 4 through 14, to be in error. The defendant's conviction is thus reversed on all counts.

J. MONEY LAUNDERING

UNITED STATES v. YUSUF
536 F.3d 178 (3rd Cir. 2008)

ROTH, Circuit Judge:

The government has appealed the District Court's pretrial order, dismissing from the indictment various counts and allegations based on international money laundering. The narrow issue on appeal is whether unpaid taxes, which were unlawfully disguised and retained by means of the filing of false tax returns through the U.S. mail, are "proceeds" of mail fraud for purposes of sufficiently stating a money laundering offense under the federal, international money laundering statute, 18 U.S.C. § 1956(a)(2). * * *

There are seven defendants in this case: (1) United Corporation, a family-owned business located in the Virgin Islands that operates a chain of three Plaza Extra Supermarket stores in St. Thomas and St. Croix; (2) Fathi Yusuf, the primary shareholder of United; * * * Because defendant United conducts business through its Virgin Islands supermarkets, it is required to comply with statutorily-mandated monthly reporting of gross receipts and payment of tax on those receipts. Section 43(a), Title 33, of the Virgin Islands Code provides, in pertinent part, that "[e]very individual and every firm, corporation, and other association doing business in the Virgin Islands shall *report their gross receipts* and *pay a tax of four percent (4%) on the gross receipts* of such business." * * *

In July 2001, the Federal Bureau of Investigation (FBI) received a suspicious activity report from the Bank of Nova Scotia in St. Thomas, U.S. Virgin Islands. The report stated that, over a four day period in April 2001, $1,920,000 (in $50 and $100 bills) was deposited into United's bank account. The FBI began an investigation which revealed that defendants allegedly conspired to avoid reporting $60,000,000 of the supermarkets' gross receipts on United's Virgin Islands gross receipts monthly tax returns and failed to pay the Virgin Islands government the 4% tax that United owed on those unreported gross receipts. The investigation further revealed that defendants allegedly engaged in various efforts to disguise and conceal the illegal scheme and its proceeds. Such efforts included allegedly depositing these monies into bank accounts, controlled by defendants, outside of the United States.

On September 9, 2004, a grand jury in the Virgin Islands returned a seventy-eight count, superseding indictment, charging various counts relating to mail fraud, tax evasion, and international money laundering. * * * Thus, the indictment relied on mail fraud as the predicate offense, or "specified unlawful activity," to support the money laundering charges against defendants. *See* 18 U.S.C. § 1956(a)(2)(B)(I). Defendants moved to dismiss the substantive money laundering charges on the basis that any unpaid taxes disguised and retained as a result of filing false tax returns through the U.S. mail do not equate to "proceeds" of mail fraud * * *

There is no dispute that the indictment sufficiently alleges mail fraud, pursuant to 18 U.S.C. § 1341. There is also no dispute that mail fraud is a predicate offense for a charge of international money laundering, pursuant to 18 U.S.C. §§ 1956(a)(2)(B)(i) (elements of international money laundering), 1956(c)(7)(A) (the term "specified unlawful activity" includes any racketeering activity under RICO) and 1961(1)(B) (mail fraud is a racketeering activity) . The narrow issue in this appeal is whether unpaid taxes unlawfully disguised and retained by means of the filing of false tax returns through the U.S. mail are "proceeds" of mail fraud for purposes of sufficiently stating an offense for money laundering. * * *

Although the federal money laundering statute does not define what constitutes "proceeds" of a specified unlawful activity, see United States v. Santos, --- U.S. ----, 128 S.Ct. 2020, 2024, 170 L.Ed.2d 912 (2008), it specifically identifies which criminal offenses constitute "specified unlawful activities." 18 U.S.C. § 1956(c)(7). The term "specified unlawful activity" covers a broad array of offenses. For example, the fraudulent *concealment* of a bankruptcy estate's assets is categorized as a "specified unlawful activity." * * * Moreover, simply because funds are *originally* procured through *lawful* activity does not mean that one cannot thereafter convert those same funds into the "proceeds" of an unlawful activity. * * * See United States v. Ladum, 141 F.3d 1328, 1340 (9th Cir.1998) (sustaining money laundering conviction where the defendant concealed rental income derived from lawfully operated retail stores); United States v. Levine, 970 F.2d 681, 686 (10th Cir.1992) (sustaining money laundering conviction where the defendant concealed corporate tax refund checks deposited in a hidden bank account). Accordingly, we reject the suggestion that to qualify as "proceeds" under the federal money laundering statute, funds must have been *directly* produced by or through a specified unlawful activity, and we agree that funds *retained* as a result of the unlawful activity can be treated as the "proceeds" of such crime.

Furthermore, the Supreme Court, in United States v. Santos, recently clarified that the term "proceeds," as that term is used in the federal money laundering statute, applies to criminal profits, not criminal receipts, derived from a specified unlawful activity. * * * The Supreme Court affirmed the trial court's decision to vacate the money laundering convictions because the transactions on which such convictions were based involved the gross receipts, as opposed to the profits, of the specified unlawful activity-the operation of an illegal lottery. The Supreme Court reasoned that the transactions upon which the money laundering charges were based could not be considered to have involved "proceeds" of the illegal lottery's operation because such transactions involved the mere payment of the illegal operation's *expenses* rather than the operation's *profits.** * * Moreover, we have previously determined that "proceeds are derived from an already completed offense, or a completed phase of an ongoing offense, before they can be laundered." United States v. Conley, 37 F.3d 970, 980 (3d Cir.1994).

Having thus elucidated the definition of "proceeds," we will next consider how the term "proceeds" relates to the predicate offense of mail fraud. * * * The particular scheme in which the defendants participated was termed "the Association." The Association organized a group of companies, all of which it controlled, into a "daisy chain," for the purpose of embezzling the excise taxes on the sale of certain kinds of fuel. Typically, the companies would sell oil down the chain in a series of paper transactions, through what was referred to as the "burn company." Eventually, the company at the bottom of the chain, the "street company," would sell the oil to a legitimate retailer, i.e., a particular gas station, for a price slightly below the tax-included market price. This retailer would pay money to the street company, which would send money back up the chain in a series of wire transfers.

This scheme was illegal because it was set up as a means to avoid excise taxes. The daisy chain was established so that the burn company was the one legally responsible for collecting the excise taxes on the fuel sales and transmitting them to the government. In the Association's scheme, the burn company would collect the taxes for a time, and then disappear without ever paying the taxes to the government. As a result, the Association could keep the money representing the excise taxes without the government being able to determine where it had gone. Id. at 803. On appeal, the defendant claimed that the money represented the "proceeds" of tax fraud, not the "proceeds" of a wire fraud, because the wiring itself had nothing to do with the Association's coming into possession of the money. We did not agree.

In affirming the trial court's judgments of conviction and sentence on the money laundering charge, we held that the money wired up through the "daisy chain" constituted "proceeds" of wire fraud based on the nature of the *entire ongoing fraudulent scheme.* * * *

Based upon the Supreme Court's decisions in *Santos, Schmuck,* and *Kann,* and our decision in *Morelli,* we hold that unpaid taxes, which are unlawfully disguised and retained by means of the filing of false tax returns through the U.S. mail, constitute "proceeds" of mail fraud for purposes of supporting a charge of federal money laundering. * * * Furthermore, the mailings of the fraudulent tax returns resulted in "proceeds" of mail fraud based on the nature of the *entire ongoing fraudulent scheme* because the unpaid taxes unlawfully retained by defendants represented the "proceeds" of a fraud that was also furthered by previous mailings. * * * Accordingly, it logically follows that the unpaid taxes, unlawfully disguised and retained through the mailing of the tax forms, were "proceeds" of defendants' overall scheme to defraud the government. This scheme was both dependent on and completed by the monthly mailing of the false Virgin Islands gross receipts tax returns. * * * Finally, in light of the Supreme Court's decision in *Santos,* we recognize that the "proceeds" from the mail fraud in this case also amount to "profits" of mail fraud. * * * By intentionally misrepresenting the total amount of Plaza Extra Supermarkets' gross receipts through the mailing of fraudulent tax returns, the defendants were able to secretly "pocket" the 4% gross receipts taxes on the unreported amounts which were the property of the Virgin Islands government. * * * Once these profits were included in the lump sums sent abroad by defendants, the offense of international money laundering was complete.

NOTES AND QUESTIONS

1. ***Money Laundering As White Collar Crime.*** Money laundering has become a significant tool used by prosecutors in white collar cases. One finds 18 U.S.C. § 1956 and § 1957 included as counts in many recent white collar indictments. See Note, Teresa E. Adams, *Tacking on Money Laundering Charges to White Collar Crimes: What Did Congress Intend, And What Are The Courts Doing?,* 17 GA. ST. L. REV. 531 (2000). The charges appear in a wide array of different contexts including mail fraud, as in *Yusuf.* See also United States v. Butler, 211 F.3d 826 (4th Cir. 2000) (bankruptcy fraud). "Money laundering, [however,] must be a crime distinct from the crime by which the money is obtained. The money laundering statute is not simply the addition of a further penalty to a criminal deed; it is a prohibition of processing the fruits of a crime or of a completed phase of an ongoing offense." United States v. Abuhouran, 162 F.3d 230 (3rd Cir. 1998); see also United States v. Seward, 272 F.3d 831 (7th Cir. 2001) ("Although it is true that the defendant must have control of the proceeds of

a fraudulent transaction before he can engage in money laundering with those proceeds, there is no requirement that the entire fraudulent scheme be complete before the defendant starts laundering the proceeds from early portions of the scheme.").

2. *Sentencing Ramifications.* The addition of money laundering can increase a defendant's sentence. Under the Federal Sentencing Guidelines, a conviction for money laundering increases the offense level used to calculate the sentence, usually resulting in a longer term of imprisonment than would be the case if mail fraud were the sole charge. See Chapter 18 for a discussion of the Federal Sentencing Guidelines. Thus, the suggestion that prosecutors add money laundering to an indictment that includes mail fraud increases the pressure on the defendant to enter a plea agreement to avoid a longer sentence.

3. *Patriot Act.* Title III of the "Uniting and Strengthening America by Providing Appropriate Tools Required to Intercept and Obstruct Terrorism (USA Patriot Act) Act of 2001" is called the "International Money Laundering Abatement and Anti-Terrorist Funding Act of 2001." This act provides for expanded obligations on the part of financial institutions. Will this new legislation offer an increased opportunity to the government to use money laundering charges in white collar prosecutions? See Gary Fields, *Antiterrorism Law Used to Seize Cash From Fraud Ring,* The Wall St. Jrl., Jan. 29, 2003, at B10.

CHAPTER SIX
THE RACKETEER INFLUENCED AND CORRUPT ORGANIZATION ACT (RICO)

A. INTRODUCTION

1. Statutes

The Racketeer Influenced and Corrupt Organization Act (RICO) was enacted by Congress as Title IX of the Organized Crime Control Act of 1970. In its early years, prosecutors seldom used RICO provisions. Today RICO is a charge used not only by federal prosecutors, but also by plaintiffs seeking civil relief. Although prosecutors initially focused on "organized crime," they later took the Act far beyond any such limitation. This was in part a product of an inability to define who and what is encompassed within the term "organized crime," and in part a product of the expanded prosecutorial authority made available through RICO. With RICO, federal prosecutors could: (1) reach certain activity that otherwise would not violate either federal or state criminal law; (2) reach activity (particularly violent activity) that otherwise would violate only state law; (3) gain enhanced penalties (including asset forfeiture) for activity that violated other provisions of the federal criminal law; and (4) gain broader joinder and more flexible venue than was available in prosecutions under other federal code provisions.

18 U.S.C.A. § 1962 enumerates the four types of prohibited conduct under this Act. RICO actions can, and often do, include more than one type of prohibited conduct. In essence, RICO requires that the defendant have invested in, maintained an interest in, participated in the affairs of an enterprise, or conspired to engage in conduct constituting a pattern of racketeering activity or collection of an unlawful debt. Case law provides interpretations of the word "enterprise," a term defined in 18 U.S.C.A. § 1961.

Each of the provisions in § 1962 allow prosecutions to be premised upon either a "pattern of racketeering" or the collection of an "unlawful debt," terms whose definitions are also outlined in RICO's definitional provision, 18 U.S.C.A. § 1961. The vast majority of RICO actions employ a pattern of racketeering as the focus of the unlawful conduct. A pattern of racketeering activity encompasses at least two acts of racketeering activity. Nine possible state offenses and over thirty federal offenses can serve as predicate acts for a RICO prosecution.

18 U.S.C.A. § 1963 provides the criminal penalties available in a RICO prosecution. These include incarceration, fines, and the forfeiture of property. Section 1963 also authorizes prosecutors to seek restraining orders

to prevent the dissipation of assets that may be subject to forfeiture. Extensive procedural rules regarding forfeiture of property and the protection of third party interests in the property are specified in this section.

18 U.S.C.A. § 1964 extends RICO outside the criminal context, allowing its use in civil proceedings. This latter provision has been the subject of significant controversy in its allowance of "garden variety" frauds to be subject to treble damages and attorney fees. Proposals have been suggested and rejected to limit RICO's application in civil actions. For example, one House Bill provided that a criminal conviction of racketeering activity or a violation under § 1962 was necessary for bringing a civil RICO action. [See H.R. 2943, 99th Cong., 1st Sess. (1985)].

2. Civil RICO

RICO actions brought by the government require prior approval from the Criminal Division. Private civil RICO cases, however, are not subject to any governmental review or restrictions. Courts have generally been hostile to private RICO claims, but the broad language of the statute makes direct restrictions on filing such actions difficult to impose. In **Sedima v. Imrex Co.**, 473 U.S. 479 (1985), a case involving a civil action brought under § 1964(c), the Court held that there is no requirement in a private civil RICO action that the defendant previously have been criminally convicted of the predicate offenses that constitute the pattern of racketeering or of the RICO violation itself. Justice White, writing for the majority, stated:

> RICO was an aggressive initiative to supplement old remedies and develop new methods for fighting crime. See generally Russello v. United States, 464 U.S. 16, 26-29 (1983). While few of the legislative statements about novel remedies and attacking crime on all fronts were made with direct reference to § 1964(c), it is in this spirit that all of the Act's provisions should be read. The specific references to § 1964(c) are consistent with this overall approach. Those supporting § 1964(c) hoped it would "enhance the effectiveness of title IX's prohibitions" and provide "a major new tool." Its opponents, also recognizing the provision's scope, complained that it provided too easy a weapon against 'innocent businessmen' and would be prone to abuse. * * *

In his dissent, Justice Marshall noted:

> * * * The Court's interpretation of the civil RICO statute quite simply revolutionizes private litigation; it validates the federalization of broad areas of state common law of frauds, and it approves the displacement of well-established federal remedial provisions. We do not lightly infer a congressional intent to effect such fundamental changes. To infer such intent here would be

untenable, for there is no indication that Congress even considered, much less approved, the scheme that the Court today defines.

The single most significant reason for the expansive use of civil RICO has been the presence in the statute, as predicate acts, of mail and wire fraud violations. Prior to RICO, no federal statute had expressly provided a private damages remedy based upon a violation of the mail or wire fraud statutes, which make it a federal crime to use the mail or wires in furtherance of a scheme to defraud. * * *

The responsible use of prosecutorial discretion is particularly important with respect to criminal RICO prosecutions—which often rely on mail and wire fraud as predicate acts—given the extremely severe penalties authorized by RICO's criminal provisions. * * * [Justice Marshall here describes the limits set forth in the Justice Department's guidelines.] In the context of civil RICO, however, the restraining influence of prosecutors is completely absent. Unlike the Government, private litigants have no reason to avoid displacing state common-law remedies. Quite to the contrary, such litigants, lured by the prospect of treble damages and attorney's fees, have a strong incentive to invoke RICO's provisions whenever they can allege in good faith two instances of mail or wire fraud. Then the defendant, facing a tremendous financial exposure in addition to the threat of being labeled a "racketeer," will have a strong interest in settling the dispute. * * * The civil RICO provision consequently stretches the mail and wire fraud statutes to their absolute limits and federalizes important areas of civil litigation that until now were solely within the domain of the States.

B. THE ENTERPRISE

1. Nature of an "Enterprise"

UNITED STATES v. TURKETTE
452 U.S. 576, 101 S.Ct. 2524, 69 L.Ed.2d 246 (1981)

Justice WHITE delivered the opinion of the Court.

* * * Count Nine of a nine-count indictment charged respondent and 12 others with conspiracy to conduct and participate in the affairs of an enterprise engaged in interstate commerce through a pattern of racketeering activities, in violation of 18 U.S.C. § 1962(d). The indictment described the enterprise as "a group of individuals associated in fact for the purpose of illegally trafficking in narcotics and other dangerous drugs, committing arsons, utilizing the United States mails to defraud insurance companies, bribing and attempting to bribe local police officers, and corruptly influencing and attempting to corruptly influence the outcome of state court proceedings

. . . ." The other eight counts of the indictment charged the commission of various substantive criminal acts by those engaged in and associated with the criminal enterprise, including possession with intent to distribute and distribution of controlled substances, and several counts of insurance fraud by arson and other means. The common thread to all counts was respondent's alleged leadership of this criminal organization through which he orchestrated and participated in the commission of the various crimes delineated in the RICO count or charged in the eight preceding counts.

After a 6-week jury trial, in which the evidence focused upon both the professional nature of this organization and the execution of a number of distinct criminal acts, respondent was convicted on all nine counts. He was sentenced to a term of 20 years on the substantive counts, as well as a 2-year special parole term on the drug count. On the RICO conspiracy count he was sentenced to a 20-year concurrent term and fined $20,000.

On appeal, respondent argued that RICO was intended solely to protect legitimate business enterprises from infiltration by racketeers and that RICO does not make criminal the participation in an association which performs only illegal acts and which has not infiltrated or attempted to infiltrate a legitimate enterprise. The Court of Appeals agreed. We reverse.   * * *

Section 1961(4) describes two categories of associations that come within the purview of the "enterprise" definition. The first encompasses organizations such as corporations and partnerships, and other "legal entities." The second covers "any union or group of individuals associated in fact although not a legal entity." The Court of Appeals assumed that the second category was merely a more general description of the first. * * * But that assumption is untenable. Each category describes a separate type of enterprise to be covered by the statute—those that are recognized as legal entities and those that are not. The latter is not a more general description of the former. The second category itself not containing any specific enumeration that is followed by a general description, *ejusdem generis* has no bearing on the meaning to be attributed to that part of § 1961(4).

A second reason offered by the Court of Appeals in support of its judgment was that giving the definition of "enterprise" its ordinary meaning would create several internal inconsistencies in the Act. With respect to § 1962(c), it was said:

> "If 'a pattern of racketeering' can itself be an 'enterprise' for purposes of section 1962(c), then the two phrases 'employed by or associated with any enterprise' and 'the conduct of such enterprise's affairs through [a pattern of racketeering activity]' add nothing to the meaning of the section. The words of the statute are coherent and logical only if they are read as applying to legitimate enterprises."

This conclusion is based on a faulty premise. That a wholly criminal enterprise comes within the ambit of the statute does not mean that a "pattern of racketeering activity" is an "enterprise." In order to secure a conviction under RICO, the Government must prove both the existence of an "enterprise" and the connected "pattern of racketeering activity." The enterprise is an entity, for present purposes a group of persons associated together for a common purpose of engaging in a course of conduct. The pattern of racketeering activity is, on the other hand, a series of criminal acts as defined by the statute. 18 U.S.C. § 1961(1). The former is proved by evidence of an ongoing organization, formal or informal, and by evidence that the various associates function as a continuing unit. The latter is proved by evidence of the requisite number of acts of racketeering committed by the participants in the enterprise. While the proof used to establish these separate elements may in particular cases coalesce, proof of one does not necessarily establish the other. The "enterprise" is not the "pattern of racketeering activity"; it is an entity separate and apart from the pattern of activity in which it engages. The existence of an enterprise at all times remains a separate element which must be proved by the Government.[5]

Apart from § 1962(c)'s proscription against participating in an enterprise through a pattern of racketeering activities, RICO also proscribes the investment of income derived from racketeering activity in an enterprise engaged in or which affects interstate commerce as well as the acquisition of an interest in or control of any such enterprise through a pattern of racketeering activity. 18 U.S.C. §§ 1962(a) and (b). The Court of Appeals concluded that these provisions of RICO should be interpreted so as to apply only to legitimate enterprises. If these two sections are so limited, the Court of Appeals held that the proscription in § 1962(c), at issue here, must be similarly limited. Again, we do not accept the premise from which the Court of Appeals derived its conclusion. It is obvious that § 1962(a) and (b) address the infiltration by organized crime of legitimate businesses, but we cannot agree that these sections were not also aimed at preventing racketeers from investing or reinvesting in wholly illegal enterprises and from acquiring through a pattern of racketeering activity wholly illegitimate enterprises such as an illegal gambling business or a loan-sharking operation. There is no inconsistency or anomaly in recognizing that § 1962 applies to both legitimate and illegitimate enterprises. Certainly the language of the statute does not warrant the Court of Appeals' conclusion to the contrary.

Similarly, the Court of Appeals noted that various civil remedies were provided by § 1964, including divestiture, dissolution, reorganization, restrictions on future activities by violators of RICO, and treble damages.

---

[5] The Government takes the position that proof of a pattern of racketeering activity in itself would not be sufficient to establish the existence of an enterprise: "We do not suggest that any two sporadic and isolated offenses by the same actor or actors *ipso facto* constitute an 'illegitimate' enterprise; rather, the existence of the enterprise as an independent entity must also be shown." * * *

These remedies it thought would have utility only with respect to legitimate enterprises. As a general proposition, however, the civil remedies could be useful in eradicating organized crime from the social fabric, whether the enterprise be ostensibly legitimate or admittedly criminal. The aim is to divest the association of the fruits of its ill-gotten gains. Even if one or more of the civil remedies might be inapplicable to a particular illegitimate enterprise, this fact would not serve to limit the enterprise concept. Congress has provided civil remedies for use when the circumstances so warrant. It is untenable to argue that their existence limits the scope of the criminal provisions.

Finally, it is urged that the interpretation of RICO to include both legitimate and illegitimate enterprises will substantially alter the balance between federal and state enforcement of criminal law. This is particularly true, so the argument goes, since included within the definition of racketeering activity are a significant number of acts made criminal under state law. 18 U.S.C. § 1961(1). But even assuming that the more inclusive definition of enterprise will have the effect suggested, the language of the statute and its legislative history indicate that Congress was well aware that it was entering a new domain of federal involvement through the enactment of this measure. Indeed, the very purpose of the Organized Crime Control Act of 1970 was to enable the Federal Government to address a large and seemingly neglected problem. * * *

Contrary to the judgment below, neither the language nor structure of RICO limits its application to legitimate "enterprises." Applying it also to criminal organizations does not render any portion of the statute superfluous nor does it create any structural incongruities within the framework of the Act. The result is neither absurd nor surprising. On the contrary, insulating the wholly criminal enterprise from prosecution under RICO is the more incongruous position.

Section 904(a) of RICO, directs that "[t]he provisions of this Title shall be liberally construed to effectuate its remedial purposes." With or without this admonition, we could not agree with the Court of Appeals that illegitimate enterprises should be excluded from coverage. We are also quite sure that nothing in the legislative history of RICO requires a contrary conclusion. * * *

The statement of findings that prefaces the Organized Crime Control Act of 1970 reveals the pervasiveness of the problem that Congress was addressing by this enactment:

"The Congress finds that (1) organized crime in the United States is a highly sophisticated, diversified, and widespread activity that annually drains billions of dollars from America's economy by unlawful conduct and the illegal use of force, fraud, and corruption; (2) organized crime derives a major portion of its power through money obtained from such illegal endeavors as syndicated gambling, loan sharking, the theft and fencing of property, the importation and distribution of narcotics and other dangerous drugs, and other forms of social exploitation; (3) this money and power are increasingly used to infiltrate and corrupt legitimate business and labor unions and to subvert and corrupt our democratic processes; (4) organized crime activities in the United States weaken the stability of the Nation's economic system, harm innocent investors and competing organizations, interfere with free competition, seriously burden interstate and foreign commerce, threaten the domestic security, and undermine the general welfare of the Nation and its citizens; and (5) organized crime continues to grow because of defects in the evidence-gathering process of the law inhibiting the development of the legally admissible evidence necessary to bring criminal and other sanctions or remedies to bear on the unlawful activities of those engaged in organized crime and because the sanctions and remedies available to the Government are unnecessarily limited in scope and impact."

In light of the above findings, it was the declared purpose of Congress "to seek the eradication of organized crime in the United States by strengthening the legal tools in the evidence-gathering process, by establishing new penal prohibitions, and by providing enhanced sanctions and new remedies to deal with the unlawful activities of those engaged in organized crime." * * *

Considering this statement of the Act's broad purposes, the construction of RICO suggested by respondent and the court below is unacceptable. Whole areas of organized criminal activity would be placed beyond the substantive reach of the enactment. * * *

Accepting that the primary purpose of RICO is to cope with the infiltration of legitimate businesses, applying the statute in accordance with its terms, so as to reach criminal enterprises, would seek to deal with the problem at its very source. Supporters of the bill recognized that organized crime uses its primary sources of revenue and power—illegal gambling, loan sharking and illicit drug distribution—as a springboard into the sphere of legitimate enterprise. * * *

As a measure to deal with the infiltration of legitimate businesses by organized crime, RICO was both preventive and remedial. Respondent's view would ignore the preventive function of the statute. If Congress had intended the more circumscribed approach espoused by the Court of Appeals, there would have been some positive sign that the law was not to reach organized criminal activities that give rise to the concerns about infiltration. The language of the statute, however—the most reliable evidence of its intent—reveals that Congress opted for a far broader definition of the word "enterprise," and we are unconvinced by anything in the legislative history that this definition should be given less than its full effect.

The judgment of the Court of Appeals is accordingly reversed.

Justice STEWART agrees with the reasoning and conclusion of the Court of Appeals as to the meaning of the term "enterprise" in this statute. See 632 F.2d 896. Accordingly, he respectfully dissents.

NOTE

Courts have permitted state and local government offices to be the enterprise in a RICO case. See United States v. Ganim, 225 F.Supp.2d 145 (D.Conn. 2002) (Office of the Mayor of Bridgeport); United States v. Cianci, 210 F.Supp.2d 71 (D.R.I. 2002) (City of Providence, Rhode Island); United States v. Genova, 187 F.Supp.2d 1015 (N.D. Ill. 2002) (Calumet City, Illinois). Although the court allowed "The Office of Governor of Tennessee" to be an enterprise in United States v. Thompson, 685 F.2d 993, 1000 (6th Cir.1982), dicta noted that it "is disruptive of comity in federal-state relations" and "may also needlessly cast unfair reflection upon innocent individuals." The court stated that preferably the indictment should be premised upon a "group of individual[s] associated in fact although not a legal entity which made use of the Office of Governor of the State of Tennessee." In United States v. Warner, 498 F.3d 666 (7th Cir. 2007), the Seventh Circuit allowed a RICO charge identifying the State of Illinois as the enterprise. The court stated, "We endorse the Sixth Circuit's call for caution. We also agree with the Sixth Circuit's ultimate conclusion that the prosecution's approach to this issue in cases such as *Thompson* and the case at hand may often not be absolutely necessary under RICO, but it is not forbidden. Some cases, however, are exceptional, and ours is one of them. In such a case, the prosecution may have no real alternative to naming the state as the RICO enterprise.

2. Association-in-Fact Enterprise

The term "enterprise" is not limited to individuals or legal entities. § 1961(4), in defining the term "enterprise," also includes "any union or group of individuals associated in fact although not a legal entity." The lower courts are in general agreement that an association-in-fact enterprise must have a common purpose and must function as a continuing unit, but from this point on, they divide. The Supreme Court is considering the issue of whether , "in order to establish the existence of an "enterprise" within the meaning of the RICO statute" " the government must prove the existence of an entity with an ascertainable structure apart from the pattern of racketeering activity in which its members engage. In **United States v. Boyle**, the Petitioner was convicted of RICO, Conspiracy to Commit RICO, and other offenses and was sentenced to 151 months imprisonment. The Supreme Court accepted certiorari from the Second Circuit. The Petitioner's Brief states:

Boyle asks the Court to make explicit what it unmistakably implied almost 30 years ago in United States v. Turkette, 452 U.S. 576 (1981): that an association-in-fact enterprise must have some sort of structure beyond that attending the pattern of racketeering activity

- the series of predicate crimes - in which its participants engage. *
* *[T]o secure a conviction under RICO, the Government must prove
both the existence of an "enterprise" and the connected "pattern of
racketeering activity." The enterprise is an entity, for present
purposes a group of persons associated together for a common
purpose of engaging in a course of conduct. The pattern of
racketeering activity is, on the other hand, a series of criminal acts
as defined by the statute. The former is proved by evidence of an
ongoing organization, formal or informal, and by evidence that the
various associates function as a continuing unit. The latter is proved
by evidence of the requisite number of acts of racketeering
committed by the participants in the enterprise. While the proof
used to establish these separate elements may in particular cases
coalesce, proof of one does not necessarily establish the other. The
"enterprise" is not the "pattern of racketeering activity"; it is an
entity separate and apart from the pattern of activity in which it
engages. The existence of an enterprise at all times remains a
separate element which must be proved by the government. * * *

To ensure the obligatory separation, most circuit courts correctly
read Turkette to require that an association-in-fact have some
perceptible operating structure aside - though permissibly inferable -
from that inherent in the predicate acts themselves. * * *
Sophistication and "access to resources" distinguish coordinated
criminality from ordinary "individual and group crime." * * * From
that premise, these courts sensibly reason that an enterprise must
be something more than just a "group of people who get together to
commit a pattern of racketeering." * * * For these courts, some
degree of structure - however proved, by the pattern or otherwise -
supplies the necessary distinguishing feature at negligible cost to
the plaintiff or prosecutor. * * * Other circuits - a distinct minority -
take a different approach, removing even that "very low hurdle"
from the government's burden. * * * Confusing the elements of an
offense with the evidence used to prove them, they have seized on
this Court's observation that pattern and enterprise proof "may in
particular cases coalesce," * * * to hold that an association-in-fact
need not have any identifiable structure. * * * And at least one
circuit - the Second, Boyle's home circuit - has decisively dropped the
Other shoe, incrementally extending that faulty premise to its
inevitable conclusion: a virtual per se rule that RICO applies "where
the enterprise [i]s, in effect, no more than the sum of the predicate
racketeering acts." * * *

In response the government states:

RICO's text and structure demonstrate that Congress defined
"enterprise" broadly to include a wide range of both formal and
informal associative groups. When the common purpose of such a
group is to pursue criminal acts, a criminal "enterprise" can exist

even if the group does not display an "ascertainable structure beyond that inherent in the commission" of those crimes * * * Congress defined "enterprise" broadly to "include[]" "any" legal entity (including "any individual, partnership, corporation, [or] association") and "any union or group of individuals associated in fact" that lacks a recognized legal existence. * * * That definition embraces a "group of individuals associated in fact" whose members are "associated together a common purpose of engaging in a [criminal] course of conduct" and who form a "formal or informal" organization whose members "function as a continuing unit." * * * Nothing in RICO's text suggests that a criminal association-in-fact must possess an ascertainable structure beyond that inherent in its members' coordinated criminal activity. Indeed, the essence of such an association is the common purpose that binds its members and prompts them to function as a unit over time to commit crimes. Petitioner's extra-textual restriction on RICO's "enterprise" concept is inconsistent with Congress's use of expansive language in Section 1961(4), which imposes "no restriction upon the associations embraced by [that] definition." * * * As this Court has recognized, RICO targets criminal associations that "extend well beyond" those traditionally understood as "organized crime" in order to apply to "a wide range of criminal activity, taking many different forms" and involving "a broad array of perpetrators operating in many different ways." * * *

An association-in-fact may be composed of as few as two members. It would therefore be anomalous for Congress to have intended that such a group must reflect the formalistic structure suggested by petitioner. Two-person enterprises do not require decision-making protocols, command structure, or fixed roles to operate effectively to pursue a common objective. Moreover, Congress expressly provided that "any individual" may constitute an enterprise. If an individual qualifies as an enterprise under RICO, there is no sound reason to conclude that an "ascertainable structure" is essential to RICO's enterprise concept. Indeed, elsewhere in the act that enacted RICO, Congress explicitly addressed the structure of an enterprise needed to trigger criminal liability, * * * but included no analogous language in RICO to limit the scope of its enterprise definition. There is no reason to disregard that presumably conscious decision in drafting RICO by importing the kind of amorphous "ascertainable structure" requirement suggested by petitioner.

Petitioner is incorrect in his suggestion that an ascertainable structure requirement is needed to avoid merging the "enterprise" concept into a RICO's "pattern of racketeering activity." An enterprise may exist absent such a pattern where, for instance, a criminal group forms to pursue non-racketeering activities. Likewise, an individual can commit a pattern of racketeering activity with a changing pool of confederates who might not form an association-in-fact. And, even when an individual participates in the conduct of the affairs of an enterprise by engaging in a pattern of racketeering, that pattern standing alone may not demonstrate the existence of the enterprise. Of course, when two or more persons associate together to coordinate their actions to commit jointly a series of related racketeering crimes that either extend over a substantial period of time or threaten such continued activity, their coordinated activities can reflect both the existence of an "enterprise" and a "pattern" of racketeering activity. * * *

NOTE

Enterprises in White Collar Crime Prosecutions. In the context of white collar crime cases, the "association-in-fact" enterprise has come in a variety of forms. For example, in **United States v. Console**, 13 F.3d 641 (3d Cir. 1993), the "government alleged that the RICO enterprise was an association-in-fact composed of [a] law firm and * * * medical practice [that was] designed 'to enrich its members through the pursuit of personal injury business.' " Appellants in *Console* argued that there was insufficient evidence of a RICO enterprise to support their convictions. "[A]ccording to appellants, '[a]ll that was shown was that the medical practice and the lawyer's office combined to commit mail fraud on an ad hoc basis.' " In rejecting appellants' arguments, the court noted that an association-in-fact can "be composed of legal as well as non-legal entities," and that the association-in-fact between a law firm and medical practice constituted a RICO enterprise under § 1961(4). See also G-I Holding, Inc. v. Baron & Budd, 238 F. Supp.2d 521, 547 (S.D.N.Y. 2002) (considering the agency relationship).

In United States v. Blandford, [p.135], the court examined an enterprise alleged to be associated-in-fact with a government office. The court found sufficient evidence of an enterprise existing in "that the defendant had several employees in his office who performed constituent service for both his constituents as Speaker of the House and his constituents as Representative for the Fourteenth District." The court noted that "[t]hese employees performed various duties for the office which constituted the enterprise, including some of the racketeering acts."

3. Distinctiveness of the Enterprise and the Defendant

CEDRIC KUSHNER PROMOTIONS, LTD. v. KING
533 U.S. 158, 121 S.Ct. 2087, 150 L.Ed.2d 198 (2001)

Justice BREYER delivered the opinion of the Court.

The Racketeer Influenced and Corrupt Organizations Act (RICO or Act), 18 U.S.C. § 1961 et seq., makes it "unlawful for any person employed by or associated with any enterprise ... to conduct or participate ... in the conduct of such enterprise's affairs" through the commission of two or more statutorily defined crimes--which RICO calls "a pattern of racketeering activity." § 1962(c). The language suggests, and lower courts have held, that this provision foresees two separate entities, a "person" and a distinct "enterprise."

This case focuses upon a person who is the president and sole shareholder of a closely held corporation. The plaintiff claims that the president has conducted the corporation's affairs through the forbidden "pattern," though for present purposes it is conceded that, in doing so, he acted within the scope of his authority as the corporation's employee. In these circumstances, are there two entities, a "person" and a separate "enterprise"? Assuming, as we must given the posture of this case, that the allegations in the complaint are true, we conclude that the "person" and "enterprise" here are distinct and that the RICO provision applies.

Petitioner, Cedric Kushner Promotions, Ltd., is a corporation that promotes boxing matches. Petitioner sued Don King, the president and sole shareholder of Don King Productions, a corporation, claiming that King had conducted the boxing-related affairs of Don King Productions in part through a RICO "pattern," i.e., through the alleged commission of at least two instances of fraud and other RICO predicate crimes. The District Court, citing Court of Appeals precedent, dismissed the complaint.* * * And the Court of Appeals affirmed that dismissal. * * * In the appellate court's view, § 1962(c) applies only where a plaintiff shows the existence of two separate entities, a "person" and a distinct "enterprise," the affairs of which that "person" improperly conducts. In this instance, "it is undisputed that King was an employee" of the corporation Don King Productions and also "acting within the scope of his authority." Under the Court of Appeals' analysis, King, in a legal sense, was part of, not separate from, the corporation. There was no "person," distinct from the "enterprise," who improperly conducted the "enterprise's affairs." And thus § 1962(c) did not apply.

Other Circuits, applying § 1962(c) in roughly similar circumstances, have reached a contrary conclusion. * * * We granted certiorari to resolve the conflict. We now agree with these Circuits and hold that the Second Circuit's interpretation of § 1962(c) is erroneous.

We do not quarrel with the basic principle that to establish liability under § 1962(c) one must allege and prove the existence of two distinct entities: (1) a "person"; and (2) an "enterprise" that is not simply the same "person" referred to by a different name. The statute's language, read as ordinary English, suggests that principle. The Act says that it applies to "person[s]" who are "employed by or associated with" the "enterprise." § 1962(c). In ordinary English one speaks of employing, being employed by, or associating with others, not oneself. See Webster's Third New International Dictionary 132 (1993) * * * In addition, the Act's purposes are consistent with that principle. Whether the Act seeks to prevent a person from victimizing, say, a small business, * * * or to prevent a person from using a corporation for criminal purposes, National Organization for Women, Inc. v.

Scheidler, 510 U.S. 249, 259, 114 S.Ct. 798, 127 L.Ed.2d 99 (1994), the person and the victim, or the person and the tool, are different entities, not the same.

The Government reads § 1962(c) "to require some distinctness between the RICO defendant and the RICO enterprise." * * * And it says that this requirement is "legally sound and workable." We agree with its assessment, particularly in light of the fact that 12 Courts of Appeals have interpreted the statute as embodying some such distinctness requirement without creating discernible mischief in the administration of RICO. * * * Indeed, this Court previously has said that liability "depends on showing that the defendants conducted or participated in the conduct of the 'enterprise's affairs,' not just their own affairs." Reves v. Ernst & Young [p. 253].

While accepting the "distinctness" principle, we nonetheless disagree with the appellate court's application of that principle to the present circumstances--circumstances in which a corporate employee, "acting within the scope of his authority," * * * allegedly conducts the corporation's affairs in a RICO-forbidden way. The corporate owner/employee, a natural person, is distinct from the corporation itself, a legally different entity with different rights and responsibilities due to its different legal status. And we can find nothing in the statute that requires more "separateness" than that. Cf. McCullough v. Suter, 757 F.2d 142, 144 (7th Cir.1985) (finding either formal or practical separateness sufficient to be distinct under § 1962(c)).

Linguistically speaking, an employee who conducts the affairs of a corporation through illegal acts comes within the terms of a statute that forbids any "person" unlawfully to conduct an "enterprise," particularly when the statute explicitly defines "person" to include "any individual ... capable of holding a legal or beneficial interest in property," and defines "enterprise" to include a "corporation." 18 U.S.C. §§ 1961(3), (4). And, linguistically speaking, the employee and the corporation are different "persons," even where the employee is the corporation's sole owner. After all, incorporation's basic purpose is to create a distinct legal entity, with legal rights, obligations, powers, and privileges different from those of the natural individuals who created it, who own it, or whom it employs. * * *

* * * Further, to apply the RICO statute in present circumstances is consistent with the statute's basic purposes as this Court has defined them. The Court has held that RICO both protects a legitimate "enterprise" from those who would use unlawful acts to victimize it, United States v. Turkette, [p. 232] and also protects the public from those who would unlawfully use an "enterprise" (whether legitimate or illegitimate) as a "vehicle" through which "unlawful ... activity is committed," * * * A corporate employee who conducts the corporation's affairs through an unlawful RICO "pattern ... of activity," § 1962(c), uses that corporation as a "vehicle" whether he is, or is not, its sole owner.

Conversely, the appellate court's critical legal distinction--between employees acting within the scope of corporate authority and those acting outside that authority – is inconsistent with a basic statutory purpose. * * * It would immunize from RICO liability many of those at whom this Court has said RICO directly aims – e.g., high-ranking individuals in an illegitimate criminal enterprise, who, seeking to further the purposes of that enterprise, act within the scope of their authority. * * *

Finally, we have found nothing in the statute's history that significantly favors an alternative interpretation. That history not only refers frequently to the importance of undermining organized crime's influence upon legitimate businesses but also refers to the need to protect the public from those who would run "organization[s] in a manner detrimental to the public interest." S.Rep. No. 91-617, at 82. This latter purpose, as we have said, invites the legal principle we endorse, namely, that in present circumstances the statute requires no more than the formal legal distinction between "person" and "enterprise" (namely, incorporation) that is present here.

In reply, King argues that the lower court's rule is consistent with (1) the principle that a corporation acts only through its directors, officers, and agents,* * * (2) the principle that a corporation should not be liable for the criminal acts of its employees where Congress so intends, * * * and (3) the Sherman Act principle limiting liability under 15 U.S.C. § 1 by excluding "from unlawful combinations or conspiracies the activities of a single firm," Copperweld Corp. v. Independence Tube Corp., 467 U.S. 752, 769-770, n. 15, 104 S.Ct. 2731, 81 L.Ed.2d 628 (1984). The alternative that we endorse, however, is no less consistent with these principles. It does not deny that a corporation acts through its employees; it says only that the corporation and its employees are not legally identical. It does not assert that ordinary respondeat superior principles make a corporation legally liable under RICO for the criminal acts of its employees; that is a matter of congressional intent not before us. * * * Neither is it inconsistent with antitrust law's intracorporate conspiracy doctrine; that doctrine turns on specific antitrust objectives. * * * Rather, we hold simply that the need for two distinct entities is satisfied; hence, the RICO provision before us applies when a corporate employee unlawfully conducts the affairs of the corporation of which he is the sole owner – whether he conducts those affairs within the scope, or beyond the scope, of corporate authority.

For these reasons, the Court of Appeals' judgment is reversed, and the case is remanded for further proceedings consistent with this opinion.

4. Interstate Commerce

1. **"Engaged In Interstate Commerce."** The different types of RICO violations in § 1962 apply to "any enterprise which is engaged in, or the activities of which affect, interstate or foreign commerce . . . ." In **United States v. Roberston**, 514 U.S. 669 (1995), the Supreme Court overturned a lower court decision finding that a claimed violation of § 1962(a) involving

a gold mining operation in Alaska did not meet the interstate commerce element. The Court summarized the defendant's interstate activities related to the mine:

> Robertson, who resided in Arizona, made a cash payment of $125,000 for placer gold mining claims near Fairbanks. He paid approximately $100,000 (in cash) for mining equipment and supplies, some of which were purchased in Los Angeles and transported to Alaska for use in the mine. Robertson also hired and paid the expenses for seven out- of-state employees to travel to Alaska to work in the mine. The partnership dissolved during the first mining season, but Robertson continued to operate the mine through 1987 as a sole proprietorship. He again hired a number of employees from outside Alaska to work in the mine. During its operating life, the mine produced between $200,000 and $290,000 worth of gold, most of which was sold to refiners within Alaska, although Robertson personally transported approximately $30,000 worth of gold out of the State.

The Court did not need to consider whether the enterprise "affected" interstate commerce, holding instead that "[w]hether or not these activities met (and whether or not, to bring the gold mine within the "affecting commerce" provision of RICO, they would have to meet) the requirement of substantially affecting interstate commerce, they assuredly brought the gold mine within § 1962(a)'s alternative criterion of 'any enterprise . . . engaged in . . . interstate or foreign commerce.'"

2. *Affecting Commerce.* If the Court had used the "affecting interstate commerce" alternative of the statute in *Robertson*, as opposed to finding the enterprise engaged in interstate commerce, what level of proof would be necessary to show that the enterprise affects interstate commerce? See United States v. Lopez [p. 15]. In the past, courts have found a sufficient nexus with interstate commerce when there is some minimal connection with interstate commerce. For example, in United States v. Joseph, 510 F. Supp. 1001 (E.D. Pa. 1981), the defendant, the Clerk of Courts of Lehigh County, Pennsylvania, was alleged to have violated RICO "by soliciting and accepting various amounts of cash from a bailbondsman in consideration for defendant's favorable recommendations and exercise of discretion in his official decisions." In rejecting defendant's motion to dismiss premised upon the indictment failing to show an affect upon interstate commerce, the court noted that "most courts do have an effect upon interstate commerce, as do sheriff's departments and the offices of prosecuting attorneys, all of which place interstate telephone calls, purchase supplies and materials through interstate commerce and involve non-citizens of the forum state in litigation."

3. *Affecting Commerce: Predicate Acts or Enterprise.* In a RICO prosecution, should a court look to whether the predicate acts or the enterprise is affecting (or is engaged in) interstate commerce? See United States v. Rone, 598 F.2d 564, 573 (9th Cir. 1981) ("The statute requires that

the activity of the 'enterprise,' not each predicate act of racketeering, have an effect on interstate commerce."); see also United States v. Bagnariol, 665 F.2d 877, 893 (9th Cir. 1981) ("The interstate commerce nexus must result from the enterprise. It is permissible to find that nexus from acts also charged as predicate acts when those constitute the activities of the enterprise.").

5. Economic Motive

NATIONAL ORGANIZATION FOR WOMEN v. SCHEIDLER
510 U.S. 249. 114 S.Ct. 798, 127 L.Ed.2d 99 (1994)

Chief Justice REHNQUIST delivered the opinion of the Court.

* * * Section 1962(c) prohibits any person associated with an enterprise from conducting its affairs through a pattern of racketeering activity. We granted certiorari to determine whether RICO requires proof that either the racketeering enterprise or the predicate acts of racketeering were motivated by an economic purpose. We hold that RICO requires no such economic motive. * * *

Petitioner National Organization For Women, Inc. (NOW) is a national nonprofit organization that supports the legal availability of abortion; petitioners Delaware Women's Health Organization, Inc. (DWHO) and Summit Women's Health Organization, Inc. (SWHO) are health care centers that perform abortions and other medical procedures. Respondents are a coalition of antiabortion groups called the Pro-Life Action Network (PLAN), Joseph Scheidler and other individuals and organizations that oppose legal abortion, and a medical laboratory that formerly provided services to the two petitioner health care centers.

Petitioners sued respondents in the United States District Court for the Northern District of Illinois, alleging violations of the Sherman Act, 15 U.S.C. § 1 et seq., and RICO's §§ 1962(a), (c), and (d), as well as several pendent state-law claims stemming from the activities of antiabortion protesters at the clinics. * * *

The amended complaint alleged that respondents were members of a nationwide conspiracy to shut down abortion clinics through a pattern of racketeering activity including extortion in violation of the Hobbs Act, 18 U.S.C. § 1951. * * *

The District Court dismissed the case pursuant to Federal Rule of Civil Procedure 12(b)(6). Citing Eastern Railroad Presidents Conference v. Noerr Motor Freight, Inc., 365 U.S. 127 (1961), it held that since the activities alleged "involve[d] political opponents, not commercial competitors, and political objectives, not marketplace goals," the Sherman Act did not apply. It dismissed petitioners' RICO claims under § 1962(a) because the "income" alleged by petitioners consisted of voluntary donations from persons opposed to abortion which "in no way were derived from the pattern of racketeering alleged in the complaint." The District Court then concluded that petitioners failed to state a claim under § 1962(c) since "an economic motive requirement exists to the extent that some profit-generating purpose must be alleged in order to state a RICO claim." Finally, it dismissed petitioners' RICO conspiracy claim under § 1962(d) since petitioners' other RICO claims could not stand.

The Court of Appeals affirmed. 968 F.2d 612 (CA7 1992).

* * * Nowhere in either § 1962(c), or in the RICO definitions in § 1961, is there any indication that an economic motive is required.   * * *

We do not believe that the usage of the term "enterprise" in subsections (a) and (b) leads to the inference that an economic motive is required in subsection (c). The term "enterprise" in subsections (a) and (b) plays a different role in the structure of those subsections than it does in subsection (c). Section 1962(a) provides that it "shall be unlawful for any person who has received any income derived, directly or indirectly, from a pattern of racketeering activity . . . to use or invest, directly or indirectly, any part of such income, or the proceeds of such income, in acquisition of any interest in, or the establishment or operation of, any enterprise which is engaged in, or the activities of which affect, interstate or foreign commerce." Correspondingly, § 1962(b) states that it "shall be unlawful for any person through a pattern of racketeering activity or through collection of an unlawful debt to acquire or maintain, directly or indirectly, any interest in or control of any enterprise which is engaged in, or the activities of which affect, interstate or foreign commerce." The "enterprise" referred to in subsections (a) and (b) is thus something acquired through the use of illegal activities or by money obtained from illegal activities. The enterprise in these subsections is the victim of unlawful activity and may very well be a "profit-seeking" entity that represents a property interest and may be acquired. But the statutory language in subsections (a) and (b) does not mandate that the enterprise be a "profit-seeking" entity; it simply requires that the enterprise be an entity that was acquired through illegal activity or the money generated from illegal activity.

By contrast, the "enterprise" in subsection (c) connotes generally the vehicle through which the unlawful pattern of racketeering activity is committed, rather than the victim of that activity. Subsection (c) makes it unlawful for "any person employed by or associated with any enterprise ... to conduct or participate ... in the conduct of such enterprise's affairs through a pattern of racketeering activity...." Consequently, since the enterprise in subsection (c) is not being acquired, it need not have a property interest that can be acquired nor an economic motive for engaging in illegal activity; it need only be an association in fact that engages in a pattern of racketeering activity. Nothing in subsections (a) and (b) directs us to a contrary conclusion.   * * *

We therefore hold that petitioners may maintain this action if respondents conducted the enterprise through a pattern of racketeering activity. The questions of whether the respondents committed the requisite predicate acts, and whether the commission of these acts fell into a pattern, are not before us. We hold only that RICO contains no economic motive requirement.

The judgment of the Court of Appeals is accordingly reversed.

Justice SOUTER, with whom Justice KENNEDY joins, concurring.

I join the Court's opinion and write separately to explain why the First Amendment does not require reading an economic-motive requirement into the RICO, and to stress that the Court's opinion does not bar First Amendment challenges to RICO's application in particular cases.   * * *

NOTE

Following the above decision, the case proceeded to a seven-week trial.

[A] six-member jury concluded that petitioners violated the civil provisions of RICO. By answering a series of special interrogatory questions, the jury found, inter alia, that petitioners' alleged "pattern of racketeering activity" included 21 violations of the Hobbs Act, 18 U.S.C. § 1951; 25 violations of state extortion law; 25 instances of attempting or conspiring to commit either federal or state extortion; 23 violations of the Travel Act, 18 U.S.C. § 1952; and 23 instances of attempting to violate the Travel Act. The jury awarded $31,455.64 to respondent, the National Women's Health Organization of Delaware, Inc., and $54,471.28 to the National Women's Health Organization of Summit, Inc. These damages were trebled pursuant to § 1964(c). Additionally, the District Court entered a permanent nationwide injunction prohibiting petitioners from obstructing access to the clinics, trespassing on clinic property, damaging clinic property, or using violence or threats of violence against the clinics, their employees, or their patients. * * *

The Supreme Court reviewed this decision to determine "whether petitioners committed extortion within the meaning of the Hobbs Act, 18 U.S.C. § 1951." The decision, written by Chief Justice Rehnquist found that "[b]ecause all of the predicate acts supporting the jury's finding of a RICO violation must be reversed, the judgment that petitioners violated RICO must also be reversed. Without an underlying RICO violation, the injunction issued by the District Court must necessarily be vacated." Scheidler v. National Organization for Women, Inc. 537 U.S.393 ,123 S.Ct. 1057, 154 L.Ed.2d 991 (2003).

The case returned to the Supreme Court a third time when the Seventh Circuit determined that it need not direct the district court to dissolve the injunction because the alleged acts of violence could be the basis for a Hobbs Act violation. **Scheidler v. National Organization for Women, Inc.**, 547 U.S. 9 (2006). The Court rejected that reading of the Hobbs Act:

> The question, as we have said, concerns the meaning of the phrase that modifies the term "physical violence," namely, the words "in furtherance of a plan or purpose to do anything in violation of this section." Do those words refer to violence (1) that furthers a plan or purpose to "affec[t] commerce ... by robbery or extortion," or to violence (2) that furthers a plan or purpose simply to "affec[t] commerce"? We believe the former, more restrictive, reading of the text-the reading that ties the violence to robbery or extortion-is correct.

> For one thing, the language of the statute makes the more restrictive reading the more natural one. The text that precedes the physical violence clause does not forbid obstructing, delaying, or affecting commerce (or the movement of any article or commodity in commerce); rather, it forbids obstructing, delaying, or affecting commerce " by robbery or extortion." Ibid. (emphasis added). This language means that behavior that obstructs, delays, or affects commerce is a "violation" of the statute only if that behavior also involves robbery or extortion (or related attempts or conspiracies). Consequently, the reference in the physical violence clause to actions or threats of violence "in furtherance of a plan or purpose to do anything in violation of this section" (emphasis added) would seem to mean acts or threats of violence in furtherance of a plan or purpose to engage in robbery or extortion, for that is the only kind of behavior that the section otherwise makes a violation.

The Court directed entry of a judgment in favor of the defendants because of the failure to allege a RICO violation through the Hobbs Act.

6. RICO Injury

ANZA v. IDEAL STEEL SUPPLY CORP.
547 U.S. 451, 126 S.Ct. 1991, 164 L.Ed.2d 720 (2006)

Justice KENNEDY delivered the opinion of the Court.

The Racketeer Influenced and Corrupt Organizations Act (RICO) prohibits certain conduct involving a "pattern of racketeering activity." One of RICO's enforcement mechanisms is a private right of action, available to "[a]ny person injured in his business or property by reason of a violation" of the Act's substantive restrictions. § 1964(c).

In Holmes v. Securities Investor Protection Corporation, 503 U.S. 258 (1992), this Court held that a plaintiff may sue under § 1964(c) only if the alleged RICO violation was the proximate cause of the plaintiff's injury. The instant case requires us to apply the principles discussed in *Holmes* to a dispute between two competing businesses.

* * * Respondent Ideal Steel Supply Corporation (Ideal) sells steel mill products along with related supplies and services. It operates two store locations in New York, one in Queens and the other in the Bronx. Petitioner National Steel Supply, Inc. (National), owned by petitioners Joseph and Vincent Anza, is Ideal's principal competitor. National offers a similar array of products and services, and it, too, operates one store in Queens and one in the Bronx.

Ideal sued petitioners in the United States District Court for the Southern District of New York. It claimed petitioners were engaged in an unlawful racketeering scheme aimed at "gain[ing] sales and market share at Ideal's expense." According to Ideal, National adopted a practice of failing to charge the requisite New York sales tax to cash-paying customers, even when conducting transactions that were not exempt from sales tax under state law. This practice allowed National to reduce its prices without affecting its profit margin. Petitioners allegedly submitted fraudulent tax returns to the New York State Department of Taxation and Finance in an effort to conceal their conduct.

Ideal's amended complaint contains, as relevant here, two RICO claims. The claims assert that petitioners, by submitting the fraudulent tax returns, committed various acts of mail fraud (when they sent the returns by mail) and wire fraud (when they sent them electronically). Mail fraud and wire fraud are forms of "racketeering activity" for purposes of RICO. Petitioners' conduct allegedly constituted a "pattern of racketeering activity," because the fraudulent returns were submitted on an ongoing and regular basis.

Ideal asserts in its first cause of action that Joseph and Vincent Anza violated § 1962(c), which makes it unlawful for "any person employed by or associated with any enterprise engaged in, or the activities of which affect, interstate or foreign commerce, to conduct or participate, directly or indirectly, in the conduct of such enterprise's affairs through a pattern of racketeering activity or collection of unlawful debt." The complaint states that the Anzas' goal, which they achieved, was to give National a competitive advantage over Ideal.

The second cause of action is asserted against all three petitioners. It alleges a violation of § 1962(a), which makes it unlawful for any person who has received income derived from a pattern of racketeering activity "to use or invest" that income "in acquisition of any interest in, or the establishment or operation of," an enterprise engaged in or affecting interstate or foreign commerce. As described in the complaint, petitioners used funds generated by their fraudulent tax scheme to open National's Bronx location. The opening of this new facility caused Ideal to lose "significant business and market share."

Petitioners moved to dismiss Ideal's complaint under Federal Rules of Civil Procedure 12(b)(6) and 9(b). The District Court granted the Rule 12(b)(6) motion, holding that the complaint failed to state a claim upon which relief could be granted. The court began from the proposition that to assert a RICO claim predicated on mail fraud or wire fraud, a plaintiff must have relied on the defendant's misrepresentations. Ideal not having alleged that it relied on petitioners' false tax returns, the court concluded Ideal could not go forward with its RICO claims.

Ideal appealed, and the Court of Appeals for the Second Circuit vacated the District Court's judgment. Addressing Ideal's § 1962(c) claim, the court held that where a complaint alleges a pattern of racketeering activity "that was intended to and did give the defendant a competitive advantage over the plaintiff, the complaint adequately pleads proximate cause, and the plaintiff has standing to pursue a civil RICO claim." This is the case, the court explained, "even where the scheme depended on fraudulent communications directed to and relied on by a third party rather than the plaintiff." [The Second Circuit reached the same conclusion regarding the § 1962(a) claim.] * * *

Our analysis begins — and, as will become evident, largely ends — with *Holmes*. That case arose from a complaint filed by the Securities Investor Protection Corporation (SIPC), a private corporation with a duty to reimburse the customers of registered broker-dealers who became unable to meet their financial obligations. SIPC claimed that the petitioner, Robert Holmes, conspired with others to manipulate stock prices. When the market detected the fraud, the share prices plummeted, and the "decline caused [two] broker-dealers' financial difficulties resulting in their eventual liquidation and SIPC's advance of nearly $13 million to cover their customers' claims." SIPC sued on several theories, including that Holmes participated in the conduct of an enterprise's affairs through a pattern of racketeering activity in violation of § 1962(c) and conspired to do so in violation of § 1962(d).

The Court held that SIPC could not maintain its RICO claims against Holmes for his alleged role in the scheme. The decision relied on a careful interpretation of § 1964(c), which provides a civil cause of action to persons injured "by reason of" a defendant's RICO violation. The Court recognized the phrase "by reason of" could be read broadly to require merely that the claimed violation was a "but for" cause of the plaintiff's injury. It rejected this reading, however, noting the "unlikelihood that Congress meant to allow all factually injured plaintiffs to recover."

Proper interpretation of § 1964(c) required consideration of the statutory history, which revealed that "Congress modeled § 1964(c) on the civil-action provision of the federal antitrust laws, § 4 of the Clayton Act." In Associated Gen. Contractors of Cal., Inc. v. Carpenters, 459 U.S. 519 (1983), the Court held that "a plaintiff's right to sue under § 4 required a showing that the defendant's violation not only was a 'but for' cause of his injury, but was the proximate cause as well."   This reasoning, the Court noted in *Holmes*,"applies just as readily to § 1964(c)."

The *Holmes* Court turned to the common-law foundations of the proximate-cause requirement, and specifically the "demand for some direct relation between the injury asserted and the injurious conduct alleged." It concluded that even if SIPC were subrogated to the rights of certain aggrieved customers, the RICO claims could not satisfy this requirement of directness. The deficiency, the Court explained, was that "the link is too remote between the stock manipulation alleged and the customers' harm, being purely contingent on the harm suffered by the broker-dealers."

Applying the principles of *Holmes* to the present case, we conclude Ideal cannot maintain its claim based on § 1962(c). Section 1962(c), as noted above, forbids conducting or participating in the conduct of an enterprise's affairs through a pattern of racketeering activity. The Court has indicated the compensable injury flowing from a violation of that provision "necessarily is the harm caused by predicate acts sufficiently related to constitute a pattern, for the essence of the violation is the commission of those acts in connection with the conduct of an enterprise." Sedima, S.P.R.L. v. Imrex Co., 473 U.S. 479 (1985).

Ideal's theory is that Joseph and Vincent Anza harmed it by defrauding the New York tax authority and using the proceeds from the fraud to offer lower prices designed to attract more customers. The RICO violation alleged by Ideal is that the Anzas conducted National's affairs through a pattern of mail fraud and wire fraud. The direct victim of this conduct was the State of New York, not Ideal. It was the State that was being defrauded and the State that lost tax revenue as a result.

The proper referent of the proximate-cause analysis is an alleged practice of conducting National's business through a pattern of defrauding the State. To be sure, Ideal asserts it suffered its own harms when the Anzas failed to charge customers for the applicable sales tax. The cause of Ideal's asserted harms, however, is a set of actions (offering lower prices) entirely distinct from the alleged RICO violation (defrauding the State). The attenuation between the plaintiff's harms and the claimed RICO violation arises from a different source in this case than in *Holmes*, where the alleged violations were linked to the asserted harms only through the broker-dealers' inability to meet their financial obligations. Nevertheless, the absence of proximate causation is equally clear in both cases.

This conclusion is confirmed by considering the directness requirement's underlying premises. One motivating principle is the difficulty that can arise when a court attempts to ascertain the damages caused by some remote action. The instant case is illustrative. The injury Ideal alleges is its own loss of sales resulting from National's decreased prices for cash-paying customers. National, however, could have lowered its prices for any number of reasons unconnected to the asserted pattern of fraud. It may have received a cash inflow from some other source or concluded that the additional sales would justify a smaller profit margin. Its lowering of prices in no sense required it to defraud the state tax authority. Likewise, the fact that a company commits tax fraud does not mean the company will lower its prices; the additional cash could go anywhere from asset acquisition to research and development to dividend payouts.

There is, in addition, a second discontinuity between the RICO violation and the asserted injury. Ideal's lost sales could have resulted from factors other than petitioners' alleged acts of fraud. Businesses lose and gain customers for many reasons, and it would require a complex assessment to establish what portion of Ideal's lost sales were the product of National's decreased prices.

The attenuated connection between Ideal's injury and the Anzas' injurious conduct thus implicates fundamental concerns expressed in *Holmes*. Notwithstanding the lack of any appreciable risk of duplicative recoveries, which is another consideration relevant to the proximate-cause inquiry, these concerns help to illustrate why Ideal's alleged injury was not the direct result of a RICO violation. Further illustrating this point is the speculative nature of the proceedings that would follow if Ideal were permitted to maintain its claim. A court considering the claim would need to begin by calculating the portion of National's price drop attributable to the alleged pattern of racketeering activity. It next would have to calculate the portion of Ideal's lost sales attributable to the relevant part of the price drop. The element of proximate causation recognized in *Holmes* is meant to prevent these types of intricate, uncertain inquiries from overrunning RICO litigation. It has particular resonance when applied to claims brought by economic competitors, which, if left unchecked, could blur the line between RICO and the antitrust laws.

The requirement of a direct causal connection is especially warranted where the immediate victims of an alleged RICO violation can be expected to vindicate the laws by pursuing their own claims. Again, the instant case is instructive. Ideal accuses the Anzas of defrauding the State of New York out of a substantial amount of money. If the allegations are true, the State can be expected to pursue appropriate remedies. The adjudication of the State's claims, moreover, would be relatively straightforward; while it may be difficult to determine facts such as the number of sales Ideal lost due to National's tax practices, it is considerably easier to make the initial calculation of how much tax revenue the Anzas withheld from the State. There is no need to broaden the universe of actionable harms to permit RICO suits by parties who have been injured only indirectly.

The Court of Appeals reached a contrary conclusion, apparently reasoning that because the Anzas allegedly sought to gain a competitive advantage over Ideal, it is immaterial whether they took an indirect route to accomplish their goal. This rationale does not accord with *Holmes*. A RICO plaintiff cannot circumvent the proximate-cause requirement simply by claiming that the defendant's aim was to increase market share at a competitor's expense. When a court evaluates a RICO claim for proximate causation, the central question it must ask is whether the alleged violation led directly to the plaintiff's injuries. In the instant case, the answer is no. We hold that Ideal's § 1962(c) claim does not satisfy the requirement of proximate causation. * * *

[The concurring opinion of Justice Scalia is deleted.]

Justice THOMAS, concurring in part and dissenting in part.

The Court today limits the lawsuits that may be brought under the civil enforcement provision of the Racketeer Influenced and Corrupt Organizations Act (RICO or Act), by adopting a theory of proximate causation that is supported neither by the Act nor by our decision in Holmes v. Securities Investor Protection Corporation, on which the Court principally relies. The Court's stringent proximate-causation requirement succeeds in precluding recovery in cases alleging a violation of § 1962(c) that, like the present one, have nothing to do with organized crime, the target of the RICO statute. However, the Court's approach also eliminates recovery for plaintiffs whose injuries are precisely those that Congress aimed to remedy through the authorization of civil RICO suits. Because this frustration of congressional intent is directly contrary to the broad language Congress employed to confer a RICO cause of action, I respectfully dissent * * * .

The language of the civil RICO provision, which broadly permits recovery by "[a]ny person injured in his business or property by reason of a violation" of the Act's substantive restrictions, § 1964(c), plainly covers the lawsuit brought by respondent. Respondent alleges that he was injured in his business, and that this injury was the direct result of petitioners' violation of § 1962(c). In *Holmes*, however, we held that a RICO plaintiff is required to show that the RICO violation "not only was a 'but for' cause of his injury, but was the proximate cause as well." We employed the term "'proximate cause' to label generically the judicial tools used to limit a person's responsibility for the consequences of that person's own acts." These tools reflect "ideas of what justice demands, or of what is administratively possible and convenient."

Invoking one of the common-law proximate-cause considerations, we held that a RICO plaintiff must prove "some direct relation between the injury asserted and the injurious conduct alleged." Today the Court applies this formulation of proximate causation to conclude that the "attenuated and uncertain relationship" between the violation of § 1962(c) and Ideal's injury "cannot, consistent with Holmes' demand for directness, sustain Ideal's claim." But the Court's determination relies on a theory of "directness" distinct from that adopted by *Holmes*.

In *Holmes*, the Court explained that "a plaintiff who complained of harm flowing merely from the misfortunes visited upon a third person by the defendant's acts was generally said to stand at too remote a distance to recover." The plaintiff in *Holmes* was indirect in precisely this sense. The defendant was alleged to have participated in a stock manipulation scheme that disabled two broker-dealers from meeting their obligations to customers. Accordingly, the plaintiff, Securities Investor Protection Corporation (SIPC), had to advance nearly $13 million to cover the claims of customers of those broker-dealers. SIPC attempted to sue based on the claim that it was subrogated to the rights of those customers of the broker-dealers who did not purchase manipulated securities. We held that the nonpurchasing customers' injury was not proximately caused by the defendant's conduct, because "the conspirators have allegedly injured these customers only insofar as the stock manipulation first injured the broker-dealers and left them without the wherewithal to pay customers' claims."

Here, in contrast, it was not New York's injury that caused respondent's damages; rather, it was petitioners' own conduct-namely, their underpayment of tax-that permitted them to undercut respondent's prices and thereby take away its business. Indeed, the Court's acknowledgment that there is no appreciable risk of duplicative recovery here, in contrast to *Holmes*, is effectively a concession that petitioners' damages are not indirect, as that term is used in *Holmes*. The mere fact that New York is a direct victim of petitioners' RICO violation does not preclude Ideal's claim that it too is a direct victim. Because the petitioners' tax underpayment directly caused respondent's injury, Holmes does not bar respondent's recovery.

The Court nonetheless contends that respondent has failed to demonstrate proximate cause. It does so by relying on our observation in *Holmes* that the directness requirement is appropriate because "[t]he less direct an injury is, the more difficult it becomes to ascertain the amount of a plaintiff's damages attributable to the violation, as distinct from other, independent, factors." In *Holmes*, we noted that it would be hard for the District Court to determine how much of the broker-dealers' failure to pay their customers was due to the fraud and how much was due to other factors affecting the broker-dealers' business success. The Court contends that here, as in *Holmes*, it is difficult to "ascertain the damages caused by some remote action."

The Court's reliance on the difficulty of ascertaining the amount of Ideal's damages caused by petitioners' unlawful acts to label those damages indirect is misguided. *Holmes* and *Associated General Contractors* simply held that one reason that indirect injuries should not be compensable is that such injuries are difficult to ascertain. We did not adopt the converse proposition that any injuries that are difficult to ascertain must be classified as indirect for purposes of determining proximate causation. * * *

As a result, after today, civil RICO plaintiffs that suffer precisely the kind of injury that motivated the adoption of the civil RICO provision will be unable to obtain relief. If this result was compelled by the text of the statute, the interference with congressional intent would be unavoidable. Given that the language is not even fairly susceptible of such a reading, however, I cannot agree with this frustration of congressional intent. * * *

[The opinion of Justice Breyer concurring in part and dissenting in part is deleted.]

C. PATTERN OF RACKETEERING

H.J. INC. v. NORTHWESTERN BELL TELEPHONE CO.
492 U.S. 229, 109 S.Ct. 2893, 106 L.Ed.2d 195 (1989)

Justice BRENNAN delivered the opinion of the Court.

* * * Petitioners, customers of respondent Northwestern Bell Telephone Co., filed this putative class action in 1986 in the District Court for the District of Minnesota. Petitioners alleged violations of §§ 1962(a), (b), (c), and (d) by Northwestern Bell and the other respondents—some of the telephone company's officers and employees, various members of the Minnesota Public Utilities Commission (MPUC), and other unnamed individuals and corporations—and sought an injunction and treble damages under RICO's civil liability provisions, §§ 1964(a) and (c).

The MPUC is the state body responsible for determining the rates that Northwestern Bell may charge. Petitioners' five-count complaint alleged that between 1980 and 1986 Northwestern Bell sought to influence members of the MPUC in the performance of their duties—and in fact caused them to approve rates for the company in excess of a fair and reasonable amount—by making cash payments to commissioners, negotiating with them regarding future employment, and paying for parties and meals, for tickets to sporting events and the like, and for airline tickets. Based upon these factual allegations, petitioners alleged in their first count a pendent state-law claim, asserting that Northwestern Bell violated the Minnesota bribery statute, Minn.Stat. § 609.42 (1988), as well as state common law prohibiting bribery. They also raised four separate claims under § 1962 of RICO. Count II alleged that, in violation of § 1962(a), Northwestern Bell derived income from a pattern of racketeering activity involving predicate acts of bribery and used this income to engage in its business as an interstate "enterprise." Count III claimed a violation of § 1962(b), in that, through this same pattern of racketeering activity, respondents acquired an interest in or control of the MPUC, which was also an interstate "enterprise." In Count IV, petitioners asserted that respondents participated in the conduct and affairs of the MPUC through this pattern of racketeering activity, contrary to § 1962(c). Finally, Count V alleged that respondents conspired together to violate §§ 1962(a), (b), and (c), thereby contravening § 1962(d).

The District Court granted respondents' Federal Rule of Civil Procedure 12(b)(6) motion, dismissing the complaint for failure to state a claim upon which relief could be granted. 648 F.Supp. 419 (Minn.1986). The court found that "[e]ach of the fraudulent acts alleged by [petitioners] was committed in furtherance of a single scheme to influence MPUC commissioners to the detriment of Northwestern Bell's ratepayers." * * * The Court of Appeals for the Eighth Circuit affirmed the dismissal of petitioners' complaint, confirming that under Eighth Circuit precedent "[a] single fraudulent effort or scheme is insufficient" to establish a pattern of racketeering activity, 829 F.2d 648, 650 (1987), and agreeing with the District Court that petitioners' complaint alleged only a single scheme. Two members of the panel suggested in separate concurrences, however, that the Court of Appeals should reconsider its test for a RICO pattern. Most Courts of Appeals have rejected the Eighth Circuit's interpretation of RICO's pattern concept to require an allegation and proof of multiple schemes, and we granted certiorari to resolve this conflict. We now reverse. * * *

In Sedima, [p.221] this Court rejected a restrictive interpretation of § 1964(c) that would have made it a condition for maintaining a civil RICO action both that the defendant had already been convicted of a predicate racketeering act or of a RICO violation, and that plaintiff show a special racketeering injury. * * * [W]e suggested that RICO's expansive uses "appear to be primarily the result of the breadth of the predicate offenses, in particular the inclusion of wire, mail, and securities fraud, and the failure of Congress and the courts to develop a meaningful concept of 'pattern' "—both factors that apply to criminal as well as civil applications of the Act. Congress has done nothing in the interim further to illuminate RICO's key requirement of a pattern of racketeering; and as the plethora of different views expressed by the Courts of Appeals since Sedima demonstrates, developing a meaningful concept of "pattern" within the existing statutory framework has proved to be no easy task. * * *

We begin, of course, with RICO's text, in which Congress followed a "pattern [of] utilizing terms and concepts of breadth." Russello v. United States, 464 U.S. 16, 21 (1983). As we remarked in Sedima, the section of the statute headed "definitions," 18 U.S.C. § 1961, does not so much define a pattern of racketeering activity as state a minimum necessary condition for the existence of such a pattern. Unlike other provisions in § 1961 that tell us what various concepts used in the Act "mean," 18 U.S.C. § 1961(5) says of the phrase "pattern of racketeering activity" only that it "requires at least two acts of racketeering activity, one of which occurred after [October 15, 1970,] and the last of which occurred within ten years (excluding any period of imprisonment) after the commission of a prior act of racketeering activity." It thus places an outer limit on the concept of a pattern of racketeering activity that is broad indeed.

Section 1961(5) does indicate that Congress envisioned circumstances in which no more than two predicates would be necessary to establish a pattern of racketeering—otherwise it would have drawn a narrower boundary to RICO liability, requiring proof of a greater number of predicates. But, at the same time, the statement that a pattern "requires at least" two predicates implies "that while two acts are necessary, they may not be sufficient."

Section 1961(5) concerns only the minimum number of predicates necessary to establish a pattern; and it assumes that there is something to a RICO pattern beyond simply the number of predicate acts involved. The legislative history bears out this interpretation, for the principal sponsor of the Senate bill expressly indicated that "proof of two acts of racketeering activity, without more, does not establish a pattern." 116 Cong.Rec. 18940 (1970) (statement of Sen. McClellan). Section § 1961(5) does not identify, though, these additional prerequisites for establishing the existence of a RICO pattern.

In addition to § 1961(5), there is the key phrase "pattern of racketeering activity" itself, from § 1962, and we must "start with the assumption that the legislative purpose is expressed by the ordinary meaning of the words used." In normal usage, the word "pattern" here would be taken to require more than just a multiplicity of racketeering predicates. A "pattern" is an "arrangement or order of things or activity," 11 Oxford English Dictionary 357 (2d ed. 1989), and the mere fact that there are a number of predicates is no guarantee that they fall into any arrangement or order. It is not the number of predicates but the relationship that they bear to each other or to some external organizing principle that renders them "ordered" or "arranged." The text of RICO conspicuously fails anywhere to identify, however, forms of relationship or external principles to be used in determining whether racketeering activity falls into a pattern for purposes of the Act.

It is reasonable to infer, from this absence of any textual identification of sorts of pattern that would satisfy § 1962's requirement, in combination with the very relaxed limits to the pattern concept fixed in § 1961(5), that Congress intended to take a flexible approach, and envisaged that a pattern might be demonstrated by reference to a range of different ordering principles or relationships between predicates, within the expansive bounds set. * * *

The legislative history, which we discussed in Sedima, shows that Congress indeed had a fairly flexible concept of a pattern in mind. A pattern is not formed by "sporadic activity," and a person cannot "be subjected to the sanctions of title IX simply for committing two widely separated and isolated criminal offenses." Instead, "[t]he term 'pattern' itself requires the showing of a relationship" between the predicates, and of "'the threat of continuing activity.'" "It is this factor of continuity plus relationship which combines to produce a pattern." (emphasis added). RICO's legislative history reveals Congress' intent that to prove a pattern of racketeering activity a plaintiff or prosecutor must show that the racketeering predicates are related, and that they amount to or pose a threat of continued criminal activity.

For analytic purposes these two constituents of RICO's pattern requirement must be stated separately, though in practice their proof will often overlap. The element of relatedness is the easier to define, for we may take guidance from a provision elsewhere in the Organized Crime Control Act of 1970 (OCCA), of which RICO formed Title IX. * * * As we noted in Sedima, Congress defined Title X's pattern requirement solely in terms of the relationship of the defendant's criminal acts one to another: "[C]riminal conduct forms a pattern if it embraces criminal acts that have the same or similar purposes, results, participants, victims, or methods of commission, or otherwise are interrelated by distinguishing characteristics and are not isolated events." § 3575(e). We have no reason to suppose that Congress had in mind for RICO's pattern of racketeering component any more constrained a notion of the relationships between predicates that would suffice.

RICO's legislative history tells us, however, that the relatedness of racketeering activities is not alone enough to satisfy § 1962's pattern element. To establish a RICO pattern it must also be shown that the predicates themselves amount to, or that they otherwise constitute a threat of, continuing racketeering activity. As to this continuity requirement, § 3575(e) is of no assistance. * * *

"Continuity" is both a closed- and open-ended concept, referring either to a closed period of repeated conduct, or to past conduct that by its nature projects into the future with a threat of repetition. It is, in either case, centrally a temporal concept—and particularly so in the RICO context, where what must be continuous, RICO's predicate acts or offenses, and the relationship these predicates must bear one to another, are distinct requirements. A party alleging a RICO violation may demonstrate continuity over a closed period by proving a series of related predicates extending over a substantial period of time. Predicate acts extending over a few weeks or months and threatening no future criminal conduct do not satisfy this requirement: Congress was concerned in RICO with long-term criminal conduct. Often a RICO action will be brought before continuity can be established in this way. In such cases, liability depends on whether the threat of continuity is demonstrated.   * * *

The limits of the relationship and continuity concepts that combine to define a RICO pattern, and the precise methods by which relatedness and continuity or its threat may be proved, cannot be fixed in advance with such clarity that it will always be apparent whether in a particular case a "pattern of racketeering activity" exists. The development of these concepts must await future cases, absent a decision by Congress to revisit RICO to provide clearer guidance as to the Act's intended scope.   * * *

Under the analysis we have set forth above, and consistent with the allegations in their complaint, petitioners may be able to prove that the multiple predicates alleged constitute "a pattern of racketeering activity," in that they satisfy the requirements of relationship and continuity. The acts of bribery alleged are said to be related by a common purpose, to influence commissioners in carrying out their duties in order to win approval of unfairly and unreasonably high rates for Northwestern Bell. Furthermore, petitioners claim that the racketeering predicates occurred with some frequency over at least a 6-year period, which may be sufficient to satisfy the continuity requirement. Alternatively, a threat of continuity of racketeering activity might be established at trial by showing that the alleged bribes were a regular way of conducting Northwestern Bell's ongoing business, or a regular way of conducting or participating in the conduct of the alleged and ongoing RICO enterprise, the MPUC.

The Court of Appeals thus erred in affirming the District Court's dismissal of petitioners' complaint for failure to plead "a pattern of racketeering activity." The judgment is reversed, and the case is remanded for further proceedings consistent with this opinion.

It is so ordered.

Justice SCALIA, with whom THE CHIEF JUSTICE, Justice O'CONNOR, and Justice KENNEDY join, concurring in the judgment.

* * * Elevating to the level of statutory text a phrase taken from the legislative history, the Court counsels the lower courts: " 'continuity plus relationship.' " This seems to me about as helpful to the conduct of their affairs as "life is a fountain." Of the two parts of this talismanic phrase, the relatedness requirement is said to be the "easier to define," yet here is the Court's definition, in toto: " '[C]riminal conduct forms a pattern if it embraces criminal acts that have the same or similar purposes, results, participants, victims, or methods of commission, or otherwise are interrelated by distinguishing characteristics and are not isolated events.' " This definition has the feel of being solidly rooted in law, since it is a direct quotation of 18 U.S.C. § 3575(e). Unfortunately, if normal (and sensible) rules of statutory construction were followed, the existence of § 3575(e)—which is the definition contained in another title of the Act that was explicitly not rendered applicable to RICO—suggests that whatever "pattern" might mean in RICO, it assuredly does not mean that. "[W]here Congress includes particular language in one section of a statute but omits it in another section of the same Act, it is generally presumed that Congress acts intentionally and purposely in the disparate inclusion or exclusion." But that does not really matter, since § 3575(e) is utterly uninformative anyway. It hardly closes in on the target to know that "relatedness" refers to acts that are related by "purposes, results, participants, victims, ... methods of commission, or [just in case that is not vague enough] otherwise." Is the fact that the victims of both predicate acts were women enough? Or that both acts had the purpose of enriching the defendant? Or that the different coparticipants of the defendant in both acts were his coemployees? I doubt that the lower courts will find the Court's instructions much more helpful than telling them to look for a "pattern"— which is what the statute already says.

The Court finds "continuity" more difficult to define precisely. "Continuity," it says, "is both a closed- and open-ended concept, referring either to a closed period of repeated conduct, or to past conduct that by its nature projects into the future with a threat of repetition." I have no idea what this concept of a "closed period of repeated conduct" means. Virtually all allegations of racketeering activity, in both civil and criminal suits, will relate to past periods that are "closed" (unless one expects plaintiff or the prosecutor to establish that the defendant not only committed the crimes he did, but is still committing them), and all of them must relate to conduct that is "repeated," because of RICO's multiple-act requirement.   * * *

It is, however, unfair to be so critical of the Court's effort, because I would be unable to provide an interpretation of RICO that gives significantly more guidance concerning its application. It is clear to me from the prologue of the statute, which describes a relatively narrow focus upon "organized crime," that the word "pattern" in the phrase "pattern of racketeering activity" was meant to import some requirement beyond the mere existence of multiple predicate acts. Thus, when § 1961(5) says that a pattern "requires at least two acts of racketeering activity" it is describing what is needful but not sufficient. * * * But what that something more is, is beyond me. As I have suggested, it is also beyond the Court. Today's opinion has added nothing to improve our prior guidance, which has created a kaleidoscope of Circuit positions, except to clarify that RICO may in addition be violated when there is a "threat of continuity." It seems to me this increases rather than removes the vagueness. There is no reason to believe that the Courts of Appeals will be any more unified in the future, than they have in the past, regarding the content of this law.

That situation is bad enough with respect to any statute, but it is intolerable with respect to RICO. For it is not only true, as Justice Marshall [dissenting opinion] commented in Sedima, that our interpretation of RICO has "quite simply revolutionize[d] private litigation" and "validate[d] the federalization of broad areas of state common law of frauds," so that clarity and predictability in RICO's civil applications are particularly important; but it is also true that RICO, since it has criminal applications as well, must, even in its civil applications, possess the degree of certainty required for criminal laws. No constitutional challenge to this law has been raised in the present case, and so that issue is not before us. That the highest Court in the land has been unable to derive from this statute anything more than today's meager guidance bodes ill for the day when that challenge is presented. * * *

NOTES AND QUESTIONS

1. *Pattern*. In **Apparel Art International Inc. v. Jacobson**, 967 F.2d 720 (1st Cir. 1992), the First Circuit considered how to define what constitutes the requisite continuity for a pattern:

> We can begin with the Supreme Court's statement that, to prove a "pattern of racketeering activity," one must show separate predicate acts that 1) are "related," and 2) "amount to or pose a threat of continued criminal activity." We can be reasonably certain that this definition does not encompass a single criminal event, a single

criminal episode, a single "crime" (in the ordinary, nontechnical sense of that word). (We deliberately employ a vague term like "episode," for we do not want to use a word such as "scheme," which might have a technical meaning.) For example, a single (interstate) bank robbery consists of several different parts (say, using a gun, threatening a teller, stealing a getaway car, perhaps abducting the teller as well, and eventually lying about participation). Some of those separate parts may themselves constitute separate criminal acts or "crimes" (in the technical sense that each, separately, violates a specific statute). Yet, those several separate criminal parts, taken together, do not generally make out a "pattern." To hold otherwise would mean that many individual bank robberies, frauds, drug sales, embezzlements, and other crimes as well would automatically fall within the scope of the RICO statute, a result contrary to RICO's basic purpose. One might express the fact that a single criminal episode, or event, is not a "pattern" by stating that its parts, taken together, do not "amount to or pose a threat of continued criminal activity." Or, one might risk circularity and simply state that those parts do not bear to each other the relevant ("pattern of racketeering") relationship. But, however courts express the point, they have consistently held that a single episode does not constitute a "pattern," even if that single episode involves behavior that amounts to several crimes (for example, several unlawful mailings).

Moving now to the opposite extreme, we can also be reasonably certain that, to show a "pattern," one must do more than simply show several different but totally "separate" instances of criminal conduct taking place over time. One 1982 securities fraud and one 1987 drug importation, for example, presumably constitute two separate instances of "racketeering activity." But, if the two separate securities fraud and drug episodes take place several years apart and involve different victims, methods, purposes, and (almost all) participants, they may well lack the requisite "racketeering" relationship to each other. Thus, they would not constitute a "pattern of racketeering activity."

In **Jackson v. BellSouth Telecommunications**, 372 F.3d 1250 (11th Cir. 2004), the Eleventh Circuit found that the closed-end pattern that lasted only nine months was insufficient to establish the continuity aspect of the pattern of racketeering activity. The court stated:

While the plaintiffs generally alleged that the defendants committed mail and wire fraud violations that extended "over a substantial period of time," the specific incidents they actually charged began only on April 22, 1997, and ended, at the very latest, sometime in January 1998. The plaintiffs maintain that no bright-line rule has been established definitively stating that nine months is too short a period to establish a "substantial period of time," for the purposes of closed-ended continuity. While the plaintiffs are correct that no court has unequivocally declared a minimum period of time that can be considered "substantial," the great weight of authority suggests that nine months is a wholly insufficient interlude. * * *

The overwhelming weight of case authority suggests that nine months is not an adequately substantial period of time. Moreover, the alleged racketeering activity was related to the settlement of a single lawsuit, and, notably, was not designed to perpetrate racketeering with respect to a series of cases. Indeed, in cases like this one, where the RICO allegations concern only a single scheme with a discrete goal, the courts have refused to find a closed-ended pattern of racketeering even when the scheme took place over longer periods of time.

2. *Relationship*. In **United States v. Indelicato**, 865 F.2d 1370 (2d Cir. 1989), the Second Circuit explained that the issue of relationship is based on the "interrelationship between acts, suggesting the existence of a pattern, [that] may be established in a number of ways. These include proof of their temporal proximity, or common goals, or similarity of methods, or repetitions. The degree to which these factors establish a pattern may depend on the degree of proximity, or any similarities in goals or methodology, or the number of repetitions." The court distinguished between proof of the pattern element and whether there was an enterprise through an association-in-fact, asserting that "relationship and continuity are necessary characteristics of a RICO enterprise. Neither the statutory definition of enterprise nor the legislative history suggests that those concepts pertain to the notion of enterprise . . . We conclude that relatedness and continuity are essentially characteristics of activity rather than of enterprise."

3. *Predicate Acts*. Both state and federal offenses can serve as predicate acts to form a pattern of racketeering. When using a state predicate offense, it is necessary that the offense be chargeable under state law and that it have a punishment of more than one year imprisonment. The label used by the state legislature to describe the offense is not crucial to it being included under RICO. For example, violations of the Illinois official misconduct statute, which prohibits "a public official or employee" from "solicit[ing] or knowingly accept[ing] for the performance of any act a fee or reward which he knows is not authorized by law," fall under bribery in § 1961(1). See United States v. Garner, 837 F.2d 1404 (7th Cir. 1987), where the court stated, "The labels placed on a state statute do not determine whether that statute proscribes bribery for purposes of the RICO statute. Congress intended for 'bribery' to be defined generically when it included bribery as a predicate act. * * * Thus any statute that proscribes conduct which could be generically defined as bribery can be the basis for a predicate act."

4. *Pleading Mail and Wire Fraud as Predicate Acts*. The two most commonly alleged predicate acts for the RICO pattern of racketeering activity are violations of the mail fraud (§ 1341) and wire fraud (§ 1343) statutes. These two provisions cover a wide array of dishonest and questionable

business practices, so they can be alleged for many business practices, such as breach of contract, overcharges, and submission of false information. Some lower courts had imposed an actual reliance requirement for civil RICO claims based on the two fraud statutes, importing this element from common law fraud even though it is not required to prove a violation of §§ 1341 and 1343. In **Bridge v. Phoenix Bond & Indemnity Co.**, 128 S.Ct. 2131 (2008), the Supreme Court rejected the actual reliance limitation on RICO in a case in which the false statements were made to a city government to obtain a greater share of properties being sold at a tax auction. While the plaintiffs did not directly receive the alleged false statements mailed by the defendants to the city, they were the victims of them, and the Court held:

> If petitioners' proposed requirement of first-party reliance seems to come out of nowhere, there is a reason: Nothing on the face of the relevant statutory provisions imposes such a requirement. Using the mail to execute or attempt to execute a scheme to defraud is indictable as mail fraud, and hence a predicate act of racketeering under RICO, even if no one relied on any misrepresentation. See Neder v. United States, 527 U.S. 1 (1999) ("The common-law requiremen[t] of 'justifiable reliance' . . . plainly ha[s] no place in the [mail, wire, or bank] fraud statutes"). And one can conduct the affairs of a qualifying enterprise through a pattern of such acts without anyone relying on a fraudulent misrepresentation.

D. THE NEXUS REQUIREMENT

REVES v. ERNST & YOUNG
507 U.S.170, 113 S.Ct. 1163, 122 L.Ed.2d 525 (1993)

Justice BLACKMUN delivered the opinion of the Court.[1]

* * * The question presented is whether one must participate in the operation or management of the enterprise itself to be subject to liability under [section 1962 (c)]. * * *

The Farmer's Cooperative of Arkansas and Oklahoma, Inc. (the Co-op), began operating in western Arkansas and eastern Oklahoma in 1946. To raise money for operating expenses, the Co-op sold promissory notes payable to the holder on demand. * * * In 1952, the board appointed Jack White as general manager.

---

[1] Justice SCALIA and Justice THOMAS do not join Part IV-A of this opinion. [Part IV-A discussed how the legislative history of § 1962 supported the Court's holding.]

In January 1980, White began taking loans from the Co-op to finance the construction of a gasohol plant by his company, White Flame Fuels, Inc. By the end of 1980, White's debts to the Co-op totalled approximately $4 million. * * * At a board meeting on November 12, 1980, White proposed that the Co-op purchase White Flame. The board agreed. One month later, however, the Co-op filed a declaratory action against White and White Flame in Arkansas state court alleging that White actually had sold White Flame to the Co-op in February 1980. The complaint was drafted by White's attorneys and led to a consent decree relieving White of his debts and providing that the Co-op had owned White Flame since February 15, 1980.

White and Kuykendall [who served as both accountant for the Co-op and White Flame] were convicted of tax fraud in January 1981. Harry Erwin, the managing partner of Russell Brown and Company, an Arkansas accounting firm, testified for White, and shortly thereafter the Co-op retained Russell Brown to perform its 1981 financial audit. Joe Drozal, a partner in the Brown firm, was put in charge of the audit and Joe Cabaniss was selected to assist him. On January 2, 1982, Russell Brown and Company merged with Arthur Young and Company, which later became respondent Ernst & Young.

One of Drozal's first tasks in the audit was to determine White Flame's fixed-asset value. * * * Drozal concluded that the Co-op had owned White Flame from the start and that the plant should be valued at $4.5 million on its books.

On April 22, 1982, Arthur Young presented its 1981 audit report to the Co-op's board. In that audit's Note 9, Arthur Young expressed doubt whether the investment in White Flame could ever be recovered. Note 9 also observed that White Flame was sustaining operating losses averaging $100,000 per month. Arthur Young did not tell the board of its conclusion that the Co-op always had owned White Flame or that without that conclusion the Co-op was insolvent.

On May 27, the Co-op held its 1982 annual meeting. At that meeting, the Co- op, through Harry C. Erwin, a partner in Arthur Young, distributed to the members condensed financial statements. These included White Flame's $4.5 million asset value among its total assets but omitted the information contained in the audit's Note 9. * * * In response to questions, Erwin explained that the Co-op owned White Flame and that the plant had incurred approximately $1.2 million in losses but he revealed no other information relevant to the Co-op's true financial health.

The Co-op hired Arthur Young also to perform its 1982 audit. The 1982 report, presented to the board on March 7, 1983, was similar to the 1981 report and restated (this time in its Note 8) Arthur Young's doubt whether the investment in White Flame was recoverable. The gasohol plant again was valued at approximately $4.5 million and was responsible for the Co-op's showing a positive net worth. * * *

In February 1984, the Co-op experienced a slight run on its demand notes. On February 23, when it was unable to secure further financing, the Co-op filed for bankruptcy. As a result, the demand notes were frozen in the bankruptcy estate and were no longer redeemable at will by the noteholders. * * *

On February 14, 1985, the trustee in bankruptcy filed suit against 40 individuals and entities, including Arthur Young, on behalf of the Co-op and certain noteholders.[a] The District Court certified a class of noteholders, petitioners here, consisting of persons who had purchased demand notes between February 15, 1980, and February 23, 1984. Petitioners settled with all defendants except Arthur Young. * * * The District Court applied the test established by the Eighth Circuit in Bennett v. Berg, 710 F.2d 1361, 1364 (en banc) (1983), that § 1962(c) requires "some participation in the operation or management of the enterprise itself." The court ruled: "Plaintiffs have failed to show anything more than that the accountants reviewed a series of completed transactions, and certified the Co-op's records as fairly portraying its financial status as of a date three or four months preceding the meetings of the directors and the shareholders at which they presented their reports. We do not hesitate to declare that such activities fail to satisfy the degree of management required by Bennett v. Berg." * * *

The narrow question in this case is the meaning of the phrase "to conduct or participate, directly or indirectly, in the conduct of such enterprise's affairs." The word "conduct" is used twice, and it seems reasonable to give each use a similar construction. As a verb, "conduct" means to lead, run, manage, or direct. Webster's Third New International Dictionary 474 (1976). Petitioners urge us to read "conduct" as "carry on," so that almost any involvement in the affairs of an enterprise would satisfy the "conduct or participate" requirement. But context is important, and in the context of the phrase "to conduct . . . [an] enterprise's affairs," the word indicates some degree of direction.

The dissent agrees that, when "conduct" is used as a verb, "it is plausible to find in it a suggestion of control." The dissent prefers to focus on "conduct" as a noun, as in the phrase "participate, directly or indirectly, in the conduct of [an] enterprise's affairs." But unless one reads "conduct" to include an element of direction when used as a noun in this phrase, the word becomes superfluous. Congress could easily have written "participate, directly or indirectly, in [an] enterprise's affairs," but it chose to repeat the word "conduct." We conclude, therefore, that as both a noun and a verb in this subsection "conduct" requires an element of direction.

---

[a] "The class alleged in its complaint that Erwin, Drozal, and Cabaniss conducted or participated in the affairs of the co-op, committing both mail fraud and securities fraud, in violation of 18 U.S.C. § 1962(c), * * *." Arthur Young & Co. v. Reves, 937 F.2d 1310 (8th Cir. 1991).

The more difficult question is what to make of the word "participate." This Court previously has characterized this word as a "ter[m] . . . of breadth." Petitioners argue that Congress used "participate" as a synonym for "aid and abet." That would be a term of breadth indeed, for "aid and abet" "comprehends all assistance rendered by words, acts, encouragement, support, or presence." Black's Law Dictionary 68 (6th ed. 1990). But within the context of § 1962(c), "participate" appears to have a narrower meaning. We may mark the limits of what the term might mean by looking again at what Congress did not say. On the one hand, "to participate . . . in the conduct of . . . affairs" must be broader than "to conduct affairs" or the "participate" phrase would be superfluous. On the other hand, as we already have noted, "to participate . . . in the conduct of . . . affairs" must be narrower than "to participate in affairs" or Congress' repetition of the word "conduct" would serve no purpose. It seems that Congress chose a middle ground, consistent with a common understanding of the word "participate"—"to take part in." Webster's Third New International Dictionary 1646 (1976).

Once we understand the word "conduct" to require some degree of direction and the word "participate" to require some part in that direction, the meaning of § 1962(c) comes into focus. In order to "participate, directly or indirectly, in the conduct of such enterprise's affairs," one must have some part in directing those affairs. Of course, the word "participate" makes clear that RICO liability is not limited to those with primary responsibility for the enterprise's affairs, just as the phrase "directly or indirectly" makes clear that RICO liability is not limited to those with a formal position in the enterprise, but some part in directing the enterprise's affairs is required. The "operation or management" test expresses this requirement in a formulation that is easy to apply. * * *

[The Court then discussed the legislative history of § 1962 and concluded that] the legislative history confirms what we have already deduced from the language of § 1962(c)—that one is not liable under that provision unless one has participated in the operation or management of the enterprise itself. * * *

RICO's "liberal construction" clause does not require rejection of the "operation or management" test. Congress directed, by § 904(a) of Pub.L. 91-452, that the "provisions of this title shall be liberally construed to effectuate its remedial purposes." This clause obviously seeks to ensure that Congress' intent is not frustrated by an overly narrow reading of the statute, but it is not an invitation to apply RICO to new purposes that Congress never intended. Nor does the clause help us to determine what purposes Congress had in mind. Those must be gleaned from the statute through the normal means of interpretation. The clause " 'only serves as an aid for resolving an ambiguity; it is not to be used to beget one.' " In this case it is clear that Congress did not intend to extend RICO liability under § 1962(c) beyond those who participate in the operation or management of an enterprise through a pattern of racketeering activity.[8] * * *

Petitioners argue that the "operation or management" test is flawed because liability under § 1962(c) is not limited to upper management but may extend to "any person employed by or associated with [the] enterprise." We agree that liability under § 1962(c) is not limited to upper management, but we disagree that the "operation or management" test is inconsistent with this proposition. An enterprise is "operated" not just by upper management but also by lower-rung participants in the enterprise who are under the direction of upper management.[9] An enterprise also might be "operated" or "managed" by others "associated with" the enterprise who exert control over it as, for example, by bribery.

The United States also argues that the "operation or management" test is not consistent with § 1962(c) because it limits the liability of "outsiders" who have no official position within the enterprise. The United States correctly points out that RICO's major purpose was to attack the "infiltration of organized crime and racketeering into legitimate organizations," but its argument fails on several counts. First, it ignores the fact that § 1962 has four subsections. Infiltration of legitimate organizations by "outsiders" is clearly addressed in subsections (a) and (b), and the "operation or management" test that applies under subsection (c) in no way limits the application of subsections (a) and (b) to "outsiders." Second, § 1962(c) is limited to persons "employed by or associated with" an enterprise, suggesting a more limited reach than subsections (a) and (b), which do not contain such a restriction. Third, § 1962(c) cannot be interpreted to reach complete "outsiders" because liability depends on showing that the defendants conducted or participated in the conduct of the "enterprise's affairs," not just their own affairs. Of course, "outsiders" may be liable under § 1962(c) if they are "associated with" an enterprise and participate in the conduct of its affairs—that is, participate in the operation or management of the enterprise itself—but it would be consistent with neither the language nor the legislative history of § 1962(c) to interpret it as broadly as petitioners and the United States urge.

In sum, we hold that "to conduct or participate, directly or indirectly, in the conduct of such enterprise's affairs," § 1962(c), one must participate in the operation or management of the enterprise itself. * * *

---

[8] Because the meaning of the statute is clear from its language and legislative history, we have no occasion to consider the application of the rule of lenity. We note, however, that the rule of lenity would also favor the narrower "operation or management" test that we adopt.

[9] * * * We need not decide in this case how far § 1962(c) extends down the ladder of operation because it is clear that Arthur Young was not acting under the direction of the Co-ops officers or board.

Both the District Court and the Court of Appeals applied the standard we adopt today to the facts of this case, and both found that respondent was entitled to summary judgment. Neither petitioners nor the United States have argued that these courts misapplied the "operation or management" test. The dissent argues that by creating the Co-op's financial statements Arthur Young participated in the management of the Co-op because " 'financial statements are management's responsibility.' " Although the professional standards adopted by the accounting profession may be relevant, they do not define what constitutes management of an enterprise for the purposes of § 1962(c).

In this case, it is undisputed that Arthur Young relied upon existing Co-op records in preparing the 1981 and 1982 audit reports. The AICPA's professional standards state that an auditor may draft financial statements in whole or in part based on information from management's accounting system. It is also undisputed that Arthur Young's audit reports revealed to the Co-op's board that the value of the gasohol plant had been calculated based on the Co-op's investment in the plant. Thus, we only could conclude that Arthur Young participated in the operation or management of the Co-op itself if Arthur Young's failure to tell the Co-op's board that the plant should have been given its fair market value constituted such participation. We think that Arthur Young's failure in this respect is not sufficient to give rise to liability under § 1962(c).

The judgment of the Court of Appeals is affirmed.

Justice SOUTER, with whom Justice WHITE joins, dissenting.

In the word "conduct," the Court today finds a clear congressional mandate to limit RICO liability under 18 U.S.C. § 1962(c) to participants in the "operation or management" of a RICO enterprise. What strikes the Court as clear, however, looks at the very least hazy to me, and I accordingly find the statute's "liberal construction" provision not irrelevant, but dispositive. But even if I were to assume, with the majority, that the word "conduct" clearly imports some degree of direction or control into § 1962(c), I would have to say that the majority misapplies its own "operation or management" test to the facts presented here. I therefore respectfully dissent.

The word "conduct" occurs twice in § 1962(c), first as a verb, then as a noun.

> "It shall be unlawful for any person employed by or associated with any enterprise engaged in, or the activities of which affect, interstate or foreign commerce, to conduct or participate, directly or indirectly, in the conduct of such enterprise's affairs through a pattern of racketeering activity or collection of unlawful debt." 18 U.S.C. § 1962(c).

Although the Court is surely correct that the cognates should receive consistent readings, and correct again that "context is important" in coming to understand the sense of the terms intended by Congress, the majority goes astray in quoting only the verb form of "conduct" in its statement of the context for divining a meaning that must fit the noun usage as well. Thus, the majority reaches its pivotal conclusion that "in the context of the phrase 'to conduct ... [an] enterprise's affairs,' the word indicates some degree of direction." To be sure, if the statutory setting is so abbreviated as to limit consideration to the word as a verb, it is plausible to find in it a suggestion of control, as in the phrase "to conduct an orchestra." * * *

In any event, the context is not so limited, and several features of the full subsection at issue support a more inclusive construction of "conduct." The term, when used as a noun, is defined by the majority's chosen dictionary as, for example, "carrying forward" or "carrying out," Webster's Third New International Dictionary 473 (1976), phrases without any implication of direction or control. The suggestion of control is diminished further by the fact that § 1962(c) covers not just those "employed by" an enterprise, but those merely "associated with" it, as well. And associates (like employees) are prohibited not merely from conducting the affairs of an enterprise through a pattern of racketeering, not merely from participating directly in such unlawful conduct, but even from indirect participation in the conduct of an enterprise's affairs in such a manner. The very breadth of this prohibition renders the majority's reading of "conduct" rather awkward, for it is hard to imagine how the "operation or management" test would leave the statute with the capacity to reach the indirect participation of someone merely associated with an enterprise. I think, then, that this contextual examination shows "conduct" to have a long arm, unlimited by any requirement to prove that the activity includes an element of direction. But at the very least, the full context is enough to defeat the majority's conviction that the more restrictive interpretation of the word "conduct" is clearly the one intended.

What, then, if we call it a tie on the contextual analysis? The answer is that Congress has given courts faced with uncertain meaning a clear tie-breaker in RICO's "liberal construction" clause, which directs that the "provisions of this title shall be liberally construed to effectuate its remedial purposes." We have relied before on this "express admonition" to read RICO provisions broadly, and in this instance, the "liberal construction" clause plays its intended part, directing us to recognize the more inclusive definition of the word "conduct," free of any restricting element of direction or control. Because the Court of Appeals employed a narrower reading, I would reverse.

Even if I were to adopt the majority's view of § 1962(c), however, I still could not join the judgment, which seems to me unsupportable under the very "operation or management" test the Court announces. If Arthur Young had confined itself in this case to the role traditionally performed by an outside auditor, I could agree with the majority that Arthur Young took no part in the management or operation of the Co-op. But the record on summary judgment, viewed most favorably to Reves, shows that Arthur

Young created the very financial statements it was hired, and purported, to audit. Most importantly, Reves adduced evidence that Arthur Young took on management responsibilities by deciding, in the first instance, what value to assign to the Co-op's most important fixed asset, the White Flame gasohol plant, and Arthur Young itself conceded below that the alleged activity went beyond traditional auditing. Because I find, then, that even under the majority's "operation or management" test the Court of Appeals erroneously affirmed the summary judgment for Arthur Young, I would (again) reverse. * * *

NOTES AND QUESTIONS

1. *"Operation or Management"*. Are mere employees within the "operation or management" of an enterprise? The majority in *Reves* notes that "operation" is not limited to upper management. Footnote 9 of this decision leaves lower courts to wrestle with the question of how far down the ladder of operation § 1962(c) will extend. In United States v. Shifman, 124 F.3d 31 (1st Cir. 1997), the First Circuit noted that the concerns in *Reves* for the liability of outside advisers was different than the issue of how far down the organizational chart RICO liability could extend. "Special care is required in translating *Reves'* concern with 'horizontal' connections-focusing on the liability of an outside adviser-into the 'vertical' question of how far RICO liability may extend within the enterprise but down the organizational ladder. In our view, the reason the accountants were not liable in Reves is that, while they were undeniably involved in the enterprise's decisions, they neither made those decisions nor carried them out; in other words, the accountants were outside the chain of command through which the enterprise's affairs were conducted. We have held, post-*Reves*, however, that a defendant who is 'plainly integral to carrying out' the enterprise's activities may be held criminally liable under RICO."

In **United States v. Cummings**, 395 F.3d 392 (7th Cir. 2005), the Seventh Circuit reversed the conviction of the defendants for RICO conspiracy based on the payment of bribes to low-level workers in the Illinois Department of Employment Security (IDES). Morris, a former worker at IDES, operated a "skip tracing" business to track down debtors for collection agencies. The database maintained by IDES contained information that would be very valuable to a skip tracer, and he paid bribes to former co-workers to obtain addresses of debtors for clients of his business. The court found the defendants did not meet the "operation or management" test:

> The charged racketeering activity was bribery — Morris paid Cummings and the others in exchange for the confidential information contained in the IDES database. The defendants candidly concede that their scheme likely violated state bribery and official misconduct laws as well as IDES policies. But defendants argue that the government failed to show that any of the scheme's participants directed or managed the enterprise as Reves requires,

and thus the evidence cannot support their convictions on the RICO count.

We agree. Regardless of which standard of review applies, the record is devoid of evidence that the defendants conspired knowingly to facilitate the activities of anyone to whom § 1962(c) would apply–namely, an operator or manager of the IDES, the charged RICO enterprise. In this regard, none of Morris's accomplices fits the bill. True, Duniver and Harris held customer service "supervisor" positions at the IDES, but nothing in the record explains the scope of their duties or the relevance of their duty titles to the RICO conspiracy with which Morris and Cummings were charged. Likewise, Cummings held a minor position in the IDES's purchasing department, and no evidence indicates that she held any position by which it may be said that she operated or managed the IDES. No evidence indicates that any of these defendants was an operator or manager of the IDES, whether by official duty position or by means of some de facto control over the agency's affairs. Certainly, nothing in the record provides any basis for the jury to have concluded that Morris's associates met the Reves operation or management test or that Morris and Cummings conspired to facilitate the activities of anyone else who might meet that test.

Notwithstanding this evidentiary shortcoming, the government also tries to characterize Morris–an outsider–as the enterprise's operator or manager. After all, *Reves* envisioned that an enterprise may be operated or managed by an outsider who "exert[s] control over it as, for example, by bribery." Moreover, a lower level defendant "may conspire to violate § 1962(c) even if that defendant could not be characterized as an operator or manager of a RICO enterprise under Reves." MCM Partners, Inc. v. Andrews-Bartlett & Assocs., Inc., 62 F.3d 967, 979 (7th Cir.1995). Thus, the government contends that Morris's bribery of the IDES employees satisfies Reves because the employees' acceptance of bribes amounted to their agreement to facilitate Morris's control of the enterprise. Even though there is no evidence that Morris exercised control over the IDES, the government explains that "an outsider who bribes a public official rarely, if ever, obtains full control of the government agency in question; rather, the purpose of the bribe is to affect the exercise of a particular function of the agency in a particular situation."

While we cannot fault this proposition as it applies to bribery generally, the government's argument is inapplicable in the RICO context. No evidence adduced at trial reveals that Morris conspired to operate or manage the affairs of the IDES through the bribery of his IDES associates. The undisputed purpose of Morris's bribes reinforces this conclusion. Morris bribed his friends at the IDES in return for confidential information to be used in his skip tracing business. He did not pay bribes in order to exert control over the

IDES's core functions of collecting insurance premiums and paying of unemployment benefits. This would be an entirely different ball game if, for example, Morris had bribed his accomplices to make payments of unemployment benefits to unqualified recipients or to falsify payment of premiums by employers. In these hypothetical situations, the bribery schemes at issue would look more like a prototypical RICO conspiracy, in which low-level government employees are bribed to facilitate an outsider's illegal control over the enterprise.

2. *"Operation or Management" & Aiding and Abetting*. After *Reves,* does "aiding and abetting" play any factor in determining if an individual participated in the "operation or management" of the enterprise? In **United States v. Viola**, 35 F.3d 37 (2d Cir. 1994), the court reversed defendants' convictions, finding an improper jury instruction in light of *Reves*. In discussing the relation of "aiding and abetting" to the "operation or management" test of *Reves*, the court noted:

In *Reves*, the Court adopted an "operation or management" test to gauge whether a defendant had a sufficient connection to the enterprise to warrant imposing liability under § 1962(c). Under the Court's interpretation, simply aiding and abetting a violation is not sufficient to trigger liability even though § 1962(c) punishes those who participate "directly or indirectly" in the enterprise's affairs. This is so because "aiding and abetting liability extends beyond persons who engage, even indirectly, in a proscribed activity; aiding and abetting liability reaches persons who do not engage in the proscribed activity at all, but who give a degree of aid to those who do." Central Bank of Denver, N.A. v. First Interstate Bank of Denver, N.A., 114 S.Ct. 1439, 1447 (1994). The Court did not determine "how far § 1962 extends down the ladder of operation," though it indicated that "[a]n enterprise is 'operated' not just by upper management but also by lower-rung participants in the enterprise who are under the direction of upper management." Some insight into the scope of the operation or management test can be discerned from the Court's intimation that while the operation or management test is more restrictive than aiding and abetting liability, it requires less than "significant" control over the enterprise.

5. *Professionals*. Do professionals, such as accountants or lawyers, who usually operate outside the "operation or management" of an organization, receive immunity from RICO actions as a result of the *Reves* decision? While the answer to that question is certainly "No," *Reves'* "operation or management" test makes it very difficult to pursue a RICO case against outside professionals based on their conduct that assists a pattern or racketeering activity so long as it is just their professional activities that is at issue. In **Department of Economic Development v. Arthur Andersen & Co.**, 924 F.Supp. 449 (S.D.N.Y. 1996), a British government

agency sued an auto manufacturers outside accounting firm and three partners under RICO. In dismissing the suit, the district court emphasized that after *Reves* courts must recognized

> the difference between actual control over an enterprise and association with an enterprise in ways that do not involve control; only the former is sufficient under *Reves* because "the test is not involvement but control . . . ." The importance of control is illustrated by the one example specifically cited by the *Reves* majority to demonstrate control over a RICO enterprise by a person outside the enterprise: bribery. Bribery is qualitatively different from mere influence or assistance because the outsider paying the bribes buys actual control over the actions of a person within the enterprise. Giving a bribe can be tantamount to gaining a management position within the enterprise, because the insider taking the bribes acts under the direction of the outsider giving them in conducting the affairs of the RICO enterprise. The Court's choice of bribery as an example of an act that might qualify as "operation or management" emphasizes how difficult it is to hold an outsider liable under § 1962(c) after *Reves*.

> An outsider who merely enjoys "substantial persuasive power to induce management to take certain actions," unlike an outsider who bribes, does not exercise control over the enterprise within the meaning of *Reves*. Similarly, it is not enough to control even fraudulent activity that is ancillary to the fraud carried out by the RICO enterprise.

F. CONSPIRACY AND RICO

BECK v. PRUPIS
529 U.S. 494, 120 S.Ct. 1608, 146 L.Ed.2d 561 (2000)

Justice THOMAS delivered the opinion of the Court.

The Racketeer Influenced and Corrupt Organizations Act (RICO) creates a civil cause of action for "[a]ny person injured in his business or property by reason of a violation of section 1962." 18 U.S.C. § 1964(c). Subsection (d) of § 1962 in turn provides that "[i]t shall be unlawful for any person to conspire to violate any of the provisions of subsection (a), (b), or (c) of [§ 1962]." The question before us is whether a person injured by an overt act done in furtherance of a RICO conspiracy has a cause of action under § 1964(c), even if the overt act is not an act of racketeering. We conclude that such a person does not have a cause of action under § 1964(c). * * *

Petitioner, Robert A. Beck II, is a former president, CEO, director, and shareholder of Southeastern Insurance Group (SIG). Respondents, Ronald M. Prupis, Leonard Bellezza, William Paulus, Jr., Ernest S. Sabato, Harry

Olstein, Frederick C. Mezey, and Joseph S. Littenberg, are former senior officers and directors of SIG. Until 1990, when it declared bankruptcy, SIG was a Florida insurance holding company with three operating subsidiaries, each of which was engaged in the business of writing surety bonds for construction contractors.

Beginning in or around 1987, certain directors and officers of SIG, including respondents, began engaging in acts of racketeering. They created an entity called Construction Performance Corporation, which demanded fees from contractors in exchange for qualifying them for SIG surety bonds. Respondents also diverted corporate funds to personal uses and submitted false financial statements to regulators, shareholders, and creditors. During most of the time he was employed at SIG, petitioner was unaware of these activities. In early 1988, however, petitioner discovered respondents' unlawful conduct and contacted regulators concerning the financial statements. Respondents then orchestrated a scheme to remove petitioner from the company. They hired an insurance consultant to write a false report suggesting that petitioner had failed to perform his material duties. The day after this report was presented to the SIG board of directors, the board fired petitioner, relying on a clause in his contract providing for termination in the event of an "inability or substantial failure to perform [his] material duties." Petitioner sued respondents, asserting, among other things, a civil cause of action under § 1964(c). In particular, petitioner claimed that respondents used or invested income derived from a pattern of racketeering activity to establish and operate an enterprise, in violation of § 1962(a); acquired and maintained an interest in and control of their enterprise through a pattern of racketeering activity, in violation of § 1962(b); engaged in the conduct of the enterprise's affairs through a pattern of racketeering activity, in violation of § 1962(c); and, most importantly for present purposes, conspired to commit the aforementioned acts, in violation of § 1962(d). With respect to this last claim, petitioner's theory was that his injury was proximately caused by an overt act – namely, the termination of his employment-done in furtherance of respondents' conspiracy, and that § 1964(c) therefore provided a cause of action. Respondents filed a motion for summary judgment, arguing * * * that employees who are terminated for refusing to participate in RICO activities, or who threaten to report RICO activities, do not have standing to sue under RICO for damages from their loss of employment. The District Court agreed and dismissed petitioner's RICO conspiracy claim. The Court of Appeals affirmed, holding that a cause of action under § 1964(c) for a violation of § 1962(d) is not available to a person injured by an overt act in furtherance of a RICO conspiracy unless the overt act is an act of racketeering. Since the overt act that allegedly caused petitioner's injury was not an act of racketeering, see § 1961(1), it could not support a civil cause of action. The court held, "RICO was enacted with an express target – racketeering activity – and only those injuries that are proximately caused by racketeering activity should be actionable under the statute." [The petitioner did not challenge the dismissal of the § 1962(a), (b), and (c) claims.]

This case turns on the combined effect of two provisions of RICO that, read in conjunction, provide a civil cause of action for conspiracy. Section 1964(c) states that a cause of action is available to anyone "injured . . . by reason of a violation of section 1962." Section 1962(d) makes it unlawful for a person "to conspire to violate any of the provisions of subsection (a), (b), or (c) of this section." To determine what it means to be "injured . . . by reason of" a "conspir[acy]," we turn to the well-established common law of civil conspiracy. As we have said, when Congress uses language with a settled meaning at common law, Congress "presumably knows and adopts the cluster of ideas that were attached to each borrowed word in the body of learning from which it was taken and the meaning its use will convey to the judicial mind unless otherwise instructed. In such case, absence of contrary direction may be taken as satisfaction with widely accepted definitions, not as a departure from them." Morissette v. United States, 342 U.S. 246 (1952).

By the time of RICO's enactment in 1970, it was widely accepted that a plaintiff could bring suit for civil conspiracy only if he had been injured by an act that was itself tortious. See, e.g., 4 Restatement (Second) of Torts § 876, Comment b (1977) ("The mere common plan, design or even express agreement is not enough for liability in itself, and there must be acts of a tortious character in carrying it into execution"); W. Prosser, Law of Torts § 46, p. 293 (4th ed. 1971) ("It is only where means are employed, or purposes are accomplished, which are themselves tortious, that the conspirators who have not acted but have promoted the act will be held liable" (footnotes omitted)) * * *.

Consistent with this principle, it was sometimes said that a conspiracy claim was not an independent cause of action, but was only the mechanism for subjecting co-conspirators to liability when one of their member committed a tortious act.

The principle that a civil conspiracy plaintiff must claim injury from an act of a tortious character was so widely accepted at the time of RICO's adoption as to be incorporated in the common understanding of "civil conspiracy." See Ballentine's Law Dictionary 252 (3d ed. 1969) ("It is the civil wrong resulting in damage, and not the conspiracy which constitutes the cause of action"); Black's Law Dictionary 383 (4th ed. 1968) ("[W]here, in carrying out the design of the conspirators, overt acts are done causing *legal* damage, the person injured has a right of action" (emphasis added)). We presume, therefore, that when Congress established in RICO a civil cause of action for a person "injured . . . by reason of" a "conspir[acy]," it meant to adopt these well-established common-law civil conspiracy principles.

Justice STEVENS does not challenge our view that Congress meant to incorporate common-law principles when it adopted RICO. Nor does he attempt to make an affirmative case from the common law for his reading of the statute by pointing to a case in which there was (a) an illegal agreement; (b) injury proximately caused to the plaintiff by a nontortious overt act in furtherance of the agreement; and (c) recovery by the plaintiff. Instead, he argues only that courts, authoritative commentators, and even dictionaries repeatedly articulated a rule with no meaning or application. We find this argument to be implausible and, accordingly, understand RICO to adopt the common-law principles we have cited. Interpreting the statute in a way that is most consistent with these principles, we conclude that injury caused by an overt act that is not an act of racketeering or otherwise wrongful under RICO, is not sufficient to give rise to a cause of action under § 1964(c) for a violation of § 1962(d). As at common law, a civil conspiracy plaintiff cannot bring suit under RICO based on injury caused by any act in furtherance of a conspiracy that might have caused the plaintiff injury. Rather, consistency with the common law requires that a RICO conspiracy plaintiff allege injury from an act that is analogous to an "ac[t] of a tortious character," see 4 Restatement (Second) of Torts § 876, Comment b, meaning an act that is independently wrongful under RICO. The specific type of act that is analogous to an act of a tortious character may depend on the underlying substantive violation the defendant is alleged to have committed. However, respondents' alleged overt act in furtherance of their conspiracy is not independently wrongful under any substantive provision of the statute. Injury caused by such an act is not, therefore, sufficient to give rise to a cause of action under § 1964(c).

Petitioner challenges this view of the statute under the longstanding canon of statutory construction that terms in a statute should not be construed so as to render any provision of that statute meaningless or superfluous. He asserts that under our view of the statute, any person who had a claim for a violation of § 1962(d) would necessarily have a claim for a violation of § 1962(a), (b), or (c). However, contrary to petitioner's assertions, our interpretation of § 1962(d) does not render it mere surplusage. Under our interpretation, a plaintiff could, through a § 1964(c) suit for a violation of § 1962(d), sue co-conspirators who might not themselves have violated one of the substantive provisions of § 1962.

We conclude, therefore, that a person may not bring suit under § 1964(c) predicated on a violation of § 1962(d) for injuries caused by an overt act that is not an act of racketeering or otherwise unlawful under the statute.
Justice STEVENS, with whom Justice SOUTER joins, dissenting.

For the purpose of decision, I assume – as I think the Court does – that petitioner has alleged an injury proximately caused by an overt act in furtherance of a conspiracy that violated 18 U.S.C. § 1962(d). In my judgment, the plain language of the Racketeer Influenced and Corrupt Organizations Act (RICO) makes it clear that petitioner therefore has a cause of action under § 1964(c), whether or not the overt act is a racketeering activity listed in § 1961(1). The common-law civil conspiracy cases relied upon by the Court prove nothing to the contrary.

A "conspiracy" is an illegal agreement. There is, of course, a difference between the question whether an agreement is illegal and the question whether an admittedly illegal agreement gives rise to a cause of action for damages. Section 1962(d), which makes RICO conspiracies unlawful, addresses the former question; § 1964(c), which imposes civil liability, concerns the latter. Section 1964(c) requires a person to be "injured in his business or property" by a violation before bringing an action for damages. And because that kind of injury only results from some form of overt act in furtherance of the conspiracy, liability under § 1964(c) naturally requires injury via an overt act. But there is nothing in either § 1962(d) or § 1964(c) requiring the overt act to be a racketeering activity as defined in § 1961(1). * * *

[B]ased on its understanding of the common law, the Court concludes that "a RICO conspiracy plaintiff [must] allege injury from an act that is analogous to an 'ac[t] of a tortious character.'" Even assuming that statement is correct, though, it is not at all clear to me why an overt act that "injure[s]" a person "in his business or property" (as § 1964(c) requires) would not be "analogous to an 'ac[t] of a tortious character'" simply because the overt act is not listed in § 1961(1). Nor do I understand why the only qualifying "tortious act" must be "an act that is independently wrongful under RICO."

And if one assumes further that the Court is correct to say that the only qualifying "'ac[t] of a tortious character'" is "an act that is independently wrongful under RICO," the analogy does not actually support what the Court has held. The majority holds that § 1964(c) liability could be imposed if the overt acts injuring the plaintiff are among those racketeering activities listed in § 1961(1) – such as murder, bribery, arson, and extortion. Racketeering activities, however, are not "independently wrongful under RICO." They are, of course, independently wrongful under other provisions of state and federal criminal law, but RICO does not make racketeering activity itself wrongful under the Act. The only acts that are "independently wrongful under RICO" are violations of the provisions of § 1962. Thus, even accepting the Court's own analogy, if petitioner were harmed by predicate acts defined in § 1961(1), that still would not, by itself, give rise to a cause of action under § 1964(c). Only if those racketeering activities also constituted a violation of § 1962(a), (b), or (c) would petitioner be harmed by "an act that is independently wrongful under RICO." And, of course, if petitioner were already harmed by conduct covered by one of those provisions, he would hardly need to use § 1962(d)'s conspiracy provision to establish a cause of action.

The plain language of RICO makes it clear that petitioner's civil cause of action under § 1964(c) for a violation of § 1962(d) does not require that he be injured in his business or property by any particular kind of overt act in furtherance of the conspiracy. * * *

NOTE

Overt Act Not Required. The Supreme Court, in **Salinas v. United States**, 522 U.S. 52 (1997), held that, "[t]here is no requirement of some overt act or specific in the statute before us, unlike the general conspiracy provision applicable to federal crimes, which requires that at least one of the conspirators have committed an 'act to effect the object of the conspiracy.' § 371. The RICO conspiracy offense in § 371." The Court also stated that, "[i]t makes no difference that the substantive offense under subsection (c) requires two or more predicate acts. The interplay between subsections (c) and (d) does not permit us to excuse from the reach of the conspiracy provision an actor who does not himself commit or agree to commit the two or more predicate acts requisite to the underlying offense."

G. FORFEITURE

1. Overview of Forfeiture

Crucial to RICO is its forfeiture provisions, allowing the government to use economic sanctions to attack the alleged criminality. The U.S.A.M. notes that "[t]he forfeiture provisions under 18 U.S.C. § 1963 are an integral part of a RICO prosecution and should be used whenever possible." U.S.A.M. § 9-110A.100. RICO forfeiture is controlled by § 1963, with subsection (a) providing enormous breadth as to what property will be subject to forfeiture. For example, a union officer's positions in a union were found to be subject to forfeiture as included within § 1963(a)'s language of "any interest, security, claim, or property or contract right." This does not, however, mean that one is permanently banned from reacquiring that office. United States v. Rubin, 559 F.2d 975 (5th Cir. 1977).

"The present RICO forfeiture statute has three basic categories of forfeitable property: (a)(1) interests acquired or maintained through racketeering; (a)(2) interests in or providing a source of influence over the racketeering enterprise; and (a)(3) proceeds of racketeering activity." Karla R. Spaulding, *"Hit Them Where It Hurts": RICO Criminal Forfeitures and White Collar Crime*, 80 J. CRIM. L. AND CRIMINOLOGY 197 (1989). It is sometimes difficult to discern the distinctions between subsections (a)(1) and (a)(2) of § 1963. Professor Craig W. Palm noted that:

> The causal connection between the racketeering activity and forfeitable property need be present only if forfeiture is sought pursuant to subsection 1963(a)(1); it is not required under subsection 1963(a)(2). Since property may be forfeitable if it falls within any of the subsections, property that lacks a causal connection to the racketeering activity may still be forfeitable under subsection 1963(a)(2) because of the property's connection with the enterprise. While subsection (a)(1) focuses on the relationship between the racketeering activity and the interests acquired or maintained by virtue of that activity, subsection (a)(2) focuses on the connection between the charged RICO enterprise and the defendant's interests in that enterprise. Subsection 1963(a)(2) does not, on its face, require that the government establish any connection between the activity and the interests in the enterprise;

a mere showing of the link between the enterprise and the interests fulfills the requirements of the section.

Craig W. Palm, *RICO Forfeiture and the Eighth Amendment: When Is Everything Too Much?*, 53 U. PITT. L. REV. 1 (1991).

In the third subsection, providing forfeiture of the "proceeds" of "racketeering activity," Congress codified the Court's holding in Russello v. United States, 464 U.S. 16 (1983). The Court held in *Russello* that "interest" as used in the statute in § 1963(a)(1) includes "profits and proceeds."

Subsection (b) of § 1963 extends the scope of property subject to forfeiture by including intangible property. Subsection (c) codifies the "relation-back" doctrine in providing that the property vests in the government at the time that § 1962 is violated. Property transferred is subject to forfeiture unless the recipient is a bona fide purchaser for value who "was reasonably without cause to believe that the property was subject to forfeiture." Temporary restraining orders or injunctions may be obtained by the government to preserve the assets subject to forfeiture. [§ 1963(d)]. Substitute assets can also be subject to forfeiture where, as a result of defendant's act or omission, the property "cannot be located," "has been transferred," "has been placed beyond the jurisdiction of the court," "has been substantially diminished in value, or has been commingled with other property which cannot be divided without difficulty." [§ 1963(m)].

2. The Relation-Back Principle

In **United States v. Angiulo**, 897 F.2d 1169 (1st Cir. 1990), the court remanded a forfeiture order for modification. In discussing the "relation-back" doctrine as applied in RICO, the court stated:

> As part of its overall verdict, the jury returned a special verdict form finding various assets of defendants to be subject to forfeiture pursuant to 18 U.S.C. § 1963. Section 1963 sets forth criminal penalties to be applied to those who have been found guilty, as defendants were, of engaging in racketeering activities in violation of 18 U.S.C. § 1962. The specific forfeiture provisions applied by the jury in this case were § 1963(a)(1) and (a)(2). * * * Determining that some assets had been acquired or maintained in violation of (a)(1) and that others had afforded a source of influence under (a)(2), the jury found that several pieces of real estate, a substantial amount of cash, six Chrysler bonds, and a yacht all were subject to forfeiture. * * *

Defendants first contend that the trial court erred in failing to instruct the jury that, before forfeiting an asset on the ground that it provided a source of influence under § 1963(a)(2), the jury had to find initially that the defendant owned the property at issue at the time of indictment. The government responds that its interest in forfeitable property vests at the time of the unlawful activity and cannot be extinguished by a subsequent transfer of the property prior to the indictment.

The government's position clearly is the accepted view with respect to forfeitures under § 1963(a)(1). Courts that have considered RICO forfeitures in this context have held that RICO forfeiture, unlike forfeiture under other statutes, "is a sanction against the individual rather than a judgment against the property itself." United States v. Ginsburg, 773 F.2d 798, 801 (7th Cir.1985). Because RICO forfeiture is an *in personam* action, rather than an *in rem* action, it has been held that the government's interest in the forfeitable property vests at the time of the unlawful activity and cannot be defeated by the defendants' subsequent transfer of the property.

Defendants acknowledge the holdings of these cases but argue that (a)(2) forfeiture should be treated differently from (a)(1) forfeiture. They, however, have cited nothing in the legislative history of RICO or anywhere else to support the proposition that RICO forfeiture under § 1963(a)(2) should be treated as an *in rem* action, in contrast to forfeiture under (a)(1), which is universally treated as an *in personam* action. The cases that we have reviewed in the (a)(1) context make no mention of such a distinction, and do not suggest that their *in personam* reasoning is limited only to (a)(1) forfeiture. Rather, they state that RICO forfeiture, presumably in general, is an *in personam* sanction.

We, therefore, reject defendants' contention that (a)(2) forfeiture can only occur when the property was owned at the time of the indictment. Due to the *in personam* nature of RICO forfeiture, we find that under (a)(2) as well as under (a)(1), the government's interest in the forfeitable property vests at the time of the unlawful activity and cannot be defeated by the defendants' subsequent transfer of the property.[24]

NOTES AND QUESTIONS

1. *In personam/In rem.* The government has the option of proceeding with criminal (*in personam*) or civil forfeiture (*in rem*). "In the civil context, the forfeiture action focuses on whether the property itself was used during the

---

[24] We note that the 1984 amendments to RICO make it explicitly clear that the government's interest vests at the time of the unlawful activity. While it can be disputed whether the actions of a later Congress provide a valid basis for discerning the intent of an earlier Congress, the 1984 amendments have been interpreted as merely confirming 'the already clearly-established legislative intent behind RICO's forfeiture provision.'

commission of a crime or whether the property constituted proceeds from a crime. In this context, the government may seek to proceed against the *res* administratively or by way of a civil suit." Arthur W. Leach & John G. Malcolm, Criminal Forfeiture: An Appropriate Solution to the Civil Forfeiture, 10 GA. ST. U. L. REV. 241 (1994). A civil forfeiture does not require that the defendant first be convicted. "Because an *in rem* action is a proceeding against the property itself, a separate civil action must be filed in each district in which the property is located. In contrast, criminal forfeiture is not limited to property within the district of the criminal prosecution." U.S.A.M. § 9-110A.100. Criminal forfeiture is a statutory creation found in statutes such as RICO, the Currency and Foreign Transactions Act, and the Continuing Criminal Enterprise statute. Criminal forfeiture provisions can also be found in statutes related to financial institutions and are clearly prevalent in drug related offenses. Since RICO forfeitures are limited to interests acquired, maintained, or used in violation of § 1962, is the effect of the forfeiture really a forfeiture *in rem*? See United States v. Grande, 620 F.2d 1026 (4th Cir. 1980) ("forfeiture under § 1963 is the functional equivalent of a forfeiture *in rem*").

2. *RICO Forfeiture.* Is there a broader reach to the forfeiture provisions in RICO than in other statutes that have forfeiture provisions? In United States v. A Parcel of Land Buildings, Appurtenances and Improvements, Known as 92 Buena Vista Avenue, Rumson, New Jersey, 507 U.S. 111 (1993), the Court found that "an owner's lack of knowledge of the fact that her home had been purchased with proceeds of illegal drug transactions" provided a defense to a forfeiture proceeding brought under the Comprehensive Drug Abuse Prevention and Control Act of 1970 (21 U.S.C.A. § 881(a)(6)). The Court noted that "the protection afforded to innocent owners is not limited to bona fide purchasers." Further, the Court held that both an amendment to the statute and the common law relation-back doctrine did not make "the Government an owner of property before forfeiture has been decreed." *Buena Vista* involved a civil *in rem* action brought by the government against a parcel of land of which there was a homeowner. "The new manual [U.S.A.M.] concedes that because of the decision, the 'relation back' doctrine can no longer stop any innocent owner, including a donee, from claiming his/her property in a civil forfeiture. But it reminds prosecutors they still should use the relation back doctrine to block similar innocent owners in criminal forfeitures unless they are 'bona fide purchasers for value.' " *Forfeiture Manual Signals Help for Victims*, 3 DOJ Alert, No.11, at 2 (1993).

RICO specifically precludes parties claiming an interest in property from "interven[ing] in a trial or appeal of a criminal case involving the forfeiture of such property." [18 U.S.C.A. § 1963(i)(1)]. Following the entry of an order of forfeiture, individuals asserting an interest in the property can "petition the court for a hearing to adjudicate the validity of the alleged interest in the property." [18 U.S.C.A. § 1963(l)(2)].

3. Forfeiture of Attorney's Fees

UNITED STATES v. SACCOCCIA
354 F.3d 9 (1st Cir. 2003)

CYR, Senior Circuit Judge.

Three attorneys who represented Stephen A. Saccoccia–a convicted drug dealer and money launderer–appeal from a district court order directing that they forfeit some of their attorney fees to the government.

[The grand jury indicted Saccoccia in November 1991, charging him with one count of RICO conspiracy under 18 U.S.C. § 1963(d) and several counts of laundering proceeds from an illegal drug trafficking operation. The government also sought the forfeiture of all the business and personal property directly or indirectly derived from Saccoccia's racketeering activities, explicitly including almost $137,000,000 in currency, and, in the alternative, sought the surrender of all non-tainted property of equivalent value (if any) should Saccoccia's tainted property have become unavailable. The district court enjoined the transfer of the forfeitable property designated in the indictment.]

Saccoccia retained Jack Hill, Esquire, and Kenneth O'Donnell, Esquire, to defend him in the RICO prosecution; he retained Stephen Finta, Esquire, to defend him against money laundering charges pending in California. * * *

Beginning in March 1992, under rather suspicious circumstances, Saccoccia caused $504,985 to be delivered to Hill, $410,000 to O'Donnell, and $469,200 to Finta, all for legal fees. Approximately one year later, Saccoccia was convicted and ordered to forfeit the $137,000,000 in currency specified in the indictment. We subsequently affirmed both the conviction and the forfeiture. Once the government discovered that Saccoccia had paid large legal fees to Hill, O'Donnell, and Finta, it submitted a motion to compel them to turn over the fees as property subject to forfeiture.

The district court granted the motion to compel, holding that (i) the government established that the legal fees paid to the appellants must have derived from Saccoccia's racketeering activity, given that Saccoccia had no legitimate sources of income, and the legal fees were paid "under especially suspicious circumstances" (viz., by "covert deliveries of large quantities of cash, made by anonymous intermediaries"); (ii) appellants met their burden of proving that they had no reasonable cause to believe that the monies Saccoccia used to pay their fees, prior to Saccoccia's conviction, were subject to forfeiture, given that an Assistant United States Attorney's pre-conviction assurances to appellants–that the government would not seek forfeiture of their legal fees–implied some government uncertainty regarding whether Saccoccia might possess sufficient non-tainted assets with which to pay his attorneys; (iii) following the trial at which Saccoccia was convicted, appellants could not have held a reasonable belief that Saccoccia's assets were not subject to forfeiture, given that the trial record made it clear that virtually all of Saccoccia's assets had been derived through illegitimate means; (iv) appellants were ordered to turn over only the portion of their legal fees received following Saccoccia's conviction; and (v) the government could not reach their pre-conviction legal fees by means of the district court's contempt power due to the fact that the government had initiated no such proceeding and the district court had already determined that appellants lacked reasonable cause to believe that the pre-conviction legal fees were subject to forfeiture, hence appellants could not have violated the post-indictment injunction willfully.

Appellants now challenge the district court order which determined that their post-conviction legal fees are subject to forfeiture.

Appellants Hill and O'Donnell contend, as they did in opposing the government's motion to compel below, that the forfeiture statute does not permit the government to reach the legal fees they received from Saccoccia, due to the fact that those fees have been expended.

The operative statutory language requires that a defendant forfeit "tainted" property, viz., property (i) acquired by committing the offense, and (ii) "constituting, or derived from, any proceeds . . . obtained, directly or indirectly" from its commission. 18 U.S.C. § 1963(a)(1), (3). Once an indictment issues, the district court may enjoin the transfer of all property "subject to forfeiture under [section 1963]." Id. § 1963(d)(1). In the event that tainted property is unavailable for forfeiture (as when it has been transferred to a third party), the government may recover "substitute" property, viz., defendant's other untainted property of equivalent value. See id. § 1963(m); United States v. Lester, 85 F.3d 1409 (9th Cir.1996) (" '[S]ubstitute property,' ... by its very nature is 'not connected to the underlying *13 crime.' ").

The operative statute enables the government to recover from the defendant "tainted" or "substitute" property in a defendant's possession, or "tainted" property held by a third party by virtue of a voidable fraudulent transfer. Id. § 1963(c). A third party may petition the court for a hearing to determine the validity of its legal interest in tainted property, id. § 1963 (l)-(2), and may defeat a forfeiture petition by establishing, inter alia, that it is a bona fide purchaser for value, "reasonably without cause to believe" that the property was subject to forfeiture at the time it was purchased, id. § 1963(l)(6)(B).

Nonetheless, the "substitute property" provision is exclusively applicable to "any other property of the defendant." Id. § 1963(m). The statutory language plainly does not afford an avenue through which the government may reach a third party's untainted assets as a substitute for tainted assets which the third party had already transferred prior to the date of forfeiture.

The government does not contend that it can recover the "tainted" property already transferred to Hill and O'Donnell by Saccoccia (i.e., the in-cash legal fees), nor does it maintain that either Hill or O'Donnell presently holds any property fairly traceable to, or acquired with the proceeds of, their legal fees. Rather, it argues that its right to recover derives from the knowing violations, by Hill and O'Donnell, of the post-indictment injunction entered pursuant to § 1963(d)(1), which constrained Saccoccia and his counsel from transferring any funds subject to forfeiture under subsection 1963(a).

The absence of language in subsection 1963(m), relating to the forfeitability vel non of a third party's substitute assets, simply forecloses one form of remedy, not all. Relief from a willful violation of a subsection 1963(d)(1) injunction may be obtained in a contempt proceeding. On the other hand, the government's initiation of contempt proceedings would significantly alter its burden in litigation. Whereas subsections 1963(c) and (l)(6) require the third party to establish that it was without reasonable cause to believe that the transferred property was subject to forfeiture under subsection 1963(a), in a criminal or civil contempt proceeding the government would bear the burden of persuasion on that issue. In a criminal contempt proceeding, moreover, the government's burden of proof would be beyond-a-reasonable-doubt, see Fed.R.Crim.P. 42; and in a civil contempt proceeding, clear and convincing evidence would be required. The district court noted, however, that "the government is not seeking to hold the attorneys in contempt."

Additionally, subsection 1963(m) would not preempt various remedies otherwise available to the government outside the forfeiture statute, which would maximize its monetary recovery from the substitute assets of culpable third parties. See United States v. Moffitt, Zwerling & Kemler, 83 F.3d 660 (4th Cir.1996) (holding that § 1963(m) does not preempt state common-law claims that enable the government to reach a third-party transferee's substitute assets). For instance, since the government's right, title, and interest in all tainted property "relates back" to the date Saccoccia committed the relevant acts, see 18 U.S.C. § 1963(c) ("All right, title, and interest in property described in subsection (a) vests in the United States upon the commission of the act giving rise to the forfeiture."), presumably it could initiate a state-law proceeding against Hill and O'Donnell for conversion of such property, and recover compensatory damages from their non-tainted assets. However, had the government brought such a tort claim in the district court, the claim presumably would be adjudicated under substantially different standards than a claim under subsection 1963(a) or (m), since the government would bear the burden of proof, and appellants might be entitled to additional procedural safeguards under state law, such as a right to jury trial.

At first blush, the present holding may appear to diverge from the stated legislative intent to accord the government extremely aggressive forfeiture remedies so as to preclude criminals from realizing the monetary benefits of their crimes. See Caplin & Drysdale, Chartered v. United States, 491 U.S.

617 (1989). On the other hand, the very potency of the forfeiture power demands that it be reasonably contained within ascertainable limits. Thus, for example, Congress provided that a non-defendant third party with rights in forfeitable property may redeem its interest by establishing either (i) that it predated the defendant's crime, or (ii) that it subsequently acquired a non-forfeitable interest under a bona fide purchase for value, see 18 U.S.C. § 1963(l)(6).

The implicit limitation in § 1963(m) – the "substitute assets" provision – that the government may reach only the defendant's substitute assets and not those of a third party–is similar in nature. Forfeiture is an in personam criminal remedy, targeted primarily at the defendant who committed the criminal offense.

Finally, the implicit limitation in § 1963(m) does not trammel the basic statutory policy by foreclosing all other remedies available to the government, nor does it enable culpable attorneys to dissipate tainted fees with impunity. Rather, the government may utilize its enforcement powers under subsection 1963(k) to "trace" tainted funds, thereby disproving the contention that appellants' cash-on-hand is neither the tainted fees, nor other property directly or indirectly derived from the tainted fees. Furthermore, absent such evidence, the government may reach other non-tainted cash of the attorneys by sustaining the somewhat weightier, though not insurmountable, burden of establishing the elements of either contempt or conversion.

As our construction of the language utilized in the forfeiture statute is one of first impression, the forfeiture award against Hill and O'Donnell must be vacated and the case must be remanded to the district court for further proceedings consistent with this opinion. Upon remand, the government is to be accorded a reasonable opportunity to determine whether it intends to institute contempt proceedings or submit conversion claims against appellants.

4. Excessiveness

In **Alexander v. United States**, 509 U.S. 544 (1993), the Supreme Court considered possible Eighth Amendment limitations on forfeiture under the Excessive Fines Clause. After a conviction for RICO violations based on selling obscene material, the defendant received a six-year prison term and $100,000 fine. In addition, the district court ordered Alexander to forfeit his wholesale and retail businesses (including all the assets of those businesses) and almost $9 million in moneys acquired through racketeering activity. In remanding the case for the lower court to consider whether the forfeiture constituted an excessive fine, the Court stated:

The personam criminal forfeiture at issue here is clearly a form of monetary punishment no different, for Eighth Amendment purposes, from a traditional "fine." Accordingly, the forfeiture in this case should be analyzed under the Excessive Fines Clause.

Petitioner contends that forfeiture of his entire business was an "excessive" penalty for the Government to exact "[o]n the basis of a few materials the jury ultimately decided were obscene." It is somewhat misleading, we think, to characterize the racketeering crimes for which petitioner was convicted as involving just a few materials ultimately found to be obscene. Petitioner was convicted of creating and managing what the District Court described as "an enormous racketeering enterprise." It is in the light of the extensive criminal activities which petitioner apparently conducted through this racketeering enterprise over a substantial period of time that the question of whether or not the forfeiture was "excessive" must be considered. We think it preferable that this question be addressed by the Court of Appeals in the first instance.

In **United States v. Bajakajian**, 524 U.S. 321 (1998) the Court held forfeiture "of the entire $357,144 that respondent failed to declare" on a customs currency reporting form to "be grossly disproportional to the gravity of his offense." The Court stated that "a punitive forfeiture violates the Excessive Fines Clause if it is grossly disproportional to the gravity of a defendant's offense." The Court further stated:

> The harm that respondent caused was also minimal. Failure to report his currency affected only one party, the Government, and in a relatively minor way. There was no fraud on the United States, and respondent caused no public loss to the public fisc. Had his crime gone undetected, the Government would have been deprived only of the information that $357,144 had left the country.

Congress, in the "Uniting and Strengthening America by Providing Appropriate Tools Required to Intercept and Obstruct Terrorism Act of 2001" (USA Patriot Act), created a bulk cash smuggling offense with new penalties for the undeclared movement of more than $10,000 across U.S. borders.

CHAPTER SEVEN
REGULATORY OFFENSES

A. INTRODUCTION

Regulatory offenses are crimes involving a violation of government regulation. The regulation will often provide specific procedures, including licensing, for maintaining activities that the government considers "a special threat to the community at large." Edmund W. Kitch, Kevin A. Russell, & Steven Duke, *Economic Crime,* 2 ENCYCLOPEDIA OF CRIMINAL JUSTICE 670, 672-73 (1983). Regulatory crimes can also be a product of a failure to comply with a regulation's reporting requirements. Id. For a discussion of the enforcement of economic regulations through criminal sanctions, see Sanford H. Kadish, *Some Observations on the Use of Criminal Sanctions in Enforcing Economic Regulations,* 30 U. CHI. L. REV. 423 (1963).

Regulatory statutes are found throughout state and federal codes. It is evident in examining recent legislation that government regulation has increased in recent years. For example, crimes relating to the environment have now received priority status by the Department of Justice. Also apparent are an increased number of prosecutions for OSHA (Occupational Health and Safety Act) violations and health offenses.

An investigation for an alleged regulatory violation usually commences with the agency overseeing the administration of the regulation. This agency will often make an initial determination as to whether the enforcement of the regulation will be through an administrative, civil, or criminal action. Parallel civil and criminal proceeding are common occurrences in the enforcement of regulatory statutes. (See Chapter 14). Cases to be pursued criminally are turned over to the DOJ Criminal Division for prosecution. In some instances the cases are resolved with civil settlement or a deferred prosecution agreement. (See Chapter 3).

NOTES AND QUESTIONS

1. ***Voluntary Disclosure.*** "It is the policy of the Department of Justice to encourage self-auditing, self-policing and voluntary disclosure of environmental violations by the regulated community by indicating that these activities are viewed as mitigating factors in the Department's exercise of criminal environmental enforcement discretion." U.S.A.M. § 5-11.301A. DOJ guidelines offer several factors to be considered by prosecutors in determining whether to proceed with a criminal prosecution when there is an

alleged environmental violation. They include "voluntary disclosure," "cooperation," and "preventive measures and compliance programs." Other considerations which may prove relevant in deciding whether to prosecute are "pervasiveness of noncompliance," "internal disciplinary action," and "subsequent compliance efforts." The DOJ clearly notes that these criteria are for internal guidance only and thus should not serve as a basis for contesting prosecutorial discretion.

2. *Prosecutorial Discretion.* To what extent do political and financial considerations impact the decision of whether a prosecutor proceeds civilly or criminally when there is an alleged violation of an environmental statute? Prosecutors also have the discretion to select the charge if proceeding criminally. The prosecution of regulatory offenses is not always limited to criminal statutes contained within one environmental act (e.g., Clean Water Act). Indictments often include charges such as conspiracy (18 U.S.C. § 371), false statements (18 U.S.C. § 1001), mail fraud (18 U.S.C. § 1341), and obstruction of justice (18 U.S.C. § 1503). Although environmental offenses are not specifically listed as predicate acts for a RICO prosecution, mail and wire fraud have served as the predicates for RICO prosecutions involving environmental offenses. See United States v. Paccione, 738 F. Supp. 691, 699 (S.D. N.Y. 1990) ("Nothing in the decisions of this Circuit suggests that mail and wire fraud, properly alleged, in the conduct of an enterprise cannot be included as racketeering activity because the enterprise is alleged to have engaged in violations of regulatory schemes which do not constitute racketeering activity on their own.") Consider the following excerpts from Philip Shabecoff, *Federal Statutes Cited In Indictment of Exxon*, N.Y.Times, Mar. 1, 1990, A14, noting how statutes from several different Acts were used in the indictment of Exxon.

> A Federal grand jury in Alaska invoked five Federal statutes on Tuesday when it indicted the Exxon Corporation and the Exxon Shipping Company on felony and misdemeanor charges in the Exxon Valdez oil spill.
>
> Following are the applicable laws and the ways the indictment charges that Exxon violated them:
>
> *The Clean Water Act* makes it illegal to discharge pollutants or hazardous substances negligently into United States waters without a permit. The indictment charges that Exxon and Exxon Shipping negligently caused pollutants, "namely 10 million gallons of crude oil,' to be discharged from the tanker Exxon Valdez into Prince William Sound, 'a navigable water of the United States," without a permit.
>
> *The Refuse Act* makes it unlawful to discharge refuse, including oil, from a ship. The indictment says the corporation and its subsidiary caused refuse matter, "namely 10 million gallons of crude oil," to be "thrown, discharged and deposited in Prince William Sound."

The Migratory Bird Treaty Act prohibits the killing of any migratory bird without a permit. The indictment did not list the number of birds killed by the Exxon Valdez spill, but a Justice Department document noted that as of last September more than 36,000 dead birds had been collected and that they were believed to be only a fraction of the actual number killed.

The Ports and Waterways Act requires that the master or anyone else in charge of a vessel insure that the wheelhouse is manned by competent people. The indictment charges that the corporation and the company, as well as the master of the tanker, Capt. Joseph J. Hazelwood, failed to assure that the vessel was in the hands of those competent to perform their duty.

The Dangerous Cargo Act makes it a felony to violate a regulation that bars from tanker crews any person known by an employer to be physically or mentally incapable of performing assigned duties. The indictment contends that Exxon "willfully and knowingly" employed people incapable of performing the duties assigned to them. * * *

B. *THE* MENS REA *ELEMENT*

There is no consistent mental state required for all of the regulatory offenses. In some cases courts have interpreted regulatory statutes to be strict liability crimes. In other instances the statutes have required a mens rea of willfulness or knowledge. In examining the mental state used in different regulatory offenses, consider whether the principles of statutory interpretation discussed in Chapter Four should differ here. Should regulatory crimes have a higher or lesser *mens rea* than traditional crimes? See Chapter 17 for a discussion of how the United States Sentencing Commission treats regulatory offenses.

1. Strict Liability

UNITED STATES v. WHITE FUEL CORPORATION
498 F.2d 619 (1st Cir. 1974)

CAMPBELL, Circuit Judge.

White Fuel Corporation was convicted after a jury-waived trial of violating Section 13 of the Rivers and Harbors Act of 1899, 33 U.S.C. § 407 (the Refuse Act).[1] White Fuel operates a tank farm abutting a small cove off

---

[1] "It shall not be lawful to throw, discharge, or deposit, or cause, suffer, or procure to be thrown, discharged, or deposited either from or out of . . . the shore [or] . . . manufacturing establishment . . . any refuse matter of any kind or description . . .

the Reserved Channel, part of Boston harbor. Both the cove and the channel are navigable waters of the United States. On May 3, 1972, the Coast Guard found oil in the water of the cove. White Fuel, which in January 1972 had been alerted by state authorities to possible oil spoilage problems, immediately undertook to clean up the oil and to trace its source. Although at first an oil-water separator and later a leaky pipe were suspected, experts called in by White Fuel finally determined that the oil was seeping from an immense accumulation (approximately half a million gallons) which had gathered under White Fuel's property. White Fuel concedes, and the court found, that it owned the oil, which continued to seep into the cove throughout the summer of 1972 even though White Fuel worked diligently to drain or divert the accumulation. By September it was successful and seepage had ceased. As part of its clean-up efforts, and to prevent the oil from spreading, White Fuel had installed booms across the mouth of the cove. There was testimony that on occasion these booms were tended improperly, so that some of the oil drifted out into the channel.

The district court found that the seepage was a violation of the Refuse Act and imposed a $1,000 fine.[3] The court denied White Fuel's motion for judgment of acquittal and, ruling that intent or scienter is irrelevant to guilt, also denied White Fuel's offer to present evidence that it had not known of the underground deposit, had not appreciated its hazards, and had acted diligently when the deposit became known. The court held that White Fuel's only defense would be to show that third parties caused the oil seepage—that "this oil escaped from a source other than that under the control of the defendant". White Fuel contends that the government was required to prove scienter or at least negligence as part of its case, and that the court erred by precluding the proffered defense. * * *

* * * [T]he sole question for us to decide is whether the conviction is supported by the undisputed fact that oil owned by White Fuel leached from its property into adjacent navigable waters. White Fuel first insists that this sort of seepage is not even covered by the Refuse Act because it did not "throw, discharge, or deposit" oil, and that since it did not know the oil was entering the cove it did not "suffer" the discharge. But a defendant which allows its own oil to be discharged, even unwittingly, seems to us in everyday language to "suffer" the discharge. That this discharge was more of an indirect percolation than a direct flow is, of course, immaterial.

There is no greater merit in White Fuel's next argument, that common law *mens rea* had to be alleged or proven. * * * In the seventy-five years since enactment, no court to our knowledge has held that there must be proof of scienter; to the contrary, the Refuse Act has commonly been termed a strict

---

into any navigable water of the United States, . . ."

[3] The offense, a misdemeanor, allows a maximum fine of $2,500 and a year's imprisonment.

liability statute.　　The offense falls within the category of public welfare offenses which

> "are not in the nature of positive aggressions or invasions, with which the common law so often dealt, but are in the nature of neglect where the law requires care, or inaction where it imposes a duty . . . . The accused, if he does not will the violation, usually is in a position to prevent it with no more care than society might reasonably expect and no more exertion than it might reasonably exact from one who assumed his responsibilities." Morissette v. United States, 342 U.S. 246, 255-56 (1952).

We do not accept White Fuel's further argument that if the government need not prove scienter it must at least prove negligence. Actually, merely by showing that White Fuel's oil escaped into public waters, the government presented facts from which negligence could be inferred. See Restatement (Second) of Torts § 328D. The real issue is not the government's prima facie case, which was sufficient by any standard, but whether due care—lack of negligence— is available as a defense. In the Federal Water Pollution Control Act Amendments of 1972, 33 U.S.C. § 1251 et seq., Congress imposed criminal penalties only upon any person who "willfully or negligently" violates its prohibitions, 33 U.S.C. § 1319(c)(1), but provided civil penalties for all violations. 33 U.S.C. § 1319(d). In the Refuse Act, on the other hand, Congress made no such distinction, and we have been told to read the latter "charitably in light of the purpose to be served," United States v. Republic Steel Corp., 362 U.S. 482, 491 (1960). The dominant purpose is to require people to exercise whatever diligence they must to keep refuse out of public waters. Given this aim, we are disinclined to invent defenses beyond those necessary to ensure a defendant constitutional due process. Specifically we reject the existence of any generalized "due care" defense that would allow a polluter to avoid conviction on the ground that he took precautions conforming to industry-wide or commonly accepted standards.

Merely to attempt to formulate, let alone apply, such standards, would be to risk crippling the Refuse Act as an enforcement tool. The defendant, if a substantial business enterprise, would usually have exclusive control of both the expertise and the relevant facts; it would be difficult indeed, and to no purpose, for the government to have to take issue with elaborate factual and theoretical arguments concerning who, why and what went wrong. A municipality may require dog owners to keep their dogs off the public streets, and the court may enforce the ordinance by criminal sanctions without paying attention, except in mitigation, to the owner's tales concerning his difficulty in getting Fido to stay home. In the present circumstances we see no unfairness in predicating liability on actual non-compliance rather than either intentions or best efforts. See O. W. Holmes, The Common Law 49 (1881). Whatever occasional harshness this could entail is offset by the moderateness of the permitted fine, the fact that the statute's command—to keep refuse out of the public waters—scarcely imposes an impossible burden, and the benefit to society of having an easily defined, enforcible standard which inspires performance rather than excuses. The President Coolidge, 101 F.2d 638 (9th Cir. 1939). As a corporate defendant like White Fuel cannot be imprisoned, we need not consider to what extent absolute liability would carry over to cases where incarceration is a real possibility.

Although there is no generalized "due care" defense, a defendant may always, of course, show that someone other than himself was responsible for the discharge. White Fuel might, for example, undertake to prove that oil had percolated through its soil from the supply of an adjacent landowner. If a plane crashed into one of its tanks causing a spill, White Fuel would not be liable. If thieves overpowered its watchmen and somehow caused a pipe to overflow, White Fuel would not be liable. Acts of God would be another legitimate defense. It might be a defense that the spill was caused by an independent contractor who was entirely outside the defendant's control. * * *

As the above instances illustrate, the law recognizes some defenses even where liability generally is predicated on the sole fact of non-compliance. One is not expected to take all conceivable measures to erect a fail-safe system which would be impregnable to sabotage, thievery, accidental intrusions, the negligence of third parties, and extreme natural disasters. Even if perfect protection could be insured, such is not the "some other course open" of which the law speaks. But, with this caveat concerning human frailty, it remains true that the standard of proof of exculpatory facts is of a much more rigorous and exceptional nature than that of reasonable care. Particularly is this true of an enterprise such as that we deal with here—an oil tank farm, with its inherent risk of spills, leaks, and seepage, abutting navigable waters. Such a high risk enterprise carries with it, even under conventional tort law, a high burden of responsibility.

Against such a requirement for exculpation, White Fuel's proffered defenses, even if proven, were inadequate. White Fuel offered to prove that its personnel did not know of the existence of the oil prior to May 3, 1972 and could not, in any event, have predicted that such oil would seep into the cove. It also wished to show its diligence in cleaning up and checking the seepage once it was discovered. But it was conceded that White Fuel owned the offending oil, that it had occupied the property continuously for years, that the accumulation was vast, and that its property bordered the cove. Given such facts, we do not think that the excluded evidence, even if true, could have demonstrated that it was so far beyond White Fuel's power to have avoided the accumulation and consequent seepage as to render the conviction and fine improper.

Affirmed.

NOTE AND QUESTION

Has the court in *White Fuel* ruled consistently with how the Supreme Court ruled in *Posters 'N' Things, Ltd*, [p.103], and *Staples*, [p.104]? Recall how Justice Thomas, in *Staples*, distinguished the National Firearms Act from "public welfare" or "regulatory offenses." Should a higher *mens rea* be required for offenses committed under the National Firearms Act than for offenses under the Refuse Act?

2. Willfulness

UNITED STATES v. DYE CONSTRUCTION COMPANY
510 F.2d 78 (10th Cir. 1975)

DOYLE, Circuit Judge.

Following the death of a workman in a trench cave-in, the appellant was charged with willfully failing to shore, sheet, brace, slope and otherwise support by means of sufficient strength sides of trenches in unstable or soft material sufficient to protect employees working within the trenches, five feet or more in depth. The cause which arose under the Occupational Safety and Health Act of 1970, 29 U.S.C. § 651 et seq.[1] was tried to a jury.   * * *

The entire thrust of the Dye argument here is that the jury should have been instructed that willfulness in terms of intent to do the act knowingly and purposefully is not enough; that an evil motive is an essential element. The instruction given reads as follows:

> The failure to comply with a safety standard under the Occupational Safety and Health Act is willful if done knowingly and purposely by an employer who, having a free will or choice, either intentionally disregards the standard or is plainly indifferent to its requirement. An omission or failure to act is willfully done if done voluntarily and intentionally.

---

[1] Section 655 of the Act authorizes the Secretary of Labor to promulgate regulations to insure that employees covered by the Act are provided with a place of employment that is free from recognized hazards that are likely to cause death or serious bodily harm.

Section 666(e) states:

> Any employer who willfully violates any standard, rule, or order promulgated pursuant to section 655 of this title, or of any regulations prescribed pursuant to this chapter, and that violation caused death to any employee, shall, upon conviction, be punished by a fine of not more than $10,000 or by imprisonment for not more than six months, or by both; . . . * * *

The Supreme Court and our court have recognized that willfulness has different meanings when used in different contexts. The distinction which is usually drawn in defining willfulness is between crimes in which moral turpitude is required and those which do not demand a moral taint. * * *

In statutes denouncing offenses involving turpitude, "willfully" is generally used to mean with evil purpose, criminal intent or the like. But in those denouncing acts not in themselves wrong, the word is often used without any such implication.

Perhaps a very clear example of this distinction appears in Spies v. United States, [317 U.S. 492 (1943)], wherein the Court considered the difference between failure to file an income tax return and tax fraud which involves moral turpitude. In the tax fraud case the Court said "willfulness" includes evil motive, but in the charge of failure to file no such element is necessary. * * *

At bar neither the statute nor the regulation requires that there be moral turpitude. The object of these provisions is prevention of injury or death and its

application is not limited to the situation in which the employer entertained a specific intent to harm the employee.   * * *

The judgment of the district court is affirmed.

NOTES

1. *No Knowledge Proviso.* A violation of the Securities Exchange Act of 1934 can become a criminal felony offense when the defendant acts willfully. The Act, however, specifically provides that "no person shall be subject to imprisonment under this section for the violation of any rule or regulation if he proves that he had no knowledge of such rule or regulation." The "no knowledge" proviso does not negate the criminal conviction, but does offer a limitation of punishment to those included within 15 U.S.C.A. § 78ff(a). This section does not serve as a defense for one who claims "no knowledge" of the "standards prescribed in the securities acts themselves." In United States v. Lilley, 291 F. Supp. 989 (S.D. Tex. 1968), the court found the "no knowledge" proviso inapplicable to defendants who pled guilty. The court stated, "These admissions by each defendant preclude him from discharging his burden of showing 'no knowledge' of Rule 10b-5."

2. *Mens Rea Determined By Misdemeanor or Felony.* The mens rea for acts under the Food, Drug, and Cosmetic Act may depend upon the level of the offense. In **United States v. Watkins**, 278 F.3d 961 (9th Cir. 2002) the court stated:

The FDCA provides two tiers of liability for misbranding violations under § 331(a).   The misdemeanor provision imposes criminal liability in the form of imprisonment, fines, or both. *See* 21 U.S.C. § 333(a)(1) ("Any person who violates [§ 331(a)(1)] shall be imprisoned for not more than one year or fined not more than $1,000, or both."). An article may be misbranded pursuant to the misdemeanor provision "without any conscious fraud at all," thus creating a form of strict criminal liability. * * * Felony misbranding, on the other hand, requires a showing that the defendant acted "with intent to defraud or mislead" * * * Thus, felony liability for misbranding requires an additional mens rea element that is absent from the broader-reaching misdemeanor provision.* * *

The court in *Watkins* also found that "felony liability for misbranding requires proof of materiality."

3. Knowingly

UNITED STATES v. BRONX REPTILES, INC.
217 F.3d 82 (2d Cir. 2000)

SACK, Circuit Judge:

* * * When a criminal statute renders unlawful an act "knowingly" undertaken by the defendant, what must the extent of the defendant's knowledge be to permit conviction?

The defendant, Bronx Reptiles, Inc., was convicted following a bench trial in the United States District Court for the Eastern District of New York * * *of violating that portion of the Lacey Act, codified as amended at 18 U.S.C. § 42(c), that makes it a misdemeanor "for any person, including any importer, knowingly to cause or permit any wild animal or bird to be transported to the United States, or any Territory or district thereof, under inhumane or unhealthful conditions or in violation of such requirements" as the Secretary of the Interior may prescribe. * * * The defendant argues on appeal that under § 42(c), the government was required to prove not only that the defendant knowingly caused the transportation to the United States of a wild animal or bird, but also that the defendant knew the conditions under which the animal or bird was transported were "inhumane or unhealthful." * * *

First, § 42(c) is a provision of a criminal statute describing behavior that it declares to be "unlawful." The reader therefore expects the sentence to tell him or her what it is that a person must do "knowingly" to perform a criminally punishable act. Reading knowingly to apply (1) to the language "to cause or permit any wild animal or bird to be transported" and (2) to the phrase "to the United States," but not to (3) the requirement that such transportation be "under inhumane or unhealthful conditions," leads to a highly unlikely result: A vast range of remarkably innocuous behavior is rendered criminal. Not only the importer but the pet store owner or the casual purchaser of pets may well become guilty of a crime by purchasing a once-wild animal or bird–* * * -knowing only that the direct or indirect result of the purchase is that a "wild animal or bird [will] be transported to the United States." To avoid this extraordinary and unlikely result, the reader is bound to read the requirement of knowledge to apply to the provision that the animal or bird be transported "under inhumane or unhealthful conditions" so that the "unlawful" act prohibited involves wrongdoing.

Second, there is nothing in the structure or punctuation of § 42(c) that signals the reader that "knowingly" does *not* apply to the phrase "under inhumane or unhealthful conditions." The statute could have been written, for example, to render it "unlawful for any person knowingly to cause or permit any wild animal or bird to be transported to the United States, *the conditions of which transportation* are inhumane or unhealthful," or "knowingly to cause or permit any wild animal or bird to be transported to the United States (*insofar as the conditions of transporting* the animal are inhumane or unhealthful)." In the former case, the comma and the word "which," and in the latter, the parentheses and the words "insofar as," indicate that "knowingly" might have been intended to apply only to causing or permitting a wild animal to be transported to the United States. But § 42(c) as written contains no punctuation or phrasing--no comma, no "which," no parentheses, no "insofar as"--to undermine the most obvious reading of § 42(c): that "knowingly" extends to the phrase "inhumane or unhealthful."

If a simple review of the language of § 42(c) does not establish that "knowingly" refers to "inhumane or unhealthful," however, the legal principle that criminal statutes are presumed to contain a *mens rea* requirement does. * * * There is, moreover, neither statutory language nor legislative history to overcome the *mens rea* presumption. We would expect that if Congress meant, contrary to the presumption, to impose liability absent a "guilty mind," it would have said so. * * * In sum, to permit the defendant to be convicted of a crime under 18 U.S.C. § 42(c) without knowledge of the "inhumane or unhealthful" conditions under which the frogs were transported to the United States would be to impose upon them guilt absent a *mens rea*. This is contrary to the fundamental presumption that *mens rea,* a "guilty mind," is a prerequisite to conviction for a crime.* * *

The government points out that in cases involving "public welfare offenses," courts have declined to read into statutes a *mens rea* requirement, concluding that Congress intended to impose a form of strict criminal liability instead. * * *

"[P]ublic welfare offenses have been created by Congress, and recognized" by courts "in limited circumstances." *   * *   Although the Supreme Court has explicitly declined to define this category of offenses precisely, * * * it has noted that cases recognizing such offenses "[t]ypically ... involve statutes that regulate potentially harmful or injurious items." * *

* Frogs are not "potentially harmful or injurious items," * * * and there is in our view nothing about transporting them that would "place[ ] [a defendant] in responsible relation to a public danger, ... alert[ing it] to the probability of strict regulation." * * * We thus decline to recognize a violation of § 42(c) as a "public welfare offense."

The government also argues that a *mens rea* requirement need not be inferred where the penalties for violating a statute are relatively small. That is simply wrong. While "a severe penalty is a further factor tending to suggest that Congress did not intend to eliminate a *mens rea* requirement," * * * it does not follow that whenever a penalty is not "severe," we may dispense with the need to prove *mens rea* as to a critical element of a crime. This is especially so where, as here, dispensing with such a requirement would "criminalize a broad range of apparently innocent conduct." * * * Because the government failed to satisfy its burden under 18 U.S.C. § 42(c), we reverse the judgment of the district court and remand with instructions to enter a judgment of not guilty.

OAKES, Senior Circuit Judge:

I respectfully dissent. * * *Bronx Reptiles imports live animals, including reptiles, into the country approximately twice a week. Since at least 1993, it has been well aware of the IATA guidelines used by the industry to determine how a specific species is to be shipped and of the container requirements listed in the guidelines. Indeed, a special agent of the U.S. Fish and Wildlife Service, Division of Law Enforcement, who spoke with Bruce Edelman, the owner of Bronx Reptiles, testified that Mr. Edelman knew of the IATA guidelines and knew that as an importer he was liable for the conditions under which wildlife entered the United States.

Despite its knowledge of IATA guidelines, Bronx Reptiles has arranged for a number of shipments that involved inadequately packed and ventilated shipments. In 1993, Bronx Reptiles arranged for an importation of iguanas and boa constrictors from Colombia that resulted in a substantial number of dead reptiles due to improper ventilation and improper labeling. Based on the two shipments from Colombia, notices of violation were issued to Bronx Reptiles and civil fines were subsequently paid. A similar incident occurred in March of 1994, involving small mammals and reptiles from Egypt in which a number of dead animals were discovered and as well a number of weaning mothers with young were improperly packaged. In March of 1995, Bronx Reptiles was cited for yet another importation of chameleons, skinks, geckos and other lizards and frogs in inhumane fashion.

There was no doubt whatsoever that the shipment of frogs from the Solomon Islands, at the center of this case, was improper. The container was shallow and the frogs were not separated. Furthermore, no damp materials or water trays were included to keep the frogs properly hydrated. This was highly improper since, as should be obvious to anyone, frogs have to have sufficient water to keep their skin from dehydrating. The former superintendent of reptiles and amphibians at the Bronx Zoo testified to the wide knowledge in the importation business of the IATA guidelines. These, of course, were violated by the shipment. He also testified to the customary practice of those in the importing business to check out the shipper, seek out references, and call the shipper to be certain that the shipper was aware of and understood the shipping requirements, including the IATA standards. Despite its vast experience in shipping and its prior violations, Bronx Reptiles did not fulfill its obligations under the guidelines.

No evidence was introduced by Bronx Reptiles to contradict any of the foregoing.

The majority holds that a violation of § 42(c) is not a public welfare offense and further holds that for a conviction under § 42(c) to stand, Bronx Reptiles had to know specifically that the frogs were improperly packed. In my view § 42(c), under the law of this Circuit, is properly treated as a public welfare statute. * * * The majority here has determined that § 42(c) is not a public welfare law, reasoning that there is nothing about transporting frogs that would "place a defendant in responsible relation to a public danger, ... [thus] alerting it to the probability of strict regulation." * * * I disagree.

The provision against inhumane transportation, which is the subject of this prosecution, has been in the law since 1948. The legislative history makes it clear that Congress knew that it could not hold foreign shippers liable for the conditions in which animals were shipped, and that it was necessary to hold the United States importer responsible for ensuring, by contract or otherwise, that the transportation would be done in a humane fashion. * * * Thus, Congress plainly contemplated that United States importers would be in a position where they could be responsible for ensuring safe transport of live animals.

The IATA guidelines themselves illustrate that the transport of live animals, including live reptiles and amphibians, is a delicate and risky business. As Congress clearly found, it is the United States importer who is in a position to take responsibility for ensuring the safe and humane transport for foreign animals. The fact that it is arranging for the transport of animals that are *alive* puts it on notice of the "probability of strict regulation." The United States importer can arrange by contract to ensure the safety of the animals. Thus, the United States importer is in responsible relation to the public danger of harm to the wildlife that it caused to be shipped to this country and should be strictly regulated. * * * I would affirm the conviction.

NOTES AND QUESTIONS

1. *Mistake of Fact.* In **United States v. Quarrell**, 310 F.3d 664 (10th Cir. 2002), the court first examined whether the Archaeological Resources

Protection Act (ARPA) required the accused to know they were excavating on public land and then decided whether a mistake was allowed. In finding that the statute did not require knowledge the court stated:

> * * * Neither the legislative history nor the purpose behind the statute directly answers the issue of whether the government must prove that the defendant knew he or she was on public land in order to establish a § 470ee(a) violation. However, extending the *mens rea* requirement to the "located on public lands" element would frustrate the purpose of the Act. For example, it would often be difficult for the government to prove that a defendant knew he was on public land unless signs were posted at or near the archaeological site. Placing signs near sites, however, would draw the attention of potential looters. Archaeological sites in the Gila National Forest are kept confidential to protect the sites from vandalism, especially since, at the time of the offenses, there were only two law enforcement officers patrolling approximately three million acres of public land. Congress' desire that land managers inform the public of the Act's requirements does not indicate that Congress intended to convict only those offenders who knew they were on public land. A public information campaign simply furthers the purpose of the Act by informing the public of ARPA's prohibitions. * * *

In deciding whether the accused should be allowed to present a mistake of fact under this statute, the court stated:

> The Quarrels argue the district court erred in not allowing them to present a defense based on their belief that they were excavating on private, not public, land. ARPA is silent as to the defenses available. * * * ARPA superseded the Antiquities Act of 1906. Therefore, we may look to this prior statute to determine whether a mistake of fact defense is available. Although the Antiquities Act is silent on this issue, its case law provides some insight.

> We * * * hold that a defendant charged with violating ARPA may present a mistake of fact defense. After the government establishes an ARPA violation, the defendant should be allowed to argue a mistake of fact defense based on his reasonable belief that he was excavating on private land *with permission*. The defendant must establish that he reasonably believed he was *lawfully* excavating on private land because such "an honest mistake of fact would not be consistent with criminal intent." * * * However, if a defendant merely argues that he thought he was excavating on private land, such a mistake of fact would not negate criminal intent because such conduct is unlawful. In addition, a defendant, * * * must present evidence that his mistake of fact was "honestly and conscientiously made."

2. *Mistake of Law.* In **United States v. Whiteside**, 285 F.3d 1345 (11th Cir. 2002), the court reversed criminal convictions and sentences for making false statements in Medicare/Medicaid and CHAMPUS reimbursement cost reports and for conspiracy to defraud the government by making false statements in those cost reports. The court stated:

> In a case where the truth or falsity of a statement centers on an interpretive question of law, the government bears the burden of proving beyond a reasonable doubt that the defendant's statement is not true under a reasonable interpretation of the law. * * * The government cannot meet its burden in this case because, despite its contention to the contrary, no Medicare regulation, administrative ruling, or judicial decision exists that clearly requires interest expense to be reported in accordance with the original use of the loan. * * * The government's position that the regulation is pellucid on this point is refuted by the relevant text of the regulation. * * * Neither the regulations nor administrative authority clearly answer the dilemma the defendants faced here.   * * * The testimony indicates that the experts disagreed as to the validity of the theory of capital reimbursement suggested by the government. This contradictory evidence lends credence to defendants' argument that their interpretation was not unreasonable. * * *

3. *Knowing Endangerment.* "Knowing endangerment" provisions are found in both the Resource Conservation and Recovery Act, 42 U.S.C.A. § 6928(e), and the Clean Water Act, 33 U.S.C.A. § 1319(c)(3)(A). In **United States v. Protex Industries, Inc.**, 874 F.2d 740 (10th Cir. 1989), the court, in affirming a criminal conviction under the "knowing endangerment" provision in RCRA, stated:

> Counts 17 through 19 of that indictment charged Protex with knowingly placing three of its employees in imminent danger of death or serious bodily injury as a result of its other alleged violations of the RCRA. The evidence showed that safety provisions for the employees in the drum recycling facility were woefully inadequate to protect the employees against the dangers of the toxic chemicals. Government experts testified that without these proper safety precautions, the employees were at an increased risk of suffering solvent poisoning. * * *
>
> Title 42, United States Code, Section 6928(e) provides that: "Any person who knowingly transports, treats, stores, disposes of, or exports any hazardous waste identified or listed under [the RCRA] in violation of [the criminal provisions of the RCRA] who knows at that time that he thereby places another person in imminent danger of death or serious bodily injury, shall [be guilty of an offense against the United States.]" Title 42, United States Code, Section 6928(f)(6) defines "serious bodily injury" as: (A) bodily injury which involves a substantial risk of death;   (B) unconsciousness;   (C)

extreme physical pain; (D) protracted and obvious disfigurement; or (E) protracted loss or impairment of the function of a bodily member, organ, or mental faculty. Protex contends that the trial court rendered section 6928(e) unconstitutionally vague by expanding the definition of "serious bodily injury" beyond that set out in section 6928(f)(6). Protex states that if the employees were placed in any "danger" at all, it was a danger of developing Type 2-A psychoorganic syndrome, a condition which does not come within the scope of subparagraphs (A)-(E) of section 6928(f)(6). Protex also argues that the enhanced "risk" of contracting some indeterminate type of cancer at some unspecified time in the future is not sufficient to constitute "serious bodily injury."

Appellant's position demonstrates a callousness toward the severe physical effect the prolonged exposure to toxic chemicals may cause or has caused to the three former employees. * * *

* * * The gist of the "knowing endangerment" provision of the RCRA is that a party will be criminally liable if, in violating other provisions of the RCRA, it places others in danger of great harm and it has knowledge of that danger. The district court conveyed this same idea to the jury in its instructions. The court rejects appellant's argument that it could not be aware that its behavior was prohibited by the "knowing endangerment" provision of the RCRA.

4. Willful Blindness

UNITED STATES v. BUCKLEY
934 F.2d 84 (6th Cir. 1991)

RYAN, Circuit Judge.

A jury convicted Paul J. Buckley of violating 42 U.S.C. §§ 7412(c)(1)(B), 7413(c)(1)(C), Clean Air Act provisions regulating the release of asbestos into the environment. The jury also convicted him of violating 42 U.S.C. § 9603(b)(3), a CERCLA provision requiring notification to authorities of any release of a reportable quantity of asbestos. Appealing both convictions, Buckley places two issues before this court. The first, is whether the jury instructions offended due process by misstating the level of scienter required for conviction under the statutes. * * *

A grand jury indicted Buckley and other parties on several counts related to the release of asbestos into the environment in the course of a demolition project. This appeal concerns only counts 4 and 5. Count 4 charged that Buckley violated 42 U.S.C. §§ 7412(c)(1)(B), 7413(c)(1)(C) by knowingly emitting certain amounts of asbestos into the environment in the process of demolishing a stationary source. Count 5 charged that Buckley violated 42 U.S.C. § 9603(b)(3) by failing to notify the appropriate federal agency of a known release of a reportable quantity of asbestos. * * *

On the element of "knowledge," the district court instructed generally as follows:

> The law provides that an individual cannot avoid knowledge by deliberately closing his eyes to what would otherwise be obvious or by failing to investigate if he is in possession of facts which cry out for investigation. Consequently, if you find beyond a reasonable doubt that the defendant acted with a conscious purpose to avoided [sic] learning the truth about the presence of asbestos, or consciously avoided investigating even though he was in possession of facts which demanded investigation, then you may find that the government has satisfied its burden of establishing knowledge.

> If you find that the defendant was aware of a high probability that asbestos was present and that the defendant acted with deliberate disregard of the facts, you may find that the defendant acted knowingly. However, if you find that the defendant actually believed that there was no asbestos on pipes or in stoves, he may not be convicted.

> It is entirely up to you whether you find that the defendant deliberately closed his eyes and any inferences to be drawn from the evidence on this issue. (Emphasis added.)

Buckley objected to these instructions on the ground that they created a strict-liability criminal offense. * * *

Buckley contends that the instructions violated due process by eliminating knowledge as an element of the crimes. He also seems to contend that due process requires the courts to define "knowledge" as awareness of wrongdoing, not awareness of the occurrence of the prohibited acts or omissions. * * *

The statutory language makes knowledge an element of the crime of violating emission standards; however, the statute requires knowledge only of the emissions themselves, not knowledge of the statute or of the hazards that emissions pose. "[W]here a statute does not specify a heightened mental element . . . , general intent is presumed to be the required element." * * *

Because of the very nature of asbestos and other hazardous substances, individuals dealing with them have constitutionally adequate notice that they may incur criminal liability for emissions-related actions. "[W]here . . . dangerous or deleterious . . . products or obnoxious waste materials are involved, the probability of regulation is so great that anyone who is aware that he is in possession of them or dealing with them must be presumed to be aware of the regulation." * * *

Here the district court properly instructed the jurors that they could not find Buckley guilty unless he *"knowingly* failed . . . to comply with . . . standards." The district court also explained the meaning of "knowledge" for the jurors.　The court noted that under the law, the government could establish Buckley's knowledge by showing that Buckley closed his eyes to obvious facts or failed to investigate when aware of facts which demanded investigation.　Finally, near the end of its explanation of knowledge, the district court noted that the jury could not convict Buckley if it found that he actually believed that the pipe and stove coverings contained no asbestos.

Accordingly, we hold that whether evaluated separately or together, these instructions accurately state the law and do not offend due process. * * *

For the foregoing reasons, Buckley's convictions are AFFIRMED.

5. Negligently

UNITED STATES v. HANOUSEK
176 F.3d 1116 (9th Cir. 1999)

DAVID R. THOMPSON, Circuit Judge.

Edward Hanousek, Jr., appeals his conviction and sentence for negligently discharging a harmful quantity of oil into a navigable water of the United States, in violation of the Clean Water Act, 33 U.S.C. §§ 1319(c)(1)(A) & 1321(b)(3). Hanousek contends that the district court erred: (1) by failing to instruct the jury that the government must prove that he acted with criminal negligence as opposed to ordinary negligence, * * * Hanousek also argues that section 1319(c)(1)(A) violates due process if it permits a criminal conviction for ordinary negligence and that, in any event, the evidence was insufficient to support his conviction.　We have jurisdiction under 28 U.S.C. § 1291 and we affirm.　* * *

Hanousek was employed by the Pacific & Arctic Railway and Navigation Company　(Pacific & Arctic) as roadmaster of the White Pass & Yukon Railroad, which runs between Skagway, Alaska, and Whitehorse, Yukon Territory, Canada.　As roadmaster, Hanousek was responsible under his contract "for every detail of the safe and efficient maintenance and construction of track, structures and marine facilities of the entire railroad ... and [was to] assume similar duties with special projects."

One of the special projects under Hanousek's supervision was a rock-quarrying project at a site alongside the railroad referred to as "6-mile," located on an embankment 200 feet above the Skagway River. * * * Pacific & Arctic hired Hunz & Hunz, a contracting company, to provide the equipment and labor for the project. * * * On the evening of October 1, 1994, Shane Thoe, a Hunz & Hunz backhoe operator, used the backhoe on the work platform to load a train with rocks. After the train departed, Thoe noticed that some fallen rocks had caught the plow of the train as it departed and were located just off the tracks in the vicinity of the unprotected pipeline. At this location, the site had been graded to finish grade and the pipeline was covered with a few inches of soil. Thoe moved the backhoe off the work platform and drove it down alongside the tracks between 50 to 100 yards from the work platform. While using the backhoe bucket to sweep the rocks from the tracks, Thoe struck the pipeline causing a rupture. The pipeline was carrying heating oil, and an estimated 1,000 to 5,000 gallons of oil were discharged over the course of many days into the adjacent Skagway River, a navigable water of the United States.

Following an investigation, Hanousek was charged with one count of negligently discharging a harmful quantity of oil into a navigable water of the United States, in violation of the Clean Water Act, 33 U.S.C. §§ 1319(c)(1)(A) & 1321(b)(3). Hanousek was also charged with one count of conspiring to provide false information to United States Coast Guard officials who investigated the accident, in violation of 18 U.S.C. §§ 371, 1001.

After a twenty-day trial, the jury convicted Hanousek of negligently discharging a harmful quantity of oil into a navigable water of the United States, but acquitted him on the charge of conspiring to provide false information. The district court imposed a sentence of six months of imprisonment, six months in a halfway house and six months of supervised release, as well as a fine of $5,000. This appeal followed.

* * * Hanousek contends the district court erred by failing to instruct the jury that, to establish a violation under 33 U.S.C. § 1319(c)(1)(A), the government had to prove that Hanousek acted with criminal negligence, as opposed to ordinary negligence, in discharging a harmful quantity of oil into the Skagway River. In his proposed jury instruction, Hanousek defined criminal negligence as "a gross deviation from the standard of care that a reasonable person would observe in the situation." See American Law Institute, Model Penal Code § 2.02(2)(d) (1985). Over Hanousek's objection, the district court instructed the jury that the government was required to prove only that Hanousek acted negligently, which the district court defined as "the failure to use reasonable care." * * *

Statutory interpretation begins with the plain language of the statute. If the language of the statute is clear, we need look no further than that language in determining the statute's meaning. "Particular phrases must be construed in light of the overall purpose and structure of the whole statutory scheme." "When we look to the plain language of a statute in order to interpret its meaning, we do more than view words or sub-sections in isolation. We derive meaning from context, and this requires reading the relevant statutory provisions as a whole."

Codified sections 1319(c)(1)(A) & 1321(b)(3) of the Clean Water Act work in tandem to criminalize the conduct of which Hanousek was convicted. Section 1319(c)(1)(A) provides that any person who negligently violates 33 U.S.C. § 1321(b)(3) shall be punished by fine or imprisonment, or both. Section 1321(b)(3) proscribes the actual discharge of oil in harmful quantities into navigable waters of the United States, adjoining shore lines or waters of a contiguous zone, as well as other specified activity.

Neither section defines the term "negligently," nor is that term defined elsewhere in the CWA.[b] In this circumstance, we "start with the assumption that the legislative purpose is expressed by the ordinary meaning of the words used." The ordinary meaning of "negligently" is a failure to use such care as a reasonably prudent and careful person would use under similar circumstances. See Black's Law Dictionary 1032 (6th ed.1990); The Random House College Dictionary 891 (Rev. ed.1980).

If Congress intended to prescribe a heightened negligence standard, it could have done so explicitly, as it did in 33 U.S.C. § 1321(b)(7)(D). This section of the CWA provides for increased civil penalties "[i]n any case in which a violation of [33 U.S.C. § 1321(b)(3)] was the result of gross negligence or willful misconduct." 33 U.S.C. § 1321(b)(7)(D). This is significant. "[W]here Congress includes particular language in one section of a statute but omits it in another section of the same Act, it is generally presumed that Congress acts intentionally and purposely in the disparate inclusion or exclusion." * * *

Hanousek argues that Congress could not have intended to distinguish "negligently" in 33 U.S.C. § 1319(c)(1)(A) from "gross negligence" in 33 U.S.C. § 1321(b)(7)(D) because the phrase "gross negligence" was only recently added to the statute in 1990. See Oil Pollution Control Act of 1990, Pub.L. No. 101-380, 104 Stat. 484 (1990). We reject this argument because Congress is presumed to have known of its former legislation and to have passed new laws in view of the provisions of the legislation already enacted. * * *

We conclude from the plain language of 33 U.S.C. § 1319(c)(1)(A) that Congress intended that a person who acts with ordinary negligence in violating 33 U.S.C. § 1321(b)(3) may be subject to criminal penalties. We

---

[b] For a statistical analysis of criminal negligence prosecutions brought under the Clean Water Act see Steven P. Solow & Ronald A. Sarachan, *Criminal Negligence Prosecutions Under the Federal Clean Water Act: A Statistical; Analysis and the Evaluation of the Impact of* Hanousek *and* Hong, 32 Envir. L. Rptr. 11153 (2002).

next consider Hanousek's argument that, by imposing an ordinary negligence standard for a criminal violation, section 1319(c)(1)(A) violates the due process clause of the Constitution.

* * * The criminal provisions of the CWA constitute public welfare legislation. * * * It is well established that a public welfare statute may subject a person to criminal liability for his or her ordinary negligence without violating due process. * * * Recognizing that our holding in *Weitzenhoff* [35 F.3d 1275 (9th Cir. 1994)] would defeat his due process argument, Hanousek attempts to distinguish *Weitzenhoff.* The attempt fails. In *Weitzenhoff,* two managers of a sewage treatment plant operating under a National Pollution Discharge Elimination System permit were convicted of knowingly discharging pollutants into a navigable water of the United States, in violation of 33 U.S.C. §§ 1311(a) & 1319(c)(2). * * * In rejecting the defendants' contention that the district court erred by failing to instruct the jury that the government had to prove that the defendants knew their acts violated the permit or the CWA, we held that the criminal provisions of the CWA constitute public welfare legislation and that the government was not required to prove that the defendants knew their conduct violated the law. We explained that, "[w]here ... dangerous or deleterious devices or products or obnoxious waste materials are involved, the probability of regulation is so great that anyone who is aware that he is in possession of them or dealing with them must be presumed to be aware of the regulation." * * *

Hanousek argues that, unlike the defendants in *Weitzenhoff* who were permittees under the CWA, he was simply the roadmaster of the White Pass & Yukon railroad charged with overseeing a rock-quarrying project and was not in a position to know what the law required under the CWA. This is a distinction without a difference. In the context of a public welfare statute, "as long as a defendant knows he is dealing with a dangerous device of a character that places him 'in responsible relation to a public danger,' he should be alerted to the probability of strict regulation."* * * Although Hanousek was not a permittee under the CWA, he does not dispute that he was aware that a high-pressure petroleum products pipeline owned by Pacific & Arctic's sister company ran close to the surface next to the railroad tracks at 6-mile, and does not argue that he was unaware of the dangers a break or puncture of the pipeline by a piece of heavy machinery would pose. Therefore, Hanousek should have been alerted to the probability of strict regulation.

In light of our holding in Weitzenhoff that the criminal provisions of the CWA constitute public welfare legislation, and the fact that a public welfare statute may impose criminal penalties for ordinary negligent conduct without offending due process, we conclude that section 1319(c)(1)(A) does not violate due process by permitting criminal penalties for ordinary negligent conduct. * * *

In light of the plain language of 33 U.S.C. § 1319(c)(1)(A), we conclude Congress intended that a person who acts with ordinary negligence in violating 33 U.S.C. § 1321(b)(3) may be subjected to criminal penalties. These sections, as so construed, do not violate due process. Accordingly, the district court properly instructed the jury on ordinary negligence. * * * AFFIRMED

C. INDIVIDUALS LIABLE

1. Persons In Charge

APEX OIL COMPANY v. UNITED STATES
530 F.2d 1291 (8th Cir. 1976)

HEANEY, Circuit Judge.

Apex Oil Company, a Missouri corporation whose business includes the transportation and storage of various types of fuel oil, appeals from a final judgment of conviction on two counts of a three-count indictment for failing to notify an appropriate agency of the United States government of a known oil spill in violation of the Water Pollution Control Act, 33 U.S.C. § 1321(b)(5). It was fined a total of $20,000 and placed on probation for three years. The execution of $15,000 of the fine was stayed on the condition that the corporation not violate any law relating to pollution during the probationary period. Two issues are raised on appeal: (1) whether the corporation is a "person in charge" within the meaning of 33 U.S.C. § 1321(b) (5), and (2) whether the evidence was sufficient to support the conviction. We affirm.

Section 1321(b)(5) of Title 33 of the United States Code, upon which the convictions are based, states in relevant part: Any person in charge of * * * an onshore facility * * * shall, as soon as he has knowledge of any discharge of oil * * * from such * * * facility in violation of paragraph (3) of this subsection, immediately notify the appropriate agency of the United States Government of such discharge. Any such person who fails to notify immediately such agency of such discharge shall, upon conviction, be fined not more than $10,000, or imprisoned for not more than one year, or both. Notification received pursuant to this paragraph or information obtained by the exploitation of such notifications shall not be used against any such person in any criminal case, except a prosecution for perjury or for giving a false statement. The appellant argues that only an individual, or natural person, and not a corporation, can be a "person in charge" within the meaning of the statute and, hence, it cannot be prosecuted.

A "person," as defined by the Act, "includes an individual, firm, corporation, association, and a partnership(.)" 33 U.S.C. § 1321(a)(7) (Emphasis supplied.) Apex Oil, thus, raises a distinction between the meaning of "person" when used alone and its meaning when used in conjunction with the words "in charge." It is a distinction which the Act does not itself make. It is, moreover, a distinction that cannot be supported by the purposes of the Act.

Section 1321(b)(5) prompts the timely reporting and discovery of oil discharges into or upon the navigable waters of the United States to facilitate the mitigation of pollution damage. It is designed to insure, so far as possible, that small discharges will not go undetected and that the possibility of effective abatement will not be lost. The purpose is best served by holding the corporation responsible under the provision of the statute. * * *

[The court rejected arguments that inclusion of the corporation within the meaning of the term "person in charge" would be inconsistent with civil penalty provisions of the Act and Coast Guard regulations.] * * * [T]he appellant argues that the government failed to prove that it was "in charge" at the time of the spills and that it had knowledge of their occurrence. * * * Each argument is meritless. The corporation is no less "in charge" of the oil facility than is its employee.

Further, the knowledge of the employees is the knowledge of the corporation. * * * The judgment of conviction on Counts two and three is affirmed.

NOTES AND QUESTIONS

1. *Corporate Liability.* What effect will the court's finding a corporation as a "person in charge" have on future corporations reporting discharges? Can there be problems in finding employees high enough in the corporation to be "in charge" who also have sufficient knowledge?

2. *Reporting Requirements.* Reporting requirements are found in other environmental statutes as well. (e.g., CERCLA, 42 U.S.C.A. § 9603(a)). Who within an organization has the burden of reporting the discharge of a hazardous substance? In **United States v. Carr**, 880 F.2d 1550 (2d Cir. 1989), the court discussed who is a person "in charge" under CERCLA's reporting requirement:

> * * * Under section 103, only those who are "in charge" of a facility must report a hazardous release. There is, however, no definition of the term "in charge" within CERCLA. Appellant argues that the district court's instruction was erroneous because Congress never intended to extend the statute's reporting requirement to those, like Carr, who are relatively low in an organization's chain of command.

> * * * The language of the statute itself sheds little light on the meaning of the term "in charge." Section 103 of CERCLA states

only that: Any person in charge of a vessel or an offshore or an onshore facility shall, as soon as he has knowledge of any release (other than a federally permitted release) of a hazardous substance from such vessel or facility in quantities equal to or greater than those determined pursuant to [42 U.S.C.A. § 9602], immediately notify the National Response Center established under the Clean Water Act [33 U.S.C.A. § 1251 et seq.] of such release. The National Response Center shall convey the notification expeditiously to all appropriate Government agencies, including the Governor of any affected State. The regulations implementing the statute fail to define the term "in charge." See 40 C.F.R. § 302 (1988) (EPA regulations). * * * The legislative history of CERCLA makes clear that Congress modeled the reporting requirements of section 103 on section 311 of the Clean Water Act, 33 U.S.C. § 1321(b)(5). Like CERCLA's section 103, the reporting requirements of section 311 of the Clean Water Act require any person "in charge" of a facility to report a release of hazardous substances. * * *

Since CERCLA's use of the term "in charge" was borrowed from section 311 of the Clean Water Act, and the two sections share the same purpose, the parallel provisions can, as a matter of general statutory construction, be interpreted to be in pari materia. * * *

The legislative history of section 311 bears out appellant's argument that CERCLA's reporting requirements should not be extended to all employees involved in a release. 'The term "person in charge" [was] deliberately designed to cover only supervisory personnel who have the responsibility for the particular vessel or facility and not to include other employees. "Indeed, as the Fifth Circuit has stated, 'to the extent that legislative history does shed light on the meaning of 'persons in charge,' it suggests at the very most that Congress intended the provisions of [section 311] to extend, not to every person who might have knowledge of [a release] (mere employees, for example), but only to persons who occupy positions of responsibility and power."

That is not to say, however, that section 311 of the Clean Water Act—and section 103 of CERCLA—do not reach lower-level supervisory employees. The reporting requirements of the two statutes do not apply only to owners and operators, but instead extend to any person who is "responsible for the operation" of a facility from which there is a release, * * *

2. Responsible Corporate Officer

UNITED STATES v. MacDONALD & WATSON WASTE OIL COMPANY
933 F.2d 35 (1st Cir. 1991)

CAMPBELL, Circuit Judge.

This appeal concerns the criminal liability of individuals and corporations under hazardous waste disposal laws.

Following a jury trial in the district court, appellants were convicted, inter alia, of having violated criminal provisions of the Resource Conservation and Recovery Act ("RCRA"), 42 U.S.C. § 6901 et seq. and the Comprehensive Environmental Response, Compensation and Liability Act ("CERCLA"), 42 U.S.C. § 9603(b). * * *D'Allesandro, the President and owner of MacDonald & Watson, contends that his conviction under RCRA, § 3008(d)(1), 42 U.S.C. § 6928(d)(1), must be vacated because the district court incorrectly charged the jury regarding the element of knowledge in the case of a corporate officer. Section 3008(d)(1) penalizes "Any person who. . . . (1) knowingly transports or causes to be transported any hazardous waste identified or listed under this subchapter . . . . to a facility which does not have a permit . . . .". (Emphasis supplied.) In his closing, the prosecutor conceded that the government had "no direct evidence that Eugene D'Allesandro actually knew that the Master Chemical shipments were coming in," i.e., were being transported to the Poe Street Lot under contract with his company. The prosecution did present evidence, however, that D'Allesandro was not only the President and owner of MacDonald & Watson but was a "hands-on" manager of that relatively small firm. There was also proof that that firm leased the Poe Street Lot from NIC, and managed it, and that D'Allesandro's subordinates had contracted for and transported the Master Chemical waste for disposal at that site. The government argued that D'Allesandro was guilty of violating § 3008(d)(1) because, as the responsible corporate officer, he was in a position to ensure compliance with RCRA and had failed to do so even after being warned by a consultant on two earlier occasions that other shipments of toluene-contaminated soil had been received from other customers, and that such material violated NIC's permit. In the government's view, any failure to prove D'Allesandro's actual knowledge of the Master Chemical contract and shipments was irrelevant to his criminal responsibility under § 3008(d)(1) for those shipments.

The court apparently accepted the government's theory. It instructed the jury as follows: When an individual Defendant is also a corporate officer, the Government may prove that individual's knowledge in either of two ways. The first way is to demonstrate that the Defendant had actual knowledge of the act in question. The second way is to establish that the defendant was what is called a responsible officer of the corporation committing the act. In order to prove that a person is a responsible corporate officer three things must be shown. First, it must be shown that the person is an officer of the corporation, not merely an employee. Second, it must be shown that the officer had direct responsibility for the activities that are alleged to be illegal. Simply being an officer or even the president of a corporation is not enough. The Government must prove that the person had a responsibility to supervise the activities in question. And the third requirement is that the officer must have known or believed that the illegal activity of the type alleged occurred. The court's phrasing of the third element at first glance seems ambiguous: it could be read to require actual knowledge of the Master Chemical shipments themselves. We are satisfied, however, that the court meant only what it literally said: D'Allesandro must have known or believed that illegal shipments of the type alleged had previously occurred. This tied into evidence that D'Allesandro had been advised of two earlier shipments of toluene- contaminated waste, and was told that such waste could not legally be received. For the court to require a finding that D'Allesandro knew of the alleged shipments themselves (i.e., the Master Chemical shipments), would have duplicated the court's earlier instruction on actual knowledge, and was not in accord with the government's theory.

D'Allesandro challenges this instruction, contending that the use of the "responsible corporate officer" doctrine is improper under § 3008(d)(1) which expressly calls for proof of knowledge, i.e., requires scienter. The government responds that the district court properly adapted the responsible corporate officer doctrine traditionally applied to strict liability offenses to this case, instructing the jury to find knowledge "that the illegal activity of the type alleged occurred,"—a finding that, together with the first two, made it reasonable to infer knowledge of the particular violation. We agree with D'Allesandro that the jury instructions improperly allowed the jury to find him guilty without finding he had actual knowledge of the alleged transportation of hazardous waste on July 30 and 31, 1986, from Master Chemical Company, Boston, Massachusetts, to NIC's site, knowledge being an element the statute requires. We must, therefore, vacate his conviction.

The seminal cases regarding the responsible corporate officer doctrine are United States v. Dotterweich, 320 U.S. 277 (1943), and United States v. Park, [p.76]. These cases concerned misdemeanor charges under the Federal Food, Drug, and Cosmetic Act, 21 U.S.C. §§ 301-392, as amended, relating to the handling or shipping of adulterated or misbranded drugs or food. The offenses alleged in the informations failed to state a knowledge element, and the Court found that they, in fact, dispensed with a scienter requirement, placing "the burden of acting at hazard upon a person otherwise innocent but standing in responsible relation to a public danger." The Court in *Park* clarified 2that corporate officer liability in that situation requires only a finding that the officer had "authority with respect to the conditions that formed the basis of the alleged violations." But while *Dotterweich* and *Park* thus reflect what is now clear and well-established law in respect to public welfare statutes and regulations lacking an express knowledge or other scienter requirement, we know of no precedent for failing to give effect to a knowledge requirement that Congress has expressly included in a criminal statute. Especially is that so where, as here, the crime is a felony carrying possible imprisonment of five years and, for a second offense, ten.

The district court, nonetheless, applied here a form of the responsible corporate officer doctrine established in *Dotterweich* and *Park* for strict liability misdemeanors, as a substitute means for proving the explicit knowledge element of this RCRA felony, 42 U.S.C. § 6928(d)(1). As an alternative to finding actual knowledge, the district court permitted the prosecution to constructively establish defendant's knowledge if the jury found the following: (1) that the defendant was a corporate officer; (2) with responsibility to supervise the allegedly illegal activities; and (3) knew or believed "that the illegal activity of the type alleged occurred." As previously stated, the third element did not necessitate proof of knowledge of the Master Chemical shipments charged in the indictment, but simply proof of earlier occasions when D'Allesandro was told his firm had improperly accepted toluene-contaminated soil.

Contrary to the government's assertions, this instruction did more than simply permit the jury, if it wished, to infer knowledge of the Master Chemical shipments from relevant circumstantial evidence including D'Allesandro's responsibilities and activities as a corporate executive. With respect to circumstantial evidence, the district court properly instructed elsewhere that knowledge did not have to be proven by direct evidence but could be inferred from the defendant's conduct and other facts and circumstances. The court also instructed that the element of knowledge could be satisfied by proof of willful blindness. These instructions allowed the jury to consider whether relevant circumstantial evidence established that D'Allesandro actually knew of the charged Master Chemical shipments. These would have sufficed had it merely been the court's purpose to point out that knowledge could be established by circumstantial evidence, although the court could, had it wished, have elaborated on the extent to which D'Allesandro's responsibilities and duties might lead to a reasonable inference that he knew of the Master Chemical transaction.

Instead, the district court charged, in effect, that proof that D'Allesandro was a responsible corporate officer would conclusively prove the element of his knowledge of the Master Chemical shipments. The jury was told that knowledge could be proven "in either of two ways." Besides demonstrating actual knowledge, the government could simply establish the defendant was a responsible corporate officer—the latter by showing three things, none of which, individually or collectively, necessarily established his actual knowledge of the illegal transportation charged. Under the district court's instruction, the jury's belief that the responsible corporate officer lacked actual knowledge of, and had not willfully blinded himself to, the criminal transportation alleged would be insufficient for acquittal so long as the officer knew or even erroneously believed that illegal activity of the same type had occurred on another occasion.

We have found no case, and the government cites none, where a jury was instructed that the defendant could be convicted of a federal crime expressly requiring knowledge as an element, solely by reason of a conclusive, or "mandatory" presumption of knowledge of the facts constituting the offense. The government's primary reliance on the Third Circuit's more limited decision in Johnson & Towers, 741 F.2d 662 (3d Cir. 1984), is misplaced. There, the court of appeals concluded that "knowingly" applies to all elements of the offense, including permit status, in RCRA § 3008(d)(2)(A). The court of appeals advised that proof of knowledge of the permit requirement and the nonexistence of the permit did not impose a great burden because such knowledge might, in a proper case, be inferred. Relying on the Supreme Court's decision in United States v. International Minerals & Chemical Corp., 402 U.S. 558, 563 (1971), the court of appeals emphasized "that under certain regulatory statutes requiring 'knowing' conduct, the government need prove only knowledge of the actions taken and not of the statute forbidding them." Thus, this case supports only the position that knowledge of the law may be inferred, and does not address knowledge of acts. * * *

We agree with the decisions discussed above that knowledge may be inferred from circumstantial evidence, including position and responsibility of defendants such as corporate officers, as well as information provided to those defendants on prior occasions. Further, willful blindness to the facts constituting the offense may be sufficient to establish knowledge. However, the district court erred by instructing the jury that proof that a defendant was a responsible corporate officer, as described, would suffice to conclusively establish the element of knowledge expressly required under § 3008(d)(1). Simply because a responsible corporate officer believed that on a prior occasion illegal transportation occurred, he did not necessarily possess knowledge of the violation charged. In a crime having knowledge as an express element, a mere showing of official responsibility under *Dotterweich* and *Park* is not an adequate substitute for direct or circumstantial proof of knowledge. * * *

NOTES AND QUESTIONS

1. *Clean Water/Clean Air Acts.* Both the Clean Water Act (33 U.S.C.A. § 1319 (c)(6)) and the Clean Air Act (42 U.S.C.A. § 7413(c)(6)) have incorporated the "responsible corporate officer" within the definition of "person." Does including the responsible corporate officer as a "person" into the statute serve to make the statute a strict liability offense when a responsible corporate officer is involved? In **United States v. Brittain**, 931 F.2d 1413, 1419 (10th Cir. 1991), the court stated:

* * * We interpret the addition of "responsible corporate officers" as an expansion of liability under the Act rather than, as defendant would have it, an implicit limitation. The plain language of the statute, after all, states that "responsible corporate officers" are liable "in addition to the definition [of persons] contained in section 1362(5) . . . ." § 1319(c)(3) (emphasis supplied). Under this interpretation, a "responsible corporate officer," to be held criminally liable, would not have to "willfully or negligently" cause a permit violation. Instead, the willfulness or negligence of the actor would be imputed to him by virtue of his position of responsibility. * * *

Should the term "responsible corporate officer" be interpreted differently, dependant upon the statute involved? For example, should a court in an action involving an environmental crime, as opposed to an FDA violation, refuse to impute liability merely on the basis of an individual being a responsible corporate officer? See Barry M. Hartman & Charles A. De Monaco, *The Present Use of the Responsible Corporate Officer Doctrine in the Criminal Enforcement of Environmental Laws*, 23 ENVIRONMENTAL L. RPTR. 10145, 10153 (1993) ["While (the responsible corporate officer doctrine) renders corporate officials criminally liable for acts of their subordinates, it does not eliminate the knowledge requirement set forth in the applicable statute."].

2. *Attributes of a Responsible Corporate Officer.* What makes a person a responsible corporate officer? Consider the following case:

UNITED STATES v. IVERSON
162 F.3d 1015 (9th Cir. 1998)

GRABER, Circuit Judge:

A jury convicted defendant of four counts of violating federal water pollution law, as embodied in the Clean Water Act (CWA), the Washington Administrative Code (WAC), and the City of Olympia's Municipal Code (Olympia code). The jury also convicted defendant of one count of conspiring to violate the WAC or the CWA. Defendant appeals, arguing that: (1) the district court misinterpreted the CWA, the WAC, and the Olympia code; (2) those provisions are unconstitutionally vague; (3) the district court erred in formulating its "responsible corporate officer" jury instruction; and (4) the district court erred by admitting evidence of defendant's prior discharges of industrial waste. We are not persuaded by any of defendant's arguments and, thus, we affirm his convictions.   * * *

Defendant was a founder of CH2O, Inc., and served as the company's President and Chairman of the Board. CH2O blends chemicals to create numerous products, including acid cleaners and heavy-duty alkaline compounds. The company ships the blended chemicals to its customers in drums.

CH2O asked its customers to return the drums so that it could reuse them. Although customers returned the drums, they often did not clean them sufficiently. Thus, the drums still contained chemical residue. Before CH2O could reuse the drums, it had to remove that residue.

To remove the residue, CH2O instituted a drum-cleaning operation, which in turn generated wastewater. In the early to mid-1980s, defendant approached the manager of the local sewer authority to see whether the sewer authority would accept the company's wastewater. The sewer authority refused, because the wastewater "did not meet the parameters we had set for accepting industrial waste. It had too high of a metal content." Thereafter, defendant and the general manager of CH2O made two other attempts to convince the sewer authority to accept the wastewater. Both times, it refused.

Beginning in about 1985, defendant personally discharged the wastewater and ordered employees of CH2O to discharge the wastewater in three places: (1) on the plant's property, (2) through a sewer drain at an apartment complex that defendant owned, and (3) through a sewer drain at defendant's home. (The plant did not have sewer access.) Those discharges continued until about 1988, when CH2O hired Bill Brady.

Brady initially paid a waste disposal company to dispose of the wastewater. Those efforts cost the company thousands of dollars each month. Beginning in late 1991, CH2O stopped its drum-cleaning operation and, instead, shipped the drums to a professional outside contractor for cleaning.

In April 1992, CH2O fired Brady. Around that same time, defendant bought a warehouse in Olympia. Unlike the CH2O plant, the warehouse had sewer access. After the purchase, CH2O restarted its drum-cleaning operation at the warehouse and disposed of its wastewater through the sewer. CH2O obtained neither a permit nor permission to make these discharges. The drum-cleaning operation continued until the summer of 1995, when CH2O learned that it was under investigation for discharging pollutants into the sewer.

A few months before CH2O restarted its drum-cleaning operation, defendant announced his "official" retirement from CH2O. Thereafter, he continued to receive money from CH2O, to conduct business at the company's facilities, and to give orders to employees. Moreover, the company continued to list him as the president in documents that it filed with the state, and the employee who was responsible for running the day-to-day aspects of the drum-cleaning operation testified that he reported to defendant.

During the four years of the operation at the warehouse, defendant was sometimes present when drums were cleaned. During those occasions, defendant was close enough to see and smell the waste.

In some instances, defendant informed employees that he had obtained a permit for the drum-cleaning operation and that the operation was on the "up and up." At other times, however, defendant told employees that, if they got caught, the company would receive only a slap on the wrist. * * *

After an eight-day trial, the jury found defendant guilty on all counts. Thereafter, the district court sentenced defendant to one year in custody, three years of supervised release, and a $75,000 fine. This timely appeal ensued. * * *

The district court instructed the jury that it could find defendant liable under the CWA as a "responsible corporate officer" if it found, beyond a reasonable doubt:

1. That the defendant had knowledge of the fact that pollutants were being discharged to the sewer system by employees of CH2O, Inc.;

2. That the defendant had the authority and capacity to prevent the discharge of pollutants to the sewer system; and

3. That the defendant failed to prevent the on-going discharge of pollutants to the sewer system.

Defendant argues that the district court misinterpreted the scope of "responsible corporate officer" liability. Specifically, defendant suggests that a corporate officer is "responsible" only when the officer in fact exercises control over the activity causing the discharge or has an express corporate duty to oversee the activity. We have not previously interpreted the scope of "responsible corporate officer" liability under the CWA. We do so now and reject defendant's narrow interpretation.

* * * The CWA defines the term "person" to include "any responsible corporate officer." See 33 U.S.C. § 1319(c)(6) ("For the purpose of this subsection, the term 'person' means, in addition to the definition contained in section 1362(5) of this title, any responsible corporate officer."). However, the CWA does not define the term "responsible corporate officer." * * * When a statute does not define a term, we generally interpret that term by employing the ordinary, contemporary, and common meaning of the words that Congress used. * * * As pertinent here, the word "responsible" means "answerable" or "involving a degree of accountability." Webster's Third New Int'l Dictionary 1935 (unabridged ed.1993). Using that meaning, "any corporate officer" who is "answerable" or "accountable" for the unlawful discharge is liable under the CWA.

The history of "responsible corporate officer" liability supports the foregoing construction. The "responsible corporate officer" doctrine originated in a Supreme Court case interpreting the Federal Food, Drug, and Cosmetic Act (FFDCA), United States v. Dotterweich, 320 U.S. 277, 64 S.Ct. 134, 88 L.Ed. 48 (1943). * * *   Because Congress used a similar definition of the term "person" in the CWA, we can presume that Congress intended that the principles of *Dotterweich* apply under the CWA. * * * Under *Dotterweich*, whether defendant had sufficient "responsibility" over the discharges to be criminally liable would be a question for the jury.

After Congress initially enacted the CWA in 1972, the Supreme Court further defined the scope of the "responsible corporate officer" doctrine under the FFDCA. In United States v. Park [p. 83], a corporate president argued that he could not be "responsible" under *Dotterweich*, because he had delegated decision- making control over the activity in question to a subordinate. The Court rejected that argument, holding that

> the Government establishes a prima facie case when it introduces evidence sufficient to warrant a finding by the trier of the facts that the defendant had, by reasons of his position in the corporation, responsibility and authority either to prevent in the first instance or promptly to correct, the violation complained of, and that he failed to do so.

Stated another way, the question for the jury is whether the corporate officer had "authority with respect to the conditions that formed the basis of the alleged violations." The Court did not, however, require the corporate officer actually to exercise any authority over the activity.

In 1987, after the Supreme Court decided *Park*, Congress revised and replaced the criminal provisions of the CWA. (Most importantly, Congress made a violation of the CWA a felony, rather than a misdemeanor.) In replacing the criminal provisions of the CWA, Congress made no changes to its "responsible corporate officer" provision. That being so, we can presume that Congress intended for Park's refinement of the "responsible corporate officer" doctrine to apply under the CWA.

Moreover, this court has interpreted similar terms in other statutes consistently with the Court's decision in *Park*. For example, the Internal Revenue Code (IRC) holds liable any "person required to collect, truthfully account for, and pay over any tax" under the IRC. 26 U.S.C. § 6672(a). The IRC defines "person" to include any "officer ... under a duty to perform the act in respect of which the violation occurs." 26 U.S.C. § 6671(b). This court consistently has interpreted the term "person" to include corporate officers with authority to pay taxes, whether or not they exercise that authority. * * *

Taken together, the wording of the CWA, the Supreme Court's interpretations of the "responsible corporate officer" doctrine, and this court's interpretation of similar statutory requirements establish the contours of the "responsible corporate officer" doctrine under the CWA. Under the CWA, a person is a "responsible corporate officer" if the person has authority to exercise control over the corporation's activity that is causing the discharges. There is no requirement that the officer in fact exercise such authority or that the corporation expressly vest a duty in the officer to oversee the activity. * * * AFFIRMED.

3. Aiding and Abetting

UNITED STATES v. DOIG
950 F.2d 411 (7th Cir. 1991)

BAUER, Chief Judge.

In this case of first impression, we must determine whether an employee may be charged with aiding and abetting his corporate employer in a criminal violation of The Occupational Health and Safety Act of 1970, 29 U.S.C. § 666(e) (1988) ("OSHA" or "the Act"). We find that Congress did not intend to subject employees to such liability under OSHA, and, therefore, affirm the district court's dismissal of criminal charges against Defendant-Appellee, Patrick J. Doig.

The S.A. Healy Company ("Healy") and Patrick J. Doig ("Doig") were charged with twelve counts of criminal OSHA violations under 29 U.S.C. § 666(e). The section imposes criminal liability on "[a]ny employer" whose willful violation of an OSHA regulation causes the death of any employee. The alleged violations occured while Healy was building a tunnel as part of the Milwaukee Metropolitan Sewerage District's water pollution abatement program. Doig was the manager of the tunnel project. An explosion in the tunnel on November 10, 1988, killed three of Healy's employees.

Healy was charged with willful violations of various safety regulations under the Act resulting in the death of the three employees. Doig was charged with aiding and abetting Healy in those violations. Specifically, the government claimed that Healy violated four OSHA regulations covering ventilation, safety training, the use of explosion-proof electrical equipment, and electrical power shutoff during a gas encounter. The government also asserted that Doig aided and abetted Healy's failure to comply with the electrical power shutoff and explosion-proof equipment regulations.

Doig moved to dismiss, asserting that because he is not an employer, he cannot be held criminally liable under § 666(e) as either a principal or an aider and abettor. The district court granted Doig's motion to dismiss. On February 20, 1991, a jury convicted Healy of all counts under the indictment. While Healy's trial was proceeding, the government appealed the district court's order dismissing Doig.

OSHA's stated purpose is "to assure so far as possible every working man and woman in the Nation safe and healthful working conditions . . . by providing that employers and employees have separate but dependent responsibilities and rights with respect to achieving safe and healthful working conditions . . . ." 29 U.S.C. § 651 (1988). In this case, the government argues that an employee may be subjected to criminal liability under § 666(e). The section provides: Any employer who willfully violates any standard, rule, or order promulgated pursuant to section 655 of this title, or of any regulations prescribed pursuant to this chapter, and that violation caused death to any employee, shall, upon conviction, be punished by a fine of not more than $10,000 or by imprisonment for not more than six months, or by both . . . . 29 U.S.C. § 666(e). The government does not argue that Doig is an employer. It maintains, however, that he may be sanctioned under § 666(e) pursuant to the provisions of 18 U.S.C.A. § 2(a) (1991). Under § 2(a), "[w]hoever commits an offense against the United States or aids, abets, counsels, commands, induces or procures its commission, is punishable as a principal."

Generally, the provisions of § 2(a) apply automatically to every criminal offense. In Pino-Perez, [870 F.2d 1230, 1233 (7th Cir.1989)], this court revisited the question of aider and abettor liability and reaffirmed its position that there must be " 'an affirmative legislative policy' to create an exemption from the ordinary rules of accessorial liability." In this case, we believe that the affirmative legislative policy placing the onus of workplace safety upon employers precludes finding that an employee may aid and abet his employer's criminal OSHA violation.

Although we have found no authority directly on point, the Third Circuit has considered whether the Occupational Safety and Health Review Commission may penalize employees who refuse to comply with OSHA regulations. It concluded that OSHA gives neither the Commission nor the Secretary of Labor the power to sanction employees. Atlantic & Gulf Stevedores v. Occupational Safety & Health Review Comm'n, 534 F.2d 541 (3d Cir.1976). * * *

* * * We agree with the Third Circuit's conclusion that sanctioning employees for OSHA violations is not part of the detailed scheme of enforcement Congress established in the statute.

One district court has considered whether a corporate officer could be liable for aiding and abetting his corporate employer's criminal violation of OSHA. United States v. Pinkston-Hollar, Inc., 4 O.S.H. Cas. (BNA) 1697, 1699 (D.Kan. Aug. 16, 1976). The Pinkston-Hollar court stated that "responsible corporate officials who have the power to prevent or correction [sic] violations of the Occupational Safety and Health Act may be prosecuted in the same sense as they may be under the Federal Food, Drug, & Cosmetic Act of 1938." Nevertheless, the court explained, it would still be necessary to find that the corporate official was an employer before applying the criminal sanctions of § 666(e).

Based upon our examination of OSHA and its legislative history, we disagree with the conclusion that any corporate employee may be found liable for aiding and abetting an employer's violation of OSHA. A corporate officer or director acting as a corporation's agent could be sanctioned under § 666(e) as a principal, because, arguably an officer or director would be an employer. Of course, the corporation would also be responsible for its officer's actions. We hold that an employee who is not a corporate officer, and thus not an employer, cannot be sanctioned under § 666(e). This does not bar state law liability for an employee whose recklessness or criminal negligence causes the death of a co- worker. OSHA's stated purpose is to force employers to ensure that employees have safe working conditions. It is not to punish employees whose reckless or willful actions injure their co-workers. State law remains the appropriate means of sanctioning such conduct.

The government asserts that our interpretation of OSHA will deprive § 666(e) of its bite. Because only employers who are sole proprietorships or partnerships will be threatened with jail terms, it argues, the section's deterrent effect will be emasculated. We disagree. First, this problem does not seem terribly significant given the small number of criminal prosecutions brought under OSHA. Second, incarceration is still a potential sanction for corporate officers. As the Supreme Court has held on numerous occasions, responsible corporate officers may be liable for a corporation's violation of a criminal law. Third, if the inability to prosecute employees under § 666(e) hampers the government's efforts to enforce OSHA, the remedy for this difficulty lies with Congress, not with the courts. "If Congress desires to go further, it must speak more clearly than it has." * * *

Our conclusion is bolstered by the particular facts in this case. The government asserts that Healy is criminally liable for the violations it allegedly committed through its agent, Doig. At the same time, it argues that Doig is criminally liable for aiding and abetting Healy's violation under 18 U.S.C. § 2(a). Thus, the government seeks to "double-count" Doig's actions. "Simply put, '[a]iding and abetting means to assist the perpetrator of the crime.'" Under the government's theory, then, Doig would have had to assist himself in violating the relevant OSHA standards, because no other individual or natural person was indicted for the offense. "[I]nherent in the evolution of the concept of accessory is the idea that the accessory and the principal are ordinarily different persons." Thus, we agree with the district court's conclusion that it is logically inconsistent to hold a corporation criminally liable because of the acts of its agent, and, at the same time to hold the agent liable for aiding and abetting the corporation.

For the foregoing reasons, we hold that an employee may not be subjected to liability as an aider and abettor under 29 U.S.C. § 666(e) and 18 U.S.C. § 2. The judgment of the district court is AFFIRMED.

NOTES AND QUESTIONS

1. *Employers Only.* In **United States v. Shear**, 962 F.2d 488 (5th Cir. 1992), the court noted that Section 666 was intended to cover employers and not employees. The court held:

> The terms "employer" and "employee" are defined in the statute. The duties of employers and employees are also carefully delineated. See 29 U.S.C. § 654. Section 654(a) requires "[e]ach employer" to "furnish to each of his employees employment and a place of employment which are free from recognized hazards that are causing or are likely to cause death or serious physical harm to his employees" and to "comply with occupational safety and health standards promulgated under this chapter." Section 654(b) requires "[e]ach employee" to "comply with occupational safety and health standards and all rules, regulations, and orders issued pursuant to this chapter which are applicable to his own actions and conduct." Section 666, entitled "Civil and Criminal Penalties," establishes the civil and criminal penalties for violating OSHA. It distinguishes between employers and broader classes of individuals in imposing liability. For example, subsection (f) imposes liability upon "[a]ny person" who gives advance notice of an inspection, and section (g) imposes liability on "[w]hoever" makes false statements or representations. In contrast, subsections (a)-(e) and (i) penalize "any employer." "[W]here Congress includes particular language in one section of a statute but omits it in another section of the same Act, it is generally presumed that Congress acts intentionally and purposely in the disparate inclusion or exclusion." This juxtaposition indicates that Congress intended to subject employers, but not employees, to criminal liability under section 666(e). * * *

2. *Third Parties.* Can a third party be held liable as an employer, for an OSHA violation, under a theory of aiding and abetting? *Shear,* supra ("We are not presented with, and do not address, the situation where a third party, or even an employee acting in some other capacity, is charged with aiding and abetting an employer's violation of section 666(e).")

3. *RCRA - Employees.* Employees have, however, been found liable under the RCRA Act. In **United States v. Dean**, 969 F.2d 187 (6th Cir. 1992) the defendant argued that subsection 6928(d)(2)(A) was not intended to reach employees who were not "owners" or "operators" of facilities. In rejecting this argument, the court noted:

> * * *"Person" is a defined term meaning "an individual, trust, firm, joint stock company, corporation (including a government corporation), partnership, association, State, municipality,

commission, political subdivision of a State, or any interstate body." 42 U.S.C. § 6903(15).

Defendant would be hard pressed to convince the court that he is not an "individual." He argues, however, that because only owners and operators of facilities are required to obtain permits, the penalty imposed for hazardous waste handling without a permit by subsection 6928(d)(2)(A) must apply only to owners and operators.

This contention is unpersuasive for numerous reasons. Of primary importance is the fact that it is contrary to the unambiguous language of the statute. We agree with the Third Circuit that "[h]ad Congress meant in § 6928(d)(2)(A) to take aim more narrowly, it could have used more narrow language." United States v. Johnson & Towers, Inc., 741 F.2d 662 (3d Cir.1984). Second, while defendant's argument at first glance has logical appeal in relation to subsection 6928(d)(2)(A), the relevant language "any person" prefaces § 6928(d) generally. A number of separate crimes are set out in § 6928(d), several of them having nothing to do with the permit requirement (e.g., failure to maintain requisite documentation or to comply with regulations). Defendant's argument would accordingly impose a limitation on all of the crimes set out in § 6928(d) on a ground relevant to few of them. Third, even the logical appeal of the assertion does not withstand scrutiny. The fact that Congress chose to impose the permit requirement upon owners and operators does not undercut the value of further assuring permit compliance by enacting criminal penalties which would lead others to make inquiry into the permit status of facilities. Given that "[s]uch wastes typically have no value, yet can only be safely disposed of at considerable cost," facilities generating hazardous waste have a strong incentive to evade the law. Moreover, clean-up of the resulting environmental damage almost always involves far greater cost than proper disposal would have, and may be limited to containing the spread of the harm. Defendant argues that employees are the least likely persons to know facilities' permit status. However, employees of a facility are more able to ascertain the relevant facts than the general public, which the statute is intended to protect. In light of these factors, it was entirely reasonable for Congress to have created broad criminal liability. Fourth, it is far from clear that defendant is in fact not an "operator" of GMF, a term defined in the regulations to mean "the person responsible for the overall operation of a facility." 40 C.F.R. § 260.10 (1991). Finally, we agree with the Court of Appeals for the Third Circuit that this result is also supported by the decision of the Supreme Court in *Dotterweich* [p.76], and by the legislative history. We conclude that employees may be criminally liable under § 6928(d).

4. *RCRA - Government Employees.* Government employees have been found criminally liable under RCRA. In **United States v. Dee**, 912 F.2d 741 (4th Cir. 1990), defendant engineers were civilian employees of the United States Army. They claimed immunity from the criminal provisions of RCRA because of their status as federal employees working at a federal facility. Circuit Judge Sprouse, in rejecting this argument stated:

> * * * The Act defines "person" as an individual, trust, firm, joint stock company, corporation (including a government corporation), partnership, association, State, municipality, commission, political subdivision of a State, or any interstate body. 42 U.S.C. § 6903(15). The definition begins with an inclusion of "an individual" as a person. The defendants, of course, were indicted, tried, and convicted as individuals, not as agents of the government. Suffice it to say that sovereign immunity does not attach to individual government employees so as to immunize them from prosecution for their criminal acts.
> * * * Even where certain federal officers enjoy a degree of immunity for a particular sphere of official actions, there is no general immunity from criminal prosecution for actions taken while serving their office. * * *

D. JUDICIAL REVIEW

ADAMO WRECKING CO. v. UNITED STATES
434 U.S. 275, 98 S.Ct. 566, 54 L.Ed.2d 538 (1978)

Justice REHNQUIST delivered the opinion of the Court.

The Clean Air Act authorizes the Administrator of the Environmental Protection Agency to promulgate "emission standards" for hazardous air pollutants "at the level which in his judgment provides an ample margin of safety to protect the public health." The emission of an air pollutant in violation of an applicable emission standard is prohibited by § 112(c)(1)(B) of the Act, 42 U.S.C. § 1857c-7(c)(1)(B). The knowing violation of the latter section, in turn, subjects the violator to fine and imprisonment under the provisions of § 113(c)(1)(C) of the Act, 42 U.S.C. § 1857c-8(c)(1)(C). The final piece in this statutory puzzle is § 307(b) of the Act, 42 U.S.C. § 1857h-5(b), which provides in pertinent part:

> "(1) A petition for review of action of the Administrator in promulgating ... any emission standard under section 112 ... . may be filed only in the United States Court of Appeals for the District of Columbia. ... Any such petition shall be filed within 30 days from the date of such promulgation, or approval, or after such date if such petition is based solely on grounds arising after such 30th day. "(2) Action of the Administrator with respect to which review could have been obtained under paragraph (1)

shall not be subject to judicial review in civil or criminal proceedings for enforcement."

It is within this legislative matrix that the present criminal prosecution arose.

Petitioner was indicted in the United States District Court for the Eastern District of Michigan for violation of § 112(c)(1)(B). The indictment alleged that petitioner, while engaged in the demolition of a building in Detroit, failed to comply with 40 CFR § 61.22(d)(2)(i) (1975). That regulation, described in its caption as a "National Emission Standard for Asbestos," specifies procedures to be followed in connection with building demolitions, but does not by its terms limit emissions of asbestos which occur during the course of a demolition. The District Court granted petitioner's motion to dismiss the indictment on the ground that no violation of § 112(c)(1)(B), necessary to establish criminal liability under § 113(c)(1)(C), had been alleged, because the cited regulation was not an "emission standard" within the meaning of § 112(c). The United States Court of Appeals for the Sixth Circuit reversed, holding that Congress had in § 307(b) precluded petitioner from questioning in a criminal proceeding whether a regulation ostensibly promulgated under § 112(b)(1)(B) was in fact an emission standard. We granted certiorari, and we now reverse.

We do not intend to make light of a difficult question of statutory interpretation when we say that the basic question in this case may be phrased: "When is an emission standard not an emission standard?" Petitioner contends, and the District Court agreed, that while the preclusion and exclusivity provisions of § 307(b) of the Act prevented his obtaining "judicial review" of an emission standard in this criminal proceeding, he was nonetheless entitled to claim that the administrative regulation cited in the indictment was actually not an emission standard at all. The Court of Appeals took the contrary view. It held that a regulation designated by the Administrator as an "emission standard," however different in content it might be from what Congress had contemplated when it authorized the promulgation of emission standards, was sufficient to support a criminal charge based upon § 112(c), unless it had been set aside in an appropriate proceeding commenced in the United States Court of Appeals for the District of Columbia Circuit pursuant to § 307(b).

The Court of Appeals in its opinion relied heavily on Yakus v. United States, 321 U.S. 414 (1944), in which this Court held that Congress in the context of criminal proceedings could require that the validity of regulatory action be challenged in a particular court at a particular time, or not at all. That case, however, does not decide this one. Because § 307(b) expressly applies only to "emission standards," we must still inquire as to the validity of the Government's underlying assumption that the Administrator's mere designation of a regulation as an "emission standard" is sufficient to foreclose any further inquiry in a criminal prosecution under § 113(c)(1)(C) of the Act. For the reasons hereafter stated, we hold that one such as respondent who is charged with a criminal violation under the Act may defend on the ground that the "emission standard" which he is charged with having violated was not an "emission standard" within the contemplation of Congress when it employed that term, even though the "emission standard" in question has not been previously reviewed under the provisions of § 307(b) of the Act.

In resolving this question, we think the statutory provisions of the Clean Air Act are far less favorable to the Government's position than were the provisions of the Emergency Price Control Act considered in *Yakus*. The broad language of that statute gave clear evidence of congressional intent that any actions taken by the Price Administrator under the purported authority of the designated sections of the Act should be challenged only in the Emergency Court of Appeals. * * *

This relatively simple statutory scheme contrasts with the Clean Air Act's far more complex interrelationship between the imposition of criminal sanctions and judicial review of the Administrator's actions. * * *

The conclusion we draw from this excursion into the complexities of the criminal sanctions provided by the Act are several. First, Congress has not chosen to prescribe either civil or criminal sanctions for violations of every rule, regulation, or order issued by the Administrator. Second, Congress, as might be expected, has imposed civil liability for a wider range of violations of the orders of the Administrator than those for which it has imposed criminal liability. Third, even where Congress has imposed criminal liability for the violation of an order of the Administrator, it has not uniformly precluded judicial challenge to the order as a defense in the criminal proceeding. Fourth, although Congress has applied the preclusion provisions of § 307(b)(2) to implementation plans approved by the Administrator, and it has in § 113(c)(1)(A) provided criminal penalties for violations of those plans, it has nonetheless required, under normal circumstances, that a violation continue for a period of 30 days after receipt of notice of the violation from the Administrator before the criminal sanction may be imposed.

These conclusions in no way detract from the fact that Congress has precluded judicial review of an "emission standard" in the court in which the criminal proceeding for the violation of the standard is brought. Indeed, the conclusions heighten the importance of determining what it was that Congress meant by an "emission standard," since a violation of that standard is subject to the most stringent criminal liability imposed by § 113(c)(1) of the Act: Not only is the Administrator's promulgation of the standard not subject to judicial review in the criminal proceeding, but no prior notice of violation from the Administrator is required as a condition for criminal liability. Since Congress chose to attach these stringent sanctions to the violation of an emission standard, in contrast to the violation of various other kinds of orders that might be issued by the Administrator, it is crucial to determine whether the Administrator's mere designation of a regulation as an "emission standard" is conclusive as to its character.

The stringency of the penalty imposed by Congress lends substance to petitioner's contention that Congress envisioned a particular type of regulation when it spoke of an "emission standard." The fact that Congress dealt more leniently, either in terms of liability, of notice, or of available defenses, with other infractions of the Administrator's orders suggests that it attached a peculiar importance to compliance with "emission standards." Unlike the situation in *Yakus,* Congress in the Clean Air Act singled out violators of this generic form of regulation, imposed criminal penalties upon them which would not be imposed upon violators of other orders of the Administrator, and precluded them from asserting defenses which might be asserted by violators of other orders of the Administrator. All of this leads us to conclude that Congress intended, within broad limits, that "emission standards" be regulations of a certain type, and that it did not empower the Administrator, after the manner of Humpty Dumpty in Through the Looking-Glass, to make a regulation an "emission standard" by his mere designation.

The statutory scheme supports the conclusion that § 307(b)(2), in precluding judicial review of the validity of emission standards, does not relieve the Government of the duty of proving, in a prosecution under § 113(c)(1)(C), that the regulation allegedly violated is an emission standard. * * *

In sum, a survey of the totality of the statutory scheme does not compel agreement with the Government's contention that Congress intended that the Administrator's designation of a regulation as an emission standard should be conclusive in a criminal prosecution. At the very least, it may be said that the issue is subject to some doubt. Under these circumstances, we adhere to the familiar rule that, "where there is ambiguity in a criminal statute, doubts are resolved in favor of the defendant." * * * The narrow inquiry to be addressed by the court in a criminal prosecution is not whether the Administrator has complied with appropriate procedures in promulgating the regulation in question, or whether the particular regulation is arbitrary, capricious, or supported by the administrative record. Nor is the court to pursue any of the other familiar inquiries which arise in the course of an administrative review proceeding. The question is only whether the regulation which the defendant is alleged to have violated is on its face an "emission standard" within the broad limits of the congressional meaning of that term. * * *

Most clearly supportive of petitioner's position that a standard was intended to be a quantitative limit on emissions is this provision of § 112(b)(1)(B): "The Administrator shall establish any such standard at the level which in his judgment provides an ample margin of safety to protect the public health from such hazardous air pollutant." (Emphasis added.) All these provisions lend force to the conclusion that a standard is an quantitative "level" to be attained by use of "techniques," "controls," and "technology." This conclusion is fortified by recent amendments to the Act, by which Congress authorized the Administrator to promulgate a "design, equipment, work practice, or operational standard" when "it is not feasible to prescribe or enforce an emission standard."

This distinction, now endorsed by Congress, between "work practice standards" and "emission standards" first appears in the Administrator's own account of the development of this regulation. Although the Administrator has contended that a "work practice standard" is just another type of emission standard, the history of this regulation demonstrates that he chose to regulate work practices only when it became clear he could not regulate emissions. The regulation as originally proposed would have prohibited all visible emissions of asbestos during the course of demolitions. In adopting the final form of the regulation, the Administrator concluded "that the no visible emission requirement would prohibit repair or demolition in many situations, since it would be impracticable, if not impossible, to do such work without creating visible emissions." Therefore the Administrator chose to "specif[y] certain work practices" instead.

The Government concedes that, prior to the 1977 Amendments, the statute was ambiguous with regard to whether a work-practice standard was properly classified as an emission standard, but argues that this Court should defer to the Administrator's construction of the Act.[5] While such deference is entirely appropriate under ordinary circumstances, in this case the 1977 Amendments to the Clean Air Act tend to undercut the administrative construction. * * * The clear distinction drawn in § 112(e) between work-practice standards and emission standards practically forecloses any such inference. * * *

* * * [W]e conclude that the work-practice standard involved here was not an emission standard. The District Court's order dismissing the indictment was therefore proper, and the judgment of the Court of Appeals is Reversed.

---

[5] Our Brother Stevens quite correctly points out, that an administrative "'contemporaneous construction'" of a statute is entitled to considerable weight, and it is true that the originally proposed regulations contain, with respect to some uses of asbestos, the sort of provisions which the Administrator and the Congress later designated as "work practice standards." It bears noting, however, that these regulations can only be said to define by implication the meaning of the term "emission standard." The Administrator promulgated both of them; both were denominated "emission standards"; and it is undoubtedly a fair inference that the Administrator thought each to be an "emission standard." But neither the regulations themselves nor the comments accompanying them give any indication of the Administrator's reasons for concluding that Congress, in authorizing him to promulgate "emission standards," intended to include "work practice standards" within the meaning of that term. * * *

Justice POWELL, concurring.

If the constitutional validity of § 307(b) of the Clean Air Act had been raised by petitioner, I think it would have merited serious consideration. This section limits judicial review to the filing of a petition in the United States Court of Appeals for the District of Columbia Circuit within 30 days from the date of the promulgation by the Administrator of an emission standard. No notice is afforded a party who may be subject to criminal prosecution other than publication of the Administrator's action in the Federal Register. The Act in this respect is similar to the preclusion provisions of the Emergency Price Control Act before the Court in *Yakus*, and petitioner may have thought the decision in that case effectively foreclosed a due process challenge in the present case.

Although I express no considered judgment, I think *Yakus* is at least arguably distinguishable. The statute there came before the Court during World War II, and it can be viewed as a valid exercise of the war powers of Congress under Art. I, § 8, of the Constitution. * * *

The 30-day limitation on judicial review imposed by the Clean Air Act would afford precariously little time for many affected persons even if some adequate method of notice were afforded. It also is totally unrealistic to assume that more than a fraction of the persons and entities affected by a regulation— especially small contractors scattered across the country—would have knowledge of its promulgation or familiarity with or access to the Federal Register. Indeed, following *Yakus*, and apparently concerned by Mr. Justice Rutledge's eloquent dissent. Congress amended the most onerous features of the Emergency Price Control Act.

I join the Court's opinion with the understanding that it implies no view as to the constitutional validity of the preclusion provisions of § 307(b) in the context of a criminal prosecution.

Justice STEWART, with whom Justice BRENNAN and Justice BLACKMUN join, dissenting.

Section 307(b)(1) of the Clean Air Act provides that a "petition for review of action of the Administrator in promulgating ... any emission standard under section 112" may be filed only in the United States Court of Appeals for the District of Columbia Circuit within 30 days of promulgation. Section 307(b)(2) of the Act provides that an "[a]ction of the Administrator with respect to which review could have been obtained under paragraph (1) shall not be subject to judicial review in civil or criminal proceedings for enforcement." Despite these unambiguous provisions, the Court holds in this case that such an action of the Administrator shall be subject to judicial review in a criminal proceeding for enforcement of the Act, at least sometimes. Because this tampering with the plain statutory language threatens to destroy the effectiveness of the unified and expedited judicial review procedure established by Congress in the Clean Air Act, I respectfully dissent.

The inquiry that the Court today allows a trial court to make—whether the asbestos regulation at issue is an emission standard of the type envisioned by Congress—is nothing more than an inquiry into whether the Administrator has acted beyond his statutory authority. But such an inquiry is a normal part of judicial review of agency action. And it is precisely such "judicial review" of an "[a]ction of the Administrator" that Congress has, in § 307(b)(2), expressly forbidden a trial court to undertake. There is not the slightest indication in the Act or in its legislative history that Congress, in providing for review of the Administrator's actions only in the Court of Appeals for the District of Columbia Circuit, meant nonetheless to allow some kinds of review to be available in other courts. To the contrary, Congress clearly ordained that "any review of such actions" be controlled by the provisions of § 307.

The Court's interpretation of § 307(b)(2) also conspicuously frustrates the intent of Congress to establish a speedy and unified system of judicial review under the Act. * * *

Finally, the Court provides no real guidance as to which aspects of an emission standard are so critical that they fall outside the scope of the exclusive judicial review procedure provided by Congress. * * * The Court today has allowed the camel's nose into the tent, and I fear that the rest of the camel is almost certain to follow.

Since I believe that the Administrator's action in promulgating this regulation could have been reviewed in the Court of Appeals for the District of Columbia Circuit under § 307(b)(1), and that such review could have included the petitioner's claim that the Administrator's action was beyond his authority under the Act, I would hold that the petitioner was barred by the express language of § 307(b)(2) from raising that issue in the present case.

Justice STEVENS, dissenting.

The reason Congress attached "the most stringent criminal liability," to the violation of an emission standard for a "hazardous air pollutant" is that substances within that narrow category pose an especially grave threat to human health. That is also a reason why the Court should avoid a construction of the statute that would deny the Administrator the authority to regulate these poisonous substances effectively.

The reason the Administrator did not frame the emission standard for asbestos in numerical terms is that asbestos emissions cannot be measured numerically. For that reason, if Congress simultaneously commanded him (a) to regulate asbestos emissions by establishing and enforcing emission standards and (b) never to use any kind of standard except one framed in numerical terms, it commanded an impossible task.

Nothing in the language of the 1970 statute, or in its history, compels so crippling an interpretation of the Administrator's authority. On the contrary, I am persuaded (1) that the Administrator's regulation of asbestos emissions was entirely legitimate; (2) that if this conclusion were doubtful, we would nevertheless be required to respect his reasonable interpretation of the governing statute; (3) that the 1977 Amendments, fairly read, merely clarified his pre-existing authority; and (4) that the Court's reading of the statute in its current form leads to the anomalous conclusion that work-practice rules, even though properly promulgated, are entirely unenforceable. * * *

CHAPTER EIGHT
PERJURY, FALSE STATEMENTS &
OBSTRUCTION

A. PERJURY

UNITED STATES v. BRONSTON
409 U.S. 352, 93 S.Ct. 595, 34 L.Ed.2d 568 (1973)

Chief Justice BURGER delivered the opinion of the Court.

* * * Petitioner is the sole owner of Samuel Bronston Productions, Inc., a company that between 1958 and 1964, produced motion pictures in various European locations. For these enterprises, Bronston Productions, opened bank accounts in a number of foreign countries; in 1962, for example, it had 37 accounts in five countries. As president of Bronston Productions, petitioner supervised transactions involving the foreign bank accounts.

In June 1964, Bronston Productions, petitioned for an arrangement with creditors under Chapter XI of the Bankruptcy Act. On June 10, 1966, a referee in bankruptcy held a § 21(a) hearing to determine, for the benefit of creditors, the extent and location of the company's assets. Petitioner's perjury conviction was founded on the answers given by him as a witness at that bankruptcy hearing, and in particular on the following colloquy with a lawyer for a creditor of Bronston Productions:

Q. Do you have any bank accounts in Swiss banks, Mr. Bronston?

A. No, sir.

Q. Have you ever?

A. The company had an account there for about six months, in Zurich. [Emphasis added]

Q. Have you any nominees who have bank accounts in Swiss banks?

A. No, sir.

Q. Have you ever?

A. No, sir.

It is undisputed that for a period of nearly five years, between October 1959 and June 1964, petitioner had a personal bank account at the International Credit Bank in Geneva, Switzerland, into which he made deposits and upon which he drew checks totaling more than $180,000. It is likewise undisputed that petitioner's answers were literally truthful. (a) Petitioner did not at the time of questioning have a Swiss bank account. (b) Bronston Productions, Inc., did have the account in Zurich described by petitioner. (c) Neither at the time of questioning nor before did petitioner have nominees who had Swiss accounts. The Government's prosecution for perjury went forward on the theory that in order to mislead his questioner, petitioner answered the second question with literal truthfulness but unresponsively addressed his answer to the company's assets and not to his own–thereby implying that he had no personal Swiss bank account at the relevant time.

At petitioner's trial, the District Court instructed the jury that the "basic issue" was whether petitioner "spoke his true belief." Perjury, the court stated, "necessarily involves the state of mind of the accused' and 'essentially consists of wilfully testifying to the truth of a fact which the defendant does not believe to be true" ; petitioner's testimony could not be found "wilfully" false unless at the time his testimony was given petitioner "fully understood the questions put to him but nevertheless gave false answers knowing the same to be false." The court further instructed the jury that if petitioner did not understand the question put to him and for that reason gave an unresponsive answer, he could not be convicted of perjury. Petitioner could, however, be convicted if he gave an answer "not literally false but when considered in the context in which it was given, nevertheless constitute(d) a false statement." [3] * * *

---

[3] The District Court gave the following example "as an illustration only ":

[I]f it is material to ascertain how many times a person has entered a store on a given day and that person responds to such a question by saying five times when in fact he knows that he entered the store 50 times that day, that person may be guilty of perjury even though it is technically true that he entered the store five times.

The illustration given by the District Court is hardly comparable to petitioner 's answer, the answer "five times" is responsive to the hypothetical question and contains nothing to alert the questioner that he may be sidetracked. Moreover, it is very doubtful that an answer which, in response to a specific quantitative inquiry, baldly understates a numerical fact can be described as even "technically true." Whether an answer is true must be determined with reference to the question it purports to answer not in isolation. An unresponsive answer is unique in this respect because its unresponsiveness by definition prevents its truthfulness from being tested in the context of the question–unless there is to be speculation as to what the

In the Court of Appeals, petitioner contended, as he had in post-trial motions before the District Court, that the key question was imprecise and suggestive of various interpretations. In addition, petitioner contended that he could not be convicted of perjury on the basis of testimony that was concededly truthful, however unresponsive. A divided Court of Appeals held that the question was readily susceptible of a responsive reply and that it adequately tested the defendant's belief in the veracity of his answer. The Court of Appeals further held that, "(f)or the purposes of 18 U.S.C. § 1621, an answer containing half of the truth which also constitutes a lie by negative implication, when the answer is intentionally given in place of the responsive answer called for by a proper question, is perjury." In this Court, petitioner renews his attack on the specificity of the question asked him and the legal sufficiency of his answer to support a conviction for perjury. The problem of the ambiguity of the question is not free from doubt, but we need not reach that issue. Even assuming, as we do, that the question asked petitioner specifically focused on petitioner's personal bank accounts, we conclude that the federal perjury statute cannot be construed to sustain a conviction based on petitioner's answer.

The statute, 18 U.S.C. § 1621, substantially identical in its relevant language to its predecessors for nearly a century, is "a federal statute enacted in an effort to keep the course of justice free from the pollution of perjury." * * * The need for truthful testimony in a § 21(a) bankruptcy proceeding is great, since the proceeding is "a searching inquiry into the condition of the estate of the bankrupt, to assist in discovering and collecting the assets, and to develop facts and circumstances which bear upon the question of discharge." Here, as elsewhere, the perpetration of perjury "well may affect the dearest concerns of the parties before a tribunal. . . ." United States v. Norris, 300 U.S. 564 (1937).

There is, at the outset, a serious literal problem in applying § 1621 to petitioner's answer. The words of the statute confine the offense to the witness who "willfully . . . states . . . any material matter which he does not believe to be true." Beyond question, petitioner's answer to the crucial question was not responsive if we assume, as we do, that the first question was directed at personal bank accounts. There is, indeed, an implication in the answer to the second question that there was never a personal bank account; in casual conversation this interpretation might reasonably be drawn. But we are not dealing with casual conversation and the statute does not make it a criminal act for a witness to willfully state any material matter that implies any material matter that he does not believe to be true.[4]

---

unresponsive answer "implies."

[4] Petitioner's answer is not to be measured by the same standards applicable to criminally fraudulent or extortionate statements. In that context, the law goes "rather far in punishing intentional creation of false impressions by a selection of literally true representations, because the actor himself generally selects and arranges the representations." In contrast, "under our system of adversary

The Government urges that the perjury statute be construed broadly to reach petitioner's answer and thereby fulfill its historic purpose of reinforcing our adversary factfinding process. We might go beyond the precise words of the statute if we thought they did not adequately express the intention of Congress, but we perceive no reason why Congress would intend the drastic sanction of a perjury prosecution to cure a testimonial mishap that could readily have been reached with a single additional question by counsel alert-- as every examiner ought to be–to the incongruity of petitioner's unresponsive answer. Under the pressures and tensions of interrogation, it is not uncommon for the most earnest witnesses to give answers that are not entirely responsive. Sometimes the witness does not understand the question, or may in an excess of caution or apprehension read too much or too little into it. It should come as no surprise that a participant in a bankruptcy proceeding may have something to conceal and consciously tries to do so, or that a debtor may be embarrassed at his plight and yield information reluctantly. It is the responsibility of the lawyer to probe; testimonial interrogation, and cross-examination in particular, is a probing, prying, pressing form of inquiry. If a witness evades, it is the lawyer's responsibility to recognize the evasion and to bring the witness back to the mark, to flush out the whole truth with the tools of adversary examination.

It is no answer to say that here the jury found that petitioner intended to mislead his examiner. A jury should not be permitted to engage in conjecture whether an unresponsive answer, true and complete on its face, was intended to mislead or divert the examiner; the state of mind of the witness is relevant only to the extent that it bears on whether "he does not believe (his answer) to be true." To hold otherwise would be to inject a new and confusing element into the adversary testimonial system we know. Witnesses would be unsure of the extent of their responsibility for the misunderstandings and inadequacies of examiners, and might well fear having that responsibility tested by a jury under the vague rubric of "intent to mislead" or "perjury by implication." The seminal modern treatment of the history of the offense concludes that one consideration of policy overshadowed all others during the years when perjury first emerged as a common-law offense: "that the measures taken against the offense must not be so severe as to discourage witnesses from appearing or testifying." Study of Perjury, reprinted in Report of New York Law Revision Commission, Legis.Doc.No.60, p. 249 (1935). A leading 19th century commentator, quoted by Dean Wigmore, noted that the English law "throws every fence round a person accused of perjury," for

> the obligation of protecting witnesses from oppression, or annoyance, by charges, or threats of charges, of having borne false testimony, is

---

questioning and cross-examination the scope of disclosure is largely in the hands of counsel and presiding officer." A.L.I. Model Penal Code § 208.20, Comment (Tent.Draft No. 6, 1957, p. 124).

far paramount to that of giving even perjury its deserts. To repress that crime, prevention is better than cure: and the law of England relies, for this purpose, on the means provided for detecting and exposing the crime at the moment of commission,–such as publicity, cross-examination, the aid of a jury, etc.; and on the infliction of a severe, though not excessive punishment, wherever the commission of the crime has been clearly proved." W. Best, Principles of the Law of Evidence s 606 (C. Chamberlayne ed. 1883).

See J. Wigmore, *Evidence* 275-276 (3d ed. 1940). * * *

Thus, we must read § 1621 in light of our own and the traditional Anglo-American judgment that a prosecution for perjury is not the sole, or even the primary, safeguard against errant testimony. While "the lower federal courts have not dealt with the question often,' and while their expressions do not deal with unresponsive testimony and are not precisely in point, 'it may be said that they preponderate against the respondent's contention." *United States v. Norris.* The cases support petitioner's position that the perjury statute is not to be loosely construed, nor the statute invoked simply because a wily witness succeeds in derailing the questioner–so long as the witness speaks the literal truth. The burden is on the questioner to pin the witness down to the specific object to the questioner's inquiry. * * *

It may well be that petitioner's answers were not guileless but were shrewdly calculated to evade. Nevertheless, we are constrained to agree with Judge Lumbard, who dissented from the judgment of the Court of Appeals, that any special problems arising from the literally true but unresponsive answer are to be remedied through the "questioner's acuity" and not by a federal perjury prosecution.

NOTES AND QUESTIONS

1. *Elements of Perjury.* Section 1621, the perjury statute, makes it a crime for someone (1) "having taken an oath before a competent tribunal, officer, or person," (2) "willfully and contrary to such oath" (3) "states or subscribes any material matter" (4) "that he does not believe to be true."

2. *Telling the Whole Truth*. Professors Bierschbach and Stein argue that the statute should be interpreted narrowly to protect an individual's right to privacy:

[E]vasive as opposed to affirmatively misleading testimony raises normatively difficult questions about the extent to which an individual's moral entitlement to privacy and nonexposure should limit her truthtelling obligations to society. From a moral (as opposed to formal legal) point of view, it is one thing to actively bring about an injustice, and it is quite another thing to withdraw one's testimonial assistance from a justice-making proceeding. From the moral perspective, only outright liars who actively mislead the court can properly be identified and condemned as perjurers.

Richard A. Bierschbach & Alex Stein, *Overenforcement*, 93 GEO. L.J. 1743 (2005).

3. **High Profile Prosecutions**. While *Bronston* makes it more difficult to win a conviction for perjury, prosecutors have been more willing to charge the offense in white collar crime cases, sometimes not filing charges related to the underlying transactions or conduct that triggered the testimony. Recent prosecutions for perjury have included I. Lewis (Scooter) Libby, former chief of staff for Vice President Cheney, and a number of prominent athletes who testified falsely about receiving steroids from Balco (Bay Area Laboratory Co-operative), including former Olympic gold medalist Marion Jones and former NFL player Dana Stubblefield.

4. *Materiality.*   Perjury requires that the statement be material. See United States v. Gremillion, 464 F.2d 901 (5th Cir. 1972) ("The test of materiality is whether the false testimony was capable of influencing the tribunal on the issue, or whether the false testimony would have the natural effect or tendency to influence, impede, or dissuade the Grand Jury from pursuing its investigation."). The impeachment of President Clinton largely involved allegations that he committed perjury in a civil deposition. In addition to questions as to what constitutes a "false" statement that permits the government to prosecute the declarant, there were also questions raised regarding the materiality of the statements.   See Alan Heinrich, Note, *Clinton's Little White Lies: The Materiality Requirement for Perjury in Civil Discovery*, 33 LOY. L.A. L. REV. 1303 (1999).

5. *Two Witness Rule.* Courts in assessing the sufficiency of the evidence in a perjury case use a two-witness rule. The policy rationale for this rule is to assure that a perjury conviction is not premised upon one person's oath against another. Although at common law the rule required two witnesses, today it is a more relaxed permitting "the testimony of two witnesses or the testimony of one witness, plus corroborating evidence." United States v. Davis, 548 F.2d 840 (9th Cir. 1977). Courts are not always in agreement on what constitutes corroborating evidence. In **United States v. Diggs**, 560 F.2d 266 (7th Cir. 1977), the court stated:

> As currently applied the two-witness rule does not literally require the direct testimony of two separate witnesses, but rather may be satisfied by the direct testimony of one witness and sufficient corroborative evidence.   * * * While this interpretation is not seriously questioned, there is an apparent division among the circuits over the precise wording of the rule to be applied in determining the sufficiency of the corroborative evidence.   In analyzing the various expressions of the rule and their application, we agree with the Second Circuit that "(t)he division in the Circuits,

judged by its results, appears to be a matter of semantics and a slight difference in emphasis."* * * No wording of the rule requires the corroborative evidence to be sufficient for conviction; nor does any phrasing permit conviction where the corroboration consists of merely peripheral testimony not tending to show the falsity of the accused's statements while under oath.

The two-witness rule is thus satisfied when there is direct testimony from one witness and additional independent evidence so corroborative of the direct testimony that the two when considered together are sufficient to establish the falsity of the accused's statements under oath beyond a reasonable doubt. "Independent" evidence in this context means evidence coming from a source other than that of the direct testimony. * * * This independent corroborating evidence must be trustworthy enough to convince the jury that what the principal witness said was correct, the ultimate determination of its credibility being an exclusive function of the jury.

But see United States v. Forrest, 639 F.2d 1224, 1226 (5th Cir. 1981) (holding that "the corroborative evidence must be inconsistent with the innocence of the accused and must tend to show the perjury independently of the testimony which it is intended to corroborate.").

6. *Literal Truth*. In **United States v. Shotts**, 145 F.3d 1289 (11th Cir. 1998), the Eleventh Circuit reversed a perjury conviction where the defendant, an attorney, provided an answer that was "literally" true. Shotts testified before the grand jury as follows:

"Q: Do you own a bail bonds business?

A: No, sir.

Q: Have you been associated in some fashion with a bail bonds business?

A: I would at this time invoke my right of self-incrimination, Your Honor.

Q: All right.

A: I have a client that is a bail bonds company.

Q: Well, have you in the past either been an officer in or had an interest in a bail bonds company, any time prior to today?

A: I would respectfully decline to answer the question on the ground it might tend to incriminate me."

In reversing the conviction under *Bronston*, the Eleventh Circuit noted that "[u]nder Alabama law, a corporation is 'owned' by its shareholders." The court stated:

> The government's argument is that Shotts ignores the "context" of his testimony. He was, "in fact", the owner even if he didn't own the stock. He had told others he "owned" the business. When asked before the grand jury if he owned a bail bond business, "he knew . . . what was meant by the question." * * *

> A perjury conviction must rest on the utterance by the accused of a false statement; it may not stand on a particular interpretation that the questioner places upon an answer. The government cannot require Shotts to interpret its question in a way that is contrary to the law of Alabama, and he may not be convicted of perjury if he does not. *Bronston* expressly places on the questioner the burden of pinning the witness down to the specific object of the inquiry.

7. *Contextual Setting*: **United States v. DeZarn.** In *Schotts*, the court rejected any reference to the context of the question or external evidence. Does the court in **United States v. DeZarn**, 157 F.3d 1042 (6th Cir. 1998), take an opposite position? In *DeZarn*, a government investigator questioned the defendant under oath about campaign contributions being made at a "Preakness Party" in 1991. During the examination, the investigator asked whether the "1991 Preakness Party" "was a political fundraising activity." The defendant answered "Absolutely not." The response was literally true because the party had occurred in 1990, but the Sixth Circuit held that the context of the question made it clear that the defendant knew the investigator was asking about the 1990 party and had misspoken when using the wrong date. In distinguishing *Bronston*, the Sixth Circuit stated:

> The question presented here, then, is whether in a perjury case in which a mistaken premise exists in one of the questions asked of the testifier, the Government is entitled to present, and the jury to consider, evidence of the context of the questioning which would establish that the Defendant – despite the false premise of the question – knew exactly what the questions meant and exactly what they were referring to. We hold that the law of perjury not only permits this, but in cases such as this, requires it.

> First, perjury must be shown to be willful, and it must be shown that the testifier did not believe his responses to be true. * * * Thus, by its very nature, perjury requires an inquiry into the Defendant's state of mind and his intent to deceive at the time the testimony was given. Indeed, the entire focus of a perjury inquiry centers upon what the testifier knew and when he knew it because in order to make a determination as to whether that person intended to testify falsely, it must be established beyond a reasonable doubt that he

knew his testimony to be false when he gave it. In order to prove this, the Government, of necessity, must present evidence of the extent of a Defendant's knowledge of the subject matter of the questioning and the circumstances surrounding how he came to that knowledge. This, of course, requires the Government to show the full context of the Defendant's activities as well as other information of which he may have had knowledge and which may have influenced him.

Thus, a perjury inquiry which focuses only upon the precision of the question and ignores what the Defendant knew about the subject matter of the question at the time it was asked, misses the very point of perjury: that is, the Defendant's intent to testify falsely and, thereby, mislead his interrogators. Such a limited inquiry would not only undermine the perjury laws, it would undermine the rule of law as a whole, as truthseeking is the critical component which allows us to determine if the laws are being followed, and it is only through the requirement that a witness testify truthfully that a determination may be made as to whether the laws are being followed. Indeed, that is the entire purpose of the sworn oath: To impress upon the testifier the need – under penalty of punishment – to testify truthfully.

This is not to say that the question to which the answer is made is not an important part of a perjury inquiry. Of course it is. A question that is truly ambiguous or which affirmatively misleads the testifier can never provide a basis for a finding of perjury, as it could never be said that one intended to answer such a question untruthfully. But, where it can be shown from the context of the question and the state of the testifier's knowledge at the time that the testifier clearly knew what the question meant, the Government must be permitted to present, and the fact-finder to consider, those contextual facts. * * *

* * * [T]he *Bronston* "literal truth" defense applies in cases where a perjury defendant responds to a question with an *unresponsive* answer. As noted, "[a]n unresponsive answer is unique . . . because its unresponsiveness ... prevents it from being tested in the context of the question – unless there is speculation as to what the unresponsive answer 'implies '." * * * [I]n this case, Defendant DeZarn gave unequivocal and directly and fully responsive answers to the questions asked * * *. Furthermore, * * * there is more than ample context and evidence to test the meaning and falsity of DeZarn's answers.

8. *Parsing the Questions*.   *Bronston* teaches that the question is as important as the answer in a perjury prosecution. Courts will often parse a series of questions very carefully to determine the exact meaning of the particular question that the government alleges formed the predicate for the

defendant's perjury. Just as the Sixth Circuit did in *DeZarn*, context is of paramount importance because it is rare that a defendant will have given a wholly untruthful answer that is easily determinable to be false. Is the level of clarity required for a question that can trigger a perjury prosecution so high that an attorney examining a witness in a grand jury investigation, deposition, or other sworn testimony cannot reasonably be expected to meet it at all times? Even if the courts examine every question as closely as *Bronston* requires, should the system expect any less from a prosecutor when a criminal violation can result simply from one's response, which may be made when the person is nervous or intimidated by the surroundings? See United States v. Serafini, 167 F.3d 812 (3rd Cir. 1999) (demonstrating the court going to great lengths to determine the meaning of the prosecutors questions and the defendant's response, refusing to look solely at a single question and answer).

9. *Leading Questions.* If an individual is charged with perjury premised upon statements made in a grand jury or during cross-examination, what arguments can the defense make to have the jury understand the context of the statements? Consider the following analysis by Professor Underwood:

> In prosecutions predicated upon false statements made before a grand jury, it must be remembered that the witness will not have had counsel's advice in the grand jury room. It's the prosecutor's turf. The prosecutor's questioning may consist entirely of leading questions, and the prosecution may be founded upon the witness' guarded responses to these questions. "This kind of interrogation always creates a great risk that the witness will misunderstand the questions or that the prosecutor will put words in the witness' mouth." * * * The same caveat may be in order when a witness is charged with committing perjury in his or her responses to leading questions in cross-examination. Indeed, one noted defense counsel has asserted that 'any witness will lie under repeated cross-examination.' ***

Richard H. Underwood: *Perjury! The Charges and the Defenses*, 36 DUQ. L. REV. 715 (1998).

10. *False Declarations.* In addition to the general perjury statute found in18 U.S.C. § 1621, there is also a false declarations statute, found in section 1623. Section 1623 makes it a crime for someone (1) "under oath... in any proceeding before or ancillary to any court or grand jury"(2) "knowingly makes" (3) "any false" (4) "material declaration." Section 1621 applies in a wide variety of circumstances, including civil depositions, while § 1623 is limited to judicial or grand jury proceedings. Both sections 1621 and 1623 require that the statement or declaration be actually false, and use the same test for materiality. Only the perjury statute, 1621 includes the "two witness rule." Unlike the perjury statute, section 1623 provides an affirmative defense of retraction. This requires the defendant to admit that the previous

statement was false, the admission of falsity must be made in the same court or grand jury proceeding, and the false declaration must not already have "substantially affected the proceeding" and it must not have "become manifest that such falsity has been or will be exposed."

11. *Other Perjury Statutes.* Specific offense related perjury statutes exist throughout the United States Code. See, e.g., 26 U.S.C. § 7206 (filing of a perjurious tax return). Is there a correlation between crimes of fraud and crimes of perjury? See Stuart P. Green, *Lying, Misleading, and Falsely Denying: How Moral Concepts Inform the Law of Perjury, Fraud, and False Statements*, 53 HASTINGS L.J. 157 (2001) ("[T]he moral concepts of lying, misleading, and falsely denying correspond, respectively, to the legal concepts of perjury, fraud, and 'exculpatory noes.'").

B. FALSE STATEMENTS

UNITED STATES v. HIXON
987 F.2d 1261 (6th Cir. 1993)

KENNEDY, Circuit Judge.

Defendant Wesley E. Hixon appeals his jury conviction and sentence for making a false and material statement and representation on claims he submitted for continuing disability compensation.

In 1974, the defendant began working for the Tennessee Valley Authority (TVA). On February 21, 1989, in an accident occurring during the performance

of his assigned duties, defendant sustained a strained right knee. As a result of this injury, defendant underwent four surgical procedures. He claimed he was unable to work because his job required him to walk on rough terrain. Between the time defendant was injured and the time he returned to work in October of 1990, defendant was considered partially or totally disabled. * * * [Defendant filed two forms with the Department of Labor (DOL), Office of Workers' Compensation Programs (OWCP), to receive temporary workers compensation for work-related injuries. Defendant wrote "not applicable" after the line on the form stating "Commission and Self-Employment. Show all activities, whether or not income resulted from your efforts." Defendant was found eligible to receive long-term benefits, and filed a different form with the OWCP that contained the following quesiton:]

> 2. *Self-Employment.* Earnings from self-employment (such as farming, sales, service, operating a store, business, etc.) must be reported. Report any such enterprise in which you worked, and from which you received revenue, even if it operated at a loss or if profits were reinvested. You must show as "rate of pay" what it

would have cost you to have hired someone to perform the work you did.

a) Were you self-employed during any time covered by this form?

Defendant filled out two of these forms, one dated November 15, 1989 and the other dated April 27, 1990. On these two forms, defendant answered "No" to both questions.

In March of 1991, the TVA Office of Inspector General, fraud division, received three phone calls regarding defendant. Thereafter, an agent, Duane Broome, began an investigation to determine whether defendant was misusing or abusing the worker's compensation program. In March, Agent Broome saw the defendant, with several of his associates, working a booth at the Dixie Deer Classic, an outdoor show where booking or travel agents display their wares in an effort to persuade potential customers to use their services. TVA agents observed the defendant carrying and setting up a portable booth with various stuffed animal heads used for wall mounts. They also saw him carrying his work table, supplies, brochures, and paraphernalia to promote his business. Subsequent investigation of defendant's business records revealed that defendant had worked numerous other shows and took several (business and) hunting trips for Woods and Water Outdoor Consultants while on disability.

Agent Broome discovered that Woods and Water Outdoor Consultants was a Georgia (Subchapter S) corporation that provided, planned, and booked fishing, hunting and outdoor vacations. Defendant was the sole stockholder (100% owner) of the corporation, as well as the President, Treasurer, registered agent, and sole member of the Board of Directors. Defendant did not receive a salary from the corporation, but allegedly earned income on commissions received from those who utilized his "travel agent type" services.

In August, 1991, Agents Broome and Derryberry went to defendant's home to interview him. In front of the house was a large red trailer bearing the name "Woods and Water Outdoor Consultants." Defendant explained to the agents that Woods and Water was a business he had started six years previously. However, defendant initially told the agents the company was his wife's business, that she attended all the shows, and that his personal involvement was nothing more than staying home and answering the phone and taking one business related trip in a year's time.

Agent Broome then confronted defendant with the information he had gathered during the course of his investigation, *e.g.,* he had read the company brochures and paperwork and the wife's name appeared nowhere; he had attended and videotaped several shows, but never saw the defendant's wife. According to Agent Broome's testimony, defendant "looked at me with a blank stare, looked back out the window and looked back at me and he said you got me." Defendant then told the agents "I've been employed since day one."

Finally, defendant broke down, cried, and asked what he had to do to get this behind him as quickly as possible. On August 30, 1991, defendant's employment at TVA was terminated due to his failure to report his activities to OWCP. [Defendant was charged with four counts of violating § 1001 for "falsely indicating that he was not self-employed and concealing his self-employment and ownership of Woods and Water Outdoor Consultants, Inc.," on the four forms he filed for workers compensation.]

Defendant * * * contends that the District Court erred in denying his motion for judgment of acquittal because he is not guilty as a matter of law. Defendant argues that the only work he performed was for Woods and Water Outdoor Consultants Corporation. He maintains that under Georgia law (and federal law) as a corporate officer he was an employee of the corporation, and as such could not, as a matter of law, be self-employed. Consequently, he did not make a false material statement or representation on his disability claim forms when he answered that he was not self-employed. This statement simply was not false.

The District Court held that whether the defendant was self-employed was a question of fact for the jury to decide. The statute, 18 U.S.C. § 1001, speaks in terms of knowingly and willfully making false material statements and representations, or concealing a material fact. It is clear that the material *fact* alleged by the indictment to have been concealed was defendant's self- employment. He was not indicted for his answer to the questions regarding employment other than self-employment. The District Court instructed the jury that whether the fact of self-employment was material was a question of law for it to decide, but it was for the jury to decide whether the defendant knowingly and willfully concealed his self-employment status or falsely stated he was not self-employed. The court instructed the jury that if it concluded beyond a reasonable doubt that because of defendant's stock ownership, his position as the corporation's president, and the actions he took on the corporation's behalf, the defendant was, in effect, the corporation, "you may disregard the existence of the corporation in your determination of whether the defendant was self-employed." We now turn to the issue whether there was sufficient evidence for the jury to convict the defendant for falsely stating he was not self-employed.

A violation of 18 U.S.C. § 1001 for the making of a false statement or representation requires: (1) the making of a statement; (2) the falsity of such statement; (3) knowledge of the falsity of such statement; (4) relevance of such statement to the functioning of a federal department or agency; and (5) that the false statement was material. Thus, a violation of section 1001 requires a determination of whether Hixon's response on his claims for continuing disability that he was not self-employed was a false representation.

The only evidence of defendant's self-employment was his presidency of Woods and Water, a Georgia Corporation, and his services to that corporation.   The Official Code of Georgia Annotated Section 14-2-140(8) reads:

> "Employee" includes an officer but not a director.   A director may accept duties that make him also an employee.

Defendant's expert witness, an Atlanta lawyer and CPA, testified that, "in my opinion, by definition, an officer of the corporation is an employee of the corporation." It is undisputed that defendant was an officer of Woods and Water. As such, he was an employee of the corporation. The government has presented no evidence that defendant personally kept any commissions for trips sold (rather than turning them over to the corporation). Admittedly, some persons may refer to themselves as self-employed when they are sole owners of a corporation. That does not make them self-employed. We see no basis for permitting the jury to conclude that defendant was self-employed simply because he owned all the stock in the corporation and was its president. Payments by a corporation for the president's services require withholding and W-2's, as with all wages. Other questions on the form asked for information regarding salaried employment and employment other than self-employment, as well as whether defendant was employed in any manner. However, defendant was not indicted for giving false answers to those questions. The indictment here simply failed to charge the making of false answers to the questions which were falsely answered but instead charged the making of false answers to the questions where the answers were not false.

The government relies on the dictionary definition of self-employed as "making a living working for oneself rather than others." Webster II New Riverside Dictionary (1988). However, where one works for a corporation, he or she works for another, namely the corporation, a distinct legal entity which must file its own separate reports to the state of incorporation and its own income tax. The corporate income tax returns of Woods and Water showed substantial receipts. There was no evidence here that the corporation was not in good standing or the corporate structure otherwise ignored so that the jury could pierce the corporate veil. The government also relies on Morgan v. Finch, 423 F.2d 551, 553 (6th Cir.1970), a social security benefits case. The wage earner, an insurance salesman, continued to work while receiving social security benefits. He reported his commissions from policies sold during the year but not on renewal commissions for policies. If he were self-employed, these commissions were required to be included under a prior administrative ruling. If he were an employee, renewal premiums would be considered as earned the year the policy was sold. The court held that whether claimant was an employee or self-employed was a question of fact to be reviewed on a substantial evidence basis.   The case does not involve the officer of a corporation. We are unable to find any evidence here that defendant, as opposed to the corporation, received any commissions. It is impossible to tell from the *Morgan* opinion just what evidence there was that Morgan was an employee.

* * * The Eighth Circuit reached an analogous conclusion when it reversed a section 1001 false statement conviction in United States v. Vesaas, 586 F.2d 101 (8th Cir.1978). In that case, the defendant was convicted for falsely reporting that he had no knowledge of property owned by his deceased mother and himself in joint tenancy. The Eighth Circuit held that defendant's denial of such ownership "cannot constitute a false statement since it is legally impossible to be a joint tenant with a decedent."

> [A] prosecution for a false statement under § 1001 ... cannot be based on an ambiguous question where the response *may* be literally and factually correct.... An indictment premised on a statement which on its face is not false cannot survive.

Here, Hixon's representation that he was not self-employed was, on its face, not a false representation.

The indictment further charges the defendant with "concealing his self-employment and ownership of Woods and Water Outdoor Consultants, Inc." A violation of section 1001 for concealment requires "knowing and willful concealment 'by any trick, scheme, or device' of a material fact." With regard to concealment, therefore, we must determine whether Hixon's self-employment was a "fact" the concealment of which was sufficient to sustain the conviction. Because we have already determined that Hixon was an employee of Woods and Water and therefore not self-employed, Hixon could not be guilty of concealing his self-employment. Nowhere was he asked if he was the owner of any corporation.[5]

Accordingly, we REVERSE Hixon's conviction for violating 18 U.S.C. § 1001.

BATCHELDER, Circuit Judge, concurring.

I concur in this case, but I write separately because my analysis of the issue in regard to the motion for acquittal differs from that of the majority.

The majority has accurately set forth what the indictment did and did not charge in this case, and what the evidence did and did not demonstrate. It is undisputed that the defendant was an officer of his corporation, Woods and Water. It is undisputed that the law applicable to this defendant's employment status is Georgia law, and that under Georgia law an officer of a corporation is an employee of that corporation. Accordingly, it seems to me

---

[5] Similarly, Hixon cannot be convicted for concealing his ownership of Woods and Water. All of Hixon's allegedly fraudulent answers pertained to questions about his employment activity. Nowhere was Hixon asked about any corporate ownership. It was Hixon's status as a corporate officer that made him a corporate employee, not his status as a corporate owner. The questions asking Hixon whether he was employed, self-employed or unemployed, did not require him to reveal his corporate ownership. Consequently, while Hixon might have been guilty of concealing his position as a corporate officer, he was only indicted for concealing his corporate ownership.

that because this defendant was an employee of the corporation, he was not, as a matter of law, self-employed. Thus his statement that he was not self-employed was not, as a matter of law, false, and therefore he was entitled to a judgment of acquittal unless the evidence permitted a finding that the corporate veil could be pierced. Here, as the majority opinion makes clear, the government simply did not present any evidence that the defendant had done any of the things with regard to the corporation which would permit such a finding. Because the actual falsity of the statement is an element of the offense, a failure of proof on that issue is fatal to a conviction. Therefore, since the evidence presented did not warrant an instruction to the jury on piercing the corporate veil, even if the instruction which the district court gave the jury had been adequate to explain what the jury must consider in determining whether to disregard the existence of the corporation, the district court erred in sending this matter to the jury at all.

It is clear that this defendant intended to make and indeed, did make a false statement to the government. However, he was not indicted for the false statement which he actually made, but for the statement which could only have been false if the government adequately established the identity between the defendant and his corporation. This the government did not do.

NOTES AND QUESTIONS

1. *Legislative History.* One of the broadest criminal statutes in the federal criminal code is 18 U.S.C. § 1001, which prohibits material false or fraudulent statements to an officer or agency of the federal government. Professor Stuart Green states:

> The statutory progenitor of Section 1001 was enacted in 1863. Entitled "An Act to Prevent and Punish Frauds Upon the Government of the United States," it prohibited the filing of "false, fictitious, or fraudulent" claims against the government. Passed in the midst of the Civil War, the statute was a response to a "spate of frauds"–particularly, procurement frauds–being committed on the U.S. Government. In 1918, this time at the end of the First World War, the statute was broadened slightly, to cover false statements made "for the purpose and with the intent of cheating and swindling or defrauding the Government of the United States."

Stuart P. Green, *Lying, Misleading, and Falsely Denying: How Moral Concepts Inform the Law of Perjury, Fraud, and False Statements*, 53 Hastings L.J. 157 (2001).

Prior to 1996, the statute prohibited false statements to departments and agencies of the federal government. Congress amended § 1001 to apply to any false statement made within the jurisdiction of the executive, legislative, or judicial branch. The amendment largely overruled the Supreme Court's decision in **Hubbard v. United States**, 514 U.S. 695 (1995), which interpreted the statute to exclude statements made to federal courts because it would chill advocacy on behalf of clients. The statute now explicitly covers false statements to all three branches, except that the submission to the legislative branch must be for administrative purposes or in connection with an investigation, and the prohibition "does not apply to a party to a judicial proceeding, or that party's counsel, for statements, representations, writings or documents submitted by such party or counsel to a judge or magistrate in that proceeding." Section 1001 has been used in a wide variety of areas, including false statements to regulatory agencies, to law enforcement agents, and on loan and aid applications.

The key issue in a § 1001 prosecution is whether the statement was "false." The statute covers more than just false statements because the prohibition reaches fraudulent misstatements or omissions.

2. *"Exculpatory No" Doctrine*. At one time, a defense to a § 1001 charge was fashioned by the lower courts known as the "exculpatory no" doctrine. Under the doctrine, a false response to a question that was limited to a denial of involvement in criminal activity was viewed as not constituting a "false" statement. The rationale of the "exculpatory no" defense was based in part on the Fifth Amendment privilege against self-incrimination, that a person should not be compelled to respond to an agent's question, so a limited denial of involvement in criminal conduct did not otherwise pervert a government function. The Supreme Court rejected the "exculpatory no" defense in **Brogan v. United States**, 522 U.S. 398 (1998), stating that "[w]hether or not the predicament of the wrongdoer run to ground tugs at the heartstrings, neither the text nor the spirit of the Fifth Amendment confers a privilege to lie."

3. *Concealment*. In addition to affirmative misstatements, § 1001 also makes it a crime to conceal information. In order to be guilty of concealment, the person must have a legal obligation to disclose the information to the government. In **United States v. Safavian**, 528 F.3d 957 (D.C.Cir. 2008), the defendant, a former deputy director of the General Services Administration (GSA), was convicted of concealing information about a golfing trip he planned to take that would be paid for by a lobbyist. The charge arose from his failure to disclose information about the lobbyist's intention to do business with the GSA to an ethics officer in connection with receiving an opinion about the propriety of taking the trip. In overturning the conviction, the D.C. Circuit noted that there was no obligation to make full disclosure to the ethics officer, and therefore no concealment under § 1001:

> [Safavian] points out that officers and employees of the executive, judicial, and legislative branches regularly seek advice from their respective ethics committees. They are encouraged to do so. The value of the advice they receive depends upon the accuracy and fullness of the information they provide. At GSA, as elsewhere in the

federal government, the officer or employee making the inquiry may or may not follow the advice of the ethics committee. That he did not follow that advice does not in itself constitute an ethical transgression. The prosecutors in this case are mistaken when they write that the GSA "ethics opinion . . . permitted [Safavian] to engage in behavior that would be prohibited if he had disclosed all relevant information." The ethics opinion did no such thing. It was not up to the GSA ethics officers to permit or forbid; their function was to offer advice. It is not apparent how this voluntary system, replicated throughout the government, imposes a duty on those seeking ethical advice to disclose-in the government's words-"all relevant information" upon pain of prosecution for violating § 1001(a)(1). As Safavian argues and as the government agrees, there must be a legal duty to disclose in order for there to be a concealment offense in violation of § 1001(a)(1), yet the government failed to identify a legal disclosure duty except by reference to vague standards of conduct for government employees.

4. *Ambiguous Questions*. Section 1001 prosecutions often arise from responses on government forms. The questions are often the problem because of their breadth, which permits a defendant to argue successfully that an answer was literally true, at least on some sense, thereby precluding a conviction. Consider **United States v. Rendon-Marquez**, 79 F.Supp.2d 1361 (N.D. Ga. 1999), involving an INS form that asked the following question: "Have you knowingly committed any crime or offense, for which you have not been arrested; or have you been arrested, cited, charged, indicted, convicted, fined, or imprisoned for breaking or violating any law or ordinance, including traffic violations?" The prescribed form asked for only yes or not answers, and the defendant answered in the negative even though he had once been arrested. The District Court granted a judgment of acquittal to a § 1001 charge for the following reason:

> * * * [T]he question that formed the basis of the indictment asked two separate and distinct questions. The form, however, provided space for only one 'yes' or "no" answer. Consequently, either way the defendant answered the question, he was answering truthfully as to one question and falsely as to the other. * * * It follows that the issue in this case could have been easily avoided had the question at issue been drafted to provide for two separate answers. The issue could have further been avoided had the question been written as one complete question which called for one distinct answer. As it now reads it is a compound question that is confusing and ambiguous. Because the defendant Rendon-Marquez's "no" response is literally and factually correct as to the first part of question three, the court finds that the government failed to provide sufficient evidence to establish the element of falsity as required under the statute. Thus, the evidence presented is insufficient to support a conclusion of defendant's guilt.

C. OBSTRUCTION OF JUSTICE

ARTHUR ANDERSEN LLP v. UNITED STATES
544 U.S. 696, 125 S.Ct. 2129, 161 L.Ed.2d 1008(2005)

Chief Justice REHNQUIST delivered the opinion of the Court.

As Enron Corporation's financial difficulties became public in 2001, petitioner Arthur Andersen LLP, Enron's auditor, instructed its employees to destroy documents pursuant to its document retention policy. A jury found that this action made petitioner guilty of violating 18 U.S.C. §§ 1512(b)(2)(A) and (B). These sections make it a crime to "knowingly us[e] intimidation or physical force, threate[n], or corruptly persuad[e] another person . . . with intent to . . . cause" that person to "withhold" documents from, or "alter" documents for use in, an "official proceeding." The Court of Appeals for the Fifth Circuit affirmed. We hold that the jury instructions failed to convey properly the elements of a "corrup[t] persuas[ion]" conviction under § 1512(b), and therefore reverse.

Enron Corporation, during the 1990's, switched its business from operation of natural gas pipelines to an energy conglomerate, a move that was accompanied by aggressive accounting practices and rapid growth. Petitioner audited Enron's publicly filed financial statements and provided internal audit and consulting services to it. Petitioner's "engagement team" for Enron was headed by David Duncan. Beginning in 2000, Enron's financial performance began to suffer, and, as 2001 wore on, worsened.[2] On August 14, 2001, Jeffrey Skilling, Enron's Chief Executive Officer (CEO), unexpectedly resigned. Within days, Sherron Watkins, a senior accountant at Enron, warned Kenneth Lay, Enron's newly reappointed CEO, that Enron could "implode in a wave of accounting scandals." She likewise informed Duncan and Michael Odom, one of petitioner's partners who had supervisory responsibility over Duncan, of the looming problems.

On August 28, an article in the Wall Street Journal suggested improprieties at Enron, and the SEC opened an informal investigation. By early September, petitioner had formed an Enron "crisis-response" team, which included Nancy Temple, an in-house counsel. On October 8, petitioner retained outside counsel to represent it in any litigation that might arise from the Enron matter. The next day, Temple discussed Enron with other

---

[2] During this time, petitioner faced problems of its own. In June 2001, petitioner entered into a settlement agreement with the Securities and Exchange Commission (SEC) related to its audit work of Waste Management, Inc. As part of the settlement, petitioner paid a massive fine. It also was censured and enjoined from committing further violations of the securities laws. In July 2001, the SEC filed an amended complaint alleging improprieties by Sunbeam Corporation, and petitioner's lead partner on the Sunbeam audit was named.

in-house counsel. Her notes from that meeting reflect that "some SEC investigation" is "highly probable."

On October 10, Odom spoke at a general training meeting attended by 89 employees, including 10 from the Enron engagement team. Odom urged everyone to comply with the firm's document retention policy.[4] He added: " '[I]f it's destroyed in the course of [the] normal policy and litigation is filed the next day, that's great .... [W]e've followed our own policy, and whatever there was that might have been of interest to somebody is gone and irretrievable.'" On October 12, Temple entered the Enron matter into her computer, designating the "Type of Potential Claim" as "Professional Practice — Government/Regulatory Inv[estigation]." Temple also e-mailed Odom, suggesting that he "'remin[d] the engagement team of our documentation and retention policy.'" On October 16, Enron announced its third quarter results. That release disclosed a $1.01 billion charge to earnings.[5] The following day, the SEC notified Enron by letter that it had opened an investigation in August and requested certain information and documents. On October 19, Enron forwarded a copy of that letter to petitioner.

On the same day, Temple also sent an e-mail to a member of petitioner's internal team of accounting experts and attached a copy of the document policy. On October 20, the Enron crisis-response team held a conference call, during which Temple instructed everyone to "[m]ake sure to follow the [document] policy." On October 23, Enron CEO Lay declined to answer questions during a call with analysts because of "potential lawsuits, as well as the SEC inquiry." After the call, Duncan met with other Andersen partners on the Enron engagement team and told them that they should ensure team members were complying with the document policy. Another meeting for all team members followed, during which Duncan distributed the policy and told everyone to comply. These, and other smaller meetings, were followed by substantial destruction of paper and electronic documents.

---

[4] The firm's policy called for a single central engagement file, which "should contain only that information which is relevant to supporting our work." The policy stated that, "in cases of threatened litigation, . . . no related information will be destroyed." It also separately provided that, if petitioner is "advised of litigation or subpoenas regarding a particular engagement, the related information should not be destroyed. Policy Statement No. 780 set forth "notification" procedures for whenever "professional practice litigation against [petitioner] or any of its personnel has been commenced, has been threatened or is judged likely to occur, or when governmental or professional investigations that may involve [petitioner] or any of its personnel have been commenced or are judged likely.

[5] The release characterized the charge to earnings as "non-recurring." Petitioner had expressed doubts about this characterization to Enron, but Enron refused to alter the release. Temple wrote an e-mail to Duncan that "suggested deleting some language that might suggest we have concluded the release is misleading."

On October 26, one of petitioner's senior partners circulated a New York Times article discussing the SEC's response to Enron. His e-mail commented that "the problems are just beginning and we will be in the cross hairs. The marketplace is going to keep the pressure on this and is going to force the SEC to be tough." On October 30, the SEC opened a formal investigation and sent Enron a letter that requested accounting documents.

Throughout this time period, the document destruction continued, despite reservations by some of petitioner's managers.[6] On November 8, Enron announced that it would issue a comprehensive restatement of its earnings and assets. Also on November 8, the SEC served Enron and petitioner with subpoenas for records. On November 9, Duncan's secretary sent an e-mail that stated: "Per Dave – No more shredding . . . . We have been officially served for our documents." Enron filed for bankruptcy less than a month later. Duncan was fired and later pleaded guilty to witness tampering.

In March 2002, petitioner was indicted in the Southern District of Texas on one count of violating §§ 1512(b)(2)(A) and (B). The indictment alleged that, between October 10 and November 9, 2001, petitioner "did knowingly, intentionally and corruptly persuade . . . other persons, to wit: [petitioner's] employees, with intent to cause" them to withhold documents from, and alter documents for use in, "official proceedings, namely: regulatory and criminal proceedings and investigations." A jury trial followed. * * * [T]he jury returned a guilty verdict. The District Court denied petitioner's motion for a judgment of acquittal.

* * * Sections 1512(b)(2)(A) and (B), part of the witness tampering provisions, provide in relevant part:

> Whoever knowingly uses intimidation or physical force, threatens, or corruptly persuades another person, or attempts to do so, or engages in misleading conduct toward another person, with intent to . . . cause or induce any person to . . . withhold testimony, or withhold a record, document, or other object, from an official proceeding [or] alter, destroy, mutilate, or conceal an object with intent to impair the object's integrity or availability for use in an official proceeding . . . shall be fined under this title or imprisoned not more than ten years, or both.

---

[6] For example, on October 26, John Riley, another partner with petitioner, saw Duncan shredding documents and told him "this wouldn't be the best time in the world for you guys to be shredding a bunch of stuff." On October 31, David Stulb, a forensics investigator for petitioner, met with Duncan. During the meeting, Duncan picked up a document with the words "smoking gun" written on it and began to destroy it, adding "we don't need this." Stulb cautioned Duncan on the need to maintain documents and later informed Temple that Duncan needed advice on the document retention policy.

In this case, our attention is focused on what it means to "knowingly . . . corruptly persuad[e]" another person "with intent to . . . cause" that person to "withhold" documents from, or "alter" documents for use in, an "official proceeding."

"We have traditionally exercised restraint in assessing the reach of a federal criminal statute, both out of deference to the prerogatives of Congress, Dowling v. United States, 473 U.S. 207, (1985), and out of concern that 'a fair warning should be given to the world in language that the common world will understand, of what the law intends to do if a certain line is passed,' McBoyle v. United States, 283 U.S. 25 (1931)." United States v. Aguilar, 515 U.S. 593 (1995).

Such restraint is particularly appropriate here, where the act underlying the conviction — "persua[sion]" — is by itself innocuous.   Indeed, "persuad[ing]" a person "with intent to . . . cause" that person to "withhold" testimony or documents from a Government proceeding or Government official is not inherently malign.   Consider, for instance, a mother who suggests to her son that he invoke his right against compelled self-incrimination, see U.S. CONST., AMDT. 5, or a wife who persuades her husband not to disclose marital confidences, see Trammel v. United States, 445 U.S. 40 (1980).

Nor is it necessarily corrupt for an attorney to "persuad[e]" a client "with intent to . . . cause" that client to "withhold" documents from the Government.   In Upjohn Co. v. United States, 449 U.S. 383 (1981), for example, we held that Upjohn was justified in withholding documents that were covered by the attorney-client privilege from the Internal Revenue Service (IRS).   No one would suggest that an attorney who "persuade[d]" Upjohn to take that step acted wrongfully, even though he surely intended that his client keep those documents out of the IRS' hands.

"Document retention policies," which are created in part to keep certain information from getting into the hands of others, including the Government, are common in business.   It is, of course, not wrongful for a manager to instruct his employees to comply with a valid document retention policy under ordinary circumstances.

Acknowledging this point, the parties have largely focused their attention on the word "corruptly" as the key to what may or may not lawfully be done in the situation presented here.   Section 1512(b) punishes not just "corruptly persuad[ing]" another, but "knowingly (3)27 corruptly persuad[ing]" another. (Emphasis added.)   The Government suggests that "knowingly" does not modify "corruptly persuades," but that is not how the statute most naturally reads.   It provides the mens rea – "knowingly" – and then a list of acts – "uses intimidation or physical force, threatens, or corruptly persuades."   We have recognized with regard to similar statutory language that the mens rea at least applies to the acts that immediately follow, if not to other elements down the statutory chain. See United States v. X-Citement Video, Inc., 513 U.S. 64 (1994) (recognizing that the "most natural grammatical reading" of 18 U.S.C. §§ 2252(a)(1) and (2) "suggests that the term 'knowingly' modifies only the surrounding verbs: transports, ships, receives, distributes, or reproduces"); see also Liparota v. United States, 471 U.S. 419 (1985).   The Government suggests that it is "questionable whether Congress would employ such an inelegant formulation as 'knowingly . . . corruptly persuades.'" Long experience has not taught us to share the Government's doubts on this score, and we must simply interpret the statute as written.

The parties have not pointed us to another interpretation of "knowingly . . . corruptly" to guide us here.[9] In any event, the natural meaning of these terms provides a clear answer. "[K]nowledge" and "knowingly" are normally associated with awareness, understanding, or consciousness. See BLACK'S LAW DICTIONARY 888 (8th ed.2004); WEBSTER'S THIRD NEW INTERNATIONAL DICTIONARY 1252-1253 (1993); AMERICAN HERITAGE DICTIONARY OF THE ENGLISH LANGUAGE 725 (1981). "Corrupt" and "corruptly" are normally associated with wrongful, immoral, depraved, or evil. Joining these meanings together here makes sense both linguistically and in the statutory scheme. Only persons conscious of wrongdoing can be said to "knowingly . . . corruptly persuad[e]." And limiting criminality to persuaders conscious of their wrongdoing sensibly allows § 1512(b) to reach only those with the level of "culpability . . . we usually require in order to impose criminal liability." *United States v. Aguilar.*

The outer limits of this element need not be explored here because the jury instructions at issue simply failed to convey the requisite consciousness of wrongdoing. Indeed, it is striking how little culpability the instructions required. For example, the jury was told that, "even if [petitioner] honestly and sincerely believed that its conduct was lawful, you may find [petitioner] guilty." The instructions also diluted the meaning of "corruptly" so that it covered innocent conduct.

The parties vigorously disputed how the jury would be instructed on "corruptly." The District Court based its instruction on the definition of that term found in the Fifth Circuit Pattern Jury Instruction for § 1503. This pattern instruction defined "corruptly" as "knowingly and dishonestly, with the specific intent to subvert or undermine the integrity" of a proceeding. The Government, however, insisted on excluding "dishonestly" and adding the term "impede" to the phrase "subvert or undermine." The District Court agreed over petitioner's objections, and the jury was told to convict if it found petitioner intended to "subvert, undermine, or impede" governmental

---

[9] The parties have pointed us to two other obstruction provisions, 18 U.S.C. §§ 1503 and 1505, which contain the word "corruptly." But these provisions lack the modifier "knowingly," making any analogy inexact.

factfinding by suggesting to its employees that they enforce the document retention policy.

These changes were significant. No longer was any type of "dishonest[y]" necessary to a finding of guilt, and it was enough for petitioner to have simply "impede[d]" the Government's factfinding ability. As the Government conceded at oral argument, "'impede'" has broader connotations than "'subvert' " or even " 'undermine,'" and many of these connotations do not incorporate any "corrupt[ness]" at all. The dictionary defines "impede" as "to interfere with or get in the way of the progress of" or "hold up" or "detract from." WEBSTER'S 3D. By definition, anyone who innocently persuades another to withhold information from the Government "get[s] in the way of the progress of" the Government. With regard to such innocent conduct, the "corruptly" instructions did no limiting work whatsoever.

The instructions also were infirm for another reason. They led the jury to believe that it did not have to find any nexus between the "persua [sion]" to destroy documents and any particular proceeding. In resisting any type of nexus element, the Government relies heavily on § 1512(e)(1), which states that an official proceeding "need not be pending or about to be instituted at the time of the offense." It is, however, one thing to say that a proceeding "need not be pending or about to be instituted at the time of the offense," and quite another to say a proceeding need not even be foreseen. A "knowingly . . . corrup[t] persaude[r]" cannot be someone who persuades others to shred documents under a document retention policy when he does not have in contemplation any particular official proceeding in which those documents might be material.

We faced a similar situation in *Aguilar*. Respondent Aguilar lied to a Federal Bureau of Investigation agent in the course of an investigation and was convicted of " 'corruptly endeavor[ing] to influence, obstruct, and impede [a] . . . grand jury investigation' " under § 1503. All the Government had shown was that Aguilar had uttered false statements to an investigating agent "who might or might not testify before a grand jury." We held that § 1503 required something more − specifically, a "nexus" between the obstructive act and the proceeding. "[I]f the defendant lacks knowledge that his actions are likely to affect the judicial proceeding," we explained, "he lacks the requisite intent to obstruct."

For these reasons, the jury instructions here were flawed in important respects. The judgment of the Court of Appeals is reversed, and the case is remanded for further proceedings consistent with this opinion.

NOTES AND QUESTIONS

1. *The Demise of Andersen.* Arthur Andersen LLP gave up its accounting licenses after the conviction and ceased doing business as an accounting and auditing firm at that time, and it has not been revived. The Department of Justice moved to dismiss the charges against the firm in November 2005 after the Supreme Court reversed the conviction. See *Move by Ex-Andersen Partner Could Affect Enron Case*, N.Y. TIMES, Nov. 24, 2005, at C9. See p. 73.

2. *Obstruction Statutes.* There are a number of obstruction of justice statutes in the federal criminal code that cover different types of proceedings, and the distinctions among them are not always clear. The broadest provision is in the Omnibus Clause of 18 U.S.C. § 1503, which reaches any person who "corruptly . . . influences, obstructs, or impedes, or endeavors to influence, obstruct, or impede, the *due administration of justice*." Section 1505 reaches any person who "corruptly . . . endeavors to influence, obstruct, or impede the due and proper administration of the law under which any *pending proceeding* is being had before any department or agency of the United States" or congressional investigation. While § 1503 applies to judicial proceedings, including civil actions, § 1505 applies to proceedings before administrative agencies in the Executive Branch and inquiries undertaken by the Legislative Branch. In **United States v. Aguilar**, 515 U.S. 593 (1995), the Supreme Court discussed the scope of the Omnibus Clause in §1503, what it described as a "catch-all" provision:

> The action taken by the accused must be with an intent to influence judicial or grand jury proceedings; it is not enough that there be an intent to influence some ancillary proceeding, such as an investigation independent of the court's or grand jury's authority. Some courts have phrased this showing as a "nexus" requirement–that the act must have a relationship in time, causation, or logic with the judicial proceedings. In other words, the endeavor must have the "natural and probable effect" of interfering with the due administration of justice. This is not to say that the defendant's actions need be successful; an "endeavor" suffices. But * * * if the defendant lacks knowledge that his actions are likely to affect the judicial proceeding, he lacks the requisite intent to obstruct.

Another provision, § 1512(c), was recently added to prohibit the destruction, alteration or concealment of records related to an official proceeding. Congress expanded the scope of § 1512 as part of the Sarbanes-Oxley Act of 2002, in response to a perceived gap in the statutory coverage in connection with the document destruction by the accounting firm Arthur Andersen in connection with the investigation of the Enron Corporation. Andersen was convicted under the prior version of § 1512, and the new provision now reaches any person who "corruptly . . . (1) alters, destroys, mutilates, or conceals a record, document, or other object, or attempts to do so, with the intent to impair the object's integrity or availability for use in an *official proceeding*; or (2) otherwise obstructs, influences, or impedes any official proceeding, or attempts to do so." Unlike § 1503, which only covers judicial and grand jury proceedings, § 1512(c) is now much broader because the statute states that "an official proceeding need not be pending or about to be instituted at the time of the offense."

The Sarbanes-Oxley Act added two additional obstruction statutes: §§ 1519 and 1520. Section 1519 covers any person who "knowingly alters, destroys, mutilates, conceals, covers up, falsifies, or makes a false entry in any record, document, or tangible object with the intent to impede, obstruct, or influence the *investigation* or proper administration of any matter within the jurisdiction of any department or agency of the United States or any case filed under title 11, or in relation to or contemplation of any such matter or case."* * * Section 1520 requires auditors of a publicly traded company to "maintain all audit or review workpapers for a period of 5 years from the end of the fiscal period in which the audit or review was concluded," and any destruction of such records is a separate criminal offense. Were these new criminal provisions necessary? The new destruction of records provision, § 1519, has been prosecuted in a few cases, but not in any corporate fraud prosecutions. Rather, this new provision has been used most prominently in child pornography cases.

It is not clear whether § 1519 extends the law to other forms of obstruction of justice. One comment asserted that the new statute is largely duplicative of other provisions: "Many of the [Sarbanes-Oxley] Act's criminal provisions duplicate the conduct and intent terms of existing provisions of the Criminal Code. The new obstruction of justice offense in 18 U.S.C. § 1519, for example, is a near facsimile of § 1505, which deals with obstruction of 'pending proceedings' before federal departments, agencies, and committees." Note, *Recent Legislation: Corporate Law–Congress Passes Corporate and Accounting Fraud Legislation.–Sarbanes-Oxley Act of 2002, Pub. L. No. 107-204, 116 Stat. 745 (Codified in Scattered Sections of 11, 15, 18, 28, and 29 U.S.C.)*, 116 HARV. L. REV. 728 (2002). Another comment, however argues that § 1519 creates a new crime of "anticipatory obstruction": "[§ 1519] can play a new and significant role in prohibiting anticipatory obstruction of justice – document destruction by individuals who are savvy enough to pre-empt an investigation by acting before they have knowledge about the specific proceeding that may demand the documents. In the area of anticipatory obstruction, the new Sarbanes-Oxley * * * provision clarifies an area of obstruction of justice that has left the courts conflicted and juries confused." Dana E. Hill, Note, *Anticipatory Obstruction of Justice: Pre-Emptive Document Destruction under the Sarbanes-Oxley Anti-Shredding Statute, 18 U.S.C. § 1519*, 89 CORNELL L. REV. 1519 (2004).

CHAPTER NINE
GRAND JURY INVESTIGATIONS

A. *THE FEDERAL GRAND JURY AS AN INVESTIGATIVE BODY*

At the time of the adoption of the United States Constitution, the grand jury was renowned as "the people's panel," serving as both the "shield" and "sword" of the criminal justice process that the colonists had brought with them from England. The grand jury served as a shield against unfounded and oppressive initiation of prosecution by refusing to issue an indictment when it viewed the Crown's evidence as insufficient or the prosecution simply appeared unjust. Exercising that screening authority, colonial grand juries had shown their independence in refusing to indict various persons who had spoken or acted in opposition to Royalist power (including twice refusing to indict Peter Zenger for seditious libel, although the Crown then proceeded against Zenger by prosecutor's information). The grand jury served as a sword when it investigated on its own initiative and brought criminal charges, even over the opposition of the Crown, by issuing a presentment (an authority colonial grand juries had exercised even against appointed Royal officials and British soldiers). Thus, it was not surprising that the grand jury's powers were given constitutional recognition in the Fifth Amendment, through the provision that no person "be held to answer for a capital or otherwise infamous crime, unless on a presentment or indictment of a Grand Jury."

During the eighteenth century, the grand jury, in many quarters, lost much of its luster. Its value as a shield was questioned by critics who contended that the grand jury was unrepresentative and inefficient, inferior to the magistrate in screening the sufficiency of the prosecution's evidence. A substantial group of states (eventually to become a majority) abolished the requirement that all felony prosecutions be initiated by indictment, thereby allowing prosecutors to proceed by information (ordinarily, only if supported by a magistrate's finding of probable cause at a preliminary hearing). In the federal system, where a constitutional amendment was not a realistic prospect, the only modification achievable by the critics was to authorize the prosecution to proceed by information in noncapital felony cases if defendant waived his right to indictment. See Fed. R. Crim. P. 7(b).

During the same period, in most states, the grand jury's investigative role was substantially reduced, though not abolished. With the growing urbanization of communities, grand jurors could no longer be expected to be familiar with the full range of local criminal activity by virtue of their ties to the community. Moreover, with the development of enforcement agencies staffed by full time professionals, investigation of most crimes was now handled more efficiently and effectively by those agencies. In the states that no longer needed the grand jury for screening (i.e., those allowing all felony prosecutions to be brought by information), many communities found that there remained so little need for the grand jury in investigations that grand juries were no longer regularly empaneled. In states where grand juries were continuously sitting for the purpose of screening, prosecutors often utilized the grand jury's subpoena authority to complement police investigations, but reliance upon the grand jury as a primary vehicle for investigation was limited to a narrow range of cases. One area of criminality that continued to be investigated through the grand jury was governmental graft and malfeasance, and it was here that grand juries on rare occasions became "runaways" and instigated investigations on their own initiative, (thereby reinforcing the public image of the grand jury as the "people's watchdog against public corruption").

In the federal system, where grand juries were regularly in session as a screening body, prosecutors over the years came to find substantially greater use for the investigative authority of the grand jury.[a] The investigative advantages of the grand jury (discussed below) fit a more substantial portion of the often complex crimes of concern to federal prosecutors than they do the crimes of concern to state prosecutors. Also, the structure of the federal grand jury process is conducive to prosecutor control of the investigation — a control also facilitated by many of the major federal investigative agencies being a part of the same executive department as the prosecutor. In general, the prosecutor can obtain subpoenas from the clerk of the court, on behalf of the grand jury, without first obtaining approval of the grand jury (or its foreperson). The grand jurors are selected from the same pool of prospective jurors as the petit jury, and thus are not likely to have any special expertise in investigation.   Professor Andrew D. Leipold described the general operation of a federal grand jury:

> The operation of a typical federal grand jury is straightforward. A pool of citizens is summoned at random from the judicial district where the jury will sit. From the group of qualified people who appear, twenty-three are chosen to serve on the jury. The jurors sit for an indefinite period not to exceed eighteen months; the number of days per month when they must actually appear depends on the

---

[a] The reference to federal "prosecutors" includes members of the local United States Attorney's Office and Department of Justice Attorneys in divisions (e.g., criminal division and antitrust divisions) that have criminal law enforcement responsibilities. Under Federal Rule 6(d), discussed in n. b, infra, only "attorneys for the government" may appear before the grand jury, and Rule 54(c) defines that term to include basically the legal staffs of the U.S. Attorneys and the Attorney General. Where needed, attorneys for federal agencies may be designated special assistants so they too then can participate, see 28 U.S.C. §§ 515, 543, but those attorneys then operate under the direction of the Department of Justice, rather than their agency.

prosecutor's case load. A district court judge administers the oath and gives the jurors general instructions about their duties. This marks the end of the judge's formal involvement in the process. From that point forward, the prosecutor dictates the course of the proceedings. The most striking feature of grand jury hearings is their secrecy. The press and public are barred from the proceedings, as are suspects and their counsel. Even judges are not allowed in the grand jury room; attendance is limited to the prosecutor, the jurors, the court reporter, and the single witness being questioned. Those who participate in the hearing [except for the witness] are sworn to secrecy, and the court may use its contempt powers to ensure that this silence is maintained even after the case is resolved. Once in session, the grand jury's primary task is to review the cases presented to it by the government. The prosecutor calls and questions witnesses, and presents documentary evidence related to the crime in question. Unlike trial jurors, grand jurors may ask questions of the witness and may discuss the case with the prosecutor as evidence is submitted. After the case is presented, the prosecutor asks the jurors to vote to return an indictment accusing the defendant of a specific crime that the prosecutor believes is supported by the evidence. The jurors then deliberate in private. If at least twelve agree that there is probable cause to believe that the suspect committed the crime, the grand jury returns a "true bill" that, when signed by the prosecutor, becomes the indictment. If the grand jury concludes that the evidence is insufficient, it returns a "no bill" (or "no true bill"), and any preliminary charges filed against the suspect are dismissed.

Andrew D. Leipold, *Why Grand Juries Do Not (and Cannot) Protect the Accused*, 80 CORNELL L. REV. 260 (1995). The investigative aspect of the grand jury is often much more important than the adjudicative role, but the individual grand jurors have no real role in the investigation.

1. *Investigative Advantages.* Compared to police investigations, grand jury investigations are expensive, time consuming, and logistically cumbersome. There are certain types of cases, however, in which prosecutors are likely to view the grand jury's investigatory assistance as either essential or highly desirable, and therefore worth the extra costs of the grand jury process. These are primarily cases in which investigators face one or more of the following tasks: unraveling a complex criminal structure, dealing with victims or witnesses reluctant to cooperate, obtaining information buried in extensive business records, controlling the information revealed about the investigation while it is ongoing and countering the likely claims of the target that the investigation is being used for the purpose of harassment or political manipulation. Criminal activities likely to present such investigative problems include almost the entire range of white collar crime.

The cornerstone of the grand jury's investigative power is its ability to use the subpoena authority of the court that impaneled it. In Branzburg v.

Hayes, 408 U.S. 665 (1972), the Supreme Court described the broad authority of the grand jury to compel the production of information to aid its investigations: "Although the powers of the grand jury are not unlimited and are subject to the supervision of a judge, the longstanding principle that 'the public . . . has a right to every man's evidence,' except for those persons protected by a constitutional, common-law, or statutory privilege, is particularly applicable to grand jury proceedings."

The grand jury may utilize the subpoena "duces tecum" to obtain tangible evidence and the subpoena "ad testificandum" to obtain testimony. These are not mere requests for assistance (as in the case of a police officer who asks a witness or suspect to make a statement). Both subpoenas are supported by the court's authority to hold in contempt any person who willfully refuses, without legal justification, to comply with a subpoena's directive. See Fed. R. Crim. P. 17(g) ("failure by any person without adequate excuse to obey a subpoena served upon that person may be deemed a contempt of the court from which the subpoena issued"). This contempt authority includes both civil and criminal contempt, although Shillitani v. United States, 384 U.S. 364 (1966), directs district courts ordinarily to look first to civil contempt. Under the civil contempt process, the recalcitrant witness is sentenced initially to imprisonment or to a fine (which may increase daily), but the recalcitrant witness may be purged of the contempt by complying with the subpoena. It is said that the recalcitrant witness held in civil contempt "carries the keys of the prison in his own pockets." Civil contemnors who refuse to purge themselves will remain under sentence until the grand jury completes its term and is discharged, although the Recalcitrant Witness Act, 28 U.S.C. § 1826, limits the term to a maximum of 18 months, less than the 36 month maximum term for an extended special grand jury. Moreover, if the information that the contemnor possesses is still needed, the contemnor may be subpoenaed by a successor grand jury and again held in contempt if there is a continual refusal to supply that information.

Courts have held that if imprisonment of a contemnor becomes punitive rather than coercive then the confinement must end. There is no bright line indicating when the nature of the confinement changes. The Recalcitrant Witness Act places an outer limit of eighteen months on the amount of time a grand jury witness can be held, which is the usual term of a grand jury. In **Armstrong v. Guccione**, 470 F.3d 89 (2d Cir. 2006), the Second Circuit explained why civil contempt in other contexts is not limited to a specific maximum period of confinement as it is for grand jury witnesses in a case in which the contemnor challenged his seven year confinement.

We also reject Armstrong's contention * * * that Congress intended the Recalcitrant Witness Statute to indicate a presumptive benchmark suggesting a limit dictated by the Due Process Clause for all coercive confinements. Section 1826(a) was carefully drafted to apply to one particular category of contemnor: A "witness . . . [who] refuses without just cause shown to comply with an order of the court to testify or provide other information." 28 U.S.C. § 1826(a);

see also Gelbard v. United States, 408 U.S. 41 (1972) (Rehnquist, J., dissenting) (stating that the statute expresses a "desire on the part of Congress to treat separately from the general contempt power of courts their authority to deal with recalcitrant witnesses in court or grand jury proceedings"). Nothing in § 1826(a) suggests that Congress intended that it apply as a presumptive benchmark, or in any other way, to contemnors who do not fit within that category.

Furthermore, we can easily appreciate that the class of contemnors for which Congress established the eighteen-month ceiling can present circumstances that understandably motivated Congress to establish such a ceiling for that particular class. Persons who go to jail rather than obey a court order to testify frequently do so in the service of some useful and socially worthwhile principle. In some cases (which invariably receive widespread publicity and therefore have surely come to the attention of Congress), it is a journalist who believes she would violate the ethical standards of her profession if she revealed a source to whom she promised confidentiality. In other cases, it is a member of some other profession – medical, legal, religious – who similarly believes that the ethical standards of her profession would be compromised by revelation of confidences (under circumstances where the court's finding of waiver of a privilege does not convince the witness that any such waiver was voluntary). In still other cases, the court's order to testify forces the witness to violate a loyalty to a family member or close friend. Even when the relationship between the witness and the subject of the testimony sought is merely that of partners in crime, our social mores are not deeply offended by the criminal who would rather spend time in jail than squeal on his partner. Accordingly, in passing a statute which imposes an eighteen-month limitation on coercive contempt confinement for recalcitrant witnesses but not for other categories of civil contemnors, Congress has not acted arbitrarily or irrationally. Although one could argue that not everyone coming within § 1826(a)'s scope is motivated by such admirable purposes, there appear to be good reasons for Congress to have selected for special treatment that class of contemnors.

We also acknowledge that there are situations where a contemnor might not come within the terms of § 1826(a) but whose circumstances nonetheless raise the same types of considerations as those of a recalcitrant witness covered by the statute. Yet Congress need not achieve a perfect fit in enacting legislation. And even if an argument could be made that such a person should benefit from the same ceiling that Congress imposed for the recalcitrant witness, that argument would do nothing for Armstrong. His case does not raise the types of considerations that led Congress to impose a ceiling for the special benefit of recalcitrant witnesses. The district court's order does not require Armstrong to choose between subservience to law and his ethical principles, nor does it require him to violate bonds of personal loyalty to a family member or friend, or even a partner in crime. According to the district court's findings, Armstrong is motivated by greed. He is willing to suffer time in jail in the hope of ending up in possession of $15 million in assets of a corporation to which he owes fiduciary duties. The Due Process Clause does not demand that the test of his obduracy end today or, for that matter, at any specific time.

If the contemnor does not respond to the civil contempt sanction, he or she also faces the threat of the additional sanction of criminal contempt. Here the court simply seeks to impose punishment for violation of its order in the same manner in which punishment is imposed for a violation of the penal code. However, there is no statutorily set maximum penalty for this offense, and the sentence imposed may be measured in years rather than months. See e.g., United States v. Brummitt, 665 F.2d 521 (5th Cir. 1981) (upholding five-year sentence). Sanctions are also available where the subpoenaed person does not directly refuse to comply, but falsely claims to be unable to comply. While a contempt citation is sometimes used in the case of evasive answers, In re Weiss, 703 F.2d 653 (2nd Cir. 1983), testimony falsely claiming a lack of memory, or falsely claiming a lack of possession of subpoenaed documents, is subject to prosecution either as perjury under 18 U.S.C. § 1621 or as a false declaration under 18 U.S.C. § 1623(e) (which eliminates both the two-witness and direct-evidence rules applicable to the proof of falsity under perjury and allows for proof of falsity by showing the defendant made two inherently inconsistent sworn statements, one of which must be false). Issues related to perjury and obstruction of justice in a grand jury investigation are discussed in Chapter 8.

Compulsory process is not the only aspect of the grand jury process that contributes to its investigative authority. The grand jury process also features lay participation, closed proceedings, immunity grants, [see p. 580] and grand jury secrecy requirements. It is the interaction of compulsory process with such features that allows the prosecution to achieve investigative objectives that either cannot be achieved, or cannot be achieved nearly so readily, through other investigative avenues. Described below are some significant objectives that can be achieved by the use of the grand jury to investigate a case.

2. *Obtaining Testimony From Reluctant Witnesses*. The grand jury subpoena is especially useful in obtaining information from persons who will not voluntarily furnish information to federal investigative agents (including both those who refuse to provide any information and those who will only give the agent so much time or so much information). Faced with compulsory process, which is backed up by a possible jail sentence for contempt, many such individuals not only will testify before the grand jury, but will do so fully (and for such period) as the prosecutor desires. Of course, if the information sought could be incriminating, the witness (unless granted immunity) may still refuse to cooperate by relying on a privilege against self-incrimination. Many persons, however, though unwilling to furnish

information voluntarily, will testify before the grand jury without even considering reliance upon the privilege, as incrimination was not their primary reason for previously refusing to cooperate. Thus, a victim of a fraud may refuse to discuss the matter with investigators out of embarrassment over the victim's gullibility or greedy objectives, yet be willing to testify before the grand jury when faced with the threat of contempt. Similarly, an employee may wish to avoid the appearance of voluntarily assisting a federal agency investigating her employer, yet testify freely when the employee can tell the employer that she was forced to do so under the compulsion of a subpoena.

The secrecy requirements of the grand jury process also may encourage the witness to be more forthcoming. The witness knows that he is in control of who will learn of what has been told to the grand jury (at least until charges are brought[b]). The witness generally is free to inform others of the testimony the witness has given, but the prosecutor's staff (including the agents from federal agencies–such as the FBI or the SEC–that are assisting the prosecutors in the grand jury investigation), the grand jurors, and all grand jury personnel (e.g., stenographers) are sworn to secrecy. An employee/witness need not inform an employer of being called to testify, or if the witness desires, inform the employer that he or she testified, but not fully reveal what was said in this testimony. Since the witness testifies out of the presence of counsel (who may be receiving his or her fee from the employer), the witness need not even tell counsel exactly what was said before the grand jury.

3. *"Fishing" For Documents.* The grand jury subpoena duces tecum offers several advantages over the primary device available to law enforcement agents to obtain records and physical evidence—the search pursuant to a warrant. Unlike the search warrant, the subpoena duces tecum can issue without a showing of probable cause. Indeed, as will be seen in the later sections of this chapter, no showing at all is required as to the likelihood that a particular crime was committed and, at most, a quite lenient standard need be met to connect the records sought to possible criminal activity. Courts recognize that the "paper trail" establishing the presence of white collar offenses is often buried in the offender's everyday business records and therefore "some exploration or fishing necessarily is inherent" in the use of the grand jury subpoena duces tecum to investigate the possible commission of those offenses. See Schwimmer v. United States, 232 F.2d 855 (8th Cir. 1956) (discussing the investigation of possible antitrust violations).

---

[b] If a prosecution is brought and if the grand jury witness is called to testify as a prosecution witness at the trial, then the defendant will have a right to discover at that point the witness' prior grand jury testimony. See 18 U.S.C. § 3500(e) (including grand jury testimony within the Jencks Act provision governing a trial witness' prior recorded statements).

Moreover, even where probable cause could be established, and a search warrant could be obtained, the grand jury subpoena duces tecum often will be preferred for its administrative advantages. For example, there may be a need to obtain so many different types of records from so many different locations that law enforcement officers would find a search highly burdensome if not absolutely impractical. With a subpoena duces tecum, the party served is required to undertake the extensive task of bringing together records from several different locations and sorting through them to collect those covered by the subpoena. At other times, there may be a need to obtain records from uninvolved third parties (e.g., a bank) and a subpoena will be preferred over a search because it will be far less disruptive to the third party's operations. Subpoenas to certain types of businesses, such as banks or internet service providers, are subject to separate restrictions on the grand jury's right to obtain evidence without notifying the account owner. On the other hand, the search warrant offers the advantage of a direct seizure of the records, in contrast to a subpoena that provides the recipient with time to respond and, possibly, to destroy records. See Chapter 12 for a discussion of the advantages and disadvantages of search warrants.

4. *Keeping The Target "In The Dark."* Grand jury secrecy requirements are commonly cited as another investigative advantage of the grand jury. Initially, those requirements are said to facilitate keeping the target of the investigation "in the dark" as to the nature of the inquiry. People may be investigated without even knowing that they are the subject of an investigation or, if they are aware of their "target" status, without knowing which of their activities are being examined or who is providing the information on those activities. This may be of assistance in gaining the cooperation of others, in ensuring that there is no tampering with physical evidence or possible witnesses, and in prosecution dealings with the target.

5. *Controlling Public Disclosure*. Grand jury secrecy requirements also are helpful in keeping an investigation from coming to the attention of the public, and where that fails, in limiting what is publicly disclosed. When the target of a possible investigation occupies a position of prominence, public disclosure of the investigation may cause irreparable harm to the target's reputation even though the investigation eventually reveals no basis for prosecution. Accordingly, if an investigation of such a person is likely to become public, a prosecutor might hesitate to initiate that investigation absent a strong indication that it will lead to a prosecution. However, if the grand jury process can keep the investigation secret, the prosecutor may be willing to undertake an investigation on the basis of suspicions that have far less grounding. If the suspicions prove erroneous, the suspect's reputation will not have been harmed; but if the suspicions prove well founded, the prosecution will have the basis for a prosecution that otherwise might never have been brought.

6. *Deflecting Claims Of Improper Motivation*. In certain types of investigations, the prosecution can expect the target to claim that the investigation is motivated by partisan influences and designed to harass. The

participation of the grand jurors — persons selected from the community "with no axes to grind" — may be used to deflect such criticism. Of course, that will not be convincing to those who see the grand jury as no more than the prosecutor's "rubber stamp," but many citizens see the grand jury as an independent shielding body that would seek the intervention of the court if it viewed the investigation as founded on improper prosecutorial motives.

B. THE GRAND JURY SUBPOENA

1. *Federal Rule of Criminal Procedure 17*. Grand jury subpoenas are governed by Federal Rule of Criminal Procedure 17, which deals with subpoenas utilized for proceedings of all types in the federal district court.[c] Subsection (a) of that Rule sets forth the basic requirements for the issuance and form of the subpoena ad testificandum. It provides that the subpoena shall be issued by the clerk under the seal of the district court, and shall be given "in blank to a party requesting it." That party in a grand jury proceeding is the prosecutor, the legal advisor to the grand jury, who then fills in the blanks — specifying first, the name of the party who is "commanded to attend and give testimony"; second, the time and place of attendance; and third, the identification of the proceeding (since a grand jury proceeding has no title, unlike a filed case, the direction here simply is to give testimony "before the grand jury").[d]

Subsection (c) of Rule 17 deals with the subpoena duces tecum. It provides:

> A subpoena may also command the person to whom it is directed to produce the books, papers, documents or other objects designated therein. The court on motion made promptly may quash or modify the subpoena if compliance would be unreasonable or oppressive. The court may direct that books, papers, documents or objects designated in the subpoena be produced before the court at a time prior to the trial or prior to the time when they are to be offered in evidence and may upon their production permit the books, papers,

---

[c] In special situations, other provisions also will bear upon the use of the grand jury subpoena. Thus, a subpoena directed to telephone companies and internet service providers for account holder information also is subject to the notice requirements of 18 U.S.C. § 2703; a subpoena directed to a financial institution for a customer's financial records is subject to the additional requirements of 12 U.S.C. §§ 3401 et seq.; a subpoena to a consumer reporting agency must meet the requirements of 15 U.S.C. §§ 1681 et seq.; and a subpoena directed to a foreign government is subject to the limitations imposed by 28 U.S.C. §§ 1602-1611.

[d] Ordinarily, the grand jury need not be consulted prior to the issuance of the subpoena. In some districts, it is the custom to inform the grand jury shortly afterwards of the subpoenas that have been issued on its behalf, and in some, the foreperson will be notified in advance and asked to initial the subpoena. See also pp. 600-01 as to special settings in which grand jury authorization prior to issuance may be required.

documents or objects or portions thereof to be inspected by the parties and their attorneys.

Very often the subpoena duces tecum and subpoena ad testificandum are combined in a single subpoena, which then directs the subpoenaed person to appear on the specified date to give testimony before the grand jury and to bring with you [the specified documents or tangible item]." Because there is limited space to list items on the subpoena itself, typically the subpoena duces tecum will direct the party to produce such items as are specified in an "attachment" to the subpoena.

Subsections (d) and (e) of Rule 17 deal with the service of the subpoena. The subpoena may be served by the U.S. Marshal or any staff member working on the investigation (a person "who is not a party and who is not less than 18 years of age"). A subpoena requiring a witness to appear at a grand jury proceeding to testify or present tangible items "may be served at any place within the United States" and may also be "directed to a witness in a foreign country" as provided in 28 U.S.C. § 1783 (authorizing foreign service as to a person who is a national or resident of the United States). A subpoena may be directed to a natural person or a legal entity. Where entity records are sought and the custodian of those records is known, the subpoena may be directed to a named person for the production of those records. Very often, however, the entity itself will be the subpoenaed party and service then may be made on any officer or managing or general agent of the entity (or where state law so provides, as it often does for corporations, on the Secretary of State of the state in which the entity is doing business).

2. *Subpoena Ad Testificandum.* The grand jury subpoena is a deceptively simple document that informs the recipient when and where they must appear, what documents or other tangible items to bring (see n.3, infra), and the name of the federal prosecutor responsible for the issuance of the subpoena. In addition, USAM § 9-11.150, prescribes the content of an "Advice of Rights" form that must be attached to a subpoena directed to a "target" or "subject" of an investigation. As a matter of practice, that form is usually attached to all subpoenas, with an additional attachment added to the subpoena duces tecum. The Advice of Rights form deals primarily with advice regarding the witness' privilege against self-incrimination and opportunity to consult with counsel. However, it also includes a brief description of the "general subject matter of the inquiry," such as the following: "The grand jury is conducting an investigation of possible violations of Federal criminal laws involving: (State here the general subject matter of inquiry, e.g., conducting an illegal gambling business in violation of 18 U.S.C. §§ 1955)." It is common practice also to send to a subpoenaed witness a letter that explains the basics of testifying before the grand jury: that the witness will testify under oath, that the only persons present will be the witness, the grand jurors, the stenographer, and the government attorneys, and that the grand jury will be composed of 16-23 persons drawn from the community. This letter also will refer to the subject of the

investigation, but typically will describe it in the same language as the "Advice of Rights" attachment.

3. *The Attachment to the Subpoena Duces Tecum*. The attachment to a subpoena duces tecum provides the critical content of the subpoena. The specific documents requested will vary with the investigation. Federal prosecutors draft the subpoenas broadly to ensure that all relevant documents are covered. The government does not need to know specifically of the existence of a particular document, although enforcement of a subpoena to an individual–as opposed to a corporation or other organization–may hinge on whether the subpoena recipient can assert the Fifth Amendment privilege against self-incrimination [see Chapter 13, infra]. The subpoena attachment below was reprinted in an appendix to the Supreme Court's opinion in United States v. Hubbell, 530 U.S. 27 (2000) [p. 408]. A grand jury investigating President Clinton's involvement in the Whitewater transactions subpoenaed personal records of Webster Hubbell to determine whether he violated the requirement of an earlier plea agreement to cooperate in the investigation. Note especially paragraphs A, B, I, J, and K, which are a good example of the breadth of the documents a grand jury subpoena duces tecum can compel a recipient to produce:

A. Any and all documents reflecting, referring, or relating to any direct or indirect sources of money or other things of value received by or provided to Webster Hubbell, his wife, or children from January 1, 1993 to the present, including but not limited to the identity of employers or clients of legal or any other type of work.

B. Any and all documents reflecting, referring, or relating to any direct or indirect sources of money of other things of value received by or provided to Webster Hubbell, his wife, or children from January 1, 1993 to the present, including but not limited to billing memoranda, draft statements, bills, final statements, and/or bills for work performed or time billed from January 1, 1993 to the present.

C. Copies of all bank records of Webster Hubbell, his wife, or children for all accounts from January 1, 1993 to the present, including but not limited to all statements, registers and ledgers, cancelled checks, deposit items, and wire transfers.

D. Any and all documents reflecting, referring, or relating to time worked or billed by Webster Hubbell from January 1, 1993 to the present, including but not limited to original time sheets, books, notes, papers, and/or computer records.

E. Any and all documents reflecting, referring, or relating to expenses incurred by and/or disbursements of money by Webster Hubbell during the course of any work performed or to be performed by Mr. Hubbell from January 1, 1993 to the present.

F. Any and all documents reflecting, referring, or relating to Webster Hubbell's schedule of activities, including but not limited to any and all calendars, day-timers, time books, appointment books, diaries, records of reverse telephone toll calls, credit card calls, telephone message slips, logs, other telephone records, minutes, databases, electronic mail messages, travel records, itineraries, tickets for transportation of any kind, payments, bills, expense backup documentation, schedules, and/or any other document or database that would disclose Webster Hubbell's activities from January 1, 1993 to the present.

G. Any and all documents reflecting, referring, or relating to any retainer agreements or contracts for employment of Webster Hubbell, his wife, or his children from January 1, 1993 to the present.

H. Any and all tax returns and tax return information, including but not limited to all W-2s, form 1099s, schedules, draft returns, work papers, and backup documents filed, created or held by or on behalf of Webster Hubbell, his wife, his children, and/or any business in which he, his wife, or his children holds or has held an interest, for the tax years 1993 to the present.

I. Any and all documents reflecting, referring, or relating to work performed or to be performed or on behalf of the City of Los Angeles, California, the Los Angeles Department of Airports or any other Los Angeles municipal Governmental entity, Mary Leslie, and/or Alan S. Arkatov, including but not limited to correspondence, retainer agreements, contracts, time sheets, appointment calendars, activity calendars, diaries, billing statements, billing memoranda, telephone records, telephone message slips, telephone credit card statements, itineraries, tickets for transportation, payment records, expense receipts, ledgers, check registers, notes, memoranda, electronic mail, bank deposit items, cashier's checks, traveler's checks, wire transfer records and/or other records of financial transactions.

J. Any and all documents reflecting, referring, or relating to work performed or to be performed by Webster Hubbell, his wife, or his children on the recommendation, counsel or other influence of Mary Leslie and/or Alan S. Arkatov, including but not limited to correspondence, retainer agreements, contracts, time sheets, appointment calendars, activity calendars, diaries, billing statements, billing memoranda, telephone records, telephone message slips, telephone credit card statements, itineraries, tickets for transportation, payment records, expense receipts, ledgers, check registers, notes, memoranda, electronic mail, bank deposit items, cashier's checks, traveler's checks, wire transfer records and/or other records of financial transactions.

K. Any and all documents related to work performed or to be performed for or on behalf of Lippo Ltd. (formerly Public Finance (H.K.) Ltd.), the Lippo Group, the Lippo Bank, Mochtar Riady, James Riady, Stephen Riady, John Luen Wai Lee, John Huang, Mark W. Grobmyer, C. Joseph Giroir, Jr., or any affiliate, subsidiary, or corporation owned or controlled by or related to the aforementioned entities or individuals, including but not limited to correspondence, retainer agreements, contracts, time sheets, appointment calendars, activity calendars, diaries, billing statements, billing memoranda, telephone records, telephone message slips, telephone credit card statements, itineraries, tickets for transportation, payment records, expense receipts, ledgers, check registers, notes, memoranda, electronic mail, bank deposit items, cashier's checks, traveler's checks, wire transfer records and/or other records of financial transactions.

4. *Subpoena Challenges*. The most common ground for refusing to comply with a grand jury subpoena is the assertion of a common law, statutory, or constitutional privilege. The full range of privileges applicable in federal courts apply to grand jury proceedings. See Fed. R. Evid. 1101(d) (noting that the Federal Rules of Evidence "other than with respect to privileges" do not apply in grand jury proceedings). The most prominent of the privileges, at least in the context of grand jury investigations, are discussed in Chapter 15. Ordinarily, claims of privilege do not challenge the subpoena in its entirety. They usually are directed at specific questions asked of the witness testifying pursuant to a subpoena ad testificandum or at specific items demanded under a subpoena duces tecum.

In determining whether to move to quash, the subpoenaed party will weigh various considerations in addition to the legal strength of its objection. In some instances, a successful objection will only result in a narrower government subpoena that will lead the prosecutors directly to what they seek. Where the government has asked for immense quantities of documents, "information control" may best be practiced by giving the government everything that could possibly fall within its demands and then counting on the lack of resources in the prosecutor's office to sort out potentially damaging material. On the other side, even when the motion to quash is not likely to be successful, making the motion may force the government to disclose information not otherwise available to the subpoenaed party, and that information may be helpful in later tactical decisions. Also, where the same judge will rule on later issues, including post-indictment objections should the subpoenaed party be prosecuted, there may be value in making a motion—even though likely to fail—where it will familiarize the judge with the questionable character of the investigation.

If the objection is made and rejected, that often ends the matter for the subpoenaed party. The denial of a motion to quash generally is not viewed as a final order, and therefore is not appealable under 28 U.S.C. § 1291, which limits appellate review to the "final decisions" of the district court. In contrast, the grant of a motion to quash is appealable by the government under 18 U.S.C. § 3731. The Supreme Court has consistently rejected the contention that a denial of a witness' motion to quash should be treated as a collateral order, separate from the ongoing proceeding and therefore a final order within § 1291. It has held that a subpoenaed party does not face such a final order unless the party continues to refuse to comply with the subpoena, notwithstanding the rejection of the motion, and the party subsequently is held in contempt. The justification for this requirement was succinctly stated in United States v. Ryan, 402 U.S. 530 (1971): "[W]e have consistently held that the necessity for expedition in the administration of the criminal law justifies putting one who seeks to resist the production of desired information to a choice between compliance with a trial court's order to produce prior to any review of that order, and resistance to that order with the concomitant possibility of an adjudication of contempt if his claims are rejected on appeal." This justification has been held equally applicable to the grand jury setting, for "it is no less important to safeguard against undue interruption of the inquiry instituted by a grand jury than to protect from delay the progress of the trial after an indictment has been found." Cobbledick v. United States, 309 U.S. 323 (1940).

The only exception recognized is for that limited class of cases where the subpoenaed party possesses documents belonging to another, has no substantial interest in challenging the subpoena, and therefore would not stand in contempt. Appellate review of the denial of a motion to quash is allowed here on the ground that insisting upon such a party standing in contempt would "render impossible any review whatsoever."

The subpoenaed party who stands in contempt after the motion to quash is denied in order to pursue his or her appeal ordinarily faces civil rather than criminal contempt. Thus, should the party lose on appeal, subsequent compliance with the grand jury subpoena will relieve the party of any further sanctions. However, the party has no assurance that the imposition of contempt sanctions will be stayed pending the appeal. The Recalcitrant Witness Act, 28 U.S.C. § 1826(a), provides: "Whenever a witness in any proceeding before * * * any grand jury of the United States refuses without just cause to comply with an order of the court * * *, the court * * * may summarily order his confinement." Courts frequently do impose the sanction of immediate confinement. Indeed, § 1826(b) notes that "no person confined pursuant to subsection (a) of this section shall be admitted to bail pending the determination of an appeal taken by him from the order of confinement if it appears that the appeal is frivolous or taken for delay." Where the contemnor is held in confinement pending appeal, § 1826(b) requires that the appeal be expedited, with its disposition coming "no later than thirty days from the filing of such appeal." Hence, the price for pursuing an appeal may be incarceration for thirty days. Note that a lawyer may be required to assert a claim on behalf of a client, including the Fifth Amendment and the attorney-client privilege, and could be forced to suffer the contempt in order to preserve the right to appeal the lower court's decision. Subpoenas to lawyers for information relating to their clients is a growing trend.

Therefore, any lawyer representing a client in an investigation runs the risk of being compelled to provide documents and testimony, and may risk his or her livelihood to vindicate the client's rights by going to jail for a substantial period of time. See also Chapter 16.

C. RULE 17(c) OBJECTIONS TO THE SUBPOENA

Rule 17(c) of the Federal Rules of Criminal Procedure permit a subpoena recipient to quash or modify a subpoena on the grounds that it is "unreasonable or oppressive." The Rule does not define that standard, and does not distinguish between subpoenas issued by a grand jury in the course of an investigation and a trial subpoena. The Supreme Court determined the standard for quashing a grand jury subpoena in the following.

UNITED STATES v. R. ENTERPRISES, INC.
498 U.S. 292, 111 S.Ct. 722, 112 L.Ed.2d 795 (1991)

Justice O'CONNOR delivered the opinion of the Court.

This case requires the Court to decide what standards apply when a party seeks to avoid compliance with a subpoena *duces tecum* issued in connection with a grand jury investigation. * * *

Since 1986, a federal grand jury sitting in the Eastern District of Virginia has been investigating allegations of interstate transportation of obscene materials. In early 1988, the grand jury issued a series of subpoenas to three companies—Model Magazine Distributors, Inc. (Model), R. Enterprises, Inc., and MFR Court Street Books, Inc. (MFR). Model is a New York distributor of sexually oriented paperback books, magazines, and videotapes. R. Enterprises, which distributes adult materials, and MFR, which sells books, magazines, and videotapes, are also based in New York. All three companies are wholly owned by Martin Rothstein. The grand jury subpoenas sought a variety of corporate books and records and, in Model's case, copies of 193 videotapes that Model had shipped to retailers in the Eastern District of Virginia. All three companies moved to quash the subpoenas, arguing that the subpoenas called for production of materials irrelevant to the grand jury's investigation and that the enforcement of the subpoenas would likely infringe their First Amendment rights.

The District Court, after extensive hearings, denied the motions to quash. As to Model, the court found that the subpoenas for business records were sufficiently specific and that production of the videotapes would not constitute a prior restraint. As to R. Enterprises, the court found a "sufficient connection with Virginia for further investigation by the grand jury." The court relied in large part on the statement attributed to Rothstein that the three companies were "all the same thing, I'm president of all three." Additionally, the court explained in denying MFR's motion to quash that it was "inclined to agree" with "the majority of the jurisdictions," which do not require the Government to make a "threshold showing" before a grand jury subpoena will be enforced. Even assuming that a preliminary showing of relevance was required, the court determined that the Government had made such a showing. It found sufficient evidence that the companies were "related entities," at least one of which "certainly did ship sexually explicit material into the Commonwealth of Virginia." * * * Notwithstanding these findings, the companies refused to comply with the subpoenas. The District Court found each in contempt and fined them $500 per day, but stayed imposition of the fine pending appeal.

The Court of Appeals for the Fourth Circuit upheld the business records subpoenas issued to Model, but remanded the motion to quash the subpoena for Model's videotapes. Of particular relevance here, the Court of Appeals quashed the business records subpoenas issued to R. Enterprises and MFR. In doing so, it applied the standards set out by this Court in United States v. Nixon, 418 U.S. 683 (1974). The court recognized that *Nixon* dealt with a trial subpoena, not a grand jury subpoena, but determined that the rule was "equally applicable" in the grand jury context. Accordingly, it required the Government to clear the three hurdles that *Nixon* established in the trial context—relevancy, admissibility, and specificity—in order to enforce the grand jury subpoenas. The court concluded that the challenged subpoenas did not satisfy the *Nixon* standards, finding no evidence in the record that either company had ever shipped materials into, or otherwise conducted business in, the Eastern District of Virginia. The Court of Appeals specifically criticized the District Court for drawing an inference that, because Rothstein owned all three businesses and one of them had undoubtedly shipped sexually explicit materials into the Eastern District of Virginia, there might be some link between the Eastern District of Virginia and R. Enterprises or MFR. It then noted that "any evidence concerning Mr. Rothstein's alleged business activities outside of Virginia, or his ownership of companies which distribute allegedly obscene materials outside of Virginia, would most likely be inadmissible on relevancy grounds at any trial that might occur," and that the subpoenas therefore failed "to meet the requirements [sic] that any documents subpoenaed under [Federal] Rule [of Criminal Procedure] 17(c) must be admissible as evidence at trial." The Court of Appeals did not consider whether enforcement of the subpoenas *duces tecum* issued to respondents implicated the First Amendment.

We granted certiorari to determine whether the Court of Appeals applied the proper standard in evaluating the grand jury subpoenas issued to respondents. We now reverse. * * *

The grand jury occupies a unique role in our criminal justice system. * * * [It] "can investigate merely on suspicion that the law is being violated, or even just because it wants assurance that it is not." * * * As a necessary consequence of its investigatory function, the grand jury paints with a broad brush. * * * A grand jury subpoena is thus much different from a subpoena issued in the context of a prospective criminal trial, where a specific offense has been identified and a particular defendant charged. * * *

This Court has emphasized on numerous occasions that many of the rules and restrictions that apply at a trial do not apply in grand jury proceedings. This is especially true of evidentiary restrictions. The same rules that, in an adversary hearing on the merits, may increase the likelihood of accurate determinations of guilt or innocence do not necessarily advance the mission of a grand jury, whose task is to conduct an *ex parte* investigation to determine whether or not there is probable cause to prosecute a particular defendant. * * * The teaching of the Court's decisions is clear: A grand jury "may compel the production of evidence or the testimony of witnesses as it considers appropriate, and its operation generally is unrestrained by the technical procedural and evidentiary rules governing the conduct of criminal trials." United States v. Calandra, 414 U.S. 338 (1974).

This guiding principle renders suspect the Court of Appeals' holding that the standards announced in *Nixon* as to subpoenas issued in anticipation of trial apply equally in the grand jury context. The multifactor test announced in *Nixon* would invite procedural delays and detours while courts evaluate the relevancy and admissibility of documents sought by a particular subpoena. We have expressly stated that grand jury proceedings should be free of such delays. * * * United States v. Dionisio, 410 U.S. 1 (1973). Additionally, application of the *Nixon* test in this context ignores that grand jury proceedings are subject to strict secrecy requirements. See Fed.Rule Crim.Proc. 6(e). Requiring the Government to explain in too much detail the particular reasons underlying a subpoena threatens to compromise "the indispensable secrecy of grand jury proceedings." Broad disclosure also affords the targets of investigation far more information about the grand jury's internal workings than the Federal Rules of Criminal Procedure appear to contemplate. * * *

The investigatory powers of the grand jury are nevertheless not unlimited. Grand juries are not licensed to engage in arbitrary fishing expeditions, nor may they select targets of investigation out of malice or an intent to harass. In this case, the focus of our inquiry is the limit imposed on a grand jury by Federal Rule of Criminal Procedure 17(c), which governs the issuance of subpoenas duces tecum in federal criminal proceedings. The Rule provides that "[t]he court on motion made promptly may quash or modify the subpoena if compliance would be unreasonable or oppressive."

This standard is not self-explanatory. As we have observed, "what is reasonable depends on the context." In *Nixon*, this Court defined what is reasonable in the context of a jury trial. We determined that, in order to require production of information prior to trial, a party must make a reasonably specific request for information that would be both relevant and admissible at trial. But, for the reasons we have explained above, the *Nixon* standard does not apply in the context of grand jury proceedings. In the grand jury context, the decision as to what offense will be charged is routinely not made until after the grand jury has concluded its investigation. One simply cannot know in advance whether information sought during the investigation will be relevant and admissible in a prosecution for a particular offense.

To the extent that Rule 17(c) imposes some reasonableness limitation on grand jury subpoenas, however, our task is to define it. In doing so, we recognize that a party to whom a grand jury subpoena is issued faces a difficult situation. As a rule, grand juries do not announce publicly the subjects of their investigations. A party who desires to challenge a grand jury subpoena thus may have no conception of the Government's purpose in seeking production of the requested information. Indeed, the party will often not know whether he or she is a primary target of the investigation or merely a peripheral witness. Absent even minimal information, the subpoena recipient is likely to find it exceedingly difficult to persuade a court that "compliance would be unreasonable." As one pair of commentators has summarized it, the challenging party's "unenviable task is to seek to persuade the court that the subpoena that has been served on [him or her] could not possibly serve any investigative purpose that the grand jury could legitimately be pursuing." Sara Sun Beale, William C. Bryson, James E. Felman, and Michael J. Elston, Grand Jury Law and Practice § 6:21 (2nd ed.).

Our task is to fashion an appropriate standard of reasonableness, one that gives due weight to the difficult position of subpoena recipients but does not impair the strong governmental interests in affording grand juries wide latitude, avoiding minitrials on peripheral matters, and preserving a necessary level of secrecy. We begin by reiterating that the law presumes, absent a strong showing to the contrary, that a grand jury acts within the legitimate scope of its authority. * * * Consequently, a grand jury subpoena issued through normal channels is presumed to be reasonable, and the burden of showing unreasonableness must be on the recipient who seeks to avoid compliance. Indeed, this result is indicated by the language of Rule 17(c), which permits a subpoena to be quashed only "on motion" and "if *compliance* would be unreasonable" (emphasis added). To the extent that the Court of Appeals placed an initial burden on the Government, it committed error. Drawing on the principles articulated above, we conclude that where, as here, a subpoena is challenged on relevancy grounds, the motion to quash must be denied unless the district court determines that there is no reasonable possibility that the category of materials the Government seeks will produce information relevant to the general subject of the grand jury's investigation. Respondents did not challenge the subpoenas as being too indefinite nor did they claim that compliance would be overly burdensome. The Court of Appeals accordingly did not consider these aspects of the subpoenas, nor do we. * * *

It seems unlikely, of course, that a challenging party who does not know the general subject matter of the grand jury's investigation, no matter how valid that party's claim, will be able to make the necessary showing that compliance would be unreasonable. After all, a subpoena recipient "cannot put his whole life before the court in order to show that there is no crime to be investigated." Consequently, a court may be justified in a case where unreasonableness is alleged in requiring the Government to reveal the general subject of the grand jury's investigation before requiring the challenging party to carry its burden of persuasion. We need not resolve this question in the present case, however, as there is no doubt that respondents knew the subject of the grand jury investigation pursuant to which the business records subpoenas were issued. In cases where the recipient of the subpoena does not know the nature of the investigation, we are confident that district courts will be able to craft appropriate procedures that balance the interests of the subpoena recipient against the strong governmental interests in maintaining secrecy, preserving investigatory flexibility, and avoiding procedural delays. For example, to ensure that subpoenas are not routinely challenged as a form of discovery, a district court may require that the Government reveal the subject of the investigation to the trial court *in camera*, so that the court may determine whether the motion to quash has a reasonable prospect for success before it discloses the subject matter to the challenging party. * * *

Applying these principles in this case demonstrates that the District Court correctly denied respondents' motions to quash. It is undisputed that all three companies—Model, R. Enterprises, and MFR—are owned by the same person, that all do business in the same area, and that one of the three, Model, has shipped sexually explicit materials into the Eastern District of Virginia. The District Court could have concluded from these facts that there was a reasonable possibility that the business records of R. Enterprises and MFR would produce information relevant to the grand jury's investigation into the interstate transportation of obscene materials. Respondents' blanket denial of any connection to Virginia did not suffice to render the District Court's conclusion invalid. A grand jury need not accept on faith the self-serving assertions of those who may have committed criminal acts. Rather, it is entitled to determine for itself whether a crime has been committed.

Both in the District Court and in the Court of Appeals, respondents contended that these subpoenas sought records relating to First Amendment activities, and that this required the Government to demonstrate that the records were particularly relevant to its investigation. The Court of Appeals determined that the subpoenas did not satisfy Rule 17(c) and thus did not pass on the First Amendment issue. We express no view on this issue and leave it to be resolved by the Court of Appeals. * * *

Justice STEVENS, with whom Justice MARSHALL and Justice BLACKMUN join, concurring in part and concurring in the judgment.

Federal Rule of Criminal Procedure 17(c) * * * requires the district court to balance the burden of compliance, on the one hand, against the governmental interest in obtaining the documents on the other. A more burdensome subpoena should be justified by a somewhat higher degree of probable relevance than a subpoena that imposes a minimal or nonexistent burden. Against the procedural history of this case, the Court has attempted to define the term "reasonable" in the abstract, looking only at the relevance side of the balance. Because I believe that this truncated approach to the Rule will neither provide adequate guidance to the district court nor place any meaningful constraint on the overzealous prosecutor, I add these comments. * * *

The moving party has the initial task of demonstrating to the Court that he has some valid objection to compliance. This showing might be made in various ways. Depending on the volume and location of the requested materials, the mere cost in terms of time, money, and effort of responding to a dragnet subpoena could satisfy the initial hurdle. Similarly, if a witness showed that compliance with the subpoena would intrude significantly on his privacy interests, or call for the disclosure of trade secrets or other confidential information, further inquiry would be required. Or, as in this case, the movant might demonstrate that compliance would have First Amendment implications.

The trial court need inquire into the relevance of subpoenaed materials only after the moving party has made this initial showing. And, as is true in the parallel context of pretrial civil discovery, a matter also committed to the sound discretion of the trial judge, the degree of need sufficient to justify denial of the motion to quash will vary to some extent with the burden of producing the requested information. For the reasons stated by the Court, in the grand jury context the law enforcement interest will almost always prevail, and the documents must be produced. I stress, however, that the Court's opinion should not be read to suggest that the deferential relevance standard the Court has formulated will govern decision in every case, no matter how intrusive or burdensome the request. * * *

NOTES AND QUESTIONS

1. **The Aftermath of R. Enterprises.** The Court's analysis makes it almost impossible to win a Rule 17(c) motion to quash, although as noted at pp. 347-51 there may be strategic reasons for bringing the motion, especially if the goal is to convince the government to limit the scope of a subpoena. How much control do the courts have over the issuance of grand jury subpoenas? Grand jury subpoenas are not self-executing, in the sense that a recipient may simply ignore the subpoena and wait to see if the government will compel the person to comply with it. To enforce a subpoena, the federal prosecutor must call on the district court to hold the recipient in contempt, at which point the person can challenge the propriety of the subpoena. Some federal courts have imposed rules governing certain types of grand jury subpoenas that federal prosecutor must comply with *before* the subpoena can be issued. This creates an additional layer of protection, although the basis for these procedural requirements is not the Constitution but the authority of the local courts to adopt rules for proceedings in the district or circuit. The notes below consider some of these requirements.

2. What Is "Unreasonable or Oppressive". In **In re Grand Jury, John Doe No. G.J. 2005-2,** 478 F.3d 581 (4th Cir. 2007), the district court quashed a grand jury subpoena issued to a police department for records of its internal investigation of a complaint filed against an officer for alleged use of excessive force as part of an investigation into possible civil rights violations. In finding the subpoena was unreasonable, the Fourth Circuit considered the police department's interests in maintaining the confidentiality of its investigations as a factor in balancing the grand jury's need for the information. The court stated:

> [T]he district court permissibly took cognizance of the City's very real concern that the Police Department preserve its ability to police itself by maintaining the confidentiality of its investigations. The internal investigation mechanism serves the same purpose as a criminal investigation by the United States Attorney's Office or Department of Justice: to uncover, and ultimately to deter, civil rights violations and other abuses. In many instances, internal investigations may offer the most effective way to pursue those goals. A police department is able to respond to a complaint quickly, while witnesses are still available and memories are still fresh. Perhaps most importantly, a strong and visible internal investigations office is in a unique position to deter misconduct in the first place. * * *

In considering the grand jury's need for the information, the court noted "that counsel for the United States repeatedly suggested that the information sought was of negligible value to the government. Counsel stated that the government merely required the internal investigation materials in order to 'close . . . the file,' as the government attorneys were "99.9 percent certain" that the complaint was "a bunch of baloney" and there was 'no expectation that it [would] turn into a prosecutable offense.'" While the district court was not required to quash the subpoena in these circumstances, its decision was not an abuse of discretion in balancing the interests of the grand jury and police department.

D. THE OVERBREADTH OBJECTION

1. Boyd v. United States. The Fourth Amendment provides: "The right of the people to be secure in their persons, houses, papers, and effects, against unreasonable searches and seizures, shall not be violated, and no Warrants shall issue, but upon probable cause, supported by Oath or affirmation, and particularly describing the place to be searched, and the persons or things to be seized." The second clause—starting with "and no Warrants shall issue" commonly is described as the "warrant" clause, while the first is sometimes described as the "reasonableness" clause. Although **Boyd v. United States**, 116 U.S. 616 (1886), is the seminal ruling on the application of the Fourth Amendment to the required production of documents by subpoena, and has been widely celebrated as a "case that will be remembered as long as civil liberties live in the United States" [see Brandeis, J., dissenting in Olmstead v. United States, 277 U.S. 438, 474 (1928)], the *Boyd* decision today has a quite limited precedential impact. Its holding would not be followed under currently applicable precedent, and its doctrinal foundation has been largely reshaped, where not entirely discarded. Still, *Boyd* remains a case commonly cited and discussed in connection with the application of both the Fourth Amendment and the self-incrimination clause of the Fifth Amendment to the subpoena of documents.

Boyd itself did not involve a traditional subpoena. At issue there was a customs forfeiture proceeding in which the government sought to utilize an 1847 statutory provision allowing it to gain documentary evidence from the importer of the property to be forfeited. The provision authorized the trial judge, on motion of the government describing a particular document and indicating what it might prove, to issue a notice directing the importer to produce that document. The petitioners in *Boyd* challenged such a notice that directed them to produce the invoice for thirty-five cases of plate glass allegedly imported by their partnership without payment of customs duties. The Supreme Court sustained their challenge, holding that the notice and the statute authorizing it violated both the Fourth Amendment and the self-incrimination clause of the Fifth Amendment. (The implications of *Boyd*'s self-incrimination ruling is discussed in Chapter 13).

Justice Bradley's opinion for the *Boyd* Court first established that the trial judge's order to produce was subject to the Fourth Amendment. Justice Bradley noted:

> [I]n regard to Fourth Amendment, it is contended that * * * [the Act of 1874], under which the order in the present case was made, is free from constitutional objection, because it does not authorize the search and seizure of books and papers, but only requires the defendant or claimant to produce them. That is so; but it declares that if he does not produce them, the allegations which it is affirmed they will prove shall be taken as confessed. This is tantamount to compelling their production; for the prosecuting attorney will always be sure to state the evidence expected to be derived from them as strongly as the case will admit of. It is true that certain aggravating incidents of actual search and seizure, such as forcible entry into a man's house and searching amongst his papers, are wanting, and to this extent the proceeding under the act of 1874 is a mitigation of that which was authorized by the former acts; but it accomplishes the substantial object of those acts in forcing from a party evidence against himself. It is our opinion, therefore, that a compulsory production of a man's private papers to establish a criminal charge against him, or to forfeit his property, is within the scope of the Fourth Amendment to the Constitution, in all cases in which a search and seizure would be; because it is a material ingredient, and effects the sole object and purpose of search and seizure.

Justice Bradley then turned to what he described as "the principle question": "Is a search and seizure, or, what is equivalent thereto, a compulsory production of a man's private papers, to be used in evidence against him in a proceeding to forfeit his property for alleged fraud against the revenue laws–is such a proceeding for such a purpose an "unreasonable search and seizure" within the meaning of the Fourth Amendment of the Constitution? or, is it a legitimate proceeding?"

The answer to this question, he argued, was obvious from the "recent history of the controversies on the subject, both in this country and in England." In the celebrated eighteenth-century English case of *Entick v. Carrington*, the English court sustained a trespass action where officials had used a general warrant to search a private home for books and papers that might be used to convict their owner of the charge of libel. This ruling, "undoubtedly familiar to the drafters of the Constitution," recognized that "papers are our owner's * * * dearest property and are so far from enduring a seizure, they will hardly bear an inspection." It was thereby established that the "essence of constitutional liberty and property" reached beyond the "concrete form" of the invasion in Entick and applied "to all invasions on the part of government * * * [into] the privacies of life." For "it is not the breaking of * * * doors, and the rummaging of * * * drawers, that constitutes the essence of the offence, but * * * the invasion of [the] indefeasible right of personal security, personal liberty, and private property." Accordingly, Justice Bradley reasoned, "any forcible and compulsory extortion of a man's * * * private papers to be used as evidence to convict him" brings into play the Fourth as well as the Fifth Amendment, which here "almost run into each other." For the "Fifth Amendment throws light on what is an 'unreasonable search and seizure' within the meaning of the Fourth Amendment," and the seizure of a man's books and papers to be used in evidence "against him" is not "substantially different from compelling him to be a witness against himself."

The Court concluded that it therefore was "of the opinion that a compulsory production of the private books and papers of the owners of goods sought to be forfeited in such a suit is compelling him to be a witness against himself within the meaning of the Fifth Amendment to the Constitution and is the equivalent of a search and seizure–and an unreasonable search and seizure–within the meaning of the Fourth Amendment." This ruling was supported by an approach to constitutional interpretation, set forth in a paragraph of Justice Bradley's opinion, that contributed largely to subsequent praise of *Boyd* as a civil liberties landmark. Justice Bradley there noted:

> Though the proceeding in question is divested of many of the aggravating incidents of actual search and seizure, yet, as before said, it contains their substance and essence, and effects their substantial purpose. It may be that it is the obnoxious thing in its mildest and least repulsive form; but illegitimate and unconstitutional practices get their first footing in that way, namely,

by silent approaches and slight deviations from legal modes of procedure. This can only be obviated by adhering to the rule that constitutional provisions for the security of person and property should be liberally construed. A close and literal construction deprives them of half their efficacy, and leads to a gradual depreciation of the right, as if it consisted more in sound than in substance. It is the duty of courts to be watchful for the constitutional rights of the citizen, and against any stealthy encroachments thereon. Their motto should be obsta principiis.

The concurring opinion of Justice Miller (joined by Chief Justice Waite) agreed that that the court order in question was "in effect a subpoena duces tecum * * * compelling a person to be a witness against himself" in violation of the Fifth Amendment. It disagreed as to the applicability of the Fourth Amendment. For "no order can be made by the court under [the 1874 Act] which requires or permits anything more than service of notice on a party to the suit." This did not have the quality of a search, which was constitutionally aimed at "searches * * * such as led to seizure when the search was successful." Here, however, the statute was "carefully framed to forbid any seizure under it."

2. **Hale v. Henkel.** Insofar as *Boyd* suggested that the Fourth Amendment prohibited searches for property the defendant was entitled to possess (i.e., property other than the fruits or instrumentalities of crime), it spawned a reading of the Fourth Amendment that received considerable support in later years but was eventually limited and then flatly rejected in Warden v. Hayden, 387 U.S. 294 (1967). Insofar as *Boyd* read the Fourth Amendment as prohibiting a search for documents, that interpretation was finally overturned in Andresen v. Maryland, 427 U.S. 463 (1976). But long before either of these developments, the Court completely restructured *Boyd*'s view of the bearing of the Fourth Amendment upon a subpoena duces tecum. That came in **Hale v. Henkel**, 201 U.S. 43 (1906), a case decided twenty years after *Boyd*.

The *Hale* Court had before it a challenge to a subpoena directing the petitioner, a corporate official, to produce before a grand jury (which was conducting an investigation into possible violations of the antitrust laws) various corporate documents. Petitioner's challenge, looking to *Boyd*, sought to rely upon the combined impact of the Fourth and Fifth Amendments, but the Court initially separated those claims. Cases subsequent to *Boyd*, it noted, had "treated the Fourth and Fifth Amendments as quite distinct, having different histories, and performing separate functions." Turning first to the petitioner's self-incrimination claim, the Court found that claim clearly unsupportable since the statute authorizing the subpoena granted petitioner immunity from prosecution (thereby eliminating his grounding for relying on the privilege [see pp. 565-630], and the corporation itself had no self-incrimination privilege [see p. 648]). The petitioner's Fourth Amendment claim did have merit, but for reasons other than what might have been assumed from *Boyd*. Speaking for the Court, Brown, J., noted:

Although * * * we are of the opinion that an officer of a corporation * * * cannot refuse to produce the books and papers of such corporation, we do not wish to be understood as holding that a corporation is not entitled to immunity, under the Fourth Amendment, against unreasonable searches and seizures. A corporation is, after all, but an association of individuals under an assumed name and with a distinct legal entity. In organizing itself as a collective body it waives no constitutional immunities appropriate to such body. * * * We are also of opinion that an order for the production of books and papers may constitute an unreasonable search and seizure within the Fourth Amendment. While a search ordinarily implies a quest by an officer of the law, and a seizure contemplates a forcible dispossession of the owner, still, as was held in the *Boyd* case, the substance of the offense is the compulsory production of private papers, whether under a search warrant or a subpoena duces tecum, against which the person, be he individual or corporation, is entitled to protection. Applying the test of reasonableness to the present case, we think the subpoena duces tecum is far too sweeping in its terms to be regarded as reasonable. It does not require the production of a single contract, or of contracts with a particular corporation, or a limited number of documents, but all understandings, contracts, or correspondence between the MacAndrews & Forbes Company, and no less than six different companies, as well as all reports made, and accounts rendered by such companies from the date of the organization of the MacAndrews & Forbes Company, as well as all letters received by that company since its organization from more than a dozen different companies, situated in seven different States in the Union.

If the writ had required the production of all the books, papers and documents found in the office of the MacAndrews & Forbes Company, it would scarcely be more universal in its operation, or completely put a stop to the business of that company. Indeed, it is difficult to say how its business could be carried on after it had been denuded of this mass of material, which is not shown to be necessary in the prosecution of this case, and is clearly in violation of the general principle of law with regard to the particularity required in the description of documents necessary to a search warrant or subpoena. Doubtless many, if not all, of these documents may ultimately be required, but some necessity should be shown, either from an examination of the witnesses orally, or from the known transactions of these companies with the other companies implicated, or some evidence of their materiality produced, to justify an order for the production of such a mass of papers. A general subpoena of this description is equally indefensible as a search warrant would be if couched in similar terms.

Justice McKenna, concurring separately in *Hale*, questioned the Court's Fourth Amendment analysis:

It is said "a search implies a quest by an officer of the law; a seizure contemplates a forcible dispossession of the owner." Nothing can be more direct and plain; nothing more expressive to distinguish a subpoena from a search warrant. Can a subpoena lose this essential distinction from a search warrant by the generality or speciality of its terms? I think not. The distinction is based upon what is authorized or directed to be done—not upon the form of words by which the authority or command is given. "The quest of an officer" acts upon the things themselves—may be secret, intrusive, accompanied by force. The service of a subpoena is but the delivery of a paper to a party—is open and aboveboard. There is no element of trespass or force in it. It does not disturb the possession of property. It cannot be finally enforced except after challenge, and a judgment of the court upon the challenge. This is a safeguard against abuse the same as it is of other processes of the law, and it is all that can be allowed without serious embarrassment to the administration of justice.

3. *Explaining the Overbreadth Doctrine*. As Judge Friendly noted in **In re Horowitz**, 482 F.2d 72 (2d Cir. 1973): "The Fourth Amendment portion of the *Boyd* decision was surely not based on the overbreadth of the Government's demand; the Government [there] sought only a single invoice of unquestionable relevance." Although relying on *Boyd*, *Hale v. Henkel* shifted the Court's underlying reasoning and "left the applicability of the Fourth Amendment to subpoena duces tecum in a most confusing state. None of the Justices seemed to think that such a subpoena could be issued only 'upon probable cause, supported by oath or affirmation,' as would be required for a search warrant. Nevertheless, except for Mr. Justice McKenna, all were of the view that an overbroad subpoena duces tecum against an individual would be an unreasonable search and seizure."

Judge Friendly suggested in *Horowitz* that the *Hale* overbreadth doctrine might find firmer support in the due process clause than in the Fourth Amendment. Although a due process grounding for the doctrine is suggested in Oklahoma Press Publishing Co. v. Walling, 327 U.S. 186 (1946) (a leading case on the application of the overbreadth doctrine to an administrative agency subpoena), later cases have referred to the doctrine as based on the Fourth Amendment.

Accepting the Court's premise that the Fourth Amendment does apply to the subpoena duces tecum, why should the overbreadth doctrine be the sole Fourth Amendment limitation as to the subpoena duces tecum? Does *Hale* reflect a determination that the requirements of the Fourth Amendment's warrant clause are inapplicable in light of the long history of subpoenas issued without regard to probable cause and the subpoena's lesser intrusion upon privacy (as compared to the traditional search), thereby leaving applicable only the Fourth Amendment's general mandate of reasonableness in its first clause? "The theory here is that the subpoena which is too sweeping, which calls for a mass of documents without regard to what is relevant, necessarily requires a sifting through the documents to obtain those that are needed. Whether that sifting takes place on the premises of the owner or in the offices of the prosecutor assisting the grand jury, it constitutes a search. Thus, *Hale* and other courts have compared the overbroad subpoena to a 'general warrant.'" WAYNE R. LAFAVE, JEROLD H. ISRAEL, NANCY J. KING, & ORIN S. KERR, CRIMINAL PROCEDURE §8.7(a) (3d ed. 2007).

E. REASONABLENESS

In addition to the Fourth Amendment's reasonableness requirement for searches, Rule 17(c) permits a subpoena recipient to challenge the demand for documents on the ground that it is unreasonable. Are the tests different? Can a defendant challenge a subpoena on both grounds? Consider the following:

In re GRAND JURY SUBPOENA *DUCES TECUM* DATED NOVEMBER 15, 1993.
846 F.Supp 11 (S.D.N.Y. 1994)

MUKASEY, District Judge.

This is a motion by a corporation and three of its executives to quash a subpoena *duces tecum* issued to the corporation by a grand jury investigating initially certain activities related to securities trading. As discussed below, a later focus of the grand jury investigation has become possible obstruction of justice and kindred offenses. Because the subpoena is unreasonably broad, and because the representatives of the grand jury oppose any modification of its reach, the motion to quash is granted.

The identities of the parties and, at the request of counsel for the movants, even the precise nature of the charges being investigated and the identities of counsel, have been omitted from this opinion so as to maintain grand jury secrecy. The subpoena at issue was addressed to a corporation that will be referred to as X Corporation. The subpoena demands that X Corporation provide the grand jury with the central processing unit (including the hard disk drive) of any computer supplied by X Corporation for the use of specified officers and employees of X Corporation, or their assistants. It demands also all computer-accessible data (including floppy diskettes) created by any of the specified officers and employees or their assistants. In addition to corporate records, personal documents are stored on the subpoenaed devices, including personal financial information, a draft of an employee's will, and legal documents relating to the Chairman's personal funding of a third party's purchase of certain goods.

Three of the specified officers of X Corporation–the owner and Chairman, the President, and the Vice President and General Counsel–and X Corporation itself have moved to quash the subpoena on three grounds: that it requests information that is not in the possession, custody or control of X Corporation; that it is overly broad; and that it requests privileged documents. * * *

The subpoena at issue here is not framed in terms of specified categories of information. Rather, it demands specified information storage devices-- namely, particular computer hard drives and floppy disks that contain some data concededly irrelevant to the grand jury inquiry. * * * As a result, there is an issue of whether the term "category of materials" used in the *R. Enterprises* standard should be applied to the information-storage devices demanded, or to the documents contained within them. If the categories of materials properly are seen to be hard disk drives and floppy disks, then the subpoena at issue would pass the *R. Enterprises* test because it is highly probable that these devices will contain some relevant information. If, on the other hand, the categories of materials properly are seen to be the various types of documents contained on these devices, then the subpoena would be unreasonably broad because there are easily separable categories of requested documents that undoubtedly contain no relevant information.

The Second Circuit has not yet addressed this issue as applied to computers and electronic documents, but it has addressed a closely related issue as applied to filing cabinets and paper documents. In *In re Horowitz,* the Second Circuit considered a Fourth Amendment challenge to the breadth of a subpoena demanding the entire contents of particular filing cabinets. Although *In re Horowitz* was not decided under Rule 17(c) expressly, the criterion applied by the Second Circuit to assess the subpoena—reasonableness—is the same criterion applicable under Rule 17(c).

The subpoena before the Second Circuit in *In re Horowitz* had been narrowed by the district court to exclude personal documents, yet the Second Circuit found that it still encompassed irrelevant documents. As a result, the Second Circuit through Judge Friendly narrowed it further, excluding from its scope categories of documents that "have no conceivable relevance to any legitimate object of investigation by the federal grand jury." Implicit in *In re Horowitz* is a determination that subpoenas properly are interpreted as seeking categories of paper documents, not categories of filing cabinets. Because it is easier in the computer age to separate relevant from irrelevant documents, Judge Friendly's ontological choice between filing cabinets and paper documents has even greater force when applied to the modern analogues of these earlier methods of storing information.

The current matter warrants a resolution similar to that in *In re Horowitz.* Government counsel have conceded on behalf of the grand jury that the subpoena demands irrelevant documents. Moreover, the government has acknowledged that a "key word" search of the information stored on the devices would reveal "which of the documents are likely to be relevant to the grand jury's investigation." It follows that a subpoena demanding documents containing specified key words would identify relevant documents without requiring the production of irrelevant documents. To the extent the grand jury has reason to suspect that subpoenaed documents are being withheld, a court-appointed expert could search the hard drives and floppy disks. Despite the suggestion that this procedure could resolve the dispute, the government opposes any modification of the subpoena, asking instead that this Court rule on the enforceability of the subpoena "as issued."

The government presses two principal arguments in favor of enforcing the subpoena without modification. First, it contends that insofar as the Fourth Amendment is the source of the constitutional prohibition on overbreadth, the movants have not established the requisite reasonable expectation of privacy. Although I am not unmindful of the privacy interests of X Corporation employees in the personal documents–such as personal financial information and a will–within the scope of the subpoena, the power to quash the subpoena pursuant to Rule 17(c), obviates recourse to the Fourth Amendment. As a result, the government's first argument need not be addressed.

Second, the government argues that the subpoena must be broader than usual because the grand jury has expanded its investigation into suspected obstruction of justice and related offenses. Specifically, it argues for "a more sweeping demand than might normally be made" because it

> has reason to believe that [X Corporation] did not fully comply with prior subpoenas *duces tecum* to it, that records in the possession of [X Corporation] were destroyed to avoid compliance with an SEC subpoena *duces tecum* and, further, that [X Corporation] would compliantly withhold from the grand jury any records demanded on the grounds that they were "personal," if asked to do so by any of its officers, even if related to [X Corporation's] business–as not "rightfully" in the possession of [X Corporation]. If this occurred, it was also possible–even likely–that such records would not be identified to the grand jury as having been withheld.

The wider grand jury investigation into obstruction and related charges indeed justifies a commensurately broader subpoena. For example, if computer directory files are relevant to the issue of whether stored documents have been tampered with or destroyed, a subpoena demanding such files would be justified.

However, the expanded investigation does not justify a subpoena which encompasses documents completely irrelevant to its scope, particularly because the government has acknowledged that relevant documents can be isolated through key-word searching.

In sum, because the subpoena at issue unnecessarily demands documents that are irrelevant to the grand jury inquiry, it is unreasonably broad under Federal Rule of Criminal Procedure 17(c). Accordingly, because this Court does not have sufficient information to identify relevant documents (including directory files) and modify the subpoena, and because the government seeks a determination of the subpoena's validity "as issued" and opposes its modification, the subpoena is quashed in its entirety, without prejudice to issuance of a narrowed subpoena *duces tecum*. To preserve the practical ability of the grand jury to issue a narrowed subpoena, X Corporation and its officers, agents and employees–including the individual movants–are directed to continue to cause the computers and related materials that were the subject of the quashed subpoena to be preserved intact in the manner specified in Judge Sweet's sealed December 1, 1993 Order.

NOTES AND QUESTIONS

1. *Volume as Proof of Unreasonableness*. Subpoena recipients often claim that a demand for a large volume of documents would be "oppressive or unreasonable" in violation of Rule 17(c). See **In re Subpoena Duces Tecum (Bailey)**, 228 F.3d 341 (4th Cir. 2000), in which the circuit court rejected the argument of a doctor being investigated for health care fraud that the subpoena was overbroad and oppressive:

> Bailey also contends that the subpoenas * * * were not relevant to the government investigation and were "overly broad and oppressive"–the second and fourth factors we have enumerated above–and therefore were constitutionally unreasonable, in violation of the Fourth Amendment. He argues that because "the government [sought] a huge volume of documents," the production "of those documents, absent a showing of relevancy and need, i.e. probable cause, [was] oppressive." Indeed, he characterizes the government's effort as a "witchhunt."
>
> The government contends, on the other hand, that the "large number of patient files and controlled substance records" responsive to its subpoenas is an "indici[um]" of the scope of fraud it is investigating. It notes that it would be "an oddity of jurisprudence" if a physician with a high-volume, government- subsidized practice could avoid complying with such subpoenas, whereas a physician with a lower volume and therefore with a narrower potential scope of fraud would have to comply. The government observes that the "volume of documents cannot be the sole criteri[on] for determining whether compliance with a subpoena is unreasonable," an observation with which Bailey agrees in the abstract. While the scope of a subpoena, if not relevant to a legitimate investigation, and overly broad and oppressive, can support a claim of unconstitutionality under the Fourth Amendment, these characteristics cannot always be determined in the abstract. The question of the permissible scope is generally "variable in relation to the nature, purposes and scope of the inquiry."
>
> Thus, if Bailey had treated 15,000 patients over a period of seven years and all of them were reimbursed on claims he submitted, a

suspicion of fraud on these claims would justify a review of Bailey's documentation of services to these patients, of the claims submitted on their behalf, and of the reimbursements collected. Even though these documents might be numerous, they would reasonably relate to and further the government's legitimate inquiry, which might be defined by any of 13 federal statutory offenses, including fraud. Bailey points out that the sheer volume of documents, the substantial expense incurred for their reproduction, and the disruption to his practice caused by their production are all indicative of the subpoenas' overbreadth and oppressiveness. But these specific burdens could have been materially reduced or avoided if Bailey had accepted the accommodation offered by the government and encompassed in the district court's order. The district court specifically stated that Bailey could retain patient files and claim-processing files, subject to the call of the U.S. Attorney expressing a "need to review particular patient files" or files relating to claim processing. Bailey specifically rejected this offer.

Yet, as a condition to maintaining the argument that an investigative subpoena is overly broad and oppressive, Bailey would have to be able to point to reasonable efforts on his behalf to reach accommodation with the government. Bailey has given no reason why the government's proffered accommodation in this case would not have alleviated the burden of compliance, nor has he explained why he did not accept the accommodation.

Finally, to define the reasonableness of a subpoena based on the volume of items identified for production would be to require the government to ascertain, before issuing a subpoena, the extent of any wrongdoing. But ascertaining the extent of wrongdoing is itself a primary purpose for the issuance of the subpoena. * * *

In sum, we cannot conclude that the subpoenas, particularly when accompanied by an offer of accommodation, were either overly broad as to be oppressive or lacking in relevance as to be unreasonable, in violation of the Fourth Amendment.

2. *Burden of Proof.* Why is the burden on the subpoena recipient to accommodate the government when the subpoena is so extensive that it may cripple the defendant's business? Fourth Amendment challenges place the burden on the government to establish there will be no constitutional violation, but in the context of a grand jury subpoena the burden is on the recipient. Is this because the claim is not really a Fourth Amendment claim, but a challenge to the reasonableness of the subpoena under Rule 17(c)? If it is really a Rule 17(c) challenge, then the presumption of regularity discussed in *R. Enterprises* may be sufficient to overcome almost any overbreadth claim. What incentive, then, does the government have to write its grand jury subpoenas more carefully?

3. *The Expense of Complying.* With the availability of photocopying and with many records already stored on computer disk, claims that document production will substantially impede the continuing operations of a subpoenaed enterprise usually focus on the cost of collecting the records rather than — as in *Hale v. Henkel* — the lost use of the records. The government generally refuses to reimburse parties for their costs in complying with subpoenas, except where the subpoena is governed by the Financial Privacy Act, 12 U.S.C. § 3415, or the Electronic Communications Privacy Act, 18 U.S.C. § 2706, which require reimbursement of subpoena recipients who produce records of their account holders. A few courts have suggested that Rule 17(c) gives the court sufficient authority to order reimbursement in cases not falling within those statutes. See In re Grand Jury Investigation, 459 F.Supp. 1335 (E.D.Pa. 1978). At the same time, those courts recognize that any such authority is to be utilized only in the most exceptional situation.

The courts note that the prevailing principle is that there is a public obligation to provide evidence and that this obligation persists no matter how financially burdensome it may be. Thus, on a subpoena requiring testimony before a grand jury, the witness cannot gain reimbursement for the true cost of testifying (such as loss of wages or income, etc.), but simply receives a standard attendance fee, plus costs of transportation. Accordingly, it is reasoned, the case for reimbursement must rest on a showing not merely that compliance will be expensive, but that it is essentially beyond the means of the subpoenaed party. See Matter of Midland Asphalt Corp., 616 F.Supp. 223 (W.D.N.Y. 1985) (showing that cost to corporations of complying with grand jury subpoena duces tecum would constitute 41% of their net operating income, but less than 2% of their operating expenses, was insufficient to establish unreasonable or oppressiveness such as to warrant government advancement or reimbursement of such costs).

4. *Subpoenas As "Seizures."* Are there any circumstances under which a grand jury subpoena might be viewed as producing "a 'seizure' in the Fourth Amendment sense"? In United States v. Dionisio, 410 U.S. 1 (1973), the Supreme Court held, "It is clear that a subpoena to appear before a grand jury is not a 'seizure' in the Fourth Amendment sense." The Court quoted the distinctions described by Judge Henry Friendly between a subpoena and an arrest or even an investigative stop: "The latter is abrupt, is effected with force or the threat of it and often in demeaning circumstances, and, in the case of arrest, results in a record involving social stigma. A subpoena is served in the same manner as other legal process; it involves no stigma whatever; if the time for appearance is inconvenient, this can generally be altered; and it remains at all times under the control and supervision of a court." United States v. Doe, 457 F.2d 895 (2d Cir. 1972).

What if the subpoena calls for "forthwith" compliance, i.e., the immediate production of evidence for presentation to the grand jury or the immediate appearance of the witness before the grand jury? Consider **United States v. Triumph Capital Group, Inc.**, 211 F.R.D. 31 (D.Conn. 2002), in which the government served a forthwith subpoena on a company's defense counsel requiring the delivery of a laptop computer to the grand jury by 5:00 p.m. that day from counsel's Boston office to the grand jury in Hartford, Connecticut. The District Court analyzed the propriety of the use of a forthwith subpoena as follows:

> The defendants have failed to show that the government had an improper purpose in using the forthwith subpoena. A grand jury subpoena must also not be used in such a way as to impinge on Fourth Amendment rights. See Boyd v. United States, 116 U.S. 616 (1886). To determine if a subpoena impinges on a defendant's Fourth Amendment rights, the focus is on the level of compulsion used when the subpoena was served, and whether the government's actions constitute an abuse of process.
>
> In this case there is no evidence that the government used any coercion, compulsion or aggressive tactics when the subpoena was served on Triumph's counsel. Accord, United States v. Wilson, 614 F.2d 1224 (9th Cir.1980) (upholding use of forthwith subpoena in the absence of evidence of abuse of process or that it was used as a ploy to facilitate office interrogation by U.S. attorneys). Cf. In re Nwamu, 421 F.Supp. 1361 (S.D.N.Y.1976) (ordering the return of evidence obtained through forthwith subpoena where executing agents used coercive methods that constituted an unlawful search and seizure).
>
> The totality of the circumstances show that the defendants' compliance with the forthwith subpoena was voluntary, not coerced. The facts that the subpoena was served on Triumph's defense attorney, who is experienced in criminal matters, and that she did not file a motion challenging its validity, support the conclusion that defendants voluntarily complied and that the use of the subpoena did not amount to an unlawful seizure. Triumph's counsel could not reasonably have been unaware of the options that were available to resist the subpoena.
>
> Indeed, the defendants were aware of their options and had ample opportunity to challenge the subpoena. Such knowledge is an essential element of effective consent and supports a finding that compliance was voluntary. * * * Moreover, the government agreed that it would not open or look at the laptop computer until Triumph's attorney had an opportunity to file a motion.
>
> The defendants had sufficient time and opportunity to file a motion and, in fact, did file one seeking protection for attorney-client privileged documents on the computer. The government did not commence its search and seizure until the issues raised in the motion were resolved. Thus, it cannot be found that the defendants were deprived of any meaningful opportunity under Fed.R.Crim.P. 17(c) to challenge the validity of the forthwith subpoena.

The government has sustained its burden of showing that compliance with the subpoena was voluntary.

In addition, there were exigent circumstances justifying the use of a forthwith subpoena. Exigent circumstances exist where there is a reasonable good faith concern that evidence might be destroyed or altered in any way.

The government had reasonable and good faith concerns that computer data and evidence could be destroyed, altered or tampered with to obstruct justice if the defendants were given advance notice.
* * *

[T]he portable nature of the laptop computer and the fact that information and data on a computer can easily be overwritten or corrupted by ordinary use, justified the government's belief that the computer could be lost or evidence it contained could be destroyed or altered if Triumph was given advance notice. Thus, the government acted reasonably in using a forthwith subpoena to immobilize the laptop computer and preserve its contents.

There is no evidence that the forthwith subpoena was improperly used to circumvent the warrant requirement. The government even assured the grand jury that it would not open or look at the laptop computer until Triumph had an opportunity to file relevant motions. The evidence shows that the government used the forthwith subpoena as a temporary measure to prevent it from being tampered with and to freeze its contents until a warrant could be obtained to search it.

3. *The Exclusionary Rule in the Grand Jury.* In **United States v. Calandra**, 414 U.S. 338 (1974), grand jury witness Calandra was asked questions about certain records (evidencing "loan-sharking" activities) that had been seized by federal agents in connection with a search of Calandra's office. Calandra initially invoked his privilege against self-incrimination, but subsequently was granted immunity. He then requested and received a postponement of the grand jury proceedings so that he could present a pre-charge motion for return and suppression of the seized evidence under Federal Rule 41(e). The district court granted the motion, holding that the search had been unconstitutional. The district court also held that "Calandra need not answer any of the grand jury's questions based on suppressed evidence," since such questions constituted the fruit of the poisonous tree. A divided Supreme Court (6-3), per Powell, J., reversed.

In deciding whether to extend the exclusionary rule to grand jury proceedings, we must weigh the potential injury to the historic role and functions of the grand jury against the potential benefits of the rule as applied in this context. It is evident that this extension of the exclusionary rule would seriously impede the grand jury. Because the grand jury does not finally adjudicate guilt or innocence, it has traditionally been allowed to pursue its investigative and accusatorial functions unimpeded by the evidentiary and procedural restrictions applicable to a criminal trial. Permitting witnesses to invoke the exclusionary rule before a grand jury would precipitate adjudication of issues hitherto reserved for the trial on the merits and would delay and disrupt grand jury proceedings. Suppression hearings would halt the orderly progress of an investigation and might necessitate extended litigation of issues only tangentially related to the grand jury's primary objective. The probable result would be "protracted interruptions of grand jury proceedings," effectively transforming them into preliminary trials on the merits. In some cases the delay might be fatal to the enforcement of the criminal law. Just last Term we reaffirmed our disinclination to allow litigious interference with grand jury proceedings. United States v. Dionisio, [p. 379].

Against this potential damage to the role and functions of the grand jury, we must weigh the benefits to be derived from this proposed extension of the exclusionary rule. * * * [The Court here considered the "incremental deterrent effect which might be achieved by extending the exclusionary rule to grand jury proceedings," and found "unrealistic" the assumption that such an extension would significantly further deterrence of illegal searches.] We therefore decline to embrace a view that would achieve a speculative and undoubtedly minimal advance in the deterrence of police misconduct at the expense of substantially impeding the role of the grand jury.

F.   CIVIL PROTECTIVE ORDERS AND GRAND JURY SUBPOENAS

White collar crime investigations frequently include civil litigation, brought by private parties and civil regulatory agencies. The authority of the federal grand jury may intersect with related civil proceedings, and the interplay can be very difficult to navigate for the criminal defense lawyer. As an initial matter, consider the authority of the grand jury to obtain evidence that is subject to a protective order issued by a judge that seals documents and prohibits the parties from disclosing information. Whose has greater authority in this circumstance: the court hearing the civil matter or the federal grand jury?

In re: GRAND JURY
286 F.3d 153 (3d Cir. 2002)

FUENTES, Circuit Judge.

This case requires us to resolve the conflict that arises when a grand jury subpoena seeks production of evidence ostensibly shielded by a civil protective order. Appellant is a target of a grand jury investigation in the District of New Jersey. The Government seeks to obtain, by way of a grand jury subpoena, testimony, documents, and other discovery material given pursuant to a protective order in a pending civil case. Appellant filed a motion to quash the subpoena on the ground that the protective order barred disclosure of the documents to the Government. The District Court denied Appellant's motion and granted the Government's cross-motion to compel production of the subpoenaed documents.

We hold that a grand jury subpoena supercedes a civil protective order unless the party seeking to avoid the subpoena demonstrates the existence of exceptional circumstances that clearly favor enforcement of the protective order. Appellant cannot meet his burden of establishing exceptional circumstances in this case, and therefore we affirm the order of the District Court denying appellant's motion to quash the subpoena and granting the Government's motion to compel production of the subpoenaed documents.

In 1998, Appellant John Doe and his wife filed a complaint in the Superior Court of New Jersey ("civil case"). The defendants in this commercial litigation removed the case to the District Court for the District of New Jersey. The parties entered into a Stipulation and Consent Order which was approved by the District Court in March 1999. The order included confidentiality provisions which limited disclosure of deposition transcripts and other documents produced in discovery. The parties agreed that the protective order was designed to avoid public disclosure of sensitive personal and corporate financial information, and that the case did not involve trade secrets or other information which normally enjoys a high level of confidentiality. After Doe added defendants to his case with whom there was no diversity of citizenship, the case was remanded to the New Jersey Superior Court in August 1999.

After remand, a Superior Court judge held a case management conference and entered a Case Management Order in October 1999 which adopted the earlier protective order entered by the District Court. Subsequent to the issuance of the state protective order, depositions, interrogatory answers, and other discovery were taken of Doe and several of his associates. The civil case, which also includes counterclaims against Doe, is still ongoing in state court and currently awaits trial.

Around April 2000, as discovery was ongoing in the civil case, the United States Attorney's Office for the District of New Jersey commenced a grand jury investigation of Doe and his wife into alleged mail fraud, wire fraud, income tax evasion, and falsification of income tax returns. These matters relate to issues raised in the civil case. On May 29, 2001, the grand jury issued a subpoena to Doe's civil case counsel. The subpoena calls for all depositions, related exhibits, interrogatory answers, and responses to requests for admissions in the civil case with respect to Doe and several other deponents. The parties agree that all the deposition testimony and other discovery sought by the subpoena was taken after the case was remanded to state court and under the state protective order. * * *

In an opinion and order filed under seal on October 25, 2001, the court denied Doe's motion to quash and granted the Government's motion to compel production. In its opinion, the court noted that a circuit split exists on the question of whether a protective order may trump a grand jury subpoena and that this Court has not decided the issue. * * *

We have not previously addressed whether, and under what circumstances, a civil protective order may shield information from a grand jury, but our sister circuits have developed three different approaches to this problem.[4] The Second Circuit has held that, absent a showing of improvidence in the grant of the protective order, or extraordinary circumstance or compelling need for the information, a protective order takes priority over a grand jury subpoena. Martindell v. International Telephone & Telegraph Corp., 594 F.2d 291 (2d Cir.1979). This presumption in favor of enforcing protective orders against grand jury subpoenas has been rejected by several courts. Three courts of appeals have announced a per se rule that a grand jury subpoena always trumps a protective order. In re Grand Jury Subpoena Served on Meserve, Mumper & Hughes, 62 F.3d 1222 (9th Cir.1995); In re Grand Jury Proceedings (Williams), 995 F.2d 1013 (11th Cir.1993); In re Grand Jury Subpoena, 836 F.2d 1468 (4th Cir.). Most recently, the First Circuit declined to adopt either the Second Circuit standard or the per se rule. It instead established a rebuttable presumption in favor of grand jury subpoenas. Under this rule, a grand jury subpoena overrides a protective order unless the party seeking to avoid the subpoena demonstrates the existence of "exceptional circumstances that clearly favor subordinating the subpoena to the protective order." In re Grand Jury Subpoena (Roach), 138 F.3d 442 (1st Cir.).

We benefit from the reasoning of these courts in announcing our rule today. We join the First Circuit in concluding that a strong but rebuttable

---

[4] We note that all the circuit cases discussed here addressed the issue in the context of protective orders issued by federal courts under Federal Rule of Civil Procedure 26(c). Here, the initial stipulated protective order was approved by the District Court, but all the materials sought by the grand jury were produced under the state court protective order, which incorporated and adopted the federal order. The interests implicated by the clash between a protective order and a grand jury subpoena are substantially the same whether the order was issued under federal or state law. Therefore, the circuit cases we discuss below are relevant, and the rule we announce applies to both federal and state protective orders.

presumption in favor of a grand jury subpoena best accommodates the sweeping powers of the grand jury and the efficient resolution of civil litigation fostered by protective orders.

In considering the tension between a grand jury subpoena and a civil protective order, we first recognize the "unique role" played by the grand jury in our system of justice. * * * Courts exercise limited control over the functioning of the grand jury and extend great deference to this historic institution and its broad powers. * * *

A civil protective order also serves important interests. Protective orders, authorized under federal law by Federal Rule of Civil Procedure 26(c) and by analogous provisions in state rules, are intended " 'to secure the just, speedy, and inexpensive determination' of civil disputes . . . by encouraging full disclosure of all evidence that might conceivably be relevant." *Martindell.* By shielding sensitive information from third parties and the public at large, protective orders "offer litigants a measure of privacy" and "aid the progression of litigation and facilitate settlements."

We ultimately conclude, however, that absent exceptional circumstances, protective orders should not serve to interfere with the unique and essential mechanism of a grand jury investigation. Other courts have rejected the Second Circuit's rule favoring protective orders because that test "tilts the scales in exactly the wrong direction" by "failing to pay proper respect" to the grand jury and its powers. While protective orders are in many cases very important facilitating devices, they are not, as the Second Circuit describes them, part of the "cornerstone of our administration of civil justice," and should almost always yield in the face of a grand jury subpoena. *See Martindell.*

The grand jury itself is a "cornerstone" of our justice system. The Fourth Circuit has cataloged the ways in which a protective order may improperly intrude upon the grand jury's functioning:

> Uncoerced testimony given in a civil action may provide important and relevant information to a grand jury investigation. In addition, the government has an interest in obtaining this information for purposes of impeachment should the deponents testify in a manner materially inconsistent with their deposition testimony in any future criminal trial. Finally, protective orders may cause the absurd result of shielding deponents from prosecutions for perjury because, while evidence of perjury would certainly be cause for modifying a protective order, the protective order itself impedes an investigation that might lead to cause for believing that perjury has occurred.

In re Grand Jury Subpoena.

It is true that under its broad powers, the grand jury may obtain evidence by means other than subpoenaing civil discovery materials. For example, it may subpoena witnesses directly, and the Government could grant these witnesses immunity if they refuse to testify. Yet in almost all cases, the grand jury should not be forced to resort to these imperfect alternatives when relevant evidence may be found in civil discovery materials. Because we give great deference to the grand jury's investigatory methods, we hesitate to dictate which methods may properly be employed. In many cases, the relevant witnesses are themselves targets of the grand jury probe and therefore a subpoena would not yield the required information because the witnesses would likely assert their Fifth Amendment privilege against self-incrimination. Allowing a protective order to prevail could all too often frustrate the grand jury's constitutionally and historically protected mission. We do not wish to allow protective orders, designed to facilitate private civil litigation, instead to delay criminal investigations which advance the public interest.

However, allowing a grand jury subpoena to override a protective order could encourage civil deponents to assert their Fifth Amendment privilege. This "may disrupt or thwart civil litigation and discovery in a wide variety of cases." Yet we agree with the Fourth Circuit that a protective order "cannot effectively deal in all instances with the problems posed by civil litigants who plead the fifth amendment during pretrial discovery," so it is "not therefore a substitute for invocation of the privilege, and it should not be afforded that status." We have held that "reliance on the Fifth Amendment in civil cases may give rise to an adverse inference against the party claiming its benefits." S.E.C. v. Graystone Nash, Inc., 25 F.3d 187 (3d Cir.1994). Therefore, concern for the Fifth Amendment right of a deponent "[does] not require, nor may it depend on, the shield of civil protective orders."

Furthermore, the Fourth Circuit has outlined several ways by which a court may "ensure [the] successful resolution of a civil action which is threatened by a deponent's privileged silence." These methods to facilitate efficient discovery include: 1) delaying discovery until any pending grand jury investigation has been completed; 2) conducting a pretrial hearing to expose any non-meritorious assertions of the Fifth Amendment privilege; 3) shifting the burden of proof to the privilege-asserting party who is in the best position to provide relevant proof and whose invocation of the privilege "contributed substantially to a party's failure of proof"; and 4) excluding testimony given at trial if the same testimony had been withheld during discovery under an assertion of privilege.

A protective order is an important device, but it is also a limited one, and is subject to modification. As the Fourth Circuit has noted:

> Even with a protective order in place, incriminating statements still create the risk that parties to a civil action will leak sealed information or materials to relevant law enforcement authorities. In the event of a leak, . . . a protective order, unlike a grant of immunity, provides no assurance that incriminating statements will not be used against a deponent in a criminal proceeding or that the

statements will not be used to obtain other relevant evidence. Moreover, a protective order . . . is normally subject to modification under Rule 26 for sufficient cause.

In re Grand Jury Subpoena. A protective order often "cannot serve as more than a stopgap measure . . . [because] incriminating information will normally be disclosed at trial even if the information is effectively suppressed prior to that time." Protective orders are limited instruments that are quite useful in facilitating the efficient disposition of litigation in the many civil cases that involve potentially embarrassing facts or sensitive commercial or other private information. Yet deponents who have reason to fear not just embarrassment or economic disadvantage, but possible criminal charges as well, should be aware that a protective order alone cannot protect them from a grand jury investigation.

Arguing for adoption of an approach akin to the Second Circuit's *Martindell* rule, Doe asserts that the Government may overcome that rule's presumption in favor of the protective order by demonstrating "compelling need" for the subpoenaed information, and therefore the harm to the esteemed role and powers of the grand jury is slight. He further contends that any impediment to the grand jury's investigation posed by quashing the subpoena can be avoided by compelling the witnesses themselves to testify, and if the witnesses elect to assert their Fifth Amendment privilege, the Government could then grant them immunity. This argument, however, does not account for the consequences that would ensue if the Government declines to grant immunity. Such consequences would likely occur in cases such as Doe's where the witness himself is the target of the grand jury probe. In addition, such a high and exacting standard as "compelling need" simply does not comport with the wide-reaching powers of the grand jury and the judicial deference shown those powers.

In the vast majority of cases, a protective order should yield to a grand jury subpoena. On the other hand, we also understand that on very rare occasions, the public interest in speedy resolution of private civil litigation could outweigh the strong public interest in favor of prosecution of criminal wrongdoing. The *per se* approach, adopted by three of our sister circuits and under which a grand jury subpoena always trumps a protective order, defers to the sweeping powers of the grand jury, but does so at the expense of flexibility. It also forecloses enforcement of a protective order in the exceptional case in which the public interest demands that the civil litigation take priority over any criminal investigation. Such a rigid test ignores "idiosyncratic circumstances" and fails to understand that "the confluence of the relevant interests–generally, those of society at large and of the parties who are seeking to keep a civil protective order inviolate–occasionally may militate in favor of blunting a grand jury's subpoena."

We therefore join the First Circuit in establishing a strong presumption that a grand jury subpoena supercedes a protective order. The party seeking to avoid the subpoena may rebut that presumption only by showing the existence of exceptional circumstances that clearly favor enforcing the protective order against the grand jury subpoena.

A court's assessment of whether a party has shown exceptional circumstances requires a case-by-case analysis of the relevant facts, and is not susceptible to easy generalization. The First Circuit outlined several factors for courts to consider in determining whether "exceptional circumstances" exist. These factors include: 1) the government's need for the information (including the availability of other sources); 2) the severity of the contemplated criminal charges; 3) the harm to society should the alleged criminal wrongdoing go unpunished; 4) the interests served by continued maintenance of complete confidentiality in the civil litigation; 5) the value of the protective order to the timely resolution of that litigation; 6) the harm to the party who sought the protective order if the information is revealed to the grand jury; 7) the severity of the harm alleged by the civil- suit plaintiff; and 8) the harm to society and the parties should the encroachment upon the protective order hamper the prosecution or defense of the civil case. We find these factors to be quite helpful and we adopt them today. We stress, however, that this list is not exhaustive; a district court need not weigh every one of these factors, and it may consider additional factors as the circumstances warrant.[e]

We cannot overemphasize that the presumption we announce today in favor of a grand jury subpoena may only be rebutted in the rarest and most important of cases. As the First Circuit stated, "[i]n the end, society's interest in the assiduous prosecution of criminal wrongdoing *almost always* will outweigh its interest in the resolution of a civil matter between private parties ... and thus, a civil protective order ordinarily cannot be permitted to sidetrack a grand jury's investigation." * * *

We recognize that the exceptional circumstances rule sacrifices some of the certainty which forms one of the most attractive features of the *per se* rule. However, we do not wish to eliminate any possibility of a court exercising its discretion in an extraordinary case. In the vast majority of cases, a grand jury subpoena should prevail. Almost always, the public interest in investigating criminal misconduct will outweigh the public interest in facilitating private civil litigation. As the Government conceded at oral argument, however, the per se rule's inherent inflexibility fails to allow for the truly exceptional case in which quashing the grand jury subpoena would be appropriate.

Finally, we share the concerns of the courts that have approved the *per se* rule that allowing a protective order to trump a grand jury subpoena, even

---

[e] Note that the factors cited by the court will weigh differently depending on the party that sought the protection of the protective order. The order may be sought by a party to the suit, or by a critical witness who would otherwise assert the Fifth Amendment privilege. It may be that the interests of the third-party witness should weigh more heavily in favor of enforcing the protective order.

in only the rarest of cases, could amount to a virtual grant of immunity and could thereby encroach upon the exclusive power of the United States Attorney, under 18 U.S.C. § 6003, to issue grants of immunity.

Our worry is alleviated because again, in almost all cases, the grand jury subpoena should prevail. We acknowledge that enforcing a protective order grants a certain degree of quasi-immunity to a deponent, because application of the protective order denies the grand jury access to statements made by the deponent, and the deponent would likely assert his Fifth Amendment privilege if subpoenaed directly. Yet a protective order is no substitute for immunity because, as we have discussed above, a protective order is inherently modifiable and does not prevent the Government from prosecuting the deponent through evidence obtained by other means. Just because the grand jury might hypothetically obtain the evidence from other available sources does not mean that it should have to resort to such imperfect alternatives. But because these potential alternatives exist, allowing a protective order to quash a grand jury subpoena in a truly exceptional case would not bar any prosecution such that enforcement of the protective order would rise to the level of a *de facto* grant of immunity. Concern with the scope of judicial power ultimately does not dissuade us from allowing some slight flexibility and entertaining the possibility that a protective order might prevail in an exceptional case. * * *

In this case, we presume that the grand jury subpoena issued to Doe's civil counsel for deposition transcripts and other discovery materials trumps the protective order under which this evidence was produced. Doe has the burden of showing the existence of exceptional circumstances that clearly favor rebutting the presumption and enforcing the protective order against the grand jury subpoena.

We need not remand this case for further consideration by the District Court and thereby further delay the pending grand jury investigation. Because the record is sufficient, we may ourselves assess whether Doe can show exceptional circumstances. In any event, the District Court's opinion included analysis quite similar to that required by the exceptional circumstances test. Although the District Court decided this case without the guidance of a clear rule from this Court, it expressly held that the public interest would not be served by enforcing the protective order because "[t]here is certainly no public interest in protecting the personal financial dealings of the [Does] in the face of a criminal investigation."

We agree. Upon consideration of the facts of this case in light of the non-exhaustive factors adopted above, we conclude that Doe cannot overcome the presumption against enforcing the protective order against the grand jury subpoena. The Government's need for the subpoenaed information is significant. Therefore, allowing the protective order to prevail could frustrate the grand jury's power to obtain evidence. The contemplated criminal charges being investigated by the grand jury are severe; the potential harm to society in allowing extensive tax evasion and fraud, and the illegal diversion of large amounts of money, without punishment, is certainly substantial. The value of the protective order to the timely resolution of the civil case is limited at best. Discovery appears mostly complete, and the civil case now awaits trial. Therefore, the protective order's value in facilitating discovery has significantly diminished, and the protected information will likely be disclosed at trial in any event. Doe may be harmed if his personal and corporate financial information is revealed to the grand jury, but because grand jury proceedings are secret, this information will not become public and risk the burden and embarrassment to Doe that protective orders are meant to avoid. Rather, any harm would result instead from the potentially self-incriminating statements contained in the subpoenaed materials. Protective orders do not serve to protect Fifth Amendment interests; any harm to such interests is comparatively slight.

Counsel for Doe asserted at oral argument that exceptional circumstances are present here because Doe is a target of the grand jury investigation which led to the subpoena. Yet, if this suffices to show exceptional circumstances, then exceptional circumstances may be found in every case. We refuse to allow "exceptional circumstances" to swallow the presumption in favor of grand jury subpoenas. Doe also contends that the Government does not have a compelling need for the subpoenaed information because it has other available sources for the information. Government need, whether it be "compelling" or otherwise, is not dispositive. It is simply one potential factor in the analysis. We have rejected the Second Circuit's *Martindell* rule partly because it placed an improper burden of showing compelling need on the Government.

The public interest in enforcing the protective order and facilitating the civil litigation simply does not outweigh the public interest in prosecuting potential criminal behavior in this case. As we stressed above, a grand jury subpoena should almost always trump a protective order, and we find no reason to rebut that strong presumption in this private commercial dispute. Doe cannot show exceptional circumstances that clearly favor subordinating the subpoena to the protective order.

NOTES AND QUESTIONS

1. *Civil Testimony.* Should a defense lawyer ever permit a client to testify or create documents in relation to a civil case if there is a reasonable chance of a criminal investigation? Did the attorney for the Does fail to anticipate the possible interest of the United States Attorney's Office? It is sometimes difficult to assess the likelihood of a criminal investigation, and not every civil case with potential criminal ramifications results in a federal grand jury investigation. The possibility of refusing to testify by asserting the Fifth Amendment privilege against self-incrimination are discussed infra in Chapter 13. Note that there may be collateral consequences from asserting the Fifth Amendment in civil litigation, including an adverse inference drawn

against the party asserting the constitutional privilege discussed in *In re: Grand Jury*. *See* infra Chapter 14.

2. *Circuit Split*. The Second Circuit continues to adhere to the rule it announced in Martindell v. International Telephone & Telegraph, 594 F.2d 291 (2d Cir. 1979). See SEC v. TheStreet.com, 273 F.3d 222 (2d Cir. 2001), in which the court reiterated that it would be "presumptively unfair for courts to modify protective orders which assure confidentiality and upon which the parties have reasonably relied." The Fourth, Ninth, and Eleventh Circuits adopted the *per se* rule requiring enforcement of the grand jury subpoena without regard to the scope or propriety of the protective order, a position completely opposed to the Second Circuit's view. Is the rebuttable presumption in favor of enforcement of the grand jury subpoena adopted by the First and Third Circuits any more than semantically different from the *per se* rule, especially given the Third Circuit's acknowledgment that in "the vast majority of cases, a protective order should yield to a grand jury subpoena" and that the presumption will be rebutted ""in the rarest and most important cases"? If the Supreme Court were to resolve the split in the circuits, what is the most likely resolution? Does the presumption of in favor of the grand jury subpoena expressed in *R. Enterprises* affect the analysis, or does that case not involve any countervailing balance?

CHAPTER TEN
THE PRODUCTION OF DOCUMENTS

The grand jury is entitled to "every man's evidence," so it has the authority to compel the production of documents absent a valid claim of privilege. The Fifth Amendment privilege against self-incrimination has been a means by which an individual can resist a subpoena to testify before the grand jury, a topic discussed in Chapter 13. At one time, the Fifth Amendment was also viewed as extending to the production of documents, based on the Supreme Court's decision in Boyd v. United States, 116 U.S. 616 (1883), that found the compelled production of incriminating business records violated the witness's right to privacy under the Fourth and Fifth Amendments. The Court stated that the Constitution prohibited "any forcible and compulsory extortion of a man's . . . private papers to be used as evidence to convict him of a crime or to forfeit his goods." The Court limited *Boyd*'s reach in Hale v. Henkel, 201 U.S. 43 (1906), when it held that the custodian subpoenaed for a corporation's records as part of an antitrust investigation could not assert the privilege against self-incrimination because that would effectively permit the organization to resist producing documents. These two decisions set up the essential framework for analyzing the production of documents pursuant to a grand jury subpoena prior to *Fisher v. United States* below.

The Supreme Court admonished that while "the powers of the grand jury are not unlimited and are subject to the supervision of a judge, the longstanding principle that 'the public . . . has a right to every man's evidence,' except for those persons protected by a constitutional, common-law, or statutory privilege, is particularly applicable to grand jury proceedings." Branzburg v. Hayes, 408 U.S. 665 (1972). The grand jury's investigative power had to give way to a Fifth Amendment claim, but the Court had been leery about extending the self-incrimination privilege to the point that investigations will be effectively thwarted. Thus, the Court had taken radically different approaches to a privilege claim under the Fifth Amendment depending on whether the demand to produce documents was made on an individual or a corporation. While the Fifth Amendment affords a measure of protection to the individual, a business or other organization was precluded from asserting the constitutional protection to resist a subpoena for records. How the Court has analyzed these issues of document production is the subject of this Chapter.

A. THE ACT OF PRODUCTION DOCTRINE

1. Personal Papers

FISHER v. UNITED STATES
425 U.S. 391, 96 S.Ct. 1569, 48 L.Ed.2d 39 (1976)

Justice WHITE delivered the opinion of the Court.

In these two cases we are called upon to decide whether a summons directing an attorney to produce documents delivered to him by his client in connection with the attorney-client relationship is enforceable over claims that the documents were constitutionally immune from summons in the hands of the client and retained that immunity in the hands of the attorney. In each case, an Internal Revenue agent visited the taxpayer or taxpayers and interviewed them in connection with an investigation of possible civil or criminal liability under the federal income tax laws. Shortly after the interviews * * *, the taxpayers obtained from their respective accountants certain documents relating to the preparation by the accountant of their tax returns. Shortly after obtaining the documents * * *, the taxpayers transferred the documents to their lawyers—each of whom was retained to assist the taxpayer in connection with the investigation. Upon learning of the whereabouts of the documents, the Internal Revenue Service served summonses on the attorneys directing them to produce documents listed therein. [Those documents were accountants' work sheets, retained copies of income tax returns, and the accountants' copies of correspondence between the accounting firm and the taxpayer]. * * * In each case, the lawyer declined to comply with the summons directing production of the documents, and enforcement actions were commenced by the Government. * * *

All of the parties in these cases and the Court of Appeals have concurred in the proposition that if the Fifth Amendment would have excused a taxpayer from turning over the accountant's papers had he possessed them, the attorney to whom they are delivered for the purpose of obtaining legal advice should also be immune from subpoena. Although we agree with this proposition for the reasons set forth * * * infra, we are convinced that, under our decision in Couch v. United States, 409 U.S. 322 (1973), it is not the taxpayer's Fifth Amendment privilege that would excuse the *attorney* from production.

The relevant part of that Amendment provides: "No person . . . shall be compelled in any criminal case to be a *witness against himself*." (Emphasis added.) The taxpayer's privilege under this Amendment is not violated by enforcement of the summonses involved in these cases because enforcement against a taxpayer's lawyer would not "compel" the taxpayer to do anything—and certainly would not compel him to be a "witness" against himself. The Court has held repeatedly that the Fifth Amendment is limited to prohibiting the use of "physical or moral compulsion" exerted on the person asserting the privilege. In *Couch*, supra, we recently ruled that the Fifth Amendment rights of a taxpayer were not violated by the enforcement of a documentary summons directed to her accountant and requiring production of the taxpayer's own records in the possession of the accountant. We did so on the ground that in such a case "the ingredient of personal compulsion against an accused is lacking." Here, the taxpayers are compelled to do no more than was the taxpayer in *Couch*. The taxpayers' Fifth Amendment privilege is therefore not violated by enforcement of the summonses directed toward their attorneys. This is true whether or not the Amendment would have barred a subpoena directing the taxpayer to produce the documents while they were in his hands.

The fact that the attorneys are agents of the taxpayers does not change this result. *Couch* held as much, since the accountant there was also the taxpayer's agent, and in this respect reflected a longstanding view. * * * "It is extortion of information from the accused which offends our sense of justice." *Couch*. Agent or no, the lawyer is not the taxpayer. The taxpayer is the "accused," and nothing is being extorted from him. Nor is this one of those situations, which *Couch* suggested might exist, where constructive possession is so clear or relinquishment of possession so temporary and insignificant as to leave the personal compulsion upon the taxpayer substantially intact. * * *

The Court of Appeals suggested that because legally and ethically the attorney was required to respect the confidences of his client, the latter had a reasonable expectation of privacy for the records in the hands of the attorney and therefore did not forfeit his Fifth Amendment privilege with respect to the records by transferring them in order to obtain legal advice. It is true that the Court has often stated that one of the several purposes served by the constitutional privilege against compelled testimonial self-incrimination is that of protecting, personal privacy. See e.g., Murphy v. Waterfront Comm'n, 378 U.S. 52 (1964). But the Court has never suggested that every invasion of privacy violates the privilege. Within the limits imposed by the language of the Fifth Amendment, which we necessarily observe, the privilege truly serves privacy interests; but the Court has never on any ground, personal privacy included, applied the Fifth Amendment to prevent the otherwise proper acquisition or use of evidence which, in the Court's view, did not involve compelled testimonial self-incrimination of some sort.

The proposition that the Fifth Amendment protects private information obtained without compelling self-incriminating testimony is contrary to the clear statements of this Court that under appropriate safeguards private incriminating statements of an accused may be overheard and used in evidence, if they are not compelled at the time they were uttered. Katz v. United States, 389 U.S. 347 (1987), and that disclosure of private information may be compelled if immunity removes the risk of incrimination. Kastigar v. United States [p. 581]. If the Fifth Amendment protected generally against the obtaining of private information from a man's mouth or pen or house, its protections would presumably not be lifted by probable cause and a warrant or by immunity. * * * We cannot cut the Fifth Amendment completely loose from the moorings of its language, and make it serve as a general protector of privacy—a word not mentioned in its text and a concept directly addressed in the Fourth Amendment. We adhere to the view that the Fifth Amendment protects against "compelled self-incrimination, not [the disclosure of] private information." * * * Insofar as private information not obtained through compelled self-incriminating testimony is legally protected, its protection stems from other sources—the Fourth Amendment's protection against seizures without warrant or probable cause and against subpoenas which suffer from "too much indefiniteness or breadth in the things required to be 'particularly described,'" the First Amendment, or evidentiary privileges such as the attorney-client privilege.[7]

* * * [While the] taxpayers have erroneously relied on the Fifth Amendment without urging the attorney-client privilege in so many words, they have nevertheless invoked the relevant body of law and policies that govern the attorney-client privilege. In this posture of the case, we feel obliged to inquire whether the attorney-client privilege applies to documents in the hands of an attorney which would have been privileged in the hands of the client by reason of the Fifth Amendment. * * * This Court and the lower courts have * * * uniformly held that pre-existing documents which could have been obtained by court process from the client when he was in possession may also be obtained from the attorney by similar process following transfer by the client in order to obtain more informed legal advice. * * * It is otherwise if the documents are not obtainable by subpoena duces tecum or summons while in the exclusive possession of the client, for the client will then be reluctant to transfer possession to the lawyer unless the documents are also privileged in the latter's hands. Where the transfer is made for the purpose of obtaining legal advice, the purposes of the attorney-client privilege would be defeated unless the privilege is applicable. * * *

Since each taxpayer [here] transferred possession of the documents in question from himself to his attorney in order to obtain legal assistance in the tax investigations in question, the papers, if unobtainable by summons from the client, are unobtainable by summons directed to the attorney by reason of the attorney-client privilege. We accordingly proceed to the question whether the documents could have been obtained by summons addressed to the taxpayer while the documents were in his possession. The only bar to enforcement of such summons asserted by the parties or the courts below is

---

[7] The taxpayers and their attorneys have not raised arguments of a Fourth Amendment nature before this Court and could not be successful if they had. The summonses are narrowly drawn and seek only documents of unquestionable relevance to the tax investigation. Special problems of privacy which might be presented by subpoena of a personal diary, United States v. Bennett, 409 F.2d 888, 897 (CA2 1969) (Friendly, J.), are not involved here. First Amendment values are also plainly not implicated in these cases.

the Fifth Amendment's privilege against self-incrimination. * * *

The proposition that the Fifth Amendment prevents compelled production of documents over objection that such production might incriminate stems from Boyd v. United States * * *. The invoice in question [there] was held to have been obtained in violation of the Fourth Amendment. The Court went on to hold that the accused in a criminal case or the defendant in a forfeiture action could not be forced to produce evidentiary items without violating the Fifth Amendment as well as the Fourth. More specifically, the Court declared, "a compulsory production of the private books and papers of the owner of goods sought to be forfeited . . . is compelling him to be a witness against himself, within the meaning of the Fifth Amendment to the Constitution." * * *

Several of *Boyd's* express or implicit declarations have not stood the test of time. The application of the Fourth Amendment to subpoenas was limited by Hale v. Henkel and more recent cases. Purely evidentiary (but "nontestimonial") materials, as well as contraband and fruits and instrumentalities of crime, may now be searched for and seized under proper circumstances, Warden v. Hayden. Also, any notion that "testimonial" evidence may never be seized and used in evidence is inconsistent with [various cases] approving the seizure under appropriate circumstances of conversations of a person suspected of crime. See Katz v. United States, supra. It is also clear that the Fifth Amendment does not independently proscribe the compelled production of every sort of incriminating evidence but applies only when the accused is compelled to make a testimonial communication that is incriminating. * * * Furthermore, despite *Boyd*, neither a partnership nor the individual partners are shielded from compelled production of partnership records on self-incrimination grounds. Bellis v. United States. It would appear that under that case the precise claim sustained in *Boyd* would now be rejected for reasons not there considered.

The pronouncement in *Boyd* that a person may not be forced to produce his private papers has nonetheless often appeared as dictum in later opinions of this Court. * * * To the extent, however, that the rule against compelling production of private papers rested on the proposition that seizures of or subpoenas for "mere evidence," including documents, violated the Fourth Amendment and therefore also transgressed the Fifth, the foundations for the rule have been washed away. In consequence, the prohibition against forcing the production of private papers has long been a rule searching for a rationale consistent with the proscriptions of the Fifth Amendment against compelling a person to give "testimony" that incriminates him. Accordingly, we turn to the question of what, if any, incriminating testimony within the Fifth Amendment's protection, is compelled by a documentary summons.

A subpoena served on a taxpayer requiring him to produce an accountant's workpapers in his possession without doubt involves substantial compulsion. But it does not compel oral testimony; nor would it ordinarily compel the taxpayer to restate, repeat, or affirm the truth of the contents of the documents sought. Therefore, the Fifth Amendment would not be violated by the fact alone that the papers on their face might incriminate the taxpayer, for the privilege protects a person only against being incriminated by his own compelled testimonial communications. The accountant's workpapers are not the taxpayer's. They were not prepared by the taxpayer, and they contain no testimonial declarations by him. Furthermore, as far as this record demonstrates, the preparation of all of the papers sought in these cases was wholly voluntary, and they cannot be said to contain compelled testimonial evidence, either of the taxpayers or of anyone else. The taxpayer cannot avoid compliance with the subpoena merely by asserting that the item of evidence which he is required to produce contains incriminating writing, whether his own or that of someone else.

The act of producing evidence in response to a subpoena nevertheless has communicative aspects of its own, wholly aside from the contents of the papers produced. Compliance with the subpoena tacitly concedes the existence of the papers demanded and their possession or control by the taxpayer. It also would indicate the taxpayer's belief that the papers are those described in the subpoena. The elements of compulsion are clearly present, but the more difficult issues are whether the tacit averments, of the taxpayer are both "testimonial" and "incriminating" for purposes of applying the Fifth Amendment. These questions perhaps do not lend themselves to categorical answers; their resolution may instead depend on the facts and circumstances of particular cases or classes thereof In light of the records now before us, we are confident that however incriminating the contents of the accountant's workpapers might be, the act of producing them—the only thing which the taxpayer is compelled to do—would not itself involve testimonial self-incrimination.

It is doubtful that implicitly admitting the existence and possession of the papers rises to the level of testimony within the protection of the Fifth Amendment. The papers belong to the accountant, were prepared by him, and are the kind usually prepared by an accountant working on the tax returns of his client. Surely the Government is in no way relying on the "truthtelling" of the taxpayer to prove the existence of or his access to the documents. The existence and location of the papers are a foregone conclusion and the taxpayer adds little or nothing to the sum total of the Government's information by conceding that he in fact has the papers. Under these circumstances by enforcement of the summons "no constitutional rights are touched. The question is not of testimony but of surrender." * * *

When an accused is required to submit a handwriting exemplar he admits his ability to write and impliedly asserts that the exemplar is his writing. But in common experience, the first would be a near truism and the latter self-evident. In any event, although the exemplar may be incriminating to the accused and although he is compelled to furnish it. his Fifth Amendment privilege is not violated because nothing he has said or done is deemed to be sufficiently testimonial for purposes of the privilege. This Court has also time and again allowed subpoenas against the custodian of corporate documents or those belonging to other collective entities such as unions and partnerships and those of bankrupt businesses over claims that the documents will incriminate the custodian despite the fact that producing the documents tacitly admits their existence and their location in the hands of their possessor. The existence and possession or control of the subpoenaed documents being no more in issue here than in the above cases, the summons is equally enforceable.

Moreover, assuming that these aspects of producing the accountant's papers have some minimal testimonial significance, surely it is not illegal to seek accounting help in connection with one's tax returns or for the accountant to prepare workpapers and deliver them to the taxpayer. At this juncture, we are quite unprepared to hold that either the fact of existence of the papers or of their possession by the taxpayer poses any realistic threat of incrimination to the taxpayer.

As for the possibility that responding to the subpoena would authenticate the workpapers, production would express nothing more than the taxpayer's belief that the papers are those described in the subpoena. The taxpayer would be no more competent to authenticate the accountant's workpapers or reports by producing them than he would be to authenticate them if testifying orally. The taxpayer did not prepare the papers and could not vouch for their accuracy. The documents would not be admissible in evidence against the taxpayer without authenticating testimony. Without more, responding to the subpoena in the circumstances before us would not appear to represent a substantial threat of self-incrimination. * * *

Whether the Fifth Amendment would shield the taxpayer from producing his own tax records in his possession is a question not involved here; for the papers demanded here are not his "private papers," see *Boyd*, supra. We do hold that compliance with a summons directing the taxpayer to produce the accountant's documents involved in this case would involve no incriminating testimony within the protection of the Fifth Amendment.

Justice BRENNAN, concurring in the judgment.

Given the prior access by accountants retained by the taxpayers to the papers involved in these cases and the wholly business rather than personal nature of the papers, I agree that the privilege against compelled self-incrimination did not in either of these cases protect the papers from production in response to the summonses. See Couch v. United States. I do not join the Court's opinion, however, because of the portent of much of what is said of a serious crippling of the protection secured by the privilege against compelled production of one's private books and papers. * * * [I]t is but another step in the denigration of privacy principles settled nearly 100 years ago in *Boyd v. United States*. * * *

Expressions are legion in opinions of this Court that the protection of personal privacy is a central purpose of the privilege against compelled self-incrimination. * * * The Court pays lip-service to this bedrock premise of privacy in the statement that "[w]ithin the limits imposed by the language of the Fifth Amendment, which we necessarily observe, the privilege truly serves privacy interests." But this only makes explicit what elsewhere highlights the opinion, namely, the view that protection of personal privacy is merely a byproduct and not, as our precedents and history teach, a factor controlling in part the determination of the scope of the privilege. This cart-before-the-horse approach is fundamentally at odds with the settled principle that the scope of the privilege is not constrained by the limits of the wording of the Fifth Amendment but has the reach necessary to protect the cherished value of privacy which it safeguards. * * * History and principle, not the mechanical application of its wording, have been the life of the amendment. * * *

History and principle teach that the privacy protected by the Fifth Amendment extends not just to the individual's immediate declarations, oral or written, but also to his testimonial materials in the form of books and papers. The common-law and constitutional extension of the privilege to testimonial materials, such as books and papers, was inevitable. An individual's books and papers are generally little more than an extension of his person. They reveal no less than he could reveal upon being questioned directly. Many of the matters within an individual's knowledge may as easily be retained within his head as set down on a scrap of paper. I perceive no principle which does not permit compelling one to disclose the contents of one's mind but does permit compelling the disclosure of the contents of that scrap of paper by compelling its production. Under a contrary view, the constitutional protection would turn on fortuity, and persons would, at their peril, record their thoughts and the events of their lives. The ability to think private thoughts, facilitated as it is by pen and paper, and the ability to preserve intimate memories would be curtailed through fear that those thoughts or the events of those memories would become the subjects of criminal sanctions however invalidly imposed. Indeed, it was the very reality of those fears that helped provide the historical impetus for the privilege. * * *

[The Court's] analysis is patently incomplete: the threshold inquiry is whether the taxpayer is compelled to produce incriminating papers. That inquiry is not answered in favor of production merely because the subpoena requires neither oral testimony from nor affirmation of the papers' contents by the taxpayer. To be sure, the Court correctly observes that "[t]he taxpayer cannot avoid compliance with the subpoena merely by asserting that the item of evidence which he is required to produce contains incriminating writing, whether his own or that of someone else." For it is not enough that the production of a writing, or books and papers, is compelled. Unless those materials are such as to come within the zone of privacy recognized by the Amendment, the privilege against compulsory self-incrimination does not protect against their production. * * *

A precise cataloguing of private papers within the ambit of the privacy protected by the privilege is probably impossible. Some papers, however, do lend themselves to classification. Production of documentary materials created or authenticated by a State or the Federal Government, such as automobile registrations or property deeds, would seem ordinarily to fall outside the protection of the privilege. They hardly reflect an extension of the person. Economic and business records may present difficulty in particular cases. The records of business entities generally fall without the scope of the privilege. But, as noted, the Court has recognized that the privilege extends to the business records of the sole proprietor or practitioner. Such records are at least an extension of an aspect of a person's activities, though concededly not the more intimate aspects of one's life. Where the privilege would have protected one's mental notes of his business affairs in a less complicated day and age, it would seem that that protection should not fall away because the complexities of another time compel one to keep business records.

Nonbusiness economic records in the possession of an individual, such as canceled checks or tax records, would also seem to be protected. They may provide clear insights into a person's total lifestyle. They are, however, like business records and the papers involved in these cases, frequently, though not always, disclosed to other parties; and disclosure, in proper cases, may foreclose reliance upon the privilege. Personal letters constitute an integral aspect of a person's private enclave. And while letters, being necessarily interpersonal, are not wholly private, their peculiarly private nature and the generally narrow extent of their disclosure would seem to render them within the scope of the privilege. Papers in the nature of a personal diary are a fortiori protected under the privilege.

The Court's treatment in the instant cases of the question whether the evidence involved here is within the protection of the privilege is, with all respect, most inadequate. The gaping hole is in the omission of any reference to the taxpayer's privacy interests and to whether the subpoenas impermissibly invade those interests. * * * For the reasons I have stated at the outset, however, I do not believe that the evidence involved in these cases falls within the scope of privacy protected by the Fifth Amendment. * * *

Justice MARSHALL, concurring in the judgment.

* * * I would have preferred it had the Court found some room in its theory for recognition of the import of the contents of the documents themselves. * * * Nonetheless, I am hopeful that the Court's new theory, properly understood and applied, will provide substantially the same protection as our prior focus on the contents of the documents. * * * Indeed, there would appear to be a precise inverse relationship between the private nature of the document and the permissibility of assuming its existence. Therefore, under the Court's theory, the admission through production that one's diary, letters, prior tax returns, personally maintained financial records, or canceled checks exist would ordinarily provide substantial

testimony. The incriminating nature of such an admission is clear, for while it may not be criminal to keep a diary, or write letters or checks, the admission that one does and that those documents are still available may quickly—or simultaneously-lead to incriminating evidence. If there is a "real danger" of such a result, that is enough under our cases to make such testimony subject to the claim of privilege. Thus, in practice, the Court's approach should still focus upon the private nature of the papers subpoenaed and protect those about which *Boyd* and its progeny were most concerned. * * *

The Court's theory will also limit the prosecution's ability to use documents secured through a grant of immunity. If authentication that the document produced is the document demanded were the only testimony inherent in production, immunity would be a useful tool for obtaining written evidence. So long as a document obtained under an immunity grant could be authenticated through other sources, as would often be possible, reliance on the immunized testimony–the authentication–and its fruits would not be necessary, and the document could be introduced. The Court's recognition that the act of production also involves testimony about the existence and possession of the subpoenaed documents mandates a different result. Under the Court's recognition that the act of production also involves testimony about the existence and possession of the subpoenaed documents mandates a different result. Under the Court's theory, if the document is to be obtained the immunity grant must extend to the testimony that the document is presently in existence. Such a grant will effectively shield the contents of the document, for the contents are a direct fruit of the immunized testimony–that the document exists–and cannot usually be obtained without reliance on that testimony. Accordingly, the Court's theory offers substantially the same protection against procurement of documents under grant of immunity that our prior cases afford.

NOTES AND QUESTIONS

1. *The Role of Privacy.* Both critics and supporters of the view that the Fifth Amendment is designed to protect a "private enclave" acknowledge that such a privacy rationale remains unpersuasive unless it offers a satisfactory explanation as to why the particular element of privacy that falls within the privilege is given absolute protection, as compared to the relative protection given other privacy interests under the Fourth and First Amendments. The answer usually offered is that the privilege protects the most significant element of individual privacy, the privacy "of the mind"; it "respects a private inner sanctum of individual feeling and thought." Couch v. United States [p. 648]. But this response only raises the further question as to why the privilege, if it is designed to protect mental privacy from state intrusion, affords such protection only as to thoughts, feelings, and beliefs that would furnish a link in the chain of evidence needed to establish criminal liability. One explanation for this limitation is that privilege seeks to protect only a "particular corner of the private enclave" that is especially significant in the

development of "moral autonomy"—the "integrity of conscience." See Robert Gerstein, *The Demise of Boyd: Self-Incrimination and Private Papers in the Burger Court*, 27 U.C.L.A. L. REV. 343 (1979). The critical element of the privilege, from this perspective, is that it preserves to the individual alone the essential right of determining whether and when to acknowledge responsibility for his actions. See also Abe Fortas, *The Fifth Amendment, Nemo Tenetur Prodere Seipsum*, 25 CLEVE. B.A.J. 95 (1954) ("*Mea culpa* belongs to a man and his God. It is a plea that cannot be extracted from free men by human authority").

Looking back to *Boyd*, can the ruling there be viewed (as suggested by Justices Brennan and Marshall) as resting upon a privacy rationale of the Fifth Amendment? The *Fisher* majority apparently subscribed to the view (held by most commentators) that the *Boyd* ruling rested on a subsequently discarded "property rights" rationale. *Boyd*, under this view, simply utilized the privilege to characterize as "unreasonable" all "searches" (which included required production) aimed at obtaining a person's personal property for possible use against him in a "criminal case" (which included a forfeiture proceeding). See Robert Heidt, *The Fifth Amendment Privilege and Documents–Cutting Fisher's Tangled Line*, 49 MO. L. REV. 440 (1984). Yet, *Boyd*, particularly because of its reliance on Entick v. Carrington and the characterization there of the individual's papers as his "dearest property" has also been viewed as suggesting a broad personal privacy grounding for the self-incrimination privilege. *Entick*, it is suggested, regards a person as being "embodied" in his papers and *Boyd* recognized that it was therefore a violation of the privilege to make his papers "speak" against him. *Entick*, however, had in mind the individual's personal political writings, while *Boyd* had before it an invoice written by another firm. *Gerstein*. See also Heidt, supra (*Boyd's* inclusion of all documents logically could be extended to make the privilege applicable to the compelled production of any property that "contained communications," including "photographs, phonograph records, and old newspapers").

2. *Sole Proprietorship Records*. In **United States v. Doe**, 465 U.S. 605 (1984) (commonly referred to as *Doe I* to distinguish it from the Court's decision in Doe v. United States, 487 U.S. 201 (1988) (*Doe II*), infra p. 405, which also involved the Fifth Amendment and obtaining records), the Court considered a challenge to subpoenas for the business records of a sole proprietorship. Respondent, the owner of several sole proprietorships, objected to a series of five subpoenas directing him to produce a broad range of business records, including billings, ledgers, cancelled checks, telephone records, contracts, and paid bills. The district court sustained the respondent's Fifth Amendment challenge, noting that the act of producing the documents had "communicative aspects" which could prove incriminating since the respondent would thereby be required to "admit that the records exist, that they are in his possession, and that they are authentic." On appeal, the Third Circuit agreed with the district court, but also added another self-incrimination ground justifying the quashing of the subpoenas. Following Fisher, that circuit had held, relying on Boyd, that an individual's private

papers, though created voluntarily, were still privileged under the self-incrimination clause. That analysis, the Third Circuit reasoned, was also applicable to the business records of a sole proprietor.

The Court stated that "[a]s we noted in *Fisher*, the Fifth Amendment only protects the person asserting the privilege only from *compelled* self-incrimination. Where the preparation of business records is voluntary, no compulsion is present." With regard to whether the sole proprietor could assert the Fifth Amendment for the act of production, the Court held:

> Although the contents of a document may not be privileged, the act of producing the document may be. *Fisher*. A government subpoena compels the holder of the document to perform an act that may have testimonial aspects and an incriminating effect. * * * In *Fisher*, the Court explored the effect that the act of production would have on the taxpayer [there] and determined that the act of production would have only minimal testimonial value and would not operate to incriminate the taxpayer. Unlike the Court in *Fisher*, we have the explicit finding of the District Court that the act of producing the documents would involve testimonial self-incrimination."[11] The Court of Appeals agreed.[12] The District Court's finding essentially rests on its determination of factual issues. Therefore, we will not overturn that finding unless it has no support in the record. Traditionally, we also have been reluctant to disturb findings of fact in which two courts below have concurred. Rogers v. Lodge, 458 U.S. 613 (1982). We therefore decline to overturn the finding of the District Court in this regard, where, as here, it has been affirmed by

---

[11] The District Court stated: "With few exceptions, enforcement of the subpoenas would compel [respondent] to admit that the records exist, that they are in his possession, and that they are authentic. These communications, if made under compulsion of a court decree, would violate [respondent's] Fifth Amendment rights. . . . The government argues that the existence, possession and authenticity of the documents can be proved without [respondent's] testimonial communication, but it cannot satisfy this court as to how that representation can be implemented to protect the witness in subsequent proceedings."

[12] The Court of Appeals stated: "In the matter sub judice, however, we find nothing in the record that would indicate that the United States knows, as a certainty, that each of the myriad documents demanded by the five subpoenas in fact is in the appellee's possession or subject to his control. The most plausible inference to be drawn from the broad-sweeping subpoenas is that the Government, unable to prove that the subpoenaed documents exist—or that the appellee even is somehow connected to the business entities under investigation—is attempting to compensate for its lack of knowledge by requiring the appellee to become, in effect, the primary informant against himself."

the Court of Appeals.[13]

*   *   * The Government, as it concedes, could have compelled respondent to produce the documents listed in the subpoena. Sections 6002 and 6003 of Title 18 provide for the granting of use immunity with respect to the potentially incriminating evidence. The Court upheld the constitutionality of the use immunity statute in Kastigar v. United States [p. 581]. The Government did state several times before the District Court that it would not use respondent's act of production against him in any way. But counsel for the Government never made a statutory request to the District Court to grant respondent use immunity. We are urged to adopt a doctrine of constructive use immunity. Under this doctrine, the courts would impose a requirement on the Government not to use the incriminatory aspects of the act of production against the person claiming the privilege even though the statutory procedures have not been followed.

We decline to extend the jurisdiction of courts to include prospective grants of use immunity in the absence of the formal request that the statute requires. As we stated in Pillsbury Co. v. Conbody, 459 U.S. 248 (1983), in passing the use immunity statute, "Congress gave certain officials in the Department of Justice exclusive authority to grant immunities." "Congress foresaw the courts as playing only a minor role in the immunizing process . . . ." Id. The decision to seek use immunity necessarily involves a balancing of the Government's interest in obtaining information against the risk that immunity will frustrate the Government's attempts to prosecute the subject of the investigation. Congress expressly left this decision exclusively to the Justice Department. If, on remand, the appropriate official concludes that it is desirable to compel respondent to produce his business records, the statutory procedure for requesting use immunity will be

---

[13] The Government concedes that the act of producing the subpoenaed documents might have had some testimonial aspects, but it argues that any incrimination would be so trivial that the Fifth Amendment is not implicated. * * * On the basis of the findings made in this case we think it clear that the risk of incrimination was "substantial and real" and not "trifling or imaginary." Respondent did not concede in the District Court that the records listed in the subpoena actually existed or were in his possession. Respondent argued that by producing the records, he would tacitly admit their existence and his possession. Respondent also pointed out that if the Government obtained the documents from another source, it would have to authenticate them before they would be admissible at trial. See Fed. R. Evid. 901. By producing the documents, respondent would relieve the Government of the need for authentication. These allegations were sufficient to establish a valid claim of the privilege against self-incrimination. This is not to say that the Government was foreclosed from rebutting respondent's claim by producing evidence that possession, existence, and authentication were a "foregone conclusion." *Fisher*. In this case, however, the Government failed to make such a showing.

available.[17]

We conclude that the Court of Appeals erred in holding that the contents of the subpoenaed documents were privileged under the Fifth Amendment. The act of producing the documents at issue in this case is privileged and cannot be compelled without a statutory grant of use immunity pursuant to 18 U.S.C. §§ 6002 and 6003. The judgment of the Court of Appeals is, therefore, affirmed in part, reversed in part, and the case is remanded to the District Court for further proceedings in accordance with this decision.

3. *The Demise of* **Boyd?** Justice O'Connor wrote a short concurring opinion in *Doe I*:

> just to make explicit what is implicit in the analysis of that opinion: that the Fifth Amendment provides absolutely no protection for the contents of private papers of any kind. The notion that the Fifth Amendment protects the privacy of papers originated in Boyd v. United States, but our decision in Fisher v. United States, sounded the death-knell for *Boyd*. "Several of Boyd's express or implicit declarations [had] not stood the test of time," *Fisher*, and its privacy of papers concept "had long been a rule searching for a rationale." Today's decision puts a long-overdue end to that fruitless search.

Justice Marshall, joined by Justice Brennan, rejected Justice O'Connor's assertion about the demise of *Boyd*:

> * * * Contrary to what Justice O'Connor contends, I do not view the Court's opinion in this case as having reconsidered whether the Fifth Amendment provides protection for the contents of "private papers of any kind." This case presented nothing remotely close to the question that Justice O'Connor eagerly poses and answers. First, as noted above, the issue whether the Fifth Amendment protects the contents of the documents was obviated by the Court of Appeals' rulings relating to the act of production and statutory use immunity. Second, the documents at stake here are business records which implicate a lesser degree of concern for privacy interests than, for example, personal diaries.

---

[17] Respondent argues that any grant of use immunity must cover the contents of the documents as well as the act of production. We find this contention unfounded. To satisfy the requirements of the Fifth Amendment, a grant of immunity need be only as broad as the privilege against self-incrimination. Murphy v. Waterfront Commission. As discussed above, the privilege in this case extends only to the act of production. Therefore. any grant of use immunity need only protect respondent from the self-incrimination that might accompany the act of producing his business records.

Were it true that the Court's opinion stands for the proposition that "the Fifth Amendment provides absolutely no protection for the contents of private papers of any kind," (O'Connor, J.), I would assuredly dissent. I continue to believe that under the Fifth Amendment "there are certain documents no person ought to be compelled to produce at the Government's request." Fisher v. United States (Justice Marshall, concurring).

Lower courts usually have found it unnecessary to decide whether anything remains of *Boyd's* Fifth Amendment analysis. "If the contents of papers are protected at all." they note, "it is only in rare situations, where compelled disclosure would break the heart of our sense of privacy." In re Steinberg, 837 F.2d 527 (1st Cir. 1988). While that might be the case for "intimate papers such as private diaries and drafts of letters or essays," it does not apply to the personal business or financial records that typically are being subpoenaed. United States v. Katin, 109 F.R.D. 406 (D. Mass. 1986). However, four courts of appeals have had before them cases in which the records being subpoenaed were of a sufficiently private character that the court deemed it appropriate to determine whether the *Boyd* analysis survives to protect voluntarily prepared personal documents. All four have held that it does not. See In re Grand Jury Subpoena Duces Tecum, 1 F.3d 87 (2d Cir. 1993) (collecting cases) ("The Supreme Court no longer views the Fifth Amendment as a general protector of privacy or private information but leaves that role to the Fourth Amendment. Self-incrimination analysis now focuses on whether the creation of the thing demanded was compelled and, if not, whether the act of production would constitute compelled testimonial communication.").

In Barrett v. Acevedo, 169 F.3d 1155 (8th Cir. 1999) (en banc), the Eighth Circuit found that *Boyd* did not prohibit a subpoena for an individual's personal journal when it was left in a public place: "Whatever the extent of Fifth Amendment protection for intensely personal and intimate documents in a defendant's possession, Barrett's journal is not entitled to such protection. * * * Barrett negligently abandoned whatever protections might inure to the contents of the journal as a personal document when he left it for perusal by any prying eyes at the fast food restaurant. The contents of the journal became known to law enforcement officers without any compulsion by the government. Accordingly, we hold that the Fifth Amendment does not protect the contents of Barrett's voluntarily created and negligently disclosed journal."

4. *Non-Testimonial Response.* In **Doe v. United States**, 487 U.S. 201 (1988) ("*Doe II*"), the Supreme Court relied upon the underlying rationale of the foregone conclusion doctrine in finding that still another form of response to a subpoena was not testimonial in character. The petitioner was the target of a grand jury investigation, and invoked the Fifth Amendment in refusing to provide documents related to bank accounts he had in the Bahamas and Cayman Islands. Branches of the banks located in the United States refused to provide account information because of bank secrecy laws in their home

country. The government moved for an order requiring Doe "to sign 12 forms consenting to disclosure of any bank records respectively relating to 12 foreign bank accounts over which the Government knew or suspected that Doe had control. The forms indicated the account numbers and described the documents that the Government wished the banks to produce." According to the government, "The form purported to apply to any and all accounts over which Doe had a right of withdrawal, without acknowledging the existence of any such account."[f]

Doe II concluded that even the act of making a verbal statement does not use to the level of a testimonial where the government's objective in forcing the subpoenaed party to make that statement is other than to have that person "relate a factual assertion or disclose information." *Doe II* held that signing the form did not compel "testimony" for Fifth Amendment purposes because "[a]s in *Fisher*, the Government is not relying upon the 'truthtelling' of Doe's directive to show the existence of, or his control over, foreign bank account records . . . By signing the form, Doe makes no statement, explicit or implicit, regarding the existence of a foreign bank account or his control over any such account. Nor would his execution of the form admit the authenticity of any records produced by the bank." This was so since the government did not seek to use the signed form itself as a factual assertion of the individual, although it intended to use the documents that might be produced by the bank in response to the signed directive as evidence against Doe in a later proceeding.

The *Doe II* Court noted that it had before it an unusual situation in which the verbal statement required of the subpoenaed party was not directed at requiring him to "convey information or assert facts." While it did

---

[f] The form the government sought to require Doe to sign stated:

I, _____, of the State of Texas in the United States of America, do hereby direct any bank or trust company at which I may have a bank account of any kind or at which a corporation has a bank account of any kind upon which I am authorized to draw, and its officers, employees and agents, to disclose all information and deliver copies of all documents of every nature in your possession or control which relate to said bank account to Grand Jury 84-2, empaneled May 7, 1984 and sitting in the Southern District of Texas, or to any attorney of the District of Texas, or to any attorney of the United States Department of Justice assisting said Grand Jury, and to give evidence relevant thereto, in the investigation conducted by Grand Jury 84-2 in the Southern District of Texas, and this shall be irrevocable authority for so doing. This direction has been executed pursuant to that certain order of the United States District Court for the Southern District of Texas issued in connection with the aforesaid investigation, dated _____. This direction is intended to apply to the Confidential Relationships (Preservation) Law of the Cayman Islands, and to any implied contract of confidentiality between Bermuda banks and their customers which may be imposed by Bermuda common law, and shall be construed as consent with respect thereto as the same shall apply to any of the bank accounts for which I may be a relevant principal.

constitute a communication, the government was directing the petitioner to do an act in a manner analogous to a directive requiring production of a handwriting sample or voice exemplar. Admittedly, the act could result in the production of evidence that would be used against the petitioner, but the directive did not "point the government toward hidden accounts or otherwise provide information that will assist the prosecution in uncovering evidence." It simply allowed the government through the directive, if accepted by the foreign bank, to seek evidence located through the government's own labor. Justice Stevens' dissent argued that the directive was no different than compelling a person to reveal the combination to his safe, but the majority characterized it as more like "requiring the individual to surrender a key to a strong box containing incriminating documents."

2. Foregone Conclusion Doctrine

As Justice Brennan noted in *Fisher*, in determining whether a witness' testimony might be viewed as incriminatory under the "link-in-the-chain" standard, courts do not look to whether the facts conveyed in the witness' testimony might be established by the government through other sources. Does the *Fisher/Doe* ruling that the privilege does not apply when "possession, existence and authentication" are a "foregone conclusion" require precisely that inquiry in determining the communicative aspects of the act of production? If so, why this special treatment for that act? Consider in this connection, Robert Mosteller, *Simplifying Subpoena Law: Taking the Fifth Amendment Seriously*, 73 VA. L. REV. 1, 32-33 (1987):

> More plausibly, the Court is suggesting [in its "foregone conclusion" analysis] that when an implicit as opposed to an explicit communication is involved, it is necessary to consider whether the government is really asking a "question" through the subpoena. Granted, the defendant's response to a documentary subpoena always reveals that the item does or does not exist; the government cannot eliminate the implicit question about the document's existence no matter how it phrases the subpoena's demand. But if the government already knows the answer to that question and is truly uninterested in the implicit answer provided by production, the witness' gratuitous communication of it should not violate the fifth amendment. In short, the *Fisher* decision suggests that constitutional rights are not violated by implicit communications that are inherent in a response to a documentary subpoena where those communications are unwanted because, though technically admissible, they are not substantially relevant to the prosecution's case given its other evidence.

UNITED STATES v. HUBBELL
530 U.S. 27, 120 S.Ct. 2037, 147 L.Ed.2d 24 (2000)

Justice STEVENS delivered the opinion of the Court.

The two questions presented concern the scope of a witness' protection against compelled self-incrimination: (1) whether the Fifth Amendment privilege protects a witness from being compelled to disclose the existence of incriminating documents that the Government is unable to describe with reasonable particularity; and (2) if the witness produces such documents pursuant to a grant of immunity, whether 18 U.S.C. § 6002 prevents the Government from using them to prepare criminal charges against him.

This proceeding arises out of the second prosecution of respondent, Webster Hubbell, commenced by the Independent Counsel appointed in August 1994 to investigate possible violations of federal law relating to the Whitewater Development Corporation. The first prosecution was terminated pursuant to a plea bargain. In December 1994, respondent pleaded guilty to charges of mail fraud and tax evasion arising out of his billing practices as a member of an Arkansas law firm from 1989 to 1992, and was sentenced to 21 months in prison. In the plea agreement, respondent promised to provide the Independent Counsel with "full, complete, accurate, and truthful information" about matters relating to the Whitewater investigation.

The second prosecution resulted from the Independent Counsel's attempt to determine whether respondent had violated that promise. In October 1996, while respondent was incarcerated, the Independent Counsel served him with a subpoena duces tecum calling for the production of 11 categories of documents before a grand jury sitting in Little Rock, Arkansas. See Appendix, infra.[a] On November 19, he appeared before the grand jury and invoked his Fifth Amendment privilege against self-incrimination. In response to questioning by the prosecutor, respondent initially refused "to state whether there are documents within my possession, custody, or control responsive to the Subpoena." Thereafter, the prosecutor produced an order, which had previously been obtained from the District Court pursuant to 18 U.S.C. § 6003(a) [p.635], directing him to respond to the subpoena and granting him immunity "to the extent allowed by law." Respondent then produced 13,120 pages of documents and records and responded to a series of questions that established that those were all of the documents in his custody or control that were responsive to the commands in the subpoena, with the exception of a few documents he claimed were shielded by the attorney-client and attorney work- product privileges.

---

[a] The Appendix to Justice Stevens' opinion set forth verbatim the "subpoena rider," which identified the 11 categories of documents in paragraphs (A)-(K). The rider is reprinted on p. 357.

The contents of the documents produced by respondent provided the Independent Counsel with the information that led to this second prosecution. On April 30, 1998, a grand jury in the District of Columbia returned a 10-count indictment charging respondent with various tax-related crimes and mail and wire fraud. The District Court dismissed the indictment relying, in part, on the ground that the Independent Counsel's use of the subpoenaed documents violated § 6002 because all of the evidence he would offer against respondent at trial derived either directly or indirectly from the testimonial aspects of respondent's immunized act of producing those documents. Noting that the Independent Counsel had admitted that he was not investigating tax-related issues when he issued the subpoena, and that he had "'learned about the unreported income and other crimes from studying the records' contents,'" the District Court characterized the subpoena as "the quintessential fishing expedition." * * *

The Court of Appeals vacated the judgment and remanded for further proceedings. The majority concluded that the District Court had incorrectly relied on the fact that the Independent Counsel did not have prior knowledge of the contents of the subpoenaed documents. The question the District Court should have addressed was the extent of the Government's independent knowledge of the documents' existence and authenticity, and of respondent's possession or control of them. It explained: "On remand, the district court should hold a hearing in which it seeks to establish the extent and detail of the [G]overnment's knowledge of Hubbell's financial affairs (or of the paperwork documenting it) on the day the subpoena issued. It is only then that the court will be in a position to assess the testimonial value of Hubbell's response to the subpoena. Should the Independent Counsel prove capable of demonstrating with reasonable particularity a prior awareness that the exhaustive litany of documents sought in the subpoena existed and were in Hubbell's possession, then the wide distance evidently traveled from the subpoena to the substantive allegations contained in the indictment would be based upon legitimate intermediate steps. To the extent that the information conveyed through Hubbell's compelled act of production provides the necessary linkage, however, the indictment deriving therefrom is tainted."

In the opinion of the dissenting judge, the majority failed to give full effect to the distinction between the contents of the documents and the limited testimonial significance of the act of producing them. In his view, as long as the prosecutor could make use of information contained in the documents or derived therefrom without any reference to the fact that respondent had produced them in response to a subpoena, there would be no improper use of the testimonial aspect of the immunized act of production. In other words, the constitutional privilege and the statute conferring use immunity would only shield the witness from the use of any information resulting from his subpoena response "beyond what the prosecutor would receive if the documents appeared in the grand jury room or in his office unsolicited and unmarked, like manna from heaven."

On remand, the Independent Counsel acknowledged that he could not satisfy the "reasonable particularity" standard prescribed by the Court of Appeals and entered into a conditional plea agreement with respondent. In essence, the agreement provides for the dismissal of the charges unless this Court's disposition of the case makes it reasonably likely that respondent's "act of production immunity" would not pose a significant bar to his prosecution. The case is not moot, however, because the agreement also provides for the entry of a guilty plea and a sentence that will not include incarceration if we should reverse and issue an opinion that is sufficiently favorable to the Government to satisfy that condition.   Despite that agreement, we granted the Independent Counsel's petition for a writ of certiorari in order to determine the precise scope of a grant of immunity with respect to the production of documents in response to a subpoena. We now affirm.

It is useful to preface our analysis of the constitutional issue with a restatement of certain propositions that are not in dispute. The term "privilege against self-incrimination" is not an entirely accurate description of a person's constitutional protection against being "compelled in any criminal case to be a witness against himself." The word "witness" in the constitutional text limits the relevant category of compelled incriminating communications to those that are "testimonial" in character.[8] As Justice Holmes observed, there is a significant difference between the use of compulsion to extort communications from a defendant and compelling a person to engage in conduct that may be incriminating. Thus, even though the act may provide incriminating evidence, a criminal suspect may be compelled to put on a shirt, to provide a blood sample or handwriting exemplar, or to make a recording of his voice. The act of exhibiting such physical characteristics is not the same as a sworn communication by a witness that relates either express or implied assertions of fact or belief. * * *

More relevant to this case is the settled proposition that a person may be required to produce specific documents even though they contain incriminating assertions of fact or belief because the creation of those documents was not "compelled" within the meaning of the privilege. [Fisher v. United States, p. 648]. * * * It is clear, therefore, that respondent Hubbell could not avoid compliance with the subpoena served on him merely because the demanded documents contained incriminating evidence, whether written

---

[8] "It is consistent with the history of and the policies underlying the Self-Incrimination Clause to hold that the privilege may be asserted only to resist compelled explicit or implicit disclosures of incriminating information. Historically, the privilege was intended to prevent the use of legal compulsion to extract from the accused a sworn communication of facts which would incriminate him. Such was the process of the ecclesiastical courts and the Star Chamber—the inquisitorial method of putting the accused upon his oath and compelling him to answer questions designed to uncover uncharged offenses, without evidence from another source. * * *" *Doe II.*

by others or voluntarily prepared by himself. * * * On the other hand, we have also made it clear that the act of producing documents in response to a subpoena may have a compelled testimonial aspect. We have held that "the act of production" itself may implicitly communicate "statements of fact" [*Doe II*]. By "producing documents in compliance with a subpoena, the witness would admit that the papers existed, were in his possession or control, and were authentic." Moreover, as was true in this case, when the custodian of documents responds to a subpoena, he may be compelled to take the witness stand and answer questions designed to determine whether he has produced everything demanded by the subpoena. The answers to those questions, as well as the act of production itself, may certainly communicate information about the existence, custody, and authenticity of the documents. Whether the constitutional privilege protects the answers to such questions, or protects the act of production itself, is a question that is distinct from the question whether the unprotected contents of the documents themselves are incriminating.

Finally, the phrase "in any criminal case" in the text of the Fifth Amendment might have been read to limit its coverage to compelled testimony that is used against the defendant in the trial itself. It has, however, long been settled that its protection encompasses compelled statements that lead to the discovery of incriminating evidence even though the statements themselves are not incriminating and are not introduced into evidence. * * * Compelled testimony that communicates information that may "lead to incriminating evidence" is privileged even if the information itself is not inculpatory. * * * It is the Fifth Amendment's protection against the prosecutor's use of incriminating information derived directly or indirectly from the compelled testimony of the respondent that is of primary relevance in this case.

Acting pursuant to 18 U.S.C. § 6002, the District Court entered an order compelling respondent to produce "any and all documents" described in the grand jury subpoena and granting him "immunity to the extent allowed by law." In Kastigar v. United States [p. 581], we upheld the constitutionality of § 6002 because the scope of the "use and derivative-use" immunity that it provides is coextensive with the scope of the constitutional privilege against self-incrimination. * * * We particularly emphasized the critical importance of protection against a future prosecution "'based on knowledge and sources of information obtained from the compelled testimony.'" * * * [W]e held that the statute imposes an affirmative duty on the prosecution, not merely to show that its evidence is not tainted by the prior testimony, but "to prove that the evidence it proposes to use is derived from a legitimate source wholly independent of the compelled testimony." * * * The "compelled testimony" that is relevant in this case is not to be found in the contents of the documents produced in response to the subpoena. It is, rather, the testimony inherent in the act of producing those documents. The disagreement between the parties focuses entirely on the significance of that testimonial aspect.

The Government correctly emphasizes that the testimonial aspect of a response to a subpoena duces tecum does nothing more than establish the existence, authenticity, and custody of items that are produced. We assume that the Government is also entirely correct in its submission that it would not have to advert to respondent's act of production in order to prove the existence, authenticity, or custody of any documents that it might offer in evidence at a criminal trial; indeed, the Government disclaims any need to introduce any of the documents produced by respondent into evidence in order to prove the charges against him. It follows, according to the Government, that it has no intention of making improper "use" of respondent's compelled testimony. The question, however, is not whether the response to the subpoena may be introduced into evidence at his criminal trial. That would surely be a prohibited "use" of the immunized act of production. But the fact that the Government intends no such use of the act of production leaves open the separate question whether it has already made "derivative use" of the testimonial aspect of that act in obtaining the indictment against respondent and in preparing its case for trial. It clearly has.

It is apparent from the text of the subpoena itself that the prosecutor needed respondent's assistance both to identify potential sources of information and to produce those sources. See Appendix [fn. a supra]. Given the breadth of the description of the 11 categories of documents called for by the subpoena, the collection and production of the materials demanded was tantamount to answering a series of interrogatories asking a witness to disclose the existence and location of particular documents fitting certain broad descriptions. The assembly of literally hundreds of pages of material in response to a request for "any and all documents reflecting, referring, or relating to any direct or indirect sources of money or other things of value received by or provided to" an individual or members of his family during a 3-year period, is the functional equivalent of the preparation of an answer to either a detailed written interrogatory or a series of oral questions at a discovery deposition. Entirely apart from the contents of the 13,120 pages of materials that respondent produced in this case, it is undeniable that providing a catalog of existing documents fitting within any of the 11 broadly worded subpoena categories could provide a prosecutor with a "lead to incriminating evidence," or "a link in the chain of evidence needed to prosecute."

Indeed, the record makes it clear that that is what happened in this case. The documents were produced before a grand jury sitting in the Eastern District of Arkansas in aid of the Independent Counsel's attempt to determine whether respondent had violated a commitment in his first plea agreement. The use of those sources of information eventually led to the return of an indictment by a grand jury sitting in the District of Columbia for offenses that apparently are unrelated to that plea agreement. What the District Court characterized as a "fishing expedition" did produce a fish, but not the one that the Independent Counsel expected to hook. It is abundantly clear that the testimonial aspect of respondent's act of producing subpoenaed documents was the first step in a chain of evidence that led to this prosecution. The documents did not magically appear in the prosecutor's office like "manna from heaven." They arrived there only after respondent asserted his constitutional privilege, received a grant of immunity, and—under the compulsion of the District Court's order—took the mental and physical steps necessary to provide the prosecutor with an accurate inventory of the many sources of potentially incriminating evidence sought by the subpoena. It was only through respondent's truthful reply to the subpoena that the Government received the incriminating documents of which it made "substantial use . . . in the investigation that led to the indictment."

For these reasons, we cannot accept the Government's submission that respondent's immunity did not preclude its derivative use of the produced documents because its "possession of the documents [was] the fruit only of a simple physical act–the act of producing the documents." It was unquestionably necessary for respondent to make extensive use of "the contents of his own mind" in identifying the hundreds of documents responsive to the requests in the subpoena. The assembly of those documents was like telling an inquisitor the combination to a wall safe, not like being forced to surrender the key to a strongbox. *Doe II*. The Government's anemic view of respondent's act of production as a mere physical act that is principally non-testimonial in character and can be entirely divorced from its "implicit" testimonial aspect so as to constitute a "legitimate, wholly independent source" (as required by *Kastigar*) for the documents produced simply fails to account for these realities.

In sum, we have no doubt that the constitutional privilege against self-incrimination protects the target of a grand jury investigation from being compelled to answer questions designed to elicit information about the existence of sources of potentially incriminating evidence. That constitutional privilege has the same application to the testimonial aspect of a response to a subpoena seeking discovery of those sources. Before the District Court, the Government arguably conceded that respondent's act of production in this case had a testimonial aspect that entitled him to respond to the subpoena by asserting his privilege against self-incrimination. * * * On appeal and again before this Court, however, the Government has argued that the communicative aspect of respondent's act of producing ordinary business records is insufficiently "testimonial" to support a claim of privilege because the existence and possession of such records by any businessman is a "foregone conclusion" under our decision in Fisher v. United States. This argument both misreads *Fisher* and ignores our subsequent decision in *Doe I*. * * * Whatever the scope of this "foregone conclusion" rationale, the facts of this case plainly fall outside of it. While in *Fisher* the Government already knew that the documents were in the attorneys' possession and could independently confirm their existence and authenticity through the accountants who created them, here the Government has not shown that it had any prior knowledge of either the existence or the whereabouts of the 13,120 pages of documents ultimately produced by respondent. The

Government cannot cure this deficiency through the overbroad argument that a businessman such as respondent will always possess general business and tax records that fall within the broad categories described in this subpoena. The *Doe I* subpoenas also sought several broad categories of general business records, yet we upheld the District Court's finding that the act of producing those records would involve testimonial self-incrimination.

Given our conclusion that respondent's act of production had a testimonial aspect, at least with respect to the existence and location of the documents sought by the Government's subpoena, respondent could not be compelled to produce those documents without first receiving a grant of immunity under § 6003. As we construed § 6002 in *Kastigar*, such immunity is co-extensive with the constitutional privilege. *Kastigar* requires that respondent's motion to dismiss the indictment on immunity grounds be granted unless the Government proves that the evidence it used in obtaining the indictment and proposed to use at trial was derived from legitimate sources "wholly independent" of the testimonial aspect of respondent's immunized conduct in assembling and producing the documents described in the subpoena. The Government, however, does not claim that it could make such a showing. Rather, it contends that its prosecution of respondent must be considered proper unless someone—presumably respondent—shows that "there is some substantial relation between the compelled testimonial communications implicit in the act of production (as opposed to the act of production standing alone) and some aspect of the information used in the investigation or the evidence presented at trial." Brief for United States 9. We could not accept this submission without repudiating the basis for our conclusion in *Kastigar* that the statutory guarantee of use and derivative-use immunity is as broad as the constitutional privilege itself. This we are not prepared to do. Accordingly, the indictment against respondent must be dismissed. The judgment of the Court of Appeals is affirmed. * * *

Chief Justice REHNQUIST dissents and would reverse the judgment of the Court of Appeals in part, for the reasons given by Judge Williams in his dissenting opinion in that court.

Justice THOMAS, with whom Justice SCALIA joins, concurring.

Our decision today involves the application of the act-of-production doctrine, which provides that persons compelled to turn over incriminating papers or other physical evidence pursuant to a subpoena duces tecum or a summons may invoke the Fifth Amendment privilege against self-incrimination as a bar to production only where the act of producing the evidence would contain "testimonial" features. I join the opinion of the Court because it properly applies this doctrine, but I write separately to note that this doctrine may be inconsistent with the original meaning of the Fifth Amendment's Self-Incrimination Clause. A substantial body of evidence suggests that the Fifth Amendment privilege protects against the compelled production not just of incriminating testimony, but of any incriminating evidence. In a future case, I would be willing to reconsider the scope and meaning of the Self-Incrimination Clause.

The Fifth Amendment provides that "[n]o person . . . shall be compelled in any criminal case to be a witness against himself." The key word at issue in this case is "witness." The Court's opinion, relying on prior cases, essentially defines "witness" as a person who provides testimony, and thus restricts the Fifth Amendment's ban to only those communications "that are 'testimonial' in character." None of this Court's cases, however, has undertaken an analysis of the meaning of the term at the time of the founding. A review of that period reveals substantial support for the view that the term "witness" meant a person who gives or furnishes evidence, a broader meaning than that which our case law currently ascribes to the term. If this is so, a person who responds to a subpoena duces tecum would be just as much a "witness" as a person who responds to a subpoena ad testificandum.[1]

Dictionaries published around the time of the founding included definitions of the term "witness" as a person who gives or furnishes evidence. Legal dictionaries of that period defined "witness" as someone who "gives evidence in a cause." * * * Such a meaning of "witness" is consistent with, and may help explain, the history and framing of the Fifth Amendment. The 18th century common-law privilege against self-incrimination protected against the compelled production of incriminating physical evidence such as papers and documents. And this Court has noted that, for generations before the framing, "one cardinal rule of the court of chancery [wa]s never to decree a discovery which might tend to convict the party of a crime." Boyd v. United States. * * * Against this common-law backdrop, the privilege against self-incrimination was enshrined in the Virginia Declaration of Rights in 1776. * * * Following Virginia's lead, seven of the other original States included specific provisions in their Constitutions granting a right against compulsion "to give evidence" or "to furnish evidence." * * * And during ratification of the Federal Constitution, the four States that proposed bills of rights put forward draft proposals employing similar wording for a federal constitutional provision guaranteeing the right against compelled self-incrimination. Each of the proposals broadly sought to protect a citizen from "be[ing] compelled to give evidence against himself." * * * Similarly worded proposals to protect against compelling a person "to furnish evidence" against himself came from prominent voices outside the conventions. See Letter of Brutus, No. 2 (1788).

---

[1]Even if the term "witness" in the Fifth Amendment referred to someone who provides testimony, as this Court's recent cases suggest without historical analysis, it may well be that at the time of the founding a person who turned over documents would be described as providing testimony. See Amey v. Long, 9 East. 472, 484, 103 Eng. Rep. 653, 658 (K.B.1808) (referring to documents requested by subpoenas duces tecum as "written ... testimony"). * * *

In response to such calls, James Madison penned the Fifth Amendment. In so doing, Madison substituted the phrase "to be a witness" for the proposed language "to give evidence" and "to furnish evidence." But it seems likely that Madison's phrasing was synonymous with that of the proposals. The definitions of the word "witness" and the background history of the privilege against self-incrimination, both discussed above, support this view. And this may explain why Madison's unique phrasing–phrasing that none of the proposals had suggested–apparently attracted no attention, much less opposition, in Congress, the state legislatures that ratified the Bill of Rights, or anywhere else. * * *

In addition, a broad definition of the term "witness"–one who gives evidence–is consistent with the same term (albeit in plural form) in the Sixth Amendment's Compulsory Process Clause. That Clause provides that "[i]n all criminal prosecutions, the accused shall enjoy the right . . . to have compulsory process for obtaining witnesses in his favor." Soon after the adoption of the Bill of Rights, Chief Justice Marshall had occasion to interpret the Compulsory Process Clause while presiding over the treason trial of Aaron Burr. Burr moved for the issuance of a subpoena duces tecum to obtain from President Jefferson a letter that was said to incriminate Burr. The Government objected, arguing that compulsory process under the Sixth Amendment permits a defendant to secure a subpoena ad testificandum, but not a subpoena duces tecum. The Chief Justice dismissed the argument, holding that the right to compulsory process includes the right to secure papers–in addition to testimony–material to the defense. This Court has subsequently expressed agreement with this view of the Sixth Amendment. See United States v. Nixon, 418 U.S. 683 (1974). Although none of our opinions has focused upon the precise language or history of the Compulsory Process Clause, a narrow definition of the term "witness" as a person who testifies seems incompatible with *Burr*'s holding. And if the term "witnesses" in the Compulsory Process Clause has an encompassing meaning, this provides reason to believe that the term "witness" in the Self-Incrimination Clause has the same broad meaning. Yet this Court's recent Fifth Amendment act-of-production cases implicitly rest upon an assumption that this term has different meanings in adjoining provisions of the Bill of Rights. * * *

This Court has not always taken the approach to the Fifth Amendment that we follow today. The first case interpreting the Self-Incrimination Clause–Boyd v. United States–was decided, though not explicitly, in accordance with the understanding that "witness" means one who gives evidence. In *Boyd*, this Court unanimously held that the Fifth Amendment protects a defendant against compelled production of books and papers. And the Court linked its interpretation of the Fifth Amendment to the common-law understanding of the self-incrimination privilege. But this Court's decision in Fisher v. United States, rejected this understanding, permitting the Government to force a person to furnish incriminating physical evidence and protecting only the "testimonial" aspects of that transfer. In so doing, *Fisher* not only failed to examine the historical backdrop to the Fifth Amendment, it also required–as illustrated by extended discussion in the opinions below in this case–a difficult parsing of the act of responding to a subpoena duces tecum. None of the parties in this case has asked us to depart from *Fisher*, but in light of the historical evidence that the Self-Incrimination Clause may have a broader reach than Fisher holds, I remain open to a reconsideration of that decision and its progeny in a proper case.

NOTES AND QUESTIONS

The Effect of Hubbell. Professor Cole noted the potential effect of the Court's analysis of the effect of a grant of immunity for the act of production on *Fisher*:

> *Hubbell* has, at least in practical effect, overruled *Fisher* and restored full, meaningful (as opposed to "act of production") Fifth Amendment protection to most private papers in the possession of an individual. After *Hubbell*, prosecutors are no longer free to use the contents of documents to prosecute a witness after they have immunized that witness's act of producing those documents. If prosecutors can show prior knowledge of the existence, location, and authenticity of the documents, then the act of production has no testimonial value, and a court must reject a witness's assertion of an act of production privilege. In that case, the prosecution can obtain the documents without an immunity grant and is free to use both the act of production and the contents of the documents to prosecute the witness.
>
> What remains of *Fisher* after *Hubbell*? Everything or nothing, depending on the case. The distinction between the contents of documents and the act of producing documents remains viable, but the significance of that distinction will vary based upon what knowledge the prosecution has when it seeks to compel production of documents. If the government can show prior knowledge of the existence, location, and authenticity of the documents, as it did in *Fisher*, then the act of production privilege is not available to the witness. In those cases, the *Fisher* distinction between contents and the act of production remains valid because the government need not show any knowledge of the contents of the documents. For example, if the government can show that it knows the witness keeps a diary and that the diary is in the witness's possession, then the government can compel production, even if the government has no idea what the diary says. On the other hand, if the government lacks knowledge of whether the witness possesses a particular document or class of documents and is merely engaged in a "fishing expedition," then a witness can assert the act of production privilege, and the three-step, post- *Hubbell* act of production analysis applies.

In those cases, little, if anything, remains of the *Fisher* distinction between contents and the act of production.

Lance Cole, *The Fifth Amendment and Compelled Production of Personal Documents After* United States v. Hubbell*: New Protection for Private Papers?*, 29 AM. J. CRIM. L. 123 (2002).

3. Proving Existence, Possession, and Authenticity

IN RE GRAND JURY SUBPOENA DATED APRIL 18, 2003
383 F.3d 905 (9th Cir. 2004)

CANBY, Circuit Judge.

Appellant John Doe was held in contempt by the district court and he appeals, challenging the district court's denial of his motion to quash a subpoena duces tecum. * * *

This appeal presents a challenge to one of several subpoenas issued in connection with the government's investigation into antitrust violations in the Dynamic Random Access Memory (DRAM) semiconductor memory chip industry. On June 17, 2002, a grand jury sitting in the Northern District of California issued subpoenas duces tecum to all the major worldwide DRAM manufacturers, including Doe's former employer (the "Corporation"). The subpoena served on the Corporation covered the period from January 1, 1998, through the date of the subpoena and requested, among other things, all documents relating to contacts and communications among competitors regarding the sale of DRAM. The subpoena also asked the Corporation for the names of all its current and former employees who had any responsibility for pricing DRAM, as well as the calendars, appointment books, telephone directories, and travel and entertainment expense records on file for those employees.

The Corporation identified Doe as an employee who was responsible for pricing DRAM. Doe worked for the Corporation from 1991 through 1998. The documents produced by the Corporation in response to the subpoena did not reveal any calendars, appointment books, notebooks, address books, or business diaries for Doe. These types of materials were found in the employee records of other DRAM salesmen, including Doe's successor.

During the government's investigation, a cooperating witness from another DRAM manufacturer provided detailed information regarding meetings and telephone conversations he had with Doe, in which they discussed the price at which the Corporation and its competitors would sell DRAM to computer manufacturers. After the government obtained this information, FBI agents interviewed Doe at his home in April 2003. During the interview, Doe indicated that he had shared DRAM pricing information with competitors, including the government's cooperating witness. Doe further stated that he had memorialized these conversations in e-mails to his supervisors. Doe stated, however, that he did not believe he had any records, notes, or documents related to the government's investigation because he had left such records at the Corporation. At the end of the interview, the agents served Doe with a subpoena duces tecum, which is the subject of this appeal. The subpoena commanded Doe to appear and testify before the grand jury and bring with him all documents in his possession "relating to the production or sale of Dynamic Random Access Memory ('DRAM') components, including but not limited to, handwritten notes, calendars, diaries, daybooks, appointment calendars, or notepads, or any similar documents." * * *

Doe, claiming a Fifth Amendment privilege against self-incrimination, informed the government that he would not testify without immunity and would not produce the subpoenaed documents. The government postponed indefinitely Doe's appearance before the grand jury, but did not relieve him of his obligation to produce the documents described in the subpoena duces tecum, nor did the government offer Doe immunity under 18 U.S.C. § 6003. Instead, the government informed counsel for the Corporation that Doe might have documents responsive to the subpoenas served on the Corporation. The Corporation requested from Doe "any company records or property" that may be in Doe's possession and covered by the Proprietary Information Agreement or the Exit Interview statement that Doe had signed. Without admitting that he had any company records in his possession, Doe declined to produce any such documents to the Corporation.

Doe then moved to quash the subpoena that had been served on him, claiming that the act of producing the documents responsive to the subpoena would violate his Fifth Amendment rights. The district court denied the motion to quash, finding that the existence of Doe's documents was a "foregone conclusion," and therefore the act of producing the documents was not testimonial in nature. Doe again refused to turn over any documents and was held in contempt by the district court pursuant to a Stipulation and Order of Contempt. Doe timely appealed, and enforcement of the contempt order has been stayed pending appeal. * * *

Where the preparation of business records is voluntary, there is no compulsion present, and consequently the contents of those records are not privileged by the Fifth Amendment. It is not contested that the documents in Doe's possession were created voluntarily during the course of his employment with the Corporation. The contents of those documents are therefore not protected by the Fifth Amendment.

Doe's claim of privilege is directed, however, not to the documents themselves but to the act of producing the documents. A witness' production of documents in response to a subpoena may have incriminating testimonial aspects. See United States v. Hubbell, 530 U.S. 27 (2000) (Hubbell II). By producing documents in compliance with a subpoena, the witness admits that the documents exist, are in his possession or control, and are authentic.

These types of admissions implicitly communicate statements of fact that may lead to incriminating evidence. Whether the act of production has a testimonial aspect sufficient to attract Fifth Amendment protection is a fact-intensive inquiry.

When the "existence and location" of the documents under subpoena are a "foregone conclusion" and the witness "adds little or nothing to the sum total of the Government's information by conceding that he in fact has the[documents]," then no Fifth Amendment right is touched because the "question is not of testimony but of surrender." Fisher. When deciding whether the government has met its burdens of production and proof, courts should look to the "quantum of information possessed by the government before it issued the relevant subpoena." United States v. Hubbell, 167 F.3d 552 (D.C.Cir. 1999) (Hubbell I).

At the time the government served the subpoena on Doe, the government possessed insufficient information to make the existence or possession of all of Doe's documents relating to the production or sale of DRAM, "including, but not limited to, handwritten notes, calendars, diaries, daybooks, appointment calendars, or notepads, or any similar documents" a foregone conclusion. The government was not required to have actual knowledge of the existence and location of each and every responsive document; the government was required, however, to establish the existence of the documents sought and Doe's possession of them with "reasonable particularity" before the existence and possession of the documents could be considered a foregone conclusion and production therefore would not be testimonial.

Although the government possessed extensive knowledge about Doe's price-fixing activities as a result of interviews with cooperating witnesses and Doe's own incriminating statements made to federal agents on April 26, 2003, it is the government's knowledge of the existence and possession of the actual documents, not the information contained therein, that is central to the foregone conclusion inquiry. The breadth of the subpoena in this case far exceeded the government's knowledge about the actual documents that Doe created or possessed during his former employment and that he retained after he terminated his employment. The government probably could identify with sufficient particularity the existence of e-mails between Doe and some of his competitors, e-mails between Doe and his superiors regarding pricing, phone records corroborating that Doe spoke to his competitors, and records establishing meetings with certain competitors because Doe made substantial admissions to investigators during his living room interview regarding these documents. The government, however, failed to draft the subpoena narrowly to identify the documents that it could establish with reasonable particularity. Thus, on the record before us, the subpoena's breadth far exceeded the reasonably particular knowledge that the government actually possessed when it served the subpoena on Doe.

The Supreme Court has stated on more than one occasion that such broad language contributes to a finding that the response to a subpoena may be testimonial. In *Hubbell*, the Supreme Court noted:

> It is apparent from the text of the subpoena itself that the prosecutor needed respondent's assistance both to identify potential sources of information and to produce those sources . . . . Given the breadth of the description of the 11 categories of documents called for by the subpoena, the collection and production of the materials demanded was tantamount to answering a series of interrogatories asking a witness to disclose the existence and location of particular documents fitting certain broad descriptions.

A subpoena such as this, which seeks all documents within a category but fails to describe those documents with any specificity indicates that the government needs the act of production to build its case against Doe.

This conclusion is supported by the timing of the subpoena in Doe's case. When the government issued its April 26, 2003, subpoena duces tecum to Doe, it had not yet served the May 19, 2003, second document subpoena on Doe's former employer, the response to which subsequently led the government to conclude that Doe possessed business records that were created during his former employment. It is the "quantum of information possessed by the government before it issue[s] the relevant subpoena" that is central to the foregone conclusion inquiry. See Hubbell I. At the time the government served the subpoena duces tecum on Doe, it had no reason to believe that Doe possessed the myriad of documents it sought. The argument that a salesman such as Doe will always possess business records describing or memorializing meetings or prices does not establish the reasonably particular knowledge required. It was therefore improper for the district court to consider evidence of Doe's business records produced by Doe's former employer in response to the May 19, 2003, subpoena to support the foregone conclusion inquiry.

The authenticity prong of the foregone conclusion doctrine requires the government to establish that it can independently verify that the compelled documents "are in fact what they purport to be." Independent verification not only requires the government to show that the documents sought to be compelled would be admissible independent of the witness' production of them, but also inquires into whether the government is compelling the witness to use his discretion in selecting and assembling the responsive documents, and thereby tacitly providing identifying information that is necessary to the government's authentication of the subpoenaed documents.

In this case, the district court simply stated it would "hold the government to its representation that [Doe's] testimony via production of these documents will not be needed for authentication," without explaining why this was an appropriate solution to overcome Doe's Fifth Amendment challenge. The subpoena commanded Doe to produce all documents "relating to the production or sale of Dynamic Random Access Memory ("DRAM") components, including but not limited to, handwritten notes, calendars, diaries, daybooks, appointment calendars, or notepads, or any similar documents." It thus sought many documents that Doe created himself. It further required him to discriminate among the many documents he might possess, requiring him specifically to identify and produce to the grand jury those that related to the production or sale of DRAM.

Although the government could probably authenticate the writing on Doe's handwritten documents through handwriting analysis, it made little effort to demonstrate how anyone beside Doe could sift through his handwritten notes, personal appointment books, and diaries to produce what Doe's attorney estimates may be 4,500 documents related to the production or sale of DRAM. Such a response by Doe would provide the government with the identifying information that it would need to authenticate these documents. Doe's notes to himself would be difficult, if not impossible, to authenticate by anyone besides Doe. * * *

In this case, the government has failed to demonstrate that it can authenticate the documents so broadly described in the subpoena without the identifying information that Doe would provide by using his knowledge and judgment to sift through, select, assemble, and produce the documents.

This case is a far cry from Fisher, where the government had prior knowledge that the documents were in the custodian's possession and the government could independently confirm their existence and authenticity through the accountants who created them. The government in Fisher did not need to rely on the "'truth-telling' of the taxpayer to prove the existence of or his access to the documents." Here, as in Hubbell, the government simply has not shown that it had prior knowledge of the existence of the estimated 4,500 documents.

The district court erred when it determined that the act of producing these documents was not testimonial because their existence, possession, and authenticity was a "foregone conclusion." We accordingly reverse its order denying on that ground Doe's motion to quash the subpoena, and its order holding Doe in contempt. * * *

NOTES

1. *Potential Incrimination.* Assuming that the government does not establish that possession, authentication, and existence are a foregone conclusion, under what circumstances will the privilege nonetheless not be applicable because the likelihood of incrimination is not "substantial and real" ? Note in this regard *Fisher*'s comments on the incriminatory aspects of producing records that were authored by another and clearly could be lawfully possessed. What did the Court mean when it said that "at this juncture," it was unwilling to hold that either the existence of the papers or

their possession posed a realistic threat of incrimination? Assuming that the contents of the papers were incriminatory, wouldn't acknowledgment of their existence pose a realistic threat of incrimination as found in *Doe I*? Assuming that the contents were incriminatory, wouldn't possession suggest knowledge of that content and thereby pose a realistic threat? Is the answer that the Court in *Fisher* may not have been willing to conclude, on the record before it in the context of an IRS investigation (rather than a grand jury investigation), that a realistic threat existed that the contents were incriminatory? In a criminal investigation, unlike a civil IRS investigation, it may be easier for the subpoena recipient to establish the potential incrimination from responding to the demand for records, and so assert the Fifth Amendment privilege.

2. *How Much Knowledge Is Required.* The need for care in providing immunity to obtain documents pursuant to a subpoena *duces tecum* was emphasized in **United States v. Ponds**, 454 F.3d 313 (D.C Cir. 2006). The District of Columbia Circuit reversed the conviction of the defendant – a criminal defense lawyer being investigated for his fee arrangements with a client who was a drug dealer – who provided documents to the grand jury only after a grant of immunity. The court stated:

> [T]he government has failed to show with reasonable particularity that it had prior knowledge of the existence and location of many of the subpoenaed documents necessary to render their existence and location a "foregone conclusion." The Supreme Court has not defined the precise amount of cognition on the part of an immunized party necessary to render a subpoena response "testimonial," but it is clear here that, as in *Hubbell*, the government "needed [Ponds'] assistance both to identify potential sources of information and to produce those sources," and "it is undeniable that providing a catalog of existing documents" rendered this subpoena response "testimony" rather than mere "surrender." So much is evident in the government's admission that it was "surprised" by some of the documents produced.

3. *Failing to Assert the Act of Production Privilege.* In **United States v. Grable**, 98 F.3d 251 (6th Cir. 1996), the Sixth Circuit stated:

> The government * * * contends that because the defendant did not assert his 'act of production' privilege at the enforcement hearing (which he neglected to attend), he was consequently precluded from asserting it at the later contempt hearing. In support of this argument, the government relies on United States v. Rylander, 460 U.S. 752 (1983), in which the Supreme Court prohibited a taxpayer from raising at a civil contempt hearing, for the first time, a defense of lack of possession and control of the corporate documents sought by an IRS summons.

The Courts of Appeals for the Fourth and Ninth Circuits appear to have rejected similar arguments. See United States v. Sharp, 920 F.2d 1167 (4th Cir.1990) (*Rylander* does not require barring a taxpayer from relying on the Fifth Amendment at a contempt hearing because he failed to assert the privilege 'in a technically proper form while unrepresented by counsel.'); United States v. Rendahl, 746 F.2d 553 (9th Cir.1984) (A defendant is not barred from claiming a Fifth Amendment privilege at a contempt hearing because of his failure to raise the claim at an enforcement hearing.).

The government's position is based either on a claim of waiver or res judicata resulting from the taxpayer's failure to claim the privilege at the enforcement hearing. Viewed either way, we cannot resolve the question from the record made in the district court. Upon remand the district court will make a determination, following such proceedings as it finds necessary, as to whether any earlier act (or failure to act) of Grable's barred him from claiming the privilege at the contempt hearing. In this regard, we note that the ruling in *Sharp* appears to have been based, in part at least, on the fact that the taxpayer was unrepresented by counsel and thus presented the defense in a form that was not technically proper. We agree that this is an important factor in determining whether a party has forfeited a constitutional privilege. It is not clear from the record before us that Grable was not represented by counsel when he failed to appear for the enforcement proceeding or the show cause hearing before the magistrate.

B. ENTITY DOCUMENTS

1. Collective Entity Doctrine

BRASWELL v. UNITED STATES
487 U.S. 99, 108 S.Ct. 2284, 101 L.Ed.2d 98 (1988)

Chief Justice REHNQUIST delivered the opinion of the Court.

This case presents the question whether the custodian of corporate records may resist a subpoena for such records on the ground that the act of production would incriminate him in violation of the Fifth Amendment. We conclude that he may not. * * *

[A federal grand jury issued a subpoena to petitioner Braswell as the president of two corporations, requiring him to produce the books and records of the two corporations, Worldwide Machinery, Inc. and Worldwide Purchasing, Inc. Petitioner had funded Worldwide Purchasing with his 100 percent interest in Worldwide Machinery and was the sole shareholder of Worldwide Purchasing. While both corporations had three directors, petitioner, his wife, and his mother, only petitioner had authority over the business affairs of the corporations. The grand jury subpoena provided that petitioner could deliver the records to the grand jury agent serving the subpoena and did not require petitioner to testify. Petitioner moved to quash the subpoena, arguing that the act or producing the records would continue a violation of his Fifth Amendment privilege against self-incrimination. The district court denied the motion and the Fifth Circuit affirmed.]

There is no question but that the contents of the subpoenaed business records are not privileged. See United States v. Doe; Fisher v. United States. Similarly, petitioner asserts no self-incrimination claim on behalf of the corporations; it is well established that such artificial entities are not protected by the Fifth Amendment. Bellis v. United States, 417 U.S. 85 (1974). Petitioner instead relies solely upon the argument that his act of producing the documents has independent testimonial significance, which would incriminate him individually, and that the Fifth Amendment prohibits government compulsion of that act. The bases for this argument are extrapolated from the decisions of this Court in *Fisher* and *Doe.* * * *

Had petitioner conducted his business as a sole proprietorship, *Doe* would require that he be provided the opportunity to show that his act of production would entail testimonial self-incrimination. But petitioner has operated his business through the corporate form, and we have long recognized that for purposes of the Fifth Amendment, corporations and other collective entities are treated differently from individuals. This doctrine—known as the collective entity rule—has a lengthy and distinguished pedigree.

The rule was first articulated by the Court in the case of *Hale v. Henkel* [p. 391]. Hale, a corporate officer, had been served with a subpoena ordering him to produce corporate records and to testify concerning certain corporate transactions. Although Hale was protected by personal immunity, he sought to resist the demand for the records by interposing a Fifth Amendment privilege on behalf of the corporation. The Court rejected that argument: "We are of the opinion that there is a clear distinction * * * between an individual and a corporation, and * * * the latter has no right to refuse to submit its books and papers for an examination at the suit of the State." The Court explained that the corporation "is a creature of the State," with powers limited by the State. As such, the State may, in the exercise of its right to oversee the corporation, demand the production of corporate records. * * *

Although *Hale* settled that a corporation has no Fifth Amendment privilege, the Court did not address whether a corporate officer could resist a subpoena for corporate records by invoking his personal privilege–Hale had been protected by immunity. In Wilson v. United States, 221 U.S. 361 (1911), the Court answered that question in the negative. * * * Wilson refused to produce [subpoenaed corporate] books, arguing that the Fifth Amendment prohibited compulsory production of personally incriminating books that he held and controlled. The Court rejected this argument, observing * * *:

"[Wilson] held the corporate books subject to the corporate duty. If the corporation were guilty of misconduct, he could not withhold its books to save it; and if he were implicated in the violations of law, he could not withhold the books to protect himself from the effect of their disclosures. The [State's] reserved power of visitation would seriously be embarrassed, if not wholly defeated in its effective exercise, if guilty officers could refuse inspection of the records and papers of the corporation. No personal privilege to which they are entitled requires such a conclusion.* * * " In a companion case, Dreier v. United States, 221 U.S. 394 (1911), the Court applied the holding in *Wilson* to a Fifth Amendment attack on a subpoena addressed to the corporate custodian. * * *

The next significant step in the development of the collective entity rule occurred in United States v. White, 322 U.S. 694 (1944), in which the Court held that a labor union is a collective entity unprotected by the Fifth Amendment. [We reasoned] that the Fifth Amendment privilege applies only to natural individuals and protects only private papers. Representatives of a "collective group" act as agents "[a]nd the official records and documents of the organization that are held by them in a representative rather than in a personal capacity cannot be the subject of the personal privilege against self-incrimination, even though production of the papers might tend to incriminate them personally." With this principle in mind, the Court turned to whether a union is a collective group:

> The test * * * is whether one can fairly say under all the circumstances that a particular type of organization has a character so impersonal in the scope of its membership and activities that it cannot be said to embody or represent the purely private or personal interests of its constituents, but rather to embody their common or group interests only. If so, the privilege cannot be invoked on behalf of the organization or its representatives in their official capacity. Labor unions—national or local, incorporated or unincorporated—clearly meet that test.

In applying the collective entity rule to unincorporated associations such as unions, the Court jettisoned reliance on the visitatorial powers of the State over corporations owing their existence to the State—one of the bases for earlier decisions.

The frontiers of the collective entity rule were expanded even further in Bellis v. United States, [p. 425], in which the Court ruled that a partner in a small partnership could not properly refuse to produce partnership records. * * * After rehearsing prior precedent involving corporations and unincorporated associations, the Court examined the partnership form and observed that is had many of the incidents found relevant in prior collective entity decisions. The Court suggested that the test articulated in *White* for determining the applicability of the Fifth Amendment to organizations was "not particularly helpful in the broad range of cases." The Court rejected the notion that the "formulation in *White* can be reduced to a simple proposition based solely upon the size of the organization. It is well settled that no privilege can be claimed by the custodian of corporate records, regardless of how small the corporation may be." *Bellis* held the partnership's financial records in a "representative capacity" and therefore "his personal privilege against compulsory self-incrimination is inapplicable."

The plain mandate of these decisions is that without regard to whether the subpoena is addressed to the corporation, or as here, to the individual in his capacity as a custodian, see *Dreier, Bellis*, a corporate custodian such as petitioner may not resist a subpoena for corporate records on Fifth Amendment grounds. Petitioner argues, however, that this rule falls in the wake of *Fisher* and *Doe*. In essence, petitioner's argument is as follows: In response to *Boyd v. United States*, with its privacy rationale shielding personal books and records, the Court developed the collective entity rule, which declares simply that corporate records are not private and therefore are not protected by the Fifth Amendment. The collective entity decisions were concerned with the contents of the documents subpoenaed, however, and not with the act of production. In *Fisher* and *Doe*, the Court moved away from the privacy based collective entity rule, replacing it with a compelled testimony standard under which the contents of business documents are never privileged but the act of producing the documents may be. Under this new regime, the act of production privilege is available without regard to the entity whose records are being sought. * * *

To be sure, the holding in *Fisher*–later reaffirmed in *Doe*–embarked upon a new course of Fifth Amendment analysis. We cannot agree, however, that it rendered the collective entity rule obsolete. The agency rationale undergirding the collective entity decisions, in which custodians asserted that production of entity records would incriminate them personally, survives. From *Wilson* forward, the Court has consistently recognized that the custodian of corporate or entity records holds those documents in a representative rather than a personal capacity. Artificial entities such as corporations may act only through their agents, and, a custodian's assumption of his representative capacity leads to certain obligations, including the duty to produce corporate records on proper demand by the Government. Under those circumstances, the custodian's act of production is not deemed a personal act, but rather an act of the corporation. Any claim of Fifth Amendment privilege asserted by the agent would be tantamount to a claim of privilege by the corporation-which of course possesses no such privilege. * * *

Indeed, the opinion in *Fisher*–upon which petitioner places primary reliance–indicates that the custodian of corporate records may not interpose a Fifth Amendment objection to the compelled production of corporate records, even though the act of production may prove personally incriminating. The *Fisher* court cited the collective entity decisions with approval and offered those decisions to support the conclusion that the production of the accountant's workpapers would "not * * * involve testimonial self-incrimination." * * * In a footnote, the Court explained: "In these cases compliance with the subpoena is required even though the books have been kept by the person subpoenaed and his producing them would itself be sufficient authentication to permit their introduction against him." *Fisher*. The Court thus reaffirmed the obligation of a corporate custodian to comply with a subpoena addressed to him.

That point was reiterated by Justice Brennan in his concurrence in *Fisher*. Although Justice Brennan disagreed with the majority as to its use of the collective entity cases to support the proposition that the act of production is not testimonial, he nonetheless acknowledged that a custodian may not resist a subpoena on the ground that the act of production would be incriminating. * * * [For] "one in control of the records of an artificial organization undertakes an obligation with respect to those records foreclosing any exercise of his privilege." Thus, whether one concludes—as did the Court—that a custodian's production of corporate records is deemed not to constitute testimonial self-incrimination, or instead that a custodian waives the right to exercise the privilege, the lesson of *Fisher* is clear: A custodian may not resist a subpoena for corporate records on Fifth Amendment grounds.

Petitioner also attempts to extract support for his contention from Curcio v. United States, 354 U.S. 118 (1957). But rather than bolstering petitioner's argument, we think Curcio substantiates the Government's position. Curcio had been served with two subpoenas addressed to him in his capacity as secretary treasurer of a local union. One subpoena required that he produce union records, the other that he testify. Curcio appeared before the grand jury, stated that the books were not in his possession, and refused to answer any questions as to their whereabouts. * * * The *Curcio* Court made clear that with respect to a custodian of a collective entity's records, the line drawn was between [that] oral testimony and other forms of incrimination. "A custodian, by assuming the duties of his office, undertakes the obligation to produce the books of which he is custodian in response to a rightful exercise of the State's visitorial [sic] powers. But he cannot lawfully be compelled, in the absence of a grant of adequate immunity from prosecution, to condemn himself by his own *oral testimony*." (Emphasis added) In distinguishing those cases in which a corporate officer was required to produce corporate records and merely identify them by oral testimony, the Court showed that it understood the testimonial nature of the act of production: "The custodian's act of producing books or records in response to a subpoena *duces tecum* is itself a representation that the documents produced are those demanded by the subpoena. Requiring the custodian to identify or authenticate the documents for admission in evidence merely makes explicit what is implicit in the production itself." In the face of this recognition, the Court nonetheless noted: "In this case petitioner might have been proceeded against for his failure to produce the records demanded by the subpoena *duces tecum*."

We note further that recognizing a Fifth Amendment privilege on behalf of the records custodians of collective entities would have a detrimental impact on the Government's efforts to prosecute "white-collar crime," one of the most serious problems confronting law enforcement authorities. "The greater portion of evidence of wrongdoing by an organization or its representatives is usually found in the official records and documents of that organization. Were the cloak of the privilege to be thrown around these impersonal records and documents, effective enforcement of many federal and state laws would be impossible." *White.* If custodians could assert a privilege, authorities would be stymied not only in their enforcement efforts against those individuals but also in their prosecutions of organizations. In *Bellis*, the Court observed: "In view of the inescapable fact that an artificial entity can only act to produce its records through its individual officers or agents, recognition of the individual's claim of privilege with respect to the financial records of the organization would substantially undermine the unchallenged rule that the organization itself is not entitled to claim any Fifth Amendment privilege, and largely frustrate legitimate governmental regulation of such organizations."

Petitioner suggests, however, that these concerns can be minimized by the simple expedient of either granting the custodian statutory immunity as to the act of production, 18 U.S.C. §§ 6002-6003, or addressing the subpoena to the corporation and allowing it to choose an agent to produce the records who can do so without incriminating himself. We think neither proposal satisfactorily addresses these concerns. Taking the last first, it is no doubt true that if a subpoena is addressed to a corporation, the corporation "must find some means by which to comply because no Fifth Amendment defense is available to it." The means most commonly used to comply is the appointment of an alternate custodian. But petitioner insists he cannot be required to aid the appointed custodian in his search for the demanded records, for any statement to the surrogate would itself be testimonial and incriminating. If this is correct, then petitioner's "solution" is a chimera. In situations such as this—where the corporate custodian is likely the only person with knowledge about the demanded documents—the appointment of a surrogate will simply not ensure that the documents sought will ever reach the grand jury room; the appointed custodian will essentially be sent on an unguided search.

This problem is eliminated if the Government grants the subpoenaed custodian statutory immunity for the testimonial aspects of his act of production. But that "solution" also entails a significant drawback. All of the evidence obtained under a grant of immunity to the custodian may of course be used freely against the corporation, but if the Government has any thought of prosecuting the custodian, a grant of act of production immunity can have serious consequences. Testimony obtained pursuant to a grant of statutory use immunity may be used neither directly nor derivatively. 18 U.S.C. § 6002. And "[o]ne raising a claim under [the federal immunity] statute need only show that he testified under a grant of immunity in order to shift to the government the heavy burden of proving that all of the evidence it proposes to use was derived from legitimate independent sources." *Kastigar.* Even in cases where the Government does not employ the immunized testimony for any purpose—direct or derivative—against the witness, the Government's inability to meet the "heavy burden" it bears may result in the preclusion of crucial evidence that was obtained legitimately.[10]

Although a corporate custodian is not entitled to resist a subpoena on the ground that his act of production will be personally incriminating, we do think certain consequences flow from the fact that the custodian's act of production is one in his representative rather than personal capacity. Because the custodian acts as a representative, the act is deemed one of the corporation and not the individual. Therefore, the Government concedes, as it must, that it may make no evidentiary use of the "individual act" against the individual. For example, in a criminal prosecution against the custodian, the Government may not introduce into evidence before the jury the fact that the subpoena was served upon and the corporation's documents were delivered by one particular individual, the custodian. The Government has the right, however, to use the corporation's act of production against the custodian. The Government may offer testimony–for example, from the process server who delivered the subpoena and from the individual who received the records–establishing that the corporation produced the records subpoenaed. The jury may draw from the corporation's act of production the conclusion that the records in question are authentic corporate records, which the corporation possessed, and which it produced in response to the subpoena. And if the defendant held a prominent position within the corporation that produced the records, the jury may, just as it would had someone else produced the documents, reasonably infer that he had possession of the documents or knowledge of their contents. Because the jury is not told that the defendant produced the records, any nexus between the defendant and the documents results solely from the corporation's act of production and other evidence in the case.[11]

Consistent with our precedent, the United States Court of Appeals for the Fifth Circuit ruled that petitioner could not resist the subpoena for

---

[10] The dissent asserts that recognition of an act of production privilege on behalf of corporate custodians will not seriously undermine law enforcement efforts directed against those custodians because only the custodian's act of production need be immunized. But the burden of proving an independent source that a grant of immunity places on the Government could, in our view, have just such a deleterious effect on law enforcement efforts.

[11] We reject the suggestion that the limitation on the evidentiary use of the custodian's act of production is the equivalent of constructive use immunity barred under our decision in *Doe*. Rather, the limitation is a necessary concomitant of the notion that a corporate custodian acts as an agent and not an individual when he produces corporate records in response to a subpoena addressed to him in his representative capacity.

We leave open the question whether the agency rationale supports compelling a custodian to produce corporate records when the custodian is able to establish, by showing for example that he is the sole employee and officer of the corporation, that the jury would inevitably conclude that he produced the records.

corporate documents on the ground that the act of production might tend to incriminate him. The judgment is therefore affirmed.

Justice KENNEDY, with whom Justice BRENNAN, Justice MARSHALL, and Justice SCALIA join, dissenting.

* * * The majority's apparent reasoning is that collective entities have no privilege and so their employees must have none either. The Court holds that a corporate agent must incriminate himself even when he is named in the subpoena and is a target of the investigation, and even when it is conceded that compliance requires compelled, personal, testimonial, incriminating assertions. I disagree with that conclusion; find no precedent for it; maintain that if there is a likelihood of personal self-incrimination the narrow use immunity permitted by statute can be granted without frustrating the investigation of collective entities; and submit that basic Fifth Amendment principles should not be avoided and manipulated, which is the necessary effect of this decision. * * *

The collective entity rule provides no support for the majority's holding. * * * In none of the collective entity cases cited by the majority, and in none that I have found, were we presented with a claim that the custodian would be incriminated by the act of production, in contrast to the contents of the documents.

The distinction is central. * * * Our decision in *Wilson*, and in later collective entity cases reflected, I believe, the Court's understandable unease with drawing too close a connection between an individual and an artificial entity. On a more practical level, the Court was also unwilling to draw too close a connection between the custodian and the contents of business documents over which he had temporary control but which belonged to his employer, often were prepared by others, and in all events were prepared voluntarily. This last factor became the focus of our analysis in *Fisher*, where we made clear that the applicability of the Fifth Amendment privilege depends on compulsion. *Fisher* put to rest the notion that a privilege may be claimed with respect to the contents of business records that were voluntarily prepared.

The act of producing documents stands on an altogether different footing. While a custodian has no necessary relation to the contents of documents within his control, the act of production is inescapably his own. Production is the precise act compelled by the subpoena, and obedience, in some cases, will require the custodian's own testimonial assertions. That was the basis of our recognition of the privilege in *United States v. Doe*. The entity processing the documents in *Doe* was, as the majority points out, a sole proprietorship, not a corporation, partnership, or labor union. But the potential for self-incrimination inheres in the act demanded of the individual, and as a consequence the nature of the entity is irrelevant to determining whether there is ground for the privilege.

* * * Recognition of the privilege here would * * * avoid adoption of the majority's metaphysical progression, which, I respectfully submit, is flawed. Beginning from ordinary principles of agency, the majority proceeds to the conclusion that when a corporate employee, or an employee of a labor union or partnership, complies with a subpoena for production of documents, his act is necessarily and solely the act of the entity. * * * [But] the heart of the matter, as everyone knows, is that the Government does not see Braswell as a mere agent at all. and the majority's theory is difficult to square with what will often be the Government's actual practice. The subpoena in this case was not directed to Worldwide Machinery Sales, Inc., or Worldwide Purchasing, Inc. It was directed to "Randy Braswell, President, Worldwide Machinery Sales, Inc., Worldwide Purchasing, Inc." and informed him that "[y]ou are hereby commanded" to provide the specified documents. The Government explained at oral argument that it often chooses to designate an individual recipient, rather than the corporation generally, when it serves a subpoena because "[we] want the right to make that individual comply with the subpoena." This is not the language of agency. By issuing a subpoena which the Government insists is "directed to petitioner personally," it has forfeited any claim that it is simply making a demand on a corporation that, in turn, will have to find a physical agent to perform its duty. What the Government seeks instead is the right to choose any corporate agent as a target of its subpoena and compel that individual to disclose certain information by his own actions.

The majority gives the corporate agent fiction a weight it simply cannot bear. In a peculiar attempt to mitigate the force of its own holdings, it impinges upon its own analysis by concluding that, while the Government may compel a named individual to produce records, in any later proceeding against the person it cannot divulge that he performed the act. But if that is so, it is because the Fifth Amendment protects the person without regard to his status as a corporate employee; and once this be admitted, the necessary support for the majority's case has collapsed. * * *

The majority's abiding concern is that if a corporate officer who is the target of a subpoena is allowed to assert the privilege, it will impede the Government's power to investigate corporations, unions. and partnerships, to uncover and prosecute white collar crimes, and otherwise to enforce its visitatorial powers. There are at least two answers to this. The first, and most fundamental, is that the text of the Fifth Amendment does not authorize exceptions premised on such rationales. Second, even if it were proper to invent such exceptions, the dangers prophesied by the majority are overstated.

Recognition of the right to assert a privilege does not mean it will exist in many cases. In many instances, the production of documents may implicate no testimonial assertions at all. In *Fisher*, for example, we held that the specific acts required by the subpoena before us "would not itself involve testimonial self-incrimination" because, in that case, "the existence and location of the papers [were] a foregone conclusion and the taxpayer adds little or nothing to the sum total of the Government's information by conceding that he in fact has the papers." Whether a particular act is testimonial and self-incriminating is largely a factual issue to be decided in each case. In the case before us, the Government has made its submission on the assumption that the subpoena would result in incriminating testimony. The existence of a privilege in future cases, however, is not an automatic result.

Further, to the extent testimonial assertions are being compelled, use immunity can be granted without impeding the investigation. Where the privilege is applicable, immunity will be needed for only one individual, and solely with respect to evidence derived from the act of production itself. The Government would not be denied access to the records it seeks, it would be free to use the contents of the records against everyone, and it would be free to use any testimonial act implicit in production against all but the custodian it selects. In appropriate cases the Government will be able to establish authenticity, possession, and control by means other than compelling assertions about them from a suspect.

In one sense the case before us may not be a particularly sympathetic one. Braswell was the sole stockholder of the corporation and ran it himself. Perhaps that is why the Court suggests he waived his Fifth Amendment self-incrimination rights by using the corporate form. One does not always, however, have the choice of his or her employer, much less the choice of the business enterprise through which the employer conducts its business. Though the Court here hints at a waiver, nothing in Fifth Amendment jurisprudence indicates that the acceptance of employment should be deemed a waiver of a specific protection that is as basic a part of our constitutional heritage as is the privilege against self-incrimination.

The law is not captive to its own fictions. Yet, in the matter before us the Court employs the fiction that personal incrimination of the employee is neither sought by the Government nor cognizable by the law. That is a regrettable holding, for the conclusion is factually unsound, unnecessary for legitimate regulation, and a violation of the Self-Incrimination Clause of the Fifth Amendment of the Constitution. For these reasons, I dissent.

NOTES AND QUESTIONS

1. *The Custodian's Obligation.* In **Curcio v. United States**, discussed in *Braswell*, the Court held that the obligation of the entity agent did not extend to explaining the whereabouts of records no longer in his possession. *Curcio* noted that lower court rulings had held that "a corporate officer who has been required by subpoena to produce corporate records may also be required, by oral testimony, to identify them," but those cases were "distinguishable" and the Court had no need "to pass on their validity." Does *Braswell* necessarily affirm those rulings? See **In re Custodian of Records of Variety**

Distributing, 927 F.2d 244 (6th Cir. 1991). Looking to *Braswell*'s discussion of *Curcio*, the Sixth Circuit there concluded that the custodian can be required to authenticate the documents for admission in evidence, as that "merely makes explicit what is implicit in the production itself." This duty existed even though the necessary statements (*e.g.*, that the custodian is familiar with the company's recordkeeping and knows the company has kept the records in the course of regular business activity) may be potentially incriminating in some situations. However, "because the custodian of corporate records is acting in a representative rather than a personal capacity, he is protected against the future evidentiary use of the testimony."

In re Grand Jury Proceedings, 471 F.Supp.2d 201 (D. Mass. 2007), criticized the approach of *Variety Distributing* that would permit a custodian to be required to provide the foundational testimony for admitting documents under the business records exception to the hearsay rule. The District Court stated:

> As an initial matter, it appears that no court other than the Variety Distributing court has ever held that corporate custodians may be compelled to provide Rule 803(6) testimony, and the case itself is based on an obviously incorrect premise.

> Furthermore, Rule 803(6) testimony, unlike authentication testimony, is not "implicit" in the act of producing a document. A witness who produces a document and testifies that the document is responsive to the subpoena has implicitly indicated that the document is genuine; it is but a tiny step from there to authentication testimony, which essentially consists of testimony to the same effect. However, to qualify a document as a business record under Rule 803(6), at a minimum there must be testimony concerning the regular record-creation and record-maintaining practices of the corporation at the relevant time. That testimony may or may not be routine, depending on the facts and circumstances, but it is never implicit in the act of producing records.

> Finally, there is no logical stopping point to the principle that a corporate custodian can be required to provide an evidentiary foundation for a document. There is no special magic in the business records exception that it should be elevated over the other hearsay exceptions, or for that matter the definition of hearsay itself set forth in Rule 801.

See also Peter J. Henning, *Finding What Was Lost: Sorting Out the Custodian's Privilege Against Self-Incrimination from the Compelled Production of Records*, 77 NEB. L. REV. 34 (1998) ("*Variety Distributing*'s extension of the custodian's duty to testify regarding the recordkeeping practices of the organization is questionable because the Sixth Circuit equated the admissibility of hearsay with authentication of records, failing to recognize the different issues addressed by the two rules of evidence. Proof of one is not necessarily proof of the other, so it is not a fair reading of *Curcio*'s erroneous endorsement of compelling authentication testimony to include statements that furnish evidentiary proof related to the introduction of documents at trial under an exception to the hearsay rule.").

2. *Personal Documents.* What characteristics should be considered in ruling on a claim that the subpoenaed records, though kept by a corporate employee, were "personal" and therefore not subject to the entity doctrine? Consider **In re Grand Jury Proceedings**, 55 F.3d. 1012 (5th Cir. 1995), in which the court adopted a "multi-factor balancing approach" to determine whether a document constituted a corporate record, and therefore government by *Braswell*, or a personal record, and therefore subject to a potential act-of-production Fifth Amendment claim under *Fisher*. In determining whether individual "daytimers" were corporate records, the court stated:

> A multi-factor balancing approach attempts to answer the key question: what is the essential nature of the document? It attempts to answer this question in light of the entire context of the ownership, preparation and use of the document. We agree with the Second Circuit that the following nonexhaustive list of criteria is relevant in this inquiry: who prepared the document; the nature of its contents; its purpose or use; who possessed it; who had access to it; whether the corporation required its preparation; and whether its existence was necessary to or in furtherance of corporate business. * * *

> We agree that the determination of the essential character of a document does not hinge upon some magical percentage of personal versus corporate entries. However, this does not mean that the ratio of personal to corporate entries is irrelevant. As a general rule, the greater proportion of personal entries, the more likely it is that the trier of fact could reasonably conclude that it was prepared, used, and maintained as a personal document. Conversely, the greater proportion of business-related entries, the more likely it is that the trier of fact could reasonably conclude that the document was prepared, used, and maintained as a corporate document. This is not to say, however, that other evidence regarding the preparation, use, and maintenance of a given document may not tilt the balance in the other direction. A multi-factor approach to the determining the nature of a document requires a court to view all relevant factors in context, giving greater or lesser weight to a given factor as the quality or quantity of evidence demands.

3. *"Required Records."* **Shapiro v. United States**, 335 U.S. 1 (1948), expanding upon some dictum in *Wilson*, held that the self-incrimination clause is not violated by requiring a person to keep records of certain business

activities and to make those records available for government inspection. Accordingly, a grand jury subpoena requiring the production of required records may not be successfully challenged on self-incrimination grounds even though the records are those of a business conducted as an individual proprietorship rather than an entity. See Grand Jury Subpoena Duces Tecum (Underhill), 781 F.2d 64 (1986) (although act of production may be incriminating, *Fisher/Doe* do not apply to required records, as nothing in these opinions casts doubt as the "continuing validity of * * * *Shapiro* and its progeny"). Business records will not be classified as required records under *Shapiro* unless three prerequisites are met: (1) the governmental requirement that records be kept must be "essentially regulatory" in nature; (2) the records must be "of a kind which the regulated party has customarily kept," and (3) the records "must have assumed some 'public aspects' which render them at least analogous to public documents." Grosso v. United States, 390 U.S. 62 (1968). In In re Grand Jury Subpoena Duces Tecum to John Doe I, 368 F.Supp.2d 846 (W.D.Tenn. 2005), the District Court found that the requirement to maintain identifying information of those participating in any depiction of sexually explicit conduct (18 U.S.C. § 2257) was essentially a criminal statute, and therefore the records did come within the required records exception that would allow compelled production over an assertion of the Fifth Amendment privilege.

2. Scope of the Collective Entity Doctrine

a. Closely-Held Business

AMATO v. UNITED STATES
450 F.3d 46 (1st Cir. 2006)

BOWMAN, Senior Circuit Judge.

Dr. Steven P. Amato appeals the denial of his motion to quash two administrative subpoenas duces tecum served on him as custodian of records for two corporations in which he was the sole shareholder, director, officer and employee. We affirm.

Amato is a chiropractor in Damariscotta, Maine. He has conducted his chiropractor business as a sole proprietorship and as a corporation. In October 1997, Amato incorporated the business as Dr. Steven Amato, D.C., P.C. ("Amato P.C.") in New York and is Amato P.C.'s sole shareholder, director, officer and employee. In September 2002, Amato incorporated Mainecures.com, Inc. ("Mainecures") in Maine. A year later, Maine dissolved Mainecures for failing to file an annual report. Amato was Mainecures's sole shareholder, director, officer and employee.

In January 2005, law enforcement, acting under the authority of a search warrant, searched Amato's office for evidence of federal health-care crimes. During the search, law enforcement served two administrative subpoenas duces tecum on Amato as the records custodian of Amato P.C. and Mainecures. The subpoenas required the records custodian to appear with the records at the United States Attorney's Office or, in lieu of an appearance, to deliver the records with certificates of authenticity to the United States Attorney's Office.

Amato moved to quash the subpoenas. Amato argued that the act-of-production doctrine protects production of the records because the testimonial aspects of the production would incriminate him. Recognizing the collective-entity doctrine, Amato nevertheless asserted that the act-of-production doctrine controls in his case. For support, Amato invoked a footnote in Braswell v. United States that left open the question of whether the collective-entity doctrine would apply if the custodian of corporate records is "able to establish, by showing for example that he is the sole employee and officer of the corporation, that the jury would inevitably conclude that he produced the records." Because Amato is his corporations' sole shareholder, director, officer and employee, he asserted his personal Fifth Amendment privilege against producing the corporate records. Amato also argued that Mainecures's records are privileged because Mainecures was a dissolved corporation.

In considering the motion to quash, the magistrate judge recognized that the collective-entity doctrine has not provided Fifth Amendment protection to custodians of corporate records because custodians act in their representative, rather than their personal, capacities when complying with a subpoena directed at the corporation. The magistrate judge declined to recognize an exception to the collective-entity doctrine that would fit Amato's situation: he is the target of an investigation, the custodian of records, and the corporation's sole shareholder, director, officer and employee. The judge reasoned that the First Circuit has rejected such an exception, see United States v. Lawn Builders of New Eng., Inc., 856 F.2d 388 (1st Cir.1988); In re Grand Jury Proceedings (The John Doe Co.), 838 F.2d 624 (1st Cir.1988), and concluded that *Braswell*'s footnote does not contradict the First Circuit's holdings. The magistrate judge also rebuffed Amato's argument that Mainecures's records are privileged because the records now belong to Amato's sole proprietorship, Mainecures having been dissolved before the subpoena issued. The judge concluded that Maine law dictates that a dissolved corporation exists for up to three years after dissolution to wind up its business affairs. Thus, the judge held that no Fifth Amendment privilege guards against the subpoena directed at Mainecures's custodian of records. * * *

It is fair to say that while the collective-entity doctrine focuses on the contents of corporate records or at least the status of the records, i.e., corporate or individual, the act-of-production doctrine focuses on whether an individual's compelled acts in producing records involve testimonial self-incrimination. This case tests Fifth Amendment boundaries when the act-of-production doctrine intersects with the collective-entity doctrine. In the present case, the issue is whether the Fifth Amendment protects Amato's act of producing the subpoenaed records in his capacity as custodian of the corporate records because the act itself would incriminate Amato personally. In other words, we ask whether the Fifth Amendment recognizes an exception to the collective-entity doctrine such that an act-of-production privilege protects a custodian of corporate records from producing those records when the custodian is the corporation's sole shareholder, director, officer and employee.

Our resolution of this issue is controlled by our decision in *John Doe Co.*, in which we decided that the act-of-production doctrine is not an exception to the collective-entity doctrine even when the corporate custodian is the corporation's sole shareholder, officer and employee. In asserting a Fifth Amendment privilege, Amato ignores the holding of *John Doe Co.* Instead, he seeks refuge in the language later used by the Supreme Court in footnote eleven in *Braswell*: "We leave open the question whether the agency rationale [behind the collective-entity doctrine] supports compelling a custodian to produce corporate records when the custodian [can] establish, by showing for example that he is the sole employee and officer of the corporation, that the jury would inevitably conclude that he produced the records." Our reading of *Braswell* and of our caselaw, however, leads us to conclude that such refuge is unavailable in this circuit.

Although *Braswell* does not directly contradict Amato's argument, the decision contains nothing that would justify our reconsideration of our holding in *John Doe Co.* * * *

Our caselaw rejects Amato's argument suggesting that we should recognize an exception to the collective-entity doctrine where the custodian of records is the corporation's sole shareholder, director, officer and employee. Four months before the Supreme Court decided *Braswell*, this court held "that the sole shareholder of a one-man corporation has no 'act of production privilege' under the fifth amendment to resist turnover of corporate documents." *John Doe Co.* In *John Doe Co.*, which is very similar to Amato's case, a grand jury investigated an individual (referred to by the court as "Owner") who was a corporation's sole shareholder, officer and employee. When the grand jury issued a subpoena to the corporation's "Keeper of the Records," the Owner's attorney provided the government some of the records, but "the corporation refused to authenticate the documents before the grand jury or to provide testimony (through Owner or by designating some other agent) that they were all the records of the corporation." The Owner also "refused to stipulate to these facts or to appoint an agent of the corporation to provide the requested testimony." Id. The government moved to compel the production of the corporate records, while the corporation moved to quash the subpoena. The district court denied the motion to compel and granted the motion to quash "on the basis that the compelled testimony would likely force Owner to incriminate himself in violation of his fifth amendment right not to be a witness against himself." This circuit reversed "on the basis that the subpoena is directed at the corporation which receives no constitutional protection from self-incrimination."

Acknowledging that "the very act of producing the documents may, in some circumstances, be a testimonial act of authentication," we nevertheless concluded that "production, including implied authentication, can be required of a corporation through a corporate officer regardless of the potential for self-incrimination." This court also concluded that a so-called "one-man corporation" fares no better under the collective-entity doctrine: "It was Owner's choice to incorporate. With that choice came all the attendant benefits and responsibilities of being a corporation. One of those responsibilities is to produce and authenticate records of the corporation when they are subpoenaed by a grand jury. How the corporation chooses to fulfill this duty is not the court's concern."

In a case argued eight days after *Braswell* was decided, this court, citing *Braswell*, reaffirmed its application of the collective-entity doctrine to a corporation where the sole shareholder was also the sole officer and employee: "even assuming [the corporation] to be a one-man corporation and [the corporate custodian] to be that one man, the corporate records are not shielded from production, nor may [the corporate custodian] resist a subpoena for those records on the ground that the act of production would impermissibly infringe on his Fifth Amendment right against self-incrimination." *Lawn Builders.* * * *

Finally, we conclude that the district court committed no error in concluding that Mainecures's records remained corporate records after the corporation's dissolution. See Me.Rev.Stat. Ann. tit. 13-C, § 1406(1) ("A dissolved corporation continues corporate existence for a period not exceeding 3 years from the effective date of the articles of dissolution ... to wind up and liquidate its business and affairs...."); 1406(2) ("Dissolution of a corporation does not: A. Transfer title to the corporation's property; ... E. Prevent commencement of a proceeding by or against the corporation in its corporate name; ... or G. Terminate the authority of the clerk of the corporation."). Mainecures was dissolved in late 2003, less than three years before the service of the subpoena in January 2005. And nothing in the record suggests that Mainecures's dissolution effected a transfer of its corporate records to Amato personally. Moreover, the Supreme Court has stated that corporate records receive no Fifth Amendment protection even after dissolution. *Bellis* (recognizing that Supreme Court decisions make "clear that the dissolution of a corporation does not give the custodian of the corporate records any greater claim to the Fifth Amendment privilege").

For the reasons discussed, we decline Amato's invitation to reconsider our prior caselaw on the applicability of the collective-entity doctrine in cases involving a records custodian who is also the corporation's sole shareholder, officer and employee. We also conclude that Mainecures's dissolution did not protect its records from the reach of the subpoena in this case. Therefore, we affirm the district court's order denying Amato's motion to quash.

NOTE

The entity in *Amato* was a professional corporation, which is treated in the same way under state corporations law as a regular corporation, such as the one used by Randy Braswell. In **United States v. Milligan**, 324 F.Supp.2d 1062 (D. Ariz. 2004), the IRS issued a summons – which is similar to a subpoena – to the president of an S-Corporation. Under the tax laws, an S-Corporation is treated as a pass-through entity, so the corporate form is disregarded for tax purposes and the owner is responsible for the taxes as if the organization did not exist. The recipient argued that this type of entity is more like a sole proprietorship, and therefore he could assert the act-of-production doctrine to resist compliance rather than being treated under the collective entity doctrine. The District Court rejected that argument:

> Milligan asserts in his Supplemental Response that, because the corporation at issue is an S Corporation, which is a "flow-through/conduit" with respect to individuals, the S Corporation should receive personal treatment for purposes of the Fifth Amendment. However, the United States Supreme Court has consistently held that the privilege against self-incrimination should be limited "to its historic function of protecting only the natural individual." *Bellis*. Milligan has not presented any authority to extend the Fifth Amendment privilege to an S Corporation. The Court finds Milligan is not entitled to assert a Fifth Amendment privilege merely because the corporation at issue is an S Corporation.

Should the same analysis apply to a limited liability company or limited liability partnership, especially if there is only a single member or partner so that it acts largely like a sole proprietorship? Why does the selection of a particular business form determine the availability of the Fifth Amendment?

b. Former Employees

If dissolution of the entity does not change the character of corporate records, then what about documents taken by a former employee from the workplace: are they corporate records, and therefore no Fifth Amendment privilege claim can be made, or are they personal records of the individual now that the person is no longer an agent of the corporation? Consider how the Second Circuit analyzed that situation.

In re THREE GRAND JURY SUBPOENAS DUCES TECUM DATED JANUARY 29, 1999 v. John Doe # 1, John Doe # 2, John Doe # 3
191 F.3d 173 (2nd Cir. 1999)

WALKER, Circuit Judge.

This case presents the question of whether an ex-employee of a corporation may assert a Fifth Amendment privilege to refuse to respond to a grand jury subpoena demanding that he produce documents belonging to his former employer on the ground that the act of producing the documents would be both testimonial and incriminating. Because we conclude that a Fifth Amendment privilege is available to the ex-employee in such circumstances, we affirm the order of the district court denying the government's motion to compel production pursuant to the subpoenas in this case. * * *

The essential facts in this appeal are undisputed. The subpoenas the government seeks to enforce were issued by a grand jury in the Southern District of New York in connection with the government's criminal investigation of a corporation and its employees. The alleged wrongdoing, which included falsification of the corporation's books and records and the misapplication of funds in the corporation's custody, occurred between 1993 and 1996 in one division of the corporation. In the spring of 1999, the corporation pled guilty to making false entries in its books and records, and, pursuant to a plea agreement, agreed to cooperate in the government's ongoing investigation of a number of individuals who may have been involved in the improper corporate activities.

Doe I, Doe II and Doe III were all officers of the corporation during the period in which the illegal activities occurred, and worked in the division where the wrongdoing took place. Before the subpoenas sought to be enforced were issued, the employees resigned from the corporation or their employment was terminated. * * * On appeal, the government contends that the district court erred in refusing to apply *Braswell* to reject a Fifth Amendment act of production privilege claim by former employees holding corporate documents. For the reasons that follow, we disagree. Some legal background is needed.

* * * In Hale v. Henkel [p. 391], the Supreme Court rejected the argument that a corporate officer served with a subpoena for corporate documents (but personally immunized) could assert a Fifth Amendment privilege on behalf of the corporation. The Court held that a corporation was "a creature of the state" with powers limited by the state, and, thus, that the state could, in its oversight of the corporation, demand production of corporate documents. *Hale* thus "carved an exception out of *Boyd* by establishing that corporate books and records are not 'private papers' protected by the Fifth Amendment." Later, in Wilson v. United States, 221 U.S. 361 (1911), the Court held that a corporate president could not refuse to

produce corporate records on the grounds that the books were personally incriminating. * * *

Later, the Court expanded the reach of the collective entity doctrine beyond the corporate circumstances presented in *Hale* and *Wilson*, by holding that entities such as labor unions, see [United States v.] White, 322 U.S. 694 (1944), and partnerships, see Bellis [v. United States], 417 U.S. 85 (1974), were bound by the collective entity rule. In doing so, "the Court jettisoned reliance on the visitorial powers of the State over corporations owing their existence to the State--one of the bases for earlier decisions." * * * Instead, the Court relied on the fact that the individual subpoenaed held the collective entity's records in " 'a representative capacity,' " rendering " 'his personal privilege against compulsory self-incrimination . . . inapplicable.' " * * *

It was against this backdrop that the Supreme Court held in 1976 in Fisher v. United States, [and] in 1984 in United States v. Doe, that the "foundations for the [*Boyd*] rule have been washed away," * * * and that the contents of voluntarily-prepared records are not protected by the Fifth Amendment against compelled production. However, in *Fisher*, the Court recognized that a person, in the act of producing a document, may communicate information apart from its contents, and that the communication may amount to compelled testimony: * * * Accordingly, it is now settled that an individual may claim an act of production privilege to decline to produce documents, the contents of which are not privileged, where the act of production is, itself, (1) compelled, (2) testimonial, and (3) incriminating. * * *

In *Braswell*, the Court addressed the question of whether a current corporate employee could claim a Fifth Amendment act of production privilege to refuse to produce corporate documents. The Court held that the employee—an officer of two closely-held corporations—who had been individually subpoenaed to produce corporate books and records, could not invoke the Fifth Amendment to refuse production even though the documents might provide the government with evidence that could incriminate him. * * * In short, the Court applied the collective entity doctrine, introduced by *Hale* and developed in *Wilson* and its progeny, to preclude the claim of an act of production privilege by a current corporate employee. In doing so, the Court employed something of a fiction—to wit, that a corporate employee acts only as an agent or custodian of the corporation when he produces corporate documents in response to a subpoena, even a subpoena directed to the employee personally. * * *

While a current employee is not entitled to raise the Fifth Amendment as a shield against producing corporate documents under the rule set forth in *Braswell*, the *Braswell* Court created a mitigating evidentiary privilege to reduce the risk that the individual will incriminate himself in the course of producing such documents. * * *

We have since had occasion to apply *Braswell* to deny to a current employee of a collective entity a Fifth Amendment privilege to decline to produce documents. In In re Grand Jury Subpoenas Dated October 22, 1991, and November 1, 1991, 959 F.2d 1158 (2d Cir.1992), following *Braswell,* we held that "the custodian of corporate records has no Fifth Amendment privilege to refuse to produce those records on the ground that the act of production itself would tend to incriminate him." * * *

The question presented by this appeal, however, is different from that presented in *Braswell.* It is whether former employees of a corporation, who have corporate documents in their possession, may claim an act of production privilege notwithstanding *Braswell.* To hold, as the government suggests, that *Braswell* governs this appeal would require an extension of *Braswell* to the former employee based upon a conception that the former corporate employee who has corporate records holds them solely in a representative capacity, and acts as the corporation's agent when he or she produces them, even though the employment relationship has ended. Such a holding would also require us to overrule our decision in *Saxon Industries,* which is otherwise on point.

Saxon Industries, 722 F.2d 981 (2d Cir.1983), involved an appeal by a former corporate officer who was held in civil contempt for his refusal to comply with a grand jury subpoena duces tecum commanding production of corporate records retained by him after he left the corporation. Though decided before *Braswell,* the *Saxon Industries* panel anticipated its holding, stating that "if the witness were still a [corporate] officer or employee he would normally be obligated as a representative of the company to produce its documents, regardless of whether they contained information incriminating him." * * * We held, however, that "[o]nce the officer leaves the company's employ, . . . he no longer acts as a corporate representative but functions in an individual capacity in his possession of corporate records." * * * Thus, in *Saxon Industries,* we remanded the case to the district court to determine "whether appellant's production of the [corporate] documents, regardless of their contents, might have [a] self-incriminatory effect." * * * We further noted that should the district court determine that the production would prove incriminatory, "the government could either by stipulation or by obtaining a grant of immunity pursuant to 18 U.S.C. §§ 6002-6003, immunize the act of production; such immunity would preserve the appellant's Fifth Amendment rights with respect to his conduct in producing the documents, Kastigar v. United States.

* * * The rule in Braswell was predicated on the rationale that corporate custodians hold and produce documents only in a representational capacity and that when a corporate custodian produces subpoenaed corporate records, at bottom, "the corporation produce[s] the documents subpoenaed." * * * It follows, as we noted in *Saxon Industries,* that once the agency relationship terminates, the former employee is no longer an agent of the corporation and is not a custodian of the corporate records. When such an individual produces records in his possession he cannot be acting in anything other than his

personal capacity. In no sense can it be said, as *Braswell* requires, that "the corporation produced the records subpoenaed." Nothing in *Braswell* convinces us otherwise, and neither the government nor the dissent has directed us to any authority for the proposition that the agency relationship between an employee and an employer somehow continues after the employment relationship ends.

Indeed, this is the crux of our difference with the dissent. In the absence of legal authority to the effect that a former employee remains an agent of the corporation, or any evidence that the corporation and the individual intended to maintain an agency relationship, the foundation upon which *Braswell* rests–that one who is currently employed by the corporation holds documents as an agent in a custodial capacity so that it is actually the corporation that is producing the records–is removed.

The government's reliance on *Bellis* and *Wheeler* is wholly misplaced. In *Bellis,* the Supreme Court held that a law partner of a dissolved partnership could not assert a Fifth Amendment privilege with respect to the contents of certain partnership records, since the partner held the records in a representational capacity. There, the Court recognized that the subpoenaed partner, unlike appellees in this case, was still an agent of the dissolved partnership, since the "dissolution of the partnership does not terminate the entity; rather it continues until the winding up of the partnership affairs is completed." * * *

In any event, it is inherent in the Fifth Amendment's privilege against self-incrimination that a greater burden is placed on law enforcement than would otherwise be the case. If our determination of the Fifth Amendment's reach turned on the policy considerations of the sort advanced by the government, the basic protection against self-incrimination that the Founders prescribed in the Fifth Amendment would be substantially undermined. It is inescapable that, because the privilege protects against self-incrimination, the greater and more varied the criminal conduct, the wider the application of the privilege. For example, in this case the individuals asserting the privilege are likely concerned about being compelled to incriminate themselves not only with respect to the original investigation but also with respect to the subsequent theft of, or failure to return, corporate documents and any resulting obstruction of justice. * * *

The Supreme Court stated long ago that "the basic purposes that lie behind the privilege against self-incrimination do not relate to protecting the innocent from conviction, but rather to preserving the integrity of a judicial system in which even the guilty are not to be convicted unless the prosecution shoulder the entire load." * * * Our recognition of the act of production privilege on the facts presented in this case comports with these purposes.

Other circuits have split on this issue. Two circuit courts have recognized *Braswell 's* inapplicability to former employees. The Third Circuit, in United States v. McLaughlin, 126 F.3d 130 (3d Cir.1997), stated in dicta that "a former employee, for example, who produces purloined corporate documents is obviously not within the scope of the *Braswell* rule." And the Ninth Circuit in In re Grand Jury Proceedings, 71 F.3d 723 (9th Cir.1995), followed *Saxon Industries* and held "that the collective entity rule . . . does not apply to a former employee of a collective entity who is no longer acting on behalf of [the] collective entity." Two other circuits have held that *Braswell* does apply in such cases. See In re Grand Jury Subpoena Dated November 12, 1991, 957 F.2d 807 (11th Cir.1992) (rejecting the analysis of *Saxon Industries*, and holding that it is the "immutable character of the records as corporate which requires their production and which dictates that they are held in a representative capacity"); In re Sealed Case (Government Records), 950 F.2d 736 (D.C.Cir.1991) ("Just as corporate records belong to the corporation and are held for the entity by the custodian in an agency capacity, so government records do not belong to the custodian, in this case the [former employee], but to the government agency. Their production thus falls outside the Fifth Amendment Privilege."). We are unpersuaded by the analysis in the latter two cases.

* * * Since Doe I, Doe II and Doe III are no longer employed by the corporation whose documents the government seeks, and therefore do not hold the corporate documents in a representational capacity, we conclude that each may claim a Fifth Amendment act of production privilege with respect to the documents called for in the 1999 subpoenas.

Affirmed.

CABRANES, Circuit Judge, dissenting.

It has been settled for more than a decade that a custodian of corporate records may not "resist a subpoena for such records on the ground that the act of production would incriminate him in violation of the Fifth Amendment." Braswell v. United States. Relying on our pre-*Braswell* decision in In re Grand Jury Subpoenas Duces Tecum Dated June 13, 1983 and June 22, 1983, 722 F.2d 981 (2d Cir.1983) ("Saxon Industries"), the majority today excepts from *Braswell* 's reach any former corporate agent who possesses corporate documents that he retained after leaving the corporation's employ. The majority does so despite the fact that all three of the former employees resisting the subpoenas in this case left the corporation after the corporation had been served with its subpoenas, and despite the fact that two of the former employees had signed severance agreements in which they accepted a continuing duty to assist the corporation in any investigation conducted by or involving the corporation.

The majority's exception to the rule of *Braswell* finds no support in Supreme Court precedent and it creates a powerful incentive for corporate employees and other agents to abscond with subpoenaed records in order to avoid judicial process. Accordingly, I dissent. * * *

As the majority opinion discusses at some length, a series of Supreme Court cases, beginning with Hale v. Henkel, and Wilson v. United States, ruled that a person who holds documents in his capacity as an agent of a "collective entity"–such as a corporation or partnership–may not claim that the Fifth Amendment prohibits compulsory production of those documents. In Wheeler v. United States, and Grant v. United States, 227 U.S. 74 (1913), the Supreme Court made it clear that the "collective entity" doctrine applies not only to current agents of the entity, but also to former agents who have retained documents that they initially held in their capacity as custodian and agent.   The Court explained that "the privilege of individuals against self-incrimination in the production of their own books and papers" does not prevent "the compulsory production of the books of a corporation with which they happen to be or have been associated. " * * * . Despite the fact that the corporation in that case had already gone out of business and despite the fact that "the books of the company had before the dissolution been made over" to the subpoenaed custodians, "this did not change the essential character of the books and papers or make them any more privileged in the investigation of crime than they were before."

These "collective entity" cases had all involved instances in which an agent or former agent sought to invoke the Fifth Amendment privilege against documents that purportedly contained incriminating information. For this reason, the scope of the "collective entity" rule was made uncertain for a time when the Supreme Court decided in Fisher v. United States, that an individual may assert an "act of production" privilege where the very act of producing the requested documents would tend to incriminate that individual. The facts in *Fisher* did not directly implicate the "collective entity" rule, as there was no suggestion that the documents at issue there were held by someone as a current or former agent of an entity. As a result, it was not immediately clear whether a custodian would be entitled, after *Fisher*, to invoke the "act of production" privilege to trump the "collective entity" rule. * * *

In *Braswell*, the Supreme Court responded to this uncertainty by disagreeing with the proposition that *Fisher* "rendered the collective entity rule obsolete." * * * The Court noted that it could have been said in prior collective entity cases–where the subpoena had been directed to a custodian, demanding that he produce records in his custody–that "the custodian's act of producing the documents would 'tacitly admi[t] their existence and their location in the hands of their possessor.' * * * While the *Braswell* Court conceded that these earlier collective entity cases had not explicitly considered (a la *Fisher*) the testimonial consequences of the act of production itself, the Court stated that it did "not think such a focus would have affected the results reached." The Court explained that the collective entity rule was extensive enough to override the "act of production" privilege because "'[i]t is well settled that no privilege can be claimed by the custodian of corporate records.'" * * *

The majority today insists on limiting *Braswell* to its facts by treating
that decision as having established a rule that applies only to current agents
of an entity. * * * But *Braswell* itself purports to apply the collective entity
rule, in full, to assertions of the "act of production" privilege. * * * And, as I
have discussed above, the collective entity rule has long applied to current
and former agents alike, continuing to treat corporate documents as such,
even when they remain in the custody of an erstwhile corporate agent whose
employment with the corporation has terminated. * * *

I recognize that our pre-*Braswell* decision in *Saxon Industries* would
have drawn precisely the distinction embraced by the majority in this case,
and thereby given former (but not current) agents the benefit of the "act of
production" privilege. In my view, however, the distinction drawn in *Saxon
Industries* runs contrary to the Supreme Court's rule in *Braswell*. Because we
obviously must apply Supreme Court precedent, even when it conflicts with
our own, earlier authority, I believe we are bound to recognize that Saxon
Industries is no longer good law.

Even if I believed that *Saxon Industries* retained its vitality, I would
disagree with the majority's refusal to distinguish it here. In the instant case,
John Doe I, John Doe II, and John Doe III were all in the corporation's
employ at the time the initial subpoena was served on the corporation. John
Doe I and John Doe II were still employed by the corporation at the time it
was served with two subsequent subpoenas, which were broader in scope. By
contrast, in *Saxon Industries*, it appears that the first subpoena issued in the
case was the one issued to the witness-appellant, who had ceased to work for
the corporation approximately one year earlier. * * * Thus, unlike the instant
case, there was little reason there to fear that the former agent had left the
corporation's employ specifically to conceal evidence relating to an ongoing
investigation.

Nor is there any indication from the *Saxon Industries* decision that the
employee there had signed an agreement under which he assumed any
post-employment obligations with respect to investigations. Significantly, in
the instant case, John Doe II and John Doe III signed severance agreements
requiring them to assist the corporation in any investigation. To be sure, as
the majority observes, the severance agreements do not purport to waive the
employees' Fifth Amendment rights.

* * * The unintended consequences of the majority opinion are not
difficult to imagine: A person who is well-informed on the state of the law,
and whose activities within a "collective entity" are under investigation,
hereafter will have a clear incentive to leave the organization, take with
him—with or without the assistance of the organization—any documents that
he knows may contain evidence of wrongdoing, and then resist production of
these documents by asserting a claim of privilege against compelled
self-incrimination. We should not be surprised if in the future, as a direct
result of today's holding, we see more "reported incidents," of this sort of

obstructionist behavior. For all of the foregoing reasons, I respectfully dissent.

NOTES AND QUESTIONS

1. *An "Incentive" to Steal Documents.* Is Judge Cabranes overstating the effect of the majority's ruling? Is it realistic to think that many corporate officers are "well-informed" about the state of the law in the area of the Fifth Amendment privilege with regard to documents to know that they might be able to assert the Act of Production privilege to shield documents? If an officer consulted an attorney, who advised the officer that she could remove corporate records and thereby shield them from production, would that constitute obstruction of justice? Even if an officer removed documents, the government could execute a search warrant for the materials if it has sufficient information regarding the location of the items to satisfy the particularity of location requirement for a valid search warrant.

2. *Former Employees and Fiduciary Duty.* Even former employees may owe a fiduciary duty to their former employer, including the duty to maintain the secrecy of confidential information. Is there a continuing duty to hold the records of a corporation that was a former employer in a representative capacity? Consider the argument advanced by Alice W. Yao, Comment, *Former Corporate Officers and Employees in the Contest of the Collective Entity and Act of Production Doctrines*, 48 U. CHI. L. REV. 1487 (2001):

> [T]he collective entity doctrine should apply to former employees in cases where there is a continuing fiduciary relationship following the termination of employment. For instance, following the dissolution of a corporation, the former business's directors have fiduciary obligations to the corporation until the resolution of all remaining corporate affairs. Consequently, these directors maintain a representative relationship with that corporation, and the collective entity doctrine should govern. However, where there is no such continuing fiduciary or other such obligation, the act of production doctrine should apply in order to protect the individual's fundamental privilege against self-incrimination. Thus, in the context of a continuing fiduciary obligation, as with current employees and officers, the documents requested may be produced, but the act of production may not be attributed to any individual. If there is no continuing obligation on the part of the former employee or officer, then the documents may not be produced by virtue of the potentially incriminating nature of the act of production.

3. *Criticism of* **Three Subpoenas.** With a clear split in the circuits, how do you think the Supreme Court would resolve the issue? In **Gloves, Inc. v Berger**, 198 F.R.D. 6 (D. Mass. 2000), the plaintiff sought the production of records under Federal Rule of Civil Procedure 34 from former officers and controlling shareholders whom it accused of engaging in illegal acts prior to

selling the corporation to its current owners. The former officers asserted the Fifth Amendment privilege to prevent being compelled to turn over the records, which the plaintiff alleged they had stolen from the company once they learned that they would be sued for their illegal conduct. In rejecting the privilege claim, the magistrate judge said the following about the analysis in *Three Subpoenas*:

> In my opinion, the reasoning of * * * Judge Cabranes' dissent is more persuasive than that of the majority in the *Three Subpoenas* case. The majority's main premise is that a person who comes into possession of corporate records as an employee holds them in a representative capacity but if the individual leaves the corporation with the records, he holds the very same records not in a representative capacity but in a personal capacity. This distinction makes no sense. The plain fact is that the person, whether a present employee or a former employee, came into possession of the documents because at the time, he or she was an agent of the corporation. The person would not have had the ability to take possession of the corporate records but for the person's status as an agent of the corporation at the time. In these circumstances, there is nothing illogical in the notion that the former employee continues to hold the documents in a representative capacity. This appears to be the rationale of the decision in *In Re Sealed Case* when the [District of Columbia Circuit] wrote that a former government employee, like a former corporate employee, could not resist producing government (or corporate) records because the records "'belong to the government' and are held for the entity only in an agency capacity . . . ." The same point is made by the Eleventh Circuit which wrote that "[w]e hold that a custodian of corporate records continues to hold them in a representative capacity even after his employment is terminated." In re Grand Jury Subpoena Dated November 12, 1991.

CHAPTER ELEVEN
CHALLENGES TO THE GRAND JURY PROCESS

The Fifth Amendment requires that "No person shall be held to answer for a capital, or otherwise infamous crime, unless on a presentment or indictment of a Grand Jury." In Wood v. Georgia, 370 U.S. 375 (1962), the Supreme Court stated that the grand jury "has been regarded as a primary security to the innocent against hasty, malicious and oppressive persecution." The grand jury has both an investigatory and an accusatory function. The authority of the body is used by the prosecutor to compel the production of documents and testimony. After the investigation is complete, a prosecutor will seek to have the grand jury issue an indictment. The prosecutor drafts the charges and advises the grand jury on the applicable legal standards. It is then up to the grand jury to decide, in secret, whether or not the evidence establishes probable cause for the charges. If so, it will approve the indictment by returning a "true bill" and, once the prosecutor signs the indictment, the criminal prosecution has been initiated. If the grand jury determines that there is not probable cause, then it issues a "no true bill." Even after a "no true bill," however, the prosecutor can present the case to a second grand jury for an independent determination of probable cause, and it can issue a valid indictment despite the decision of the prior grand jury.

The Supreme Court has been highly protective of the grand jury's screening function by rejecting challenges of defendants to the probable cause determination. **United States v. Costello**, 350 U.S. 359 (1956), rejected a defendant's request to overturn a conviction on the ground that the grand jury did not have sufficient admissible evidence to charge him with a crime. The Court stated that "neither the Fifth Amendment nor any other constitutional provision prescribes the kind of evidence upon which grand juries must act * * * An indictment returned by a legally constituted and unbiased grand jury * * * if valid on its face, is enough to call for trial of the charge on the merits."

Costello effectively rules out challenges to the evidentiary basis for an indictment, and requires a defendant to go to trial to test the government's case. The Supreme Court relied on *Costello's* analysis in *United States v. Williams*, [p. 451], to limit the authority of lower courts to impose rules on the prosecutor's conduct before the grand jury because any challenge would call into question the evidence the grand jury considered in making its probable cause assessment.

The effectiveness of the grand jury as a screen on the prosecutor has been strongly criticized because they rarely, if ever, reject the prosecutor's request to return an indictment. Professor Andrew D. Leipold analyzed the problem in this way:

> The barriers to a grand jury's ability to screen are not obvious, because its task seems so simple. Jurors listen to the prosecutor's case and then are asked to answer a single question: is there probable cause to believe that the suspect committed the specified crime? Stated simply, grand jurors are not qualified to answer this question. Whether probable cause exists is ultimately a legal determination about the sufficiency of the evidence: whether the prosecutor put forth enough information to surpass the legal threshold established by the probable cause standard. In submitting a case to the grand jury we are asking nonlawyers with no experience in weighing evidence to decide whether a legal test is satisfied, and to do so after the only lawyer in the room, the prosecutor, has concluded that it has. Because jurors lack any experience or expertise in deciding whether probable cause exists, it becomes not only predictable but also logical that the jurors will return a true bill. This is not because they are a rubber stamp, but because they have no benchmark against which to weigh the evidence, and thus no rational basis for rejecting the prosecutor's recommendation to indict.

Andrew D. Leipold, *Why Grand Juries Do Not (and Cannot) Protect the Accused*, 80 CORNELL L. REV. 260 (1995).

Why is the Supreme Court so protective of the grand jury? Should the process be reformed? Section A reviews challenges to the prosecutor's use of the grand jury in the pre-indictment phase of a case, and Section B reviews challenges to misuse of the grand jury after it has returned an indictment. Note that the grand jury's authority pre-indictment is much less constrained by judicial review than when it is used post-indictment to gather information. Section C reviews the strict rule of grand jury secrecy, and Section D considers a new law—the Hyde Amendment—that permits exonerated defendants to seek attorneys fees for prosecutorial misconduct.

A. *SUPERVISORY POWER OVER THE CONDUCT OF THE GRAND JURY*

UNITED STATES v. WILLIAMS
504 U.S. 36, 112 S.Ct. 1735, 118 L.Ed.2d 352 (1992)

Justice SCALIA delivered the opinion of the Court.

The question presented in this case is whether a district court may dismiss an otherwise valid indictment because the Government failed to disclose to the grand jury "substantial exculpatory evidence" in its possession. * * * On May 4, 1988, respondent John H. Williams, Jr., a Tulsa, Oklahoma, investor, was indicted by a federal grand jury on seven counts of "knowingly mak[ing] [a] false statement or report . . . for the purpose of influencing . . . the action [of a federally insured financial institution]," in violation of 18 U.S.C. § 1014 (1988 ed., Supp. II). According to the indictment, between September 1984 and November 1985 Williams supplied four Oklahoma banks with "materially false" statements that variously overstated the value of his current assets and interest income in order to influence the banks' actions on his loan requests.

Williams' misrepresentation was allegedly effected through two financial statements provided to the banks, a "Market Value Balance Sheet" and a "Statement of Projected Income and Expense." The former included as "current assets" approximately $6 million in notes receivable from three venture capital companies. Though it contained a disclaimer that these assets were carried at cost rather than at market value, the Government asserted that listing them as "current assets"—i.e., assets quickly reducible to cash—was misleading, since Williams knew that none of the venture capital companies could afford to satisfy the notes in the short term. The second document—the Statement of Projected Income and Expense—allegedly misrepresented Williams' interest income, since it failed to reflect that the interest payments received on the notes of the venture capital companies were funded entirely by Williams' own loans to those companies. The Statement thus falsely implied, according to the Government, that Williams was deriving interest income from "an independent outside source." Brief of the United States 3.

Shortly after arraignment, the District Court granted Williams' motion for disclosure of all exculpatory portions of the grand jury transcripts, see Brady v. Maryland, 373 U.S. 83 (1963). Upon reviewing this material, Williams demanded that the District Court dismiss the indictment, alleging that the Government had failed to fulfill its obligation under the Tenth Circuit's prior decision in United States v. Page, 808 F.2d 723, 728 (1987), to present "substantial exculpatory evidence" to the grand jury (emphasis omitted). His contention was that evidence which the Government had chosen not to present to the grand jury—in particular, Williams' general ledgers and tax returns, and Williams' testimony in his contemporaneous Chapter 11 bankruptcy proceeding—disclosed that, for tax purposes and otherwise, he had regularly accounted for the "notes receivable" (and the interest on them) in a manner consistent with the Balance Sheet and the Income Statement. This, he contended, belied an intent to mislead the banks, and thus directly negated an essential element of the charged offense.

The District Court initially denied Williams' motion, but upon reconsideration ordered the indictment dismissed without prejudice. It found, after a hearing, that the withheld evidence was "relevant to an essential element of the crime charged," created " 'a reasonable doubt about [respondent's] guilt,' " and thus "render[ed] the grand jury's decision to indict gravely suspect." Upon the Government's appeal, the Court of Appeals affirmed the District Court's order, following its earlier decision in *Page*. It first sustained as not "clearly erroneous" the District Court's determination that the Government had withheld "substantial exculpatory evidence" from the grand jury. It then found that the Government's behavior " 'substantially influence[d]' " the grand jury's decision to indict, or at the very least raised a " 'grave doubt that the decision to indict was free from such substantial influence,' " (quoting Bank of Nova Scotia v. United States, 487 U.S. 250, 263 (1988)). Under these circumstances, the Tenth Circuit concluded, it was not an abuse of discretion for the District Court to require the Government to begin anew before the grand jury. We granted certiorari. * * *

Respondent does not contend that the Fifth Amendment itself obliges the prosecutor to disclose substantial exculpatory evidence in his possession to the grand jury. Instead, building on our statement that the federal courts "may, within limits, formulate procedural rules not specifically required by the Constitution or the Congress," United States v. Hasting, 461 U.S. 499, 505 (1983), he argues that imposition of the Tenth Circuit's disclosure rule is supported by the courts' "supervisory power." We think not. Hasting, and the cases that rely upon the principle it expresses, deal strictly with the courts' power to control their own procedures. That power has been applied not only to improve the truth-finding process of the trial, but also to prevent parties from reaping benefit or incurring harm from violations of substantive or procedural rules (imposed by the Constitution or laws) governing matters apart from the trial itself, see, e.g., Weeks v. United States, 232 U.S. 383 (1914). Thus, Bank of Nova Scotia v. United States makes clear that the supervisory power can be used to dismiss an indictment because of misconduct before the grand jury, at least where that misconduct amounts to a violation of one of those "few, clear rules which were carefully drafted and approved by this Court and by Congress to ensure the integrity of the grand jury's functions," United States v. Mechanik, 475 U.S. 66 (1986) (O'Connor, J., concurring in judgment).[6]

---

[6] Rule 6 of the Federal Rules of Criminal Procedure contains a number of such rules, providing, for example, that "no person other than the jurors may be present while the grand jury is deliberating or voting," Rule 6(d)(2), and placing strict controls on disclosure of "matters occurring before the grand jury," Rule 6(e)(2)(B). Additional standards of behavior for prosecutors (and others) are set forth in the United States Code. See 18 U.S.C. §§ 6002, 6003 (setting forth procedures for granting a witness immunity from prosecution); § 1623 (criminalizing false declarations before grand jury); § 2515 (prohibiting grand jury use of unlawfully intercepted wire or oral communications); § 1622 (criminalizing subornation of perjury). That some of the misconduct alleged in Bank of Nova Scotia v. United States was not specifically proscribed by Rule, statute, or the Constitution does not make the case stand for a judicially prescribable grand jury code, as the dissent suggests. All of the allegations of violation were dismissed by the Court—without considering their validity in law—for failure to meet *Nova Scotia 's* dismissal standard.

We did not hold in *Bank of Nova Scotia*, however, that the courts' supervisory power could be used, not merely as a means of enforcing or vindicating legally compelled standards of prosecutorial conduct before the grand jury, but as a means of prescribing those standards of prosecutorial conduct in the first instance–just as it may be used as a means of establishing standards of prosecutorial conduct before the courts themselves. It is this latter exercise that respondent demands. Because the grand jury is an institution separate from the courts, over whose functioning the courts do not preside, we think it clear that, as a general matter at least, no such "supervisory" judicial authority exists, and that the disclosure rule applied here exceeded the Tenth Circuit's authority. * * *

"[R]ooted in long centuries of Anglo-American history," the grand jury is mentioned in the Bill of Rights, but not in the body of the Constitution. It has not been textually assigned, therefore, to any of the branches described in the first three Articles. It "'is a constitutional fixture in its own right.'" United States v. Chanen, 549 F.2d 1306 (9th Cir. 1977). In fact the whole theory of its function is that it belongs to no branch of the institutional government, serving as a kind of buffer or referee between the Government and the people. Although the grand jury normally operates, of course, in the courthouse and under judicial auspices, its institutional relationship with the judicial branch has traditionally been, so to speak, at arm's length. Judges' direct involvement in the functioning of the grand jury has generally been confined to the constitutive one of calling the grand jurors together and administering their oaths of office.

The grand jury's functional independence from the judicial branch is evident both in the scope of its power to investigate criminal wrongdoing, and in the manner in which that power is exercised. "Unlike [a] [c]ourt, whose jurisdiction is predicated upon a specific case or controversy, the grand jury 'can investigate merely on suspicion that the law is being violated, or even because it wants assurance that it is not.'" United States v. R. Enterprises, [p. 361]. It need not identify the offender it suspects, or even "the precise nature of the offense" it is investigating. Blair v. United States, 250 U.S. 273 (1919). The grand jury requires no authorization from its constituting court to initiate an investigation, nor does the prosecutor require leave of court to seek a grand jury indictment. And in its day-to-day functioning, the grand jury generally operates without the interference of a presiding judge. It swears in its own witnesses, Fed. Rule Crim. Proc. 6(c), and deliberates in total secrecy.

True, the grand jury cannot compel the appearance of witnesses and the production of evidence, and must appeal to the court when such compulsion is required. And the court will refuse to lend its assistance when the compulsion the grand jury seeks would override rights accorded by the Constitution, see, e.g., Gravel v. United States, 408 U.S. 606 (1972) (grand jury subpoena effectively qualified by order limiting questioning so as to preserve Speech or Debate Clause immunity), or even testimonial privileges recognized by the common law, see In re Grand Jury Investigation of Hugle,

754 F.2d 863 (9th Cir. 1985) (same with respect to privilege for confidential marital communications) (opinion of Kennedy, J.). Even in this setting, however, we have insisted that the grand jury remain "free to pursue its investigations unhindered by external influence or supervision so long as it does not trench upon the legitimate rights of any witness called before it." United States v. Dionisio. Recognizing this tradition of independence, we have said that the Fifth Amendment's "constitutional guarantee presupposes an investigative body 'acting independently of either prosecuting attorney or judge '. . . ." *Dionisio* (emphasis added).

No doubt in view of the grand jury proceeding's status as other than a constituent element of a "criminal prosecutio[n]," U.S. Const., Amdt. VI, we have said that certain constitutional protections afforded defendants in criminal proceedings have no application before that body. The Double Jeopardy Clause of the Fifth Amendment does not bar a grand jury from returning an indictment when a prior grand jury has refused to do so. We have twice suggested, though not held, that the Sixth Amendment right to counsel does not attach when an individual is summoned to appear before a grand jury, even if he is the subject of the investigation. See United States v. Mandujano [p. 567]. And although "the grand jury may not force a witness to answer questions in violation of [the Fifth Amendment's] constitutional guarantee" against self-incrimination, our cases suggest that an indictment obtained through the use of evidence previously obtained in violation of the privilege against self-incrimination "is nevertheless valid." *Calandra.*

Given the grand jury's operational separateness from its constituting court, it should come as no surprise that we have been reluctant to invoke the judicial supervisory power as a basis for prescribing modes of grand jury procedure. Over the years, we have received many requests to exercise supervision over the grand jury's evidence-taking process, but we have refused them all, including some more appealing than the one presented today. In *Calandra*, a grand jury witness faced questions that were allegedly based upon physical evidence the Government had obtained through a violation of the Fourth Amendment; we rejected the proposal that the exclusionary rule be extended to grand jury proceedings, because of "the potential injury to the historic role and functions of the grand jury." In Costello v. United States, 350 U.S. 359 (1956), we declined to enforce the hearsay rule in grand jury proceedings, since that "would run counter to the whole history of the grand jury institution, in which laymen conduct their inquiries unfettered by technical rules."

These authorities suggest that any power federal courts may have to fashion, on their own initiative, rules of grand jury procedure is a very limited one, not remotely comparable to the power they maintain over their own proceedings. It certainly would not permit judicial reshaping of the grand jury institution, substantially altering the traditional relationships between the prosecutor, the constituting court, and the grand jury itself. * * * As we proceed to discuss, that would be the consequence of the proposed rule here. * * *

Respondent argues that the Court of Appeals' rule can be justified as a sort of Fifth Amendment "common law," a necessary means of assuring the constitutional right to the judgment "of an independent and informed grand jury," Wood v. Georgia, 370 U.S. 375, 390 (1962). Respondent makes a generalized appeal to functional notions: Judicial supervision of the quantity and quality of the evidence relied upon by the grand jury plainly facilitates, he says, the grand jury's performance of its twin historical responsibilities, i.e., bringing to trial those who may be justly accused and shielding the innocent from unfounded accusation and prosecution. We do not agree. The rule would neither preserve nor enhance the traditional functioning of the institution that the Fifth Amendment demands. To the contrary, requiring the prosecutor to present exculpatory as well as inculpatory evidence would alter the grand jury's historical role, transforming it from an accusatory to an adjudicatory body.

It is axiomatic that the grand jury sits not to determine guilt or innocence, but to assess whether there is adequate basis for bringing a criminal charge. That has always been so; and to make the assessment it has always been thought sufficient to hear only the prosecutor's side. As Blackstone described the prevailing practice in 18th-century England, the grand jury was "only to hear evidence on behalf of the prosecution[,] for the finding of an indictment is only in the nature of an enquiry or accusation, which is afterwards to be tried and determined." 4 W. Blackstone, Commentaries 300 (1769). So also in the United States. According to the description of an early American court, three years before the Fifth Amendment was ratified, it is the grand jury's function not "to enquire . . . upon what foundation [the charge may be] denied," or otherwise to try the suspect's defenses, but only to examine "upon what foundation [the charge] is made" by the prosecutor. Respublica v. Shaffer, 1 U.S. (1 Dall.) 236 (Philadelphia Oyer and Terminer 1788); see also F. Wharton, Criminal Pleading and Practice § 360, pp. 248-249 (8th ed. 1880). As a consequence, neither in this country nor in England has the suspect under investigation by the grand jury ever been thought to have a right to testify, or to have exculpatory evidence presented.

Imposing upon the prosecutor a legal obligation to present exculpatory evidence in his possession would be incompatible with this system. If a "balanced" assessment of the entire matter is the objective, surely the first thing to be done—rather than requiring the prosecutor to say what he knows in defense of the target of the investigation—is to entitle the target to tender his own defense. To require the former while denying (as we do) the latter would be quite absurd. It would also be quite pointless, since it would merely invite the target to circumnavigate the system by delivering his exculpatory evidence to the prosecutor, whereupon it would have to be passed on to the grand jury—unless the prosecutor is willing to take the chance that a court will not deem the evidence important enough to qualify for mandatory disclosure. * * *

Respondent acknowledges (as he must) that the "common law" of the grand jury is not violated if the grand jury itself chooses to hear no more evidence than that which suffices to convince it an indictment is proper. Thus, had the Government offered to familiarize the grand jury in this case with the five boxes of financial statements and deposition testimony alleged to contain exculpatory information, and had the grand jury rejected the offer as pointless, respondent would presumably agree that the resulting indictment would have been valid. Respondent insists, however, that courts must require the modern prosecutor to alert the grand jury to the nature and extent of the available exculpatory evidence, because otherwise the grand jury "merely functions as an arm of the prosecution." We reject the attempt to convert a nonexistent duty of the grand jury itself into an obligation of the prosecutor. The authority of the prosecutor to seek an indictment has long been understood to be "coterminous with the authority of the grand jury to entertain [the prosecutor's] charges." United States v. Thompson, 251 U.S. 407 (1920). If the grand jury has no obligation to consider all "substantial exculpatory" evidence, we do not understand how the prosecutor can be said to have a binding obligation to present it.

There is yet another respect in which respondent's proposal not only fails to comport with, but positively contradicts, the "common law" of the Fifth Amendment grand jury. Motions to quash indictments based upon the sufficiency of the evidence relied upon by the grand jury were unheard of at common law in England. And the traditional American practice was described by Justice Nelson, riding circuit in 1852, as follows:

> "No case has been cited, nor have we been able to find any, furnishing an authority for looking into and revising the judgment of the grand jury upon the evidence, for the purpose of determining whether or not the finding was founded upon sufficient proof, or whether there was a deficiency in respect to any part of the complaint . . . ." United States v. Reed, 27 Fed. Cas. 727, 738 (No. 16,134) (C.C. N.D.N.Y. 1852).

We accepted Justice Nelson's description in Costello, where we held that "it would run counter to the whole history of the grand jury institution" to permit an indictment to be challenged "on the ground that there was incompetent or inadequate evidence before the grand jury." And we reaffirmed this principle recently in *Bank of Nova Scotia*, where we held that "the mere fact that evidence itself is unreliable is not sufficient to require a dismissal of the indictment," and that "a challenge to the reliability or competence of the evidence presented to the grand jury" will not be heard. It would make little sense, we think, to abstain from reviewing the evidentiary support for the grand jury's judgment while scrutinizing the sufficiency of the prosecutor's presentation. A complaint about the quality or adequacy of the evidence can always be recast as a complaint that the prosecutor's presentation was "incomplete" or "misleading."[8] Our words in Costello bear repeating: Review of facially valid indictments on such grounds "would run counter to the whole history of the grand jury institution[,] [and] [n]either justice nor the concept of a fair trial requires [it]." * * *

Echoing the reasoning of the Tenth Circuit in United States v. Page, respondent argues that a rule requiring the prosecutor to disclose exculpatory evidence to the grand jury would, by removing from the docket unjustified prosecutions, save valuable judicial time. That depends, we suppose, upon what the ratio would turn out to be between unjustified prosecutions eliminated and grand jury indictments challenged–for the latter as well as the former consume "valuable judicial time." We need not pursue the matter; if there is an advantage to the proposal, Congress is free to prescribe it. For the reasons set forth above, however, we conclude that courts have no authority to prescribe such a duty pursuant to their inherent supervisory authority over their own proceedings. The judgment of the Court of Appeals is accordingly reversed and the cause remanded for further proceedings consistent with this opinion. * * *

Justice STEVENS, with whom Justice BLACKMUN and Justice O'CONNOR join, and with whom Justice THOMAS joins as to Parts II and III, dissenting.[b]

* * * Like the Hydra slain by Hercules, prosecutorial misconduct has many heads. * * * [It has not] been limited to judicial proceedings: the reported cases indicate that it has sometimes infected grand jury proceedings as well. The cases contain examples of prosecutors presenting perjured testimony, questioning a witness outside the presence of the grand jury and then failing to inform the grand jury that the testimony was exculpatory, failing to inform the grand jury of its authority to subpoena witnesses, operating under a conflict of interest, misstating the law, and misstating the facts on cross-examination of a witness.

---

[8] In Costello, for example, instead of complaining about the grand jury's reliance upon hearsay evidence the petitioner could have complained about the prosecutor's introduction of it. See, e.g., United States v. Estepa, 471 F.2d 1132 (2d Cir. 1972) (prosecutor should not introduce hearsay evidence before grand jury when direct evidence is available); see also Arenella, Reforming the Federal Grand Jury and the State Preliminary Hearing to Prevent Conviction Without Adjudication, 78 MICH.L.REV. 463, 540 (1980) ("[S]ome federal courts have cautiously begun to . . . us[e] a revitalized prosecutorial misconduct doctrine to circumvent Costello 's prohibition against directly evaluating the sufficiency of the evidence presented to the grand jury").

[b] Part I of Justice Stevens' opinion, deleted here, argued that certiorari was improvidently granted. That portion of the majority's opinion responding to this argument also has been deleted.

* * * [T]he prosecutor's duty to protect the fundamental fairness of judicial proceedings assumes special importance when he is presenting evidence to a grand jury. As the Court of Appeals for the Third Circuit recognized, "the costs of continued unchecked prosecutorial misconduct" before the grand jury are particularly substantial because there

> "the prosecutor operates without the check of a judge or a trained legal adversary, and virtually immune from public scrutiny. The prosecutor's abuse of his special relationship to the grand jury poses an enormous risk to defendants as well. For while in theory a trial provides the defendant with a full opportunity to contest and disprove the charges against him, in practice, the handing up of an indictment will often have a devastating personal and professional impact that a later dismissal or acquittal can never undo. Where the potential for abuse is so great, and the consequences of a mistaken indictment so serious, the ethical responsibilities of the prosecutor, and the obligation of the judiciary to protect against even the appearance of unfairness, are correspondingly heightened." United States v. Serubo, 604 F.2d 807, 817 (3d Cir. 1979). * * *

The standard for judging the consequences of prosecutorial misconduct during grand jury proceedings is essentially the same as the standard applicable to trials. In *Mechanik*, [p. 465] we held that there was "no reason not to apply [the harmless error rule] to 'errors, defects, irregularities, or variances' occurring before a grand jury just as we have applied it to such error occurring in the criminal trial itself." We repeated that holding in *Bank of Nova Scotia*, when we rejected a defendant's argument that an indictment should be dismissed because of prosecutorial misconduct and irregularities in proceedings before the grand jury. Referring to the prosecutor's misconduct before the grand jury, we "concluded that our customary harmless-error inquiry is applicable where, as in the cases before us, a court is asked to dismiss an indictment prior to the conclusion of the trial." Moreover, in reviewing the instances of misconduct in that case, we applied precisely the same standard to the prosecutor's violations of Rule 6 of the Federal Rules of Criminal Procedure and to his violations of the general duty of fairness that applies to all judicial proceedings. * * * Unquestionably, the plain implication of that discussion is that if the misconduct, even though not expressly forbidden by any written rule, had played a critical role in persuading the jury to return the indictment, dismissal would have been required.

In an opinion that I find difficult to comprehend, the Court today repudiates the assumptions underlying these cases and seems to suggest that the court has no authority to supervise the conduct of the prosecutor in grand jury proceedings so long as he follows the dictates of the Constitution, applicable statutes, and Rule 6 of the Federal Rules of Criminal Procedure. The Court purports to support this conclusion by invoking the doctrine of separation of powers and citing a string of cases in which we have declined to impose categorical restraints on the grand jury. Needless to say, the Court's reasoning is unpersuasive.

Although the grand jury has not been "textually assigned" to "any of the branches described in the first three Articles" of the Constitution, it is not an autonomous body completely beyond the reach of the other branches. Throughout its life, from the moment it is convened until it is discharged, the grand jury is subject to the control of the court. As Judge Learned Hand recognized over sixty years ago, "a grand jury is neither an officer nor an agent of the United States, but a part of the court." Falter v. United States, 23 F.2d 420, 425 (2d Cir. 1928). This Court has similarly characterized the grand jury: * * * "A grand jury is clothed with great independence in many areas, but it remains an appendage of the court, powerless to perform its investigative function without the court's aid, because powerless itself to compel the testimony of witnesses. It is the court's process which summons the witness to attend and give testimony, and it is the court which must compel a witness to testify if, after appearing, he refuses to do so." Brown v. United States.

* * * [T]he Court has recognized that it has the authority to create and enforce limited rules applicable in grand jury proceedings. Thus, for example, the Court has said that the grand jury "may not itself violate a valid privilege, whether established by the Constitution, statutes, or the common law." And the Court may prevent a grand jury from violating such a privilege by quashing or modifying a subpoena, or issuing a protective order forbidding questions in violation of the privilege. Moreover, there are, as the Court notes, a series of cases in which we declined to impose categorical restraints on the grand jury. In none of those cases, however, did we question our power to reach a contrary result.

Although the Court recognizes that it may invoke its supervisory authority to fashion and enforce privilege rules applicable in grand jury proceedings, and suggests that it may also invoke its supervisory authority to fashion other limited rules of grand jury procedure, it concludes that it has no authority to "prescrib[e] standards of prosecutorial conduct before the grand jury," because that would alter the grand jury's historic role as an independent, inquisitorial institution. I disagree.

We do not protect the integrity and independence of the grand jury by closing our eyes to the countless forms of prosecutorial misconduct that may occur inside the secrecy of the grand jury room. After all, the grand jury is not merely an investigatory body; it also serves as a "protector of citizens against arbitrary and oppressive governmental action." *Calandra.* * * * It blinks reality to say that the grand jury can adequately perform this important historic role if it is intentionally misled by the prosecutor—on whose knowledge of the law and facts of the underlying criminal investigation the jurors will, of necessity, rely.

Unlike the Court, I am unwilling to hold that countless forms of prosecutorial misconduct must be tolerated—no matter how prejudicial they may be, or how seriously they may distort the legitimate function of the grand jury—simply because they are not proscribed by Rule 6 of the Federal Rules of Criminal Procedure or a statute that is applicable in grand jury proceedings. Such a sharp break with the traditional role of the federal judiciary is unprecedented, unwarranted, and unwise. Unrestrained prosecutorial misconduct in grand jury proceedings is inconsistent with the administration of justice in the federal courts and should be redressed in appropriate cases by the dismissal of indictments obtained by improper methods. * * *

What, then, is the proper disposition of this case? I agree with the Government that the prosecutor is not required to place all exculpatory evidence before the grand jury. A grand jury proceeding is an ex parte investigatory proceeding to determine whether there is probable cause to believe a violation of the criminal laws has occurred, not a trial. Requiring the prosecutor to ferret out and present all evidence that could be used at trial to create a reasonable doubt as to the defendant's guilt would be inconsistent with the purpose of the grand jury proceeding and would place significant burdens on the investigation. But that does not mean that the prosecutor may mislead the grand jury into believing that there is probable cause to indict by withholding clear evidence to the contrary. I thus agree with the Department of Justice that "when a prosecutor conducting a grand jury inquiry is personally aware of substantial evidence which directly negates the guilt of a subject of the investigation, the prosecutor must present or otherwise disclose such evidence to the grand jury before seeking an indictment against such a person." U.S. Dept. of Justice, United States Attorneys' Manual, Title 9, ch. 11, § 9-11.233, 88 (1988).

Although I question whether the evidence withheld in this case directly negates respondent's guilt, I need not resolve my doubts because the Solicitor General did not ask the Court to review the nature of the evidence withheld. Instead, he asked us to decide the legal question whether an indictment may be dismissed because the prosecutor failed to present exculpatory evidence. Unlike the Court and the Solicitor General, I believe the answer to that question is yes, if the withheld evidence would plainly preclude a finding of probable cause. I therefore cannot endorse the Court's opinion. * * *

NOTES AND QUESTIONS

1. *The Effect of* **Williams**. Prior to *Williams*, federal lower courts had characterized a broad range of prosecutorial actions and inactions as "misconduct" that would lead to dismissal of an indictment unless that misconduct constituted harmless error. Lower courts have recognized that *Williams* cuts deeply into the prior precedent on other types of misconduct

claims. See United States v. Gillespie, 974 F.2d 796 (7th Cir. 1992) ("after Williams, then, nothing short of a violation of laws or procedural rules regulating grand jury matters will permit a court to exercise its supervisory authority in the grand jury area"). Based on *Williams*, the Fifth Circuit overturned the district court's dismissal of an indictment when the government allegedly used perjured testimony to obtain it: "[W]e are persuaded that perjury before the grand jury that was not knowingly sponsored by the government may not form the basis for a district court's dismissal of an indictment under its supervisory power." United States v. Strouse, 286 F.3d 767 (5th Cir. 2002). In United States v. Breslin, 916 F.Supp. 438 (E.D. Pa. 1996), however, the court dismissed an indictment without prejudice under its supervisory power for the "cumulative effect of the many instances of misconduct" before the grand jury. One of the concerns with the prosecutor's presentation to the grand jury included his attempt to bond with the grand jury by providing donuts at one of the meetings. The court found "that it is inappropriate for the prosecutor to provide snacks to a grand jury, and that his suggestion that the donuts were provided because the task they were about to start was unpleasant made the situation worse." Did the district court miss the implications of *Williams* in using its supervisory power to dismiss an indictment even though no single violation supported such a remedy? A different grand jury later reindicted the defendant on the same charges, and the district court refused to dismiss the indictment because of the earlier misconduct. United States v. Breslin, 1997 WL 50422 (E.D. Pa. 1997).

The Department of Justice maintains a policy that its prosecutors should provide the grand jury with any exculpatory evidence, as Justice Stevens noted in his dissent in *Williams*. The U.S. Attorney's Manual now provides:

> In *United States v. Williams*, the Supreme Court held that the Federal courts' supervisory powers over the grand jury did not include the power to make a rule allowing the dismissal of an otherwise valid indictment where the prosecutor failed to introduce substantial exculpatory evidence to a grand jury. It is the policy of the Department of Justice, however, that when a prosecutor conducting a grand jury inquiry is personally aware of substantial evidence that directly negates the guilt of a subject of the investigation, the prosecutor must present or otherwise disclose such evidence to the grand jury before seeking an indictment against such a person. While a failure to follow the Department's policy should not result in dismissal of an indictment, appellate courts may refer violations of the policy to the Office of Professional Responsibility for review.

U.S.A.M. § 9-11.233.

2. *The Fifth Amendment Grand Jury Right.* As the Court noted in *Williams*, there was no claim that the alleged prosecutorial misconduct amounted to a constitutional violation. The Supreme Court has said very

little about what prosecutorial action before a grand jury would constitute a violation of the Fifth Amendment right to a grand jury indictment that would justify dismissing an indictment. In *Bank of Nova Scotia,* [p. 465], the defendant claimed that the prosecutor had "violated the Fifth Amendment by calling a number of witnesses [associated with the target] for having them assert their privilege against self-incrimination," but the Court found no need to rule explicitly on whether the target's constitutional rights would be violated by such action if aimed at having the grand jury draw adverse inferences against the target based on the witnesses' assertion of the privilege. It agreed with the Court of Appeals that there had been "no error" in the handling of these particular witnesses. The government "was not required to take at face value" the witnesses earlier assertions that they would invoke the privilege if called to testify, the questioning before the grand jury ceased as soon as the witnesses asserted the privilege, and "throughout the proceedings, the prosecution repeated the caution to the grand jury that it was not to draw an adverse inference from a witness' invocation of the Fifth Amendment." Lower court rulings have dealt more extensively with the question of what prosecutorial misconduct reaches the level of a constitutional violation. The intentional prosecutorial introduction of perjured testimony on a critical issue has been characterized by several courts as a constitutional violation. Consider also SARA SUN BEALE, WILLIAM C. BRYSON, JAMES E. FELMAN, & MICHAEL J. ELSTON , GRAND JURY LAW AND PRACTICE § 9.31 (2nd ed.):

> As several courts have explicitly recognized, the goal of constitutional or supervisory power analysis is generally the same: to protect the integrity of the judicial process from unfair or improper prosecutorial conduct. Supervisory power may be exercised if the prosecutor's conduct threatens the impartiality or independence of the grand jury's processes. The requirement of an impartial and independent grand jury is ultimately derived from the grand jury clause of the Fifth Amendment. Supervisory power cases not infrequently recognize this point implicitly, citing constitutional decisions such as *Costello v. United States* and *Stirone v. United States* to explain that the grand jury's function requires it to act independently of either the prosecutor or judge. Thus supervisory power cases can be seen as simply enforcing the requirements of the grand jury clause, rather than as defining new nonconstitutional standards for prosecutorial conduct. This interpretation of the function of supervisory power in grand jury cases would be consistent with its use in other contexts.

In United States v. Storey, 2 F.3d 1037 (10th Cir. 1993), the court rejected the defendant's appeal of a district court's denial of a motion to dismiss charges because the prosecutorial misconduct amounted to a denial of the Fifth Amendment right to a grand jury indictment. The court stated that the "alleged Rule 6(e)(2) violations do not raise a right not to be tried, and we disagree with Appellants that the other alleged misconduct either made the grand jury not a grand jury, or the indictment not an indictment. The district court expressed dissatisfaction with the conduct of the Government, but evinced no concern with the conduct, independence, or product of the grand jury."

3. *State Court Rejection of* **Williams**. While *Williams* is the rule for federal courts, the states interpret their own constitutions, or apply their own supervisory authority, to impose a rule similar to the one rejected by the Supreme Court. In State v. Hogan, 676 A.2d 533 (N.J. 1996), the New Jersey Supreme Court rejected *Williams* and used its supervisory power over the lower courts to require prosecutors to present exculpatory evidence to a grand jury. The New Jersey Supreme Court extended the rule in a later case involving a different defendant with the same last name, State v. Hogan, 764 A.2d 1012 (N.J. 2001), to recognize "a prosecutor's obligation to instruct the grand jury on possible defenses is a corollary to his responsibility to present exculpatory evidence. The extent of the prosecutor's duty must be defined with reference to the role of the grand jury–to protect the innocent, and bring to trial those who may be guilty. Viewed from this perspective, the question of whether a particular defense need be charged depends upon its potential for eliminating a needless or unfounded prosecution. The appropriate distinction for this purpose is between exculpatory and mitigating defenses. An exculpatory defense is one that would, if believed, result in a finding of no criminal liability, i.e., a complete exoneration." Other states that require prosecutors to disclose exculpatory evidence to the grand jury include California (Johnson v. Superior Court, 539 P.2d 792 (1975) (requiring production of any evidence that reasonably tends to negate guilt)), and Massachusetts (Commonwealth v. LaVelle, 605 N.E.2d 852 (1993) (evidence that would greatly undermine credibility of evidence likely to affect grand jury's decision to indict).

4. *Grand Jury Independence*. The grand jury is independent of both the judiciary and the prosecutor, but the prosecutor plays a key role in providing legal advice and drafting the indictment that the grand jury may consider. How much involvement can a prosecutor have in the process before the grand jury's independence is undermined? If there is prosecutorial misconduct in the grand jury's consideration of whether probable cause exists to indict, does that violate a defendant's Fifth Amendment right to a grand jury indictment? In United States v. Navarro-Vargas, 408 F.3d 1184 (9th Cir. 2005), the Ninth Circuit, sitting en banc, rejected the claim that the grand jury instructions provided at the start of the term of service must include a specific statement that it need not return an indictment even if they found probable cause that the defendant committed the offense. The majority stated that the "instruction does not violate the grand jury's independence. The language of the model charge does not state that the jury 'must' or 'shall' indict, but merely that it 'should' indict if it finds probable cause. As a matter of pure semantics, it does not eliminate discretion on the part of the grand jurors, leaving room for the grand jury to dismiss even if it finds probable cause." A dissenting opinion by Judge Hawkins argued against "the essential hypocrisy of the government's position. Standing firmly in the defense of its exercise of discretion (amounting at times to nullification), it just as firmly argues that

grand jurors are without authority to make similar judgments about which laws deserve vigorous enforcement and which ones do not, in deciding whom to indict, and on what charges. In the government's eye, the grand jury is a mere instrument of prosecutorial will, a probable cause screening device obligated to act at the direction of the prosecutor and then only when the prosecutor has decided whom and how much to charge."

5. *The Dismissal Remedy*: **Mechanik** *and* **Bank of Nova Scotia**. In **United States v. Mechanik**, 475 U.S. 66 (1986), the defense learned during its cross-examination of a government agent that the agent had appeared together with another agent before the grand jury, where they had testified in tandem. The defense then moved for dismissal of the indictment on the ground that this practice violated Rule 6(d), which specifies those persons who may be present at grand jury proceedings and refers only to "the witness under examination" (emphasis added). Although Rule 12(b)(2) requires that such motions to dismiss ordinarily be raised before trial, an exception is made where there is "good cause" for the late objection. The trial judge took the motion under advisement until after the trial. It was then considered, after the jury had returned its verdict of guilty, with the trial judge ruling that Rule 6(d) had been violated but the violation was harmless because it had no impact upon the grand jury's decision to indict. The Court of Appeals reversed, holding that a Rule 6(d) violation should require automatic reversal. That ruling was then reversed by the Supreme Court, and the conviction reinstated.

Three different approaches were advanced in the three opinions in *Mechanik*. Justice Marshall, in dissent, adopted the analysis of the Court of Appeals. Three concurring judges (in an opinion by Justice O'Connor) agreed with the trial judge's conclusion that the critical question was whether the violation was harmless as it impacted upon the grand jury's decision to indict. The opinion for the Court (per Rehnquist, C.J.) argued that the impact of the Rule 6(d) violation should be evaluated in light of the supervening jury verdict. It reasoned:

Both the District Court and the Court of Appeals observed that Rule 6(d) was designed, in part, "to ensure that grand jurors, sitting without the direct supervision of a judge, are not subject to undue influence that may come with the presence of an unauthorized person." The Rule protects against the danger that a defendant will be required to defend against a charge for which there is no probable cause to believe him guilty. The error involving Rule 6(d) in these cases had the theoretical potential to affect the grand jury's determination whether to indict these particular defendants for the offenses for which they were charged. But the petit jury's subsequent guilty verdict not only means that there was probable cause to believe that the defendants were guilty as charged, but that they are in fact guilty as charged beyond a reasonable doubt. Measured by the petit jury's verdict, then, any error in the grand jury proceeding connected with the charging decision was harmless beyond a reasonable doubt.

It might be argued in some literal sense that because the Rule was designed to protect against an erroneous charging decision by the grand jury, the indictment should not be compared to the evidence produced by the Government at trial, but to the evidence produced before the grand jury. But even if this argument was accepted, there is no simple way after the verdict to restore the defendant to the position in which he would have been had the indictment been dismissed before trial. He will already have suffered whatever inconvenience, expense, and opprobrium that a proper indictment may have spared him. In courtroom proceedings as elsewhere, "the moving finger writes, and having writ moves on." Thus reversal of a conviction after a trial free from reversible error cannot restore to the defendant whatever benefit might have accrued to him from a trial on an indictment returned in conformity with Rule 6(d). * * *

We express no opinion as to what remedy may be appropriate for a violation of Rule 6(d) that has affected the grand jury's charging decision and is brought to the attention of the trial court before the commencement of trial. We hold only that however diligent the defendants may have been in seeking to discover the basis for the claimed violation of Rule 6(d), the petit jury's verdict rendered harmless any conceivable error in the charging decision that might have flowed from the violation. In such a case, the societal costs of retrial after a jury verdict of guilty are far too substantial to justify setting aside the verdict simply because of an error in the earlier grand jury proceedings. * * * [d]

---

[d] As to those costs, the Court noted:

The reversal of a conviction entails substantial social costs: it forces jurors, witnesses, courts, the prosecution, and the defendants to expend further time, energy, and other resources to repeat a trial that has already once taken place; victims may be asked to relive their disturbing experiences. The "[p]assage of time, erosion of memory, and dispersion of witnesses may render retrial difficult, even impossible." * * *. Thus, while reversal "may, in theory, entitle the defendant only to retrial, in practice it may reward the accused with complete freedom from prosecution," and thereby "cost society the right to punish admitted offenders." * * * Even if a defendant is convicted in a second trial, the intervening delay may compromise society's "interest in the prompt administration of justice," * * * and impede accomplishment of the objectives of deterrence and rehabilitation. These societal costs of reversal and retrial are an acceptable and often necessary consequence when an error in the first proceeding has deprived a defendant of a fair determination of the issue of guilt or innocence. But the balance of interest tips decidedly the other way when an error has had no effect on the outcome of the trial.

In **Bank of Nova Scotia v. United States**, 487 U.S. 250 (1988), the Supreme Court spelled out the governing standard for the dismissal of an indictment prior to conviction. *Bank of Nova Scotia* was decided prior to *Williams* and dealt with some prosecutorial actions that would not constitute cognizable misconduct under *Williams* [see p. 451]. *Bank of Nova Scotia* applied the same standard to actions that would be subject to a supervisory-authority dismissal under *Williams*, and *Williams* itself assumed the applicability of the *Bank of Nova Scotia* standard to such misconduct.

The trial court in *Bank of Nova Scotia* had dismissed the indictment pretrial on the basis of numerous prosecutorial actions characterized as misconduct, including The district court in the Bank of Nova Scotia case had based its dismissal order on several instances of alleged misconduct that included: (1) various violations of Rule 6(e) secrecy provisions through disclosures of grand jury materials to government agents and potential witnesses and through instructions to witnesses not to disclose their testimony to the target; (2) violations of Rule 6(d) in allowing joint appearances by IRS agents reading transcripts to the grand jury; (3) alleged violation of 18 U.S.C. § 6002 in the use of "pocket immunity"; (4) causing government agents to mischaracterize prior testimony that they summarized for the grand jury; (5) calling witnesses associated with the target for the sole purpose of having them assert their privilege against self-incrimination before the grand jury; and (6) administering unauthorized oaths to IRS agents, characterizing them as agents of the grand jury, in violation of Rule 6(e). The district court found that dismissal was appropriate to declare "with unmistakable intention" that "such conduct * * * will not be tolerated." A divided Court of Appeals reversed the dismissal order. It concluded that the prosecutorial actions had not "significantly infringe[d] on the grand jury's ability to exercise independent judgment" and that "without a showing of such infringement," federal supervisory authority could not be used to dismiss an indictment. A dissenting judge disagreed with "the view of the majority that prejudice to the defendant must be shown before a court can exercise its supervisory power to dismiss an indictment on the basis of egregious prosecutorial misconduct." The Supreme Court, with only Justice Marshall dissenting, held in an opinion by Justice Kennedy that the Court of Appeals majority had been correct in insisting upon a prejudicial impact and in finding no such impact here. Speaking first to the requisite showing of prejudice, Justice Kennedy articulated a standard somewhat differently than the Court of Appeals. He noted:

> We hold that, as a general matter, a District Court may not dismiss an indictment for errors in grand jury proceedings unless such errors prejudiced the defendants. * * * In the exercise of its supervisory authority, a federal court "may, within limits, formulate procedural rules not specifically required by the Constitution or the Congress." United States v. Hasting, 461 U.S. 499 (1983). Nevertheless, it is well established that "[e]ven a sensible and efficient use of the supervisory power . . . is invalid if it conflicts with constitutional or statutory provisions." * * * . Our previous cases

have not addressed explicitly whether this rationale bars exercise of a supervisory authority where, as here, dismissal of the indictment would conflict with the harmless error inquiry mandated by the Federal Rules of Criminal Procedure. * * * We now hold that a federal court may not invoke supervisory power to circumvent the harmless error inquiry prescribed by Federal Rule of Criminal Procedure 52(a). Rule 52(a) provides that "[a]ny error, defect, irregularity or variance which does not affect substantial rights shall be disregarded." * * * Rule 52 is, in every pertinent respect, as binding as any statute duly enacted by Congress, and federal courts have no more discretion to disregard the Rule's mandate than they do to disregard constitutional or statutory provisions. * * *

Having concluded that our customary harmless-error inquiry is applicable where, as in the case before us, a court is asked to dismiss an indictment prior to the conclusion of the trial, we turn to the standard of prejudice that courts should apply in assessing such claims. We adopt for this purpose, at least where dismissal is sought for nonconstitutional error, the standard articulated by Justice O'Connor in her concurring opinion in United States v. Mechanik. Under this standard, dismissal of the indictment is appropriate only "if it is established that the violation substantially influenced the grand jury's decision to indict," or if there is "grave doubt" that the decision to indict was free from the substantial influence of such violations. This standard is based on our decision in Kotteakos v. United States, 328 U.S. 750 (1946), where, in construing a statute later incorporated into Rule 52(a), we held that a conviction should not be overturned unless, after examining the record as a whole, a court concludes that an error may have had "substantial influence" on the outcome of the proceeding.

To be distinguished from the cases before us are a class of cases in which indictments are dismissed, without a particular assessment of the prejudicial impact of the errors in each case, because the errors are deemed fundamental. These cases may be explained as isolated exceptions to the harmless error rule. We think, however, that an alternative and more clear explanation is that these cases are ones in which the structural protections of the grand jury have been so compromised as to render the proceedings fundamentally unfair, allowing the presumption of prejudice. * * * "

In the cases before us we do not inquire whether the grand jury's independence was infringed. Such an infringement may result in grave doubt as to a violation's effect on the grand jury's decision to indict, but we did not grant certiorari to review this conclusion. We note that the Court of Appeals found that the prosecution's conduct was not "a significant infringement on the grand jury's ability to exercise independent judgment," and we accept that conclusion here. Finally, we note that we are not faced with a history of prosecutorial misconduct, spanning several cases, that is so systematic and pervasive as to raise a substantial and serious question about the fundamental fairness of the process which resulted in the indictment.

The Court concluded that there was no factual basis for some of the alleged violations, that the alleged Rule 6(e) violations clearly "could not have affected the charging decision," and that as to those that could conceivably have had an impact, the circumstances under which they occurred did not pose the requisite likelihood of prejudicial effect to escape being characterized as "harmless error."

6. ***The Scope of* Mechanik**. Federal lower courts have disagreed as to how broadly *Mechanik* should be read. The Tenth Circuit has reasoned that *Mechanik* was "carefully crafted along very narrow lines" and involved misconduct that "at worst, was [a] technical [violation]." It would hold postconviction review available for allegations of misconduct suggesting the prosecutor "attempted to unfairly sway the grand jury or to otherwise affect the accusatory process" or misconduct that "transgressed the defendant's right to fundamental fairness." United States v. Taylor, 798 F.2d 1337 (10th Cir. 1986) (finding reviewable a pre-*Williams* "totality of the circumstances" challenge that cited the prosecutor's failure to present exculpatory evidence, use of inadmissible and inflammatory evidence, violation of the attorney-client privilege, and unauthorized use of state officers in the grand jury's investigation). In United States v. Colon-Munoz, 192 F.3d 210 (1st Cir. 1999), the defendant sought to overturn his conviction because the appointment of an interim United States Attorney by the district court violated the Appointments Clause, and therefore the grand jury indictment was invalid. The First Circuit stated, "As a matter of law, any error in the charging decision of the grand jury was rendered harmless by the verdict and Colon cannot claim that Gil's presence before the grand jury entitles him to a dismissal of the indictment. We caution, however, that this conclusion implies no judgment about the importance of the issues raised by Colon or the Association in their challenge to the constitutionality of the lengthy interim judicial appointment of the United States Attorney."

7. ***Interlocutory Appeal.*** Justice Marshall, in his dissent in *Mechanik*, complained that the majority was leaving the enforcement of Rule 6(d) to the "unreviewable largesse of the district courts." He noted that if a judge should rule against a defendant on a pretrial motion to dismiss, that ruling might not be subject to appeal until after the trial, where a conviction would then preclude any relief under the majority's view. He offered the possibility of viewing the denial of the pretrial motion as a collateral order, so that it would be immediately appealable. The Court rejected that position in Midland Asphalt Corp. v. United States, 489 U.S. 794 (1989), holding that the trial court's refusal to dismiss an indictment because of the improper disclosure of grand jury material in violation of Federal Rule of Criminal Procedure 6(e) was not appealable under the collateral order doctrine.

Justice Marshall also suggested that the district court might simply defer ruling on a motion until after trial, thereby basically avoiding the need for a ruling on the merits of the motion, since an acquittal would render the motion moot and a conviction would render the error per se harmless. While the trial judge did defer ruling on the motion made in *Mechanik*, that motion was made during trial, and it generally is assumed that deferral is inappropriate where motions are made pretrial. This has led to increased efforts by defense counsel to gain pretrial disclosure of possible grand jury misconduct, so that challenges can be presented pretrial.   However, as discussed below, that is not easily done.

8. *Establishing Misconduct*. How does a defendant first discover, and then establish, that there was prosecutorial misconduct? The best source for determining what happened before the grand jury usually is the transcript of the grand jury proceedings. Under Federal Rule 6(e)(3)(C)(ii), that transcript can be obtained "when permitted by the court at the request of the defendant, upon a showing that grounds may exist for a motion to dismiss the indictment because of matters occurring before the grand jury." Federal courts generally hold that disclosure will not be permitted under this provision unless the defense first makes a preliminary showing, from the sources available to it, of likely misconduct that might justify dismissal. See, e.g., Beatrice Foods Co. v. United States, 312 F.2d 29 (8th Cir. 1963). But see United States v. Singer, 660 F.2d 1295 (8th Cir. 1981) (district court has discretion to examine the transcript *in camera* even if the requisite showing is not made). Courts have generally been unwilling to grant defense requests to review grand jury transcripts for only potential misconduct claims.. See BEALE ET AL., GRAND JURY LAW AND PRACTICE § 5.11 ("In order to make the preliminary showing that is a prerequisite to obtaining disclosure under Rule 6(e)(3)(C)(ii), the defendant must point to more than 'mere speculation' that improprieties may have occurred before the grand jury. Defendants have not succeeded in obtaining disclosure under this rule when they have argued that the grand jury materials, if disclosed, might reveal improprieties. Courts denying motions for disclosure have been unsympathetic to claims that it is impossible to determine whether grand jury abuses might have occurred without first having access to the grand jury record.").

The preliminary-showing requirement is most likely to be met where the misconduct occurred while a witness was present. A friendly witness, not being sworn to secrecy, may call the misconduct to the attention of the defense, and provide the testimony needed to make the preliminary showing. Even if the witness is not friendly, should the grand jury witness later testify at trial, the defense will be given access at the trial to the witness' recorded grand jury testimony, which may suggest (in the prosecutor's comments and questions) the likely misconduct. Of course, at this point, the trial judge may put off the misconduct inquiry, as was done in *Mechanik*. If only the jurors and the prosecutor were present when the misconduct occurred, the defense counsel faces what may be an insurmountable task in ever making a preliminary showing.[e]

B. CHALLENGES TO USE OF THE GRAND JURY

UNITED STATES v. ARTHUR ANDERSEN, L.L.P.
Crim. Action No. H-02-0121 (S.D. Texas April 9, 2002)

Unpublished Order

[HARMON, District Judge.]

Pending before the Court in the above referenced action is Defendant Arthur Andersen L.L.P.'s motion to quash subpoenas and limit grand jury proceedings.

Defendant contends that once an indictment has been returned, the government is prohibited from using the grand jury to conduct discovery or otherwise prepare its case for trial. United States v. Beasley, 550 F.2d 261 (5th Cir. 1977) ("prosecutorial agents many not use the Grand Jury for the primary purpose of strengthening [their] case on a pending indictment or as a substitute for discovery"); In re Grand Jury Subpoena Duces Tecum Dated January 2, 1985 ("Simels"), 767 F.2d 26 (2nd Cir. 1985) (the government may not use the grand jury to prepare "an already pending indictment for trial"). Defendant charges that the government is abusing the grand jury process by seeking to use the grand jury to assist in its trial preparation and to conduct discovery and "freeze" testimony. Defendant complains that only now, after obtaining the indictment on March 7, 2002, charging it with obstruction of justice in violation of 18 U.S.C. § 1512(b)(2), and after Defendant refused to plead guilty, is the government impermissibly subpoenaing Arthur Andersen personnel as fact witnesses to testify under oath about evidence relating to the obstruction of justice charge to strengthen its case, to "lock in–for trial purposes–those witnesses previously furnished through their voluntary interviews." Defendant argues that not only the timing of these delayed subpoenas, but also the implausibility of the government's claim that it is now seeking to investigate whether to indict individuals in addition to the accounting institution, its subpoenas for Arthur Andersen witnesses whose

---

[e] *Bank of Nova Scotia* presented an unusual situation in this regard, as explained in James Stewart, *The Prosecutors* 361 (1987):

[O]ne of the witnesses, * * * a lawyer who advised Kilpatrick on one of the tax shelter programs, was left alone by [the prosecutors] * * * in the office where secret exhibits and transcripts related to the investigation were stored * * * [and] he took the opportunity to read through much of the material. As a result, defense lawyers were able to mount an unusually detailed assault on the prosecutors handling of the grand jury investigation.

testimony might constitute admissions attributable to their employer at trial support Defendant's charge of abuse by the government. Moreover, urges Defendant, the imminence of the trial setting eliminates any need to place witnesses before the grand jury now. Finally, Defendant asserts that "the government . . . made this bed; having rushed to indict on an extraordinarily expedited schedule, the Justice Department is in no position to complain if temporary restrictions on the grand jury are necessary to prevent the government from obtaining an unfair and improper advantage at trial."

In its memorandum in opposition, the government reiterates a point made in open court, *i.e.*, that Andersen urged the Department of Justice to expedite a decision about whether to indict the firm for obstruction of justice based on document destruction; then after Defendant was indicted, Andersen reversed its position and asked the government to delay investigating individual employees, including those that Andersen has publicly blamed for the destruction of documents. The government further complains that in light of Andersen's campaign to enlist public sympathy by slanted statements and demonstrations, to influence the potential jury pool, and to signal its desired factual stance to current and former employees, including potential targets, subjects or witnesses in the grand jury investigation, expeditious investigation by the grand jury of current and former employees is necessary.

Emphasizing that the grand jury, charged with determining whether a crime has been committed and, if so, uncovering its perpetrators, is a separate entity from the courts, which have only a "very limited" supervisory power over grand jury proceedings. *United States v. Williams* * * * also underscores that grand jury proceedings are entitled to a presumption of regularity. The government points to the long settled principle that "where the primary purpose of the investigation is to determine whether others not indicted were involved in the same criminal activity, or whether the indicted party committed still other crimes, the government may go forward with the inquiry even though one result may be the production of evidence that could then be used at the trial of the pending indictment." Wayne R. LaFave, Jerold H. Israel & Nancy J. King. 3 *Criminal Procedure* § 8.8 (f) at 173 (2d ed. 1999). Thus a grand jury subpoena may issue to assist the grand jury in its investigation even where the incidental effect might be that the prosecutor will use any information obtained for purposes other than that grand jury's investigation. See also Port v. Heard, 594 F. Supp. 1212 (S.D. Tex. 1984) (fact that "some pretrial discovery" may follow from proper grand jury investigation provides no basis for court intervention). Furthermore, the government highlights the fact that it is Defendant's burden to prove that the government's primary purpose for proceeding before the grand jury is to collect evidence relating to the pending indictment against Arthur Andersen L.L.P. *R. Enterprises, Inc.* The government contends that Defendant has failed to meet that burden.

In support of its response, the government submits two declarations from attorneys working with the Enron Task Force, investigating all criminal matters associated with the collapse of Enron Corporation. The first, filed ex parte and under seal, was made by an Assistant United States Attorney ("AUSA") and explains in detail that the challenged subpoenas were issued by a different grand jury than the one that indicted Defendant and were properly issued to investigate uncharged criminal conduct by individuals and entities. A second, unsealed declaration by AUSA Leslie Caldwell delineating the procedural steps and negotiations between the government and Defendant up to the unsealing of the indictment for the instant case on March 14, 2002.

The Court has reviewed the applicable law and the record before it. A court should not intervene in the grand jury process absent a compelling reason. The existence of a pending indictment does not per se bar the government from using the grand jury to make a good faith, continuing inquiry into charges not included in that pending indictment. Abuse of the grand jury process occurs only when the government's sole or dominant purpose in convening a grand jury is to gather evidence for an already pending litigation. This sole or dominant purpose rule serves obvious purposes. It allows grand juries to continue investigations without having to wait to indict individuals or entities against which sufficient information to indict has already been uncovered, as well as to investigate additional individuals or entities who become suspects only after the indictment has been returned.

The government has explained with particularity and with documentary support that the government's expedited indictment was due to Arthur Andersen's urging. Thus the timing of the subpoenas is not a factor bolstering Defendant's argument, as it was in *Simels*. Other than conclusory statements, Defendant has failed to show that the government's investigation in subpoenaing the Defendant's employees as witnesses is for the sole and dominant purpose of developing evidence for trial on its pending destruction-of-documents obstruction charge against Arthur Andersen L.L.P. The Court finds that the government's affidavits have that shown it is acting in good faith to investigate unindicted charges against individuals and entities. As anyone following the news is fully aware, the collapse of Enron has spawned a complex and seemingly ever expanding investigation involving a wide range of parties and potential causes of action. The Court finds that there has been no abuse of grand jury process here. For these reasons the Court ORDERS that Defendant's motion to quash subpoenas and limit grand jury proceedings is DENIED.

NOTES AND QUESTIONS

1. **Scope**. The misuse objection alleged in *Arthur Andersen*–that the prosecution's primary purpose in utilizing the grand jury's investigative authority was helping it prepare for trial on indictments already brought–is one member of a family of objections centering on use of the grand jury's investigative powers for purposes other than determining whether to issue

an indictment. Other objections in the same family include the use of the grand jury (1) to gather evidence for use in a pending or future civil action (note 2, infra); (2) to gather evidence to further independent investigations by law enforcement agencies (note 3, infra); and, (3) to "harass" witnesses by forcing an unneeded personal appearance or placing a witness in a situation where he or she is likely to commit perjury (note 4, infra).

2. *Use for Civil Discovery.* In **United States v. Procter & Gamble**, 356 U.S. 677 (1958), the district court had granted broad disclosure of grand jury testimony to defendants in a civil antitrust action brought by the government. That ruling was apparently influenced in large part by the district court's belief that the government had used the grand jury investigation at which the testimony was given "to elicit evidence" for its subsequent civil action. The Supreme Court rejected the district court's disclosure order as not supported by a showing of particularized need, but it also acknowledged that the alleged government use of the grand jury process to prepare a civil case would have been improper. If the grand jury had been employed in that fashion, the Court noted, the government clearly would have been guilty of "flouting the policy of the law," both in using the grand jury for a purpose other than criminal investigation and in circumventing limits that would be placed upon a plaintiff in civil discovery. The Court added, however, that if the grand jury investigation was aimed at developing evidence for the possible issuance of an indictment, then there was no need to deny the government the incidental benefit of civil use of properly acquired evidence.

Lower courts applying the civil misuse standard of *Procter & Gamble* agree that whether or not an abuse exists depends upon the government's purpose in using the grand jury process, rather than the relevancy of the requested information to possible civil litigation. They recognize that a proper criminal investigation may readily encompass elements that also relate to civil cases, and that in some areas of the law (e.g., antitrust), the overlap between the criminal and civil investigation will be substantial. Some disagreement appears to exist, however, as to exactly how "pure" the government's purpose must be. Several courts have suggested that the *Procter & Gamble* standard is violated only when the investigation was aimed "primarily" at civil discovery. The issue, as they see it, is whether the grand jury proceedings are simply a "cover" or "subterfuge" for a civil investigation. Under this view, an investigation directed at concurrent criminal and civil uses is acceptable, provided the criminal use is at least equal in significance. In In re Grand Jury Subpoena Under Seal, 175 F.3d 332 (4th Cir. 1999), the Fourth Circuit stated that when "a showing of relevance [to a criminal investigation] can be made, a subpoena will issue even if the subpoena is also being sought for another, illegitimate purpose."

3. *Harassment.* Opinions upholding broad investigatory powers of the grand jury frequently add that, "of course," any use of those powers for the purpose of "harassment" will be subject to judicial remedy. See e.g., Branzburg v. Hayes, 408 U.S. 665 (1972). Such statements usually do not indicate precisely

what is meant by "harassment," but the reference apparently is to something more than simply using the grand jury process for some unauthorized purpose, such as civil discovery. Courts that have offered illustrations of harassment tend to stress a vindictive element in the use of the grand jury, usually a use designed to intimidate the witness. Thus, one court cited the "bad faith harassment of a political dissident" by imposing the burdens (political and otherwise) of a grand jury appearance with "no expectation that any testimony concerning a crime would be forthcoming." In re Santiago, 533 F.2d 727 (1st Cir. 1976). Similarly, repeated subpoenas to appear before one grand jury after another, without any additional investigative need, would constitute harassment. See In re Grand Jury (Schmidt), 619 F.2d 1022 (1988). So too would purposeful leaks to the press designed to create adverse publicity. See In re Grand Jury Investigation (Lance), 610 F.2d 202 (5th Cir. 1980). It has also been argued that calling a witness before the grand jury solely to trap him into committing perjury constitutes a form of harassment. United States v. Howard, 867 F.2d 548 (9th Cir. 1989). In large part, courts recognizing that such uses would constitute harassment have also found that the objecting party has failed to establish that the subpoena authority was being used in that fashion. An objecting party here bears an especially heavy burden.

C. GRAND JURY SECRECY

1. *Preventing Disclosure of Grand Jury Information*. Federal Rule of Criminal Procedure 6(e) imposes a strict secrecy requirement on all participants in the grand jury process, except witnesses. Rule 6(e)(2)(A) provides that "[n]o obligation of secrecy may be imposed on any person except in accordance with Rule 6(e)(2)(B)." Can a court exercise its supervisory authority to impose a secrecy bar on a grand jury witness, or does the Rule prohibit such a prohibition? Consider In re Subpoena to Testify Before Grand Jury Directed to Custodian of Records, 864 F.2d 1559 (11th Cir. 1989), which involved a federal grand jury subpoena to the University of Florida to produce certain records of the Florida Athletic program. After producing the records, the University "felt compelled by the Florida Public Records Law * * * to release to the press copies of motions and other documents filed with the district court in connection with the subpoena." At the request of the government, the district court then issued a "closure order" directing the University "not to reveal any information contained in such pleadings or memoranda, or any other information relating to the subject Grand Jury investigation, including but not limited to any documents produced pursuant to a Grand Jury subpoena, or testimony or other information obtained as a result of the subject Grand Jury investigation." Upon a challenge to that order by four intervening newspapers, the Eleventh Circuit held: (1) that the press has no standing because there is no First Amendment right of access to grand jury proceedings; (2) under Fed. R. Crim. P. 6(e)(5) (permitting the closing of hearings "to the extent necessary to prevent disclosure of [a] matter[] occurring before the grand jury"), the district court had properly

closed its hearing on the closure order, in which the government and the University participated; and (3) the inherent authority of the court to "protect the integrity of the grand jury process" sustained the closure order. As to the latter ruling, the Eleventh Circuit noted that the district court had found "compelling necessity" for its order, which only extended to secret aspects of the grand jury (including not only documents prepared for the grand jury and statements presented in the grand jury proceedings, but also "the names of individuals being investigated or those who might be expected to testify before the grand jury"). While the district court "could have written a less restrictive order," it was not "compelled * * * to take the least restrictive means available to protect the secrecy of the grand jury proceedings during the pendency of those proceedings."

2. ***Disclosure to Other Government Personnel.*** Under Rule 6(e)(3)(A)(ii), grand jury matter may be disclosed without a court order to "such government personnel (including personnel of a state or subdivision of a state) as are deemed necessary by an attorney for the government to assist an attorney for the government in the performance of such attorney's duty to enforce federal criminal law." "Government personnel" for this purpose includes not only federal criminal investigators, such as FBI agents, but also employees from administrative agencies or other executive departments who are on loan to the U.S. Attorney for the purpose of assisting in the grand jury investigation. The decision as to which personnel is needed for this purpose lies within the discretion of the prosecutor and need not be justified to the court. In re Perlin, 589 F.2d 260, 268 (7th Cir. 1978). However, under 6(e)(3)(B), the prosecutor must furnish to the supervising judge a listing of the personnel to whom grand jury matter will be disclosed and must also certify that those persons have been advised of their secrecy obligation. In 2000, Congress amended Rule 6(e) in the Civil Asset Forfeiture Reform Act to allow disclosure of grand jury material to government attorneys "in connection with any civil forfeiture provision of Federal law." 18 U.S.C. § 3322.

Since agency personnel receiving grand jury information under Rule 6(e)(3)(A)(i) are restricted to using that information only in the assistance of the government attorney's "duty to enforce federal criminal law," they may not disclose that information to their administrative agency absent a Rule 6(e)(3)(C)(i) court order. This limitation is stressed in USAM, § 9-11.251, which provides: "Strict precautions should be taken when employing personnel from agencies which have a civil function, such as the Securities and Exchange Commission, the Environmental Protection Agency, or the Internal Revenue Service, to ensure that knowledge of the grand jury investigation or documents subpoenaed by the grand jury are not used improperly for civil purposes by the agency. Grand jury documents should be segregated and personnel assisting the grand jury investigation should not work on a civil matter involving the same subjects unless a court order has been obtained authorizing such use." See Chapter 14, p. 628.

3. *Grand Jury Leaks.* Most grand jury secrecy issues do not involve the imposition of secrecy in the grand jury process, but challenging improper disclosure of information in violation of Federal Rule of Criminal Procedure 6(e) The Rule provides that, *inter alia*, prosecutors "must not disclose a matter occurring before the grand jury," and Rule 6(e)(7) provides "A knowing violation of Rule 6 may be punished by contempt." What constitutes a "matter occurring before the grand jury" is a "term of art" that is by no means clear (infra., p. 487). Disclosures of grand jury information tend to fall into two categories. First, there are disclosures openly made by government personnel in the belief that their disclosures do not violate Rule 6(e). These are usually cases in which the government contends that the information disclosed did not fit within the Rule 6(e)(2) secrecy requirement because it did not reveal "matters occurring before the grand jury," or that disclosure is of grand jury matter but is authorized under one of the "exceptions" in Rule 6(e)(3) permitting disclosure without a court order [see p. 480]. The central issue is the legal question of whether the disclosure did or did not violate Rule 6(e). Ordinarily, the remedy for a violation is to order that improper disclosure cease, although courts have noted that an exclusionary remedy may also be appropriate when the disclosure was to a party who now desires to use the improperly revealed information in a civil proceeding against the subject of the disclosure. See United States v. Couhlan, 842 F.2d 737 (4th Cir. 1988) (material given to government's civil attorney without the required Rule 6(e)(3)(c) order).

The second group of challenged disclosures are of a quite different order, and potentially more serious for those being investigated by the grand jury. They involve the alleged "leaking" of grand jury matter to the press. Here, the disclosure would clearly violate Rule 6(e), and the central issue is whether there was in fact a leak by government personnel subject to the secrecy requirement.

FINN v. SCHILLER
72 F.3d 1182 (4th Cir. 1996)

CHAPMAN, Senior Circuit Judge.

Mark T. Finn filed suit in the United States District Court for the Eastern District of Virginia against S. David Schiller, Assistant United States Attorney, alleging an ongoing pattern of prosecutorial misconduct including violations of Federal Rule of Criminal Procedure 6(e)(2) and seeking injunctive relief so as to prevent Schiller from disclosing grand jury material. The district court determined that only criminal contempt of court is provided by the Rule and, therefore, that only the court or the United States Attorney may institute contempt proceedings thereunder. The district court dismissed the suit, and Finn appeals. For the reasons discussed below, we affirm the dismissal under Rule 12(b)(6) for failure to state a claim upon which relief can be granted. However, we conclude that Rule 6(e)(2) provides both civil and criminal contempt but does not create a private cause of action. Accordingly, we remand for further proceedings consistent with this opinion.

Finn served on the Virginia Retirement System ("VRS") Board of Trustees in the early 1990s. From May 1990 until August 1990, the VRS increased its stock ownership in the Richmond, Fredericksburg & Potomac Railroad Corporation through open-market purchases. After learning of these stock purchases, Schiller, an Assistant United States Attorney, commenced a grand jury inquiry into the VRS's actions to determine if there had been securities laws violations.

On September 19, 1994, Schiller filed a plea agreement and a three page criminal information charging Patrick Bynum with a federal mail fraud violation. The information did not mention Finn. On September 23, 1994, Schiller signed and filed an eighty-three page statement (the "Statement") in the criminal proceeding against Bynum. Only six pages of the Statement dealt with the guilty plea of Bynum, and the remainder of the Statement generally alleged that Finn and other VRS officials conspired to commit mail, wire, and securities fraud in acquiring the railroad stock. Finn was mentioned by name over 370 times in the Statement.

On September 30, 1994, at Bynum's arraignment, his counsel informed the court that Bynum did not accept the Statement for several reasons, including the fact that "the majority of the information contained therein is not associated with Mr. Bynum." Schiller then filed a one-and-one-half page stipulation of facts (the "Stipulation") as the factual predicate for Bynum's plea.[1] When the court asked Schiller why he filed both the Statement and the Stipulation, Schiller responded that the Stipulation reflects "the essential elements for today," while the Statement "is the government's proffer as to the entire matter."

As a result of Schiller filing the Statement, Finn's picture appeared on the front page of the *Richmond Times Dispatch* the next day under the heading "Fraud Alleged in VRS Takeover of RF & P." The *Washington Post* featured a similar article the same day in its front page headlines.[3] Articles referring to or quoting from the Statement continued to appear in newspapers throughout October 1994.[4] The last newspaper article appeared

---

[1] Finn's name does not appear in the Stipulation.

[3] The *Washington Post* article discussed alleged violations of state and federal law by three senior officials of VRS: Jacqueline Epps, Mark Finn, and Glen Pond. The article cited the Statement as the source for the information contained therein. The article quoted from the Statement that all three officials "sought to enrich themselves financially, reputationally, politically and obtain business benefits for their careers."

[4] A *Richmond Times Dispatch* article on September 27, 1994 stated that the Statement implicated Finn. The same day, another article from the same newspaper stated:

Now the federal government has alleged that in a scheme to hide the VRS takeover of the RF & P, three former officials of the VRS--Jacqueline Epps, Mark Finn, and Glen Pond--broke securities laws, mail- and wire-fraud laws,

on October 12, 1994 and featured a picture of Finn with a caption under the picture that read: "The U.S. attorney ... alleges that Mark T. Finn ..., president of a Virginia Beach money-management firm and a former board member of the [VRS], plotted with a former board chairman to have the pension fund illegally take control of RF & P Corp." A magazine article in the December 1994 issue of *Managed Derivatives* incorrectly stated that "Mark Finn ... pleaded guilty to charges of felony mail fraud."

Finn claims that the release of the Statement and the resulting media coverage have harmed his reputation and his business. On October 7, 1994, Finn filed suit alleging that because the Statement disclosed matters occurring before the grand jury, Schiller had violated Federal Rule of Criminal Procedure 6(e) and had violated his constitutional rights under the Fifth and Sixth Amendments. Finn sought both preliminary and permanent injunctions to enjoin Schiller from further violations of Rule 6(e) and from an ongoing pattern of prosecutorial misconduct. Also, Finn requested the district court to strike the Statement from the record in United States v. Bynum. Finally, Finn asked the court to poll the grand jurors to determine if they could continue deliberations in an unbiased manner. In response, Schiller filed a motion to dismiss.

The district court heard the motions on October 20, 1994 and noted that it had never seen a stipulation of facts, accompanying a plea, that accused individuals of criminal activity who were not included in the indictment. The court asked Schiller's counsel if the United States Attorney was "initiating some new technique of *in terrorem* tactics in the Eastern District of Virginia that is going to create a lot of stressors for district judges like myself?" However, the court concluded that without an indictment, Finn could not establish that the Statement prejudiced him and that the contempt of court remedy provided by Rule 6(e)(2) was limited to criminal contempt. The district court dismissed Finn's complaint, finding that it lacked jurisdiction over Finn's civil claims and that the complaint did not state a claim upon which relief could be granted. The judge indicated that Finn could file a motion to strike the Statement from the public record in United States v. Bynum. On October 27, 1994, Finn filed an application to intervene in *Bynum* for the limited purpose of moving to strike the Statement. On November 2, 1994, the government filed a motion seeking to withdraw the Statement from the *Bynum* record on the ground that the Stipulation rendered the Statement superfluous. Concurrently, the government moved to dismiss Finn's motion to strike as moot. On November 4, 1994, Finn responded to the government's motion to dismiss and claimed that because

---

and state statutes concerning prohibitions against secret meetings, perjury, misuse of public funds, falsification of records, and more. The document is not an indictment, although federal prosecutors say they expect to file criminal charges.

The newspaper articles appearing throughout October continued to discuss the charges against Finn and the others.

the Statement was filed for an improper purpose,[5] the district court should strike it from the record. On November 14, 1994, the district court granted Finn's motion to intervene, granted the government's motion to withdraw the Statement from the record, and found moot Finn's motion to strike. Finn appealed the district court's final order dismissing his suit. * * *

The central issue in this appeal is whether Federal Rule of Criminal Procedure 6(e) provides a civil remedy for its violation. Rule 6(e)(2) provides:

> **General Rule of Secrecy.** A grand juror, an interpreter, a stenographer, an operator of a recording device, a typist who transcribes recorded testimony, an attorney for the government, or any person to whom disclosure is made under paragraph (3)(A)(ii) of this subdivision shall not disclose matters occurring before the grand jury, except as otherwise provided for in these rules. No obligation of secrecy may be imposed on any person except in accordance with this rule. A knowing violation of Rule 6 may be punished as a contempt of court.[c]

At the heart of the present controversy is the last line of the Rule. We must decide whether this language creates a private cause of action–that is, whether a private person who claims damage because of a violation of this general rule of grand jury secrecy may bring an action against a violator of the rule to enjoin such violation or any threatened future violations and seek sanctions for contempt. We conclude that Rule 6(e)(2) does not establish a private cause of action, but a person claiming damage as a result of a violation of the rule has the right to call such violation to the court's attention, and the court shall take action as hereinafter directed. Notice to the court may be by way of petition or by letter to the district judge.

Plaintiff argues that if the rule provides for civil contempt then it follows that a private cause of action may be maintained thereunder. Several [circuit] courts have adopted this reasoning. [p. 481] * * *

We find that the question of whether this rule of grand jury secrecy creates a private cause of action is not determined by the nature of the contempt provided therein. The rule does not modify contempt as being either civil or criminal or both.

---

[5] Finn claims that Schiller filed the Statement in an effort to pressure him into a plea agreement. Based on the record before us, this is certainly a reasonable conclusion.

[c] The second sentence of Rule 6(e)(2) permitting a contempt for knowing violation of the Rule was moved to Rule 6(e)(7) in a revision of the Federal Rules of Criminal Procedure that became effective on December 1, 2002. The language remains identical, and the Fourth Circuit's discussion of Rule 6(e)(2)'s contempt sanction is unaffected by the change in the Rule.

In Gompers v. Buck's Stove & Range Co., 221 U.S. 418 (1911), the United States Supreme Court held:

> Contempts are neither wholly civil nor altogether criminal. And "it may not always be easy to classify a particular act as belonging to either one of these two classes. It may partake of the characteristics of both." But in either event, and whether the proceedings be civil or criminal, there must be an allegation that in contempt of court the defendant has disobeyed the order, and a prayer that he be attached and punished therefor. It is not the fact of punishment, but rather its character and purpose, that often serve to distinguish between the two classes of cases. If it is for civil contempt the punishment is remedial, and for the benefit of the complainant. But if it is for criminal contempt the sentence is punitive, to vindicate the authority of the court. It is true that punishment by imprisonment may be remedial as well as punitive, and many civil contempt proceedings have resulted not only in the imposition of a fine, payable to the complainant, but also in committing the defendant to prison. But imprisonment for civil contempt is ordered where the defendant has refused to do an affirmative act required by the provisions of an order which, either in form or substance, was mandatory in its character. Imprisonment in such cases is not inflicted as a punishment, but is intended to be remedial by coercing the defendant to do what he had refused to do.

Guided by this reasoning and by the fact that Rule 6 does not modify or qualify in any way the phrase "contempt of court", we conclude that the rule provides for both civil and criminal contempt.

If Plaintiff's allegations are true, both civil and criminal contempt may be required to afford complete relief. Plaintiff alleges a continuing pattern of prosecutorial misconduct that includes release of grand jury material in violation of Rule 6(e)(2). An injunction to stop further or future release of grand jury material would be remedial and civil in nature. However, Plaintiff also alleges that Defendant has already violated the rule by making public the eighty-three page Statement. If this were proved, a finding of criminal contempt would be proper as punishment for the past violation of the rule and to vindicate the authority of the court.

Although we find that the language of the rule provides both civil and criminal contempt, it does not follow that the rule creates a private cause of action. A claimant may notify the court of a violation of the rule or may petition the court to investigate an alleged violation, but such complainant may not proceed by way of a civil action against the alleged violator. * * *

The rule by its clear language does not indicate that there is a right of private enforcement, and we find that such a right may not be implied. "The federal judiciary will not engraft a remedy on a statute, no matter how salutary, that Congress did not intend to provide." California v. Sierra Club,

451 U.S. 287, 297 (1981). This reluctance is more pronounced when one contemplates adding a remedy to a rule of court.

Even if it may be argued that a civil remedy under Rule 6(e)(2) would not be inconsistent with the congressional scheme, this is not sufficient to justify a court-created cause of action where Congress has not affirmatively indicated that it intended such.

In Cort v. Ash, 422 U.S. 66 (1975), the Supreme Court established the preferred approach for determining whether a private right of action should be implied from a federal statute. The Court listed four factors to be considered:

> First, is the plaintiff "one of the class for whose *especial benefit* the statute was enacted,"--that is, does the statute create a federal right in favor of the plaintiff? Second, is there any indication of legislative intent, explicit or implicit, either to create such a remedy or to deny one? Third, is it consistent with the underlying purposes of the legislative scheme to imply such a remedy for the plaintiff? And finally, is the cause of action one traditionally relegated to state law, in an area basically the concern of the states, so that it would be inappropriate to infer a cause of action based solely on federal law?
> * * *

A consideration of the first two *Cort* factors is dispositive. The language of the rule does not suggest that Congress intended to create a federal right for the special benefit of a class of persons; rather, the rule was established to protect the grand jury process and to codify "a practice the district courts had been following for eighty years."

Under the second step of the analysis, there is no evidence that Congress anticipated that there would be a private remedy. Therefore, it is unnecessary to inquire further because factors three and four are only relevant "if the first two factors give indication of congressional intent to create the remedy." California v. Sierra Club.

Our decision that Finn may not bring a private action under Rule 6 does not preclude the district court from granting relief. To the contrary, once an alleged Rule 6(e)(2) violation is brought to the court's attention, it is the district court's duty to investigate the matter and impose contempt sanctions when it finds a violation has occurred. Because the victim of a breach of grand jury secrecy cannot bring suit on his or her own behalf, the district court has an inherent duty to preserve the integrity of Rule 6 by instituting contempt proceedings when presented with a prima facie case of a violation. The United States Attorney has a similar duty to preserve the integrity of the Rule and to act promptly when he has information of a violation.

At first glance, criminal contempt may appear to be a harsh remedy, but compromising grand jury secrecy is a serious matter. It can endanger the lives of witnesses and law enforcement officers and undermine the grand jury system. Courts must not tolerate violations of Rule 6(e) by anyone, especially United States Attorneys who, as alleged in this case, may do so in an effort to pressure a target into a plea agreement. Overzealous prosecutors must not be allowed to file sweeping statements of fact alleging violations of various laws by unindicted individuals. A primary purpose of Rule 6 is to protect the unindicted, and the United States Attorney has a duty to protect the innocent as well as to prosecute those indicted by the grand jury.

The Rule is intended to protect grand jury secrecy, and one of the purposes of grand jury secrecy is to "assure that persons who are accused but exonerated by the grand jury will not be held up to public ridicule." *Douglas Oil.* We hold that upon a prima facie showing to the district court of an alleged Rule 6(e) violation, the court *must* take appropriate steps to determine whether a violation has occurred. If the court finds that a violation has, in fact, occurred, the court should take appropriate action to prevent further violations and to sanction the violator as provided by the Rule. * * *

Next, we turn to Finn's assertion that, independent of any statutory authority, the district court retains jurisdiction over his private action pursuant to the court's inherent supervisory power over grand jury proceedings.

Schiller maintains that the Fourth Circuit should decline to consider Finn's argument that the district court's inherent supervisory authority is a basis for jurisdiction, because Finn never pursued this issue in the district court. However, a review of the pleadings reveals that Finn cites, as a basis for jurisdiction, the "inherent authority of this court to supervise grand jury proceedings." In addition, Finn raised the issue in his brief in support of his petition to strike the Statement and to have the court interview the grand jurors to determine if they could continue deliberations in an unbiased manner. We find that Finn adequately presented the issue to the district court.

* * * In Chambers v. NASCO, Inc., 501 U.S. 32 (1991), the Supreme Court noted that

> when there is bad-faith conduct in the course of litigation that could be adequately sanctioned under the Rules, the court ordinarily should rely on the Rules rather than the inherent power. But if in the informed discretion of the court, neither the statute nor the Rules are up to the task, the court may safely rely on its inherent power.

The district court's inherent supervisory power over grand jury proceedings is sufficient for it, upon proper proof, to impose either civil or criminal contempt sanctions because its inherent powers are not proscribed by Rule 6. However, the court's supervisory power does not authorize a private cause of action because such power is vested in the court, and only the court may invoke it. * * *

Finally, we turn to Finn's assertion that the district court has jurisdiction over his complaint directly under the Fifth Amendment. Finn argues that the Due Process Clause of the Fifth Amendment guarantees that he will not be charged with criminal misconduct by a U.S. Attorney or by a grand jury absent a proper indictment, and he claims that the district court erred in dismissing his complaint for lack of subject matter jurisdiction because the district court has "original jurisdiction of all civil actions arising under the Constitution, laws or treaties of the United States." 28 U.S.C. § 1331.

In response, Schiller asserts that Finn did not request relief based upon alleged due process violations, but rather limited his request for relief to alleged violations of Rule 6(e). Therefore, Schiller argues, we should not consider this jurisdictional claim because it was not raised below. Under a liberal reading of the complaint, one might find a constitutional question presented, and Finn did mention due process in his argument and in his brief before the district court, but the district judge did not mention this claim of jurisdiction in his ruling. Because this matter is being remanded, we will not consider the due process claim and allow the district court the opportunity to first consider it.

For the foregoing reasons, we find that the district court correctly dismissed Finn's complaint under Rule 12(b)(6) because neither Rule 6(e)(2) nor the district court's inherent power creates or provides a private cause of action for its enforcement. However, we find that the district court has a duty to protect the integrity of grand jury proceedings. Upon remand, the district court must investigate the matter to determine whether the information contained in the statement violates Rule 6(e)(2). If so, the court shall impose such sanctions as it may find appropriate. Additionally, the district court may, under its inherent power impose either civil or criminal contempt sanctions if it finds that sanctions under Rule 6(e)(2) are not appropriate. Also, the district court shall, on remand, consider Finn's claim of jurisdiction for denial of due process. Consequently, the district court's order is Affirmed but Remanded for Further Proceedings Consistent with this Opinion.

NOTES AND QUESTIONS

1. *Sufficient Evidence to Trigger an Investigation. In re U.S.,* 441 F.3d 444 (1st Cir. 2006), refused to adopt any specific test for triggering an investigation of pre-indictment leaks of grand jury material. The First Circuit stated:

> [T]here must be some reasonable basis for a district court to launch an inquiry into claims that the prosecutor has engaged in grand jury

misconduct. Some courts have adopted a rule that a prima facie case must be shown first. We are reluctant to use such a test. The "prima facie case" test is used in many different ways and means many different things. Further, a formulaic approach helps little: the varieties of possible misconduct and the factual variations are myriad. Depending on context, mere suspicion may be enough to cause further inquiry into violation of a well-established rule, particularly where infringement of a defendant's constitutional rights is potentially involved.

While the district court's initial investigation of leaks was justified, its later order halting trial a year after the leaks ended was not justified under Rule 6(e). The First Circuit found that "the court's actions in launching an investigation of the government as a source of the pre-indictment leaks, more than a year after the leaks had stopped and after a decision had been made de facto not to investigate leaks further, were unjustified in this context."

2. *Recognizing a Civil Cause of Action*. Unlike the Fourth Circuit, the Fifth and District of Columbia Circuits recognize that an individual who is the subject of a grand jury leak can pursue a civil cause of action for relief under Rule 6(e). **In re Grand Jury Investigation (Lance)**, 610 F.2d 202 (5th Cir. 1980), involved a claim by Bert Lance, a former senior official in the Carter administration, who sought relief, including dismissal of the grand jury and termination of the investigation, because of information published about the grand jury's investigation of his conduct in connection with a national bank. The court set out a five factor test to determine is the claimant established a prima facie violation of Rule 6(e), which would require the district court to hold an evidentiary hearing to determine whether there was a violation: (1) the court must have before it news reports that "clearly indicate * * * [disclosure of] information about matters occurring before the grand jury"; (2) the reports must also indicate that the source of such information was "one of those [persons] proscribed from disclosing such matter" by Rule 6(e)(2) (i.e., government personnel, jurors, or jury personnel); (3) in "assessing the what and who of disclosure at the prima facie case stage, the court must assume that all statements in the news reports are correct"; (4) the "court must consider the nature of the relief requested and the extent to which it interferes with the grand jury process," requiring a "lesser showing for a prima facie case" on a request for contempt sanctions than on a request to dismiss the grand jury; and (5) "the court must weigh any evidence presented by the government to rebut the assumed truthfulness of reports which otherwise make a prima facie case of misconduct."

In **Barry v. United States**, 865 F.2d 1317 (D.C. Cir. 1989), former District of Columbia Mayor Marion Barry filed a complaint for equitable relief and contempt sanctions against the Attorney General of the United States, the United States Attorney for the District of Columbia, and other federal officials, claiming that they had unlawfully disclosed matters occurring before the grand jury that was investigating allegations of governmental corruption. The District of Columbia Circuit found that one newspaper article disclosed information about matters occurring before the grand jury and indicated that the sources of the information included attorneys and agents of the government. It ordered the district court to conduct an evidentiary hearing on the claim, "which, if proven, would justify civil contempt sanctions and/or injunctive relief under Rule 6(e)(2)." In **In re Sealed Case**, 151 F.3d 1059 (D.C. Cir. 1998), the court explained the process for pursuing a Rule 6(e) complaint:

> Barry thus envisions that a two-step analysis will be employed to determine whether a violation of Rule 6(e)(2) has occurred. First, the district court must determine whether the plaintiff has established a prima facie case. This determination will typically be based solely on an assessment of news articles submitted by the plaintiff; indeed, we acknowledged in Barry that a Rule 6(e)(2) plaintiff could not be "expected to do more at this juncture of the litigation" given that he or she would "almost never have access to anything beyond the words of the [news] report." Second, if the court determines that a prima facie case has been established, the burden shifts to the government to "attempt to explain its actions" in a show cause hearing. If the government fails to rebut the prima facie case, a violation of Rule 6(e)(2) is deemed to have occurred. The court then determines what remedy will be sufficient to deter further leaks. The remedy may be the imposition of civil contempt sanctions or equitable relief or both, "depending upon the nature of the violation and what the trial court deems necessary to prevent further unlawful disclosures of matters before the grand jury." Significantly, in establishing this two- step framework, Barry said nothing about the burden shifting back to the plaintiff after the government's presentation or about the plaintiff retaining the burden of persuasion after a prima facie case has been established. Under Barry, then, the plaintiff's burden is minimal; the responsibility of coming forward with evidence to rebut the accusation of unauthorized disclosure lies squarely with the government, the party in "the best position to know whether [it is] responsible for a violation of the Rule." If, of course, the government convinces the trial judge that no violation of Rule 6(e)(2) has occurred, that is the end of the proceeding.

3. *Strategic Considerations.* The Rule 6(e) challenges to alleged disclosure of secret grand jury information are very difficult to prove, if the courts in that circuit can even hear the case. Are their strategic reasons for raising the issue, even if it is unlikely to succeed? The claim that the grand jury's strict rule of secrecy has been violated will likely result in an end to leaks, if they came from the prosecutor's office or the criminal investigators. If the Rule 6(e) claim will be heard by the same judge who would also be responsible for a subsequent prosecution, then bringing potential violations to the court's attention can alert the judge to possible governmental misconduct. Moreover, as discussed below in Section D, a defendant who is acquitted may be able to bring a suit against the government for attorney's fees if the government's

conduct in prosecuting the case can be shown to be "vexatious, frivolous, or in bad faith." Proof of a Rule 6(e) violation would help to establish that the government's conduct warrants such an award.

4. *"Matters Occurring Before the Grand Jury."* Rule 6(e)(2)(B) does not define what constitutes a "matters occurring before the grand jury," and the phrase can be interpreted broadly—anything related to the grand jury investigation or obtained pursuant to its authority, or narrowly—only those things that actually take place in the presence of the grand jury. The District of Columbia Circuit considered the threshold question in relation to a claim by President Clinton that the Office of Independent Counsel (OIC) had improperly leaked information to the New York Times that involved "matters occurring before the grand jury," specifically whether the OIC planned to indict the President.

In re: SEALED CASE NO. 99-3091
(Office of Independent Counsel Contempt Proceeding)
192 F.3d 995 (D.C. Cir. 1999)

PER CURIAM.

On January 31, 1999, while the Senate was trying President William J. Clinton on articles of impeachment, the New York Times published a front page article captioned "Starr is Weighing Whether to Indict Sitting President." * * * The next day, the Office of the President (the White House) and Mr. Clinton jointly filed in district court a motion for an order to show cause why OIC, or the individuals therein, should not be held in contempt for disclosing grand jury material in violation of Federal Rule of Criminal Procedure 6(e). The White House and Mr. Clinton pointed to several excerpts from the article as evidence of OIC's violations of the grand jury secrecy rule. * * * OIC responded that the matters disclosed in the article merely rehashed old news reports and, in any event, did not fall within Rule 6(e)'s definition of "matters occurring before the grand jury." * * *

A prima facie violation based on a news report is established by showing that the report discloses "matters occurring before the grand jury" and indicates that sources of the information include government attorneys. See Barry v. United States, [p. 485]. Because OIC has withdrawn its argument that none of its attorneys was the source of the disclosures in the New York Times article at issue here, the only remaining issue is whether those disclosures qualify as "matters occurring before the grand jury." Fed.R.Crim.P. 6(e)(2).

The district court concluded that only one excerpt from the New York Times article constituted a prima facie violation of Rule 6(e). That excerpt, * * * disclosed the desire of some OIC prosecutors to seek, not long after the conclusion of the Senate trial, an indictment of Mr. Clinton on perjury and obstruction of justice charges, including lying under oath in his deposition in the Paula Jones matter and in his grand jury testimony. These statements, according to the district court, reveal a specific time frame for seeking an indictment, the details of a likely indictment, and the direction a group of prosecutors within OIC believes the grand jury investigation should take. Not surprisingly, Mr. Clinton and the White House agree with the district court's expansive reading of Rule 6(e). OIC takes a narrow view of the Rule's coverage, arguing that matters occurring outside the physical presence of the grand jury are covered only if they reveal grand jury matters. DOJ generally supports OIC with respect to the Rule's coverage, but emphasizes the importance of the context and concreteness of disclosures.

The key to the district court's reasoning is its reliance on this court's definition of "matters occurring before the grand jury." In In re Motions of Dow Jones & Co., 142 F.3d 496, 500 (D.C.Cir.), we noted that this phrase encompasses "not only what has occurred and what is occurring, but also what is likely to occur," including "the identities of witnesses or jurors, the substance of testimony as well as actual transcripts, the strategy or direction of the investigation, the deliberations or questions of jurors, and the like." In the earlier contempt proceeding against Independent Counsel Starr, however, we cautioned the district court about "the problematic nature of applying so broad a definition, especially as it relates to the 'strategy or direction of the investigation,' to the inquiry as to whether a government attorney has made unauthorized disclosures." In re Sealed Case No. 98-3077, 151 F.3d at 1071 n. 12. Despite the seemingly broad nature of the statements in Dow Jones, we have never read Rule 6(e) to require that a "veil of secrecy be drawn over all matters occurring in the world that happen to be investigated by a grand jury." * * * Indeed, we have said that "[t]he disclosure of information 'coincidentally before the grand jury [which can] be revealed in such a manner that its revelation would not elucidate the inner workings of the grand jury' is not prohibited." * * * Thus, the phrases "likely to occur" and "strategy and direction" must be read in light of the text of Rule 6(e)–which limits the Rule's coverage to "matters occurring before the grand jury"–as well as the purposes of the Rule.

As we have recited on many occasions,

Rule 6(e) . . . protects several interests of the criminal justice system: "First, if preindictment proceedings were made public, many prospective witnesses would be hesitant to come forward voluntarily, knowing that those against whom they testify would be aware of that testimony. Moreover, witnesses who appeared before the grand jury would be less likely to testify fully and frankly, as they would be open to retribution as well as to inducements. There also would be the risk that those about to be indicted would flee, or would try to influence individual grand jurors to vote against indictment. Finally, by preserving the secrecy of the proceedings, we assure that persons who are accused but exonerated by the grand jury will not be held up to public ridicule."

In re Sealed Case No. 98-3077, 151 F.3d 1059 (D.C.Cir.1998) (quoting Douglas Oil Co. v. Petrol Stops Northwest, 441 U.S. 211 (1979)). These purposes, as well as the text of the Rule itself, reflect the need to preserve the secrecy of the grand jury proceedings themselves. It is therefore necessary to differentiate between statements by a prosecutor's office with respect to its own investigation, and statements by a prosecutor's office with respect to a grand jury's investigation, a distinction of the utmost significance upon which several circuits have already remarked. * * *

Information actually presented to the grand jury is core Rule 6(e) material that is afforded the broadest protection from disclosure. Prosecutors' statements about their investigations, however, implicate the Rule only when they directly reveal grand jury matters. To be sure, we have recognized that Rule 6(e) would be easily evaded if a prosecutor could with impunity discuss with the press testimony about to be presented to a grand jury, so long as it had not yet occurred. Accordingly, we have read Rule 6(e) to cover matters "likely to occur." And even a discussion of "strategy and direction of the investigation" could include references to not yet delivered but clearly anticipated testimony. * * * But that does not mean that any discussion of an investigation is violative of Rule 6(e). Indeed, the district court's Local Rule 308(b)(2), which governs attorney conduct in grand jury matters, recognizes that prosecutors often have a legitimate interest in revealing aspects of their investigations "to inform the public that the investigation is underway, to describe the general scope of the investigation, to obtain assistance in the apprehension of a suspect, to warn the public of any dangers, or otherwise aid in the investigation."

It may often be the case, however, that disclosures by the prosecution referencing its own investigation should not be made for tactical reasons, or are in fact prohibited by other Rules or ethical guidelines. For instance, prosecutors may be prohibited by internal guidelines, see, e.g., United States Attorney Manual § 1-7.530, from discussing the strategy or direction of their investigation before an indictment is sought. This would serve one of the same purposes as Rule 6(e): protecting the reputation of innocent suspects. But a court may not use Rule 6(e) to generally regulate prosecutorial statements to the press. The purpose of the Rule is only to protect the secrecy of grand jury proceedings.

Thus, internal deliberations of prosecutors that do not directly reveal grand jury proceedings are not Rule 6(e) material. * * * It may be thought that when such deliberations include a discussion of whether an indictment should be sought, or whether a particular individual is potentially criminally liable, the deliberations have crossed into the realm of Rule 6(e) material. This ignores, however, the requirement that the matter occur before the grand jury. Where the reported deliberations do not reveal that an indictment has been sought or will be sought, ordinarily they will not reveal anything definite enough to come within the scope of Rule 6(e).

For these reasons, the disclosure that a group of OIC prosecutors "believe" that an indictment should be brought at the end of the impeachment proceedings does not on its face, or in the context of the article as a whole, violate Rule 6(e). We acknowledge, as did OIC, that such statements are troubling, for they have the potential to damage the reputation of innocent suspects. But bare statements that some assistant prosecutors in OIC wish to seek an indictment do not implicate the grand jury; the prosecutors may not even be basing their opinion on information presented to a grand jury.

The fact that the disclosure also reveals a time period for seeking the indictment of "not long after the Senate trial concludes" does not in any way indicate what is "likely to occur" before the grand jury within the meaning of Rule 6(e). That disclosure reflects nothing more than a desire on the part of some OIC prosecutors to seek an indictment at that time, not a decision to do so. The general uncertainty as to whether an indictment would in fact be sought (according to the article, only some prosecutors in OIC thought one should be) leads us to conclude that this portion of the article did not reveal anything that was "occurring before the grand jury."

Nor does it violate the Rule to state the general grounds for such an indictment–here, lying under oath in a deposition and before the grand jury–where no secret grand jury material is revealed. In ordinary circumstances, Rule 6(e) covers the disclosure of the names of grand jury witnesses. Therefore, the statement that members of OIC wished to seek an indictment based on Mr. Clinton's alleged perjury before a grand jury would ordinarily be Rule 6(e) material. In this case, however, we take judicial notice that the President's status as a witness before the grand jury was a matter of widespread public knowledge well before the New York Times article at issue in this case was written; the President himself went on national television the day of his testimony to reveal this fact. * * * Where the general public is already aware of the information contained in the prosecutor's statement, there is no additional harm in the prosecutor referring to such information. * * * Therefore, it cannot be said that OIC "disclosed" the name of a grand jury witness, in violation of Rule 6(e), by referring to the President's grand jury testimony.

Similarly, it would ordinarily be a violation of Rule 6(e) to disclose that a grand jury is investigating a particular person. Thus, the statement that a grand jury is "hearing the case against Mr. Clinton" would be covered by Rule 6(e) if it were not for the fact that the New York Times article did not reveal any secret, for it was already common knowledge well before January 31, 1999, that a grand jury was investigating alleged perjury and obstruction of justice by the President. Once again, the President's appearance on national television confirmed as much. * * *

In light of our conclusion that the excerpt from the New York Times article does not constitute a prima facie violation of Rule 6(e), we reverse and remand with instructions to dismiss the Rule 6(e) contempt proceedings against OIC. * * *

D. ATTORNEY'S FEES FOR THE GOVERNMENT'S MISCONDUCT

The Supreme Court in *Bank of Nova Scotia* noted there were other means of remedying errors that did not have a prejudicial impact. They cited as illustrations of alternative remedies the punishment of a prosecutor's knowing violation of Rule 6 as contempt of court, requesting the bar or department of justice to initiate discipline proceedings, and the court "chastis[ing] the prosecutor in a published opinion." "Such remedies," it noted, "allow the court to focus on the culpable individual rather than granting a windfall to the unprejudiced defendant." Anne Poulin, *Supervision of the Grand Jury: Who Watches the Guardian?*, 68 WASH. U.L.Q. 885 (1990), is sharply critical of the Court's reliance upon such sanctions, noting that several factors limit their effectiveness. The "victim may have minimal incentive to invoke the sanction" since it will not address "the harm to the victim and the victim's reputation." Second, sanctions against the prosecutor "will only reach a narrow sub-group of abuses." As a practical matter, for various types of misconduct, such as leaks to the press, the victim will be unable to establish which government personnel engaged in the conduct. As to others, even if the abuser is identified, the victim will be unable to establish the element of bad faith that typically is a prerequisite to imposing the sanctions cited by the court. Finally, the "sanctions will have limited deterrent effect," as they are "unlikely to exert institutional pressure" beyond the individual sanctioned. The author suggests that, in the wake of *Bank of Nova Scotia* and *Mechanik*, "equitable intervention in the grand jury process may offer the only opportunity to address abusive grand jury practice." Would such intervention be permissible in light of *Williams*, apart from instances of violation of Rule 6 or statutory prohibitions? See Peter J. Henning, *Prosecutorial Misconduct in Grand Jury Investigations*, 51 S.C. L. REV. 1 (1999) ("The Supreme Court has eliminated direct judicial review of prosecutorial misconduct in the proceeding in which the misconduct occurred. If a grand jury indicts a defendant, the only means of seeking vindication is a trial in which a jury or a judge determines whether the government introduced proof beyond a reasonable doubt that the defendant committed a crime.").

In 1998, Congress adopted the Hyde Amendment, 18 U.S.C. § 3006A, to permit defendants subjected to improper federal prosecution to sue for attorneys fees after their exoneration. The statute permits a fee claim if the government's position was "vexatious, frivolous, or in bad faith." The statute does not define any of the three bases for an award of attorneys fees, and the legislative history sheds minimal light on the meaning of the terms. Therefore, the courts have been left to determine their meaning and apply them to claims of prosecutorial and investigatory misconduct in the wide variety of setting in which such misconduct arises including, *inter alia*, misconduct in obtaining a grand jury indictment.

UNITED STATES v. BRAUNSTEIN
281 F.3d 982 (9th Cir. 2002)

PREGERSON, Circuit Judge.

Appellant David T. Braunstein ("Braunstein") appeals the district court's order denying his motion for attorney's fees pursuant to the Hyde Amendment. Braunstein asserts that he incurred approximately $200,000 in attorney's fees defending against sixteen federal criminal charges of wire fraud, interstate transportation of goods obtained by fraud, and money laundering. He claims that under the Hyde Amendment, the government is required to pay his attorney's fees because the prosecution was "vexatious, frivolous, or in bad faith." * * *

Braunstein is a businessman who bought and sold computers, often through two companies he owned, Pacific Rim Technologies Corporation and Almacen. Braunstein maintained a computer distribution company in California and a computer retail store and refurbishing plant in Tijuana, Mexico. From September 1993 through April 1996, Braunstein bought computers from the Apple Latin America Company ("ALAC"). ALAC is a subdivision of Apple Computer, Inc. ("Apple"), an international computer manufacturer and sales company headquartered in the United States. ALAC is responsible for the sale of Apple products to Mexico, Central America, South America, and the Caribbean.

Braunstein's business relationship with ALAC consisted primarily of buying excess or obsolete Apple computers at greatly reduced prices. ALAC would ship the computers from Apple's warehouses in Chicago, California, and Canada to Braunstein's warehouse in San Diego. Although Braunstein was known as an ALAC distributor whose sales territory was Mexico, Braunstein sold most of his ALAC inventory within the United States, to an Arizona businessman named Alan Kaplan ("Kaplan"). Kaplan, in turn, sold the ALAC computers to other Apple resellers and wholesalers in the United States at prices substantially below Apple's listed wholesale price for such products. ALAC's former Sales Director referred to distributors like Braunstein and Kaplan as "the Marshalls or the T.J. Maxx of the computer industry."[4]

When purchasing Apple products, Braunstein dealt directly with Lopez and Carlos Valladeros ("Valladeros"), ALAC's regional sales representative

---

[4] The type of sales transacted between ALAC and Braunstein were alternately described as ALAC's method of "flushing" and "dumping" unwanted excess product.

for northern Latin America. In addition, Braunstein's business ventures with ALAC were overseen by Rubio.

Braunstein always paid ALAC up front, in cash. In exchange, he received an additional one percent discount. Lopez estimated that Braunstein's purchases brought ALAC "about a million dollars a month, which could be about five percent of the sales for Apple Latin America. It could have gone as high as 55 percent of the overall sales of Apple Latin America." Braunstein's dealings with ALAC were not, however, formalized by written contract; instead, the parties reached an oral understanding for each deal as to quantity and price. Lopez testified that it was unusual to conduct business with a distributor without a contract, but that "[i]t was done sometimes."

According to internal and external reports, ALAC "was under pressure to generate high sales volume," and deals such as the one with Braunstein facilitated that goal. Some of this pressure appears to stem from the fact that ALAC employees worked on commission. According to the postal inspector's report, if ALAC employees "made their gross margin, unit mix, and revenue, a bonus would be given." * * *

ALAC's deals with Braunstein benefitted ALAC in the short term by increasing the sales volume of products for which there were few, if any, other buyers. But the deals hurt Apple in the long-term by undercutting its ability to generate profitable sales in the United States. ALAC's business dealings effectively put ALAC's own distributors (whose sales area was limited to Latin America and the Carribean) into direct competition with Apple's United States distributors. Moreover, Braunstein and Kaplan were selling their Apple inventory within the United States at a much cheaper price than the other United States distributors were offering, which hurt the sales of those distributors and caused confusion and resentment in the market.

In August 1996, Apple's management became concerned about the systemic underselling of Apple's United States distributors by ALAC distributors. Specifically, Apple was concerned that ALAC distributors were engaging in "gray marketing," which involves the sale of Apple products outside the territory for which they are intended, and at a lower price than Apple would have authorized. Apple hired Kroll Associates ("Kroll"), an international private investigation firm, to look into ALAC's business practices.

Kroll issued its findings in a fifteen-page written report, on January 7, 1997. The report concluded that, "a potentially significant gray market problem existed" at ALAC and that "[t]here also appear to be a number of issues internal to ALAC which were contributing to the gray market problem." Kroll based this conclusion on its "preliminary findings, [which] consisted of specialized audits, interviewing selected persons, and reviewing pertinent documentation."

For reasons that are somewhat unclear from the record, the United States Attorney's Office in Arizona began investigating ALAC's business deals with Braunstein in the fall of 1997.[6] In August 1997, the Assistant United States Attorney ("AUSA") assigned to the ALAC case alerted Braunstein that he had become a target of a federal criminal investigation, and Braunstein retained Michael L. Lipman ("Lipman") as counsel.

In August, September, and October 1997, the AUSA conducted telephone interviews of several ALAC employees who had dealt directly with Braunstein, including Valladeros. The AUSA also interviewed Lopez. * * *

On September 23, 1997, Lipman wrote the AUSA a twenty-two page letter, in which he set forth in detail the legal and factual bases for his belief that Braunstein had done nothing illegal. * * * Lipman wrote:

> We believe that our client did not have a valid contract with Apple Latin America at any time during these transaction[s]; that Apple Latin America was aware that there were no legal restrictions on my client's resale of product; and that Apple Latin America knew, or should have known, that my client was selling the bulk of the product to a reseller in the U.S. Furthermore, Apple Latin America was more than happy to have these transactions occur because they created a material increase in their revenues.

Lipman continued, "To the degree that particular employees or former employees of Apple Latin America contend that they thought Mr. Braunstein was selling his product in Mexico, we submit that Apple's own financial documents will disprove these contentions." Lipman then detailed ALAC's financial woes and its efforts to "rebuild its distribution network," including its development of the "Alternate Channel Concept." He explained:

> [T]he "alternate channel" concept called for Apple Latin America to recruit United States distributors in the "border states" (primarily California, Texas and Florida). These distributors would be offered lower prices than U.S. distributors with the expectation that they could "recapture" the Latin American reseller market for ALAC.... This program was established so the U.S. distributors could not undercut the Latin American in-country distributors (and take away sales from the Apple Latin America division) and effectively "gray market" product into Latin America. Under the "alternate channel" concept, these distributors could sell to, among others, United States

---

[6] The most plausible reason for the investigation is that Apple alerted the United States Attorney's Office to the problem. The United States Attorney's Office in Arizona may have gotten involved because it was already investigating criminal fraud allegations against Kaplan. The Arizona United States Attorney's Office obtained an indictment against Kaplan in the fall of 1997 for conducting "a fraudulent rebate scheme involving Apple Powerbook 5300's." The government has never accused Braunstein of any involvement in that rebate scheme.

businesses with operations in Latin America. Thus, the program itself provided for sales of computers inside the United States. Additionally, it was anticipated by ALAC, and ALAC was willing to accept, that some "gray marketing" would occur into United States markets.

Lipman informed the AUSA that she could find confirmation of the alternative channel concept in "pricing studies performed by Apple Latin America," memos between ALAC and other Apple divisions, and internal documentation and memoranda within ALAC. Lipman also explained in detail Braunstein's relationship with ALAC and told the AUSA that internal ALAC documents would confirm that Braunstein was an alternate channel distributor who generated over $25 million in revenue for ALAC and that "ALAC had Braunstein existing entirely outside its normal distribution network for two years."

In a separate section of the letter, entitled "Apple's Knowledge Regarding Braunstein's Sales," Lipman listed "numerous sources of information and documentation" in Apple's possession that he believed would demonstrate that ALAC knew that Braunstein was selling its product in the United States. * * * Lipman concluded his letter by telling the AUSA: "You invited us to provide you evidence to support our theories; unfortunately, this documentation is at Apple, and *only you can gain access to it*." (Emphasis added). [The court discussed other conversations and documents within the possession of the government.].

* * * The AUSA convened a grand jury in the District of Arizona to present her case against Braunstein. On August 21, 1997, the same day that the AUSA interviewed Valladeros by telephone, Valladeros appeared as a witness before the grand jury and testified about his business dealings with Braunstein. Valladeros testified that, as an ALAC sales representative, he sold computers to Braunstein from 1993 until Valladeros left the company in 1995. Responding to repeated questions from the AUSA as to whether Braunstein was told that he could only sell Apple products in Mexico, Valladeros stated that he did not recall. The AUSA then asked: "If [Braunstein] told you that the [Apple] product was going to stay in the United States and be shipped to Nebraska, for example, would you have sold him the product?" Valladeros replied: "No." Several transcript pages later, the following exchange occurred:

AUSA: And did you explain to [Braunstein] he could not sell [Apple products] inside the United States?

VALLADEROS: Again, when I explained to him the concept, I do not recall if I was explicit to him telling him that he could not sell in the United States.... And to be honest with you, having dealt in Latin America for eight, nine years, it never crossed my mind the fact that, you know, illegally selling product into the U.S., because it didn't make sense.

AUSA: So you assumed when you were negotiating with [Braunstein] that because you're Apple Latin America, this is all going to be exported to Latin America?
VALLADEROS: Correct.

The AUSA later asked Valladeros, "[D]o you know of anyone at Apple, either Apple Latin America or Apple America, who told Mr. Braunstein he could sell the product within the U.S. and not export it?" Valladeros replied, "Not to my knowledge."

This grand jury testimony by Valladeros flatly contradicted his answers to the AUSA's questions during the telephone conversation they had earlier *that same day.* In the telephone interview, Valladeros told the AUSA that "Braunstein could sell in his area of San Diego and sell to other U.S. companies who had dealings with Apple and exported products." Valladeros also told the AUSA that he and Braunstein "spoke extensively" about Braunstein's United States sales and that Valladeros "gave [a] report to Apple" about these conversations.

The AUSA also called Rubio and Lopez as grand jury witnesses. Both Lopez and Rubio testified that they were laid off by Apple in 1997 and that Braunstein was only authorized to sell Apple products within Latin America. On December 11, 1997, the grand jury returned an indictment charging Braunstein with multiple counts of wire fraud, in violation of 18 U.S.C. § 1343; interstate transportation of goods obtained by fraud, in violation of 18 U.S.C. § 2314; and money laundering, in violation of 18 U.S.C. § 1956. * * *

* * * On February 12, 1999, Philip H. Stillman, ("Stillman") who had replaced Lipman as Braunstein's counsel, subpoenaed various documents and records from Apple. Apple, represented by John J. Steele, ("Steele") moved to quash the subpoena as overly broad, and the government joined in the motion. On February 23, 1999, the district court granted the motion to quash and ordered Stillman to meet with Steele to "narrow down the number of areas of documents that you seek." The court also ordered Steele to "turn over the Kroll Report unredacted." * * * On March 8, 1999, the parties were back in court arguing over the subpoenas, and the district court was getting impatient with Apple * * *On March 12, 1999, Apple still had not turned over the Kroll report or any of the other subpoenaed documents. On March 22, Stillman moved for a continuance of the trial. On March 29, the court granted the motion and reset the trial date for May 11. On the same day, the court told Apple to turn over the subpoenaed documents "to the chambers of this court" no later than April 1. Apple did not comply with the order.

After joining in the first motion filed by Apple to quash the subpoena, the United States Attorney's Office was not involved in the discovery battle. Instead, as the AUSA later told the district court, "We remained silent."

On April 14, 1999, less than a month before the trial date, Apple turned over the subpoenaed documents to Braunstein. Among the documents that

Apple turned over were memos written by Lopez and Rubio in which they openly acknowledged the existence of gray market practices among ALAC's distributors. * * * On April 21, 1999, the AUSA moved for a continuance of the trial date. The court denied the motion. On May 3, 1999, the AUSA moved to dismiss the indictment without prejudice. The court granted the motion.

On July 2, 1999, Braunstein filed a motion for attorney's fees pursuant to the Hyde Amendment. The government filed an opposition, and a hearing was held on April 5, 2000. At the hearing, Stillman argued that the AUSA knew about the Lopez-Rubio memos detailing ALAC's knowledge of the gray market practices of its distributors. Specifically, Stillman pointed out that: (1) Lipman, told the AUSA about the Lopez-Rubio memos in his September 23, 1997 letter; (2) Lopez told the AUSA about the memos during their telephone interview on October 15, 1997; and (3) the Kroll report referred to the memos. Stillman stated:

> This was not a needle in a haystack. These documents came from Mr. Lopez's and Mr. Rubio's personnel files. There was a personnel file. It would have taken one phone call from [the AUSA]. [The AUSA] got stacks and stacks of documents, all sales invoices and so forth.... She could have made one phone call to Apple, who was cooperating with [the AUSA] for three years, providing logistic support, document support, and factual support, could have called them on the telephone and said, I want to see Lopez's personnel file.

The AUSA responded by stating that "the Government never alleged this as a gray market case. This is a fraud case ...." She continued:

> Now [the documents] may help the defendant put on his theory of the case which is that gray marketing was a problem at Apple. But they certainly do not constitute Brady material under the Government's theory of the case which is represented in the Indictment, and that is that the defendant engaged in fraudulent activity. He made misrepresentations to Apple repeatedly about where this product was going, and therein lie[s] the fraud.

The AUSA then stated that she received the documents that Stillman subpoenaed from Apple on April 14, 1999, the same day that Stillman did. She continued, "Did we know about a gray marketing issue? Well, obviously, we did, because we had the Kroll Report. But since gray marketing has nothing to do with wire fraud, mail fraud, interstate transportation of goods taken by fraud and money laundering, it's not exculpatory."

Stillman responded: "[T]he concept that gray marketing was not an issue in this case is simply gas. I mean it's–it's the core of the case. If Apple's condoning sales outside the territory, that's it. It's [the] end of [the] story."

On October 3, 2000, the district court entered its five-page order denying Braunstein's motion for attorney's fees. The court concluded that the government's case was not "contrary to established law on fraud ... [and] based on the facts as they evolved, was not frivolous." This appeal followed.
* * *

The Hyde Amendment was enacted by Congress as part of a 1998 appropriations bill and is located in a statutory note to 18 U.S.C. § 3006A. It provides, in relevant part, that courts may award attorney's fees and other litigation expenses to prevailing criminal defendants "where the court finds that *the position of the United States was vexatious, frivolous, or in bad faith,* unless the court finds that special circumstances make the award unjust." Pub.L. No. 105-119,111 Stat. 2440, 2519 (1997) (reprinted in 18 U.S.C. § 3006A, historical and statutory notes) (emphasis added).[8] The defendant bears the burden of proof, "as well as establishing that he is otherwise qualified for the award under the law."[9] * * * The key terms of the Hyde Amendment, "vexatious, frivolous, or in bad faith," are not defined in the statute.

Because the district court based its ruling on a finding that the prosecution was not frivolous in instituting the criminal proceeding against Braunstein, our analysis will focus on that prong of the Hyde Amendment. United States v. Sherburne, 249 F.3d 1121 (9th Cir.2001), stated in a footnote that "frivolous" has only an objective component. No further guidance was given. Therefore, the Hyde Amendment's legislative history and out-of-circuit authority will be considered to provide helpful guidance in deciphering

---

[8] The full text of the Hyde Amendment provides: During fiscal year 1998 and in any fiscal year thereafter, the court, in any criminal case (other than the case in which the defendant is represented by assigned counsel paid for by the public) pending on or after the date of the enactment of this Act [Nov. 26, 1997], may award to a prevailing party, other than the United States, a reasonable attorney's fee and other litigation expenses, where the court finds that the position of the United States was vexatious, frivolous, or in bad faith, unless the court finds that special circumstances make such an award unjust. Such awards shall be granted pursuant to the procedures and limitations (but not the burden of proof) provided for an award under section 2412 of title 28, United States Code. To determine whether or not to award fees and costs under this section, the court, for good cause shown, may receive evidence ex parte and in camera ... and evidence or testimony so received shall be kept under seal. Fees and other expenses awarded under this provision to a party shall be paid by the agency over which the party prevails from any funds made available to the agency by appropriation. No new appropriations shall be made as a result of this provision.

[9] Specifically, as a threshold matter, the defendant must show that: (1) the case against him was pending on or after the enactment of the Hyde Amendment; (2) his net worth is less than $2 million; (3) he was the prevailing party in a criminal prosecution; (4) he was not represented by assigned counsel paid for by the public; (5) his attorney's fees were reasonable; and (6) no special circumstances exist to make the award unjust. United States v. Adkinson, 247 F.3d 1289, 1291 n.2 (11th Cir.2001).

the meaning of "frivolous." United States Representative Henry Hyde, who wrote the original version of the Amendment, explained that successful claimants under the Hyde Amendment must show that the prosecutors "are not just wrong, they are willfully wrong, they are frivolously wrong. They keep information from you that the law says they must disclose. They hide information. They do not disclose exculpatory information to which you are entitled." 143 Cong. Rec. H7786-04, HH7791 (Sept. 24, 1997) (statement of Rep. Hyde).[10] Thus, it is clear that, "[e]ven in its earliest form, the Hyde Amendment was targeted at prosecutorial misconduct, not prosecutorial mistake."

In [United States v.] Gilbert, the Eleventh Circuit interpreted "frivolous" using the "ordinary meaning" of the word as provided in Black's Law Dictionary. The court determined that "frivolous" means "groundless . . . with little prospect of success; often brought to embarrass or annoy the defendant." * * * Because the Eleventh's Circuit's approach to defining "frivolous" and "bad faith" is clear and well-reasoned, we [adopt] it.

To show that the criminal prosecution was "frivolous," Braunstein must demonstrate that the government's position was "foreclosed by binding precedent or so obviously wrong as to be frivolous."

The AUSA obtained an indictment against Braunstein for the federal crimes of wire fraud, interstate transportation of goods obtained by fraud, and money laundering. 18 U.S.C. §§ 1343, 2314, and 1956. * * *

To succeed in prosecuting Braunstein under any of the[se] statutes, * * * the government had to prove that Braunstein engaged in fraud; namely, that he obtained the computers from ALAC through false promises or representations. As the AUSA informed the district court during the argument on the Hyde Amendment motions, "this is a fraud case." Thus, the government's prosecution of Braunstein depended entirely on whether it could prove that he defrauded Apple.

The evidence in the record supports the conclusion that the government's position was so obviously wrong as to be frivolous. First, there was never an enforceable contract between Braunstein and ALAC. Thus, the AUSA's allegations of fraud were dependent on oral misrepresentations by Braunstein. Significantly, none of the grand jury witnesses testified that Braunstein made any such misrepresentations. More importantly, however,

---

[10] The legislation was motivated by Representative Hyde and his colleagues' outrage over the prosecution of former Labor Secretary Ray Donovan and former Congressman Joseph McDade. Both Donovan and McDade were subjected to lengthy federal criminal prosecutions and ultimately were acquitted. Gilbert, 198 F.3d at 1299-1300. The intent of the legislation was to ensure that innocent people would not bankrupt themselves defending against frivolous and bad faith prosecutions. Id. at 1300 (quoting Rep. Hyde as stating, "at least, if the Government tries to bankrupt someone because of attorney's fees, they ought to pay that").

the AUSA had reason to believe, based on information from four independent sources, that employees at ALAC knowingly sold computer products to distributors who resold the same products on the "gray market"; i.e., outside of Latin America, the intended territory.

First, there is the AUSA's interview with Valladeros. According to the AUSA's notes, Valladeros told her that "it was his understanding that Braunstein could sell in his area of San Diego and sell to other U.S. companies who had dealings with Apple." Valladeros made this statement to the AUSA on August 21, 1997, *over three months before the AUSA obtained the indictment against Braunstein.* [Emphasis in original] Second, the AUSA was aware that ALAC employees knew that their customers were selling Apple products in the United States through her interview with Lopez, Valladeros's supervisor. According to the AUSA's notes "there were pages and pages of hard copy documents sent between [Lopez] and Luis Rubio regarding this problem."

Third, the AUSA had in her possession the letter from Braunstein's attorney which detailed the defense to the fraud charges and directed her to sources within Apple and ALAC. Specifically, the letter stated that Apple had records of receiving registration records, warranty forms, and damage claims for the computers sold by Braunstein to United States distributors that were returned to Apple. The letter also described records of memoranda among its employees corroborating ALAC's participation in and dependence upon gray marketing. Fourth, the AUSA had the Kroll report, which supported the allegations that ALAC employees participated in gray market deals to boost their sales volume at the expense of long-term profits for Apple.

All of this information was in the AUSA's possession prior to her decision to seek a grand jury indictment against Braunstein. To the extent there was any confusion regarding the extent of gray market awareness on the part of ALAC employees, the AUSA could have clarified the matter by examining documents within the possession and control of Apple, described by the district court as a "complaining party."

ALAC's well-documented participation in gray marketing negated any well-founded prosecution based on fraud because ALAC could not be deceived about practices it actively endorsed. Accordingly, the government's case against Braunstein was frivolous. Braunstein is entitled to attorney's fees under the Hyde Amendment.

* * * We reverse the district court's denial of attorney's fees pursuant to the Hyde Amendment, finding that the court abused its discretion in denying Braunstein's motion. We hold that Braunstein, as the prevailing party in a criminal prosecution that was "frivolous" is entitled to an award of his attorney's fees.

NOTES AND QUESTIONS

1. *"Vexatious" and "Bad Faith."* *Braunstein* adopted the standard for whether the charges sought by the government were "frivolous." In United States v. Gilbert, 198 F.3d 1293 (11th Cir. 1999), the Eleventh Circuit defined "bad faith" as "not simply bad judgment or negligence, but rather it implies the conscious doing of a wrong because of dishonest purpose or moral obliquity; ... it contemplates a state of mind affirmatively operating with furtive design or ill will." Determining whether a prosecution was "vexatious" "has both a subjective and objective element: subjectively, the Government must have acted maliciously or with an intent to harass Appellants; objectively, the suit must be deficient or without merit. To prove vexatiousness, the defendant must show the Government had some 'ill intent.'" United States v. Manchester Farming Partnership, 315 F.3d 1176 (9th Cir. 2003).

Unlike a "frivolous" prosecution, a claim of vexatiousness and bad faith require proof of the individual prosecutor's subjective intent—"ill intent" or "conscious doing of a wrong." In United States v. Sherburne, 506 F.3d 1187 (9th Cir. 2007), the Ninth Circuit overturned a district court decision to award attorney's fees because the prosecutors did not understand their theory of the case. The appellate court noted that prosecutors lost much of their evidence of the defendant's involvement in the fraudulent scheme due to a suppression motion, and that "subjective intent to harass does not arise from merely factual mistakes or mistakes concerning the legal merit of the government's position."

While courts stress that each of the three elements of a Hyde Amendment claim define a separate type of prosecutorial misconduct, they are not easily distinguishable and claimants frequently allege violations under more than one prong of the statute. To prove the prosecutor's intent, to what extent should a court rely on circumstantial evidence? Can courts use the Hyde Amendment to police prosecutorial misconduct in a way that is denied under the Supreme Court's preclusion of the exercise of supervisory authority over the grand jury in *Williams*? Will an assessment of costs against a United States Attorney's Office have a deterrent effect on individual prosecutors?

2. *Proving a Hyde Amendment Claim.* The Hyde Amendment provides that claims must be made "pursuant to the procedures and limitations (but not the burden of proof) provided for an award under section 2412 of title 28, United States Code," the Equal Access to Justice Act (EAJA). "[T]he Hyde Amendment has a more demanding burden of proof than the EAJA. Under the EAJA, a defendant will prevail unless the government can prove its position was substantially justified. However, recovering attorney fees and costs under the Hyde Amendment requires a stronger showing. Under the Hyde Amendment, the burden is on the defendant in the underlying case to prove the Government's position was vexatious, frivolous, or in bad faith." *Manchester Farming Partnership.* Similar to the EAJA, a "prevailing party"

is one who has received at least some relief on the merits of the claim. Dismissal of charges after a defendant enters a diversion program and repays the government for its loss due to his conduct means the defendant was not a "prevailing party." United States v. Campbell, 291 F.3d 1169 (9th Cir. 2002).

CHAPTER TWELVE
SEARCHES

A. *THE USE OF SEARCHES IN WHITE COLLAR CRIME INVESTIGATIONS*

1. *Current practice.* Federal prosecutors, in the past 15 years, have increased dramatically their use of physical searches, authorized by warrants, as a tool of investigation in white collar cases. Some practitioners attribute the increased utilization of searches to their highly publicized and quite successful deployment during the late 1980s in the investigation of procurement fraud by defense contractors. Still others cite the Supreme Court's establishment in 1984 of an "objective good faith" exception to the exclusionary rule for searches conducted under a warrant. In large part, the searches in white collar cases are directed at seizing documents, although occasionally they may be aimed at obtaining other items (e.g., improperly acquired goods or equipment). The use of search warrants has been especially noticeable in investigations involving health care fraud and investigations involving records stored on personal computers.[a] While subpoenas are the more common method for obtaining documents, especially from third-parties who are not involved in the underlying wrongdoing, the search warrant is readily available as an alternative, and sometimes superior, means of gathering records.

2. *Costs.* The search pursuant to a warrant has obvious costs and restrictions not applicable to the subpoena. First, the search is not as readily available to the prosecutor as the subpoena. To obtain a warrant authorizing a search for documents, a prosecutor must persuade a federal judicial officer that there is probable cause to believe that a crime has been committed and that specific documents which would constitute evidence of the crime can be found in a particular place (typically a business office or residence). This is a far more demanding grounding than the showing required when a subpoena is challenged.

Second, the affidavit presented to the magistrate to show probable cause is presumed to be open to the public (and press). See Baltimore Sun Co. v. Goetz 886 F.2d 60 (4th Cir. 1989). Upon a proper showing of need by the

---

[a] Under the Electronic Communications Privacy Act, 18 U.S.C. § 2703(a), the government must obtain a warrant if it seeks the contents of a wire or electronic communication from the provider of a remote computing service if it has been held in an electronic storage system for 180 days or less. See WAYNE R. LAFAVE, JEROLD H. ISRAEL, NANCY J. KING, & ORIN S. KERR, CRIMINAL PROCEDURE 3D § 4.8 (d)(2007).

prosecutor, the court may place the search warrant affidavit under seal. See In re Search Warrant for Secretarial Area Outside Office of Gunn, 855 F.2d 569 (8th Cir. 1988) (sealing must be justified by a "compelling government need"). Even if the sealing is ordered, however the subject of the search will eventually gain access to the affidavit in filing a Rule 41(g) motion challenging the search and asking that the seized property be returned.[b] This will give the subject far more information as to the scope and character of the government's investigation than would be obtained on a challenge to a subpoena. See *R. Enterprises*, p. 361.

Third, the remedy for conducting an unconstitutional search can be far more harsh than the remedy for issuing an illegal subpoena. If a subpoena is challenged and the court holds that it is overbroad or otherwise invalid, the subpoena is quashed, and the government can seek to fashion a new subpoena that meets the court's objections. If a search is conducted and a court subsequently holds that the search was invalid, the usual Fourth Amendment remedy is the "exclusionary rule" remedy. Under that remedy, the government is precluded from using the matter seized–and any other evidence obtained as a fruit of that illegal search (e.g., documents later discovered through information gleaned from the documents seized during the search)–in its case-in-chief in any subsequent prosecution against individuals or entities whose privacy was violated by the unconstitutional search.

Fourth, a search ordinarily entails considerably greater administrative costs than a subpoena duces tecum. With the subpoena, the recipient of the subpoena has the responsibility of collecting the documents identified in the subpoena and delivering them in accordance with the subpoena's directive. See chapter 15. With a search, the executing officers have the responsibility of finding and collecting the documents specified in the warrant. That can be a time consuming task where the search is conducted at a business that has voluminous records and many different documents are specified in the warrant. The search can also disrupt ongoing business activities on the premises being searched, antagonizing the employees as well as the employer.

---

[b] Fed. R. Crim. P. 41(g) provides:

(g) Motion to Return Property. A person aggrieved by an unlawful search and seizure of property or by the deprivation of property may move for the property's return. The motion must be filed in the district where the property was seized. The court must receive evidence on any factual issue necessary to decide the motion. If it grants the motion, the court must return the property to the movant, but may impose reasonable conditions to protect access to the property and its use in later proceedings.

In white collar cases, there often is a substantial time interval between a search and any subsequent indictment, so the challenge to the search is most likely to be first presented by a Rule 41(g) motion rather than a motion to suppress.

3. *Advantages*. Offsetting the costs and limitations of utilizing a search are various attributes of the search that may be viewed as advantages–at least in some types of investigations. These include the following:

(a) Unlike the subpoena duces tecum, the search does not afford the party in possession of the documents the opportunity to destroy, conceal, or alter those documents. Of course, a "forthwith subpoena" can be used where destruction is a distinct possibility. However, the forthwith subpoena may be treated as a Fourth Amendment search if the agents themselves seize the documents, and if they do not, the subpoenaed party may not necessarily produce all the documents specified. Also, access may be delayed as the subpoenaed party may insist upon depositing the documents with the court and having them kept there until the party has the opportunity to present its challenge to the subpoena.

(b) A search gives the prosecutor immediate access to the documents seized. With a subpoena, the party in possession initially must be given sufficient time to produce the documents, and then may delay access further by obtaining an extension or challenging the subpoena.

(c) With a subpoena, specified documents are demanded and those documents are all that will be produced. With a search, there is the possibility of discovering and seizing documents beyond those specified in the warrant. That potential stems from the "plain view" doctrine. Under that doctrine, if an officer, in the course of the executing the search authorized by the warrant, should come across other matter in plain view and has probable cause to believe that matter constitutes evidence of a crime, the officer may seize that matter even though it is not among the items specified in the warrant.

(d) A person subpoenaed to produce documents may assert the self-incrimination privilege where the act of producing the documents is testimonial and potentially incriminatory. A search, however, does not compel the person in possession to produce anything; the documents are seized by the officers executing the search. Hence the Supreme Court held in Andresen v. Maryland, 427 U.S. 463 (1976), that the self-incrimination privilege was not a valid grounding for challenging a search. The same is not true, however, of other privileges, such as the lawyer-client privilege. Here the search warrant provides no advantage over the subpoena. However, such privileges are limited by exceptions, such as the crime-fraud exception under the lawyer-client privilege which often will render documentary evidence subject to seizure even though it would otherwise have been privileged.

(e) A search places investigators on the scene, where they can readily question employees. Such "on the spot" questioning often may be more productive than questioning pursuant to subpoena or prearranged interviews. The questioning comes without advance notice and usually before the employer has a chance to speak to the employees about the investigation and their rights, and to offer them the assistance of legal counsel. See United States v. Hampton, 153 F.Supp.2d 1262 (D. Kan. 2001) (rejecting defendant's claim that her interview with a government investigator while her company was being searched violated *Miranda* because it was a custodial interrogation when the agent twice told her she was free to leave and she consulted with her counsel during the interview; "Further, the mere fact that the defendants were the focus of an investigation does not indicate that they were in custody during the questioning.").

(f) The disruptive impact of a search can convey a special sense of urgency to those involved. The agents executing the warrant (often armed) will enter an office without previous warning, direct employees to immediately leave the room or stay off to the side, and proceed to go through desks and files. All of this may "throw a little scare" into employees and executives, leading to greater cooperation in subsequent requests for information, and possibly producing additional pressures on the subject to reach a swift settlement.

(g) The use of searches may be useful in conveying to the public the message that prosecutors are adopting a "tough, aggressive stance" in combating white collar crime. They are subjecting white collar suspects to the same intrusions on privacy as persons suspected of street crimes.

(h) The search warrant, the affidavit, and the evidence seized are not subject to the secrecy requirements that attach to a grand jury subpoena duces tecum . This can offer several additional advantages. At times, the prosecutor may desire to make an investigation, its grounding, and its current findings a matter of public record. That may put pressure on a target to reach a fast settlement and thereby minimize the impact of the bad publicity. Also, at times, the prosecutor may desire to share the product of the search with other agencies. In contrast to documents obtained by grand jury subpoena, documents obtained by an independently generated search may be shared without a Rule 6(e) order.

4. *Mitigating the Effect of a Search.* Recognizing that some of these advantages of a warrant can be limited (or even precluded) by certain action taken by the person in charge of the premises that are searched, counsel will advise clients of several steps they should take if agents suddenly appear on their property with a search warrant. These include: (1) immediate notification of counsel and hopefully delaying the search until counsel arrives; (2) sending employees home for the day (and thereby avoiding incidental questions in the course of the search); (3) demanding a copy of the warrant, and informing agents as to where the specified documents are located; (4) protesting any screening of other files where the documents are not located; (5) identifying files containing lawyer-client and other privileged material and demanding that they be sealed and not read until a court can determine their status; (6) monitoring the search, paying particular attention to the sequence of the search (e.g., did the officers first look in those places where the documents were most likely to be found, did they terminate the

search upon finding the documents specified in the warrant); (7) keeping track of all documents examined, whether or not seized; and (8) keeping a record of all matter seized and comparing it to the inventory that officers are required to leave with the person in charge of the premises under Rule 41(d).

5. *Warrants Directed at Non-Suspects.* In **Zurcher v. Stanford Daily**, 436 U.S. 547 (1978), the Supreme Court held that the Fourth Amendment does not prevent the government from seeking a warrant to search for evidence just because the owner or possessor of the place to be searched is not suspected of being involved in the underlying criminal conduct that is under investigation. In *Zurcher*, the police searched the offices of the *Stanford Daily*, a student newspaper, for photographs of those who had been involved in a protest in which officers were attacked. The district court held that because the newspaper was not suspected of any wrongdoing, the government was restricted to using a subpoena duces tecum to obtain the evidence rather than a search warrant. The Supreme Court, per Justice White writing for the majority, rejected the contention that the district court's reasoning found support in the broad underlying policy objectives of the Fourth Amendment:

> [W]e are unpersuaded that the District Court's new rule denying search warrants against third parties and insisting on subpoenas would substantially further privacy interests without seriously undermining law enforcement efforts. Because of the fundamental public interest in implementing the criminal law, the search warrant, a heretofore effective and constitutionally acceptable enforcement tool, should not be suppressed on the basis of surmise and without solid evidence supporting the change. As the District Court understands it, denying third-party search warrants would not have substantial adverse effects on criminal investigations because the nonsuspect third party, once served with a subpoena, will preserve the evidence and ultimately lawfully respond. The difficulty with this assumption is that search warrants are often employed early in an investigation, perhaps before the identity of any likely criminal and certainly before all the perpetrators are or could be known. The seemingly blameless third party in possession of the fruits or evidence may not be innocent at all; and if he is, he may nevertheless be so related to or so sympathetic with the culpable that he cannot be relied upon to retain and preserve the articles that may implicate his friends, or at least not to notify those who would be damaged by the evidence that the authorities are aware of its location. In any event, it is likely that the real culprits will have access to the property and the delay involved in employing the subpoena duces tecum, offering as it does the opportunity to litigate its validity, could easily result in the disappearance of the evidence, whatever the good faith of the third party.

B. FOURTH AMENDMENT PRINCIPLES

1. *The Fourth Amendment*.

> The right of the people to be secure in their persons, houses, papers, and effects, against unreasonable searches and seizures, shall not be violated, and no Warrants shall issue, but upon probable cause, supported by Oath or affirmation, and particularly describing the place to be searched, and the persons or things to be seized.

Only the second clause of the Amendment refers to warrants, and the Supreme Court has held that a variety of searches may be deemed reasonable under the first clause even though executed without a warrant. In general, conducting a search without first obtaining the "neutral and detached" probable-cause determination provided by the warrant process is justified either by "exigent circumstances," a "diminished expectation of privacy" in the area searched, or historical tradition. None of these justifications, however, bear upon the search of a business or residence to obtain documents believed to constitute evidence of a crime. Accordingly, such searches almost invariably are conducted pursuant to a warrant.

Although the constitutional law governing the issuance and execution of search warrants has numerous elements, three stand out as having the greatest significance for the document searches utilized in white collar crime investigations. They are: (1) the requirement that the warrant be issued only upon a showing of probable cause before the magistrate; (2) the requirement that the warrant "particularly describ[e] * * * the * * * things to be seized"; and (3) the *Leon* exception to the remedy of exclusion of evidence obtained through a search that violates the Fourth Amendment.[a] The excerpts reprinted below set forth the guiding principles that govern each of those elements.

2. *Probable Cause*. **Illinois v. Gates**, 462 U.S. 213 (1983), involved the issuance of search warrant based upon a probable cause finding that relied in part upon a letter written to police by an anonymous informant. The Court majority (per Rehnquist, J.) said the following in the course of abandoning a previously adopted two-pronged standard for utilizing information from an informant:

---

[a] Other elements of Fourth Amendment law relating to search warrants include: the requirement that the magistrate issuing the warrant be "neutral and detached"; the requirement that the warrant be supported by "oath or affirmation"; the requirement that the warrant "particularly describ[e] *** the place to be searched"; the requirement that the warrant be executed in a reasonable manner; and the allowable seizure of items not named in the warrant under the "plain view" doctrine. See WAYNE R. LAFAVE, JEROLD H. ISRAEL, NANCY J. KING, & ORIN S. KERR, CRIMINAL PROCEDURE 3D § 3.4 (2007).

Perhaps the central teaching of our decisions bearing on the probable cause standard is that it is a "practical, nontechnical conception." Brinegar v. United States, 338 U.S. 160 (1949). 'In dealing with probable cause, * * * as the very name implies, we deal with probabilities. These are not technical; they are the factual and practical considerations of everyday life on which reasonable and prudent men, not legal technicians, act.' Our observation in United States v. Cortez, 449 U.S. 411 (1981), regarding "particularized suspicion," is also applicable to the probable cause standard:

> The process does not deal with hard certainties, but with probabilities. Long before the law of probabilities was articulated as such, practical people formulated certain common-sense conclusions abut human behavior; jurors as fact finders are permitted to do the same--and so are law enforcement officers. Finally, the evidence thus collected must be seen and weighed not in terms of library analysis by scholars, but as understood by those versed in the field of law enforcement.

As these comments illustrate, probable cause is a fluid concept–turning on the assessment of probabilities in particular factual contexts–not readily, or often usefully, reduced to a neat set of legal rules. Informants' tips doubtless come in many shapes and sizes from many different types of persons. * * * Rigid legal rules are ill-suited to an area of such diversity. "One simple rule will not cover every situation." * * *

We also have recognized that affidavits are "normally drafted by non-lawyers in the midst and haste of a criminal investigation. Technical requirements of elaborate specificity once exacted under common law pleading have no proper place in this area." Likewise, search and arrest warrants long have been issued by persons who are neither lawyers nor judges, and who certainly do not remain abreast of each judicial refinement of the nature of "probable cause."

Similarly, we have repeatedly said that after-the-fact scrutiny by courts of the sufficiency of an affidavit should not take the form of *de novo* review. A magistrate's "determination of probable cause should be paid great deference by reviewing courts. * * *" A grudging or negative attitude by reviewing courts toward warrants' is inconsistent with the Fourth Amendment's strong preference for search conducted pursuant to a warrant; "courts should not invalidate * * * warrant[s] by interpreting affidavit[s] in a hypertechnical, rather than a commonsense, manner." * * * Reflecting this preference for the warrant process, the traditional standard for review of an issuing magistrate's probable-cause determination has been that so long as the magistrate had a "substantial basis for ... conclud[ing]" that a search would uncover evidence of wrongdoing, the Fourth Amendment requires no more.

* * * [W]e reaffirm the task of the issuing magistrate is simply to make a practical, common-sense decision whether, given all the circumstances set forth in the affidavit before him, including the "veracity" and "basis of knowledge" of persons supplying hearsay information, there is a fair probability that contraband or evidence of a crime will be found in a particular place.[b] And the duty of a reviewing court is simply to ensure that the magistrate had a "substantial basis for * * * conclud[ing]" that probable cause existed. Our earlier cases illustrate the limits beyond which a magistrate may not venture in issuing a warrant. A sworn statement of an affiant that "he has cause to suspect and does believe" that liquor illegally brought into the United States is located on certain premises will not do. Nathanson v. United States, 290 U.S. 41 (1933). An affidavit must provide the magistrate with a substantial basis for determining the existence of probable cause, and the wholly conclusory statement at issue in *Nathanson* failed to meet this requirement. * * * Sufficient information must be presented to the magistrate to allow that official to determine probable cause; his action cannot be a mere ratification of the bare conclusions of others. In order to ensure that such as abdication of the magistrate's duty does not occur, courts must continue to conscientiously review the sufficiency of affidavits on which warrants are issued. But when we move beyond the "bare bones" affidavits presented in cases such as *Nathanson* * * * , this area simply does not lend itself to a prescribed set of rules * * * ."

3. *Particularity of Description*. A significant issue for determining the validity of a search warrant in a white collar crime investigation is whether the warrant contains sufficient particularity regarding the place to be searched and the items that may be seized. In Marron v. United States, 275 U.S. 192 (1927), the Supreme Court stated, ""The requirement that warrants shall particularly describe the things to be seized makes general searches under them impossible and prevents the seizure of one thing under a warrant describing another." To avoid the problem of general warrants, there are

---

[b] In a later footnote, in the course of discussing the significance of police verification of details mentioned by the informant, even where those details deal with innocent activity, the *Gates* Court offered the following comment on this probability: "As discussed previously, probable cause requires only a probability or substantial chance of criminal activity, not an actual showing of such activity."

certain factors a court will consider in assessing the particularity of the description in the warrant:

Consider:

> [There] are certain general principles which may be distilled from the decided cases in this area. They are: (1) A greater degree of ambiguity will be tolerated when the police have done the best that could be expected under the circumstances, by acquiring all the descriptive facts which reasonable investigation of this type of crime could be expected to uncover and by ensuring that all of those facts were included in the warrant. (2) A more general type of description will be sufficient when the nature of the objects to be seized are such that they could not be expected to have more specific characteristics. (3) A less precise description is required of property which is, because of its particular character, contraband. (4) Failure to provide all of the available descriptive facts is not a basis for questioning the adequacy of the description when the omitted facts could not have been expected to be of assistance to the executing officer. (5) An error in the statement of certain descriptive facts is not a basis for questioning the adequacy of the description if the executing officer was nonetheless able to determine, from the other facts provided, that the object seized was that intended by the description. (6) Greater care in description is ordinarily called for when the type of property sought is generally in lawful use in substantial quantities. (7) A more particular description than otherwise might be necessary is required when other objects of the same general classification are likely to be found at the particular place to be searched. (8) The greatest care in description is required when the consequences of a seizure of innocent articles by mistake is most substantial, as when the objects to be seized are books or films or the papers of a newsgathering organization.

Wayne R. LaFave, Jerold H. Israel, Nancy J. King, & Orin S. Kerr, Criminal Procedure 3d §3.4(e)-(f) (2007).

4. *The Exclusionary Rule and the* Leon *Exception*. Because warrantless searches are comparatively rare in white collar crime cases, the focus is on searches pursuant to a warrant. The Supreme Court's decision in United States v. Leon, 468 U.S. 897 (1984), has a significant impact on the application of the exclusionary rule to searches in which the warrant that was not based on sufficient probable cause. In *Leon*, the Court stated that "[p]enalizing the officer for the magistrate's error, rather than his own, cannot logically contribute to the deterrence of Fourth Amendment violations." Therefore, application of the exclusionary rule to suppress evidence obtained pursuant to a warrant should be ordered "only in those unusual cases in which exclusion will further the purposes of the exclusionary rule." If officers act in good faith in executing a search warrant

that appears facially valid, then the exclusionary rule does not apply.

Leon identified four circumstances in which a flaw in the warrant would still result in the application of the exclusionary rule: (1) where the officer presented knowing or reckless falsehoods to obtain the warrant; (2) "where the issuing magistrate wholly abandoned his judicial role"; (3) where the warrant was "so facially deficient – i.e., in failing to particularize the place to be searched or the things to be seized – that the executing officers cannot reasonably presume it to be valid"; and (4) where the affidavit supporting the warrant application was "so lacking in indicia of probable cause as to render official belief in its existence entirely unreasonable." *Leon* applies only to reasonable reliance on an invalid warrant, not when there are Fourth Amendment violations in the execution of the warrant unrelated to its validity or invalidity.

The issue in white collar cases is usually the lack of particularity in the warrant and supporting affidavit, and the following case illustrates the application of *Leon*.

UNITED STATES v. TRAVERS
233 F.3d 1327 (11th Cir. 2000)

HILL, Circuit Judge.

Joseph Travers was convicted on several counts of mail fraud, equity skimming, money laundering and bankruptcy fraud. * * *

Between 1991 and 1995, Joseph Travers obtained title to more than 97 houses by assuming Veterans Administration (VA) and Federal Housing Association (FHA) guaranteed home loans. He did so under a variety of false names and aliases. Travers collected the rents on these properties but never paid on any of the mortgages. He used a series of names on the deeds and filed successive bankruptcy petitions for each name in a successful attempt to forestall foreclosure during which time he would continue to collect the rents. Travers used a series of false identities and mail drops to hide his identity and avoid detection. During the two-year investigation of his activities, federal agents compiled a list of at least 40 VA and FHA mortgages that Travers had assumed, aliases he used in those transactions, mailboxes he had rented, and fraudulent bankruptcy proceedings that he had filed.

Agents arrested Travers on May 8, 1996. On the same day, they executed search warrants at his two properties on Bay Harbor Island, Florida. The agents seized voluminous boxes of documents detailing Travers' equity skimming operation.

Before trial, Travers filed a motion to suppress the evidence found during the searches of his residence and office on the grounds that the warrant authorizing the searches was unconstitutionally overbroad and the resulting searches general rather than limited. After an evidentiary hearing, the district court denied the motion, holding that, while the warrant was overly broad, "the agents acted in good faith in drafting and executing the warrant." * * *

The requirement that warrants particularly describe the place to be searched and the things to be seized makes general searches under them impossible. A warrant which fails to sufficiently particularize the place to be searched or the things to be seized is unconstitutionally over broad. The resulting general search is unconstitutional. In order to deter such warrants and searches, the Court has held that any evidence so seized must be excluded from the trial of the defendant. Stone v. Powell, 428 U.S. 465 (1976).

The exclusionary rule's deterrent effect is negated, however, where law enforcement officers act in the "objectively reasonable belief that their conduct does not violate the Fourth Amendment." United States v. Leon, 468 U.S. 897 (1984). When an officer has in good faith obtained a search warrant from a judge or magistrate and acted within its scope, "there is no police illegality and thus nothing to deter." In *Leon*, therefore, the Court carved out an exception to the exclusionary rule for evidence obtained in such a search.

* * * The United States does not contest the district court's holding that the warrant was overbroad. Therefore, the issue for our review is whether the good faith exception applies in this case to excuse the unconstitutionally over broad warrant. We conclude that it does.

The good faith exception may be applied to a search conducted pursuant to an overly broad warrant. The officers do not act in objective good faith, however, if the warrant is so overly broad on its face that the executing officers could not reasonably have presumed it to be valid.

The warrant in this case permitted the officers to search for all documents involving real estate, litigation, property, mailings, photographs and any other material reflecting identity, and anything reflecting potential fraud. Pursuant to the warrant, the executing officers seized copies of warranty deeds and other documents reflecting Travers' use of false identities to purchase properties; notary public seals for signatures that Travers forged on various deeds and other legal documents; passports, birth certificates, drivers licenses, and credit cards issued in various names; business cards for businesses in various names; letters to tenants written by Travers using both his names and aliases; copies of bankruptcy pleadings, letters to bankruptcy courts, and other filings reflecting Travers' attempts to delay foreclosures; and various other documents concerning Travers' use of aliases, mail drop boxes, and false addresses to avoid detection.

Although the district court ultimately held the warrant overly broad, it characterized its conclusion as a "close call." We agree. This case involves a complex scheme to commit financial fraud concerning real property. The charges include mail fraud, bankruptcy fraud, equity skimming, and money laundering. A wide variety of documents were relevant to prove this scheme-deeds, loan papers, legal pleadings, identity papers and cards, and mailing receipts and papers. Thus, the agents applied for and received a warrant which cut a wide swath through Travers' papers and documents. In [United States v. Accardo, 749 F.2d 1477 (11th Cir. 1985)], we recognized that cases involving "complex financial fraud . . . justify a more flexible reading of the fourth amendment particularity requirement." Thus, the warrant in this case, even if subsequently determined by the district court to be overly broad, was not "so facially deficient – i.e., failing to particularize the place to be searched or the things to be seized-that the executing officers could not have reasonably presumed it to be valid." The application of the good faith exception to the exclusionary rule, therefore, is not precluded in this case by a warrant that no reasonable officer could have relied upon.

Travers also contends that the district erred in finding that the agents obtained and executed the warrant in subjective good faith. He claims that the agents intentionally deceived the issuing magistrate by omitting details of their investigation thereby inducing him to grant an overly broad warrant. He also alleges that they deliberately exceeded the scope of their warrant in the items seized.

Whether the officers acted in subjective good faith in obtaining and executing the warrant is a mixed question of fact and law. While the ultimate conclusion of good faith is a legal one, findings of fact serve as the predicate for this conclusion. In order to hold that the officers acted in good faith in this case, the district court necessarily found as a matter of fact that the agents neither intentionally deceived the issuing magistrate by omitting details regarding the nature of their investigation, nor deliberately exceeded the scope of their warrant in the items seized during the searches. The agents testified unequivocally that they consulted with the United States Attorney in drafting the warrant application and included all information that they and she believed necessary to establish sufficient probable cause to support the warrant application. The supervising agent testified that he instructed the other agents regarding items to be seized according to his understanding of the warrant. The searching agents testified that there were documents strewn throughout Travers' residence and office with no apparent organization. In their effort to take only what was authorized by the warrant, they reviewed documents. The district court credited all this testimony. We find nothing in the record that would indicate that these factual findings that the officers obtained the warrant in cooperation with the United States Attorney who advised them on the requirements for showing probable cause and conducted their search in a conscious effort to stay within its limits are clearly erroneous. Nor do we disagree with the district court's legal conclusion that the officers, therefore, acted in good faith.

We hold that the district court did not err in holding that the good faith exception to the exclusionary rule applies to excuse the overly broad warrant at issue in this case. We find no merit in Travers' other allegations of error. Accordingly, Travers' conviction and sentence are due to be AFFIRMED.

C. SEARCH OF A BUSINESS

1. Standing and the Warrant Requirements

If a business or other organization directly engages in questionable activity, then the government will seek a wide range of documents that may ultimately involve nearly all the records of an organization. How specific does a warrant have to be in that type of situation? In United States v. Hickey, 16 F.Supp.2d 223 (E.D.N.Y. 1998), the District Court found that a warrant was overbroad in its description of the items to be seized: "[T]the officers were simply furnished with warrants that directed the seizure of "all business records" of the four corporate defendants found at any one of the five search locations, absent any explicit or implicit reference points. That direction is followed by a list of items subject to seizure, many generic (e.g., "[b]ank records of any kind," "corporate resolutions," "ledgers," "invoices," "computer files," "computer software," and "correspondence files"), preceded by the troubling instruction that the searches were "not limited to" those items. In essence–given the format of the warrants–the officers were directed to search all of the business records of each of the defendant corporations and to seize any items that constituted evidence of any crime regardless of its nature or when it occurred."

When a search warrant is executed at a business, it may result in the seizure of evidence that will be used against individual officers of the organization. To what extent can they challenge a warrant on the ground that it fails to meet the specificity requirement of the Fourth Amendment? Consider the following case:

UNITED STATES v. SDI FUTURE HEALTH, INC.
553 F.3d 1246 (9th Cir. 2009)

O'SCANNLAIN, Circuit Judge:

We must decide whether corporate executives may challenge a police search of company premises not reserved for the executives' exclusive use.

After a nearly two-year investigation spearheaded by the Internal Revenue Service ("IRS") with the participation of four other federal and Nevada state agencies, investigators concluded that SDI Future Health, Inc. ("SDI"), a California corporation, had engaged in wide-ranging Medicare fraud. In addition, they believed that both SDI and Todd Stuart Kaplan, its president and part-owner, had committed extensive tax fraud. On January 28, 2002, based on the information obtained during the investigation, IRS Special Agent Julie Raftery applied for a warrant to search SDI's premises.

The warrant relied on an affidavit sworn by Raftery, which contained information she had learned from three former employees and two business associates of SDI. The affidavit alleged that SDI, Kaplan and Jack Brunk, also an officer and part-owner of SDI, participated in a conspiracy with physicians and cardiac diagnostic companies to defraud the Medicare program, the Federal Employees Health Benefit Program, and private healthcare insurance carriers by seeking payment for services that SDI never rendered. According to the affidavit, they sometimes billed twice for such services and made kickback payments to physicians who participated in the scheme. It alleged specifically that SDI employees who were placed in participating doctors' offices would induce patients to participate in a sleep study. While cardiac diagnostic companies affiliated with SDI would purport to complete a report of the results of each sleep study, officers of SDI would instead affix a signature stamp bearing the signatures of staff physicians on reports that other SDI employees had actually completed. Referring physicians were instructed to bill for time spent reviewing the reports, a task the physicians never actually performed. Frequently, SDI would then recommend that a patient participate in further studies, usually in cases where the patient's health insurer would pay for them.

The affidavit also revealed incidents of alleged tax fraud. It noted that Kaplan and his wife reported negative gross income and, consequently, paid no taxes in the years 1996, 1998 and 1999, and reported relatively low income in 1997 and 2000. During the same period, however, the couple purchased several expensive automobiles and watercraft and supported a home mortgage. This discrepancy, according to the affidavit, provided the probable cause to support the investigators' belief that Kaplan and his wife substantially underreported their gross income during those years. The government also alleged that SDI had violated federal tax laws by under-reporting its sales revenue and its income at least for the years 1996-2000.

The government submitted a proposed warrant with its affidavit. Appendix A of the warrant stated that the premises to be searched were SDI's corporate headquarters, principal business offices, and computers. Appendix B provided 24 categories of items to be seized and gave specific instructions concerning retrieving and handling of electronic data and other technical equipment.[2]

---

[2] The categories of items to be seized are as follows: 1. Documents relating to patient lists; 2. Documents relating to billing procedures, billing manuals, and billing materials; 3. Documents relating to lists of referring physicians both active and inactive; 4. Documents relating to billing records and records of payments received; 5. Documents relating to contracts or "purchase service agreements" with referring physicians; 6. Documents relating to contracts and agreements with cardiac diagnostic companies; 7. Documents relating to non-privileged correspondence with consultants; 8. Documents relating to correspondence with Medicare intermediaries and private insurance companies; 9. Documents relating to non-privileged internal memoranda and E-mail; 10. Documents relating to bank accounts, brokerage

* * * The day before the execution of the search warrant, Special Agent Raftery met with the forty-two agents who would make up the search team. She distributed copies of the affidavit and gave them time to read it. She then conducted a "verbal briefing," explaining the probable cause for the search warrant and "the items that [the search team was] searching for and the items to be seized." All members of the search team were to have the cellular phone number of Special Agent Raftery during the search.

The team executed the search early the following morning, on January 31, 2002. Upon arriving at the scene, Special Agent Raftery met with one of SDI's executive officers and delivered a copy of the search warrant, but not a copy of the affidavit because it had been sealed by the district court. The affidavit was, however, available to the members of the search team. Kaplan also received a copy of the warrant, and he consented to allow investigators to search an off-site storage warehouse used by SDI.

About three years after the search, a federal grand jury in the District of Nevada returned an indictment charging SDI, Kaplan and Brunk with one count of conspiracy, in violation of 18 U.S.C. § 371 – specifically conspiracy to commit health care fraud, in violation of 18 U.S.C. § 1347, and to provide illegal kickback payments, in violation of 42 U.S.C. § 1320a-7b(b); 124 counts of health care fraud, in violation of 18 U.S.C. § 1347; one count of illegal kickbacks, in violation of 42 U.S.C. § 1320a-7b(b); one count of conspiracy to commit money laundering, in violation of 18 U.S.C. §§ 1956(a)(1)(A)(i) and 1956(h); and three counts of attempting to evade or defeat taxes, in violation of 26 U.S.C. § 7201. Additionally, Kaplan and Brunk were each individually indicted for three and four counts, respectively, of attempting to evade or defeat taxes, in violation of 26 U.S.C. § 7201. * * *

---

accounts, trusts; 11. Checking, savings, and money market account records including check registers, canceled checks, monthly statements, wire transfers, and cashier's checks; 12. Documents relating to personnel and payroll records; 13. Documents relating to accounting records; 14. Patient records including patient questionnaires, sleep study referrals, results of cardiac risk assessment tests, results of sleep studies, and sleep study reports; 15. Documents relating to raw sleep study data; 16. Documents relating to all state and federal income tax returns including personal, corporate, trust, estate, and partnership, and information relating to the preparation of those returns for the following: (a) Todd Stuart Kaplan, (b) Denise Kaplan, (c) SDI; 17. Signature stamps for Dr. Gavin Awerbuch, Dr. Susan Sprau, and any other physician signature stamps; 18. Computer zip discs containing sleep study data; 19. Documents relating to mailing or shipping records between physicians and SDI; 20. Documents relating to employee training materials regarding health service coordinator ("HSC") program, cardiac risk assessment program, and/or physician practice enhancement program; 21. Documents relating to presentations and/or training materials used to solicit patient referrals from physicians, and/or placement of HSCs in the physician's offices; 22. Holter monitor tapes containing cardiac monitor data; 23. Documents relating to material that provides instructions or examples concerning the operation of the computer system, computer software, and/or related device; and 24. Rolodexes, address books and calendars.

On December 2, 2005, SDI, Kaplan and Brunk filed a motion to suppress evidence obtained from the search warrant, arguing that the warrant was vague and overbroad in violation of the Fourth Amendment. On June 26, 2006, a magistrate judge entered a Findings and Recommendation, in which he recommended that the motion to suppress be granted in part.

On April 4, 2007, the district court adopted the magistrate judge's factual findings, but entered an order granting the defendants' motion to suppress in full rather than in part. The district court first held that Kaplan and Brunk had standing to challenge the search of SDI's business premises, because they "had significant ownership interests in SDI," "exercised a high level of authority over the operations of the company including the authority to set and control policy regarding access to SDI's business records and computer systems," "maintained offices at SDI's corporate headquarters and were present during the execution of the Search Warrant," and because SDI "maintained a level of security and confidentially [sic] practices regarding its premises and records that one would reasonably expect of a health care provider."

The district court concluded that items 7, 9-13, and 24 of the search warrant were overbroad and lacked sufficient particularity because "[t]he search warrant did not limit these general categories of business documents and financial records to the seizure of records relating to the criminal activity described in the affidavit," and because they lacked "any time restriction." Similarly, the district court noted that items 2, 4, 8, and 19, of the search warrant were "borderline in acceptability," but nevertheless violated the Fourth Amendment because "some additional description could and should have been provided regarding these categories." Lastly, the district court concluded that the "good faith exception" did not apply in this case based on its conclusion that the affidavit was not incorporated into the warrant. Without the affidavit, the court concluded, the agents' reliance on the warrant alone was not objectively reasonable, since it "did not contain any description of the alleged criminal activity relating to the listed categories of documents." * * *

The government first argues that Kaplan and Brunk lack standing to challenge the search and seizure of materials from SDI's premises.[3] According to the government, their mere ownership and management of SDI, and the

---

[3] Wisely, the government does not argue that SDI itself lacks standing to challenge the underlying search and seizure. See United States v. Leary, 846 F.2d 592, 596 (10th Cir.1988) ("[A] corporate defendant has standing with respect to searches of corporate premises and seizure of corporate records." (internal citation and quotation marks omitted)). We therefore only consider the Fourth Amendment standing of Kaplan and Brunk. Insofar as they do indeed lack standing, all evidence is admissible as to charges against them. By contrast, insofar as we affirm the district court's suppression of some evidence, such evidence will be inadmissible against SDI. Standing, therefore, makes a difference in this case.

steps SDI took to preserve the security of its business files, are inadequate to support the conclusion that Kaplan and Brunk personally had an expectation of privacy in the searched areas and seized materials. While "[i]t has long been settled that one has standing to object to a search of his office, as well as of his home," Mancusi v. DeForte, 392 U.S. 364 (1968), this case presents the novel issue of the extent to which a business employee may have standing to challenge a search of business premises generally.

The Fourth Amendment ensures that "[t]he right of the people to be secure in their persons, houses, papers, and effects, against unreasonable searches and seizures, shall not be violated, and no Warrants shall issue, but upon probable cause, supported by Oath or affirmation, and particularly describing the place to be searched, and the persons or things to be seized." U.S. Const. amend. IV. A person has standing to sue for a violation of this particular "right of the people" only if there has been a violation "as to him," personally. *Mancusi.* In other words, Fourth Amendment standing, unlike Article III standing, "is a matter of substantive [F]ourth [A]mendment law; to say that a party lacks [F]ourth [A]mendment standing is to say that his reasonable expectation of privacy has not been infringed." United States v. Taketa, 923 F.2d 665 (9th Cir.1991). This follows from the Supreme Court's famous observation that the Fourth Amendment "protects people, not places," Katz v. United States, 389 U.S. 347 (1967).

To show the government has violated his Fourth Amendment rights, an individual must have "a legitimate expectation of privacy in the invaded place," United States v. Crawford, 323 F.3d 700 (9th Cir.2003). Defendants must demonstrate "a subjective expectation of privacy in the area searched, and their expectation must be one that society would recognize as objectively reasonable." United States v. Sarkisian, 197 F.3d 966 (9th Cir.1999).

As a logical extension of this approach, "[p]roperty used for commercial purposes is treated differently for Fourth Amendment purposes from residential property." Minnesota v. Carter, 525 U.S. 83 (1998). Of course, individuals may still have a "reasonable expectation of privacy against intrusions by police" into their offices. O'Connor v. Ortega, 480 U.S. 709 (1987) ("Within the workplace context, . . . an expectation [of privacy] in one's place of work is based upon societal expectations that have deep roots in the history of the Amendment."). But, unlike the nearly absolute protection of a residence, the "great variety of work environments" requires analysis of reasonable expectations "on a case-by-case basis."

Our precedents provide numerous guideposts, however. For starters, it is crucial to Fourth Amendment standing that the place searched be "given over to [the defendant's] exclusive use." Schowengerdt v. General Dynamics Corp., 823 F.2d 1328 (9th Cir.1987). We have thus held that mere access to, and even use of, the office of a co-worker "does not lead us to find an objectively reasonable expectation of privacy." *Taketa.* By the same token, we have rejected managerial authority alone as sufficient for Fourth Amendment standing. In United States v. Cella, we held the corporate officer of a hospital, whom we described as the "de facto controlling force in [its] management," did not have standing to challenge the seizure of records from the hospital print shop. 568 F.2d 1266 (9th Cir.1977). Even though the defendant "had access to and control of the print shop operations, his rights did not include any expectation of privacy over documents which were kept at the print shop premises but over which [he] did not show an independent possessory or proprietary interest."

It thus appears that an employee of a corporation, whether worker or manager, does not, simply by virtue of his status as such, acquire Fourth Amendment standing with respect to company premises. Similarly, and notwithstanding the reference to "an independent . . . proprietary interest" in *Cella*, to be merely a shareholder of a corporation, without more, is also not enough.[5] As always, a reasonable expectation of privacy does not arise ex officio, but must be established with respect to the person in question.

We took this approach in United States v. Gonzalez, in which we held that the directors of a small, family-run corporation had standing to challenge a wiretap in one of the company's buildings. That holding relied on the facts of the case:

> [W]e simply hold that because the [defendants] were corporate officers and directors who not only had ownership of the [premises] but also exercised full access to the building as well as managerial control over its day-to-day operations, they had a reasonable expectation of privacy over calls made on the premises.

412 F.3d 1102 (9th Cir.2005).

Kaplan and Brunk argue that *Gonzalez* supports their claim of Fourth Amendment standing, but their argument rests on an overbroad reading of our opinion. We explicitly tied the defendants' standing to the "nature of the [business]." The defendants exercised "managerial control over [the] day-to-day operations" of the office where the conversations the wiretap "seized" took place, they owned the building where the office was located, and they not only could access the office but actually "exercised full access to the

---

[5] The Second Circuit summarized this point memorably in language quoted heavily by this and other circuits:

> When a man chooses to avail himself of the privilege of doing business as a corporation, even though he is its sole shareholder, he may not vicariously take on the privilege of the corporation under the Fourth Amendment; documents which he could have protected from seizure, if they had been his own, may be used against him, no matter how they were obtained from the corporation. Its wrongs are not his wrongs; its immunity is not his immunity.

Hill v. United States, 374 F.2d 871, 873 (9th Cir.1967).

building." Finally, the business in question was "a small, family-run business housing only 25 employees at its peak." In our detailed factual analysis, therefore, we made clear that it does not suffice for Fourth Amendment standing merely to own a business, to work in a building, or to manage an office. Since no one contends that Kaplan and Brunk operated SDI on a daily basis as a family-owned business like the defendants in *Gonzalez*, that precedent does not control here. * * *

In United States v. Anderson, the Tenth Circuit laid out a test to deal with situations in which a corporate employee does not work on a regular basis in the area searched. See 154 F.3d 1225 (10th Cir.1998). Given our case law, *Anderson* suggests three factors a court should consider in cases where an employee has not established that the area searched is "given over to [his] exclusive use." The Tenth Circuit's *Anderson* test looks to "(1) the employee's relationship to the item seized; (2) whether the item was in the immediate control of the employee when it was seized; and (3) whether the employee took actions to maintain his privacy in the item."

Though phrased vaguely, the first factor really addresses whether the item seized was personal property without any relationship to work. In addition, we note that the third factor involves actions the employee takes on his own behalf, not as an agent of the corporation.

Reading *Anderson* alongside our own precedent, we conclude that, except in the case of a small, family-run business over which an individual exercises daily management and control, an individual challenging a search of workplace areas beyond his own internal office must generally show some personal connection to the places searched and the materials seized. To adapt *Anderson*, although all the circumstances remain relevant, we will specifically determine the strength of such personal connection with reference to the following factors: (1) whether the item seized is personal property or otherwise kept in a private place separate from other work-related material;[7] (2) whether the defendant had custody or immediate control of the item when officers seized it; and (3) whether the defendant took precautions on his own behalf to secure the place searched or things seized

---

[7] In light of the Supreme Court's opinion in *O'Connor*, it cannot suffice for Fourth Amendment standing to challenge the seizure of an item in the workplace that the item is the personal property of an individual. See 480 U.S. at 715-16 (noting that "[t]he workplace includes those areas and items that are related to work and are generally within the employer's control," such as "the hallways, cafeteria, offices, desks and file cabinets," "even if the employee has placed personal items in them, such as a photograph placed in a desk"). Therefore, though personal ownership is important, Supreme Court precedent precludes us from considering it sufficient by itself to confer standing in this context.

from any interference without his authorization.[8] Absent such a personal connection or exclusive use, a defendant cannot establish standing for Fourth Amendment purposes to challenge the search of a workplace beyond his internal office.

The district court relied on three facts in concluding that Kaplan and Brunk had Fourth Amendment standing: their ownership of SDI, their management of SDI from offices in the building searched, and the security measures SDI took to secure its business records. Our review of relevant precedent indicates that these facts are too broad and generalized to support the district court's conclusion. The security measures that SDI took to ensure the privacy of its business records are relevant only to the standing of the corporation itself, not of its officers. As for Kaplan and Brunk, their ownership and management do not necessarily show a legitimate expectation of privacy. Because neither claims to enjoy "exclusive use" of the places searched – that is, the entire SDI office – they each must show a personal connection, along the lines we have drawn out of *Anderson*, to justify an expectation of privacy.

Lacking precedent on what is admittedly a novel issue of law, the district court did not adequately develop the record. Therefore, the district court's grant of the motion to suppress must be reversed and the matter remanded for further fact-finding. It seems that none of the items seized were the personal property of Kaplan or Brunk, nor were they in the custody of either. Therefore, on remand, the district court should focus its inquiry on, but need not confine it to, whether either Kaplan or Brunk took measures, each on his or the pair's personal behalf, to keep the items private and segregated from other general business materials. Of course, Kaplan and Brunk do have standing to challenge the admission of any evidence obtained from their own personal, internal offices. * * *

[The court turned to SDI's challenge to the warrant.] Evaluating the warrant (including the affidavit) to determine whether it met the demands of the Fourth Amendment, we start with the relevant language, which, of course, provides that "no Warrants shall issue, but upon probable cause . . . and particularly describing the place to be searched, and the persons or things to be seized." U.S. Const. amend. IV. Our cases describe this requirement as one of "specificity" and we have distinguished its "two aspects": "particularity and breadth . . . . Particularity is the requirement that the warrant must clearly state what is sought. Breadth deals with the requirement that the scope of the warrant be limited by the probable cause on which the warrant is based." In re Grand Jury Subpoenas Dated Dec. 10,

---

[8] We add that this list of factors is not exclusive, though it indicates what kind of factors are relevant. The law of Fourth Amendment standing in general, and of our cases on employee standing in particular, emphasize that a defendant must show a personal connection to the place searched and item seized; therefore we will only consider factors that relate to such inquiry.

1987, 926 F.2d 847 (9th Cir.1991).

Particularity means that "the warrant must make clear to the executing officer exactly what it is that he or she is authorized to search for and seize." Id. "'The description must be specific enough to enable the person conducting the search reasonably to identify the things authorized to be seized.'" United States v. Smith, 424 F.3d 992 (9th Cir.2005). * * *

Particularity is not the problem with the warrant in this case. Even the most troubling items on the list, such as "[r]olodexes, address books and calendars," are particular in that they "enable the person conducting the search reasonably to identify the things authorized to be seized." *Smith*. The officers could tell from the warrant that, should they happen upon a rolodex, they should seize it. Because the warrant was not vague as to what it directed law enforcement officers to search for and to seize, we are satisfied that it did not lack particularity for Fourth Amendment purposes.

The district court only made one inquiry, which explicitly conflated particularity and overbreadth. The court found that the warrant "at issue here was unconstitutionally overbroad because the lack of particularity provided no guidance in limiting the search and no direction to government agents regarding the purpose of the search or what types of records were within its scope." This error is quite understandable, given that some of our own opinions have been unclear on the difference between particularity and overbreadth. However, we now insist that particularity and overbreadth remain two distinct parts of the evaluation of a warrant for Fourth Amendment purposes.

A warrant must not only give clear instructions to a search team, it must also give legal, that is, not overbroad, instructions. Under the Fourth Amendment, this means that "there [must] be probable cause to seize the particular thing[s] named in the warrant." In re Grand Jury Subpoenas. "[P]robable cause means a fair probability that contraband or evidence of a crime will be found in a particular place, based on the totality of circumstances." United States v. Diaz, 491 F.3d 1074 (9th Cir.2007). "The number of files that could be scrutinized . . . is not determinative. The search and seizure of large quantities of material is justified if the material is within the scope of the probable cause underlying the warrant." United States v. Hayes, 794 F.2d 1348 (9th Cir.1986).

We turn now to the specific items with respect to which the district court found the warrant invalid, keeping in mind the warrant's incorporation of the affidavit. First, the district court, adopting the findings and recommendations of the magistrate judge, pointed to four categories of materials that it concluded were "borderline in acceptability," but nevertheless invalid: "2. Documents relating to billing procedures, billing manuals, and billing materials. 4. Documents relating to billing records and records of payments received. 8. Documents relating to correspondence with

Medicare intermediaries and private insurance companies. 19. Documents relating to mailing and shipping records between physicians and SDI."

The magistrate judge recognized that "SDI's entire business appears to have been the conducting of sleep studies, and the affidavit supported the conclusion that SDI's allegedly fraudulent conduct was routine."[12] All the same, he concluded that these categories were "overbroad and vague . . . and not adequately limited to seizure of documents relating to the fraudulent scheme under investigation."

In light of the warrant's incorporation of the affidavit, we reject this conclusion. According to the affidavit, SDI's entire business involved sleep studies, and billing for phony sleep studies lay at the core of its scheme. There was probable cause, therefore, to support Category 2, in that any and all documents related to billing practices would have information relevant to whether SDI trained its employees to commit fraud or otherwise engaged in fraudulent billing. The same applies to Category 8. While the magistrate judge faulted the government for failing to specify that it sought "billing and payments for sleep studies," such criticism relied on the nonincorporation of the affidavit into the warrant. Including the affidavit as part of the warrant moots this concern. The affidavit also alleged that SDI engaged in both tax fraud and Medicare fraud, providing probable cause to support the seizure of all documents within the purview of category 4. Finally, in light of the government's allegation that SDI was engaging in mail fraud and providing illegal kickback payments to referring physicians, we conclude that Category 19 adequately limited the search to documents related to the mailing and shipping records with physicians (i.e., as opposed to allowing the seizure of all mailing and shipping records). It did not have to be any more restrictive.

The magistrate judge also pointed to seven categories that, he believed, more clearly violated the Fourth Amendment: "7. Documents relating to non-privileged correspondence with consultants. 9. Documents relating to non-privileged internal memoranda and E-mail. 10. Documents relating to bank accounts, brokerage accounts, trusts. 11. Checking, savings, and money market account records, including check registers, cancelled checks, monthly statements, wire transfers, and cashier's checks. 12. Documents relating to personnel and payroll records. 13. Documents relating to accounting records. 24. Rolodexes, address books and calendars."

---

[12] The government does not expressly challenge the magistrate judge's conclusion that the "permeated with fraud" exception does not apply in this case, but it cites and applies cases setting forth such principle. To dispel any uncertainty, we confirm that the exception does not apply to this case. We have held that a generalized seizure of business documents may be justified if the government establishes probable cause to believe that the entire business is merely a scheme to defraud or that all of the business's records are likely to evidence criminal activity. However, in this case the affidavit did not allege that SDI's entire business was fraudulent, and therefore such exception is inapplicable.

Certainly, the district court had better justification finding these categories invalid under the Fourth Amendment. Indeed, we disagree with the district court only with respect to Categories 7 and 13.

Category 7 involves the "non-privileged correspondence of consultants." Consultants are contract counter-parties outside of a firm who assist it with one or another part of its business. Since, again, SDI's entire business involved sleep studies, it would have been difficult to specify beforehand which consultants were complicit in the fraudulent sleep studies.

Category 9, on the other hand, makes no attempt to limit the search team's reach to internal memoranda related to the sleep studies. Since internal documents typically cover a subject-matter far wider than do external communications, this failure constitutes an invitation to a general, "exploratory rummaging in a person's belongings." *United States v. Holzman*, 871 F.2d 1496 (9th Cir.1989). It is true that the affidavit stated that "SDI likely will have contracts, memoranda, Email and/or other documents explaining the relationship between SDI and [cardiac diagnostic companies] and the reasons for . . . payments." But even though we find the warrant incorporated the affidavit, this does not mean that every chance remark buried in its thirty-five pages can cure plain defects in the warrant.

Categories 10, 11, and 12 pose a similar problem. Companies keep documents relating to the bank and checking accounts or other financial information of most of their employees. In other words, by failing to describe the crimes and individuals under investigation, the warrant provided the search team with discretion to seize records wholly unrelated to the finances of SDI or Kaplan.

Although SDI's entire business revolved around sleep studies, that does not mean, and no one has suggested, that its entire business was a sham. As we noted above, the "permeated with fraud" exception to the specificity requirements of the warrant does not apply here. This makes Category 13 problematic. However, especially considering the allegations that SDI engaged in tax fraud by understating its earnings, it would be difficult to distinguish in the warrant between those records which would provide evidence of the alleged fraud and those that would not. Category 13, then, more closely resembles Category 4 rather than Categories 10-12. That is to say, the only accounting records companies typically keep are those of their business dealings; they do not keep accounting records of their employees' personal finances. Since SDI's entire business involved sleep studies, all of its accounting records could potentially reveal evidence of the alleged fraud.

Finally, Category 24 – SDI's rolodexes, address books, and calendars – amounts to the laziest of gestures in the direction of specificity. Again, this category practically begs the search team to find and to seize the contact information of every person who ever dealt with SDI. It would have been far more sensible, as well as constitutional, to limit the search to information relating to consultants, physicians, and health insurance companies, or some other group likely to turn up conspirators in the alleged fraud.

We therefore conclude that Categories 9, 10, 11, 12, and 24 were overbroad because probable cause did not exist to seize all items of those particular types.

[The court rejected the government's argument under *United States v. Leon*, 468 U.S. 897 (1984), that the good faith reliance exception to the exclusionary rule applied because the government failed to show that the officers executing the warrant actually relied on the affidavit. It upheld the suppression of the documents seized pursuant to the overbroad categories in the warrant.]

NOTE

Specificity of Time. When the government searches for records related to ongoing business transactions, how specific does the warrant have to be regarding the dates of the records? The government may argue that the it needs records beyond just the time in which particular transactions under investigation occurred because the events can take place over a broader period. Courts have rejected warrants that cover an extensive period of time if there is no probable cause that improper activity took place during the entire period. In **United States v. Ford**, 184 F.3d 566 (6th Cir. 1999), the warrant included broad descriptions of financial records without any time limitation, and the officers seized "several file cabinets and eleven boxes of documents" in connection with an illegal bingo operation. The court found the warrant lacked the requisite specificity regarding the time period for the items to be seized:

> [The warrant] authorized a broader search than was reasonable given the facts in the affidavit supporting the warrant. The affidavit stated that the first of Ford's RVA posts was incorporated in December 1991, and there was no indication in the affidavit of criminal activity before that date. The affidavit described an investigation beginning on April 24, 1992. It also reported an interview with Clay Ballinger, who said he had operated the bingo himself but had "sold the Arcade Plaza Bingo back to Mr. Ford in 1991." However, the police seized promissory notes, deeds, and related papers dated between 1984 and 1988, which had no relation to the bingo operation. * * *

> The government argues that it was necessary to seize documents antedating the bingo operation to establish what money Ford had before the bingo business started. This would help the government to identify which of his present assets could be bingo proceeds. This argument would allow virtually unlimited seizure of a lifetime's worth of documentation, which is extremely intrusive. Moreover, the

impracticability of tracing the origin of every dollar Ford owned to show whether it came from some enterprise other than bingo, casts doubt on whether the government really means to take on such a herculean task. At any rate, this rationale was not articulated in the affidavit, and therefore we need not decide whether it would have provided a justification for the warrant if it had been presented to the magistrate. * * *

The government further argues that there was probable cause to seize all the documents at the RVA Hall because the business carried on there was "permeated with fraud." * * * The affidavit definitely contained evidence that Ford was abusing the form of charitable organizations in order to run bingo games for personal profit. However, the affidavit did not disclose any reason to believe that the scheme began before December 1991, the date given in the affidavit as the date when Ford reactivated his first RVA post. Even if one business carried on at a site is permeated with fraud, if other businesses run at the same site are separable and are not shown to be related to the suspected crime, a warrant permitting seizure of all documents at the site is not justified.[a]

2. Business Pervaded by Fraud

The Fourth Amendment requires that a warrant specify the place to be searched and the items to be seized. When the government executes a search for the records of a business, the documents and computers could be in a wide variety of locations within a business, and even at different offices in various parts of the country. Similarly, evidence of criminality will often consist of voluminous records of regularly conducted activities, so it will be difficult to specify at the outset exactly which records are related to the suspected criminal activity. If the operation of an entire business is tainted by suspected illegal activity—such as a boiler room operation selling worthless securities or an advanced-loan scheme operated out of a remote location—can the government simply seize all of the records of a business on the ground that every item is relevant to prove criminality?

Once the government seizes a large volume of records, the business may be crippled if it cannot get access to billing records, order forms, etc. There may be a substantial gap in time between when the government seizes records under a search warrant and when, if ever, it files criminal charges that would permit the defendant to challenge a search. Federal Rule of Criminal Procedure 41(g) provides an avenue to challenge the propriety of the government's seizure of documents and evidence, and motions brought

---

[a] The government failed to argue that, under *Leon*, the agents' good faith reliance on the warrant should block application of the exclusionary rule.

under the Rule are only seen in cases involving white collar crimes and not illegal narcotics or other types or organized crime cases.

In re GRAND JURY INVESTIGATION CONCERNING SOLID STATE DEVICES, INC.
130 F.3d 853 (9th Cir. 1997)

D.W. NELSON, Circuit Judge.

Solid State Devices, Inc. and Unisem International (collectively "SSDI") appeal the district court's decision to deny their petition for return of property, filed pursuant to Federal Rule of Criminal Procedure 41(e). SSDI's property was seized in connection with a Department of Defense ("DoD") investigation of alleged fraudulent practices. SSDI challenges the legality of the seizure, arguing that the warrants executed against it were insufficiently specific.

SSDI supplies semiconductor devices to the DoD and to a number of DoD contractors. Because SSDI's semiconductors are used in sophisticated military, aerospace, and space programs, the Government requires that they be manufactured in conformity with exacting standards and tested to assure a high degree of reliability.

Since 1995, SSDI has been under investigation by agents of the Defense Criminal Investigative Service ("DCIS"), an investigative agency within the DoD. On May 17, 1995, Craig N. Wyckoff, a DCIS Special Agent, presented an affidavit to United States Magistrate Judge Virginia Phillips in support of the issuance of warrants to search SSDI. Based on interviews with two SSDI employees, SSDI clients, and government experts, Wyckoff alleged that SSDI had acquired commercial-grade semiconductors that did not comply with the standards and specifications required under SSDI's government contracts. He alleged that SSDI then falsely labeled these parts as SSDI-manufactured components, falsified test results certifying that the parts had undergone the necessary quality inspections, and sold the parts to the government at "high reliability" component prices. Because Wyckoff's affidavit reveals sensitive information, including the identities of informants, Wyckoff filed it under seal and requested that its contents not be disclosed to SSDI.

On May 23, 1995, federal agents of the FBI, DCIS and NASA executed search warrants on the premises of SSDI. The warrants, the validity of which is at issue on this appeal, authorized the seizure of a broad array of documents and data storage equipment, including the following:

a. Contracts, subcontracts, purchase orders, sales orders, invoices and correspondence, Certificates of Quality Conformance/Compliance (COQC), and memoranda relating to agreements between Solid State Devices, Inc., (SSDI), and any governmental or non-governmental entity regarding the manufacture, testing or inspection of semi-conductor devices supplied for U.S. Department of Defense (DoD) or other governmental programs from May 1, 1990 to the present.

k. Electronic data processing and storage devices, computers and computer systems including central processing units; internal and peripheral storage devices such as fixed disks, floppy disk drives and diskettes, tape drives and tapes, optical storage devices or other memory storage devices; peripheral input/output devices such as keyboards, printers, video display monitors, optical readers, and related communications devices such as modems; together with system documentation, operating logs and documentation, software and instruction manuals, all passwords, test keys, encryption codes or similar codes that are necessary to access computer programs, data or other information or to otherwise render programs or data into a usable form.

The warrants made no reference either to any statutes allegedly violated or, with one minor exception,[1] to any illegal acts. Moreover, no one at SSDI has been permitted to see the affidavit on which the warrants were based.

Pursuant to the search warrants, the agents seized computers, computer storage media, and more than 2,000 file drawers and file boxes containing business records. SSDI claims that nearly ninety percent of all of the documents and items at SSDI dealing with contracts over a five-year period were seized. These items have been stored since their seizure in May 1995 at DCIS offices in El Toro, California. In March 1996, SSDI filed a petition for return of seized property pursuant to Federal Rule of Criminal Procedure 41(e). The district court denied the petition, and SSDI timely appeals.

Federal Rule of Criminal Procedure 41(e) provides, in part, "A person aggrieved by an unlawful search and seizure or by the deprivation of property may move the district court . . . for the return of the property on the ground that such person is entitled to lawful possession of the property."[a] A Rule 41(e) motion therefore should be granted either when the movant is aggrieved by an unlawful seizure or, if the seizure was lawful, when the movant is aggrieved by the government's continued possession of the seized property. On this appeal, SSDI confines itself to challenging the legality of the Government's seizure of its property.

---

[1] The warrants authorized the seizure of fourteen categories of materials. Only one of the categories specifically referred to illegal acts:

j. Hewlett Packard computer utilized in the falsification of test results of the pre and post burn-in testing on Westinghouse semi-conductor parts.

[a] Rule 41 was revised in 2002, and the applicable provision is now Rule 41(g).

The Fourth Amendment provides that "no Warrants shall issue, but upon probable cause, supported by Oath or affirmation, and particularly describing the place to be searched, and the persons or things to be seized." U.S. Const. amend. IV. * * * In assessing whether a warrant passes constitutional muster, a court therefore is obliged to make two inquiries: first, whether the scope of the search authorized by the warrant was justified by probable cause and, second, whether the warrant was sufficiently particular to limit the discretion of the officers executing it. Because we find that the scope of the search exceeded the Government's showing of probable cause, however, we do not reach the particularity analysis. * * *

The warrants executed against SSDI were exceptionally broad in scope. Indeed, the only limitations imposed by the warrants were that the records relate to the supply of semiconductors to government programs and that they date from 1990 to 1995. The Government acknowledges, however, that the vast majority of SSDI's business relates directly or indirectly to the supply of semiconductors for government programs. Moreover, the Government nowhere provides a rationale for the dates chosen. Under these circumstances, such limitations are not meaningful.

The Government does not dispute that the warrants served on SSDI were broad in scope. It simply contends that Wyckoff's affidavit indicates that SSDI was so pervaded by fraud that there was probable cause to seize the majority of its documents. Under the law of this circuit, it is well-settled that "[a] generalized seizure of business documents may be justified if the government establishes probable cause to believe that the entire business is merely a scheme to defraud or that all of the business's records are likely to evidence criminal activity." See generally United States v. Offices Known as 50 State Distrib. Co., 708 F.2d 1371 (9th Cir.1983) (finding breadth of warrant justified by breadth of probable cause in view of fact that affidavit evidenced "pervasively fraudulent operation").

SSDI, however, is substantially different from the types of businesses to which this Court has applied the "pervaded by fraud" exception in the past. This circuit first adopted the exception in *50 State,* relying on the First Circuit's decision in United States v. Brien, 617 F.2d 299 (1st Cir.1980). In both *50 State* and *Brien* the affidavits supporting the warrants at issue showed that the companies involved were little more than "boilershop" sales operations engaged only negligibly in legitimate business activities. Although Wyckoff's affidavit alleges that SSDI has routinely engaged in fraudulent practices, it does not provide cause to believe that the majority of SSDI's operations are fraudulent. To the contrary, the record indicates that SSDI has received an impressive array of awards and certificates from a variety of clients, commending its contributions to their projects. Where a business appears, as SSDI does here, to be engaged in some legitimate activity, this Court has required a more substantial showing of pervasive fraud than that provided by the Government in the instant case.

Thus, while Wyckoff's affidavit very likely would have provided probable cause for a narrower, more carefully-defined search, we find it to have been an insufficient basis for the broad scope of the warrants executed against SSDI.

For the foregoing reasons, we REVERSE the district court's order denying the plaintiffs' Rule 41(e) motion for return of property and REMAND with instructions to the district court to grant the plaintiffs' Rule 41(e) motion.

NOTES AND QUESTIONS

1. *Effect on Future Use of the Evidence at Trial.* Even if the court grants the Rule 41(g) motion, is the government precluded from offering the content of the records in evidence? While the seizure may be improper, requiring the return of the records, the government could still rely on *Leon* to argue that suppression is not the appropriate remedy. Would the "fruit of the poisonous tree" doctrine prohibit the government from obtaining the documents returned after the Rule 41(g) motion? Could the government just subpoena the same records it seized pursuant to the illegal warrant? Consider the Supreme Court's statement in **Silverthorne Lumber Co. v. United States**, 251 U.S. 385 (1920), in which federal officers unlawfully seized certain documents and, after a district court ordered their return, the grand jury issued subpoenas to the defendants to produce the very same documents:

> The essence of a provision forbidding the acquisition of evidence in a certain way is that not merely evidence so acquired shall not be used before the Court but that it shall not be used at all. Of course this does not mean that the facts thus obtained become sacred and inaccessible. If knowledge of them is gained from an independent source they may be proved like any others, but the knowledge gained by the Government's own wrong cannot be used by it in the way proposed.

If *Leon* would allow the use of derivative evidence notwithstanding the Rule 41(g) ruling, then why not give the government the means to reobtain the documents seized illegally? If the government in *Solid State* had shown that it intended to proceed with an indictment and the illegal search met the good faith standard of Leon, should that have precluded return of the property? Was *Solid State* assuming that the warrant there met the facially deficient exception of *Leon*? If *Leon* applies, then the target may not be able to get a Rule 41(g) "exception" by making a motion for return prior to indictment. The government can return copies of documents seized in a search to comply with an order to return property under Rule 41(g). In In re Search of Office of Tylman, 245 F.3d 978 (7th Cir. 2001), the circuit court noted that "the district court ordered the government to return copies of the seized documents. That was done. We have been given no compelling reason to think that this solution is not an adequate remedy for the appellants."

2. *Pervasively Fraudulent Organization*. The Ninth Circuit asserted that a broad warrant permitting the seizure of all of an organization's documents might be permissible if the business were entirely criminal, although that was not the case in *Solid State*. In **United States v. Johnson**, 886 F.Supp. 1057 (W.D.N.Y. 1995), the District Court upheld a warrant for "any and all books and records * * * for the period 1982 to the present, including ledgers, journals, receipts, balance sheets, deeds, mortgages, contracts, invoices, bills, bank statements, financial statements, tax returns, stocks bonds and treasury notes" of four interrelated corporations involved in hazardous waste disposal. The court found that "although the search warrants at issue were broad, they were not unconstitutionally overbroad, as the businesses involved were shown to be sufficiently permeated with fraud to justify the wide scope of the warrant." In reviewing the warrant, the court noted that "[a]lthough a mere allegation of fraud is not enough to authorize the seizure of all business records, given the closely-connected nature of the Defendants' businesses here, it would not have been possible 'through a more particular description to segregate those business records that would be evidence of fraud from those that would not . . . .'"

3. *Overbroad Warrants to Search a Business*. The Tenth Circuit rejected that position in **Voss v. Bergsgaard**, 774 F.2d 402 (10th Cir. 1985):

> To the extent that * * * cases can be read as allowing the seizure of all of an organization's records when there is probable cause to believe the organization is pervasively criminal, whether or not those records are relevant to an alleged crime, we decline to follow them. This is not to say that a search may never properly result in the seizure of all of an organization's records. Where a warrant authorizes the seizure of particularly described records relevant to a specific crime and all of an organization's records, in fact, fall into that category, they may all lawfully be seized. However, a warrant that simply authorizes the seizure of all files, whether or not relevant to a specified crime, is insufficiently particular.

Circuit Judge Logan, in a concurring opinion, stated:

> I do not accept the majority's disapproval of [cases that] * * * permitted an all records search. These cases hold that if an entire business enterprise is permeated with a scheme to defraud, and the government properly supports its probable cause determination, a warrant seeking all business records is not overbroad. In such a case the government's agents' discretion in the execution of the warrant is properly confined, and all of the organization's business records are likely to be relevant to the crime being investigated.

The scope of the organization's criminality does not create an exception to the Fourth Amendment so much as it makes it easier for the government to establish that the description is sufficient to meet the particularity requirement for a valid warrant. What level of proof is needed to establish that a business is pervaded by fraud? If a business successfully challenges that conclusion, should a court suppress the evidence because the warrant did not have the requisite specificity?

C. COMPUTER SEARCHES

A significant volume of the information that will assist the government in an investigation of any complex business transaction most likely was created and stored on a computer. Business records, memoranda, reports, spreadsheets, financial and tax records, and correspondence are just a few of the types of records that can be found on a computer. Of particular interest to investigators are the internal e-mail messages of corporate employees, which often give contain unguarded statements of the reasons for an action or decision, and they usually are contemporaneous with the transactions under investigation. "For prosecutors, [e-mail] has become the star witness—or perhaps an even better weapon than that. Think of e-mail as the corporate equivalent of DNA evidence . . . So ubiquitous has the smoking e-mail become that some lawyers have taken to calling it 'evidence mail.'" Nicholas Varchaver, *The Perils of E-Mail*, FORTUNE, Feb. 17, 2003, at 96. Individuals use Personal Digital Assistants and other portable electronic devices to store calendars, schedules, notes, documents, and e-mail, so that the amount of information held by an individual is much greater than when information was only in documentary form.

Businesses often back-up their computer data on a regular basis, so records may be available from multiple locations. Data stored on a computer is not easily destroyed, so that even a concerted effort to eliminate all documentary evidence of a transaction may not be completely effective. The government has focused its attention to a much greater degree obtaining evidence from internal corporate computer systems, and with much greater frequency seize individual computers and memory devices. The Department of Justice recognizes the importance of obtaining evidence from computers, and the Computer Crime and Intellectual Property Section of its Criminal Division published a detailed manual on issues related to computer searches. U.S. Dept. of Justice, SEARCHING AND SEIZING COMPUTERS AND OBTAINING ELECTRONIC EVIDENCE IN CRIMINAL INVESTIGATIONS (2002) ("Searching and Seizing Computers"). The Department of Justice explains:

> In the last decade, computers and the Internet have entered the mainstream of American life. Millions of Americans spend several hours every day in front of computers, where they send and receive e-mail, surf the Web, maintain databases, and participate in countless other activities. Unfortunately, those who commit crime

have not missed the computer revolution. An increasing number of criminals use pagers, cellular phones, laptop computers and network servers in the course of committing their crimes. In some cases, computers provide the means of committing crime. For example, the Internet can be used to deliver a death threat via e-mail; to launch hacker attacks against a vulnerable computer network; to disseminate computer viruses; or to transmit images of child pornography. In other cases, computers merely serve as convenient storage devices for evidence of crime. For example, a drug kingpin might keep a list of who owes him money in a file stored in his desktop computer at home, or a money laundering operation might retain false financial records in a file on a network server. The dramatic increase in computer-related crime requires prosecutors and law enforcement agents to understand how to obtain electronic evidence stored in computers. Electronic records such as computer network logs, e-mails, word processing files, and ".jpg" picture files increasingly provide the government with important (and sometimes essential) evidence in criminal cases. * * *

The most basic Fourth Amendment question in computer cases asks whether an individual enjoys a reasonable expectation of privacy in electronic information stored within computers (or other electronic storage devices) under the individual's control. For example, do individuals have a reasonable expectation of privacy in the contents of their laptop computers, floppy disks or pagers? If the answer is "yes," then the government ordinarily must obtain a warrant before it accesses the information stored inside.

When confronted with this issue, courts have analogized electronic storage devices to closed containers, and have reasoned that accessing the information stored within an electronic storage device is akin to opening a closed container. Because individuals generally retain a reasonable expectation of privacy in the contents of closed containers, see United States v. Ross, 456 U.S. 798, 822-23 (1982), they also generally retain a reasonable expectation of privacy in data held within electronic storage devices. Accordingly, accessing information stored in a computer ordinarily will implicate the owner's reasonable expectation of privacy in the information. * * *

Individuals who retain a reasonable expectation of privacy in stored electronic information under their control may lose Fourth Amendment protections when they relinquish that control to third parties. For example, an individual may offer a container of electronic information to a third party by bringing a malfunctioning computer to a repair shop, or by shipping a floppy diskette in the mail to a friend. Alternatively, a user may transmit information to third parties electronically, such as by sending data across the Internet. When law enforcement agents learn of information possessed by third parties that may provide evidence of a crime, they may wish to inspect it. Whether the Fourth Amendment requires them to obtain a warrant before examining the information depends first upon whether the third-party possession has eliminated the individual's reasonable expectation of privacy.

To analyze third-party possession issues, it helps first to distinguish between possession by a carrier in the course of transmission to an intended recipient, and subsequent possession by the intended recipient. For example, if A hires B to carry a package to C, A's reasonable expectation of privacy in the contents of the package during the time that B carries the package on its way to C may be different than A's reasonable expectation of privacy after C has received the package. During transmission, contents generally retain Fourth Amendment protection. The government ordinarily may not examine the contents of a package in the course of transmission without a warrant. Government intrusion and examination of the contents ordinarily violates the reasonable expectation of privacy of both the sender and receiver.

SEARCHING AND SEIZING COMPUTERS, § I.B.

Searches of computers can raise thorny Fourth Amendment issues in the application of traditional Fourth Amendment doctrines to developing electronic devices, especially the particularity requirement for a valid warrant and the authority of a government agent under the "plain view" doctrine to look at materials stored on a computer or other electronic device to determine their relevance. The case below presents the issue of the scope of the government agent's right to view materials on a seized computer under the Fourth Amendment.

UNITED STATES v. ADJANI
452 F.2d 1140 (9th Cir. 2006)

FISHER, Circuit Judge:

While executing a search warrant at the home of defendant Christopher Adjani to obtain evidence of his alleged extortion, agents from the Federal Bureau of Investigation seized Adjani's computer and external storage devices, which were later searched at an FBI computer lab. They also seized and subsequently searched a computer belonging to defendant Jana Reinhold, who lived with Adjani, even though she had not at that point been identified as a suspect and was not named as a target in the warrant. Some of the emails found on Reinhold's computer chronicled conversations between her and Adjani that implicated her in the extortion plot. Relying in part on the incriminating emails, the government charged both Adjani and Reinhold with conspiring to commit extortion in violation of 18 U.S.C. § 371 and transmitting a threatening communication with intent to extort in violation of 18 U.S.C. § 875(d).

The defendants brought motions to suppress the emails, arguing that the warrant did not authorize the seizure and search of Reinhold's computer and its contents; but if it did, the warrant was unconstitutionally overbroad or, alternatively, the emails fell outside the scope of the warrant. The district court granted the defendants' motion to suppress the email communications between Reinhold and Adjani, finding that the agents did not have sufficient probable cause to search Reinhold's computer, and that once they discovered information incriminating her, the agents should have obtained an additional search warrant. The government appeals this evidentiary ruling, but only with respect to three emails dated January 12, 2004. * * *

Adjani was once employed by Paycom Billing Services Inc. (formerly Epoch), which facilitates payments from Internet users to its client websites. As a payment facilitator, Paycom receives and stores vast amounts of data containing credit card information. On January 8, 2004, a woman (later identified as Reinhold) delivered envelopes to three Paycom partners, Christopher Mallick, Clay Andrews and Joel Hall. Each envelope contained a letter from Adjani advising that he had purchased a copy of Paycom's database containing its clients' sensitive financial information. The letter threatened that Adjani would sell the Paycom database and master client control list if he did not receive $3 million. To prove his threats were real, Adjani included samples of the classified data. He directed the Paycom partners to sign an enclosed agreement attesting to the proposed quid pro quo and fax it back to him by January 12. The letter included Adjani's email address, cadjani@mac.com, and a fax number. Agents later learned that Adjani's email address was billed to Reinhold's account.

Evidence suggested that Adjani left Los Angeles on January 9, 2004, and ultimately ended up in Zurich, Switzerland. From Switzerland, Adjani sent an email on January 12 to Joel Hall to confirm that Hall and the others had received the envelopes. Adjani followed up on this email on January 13 by instructing Hall to contact him through AOL/Mac iChat instant messaging if he wanted to discuss the settlement agreement. With the FBI monitoring, Hall conversed several times with Adjani on the Internet and over the telephone. In spite of Adjani's insistence that he remain overseas, Hall convinced him to come to Los Angeles on January 26 to pick up $2.5 million in exchange for the database.

Adjani returned to Los Angeles on January 22, under FBI surveillance. Reinhold, driving in a car that the FBI had earlier identified as Adjani's, was observed leaving Adjani's residence in Venice, California, picking him up from the airport and returning to his residence. The FBI also observed Reinhold using an Apple computer, the same brand of computer Adjani used to email and chat with Paycom.

On January 23, 2004, based on the facts recited above and attested to in FBI Agent Cloney's affidavit (which was affixed to the warrant), a federal magistrate judge granted the government an arrest warrant for Adjani and a search warrant covering Adjani's Venice residence, his vehicle, his person and the residence of the individual who had stolen the confidential information from Paycom. The warrant specifically sought "evidence of violations of [18 U.S.C. § 875(d)]: Transmitting Threatening Communications With Intent to Commit Extortion." Further, the warrant expressly authorized seizure of:

> 5g. Records, documents and materials containing Paycom's or Epoch's master client control documents, Paycom's or Epoch's email database, or other company information relating to Paycom or Epoch.

> 5h. Records, documents and materials which reflect communications with Christopher Mallick, Clay Andrews, Joel Hall or other employees or officers of Paycom or Epoch.

> 5i. Any and all evidence of travel, including hotel bills and receipts, gasoline receipts, plane tickets, bus tickets, train tickets, or any other documents related to travel from January 8, 2004 to the present. * * *

> 5k. Computer, hard drives, computer disks, CD's, and other computer storage devices.

With respect to the computer search, the warrant prescribed the process to be followed: "In searching the data, the computer personnel will examine all of the data contained in the computer equipment and storage devices to view their precise contents and determine whether the data falls within the items to be seized as set forth herein." Additionally, it noted that "[i]n order to search for data that is capable of being read or intercepted by a computer, law enforcement personnel will need to seize and search * * * [a]ny computer equipment and storage device capable of being used to commit, further, or store evidence of the offense listed above."

On January 26, 2004, * * * agents executed the search warrant for Adjani's Venice residence. There they found and seized various computers and hard drives, including Reinhold's computer, which were later sent to an FBI computer lab to be searched. During that search process, the hard drive from Reinhold's computer revealed certain email correspondence between Reinhold and Adjani, implicating Reinhold in the extortion plot and supporting a charge of conspiracy against both of them.

Probable Cause

The government principally argues that contrary to the district court's finding and the defendants' assertions, the search warrant affidavit established probable cause to search all instrumentalities that might contain "evidence of violations of" 18 U.S.C. § 875(d), including Reinhold's computer and emails. Reinhold counters that the affidavit may have generally established probable cause, but did not do so with respect to her computer, because "[i]n the affidavit, Reinhold was not labeled as a target, suspect, or co-conspirator."

* * * The warrant here was supported by probable cause, because the affidavit submitted to the magistrate judge established that "there [was] a fair probability that contraband or evidence of a crime [would] be found in" computers at Adjani's residence. See Illinois v. Gates, 462 U.S. 213 (1983). The extensive 24-page supporting affidavit described the extortion scheme in detail, including that Adjani possessed a computer-generated database and communicated with Paycom over email, requiring the use of a computer. Furthermore, the agent's affidavit explained the need to search computers, in particular, for evidence of the extortion scheme: "I know that considerable planning is typically performed to construct and consummate an extortion. The plan can be documented in the form of a simple written note or more elaborate information stored on computer equipment."

* * * The crime contemplated by the warrant was transmitting a threatening communication with intent to extort. See 18 U.S.C. § 875(d). To find evidence of extortion, the government would have probable cause to search for and seize instrumentalities likely to have been used to facilitate the transmission. The magistrate judge could rightfully assume that there was a "fair probability" that such evidence could be contained on computers or storage devices found in Adjani's residence.

Having held that the affidavit supporting the warrant established probable cause to search for and seize instrumentalities of the extortion (including records, files and computers) in Adjani's residence, we turn to Reinhold's contention that the probable cause for the Adjani warrant did not extend so far as to permit a search of her property. We disagree. The agents, acting pursuant to a valid warrant to look for evidence of a computer-based crime, searched computers found in Adjani's residence and to which he had apparent access. That one of the computers actually belonged to Reinhold did not exempt it from being searched, especially given her association with Adjani and participation (however potentially innocuous) in some of his activities as documented in the agent's supporting affidavit. The officers therefore did not act unreasonably in searching Reinhold's computer as a source of the evidence targeted by the warrant.

Reinhold's argument that there was no probable cause to search her computer, a private and personal piece of property, because the warrant failed to list her as a "target, suspect, or co-conspirator" misunderstands Fourth Amendment jurisprudence.[5] Although individuals undoubtedly have

_____

[5] The district court appears to have agreed with Reinhold's argument when it noted that "[t]here's not probable cause of any kind mentioned in the search warrant itself to deal with any property of Ms. Reinhold." However, as we explain below, probable cause analysis focuses not on the owner of the property, but rather on

a high expectation of privacy in the files stored on their personal computers, we have never held that agents may establish probable cause to search only those items owned or possessed by the criminal suspect. The law is to the contrary. "The critical element in a reasonable search is not that the owner of the property is suspected of crime but that there is reasonable cause to believe that the specific 'things' to be searched for and seized are located on the property to which entry is sought." Zurcher v. Stanford Daily, 436 U.S. 547 (1978)

* * * [T]here was no need here for the agents expressly to claim in the affidavit that they wanted to arrest Reinhold, or even that Reinhold was suspected of any criminal activity. The government needed only to satisfy the magistrate judge that there was probable cause to believe that evidence of the crime in question-here extortion-could be found on computers accessible to Adjani in his home, including – as it developed – Reinhold's computer. By setting forth the details of the extortion scheme and the instrumentalities of the crime, augmented by descriptions of Reinhold's involvement with Adjani, the government satisfied its burden. The magistrate judge therefore properly approved the warrant, which in turn encompassed all the computers found at Adjani's residence.

Specificity Requirement

The defendants argue that if the warrant did authorize a search that properly included Reinhold's computer, the warrant was fatally overbroad, justifying the district court's exclusion of the Reinhold emails. The government counters that the warrant satisfied the particularity standards articulated by this court, so exclusion was improper.

The Fourth Amendment's specificity requirement prevents officers from engaging in general, exploratory searches by limiting their discretion and providing specific guidance as to what can and cannot be searched and seized. However, the level of detail necessary in a warrant is related to the particular circumstances and the nature of the evidence sought. See United States v. Spilotro, 800 F.2d 959 (9th Cir.1986) ("Warrants which describe generic categories of items are not necessarily invalid if a more precise description of the items subject to seizure is not possible.").

* * * *Spilotro* involved a warrant issued against individuals suspected of loan sharking and gambling activities. The warrant authorized "the seizure of address books, notebooks, notes, documents, records, assets, photographs, and other items and paraphernalia evidencing violations of the multiple criminal statutes listed." It failed, however, to state the "precise identity, type, or contents of the records sought." Partly because of this reason, we

---

whether evidence of the crime can be found on the property given the circumstances.

held that the warrant was not sufficiently specific to pass muster under the Fourth Amendment. More could have been done to tie the documents sought to the crimes alleged by, for example, stating that the police were searching for "records relating to loan sharking and gambling, including pay and collection sheets, lists of loan customers, loan accounts and telephone numbers . . . ."

In contrast to *Spilotro*, the warrant to search Adjani's residence satisfied our specificity criteria. First, we have already held that there was probable cause to search the computers. As to the second factor, the warrant objectively described the items to be searched and seized with adequate specificity and sufficiently restricted the discretion of agents executing the search. The warrant affidavit began by limiting the search for evidence of a specific crime-transmitting threatening communications with intent to commit extortion. Further, unlike in *Spilotro*, the Adjani warrant provided the "precise identity" and nature of the items to be seized. For example, paragraph 5h of the warrant instructed agents to search for documents reflecting communications with three individuals or other employees of a specific company. Also, paragraph 5i authorized seizure of "any" evidence of travel but provided a specific, though not exhaustive, list of possible documents that fell within this category and temporally restricted the breadth of the search. Moreover, the extensive statement of probable cause in the affidavit detailed the alleged crime and Adjani's unlawful scheme.

With respect to the final *Spilotro* factor, we conclude that the government described the items to be searched and seized as particularly as could be reasonably expected given the nature of the crime and the evidence it then possessed. The Adjani warrant described in great detail the items one commonly expects to find on premises used for the criminal activities in question.

Center Art Galleries-Hawaii, Inc. v. United States, 875 F.2d 747 (9th Cir.1989), the principal case defendants rely upon in making their overbreadth argument, is distinguishable. In that case, we held that a warrant providing for "the almost unrestricted seizure of items which are 'evidence of violations of federal criminal law' without describing the specific crimes suspected is constitutionally inadequate." In contrast, the government here did describe at some length both the nature of and the means of committing the crime. Further, unlike in Center Art Galleries, the affidavit was expressly incorporated into the warrant.[7]

---

[7] The supporting affidavit attached to the warrant set forth a detailed computer search protocol, including instructions as to when the computers should be searched on-site rather than taken off-site and procedures for screening the data to determine what data could be searched and seized under the terms of the warrant. See also U.S. Dep't of Justice, Searching and Seizing Computers and Obtaining Electronic Evidence in Criminal Investigations 43, 69 (July 2002) (detailing what FBI agents should include in warrants when they contemplate the need to search computers). Such specificity increases our confidence that the magistrate judge was well aware of what

We understand the heightened specificity concerns in the computer context, given the vast amount of data they can store. As the defendants urge, the warrant arguably might have provided for a "less invasive search of Adjani's [email] 'inbox' and 'outbox' for the addressees specifically cited in the warrant, as opposed to the wholesale search of the contents of all emails purportedly looking for evidence' reflecting' communications with those individuals." Avoiding that kind of specificity and limitation was not unreasonable under the circumstances here, however. To require such a pinpointed computer search, restricting the search to an email program or to specific search terms, would likely have failed to cast a sufficiently wide net to capture the evidence sought. Moreover, agents are limited by the longstanding principle that a duly issued warrant, even one with a thorough affidavit, may not be used to engage in a general, exploratory search.

Computer files are easy to disguise or rename, and were we to limit the warrant to such a specific search protocol, much evidence could escape discovery simply because of Adjani's (or Reinhold's) labeling of the files documenting Adjani's criminal activity. The government should not be required to trust the suspect's self-labeling when executing a warrant.

Scope of the Warrant

Even assuming that the warrant was supported by probable cause and was adequately specific such that a search of Reinhold's computer and emails were permissible, Reinhold argues that the actual emails sought to be introduced into evidence were outside the scope of the warrant. Again, we disagree.

The three seized emails the government seeks to admit clearly fall within the scope of paragraph 5h of the warrant affidavit, authorizing seizure of "[r]ecords, documents and materials which reflect communications with Christopher Mallick, Clay Andrews, Joel Hall or other employees or officers of Paycom or Epoch," which are relevant evidence of violations of 18 U.S.C. § 875(d). Each email specifically refers to communication with Joel Hall or one of the stated companies (identifying them by name). Reinhold's argument that the term "reflect communications with" should be read narrowly to cover only those emails sent between one of the named Paycom employees and Adjani is nonsensical. The government already had the emails sent between the victims of the extortion and Adjani-obtained from the victims themselves. The purpose of the warrant was to obtain further and corroborating evidence of the extortion scheme and Adjani's criminal intent

---

he was authorizing and that the agents knew the bounds of their authority in executing the search. * * * The protocol, of course, does not eliminate the necessity that the protocol procedures and the materials seized or searched fall within the scope of a properly issued warrant supported by probable cause.

in communicating with the victims, and the three emails plainly "reflect" the relevant communications specified in paragraph 5h.

To the extent Reinhold argues that the emails were outside the scope of the warrant because they implicated her in the crime and supported a charge of conspiracy to commit extortion (a crime not specifically mentioned in the warrant), we reject the argument. There is no rule, and Reinhold points to no case law suggesting otherwise, that evidence turned up while officers are rightfully searching a location under a properly issued warrant must be excluded simply because the evidence found may support charges for a related crime (or against a suspect) not expressly contemplated in the warrant.

In United States v. Beusch, 596 F.2d 871 (9th Cir.1979), the defendants argued that certain seized items, including two ledgers and a file, should be excluded because they contained information unrelated to the suspect identified in the warrant. The defendants claimed that the officers impermissibly engaged in a general search by not segregating out those items implicating a third individual in the crime. We rejected this proposition and refused to impose the burden of segregation on the police. In so doing we held,

> All three items admittedly contained information seizable under the terms of the warrant and they therefore met the particularity requirement of the Fourth Amendment. As long as an item appears, at the time of the search, to contain evidence reasonably related to the purposes of the search, there is no reason absent some other Fourth Amendment violation to suppress it. The fact that an item seized happens to contain other incriminating information not covered by the terms of the warrant does not compel its suppression, either in whole or in part. In so holding we are careful to point out that we are discussing single files and single ledgers, i.e., single items which, though theoretically separable, in fact constitute one volume or file folder.

Beusch is analogous to the situation at hand. The agents were rightfully searching Reinhold's computer for evidence of Adjani's crime of extortion. They were looking in Reinhold's email program when they came across information that was both related to the purposes of their search and implicated Reinhold in the crime. That the evidence could now support a new charge against a new (but already identified) person does not compel its suppression. On these facts, we disagree with the district court's conclusion that the officers should have obtained a new search warrant when they came across the incriminating emails. In so concluding, we are careful to note that in this case the evidence discovered was clearly related to the crime referred to in the warrant. We need not decide to what extent the government would be able to introduce evidence discovered that the police knew, at the time of discovery, was not related to the crime cited in the warrant.

Conclusion

"The Fourth Amendment incorporates a great many specific protections against unreasonable searches and seizures." *Beusch*. The contours of these protections in the context of computer searches pose difficult questions. Computers are simultaneously file cabinets (with millions of files) and locked desk drawers; they can be repositories of innocent and deeply personal information, but also of evidence of crimes. The former must be protected, the latter discovered. As society grows ever more reliant on computers as a means of storing data and communicating, courts will be called upon to analyze novel legal issues and develop new rules within our well established Fourth Amendment jurisprudence. The fact of an increasingly technological world is not lost upon us as we consider the proper balance to strike between protecting an individual's right to privacy and ensuring that the government is able to prosecute suspected criminals effectively. In this era of rapid change, we are mindful of Justice Brandeis's worry in Olmstead v. United States,

> Ways may some day be developed by which the Government, without removing papers from secret drawers, can reproduce them in court, and by which it will be enabled to expose to a jury the most intimate occurrences of the home * * *. Can it be that the Constitution affords no protection against such invasions of individual security?

277 U.S. 438 (1928) (Brandeis, J., dissenting).

We do not now have occasion to address the myriad complex issues raised in deciding when a court should exclude evidence found on a computer, but are satisfied that the agents in this case acted properly in searching Reinhold's computer and seizing the emails in question here. The district court erred in excluding these emails. Therefore, the district court's ruling on the motion to suppress is reversed, and this matter is remanded for further proceedings consistent with this opinion.

NOTES AND QUESTIONS

1. *The "File Cabinet" Theory*. In **United States v. Carey**, 172 F.3d 1268 (10th Cir. 1999), the Tenth Circuit focused on how computer files are different from documents stored at a business, and therefore how the Fourth Amendment analysis will differ.

> In our judgment, the case turns upon the fact that each of the files containing pornographic material was labeled "JPG" and most featured a sexually suggestive title. Certainly after opening the first file and seeing an image of child pornography, the searching officer

was aware—in advance of opening the remaining files—what the label meant. When he opened the subsequent files, he knew he was not going to find items related to drug activity as specified in the warrant, just like the officer in Turner knew he was not going to find evidence of an assault as authorized by the consent.

At oral argument the government suggested this situation is similar to an officer having a warrant to search a file cabinet containing many drawers. Although each drawer is labeled, he had to open a drawer to find out whether the label was misleading and the drawer contained the objects of the search. While the scenario is likely, it is not representative of the facts of this case. This is not a case in which ambiguously labeled files were contained in the hard drive directory. It is not a case in which the officers had to open each file drawer before discovering its contents. Even if we employ the file cabinet theory, the testimony of Detective Lewis makes the analogy inapposite because he stated he knew, or at least had probable cause to know, each drawer was properly labeled and its contents were clearly described in the label.

Further, because this case involves images stored in a computer, the file cabinet analogy may be inadequate. * * * Where officers come across relevant documents so intermingled with irrelevant documents that they cannot feasibly be sorted at the site, the officers may seal or hold the documents pending approval by a magistrate of the conditions and limitations on a further search through the documents. The magistrate should then require officers to specify in a warrant which type of files are sought.

2. *Plain View Doctrine.* While many of the exceptions to the warrant requirement, such as the automobile and border search exceptions, are irrelevant in white collar crime cases, the plain view doctrine can play a significant role when agents are executing a search warrant and review documents or computer files that may be relevant. In **Texas v. Brown**, 460 U.S. 730 (1983), the Supreme Court explained the requirements that allow the seizure of an item in plain view:

First, the police officer must lawfully make an initial intrusion or otherwise properly be in a position from which he can view a particular area. Second, the officer must discover incriminating evidence inadvertently, which is to say, he may not know in advance the location of certain evidence and intend to seize it, relying on the plain view doctrine only as a pretext. Finally, it must be immediately apparent to the police that the items they observe may be evidence of a crime, contraband, or otherwise subject to seizure.

The prerequisite for application of the plain view doctrine to seize an item is that the officer be lawfully present when the observation occurs. In white collar cases, this usually occurs during the execution of a search warrant, when agents may review files to determine whether they come within the scope of the warrant. As *Brown* noted, "'Plain view' is perhaps better understood, therefore, not as an independent 'exception' to the warrant clause, but simply as an extension of whatever the prior justification for an officer's 'access to an object' may be."

In computer searches, the agents will often review all the files in the memory to determine which ones come within the warrant. In **United States v. Gray**, 78 F.Supp.2d 524 (E.D.Va. 1999), the district court rejected a defendant's challenge to the government's discovery of child pornography while agents were executing a warrant that allowed them to review his computer for files related to a computer intrusion at a government facility. The district court stated:

> The Fourth Amendment requires that a search warrant describe the things to be seized with sufficient particularity to prevent a general exploratory rummaging in a person's belongings. To prevent such rummaging, therefore, a "warrant must enable the executing officer to ascertain and identify with reasonable certainty those items that the magistrate has authorized him to seize." United States v. George, 975 F.2d 72 (2d Cir.1992). In some searches, however, it is not immediately apparent whether or not an object is within the scope of a search warrant; in such cases, an officer must examine the object simply to determine whether or not it is one that he is authorized to seize. Searches of records or documents present a variant of this principle, as documents, unlike illegal drugs or other contraband, may not appear incriminating on their face. As a result, in any search for records or documents, "innocuous records must be examined to determine whether they fall into the category of those papers covered by the search warrant." United States v. Kufrovich, 997 F.Supp. 246 (D.Conn.1997). Although care must be taken to minimize the intrusion, records searches require that many, and often all, documents in the targeted location be searched because "few people keep documents of their criminal transactions in a folder marked 'crime records.'" United States v. Hunter, 13 F.Supp.2d 574 (D.Vt.1998). Thus, agents authorized by warrant to search a home or office for documents containing certain specific information are entitled to examine all files located at the site to look for the specified information. So it is not surprising, then, that in the course of conducting a lawful search pursuant to a search warrant, law enforcement agents often discover evidence of criminal activity other than that which is the subject of the warrant. If an agent sees, in plain view, evidence of criminal activity other than that for which she is searching, this does not constitute an unreasonable search under the Fourth Amendment, for "[v]iewing an article that is already in plain view does not involve an invasion of privacy." United States v. Jackson, 131 F.3d 1105 (4th Cir.1997). Further, such evidence may be seized under the "plain view" exception to the

warrant requirement, provided that "(1) the officer is lawfully in a place from which the object may be plainly viewed; (2) the officer has a lawful right of access to the object itself; and (3) the object's incriminating character is immediately apparent." *Jackson*. These principles applied in the context of a document or record search means that, if an agent searching files pursuant to a search warrant discovers a document that contains evidence of another crime, that document can be seized under the "plain view" exception to the warrant requirement.

3.   *Warrantless Workplace Searches*.   "The rules for conducting warrantless searches and seizures in private-sector workplaces generally mirror the rules for conducting warrantless searches in homes and other personal residences. Private company employees generally retain a reasonable expectation of privacy in their workplaces. As a result, searches by law enforcement of a private workplace will usually require a warrant unless the agents can obtain the consent of an employer or a co-worker with common authority." SEARCHING AND SEIZING COMPUTERS § I.D.1. Public employer workplace searches, including computers, are much murkier. In **O'Connor v. Ortega**, 480 U.S. 709 (1987), Justice O'Connor's plurality decision offered a totality-of-the-circumstances test for determining when a public employer could search the office or workspace of a public employee. In *O'Connor*, the plaintiff, Dr. Ortega, filed a § 1983 suit against the public hospital where he worked because a search of his office violated his Fourth Amendment rights. The plurality analyzed whether a public employee has a reasonable expectation of privacy in the workplace in this way:

> [I]t is essential first to delineate the boundaries of the workplace context. The workplace includes those areas and items that are related to work and are generally within the employer's control. At a hospital, for example, the hallways, cafeteria, offices, desks, and file cabinets, among other areas, are all part of the workplace. These areas remain part of the workplace context even if the employee has placed personal items in them, such as a photograph placed in a desk or a letter posted on an employee bulletin board.

> Not everything that passes through the confines of the business address can be considered part of the workplace context, however. An employee may bring closed luggage to the office prior to leaving on a trip, or a handbag or briefcase each workday. While whatever expectation of privacy the employee has in the existence and the outward appearance of the luggage is affected by its presence in the workplace, the employee's expectation of privacy in the *contents* of the luggage is not affected in the same way. The appropriate standard for a workplace search does not necessarily apply to a piece of closed personal luggage, a handbag or a briefcase that happens to be within the employer's business address.

Within the workplace context, this Court has recognized that employees may have a reasonable expectation of privacy against intrusions by police. * * *

[W]e reject the contention made by the Solicitor General and petitioners that public employees can never have a reasonable expectation of privacy in their place of work. Individuals do not lose Fourth Amendment rights merely because they work for the government instead of a private employer. The operational realities of the workplace, however, may make *some* employees' expectations of privacy unreasonable when an intrusion is by a supervisor rather than a law enforcement official. Public employees' expectations of privacy in their offices, desks, and file cabinets, like similar expectations of employees in the private sector, may be reduced by virtue of actual office practices and procedures, or by legitimate regulation. * * * The employee's expectation of privacy must be assessed in the context of the employment relation. An office is seldom a private enclave free from entry by supervisors, other employees, and business and personal invitees. Instead, in many cases offices are continually entered by fellow employees and other visitors during the workday for conferences, consultations, and other work-related visits. Simply put, it is the nature of government offices that others—such as fellow employees, supervisors, consensual visitors, and the general public—may have frequent access to an individual's office. We agree with Justice Scalia that "[c]onstitutional protection against *unreasonable* searches by the government does not disappear merely because the government has the right to make reasonable intrusions in its capacity as employer," but some government offices may be so open to fellow employees or the public that no expectation of privacy is reasonable. [The Court determined that Dr. Ortega had a reasonable expectation of privacy in his desk and file cabinets.] * * *

The legitimate privacy interests of public employees in the private objects they bring to the workplace may be substantial. Against these privacy interests, however, must be balanced the realities of the workplace, which strongly suggest that a warrant requirement would be unworkable. While police, and even administrative enforcement personnel, conduct searches for the primary purpose of obtaining evidence for use in criminal or other enforcement proceedings, employers most frequently need to enter the offices and desks of their employees for legitimate work-related reasons wholly unrelated to illegal conduct. Employers and supervisors are focused primarily on the need to complete the government agency's work in a prompt and efficient manner. An employer may have need for correspondence, or a file or report available only in an employee's office while the employee is away from the office. Or, as is alleged to have been the case here, employers may need to safeguard or identify state property or records in an office in connection with a pending investigation into suspected employee misfeasance.

In our view, requiring an employer to obtain a warrant whenever the employer wished to enter an employee's office, desk, or file cabinets for a work-related purpose would seriously disrupt the routine conduct of business and would be unduly burdensome. Imposing unwieldy warrant procedures in such cases upon supervisors, who would otherwise have no reason to be familiar with such procedures, is simply unreasonable. In contrast to other circumstances in which we have required warrants, supervisors in offices such as at the Hospital are hardly in the business of investigating the violation of criminal laws. Rather, work-related searches are merely incident to the primary business of the agency. Under these circumstances, the imposition of a warrant requirement would conflict with "the common-sense realization that government offices could not function if every employment decision became a constitutional matter." Connick v. Myers, 461 U.S. 138 (1983).***

As an initial matter, it is important to recognize the plethora of contexts in which employers will have an occasion to intrude to some extent on an employee's expectation of privacy. Because the parties in this case have alleged that the search was either a noninvestigatory work-related intrusion or an investigatory search for evidence of suspected work-related employee misfeasance, we undertake to determine the appropriate Fourth Amendment standard of reasonableness *only* for these two types of employer intrusions and leave for another day inquiry into other circumstances. * * *

In our view, therefore, a probable cause requirement for searches of the type at issue here would impose intolerable burdens on public employers. The delay in correcting the employee misconduct caused by the need for probable cause rather than reasonable suspicion will be translated into tangible and often irreparable damage to the agency's work, and ultimately to the public interest. * * * It is simply unrealistic to expect supervisors in most government agencies to learn the subtleties of the probable cause standard. * * *

In sum, we conclude that the "special needs, beyond the normal need for law enforcement make the . . . probable-cause requirement impracticable," for legitimate work-related, noninvestigatory intrusions as well as investigations of work-related misconduct. A standard of reasonableness will neither unduly burden the efforts of government employers to ensure the efficient and proper operation of the workplace, nor authorize arbitrary intrusions upon the privacy of public employees. We hold, therefore, that public employer intrusions on the constitutionally protected privacy interests of government employees for noninvestigatory, work-related purposes, as well as for investigations of work- related misconduct, should be judged by the standard of reasonableness under all the circumstances. Under this reasonableness standard, both the inception and the scope of the intrusion must be reasonable[.] * * *

Justice Scalia concurred in the judgment, but criticized the vagueness of the plurality's approach to determining whether a public employee has a legitimate expectation of privacy in the workplace and whether the search was reasonable:

> The plurality opinion instructs the lower courts that existence of Fourth Amendment protection for a public employee's business office is to be assessed "on a case-by-case basis," in light of whether the office is "so open to fellow employees or the public that no expectation of privacy is reasonable." No clue is provided as to how open "so open" must be; much less is it suggested how police officers are to gather the facts necessary for this refined inquiry. * * *

> Even if I did not disagree with the plurality as to what result the proper legal standard should produce in the case before us, I would object to the formulation of a standard so devoid of content that it produces rather than eliminates uncertainty in this field. * * *

> I cannot agree, moreover, with the plurality's view that the reasonableness of the expectation of privacy (and thus the existence of Fourth Amendment protection) changes "when an intrusion is by a supervisor rather than a law enforcement official." The identity of the searcher (police v. employer) is relevant not to whether Fourth Amendment protections apply, but only to whether the search of a protected area is reasonable.

Can a public employee ever have a reasonable expectation of privacy in files stored on a computer used in a public workplace, even if that person is the only one who uses the computer? What if the files were protected by a password known only to the employee, and did not include any material for use in the agency's public function? If the use of a public employer's computer for private purposes is prohibited–which is normally the case–then that misconduct would seem to permit a supervisor to access any files on the computer in an investigation of "work-related employee misfeasance" under the plurality's analysis in O'Connor v. Ortega.

4. *Inventory Searches.* The government may conduct an inventory search of any containers that were properly impounded at the time a person is arrested. If computer disks or other storage media are among the items the defendant carried at the time of the arrest, can the government inventory the contents of the computer material by opening and inspecting the files? The answer appears to be that this would fall outside the scope of the inventory

search exception to the warrant requirement. See United States v. O'Razvi, 1998 WL 405048, at *7 (S.D.N.Y. July 17, 1998) ("the Government has not represented that the Secret Service inventory procedures provide for the inspection of computer disks, or analogous 'opening' of closed containers. The Court's review of the pertinent procedures similarly suggests that the Secret Service procedures do not provide for the inspection of closed materials. Indeed, the Government has conceded that a warrant was required for the examination of the contents of the disks, although it has not indicated on what legal authority it relies in making this concession."). If the government does not have any information about the contents of the computer files, will it have probable cause to secure a warrant to inspect the disks or storage media?

D. LAW OFFICE SEARCHES

Attorneys may be involved in the crimes of their clients, either as direct participants or in advising them how to avoid detection. The issue of searching a law office for evidence is complex because of the presence of documents subject to protection from disclosure under the attorney-client privilege and the work product doctrine. The prospect of government agents rummaging through a law firm's files, searching for evidence of wrongdoing, is a particularly chilling thought.

The Department of Justice sought to balance the need to fully investigate wrongdoing by allowing searches of law offices with the need to be sensitive to confidentiality concerns not encompassed by the Fourth Amendment's warrant requirement. The *U.S. Attorney's Manual* § 9-13.420 requires that prosecutors and investigators follow procedures to limit the possibility that confidential documents and information that falls outside the scope of the search warrant will be reviewed by the government. Section 9-13.420 covers cases involving "a search warrant for the premises of an attorney who is a suspect, subject or target of a criminal investigation where information relating to the representation of clients is likely to be present and subject to search . . . [T]o avoid impinging on valid attorney-client relationships, prosecutors are expected to take the least intrusive approach consistent with vigorous and effective law enforcement when evidence is sought from an attorney actively engaged in the practice of law." Accordingly, consideration should be given to "alternatives to search warrants", such as "obtaining information from other sources or through the use of a subpoena." Where the prosecutor concludes that a warrant is needed, the Department of Justice requires that the application for the warrant be approved by "the United States Attorney or pertinent Assistant Attorney General." Ordinarily, authorization will be granted "only when there is a strong need for the information or material and less intrusive means have been considered and rejected."

In addition to the required authorization, prior consultation with the Criminal Division is required. The prosecutor is directed to submit to that office a form explaining why the search is desired, why alternatives means have been rejected, and what procedures are to be followed "to protect privilege and to ensure the prosecution is not tainted." The policy directive adds the following commentary on what is expected in conducting the search:

Safeguarding Procedures and Contents of the Affidavit. Procedures should be designed to ensure that privileged materials are not improperly viewed, seized or retained during the course of the search. While the procedures to be followed should be tailored to the facts of each case and the requirements and judicial preferences and precedents of each district, in all cases a prosecutor must employ adequate precautions to ensure that the materials are reviewed for privilege claims and that any privileged documents are returned to the attorney from whom they were seized.

Conducting the Search. The search warrant should be drawn as specifically as possible, consistent with the requirements of the investigation, to minimize the need to search and review privileged material to which no exception applies.

While every effort should be made to avoid viewing privileged material, the search may require limited review of arguably privileged material to ascertain whether the material is covered by the warrant. Therefore, to protect the attorney-client privilege and to ensure that the investigation is not compromised by exposure to privileged material relating to the investigation or to defense strategy, a "privilege team" should be designated, consisting of agents and lawyers not involved in the underlying investigation.

Instructions should be given and thoroughly discussed with the privilege team prior to the search. The instructions should set forth procedures designed to minimize the intrusion into privileged material, and should ensure that the privilege team does not disclose any information to the investigation/prosecution team unless and until so instructed by the attorney in charge of the privilege team. Privilege team lawyers should be available either on or off-site, to advise the agents during the course of the search, but should not participate in the search itself.

The affidavit in support of the search warrant may attach any written instructions or, at a minimum, should generally state the government's intention to employ procedures designed to ensure that attorney-client privileges are not violated.

If it is anticipated that computers will be searched or seized, prosecutors are expected to follow the procedures set forth in

Federal Guidelines for Searching and Seizing Computers (July 1994), published by the Criminal Division Office of Professional Training and Development.

Review Procedures. The following review procedures should be discussed prior to approval of any warrant, consistent with the practice in your district, the circumstances of the investigation and the volume of materials seized.

• Who will conduct the review, i.e., a privilege team, a judicial officer, or a special master.

• Whether all documents will be submitted to a judicial officer or special master or only those which a privilege team has determined to be arguably privileged or arguably subject to an exception to the privilege.

• Whether copies of all seized materials will be provided to the subject attorney (or a legal representative) in order that: a) disruption of the law firm's operation is minimized; and b) the subject is afforded an opportunity to participate in the process of submitting disputed documents to the court by raising specific claims of privilege. To the extent possible, providing copies of seized records is encouraged, where such disclosure will not impede or obstruct the investigation..

• Whether appropriate arrangements have been made for storage and handling of electronic evidence and procedures developed for searching computer data (i.e., procedures which recognize the universal nature of computer seizure and are designed to avoid review of materials implicating the privilege of innocent clients).

The use of a "privilege team " or "taint team" comprised of federal prosecutors has been criticized as not being fully protective of the attorney-client privilege. **In re Grand Jury Subpoenas**, 454 F.3d 511 (6th Cir. 2006), considered the use of a taint team in connection with a grand jury subpoena to a company as part of an investigation of its former owner, who claimed that certain materials at the company contained communications protected by the attorney-client privilege. In rejecting the government's suggestion that a taint team should review the subpoenaed materials to determine what was privileged, the court noted:

Yet the taint team procedure would present a great risk to the appellants' continued enjoyment of privilege protections. In the first place, government taint teams seem to be used primarily in limited, exigent circumstances in which government officials have already obtained the physical control of potentially-privileged documents through the exercise of a search warrant. In such cases, the potentially-privileged documents are already in the government's possession, and so the use of the taint team to sift the wheat from the chaff constitutes an action respectful of, rather than injurious to, the protection of privilege. But the government does not actually possess the potentially-privileged materials here, so the exigency typically underlying the use of taint teams is not present.

Furthermore, taint teams present inevitable, and reasonably foreseeable, risks to privilege, for they have been implicated in the past in leaks of confidential information to prosecutors. That is to say, the government taint team may have an interest in preserving privilege, but it also possesses a conflicting interest in pursuing the investigation, and, human nature being what it is, occasionally some taint-team attorneys will make mistakes or violate their ethical obligations. It is thus logical to suppose that taint teams pose a serious risk to holders of privilege, and this supposition is substantiated by past experience. In *United States v. Noriega*, 764 F.Supp. 1480 (S.D.Fla.1991), for instance, the government's taint team missed a document obviously protected by attorney-client privilege, by turning over tapes of attorney-client conversations to members of the investigating team. This Noriega incident points to an obvious flaw in the taint team procedure: the government's fox is left in charge of the appellants' henhouse, and may err by neglect or malice, as well as by honest differences of opinion.

It is reasonable to presume that the government's taint team might have a more restrictive view of privilege than appellants' attorneys. But under the taint team procedure, appellants' attorneys would have an opportunity to assert privilege only over those documents which the taint team has identified as being clearly or possibly privileged. As such, we do not see any check in the proposed taint team review procedure against the possibility that the government's team might make some false negative conclusions, finding validly privileged documents to be otherwise; that is to say, we can find no check against Type II errors in the government's proposed procedure. On the other hand, under the appellants' proposal, which incidentally seems to follow a fairly conventional privilege review procedure employed by law firms in response to discovery requests, the government would still enjoy the opportunity to challenge any documents that appellants' attorneys misidentify (via the commission of Type I errors) as privileged. We thus find that, under these circumstances, the possible damage to the appellants' interest in protecting privilege exceeds the possible damage to the government's interest in grand jury secrecy and exigency in this case.

NOTES

1. *ALI Procedures.* The American Law Institute (ALI) adopted in 1975 a Model Code of Pre-Arraignment Procedure that includes a section entitled "Execution and Return of Warrants for Documents" that provides procedures for seizing records, including those from a law office:

> (1) *Identification of Documents to Be Seized.* If the warrant authorizes documentary seizure *** the executing officer shall endeavor by all appropriate means to search for and identify the documents to be seized without examining the contents of documents not covered by the warrant. * * *

> (2) *Intermingled Documents.* If the documents to be seized cannot be searched for or identified without examining the contents of other documents, or if they constitute item or entries in account books, diaries, or other documents containing matter not specified in the warrant, the executing officer shall not examine the documents but shall either impound them under appropriate protection where found, or seal and remove them for safekeeping pending further proceedings pursuant to Subsection (3) of this Section.

> (3) *Return of intermingled Documents.* An executing officer who has impounded or removed documents pursuant to Subsection (2) of this Section shall, as promptly as practicable, report the fact and circumstances of the impounding or removal to the issuing official. As soon thereafter as the interests of justice permit, and upon due and reasonable notice to all interested persons, a hearing shall be held before the issuing official, *** at which the person from whose possession or control the documents were taken, and any other person asserting any right or interest in the document, may appear, in person or by counsel, and move (a) for the return of the documents, *** in whole or in part, or (b) for specification of such conditions and limitations on the further search for the documents to be seized as may be appropriate to prevent unnecessary or unreasonable invasion of privacy. * * * If the motion is not granted, the search shall proceed under such conditions and limitations as the order shall prescribe. * * *

In **United States v. Mittelman**, 999 F.2d 440 (9th Cir. 1992), an FBI agent assured the federal magistrate in seeking a warrant that the government would comply with the ALI procedures, but then failed to follow them as promised. The district court ordered that suppression of the evidence seized pursuant to the warrant under Franks v. Delaware because the agent knowingly or recklessly made false statements to the magistrate. The Ninth Circuit reversed, noting:

[W]hile we agree that special care should be taken when conducting a search of law offices, separate legal rules are not necessary for remedying such searches when they exceed the scope of the warrant. [The exclusionary rule is] fully applicable to law office searches, [and] provide[s] ample protection and relief. *Tamura* is an instructive example in this regard. After suggesting the use of [the ALI] procedures designed to protect privacy interests during document searches, we nonetheless applied the traditional remedy for searches which exceed the scope of the warrant: we first examined whether the government had engaged in "indiscriminate fishing," and having determined it did not, we concluded that suppression was required of only that evidence seized outside the scope of the warrant. We vacate the suppression order and remand to allow the district court to determine first whether the search of Reeves's law office amounted to an "impermissible general search." If it did, suppressing all of the evidence seized during the search is appropriate. If the violations of the search warrant were not so extreme as to justify this extraordinary remedy, the district court should determine what evidence, if any, was seized in violation of the warrant and order the suppression of that evidence only.

2. *Right to Practice Law*. In **Conn v. Gabbert**, 526 U.S. 286 (1999), the Supreme Court unanimously rejected the Ninth Circuit's holding that a search warrant served on a lawyer, which was designed to interfere with his representation of a client currently testifying before a grand jury, violated the lawyer's Fourteenth Amendment right to practice his profession and therefore states a claim for damages under § 1983. The Court stated, "We hold that the Fourteenth Amendment right to practice one's calling is not violated by the execution of a search warrant, whether calculated to annoy or even to prevent consultation with a grand jury witness. In so holding, we thus of course pretermit the question whether such a right was 'clearly established' as of a given day."

CHAPTER THIRTEEN
SELF-INCRIMINATION PRIVILEGE

A. THE PRIVILEGE AGAINST SELF-INCRIMINATION

At trial, A criminal defendant exercises the Fifth Amendment privilege against self-incrimination by declining to testify. The prosecution may not call the defendant as a witness at the defendant's own trial and force the defendant to claim the privilege in response to each question asked by the prosecutor. While the Fifth Amendment also applies in the grand jury, federal courts have long held that the grand jury is not similarly prohibited from calling to testify a person that it expects to indict and thereby forcing that person to exercise the privilege as to individual questions.

The privilege against self-incrimination only applies if the testimony of the person claiming the privilege would be "incriminating." What standard determines whether testimony has that quality and who makes that determination? Both of these critical questions were largely resolved in **Hoffman v. United States**, 341 U.S. 479 (1951). In that case, a witness subpoenaed before a federal grand jury relied on the privilege in refusing to answer questions as to his current occupation and his contacts with a fugitive witness. The district court found that there was "no real and substantial danger of incrimination" and the privilege therefore was inapplicable. When the witness persisted in his claim, he was held in contempt. In reversing that conviction, the Supreme Court (per Clark, J.) set forth the following guidelines for the district court:

> This provision of the [Fifth] Amendment must be accorded liberal construction in favor of the right it was intended to secure. The privilege afforded not only extends to answers that would in themselves support a conviction under a federal criminal statute but likewise embraces those which would furnish a link in the chain of evidence needed to prosecute the claimant for a federal crime. But this protection must be confined to instances where the witness has reasonable cause to apprehend danger from a direct answer. The witness is not exonerated from answering merely because he declares that in so doing he would incriminate himself–his say-so does not of itself establish the hazard of incrimination. It is for the court to say whether his silence is justified, and to require him to answer if 'it clearly appears to the court that he is mistaken.' However, if the witness, upon interposing his claim, were required to prove the hazard in the sense in which a claim is usually required to be established in court, he would be compelled to surrender the very protection which the privilege is designed to guarantee. To

sustain the privilege, it need only be evident from the implications of the question, in the setting in which it is asked, that a responsive answer to the question or an explanation of why it cannot be answered might be dangerous because injurious disclosure could result.

Applying these guidelines, the Supreme Court concluded that the privilege clearly was available to the witness Hoffman. Since the district court was aware that the grand jury was investigating racketeering, it should have recognized that questions concerning Hoffman's current occupation might require answers relating to violations of federal gambling laws. It also should have recognized that the questions concerning Hoffman's contacts with the fugitive witness might relate to efforts to hide that witness.

Under the *Hoffman* guidelines it will be a rare case in which a court can properly reject a witness' assertion of the privilege. Is the case that follows such a situation?

In re MORGANROTH v. FITZSIMMONS
718 F.2d 161 (6th Cir. 1983)

KENNEDY, Circuit Judge.

Petitioner Morganroth seeks review of an order directing him to answer deposition questions to which he asserted his fifth amendment right to remain silent on the ground that his answers might tend to subject him to criminal liability. In 1975 the Central States, Southeast & Southwest Areas Pension Fund made a loan to Indico Corporation of $7,000,000. Morganroth was president of Indico Corporation at that time. Subsequently, Indico defaulted on the loan and as a result the Pension Fund suffered significant losses on its investment. Morganroth has since been involved in a number of lawsuits. He was indicted by a federal grand jury on conspiracy and mail and wire fraud charges arising out of this loan transaction with the Pension Fund. On October 20, 1979, subsequent to his indictment, Morganroth was deposed in a civil action * * * then pending in a Florida state court. This civil case was a foreclosure proceeding in connection with the same loan. At that deposition Morganroth appeared voluntarily and answered all questions put to him. Morganroth is himself an attorney. In March 1980, Morganroth was acquitted of the federal criminal charges. It appears that after his acquittal, Morganroth was subpoenaed to appear before a New York federal grand jury and was asked the same set of questions which he voluntarily answered in the Florida state foreclosure proceeding. Morganroth asserted his fifth amendment privilege to these same questions. Immunity was conferred upon Morganroth, his testimony given, and thereafter he was advised by one of the prosecutors that his testimony was in serious conflict with that of others appearing before the grand jury.

Subsequent to his acquittal and the immunized testimony before the New York federal grand jury, the Secretary of Labor subpoenaed Morganroth to appear for a deposition as a non-party witness in this civil action * * *. [T]he Secretary has alleged that defendants, who are former trustees and officials of the * * * Pension Fund, imprudently made, administered and monitored certain investments on behalf of the Fund in violation of their fiduciary obligations under the Employee Retirement Income Security Act. At the deposition, Morganroth was represented by counsel. He answered questions under oath. After providing information as to his name, address and occupation, Morganroth individually refused to answer each question propounded to him by counsel for the Secretary of Labor on the ground that each answer might tend to incriminate him, without elaborating further. The questions he refused to answer * * * covered the same aspects of the Indico loan transaction with the * * * Pension Fund about which he had previously given deposition answers voluntarily in the Florida state foreclosure proceeding * * * and pursuant to the grant of immunity in the New York federal grand jury proceeding. As a result, the Secretary of Labor moved the District Court * * * for an order pursuant to Fed.R.Civ.P. 37(a) compelling Morganroth to answer these questions on the grounds that he had waived any Fifth Amendment right he had with respect to these questions by answering virtually identical questions in the Florida state foreclosure proceeding and that he had no legitimate Fifth Amendment right to assert because there was no reasonable likelihood of criminal prosecution, given his acquittal in March 1980, that would flow from the answers requested. The District Court ordered Morganroth to testify [relying upon the waiver ground] * * *. The District Court did, however, confine the Secretary of Labor to asking only the identical questions asked at the prior deposition.

Morganroth then filed for certification under 28 U.S.C. § 1292(b) [and the] * * * District Court granted the motion and certified the [waiver] question * * *. In granting Morganroth's petition for leave to appeal, this Court stated that it may consider other issues raised in the order of the District Court even though they were not included in the certified question formulated by the District Court.* * *

In this appeal, Morganroth urges that this Court reject the "minority" rule [on waiver] adopted by the District Court, or its application of that rule, and adopt the "majority" rule that waiver of the privilege and voluntary testimony in response to specific questions or a particular subject matter in one proceeding does not constitute a waiver of the fifth amendment privilege with respect to identical questions or a particular subject matter in a second proceeding if the witness remains at risk for the same offense. * * * The policy behind the majority rule that the privilege is "proceeding specific" and not waived in a subsequent proceeding by waiver in an earlier one, rests on the thought that during the period between the successive proceedings conditions might have changed creating new grounds for apprehension, e.g., the passage of new criminal law, or that the witness might be subject to different interrogation for different purposes at a subsequent proceeding, or that repetition of testimony in an independent proceeding might itself be incriminating, even if it merely repeated or acknowledged the witness' earlier testimony, because it could constitute an independent source of evidence against him or her.

The Secretary of Labor urges that the District Court correctly adopted and applied the minority rule set forth in Ellis v. United States, 416 F.2d 791 (D.C.Cir.1969). In *Ellis*, the court held that a waiver of the assertion of a valid privilege in one proceeding, where a witness places himself or herself at risk of prosecution for a particular offense, constitutes a waiver of the privilege in all subsequent proceedings in response to the identical questions or the same general subject matter where the risk of prosecution for the identical offense remains the same. * * * The rationale behind the minority view of Ellis is that, absent intervening circumstances, a witness' repetition of the same information in a subsequent proceeding for which he originally placed himself at risk of prosecution in an earlier proceeding would not expose him to any real danger of legal harm to which he had not already exposed himself by virtue of his prior voluntary testimony. The rationale of the minority view of *Ellis* applies only where the witness faces the identical risk of prosecution in both proceedings in which he is called upon to testify. The *Ellis* court's exception recognizes this limitation.

We need not reach the issue of whether this Circuit should adopt the majority or minority view on waiver * * * because we find neither applicable to a factual situation where a fifth amendment privilege is asserted solely because the witness alleges he is apprehensive of providing incriminating evidence in regard to a possible perjury charge stemming from responses in an earlier proceeding under oath.[1] The District Court's adoption and application of the minority view is inappropriate in this case because the minority view presumes that the witness is facing identical risks in both proceedings. In contrast, as in this case, once a witness has testified under oath initially, the risk of prosecution which the witness faced in the earlier proceeding is not identical even though the questions may be the same in a subsequent proceeding or the same subject matter covered. Once a witness has testified under oath, he risks the possibility of perjury charges in addition to any risk he may face for prosecution for non-perjury offenses suggested by his testimony. * * * The risk of prosecution for which Morganroth has articulated a fear of prosecution in this case is that for perjury in his prior testimony. This possibility of prosecution exists independently of and is unaffected by his acquittal of federal conspiracy and mail and wire fraud charges. It is unclear whether he fears perjury charges stemming from his deposition testimony in the Florida state foreclosure proceeding or his New

---

[1] We also note that the Supreme Court's recent decision in Pillsbury Co. v. Conboy, 459 U.S. 248 (1983), raises doubt as to the continued validity of the *Ellis* Court's view. In *Conboy*, the Supreme Court emphasized that: "Questions do not incriminate; answers do." The Court reasoned that "answers to such questions 'are derived from the deponent's current, independent memory of events' and thus 'necessarily create a new source of evidence' that could incriminate a witness and could be used in a subsequent criminal prosecution against him."

York federal grand jury testimony. Either could provide a basis for a valid assertion of the privilege. * * * Therefore, because Morganroth alleges he is presently at risk for a different crime than those for which he initially faced a reasonable risk of prosecution, the question of whether the minority view should control the waiver issue is not properly raised by the facts.

We do, however, consider another issue raised by the order of the District Court even though not included in the certified question. At issue is what sort of showing must be made by a witness to justify the invocation of the fifth amendment privilege when the only possible risk of prosecution which might flow from testimony in a subsequent proceeding is for perjury.

We conclude that it is not enough that Morganroth answer each deposition question propounded by the Secretary of Labor with the conclusory statement: "I refuse to answer on the ground that the answer might tend to incriminate me." Morganroth must supply such additional statements under oath and other evidence to the District Court in response to each question propounded so as to enable the District Court to reasonably identify the nature of the criminal charge for which Morganroth fears prosecution, i.e., perjury and to discern a sound basis for the witness' reasonable fear of prosecution.

Before a witness, such as Morganroth, is entitled to remain silent, there must be a valid assertion of the fifth amendment privilege. It is for the court to decide whether a witness' silence is justified and to require him to answer if it clearly appears to the court that the witness asserting the privilege is mistaken as to its validity. *Hoffman.* A valid assertion of the fifth amendment privilege exists where a witness has reasonable cause to apprehend a real danger of incrimination. Id. A witness must, however, show a "real danger," and not a mere imaginary, remote or speculative possibility of prosecution. * * * While the privilege is to be accorded liberal application, the court may order a witness to answer if it clearly appears that he is mistaken as to the justification for the privilege in advancing his claim as a subterfuge. *Hoffman.* A blanket assertion of the privilege by a witness is not sufficient to meet the reasonable cause requirement and the privilege cannot be claimed in advance of the questions. The privilege must be asserted by a witness with respect to particular questions, and in each instance, the court must determine the propriety of the refusal to testify. See *Hoffman.*

A witness risks a real danger of prosecution if an answer to a question, on its face, calls for the admission of a crime or requires that the witness supply evidence of a necessary element of a crime or furnishes a link in the chain of evidence needed to prosecute. In *Hoffman*, the Supreme Court held that a real danger of prosecution also exists where questions, which appear on their face to call only for innocent answers, are dangerous in light of other facts already developed. In such a situation a witness bears no further burden of establishing a reasonable cause to fear prosecution beyond asserting the privilege and identifying the nature of the criminal charge or supplying sufficient facts so that a particular criminal charge can reasonably be identified by the court. The witness has met his burden and the court does not need to inquire further as to the validity of the assertion of the privilege, if it is evident from the implications of a question, in the setting in which it is asked, that a responsive answer might be dangerous to the witness because an injurious disclosure could result. * * *

The facts of this case make the *Hoffman* approach to a witness' burden of establishing a foundation for the reasonable cause determination, or rather lack of it, inapplicable. Morganroth is allegedly raising the specter of a perjury prosecution; i.e., his proposed truthful testimony might provide evidence that he had perjured himself in earlier proceedings under oath. Like *Hoffman*, the questions propounded to Morganroth appear on their face to be innocent. Unlike *Hoffman*, the present setting, in which the questions were propounded and representations made, sheds no light whatsoever on whether Morganroth's proposed truthful answers would constitute injurious disclosures in light of his previous testimony on the same subject matter in earlier proceedings.

The *Hoffman* guidelines for determining whether an assertion of the privilege against self-incrimination should be respected works well in cases in which an individual is at risk of prosecution on substantive charges or in which an individual expresses a concern of perjury prosecution stemming from statements made in earlier proceedings in which the trial judge has a personal familiarity. The *Hoffman* guidelines, however, are of little help in a case such as the one on appeal where the District Court making the privilege determination has no personal knowledge of the scope of content of prior proceedings and where the only possible prosecution for which the witness is at risk is perjury. This is due to the nature of the perjury offense in relation to the assertion of the privilege and the inability of the trial court, in this case and others like it, to draw upon its own knowledge of the case. In *Hoffman*, the Supreme Court stressed facts within the knowledge of the trial court. There the trial court was instructed that the privilege be "evident from the implications of the question in the setting in which it was asked," that the determination be governed "as much by his [trial judge's] personal perception of the particularities of the case as by the facts actually in evidence," and that it consider the "circumstances" of the case. *Hoffman*. *Hoffman* is typical of subsequent cases applying the *Hoffman* guidelines. As in *Hoffman*, those cases, in contrast to the one on appeal, reveal a superior knowledge by the trial court of the "setting in which it [the questions to which the privilege is sought] is asked." * * *

This case is in sharp contrast to *Hoffman* * * *. The trial court did not have any background familiarity with the setting in which the assertion was raised. The District Court had not participated in either the grand jury matter in New York or the Florida foreclosure proceeding. With respect to the New York grand jury statements, he did not even know the substance of those statements, the nature of the conflicting testimony by other witnesses or contradictory documentary evidence which might tend to show that Morganroth had perjured himself in that proceeding. Nor did Morganroth apprise the District Court that his testimony or deposition answers would differ from statements given in the earlier proceedings. The District Court in this case was merely informed by Morganroth's attorney that there was a possibility that material inconsistencies would exist between his proposed testimony, based on his current memory of the loan transactions, and prior testimony. This possibility, however, exists in every case in which a witness has given prior testimony. Thus, perjury prosecutions which are prospective and possible in nature present special problems in determining appropriate invocation of the fifth amendment right.

Whether a witness risks a "real danger" of prosecution from questions which appear on their face to call for only innocent answers and where the incriminating nature of the answer is not evident from the implications of the question in the setting in which it is asked, is a difficult question left unanswered by *Hoffman*. On one hand, while it is clear that a witness, upon interposing his claim of privilege, is not required to prove the hazard in the sense in which a claim is usually required to be established in court, it is equally clear that a witness' "say so" does not by itself establish the hazard of incrimination. *Hoffman*. Where there is nothing suggestive of incrimination about the setting in which a seemingly innocent question is asked, the burden of establishing a foundation for the assertion of the privilege should lie with the witness making it. We do not hold, however, that a witness has the burden of proof on this issue. A witness presents sufficient evidence to establish a foundation for the assertion of the privilege and shows a real danger of prosecution if it is not perfectly clear to the court "from a careful consideration of all of the circumstances in the case, that a witness is mistaken, and that the answer[s] cannot possibly have such a tendency to incriminate." *Hoffman*. Stated differently, sufficient evidence is presented by a witness if a court can, by the use of reasonable inference or judicial imagination, conceive a sound basis for a reasonable fear of prosecution. Short of uttering statements or supplying evidence that would be incriminating, a witness must supply personal statements under oath or provide evidence with respect to each question propounded to him to indicate the nature of the criminal charge which provides the basis for his fear of prosecution[2] and, if necessary to complement non-testimonial evidence,

---

[2] With respect to each question for which the privilege is asserted, it is important to the court's reasonable cause determination that Morganroth swear under oath or provide other evidence that the criminal charge for which he has reasonable cause to fear prosecution is perjury. Here he stated only that the issue would tend to incriminate him. This fear may have been based on the mistaken belief he could still be prosecuted for some statute of limitations barred offense. While no ritualistic formula or talismanic phrase is necessary to invoke the privilege, a court cannot be asked to scan all of the law for a possible connection between a question and a criminal offense. To impose such a duty on courts in response to a mere assertion of the privilege, without elaboration, in response to seemingly innocent questions devoid of a setting suggestive of producing injurious disclosures would result in a guessing game in which the witness is the final judge of the claim of privilege.

personal statements under oath to meet the standard for establishing reasonable cause to fear prosecution under this charge. Statements under oath, in person or by affidavit, are necessary because the present penalty of perjury may be the sole assurance against a spurious assertion of the privilege. Argument may be supplied by counsel but not the facts necessary for the court's determination.

Public policy also requires that a witness bear the burden of establishing the foundation of the privilege beyond his mere "say so." Unless something more is required in situations such as the one on appeal where seemingly innocent questions exist in a setting presently devoid of incriminating overtones, witnesses such as Morganroth will be the final arbiters of the validity of their asserted privileges. A litigant's right to information must be balanced against a witness' constitutional right to invoke the privilege. Only where there is some real danger can the loss of information to a litigant or to the judicial system be justified. In addition, unless some additional showing beyond the mere assertion of the privilege is required, no witness would ever have to testify twice regarding the same subject matter because the possibility of perjury would always exist in theory.

From the record on appeal, it appears that Morganroth has not met this burden of establishing a foundation necessary for the valid assertion of the privilege based on his alleged fear of a perjury prosecution. Accordingly, we remand this case to the District Court for further proceedings consistent with this opinion.

JONES, Circuit Judge, dissenting.

The majority reasons that the considerations that were before the Supreme Court in Pillsbury Co. v. Conboy, 459 U.S. 258 (1983), are not implicated in the instant case because of the particular offense for which appellant-Morganroth fears prosecution. The clear holding in *Conboy* is that a district court cannot compel a witness to answer deposition questions over a valid assertion of his Fifth Amendment right, absent a duly authorized grant of immunity at the time the testimony is sought. Thus, when a witness or deponent is accorded a grant of immunity for testimony that is given during one proceeding, a subsequent interrogation pertaining to the same subject matter must be accompanied by a new grant of immunity. The majority concludes that this rule is not applicable to the facts sub judice because the witness' attempt to invoke his Fifth Amendment privilege was based upon his fear of prosecution for perjury. * * * It is upon this basis that I enter my dissent.

My review of the proceedings below indicates that the appellant's response to the numerous questions that were propounded to him was "I refuse to answer on the ground it may incriminate me." During these proceedings, Morganroth's attorney advised the court that if the appellant testified, he ran the risk of possible prosecution for tax evasion. The majority apparently assumed that since the prosecutor informed the appellant that his answers during the grand jury proceeding contradicted the testimony of other witnesses, the appellant was invoking his right to remain silent in order that he would not perjure himself. However, the appellant declares that he invoked his Fifth Amendment privilege because of the possible threat of perjury and criminal tax evasion.* * *

B. THE PRIVILEGE IN THE GRAND JURY

1. *Targets and Subjects of Grand Jury Investigations*. The United States Attorney's Manual (USAM) § 9-11.151 defines a target as "a person as to whom the prosecutor or the grand jury has substantial evidence linking him or her to the commission of a crime and who, in the judgment of the prosecutor, is a putative defendant." A "subject" of the grand jury investigation is "a person whose conduct is within the scope of the grand jury's investigation.

All witnesses called before a grand jury may exercise the privilege against self-incrimination only by taking the witness stand and refusing to answer individual questions on the basis of the privilege. Various explanations have been offered as to why a grand jury witness, even if a "putative defendant," cannot exercise the privilege in the same manner as a defendant at trial. They include: (1) the right of the defendant to refrain from appearing as a witness at trial grew out of the early common law rule deeming the parties to an action incompetent to testify (a rule never applicable to a grand jury witness), as the defendant's right of silence was created as a means of retaining the procedural benefits of that rule for the criminal defendant once the concept of party incompetency was overturned; (2) the defendant's right not to take the stand at trial is aimed, in part, at protecting the defendant from being placed in a position where he may be forced to refuse to answer questions on self-incrimination grounds in the presence of the jury (who may conclude that he therefore has something to hide), but that protective feature has less significance in the grand jury setting since that body does no more than charge and its proceedings therefore need not be conducted "with the assiduous regard for the preservation of procedural safeguards which normally attends the ultimate trial of the issues"; (3) the grand jurors, having an obligation to "shield the innocent," must be able to seek the testimony even of a person they anticipate indicting to determine whether that person's testimony might not "explain away" the evidence against him; and, (4) the grand jury, having an obligation to pursue every possible source of evidence, cannot ignore the possibility that one participant in a criminal enterprise, though unwilling to furnish evidence that directly incriminates himself, may be willing to furnish information that leads to other participants.

USAM § 9-11.150 places internal restraints on federal prosecutors subpoenaing a target to testify. It provides:

A grand jury may properly subpoena a subject or a target of the investigation and question the target about his or her involvement in the crime under investigation.   However, in the context of particular cases such a subpoena may carry the appearance of unfairness. Because the potential for misunderstanding is great, before a known "target" (as defined in USAM 9-11.151) is subpoenaed to testify before the grand jury about his or her involvement in the crime under investigation, an effort should be made to secure the target's voluntary appearance. If a voluntary appearance cannot be obtained, the target should be subpoenaed only after the grand jury and the United States Attorney or the responsible Assistant Attorney General have approved the subpoena. In determining whether to approve a subpoena for a "target," careful attention will be paid to the following considerations:

- The importance to the successful conduct of the grand jury's investigation of the testimony or other information sought;

- Whether the substance of the testimony or other information sought could be provided by other witnesses; and

- Whether the questions the prosecutor and the grand jurors intend to ask or the other information sought would be protected by a valid claim of privilege.

2. *Inviting the Target to Testify*.   USAM § 9-11.151 states that "[i]t is the policy of the Department of Justice to advise a grand jury witness of his or her rights if such witness is a 'target' or 'subject' of a grand jury investigation." USAM § 9-11.153 provides:

When a target is not called to testify pursuant to USAM 9-11.150, and does not request to testify on his or her own motion (*see* USAM 9-11.152), the prosecutor, in appropriate cases, is encouraged to notify such person a reasonable time before seeking an indictment in order to afford him or her an opportunity to testify before the grand jury, subject to the conditions set forth in USAM 9-11.152.

The USAM contains a "Sample Target Letter" that provides an invitation to a target of the grand jury investigation to testify, which is almost always declined:

This letter is supplied to a witness scheduled to appear before the federal Grand Jury in order to provide helpful background information about the Grand Jury. The Grand Jury consists of from sixteen to twenty-three persons from the District of ___. It is their responsibility to inquire into federal crimes which may have been committed in this District.

As a Grand Jury witness you will be asked to testify and answer questions, and to produce records and documents. Only the members of the Grand Jury, attorneys for the United States and a stenographer are permitted in the Grand Jury room while you testify.

We advise you that the Grand Jury is conducting an investigation of possible violations of federal criminal laws involving, but not necessarily limited to * * *. You are advised that the destruction or alteration of any document required to be produced before the grand jury constitutes serious violation of federal law, including but not limited to Obstruction of Justice.

You are advised that you are a target of the Grand Jury's investigation. You may refuse to answer any question if a truthful answer to the question would tend to incriminate you. Anything that you do or say may be used against you in a subsequent legal proceeding. If you have retained counsel, who represents you personally, the Grand Jury will permit you a reasonable opportunity to step outside the Grand Jury room and confer with counsel if you desire.

U.S. Department of Justice *Criminal Resource Manual* No. 160.

USAM 9-11.152 discusses the situation where a target asks to testify before the grand jury, and requests that the prosecutor all additional witnesses. As the Supreme Court made clear in *Williams*, there is no requirement that a prosecutor permit a target to testify or present exculpatory evidence, but the Department of Justice recognizes that in certain instances the prosecutor should afford a target the opportunity to present their side of the case:

> While the prosecutor has no legal obligation to permit such witnesses to testify, a refusal to do so can create the appearance of unfairness. Accordingly, under normal circumstances, where no burden upon the grand jury or delay of its proceedings is involved, reasonable requests by a "subject" or "target" of an investigation, as defined above, to testify personally before the grand jury ordinarily should be given favorable consideration, provided that such witness explicitly waives his or her privilege against self-incrimination, on the record before the grand jury, and is represented by counsel or voluntarily and knowingly appears without counsel and consents to full examination under oath.

3. *Advance Assertion of the Privilege.* Upon receipt of a subpoena, a witness may inform the prosecutor that he or she will exercise the privilege as to all questions posed by the grand jury (apart from simple identification questions, e.g., name, address). While the grand jury may insist upon the appearance of such a witness, here again the internal guidelines of the

Department of Justice suggest some restraint in exercising that authority. USAM § 9-11.154 provides, "If a 'target' of the investigation and his or her attorney state in a writing, signed by both, that the 'target' will refuse to testify on Fifth Amendment grounds, the witness ordinarily should be excused from testifying unless the grand jury and the United States Attorney agree to insist on the appearance."

4. *Self-Incrimination Warnings*. In **United States v. Mandujano**, 425 U.S. 564 (1976), the Court found it unnecessary to decide whether the Fifth Amendment required that a witness called before the grand jury initially be advised of the right to exercise the self-incrimination privilege, but there was considerable discussion of that issue by six of the Justices. The defendant Mandujano, known by the prosecutor to be a narcotics user, was called before the grand jury in the hope that he would furnish information about significant dealers. Instead, he steadfastly denied any involvement in the sale of narcotics and specifically disclaimed having sought within the year to make a purchase for a third-party for $650.00. The latter statement was a lie since (as the prosecutor already knew) Mandujano had recently tried to make such a purchase for a person who was actually an undercover agent. Subsequently prosecuted for perjury, Mandujano moved to suppress the grand jury testimony which was the basis of the charge. The trial court granted the motion on the ground that Mandujano had not been given full *Miranda* warnings prior to testifying. He had been informed of his privilege against self-incrimination and had been advised that he could have a retained lawyer located outside the grand jury room for the purpose of consultation. However, he had not been told that a lawyer could be appointed at the government's expense even though he had informed the prosecutor that he could not afford to hire a lawyer. The Court unanimously rejected the lower court's ruling. All the Justices agreed that, even if adequate warnings had not been given, that failure could not constitute a defense to a perjury charge.

Speaking for himself and three other members of the Court, Chief Justice Burger also commented on the adequacy of the warnings given to Mandujano. The Chief Justice concluded that those warnings clearly were adequate under even the broadest reading of the Fifth Amendment. The *Miranda* warnings were prescribed in Miranda v. Arizona, 384 U.S. 436 (1966), for custodial police interrogation, and were designed specifically to negate the "compulsion" thought to be inherent in that setting. *Miranda* itself recognized "that many official investigations, such as grand jury questioning, take place in a setting wholly different from custodial police interrogation." To extend a standard devised to combat "police coercion" found in such practices as the "third degree" to "questioning before a grand jury inquiry into criminal activity under the guidance of a judge" would be "an extravagant expansion never remotely contemplated by this Court in *Miranda*." Justice Brennan, joined by Justice Marshall, responded to what he viewed as a "denigration of the privilege against self-incrimination" in the Chief Justice's opinion.

5. *Warnings to Grand Jury Targets and Subjects.* USAM § 9-11.151 directs federal prosecutors to advise a target or subject of the investigation of the following:

Advice of Rights

A. The grand jury is conducting an investigation of possible violations of federal criminal laws involving: (State here the general subject matter of inquiry, e.g., the conducting of an illegal gambling business in violation of 18 U.S.C. § 1955).

B. You may refuse to answer any question if a truthful answer to the question would tend to incriminate you.

C. Anything that you do say may be used against you by the grand jury or in a subsequent legal proceeding.

D. If you have retained counsel, the grand jury will permit you a reasonable opportunity to step outside the grand jury room to consult with counsel if you do so desire.

In **United States v. Washington**, 431 U.S. 181 (1977), the Court answered another question left open in *Mandujano*: whether a witness who is the target of a grand jury investigation constitutionally is entitled to notification of that status when called before the grand jury. Defendant Washington had been questioned by District of Columbia police officers regarding a stolen motorcycle found in his truck. He subsequently was questioned by a prosecuting attorney, who served him with a subpoena to testify before a grand jury. When Washington appeared before the grand jury, the prosecuting attorney did not tell him that he might be indicted on a stolen motorcycle charge (although he had been called to testify because the prosecutor and police were "more than a little skeptical" of his explanation of the presence of the motorcycle). The prosecutor did, however, give Washington a complete set of warnings, even going beyond the usual federal practice (Washington was told that a lawyer would be provided if he could not afford one). Washington stated that he understood his rights, and proceeded to testify, repeating the story he had told to the police and prosecutor. When subsequently indicted for the theft of the motorcycle, he argued that his testimony before the grand jury should be suppressed as he had been unable to intelligently waive his self-incrimination privilege due to the prosecutor's failure to advise him that he was a potential defendant. Rejecting that argument, the Supreme Court majority (per Burger, C.J.) reasoned:

> Even in the presumed psychologically coercive atmosphere of police custodial interrogation, *Miranda* does not require that any additional warnings be given simply because the suspect is a potential defendant; indeed, such suspects are potential defendants more often than not. Respondent points out that unlike one subject

to custodial interrogation, whose arrest should inform him only too clearly that he is a potential criminal defendant, a grand jury witness may well be unaware that he is targeted for possible prosecution. While this may be so in some situations, it is an overdrawn generalization. * * * [E]vents here clearly put respondent on notice that he was a suspect in the motorcycle theft. * * * However, all of this is largely irrelevant, since we do not understand what constitutional disadvantage a failure to give potential defendant warnings could possibly inflict on a grand jury witness, whether or not he has received other warnings. * * * Because target witness status neither enlarges nor diminishes the constitutional protection against compelled self-incrimination, potential defendant warnings add nothing of value to protection of Fifth Amendment rights.

Although *Washington* does not require giving warnings to a grand jury witness, the Department of Justice's position is that

[a]lthough the Court in *Washington* held that "targets" of the grand jury's investigation are entitled to no special warnings relative to their status as "potential defendant(s)," the Department of Justice continues its longstanding policy to advise witnesses who are known "targets" of the investigation that their conduct is being investigated for possible violation of Federal criminal law. This supplemental advice of status of the witness as a target should be repeated on the record when the target witness is advised of the matters discussed in the preceding paragraphs.

U.S.A.M. § 9-11.151.

6. *Subsequent Impeachment.* **Grunewald v. United States**, 353 U.S. 391 (1957), held that where a defendant exercised his privilege during grand jury questioning and then testified at his trial, answering some of the same questions and offering explanations consistent with his innocence, the government should not have been allowed to bring out on cross-examination the fact that he had previously refused on the basis of the privilege to answer the same questions. This was so even though the trial judge had told the petit jury that the defendant's previous exercise of the privilege could be taken only as reflecting upon his credibility in answering the same questions at trial and that no inference as to guilt could be drawn therefrom. The Court (per Harlan, J.) reasoned:

It is, of course, an elementary rule of evidence that prior statements may be used to impeach the credibility of a criminal defendant or an ordinary witness. But this can be done only if the judge is satisfied that the prior statements are in fact inconsistent. 3 Wigmore, Evidence, § 1040. And so the threshold question here is simply whether, in the circumstances of this case, the trial court erred in holding that [defendant] Halperin's plea of the Fifth Amendment privilege before the grand jury involved such inconsistency with any of his trial testimony as to permit its use against him for impeachment purposes. * * * [W]e deem it evident that Halperin's claim of the Fifth Amendment privilege before the Brooklyn grand jury in response to questions which he answered at the trial was wholly consistent with innocence. Had he answered the questions put to him before the grand jury in the same way he subsequently answered them at trial, this nevertheless would have provided the Government with incriminating evidence from his own mouth. For example, had he stated to the grand jury that he knew Grunewald, the admission would have constituted a link between him and a criminal conspiracy, and this would be true even though he was entirely innocent and even though his friendship with Grunewald was above reproach. There was, therefore, as we see it, no inconsistency between Halperin's statement to the grand jury that answering the question whether he knew Grunewald would tend to furnish incriminating evidence against him, and his subsequent testimony at trial that his acquaintance with Grunewald was free of criminal elements.

The *Grunewald* Court noted that a target of a grand jury investigation may have a very powerful reason for asserting the Fifth Amendment in the investigation even though the defendant maintains his innocence: "[M]any innocent men who know that they are about to be indicted will refuse to help create a case against themselves under circumstances where lack of counsel's assistance and lack of opportunity for cross-examination will prevent them from bringing out the exculpatory circumstances in the context of which superficially incriminating acts occurred." Does this analysis argue in favor of allowing defense counsel in the grand jury room to at least monitor the proceeding and provide some measure of assistance to the witness?

7. *Sanctions for Asserting the Privilege in the Grand Jury.* Gardner v. Broderick, 392 U.S. 273 (1968), held that a state could not discharge a state employee because he exercised the privilege before a grand jury inquiring into possible criminality in the performance of his duties. In that case, involving a state grand jury proceeding under which witnesses received automatic immunity, the employee refused to waive that immunity, and was discharged under a statute making that refusal (or the exercise of the privilege) grounds for dismissal. The Court noted that, if the employee had been required as an obligation of his employment to "answer questions specifically, directly, and narrowly relating to performance of his official duties, without being required to waive his immunity with respect to the use of his answers or the fruits thereof in a criminal prosecution of him, * * * the privilege against self-incrimination would not have been a bar to dismissal." However, a dismissal based on his exercise of the privilege (or refusal to waive the immunity to which a witness was entitled under state law) imposed an impermissible burden on the exercise of a constitutional right. In Lefkowitz v. Turley, 414 U.S. 70 (1973), the Court similarly held that a state could not impose a penalty upon a contractor (here a five years

disqualification from doing business with the state) based upon the contractor's exercise of the privilege (or refusal to waive automatic witness immunity) when called to testify before a grand jury.

C. WAIVER

ROGERS v. UNITED STATES
340 U.S. 367, 71 S.Ct. 438, 95 L.Ed. 344 (1951)

Chief Justice VINSON delivered the opinion of the Court.

This case arises out of an investigation by the regularly convened grand jury of the United States District Court for the District of Colorado. The books and records of the Communist Party of Denver were sought as necessary to that inquiry and were the subject of questioning by the grand jury. In September, 1948, petitioner, in response to a subpoena, appeared before the grand jury. She testified that she held the position of Treasurer of the Communist Party of Denver until January, 1948, and that, by virtue of her office, she had been in possession of membership lists and dues records of the Party. Petitioner denied having possession of the records and testified that she had turned them over to another. But she refused to identify the person to whom she had given the Party's books, stating to the court as her only reason: "I don't feel that I should subject a person or persons to the same thing that I'm going through.' The court thereupon committed petitioner to the custody of the marshal until ten o'clock the next morning, expressly advising petitioner of her right to consult with counsel.

The next day, counsel for petitioner informed the court that he had read the transcript of the prior day's proceedings and that, upon his advice, petitioner would answer the questions to purge herself of contempt. However, upon reappearing before the grand jury, petitioner again refused to answer the question. The following day she was again brought into court. Called before the district judge immediately after he had heard oral argument concerning the privilege against self-incrimination in another case, petitioner repeated her refusal to answer the question, asserting this time the privilege against self-incrimination. After ruling that her refusal was not privileged, the district judge imposed a sentence of four months for contempt. The Court of Appeals for the Tenth Circuit affirmed, and we granted certiorari.

* * * [T]he decisions of this Court are explicit in holding that the privilege against self-incrimination "is solely for the benefit of the witness," and "is purely a personal privilege of the witness." Petitioner expressly placed her original declination to answer on an untenable ground, since a refusal to answer cannot be justified by a desire to protect others from punishment, much less to protect another from interrogation by a grand jury. Petitioner's claim of the privilege against self-incrimination was pure afterthought. Although the claim was made at the time of her second refusal to answer in the presence of the court, it came only after she had voluntarily testified to her status as an officer of the Communist Party of Denver. To uphold a claim of privilege in this case would open the way to distortion of facts by permitting a witness to select any stopping place in the testimony.

The privilege against self-incrimination, even if claimed at the time the question as to the name of the person to whom petitioner turned over the Party records was asked, would not justify her refusal to answer. As a preliminary matter, we note that petitioner had no privilege with respect to the books of the Party, [which she kept] in "a representative rather than a personal capacity." United States v. White [p. 426]. Since petitioner's claim of privilege cannot be asserted in relation to the books and records sought by the grand jury, the only claim for reversal of her conviction rests on the ground that mere disclosure of the name of the recipient of the books tends to incriminate.

In Blau v. United States, 340 U.S. 159 (1950), we held that questions as to connections with the Communist Party are subject to the privilege against self-incrimination as calling for disclosure of facts tending to criminate under the Smith Act, 18 U.S.C. § 2386. But petitioner's conviction stands on an entirely different footing, for she had freely described her membership, activities and office in the Party. Since the privilege against self-incrimination presupposes a real danger of legal detriment arising from the disclosure, petitioner cannot invoke the privilege where response to the specific question in issue here would not further incriminate her. Disclosure of a fact waives the privilege as to details. As this Court stated in Brown v. Walker, 161 U.S. 591 (1896): "Thus, if the witness himself elects to waive his privilege, as he may doubtless do, since the privilege is for his protection and not for that of other parties, and discloses his criminal connections, he is not permitted to stop, but must go on and make a full disclosure."

* * * Requiring full disclosure of details after a witness freely testifies as to a criminating fact does not rest upon a further "waiver" of the privilege against self-incrimination. Admittedly, petitioner had already "waived" her privilege of silence when she freely answered criminating questions relating to her connection with the Communist Party. But when petitioner was asked to furnish the name of the person to whom she turned over Party records, the court was required to determine, as it must whenever the privilege is claimed, whether the question presented a reasonable danger of further crimination in light of all the circumstances, including any previous disclosures. As to each question to which a claim of privilege is directed, the court must determine whether the answer to that particular question would subject the witness to a 'real danger' of further crimination. After petitioner's admission that she held that office of Treasurer of the Communist Party of Denver, disclosure of acquaintance with her successor presents no more than a "mere imaginary possibility" of increasing the danger of prosecution.

Petitioner's contention in the Court of Appeals and in this Court has been that, conceding her prior voluntary crimination as to one element of proof of a Smith Act violation, disclosure of the name of the recipient of the Party records would tend to incriminate as to the different crime of conspiracy to violate the Smith Act. Our opinion in Blau v. United States, explicitly rejects petitioner's argument for reversal here in its holding that questions relating to activities in the Communist Party are criminating both as to "violation of (or conspiracy to violate) the Smith Act." Of course, at least two persons are required to constitute a conspiracy, but the identity of the other members of the conspiracy is not needed, inasmuch as one person can be convicted of conspiring with persons whose names are unknown. Affirmed.

Justice BLACK, with whom Mr. Justice FRANKFURTER and Justice DOUGLAS concur, dissenting.

* * * In the case of this petitioner, there is no evidence that she intended to give up her privilege of silence concerning the persons in possession of the Communist Party records. To the contrary, the record—as set out in the Court's opinion—shows she intended to avoid answering the question on whatever ground might be available and asserted the privilege against self-incrimination at the first moment she became aware of its existence. This fact and the cases which make it crucial are ignored in the decision today.

* * * Apparently, the Court's holding is that at some uncertain point in petitioner's testimony, regardless of her intention, admission of associations with the Communist Party automatically effected a 'waiver' of her constitutional protection as to all related questions. To adopt such a rule for the privilege against self-incrimination, when other constitutional safeguards must be knowingly waived, relegates the Fifth Amendment's privilege to a second-rate position. Moreover, today's holding creates this dilemma for witnesses: On the one hand, they risk imprisonment for contempt by asserting the privilege prematurely; on the other, they might lose the privilege if they answer a single question. The Court's view makes the protection depend on timing so refined that lawyers, let alone laymen, will have difficulty in knowing when to claim it. In this very case, it never occurred to the trial judge that petitioner waived anything. And even if voluntary testimony can under some circumstances work a waiver, it did not do so here because what petitioner stated to the grand jury 'standing alone did not amount to an admission of guilt or furnish clear proof of crime * * *.' Arndstein v. McCarthy, 254 U.S. 71 (1920).

Furthermore, unlike the Court, I believe that the question which petitioner refused to answer did call for additional incriminating information. She was asked the names of the persons to whom she had turned over the Communist Party books and records. Her answer would not only have been relevant in any future prosecution of petitioner for violation of the Smith Act but also her conviction might depend on testimony of the witnesses she was thus asked to identify. For these reasons the question sought a disclosure which would have been incriminating to the highest degree. * * *

NOTES AND QUESTIONS

1. *Scope of the Waiver.* *Rogers* has led counsel to direct witnesses intending to invoke the privilege to provide the civilian counterpart of "name, rank, and serial number" and then turn to the privilege. Is that an appropriate employment of the privilege? Consider the analysis in Sara Sun Beale, William C. Bryson, James E. Felman, & Michael J. Elston, GRAND JURY LAW & PRACTICE § 6:10 (2d ed. 2000):

> The lower courts have tended to give the Rogers decision a fairly narrow interpretation, focusing on the rationale of the decision, not merely on whether the witness has already disclosed a "fact" and should be required to disclose the supporting details. Although there are lower court decisions denying the privilege on the basis of a finding that no further incrimination would result, many lower courts have taken a liberal approach toward identifying danger of further incrimination.

> If the witness is justified in claiming the privilege, the prosecutor has two options. If the witness's testimony is not critical, the prosecutor may excuse the witness after he has given any testimony that is not covered by the privilege. If the witness's testimony is vital, the prosecutor may wish to grant the witness immunity. * * * If immunity is granted and the witness persists in his refusal to testify, the witness may be held in contempt.

As discussed in *Morganroth*, most federal courts take the position that giving testimony in one proceeding does not waive the claim in a later proceeding, even though the questioning relates to the same topic and the proceedings are related. The D.C. Court of Appeals, however, continues to adhere to its position in Ellis v. United States, 416 F.2d 791 (D.C.Cir.1969), that "a witness who voluntarily testifies before a grand jury without invoking the privilege against self-incrimination of which he has been advised, waives the privilege and may not thereafter claim it when he is called to testify as a witness on the indictment returned by the grand jury, where the witness is not the defendant or under indictment." United States v. Miller, 904 F.2d 65 (D.C. Cir. 1990). Note that the *Ellis* rules only applies to a witness, and not the defendant in the case. Of course, in a jurisdiction in which that position is rejected, the witness' exercise of the privilege at trial makes the witness "unavailable," and while the witness' grand jury testimony was not subject to cross-examination, the prosecution may still seek to have it admitted under Fed.R.Evid 804(b)(5) (residual hearsay exception allowing admission where prior statement of unavailable witness was made under circumstances guaranteeing trustworthiness, constitutes evidence more probative than other evidence, and admission serves interest of justice). See United States v. Barlow, 693 F.2d 954 (6th Cir. 1982).

2. *Incrimination Under the Laws of Another Sovereign.* For many years, American courts took the position that the privilege protected only against incrimination under the laws of the sovereign which was compelling the incriminating testimony. As applied to the state and the federal systems, the practical impact of this separate-sovereign doctrine related primarily to immunity. The overlap of federal and state criminal law is such that only rarely would a defendant's testimony not meet the *Hoffman* standard as to potential incrimination in one of those jurisdictions, yet meet that standard as to the other. That situation was only likely to exist where the testimony would not be incriminating in the jurisdiction compelling the response because it concerned an offense on which the witness had already been convicted or acquitted in that jurisdiction. Far more frequently the separate-sovereign doctrine came into play in the granting of witness immunity, as it allowed one jurisdiction to compel testimony by granting immunity only as to that jurisdiction, with no prohibition against the other jurisdiction using that testimony to prosecute the person under its law. This state of affairs was overturned in **Murphy v. Waterfront Comm'n**, 378 U.S. 52 (1964). The Supreme Court there rejected the separate-sovereign doctrine as applied to state and federal inquiries. Noting that a separate-sovereign limitation would permit a witness to be "whip-sawed into incriminating himself under both state and federal law," the Court concluded that the "policies and purposes" of the Fifth Amendment required that the privilege protect "a state witness against incrimination under federal as well as state law and a federal witness against incrimination under state as well as federal law."

Does it follow from *Murphy* that the privilege should be available where the witness' testimony would be incriminating only in a foreign country? In Zicarelli v. New Jersey Investigation Commission, 406 U.S. 472 (1972), the Supreme Court left that issue unresolved, noting that it would only be presented where a witness given immunity in this country could point to a "real" rather than a hypothetical risk of foreign prosecution. The Supreme Court resolved the issue in United States v. Balsys, 524 U.S. 666 (1998), when it held that "concern with foreign prosecution is beyond the scope of the Self-Incrimination Clause." The case involved an "administrative subpoena [issued by] the Office of Special Investigations of the Criminal Division of the United States Department of Justice (OSI) [that] sought testimony from the respondent, Aloyzas Balsys, about his wartime activities between 1940 and 1944 and his immigration to the United States in 1961. Balsys declined to answer such questions, claiming the Fifth Amendment privilege against self-incrimination, based on his fear of prosecution by a foreign nation." See Dianne Marie Amann, *A Whipsaw Cuts Both Ways: The Privilege Against Self-Incrimination In An International Court*, 45 U.C.L.A. L. REV. 1201 (1998) (international law arguments that still may remain available).

D. THE PRIVILEGE IN CIVIL AND ADMINISTRATIVE PROCEEDINGS

A person can invoke the Fifth Amendment privilege against self-incrimination in any proceeding so long as the statement might incriminate the person in a subsequent criminal prosecution. What is the effect of an invocation of the privilege in a non-criminal proceeding? Asserting the Fifth Amendment cannot, standing along, be a basis for depriving a person of a license or job. In Spevack v. Klein, 385 U.S. 511 (1967), the Court found that the disbarment of a lawyer because of his assertion of the privilege against self-incrimination in response to a subpoena issued in a disciplinary proceeding was impermissible because "[t]he threat of disbarment and the loss of professional standing, professional reputation, and of livelihood are powerful forms of compulsion to make a lawyer relinquish the privilege. That threat is indeed as powerful an instrument of compulsion as 'the use of legal process to force from the lips of the accused individual the evidence necessary to convict him * * *.'" Similarly, in the companion case of Garrity v. New Jersey, 385 U.S. 493 (1967), the Court overturned a state statute that required police officers to cooperate in an investigation or lose their jobs automatically because it violated the Fifth Amendment rights of the officers. The Court stated, "The choice given petitioners was either to forfeit their jobs or to incriminate themselves. The option to lose their means of livelihood or to pay the penalty of self-incrimination is the antithesis of free choice to speak out or to remain silent."

In Baxter v. Palmigiano, 425 U.S. 308 (1976), however, the Supreme Court considered a prison disciplinary policy under which "Palmigiano was advised that he was not required to testify at his disciplinary hearing and that he could remain silent but that his silence could be used against him." The Court held that "the prevailing rule [is] that the Fifth Amendment does not forbid adverse inferences against parties to civil actions when they refuse to testify in response to probative evidence offered against them: the Amendment 'does not preclude the inference where the privilege is claimed by a party to a Civil cause.' 8 J. Wigmore, Evidence 439 (McNaughton rev. 1961)."

When a person exercises the privilege in a civil or administrative proceeding, it may entail certain costs that would not arise in a criminal prosecution. While a court or administrative tribunal cannot punish a person for asserting the Fifth Amendment privilege, it can take steps to remedy the harm to an opposing party deprived of a useful source of information. For example, a party claiming the privilege may be precluded from offering evidence to support her side of the case, which may result in a grant of summary judgment. The finder of fact may be allowed to draw an adverse inference against the party asserting the privilege as to the withheld information, such as find that an answer not given would have been unfavorable to the party refusing to respond. When a non-party witness invokes the privilege, an adverse inference should not be drawn against either party unless the witness is so closely connected to a party that the person is within its control, such as the officers of a corporation who have particular knowledge of its activities.

What are the limits in a civil proceeding on the use of an individual's assertion of the Fifth Amendment as substantive proof that the person engaged in alleged misconduct? How much "compulsion" will a court permit? The issue is especially troublesome for attorneys, who are required under state ethics rules to cooperate in an investigation. Consider how the Maine Supreme Court analyzed this issue in the following case.

STATE v. HORTON
561 A.2d 488 (Me. 1989)

McKUSICK, Chief Justice.

Defendant James S. Horton, a lawyer, was indicted on April 4, 1988, on one count of theft by unauthorized taking, for the alleged misappropriation of $10,000 left with him by a client, the late Muriel Hall. The Superior Court granted defendant's motion to suppress statements made by him during an inquiry by the Board of Overseers of the Bar relating to the same alleged misappropriation. The question presented on the State's appeal from the suppression order is whether the statements Horton made to the Board during its disciplinary proceedings were compelled, so that use of those statements in this criminal prosecution would violate the guarantees against self-incrimination contained in both the United States and Maine Constitutions. Because we conclude that the suppression justice erred as a matter of law in finding that Horton was compelled to make those statements, we vacate the suppression order.

In 1983 the Board received a complaint alleging that Horton had misappropriated $10,000 that Mrs. Hall had entrusted to him for investment.[1] Bar Counsel notified Horton of the complaint and requested that he produce all documents relating to the matter. In response to a subpoena, Horton accompanied by counsel spoke to Bar Counsel in March of 1983. Without asserting or even mentioning his privilege against self-incrimination, Horton explained to Bar Counsel what had happened to Mrs. Hall's money. Horton later spoke to an investigator for the Board and still later testified voluntarily at a public hearing held by a panel of the Board's Grievance Commission in February of 1988. At no time did Horton or his

---

[1] Mrs. Hall was the step-grandmother of Horton's wife and Horton had drafted her will. Horton, however, characterizes his transaction with Mrs. Hall with regard to the $10,000 as a family matter not involving legal representation.

counsel discuss with anyone connected with the Board the possibility of his invoking the privilege.[2]

Meanwhile, in 1987 the Attorney General, having received a complaint from one of the beneficiaries under Mrs. Hall's will, initiated a criminal investigation of Horton's conduct. On April 4, 1988, the Penobscot County grand jury indicted Horton for theft. Horton then moved in the Superior Court to suppress all statements he had made to the Board or anyone connected with it, arguing that those statements were involuntary and obtained in violation of the federal and state constitutions.

At issue in this appeal is the suppression justice's interpretation of Maine Bar Rule 2(c). That rule provides, in relevant part:

> The failure without good cause to comply with any rule, regulation or order of the Board or the Grievance Commission or to respond to any inquiry by the Board, the Grievance Commission or Bar Counsel shall constitute misconduct and shall be grounds for appropriate discipline.

The suppression justice concluded that Rule 2(c) forces lawyers to make statements to the Board at the risk of disciplinary sanctions including even disbarment, and that the threat of such sanctions has the effect of depriving lawyers of the freedom to invoke their constitutional privilege against self-incrimination. Concluding that Horton's statements made in these circumstances were involuntary, the justice ruled that using those statements in this criminal prosecution would be unconstitutional.

The suppression justice's conclusion, however, is based on a flawed premise: that Rule 2(c) forces a lawyer receiving an inquiry from the Board to make statements or suffer disciplinary sanction. It is a fundamental principle of statutory construction that when we can reasonably interpret the words of a statute to uphold its constitutionality, we will do so. Under Rule 2(c) a lawyer is subject to discipline if he fails "without good cause" to "respond" to a Board inquiry. Giving those words their plain and ordinary meaning, we conclude that if a lawyer invokes his privilege against self-incrimination, communication to the Board of that decision constitutes itself a response to the Board's inquiry and he has not failed to respond within the meaning of Rule 2(c). Alternatively, even if one were to treat the invocation of the privilege as a failure to respond, that failure is for "good cause" within the meaning of Rule 2(c). If a lawyer chooses to invoke his constitutional privilege because he fears that his answers might incriminate him, the

---

[2] Bar Counsel has filed an information, pursuant to Maine Bar Rule 7(e)(6), recommending that the Supreme Judicial Court discipline Horton for misapplication of funds, but that disciplinary proceeding has been stayed pending resolution of this criminal case.

reason for his choice to remain silent constitutes the kind of "good cause" that excuses any other response to the Board's inquiry.

An interpretation of Rule 2(c) that allowed sanctions to be imposed on a lawyer for invoking the privilege against self-incrimination would be unconstitutional. In Spevack v. Klein, 385 U.S. 511 (1967), the United States Supreme Court, noting that a citizen may not be penalized for asserting this constitutional right, declared unconstitutional the disbarment of a lawyer for invoking his Fifth Amendment privilege. In a companion case handed down the same day, the Court held that when a New Jersey statute gave police officers under investigation by the state attorney general a choice between answering questions with no grant of immunity or losing their jobs, any statements made were "infected [with] coercion" and not voluntary. Garrity v. New Jersey, 385 U.S. 493 (1967). Faced with a choice between self-incrimination and job forfeiture, the Court found, the officers did not waive their constitutional privilege even though they did not object to use of the statements until their subsequent criminal prosecutions. See also Lefkowitz v. Cunningham, 431 U.S. 801 (1977) ("State may not impose substantial penalties because a witness elects to exercise his Fifth Amendment right not to give incriminating testimony against himself").

Horton has made no showing that either Rule 2(c) or any action by the Board subjected him to pressures such as were present in *Spevack* and *Garrity*. Absent that or any other compulsion, a lawyer who chooses to make statements in the Board proceedings without invoking his privilege to remain silent has done so voluntarily, and there is no constitutional barrier to using those statements in a subsequent criminal prosecution.

The situation here is unlike that in Moffett v. City of Portland, 400 A.2d 340 (Me.1979), where police officers were told that failure to answer questions in an internal police disciplinary proceeding could result in "disciplinary action." In the face of such a threat, we found that the officers were deprived of their free choice in deciding whether to speak or remain silent. But neither the actions of the Board nor the terms of Rule 2(c) compelled Horton to answer questions at the risk of disciplinary action. The circumstances of the case at bar are closer to those of United States v. Indorato, 628 F.2d 711 (1st Cir.), in which the First Circuit held that a police officer's statements in response to questioning by his superiors were not coerced when he failed to assert the privilege, he was not told he would be dismissed if he failed to answer, he was not asked to waive any immunity, and no statute required his dismissal for refusing to answer. The court there noted:

> In all of the cases flowing from *Garrity*, there are two common features: (1) the person being investigated is explicitly told that failure to waive his constitutional right against self-incrimination will result in his discharge from public employment (or a similarly severe sanction imposed in the case of private citizens); and (2) there is a statute or municipal ordinance mandating such procedure. In

this case, there was no explicit "or else" choice and no statutorily mandated firing is involved. We do not think that the subjective fears of defendant as to what might happen if he refused to answer his superior officers are sufficient to bring him within *Garrity's* cloak of protection.

Contrary to Horton's contention, the fact that a lawyer's decision to invoke the privilege and remain silent can be used as evidence in the disciplinary proceeding does not render the lawyer's decision to speak involuntary. Disciplinary proceedings are civil in nature, and a lawyer has no constitutional right to prevent the factfinder in that proceeding from considering the implications of his silence, along with other evidence against him, in making a determination. If he chooses to invoke his Fifth Amendment privilege and remain silent, a lawyer might be disciplined for the underlying misconduct charged by the Board, but that does not mean he is compelled to speak rather than assert his privilege. See Arthurs v. Stern, 560 F.2d 477 (1st Cir.1977) (there is nothing "inherently repugnant to due process in requiring the doctor to choose between giving testimony at the disciplinary hearing, a course that may help the criminal prosecutors, and keeping silent, a course that may lead to the loss of his license").

In this case Horton, appearing before representatives of the Board, chose to tell his story. A lawyer himself, Horton was also represented by counsel at his first meeting with Bar Counsel. At no time did he bring up the possibility of claiming his privilege against self-incrimination even though he was charged with misappropriation of funds, a charge he knew or should have known could lead to criminal prosecution. Whatever Horton's subjective interpretation of Rule 2(c) may have been, nothing in that rule would allow disciplinary sanctions to be imposed on a lawyer for invoking his constitutional right to remain silent. In these circumstances Horton's election to tell his story to the Board was a voluntary one, and his statements should not be suppressed in this criminal prosecution.

E. IMMUNITY

Under 18 U.S.C § 6002, the United States can grant a witness immunity from prosecution and compel the person to testify. The immunity provided under the statute is called "use/fruits" immunity, and provides that at the request of the government, the court will issue an order that "the witness may not refuse to comply with the order on the basis of his privilege against self-incrimination; but no testimony or other information compelled under the order (or any information directly or indirectly derived from such testimony or other information) may be used against the witness in any criminal case, except a prosecution for perjury, giving a false statement, or otherwise failing to comply with the order." The other form of immunity that the government can offer is known as "transactional immunity," which grants the witness full immunity from any later prosecution for any crimes about which the witness testifies. For any number of reasons, prosecutors are reluctant to grant a witness transactional immunity because the person cannot be prosecuted at any point, while use/fruits immunity does not prevent a subsequent prosecution of the immunized witness. In **Kastigar v. United States**, 406 U.S. 441 (1972), the Court discussed the history of the immunity statute and the effect of an order of immunity on a subsequent prosecution of the witness.

> The power of government to compel persons to testify in court or before grand juries and other governmental agencies is firmly established in Anglo-American jurisprudence. * * * But the power to compel testimony is not absolute. There are a number of exemptions from the testimonial duty, the most important of which is the Fifth Amendment Privilege against compulsory self-incrimination. The privilege reflects a complex of our fundamental values and aspirations, Murphy v. Waterfront Comm'n, and marks an important advance in the development of our liberty. * * *

> Immunity statutes, which have historical roots deep in Anglo-American jurisprudence, are not incompatible with these values. Rather, they seek a rational accommodation between the imperatives of the privilege and the legitimate demands of government to compel citizens to testify. The existence of these statutes reflects the importance of testimony, and the fact that many offenses are of such a character that the only persons capable of giving useful testimony are those implicated in the crime. Indeed, their origins were in the context of such offenses, and their primary use has been to investigate such offenses. Congress included immunity statutes in many of the regulatory measures adopted in the first half of this century. Indeed, prior to the enactment of the statute under consideration in this case, there were in force over 50 federal immunity statutes. In addition, every State in the Union, as well as the District of Columbia and Puerto Rico, has one or more such statutes. The commentators, and this Court on several occasions, have characterized immunity statutes as essential to the effective enforcement of various criminal statutes. * * *

> The statute's explicit proscription of the use in any criminal case of "testimony or other information compelled under the order (or any information directly or indirectly derived from such testimony or other information)" is consonant with Fifth Amendment standards. We hold that such immunity from use and derivative use is coextensive with the scope of the privilege against self-incrimination, and therefore is sufficient to compel testimony over a claim of the privilege. While a grant of immunity must afford protection commensurate with that afforded by the privilege, it need not be broader. Transactional immunity, which accords full immunity from prosecution for the offense to which the compelled testimony relates, affords the witness considerably broader protection than does the Fifth Amendment privilege. The privilege has never been construed to mean that one who invokes it cannot

subsequently be prosecuted. Its sole concern is to afford protection against being "forced to give testimony leading to the infliction of 'penalties affixed to * * * criminal acts.'" Immunity from the use of compelled testimony, as well as evidence derived directly and indirectly therefrom, affords this protection. It prohibits the prosecutorial authorities from using the compelled testimony in *any* respect, and it therefore insures that the testimony cannot lead to the infliction of criminal penalties on the witness. * * *

Although an analysis of prior decisions and the purpose of the Fifth Amendment privilege indicates that use and derivative-use immunity is coextensive with the privilege, we must consider additional arguments advanced by petitioners against the sufficiency of such immunity. * * * Petitioners argue that use and derivative-use immunity will not adequately protect a witness from various possible incriminating uses of the compelled testimony: for example, the prosecutor or other law enforcement officials may obtain leads, names of witnesses, or other information not otherwise available that might result in a prosecution. It will be difficult and perhaps impossible, the argument goes, to identify, by testimony or cross-examination, the subtle ways in which the compelled testimony may disadvantage a witness, especially in the jurisdiction granting the immunity.

This argument presupposes that the statute's prohibition will prove impossible to enforce. The Statute provides a sweeping proscription of any use, direct or indirect, of the compelled testimony and any information derived therefrom. * * * This total prohibition on use provides a comprehensive safeguard, barring the use of compelled testimony as an "investigatory lead," and also barring the use of any evidence obtained by focusing investigation on a witness as a result of his compelled disclosures. A person accorded this immunity under 18 U.S.C. § 6002, and subsequently prosecuted, is not dependent for the preservation of his rights upon the integrity and good faith of the prosecuting authorities. As stated in *Murphy* [*v. Waterfront Comm'n*, 378 U.S. 52 (1964)]:

> Once a defendant demonstrates that he has testified, under a state grant of immunity, to matters related to the federal prosecution, the federal authorities have the burden of showing that their evidence is not tainted by establishing that they had an independent, legitimate source for the disputed evidence.

This burden of proof, which we reaffirm as appropriate, is not limited to a negation of taint: rather, it imposes on the prosecution the affirmative duty to prove that the evidence it proposes to use is derived from a legitimate source wholly independent of the compelled testimony.

This is very substantial protection, commensurate with that resulting from invoking the privilege itself. The privilege assures that a citizen is not compelled to incriminate himself by his own testimony. It usually operates to allow a citizen to remain silent when asked a question requiring an incriminatory answer. This statute, which operates after a witness has given incriminatory testimony, affords the same protection by assuring that the compelled testimony can in no way lead to the infliction of criminal penalties. The statute, like the Fifth Amendment, grants neither pardon nor amnesty. Both the statute and the Fifth Amendment allow the Government to prosecute using evidence from legitimate independent sources.

NOTES AND QUESTIONS

1. *Administrative Investigations.* A decision whether to grant federal immunity is the prerogative of the Executive Branch, and as a general rule, only the Attorney General or a designated officer of Department of Justice has authority to grant use immunity. Section 6004 also provides that an administrative agency may issue an immunity order to compel testimony in connection with agency proceedings "with the approval of the Attorney General." The statute requires that the agency seeking immunity determine that "(1) the testimony or other information from such individual may be necessary to the public interest; and (2) such individual has refused or is likely to refuse to testify or provide other information on the basis of his privilege against self-incrimination."

2. *Prosecuting the Immunized Witness.* While § 6002 immunity holds open the possibility of prosecuting an immunized witness for offenses that are the subject of the witness' testimony, the United States Attorney's Manual indicates that the prosecutorial decision to proceed on such a case involves considerations beyond the availability of independently obtained evidence that would sustain a conviction. It provides that the prosecutor must obtain express written authorization from the Attorney General, and "[t]he request to prosecute should indicate the circumstances justifying prosecution and the method by which the government will be able to establish that the evidence it will use against the witness will meet the government's burden under *Kastigar v. United States*." USAM § 9-23.400.

3. *Prosecution's Burden.* Lower courts have held that the prosecution's burden of establishing that its evidence was derived from an independent source, and not from the defendant's immunized testimony, is governed by a preponderance of the evidence standard (rather than a higher burden of persuasion, such as "clear and convincing"). The burden is placed at this level because the same standard is used in other settings that the courts view as analogous—the government's burden in establishing a *Miranda* waiver and in establishing the voluntariness of a confession. See United States v. Byrd, 765 F.2d 1524 (11th Cir. 1985); United States v. Abanatha, 999 F.2d 1246

(8th Cir. 1993). This burden is placed on the government only after the defendant meets the threshold requirement of establishing that he or she testified under immunity on matters that could conceivably relate to the current prosecution. As a practical matter, however, almost any immunized testimony, whether or not in the jurisdiction of prosecution, will serve that function.

4. *The* Kastigar *Hearing*. "[A] trial court may hold a *Kastigar* hearing pre-trial, post-trial, mid-trial (as evidence is offered) or it may employ some combinations of these methods." United States v. North, 910 F.2d 843 (D.C. Cir. 1990) (noting that the pre-trial hearing is the "most common choice"). Courts favoring the pretrial hearing argue that the defendant should not be forced to trial unless the government can first establish that it can meet the independent source burden. See United States v. Smith, 580 F.Supp. 1418 (D.N.J. 1984). Defendants commonly favor a pretrial hearing because, even if the government succeeds, the hearing will provide the defense with valuable discovery as the government identifies the evidence it intends to use and cites its independent source. But note United States v. Byrd, supra (government may be allowed to make a partial in camera showing as to independent sources where it has good cause, e.g., to protect grand jury secrecy). Since the taint hearing will require a review of the immunized testimony, comparing it to the government's evidence, one disadvantage of a pretrial hearing is that it may make that testimony known to the government's trial prosecutors, who previously may have been shielded from the testimony by a wall. According to Sara Sun Beale, William C. Bryson, James E. Felman, & Michael J. Elston, GRAND JURY LAW & PRACTICE § 7:20:

> If a hearing is held prior to trial, and the prosecutor reads the immunized testimony in preparation for that hearing, the prosecutor's exposure to the immunized testimony at that time will ordinarily not be held to result in the kind of taint that requires dismissal of the indictment. On the other hand, the fact that the prosecutor will almost certainly be exposed to the immunized testimony or facts derived from the immunized testimony in preparation for and during the taint hearing provides a good reason for the court to postpone that hearing until after the trial.

Another argument advanced against the pretrial hearing is that a ruling there in the government's favor cannot be final, for even if the trial court finds independent sources for the evidence that the government intends to use, there remains the question of whether the government nonetheless used the immunized testimony in another fashion, and that determination can be made only after the trial is completed. In United States v. Cantu, 185 F.3d 298 (D.C. Cir. 1999), the District of Columbia Circuit held that "the substantial burden of *Kastigar* does require the government to give the defendant a chance to cross-examine relevant witnesses, to ensure the lack of tainted evidence. Where, however, the government offers such a witness at a hearing, and supplements that witness's testimony with documentation, we can not find a violation of the defendant's *Kastigar* rights. The focus of the

Kastigar inquiry should remain on whether the evidence was tainted, and not on the procedures by which the court comes to this conclusion."

5. *"But For" Discovery*. Is evidence "derived" from the immunized testimony if it would not have been discovered but for that testimony, no matter how attenuated the causal connection? Looking to *Kastigar's* reference to investigative leads, several lower courts have stated that a strict "but for" test applies. See e.g., In re Grand Jury Proceedings, 497 F.Supp. 979 (E.D. Pa. 1980). Illustrative is United States v. Kristel, 762 F.Supp. 1100 (S.D.N.Y. 1991), in which an F.B.I. agent investigating a padded billing scheme initially assumed the role of the defendant simply was that of a victim of extortion. However, he shifted the investigation to consider the possibility that defendant had used bribery to initiate the scheme (a shift that led to defendant's eventual prosecution for that bribery) when another agent, fortuitously overhearing a reference to defendant, commented that he had worked on another case in which defendant had cooperated (after being given immunity) and had acknowledged bribing a federal official. The district court concluded that "Mr. Kristel's immunized admissions in the [bribery of the federal official] assisted the Government in deciphering otherwise unintelligible or inconclusive information and evidence [relating to the padded commercial billings] and caused the Government to 'focus' its investigation in this matter as a bribe giver, in violation of the principles adopted by the Supreme Court in *Kastigar*."

In **United States v. Blau**, 159 F.3d 68 (2nd Cir. 1998), the Second Circuit again found the "but for" causation chain too attenuated to establish a *Kastigar* claim:

> Blau's "chain of taint" argument rests on the following logic: Blau's immunized testimony, by buttressing the case against Lupo, led to Lupo's decision to plead guilty. Lupo's guilty plea led to his decision to cooperate and to implicate Blau and Levin. This in turn led to the cooperation and testimony of Roger Levin against Blau. Blau's series of "but for" causation connections between his immunized proffer and his ultimate conviction is insufficient to make out a viable Kastigar claim. To make out a Fifth Amendment violation, Blau would have to demonstrate that Blau's proffer motivated Lupo and Levin to testify against him. We see no basis for disturbing the district court's finding that no such showing was made. The district court, relying on the record developed at trial and in Blau's post-trial motion, found that Lupo chose to plead guilty and then to cooperate and provide evidence against Blau for reasons unrelated to Blau's immunized proffer.

6. *Nonevidentiary Use*. Lower courts have divided over whether and how *Kastigar* applies to nonevidentiary uses–i.e., to prosecutorial consideration of immunized testimony in strategic decisions that do not deal directly with the production of evidence. Initially, there is a division as to whether the nonevidentiary category extends to such decisions as (1) deciding which

witnesses to call, (2) planning cross-examination, and (3) interpreting previously discovered evidence. Compare United States v. McDaniel, 423 F.2d 305 (8th Cir. 1975) (characterizing such decisions as nonevidentiary). At least where decisions are uncontestably nonevidentiary (as in the case of the decision not to plea bargain), some courts suggest that *Kastigar* either does not apply or applies with, at most, a very limited impact. They note that *Kastigar* described the requisite scope of the immunity as placing the individual in "substantially the same position" as if he had claimed the privilege, and that nonevidentiary uses are often so tangential to the presentation of the prosecution as to hardly alter the strength of a case against the defendant. While these courts often do not flatly reject the possibility that a nonevidentiary use can violate *Kastigar*, they would at least shift the *Kastigar* burden and require the defense to show that a specific trial strategy was formed by reference to the immunized testimony and had a measurable bearing upon the strength of the case presented by the prosecution. See United States v. Mariani, 851 F.2d 595 (2d Cir. 1988).

Other courts conclude that neither the statute nor the reasoning of *Kastigar* permits a distinction to be drawn between evidentiary and nonevidentiary uses–i.e., both must be barred. See United States v. McDaniel, supra; United States v. Semkiw, 712 F.2d 891 (3d Cir. 1983). They note that the immunity statute refers to prohibiting use of "information" derived from immunized testimony, and that *Kastigar* spoke of that immunity as "prohibit[ing] the prosecutorial authorities from using the compelled testimony in *any* respect." They further note that "if the immunity protection is to be coextensive with the Fifth Amendment privilege," as *Kastigar* demanded, "then it must forbid all prosecutorial use of the testimony, not merely that which results in the presentation of evidence before the jury." United States v. McDaniel, supra.

7. *Granting Immunity to Defense Witnesses*. The Department of Justice has the sole authority to request immunity under § 6002, and courts generally will not grant immunity without government request. In some cases, a witness may have information favorable to a defendant, but refuses to testify unless the government grants immunity because of the person's fear of prosecution. Because the defense cannot grant immunity, and the government may be uninterested in helping a defendant, can a court order immunity under § 6002 despite the government's refusal to request immunity? Courts are quite reticent to do so, although in an extreme case in which the refusal to grant immunity will significantly hinder the ability to determine the truth a court can grant immunity to protect the defendant's due process rights. In **United States v. Ebbers**, 458 F.3d 110 (2nd Cir. 2006), the Second Circuit set for the test for evaluating a claim that the refusal to grant immunity impermissibly harmed the defense:

> In an extreme case, a court might hold that the absence of the non-immunized witness caused the government's evidence to fall short of proof beyond a reasonable doubt. In addition, a court may

order the prosecution to choose between forgoing the testimony of an immunized government witness or granting use immunity to potential defense witnesses. To obtain such an order, a defendant must make a two-pronged showing.

First, the defendant must show that the government has used immunity in a discriminatory way has forced a potential witness to invoke the Fifth Amendment through "overreaching" or has deliberately denied immunity for the purpose of withholding exculpatory evidence and gaining a tactical advantage through such manipulation.

We have said that a discriminatory grant of immunity arguably may be no more than "a decision ... to confer immunity on some witnesses and not on others." [*United States v. Dolah*, 245 F.3d 98 (2nd Cir. 2001)]. However, it may also be the case that the immunity decisions in question are so obviously based on legitimate law enforcement concerns-e.g., granting immunity to a witness who has pleaded guilty and has been sentenced to substantial jail time while denying it to a principal target of the ongoing criminal investigation-that it is clear that a court cannot intervene without substantially hampering the administration of justice.

Prosecutorial "overreaching" can be shown through the use of "threats, harassment, or other forms of intimidation [which have] effectively forced the witness to invoke the Fifth Amendment." *Blissett v. Lefevre*, 924 F.2d 434 (2nd Cir. 1991). The "manipulation" standard overlaps to a degree with the discrimination test but involves an express finding of a tactical purpose on the government's part.

Second, the defendant must show that the evidence to be given by an immunized witness will be material, exculpatory and not cumulative and is not obtainable from any other source. In that regard, exculpatory evidence is material when it tends to show that the accused is not guilty. The bottom line at all times is whether the non-immunized witness's testimony would materially alter the total mix of evidence before the jury.

The Ninth Circuit stated a defendant "may prove that the prosecution acted with a certain purpose merely by demonstrating that the prosecution committed a set of acts (the selective denial of use immunity described) that had the effect of distorting the fact-finding process." *United States v. Straub*, 538 F.3d 1147 (9th Cir. 2008).

8. *Corporate Antitrust Immunity*.   The Antitrust Division of the Department of Justice has a Corporate Leniency Policy that permits a company reporting its own misconduct to avoid being charged with a crime.

Unlike individual immunity, in which the person can be compelled to testify, the company gains the benefit of not being prosecuted even though it has no Fifth Amendment privilege. The Policy provides:

> The Division has a policy of according leniency to corporations reporting their illegal antitrust activity at an early stage, if they meet certain conditions. "Leniency" means not charging such a firm criminally for the activity being reported. (The policy also is known as the corporate amnesty or corporate immunity policy.)

A. Leniency Before an Investigation Has Begun

Leniency will be granted to a corporation reporting illegal activity before an investigation has begun, if the following six conditions are met:

1. At the time the corporation comes forward to report the illegal activity, the Division has not received information about the illegal activity being reported from any other source;

2. The corporation, upon its discovery of the illegal activity being reported, took prompt and effective action to terminate its part in the activity;

3. The corporation reports the wrongdoing with candor and completeness and provides full, continuing and complete cooperation to the Division throughout the investigation;

4. The confession of wrongdoing is truly a corporate act, as opposed to isolated confessions of individual executives or officials;

5. Where possible, the corporation makes restitution to injured parties; and

6. The corporation did not coerce another party to participate in the illegal activity and clearly was not the leader in, or originator of, the activity.

In 2004, the Antitrust Division informed Stolt-Nielsen, S.A., that it was revoking its immunity under the Corporate Leniency Policy because the company allegedly continued its illegal activity after entering into an agreement with the Department of Justice that required it to avoid future violations. After the indictment of the company and its executives in 2006, the District Court dismissed the charges in **United States v. Stolt-Nielsen, S.A.**, 524 F.Supp.2d 609 (E.D.Pa. 2007). In finding that Stolt-Nielsen had not breached its agreement, the court discussed the standard of review for revocation of a corporate immunity agreement:

While non-prosecution agreements are binding contracts and their interpretation is guided by general principles of contract law, "such agreements are unique and are to be construed in light of 'special due process concerns.' " *United States v. Baird*, 218 F.3d 221 (3d Cir.2000). Mindful of the fact that parties who enter into non-prosecution agreements frequently forego valuable constitutional rights, the Court must determine whether the Government's conduct comported with "what was reasonably understood by defendant when entering" the Agreement.

* * * The Division bears the burden of demonstrating that Stolt-Nielsen materially breached the Agreement. The Division urges the Court to apply a "preponderance of the evidence" standard, a standard applied by a number of courts evaluating alleged breaches of plea agreements. Defendants propose a "clear and convincing" standard of proof. The Court's findings of fact and conclusions of law would be unchanged regardless of which of the two standards is applied.

In determining whether a non-prosecution agreement has been breached, the Court must consider whether the non-breaching party received the benefit of the bargain, as well as the incriminating nature of the information provided by the defendant.

F. THE PROFFER AND LIMITED IMMUNITY

For many potential defendants, an immunity grant is the best for which one can hope. Very often, however, more than one potential defendant will have that same hope, and the prosecutor has no need to grant immunity to all of those persons. The government will need the testimony of an inside participant to make its case, and the inside participants will be competing with each other to see who will win the "immunity sweepstakes." How are the Department of Justice's guidelines helpful to the participant's counsel in suggesting those factors that should be emphasized in convincing the government's attorney to grant immunity to counsel's client? To what extent may the critical factor be which participant contacts the prosecutor first, especially in a situation where all participants up to that point have asserted the self-incrimination privilege (following the not always sound aphorism, "nobody talks, everybody walks")?

Obviously, the government attorney will be hesitant to grant immunity to a person without knowing a good deal about what kind of testimony that person can provide and the extent of the person's participation in the illegality. Thus, the prosecutor commonly will require that the individual's counsel make a "proffer" as to the individual's participation and the information that he/she can provide. One concern here is the possible waiver of the lawyer-client privilege, and counsel will often first obtain an agreement in writing that the proffer will not constitute such a waiver. Another concern is that the proffer will be used by the government as a lead to evidence which might then be used without granting the client immunity. Thus, where a proffer includes a reference to incriminating documents that the client can identify, it may give the government information about the existence and location of the documents that it would not otherwise have had, and thus allow the government to obtain those documents by subpoena.

In some instances the government attorney may want to interview the witness before deciding on an immunity grant. An interview often is desired to test the witness' credibility and to determine how he or she will perform in a courtroom setting. Federal Rule of Criminal Procedure 11(f) provides that "[t]he admissibility or inadmissibility of a plea, a plea discussion, and any related statement is governed by Federal Rule of Evidence 410." Rule 410 provides in turn that "any statement made in the course of plea discussions with an attorney for the prosecuting authority which do not result in a plea of guilty or which result in a plea of guilty later withdrawn" cannot be admitted in evidence against the person making the statement, with one exception being a perjury prosecution. Should the same rule apply to statements made in the course of negotiations for a grant of use/fruits immunity? Counsel commonly insist upon an agreement to that effect prior to allowing the client to be interviewed, often asking as well for a commitment that the statement made by the client similarly will not be used for civil purposes. The government may insist that the proffer at least be available to it for use to impeach the individual should he or she later be prosecuted and offer contrary testimony at trial.

In **United States v. Mezzanatto**, 513 U.S. 196 (1995), the Supreme Court considered the validity of a pre-indictment agreement reached as part of plea negotiations "that any statements he made during the meeting could be used to impeach any contradictory testimony he might give at trial if the case proceeded that far." The defendant then stated that he knew a package he tried to sell to an undercover officer contained methamphetamine, but attempted to minimize his role in a drug manufacturing operation. The government had evidence of more extensive involvement, and ultimately no plea agreement was reached. At trial, the defendant denied any involvement in selling drugs, and the prosecutor cross-examined him with the statements from the earlier meeting. The Court, per Thomas, J., upheld the validity of agreements waiving the protections of Rule 11(f) as a condition for negotiating a plea bargain, stating:

> Prosecutors may be especially reluctant to negotiate without a waiver agreement during the early stages of a criminal investigation, when prosecutors are searching for leads and suspects may be willing to offer information in exchange for some form of immunity or leniency in sentencing. In this "cooperation" context, prosecutors face "painfully delicate" choices as to "whether to proceed and prosecute those suspects against whom the already produced evidence makes a case or whether to extend leniency or full immunity to some suspects in order to procure testimony against

other, more dangerous suspects against whom existing evidence is flimsy or nonexistent." Hughes, Agreements for Cooperation in Criminal Cases, 45 Vand.L.Rev. 1 (1992). Because prosecutors have limited resources and must be able to answer "sensitive questions about the credibility of the testimony" they receive before entering into any sort of cooperation agreement, prosecutors may condition cooperation discussions on an agreement that the testimony provided may be used for impeachment purposes. See Thompson & Sumner, Structuring Informal Immunity, 8 Crim.Just. 16 (spring 1993). If prosecutors were precluded from securing such agreements, they might well decline to enter into cooperation discussions in the first place and might never take this potential first step toward a plea bargain.

Indeed, as a logical matter, it simply makes no sense to conclude that mutual settlement will be encouraged by precluding negotiation over an issue that may be particularly important to one of the parties to the transaction. A sounder way to encourage settlement is to permit the interested parties to enter into knowing and voluntary negotiations without any arbitrary limits on their bargaining chips. To use the Ninth Circuit's metaphor, if the prosecutor is interested in "buying" the reliability assurance that accompanies a waiver agreement, then precluding waiver can only stifle the market for plea bargains. A defendant can "maximize" what he has to "sell" only if he is permitted to offer what the prosecutor is most interested in buying. And while it is certainly true that prosecutors often need help from the small fish in a conspiracy in order to catch the big ones, that is no reason to preclude waiver altogether. If prosecutors decide that certain crucial information will be gained only by preserving the inadmissibility of plea statements, they will agree to leave intact the exclusionary provisions of the plea-statement Rules.

In sum, there is no reason to believe that allowing negotiation as to waiver of the plea-statement Rules will bring plea bargaining to a grinding halt; it may well have the opposite effect. Respondent's unfounded policy argument thus provides no basis for concluding that Congress intended to prevent criminal defendants from offering to waive the plea-statement Rules during plea negotiation.

Justice Ginsburg concurred in *Mezzanatto*, but noted that "[i]t may be, however, that a waiver to use such statements in the case in chief would more severely undermine a defendant's incentive to negotiate, and thereby inhibit plea bargaining. As the Government has not sought such a waiver, we do not here explore this question."

For various reasons, a prosecutor may prefer to utilize a limited immunity to learn what the person can offer to assist the government's investigation and prosecution. This type of agreement–sometimes referred to as "Queen for a Day" immunity–grants the witness much less protection than a full grant of immunity. In **United States v. Lauersen**, 2000 WL 1693538 (S.D.N.Y. 2000), the district court described this form used in the Southern District of New York:

> A "Queen for a Day" agreement is a limited use immunity agreement where the suspect agrees to provide information in exchange for a promise from the Government that any statements made during the proffer will not be used against the profferor. Where plea negotiations break down or an immunity deal is rejected, the standard form Queen for a Day used in the Southern District of New York permits a prosecutor to use the proffered statements in a number of circumstances, including to pursue leads, to cross-examine the defendant if she testifies, and for purposes of rebuttal.

A grant of use/fruits immunity can be forced upon a witness who would prefer to exercise the privilege, but without a proffer the government may be granting immunity to a person it would not otherwise have entered into such an agreement with because of their involvement in criminal activity. A limited immunity agreement requires that the witness be willing to forego exercise of the privilege in return for what the agreement offers, thereby allowing the government to preview what the witness has to offer without fully committing to immunity or some type of plea bargain. Quite often, a person who can offer important assistance will be willing to enter into such an agreement. In some cases that may be because the person feels that he is gaining more than would be gained by an immunity grant. More often, the person is aware that he may be getting less, but that is the best he can expect to achieve (especially where there is a competition among various insiders to get the benefit of what the prosecutor might offer).

The government has become increasingly aggressive in offering fewer protections in these limited immunity agreements to individuals seeking to make a deal in exchange for cooperation. In *Mezzanatto*, the Supreme Court upheld an agreement that permitted the government to use the defendant's statements for impeachment if the defendant testified inconsistently. How far can the government go in limiting the protection afforded an individual? Consider the following case to see how the limited immunity agreement can permit the government to use the defendant's statements in its case-in-chief and not merely to impeach a defendant who testifies inconsistently with a prior statement.

UNITED STATES v. KRILICH
159 F.3d 1020 (7th Cir. 1999)

EASTERBROOK, Circuit Judge.

A golfer's dream came true for Andy Sarallo. On June 19, 1985, Andy lined up at the ninth tee at Country Lakes Country Club and struck the ball; an observer on the ninth green pulled Andy's ball out of the hole. Andy's foursome jumped up and down and shouted for joy. Because the ninth hole at Country Lakes was the subject of a hole-in-one contest that day, Andy had just won his choice of a 1931 Cadillac or a check for $40,000!

A hole-in-one is quite a thrill because it happens so infrequently–perhaps one chance in 40,000, rarer than a 300 game in bowling. But Andy's chances were close to 100%, because his father was mayor of Oakbrook Terrace, Illinois, and the mayor's support was needed for a bond offering to finance an apartment complex to be built by Robert Krilich–who sponsored the contest, pulled the ball out of the hole, and became the defendant in this criminal case. Krilich and Mayor Sarallo agreed to use the golf tournament as the vehicle for a payoff. Krilich palmed one of Andy's golf balls, put his hand into the cup, and displayed the ball. Delivering the bribe in this way enabled Krilich to shift the cost to the National Hole-In-One Association, which provided insurance. Thus fraud and bribery were coupled. Krilich admitted this scheme in a proffer to the United States Attorney, and he also conceded bribing the mayor to alter the zoning of some land and orchestrating the extraction of funds from municipal bond offerings. The bonds–Industrial Revenue Bonds, interest on which is not taxable to the investors–were sold to finance Krilich's developments. Because the bonds were limited to specific projects (tax exemption depended on that link), the funds were placed in trust, and the trustee banks were to release the money only to reimburse expenses associated with the projects. Preferring to use the money elsewhere, such as for payments on his yacht, Krilich instructed vendors to falsify their invoices and had those bogus invoices sent to the banks for payment out of the trust accounts.

Krilich was convicted of conspiracy to violate the Racketeer Influenced and Corrupt Organizations statute, 18 U.S.C § 1962(d) (RICO), and a fraud statute, 18 U.S.C. § 1014. Krilich maintains on appeal that the district court erred by permitting the prosecutor to use some of the proffer's contents at his trial. * * *

Statements made during plea negotiations are inadmissible, Fed.R.Evid. 410; Fed.R.Crim.P. 11(e)(6), but a defendant may waive the right to prevent their use. *Mezzanatto.* The agreement Krilich signed contains a conditional waiver:

[S]hould [Krilich] subsequently testify contrary to the substance of the proffer or otherwise present a position inconsistent with the proffer, nothing shall prevent the government from using the substance of the proffer at sentencing for any purpose, at trial for impeachment or in rebuttal testimony, or in a prosecution for perjury.

By authorizing the prosecutor to use his statements if he should contradict himself, Krilich made his representations more credible and thus strengthened his hand in negotiations. A prosecutor may be reluctant to negotiate; what has the defendant to offer? A statement that shows how the defendant's aid could assist the prosecutor in other cases (or lead to the appropriate sentence in this one) may get negotiations under way and set the stage for a favorable bargain. But a prosecutor needs assurance that the defendant is being candid. A conditional waiver of the kind Krilich signed tends to keep the defendant honest, which makes the proffer device more useful to the both sides. For this strategy to work the conditional waiver must be enforceable; its effect depends on making deceit *costly*. We therefore reject the argument that waivers should be construed against prosecutors; that might help Krilich today but would hinder bargaining for other defendants tomorrow. We give this waiver neither a stingy reading nor a generous one, but a natural reading, which leaves the parties in control through their choice of language.

This agreement allowed the prosecutor to use the proffer as evidence if Krilich were to "testify contrary to the substance of the proffer or otherwise present a position inconsistent with the proffer". Introduction of the statements thus was proper if either his testimony, or evidence that he presented through the testimony of others, contradicted the proffer. Because Krilich did not testify, only the second clause is at issue. Krilich wants us to limit this clause to evidence presented through his own witnesses; evidence obtained by cross-examination of the prosecution's witnesses does not count, he insists. But that would be an unnatural reading of the language. Evidence is evidence, whether it comes out on direct or cross-examination. One can "otherwise present" a position through arguments of counsel alone, so it is easy to see how a position can be "presented" by evidence developed on cross-examination and elaborated by counsel. When the prosecution's witnesses are inclined to accommodate the defense, as many were in this case, developing one's position through cross-examination is especially attractive.

The prosecutor's position about the effect of the language is as unrealistic as Krilich's. According to the prosecutor, putting on *any* defense permits the United States to introduce the statements. A plea of not guilty followed by passivity at trial is about all the defense can do, the prosecutor contends–though, when pressed at oral argument, the prosecutor allowed that Krilich could have avoided introduction of the statements if he had limited his cross-examination to "the credibility, weight and sufficiency of the government's evidence in ways that were extrinsic to the facts of the case." On this understanding, asking a witness on cross-examination whether he had been convicted of perjury would be "extrinsic to the facts of the case," but asking the witness whether he had been in a position to see what happened at the ninth green on June 19 would open the door to the use of the proffer.

Such a distinction makes sense of neither the language in the contract nor the reason why the waiver was *conditional*. The prosecutor wanted to give Krilich an incentive to tell the truth; Krilich wanted assurance that he could defend himself at trial if bargaining collapsed (for otherwise he was delivering himself into the prosecutor's hands); conditioning the use of the proffer statements on the presentation of a position "inconsistent with the proffer" does both of those things only if the judge must find genuine inconsistency before allowing use of the statements.

Impeachment of a witness need not be "contrary to" or "inconsistent with" a defendant's admission of guilt in a bargaining proffer. To take a simple example, the statements "I faked the hole-in-one on the ninth hole" (Krilich, in the proffer) and "I did not see Krilich palm a golf ball at the ninth hole on June 19" (a witness, on cross-examination) are not inconsistent. Investigation via cross-examination of witnesses' ability (or willingness) to observe and recount the facts they claim to have observed therefore could not have justified introduction of the proffer statements. Millions of people who live in Illinois did not see what happened at the ninth green on June 19; others who did see what happened may have had reasons to misrepresent what they saw; proof that a given person who took the stand at trial was in the set of non-observers (or liars) is not "inconsistent" with the proffer. Statements are inconsistent only if the truth of one implies the falsity of the other. The statements "Krilich pulled a palmed ball from the cup at the ninth hole" and "Krilich wasn't at the ninth hole when Andy hit his shot" are inconsistent because the former statement cannot be true if the latter is. This appeal turns on whether Krilich elicited such inconsistent testimony. The district judge concluded that he had, and that assessment is not clearly erroneous.

Several witnesses testified, in response to questions from Krilich's attorney, that the ninth hole at Country Lakes Country Club is close to the clubhouse and easily observed. Krilich wanted the jury to infer that no one would attempt to fake a hole-in-one there; that implication is inconsistent with the proffer. Defense counsel got two witnesses to say that they were at the ninth hole when Andy hit the shot but didn't think that Krilich was at the ninth hole then. This line of cross-examination was not designed to cast doubt on the witnesses' ability to see clearly or suggest that they are not trustworthy. Their testimony implied that Krilich did not fake the hole-in-one, contrary to what he admitted in his proffer. Similarly, in response to evidence that Krilich paid a bribe to obtain favorable zoning, his lawyer elicited testimony on cross-examination that no bribe was required because the city attorney thought the new zoning to be correct. Counsel likewise led witnesses to testify that the procedures followed for altering the zoning were not exceptional. Krilich's attorney also had the vice president of his company testify that he was not aware of *any* bribes paid to *any* public official in connection with *any* project. The implication was that if someone so close to Krilich (and the projects) was unaware of bribes, there must not have been any. These statements go well beyond casting doubt on the prosecutor's evidence; they advance a position inconsistent with the proffer–or so the trial judge sensibly could conclude.

Krilich insists that if the conditional waiver means what we think it means, then it is unenforceable because involuntary. *Mezzanatto* says that waivers of the plea-statement rules are unenforceable if given "unknowingly or involuntarily," but this is a far cry from saying that waivers mean whatever the defendants say they understood them to mean; no party to a contract has Humpty Dumpty's power over language either directly or through the gambit that unanticipated consequences render the agreement "involuntary." A waiver is voluntary in the absence of coercion, and is knowing if made "with a full awareness of both the nature of the right being abandoned and the consequences of the decision to abandon it." Krilich does not contend that his assent was coerced and offers no support for a conclusion that he didn't understand the rights that Rules 410 and 11(e)(6) confer. A defendant's understanding of the *consequences* of his waiver need not be perfect; it was Krilich's understanding of the rights being relinquished, not of all possible repercussions of relinquishing them, that made his waiver knowing. [The court affirmed the defendant's conviction.]

NOTES AND QUESTIONS

1. *Inconsistent Positions.* When has a defendant taken an "inconsistent" position that permits the government to introduce statements made at a proffer subject to the limited immunity agreement? The defendant's statements can have a devastating effect on any defense, especially if the government can use it in its case-in-chief to undermine the defendant's credibility even before the defense can mount its case. The scope of the waiver in the limited immunity agreement is the key, and prosecutors have been seeking ever broader waivers. In **United States v. Barrow**, 400 F.3d 109 (2d Cir. 2005), the Second Circuit considered whether defense counsel's opening statement and cross-examination of a prosecution witness allowed the government to introduce the defendant's statements made a proffer session. The agreement provided that the government could use the statements "as substantive evidence to rebut any evidence offered or elicited, or factual assertions made, by or on behalf of [defendant] at any stage of a criminal prosecution (including but not limited to detention hearing, trial or sentencing)." This is broader than the waiver in *Krilich*, which was triggered if Krilich presented "a position inconsistent with the proffer." Analyzing the scope of the waiver, the court stated:

> The mere fact that a defendant pleads not guilty and stands trial is not a factual assertion that triggers the proffer agreement waiver, and the government certainly does not contend otherwise. See *United States v. Krilich.* Nor are defense arguments that attempt to demonstrate why the facts put in evidence by the prosecution are insufficient to permit the jury to find the elements of the crime proved. Thus, a defense argument that simply challenged the

sufficiency of government proof on elements such as knowledge, intent, identity, etc., would not trigger the waiver here at issue. On the other hand, a statement of fact in a defense opening, such as the statement in this case unequivocally identifying Jamal Barrow as the real perpetrator of the charged crimes, does qualify as a factual assertion within the four corners of the waiver provision. Thus, we conclude that the waiver's "factual assertion" requirement was satisfied in this case.

We note, however, that such a conclusion may not be reached so easily when counsel's arguments or questions assert facts implicitly rather than directly. For example, a cross-examination question challenging a witness's perception or recollection of an event does not necessarily imply that the event did not occur, only that the witness may not have seen or reported it accurately. On the other hand, a question accusing a witness of fabricating an event, such as counsel in this case put to Det. Campana with respect to the April 19, 2001 meeting with the confidential informant, does implicitly assert that no such meeting ever took place. Thus, when confronted with a government argument that a defense opening or cross-examination implicitly satisfies the factual assertion requirement for waiver, a district court may well have to consider carefully what fact, if any, has actually been implied to the jury before deciding whether proffer statements fairly rebut it.

We further note that even when a district court is satisfied that a factual assertion triggering a Rule 410 waiver has been made, whether directly or implicitly, that conclusion does not mandate receipt of the proffer statements in evidence. A waiver agreement between the parties does not divest a district court of its considerable discretion to exclude relevant evidence that may inject "unfair prejudice" or "confusion" into the jury's resolution of the issues in dispute.

2. *Other Uses*. While the use of a defendant's prior proffer statement can be most damaging at trial, the agreement with the prosecutor may allow for other uses, even if they are not specifically addressed in the written terms. In **United States v. Schwartz**, 541 F.3d 1331 (11th Cir. 2008), an agent testified before the grand jury as to the substance of the proffer interviews with defendant Meyer. The relevant provision of the agreement provided: "The United States may make derivative use of the statements [Meyer] makes during the proffer and may pursue investigative leads therefrom, and would not be required to prove an independent source at any *Kastigar* or other hearing held thereon. By signing this agreement [Meyer] agrees to waive any right to a *Kastigar* hearing in the future." The Eleventh Circuit rejected the defendant's argument that the grand jury indictment should be dismissed because the government violated his rights under the proffer agreement:

Although the agreement does not state explicitly that the Government may use Meyer's statement directly before the grand jury, we think it is nonetheless clear when read holistically. Meyer waived his right to a Kastigar hearing. Put differently, he waived his right to challenge the Government's use of his statements before the grand jury. We cannot conclude that he left himself vulnerable to what he characterizes as a Fifth Amendment violation but voluntarily waived his right to learn about and seek a remedy for that violation. The only reasonable inference is that Meyer intended to waive his Fifth Amendment privilege against use of his statements before the grand jury.

That inference is strengthened by an application of the interpretive doctrine of *noscitur a sociis*, or a phrase is "known by its associates." In paragraph three of the agreement Meyer first voluntarily waives his Fifth Amendment privilege against derivative use of his statement against him at trial. In the next sentence he waives his right to a Kastigar hearing. We think the parties intended paragraph three to list ways the Government could use Meyer's statements notwithstanding the Fifth Amendment.

3. *Knowing and Voluntary Waiver.* In United States v. Plummer, 941 F.2d 799 (9th Cir. 1991), the Ninth Circuit applied "ordinary contract principles" in construing the limited immunity agreement, and found that the terms should be construed narrowly when the government drafted the agreement. Therefore, in determining the scope of immunity, the circuit court stated that "use immunity presumptively includes derivative use immunity, unless the government can demonstrate in a given case that, at the time the agreement was made, it expressly clarified that only direct use immunity was offered." In United States v. Aleman, 286 F.3d 86 (2d Cir. 2002), the court noted that the contract interpretation also involved basic principles of fairness:

Due process concerns color our interpretation of a contract involving defendant's constitutional rights. Due process not only requires that the government adhere to the terms of any plea bargain or immunity agreement it makes, but also requires us to construe agreements strictly against the government in recognition of its superior bargaining power and to presume that both parties to the agreement contemplated that all promises made were legal. Sometimes general fairness principles will require us to invalidate particular agreement terms.

In United States v. Young, 223 F.3d 905 (8th Cir. 2000), the Eighth Circuit found that a defendant waived his rights to exclude an affidavit he executed–acknowledging his involvement in criminal activity–as part of the entry of a plea agreement which he later breached. Although the plea agreement did not specifically state that the affidavit could be used against him at trial, it did provide that in the event of a breach "all testimony and other information he has provided at any time to attorneys, employees or law enforcement officers of the government, to the court, or to the federal grand jury, may and will be used against him in any prosecution or proceedings." Furthermore, the agreement stated that defendant had reviewed the agreement with his counsel and that "[h]e has discussed the case and his constitutional and other rights with his attorney." The circuit court stated, "We do not believe that the failure to include a rote recitation of the rules in the plea agreement constitutes an 'affirmative indication that the agreement was entered into unknowingly or involuntarily' [quoting *Mezzanatto*]."

4. *Sixth Amendment*. Recall Justice Ginsburg's concurrence in *Mezzanatto*, [p. 590], in which she noted that the Court was not considering a waiver that would permit the government to use proffer statements in its case-in-chief. Can the government's demand for a waiver of the Rule 11(f) protections as a condition of considering a plea bargain violate the defendant's Sixth Amendment rights? In United States v. Duffy, 133 F.Supp. 213 (E.D.N.Y. 2001), District Judge Gershon ruled that a limited immunity agreement that permitted the government to use the defendant's statements "as substantive evidence to rebut any evidence offered or elicited, or factual assertions made, by or on behalf of [Duffy] at any stage of a criminal prosecution" violated the Sixth Amendment right to the effective assistance of counsel because it complete hamstrings any effort by counsel to represent the defendant. The Second Circuit rejected that position in **United States v. Velez** , 354 F.3d 190 (2d Cir. 2004). The defendant argued "that the waiver provision in the proffer agreement–which permits the Government to offer a proffer admission by the defendant in rebuttal to contradictory evidence or argument–violates defendant's constitutional rights to mount a defense, to the effective assistance of counsel, and to a fair trial." In rejecting this position, Circuit Judge Cabranes stated:

> In contending that the agreement is unenforceable, defendant relies principally on *United States v. Duffy*, 133 F.Supp.2d 213 (E.D.N.Y.2001), in which the district court refused to enforce a waiver provision in a proffer agreement similar to the one we consider here. The *Duffy* ruling determined that the waiver provision "prevent[ed defense counsel] from making any sort of meaningful defense," and that it "exploit[ed]" a disparity of bargaining power between the Government and the defendant. The court stated: "After signing the standard proffer agreement, the terms of which are dictated by the government, the only thing that a defendant is guaranteed is the chance to convince the prosecutor to enter a deal. At the same time, the defendant bears all of the risk." Concluding that the waiver provision effectively forfeited the defendant's fundamental rights to present a defense and to the effective assistance of counsel and, in doing so, implicated important public interests, the district court held the waiver provision unenforceable.

For the reasons that follow, we respectfully decline to adopt the position advanced in *Duffy*, and we note with approval the recent, contrasting opinion in *United States v. Gomez*, 210 F.Supp.2d 465 (S.D.N.Y.2002), which found enforceable a proffer agreement containing a waiver provision identical to the one at issue in this case.

As the *Gomez* ruling points out, "fairness dictates that the agreement be enforced [. . .] If the proffer agreement is not enforced, a defendant will have less incentive to be truthful, for he will know that his proffer statements cannot be used against him at trial as long as he does not testify, even if he presents inconsistent evidence or arguments." See also *United States v. Krilich* (stating that, in proffer sessions, "a prosecutor needs assurance that the defendant is being candid" and that "[f]or this strategy to work the conditional waiver must be enforceable; its effect depends on making deceit costly ").

In addition, invalidating a waiver provision like the one before us would clearly interfere with plea bargaining and cooperation efforts–in direct contravention of the criminal justice system's legitimate goal of encouraging plea bargaining in appropriate circumstances. The Supreme Court has noted that, "[i]f prosecutors were precluded from securing [waiver] agreements, they might well decline to enter into cooperation discussions in the first place and might never take this potential first step toward a plea bargain." *Mezzanatto*; see also *Gomez*, ("Prosecutors will be reluctant to enter into cooperation agreements if they cannot obtain some assurance that the defendant will tell the truth.").

We do not lightly dismiss the observation in *Duffy* that the Government holds significant bargaining power in arranging proffer sessions and securing a waiver provision as a prerequisite for a defendant's participation. However, "[t]he mere potential for abuse of prosecutorial bargaining power is an insufficient basis for foreclosing negotiation altogether." * * * We thus reject the argument that defendant, relying on *Duffy*, makes in this case–that the asserted disparity of power between the Government and a defendant in proffers renders waiver provisions in proffer agreements unenforceable.

Finally, a defendant remains free to present evidence inconsistent with his proffer statements, with the fair consequence that, if he does, "the Government [is] then . . . permitted to present the defendant's own words in rebuttal." *Gomez*. With this avenue open to him, a defendant who has consented to a waiver provision like the one at issue here has not forfeited his constitutional right to present a defense, to the effective assistance of his counsel, or to a fair trial.

Accordingly, we reject defendant's claim that the waiver provision is unconstitutional, and we hold that, where a proffer agreement is entered into knowingly and voluntarily, a provision in which defendant waives his exclusionary privilege under Federal Rule of Evidence 410 by permitting the Government to introduce defendant's proffer statements to rebut contrary evidence or arguments presented by the defense, whether or not defendant testifies, is enforceable.

CHAPTER FOURTEEN
AGENCY INVESTIGATIONS AND THE
PROBLEM OF PARALLEL PROCEEDINGS

The federal administrative agencies have developed enforcement staffs–comprised of both lawyers and investigators–with expertise in the intricacies of their particular fields. Unlike the United States Attorneys Offices, which deal with a broad range of cases from violent crime to sophisticated frauds, these enforcement officials are familiar with the inner workings of the industry they regulate and can ferret out wrongdoing that might not be apparent to the untrained eye. Quite often, federal prosecutors will rely on investigations by the administrative agencies to provide the details of the underlying misconduct, and agency lawyers may be appointed as"Special" Assistant United States Attorneys to assist in the presentation of a case to the grand jury and subsequent prosecution. 28 U.S.C. § 515.[a]

Of increasing importance in the field of administrative investigations are the Inspector Generals in now found in most federal agencies. The Inspector General Act, 5 U.S.C.App. 3 § 4(a)(1), created the office "to conduct, supervise, and coordinate audits and investigations relating to the programs and operations of" the agency." The idea of an Inspector General who independently audits the work and conduct of an agency and its enforcement of the law was adopted by the Continental Congress during the Revolutionary War. The adoption of the Inspector General Act in 1978 came during an era in which the need for independent review of agency conduct was strong, and they are an important component in the law enforcement programs of many federal agencies, such as the Department of Health and Human Services, which is responsible for the oversight of programs with significant budgets, including Medicare and Medicaid. Professor Hartmus described the duties of the Inspector Generals:

> The Inspector General Act of 1978 charges IGs with five main duties. First, they are to conduct and supervise audits and investigations relating to the programs and operations of their agency. Second, they are to review existing and proposed legislation relating to their agencies, and to make recommendations regarding

---

[a] "The Attorney General or any other officer of the Department of Justice, or any attorney specially appointed by the Attorney General under law, may, when specifically directed by the Attorney General, conduct any kind of legal proceeding, civil or criminal, including grand jury proceedings and proceedings before committing magistrate judges, which United States attorneys are authorized by law to conduct, whether or not he is a resident of the district in which the proceeding is brought."

the impact of such legislation on the economy and efficiency of the agency. Third, they are to recommend policies to promote economy, efficiency and effectiveness, and to provide leadership and coordination with other federal, state and local agencies. Fourth, they are to prevent and detect fraud and abuse in the programs and operations of their agencies. Fifth, they are to provide a means for keeping the head of the agency and the Congress informed about problems and deficiencies in the administration of their agencies' programs and operations, as well as the necessity for, and the progress of, corrective action.

Diane M. Hartmus, *Inspection and Oversight in the Federal Courts: Creating an Office of Inspector General*, 35 CALIF. WEST. L. REV. 243 (1999). The authority of the Inspector Generals includes investigations of misconduct by those outside the agency. In Adair v. Rose Law Firm, 867 F.Supp. 1111 (D.D.C. 1994), the District Court found that:

> the "relating to" language [in the Inspector General Act is] a broad grant of authority rather than a limitation. This language is expansive enough to extend the IG's authority beyond investigations of the agency itself to investigations of individuals and entities outside the agency involved with an agency's programs. Furthermore, other sections of the Inspector General Act clarify, if clarification is needed, that the IG's authority extends to conducting audits and investigations of programs that the agency finances, including investigations into alleged fraud, abuse and waste by government contractors and other recipients of government funds in connection with those programs. * * * It is obvious that the IG could not fulfill many of its responsibilities under * * * the Act * * * without investigating fraud, abuse and waste by both the agency administering and financing the program and the participants in the program.

In creating this broad administrative apparatus, Congress gave the regulatory authorities the power to compel the production of records and testimony that is, in many ways, similar to the investigative authority of the federal grand jury. As the Supreme Court discussed in **United States v. Morton Salt**, 338 U.S. 632 (1950):

> Because judicial power is reluctant if not unable to summon evidence until it is shown to be relevant to issues in litigation, it does not follow that an administrative agency charged with seeing that the laws are enforced may not have and exercise powers of original inquiry. It has a power of inquisition, if one chooses to call it that, which is not derived from the judicial function. It is more analogous to the Grand Jury, which does not depend on a case or controversy for power to get evidence but can investigate merely on suspicion that the law is being violated, or even just because it

wants assurance that it is not. When investigative and accusatory duties are delegated by statute to an administrative body, it, too, may take steps to inform itself as to whether there is probable violation of the law.

The authority of an agency to conduct investigations and pursue administrative remedies is governed by particular statutes. Judicial oversight of administrative agencies will involve reviewing an agency's specific legislative authority, and also by reference to more general principles of fairness and due process. The Internal Revenue Service (IRS) is the most closely scrutinized federal agency because it deals with such highly sensitive information. Courts have been very careful in deciding whether to enforce the efforts of the IRS to gather information, and Congress has enacted detailed requirements for the agency to obtain information from a taxpayer and from third parties. The next section deals with the IRS investigations. The following sections treat other federal agencies, and consider the standards applied to those investigations and how courts have not scrutinized those agencies to the same degree as the IRS. This is especially notable in the area of concurrent civil and criminal investigations, and the use of a civil regulatory agency to gather information for use in a grand jury investigation. The Chapter reviews the administrative remedies available to an agency that finds a violation of the laws it is charged with administering, and concludes with consideration of the problems that can arise from parallel civil and criminal investigations.

A. INTERNAL REVENUE SERVICE INVESTIGATIONS

1. *Civil and Criminal Investigations*. The Internal Revenue Service (IRS) is responsible for the collection of taxes and enforcement of the federal tax code, which reaches virtually every business and adult in the country. In **United States v. Peters**, 153 F.3d 445 (7th Cir. 1998), the Seventh Circuit explained how the IRS divides its investigatory authority into civil and criminal components:

> The IRS splits the responsibility for enforcing the nation's tax laws between its two investigative divisions. The Criminal Investigative Division ("CID") is charged with investigating criminal violations of the tax code and related federal statutes. CID investigators are called "special agents." Like many other criminal law enforcement agents, they carry firearms and badges. In addition, special agents must recite an administrative warning prior to soliciting information from taxpayers.

> On the other hand, the Examination Division of the IRS is responsible for conducting civil tax audits. Examination Division investigators are known as "revenue agents." In contrast to special agents, revenue agents do not carry firearms; nor are they required

to provide taxpayers with an administrative warning. Although an Examination Division audit typically concludes with some sort of civil settlement between the IRS and the taxpayer, such an audit may uncover evidence that causes the revenue agent to refer the case to the CID for criminal investigation. Under IRS regulations, a revenue agent who uncovers a "firm indication of fraud on the part of the taxpayer" must immediately suspend her audit and refer the case to the CID.

If the IRS uncovers evidence of what it believes is a criminal violation of the tax laws, then the case is referred to the Tax Division of the Department of Justice, which is responsible for the any resulting criminal prosecution of the case. The IRS remains involved in the criminal case because its CID agents assist in the investigation, in much the same way the FBI or Secret Service agents assist prosecutors in investigations.

The Internal Revenue Manual describes the process by which the agency determines whether to make a criminal referral in a matter under investigation:

(1) This section discusses the fact that fraud case begins with the recognition of affirmative indications and acts of fraud by the taxpayer. Further development of these "indicators" assists the employee in establishing the firm indications necessary for a successful fraud case.

(2) When initial indications of fraud are uncovered, the compliance employee should initiate a discussion with his/her group manager. A plan of action should be developed as early as possible to document firm indications of fraud. An integral part of the plan is establishing that sufficient affirmative acts exist which confirm fraud. * * *

(3) When first alerted to the possibility of fraud, the compliance employee must know when to suspend action on the case and prepare a criminal referral. If the compliance employee stops too soon all the information necessary to document firm indications of fraud may not be developed sufficiently for the Criminal Investigation (CI) function.

(4) The minimum plan of development should include following up on all leads indicated as fraud indicators, securing copies of all relevant data relating to indicators of fraud and noting from whom and when obtained. Documents obtained from the taxpayer or other third parties should not be annotated with any comments by the compliance employee. It is critical for the employee to secure the taxpayer's explanations for any discrepancies.

(5) An understatement of the tax liability alone is not fraud. In order to sustain the penalty or make a criminal referral, the compliance employee must establish the intent was to defraud.

Internal Revenue Manual Ch. 21.1.3.

Criminal tax prosecutions are comparatively rare, especially given the large number of tax returns filed every year by businesses and individuals, so the opportunities to avoid punishment for the evasion of taxes are significant. The IRS and the Tax Division of the Department of Justice have limited resources, and tax cases are considered among the most difficult to prosecute because of their complexity and perceived lack of jury appeal. Quite often, tax charges are brought as an adjunct to other substantive charges. For example, in McCormick v. United States [p. 117], the government charged the defendant with tax fraud for failing to report the payments from the foreign doctors that he asserted were campaign contributions, in addition to the Hobbs Act charge. For other tax prosecutions, the government targets its resources to achieve the greatest effect.

> As a practical matter the Service may be more likely to press a case involving a locally prominent taxpayer than a relatively obscure person. The basic reason for this is that the maximum deterrent, in the view of the Service, comes from prosecution of the otherwise reputable taxpayer. Similarly, in the case of celebrities or nationally prominent persons, indictment will be sought for their national publicity and deterrent value although the process of internal review is apparently more stringent in such instances.

Ray A. Knight & Lee G. Knight, *Criminal Tax Fraud: An Analytical Review*, 57 MO. L. REV. 175 (1992).

2. **The *Powell* Test.** The IRS has the authority to issue a summons to obtain information to determine whether a taxpayer has properly paid taxes. A summons is similar to a grand jury subpoena in that it compels the recipient to do any of the following:

(1) To examine any books, papers, records, or other data which may be relevant or material to such inquiry;

(2) to summon the person liable for tax or required to perform the act, or any officer or employee of such person, or any person having possession, custody, or care of books of account containing entries relating to the business of the person liable for tax or required to perform the act, or any other person the Secretary may deem proper, to appear before the Secretary at a time and place named in the summons and to produce such books, papers, records, or other data, and to give such testimony, under oath, as may be relevant or

material to such inquiry; and

(3) To take such testimony of the person concerned, under oath, as may be relevant or material to such inquiry.

26 U.S.C. § 7602(a). If the summons recipient refuses to comply, the IRS must apply to the court for an order compelling compliance with the summons. Unlike a proceeding to enforce a grand jury subpoena, a summons enforcement proceeding is treated as a separate civil proceeding, and an enforcement order is directly appealable by the taxpayer as a final decision under 28 U.S.C.A. § 1291. See Church of Scientology of California v. United States, 506 U.S. 9 (1992). The same is true for enforcement of subpoenas issued on behalf of other administrative agencies. Moreover, compliance with the enforcement order does not render moot a subsequent appeal, as the appellate court can order the return to the taxpayer of the subpoenaed material and destruction of all copies made by the agency. Church of Scientology of California v. United States.

In **United States v. Powell**, 379 U.S. 48 (1964), the Supreme Court established a four-part test to determine whether enforcement of an IRS summons is proper: "[The IRS] must show that the investigation will be conducted pursuant to a legitimate purpose, that the inquiry may be relevant to the purpose, that the information sought is not already within the Commissioner's possession, and that the administrative steps required by the Code have been followed." The *Powell* test has been further refined, as explained by the First Circuit in **United States v. Gertner,**[b] 65 F.3d 963 (1st Cir.1995):

---

[b] *Gertner* arose in the following context:

At various times in 1991 and 1992, respondents Nancy Gertner and Jody Newman, then partners in a Boston law firm, filed forms reflecting four successive payments of hefty cash fees to the firm by a single client. Each of the forms was essentially complete except for the name of the client. The respondents advised the IRS that they were withholding the client's identity on the basis of ethical obligations, attorney-client privilege, and specified constitutional protections. * * *

The parties remained deadlocked and the IRS issued summonses purporting to direct the respondents to furnish certain records and testimony anent the client's identity. The respondents declined to comply. The government then brought an enforcement action pursuant to I.R.C. §§ 7402(a) & 7604(a), claiming that it wanted the information in connection with an investigation of the law firm's tax liability.

The First Circuit noted the "remarkably thin prima facie case established by Agent Ameno's declaration provides a shallow foundation for a presumption in favor of the government."

* * * This court has constructed a three-tiered framework for [enforcement] determinations. To mount the first tier, the IRS must make a prima facie showing that it is acting in good faith and for a lawful purpose. * * * [That may be satisfied by] an affidavit of the investigating agent attesting to satisfaction of the four *Powell* elements * * *. Once this minimal showing surfaces, the burden shifts to the taxpayer to rebut the good-faith presumption that arises in consequence of the government's prima facie case. The taxpayer is not at this stage required to *disprove* the government's profession of good faith. She must, however, shoulder a significant burden of production: in order to advance past the first tier, the taxpayer must articulate specific allegations of bad faith and, if necessary, produce reasonably particularized evidence in support of those allegations. This showing does not demand that the taxpayer conclusively give the lie to the prima facie case, but only that she create a "substantial question in the court's mind regarding the validity of the government's purpose." To reach this goal, it is not absolutely essential that the taxpayer adduce additional or independent evidence; she may hoist her burden either by citing new facts or by bringing to light mortal weaknesses in the government's proffer. * * * If the taxpayer satisfies this burden of production, the third tier beckons. At this stage, the district court weighs the facts, draws inferences, and decides the issue. To do so, the court frequently will proceed to an evidentiary hearing, taking testimony and exhibits from both sides. But there is no hard-and-fast rule compelling an evidentiary hearing. A district court may, in appropriate circumstances, forgo such a hearing and decide the issues on the existing record.

A question lingers at the third tier as to the continuing viability of the original presumption in favor of the IRS. The case law seems to suggest that the presumption endures and serves at this stage to saddle the taxpayer with the burden of persuading the judge, *qua* factfinder, that at least one of the *Powell* elements is missing. * * * [The usual treatment of presumptions], codified in the Federal Rules of Evidence * * * [is that] "a presumption imposes on the party against whom it is directed the burden of going forward with evidence to rebut or meet the presumption, but does not shift to such party the burden of proof in the sense of the risk of nonpersuasion, which remains throughout the trial upon the party on whom it was originally cast." Fed. R. Evid. 301.* * * We are hard-pressed to fathom why IRS enforcement proceedings should diverge from this principle. It is the IRS, not the taxpayer, that seeks to invoke the processes of the court; and, in a related vein, the court is instructed to grant the requested relief only when "sufficient proof is made." § 7604(b). Though it certainly can be argued that "strong reasons of public policy" justify a burden-shifting scheme, it would seem that the IRS's legitimate interest in obtaining summary enforcement is satisfactorily addressed by the particularized burden of production imposed on the taxpayer, without going the whole hog. * * * [But] we defer a definitive decision on * * * [this question] to a different day. After all, the respondents concede that the district court tacitly required them to prove improper purpose by a preponderance of the evidence, and they accepted the burden of proof without any objection. * * *

The Ninth Circuit rejected the burden-shifting analysis advanced in *Gertner*, which it described as "*dicta*," and leaves the burden on the taxpayer once the IRS meets its initial "slight" burden of meeting the four-part *Powell* test. United States v. Crystal, 172 F.3d 1141 (9th Cir. 1999).

3. *Third-Party Summons*. If the IRS issues a summons to a third-party to obtain information as part of an examination of a taxpayer, and the summons identifies the person whose information is the subject of the summons, then the IRS must provide a copy of the summons to the identified person. In addition, that person has a right to file a motion to quash the summons or intervene in a proceeding to enforce the summons. 26 U.S.C. § 7609(a).

The IRS can also issue what is known as a "John Doe Summons" in which the particular taxpayer who is the subject of the examination is not identified. Under 26 U.S.C. § 7609(f), the IRS must comply with the following procedures before the summons can be issued:

Any summons * * * which does not identify the person with respect to whose liability the summons is issued may be served only after a court proceeding in which the Secretary establishes that--

(1) the summons relates to the investigation of a particular person or ascertainable group or class of persons,

(2) there is a reasonable basis for believing that such person or group or class of persons may fail or may have failed to comply with any provision of any internal revenue law, and

(3) the information sought to be obtained from the examination of the records or testimony (and the identity of the person or persons with respect to whose liability the summons is issued) is not readily available from other sources.

4. *Judicial Review of Internal IRS Decisions*. In **United States v. Peters**, 153 F.3d 445 (7th Cir. 1998), the Seventh Circuit discussed the problem with the judicial role in determining whether the IRS agent had a "firm indication of fraud" such that the civil audit should have been terminated:

[T]he "firm indications of fraud" standard is a difficult standard for federal courts to apply because it is inherently vague and depends, in large part, on the good faith and professional judgment of the revenue agents conducting the investigation at issue. When applying this standard, federal courts must navigate between two perils. On the one side, courts face the Scylla of judicial micromanagement of the inner functionings of an administrative agency, a peril recognized by many of the courts that have addressed this issue. Yet, on the other side, courts face the Charybdis of judicial abdication of their Article III duty to protect the constitutional rights of criminal defendants. As the district court recognized, this latter peril will be realized if the courts are forced to rely solely on the after-the-fact assessments of revenue agents who may have an incentive to use the discretionary nature of the "firm indications" rule to shield their actions from judicial scrutiny.

In navigating the narrow course necessitated by these two perils, courts must remember that the "firm indications of fraud" rule is but a tool for courts to utilize in determining whether the revenue agents made an affirmative misrepresentation to a defendant or her representatives concerning the nature of their investigation.

5. *Constitutional Protections in IRS Audits*. The IRS Manual does not explicitly refer to any rights of a taxpayer in describing when a case should be referred for further criminal investigation and possible prosecution. In United States v. McKee, 192 F.3d 636 (6th Cir. 1999), the circuit court stated that "an affirmative representation by an IRS agent that the investigation is routine when in fact it is a criminal investigation requires suppression of evidence." *McKee* referred to the Fourth and Fifth Amendment rights of the taxpayers, but those rights are not implicated in any traditional sense during an IRS civil audit. The Fifth Amendment right against self-incrimination only applies to compelled testimony or custodial interrogations, neither of which are present in a tax audit. Moreover, while the taxpayer may be compelled to produce records, the Fifth Amendment does not apply to pre-existing documents. Similarly, the Fourth Amendment applies to searches and seizures, but the IRS summons is equivalent to a grand jury subpoena and is not a search. Is the court's concern grounded more in the nature of the tax system, that taxpayers are expected to voluntarily report their income, so that instances of misleading conduct or misrepresentations by an IRS agent will have a detrimental effect on the operation of the tax system? See United States v. Grunewald, 987 F.2d 531 (8th Cir. 1993)("It would be a flagrant disregard of individuals' rights to deliberately deceive, or even lull, taxpayers into incriminating themselves during an audit when activities of an obviously criminal nature are under investigation."). The police are usually permitted to engage in deceptive actions to gather evidence, and in a voluntary interview, the government is not required to reveal whether a person is suspected of criminal behavior, so why would conduct by an IRS

agent that "lulls" a taxpayer into revealing information be a constitutional violation?

7. *Effect on Other Agencies.* The solicitude of courts for the rights of taxpayers apparently springs from concern that the IRS may abuse its enormous authority in an area that touches virtually all citizens and involves some of the most intimate details of their lives. The restrictive approach to IRS civil audits does not translate to civil law enforcement investigations by other agencies of the federal government. See SEC v. Dresser Industries, 628 F.2d 1368 (D.C. Cir. 1980)(discussed in Note 4, p. 625).

B. CIVIL LAW ENFORCEMENT AGENCY INVESTIGATIONS

1. Distinguishing Between IRS and Other Agency Investigations

The subject of administrative investigations argued that the four-part *Powell* test required the Securities and Exchange Commission to notify the subject of its investigation that the agency issued a subpoena to a third party for records. The Supreme Court firmly rejected that position in **Securities and Exchange Commission v. Jerry T. O'Brien, Inc.**, 467 U.S. 735 (1984):

> There are several tenuous links in respondents' argument. Especially debatable are the proposition that a target has a substantive right to be investigated in a manner consistent with the *Powell* standards and the assertion that a target may obtain a restraining order preventing voluntary compliance by a third party with an administrative subpoena. Certainly we have never before expressly so held. For the present, however, we may assume, *arguendo*, that a target enjoys each of the substantive and procedural rights identified by respondents. Nevertheless, we conclude that it would be inappropriate to elaborate upon those entitlements by mandating notification of targets whenever the Commission issues subpoenas.
>
> Two considerations underlie our decision on this issue. First, administration of the notice requirement advocated by respondents would be highly burdensome for both the Commission and the courts. The most obvious difficulty would involve identification of the persons and organizations that should be considered "targets" of investigations. The SEC often undertakes investigations into suspicious securities transactions without any knowledge of which of the parties involved may have violated the law.[a] To notify all

---

[a] So, for example, the Commission is sometimes called upon to investigate unusually active trading in the stock of a company during the period immediately preceding a tender offer for that stock. In such a case, the Commission may have no

potential wrongdoers in such a situation of the issuance of each subpoena would be virtually impossible. The Commission would thus be obliged to determine the point at which enough evidence had been assembled to focus suspicion on a manageable subset of the participants in the transaction, thereby lending them the status of "targets" and entitling them to notice of the outstanding subpoenas directed at others. The complexity of that task is apparent. Even in cases in which the Commission could identify with reasonable ease the principal targets of its inquiry, another problem would arise. In such circumstances, a person not considered a target by the Commission could contend that he deserved that status and therefore should be given notice of subpoenas issued to others. To assess a claim of this sort, a district court would be obliged to conduct some kind of hearing to determine the scope and thrust of the ongoing investigation. Implementation of this new remedy would drain the resources of the judiciary as well as the Commission.

Second, the imposition of a notice requirement on the SEC would substantially increase the ability of persons who have something to hide to impede legitimate investigations by the Commission. A target given notice of every subpoena issued to third parties would be able to discourage the recipients from complying, and then further delay disclosure of damaging information by seeking intervention in all enforcement actions brought by the Commission. More seriously, the understanding of the progress of an SEC inquiry that would flow from knowledge of which persons had received subpoenas would enable an unscrupulous target to destroy or alter documents, intimidate witnesses, or transfer securities or funds so that they could not be reached by the Government. Especially in the context of securities regulation, where speed in locating and halting violations of the law is so important, we would be loathe to place such potent weapons in the hands of persons with a desire to keep the Commission at bay.

We acknowledge that our ruling may have the effect in practice of preventing some persons under investigation by the SEC from asserting objections to subpoenas issued by the Commission to third parties for improper reasons. However, to accept respondents' proposal "would unwarrantedly cast doubt upon and stultify the [Commission's] every investigatory move,' *Donaldson v. United States*. Particularly in view of Congress' manifest disinclination to require the Commission to notify targets whenever it seeks information from others, we refuse so to curb the Commission's exercise of its statutory power.

---

idea which (if any) of the thousands of purchasers had improper access to inside information.

2. Enforcement of Agency Subpoenas

In re ADMINISTRATIVE SUBPOENA JOHN DOE, D.P.M.
253 F.3d 256 (6th Cir. 2001)

MOORE, Circuit Judge.

Petitioner-Appellant John Doe ("Doe" or "petitioner") appeals the district court's order denying his motion to quash an administrative subpoena issued by the Department of Justice pursuant to a health care fraud investigation. Doe, a podiatrist, is under investigation for an alleged kickback arrangement with two medical testing laboratories. The administrative subpoena, issued pursuant to the Department of Justice's authority under § 248 of the Health Insurance Portability & Accountability Act ("HIPAA"), ordered Doe to turn over a number of documents, including:

> records relating to his professional education and ethical training; personal and business financial records; records evidencing any asset transfers by Doe to his children; and various patient files.

John Doe, D.P.M., a podiatrist operating a clinic in the Cleveland metropolitan area, is under investigation by the FBI and a federal grand jury for an alleged "kickback" arrangement with two medical testing laboratories. More specifically, it is alleged that Doe received payments from these labs for referring his patients to them for medically unnecessary vascular and electrodiagnostic tests. The government alleges that these kickbacks were disguised as rental payments that the labs made to Doe for the periodic use of one room in his clinic. The government has obtained documents through previous subpoenas evidencing lease agreements with the labs that show that, in less than three years, approximately $10,000 was paid to Doe for the use of a single room in his clinic for a few hours each month. By contrast, Doe himself only paid about $16,800 in rent for the entire office over that same period of time. The government claims that, based on information discovered thus far, Doe may have aided one of the laboratories in submitting false claims approximating $150,000 to various health care benefit programs. These programs paid approximately $57,000 on the claims.

The government also has evidence from independent medical experts stating that one of the labs to which Doe referred patients was performing a grossly excessive amount of electrodiagnostic testing. * * *

Pursuant to the DOJ's investigation, a series of subpoenas were issued to Doe requesting various documents. In the first subpoena, issued August 5, 1998, the DOJ requested lease agreements between Doe and the labs, any payments made to Doe by any medical service provider, including laboratories, and information on tests performed on patients by any medical service provider. The second subpoena, issued May 25, 1999, requested information on various patients. The third subpoena, an administrative subpoena and the subpoena at issue in this case, was ordered pursuant to the DOJ's authority under § 248 of the HIPAA, which allows the Attorney General or her designee to issue subpoenas requiring the production of records "which may be relevant to" a "Federal health care offense" investigation. 18 U.S.C. § 3486(a)(1)(A).[1]

The administrative subpoena ordered Doe's records custodian to turn over a number of documents by August 28, 2000.[a] * * * Doe did not turn over these documents. Instead, on August 29, 2000, Doe filed in the district court a motion to quash the subpoena, or, in the alternative, to issue a protective order. In this motion, Doe called the government's latest document request "unreasonably burdensome" and questioned its relevance.

---

[1] On December 19, 2000, several months after the subpoena was issued in this case, the Presidential Threat Protection Act of 2000, Pub.L. No. 106-544, 114 Stat. 2715, altered the precise statutory language authorizing the Attorney General to issue administrative subpoenas pursuant to federal health care investigations. Although we apply § 3486 as it existed at the time the subpoena was issued, we note that the changes made in the language of § 3486 would not alter the ultimate outcome in this case.

[a] Similar to the broad grand jury subpoenas duces tecum discussed in Chapter _ supra., the administrative subpoena here sought voluminous documents from Doe, including five years of patient files if they were referred to a testing laboratory for certain tests:

1) all professional journals, magazines, and newsletters subscribed to or received by Doe from January 1990 through March 1998;
2) copies of recent bank and other financial records showing the current location, amount, and value of all Doe's personal and health care-related business assets, whether jointly or individually held;
3) copies of recent bank and other financial records showing the current location, amount, and value of all Doe's children's assets insofar as those assets were provided or derived from the individual or jointly held assets of Doe;
4) all documents and patient files evidencing Doe's referral of patients for certain electrodiagnostic tests after April 2, 1998;
5) all documents and patient files after January 1, 1993 evidencing Doe's referral of patients to a specific medical testing laboratory for certain diagnostic ultrasound tests;
6) complete academic transcripts and records from medical or podiatric school, as well as any other post-graduate training;
7) all documents concerning the extent of Doe's continuing medical education, including a list and description of courses taken, credit hours earned, and any materials provided in those courses;
8) all documents concerning ethics, professional responsibility, and medical-billing issues in Doe's custody; and
9) retained copies of federal, state, and local tax returns both for Doe and any of his businesses from 1993 to the present.

* * * The district court denied the motion to quash because "the subpoena was issued within the authority of the U.S. Attorney General, the records sought [were] relevant to the government's health-care fraud investigation, the materials [were] not already in the possession of the Department of Justice, and [because the] Court's process would not be abused by enforcement of the subpoena." * * *

As noted in its heading, 18 U.S.C. § 3486 authorizes the Attorney General or her designee to issue "[a]dministrative subpoenas in [f]ederal health care investigations[.]" Doe claims that, by enforcing the DOJ's administrative subpoena in this case, his Fourth Amendment right to be free from unreasonable searches and seizures has been violated.

This circuit has noted that a district court plays only a limited role in the enforcement of an administrative subpoena. All the district court must do in deciding whether to enforce an administrative subpoena is 1) determine whether the administrative agency to which Congress has granted the subpoena power, in this case the DOJ, has satisfied the statutory prerequisites to issuing and enforcing the subpoena, and 2) determine whether the agency has satisfied the judicially created standards for enforcing administrative subpoenas. We first turn to the judicially created standards that must be met for an administrative subpoena to be enforced.

In Oklahoma Press Publishing Co. v. Walling, 327 U.S. 186 (1946), one of the Supreme Court's first major cases addressing the constitutionality of an administrative subpoena under the Fourth Amendment, the Court created standards for the enforcement of administrative subpoenas that are still used today. In *Oklahoma Press,* the Court held that a subpoena duces tecum for corporate records issued by the Department of Labor would comply with the Constitution so long as the demand for documents

> is authorized by Congress, is for a purpose Congress can order, and the documents sought are relevant to the inquiry. Beyond this the requirement of reasonableness, including particularity in describing the place to be searched, and the persons or things to be seized ... comes down to [whether] specification of the documents to be produced [is] adequate, but not excessive, for the purposes of the relevant inquiry. Necessarily, ... this cannot be reduced to formula; for relevancy and adequacy or excess in the breadth of the subpoena are matters variable in relation to the nature, purposes and scope of the inquiry.

Put more succinctly in United States v. Morton Salt Co., 338 U.S. 632 (1950), another case involving a request for corporate documents, the Court stated that an agency's request for documents should be approved by the judiciary so long as it "is within the authority of the agency, the demand is not too indefinite and the information sought is reasonably relevant." In other words, the agency request must be reasonable.

It is from the last major Supreme Court case on the issue, United States v. Powell, 379 U.S. 48 (1964), that the basic language of the "reasonable relevance" test employed by this circuit emanates. * * *

The *Powell* Court was concerned that requiring the IRS to show probable cause that a tax fraud had been committed would seriously hinder the agency's ability to conduct these kinds of investigations. Thus, rather than probable cause, the Court held that all the IRS need show to obtain judicial enforcement of a summons is "that the investigation will be conducted pursuant to a legitimate purpose, that the inquiry may be relevant to the purpose, that the information sought is not already within the Commissioner's possession, and that the administrative steps required by the Code have been followed[.]" We still use this test today when examining administrative subpoenas. As this circuit has summarized, "[w]hile the court's function is neither minor nor ministerial" when deciding whether to enforce an administrative subpoena, "the scope of the issues which may be litigated in an enforcement proceeding must be narrow, because of the important governmental interest in the expeditious investigation of possible unlawful activity."

Following *Powell* and the precedent of this circuit, we hold that the DOJ need not make a showing of probable cause to issue an administrative subpoena under 18 U.S.C. § 3486, nor does petitioner argue for such a standard on appeal. In In re Subpoena Duces Tecum, 228 F.3d 341 (4th Cir.2000), the U.S. Court of Appeals for the Fourth Circuit was the first circuit court to address administrative subpoenas issued under § 3486. As the Fourth Circuit explained, whereas the Fourth Amendment mandates a showing of probable cause for the issuance of search warrants, subpoenas are analyzed only under the Fourth Amendment's general reasonableness standard. One primary reason for this distinction is that, unlike "the immediacy and intrusiveness of a search and seizure conducted pursuant to a warrant[,]" the reasonableness of an administrative subpoena's command can be contested in federal court before being enforced. * * *

We agree with the Fourth Circuit that the reasonable relevance test should apply to administrative subpoenas under § 3486. Both the Supreme Court and this circuit have long applied this test when reviewing administrative subpoena requests, and we see no convincing basis upon which to distinguish these binding precedents simply because this subpoena was issued pursuant to a criminal, as opposed to civil, investigation.

Following Supreme Court precedent on the enforcement of administrative subpoenas, this circuit has held that a subpoena is properly enforced if 1) it satisfies the terms of its authorizing statute, 2) the documents requested were relevant to the DOJ's investigation, 3) the information sought is not already in the DOJ's possession, and 4) enforcing the subpoena will not constitute an abuse of the court's process.

* * * [T]he administrative subpoena at issue in this case requested nine categories of documents [see footnote a supra]. Of these, two involve requests for the files of patients who were referred to outside labs for additional testing. Doe no longer disputes the reasonableness of the government's request for patient documents, however, and thus we will not address this aspect of the subpoena. Of the remaining categories, four encompass documents related to Doe's professional education and the extent of his ethical training, two involve Doe's personal and business financial records, and the final request seeks those bank and other financial records of Doe's children showing any assets that "were provided or derived from individual or jointly held assets of [John Doe.]"

We will now address whether the requirements for enforcing an administrative subpoena have been met in this case, focusing on each of the different categories of documents in turn. * * * Petitioner does not argue that this administrative subpoena fails to comply with the statutory requirements of § 3486. Indeed, to do so would be difficult given the broad subpoena power that the statute gives to the Attorney General and her designees. The provision states:

> In any investigation relating to any act or activity involving a Federal health care offense, . . . the Attorney General or the Attorney General's designee may issue in writing and cause to be served a subpoena . . . requiring the production of any records (including any books, papers, documents, electronic media, or other objects or tangible things), which may be relevant to an authorized law enforcement inquiry, that a person or legal entity may possess or have care, custody, or control[.]

18 U.S.C. § 3486(a)(1)(A). The Code broadly defines a "Federal health care offense" as a violation of, or a conspiracy to violate, a number of health-care related offenses, including 18 U.S.C. § 1035 (false statements relating to health care matters) and 18 U.S.C. § 1347 (health care fraud). 18 U.S.C. § 24(a)(1). A federal health care offense also encompasses a variety of general criminal violations (*e.g.,* mail and wire fraud under 18 U.S.C. §§ 1341 and 1343), if those violations "relate[ ] to a health care benefit program." 18 U.S.C. § 24(a)(2).

Section 3486 also requires that any subpoena issued describe the objects to be produced and allow a reasonable period of time for the items to be assembled. 18 U.S.C. § 3486(a)(2). The subpoenaed party need not deliver any documents requested pursuant to § 3486 more than 500 miles from the place where it was served. 18 U.S.C. § 3486(a)(3).

There is no dispute that the investigation at issue in this case relates to a potential federal health care offense. While Doe does describe the subpoena as "overly burdensome[,]" he does not argue that the length of time given him to comply with the subpoena or the designated delivery location for the requested documents are beyond the scope of the authority granted in § 3486.

Instead, the primary point of contention in this case is whether the documents requested are relevant to the DOJ's investigation of Doe. Because § 3486 authorizes subpoena requests for documents "which *may be relevant* to an authorized law enforcement inquiry," § 3486(a)(1)(A) (emphasis added), the question of the relevance of the documents requested is inherently a question of whether the DOJ had the statutory authority to issue this subpoena. Nevertheless, because the second element of our test for determining the enforceability of an administrative subpoena focuses on the relevance of the documents to the agency's investigation, we will address this issue under that heading. Thus, aside from the question of relevance, we are confident that the DOJ has satisfied § 3486's statutory requirements for issuing this administrative subpoena.

While we have no circuit precedent addressing the administrative subpoena relevance requirement as it relates to documents requested under § 3486, other administrative subpoena cases in this circuit, as well as Supreme Court precedent, hold that relevance should be construed broadly. First, we note that the language of § 3486 indicates that the question of an administrative subpoena's relevance is not a question of evidentiary relevance, but rather is simply a question of whether the documents requested pursuant to the subpoena are relevant to the health care fraud investigation being undertaken. 18 U.S.C. § 3486(a)(1)(A). Furthermore, in *Markwood,* while we did not have to engage in a discussion of the relevance of the documents requested through the administrative subpoena, we did note often the deference that courts must show to the statutory authority of the administrative agency, stating that subpoenas should be enforced when " 'the evidence sought by the subpoena [is] not plainly incompetent or irrelevant to any lawful purpose of the [agency] in the discharge of [its] duties.' "

In EEOC v. Ford Motor Credit Co., 26 F.3d 44 (6th Cir.1994), this court discussed the relevance requirement as it related to administrative subpoenas issued by the EEOC. Following Supreme Court precedent, we explained that the term "relevant" in the statute authorizing the EEOC to issue administrative subpoenas had been construed broadly so as to allow "the Commission access to virtually any material that might cast light on the allegations against the employer." We noted that this broad interpretation of relevance was influenced by Congress's intent that the EEOC have the authority to demand documents that it deemed relevant to its investigation. We stated, however, that, while relevance should be viewed broadly, because the court was given the duty of reviewing the agency's decision to issue a subpoena, it did not simply have to accept the agency's opinion as to what is and is not relevant to agency investigations. Ultimately, we decided that, in reviewing whether an administrative subpoena should be enforced, we would "weigh the likely relevance of the requested material to the investigation against the burden . . . of producing the material."

As with the EEOC's subpoena power, it appears clear, both from the language of the statute and from Congress's intent in enacting HIPAA, that the DOJ's subpoena power in investigating federal health care offenses is meant to be broad. Section 3486 authorizes the Attorney General or her designee to subpoena any records "which *may be relevant*" to an authorized investigation, thus illustrating the substantial scope of the subpoena power Congress intended to give to the Attorney General. 18 U.S.C. § 3486(a)(1)(A) (emphasis added).

Aside from the statutory language, other evidence of Congress's intent to grant the Attorney General a broad subpoena power can be found in HIPAA's legislative history. One of the main legislative purposes of HIPAA was to prevent[ ] health care fraud and abuse. H.R.Rep. No. 104-496, at 67 (1996). As the House Ways and Means Committee Report stated in recommending that HIPAA be passed:

> In order to address the problem of health care cost inflation and make insurance more affordable, it is important to focus on key sources affecting levels of the underlying health care costs. Two key sources of excessive cost are medical fraud and abuse, and the current medical paperwork burden.

> According to the General Accounting Office (GAO), as much as 10 percent of total health care costs are lost to fraudulent or abusive practices by unscrupulous health care providers. The GAO reports that only a small fraction of the fraud and abuse committed in the health care system is identified and dealt with. Federal funding for prevention, detection, and prosecutions of the perpetrators of health care fraud and abuse has not kept pace with the problem. Coordination of the various law enforcement agencies at the federal and state levels has been insufficient, and law enforcement agencies agree that penalties for health care fraud and abuse should be increased.

H.R.Rep. No. 104-496. It is safe to assume that Congress, in passing HIPAA, recognized the serious problem that health care fraud had become, and that, through this legislation, Congress was intending to strike back at this problem. Accordingly, in light of both the statutory language and legislative history of § 3486, it appears that Congress intended to give the Attorney General broad authority to conduct health care fraud investigations, thus entailing a less restricted interpretation of what records may be subpoenaed under § 3486 because they are "relevant" to a health care investigation.

While the *Ford Motor* court's decision to weigh the likely relevance of requested material against the burden of producing that material came in the context of an EEOC administrative subpoena, we did not confine our reasoning only to that type of administrative subpoena, nor is there any basis for following a different course in this case. The administrative subpoena powers under both Title VII and HIPAA are broadly defined, and the *Ford Motor* court's approach of balancing the likely relevance of documents against the burden of their production clearly appears applicable in this case. With this background in mind, we now turn to an analysis of the relevance of the various materials requested in this subpoena.

As noted earlier, of the nine categories of documents subpoenaed by the DOJ, four categories request documents relating to Doe's professional education and training regarding ethical issues. * * *

The government claims that these documents are relevant to its investigation because they go to show Doe's intent. If it were to prosecute Doe for these alleged kickback agreements, the government states that it would have to prove that "[Doe] knew as a general matter that the concept of remuneration for referrals was somehow wrongful (whether illegal or unethical)[.]" The government further states that its request for documents relating to Doe's medical training will aid it in learning the extent to which Doe may have known that the tests to which he was subjecting his patients were medically unnecessary.

The government, through its proffered reasons for requesting documents relating to Doe's professional education and ethical training, has sufficiently shown how these documents are relevant to its underlying health care fraud investigation. The extent to which Doe knew that these tests were medically unnecessary and the extent to which he knew that kickback arrangements were illegal or unethical are not ancillary or unimportant issues in an investigation of possible health care fraud. Thus, this request falls within the broad concept of relevance intended by Congress in § 3486.

As this circuit has stated, however, this court must weigh against the relevance of the requested material the burden that would be placed on Doe in producing it. *Ford Motor.* The extent of Doe's argument regarding the burden imposed by this request is his statement that he "would have to literally put his life on hold and search for papers and documents which stretch *ten years* into the past[,][w]ell beyond any statute of limitations that the Government may apply to any alleged health care offenses." Of the four categories of documents currently under consideration, however, only one, the request for all professional journals, magazines, and newsletters subscribed to or received by Doe from January 1990 through March 1998, has the potential to pose any meaningful burden on Doe. Nevertheless, Doe has made no attempt to reach a reasonable accommodation with the government regarding this aspect of the subpoena, an effort the Supreme Court has suggested should be expected before a court is willing to hold an administrative subpoena overly burdensome. * * * Nor has Doe given us anything but a general and conclusory statement as to why this request constitutes an undue burden. Although Doe's arguments regarding the burden of this subpoena are rather general and conclusory, we do note that the government's investigation of Doe has gone on for more than two years, and that this is the third subpoena requesting documents from Doe issued over this time. While we do not believe that the length of the investigation or the number of subpoenas previously issued to Doe make any further request for documents unreasonable in this case, such factors may be taken into account when deciding whether an administrative subpoena is unduly burdensome.

In sum, we believe that the strong likelihood of the requested documents' relevance to the government's health care fraud investigation outweighs any burden imposed on Doe in producing these documents. Accordingly, this aspect of the government's administrative subpoena will be enforced so long as the final two elements of our administrative subpoena test are met.

The government's subpoena also requested "[c]opies of recent bank and other financial records sufficient to completely show current location, amount, and value of all assets for [John Doe], D.P.M., and/or his health care related businesses," as well as copies of Doe's business and personal tax returns from 1993 to the present. The government asserts that these documents are relevant because they go to show "[Doe]'s profit motive for alleged criminal activity, the degree to which [Doe] profited from illegal activity, and the assets that may be forfeitable as a result of criminal activity." Again, Doe offers no specific reason why the production of these documents would be overly burdensome.

Several courts have recognized that heightened privacy interests are at stake when dealing with personal, as opposed to corporate, financial records. Despite these heightened privacy concerns, the U.S. Courts of Appeals for the Second, Ninth, and District of Columbia Circuits have held that the same standard of reasonable relevance applied to corporate records when requested pursuant to the administrative subpoena power granted to the FDIC and the now-defunct Resolution Trust Corporation ("RTC") to investigate fraudulent asset transfers should also be applied to requests for the private financial records of corporate officials. * * *

We agree with the reasoning of these circuits applying the reasonable relevance standard to subpoenas requesting the personal financial documents of corporate officials, and believe that applying the reasonable relevance standard is particularly appropriate in light of the facts of this case. Doctors operating their own medical clinics or practices, as appears to be the case with Doe, can easily transfer assets from business accounts to personal accounts, arguably even more readily than the corporate officers whose personal financial documents were requested pursuant to the FDIC and RTC subpoenas. To apply a more stringent standard to Doe's personal financial records in this case, in light of the ease with which personal and corporate assets could be commingled and shuttled from one account to another, would be inconsistent with the Congressional mandate given the Attorney General in § 3486 to uncover information relevant to its health care fraud investigation.

Applying the reasonable relevance standard to the government's requests for Doe's personal and business financial records, we again hold that the likely relevance of these documents outweighs the burden imposed on Doe in producing them. Doe has not explained why producing documents related to this portion of the subpoena would burden him, nor has he proffered any argument to refute the government's explanation of the documents' relevance. So long as the remaining elements of the reasonable relevance test are met, we will enforce this aspect of the government's administrative subpoena.[5]

In addition to Doe's personal financial records, the DOJ's administrative subpoena also requested "[c]opies of recent bank and other financial records sufficient to show current location, amount, and value of all assets for any and all children of [John Doe], D.P.M., insofar as those assets were provided or derived from individual or jointly held assets of John Doe, D.P.M." The government requests these documents for many of the same reasons it requested Doe's personal and business financial documents: to determine the degree to which Doe profited from this potentially illegal activity, and the assets that may be forfeitable as a result.

We are more troubled by the government's request for personal financial documents of the children of the target of a health care fraud investigation. Indeed, in other administrative subpoena cases, the U.S. Courts of Appeals for the Second and Ninth Circuits have recognized that family members of an investigation's target "have a greater reasonable expectation of privacy in their personal financial affairs than do those individuals who do participate in such matters."

Although we are more reluctant to enforce this aspect of the administrative subpoena, we believe that it is sufficiently narrowly-tailored to pass the reasonable relevance standard. The DOJ's request for Doe's children's financial documents explicitly limits its reach to only those records concerning assets "provided or derived from individual or jointly held assets of [John Doe], D.P.M." Further evidence of the government's efforts to confine the scope of this portion of the subpoena can be found in correspondence between the government and Doe's attorney following the issuance of the subpoena, in which the government stated that "the request concerning [Doe's] children's assets is limited to information relating to

---

[5] Even if we imposed a higher standard than reasonable relevance for the request of Doe's personal financial documents, we are confident that this standard would be met in this case. The most difficult standard for subpoenaing personal financial records announced by any court of appeals was that in the withdrawn First Circuit decision in *[United States v.] Parks,* in which the court held that an agency would have to show "a reasonable suspicion of wrongdoing[.]" *Parks,* 1995 WL 529629, at *8. In this case, the DOJ has articulated a reasonable suspicion of wrongdoing on the part of Doe. The government has evidence of medical testing laboratories making unusual rental payments to Doe, as well as evidence from independent medical experts stating that one of the labs to which Doe referred patients was performing excessive and unnecessary electrodiagnostic testing. Thus, even under a standard requiring a reasonable suspicion of wrongdoing before a subpoena can be enforced, the government has made a sufficient showing to request Doe's personal financial records.

assets/moneys where [Doe] was the source, and where, presumably, the source of that money was his health-care business."

As his attorney acknowledged at oral argument, Doe's children are minors. Just as Doe could easily commingle assets between his personal and business financial accounts, so also could he transfer ill-gotten gains into the personal accounts of his unsuspecting minor children. Because the government has been careful to avoid a sweeping exploration of Doe's children's assets, we hold that the likely relevance of these documents to the government's health care fraud investigation outweighs the children's heightened privacy interests in guarding this information. Doe has made no other showing of why the production of these documents would be unduly burdensome, and, assuming the final elements of the reasonable relevance test are met, we will enforce the government's narrowly tailored request for specific personal financial documents belonging to Doe's children.

Having concluded our analysis of the relevance of the requested documents to the government's health care fraud investigation, we now proceed to the remaining elements of the reasonable relevance test. * * *

The Supreme Court has stated that a court's process is abused where the subpoena is "issued for an improper purpose, such as to harass the [investigation's target] or to put pressure on him to settle a collateral dispute, or for any other purpose reflecting on the good faith of the particular investigation." *Powell.* Furthermore, in *United States v. LaSalle,* the Court held that any bad faith asserted by a plaintiff may not be based on the improper motives of an individual agency employee, but instead must be founded upon evidence that the agency itself, in an institutional sense, acted in bad faith when it served the subpoena.

Doe asserts that, because this is the third subpoena served to him in two years, it constitutes harassment. While we are troubled by the fact that the government, after two years of investigation and two subpoenas, has now imposed yet another document request on Doe, Doe has proffered no evidence, nor is there any in the record, that would support a conclusion that the DOJ was motivated by an improper purpose when issuing this subpoena. Doe has not met his "heavy" burden of showing institutional bad faith in this case.

Thus, because all the requirements for enforcing an administrative subpoena have been met in this case, we AFFIRM the district court's decision enforcing the administrative subpoena.

NOTES AND QUESTIONS

1. *Reviewing Subpoenas*. Note that the court relied on *Powell*'s four-part test, adopted to determine the propriety of an IRS summons, to review a

subpoena issued by a different administrative agency operating under HIPPA's broader grant of authority. The *Powell* test provides courts with a meaningful, although deferential, standard to review the propriety of an agency subpoena, and the initial burden is on the government to meet show that the subpoena meets the requirements for enforcement. In *R. Enterprises* [p. 361], on the other hand, the Supreme Court largely precluded judicial review of a grand jury subpoena by stating that the subpoena is presumed to have been properly issued unless the recipient could demonstrate that it was unreasonable or oppressive. While *Powell* and its progeny place the initial burden on the government to justify its effort to gather documents, the heavy burden is on the recipient challenging a grand jury subpoena. Is the difference based on the source of the different tests for enforcement? The test for reviewing a grand jury subpoena is Rule 17(c)–"unreasonable or oppressive"–while the court in *John Doe* referred to the Fourth Amendment as the basis for imposing the *Powell* test for enforcement of an administrative subpoena. Is that a meaningful distinction, especially when the production of records pursuant to a subpoena is usually not considered a search subject to the requirements of the Fourth Amendment? Are courts concerned that civil investigations may be more intrusive because there is a much greater degree of regulation of businesses and individuals than there are criminal investigations and prosecutions? Are the privacy concerns expressed in *Boyd* [supra, p. 368] more applicable to a civil investigation than criminal proceedings, in which there are explicit constitutional protections for the accused?

2. *Administrative Subpoenas for Personal Financial Information*. Courts have adopted an even higher level of review for an administrative subpoena compelling an individual to produce their private financial information. The Second Circuit, in **In re McVane**, 44 F.3d 1127 (2d Cir. 1995), refused to enforce a Federal Deposit Insurance Corporation subpoena seeking personal financial records from family members of directors of a failed bank. The court stated:

> [W]e conclude that administrative subpoenas issued pursuant to an agency investigation into corporate wrongdoing, which seek personal records of persons who are not themselves targets of the investigation and whose connection to the investigation consists only of their family ties to corporate participants, must face more exacting scrutiny than similar subpoenas seeking records solely from corporate participants. With regard to subpoenas seeking such material * * * 'an administrative agency is not automatically entitled to obtain all material that may in come way be relevant to a proper investigation. Rather . . . the agency must make some showing of need for the material sought beyond its mere relevance to a proper investigation. (Quoting FEC v. LaRouche Campaign, 817 F.2d 233 (2d Cir. 1987).

In FDIC v. Garner, 126 F.3d 1138 (9th Cir. 1997), the Ninth Circuit accepted the reasoning of *In re McVane* but still enforced the subpoena because there was information indicating that the family members received benefits from the failed bank and so the personal financial records were relevant to the investigation. In Resolution Trust Corporation v. Walde, 18 F.3d 943 (D.C. Cir. 1994), the District of Columbia Circuit refused to enforce a subpoena for personal financial records of former officers and directors of a failed savings bank, holding that "where the RTC has no articulable suspicion to believe that the former officer or director is liable to an S&L in its custody, the RTC may not subpoena his personal financial information for the purpose of assessing the cost-effectiveness of prospective litigation." The same court applied the "articulable suspicion" standard to a subpoena for personal financial records in In re Sealed Case (Administrative Subpoena), 42 F.3d 1412 (D.C Cir. 1994), rejecting the agency's claim that the subpoena sought to uncover "other wrongdoing, as yet unknown" was sufficient to meet the standard for enforcement. The Seventh Circuit, in CFTC v. Collins, 997 F.2d 1230 (7th Cir. 1993), refused to enforce a subpoena for personal tax return information, noting that the agency "asked for and obtained the enforcement of the subpoenas as a matter of rote, upon its bare representation that the tax returns might contain information germane to the investigation. That is not enough, if an appropriate is to be struck between the privacy of income tax returns and the needs of law enforcement."

3. *Third-Party Subpoenas under the RFPA and ECPA*. The Right to Financial Privacy Act requires prior notice to the customer whose information is sought by an administrative subpoena, and that person can challenge the subpoena.   12 U.S.C. § 3410.   Similarly, under the Electronic Communications Privacy Act, the government must provide notice to the person whose stored electronic communications it seeks to obtain by an administrative subpoena, and the person can challenge the subpoena. 18 U.S.C. § 2703.

4. *Continuing the Civil Investigation*. Unlike the limitation on the use of civil investigative authority by the IRS once a criminal referral has been made, other federal agencies may cooperate with the prosecutors and continue the civil investigation while also providing information to the criminal investigators. Recipients of agency subpoenas sought to extend the Supreme Court's decision in *LaSalle National Bank*–now codified in 26 U.S.C. § 7602(b)–that prohibits the IRS from continuing a civil audit once a criminal referral to the Department of Justice has been made, to block enforcement of subpoenas issued after the commencement of a criminal investigation. In **SEC v. Dresser Industries**, 628 F.2d 1368 (D.C. Cir. 1980), the District of Columbia Circuit rejected the argument that the court should deny enforcement of a Securities and Exchange Commission subpoena because the agency had forwarded information to the Department of Justice for use in a grand jury investigation of the same transactions:

> Dresser principally relies on an analogy to *United States v. LaSalle Nat'l Bank*, in which the Supreme Court said in dictum that the Internal Revenue Service (IRS) may not use its summons authority

to investigate possible violations of the tax laws after it has referred those violations to Justice for criminal prosecution. Dresser argues that the SEC's transmittal of Dresser's file to Justice was equivalent to a "referral" under *LaSalle*, and thus that the SEC's power to enforce investigative subpoenas against Dresser in connection with that file lapsed at that time. Alternatively, Dresser suggests that, even if transmittal of the file was not analogous to a "referral" under *LaSalle*, initiation of the grand jury investigation precluded subsequent enforcement of SEC investigative subpoenas into the same matters.

These two alternatives are vulnerable to the same objection: the *LaSalle* rule applies solely to the statutory scheme of the Internal Revenue Code, in which the IRS's civil authority ceases for all practical purposes upon referral of a taxpayer's case to Justice; it does not apply to the securities laws, in which the SEC's civil enforcement authority continues undiminished after Justice initiates a criminal investigation by the grand jury. * * *

Dresser asks this court to extend the reasoning of *LaSalle* to govern the conduct of the SEC under the securities laws. But IRS investigative and enforcement proceedings are not analogous to those of the SEC. The language of the securities laws and the nature of the SEC's civil enforcement responsibilities require that the SEC retain full powers of investigation and civil enforcement action, even after Justice has begun a criminal investigation into the same alleged violations.

The investigative provisions of the securities laws are far broader than Section 7602 of the Internal Revenue Code, as interpreted in *LaSalle*. SEC investigations are not confined to "four purposes only." Rather, the SEC may, "*in its discretion*, make such investigations as *it deems necessary* to determine whether any person has violated, is violating, or is about to violate any provision" of the '34 Act, Section 21(a). Moreover, the SEC is "authorized *in its discretion* * * * to investigate *any* facts, conditions, practices, or matters which *it may deem necessary or proper* to aid in the enforcement of such provisions, in the prescribing of rules and regulations under this chapter, or in securing information to serve as a basis for recommending further legislation concerning matters to which this chapter relates." (emphasis added). Given this broad statutory mandate, there is virtually no possibility that in issuing this subpoena the SEC was acting *ultra vires*. The investigation of Dresser based as it was on the staff's conclusion that Dresser may have engaged in conduct seriously contravening the securities laws falls squarely within the Commission's explicit investigatory authority. Unlike the Internal Revenue Code as interpreted in *LaSalle*, the securities laws offer no suggestion that the scope of the SEC's investigative authority shrinks when a grand jury begins to investigate the same matters. Since the validity of summonses or subpoenas "depend(s) ultimately on whether they were among those authorized by Congress," *United States v. LaSalle Nat'l Bank*, we conclude that this subpoena is enforceable under the rule of that case.

Fulfillment of the SEC's civil enforcement responsibilities requires this conclusion. Unlike the IRS, which can postpone collection of taxes for the duration of parallel criminal proceedings without seriously injuring the public, the SEC must often act quickly, lest the false or incomplete statements of corporations mislead investors and infect the markets. Thus the Commission must be able to investigate possible securities infractions and undertake civil enforcement actions even after Justice has begun a criminal investigation. For the SEC to stay its hand might well defeat its purpose.[a]

5. ***Prosecutorial Use of Information***. An agency ordinarily faces no significant obstacles in sharing with the United States Attorney information it has obtained through its subpoena power, while the United States Attorney must obtain a court order based on a showing of "particularized need" to share "grand jury matter" with an agency. It therefore is not surprising that some United States Attorneys will encourage agencies to carry potential criminal investigations as far forward as possible, rather than have the investigation shifted earlier to the grand jury, so that the information obtained by compulsory process will be readily available to the agency as well as the federal prosecutors. Indeed, such an approach has at times been encouraged by the Department of Justice. Professor Hughes comments:

> Little appears to be left of the old incantation that pursuit of a criminal violation through civil process would be an illegitimate usurpation of the role of the grand jury. If the governing statute clearly bestows on a regulatory agency or on the investigative arm of government the power to investigate criminal violations, the statute will prevail, since courts have rightly acknowledged that no constitutional right is endangered. At the same time, as the cases discussed below demonstrate, the civil agency often may make its

---

[a] Following *Jerry T. O'Brien, Inc.* and *Dresser*, federal courts have similarly rejected the applicability of IRS-type limitations on the exercise of subpoena power by various other governmental agencies. *See* United States v. Aero-Mayflower Transit Co., 831 F.2d 1142 (D.C. Cir. 1987) (subpoena authority of Inspector General of Department of Defense); Donovon v. Spaeda, 757 F.2d 74 (3d Cir. 1985) (Department of Labor Subpoenas); United States v. Merit Petroleum, 731 F.2d 901 (Temp.Emer.Ct.App. 1984) (Department of Energy subpoena); United States v. Gel Spice Co., 773 F.2d 427 (2d Cir. 1985) (F.D.A. inspections); In re Equal Opportunity Employment Commission, 709 F.2d 372 (5th Cir. 1983) (EEOC discovery); United States v. Medic House, Inc., 736 F.Supp. 1531 (W.D. Mo. 1989) (Department of Health and Human Services discovery).

files and the fruit of its compulsory process fully available to a prosecutor, at least until an indictment has been returned. If civil process were more intrusive than grand jury investigation, a sensitive situation would arise, but since the grand jury is the most powerful inquisitorial engine in our system, no problem exists.

Graham Hughes, *Administrative Subpoenas and the Grand Jury: Converging Streams of Criminal and Civil Compulsory Process*, 47 VAND. L. REV. 573 (1994).

6. *Coordinating Civil and Criminal Investigations.* In **United States v. Educational Development Network Corp.**, 884 F.2d 737 (3d Cir. 1989), the Third Circuit rejected a claim that such a maneuver, where designed to avoid the restrictions of grand jury secrecy, constituted an abuse of the agency's subpoena authority. The United States Attorney's office (USAO) had received sufficient information pointing to possible fraudulent practices by a defense contractor to open a grand jury file. The grand jury, however, did not proceed with the investigation. The office of the Inspector General (IG) of the Department of Defense was informed of the information received by the USAO, and the IG subsequently issued a subpoena demanding that the contractor produce various documents. The IG also obtained a search warrant allowing it to search the contractor's facilities and seize many of the same documents. The information obtained by the IG was shared with the USAO, which later presented it to the grand jury and obtained an indictment. The contractor then filed a "motion to compel discovery in aid of a suppression motion alleging that the USAO acted in 'bad faith' when it used IG subpoenas and a search warrant to gather evidence during a joint grand jury/criminal/civil/ administrative/military investigation." The district court held that the defendant had "failed to make out a prima facie case showing of grand jury abuse" and denied the motion (as well as a subsequent motion to suppress). Affirming that ruling, the Third Circuit noted:

> * * * The government candidly admits on appeal that the USAO and DOD agreed to conduct a joint investigation and to use DOD IG subpoenas so that the agencies could share the evidence obtained. * * * [But the appellants contend] that once the USAO's criminal division impaneled the grand jury and filed a notice of disclosure under Rule 6(e) [informing the district court that it intended to utilize certain investigative personnel, who would be bound by Rule 6(e) secrecy], the agency was not free to ignore the grand jury subpoena process and its secrecy requirements in favor of the IG subpoena process. * * *

In presenting their argument appellants place great reliance on Federal Rule of Criminal Procedure 6(e)(2). However, we do not believe Rule 6(e) bars the USAO's criminal division from participating in other agencies' investigations before it actually begins presentation of evidence to the grand jury, and appellants refer us to no statutory or case law to the contrary. * * * In this case the USAO did not present any evidence to the grand jury until January 13, 1988. Therefore, the secrecy requirements of Rule 6(e) did not attach until that time, and the USAO was free to share information uncovered in the joint investigation with the DOD and the Army. What occurred here is the USAO's disclosure of information obtained by the DOD to the grand jury, not the USAO's disclosure of information obtained by the grand jury to the DOD. Therefore Rule 6(e), requiring grand jury secrecy, would seem to have no application. * * *

Appellants also argue that the evidence must be suppressed because the USAO's criminal division obtained it pursuant to subpoenas and a search warrant it had caused to be issued in a bad faith attempt to do an end run around the constitutional requirement that indictments be secured only through a grand jury. EDN and Kress base this argument on the fact that the USAO was involved in the investigation and controlled, at least partially, the issuance of the IG subpoenas. We do not minimize the concerns appellants express about the USAO's criminal division's conceded express avoidance of the grand jury by choosing instead to use the Inspector General's civil investigative powers in the investigation of crime, but they fail to direct us to any statutory, regulatory, or case law that prevents the USAO from doing so. * * *

In denying appellants' request for a hearing and suppression of the evidence, the district court relied on United States v. Aero Mayflower Transmit Co. [supra]. In that case, the Antitrust Division of the Justice Department was investigating the moving and storage industry. In September 1985, the Department of Defense Inspector General began his own investigation of DOD contractors. The Antitrust Division and the FBI contacted the Inspector General and suggested a "cooperative investigation." The Inspector General then issued subpoenas to the appellants, who refused to comply. They argued that the Inspector General had "rubber stamped" the subpoenas and that the real investigator was the Justice Department which should have gotten its subpoenas from a grand jury. The Inspector General's subpoenas, they argued, were therefore issued for an improper purpose. * * * On appeal, the United States Court of Appeals for the District of Columbia Circuit made clear that the Justice Department was free to guide or influence the Inspector General and his subpoenas, "[s]o long as the Inspector General's subpoenas seek information relevant to the discharge of his duties." * * * It said that "no body of law, whether statutory or regulatory, explicitly or implicitly restricts the Inspector General's ability to cooperate with divisions of the Justice Department exercising criminal prosecutorial authority." * * *

* * * Whatever our reservations regarding the USAO's use of IG subpoenas and its degree of involvement in the DOD and Army investigation, appellants' arguments are more properly addressed to the Congress than to a court. * * * Although the USAO's criminal division is traditionally restricted to conducting investigations before a grand jury, on this record we see no law or principle that would prevent it from presenting to the grand jury facts properly uncovered in the course of lawful investigations by another agency.

7. **Sharing Information Not Subject to Grand Jury Secrecy.** The grand jury secrecy obligation of Rule 6(e) applies only to "matter occurring before the grand jury." Recall *In re: Sealed Case No. 99-3091*, p. 487 supra, in which the District of Columbia Circuit discussed what constitutes information subject to the Rule, which was not construed literally as encompassing only events actually taking place before the grand jury. A Department of Justice publication, *Guide on Rule 6(e) After Sells and Baggot* 52-57 (1984), advised government attorneys wishing to share information without obtaining a Rule 6(e)(3)(E)(i) order to gather information "independently" of the grand jury. [See p. 666] One suggested possibility was to encourage an administrative agency interested in the same events to obtain documents and testimony through its subpoena power. Another was the use of search warrants. Consider, however, **In re Grand Jury Subpoena (U.S. v. Under Seal)**, 920 F.2d 235 (4th Cir. 1990), where documents were obtained by IRS agents through a search warrant, prior to the service of grand jury subpoenas, that alone is not dispositive as the court could "easily visualize * * * circumstances where a government investigating agent may, in pursuing an investigation * * * became an agent of the grand jury," with "search warrants and subpoenas * * * used indiscriminately to obtain the targeted information"; here, however, the IRS investigation and the grand jury investigation were not "indiscriminately merged" and the search warrant was based on the "debriefing of informants and surveillance on the targeted residence * * * which was earlier than or apart from the grand jury proceedings".

8. *Public Disclosure of Information.* After an investigation is completed, information obtained by an agency through either compulsory process or voluntary disclosure may be discoverable by private parties under the Freedom of Information Act. 5 U.S.C.A. § 552. The FOIA contains an exemption in § 552(b)(7) for agency "records or information compiled for law enforcement purposes" (applicable to both civil and criminal law enforcement), but that exemption is limited to situations in which disclosure:

(A) could reasonably be expected to interfere with enforcement proceedings, (B) would deprive a person of a right to a fair trial or an impartial adjudication, (C) could reasonably be expected to constitute an unwarranted invasion of personal privacy, (D) could reasonably be expected to disclose the identity of a confidential source including a State, local, or foreign agency or authority or any private institution which furnished information on a confidential basis, * * * (E) would disclose techniques and procedures for law enforcement investigations or prosecutions, or would disclose guidelines for law enforcement investigations or prosecutions if such disclosure could reasonably be expected to risk circumvention of the law, or (F) could reasonably be expected to endanger the life or physical safety of any individual.

As long as the investigation is continuing or an enforcement proceeding is active or can still reasonably be anticipated, the § 552(b)(7)(A) exemption is likely to be available against an FOIA request. See Kay v. F.C.C., 867 F.Supp. 11 (D.D.C. 1994) (interference present in revealing the strength of government's case or the scope of its investigation); Manna v. U.S. Dept. of Justice, 51 F.3d 1158 (3d Cir. 1995) (exemption for records or information compiled for law enforcement purposes, even if government initially compiles records for nonlaw enforcement purposes after request is made but later transfers documents to law enforcement agency seeking to use them for law enforcement purposes, documents satisfy exemption's initial threshold requirement that documents be compiled for law enforcement purposes). But once the matter is closed, settled, or adjudicated, disclosure will ordinarily be available unless some other exemption applies. See James T. O'Reilly, *Federal Information Disclosure* § 17.07 (3d ed. 2002) (noting, however, that "factual interference, not a mere closed status is the issue under (7)(A)" and that such interference is possible where the files on a closed case relate to another, ongoing enforcement proceeding). The "unwarranted-invasion-of-privacy" exemption in (7)(c) relates to "personal matters" not likely to be involved in white collar cases. See United States Department of Justice v. Reporters Committee, 489 U.S. 749 (1989). So too, in the white collar case, the other exemptions noted in (b)(7) apply only under fairly unusual circumstances. See e.g., Church of Scientology International v. U.S. Department of Justice, 30 F.3d 224 (1st Cir. 1994) (exemptions based on government employee privacy, confidential source, and other (b)(7) provisions claimed in response to request for documents by victim of check fraud scheme as to which prosecution had been completed).

More frequently applicable is a separate exemption provision for "trade secrets and commercial or financial information obtained from a person and privileged or confidential." See § 552(b)(4). Where documents might fall in this category they commonly are identified by the party producing the documents as being subject to "FOIA Confidential Treatment," see e.g., In re Steinhardt Partners, L.P., 9 F.3d 230 (2d Cir. 1993). Some agencies have procedures allowing a person making a voluntary submission to obtain an advance agency determination as to whether that information will be viewed by the agency as confidential under this exemption. See 16 C.F.R. § 1101.25 (Consumer Product Safety Commission); 17 C.F.R. 240.24b-2 (Securities & Exchange Commission).

When an agency compels the production of documents that may contain trade secrets or other confidential information, the Supreme Court recognized in Chrysler Corp. v. Brown, 441 U.S. 281 (1979), the right of the party producing such records to intervene and file a "reverse FOIA" claim to block disclosure. The agency may also enter into an agreement with subpoenaed party to provide notice and an opportunity to participate in litigation related to a FOIA claim for confidential information. In **United States v. Chevron U.S.A., Inc.**, 186 F.3d 644 (5th Cir. 1999), a confidentiality agreement proffered by the government to limit disclosure of trade secrets was a basis for the court's determination that enforcement of the administrative subpoena was proper. As described by the court:

> Under protective order ¶ 1, "Protected Competitive Material" (designated pursuant to protective order-procedures) is not to "be disclosed to any other person except in accord with [the protective order] or as may otherwise be required by law." As we directed at oral argument, the Government's post-argument submittal covers its "obligations to preserve the confidentiality of documents obtained through [the IG's] subpoenas."
>
> Concerning the above quoted disclosure-proscription, the Government has stipulated that it "will not disclose Protected Competitive Material to any private party unless compelled to do so by a judicial order entered by a court of competent jurisdiction." In explaining why it has so stipulated, even though a disclosure-order is not explicitly required by the protective order, the Government states in its post-argument submittal that it "construe[s] these [protective order ¶ 1] provisions as barring voluntary governmental disclosure of Protected Confidential Material to Chevron's business competitors or to any other private party." In that the Government has stipulated to no non-order disclosure, and in that, pursuant to protective order ¶ 10, Chevron must be given pre-disclosure notice, it may well be that the court considering disclosure vel non will allow Chevron to first object. In any event, as noted, prior to such disclosure, the Government is to resist to the extent permitted by law and "Chevron [is to] be given as much notice as practical," offering it opportunity to intervene and, inter alia, make a reverse Freedom of Information Act claim.

When a party cooperates with a government investigation by providing otherwise privileged communications or work product to the government, then that will usually constitute a voluntary waiver of the privilege. See Chapter 16.

C. COOPERATION AND DECEPTION

There is often a close collaboration between investigators for a civil agency and prosecutors from the Department of Justice. The administrative agency usually has far superior expertise in the subject matters it regulates, and so can provide valuable assistance to criminal investigators and prosecutors. The agency may have greater access to documents and other materials because of its authority to compel the disclosure of certain information from a regulated entity. The administrative agency may be less threatening to the companies it deals with on a regular basis, and a civil subpoena does not necessarily mean there is a criminal investigation, while a grand jury subpoena or execution of search warrant means a criminal investigation is under way. The targets and subjects of the criminal investigation likely will be much less forthcoming if they are aware of a criminal investigation, so it may be in the interests of prosecutors to use the civil investigation as a means to gather evidence that will be useful in a subsequent criminal prosecution. While some measure of deception on the government's part may be acceptable, questions have been raised when the government uses subterfuge to obtain information through an administrative agency that is misleading about the potential for criminal prosecution. In *S.E.C. v. ESM Government Securities, Inc.*, 645 F.2d 310 (5th Cir. 1981), the court discussed the need for the government to be honest in its dealings with those who it regulates and seeks information from:

> The key to both these cases, we believe, is the nature of the relationship between the government agent and the private citizen. We recognize that much law enforcement activity relies on the use of sanctions by the government. The police officer, the undercover agent, the FBI investigator, all threaten the potential miscreant with discovery and penalties. Thus people obey the law from fear of punishment. Many governments, indeed, depend exclusively on fear for their authority.

> In this country, while we have recognized the importance of sanctions, we have never been willing to rely on them exclusively. Inherent in our democracy is a belief that, since the government represents the will of the people, the people will accept its dictates voluntarily. There is a sense of trust between the government and the people. * * *

> We believe that a private person has the right to expect that the government, when acting in its own name, will behave honorably. When a government agent presents himself to a private individual, and seeks that individual's cooperation based on his status as a government agent, the individual should be able to rely on the agent's representations. We think it clearly improper for a government agent to gain access to records which would otherwise be unavailable to him by invoking the private individual's trust in his government, only to betray that trust. When that government agency then invokes the power of a court to gather the fruits of its deception, we hold that there is an abuse of process. * * *

In holding that fraud, deceit or trickery is grounds for denying enforcement of an administrative subpoena, we exercise the well-established power of the courts to prevent abuse of process. * * * The Supreme Court's directives in *Powell* and *LaSalle* leave no doubt that this power may be properly invoked in cases involving the enforcement of administrative subpoenas. We note that this power is associated with our supervisory power which is distinct from the fourth amendment exclusionary rule, although the goals may sometimes overlap. * * * Consequently, the court should not invoke an automatic exclusionary rule. "The correct approach for determining whether to enforce a summons requires that court to evaluate the seriousness of the violation under all the circumstances, including the government's good faith and the degree of harm imposed by the unlawful conduct." United States v. Bank of Moulton, 614 F.2d 1063 (5th Cir. 1980). Each case must be examined on its facts.

While *E.S.M. Government Securities* spoke of the need to avoid "deceit, fraud, or trickery" when the government deals with a regulated entity, how much of a disclosure duty should the administrative agency have to warn a potential target of a criminal prosecution that an investigation is under way? **In United States v. Medic House, Inc.,** 736 F.Supp. 1531 (W.D. Mo. 1989), the recipient of an administrative subpoena alleged that the investigatory agent made "friendly overtures" to officers of the company and failed to disclose a pending formal criminal investigation when he met with the officers. The District Court found that the government did not engage in improper conduct, stating that "[s]ome kind of affirmative action (or inaction when there was a duty to act) is necessary before fraud, deceit or trickery can be found." At what point does the failure to disclose the fact that a criminal investigation has commenced become actively misleading to a cooperating individual or company? Should the recipient of an administrative subpoena always assume that a criminal investigation may be taking place? Consider the following case.

UNITED STATES v. STRINGER
521 F.3d 1189 (9th Cir. 2008)

SCHROEDER, Circuit Judge:

The United States appeals from a final order of the district court dismissing criminal indictments against three individual defendants charging counts of criminal securities violations. The dismissal was premised on the district court's conclusion that the government had engaged in deceitful conduct, in violation of defendants' due process rights, by simultaneously pursuing civil and criminal investigations of defendants' alleged falsification of the financial records of their high-tech camera sales company. Foreseeing the possibility of an appeal, the district court held that the indictments must be dismissed, but ruled in the alternative that, should there be a criminal trial, all evidence provided by the individual defendants in response to Securities and Exchange Commission ("SEC") subpoenas should be suppressed. * * *

Accepting the district court's factual findings under the clear error standard, we hold that the government's conduct does not amount to a constitutional violation under either the Fourth or Fifth Amendments. We vacate the dismissal of the indictments because in a standard form it sent to the defendants, the government fully disclosed the possibility that information received in the course of the civil investigation could be used for criminal proceedings. There was no deceit; rather, at most, there was a government decision not to conduct the criminal investigation openly, a decision we hold the government was free to make. There is nothing improper about the government undertaking simultaneous criminal and civil investigations, and nothing in the government's actual conduct of those investigations amounted to deceit or an affirmative misrepresentation justifying the rare sanction of dismissal of criminal charges or suppression of evidence received in the course of the investigations. * * *

Background

Prior to the criminal action that forms the basis of this appeal, the SEC began investigating the defendants, J. Kenneth Stringer, III, J. Mark Samper, and William N. Martin, and their company for possible civil securities fraud violations. The company was FLIR Systems, Inc. ("FLIR"), an Oregon corporation headquartered in Portland that sells infrared and heat-sensing cameras for military and industrial use. The SEC began the investigation on June 8, 2000. About two weeks later, the SEC held the first of a series of meetings with the Oregon United States Attorney's Office ("USAO") to coordinate the ongoing SEC investigation with a possible criminal investigation. An SEC Assistant Director and an SEC Staff Attorney met with the supervisor of the white collar crime section of the USAO to discuss the possibility of opening a criminal investigation. The meeting apparently convinced the USAO supervisor to investigate. Within days, the USAO and the Federal Bureau of Investigation ("FBI") opened a criminal investigation.

Federal securities laws authorize the SEC to transmit evidence it has gathered to the USAO to facilitate a criminal investigation by the USAO. To gather evidence for its criminal investigation, the Oregon USAO in June of 2000 sent a letter to the SEC (the "Access Letter") requesting access to the SEC's non-public investigative files, and the SEC promptly granted access.

The civil and criminal investigations proceeded in tandem and the SEC continued to meet and communicate with the USAO and FBI. The SEC turned over documents the SEC collected through its civil investigation.

At the beginning of the criminal investigation, the USAO identified two of the three defendants, FLIR's former CEO, Stringer, and former CFO,

Samper, as possible targets, and named them in the USAO's Access Letter to the SEC. A few months later, in October 2000, the Assistant United States Attorney ("AUSA") assigned to the case made a list of the subjects of the investigation and placed asterisks and the comment "knew what [was] going on" next to the entries for Samper and Stringer. A month later, the AUSA stated in his handwritten notes that Stringer had "lied [about] his role in" the company. In April 2001, an e-mail from the SEC Staff Attorney to the SEC Assistant Director stated the AUSA "define[d] [the] targets as Ken Stringer and Mark Samper."

The district court concluded that the third defendant, Martin, former VP of Sales, was also an early potential target of the criminal investigation. Martin appears on the AUSA's early list of the subjects of the investigation above the comment "knew pushing up sales." During a January 2001 meeting, the SEC advised the USAO and FBI that FLIR was blaming Stringer and Martin for the fraudulent conduct at the heart of the investigation.

Early in the criminal investigation, the USAO decided the investigation should remain confidential. At an October 2000 meeting between the SEC, USAO, and FBI, the AUSA advised that the evidence collected by the SEC might support criminal wire fraud charges. Nonetheless, an internal FBI memo issued in late October stated that the AUSA had concluded, based on the defendants' cooperation with the SEC at that point, that the SEC should investigate "without the assistance or inclusion of the FBI." At the January 2001 meeting between the SEC, FBI, and USAO, the SEC revealed that FLIR was cooperative and was providing evidence that was damaging to Stringer and Martin.

By June 2001, the USAO was not yet ready to convene a grand jury and issue indictments. The SEC and USAO believed that FLIR and defendant Samper would settle with the SEC so long as the U.S. Attorney was not directly involved. During a December 2001 phone conversation between the AUSA assigned to the case and the SEC Assistant Director, the AUSA continued to believe it was "premature [sic] to surface" and that the presence of an AUSA would "impede" a meeting between the SEC and defendants. During a December 2002 phone call, the SEC and USAO decided that the USAO would not "surface", i.e., convene a grand jury and issue indictments, until the "end of Jan/early Feb" 2003.

The SEC facilitated the criminal investigation in a number of ways. The SEC offered to conduct the interviews of defendants so as to create "the best record possible" in support of "false statement cases" against them, and the AUSA instructed the SEC Staff Attorney on how best to do that. The AUSA asked the relevant SEC office, located in Los Angeles, to take the depositions in Oregon so that the Portland Office of the USAO would have venue over any false statements case that might arise from the depositions, and the SEC did so. Both the SEC and USAO wanted the existence of the criminal investigation kept confidential. The SEC Staff Attorney, at one of the

Portland depositions, made a note that she wanted to "make sure [the] court reporters won't tell [FLIR's Attorney]" that there was an AUSA assigned to the case.

The SEC, however, did not hide from the defendants the possibility – even likelihood – of such an investigation. The SEC sent each of the defendants subpoenas in the summer of 2001, and attached to each was Form 1662, a form sent to all witnesses subpoenaed to testify before the SEC. Under the header "Routine Uses of Information," the four-page form states that "[t]he Commission often makes its files available to other governmental agencies, particularly the United States Attorneys and state prosecutors. There is a likelihood that information supplied by you will be made available to such agencies where appropriate."

Form 1662 also advises witnesses of their Fifth Amendment rights. After the heading "Fifth Amendment and Voluntary Testimony," the form states that:

> Information you give may be used against you in any federal . . . civil or criminal proceeding brought by the Commission of any other agency. You may refuse, in accordance with the rights guaranteed to you by the Fifth Amendment of the Constitution of the United States, to give any information that may tend to incriminate you or subject you to fine, penalty, or forfeiture.

None of the defendants invoked his right against self-incrimination during his deposition, and all proceeded to testify in compliance with the subpoena. Each of the defendants was represented by counsel when he testified.

During the course of Stringer's deposition, taken in Portland in October 2001, Stringer's attorney actually questioned the SEC Staff Attorney about the involvement of the USAO. In response to those questions, the SEC Staff Attorney answered as follows:

> MR. MARTSON: My first question is whether Mr. Stringer is a target of any aspect of the investigation being conducted by the SEC.

> STAFF ATTORNEY: The SEC does not have targets in this investigation.

> MR. MARTSON: The other questions I have relate to whether or not, in connection with your investigation, the SEC is working in conjunction with any other department of the United States, such as the U.S. Attorney's Office in any jurisdiction, or the Department of Justice.

> STAFF ATTORNEY: As laid out in the 1662 form, in the "routine use of" section there are routine uses of our investigation, and it is

the agency's policy not to respond to questions like that, but instead, to direct you to the other agencies you mentioned.

MR. MARTSON: And which U.S. Attorney's Office might I inquire into?

STAFF ATTORNEY: That would be a matter up to your discretion.

The record does not show the SEC did anything to impede an inquiry, nor does it disclose that any inquiry was made. The record reflects that the government never furnished defendants with any false information concerning the existence of a criminal investigation.

In September 2002, a year before the criminal indictments, defendants Samper and Martin entered into consent decrees in the civil action, agreeing to pay penalties, disgorgement, and pre-judgment interest. * * *

On September 17, 2003, a grand jury returned an indictment charging Stringer, Samper, and Martin with securities, mail, and wire fraud. Defendants filed motions to dismiss the indictments and to suppress statements they made to the SEC. The district court dismissed the indictments and suppressed the SEC statements because it concluded that the government, in violation of the due process clause, abused its authority to conduct parallel proceedings. The district court held that the government violated defendants' Fifth Amendment due process rights by using trickery and deceit to conceal the criminal investigation from defendants, and conducting a criminal investigation under the auspices of a civil investigation. * * *

Discussion

The Supreme Court has held that the government may conduct parallel civil and criminal investigations without violating the due process clause, so long as it does not act in bad faith. See United States v. Kordel, 397 U.S. 1 (1970). In *Kordel*, the Supreme Court held that the government did not violate the due process rights of corporate executives when it used evidence it obtained from an FDA civil investigation to convict them of criminal misbranding. The Court explained that the FDA did not act in bad faith when it made a request for information, which ultimately was used in the criminal investigation, for the agency made similar requests as a matter of course in 75% of its civil investigations. The Court suggested that the government may act in bad faith if it brings a civil action solely for the purpose of obtaining evidence in a criminal prosecution and does not advise the defendant of the planned use of evidence in a criminal proceeding. The Court thus distinguished the *Kordel* investigation from bad faith cases where

the [g]overnment has brought a civil action solely to obtain evidence for its criminal prosecution or has failed to advise the defendant in its civil proceeding that it contemplates his criminal prosecution; . . . [or] any other special circumstances ... might suggest the unconstitutionality or even the impropriety of this criminal prosecution.

The Supreme Court has not had occasion to address such issues since Kordel, but lower courts have. In SEC v. Dresser Industries, Inc., the D.C. Circuit applied the principles laid down in *Kordel* to a case involving parallel SEC civil and Department of Justice criminal investigations. See 628 F.2d 1368, (D.C.Cir.1980) (en banc). The court emphatically upheld the propriety of such parallel investigations. "Effective enforcement of the securities laws requires that the SEC and Justice be able to investigate possible violations simultaneously." The court said it would refuse to bar such investigations absent unusual circumstances. Id. It said courts should refuse to "block parallel investigations by these agencies in the absence of 'special circumstances' in which the nature of the proceedings demonstrably prejudices substantial rights of the investigated party or of the government."

District courts have occasionally suppressed evidence or dismissed indictments on due process grounds where the government made affirmative misrepresentations or conducted a civil investigation solely for purposes of advancing a criminal case. See, e.g., United States v. Posada Carriles, 486 F.Supp.2d 599, 615 (W.D.Tex. 2007); United States v. Rand, 308 F.Supp. 1231, 1233 (N.D.Ohio 1970).

In this case, the district court concluded that the government should have told defendants of the criminal investigation and that it violated the standards laid down in *Kordel* when it failed to "advise defendants that it anticipated their criminal prosecution." It held that the government engaged in "trickery and deceit" when the SEC staff attorney instructed court reporters to refrain from mentioning the AUSA's involvement. When the SEC staff attorney responded to Stringer's attorney's question, during Stringer's deposition, by directing him to the U.S. Attorney, the district court concluded that the SEC attorney "evaded the question."

In its appeal, the government argues that it had no legal duty to make any further disclosure of the existence of the pending criminal investigation. It points to the warnings in Form 1662 in which the government disclosed the possibility of criminal prosecution, and it stresses that it did not make any affirmative misrepresentations. It maintains the SEC attorney's answer was appropriate and truthful.

The defendants argue that the district court properly held that the use of the evidence obtained by the SEC in a criminal prosecution would violate defendants' Fifth Amendment privilege against self-incrimination. The defendants were advised that the evidence could be used in a criminal investigation, but defendants did not invoke their Fifth Amendment privilege during the SEC investigation. The government on appeal correctly contends that defendants waived or forfeited their Fifth Amendment right against self-incrimination.

The privilege against self-incrimination protects an individual from being forced to provide information that might establish a direct link in a chain of evidence leading to his conviction. Hoffman v. United States, 341 U.S. 479, 486 (1951). It may be waived if it is not affirmatively invoked. In *Minnesota v. Murphy*, the Supreme Court stressed that the privilege is lost if not affirmatively invoked, even if the defendant did not make a knowing and intelligent waiver. 465 U.S. 420 (1984). * * *

The district court therefore erred in holding that defendants' waivers of the privilege were ineffective because they were not told of the U.S. Attorney's active involvement. The SEC Form 1662 used in this case alerts SEC investigative witnesses that the information can be used in a criminal proceeding. Defendants were on sufficient notice, and so were their attorneys. As one federal court has explained, all that was required was "sufficient notice . . . that any information could be used against [them] in a subsequent criminal proceeding." United States v. Teyibo, 877 F.Supp. 846 (S.D.N.Y.1995). That court emphasized that "SEC Form 1662 stated in no uncertain terms that the [g]overnment's request for information could be refused pursuant to the Fifth Amendment's protection against compelled self-incrimination." We agree.

The SEC here went even further, warning each defendant at the beginning of each deposition that "the facts developed in this investigation might constitute violations of . . . criminal laws." Nonetheless, defendants proceeded to testify and failed to invoke their privilege against self-incrimination. Defendants have forfeited any claims that the use of their testimony against them in the criminal proceedings violates the privilege against self-incrimination.

The defendants next contend that the district court properly concluded that the government used the civil investigation solely to obtain evidence for a subsequent criminal prosecution, in violation of due process. The Supreme Court in *Kordel* made it clear that dual investigations must meet the requirements of the Fifth Amendment Due Process Clause. While holding that "[i]t would stultify the enforcement of federal law" to curtail the government's discretion to conduct dual investigations strategically, the Court suggested that a defendant may be entitled to a remedy where "the [g]overnment has brought a civil action solely to obtain evidence for its criminal prosecution." In this case, the government argues that it did not violate defendants' due process rights because the civil investigation was not commenced solely to obtain evidence for a criminal prosecution.

It is significant to our analysis that the SEC began its civil investigation first and brought in the U.S. Attorney later. This tends to negate any likelihood that the government began the civil investigation in bad faith, as, for example, in order to obtain evidence for a criminal prosecution. In *United*

States v. Unruh, 855 F.2d 1363 (9th Cir. 1987), we held that a defendant was not entitled to dismissal of his indictment when the U.S. Department of the Treasury instituted its investigation before any indictment and in order to file its own civil complaint.

United States v. Posada Carriles, 486 F.Supp.2d 599, 619-21 (W.D.Tex.2007), on the other hand, is a clear example of government bad faith. The district court dismissed an indictment because the U.S. Citizenship and Immigration Services ("USCIS") interviewed the defendant solely to collect evidence in support of a criminal case against him. The defendant, a Cuban national, filed an application for naturalization. Although USCIS had already determined that the defendant was not eligible for citizenship, the agency nonetheless invited him to a pre-citizenship interview in order to collect evidence for a crimina false statements case. The interview protocol was altered in so many ways to serve the needs of the criminal investigation that it became an interrogation. The court described the "interview" as follows:

> (1) it lasted eight hours over the course of two days as opposed to the usual maximum of thirty minutes, (2) it involved two interviewers, (3) the [g]overnment provided an interpreter, (4) there were a total of four attorneys present-two defense attorneys and two Government attorneys, and (5) it was both audio and videotaped.

Because the "entire interview was . . . a pretext for a criminal investigation," the district court dismissed the indictment.

Our case is not remotely similar to *Posada Carriles*. In this case the SEC's civil investigation was opened first, led to SEC sanctions and was conducted pursuant to the SEC's own civil enforcement jurisdiction. It was not a pretext for the USAO's criminal investigation of defendants. Congress has expressly authorized the SEC to share information with the Department of Justice to facilitate the investigation and prosecution of crimes. We must conclude the SEC interviewed the defendants in support of a bona fide civil investigation. There was no violation of due process.

Defendant appellees finally contend that the district court properly concluded that dismissal or, in the alternative, suppression, was warranted because the government lulled the defendants into turning over incriminating evidence by engaging in "trickery and deceit." It was dispositive for the district court that the SEC staff attorney instructed court reporters to refrain from mentioning the AUSA's involvement and that the SEC gave evasive answers to questions about the imminence of a dual investigation. We have previously applied the Fourth Amendment's bar to unreasonable searches and seizures in the context of dual investigations by the civil and criminal branches of the IRS, where review of documentary evidence is inherent in the investigation. We have thus held that a search is unreasonable, even if consensual, if the consent is obtained by trickery or deceit. While not every SEC and USAO dual investigation will necessarily involve a search and seizure, to the extent that the individual defendants may have been led through trickery or deceit to turn over documentary or physical evidence in their possession or to use their official authority to turn over evidence in the possession of the corporation, the defendants could state a claim under the Fourth Amendment.

Other circuits have agreed that Fourth Amendment and possible due process limitations may be implicated in a dual investigation. See United States v. Peters, 153 F.3d 445 (7th Cir.1998) ("A consensual search is unreasonable under the Fourth Amendment or violative of due process under the Fifth Amendment if the consent was induced by fraud, deceit, trickery or misrepresentation."). Almost every other circuit has denied suppression, even when government agents did not disclose the possibility or existence of a criminal investigation, so long as they made no affirmative misrepresentations.

The district court in this case relied on the Eighth Circuit's opinion in [United States v. Grunewald, 987 F.2d 531 (8th Cir.1993)], which said it would be a "flagrant disregard of individuals' rights" to "deliberately deceive, or even lull" a person into incriminating themselves in a criminal investigation being pursued under the guise of a civil one. The Eighth Circuit was referring to the criminal defendant's argument that he was the victim of a criminal investigation being pursued in the guise of a civil tax audit. The court rejected the argument and affirmed the district court's denial of suppression because there had been no deceit. * * *

In this case, the SEC made no affirmative misrepresentations. The SEC did advise defendants of the possibility of criminal prosecution. The SEC engaged in no tricks to deceive defendants into believing that the investigation was exclusively civil in nature. The SEC's Form 1662 explicitly warned defendants that the civil investigation could lead to criminal charges against them: "Information you give may be used against you in any federal . . . civil or criminal proceeding brought by the Commission or any other agency." Defendants were represented by counsel, and the government provided counsel, so far as this record reflects, with accurate information. The standard we laid down in Robson was not violated.

The defendant-appellees point to a number of collateral facts they argue demonstrate trickery or deliberate misleading. They argue the SEC Staff Attorney affirmatively misled Stringer's attorney when, in response to the attorney's question about other agency involvement, she directed him to the provision in Form 1662 that warned that the SEC would likely turn over to the USAO evidence it collected at the depositions. The Staff Attorney, during the deposition taken in Portland, declined to direct defense counsel to a specific U.S. Attorney's Office, which would have been the Portland Office, but there was nothing false or misleading in her response that it was up to the defendant to decide where to direct his inquiries.

The defendant-appellees also point to the Staff Attorney's request to the court reporters not to mention the AUSA in the presence of defendants' attorneys. While this indicates an intent to prevent disclosure to defendants of the actual criminal investigation, the possibility of criminal investigation should have been well known to both the defendants and their counsel. The request to the court reporters to, in effect, mind their own business did not mislead or misinform defendants about the existence of an investigation. Thus, to the extent that the Fourth Amendment may have been implicated by the dual investigation, the district court erred in concluding that the government's actions in this case constituted an unreasonable search or seizure. * * *

For the foregoing reasons, we conclude that there was no deception or affirmative misconduct on the part of the government in the course of the SEC and U.S. Attorney investigations that warranted dismissal of the indictment or suppression of any of the evidence in question. In addition, defendants' Fifth Amendment rights were not violated.

D. PARALLEL PROCEEDINGS

1. Types of Parallel Proceedings

White collar criminal offenses frequently involve common law torts or violations of statutes or administrative codes that can lead to administrative sanctions, civil fines, or civil damage actions. A substantial potential exists for simultaneous or seriatim criminal, civil, and administrative proceedings based upon essentially the same activities. Such "parallel proceedings" present a variety of legal questions, such as whether voluntarily providing information waives the attorney-client privilege (see Chapter 15), but the one that has attracted the most attention is the extent to which parallel proceedings can be utilized to develop information in one type of proceeding that will be available to litigants in another.

The "parallel proceedings" problem can arise in almost any type of litigation, in addition to administrative agency investigations. For example, evidence developed in private litigation involving securities fraud, *qui tam* actions for defrauding the government, and consumer fraud class actions is often used by the government in subsequent enforcement actions. In other cases, plaintiffs or defendants in civil actions will learn about a governmental investigation after the civil case commences, which will raise issues regarding whether to provide information that may be incriminating and whether civil discovery may be used to gain information related to a criminal investigation that might not otherwise be available. The problem is not limited to parties to litigation. Consider In re Grand Jury Subpoena, 836 F.2d 1468 (4th Cir. 1988), in which third-party deponents in one state refused to testify in a federal civil suit in another state until the court issued a protective order ostensibly prohibiting disclosure of their deposition transcripts. The Fourth

Circuit held in that case that the grand jury in another state has a per se right to obtain evidence regardless of the protective order, which makes it even more likely that a witness will assert the Fifth Amendment rather than testify if there is any possibility that the information will be incriminating. The efficacy of protective orders in civil litigation is discussed in Chapter Nine, supra.

This chapter considers information sharing as it relates to the civil case presented simultaneously with, or in advance of, a criminal investigation or prosecution (Section B), and the grand jury investigation that is followed by civil or administrative proceedings (Section C).

2. Use of Civil Discovery in a Criminal Prosecution

In **United States v. Kordel**, 397 U.S. 1 (1970), the Supreme Court rejected two constitutional challenges to parallel civil and criminal proceedings, which had been brought by the United States Attorney. Initially, the United States Attorney, following an investigation by the Food and Drug Administration, instituted a civil in rem action against two food products produced by the corporation of which Kordel and Feldten were president and vice president. The in rem action sought to seize and condemn the products on the ground that they were being distributed in violation of the Food, Drug, and Cosmetic Act. In connection with that suit, the United States Attorney served on the corporation, pursuant to Rule 33 of the Federal Rules of Civil Procedure, extensive interrogatories that had been pprepared by FDA personnel. Shortly thereafter, the FDA served notice upon the corporation and its two officers informing them that the agency was contemplating recommending a criminal prosecution and that they had the opportunity to present their views in opposition. The corporation immediately moved to stay further proceedings in the civil action, or in the alternative to extend its time for answering the interrogatories until after the disposition of the anticipated criminal proceedings. The motion was denied, however, and the corporation was ordered to answer the interrogatories, which was done through Feldten. The civil case was subsequently settled, and Feldten and Kordel were thereafter prosecuted and convicted at a trial in which the government utilized Feldten's answers to the interrogatories to "provid[e] evidence or leads useful to the Government."

Finding no Fifth Amendment violation in the use of the civil discovery as evidence in the criminal prosecution, Justice Stewart's opinion for the Court stated:

> Feldten need not have answered the interrogatories. Without question he could have invoked his Fifth Amendment privilege against compulsory self-incrimination. Surely Feldten was not barred from asserting his privilege simply because the corporation had no privilege of its own, or because the proceeding in which the Government sought information was civil rather than criminal in

character. To be sure, service of the interrogatories obliged the corporation to "appoint an agent who could, without fear of self-incrimination, furnish such requested information as was available to the corporation." The corporation could not satisfy its obligation under Rule 33 simply by pointing to an agent about to invoke his constitutional privilege. * * * Such a result would effectively permit the corporation to assert on its own behalf the personal privilege of its individual agents. * * * The respondents press upon us the situation where no one can answer the interrogatories addressed to the corporation without subjecting himself to a "real and appreciable" risk of self-incrimination. For present purposes we may assume that in such a case the appropriate remedy would be a protective order under Rule 30(b), postponing civil discovery until termination of the criminal action. But we need not decide this troublesome question. For the record before us makes clear that even though the respondents had the burden of showing that the Government's interrogatories were improper, they never even asserted, let alone demonstrated, that there was no authorized person who could answer the interrogatories without the possibility of compulsory self-incrimination. * * *

For a prospective criminal defendant, the perils of responding to civil discovery go beyond possibly providing leads to incriminatory information that could help the prosecution in building its criminal case-in-chief. Even where the privilege against self-incrimination would not be available legally because the information sought in the civil discovery presents no "real and appreciable" risk of providing a "link in the chain" of a prosecutor's proof of a crime, there remains the tactical disadvantage of exposing at this early point the basis of a defense that, in all likelihood, would not have to be revealed in the criminal prosecution until the trial itself. Where the opposing litigant is the government, however, the prospective defendant may find that disadvantage more than offset by the potential for using civil discovery to obtain information about the government's case that would not be available through pretrial criminal discovery. Federal Rule of Criminal Procedure 16 governs discovery in criminal cases, and it provides significantly less discovery than the Federal Rules of Civil Procedure.

3. *Qui Tam* Actions

Parallel civil actions brought by private parties take many forms. Of special concern to those entities selling goods or services to the federal government is a whistleblower's *qui tam* action. The *qui tam* action is authorized under the Civil False Claims Act, 31 U.S.C.A. § 3729, which creates civil and criminal liability for a broad range of "false claims" against the government (e.g., knowingly presenting false invoices or supporting documents, knowingly shorting the government in the delivery of property, and knowingly using false records to conceal or decrease an obligation owed to government). The *qui tam* action is a civil action for violation of the False Claims Act brought on behalf of the *qui tam* relator as an individual and on behalf of the government by the relator. The term *"qui tam"* derives from the Latin *"qui tam pro domino rege quam pro sic ipso in hoc parte sequitur,"* meaning "who as well for the king as for himself sues in this manner." See Michelle D. Bernard, *Qui Tam Litigation Under the Civil and Criminal False Claims Act,* 1994 *Complex Crimes Journal* 193.

The filing of the *qui tam* action makes the *qui tam* relator and the government co-plaintiffs in the action. Upon filing, the relator must serve upon the government both the complaint and a "written disclosure of substantially all material evidence and information the person possesses." The government then has at least 60 days to decide whether to take over the action. During that period, the complaint, which is filed *in camera,* must remain under seal. If the government chooses to intervene in the action, it has the primary responsibility for prosecuting the action and is not bound by an act of the *qui tam* relator. The relator has the right to continue as a party to the action, but the government may limit the relator's authority to call witnesses and cross-examine adverse witnesses, and may dismiss or settle the action without the relator's consent.

If the government declines to intervene, the relator has the right to conduct the action and no person other than the government may intervene or bring a related action based on the same underlying facts. The government may also take steps that, in effect, splinter the action. This is done when it files an amended complaint that includes some but not all of the claims contained in the relator's complaint. The unadopted claims, if the government does not move to dismiss them, can then be removed from under seal with the approval of the court, allowing the relator to proceed upon them. This leaves the defendant subject to two complaints, with one under the control of the government and the other under the control of the relator. But see Bernard, supra, at 209 (noting the Department of Justice's position that "relators are jurisdictionally barred under § 3730(e)(3) from separately continuing unadopted claims that arise out of the same facts and transactions as the claims adopted by the government").

Where the government decides to intervene, the *qui tam* relator will receive between 15-25% of the proceeds of any judgment or settlement, depending upon the "extent to which the relator substantially contributed to the prosecution of the action." § 3730(d)(1). If the government chooses not to participate the relator ordinarily receives "an amount which the court decides is reasonable for collecting the civil penalty or damages" which must be at least twenty-five percent but not more than thirty percent of the proceeds of the action or any settle. §3730(d)(2).[b]

---

[b] Under certain circumstances, the relator's share may be reduced below these general ranges. If a case was based "primarily" (but not entirely) on specific information that had been publicly disclosed and the government has intervened, "the court may award such sums as it considers appropriate, but in no case more than ten percent of the proceeds, taking into account the significance of the information and the role of the person bringing the action in advancing the case to litigation." §

4. Shareholder Derivative Suits

It is common for shareholders of a corporation to file a derivative action related to wrongdoing in the business alleging the directors and officers breached their fiduciary duties to the company. While the attorney-client privilege, which is discussed in greater detail in Chapter Fifteen, usually protects internal communications related to an internal investigation of the company, shareholders can seek to obtain otherwise privileged communications as part of the derivative litigation. There is a risk that the privileged information could be disclosed to prosecutors and civil investigative agencies. In describing whether the corporation can be compelled to disclose communications protected by the attorney-client privilege to shareholders, the Fifth Circuit in *Garner v. Wolfinbarger*, 430 F.2d 1093 (5th Cir.1970) stated:

> The attorney-client privilege still has viability for the corporate client. The corporation is not barred from asserting it merely because those demanding information enjoy the status of stockholders. But where the corporation is in suit against its stockholders on charges of acting inimically to stockholder interests, protection of those interests as well as those of the corporation and of the public require that the availability of the privilege be subject to the right of the stockholders to show cause why it should not be invoked in the particular instance.

E. *DELAYING THE PARALLEL CIVIL ACTION*

A party in a civil suit who faces the possibility of a parallel criminal proceeding may seek to stay the civil proceeding pending the outcome of the criminal proceeding. The general principles that guide a court's decision as to whether to grant such a stay are analyzed in a widely cited article by District Judge Milton Pollack:

> Generally, the courts have great discretion in regard to this question and, as you may expect, must balance the competing concerns of the private (or Government) plaintiff with the harm to the defendant by letting both proceedings go forward at once under special circumstances. In addition, a court should consider any prejudice which would be caused to both parties and non-parties if the civil suit is delayed and should consider the convenience to the courts as

---

3730(d)(1). If the government has declined to intervene in such a case, there is no such limitation. Also, if the relator "planned and initiated" the fraudulent activity that is the subject of the case, the court may reduce the relator's award to the extent the court considers appropriate, "taking into account the role of that person in advancing the case to litigation and any relevant circumstances pertaining to the violation." If the relator is convicted of criminal conduct arising from his or her role in the violation, then no share of the proceeds can go to the relator. § 3730(d)(3).

well. * * * In more practical terms, the courts generally treat four factors as significant, if not dispositive, weights which can tip the balance either in favor of or against a stay of the plaintiff's quest for discovery. These four factors are: (1) the commonality of transactions or issues, (2) the timing of the motion, (3) judicial efficiency, and (4) the public interest.

First. The most important factor at the threshold is the degree to which the civil issues overlap with the criminal issues. Some civil issues are irrelevant to related criminal proceedings. For example, the issue of damages for wrongful death would not arise in most related criminal negligence prosecutions; in such a case, a stay of the civil proceedings on the issue of damages would rarely be appropriate.

Second. The current stage of the parallel criminal proceeding will often substantially affect the net balance of equities. Is resolution nearby or remote in time? * * * The strongest case for a stay of discovery in the civil case occurs during a criminal prosecution after an indictment is returned. * * * The potential for self-incrimination is greatest during this stage, and the potential harm to civil litigants arising from delaying them is reduced due to the promise of a fairly quick resolution of the criminal case under the Speedy Trial Act. See, e.g., *Dresser* [p. 625].

The chances of the defendant's procuring a stay are less favorable (but still possible) if the government is conducting an active parallel criminal *investigation* in which an indictment or information has not yet been filed. * * * If no indictment has been returned and no known investigation is underway, the case for a stay of discovery, no matter at whose instance, is "far weaker." * * * If criminal proceedings are over or there is no substantial criminal exposure, the courts are most likely to deny a delay of plaintiff's discovery or other pre-trial relief. The accused's trial tactics have already been exposed, and the likelihood of self-incrimination may be diminished, particularly if the defendant has testified at trial. And, the appeal process is an uncertain, potentially long-ranging, process. Only unusual circumstances would justify an order staying a post-conviction civil proceeding. * * *

Third. Judicial efficiency is also a factor in the balancing analysis. Resolution of the criminal case may increase prospects for settlement of the civil case. Due to differences in the standards of proof between civil suits and criminal prosecutions, the possibility always exists for a collateral estoppel or res judicata effect on some or all of the overlapping issues. Conviction of a defendant in a parallel criminal case may effectively dispose of all common issues in a subsequent civil action, although the reverse is not true. Thus, it was held that a district court did not abuse its discretion in deciding that judicial economy was best served by granting a stay of the civil case, where the proceedings involved substantial overlap of issues such that "resolution of the criminal case would moot, clarify, or otherwise affect various contentions in the civil case." United States v. Mellon Bank, N.A., 545 F.2d 869, 873 (3d Cir. 1976). This, however, might be thought to assume that the criminal proceedings will result in a conviction of the defendant, which as you know should not and cannot be predicted prematurely. And again, the degree to which the issues in the two proceedings overlap will greatly influence the extent to which such issues may later be precluded at all.

Fourth. The effect of a stay of the civil case upon the "public interest" is perhaps the most important factor in the equation, albeit the one hardest to define. As I noted before, both plaintiffs and defendants have an interest in a timely judgment. In civil securities actions, the public has an interest in the maintenance of and preservation of the integrity of the securities market. These interests can be substantially prejudiced by stays imposing significant delays upon the civil proceeding. To this end it would behoove both the litigants and the court to tailor a stay at the instance of the defendant (if one is to be granted) to minimize any delays upon the process.

One additional, although relatively uncommon, factor which almost inevitably results in a denial of a motion for a stay is where the movant intentionally creates the impediment which he seeks to erect as a shield. Thus, where a criminal defendant pleads guilty to criminal charges and agrees to assist the government's prosecution of others while keeping such matters confidential, it is questionable whether at his insistence the civil proceedings against him should be held in abeyance because he purportedly cannot disclose confidential information in his answer to a civil complaint pursuant to his agreement with the Department of Justice and pursuant to the Fifth Amendment. See Arden Way Associates v. Boesky, 660 F.Supp. 1494 (S.D.N.Y. 1987). * * *

Judge Milton Pollack, *Parallel Civil Criminal Proceedings*, 129 F.R.D. 201 (1989). Consider how the court balanced the competing equities in the following opinion.

AFRO-LECON, INC. v. UNITED STATES
820 F.2d 1198 (Fed. Cir. 1987)

NICHOLS, Senior Circuit Judge.

Afro-Lecon, Inc. (Afro-Lecon) appeals the final decision of the General Services Administration Board of Contract Appeals (board), denying Afro-Lecon's motion to stay proceedings in its civil action relating to United States contract No. SB2-10-8(a)80C-045 until after the completion of related criminal proceedings against Afro-Lecon and dismissing the civil claim with prejudice. We vacate and remand.

The Small Business Administration awarded a subcontract to Afro-Lecon on February 29, 1980, to supply 18,298 filing cabinets for the General Services Administration (GSA). After disputes developed concerning the contract, the parties entered into a settlement agreement in October 1982 that terminated the contract without termination costs and preserved Afro-Lecon's right to assert claims concerning the delivered portion of the contract.

On June 8, 1983, Afro-Lecon submitted a certified claim, pursuant to this agreement, for costs through October 12, 1982. The basis of the claim was that the GSA delayed issuing purchase orders and bills of lading thereby increasing the company's costs. The contracting officer denied the claim on April 11, 1984, and Afro-Lecon appealed to the board.

The GSA, in preparation of its case before the board, requested discovery of the dates of the delay periods, the costs incurred during these periods, and the causal relationship between the government's actions and the claimed costs. Afro-Lecon did not respond to the satisfaction of the GSA. The GSA then issued a second set of interrogatories and a second document request. Afro-Lecon objected to the second discovery request and the agency then filed a motion to compel discovery, which the board granted on May 9, 1985. The responses provided by Afro-Lecon continued to be unacceptable to the GSA. On July 3, 1985, the board issued an order on accounting, which required Afro-Lecon to provide a detailed account of its claim with a response due by September 4, 1985.

In late July 1985, Afro-Lecon learned that it was the subject of a grand jury investigation regarding the civil claims before the board. On September 4, 1985, Afro-Lecon moved to suspend the civil proceedings because key witnesses such as officers, former employees, and consultants, were advised by counsel not to participate in the response to the order on accounting or in any portion of the civil litigation in order to avoid incrimination in the criminal proceedings. On October 17, 1985, the Assistant U.S. Attorney for the Western District of New York notified Afro-Lecon that the company and its president, Benjamin Okumabua, were potential defendants in a grand jury investigation into whether the company's claims were false, in violation of 18 U.S.C. §§ 641 and 1001.

On January 17, 1986, the board denied Afro-Lecon's September 4 motion for a stay of the civil appeal and required the company to respond to the order on accounting by February 18, 1986. In early February the grand jury, empaneled in the United States District Court for the Western District of New York, indicted Afro-Lecon and Okumabua for making false claims against the government. On February 15, 1986, Afro-Lecon renewed its motion to stay the civil proceedings in view of the indictment. The board denied the stay and dismissed the company's civil appeal on April 11, 1986. The board, in reaching this conclusion, noted that the refusal of crucial Afro-

Lecon witnesses to testify made it impossible for Afro-Lecon to comply with the order on accounting. The board decided, however, that Afro-Lecon, as the party asserting the civil claim, could not use the fifth amendment as a basis to defer civil proceedings. * * *

The question in this case is whether the board properly denied Afro-Lecon's motion to stay the company's civil claim until completion of the criminal trial which concerned the same facts. This turns on whether the board has a right and duty to proceed in these circumstances and whether Afro-Lecon can maintain its civil suit and, at the same time, claim the fifth amendment privilege against self-incrimination. * * * We conclude that the board, in the exercise of its undoubted discretion, was mistaken in its analysis of the applicable legal standards in this case, and to Afro-Lecon's prejudice. * * *

Although the fifth amendment claims per se are not, as we shall show, the only consideration in the analysis of the propriety of parallel proceedings, we address the fifth amendment claims first in view of the emphasis placed on the fifth amendment claims by the parties and the board.

The fifth amendment provides that "[n]o person * * * shall be compelled in any criminal case to be a witness against himself * * *. U.S. Const. amend. V. The board, citing United States v. Rylander, 460 U.S. 752 (1983) and Smith v. Black Panther Party, 458 U.S. 1118 (1982), concluded that in a civil suit, a party placing facts in issue may not rely upon the fifth amendment to avoid disclosure of such facts and still maintain the suit. [The court declined "to accept the interpretation of Black Panther as suggested by the board."].

* * * The second case relied on by the board, Rylander, did not concern the issue of parallel criminal and civil proceedings. The Court in Rylander considered the evidentiary effect of a fifth amendment claim and concluded that the fifth amendment does not excuse a claimant from meeting the appropriate burden of proof in his case. In the case at bar, Afro-Lecon recognizes that it is not possible to establish its civil case without producing the appropriate evidence and, therefore, requests only a stay of the civil proceedings. It does not ask to be excused from producing evidence before it can recover.

The board's scenario of the appellant waving its sword, the contract claim, over the government's head, while unfairly invoking the privilege against self- incrimination to deny the government access to evidence essential as its shield, is overstrained. In the first place, the government already has the evidence it improperly seized for the criminal trial. In the second place, the government has the money in dispute, which it retains while the stay, if granted, lasts. In the third place, a proceeding in a board of contract appeals is not precisely a combat arena. It is a mode of dispute resolution resorted to by election of the parties in a tribunal which is part of the government's own executive branch. The appellant is not necessarily waving the sword because the government may be seeking money from the appellant, not the other way around. If an appellant seeking money is willing to await the outcome of the criminal trial, the board does not point out how the government is prejudiced by delay. It is the government which wishes to deny the mode of dispute resolution it has contracted for, as a price for asserting a constitutional right.

We now consider the appropriate standards for determining whether a stay of the civil proceedings should have been granted in this case. The Constitution does not require a stay of civil proceedings pending the outcome of criminal proceedings. A court, however, has the discretion to stay civil proceedings, postpone civil discovery, or impose protective orders and conditions "when the interests of justice seem[ ] to require such action, sometimes at the request of the prosecution, * * * sometimes at the request of the defense[.]" United States v. Kordel, 397 U.S. 1 (1970).

* * * [T]he circumstances that weigh in favor of granting a stay include malicious prosecution, the absence of counsel for defendant during depositions, agency bad faith, malicious government tactics, and "other special circumstances." * * *

The court in [SEC v. Dresser Industries, 628 F.2d 1368 (D.C. Cir. 1980, supra p. 625] outlined the circumstances of parallel proceedings in clear terms:

> Other than where there is specific evidence of agency bad faith or malicious governmental tactics, the strongest case for deferring civil proceedings until after completion of criminal proceedings is where a party under indictment for a serious offense is required to defend a civil or administrative action involving the same matter. The noncriminal proceeding, if not deferred, might undermine the party's Fifth Amendment privilege against self-incrimination, expand rights of criminal discovery beyond the limits of Federal Rule of Criminal Procedure 16(b), expose the basis of the defense to the prosecution in advance of criminal trial, or otherwise prejudice the case. If delay of the noncriminal proceeding would not seriously injure the public interest, a court may be justified in deferring it.

We agree with the court's assessment in *Dresser* that parallel proceedings may result in the abuse of discovery. We discuss, infra, the question of whether the position of the claimant, e.g., as plaintiff or defendant, is relevant. Although the government does not concede that discovery abuse is a concern in this case, it does admit on appeal that the evaluation of the motion to stay is multifaceted and not limited to the narrow issue of whether a corporation has a fifth amendment right.

The scope of civil discovery is broad and requires nearly total mutual disclosure of each party's evidence prior to trial. Hickman v. Taylor, 329 U.S. 495 (1947). Rule 26 broadly authorizes discovery of "any matter, not privileged, which is relevant to the subject matter involved in the pending action[.]" Fed.R.Civ.P. 26(b)(1). The information sought during discovery in a civil case need not be admissible at trial and need only be reasonably calculated to lead to discovery of admissible evidence.

Criminal "discovery" under the federal rules, in contrast, is highly restricted. For example, Rule 15 controls the deposition process and permits a party to an action to depose only its own witnesses and then only pursuant to a court order in "exceptional circumstances." Fed.R.Crim.P. 15(a). The civil rules, in contrast, allow depositions of all parties to the action and any other person necessary to obtain testimony relevant to the subject matter of the action. Fed.R.Civ.P. 26. Rule 15 also provides that the defendant cannot be deposed without his consent and that the scope of cross-examination must be the same as at trial. Fed.R.Crim.P. 15(d). Rule 16 also significantly restricts discovery in criminal cases by describing what is discoverable with specificity and detail.

The broad scope of civil discovery may present to both the prosecution, and at times the criminal defendant, an irresistible temptation to use that discovery to one's advantage in the criminal case. Such unconstitutional uses may begin with the surreptitious planting of criminal investigators in civil depositions, as in the case at bar, and end with passive abuses, such as when the civil party, who asserts fifth amendment rights, is compelled to refuse to answer questions individually, revealing his weak points to the criminal prosecutor. This point-by-point review of the civil case may lead to a "link in the chain of evidence" that unconstitutionally contributes to the defendant's conviction.

In Peden v. United States, 512 F.2d 1099 (Ct.Cl.1975), the court noted the dangers of parallel proceedings in a civil service action where the same circumstances were subject to both civil and criminal proceedings:

> [A] CSC [Civil Service Commission] hearing that is in the nature of a dress rehearsal for a criminal trial, in which all the Government witnesses testify and are cross-examined at length, but the defendant to be does not, is potentially a big lift to the criminal defense and could well be decisive in securing an acquittal, if anything could.

The court noted the remedy for the problem presented by this situation:

> [I]t has long been the practice to "freeze" civil proceedings when a criminal prosecution involving the same facts is warming up or under way. In the context of appeals from civil service adverse actions, we have repeatedly approved this practice.

The court in *Peden* suggested that postponement of civil proceedings is desirable not only for fifth amendment reasons, but also for the protection of the integrity of two separate processes:

The "freeze" we think is not for the protection of the employee only, but also rises out of a sense that deferrable civil proceedings constitute improper interference with the criminal proceedings if they churn over the same evidentiary material.

* * * In the case at bar, the dangers of parallel proceedings have already been realized. Afro-Lecon's motion to suppress the fruits of the discovery abuses has been granted in part and denied in part. In this order, the court criticized the government:

> This Court is not approbatory of the prosecution's utilization of the ploy of having a criminal investigator "sit in" on and participate in a non-criminal conference or interview when criminal prosecution was, as here, eminently predictable and without advising the "target" of the investigator's role and purpose.

The district court concluded that, in regard to the documents involved, there was no harm to the defendants because their existence was known prior to the conference and would have properly become available through a *subpoena duces tecum*. Verbal statements, however, made by the defendants, the court noted, could not be used against the defendants because of the improper tactics employed by the prosecution. The district court noted:

> Suppression * * * is merited not only by equity and good conscience but also by the salutary aspect of impressing upon the prosecution that such overreaching is not compatible with evenhanded justice which, rather than achieving convictions, should be a prosecutor's goal.

The abuse of civil discovery sanctioned by the district court is now fait accompli. On remand, we ask the board to evaluate in view of the precedent cited whether there is any additional danger of abuse of discovery or whether there is any likelihood that the civil case, if proceeded with, will interfere with the administration of the criminal proceedings.

As Judge Friedman noted in Zenith Radio Corporation v. United States, 764 F.2d 1577 (Fed. Cir. 1985), there are three schools of thought in treating privileges asserted by plaintiffs. The first approach considers that the party automatically waives his privilege by pursuing judicial relief. The second approach balances the need for discovery against the need for secrecy. The third theory denies a plaintiff the privilege if he places the matter subject to the privilege in issue and the information is vital to the defendant's case.

The board adopted the "automatic waiver" theory. We believe that this approach is too rigid and choose instead the balancing approach * * *. This is particularly appropriate where the civil case is not in court but in a tribunal provided by defendant itself for dispute resolution. We conclude that there may be greater reasons to postpone civil proceedings when even an appellant requests it where there is a parallel criminal suit.

In *Kordel* the Court noted the strong policy interest in allowing both the civil and criminal cases brought by the *government* to go forward:

> It would stultify enforcement of federal law to require a governmental agency such as the FDA invariably to choose either to forgo recommendation of a criminal prosecution once it seeks civil relief, or to defer civil proceedings pending the ultimate outcome of a criminal trial.

This important government interest is absent when the civil case is not initiated by the government. Although there are other interests of possible harm to the civil defendant, which we will address *infra,* the harm discussed in *Kordel* is not at issue at present.

Essentially, the board concludes that one may not bring a suit, "wave the sword" of the fifth amendment, and then maintain the suit. We agree that a party may not claim a fifth amendment privilege and *proceed* with his suit. Afro-Lecon, however, asks for a *stay* of civil proceedings and, as a result, does not raise the problem of placing the defendant in the position of maintaining a defense without necessary discovery.

In Wehling v. Columbia Broadcasting System, 608 F.2d 1084 (5th Cir. 1979), the [Fifth Circuit] considered circumstances very much like those at issue in the case at hand. In *Wehling,* the plaintiff appealed the dismissal of his libel action against CBS where his refusal to testify deprived CBS of information essential to its defense. Wehling was required to appear before a grand jury and believed that he was the subject of their investigation.

The court in *Wehling* concluded that the federal rules do not permit a court to punish a party who resists discovery by asserting a valid claim of privilege and that dismissing a plaintiff's action with prejudice solely because he exercises his privilege against self-incrimination is constitutionally impermissible. The basis of this decision was the principle articulated by the Court in Simmons v. United States, 390 U.S. 377 (1968), and elsewhere, that procedures should not require a party to surrender one constitutional right in order to assert another one. * * *

In *Wehling,* CBS advocated, as does the government here, agreed with by the board, that one who brings suit and then claims fifth amendment privileges is akin to the spoiled child who wants the cake and the right to consume it as well. In *Wehling,* the court properly addressed this misguided idea:

> It is true that, as a voluntary litigant, the civil plaintiff has created the situation which requires him to choose between his silence and his lawsuit. In most cases, however, a party "voluntarily" becomes a plaintiff only because there is no other means of protecting legal rights. As one commentator has observed, although the plaintiff-

defendant "distinction is superficially appealing, * * * civil plaintiffs seldom voluntarily seek situations requiring litigation."

* * * We agree with the Fifth Circuit and decline to accept the wooden plaintiff-defendant distinction.

We now address the appropriate analysis for parallel proceedings. Neither the court in *Wehling* nor this court concludes that there is a per se right to postponement of civil proceedings under the circumstances of these two cases. Rather, a balancing must occur of the interest of the appellant in postponement, which is strong, against the possible prejudice to the appellee by way of important evidence that will be lost over time. The court in *Wehling* found that the district court abused its discretion by not granting the stay, yet noted that the district court could dismiss the plaintiff's case at any future point if crucial avenues of discovery were shown to be closing during the three-year period of the stay. We remand to the board to assess the sources of evidence for the order on accounting and to find whether the requested postponement will create an appreciable prejudice to the defendant's case. * * *

NIES, Circuit Judge, concurring.

I concur because I see the issue somewhat differently. Appellant sought a stay of board proceedings on the ground that at the time its response was due to the board's Order on Accounting, it was impossible to respond because the persons who could provide the explanation for its claim were potential defendants in a criminal case and allegedly refused, on advice of counsel, to cooperate. The board accepted that explanation stating, "The immediate effect of their refusal to cooperate is the inability of appellant to satisfactorily comply with the Board's Order on Accounting." Under such circumstances, appellant is guilty of no willful disobedience or even gross negligence in failing to respond to the board's order. A dismissal of its claim with prejudice would have been an abuse of discretion in my view. Notably, however, the board did not dismiss the claim as a matter of *discretion.* The board held, as a matter of *law,* "that in a civil suit a party placing facts in issue may not rely upon the fifth amendment to avoid disclosure of such facts and still maintain his suit." From that legal premise, the board concluded that appellant was not entitled to a stay.

The board's premise, i.e., that a party may not maintain its claim and at the same time assert the fifth amendment, even if correct, does not apply here. Appellant sought a stay of the order because of an impossibility in complying, not because of its assertion of a fifth amendment privilege. Indeed, as far as the record here is concerned, no one has asserted fifth amendment rights *in this proceeding.* Such rights have merely been alluded to by appellant's counsel as the explanation for the appellant's failure to respond. The board, nevertheless, treated counsel's statements as sufficient to establish that it was impossible for appellant to comply with its order. At this moment in these proceedings, that is its ruling.

Thus, I agree that the board's order must be vacated and the matter remanded. Having found impossibility of compliance with its order, the board should not have dismissed but, rather, should have granted a stay for a reasonable period. The government would be, of course, free at any time to seek to have the stay lifted if the impossibility is removed in the interim. At the end of the stay appellant would be required to proceed or to put forth satisfactory grounds for a continuance, at which time the matter would be re-evaluated in light of subsequent developments and the prejudice to the government caused by further delay.

NOTES AND QUESTIONS

1. *Granting a Stay.* The decision to stay is not simply an issue for trial courts. As *Afro-Lecon* shows, administrative bodies will have to determine whether to halt their proceedings until the criminal action is complete. Note that this may involve cases in different jurisdictions, such as a state license boards and federal grand jury investigations. See J. Cal McCastlain and Steven Schooner, *To Stay or Not To Stay: Difficult Decisions For Boards of Contract Appeals Confronted With Parallel Proceedings*, 16 PUB.CONT.L.J. 418 (1987).

2. *Effect of Denying a Stay.* If a party fails to obtain a stay in a civil suit, what is the effect on discovery in that action if the party asserts the Fifth Amendment? Consider the analysis of the Fourth Circuit in **In re Grand Jury Subpoena**, 836 F.2d 1468 (4th Cir. 1988):

> In many civil cases the burden placed on a person's silence may be unavoidable. Where a plaintiff has gathered sufficient evidence to establish a claim prior to discovery, a defendant who risks incrimination by speaking will inevitably face the choice of forsaking silence or losing a civil judgment, even if the defendant's silence is not used against him. See 8 Wright & Miller, Federal Practice & Procedure §2018 & n. 49 (1970) [noting that where there is no evidence to support the defendant's case, by virtue of the claim of the privilege, a "directed verdict or grant of summary judgment will be proper"]. A plaintiff whose claim requires incriminating testimony will likewise always face the choice of speaking or forsaking his prayer for redress. In either case, a district court may reduce the risk of a party's silence by not dismissing an action for failing to cooperate with discovery, but the party will nonetheless face the inevitable judgment of the trier of fact who must make a decision based on an imbalanced presentation of the evidence.

For a discussion of how an assertion of the Fifth Amendment can be used in an attorney disciplinary proceeding, see Chapter 17.

3. *Balancing the Factors.* Although district court rulings on private-party stay requests are tied to the facts of the particular case, they sometimes reflect, as evidenced by the two rulings discussed below, considerable

difference in guiding philosophy. **Brock v. Toklow,** 109 F.R.D. 116 (E.D.N.Y. 1985), involved an action brought by the Secretary of Labor against the trustees of an employee benefit plan for violations of their fiduciary obligations. The trustees moved for a stay of discovery pending the "completion of criminal proceedings against all Trustee Defendants who may be indicted as a result of the current investigation by the [Department of Justice's] Organized Crime and Racketeering Section." The trustees noted in this connection that a grand jury operated by that Section had recently demanded production of a variety of documents relating to the "same facts" as the complaint filed by the Secretary of Labor. The trustees stated that they feared that any testimony given in depositions in the civil case would be shared with the DOJ and used in the grand jury investigation. They argued further that they were not truly free to invoke their self-incrimination privileged in response to the depositions because that could "hamper their ability to defend the civil suit." In granting the stay, District Judge McLaughlin cited several factors: (1) the "ongoing criminal investigation * * * involved the same subject matter as the civil case" and both actions were being "brought by the government"; (2) though no indictments had yet been issued, pre-indictment criminal inquiries, such as a grand jury investigation, also could make a stay appropriate; (3) the trustee defendants did not seek "a stay of the entire civil case," but were asking only that discovery be deferred—"in all other respects the civil case will go forward"; (4) a stay of discovery would cause no serious damage to the public interest, for while "this case alleges serious violations of ERISA, there is no allegation that, for example, plan beneficiaries are not receiving benefits to which they are currently entitled," and "possible mismanagement of a pension fund does not present the same danger to the public interest as the distribution of misbranded drugs [at issue in *Kordel*, p. 644] or the dissemination of false information to the investing public [at issue in *Dresser*, p. 625]"; (5) the government could not point to any evidence that might be lost if civil discovery were stayed; (6) "resolution of the criminal case might reduce the scope of discovery in the civil case or otherwise simplify the issues"; and (7) while it "concededly * * * does not offend the Constitution if a defendant in a civil case is asked questions the answers to which might incriminate him," even though that creates a dilemma due to possible adverse civil suit consequences in refusing to answer on self-incrimination grounds, "a court can exercise its discretion to enable a defendant to avoid this unpalatable choice when to do so would not seriously hamper the public interest."

In **Sterling National Bank v. A-1 Hotels International, Inc.,** 175 F.Supp.2d (S.D.N.Y. 2001), the defendants sought to stay a civil RICO action because the corporation received a grand jury subpoena for records related to the transactions in the RICO suit and "subsequent inquiries by a special agent of the Federal Bureau of Investigation." The district court refused to grant the stay:

> Nevertheless, defendants here can point to nothing that suggests that the dilemma they face is more pointed or difficult than in any other case of parallel proceedings, and it is universally agreed that

the mere pendency of a criminal investigation standing alone does not require a stay. * * * There is no indication whatever that the grand jury's investigation has reached a critical stage; only one document subpoena, issued in January 2001, and some investigative inquiries by an FBI agent, have been called to the Court's attention; defendants do not assert that the government has sought to subpoena or interview the individual defendants, there is nothing to suggest that indictments are imminent. While it can be assumed on this record that there is substantial overlap between the allegations in this complaint and the grand jury's investigation, which defendants assert was triggered by the filing of a suspicious activity report by Sterling, the Court has no way of knowing whether the grand jury's inquiry has expanded or will expand beyond these allegations. Moreover, since depositions have not yet taken place, there is no way of measuring with any precision what questions defendants may refuse to answer, or what damage may be done to their position in the civil case by any assertions of privilege they might choose to make. Perhaps at some later stage of this litigation, the Court will be in a better position to "further the goal of permitting as much testimony as possible to be presented in the civil litigation, despite the assertion of the privilege." At this point, however, the nature of the threat to defendants' Fifth Amendment rights is necessarily still imprecise.

Moreover, this is not a case in which the government itself has an opportunity to escalate the pressure on defendants by manipulating simultaneous civil and criminal proceedings, both of which it controls. In such circumstances, there is a special danger that the government can effectively undermine rights that would exist in a criminal investigation by conducting a de facto criminal investigation using nominally civil means. In that special situation, the risk to individuals' constitutional rights is arguably magnified. Defendants here attempt to raise a similar specter by pointing out that the plaintiff, as the alleged crime victim, may choose to share information it obtains with the government. But that is hardly the same thing. Plaintiff is a private entity, with interests distinct from those of the government. There is no reason to assume that its civil case is simply a stalking horse for the government's criminal inquiry, rather than a good faith effort to obtain compensation for its own private injuries.

4. *Prosecutorial Request for Stay During Grand Jury Investigation*. Although many requests for a stay are brought by individuals seeking to avoid discovery, the government may request that a civil action—including those brought by federal administrative agencies—be stayed pending completion of the criminal investigation. The reason given is that the defendant in the civil case will obtain discovery of materials otherwise unavailable in a criminal investigation. A defendant in a civil enforcement action can use the discovery tools afforded by the Federal Rules of Civil

Procedure to take the deposition of witnesses–especially those who may be cooperating with the criminal investigators–to learn what has been revealed to the criminal investigators. In **Securities & Exchange Commission v. HealthSouth Corp.**, 261 F.Supp.2d 1298 (N.D. Ala. 2003), the SEC sought a freeze on the assets of a corporation's former CEO, Richard Scrushy, pending resolution of a civil securities fraud action while the criminal investigation proceeded. The SEC sought to use the plea agreements of 11 former company officers as evidence of Scrushy's involvement in the underlying fraud, but the former officers asserted the Fifth Amendment in response to questions from defense counsel. In response to efforts by Scrushy to obtain information about the criminal investigation, the United States Attorney and the Department of Justice sought a 60 day stay in the proceeding "as alternative relief for the purpose of 'permitting the grand jury to complete its investigation and the Government to properly pursue its criminal prosecution.'" The SEC, however, pressed forward with its request for the asset freeze, which the district court denied. In granting a stay, the district court emphasized the impact of the ongoing criminal investigation on the civil suit:

> The government having repeatedly asked the court to stay this matter raised the very question with which this court is now confronted, that being defendant Scrushy's inherent inability to present evidence in his defense due to the ongoing criminal investigation. Although the SEC repeatedly represented that it was not offering the plea colloquies for the truth of the matters asserted therein, counsel's statements in closing argument contradict that representation. Because the individual witnesses who had already entered pleas, or already arranged to enter pleas, when called by defendant Scrushy to testify, stated only that they invoked their Fifth Amendment privilege against self-incrimination, defendant Scrushy was effectively denied his right to cross examine these witnesses. Additionally, defendant Scrushy was denied the right to explore these witnesses' motives or reasons for entering guilty plea agreements. Because the SEC then represented to the court in its closing argument that these plea colloquies implicate the defendant, cross examination was critical to the defendant's right to a fair hearing. Further adding to this inability to engage in cross examination was [U.S. Department of Justice attorney] Mr. Richard Smith's representation to the court that should Bill Owens be called to the stand, he would be forced to file another motion to intervene to object to the defendant "attempting to put on a witness in a criminal case in a civil proceeding." He made similar motions with regard to every individual who was called to testify by defendant Scrushy who had already entered into a plea bargain arrangement with the U.S. Attorney's Office.

> * * * As long as a criminal investigation is ongoing and the individuals who have pled guilty have not yet been sentenced, the key witnesses to defendant Scrushy's involvement or lack thereof

will refuse to answer the very questions that would either support or rebut the SEC's allegations. Yet these are the same witnesses upon which the SEC relies to keep the asset freeze in place. This court has no way to predict when the criminal case may be resolved so that this case may proceed without these crucial witnesses who are taking the Fifth Amendment.

Because of the ongoing criminal investigation, defendant Scrushy has been placed in the precarious position of either waiving his Fifth Amendment rights and defending himself in the matter before this court, or asserting the privilege and probably losing this civil proceeding. While such a choice may not be unconstitutional, this court may still exercise its discretion to stay this case in the interest of justice.

* * * [T]he SEC's other evidence of an alleged fraud on the part of defendant Scrushy was obtained from both FBI and from the parallel criminal investigation. Although the SEC, since the conclusion of the hearing on whether or not the asset freeze should remain in full force and effect, has filed a "motion to supplement the record with the guilty pleas of Michael Martin and Malcom McVay," such motion further supports defendant's argument that the SEC's investigation into this civil matter is in fact a precursor for a setup to the criminal indictment and this court's conclusion that the SEC has no evidence other than what stems from the parallel criminal investigation. Allowing those pleas as evidence of defendant Scrushy's involvement in the alleged securities fraud, without allowing defense counsel to cross-examine these witnesses, is just another reason to support the court's conclusion that this matter should be stayed pending completion of the criminal investigation or until such witnesses have been sentenced and can no longer invoke their privilege pursuant to Fifth Amendment of the United States Constitution.

* * * The court finds the criminal and civil cases overlap completely. The issues in both are identical. Although defendant Scrushy has not yet been indicted, no one has represented to the court that such indictment is anything but an eventuality. During this court's hearing, the U.S. Attorney's Office intervened repeatedly in an attempt to prevent defendant Scrushy from obtaining any evidence in this civil proceeding that he would not be entitled to in a criminal proceeding. Although the plaintiff does have an interest in the expeditious resolution of this case, the court finds the harm to defendant Scrushy from blindly pushing ahead with this matter to greatly outweigh the prejudice to the SEC from a stay of this civil proceeding. Given that the evidence presented by the SEC was that obtained from the FBI pursuant to the criminal investigation, and the guilty pleas already entered, the court actually finds the SEC may actually benefit from a stay to allow the FBI to continue

gathering evidence. The court finds, in the same vein, that both the SEC and defendant Scrushy would benefit from a stay of this case until all those who pled guilty have been sentenced, so that testimony may be obtained from them at the final hearing in this case, rather than repeated insistence by these individuals on their Fifth Amendment rights. This is especially true given the U.S. Attorney's Office's great efforts to prevent the testimony of "Owens, Livesay, Smith, Harris, or Morgan, or any other witness with knowledge about matters being criminally investigated . . ." Additionally, the plaintiff here is not an individual who has been wronged, but the SEC, which is a governmental body.

While a stay in a civil proceeding when no indictment has yet issued in the criminal proceeding is rare, issuing such a stay is within this court's inherent powers.

* * * The court's role in a civil proceeding such as that before it is to ensure that fairness permeates the proceeding and to try to ascertain the truth.[48] The court is unable to accomplish either of these purposes here, as the witnesses who could testify as to the allegations in the SEC's complaint have refused to do so, by invoking their Fifth Amendment rights. Although the court may draw inferences from such use of the Fifth Amendment in a civil proceeding, the inferences here are too speculative to draw.[50] These

---

[48] The Ninth Circuit Court of Appeals has wisely noted that "[i]n highly publicized cases, such as the one at hand, judicial . . . decisionmakers need to be especially careful that undue consideration is not given a proceeding's impact on the public. Governmental entities are frequently aware of the need to reassure the public that they are taking prompt action in response to a crisis. In such high visibility situations, it is especially necessary to guard the rights of defendants, and concern for the public deterrence value of an enforcement proceeding must not be allowed to override the individual defendant's due process rights." Keating v. Office of Thrift Supervision, 45 F.3d 322 (9th Cir.1994).

[50] Each of the witnesses in this case who have entered guilty pleas have entered plea bargains with the government. Each has agreed to provide "substantial assistance" to the U.S. Attorney's office in its ongoing investigation in exchange for a downward departure upon sentencing. Each has taken the Fifth in response to questions about his or her, or defendant Scrushy's role in the allegations. The court has considered what motivations a witness, who has already entered a plea, but not yet been sentenced, may have to invoke the Fifth Amendment in response to information stated by him or her in open court upon entering a plea of guilty. The court has considered perhaps the prosecutor's desire to not reveal its hand during this civil proceeding, evidence of additional, uncharged crimes, and even possible future perjury charges as motivating factors. Given these uncertainties, the court is unable to draw any inferences adverse to defendant Scrushy from such testimony. The court notes issues such as this should resolve themselves upon these witnesses giving their testimony during the criminal proceeding and being sentenced. At least then, defendant Scrushy will have some factual basis to determine how best to defend himself, or whether to defend himself at all.

problems are further compounded by the U.S. Attorney's Office and Department of Justice's efforts to prevent defendant Scrushy from obtaining any discovery. These entities argued that "to permit any depositions to be conducted by the defendants in this civil action would result in disclosure of sensitive information critical to the criminal investigation and to an anticipated trial. For these reasons, the Government requests that it be permitted to intervene and that this Court either quash any and all subpoenas issued by Defendant Scrushy to the above-named specific individuals and to any and all witnesses who may be called who have knowledge about the criminal investigation in this case, and prohibit their compelled testimony, or in the alternative, that these civil proceedings be stayed in their entirety."

* * * This case is stayed pending the resolution of any criminal charges against defendant Scrushy, or notification by either party that such charges will not be forthcoming.

5. ***Prosecutorial Request for Stay After Indictment.*** When the government indicts a defendant who is also the subject of a civil enforcement action, the defendant may try to take advantage of the more liberal civil discovery rules to gather information about the criminal case that would not be as readily available through the criminal discovery rules. Is the prosecutor's interests in preventing discovery of the criminal case sufficient to warrant a stay? Consider the analysis in **Securities & Exchange Comm'n v. Doody**, 186 F.Supp.2d 379 (S.D.N.Y. 2002), in which only one defendant in an SEC civil suit was charged in the criminal case, and the prosecutor sought a stay of discovery in the civil case pending completion of the criminal matter:

On November 8, 2001, a grand jury sitting in this district returned an indictment charging Joseph F. Doody, IV, with securities fraud. The charge, in substance, is that Doody traded on material inside information regarding an impending merger between BetzDearborn, Inc. and Hercules Incorporated which he obtained from his girlfriend, Diane Neiley.

On the same date, the SEC brought this civil action against Doody, his father, Joseph F. Doody ("Doody Sr."), and Neilly charging the same insider trading scheme. Doody is alleged to have tipped Doody Sr. on the basis of the tips he received from Neilly, and Doody Sr. is alleged to have traded on that information as well. The SEC seeks an injunction and other relief.

The trial of the criminal case now is set * * *. In the meantime, Doody Sr. has commenced an ambitious discovery program in this action, seeking answers to interrogatories from and production of documents by the SEC which, the government says, would result in premature disclosure of the evidence upon which it hopes to rely in the criminal case. In addition, Doody Sr. has noticed Neilly's deposition, and the government apprehends that he will seek to depose individuals who are likely to be witnesses in the criminal trial, thus further tipping the government's hand and, in effect, giving Doody an extra opportunity to cross-examine the government's witnesses.

The government has made a persuasive case that its interest in protecting its criminal case justifies its intervention here, and Doody makes no serious argument to the contrary. Accordingly, the government will be permitted to intervene for the purpose of seeking relief against discovery in this case pending the completion of the criminal trial. The question is whether it is entitled to that relief.

Once an indictment has been returned, the government often moves for and frequently obtains relief preventing a criminal defendant from using parallel civil proceedings to gain premature access to evidence and information pertinent to the criminal case. In granting such relief, courts must weigh competing interests, including "the interests of the defendants, the interests of the plaintiffs in proceeding with the litigation, the public interest, and the interests of the courts and of third parties."

Doody Sr. argues that the abundance of authority is not controlling or, arguably, even pertinent here because he is not a defendant in the criminal case and, moreover, has a compelling need to proceed expeditiously in the civil case. The need is said to stem from the fact that he is employed by Enron, is likely soon to be out of a job and, absent speedy disposition of the civil case, would have difficulty finding employment with the stigma from the SEC's charges against him hanging over his head.

To be sure, most cases involving stays of civil actions pending the completion of parallel criminal proceedings have involved common defendants. This case therefore is different to the extent that it is Doody Sr. who is leading the charge toward discovery in this civil case. But the Court would have to be unimaginably naive to suppose that Doody Sr. is not a stalking horse for Doody himself. Whether Doody Sr. discovers the government's case against his son or his son's attorneys do it by exercising their right, as counsel to a co-defendant in the civil case, to participate in discovery here is immaterial. The fact is that discovery here that would afford Doody access to information to which he would not be entitled in his defense of the criminal case almost surely would occur absent some relief.

Doody Sr. is at least arguably right also in saying that this case is unusual in that he would be subjected to some prejudice by a delay of civil discovery different than anything that might be claimed by one who is a defendant in both cases. But he has failed to demonstrate that he will suffer prejudice that outweighs the government's interest in obtaining a stay. Perhaps he will lose his job, and perhaps he will have some difficulty finding new employment while this action is pending. But the fact is that he has not lost it yet and may not lose it. Even if he does, the criminal case is scheduled for trial in approximately four weeks. Doody Sr. has provided no information concerning his financial situation, so there is no basis whatever to suppose that a delay of discovery in this case for, say, six weeks would mean the difference between his putting food on the table and starvation. Thus, Doody Sr.'s position is based on unfounded assumptions and inappropriate exaggerations. But he is not alone in having overstated his case.

The relief the government seeks is virtually a blanket stay of all disclosure in this case. Perhaps no discovery could be provided here without implicating its legitimate concerns in the criminal case, but that is not self evident. In consequence, the Court is left guessing as to just what protection the government legitimately requires. After having weighed the competing interests of the various parties, it therefore must make the best judgments it can in the circumstances.

* * * The following discovery is stayed until the earliest of (i) the entry of a plea of guilty, (ii) the completion of the trial of the criminal case, and (iii) March 20, 2002:

(1) Rule 26(a)(i)(A) discovery.

(2) Production of transcripts of SEC testimony and notes of interviews of any person whom the United States Attorney's office certifies may be called as a witness in the criminal case.

(3) Depositions of any person whom the United States Attorney's office certifies may be called as a witness in the criminal case.

F. DISCLOSURE OF INFORMATION OBTAINED IN THE COURSE OF A GRAND JURY INVESTIGATION FOR USE IN A CIVIL OR AGENCY PROCEEDING

1. Disclosure to Private Parties

Under Rule 6(e)(3)(E)(i), a private party involved in a civil litigation may petition the federal district court to order disclosure to it of matters occurring before the grand jury. The applicable guidelines for ordering disclosure on such a request were set forth in **Douglas Oil Co. of California v. Petrol Stops Northwest**, 441 U.S. 211 (1979). In that case, respondents, independent gasoline dealers, brought civil antitrust actions against several large oil companies who had been indicted for price-fixing and had entered nolo contendere pleas. After civil interrogatories proved unavailing in obtaining evidence of alleged communications between the oil companies relating to their setting of wholesale prices, the respondents sought disclosure of the grand jury transcripts of the testimony of the oil company employees (the oil companies themselves had received copies of that testimony prior to entry of their pleas). The Justice Department expressed no opposition to such disclosure, and it was ordered by the district court. The Supreme Court, on subsequent review, concluded that the district court had not erred in the standard it had applied to the respondents' request. The Court, per Powell, J., noted:

> In United States v. Procter & Gamble Co., 356 U.S. 677 (1958) [p. 412], the Court sought to accommodate the competing needs for secrecy and disclosure by ruling that a private party seeking to obtain grand jury transcripts must demonstrate that "without the transcript a defense would be greatly prejudiced or that without reference to it an injustice would be done." Moreover, the Court required that the showing of need for the transcripts be made "with particularity" so that "the secrecy of the proceedings [may] be lifted discretely and limitedly." In Dennis v. United States, 384 U.S. 855 (1966), the Court considered a request for disclosure of grand jury records in quite different circumstances. It was there held to be an abuse of discretion for a District Court in a criminal trial to refuse to disclose to the defendants the grand jury testimony of four witnesses who some years earlier had appeared before a grand jury investigating activities of the defendants. The grand jury had completed its investigation, and the witnesses whose testimony was sought already had testified in public concerning the same matters. The Court noted that "[n]one of the reasons traditionally advanced to justify nondisclosure of grand jury minutes" was significant in those circumstances, whereas the defendants had shown it to be likely that the witnesses' testimony at trial was inconsistent with their prior grand jury testimony.

> From *Procter & Gamble* and *Dennis* emerges the standard for determining when the traditional secrecy of the grand jury may be broken: Parties seeking grand jury transcripts under Rule 6(e) must show that the material they seek is needed to avoid a possible injustice in another judicial proceeding, that the need for disclosure is greater than the need for continued secrecy, and that their request is structured to cover only material so needed.[12] Such a

---

[12] As noted in United States v. Procter & Gamble Co., 356 U.S., at 683, the typical showing of particularized need arises when a litigant seeks to use "the grand jury transcript at the trial to impeach a witness, to refresh his recollection, to test his credibility and the like." Such use is necessary to avoid misleading the trier of fact. Moreover, disclosure can be limited strictly to those portions of a particular witness' testimony that bear upon some aspect of his direct testimony at trial. Under the Jencks Act, 18 U.S.C.A. § 3500(a), the defendant in a criminal case now has an automatic right to that prior grand jury testimony of a trial witness "which relates

showing must be made even when the grand jury whose transcripts are sought has concluded its operations, as it had in *Dennis*. For in considering the effects of disclosure on grand jury proceedings, the courts must consider not only the immediate effects upon a particular grand jury, but also the possible effect upon the functioning of future grand juries. Persons called upon to testify will consider the likelihood that their testimony may one day be disclosed to outside parties. Fear of future retribution or social stigma may act as powerful deterrents to those who would come forward and aid the grand jury in the performance of its duties. Concern as to the future consequences of frank and full testimony is heightened where the witness is an employee of a company under investigation. Thus, the interests in grand jury secrecy, although reduced, are not eliminated merely because the grand jury has ended its activities.[13]

It is clear from *Procter & Gamble* and *Dennis* that disclosure is appropriate only in those cases where the need for it outweighs the public interest in secrecy, and that the burden of demonstrating this balance rests upon the private party seeking disclosure. It is equally clear that as the considerations justifying secrecy become less relevant, a party asserting a need for grand jury transcripts will have a lesser burden in showing justification. In sum, as so often is the situation in our jurisprudence, the court's duty in a case of this kind is to weigh carefully the competing interests in light of the relevant circumstances and the standards announced by this Court. And if disclosure is ordered, the court may include protective limitations on the use of the disclosed material, as did the District Court in this case.[a] Moreover, we emphasize that a court called upon

---

to the subject matter as to which the witness has testified" at trial.

[13] The transcripts sought by respondents already had been given to the target companies in the grand jury investigation. Thus, release to respondents will not enhance the possibility of retaliatory action by employers in this case. But the other factors supporting the presumption of secrecy remain and must be considered.

[See also In re Grand Jury Proceedings, GJ-76-4 and GJ-75-3, 800 F.2d 1293 (4th Cir. 1986) (even where there has been disclosure to the investigated parties, there may be need to protect from "public opprobrium" those grand jury witnesses "whose identity has not yet been publicly disclosed").].

[a] The Court earlier had noted "several protective conditions" imposed by the district court: "the transcripts were to 'be disclosed only to counsel for [respondents] in connection with the two civil actions' pending in Arizona. Furthermore, under the court's order the transcripts of grand jury testimony 'may be used . . . solely for the purpose of impeaching that witness or refreshing the recollection of a witness, either in deposition or at trial' in the Arizona actions. Finally, the court forbade any further reproduction of the matter turned over to respondents, and ordered that the material be returned to the Antitrust Division 'upon completion of the purposes authorized by this Order.'"

to determine whether grand jury transcripts should be released necessarily is infused with substantial discretion.

2. Disclosure to Agencies and Civil Attorneys

In **United States v. Sells Engineering**, 463 U.S. 418 (1983), involving a disclosure by federal prosecutors to attorneys in the Justice Department's Civil Division, the Court rejected the contention that such intra-governmental disclosures should be allowed without regard to the standards set forth in *Douglas Oil*. At the same time, however, the Court indicated that the balancing process required by *Douglas Oil* would be applied somewhat differently for disclosures to governmental units. The Court characterized as "overstated," but nonetheless having "some validity," the government's contention that "disclosure of grand jury materials to government attorneys typically implicates few, if any, of the concerns that underlie the policy of grand jury secrecy." Prosecutors ordinarily will initiate such disclosures only after the "criminal aspect of the matter is closed." Where, as here, such disclosure was to be made to another unit of the Justice Department, a district court "might reasonably consider" that the disclosure "poses less risk of further leakage or improper use than would disclosure to private parties or the general public." However, even though these factors weighed in favor of disclosure, they did not justify simply dispensing with the prerequisite of a showing of particularized need as mandated in *Douglas Oil*.

In **United States v. John Doe, Inc. I**, 481 U.S. 102 (1987), the Supreme Court concluded that the Court of Appeals had erred in rejecting the government's particularized need showing "because the same information could eventually have been obtained through civil discovery." The requested disclosure in *Doe* was aimed at allowing the Antitrust Division to gain the views of Civil Division attorneys in determining whether a contemplated civil suit should be brought, and, as such, it could have "sav[ed] the Government, the potential defendants, and witnesses, the pains of costly and time consuming depositions and interrogatories which might later have turned out to be wasted if the Government decided not to file a civil action after all." Admittedly, "not every instance of 'saving time and expense' justifies disclosure," but that factor prevailed here, as the requested disclosure involved none of the "three types of dangers" noted in *Sells*. First, there was no concern as to a dramatic increase in "the number of persons as to whom the information is available" or as to chilling the "willingness of witnesses to come forward and to testify fully and candidly"; the disclosure was to named government attorneys for a limited purpose that "would not directly result in any witness' testimony being used against him or her in a civil proceeding." Second, there was no concern as to creating an incentive for possible DOJ misuse of the "grand jury's powerful investigative tools" to "root out additional evidence in a civil suit, or even to start or continue a grand jury inquiry where no criminal prosecution is likely." This was not a request to give the Civil Division "unfettered access to grand jury materials," but a request supported by a showing of need and the filing of an "affidavit attesting to the Department's good faith in conducting the grand jury investigation."[b] Third, the use involved did not threaten to "subvert the limitations applied outside the grand jury's context on the Government's powers of discovery and investigation" as the requested disclosure was not for use "in an actual adversarial proceeding."

The Court of Appeals in *Doe* also had relied upon the assumption that the Antitrust Division could use its Civil Investigative Deposition authority to obtain virtually all of the relevant information prior to filing a civil suit (and could then share that information with Civil Division attorneys). The *Doe* Court acknowledged that a federal agency's capacity to obtain the same information through its own investigative authority is a consideration weighing against the need for disclosure of grand jury matter, but stressed that such capacity was not a per se bar against authorizing disclosure. Rather, the availability of an alternative means of obtaining the information must be weighed against "the delay and expense that would be caused by such duplicative discovery."

3. The Mechanics of Disclosure Orders

Rule 6(e)(3)(F) and 6(e)(3)(G) govern the mechanics of seeking and obtaining disclosure orders under Rule 6(e)(3)(E)(i). These rules adopt the procedure suggested in *Douglas Oil Co. v. Petrol Stops Northwest* for assigning venue where disclosure is sought for use in a judicial proceeding instituted in a different district from that in which the grand jury sat. Initially, the party seeking disclosure must file a motion for disclosure before the court in the district where the grand jury sat (the grand jury court). Next, the grand jury court must determined the need for continued secrecy. It has authority too deny the motion should there be a strong need for continued secrecy (e.g., protect an ongoing investigation) which would outweigh any showing of need. If the grand jury court decides that is not the case and that disclosure may be appropriate, it then transfers the requested materials with a statement evaluating the need for continued secrecy to the court where the "preliminary-to" judicial proceeding is located. That court then determines the particularized need and balances it against the need for continued secrecy as stated by the grand jury court.

Where the person seeking disclosure is a private party or state agency, Rule 6(e)(3)(F)(iii) requires notice to, and the opportunity to be heard for, the attorney for the government, the parties to the judicial proceeding, and "any other person whom the court may designate." In its Notes to the 1983 Amendment of Rule 6, the Advisory Committee for the Federal Rules of Criminal Procedure indicated that this last clause was designed to authorize court-ordered notification of non-litigants who might suffer reputational or other injury from a disclosure. Offered as illustrations of persons in that position were the grand jury witness fearful of economic retribution if her

---

[b] As to challenges to disclosure based on alleged governmental misuse of the grand jury process to obtain civil discovery, see p.644, Note 2.

identity became known to one of the litigants and the target of an investigation who was never indicted and could be stigmatized by public disclosure that he had been a target.

It is common practice for the government to file their motions for disclosure without notification to other interested parties, to request that the court consider the motion ex parte, to request further that any hearing on the motion be in camera as provided in Rule 6(e)(5), and to ask that the motion, any supporting affidavits, and the disclosure order itself be kept under seal, as allowed under Rule 6(e)(6), until the anticipated judicial proceeding is filed. Anticipating the government's practice, counsel for a target subject to a parallel civil action often will file with the court a request to be notified if anyone files a petition for court ordered disclosure, so that the target can at least be heard on the issue, even if the contents of the government's statement of particularized need is not disclosed. If counsel has any basis for believing that the grand jury authority was used to develop information for civil discovery, that basis will be noted in the request.

G. ADMINISTRATIVE SANCTIONS

In addition to the authority to investigate possible violations, the civil law enforcement agencies can impose various sanctions for violations. These penalties may be imposed after a administrative hearing or be ordered by a federal court after a judicial determination that a violation has occurred. The sanctions may be imposed after the completion of a criminal prosecution, although a conviction is not a prerequisite to the administrative agency pursuing its own remedies. Quite often, an individual or company will settle the agency action and accept a civil penalty as part of a global settlement of a parallel criminal investigation that may result in a guilty plea or, for a corporation, a deferred or non-prosecution agreement. The penalties an agency can impose are established by statute, and can include monetary penalties, suspension or revocation of a license, forfeiture of goods or money, and prohibition on future participation in government programs or contracts.

At one point, the imposition of civil penalties raised potential problems in parallel criminal cases under the Double Jeopardy Clause of the Fifth Amendment. In **United States v. Halper**, 490 U.S. 435 (1989), the Supreme Court held that a fixed civil penalty imposed after the defendant's criminal conviction arising from the same underlying conduct violated the multiple punishment prong of the prohibition on double jeopardy because the civil penalty was punitive and not remedial. The Court overruled *Halper* in **Hudson v. United States**, 522 U.S. 93 (1997), stating that "*Halper*'s deviation from longstanding double jeopardy principles was ill considered." After *Hudson*, the test for determining whether the Double Jeopardy Clause applies is whether the statute is civil or criminal, based on whether Congress designated the provision as criminal or civil, or whether it intended a criminal provision. The Eighth Amendment's proscription on excessive fines applies to both civil and criminal penalties, and in **United States v. Bajakajian**, 524 U.S. 321 (1998), the Court found the civil forfeiture of $357,

144 of undeclared currency to be excessive and in violation of the Eighth Amendment.

When an administrative agency imposes sanctions for a violation, what standard applies to judicial enforcement of that determination?

BURKE v. ENVIRONMENTAL PROTECTION AGENCY
127 F.Supp.2d 235 (D.D.C. 2001)

KENNEDY, District Judge.

* * * Plaintiff Paul M. Burke ("Burke") challenges the decision of the United States Environmental Protection Agency ("EPA" or "the agency") to debar him from contracting with the federal government and from participating in federal assistance, loans, and benefit programs for a period of five (5) years. Burke claims that EPA's debarment decision was arbitrary and capricious, an abuse of discretion, and not in accordance with law, all of which EPA denies. * * *

From 1989 to 1998, Burke was the president and sole shareholder of ACMAR Regional Landfill, Inc. ("ACMAR"), and the majority shareholder of Acmar Landfill, a Partnership ("the Partnership"). ACMAR and the Partnership owned and operated the ACMAR Regional Landfill ("the Landfill") located in Moody, Alabama. The Landfill accepted residential and industrial waste and bordered on the Big Black Creek, which flows into the Cahaba River, a source of drinking water for the residents of Birmingham, Alabama. In March 1990, the Alabama Department of Environmental Management ("ADEM") issued a permit to ACMAR for the disposal of solid waste within a fifty-acre, cigar-shaped parcel of land, referred to as the "cigar parcel." ADEM also issued to ACMAR a National Pollution Discharge Elimination System ("NPDES") permit, which authorized the release of storm water runoff that does not contain leachate[1] into the Big Black Creek.

On February 24, 1998, an information was filed in the United States District Court for the Northern District of Alabama, Middle Division, charging Burke with violating the Clean Water Act ("CWA"), 33 U.S.C. § 1319(c)(1)(A), for the negligent discharge of leachate into the Big Black Creek. The discharge occurred almost five years earlier on March 30, 1993. Burke pled guilty to violating the CWA, was fined $10,000, and was sentenced to eight months in prison, four months at a halfway house, and one year supervised release if he continued to own or work for ACMAR or the Partnership at the time of his release from custody. In addition, ACMAR pled guilty to conspiring to defraud the United States through the illegal

---

[1] Leachate is a liquid by-product produced in landfills when either precipitation or other fluid mixes with contaminants found in the waste, thereby, creating a biological reaction. Depending on the amount of decomposition or available oxygen, the leachate leads to the production of additional contaminants in downward moving water. Leachate also stains the ground as it seeps back into the soil.

expansion of the Landfill, the disposal of solid waste in an unpermitted area, and the defrauding of landfill clients. ACMAR was fined $1.8 million and was ordered to develop an effective environmental compliance plan. Pursuant to his plea agreement, Burke sold ACMAR to Superior Star Ridge in March 1998.

On July 16, 1998, the EPA Suspension and Debarment Division ("SDD") requested, through an Action Referral Memorandum ("ARM"), that Burke be suspended immediately, pending a proposed five-year debarment based on his conviction for violating the Clean Water Act. Robert F. Meunier, EPA Debarring Official, issued the notice of suspension on August 4, 1998[.] Burke timely contested the notice and requested an oral hearing, which was held on April 27, and 28, 1999.

On August 30, 1999, Meunier officially debarred Burke from participating in federal assistance, loans, and benefit programs and from contracting with the federal government for a five-year period, measured from the date of his suspension. In the Decision, EPA concluded that Burke's criminal conviction provided cause for debarment and that Burke did not demonstrate sufficient mitigating factors or remedial measures showing that debarment was unnecessary. EPA also found that a five-year, as opposed to a three-year, period of debarment was warranted under the circumstances. This action followed. * * *

Judicial review of EPA's Decision is available pursuant to the Administrative Procedure Act ("APA"), 5 U.S.C. § 701 *et seq.* The APA provides that the reviewing court shall hold unlawful an agency action that is "arbitrary, capricious, an abuse of discretion, or otherwise not in accordance with law." 5 U.S.C. § 706(2)(A). * * * The arbitrary and capricious standard is highly deferential and presumes the agency action to be valid. It is also well established that when reviewing matters under this standard, the court may not substitute its judgment for that of the agency officials. Rather, the court's inquiry is limited to determining whether the agency examined the case facts and articulated a satisfactory explanation for its decision, including a "rational connection between the facts found and the choice made." * * *

Debarment is a discretionary measure taken to protect the public interest and to promote an agency's policy of conducting business only with responsible persons. Debarment cannot be used to punish an individual; rather, it serves a remedial purpose of protecting the federal government from the business risk of dealing with an individual who lacks "business integrity or business honesty." The initiation of a debarment proceeding requires the existence of past misconduct; however, the final decision to debar an individual must focus on that individual's present business responsibility. In addition, the debarring official must determine whether any mitigating factors show that the business risk to the government has been eliminated to the extent that debarment would be unnecessary.

EPA found that Burke's criminal conviction for a negligent violation of the Clean Water Act established cause for debarment under 40 C.F.R. § 32.305(a)(4)[4] because the offense indicates a lack of business integrity that directly affects Burke's present responsibility. The agency also found an alternative cause for debarment under 40 C.F.R. § 32.305(d)[5] because the "factual misconduct" providing the basis for Burke's conviction "shows a serious lack of business responsibility."

Burke offers several arguments in support of his claim that EPA's determination was "arbitrary, capricious, an abuse of discretion, or otherwise not in accordance with law." First, Burke argues that the Decision erred as a matter of law by concluding that his criminal conviction established an offense-based cause for debarment. Burke contends that his conviction for the negligent discharge of leachate is neither one of the specified offenses listed in 40 C.F.R. § 32.305(a)(1-3) nor within the "nature and character" of offenses generally described in 40 C.F.R. § 32.305(a)(4). EPA responds by pointing out that it interprets 40 C.F.R. § 32.305(a)(4) to include environmental crimes where there is a reasonable connection between the participant's misconduct and his business integrity. Burke does not challenge EPA's interpretation of Section 32.305; rather, he contends that his case does not fall within the parameters of that interpretation.

* * * [T]here is no basis for concluding that EPA's interpretation of the parameters of Section 32.305 is wrong. EPA evaluated the relevant case facts and discerned a reasonable connection between Burke's misconduct and his business integrity:

> Operation of landfills in an environmentally compliant manner protects the environment and human health and safety. The negligent discharge of leachate, in the course of Mr. Burke's commercial operation of Acmar, raises serious questions about his business integrity.

Moreover, the administrative record contains substantial evidence to support EPA's finding that a nexus exists between Burke's criminal

---

[4] 40 C.F.R. § 32.305(a) states: "Debarment may be imposed in accordance with the provisions of §§ 32.300 through 32.314 for (a) Conviction of or civil judgment for: (1) Commission of fraud or a criminal offense in connection with obtaining, attempting to obtain, or performing a public or private agreement or transaction; (2) Violation of Federal or State antitrust statutes, including those proscribing price fixing between competitors, allocation of customers between competitors, and bid rigging; (3) Commission of embezzlement, theft, forgery, bribery, falsification or destruction of records, making false statements, receiving stolen property, making false claims, or obstruction of justice; or (4) *Commission of any other offense indicating a lack of business integrity or business honesty that seriously and directly affects the present responsibility of a person.*" (emphasis added).

[5] 40 C.F.R. § 32.305(d) provides for debarment for "[a]ny other cause of so serious or compelling a nature that it affects the present responsibility of a person." Id.

conviction and his business integrity. As a result of his guilty plea, Burke was fined $10,000 and sentenced to eight months in prison, four months in a halfway house, and twelve months supervised release if he continued his relationship with ACMAR. The details of the plea agreement, along with the fact that Burke was essentially compelled to discontinue his relationship with ACMAR, adequately support EPA's conclusion that Burke's criminal conviction reflected, to a significant degree, on his business integrity.

In addition, EPA properly evaluated Burke's criminal offense in light of ACMAR's fraud and deceit. Here the totality of the circumstances–especially the fact that Burke was the president and sole owner of ACMAR, which pled guilty to criminal conspiracy and was fined $1.8 million–gives rise to adverse inferences regarding Burke's business practices. The administrative record also confirms that Burke's guilty plea and fine were considered as part of the overall plea agreement with ACMAR. Even though Burke's individual conviction *alone* provides sufficient cause for debarment, it was hardly arbitrary and capricious for EPA to consider Burke's criminal offense in light of his company's related criminal fraud.

Before imposing a debarment, EPA must ascertain whether any mitigating factors or remedial measures show that the business risk of dealing with the individual has been eliminated to the extent that debarment is unnecessary. Federal Acquisition Regulations ("FARs") set forth relevant mitigating factors the agency should consider. The respondent has the burden of demonstrating–to the satisfaction of the debarring official–that sufficient mitigating factors make debarment unnecessary, however. Burke argues that EPA failed to consider substantial mitigating evidence in concluding that he should be debarred and failed to evaluate properly the seriousness of his conduct.

Burke first points to testimony in the administrative record indicating that the leachate violations were eliminated before the government informed Burke or ACMAR of the problem. Burke also contends that the off-site disposal was the result of a mere "misunderstanding" with the state regulatory agency. According to Burke, the circumstances of the off-site disposal prove that his conduct was "hardly serious enough to warrant debarment." Burke next asserts that he did not have a high degree of relative culpability, as EPA claimed, because he tried to make sure that the leachate problem was addressed and because other staff members were more responsible for the day-to-day activities at the Landfill. Finally, Burke claims that his overall character, the time period since his violation, and his compliance with court-ordered sanctions all demonstrate that debarment is unnecessary.

It is apparent that Burke seeks to expand the court's limited standard of review. However, we can neither perform a de novo review of the record, nor substitute our judgment for that of agency officials. Based on our evaluation of the administrative record and EPA's Decision, the court cannot conclude that the agency was arbitrary and capricious in considering the relevant mitigating factors. The Decision clearly indicates that EPA evaluated each mitigating factor Burke raised. Moreover, there is substantial evidence in the record to support EPA's assessment of each factor and the relative *weight* assigned to each factor. While there are some aspects of the record that support Burke's position, EPA's determination that such evidence is outweighed by other evidence in the record is reasonable and must be upheld under the applicable standard of review.

Burke argues that the administrative record does not support EPA's conclusion that a five-year, as opposed to three-year, debarment is warranted. Federal regulations provide that debarment shall be for a period of time commensurate with the seriousness of the cause and in consideration of any mitigating factors. Debarment is generally imposed for a three-year period, though a longer time frame is permitted "[w]here circumstances warrant." Here EPA determined that the seriousness of Burke's misconduct, "based on the fact that Mr. Burke was the sole shareholder and president of Acmar; that he knew that Acmar was not acting in accordance with their permit; and that he misrepresented to customers that solid waste would be disposed of in accordance with state and federal regulations," warrants a five year debarment period. EPA also imposed the five-year debarment because "[o]nly when Mr. Burke was forced into a position of compliance by ADEM did he begin to implement actions that should have been a part of the daily operation of Acmar . . . [and because] Mr. Burke has not presented persuasive evidence of altered personal business conduct which demonstrates that he now does not pose a risk to the government."

Burke challenges the length of his debarment on several grounds. First, he argues that EPA misstated the facts when it claimed that he implemented remedial actions only after the ADEM forced him into compliance. Second, Burke contends that his criminal conviction resulted from a one-day violation, rather than multiple violations extending over several years, as EPA implies. Third, Burke again claims that the agency failed to consider evidence that he undertook voluntary compliance efforts "more and more seriously, and more and more proactively, over time."

EPA responds that it properly weighed the circumstances surrounding Burke's conviction and any relevant mitigating factors. Though EPA acknowledges that its Decision misstated certain aspects of Burke's offense, this mistake was not a "grossly erroneous mischaracterization" that warrants reversal, as Burke contends. In fact, in the Decision's very next paragraph, EPA correctly notes that "Mr. Burke pled guilty to a *one* count violation of the CWA."

EPA has discretion to impose debarment periods consistent with the case circumstances and mitigating factors. This court's only responsibility then is to ensure that such discretion was exercised non-arbitrarily and that EPA's Decision was supported by the administrative record. Even if the Decision was "of less than ideal clarity," the court must nonetheless uphold it "if the agency's path may reasonably be discerned." This is the case here.

EPA provided several valid reasons in support of its determination that a five-year, as opposed to three-year, debarment was appropriate. The seriousness of Burke's criminal conviction, his failure to take personal responsibility for his offense, and his direct control of and involvement with ACMAR and the Landfill[9] each provided an independent basis for EPA's conclusion. In addition, EPA adequately demonstrated that it considered–though found unpersuasive–Burke's arguments concerning his past "misunderstandings" with environmental regulators. EPA also properly entertained Burke's alternative argument that other EPA debarment decisions suggest that a longer debarment period is unwarranted. Because there is no clear error of judgment or failure to consider relevant factors, this court concludes that EPA's imposition of a five-year, as opposed to a three-year, debarment was not arbitrary and capricious.

After reviewing the EPA Decision and administrative record, the court cannot conclude that the agency's five-year debarment of Burke was arbitrary, capricious, an abuse of discretion, or otherwise not in accordance with the law. There was substantial evidence to support Burke's debarment, and EPA articulated a rational connection between the facts found and the decision made. Also, there was no clear error of judgment. The court, therefore, denies Burke's motion for summary judgment and enters judgment on all counts in favor of EPA. An appropriate order accompanies this memorandum.

NOTES AND QUESTIONS

1. *Debarment and Suspension*. Suspension and debarment are administrative actions that prohibit or limit an individual or business from doing future business with the federal government. Designed to protect the government by ensuring that it contracts only with "presently responsible" contractors, these sanctions may be imposed on those who engaged in wrongful conduct, including a criminal conviction, or who violated the requirements of a contract or program. Debarment means the person or business is prohibited from doing business with the government for a defined period, with three years being the usual maximum. A suspension is a temporary exclusion imposed upon a suspected wrongdoer pending the outcome of an investigation and any ensuing judicial or administrative proceedings. 48 C.F.R. § 9.406.

---

[9] Burke strongly argues that his business conduct should not be evaluated in the context of ACMAR, a company Burke controlled and directed. But as the agency rightly points out, Burke tries to have it both ways: he takes credit for the positive attributes at ACMAR (its "state-of-the-art facilities"), while distancing himself from its negative history (its guilty plea to criminal conspiracy and $1.8 million fine). Burke also takes an extremely narrow view of his conviction and fails to recognize that his punishment was considered as part of the overall plea agreement with ACMAR. Moreover, the record includes substantial evidence that Burke was intimately involved with ACMAR and that he directly benefitted from the company's criminal conspiracy.

Federal procurement regulations provide that a contractor can be debarred based on a conviction or civil judgment for:

(1) Commission of fraud or a criminal offense in connection with (i) obtaining, (ii) attempting to obtain, or (iii) performing a public contract or subcontract;

(2) Violation of Federal or State antitrust statutes relating to the submission of offers;

(3) Commission of embezzlement, theft, forgery, bribery, falsification or destruction of records, making false statements, tax evasion, or receiving stolen property;

(4) Intentionally affixing a label bearing a "Made in America" inscription (or any inscription having the same meaning) to a product sold in or shipped to the United States or its outlying areas, when the product was not made in the United States or its outlying areas (see Section 202 of the Defense Production Act (Public Law 102-558)); or

(5) Commission of any other offense indicating a lack of business integrity or business honesty that seriously and directly affects the present responsibility of a Government contractor or subcontractor.

48 C.F.R. § 9.406.2(a). Other types of conduct that can lead to debarment include willful failure to perform a contract, drug violations by the contractor, a failure to comply with the Immigration and Nationality Act employment provisions, and unfair trade practices under the Defense Production Act. There is also a general catch-all provision that authorizes debarment "based on any other cause of so serious or compelling a nature that it affects the present responsibility of the contractor or subcontractor." 48 C.F.R. § 9.406.2(b)-(c). Just the threat of debarment or suspension "often causes a much greater concern than either a criminal prosecution or civil action, because a contractor or participant might be disqualified immediately from dealing with the government, even before the criminal or civil matter is resolved." *ABA Practitioner's Guide to Suspension and Debarment* 6 (1994).

2. *"Present Responsibility."*. The principal of corporate criminal liability for the misconduct of an agent acting in the course of employment is firmly established by the Supreme Court's holding in *New York Central* [Chapter 3]. To what extent should the corporation be *punished* for actions of an agent who no longer holds a position with the company? If a company has "present responsibility," then debarment is not appropriate. Note that the administrative sanction is remedial and not just punitive, so if a contractor can demonstrate present responsibility the sanction may not be appropriate.

In **Robinson v. Cheney**, 876 F.2d 152 (D.C. Cir. 1989), the Defense Logistics Agency (DLA) debarred the Francis E. Heydt Company (FHC), a manufacturer of military apparel, from bidding on any contract or subcontract with any agency in the Executive Branch for three years. Although the sole shareholder of the corporation, Francis E. Heydt, was not indicted, he was implicated in bid-rigging. To avoid debarment, Heydt placed his company in a blind trust to be administered by Robinson, who argued that the removal of Heydt from the operations of the company meant that it was now "presently responsible" to receive government contracts. The District of Columbia Circuit upheld the debarment of the corporation under the following analysis:

> [A] corporation cannot act except through the human beings who may act for it. Thus, it contemplates that a corporate contractor may be held responsible for the wrongful act of its agent, even though "the corporation" was not "aware" (as a practical matter, through its other agents) of the wrong and thus cannot specifically deny that it took place. The regulation puts FHC in a difficult but by no means an unusual position, since a rule of vicarious responsibility will inevitably result in situations in which a company charged with the acts of its agent is compromised in defending itself because it cannot compel the agent to speak in the company's defense. The Government cannot be required to suspend its rule of imputed misconduct, however, in every case in which a contractor lacks access to a witness whose testimony might exonerate it.
>
> First, the Government must be able to fulfill its statutory duty of dealing only with responsible contractors. Once a credible charge of improper conduct comes to the DLA's attention and the regulatory scheme for resolving such charges is set in motion, the responsible officer must make a decision based upon the available evidence. If the record contains evidence that, standing alone, indicates to the officer that improper conduct more likely than not occurred, and no evidence to the contrary is available, we cannot deem it arbitrary for the officer to conclude that the alleged conduct did occur. The decisionmaker must protect the Government's interests—both in rooting out irresponsible contractors and in not disqualifying responsible contractors that compete for its business—and its interests would not be served by a rule requiring him to ignore evidence of wrongdoing simply because the alleged wrongdoer is unable or unwilling to come forward to deny the charges."
>
> Second, adhering to a rule of imputed misconduct in a case where the wrongdoing agent is unavailable to testify does not leave the contractor without recourse, since even if it is unable to demonstrate that the improper act did not occur, it may still show that it is nonetheless presently responsible. * * *
>
> Under the applicable regulations, the ultimate inquiry as to "present responsibility" relates directly to the contractor itself, not to the agent or former agent personally responsible for its past misdeeds.

Thus, the contractor can meet the test of present responsibility by demonstrating that it has taken steps to ensure that the wrongful acts will not recur. * * * Affording the contractor this opportunity to overcome a blemished past assures that the agency will impose debarment only in order to protect the Government's proprietary interest and not for the purpose of punishment.

In this case, Robinson argues that the DLA should have credited the trust arrangement as sufficient, notwithstanding Heydt's past conduct, to establish the company's present responsibility to do business with the Government. Robinson points both to the trust agreement, which gives him full management authority over the company, and to the affidavits of the management employees of FHC stating that Heydt has removed himself from FHC's premises and, to their knowledge, has had no business contact with the company since the effective date of the trust agreement. * * * First, although the trust agreement gives Robinson direct authority over all company operations, it contains no specific term barring Heydt from either acting on behalf of the company or participating in its management. * * * Second, and more important, nothing in either the trust agreement or in any other submission by the company gave the Government any assurance that Heydt would not conduct illicit dealings on behalf of FHC entirely outside company channels. * * * [W]e hold that the DLA reasonably found the trust agreement inadequate to assure that Heydt would not continue to act improperly in FHC's interest as a government contractor * * *.

3. ***Professional Practice Exclusion.*** The Securities and Exchange Commission adopted Rule 2(e) that permits it to exclude an accountant from practicing before it if the person acts improperly. The Rule provides:

e) Suspension and disbarment.

(1) Generally. The Commission may censure a person or deny, temporarily or permanently, the privilege of appearing or practicing before it in any way to any person who is found by the Commission after notice and opportunity for hearing in the matter:

(i) Not to possess the requisite qualifications to represent others; or

(ii) To be lacking in character or integrity or to have engaged in unethical or improper professional conduct; or

(iii) To have willfully violated, or willfully aided and abetted the violation of any provision of the Federal securities laws or the rules and regulations thereunder.

(iv) With respect to persons licensed to practice as accountants, "improper professional conduct" under § 201.102(e)(1)(ii) means:

(A) Intentional or knowing conduct, including reckless conduct, that results in a violation of applicable professional standards; or

(B) Either of the following two types of negligent conduct:

(1) A single instance of highly unreasonable conduct that results in a violation of applicable professional standards in circumstances in which an accountant knows, or should know, that heightened scrutiny is warranted.

(2) Repeated instances of unreasonable conduct, each resulting in a violation of applicable professional standards, that indicate a lack of competence to practice before the Commission.

17 C.F.R. § 201.102(e). In **Touche Ross & Co. v. Securities and Exchange Commission**, 609 F.2d 570 (2d Cir. 1979), the Second Circuit upheld the validity of Rule 2(e), finding that

> Rule 2(e) thus represents an attempt by the SEC essentially to protect the integrity of its own processes. If incompetent or unethical accountants should be permitted to certify financial statements, the reliability of the disclosure process would be impaired. * * *

> * * * [W]e reject appellants' assertion that the Commission acted without authority in promulgating Rule 2(e). Although there is no express statutory provision authorizing the Commission to discipline professionals appearing before it, Rule 2(e), promulgated pursuant to its statutory rulemaking authority, represents an attempt by the Commission to protect the integrity of its own processes. It provides the Commission with the means to ensure that those professionals, on whom the Commission relies heavily in the performance of its statutory duties, perform their tasks diligently and with a reasonable degree of competence. As such the Rule is 'reasonably related' to the purposes of the securities laws. Moreover, we hold that the Rule does not violate, nor is it inconsistent with, any other provision of the securities laws. We therefore sustain the validity of the Rule as a necessary adjunct to the Commission's power to protect the integrity of its administrative procedures and the public in general.

CHAPTER FIFTEEN
ATTORNEY-CLIENT PRIVILEGE AND
WORK PRODUCT DOCTRINE

A. SCOPE OF LAWYER-CLIENT PRIVILEGE AND WORK PRODUCT DOCTRINE

1. Upjohn v. United States

While corporations can be charged with crimes under the Due Process Clause, and are protected by the Fourth Amendment from unreasonable searches, a collective entity cannot assert the Fifth Amendment privilege to avoid producing its business records. Outside of the constitutional protections, can a corporation assert the attorney-client privilege? The answer is "yes," but the issue is complicated by the fact that the actual communications between the corporate client and its attorney protected by the privilege will take place with individual officers and employees. Unlike the classic lawyer-client relationship, which involves two individuals meeting alone, a corporation can have thousands of employees, each of whom may bind the corporation and subject it to criminal liability. Does the attorney-client privilege extend to any communication between a lawyer and a corporate employee or agent? The Supreme Court dealt with this question in the following case.

UPJOHN CO. v. UNITED STATES
449 U.S. 383, 101 S.Ct. 677, 66 L.Ed.2d 584 (1981)

Justice REHNQUIST delivered the opinion of the Court.

[The Upjohn Company conducted an internal investigation into potentially illegal payments made to third parties by employees of the company's foreign subsidiaries. As described by the Court, "As part of this investigation the attorneys prepared a letter containing a questionnaire which was sent to 'All Foreign General and Area Managers' over the Chairman's signature. The letter began by noting recent disclosures that several American companies made 'possibly illegal' payments to foreign government officials and emphasized that the management needed full information concerning any such payments made by Upjohn. The letter indicated that the Chairman had asked Thomas, identified as 'the company's General Counsel,' 'to conduct an investigation for the purpose of determining the nature and magnitude of any payments made by the Upjohn Company or any of its subsidiaries to any employee or official of a foreign government.'"

After completing its investigation, the company submitted its findings of possible illegal conduct to the SEC and IRS. The IRS then issued a summons requiring Upjohn to produce the documents generated in its internal investigation.

The company objected on the grounds that the documents were protected by the attorney-client privilege and the work product doctrine. The government argued that communications with lower-level employees who were not part of the company's "control group" fell outside the privilege and the protection afforded attorney work product. The opinion for a unanimous Court, by then-Justice Rehnquist, rejected the control group test and presented a flexible analysis of how far the privilege can extend].

Federal Rule of Evidence 501 provides that "the privilege of a witness . . . shall be governed by the principles of the common law as they may be interpreted by the courts of the United States in light of reason and experience." The attorney-client privilege is the oldest of the privileges for confidential communications known to the common law. 8 J. Wigmore, Evidence § 2290 (McNaughton rev. 1961). Its purpose is to encourage full and frank communication between attorneys and their clients and thereby promote broader public interests in the observance of law and administration of justice. The privilege recognizes that sound legal advice or advocacy serves public ends and that such advice or advocacy depends upon the lawyer's being fully informed by the client. * * * Admittedly complications in the application of the privilege arise when the client is a corporation, which in theory is an artificial creature of the law, and not an individual; but this Court has assumed that the privilege applies when the client is a corporation, and the Government does not contest the general proposition. * * *

The Court of Appeals, however, considered the application of the privilege in the corporate context to present a "different problem," since the client was an inanimate entity and "only the senior management, guiding and integrating the several operations, . . . can be said to possess an identity analogous to the corporation as a whole." * * * Such a view, we think, overlooks the fact that the privilege exists to protect not only the giving of professional advice to those who can act on it but also the giving of information to the lawyer to enable him to give sound and informed advice. * * *

In the case of the individual client the provider of information and the person who acts on the lawyer's advice are one and the same. In the corporate context, however, it will frequently be employees beyond the control group * * *. Middle-level—and indeed lower-level—employees can, by actions within the scope of their employment, embroil the corporation in serious legal difficulties, and it is only natural that these employees would have the relevant information needed by corporate counsel if he is adequately to advise the client with respect to such actual or potential difficulties. * * *

The control group test adopted by the court below thus frustrates the very purpose of the privilege by discouraging the communication of relevant information by employees of the client to attorneys seeking to render legal advice to the client corporation. The attorney's advice will also frequently be more significant to noncontrol group members than to those who officially sanction the advice, and the control group test makes it more difficult to convey full and frank legal advice to the employees who will put into effect the client corporation's policy. * * * The communications at issue were made by Upjohn employees[3] to counsel for Upjohn acting as such, at the direction of corporate superiors in order to secure legal advice from counsel. * * *

Application of the attorney-client privilege to communications such as those involved here, however, puts the adversary in no worse position than if the communications had never taken place. The privilege only protects disclosure of communications; it does not protect disclosure of the underlying facts by those who communicated with the attorney:

> [T]he protection of the privilege extends only to *communications* and not to facts. A fact is one thing and a communication concerning that fact is an entirely different thing. The client cannot be compelled to answer the question, "What did you say or write to the attorney?" but may not refuse to disclose any relevant fact within his knowledge merely because he incorporated a statement of such fact into his communication to his attorney. Philadelphia v. Westinghouse Electric Corp., 205 F. Supp. 830, 831.

* * * Here the Government was free to question the employees who communicated with Thomas and outside counsel. Upjohn has provided the IRS with a list of such employees, and the IRS has already interviewed some 25 of them. While it would probably be more convenient for the Government to secure the results of petitioner's internal investigation by simply subpoenaing the questionnaires and notes taken by petitioner's attorneys, such considerations of convenience do not overcome the policies served by the attorney-client privilege. * * *

Needless to say, we decide only the case before us, and do not undertake to draft a set of rules which should govern challenges to investigatory subpoenas. * * * While such a "case-by-case" basis may to some slight extent undermine desirable certainty in the boundaries of the attorney-client privilege, it obeys the spirit of the Rules. * * *

---

[3] Seven of the eighty-six employees interviewed by counsel had terminated their employment with Upjohn at the time of the interview. Petitioners argue that the privilege should nonetheless apply to communications by these former employees concerning activities during their period of employment. Neither the District Court nor the Court of Appeals had occasion to address this issue, and we decline to decide it without the benefit of treatment below.

NOTES

1. *Scope of* **Upjohn.** The Supreme Court notes a number of factors in support of extending the privilege to the communications between the company employees and corporate counsel: (1) communications were made and sought by counsel in connection with rendering legal advice; (2) corporate superiors directed employees to provide information to counsel; (3) employees were "sufficiently aware that they were being questioned in order that the corproation could obtain legal advice"; (4) "the communications concerned matters within the scope of the employees' corporate duties"; (5) the information provided was "not available from upper echelon management" and "was needed to supply a basis for legal advice"; and (6) the company informed employees that the communications were "highly confidential" and were subsequently "kept confidential by the company." It is not clear whether the application of the privilege requires all of the factors, or whether some are more important than others.

2. *Former Employees.* In footnote 3 in *Upjohn*, the Supreme Court did not rule on whether the corporation's attorney-client privilege extended to communications with former employees. When the attorney's communications with the former employee concern matters that arose while the person was an employee, courts generally view the discussions as coming within the privilege. In In re Allen, 106 F.3d 582 (4th Cir. 1997), the Fourth Circuit stated:

> The Supreme Court has explained that the attorney-client privilege "rests on the need for the advocate and counselor to know all that relates to the client's reasons for seeking representation if the professional mission is to be carried out." Trammel v. United States, 445 U.S. 40 (1980). The Court reiterated this "need to know" focus in *Upjohn*: "the privilege exists to protect not only the giving of professional advice to those who can act on it but also the giving of information to the lawyer to enable him to give sound and informed advice." In rejecting the "control group" test for determining which employees are within the scope of a corporation's attorney-client privilege, the Upjohn Court recognized that "it will frequently be employees beyond the control group . . . who will possess the information needed by the corporation's lawyers." Accordingly, we hold that the analysis applied by the Supreme Court in *Upjohn* to determine which employees fall within the scope of the privilege applies equally to former employees.

When the communication does not relate to actions while the person was an employee, but only after the employment relationship has ended, then it is much less likely to be protected by the corporation's attorney-client privilege and instead viewed as a communication with a third party absent special circumstances. See, e.g., Infosystems, Inc. v. Ceridian Corp., 197 F.R.D. 303 E.D. Mich. 2000) ("there may be situations where the former employee retains a present connection or agency relationship with the client corporation, or where the present-day communication concerns a confidential matter that was uniquely within the knowledge of the former employee when he worked for the client corporation, such that counsel's communications with this former employee must be cloaked with the privilege in order for meaningful fact-gathering to occur. ").

2. Attorney-Client Privilege – Underlying Facts

The Court in *Upjohn* noted that the attorney-client privilege "did not protect disclosure of the underlying facts by those who communicated with the attorney." Is the government, therefore, permitted to ask any questions pertaining to the underlying facts?

IN RE SIX GRAND JURY WITNESSES
979 F.2d 939 (2d Cir. 1992)

CARDAMONE, Circuit Judge:

Believing it had been deliberately defrauded by a subcontractor under a government contract, the United States commenced a criminal investigation and summoned several company employees to testify before a grand jury. When the contractor corporation learned it was the target of a criminal investigation it retained counsel, consulted with company officials and implemented an approach to evaluating the work performed that it believed would demonstrate that the government had received fair value for the equipment furnished. The employees responsible for monitoring the costs on the subject government project and who performed the analysis for defense counsel are the ones called before the grand jury. Their refusal to answer certain questions based on their corporate employer's assertion of the attorney-client privilege and the attorney's work product privilege precipitated this appeal.

Squarely presented for reconciliation are the seemingly conflicting interests of disclosure and secrecy. Discovery, designed to advance the pursuit of truth, takes the "sporting" element out of litigation by eliminating surprise. The inviolability of confidential communications between attorney and client and the protected privacy of the attorney's work product also contribute to the efficient functioning of the adversarial system's search for truth. Each ceases to be a privilege when it ceases to be a secret. The question before us asks to what extent may the prosecution obtain access to information defendant counsel alleges it has gathered; or, to phrase it another way, may these employees be compelled-despite the company's assertion of the two privileges-to testify before the grand jury with respect to their activities. With a few exceptions, we think they may be so compelled.

The facts in this case are straightforward and undisputed. XYZ Corporation designs and builds timing devices for, among other uses, navigating satellites. A grand jury in the Eastern District of New York is investigating allegations that XYZ and its president, Richard Roe, conspired to defraud the United States in violation of 18 U.S.C. §§ 286 and 371 and committed major fraud against the United States in violation of § 1031 by submitting claims containing false statements in violation of § 1001. The investigation concerns XYZ's performance under contracts to design and build a frequency source amplifier, a voltage controlled crystal oscillator, a frequency multiplier power amplifier, a calibration upconverter, a reference generator unit, and a surface acoustic wave oscillator. The government believes XYZ illegally inflated its costs when submitting vouchers for work performed as a subcontractor on contracts called the "Fox" contracts that XYZ had with a prime government contractor producing this sophisticated space equipment.

The investigation of XYZ for making false and inflated claims for payment under the Fox contracts started after "stop work" orders were issued in February 1988. Subsequently, certain of the Fox contracts were terminated altogether; others were renegotiated and continued on a reduced scale. XYZ's payment claims relate to the work it performed up to the date of the stop-work orders. It also made proposals on the reconfigured continuing contracts. The government alleges that XYZ created false books and records in support of its termination payment claims and proposals and that its original corporate records on these contracts were either destroyed or discarded. At the commencement of its investigation in 1990 the government obtained two broad search warrants and a subpoena for "all documents related to the Fox contracts," resulting in its gathering truckloads of documents from XYZ amounting to at least 170 boxes of corporate records.

XYZ retained counsel to represent it in connection with the investigation. In January 1991 defense counsel requested that an analysis of costs be made by certain high-ranking employees—John Does # 1 through # 6. These employees were engineering manager, program manager, microwave systems manager, director of marketing, program administrator, and vice-president of systems engineering, respectively. As such, they were the employees responsible for monitoring XYZ's costs and were familiar with the Fox contracts. In conducting their analysis each of them chose what documents they would review. In early 1992 all six employees appeared before the grand jury.

During the course of their grand jury testimony John Does # 1, # 3, # 5 and # 6 refused to answer questions with respect to the analysis they had made of the Fox contracts because this work had been done at the direction of XYZ's counsel. The witnesses read a statement setting forth their understanding that the corporation was asserting the confidentiality of the attorney-client privilege with respect to the witnesses' communication with defense counsel and also the confidentiality under the work product privilege of "all information and materials generated" at the direction of counsel.* * *

Appellants contend that they may rightfully refuse to answer the questions * * * because the information gathered in the employees' analysis is protected by the attorney-client privilege, and that absent a waiver, the prosecutor has no right to discover the communications of these analyses to defense counsel no matter how great the need. Appellants also assert this information is immune from grand jury inquiry under the attorney's work product doctrine. Specifically, they assert that these privileges protect the "substance" of the work product, not simply the written analysis, which the government concedes it is not entitled to. The government responds that the information it seeks is limited to underlying facts and opinions * * * within the knowledge of these witnesses and that it is entitled to their testimony before the grand jury because neither the attorney-client privilege nor the work product doctrine protects the requested information. * * *

We recognize that the availability of advice from an attorney is essential if corporations are to comply with the ever-increasing complexities of federal law; and, if that advice is to be sought and given there must be predictable certainty as to which communications will be protected. Where the client is a corporation, as here, the privilege extends to communications between a lawyer and his or her client—both information provided to the lawyer by the client and professional advice given by an attorney that discloses such information. Yet, the cloak of the privilege simply protects the communication from discovery, the underlying information contained in the communication is not shielded from discovery.* * *

Whether the work product of counsel gathered and devised in preparation for litigation, such as facts, legal contentions or trial tactics, may be discovered is a highly controversial area of the law, as this case illustrates. The boundaries of the doctrine are far from fixed. * * * From [*Hickman v. Taylor*], it can be gleaned that the work product doctrine provides a zone of privacy for a lawyer; the doctrine grants counsel an opportunity to think or prepare a client's case without fear of intrusion by an adversary. While unwarranted questions probing the attorney's files and theory of the case are barred in criminal as well as civil litigation, relevant, non-privileged facts may be discovered from an attorney's files where their production is essential to the opponent's preparation of its case. * * * Both common law principles embodied in the attorney-client privilege and the work product doctrine are to be applied in a common sense way in light of reason and experience as determined on a case-by-case basis. * * *

We turn to the pending questions. To begin with it seems plain that merely by asking witnesses to conduct an analysis defense counsel may not thereby silence all the key witnesses on the cost aspects of the * * * contracts under either claim of privilege. Were counsel to succeed in such a tactic, the government would never be able to conduct a full and complete investigation of an alleged crime because the critical witnesses would have been effectively silenced, nor for the same reason would the government be able to present all the evidence at trial regarding a defendant's guilt or innocence.

Examining the 23 questions we see no trampling of either privilege, except in four questions.[a] Question # 8 "With whom did you discuss this analysis," # 9 "What was said [other than to counsel]," # 14 "What information did you give them [anyone other than [XYZ's] attorney]," and question # 15 "When did you give this information to anyone other than [XYZ's] attorney." The form of these four questions, considered in sequence, risks violation of the attorney-client privilege because the witness, in responding, might be understood to be implying to the grand jury that he had conveyed privileged information to the lawyer. Appellee's efforts now to include bracketed exclusions of communications to counsel minimize the risk, but a rephrasing of the questions is preferable to avoid suggesting that the witness is being asked about any aspect of any communication he might have had with the lawyer.

Although an attorney-client communication is privileged and may not be divulged, the underlying information or substance of the communication is not, as appellants incorrectly believe, so privileged. Further, the remaining 19 questions seek underlying factual information to which the prosecutor is clearly entitled.   The factual information is not protected by the attorney-client privilege just because the information was developed in anticipation of litigation.* * *

As a consequence, there is no common law privilege barring the government from obtaining answers to these 19 questions from the * * * witnesses.

3. Attorney-Client Privilege – Hiring Experts

White collar crime practitioners – whether in the Department of Justice or private practice – are primarily trial lawyers, and do not have expertise in specialized areas that may come up in a wide range of cases, such as medical procedures, accounting principles, or the valuation of complex securities. They will frequently retain outside experts to advise them on the technical

---

[a] In an appendix, the court set forth all 23 questions, dividing them into 3 groups: (1) questions which witnesses refused to answer on privilege grounds, as set forth in a letter of the U.S. Attorney dated March 17, 1992; (2) additional questions which the U.S. Attorney intended to ask when the witnesses were recalled, also set forth in that letter; (3) further questions submitted by the U.S. Attorney on May 4, 1992. The first group, containing questions 1-6, asked about the character of the internal analysis that had evaluated the work performed under the contract (e.g., the witness' role in the analysis, the general nature of the analysis). The second group, containing questions 7-17, included the 4 questions discussed by the court. It also included various questions relating to details of the analysis (what records were reviewed, what information was furnished by employees, what conclusions were drawn). Group 3 contained questions 18-23, which related to the information needed to conduct an accurate analysis of the total costs under the contract (e.g., what documents would be needed, what questions would have to be answered, who were possible sources of information) and the witness' estimate of those costs.

issues that may arise in a case, and in some instances use the expert to testify at trial. In **United States v. Kovel**, 296 F.2d 918 (2d Cir. 1961), the court held that the attorney-client privilege extended to counsel's consultations with an accountant retained to assist the attorney in understanding the client's financial transactions. Comparing an outside expert to an interpreter who can translate foreign documents, the Second Circuit stated, "Accounting concepts are a foreign language to some lawyers in almost all cases, and to almost all lawyers in some cases. Hence the presence of an accountant, whether hired by the lawyer or by the client, while the client is relating a complicated tax story to the lawyer, ought not destroy the privilege, any more than would that of the linguist in the second or third variations of the foreign language theme discussed above; the presence of the accountant is necessary, or at least highly useful, for the effective consultation between the client and the lawyer which the privilege is designed to permit."

The practice of including outside experts on the defense team, and therefore communications with them come within the protections of the attorney-client privilege, is referred to as "*Kovelling*" the expert. The use of an outside expert by an attorney is not automatically protected by the attorney-client privilege, however, as the Second Circuit noted in United States v. Ackert, 169 F.3d 136 (2d Cir. 1999): "[A] communication between an attorney and a third party does not become shielded by the attorney-client privilege solely because the communication proves important to the attorney's ability to represent the client." Similarly, in Cavallaro v. United States, 284 F.3d 236, 240 (1st Cir. 2002), the First Circuit held that because the hiring of the Ernst & Young accounting firm was not related to any effective consultation between the client and the lawyer, the attorney-client privilege did not extend to the documents in question. The Court did "not decide whether, in all instances, the attorney or client (as opposed to some third party) must hire the accountant in order to sustain a privilege * * *." The Court further noted that "an attorney, merely by placing an accountant on her payroll, does not, by this action alone, render communications between the attorney's client and the accountant privileged."

In **In re Grand Jury Subpoena Dated March 24, 2003**, 265 F. Supp.2d 321 (S.D.N.Y. 2003), the Court applied both the attorney-client privilege and the work product protection to communications between a prospective defendant in a criminal case, her lawyers, and a public relations firm hired by the lawyers to aid in avoiding an indictment. The P.R. firm's activities included not just advising the target and her lawyers, but also spoke to members of the media on behalf of the attorney. The Court focused on "the effective operation of the attorney-client privilege of a client and lawyer under conditions where the lawyer needs outside help." The district court noted that the communications between the target and the P.R. firm would not have been privileged if she had simply gone out and hired public relations counsel; in this case the attorneys hired the P.R. firm. The Court resolved in favor of the target, the "ultimate issue" – "whether attorney efforts to influence public opinion in order to advance the client's legal position– in this case by neutralizing what the attorneys perceived as a climate of opinion pressing prosecutors and regulators to act in ways adverse to Target's interests–are services, the rendition of which also should be facilitated by applying the privilege to relevant communications which have this as their object." The Court applied the protections not just to Target's communications with the P.R. firm that took place in the presence of lawyers, but also to those between the Target and the firm, provided they were directed at giving or obtaining legal advice. Finally, the court noted that the presence of the Target's spouse during some of the conversations did not destroy any applicable privilege, because disclosure of communications protected by the attorney-client privilege in the context of another privilege (spouse) does not constitute waiver of the attorney-client privilege.

4. Work Product

The protection afforded the work product of an attorney is distinct from, and in some cases broader than, the privilege for communications between a lawyer and client.

> Privileged information is immune totally from discovery, no matter how compelling the need for the information seems to be. Information that is collected in anticipation of litigation or trial is protected from discovery, but that protection may yield to a showing of need on the part of the requesting party. Mental impressions of the attorney enjoy the highest level of protection under the work product doctrine, but * * * even they may be revealed, at least in part, upon a sufficient showing. Thus, the application of the work product rule often requires a balancing of the competing needs of the parties, as well as an inquiry into whether the material involved properly falls within the concerns that originally produced this discovery exception.

JACK H. FRIEDENTHAL, MARY KAY KANE, & ARTHUR R. MILLER, CIVIL PROCEDURE 387 (2d ed. 1993). The Supreme Court in *Upjohn* discussed the scope of the work product protection:

> Our decision that the communications by Upjohn employees to counsel are covered by the attorney-client privilege disposes of the case so far as the responses to the questionnaires and any notes reflecting responses to interview questions are concerned. The summons reaches further, however, and Thomas has testified that his notes and memoranda of interviews go beyond recording responses to his questions. To the extent that the material subject to the summons is not protected by the attorney-client privilege as disclosing communications between an employee and counsel, we must reach the ruling by the Court of Appeals that the work-product doctrine does not apply to summonses issued under 26 U.S.C. § 7602.

The Government concedes, wisely, that the Court of Appeals erred and that the work-product doctrine does apply to IRS summonses. This doctrine was announced by the Court over 30 years ago in Hickman v. Taylor, 329 U.S. 495 (1947). In that case the Court rejected "an attempt, without purported necessity or justification, to secure written statements, private memoranda and personal recollections prepared or formed by an adverse party's counsel in the course of his legal duties." The Court noted that "it is essential that a lawyer work with a certain degree of privacy" and reasoned that if discovery of the material sought were permitted

> much of what is now put down in writing would remain unwritten. An attorney's thoughts, heretofore inviolate, would not be his own. Inefficiency, unfairness and sharp practices would inevitably develop in the giving of legal advice and in the preparation of cases for trial. The effect on the legal profession would be demoralizing. And the interests of the clients and the cause of justice would be poorly served. [Hickman v. Taylor].

The "strong public policy" underlying the work-product doctrine was reaffirmed recently in United States v. Nobles, 422 U.S, 225 (1975) and has been substantially incorporated in Federal Rule of Civil Procedure 26(b)(3).

As we stated last Term, the obligation imposed by a tax summons remains "subject to the traditional privileges and limitations." United States v. Euge, 444 U.S. 707 (1980). Nothing in the language of the IRS summons provisions or their legislative history suggests an intent on the part of Congress to preclude application of the work-product doctrine. Rule 26(b)(3) codifies the work-product doctrine, and the Federal Rules of Civil Procedure are made applicable to summons enforcement proceedings by Rule 81(a)(3). While conceding the applicability of the work-product doctrine, the Government asserts that it has made a sufficient showing of necessity to overcome its protections. * * *

Rule 26 accords special protection to work product revealing the attorney's mental processes. The Rule permits disclosure of documents and tangible things constituting attorney work product upon a showing of substantial need and inability to obtain the equivalent without undue hardship. * * * Rule 26 goes on, however, to state that "[i]n ordering discovery of such materials when the required showing has been made, the court shall protect against disclosure of the mental impressions, conclusions, opinions or legal theories of an attorney or other representative of a party concerning the litigation." Although this language does not specifically refer to memoranda based on oral statements of witnesses, the *Hickman* court stressed the danger that compelled disclosure of such memoranda would reveal the attorney's mental processes. It is clear that this is the sort of material the draftsmen of the Rule had in mind as deserving special protection. * * *

Based on the foregoing, some courts have concluded that no showing of necessity can overcome protection of work product which is based on oral statements from witnesses. * * * Those courts declining to adopt an absolute rule have nonetheless recognized that such material is entitled to special protection. * * *

We do not decide the issue at this time. It is clear that the Magistrate applied the wrong standard when he concluded that the Government had made a sufficient showing of necessity to overcome the protections of the work-product doctrine. The Magistrate applied the "substantial need" and "without undue hardship" standard articulated in the first part of Rule 26(b)(3). The notes and memoranda sought by the Government here, however, are work product based on oral statements. If they reveal communications, they are, in this case, protected by the attorney-client privilege. To the extent they do not reveal communications, they reveal the attorneys' mental processes in evaluating the communications. As Rule 26 and *Hickman* make clear, such work product cannot be disclosed simply on a showing of substantial need and inability to obtain the equivalent without undue hardship.

While we are not prepared at this juncture to say that such material is always protected by the work-product rule, we think a far stronger showing of necessity and unavailability by other means than was made by the Government or applied by the Magistrate in this case would be necessary to compel disclosure. Since the Court of Appeals thought that the work-product protection was never applicable in an enforcement proceeding such as this, and since the Magistrate whose recommendations the District Court adopted applied too lenient a standard of protection, we think the best procedure with respect to this aspect of the case would be to reverse the judgment of the Court of Appeals for the Sixth Circuit and remand the case to it for such further proceedings in connection with the work-product claim as are consistent with this opinion. * * *

The work product doctrine is "now codified in part in Rule 26(b)(3) of the Federal Rules of Civil Procedure and Rule 16(b)(2) of the Federal Rules of Criminal Procedure." In re Grand Jury Subpoenas, 318 F.3d 379, 383 (2d Cir. 2003). In In re Grand Jury Subpoena, 220 F.R.D. 130, 141 (D. Mass. 2004), the court noted:

There are important differences between the doctrine articulated in Hickman [v. Taylor, 329 U.S. 495 (1947)] and the text of Rule 26(b)(3) . . . . for example, unlike Hickman, Rule 26(b)(3) does not reach "intangible" work product, but Rule 26(b)(3) more clearly protects non-attorney work product than Hickman does.

See Special Project, *The Work Product Doctrine*, 68 CORNELL L. REV. 760, 766-73 (1983).

5. Work Product – "In Anticipation of Litigation"

In In re Grand Jury Subpoenas Dated March 9, 2001, 179 F.Supp.2d (S.D.N.Y. 2001), the district court enforced subpoenas to five attorneys for two men, Marc Rich and Pincus Green, who had obtained a pardon from President Clinton on his last day in office. The pardon's were "highly controversial and generated much public outcry" because the defendants had fled the United States after their indictment and could not be extradited to stand trial. The attorneys argued that they did not have to comply with the subpoenas, *inter alia*, because the documents constituted work product. The district court rejected that argument, stating that the "reliance on the work product doctrine is misplaced because the process by which Rich and Green sought their pardons here was not an adversarial one; rather, it was an *ex parte* process that did not anticipate further litigation because it was clear that Rich and Green were never going to return to face the charges." Rich and Green avoided dealing directly with the Department of Justice–*i.e.* litigation–and concentrated their efforts on the White House–*i.e.* Executive authority.

How likely does the litigation have to be to invoke the protection of the work product doctrine? Consider the following case involving advice from a lawyer that involves a pending business decision and potential related litigation.

UNITED STATES v. ADLMAN
134 F.3d 1194 (2nd Cir. 1998)

LEVAL, Circuit Judge:

This appeal concerns the proper interpretation of Federal Rule of Civil Procedure 26(b)(3) ("the Rule"), which grants limited protection against discovery to documents and materials prepared "in anticipation of litigation." Specifically, we must address whether a study prepared for an attorney assessing the likely result of an expected litigation is ineligible for protection under the Rule if the primary or ultimate purpose of making the study was to assess the desirability of a business transaction, which, if undertaken, would give rise to the litigation. We hold that a document created because of anticipated litigation, which tends to reveal mental impressions, conclusions, opinions or theories concerning the litigation, does not lose work-product protection merely because it is intended to assist in the making of a business decision influenced by the likely outcome of the anticipated litigation. Where a document was created because of anticipated litigation, and would not have been prepared in substantially similar form but for the prospect of that litigation, it falls within Rule 26(b)(3).

The district court ruled that the document sought by the IRS in this case did not fall within the scope of Rule 26(b)(3) and ordered its production. Because we cannot determine whether the district court used the correct standard in reaching its decision, we vacate the judgment and remand for reconsideration. * * *

Sequa Corporation is an aerospace manufacturer with annual revenues of nearly $2 billion. Prior to 1989, Atlantic Research Corporation ("ARC") and Chromalloy Gas Turbine Corporation ("Chromalloy") were wholly-owned Sequa subsidiaries. Appellant Monroe Adlman is an attorney and Vice President for Taxes at Sequa.

In the spring of 1989, Sequa contemplated merging Chromalloy and ARC. The contemplated merger was expected to produce an enormous loss and tax refund, which Adlman expected would be challenged by the IRS and would result in litigation. Adlman asked Paul Sheahen, an accountant and lawyer at Arthur Andersen & Co. ("Arthur Andersen"), to evaluate the tax implications of the proposed restructuring. Sheahen did so and set forth his study in a memorandum (the "Memorandum"). He submitted the Memorandum in draft form to Adlman in August 1989. After further consultation, on September 5, 1989, Sheahen sent Adlman the final version. The Memorandum was a 58-page detailed legal analysis of likely IRS challenges to the reorganization and the resulting tax refund claim; it contained discussion of statutory provisions, IRS regulations, legislative history, and prior judicial and IRS rulings relevant to the claim. It proposed possible legal theories or strategies for Sequa to adopt in response, recommended preferred methods of structuring the transaction, and made predictions about the likely outcome of litigation.

Sequa decided to go ahead with the restructuring, which was completed in December 1989 in essentially the form recommended by Arthur Andersen. Sequa sold 93% of its stock in ARC to Chromalloy for $167.4 million, and the remaining 7% to Bankers Trust for $12.6 million. The reorganization resulted in a $289 million loss. Sequa claimed the loss on its 1989 return and carried it back to offset 1986 capital gains, thereby generating a claim for a refund of $35 million.

In an ensuing audit of Sequa's 1986-1989 tax returns, the IRS requested a number of documents concerning the restructuring transaction. Sequa acknowledged the existence of the Memorandum, but cited work-product privilege as grounds for declining to produce it. On September 23, 1993, the IRS served a summons on Adlman for production of the Memorandum.

When Adlman declined to comply, the IRS instituted an action in the United States District Court for the Southern District of New York to enforce the subpoena. Adlman defended on the grounds that the Memorandum was protected by both the attorney-client and work-product privileges. The district court (Knapp, J.) in its first decision rejected Adlman's claim that the Memorandum was protected by attorney-client privilege, finding that Adlman had not consulted Arthur Andersen in order to obtain assistance in furnishing legal advice to Sequa. * * * It rejected Adlman's claim of work-product privilege because the Memorandum was prepared for litigation based on actions or events that had not yet occurred at the time of its creation. The court granted the IRS's petition to enforce the summons.

On appeal, we affirmed denial of Adlman's claim of attorney-client privilege. United States v. Adlman, 68 F.3d 1495 (2d Cir.1995). We vacated the district court's enforcement order, however, because the district court had evaluated Adlman's claim of work-product privilege under the wrong standard. Although the non-occurrence of events giving rise to litigation prior to preparation of the documents is a factor to be considered, we explained, it does not necessarily preclude application of work-product privilege. * * *

On remand, Adlman argued that the Memorandum was protected by Rule 26(b)(3) because it included legal opinions prepared in reasonable anticipation of litigation. * * * The district court again rejected the claim of work-product privilege, concluding that the Memorandum was not prepared in anticipation of litigation. * * * Adlman appeals.

* * * The work-product doctrine, codified for the federal courts in Fed.R.Civ.P. 26(b)(3), is intended to preserve a zone of privacy in which a lawyer can prepare and develop legal theories and strategy "with an eye toward litigation," free from unnecessary intrusion by his adversaries. Hickman v. Taylor, 329 U.S. 495 (1947). Analysis of one's case "in anticipation of litigation" is a classic example of work product, * * * and receives heightened protection under Fed.R.Civ.P. 26(b)(3).

This case involves a question of first impression in this circuit: whether Rule 26(b)(3) is inapplicable to a litigation analysis prepared by a party or its representative in order to inform a business decision which turns on the party's assessment of the likely outcome of litigation expected to result from the transaction. Answering that question requires that we determine the proper interpretation of Rule 26(b)(3)'s requirement that documents be prepared "in anticipation of litigation" in order to qualify for work-product protection. * * *

The first problem we face is to determine the meaning of the phrase prepared "in anticipation of litigation." The phrase has never been interpreted by our circuit; furthermore, courts and commentators have expressed a range of views as to its meaning. It is universally agreed that a document whose purpose is to assist in preparation for litigation is within the scope of the Rule and thus eligible to receive protection if the other conditions of protection prescribed by the Rule are met. The issue is less clear, however, as to documents which, although prepared because of expected litigation, are intended to inform a business decision influenced by the prospects of the litigation. The formulation applied by some courts in determining whether documents are protected by work-product privilege is whether they are prepared "primarily or exclusively to assist in litigation"–a formulation that would potentially exclude documents containing analysis of expected litigation, if their primary, ultimate, or exclusive purpose is to assist in making the business decision. Others ask whether the documents were prepared "because of" existing or expected litigation–a formulation that would include such documents, despite the fact that their purpose is not to "assist in" litigation. Because we believe that protection of documents of this type is more consistent with both the literal terms and the purposes of the Rule, we adopt the latter formulation. * * *

We believe that a requirement that documents be produced primarily or exclusively to assist in litigation in order to be protected is at odds with the text and the policies of the Rule. Nowhere does Rule 26(b)(3) state that a document must have been prepared to aid in the conduct of litigation in order to constitute work product, much less primarily or exclusively to aid in litigation. Preparing a document "in anticipation of litigation" is sufficient.

The text of Rule 26(b)(3) does not limit its protection to materials prepared to assist at trial. To the contrary, the text of the Rule clearly sweeps more broadly. It expressly states that work-product privilege applies not only to documents "prepared . . . for trial" but also to those prepared "in anticipation of litigation." If the drafters of the Rule intended to limit its protection to documents made to assist in preparation for litigation, this would have been adequately conveyed by the phrase "prepared . . . for trial." The fact that documents prepared "in anticipation of litigation" were also included confirms that the drafters considered this to be a different, and broader category. Nothing in the Rule states or suggests that documents prepared "in anticipation of litigation" with the purpose of assisting in the making of a business decision do not fall within its scope.

In addition, the Rule takes pains to grant special protection to the type of materials at issue in this case–documents setting forth legal analysis. While the Rule generally withholds protection for documents prepared in anticipation of litigation if the adverse party shows "substantial need" for their disclosure and inability to obtain their equivalent by other means, even where the party seeking disclosure has made such a showing the Rule directs that "the court shall protect against disclosure of the mental impressions, conclusions, opinions, or legal theories of . . . [a party or its representative] concerning the litigation." Fed.R.Civ.P. 26(b)(3) (emphasis added). As the Advisory Committee notes indicate, Rule 26(b)(3) is intended to ratify the principles that "each side's informal evaluation of its case should be protected, that each side should be encouraged to prepare independently, and that one side should not automatically have the benefit of the detailed preparatory work of the other side." Where the Rule has explicitly established a special level of protection against disclosure for documents revealing an attorney's (or other representative's) opinions and legal theories concerning litigation, it would oddly undermine its purposes if such documents were excluded from protection merely because they were prepared to assist in the making of a business decision expected to result in the litigation.

Admittedly, there are fragmentary references in the caption to the Rule and in its commentary that can be read to lend support to a contrary interpretation. The caption, for example, refers to "Trial Preparation," and the Advisory Committee Notes make occasional reference to "trial preparation materials." We attach small importance to those references. Given that the text of the Rule (and of the commentary) expressly goes beyond documents "prepared . . . for trial" to encompass also those documents "prepared in anticipation of litigation," we cannot read the references in the caption and commentary as overriding the text of the Rule. * * *

In addition to the plain language of the Rule, the policies underlying the work-product doctrine suggest strongly that work-product protection should not be denied to a document that analyzes expected litigation merely because it is prepared to assist in a business decision. Framing the inquiry as whether the primary or exclusive purpose of the document was to assist in litigation threatens to deny protection to documents that implicate key concerns underlying the work-product doctrine. * * *

* * * The formulation of the work-product rule used by the Wright & Miller treatise, and cited by the Third, Fourth, Seventh, Eighth and D.C. Circuits, is that documents should be deemed prepared "in anticipation of litigation," and thus within the scope of the Rule, if "in light of the nature of the document and the factual situation in the particular case, the document can fairly be said to have been prepared or obtained because of the prospect of litigation." * * *

* * * [W]e find that the Wright & Miller "because of" test appropriately focuses on both what should be eligible for the Rule's protection and what should not. We believe this is the proper test to determine whether a document was prepared "in anticipation of litigation" and is thus eligible for protection depending on the further findings required by the Rule. * * * We cannot determine from the district court's opinion what test it followed in concluding that the Memorandum was ineligible for protection.

There are indications that the district court may have followed the "primarily to assist in litigation" test, which we here reject. * * * On the other hand, the tenor of the discussion in the court's opinion suggests it may have focused properly on the question whether the Memorandum studying the tax implications of the contemplated restructuring would have been prepared in substantially similar form regardless whether litigation was contemplated, and thus was not prepared "because of" the expected litigation.

We remand with instructions to the district court to reconsider the issue under the Wright & Miller test of whether "the document can fairly be said to have been prepared . . . because of the prospect of litigation." There is little doubt under the evidence that Sequa had the prospect of litigation in mind when it directed the preparation of the Memorandum by Arthur Andersen. Whether it can fairly be said that the Memorandum was prepared because of that expected litigation really turns on whether it would have been prepared irrespective of the expected litigation with the IRS.

If the district court concludes that substantially the same Memorandum would have been prepared in any event–as part of the ordinary course of business of undertaking the restructuring–then the court should conclude the Memorandum was not prepared because of the expected litigation and should adhere to its prior ruling denying the protection of the Rule.

On the other hand, if the court finds the Memorandum would not have been prepared but for Sequa's anticipation of litigation with the IRS over the losses generated by the restructuring, then judgment should be entered in favor of Sequa. * * *

KEARSE, Circuit Judge, dissenting.

I respectfully dissent. It does not appear to me that the district court applied an erroneous standard in this case. Accordingly, I would affirm. * * * I disagree with the majority's expansion of the work-product privilege to afford protection to documents not prepared in anticipation of litigation but instead prepared in order to permit the client to determine whether to undertake a business transaction, where there will be no anticipation of litigation unless the transaction is undertaken.

6. Work Product – Dual Purpose Documents

The Second Circuit's adoption of the Wright & Miller "because of" test in Adlman requires courts to determine the purpose for the document's creation, which may be difficult to ascertain. The attorney asserting the work product protection will emphasize its relationship to litigation while the opposing party–often the grand jury seeking to obtain the record–will focus on its use for a company's business. What happens when the company operates in a heavily regulated area, and the document was created in response to the settlement of an action with the regulator that requires the company to gather information about its operation to assure future compliance with the law? Is that document created "for or because of" future litigation against the company, or is it merely the record of a company that is required to create such information in order to conduct its business?

In re GRAND JURY SUBPOENA (TORF)
357 F.3d 900 (9th Cir. 2004)

DAVID R. THOMPSON, Senior Circuit Judge.

[Ponderosa Paint Manufacturing, Inc. hired an attorney, McCreedy, to represent it in connection with an investigation by the Environmental Protection Agency about disposal of waste material at one of its plants. McCreedy then hired Torf to investigate possible violations and provide a report to assist McCreedy in representing the company in the investigation. To avoid litigation with the EPA, Ponderosa later entered into an Information Request and Consent Order that required it to "preserve all documents and information related to work performed under this Order or relating to hazardous substances found on or released from this Site." McCreedy continued to advise the company on its compliance, and he used Torf to assist him. Believing the company may have continued violating the law, a grand jury subpoenaed Torf for all records related to "disposal of waste material" by Ponderosa, including documents created after entry of the Consent Order. Ponderosa asserted a work product claim to prevent disclosure of Torf's reports prepared for McCreedy.]

The "because of" standard does not consider whether litigation was a primary or secondary motive behind the creation of a document. Rather, it considers the totality of the circumstances and affords protection when it can fairly be said that the "document was created because of anticipated litigation, and would not have been created in substantially similar form but for the prospect of that litigation[.]" *Adlman*. Here, there is no question that all of the documents were produced in anticipation of litigation. McCreedy hired Torf because of Ponderosa's impending litigation and Torf conducted his investigations because of that threat. The threat animated every document Torf prepared, including the documents prepared to comply with the Information Request and Consent Order, and to consult regarding the cleanup.

The government argues, however, that the withheld documents would have been created in substantially similar form in any event to comply with the Information Request and the Consent Order, and therefore are not protected by the work product doctrine. The government relies on language in Adlman which states: "the 'because of' formulation . . . withholds protection from documents . . . that would have been created in essentially similar form irrespective of the litigation." We do not view this language as eviscerating work product protection for the documents withheld in this case.

The question of entitlement to work product protection cannot be decided simply by looking at one motive that contributed to a document's preparation. The circumstances surrounding the document's preparation must also be considered. In the "because of" Wright & Miller formulation, "the nature of the document and the factual situation of the particular case" are key to a determination of whether work product protection applies. When there is a true independent purpose for creating a document, work product protection is less likely, but when two purposes are profoundly interconnected, the analysis is more complicated.

Here, Ponderosa's response to the Information Request and its accession to the Consent Order were done under the direction of an attorney in anticipation of litigation. By cooperating with the EPA, Ponderosa sought to avoid litigation with the government. Having chosen to pursue a criminal investigation, the government now seeks to capitalize on Ponderosa's earlier cooperation and obtain all of Torf's documents pertaining to the disposal of Ponderosa's waste material. The withheld documents, however, just like the others, were prepared by Torf, at least in part, to help McCreedy advise and defend Ponderosa in anticipated litigation with the government. Thus, the withheld documents fall within the broad category of documents that were prepared for the overall purpose of anticipated litigation.

To the extent that Adlman suggests there is no work product protection when, viewed in isolation of the facts of the case, a document can be said to have been created for a nonlitigation purpose, we believe the better view is set forth in two Seventh Circuit cases. In the first, In re Special September 1978 Grand Jury, 640 F.2d 49 (7th Cir. 1980) ("*Special September*"), the court extended work product protection to materials that were produced both in anticipation of litigation and for the filing of Board of Elections reports required under state law. Work product protection was proper because, by the time the law firm's client received the Board's request for the required reports, the client had already received a subpoena from a federal grand jury. The so-called "independent" purpose of complying with the Board's request was grounded in the same set of facts that created the anticipation of litigation, and it was the anticipation of litigation that prompted the law firm's work in the first place.

In the later case, United States v. Frederick, 182 F.3d 496 (7th Cir. 1999), the Seventh Circuit held that "a dual-purpose document–a document prepared for use in preparing tax returns and for use in litigation–is not privileged; otherwise, people in or contemplating litigation would be able to invoke, in effect, an accountant's privilege, provided that they used their lawyer to fill out their tax returns."

Frederick does not discuss or distinguish *Special September*, but the two cases can be reconciled by the extent to which the so-called independent purpose is truly separable from the anticipation of litigation. In Frederick, at issue were accountants' worksheets, albeit prepared by a lawyer, in preparation of his clients' tax returns. Although his clients were under investigation (which the court acknowledged was a "complicating factor"), work product protection was ultimately inappropriate because tax return preparation is a readily separable purpose from litigation preparation and "using a lawyer in lieu of another form of tax preparer" does nothing to blur that distinction. In Special September, on the other hand, the materials used to prepare the Board of Elections reports were compiled by lawyers and were necessarily created in the first place because of impending litigation.

Similarly here, by hiring McCreedy who in turn hired Torf, Ponderosa was not assigning an attorney a task that could just as well have been performed by a non-lawyer. The company hired McCreedy only after learning that the federal government was investigating it for criminal wrongdoing; a circumstance virtually necessitating legal representation. Torf assisted McCreedy in preparing Ponderosa's defense. He also acted as an environmental consultant on the cleanup. Although in that capacity he could have been retained by Ponderosa directly, this circumstance does not preclude the application of the work-product privilege to documents produced in that capacity, if the documents were also produced "because of" litigation. The challenged documents were prepared under the direction of McCreedy, who was providing legal advice to Ponderosa in anticipation of the impending litigation.

We conclude that the withheld documents, notwithstanding their dual purpose character, fall within the ambit of the work product doctrine. The documents are entitled to work product protection because, taking into account the facts surrounding their creation, their litigation purpose so permeates any non-litigation purpose that the two purposes cannot be discretely separated from the factual nexus as a whole.

7. Work Product – Substantial Need

Unlike privileged attorney-client communications, a court can order the production of work product if the party seeking the information can establish both a substantial need and the inability to obtain the equivalent without undue hardship. What constitutes "substantial need"? Consider **In re Grand Jury Subpoena Dated October 22, 2001**, 282 F.3d 156 (2d Cir. 2002), in which the government sought the compel an attorney to testify before the grand jury about statements made by the general counsel for her corporate client. Four years earlier, in connection with a government investigation of possible tax fraud by the corporation, the attorney attended an interview of the general counsel with two IRS agents, one of whom subsequently died. The grand jury was investigating the general counsel for false statements in violation of § 1001 and possible participation in the tax fraud four years earlier, and subpoenaed the attorney to recount what the general counsel said to the IRS agents. The court found that the work product doctrine applied if the government sought the attorney's testimony to establish the fraud charge:

> If the use of Attorney's testimony were limited to proving that General Counsel committed the crime of false statements in Attorney's presence, the Government would have strong arguments that the work product privilege should not bar a prosecutor's access to eyewitness testimony of the commission of criminal acts.

> On the other hand, the Government's argument seems much less persuasive when the work product privilege is invoked to bar an order compelling the attorney's testimony to admissions made by her client in her presence when that testimony will be used to prove the client's commission of the very crimes concerning which the attorney was representing him at the time.

> The work product doctrine is suffused with policy considerations relating to the appropriate role of the attorney and the relationship

between client and attorney. It is one thing for a client to recognize that if he commits a crime in his attorney's presence, the attorney may be compelled to testify to the criminal acts she witnessed. It seems to us quite different for the client to accept that if he hires an attorney to represent him with respect to his past commission of a crime, the attorney may be compelled to testify against him as to admissions (or denials) he made in his attorney's presence that tend to prove his guilt with respect to that past crime.

We see no reason why the work product privilege is not properly invoked to bar the compulsion of that testimony. It falls comfortably within the black letter definition of work product. Furthermore, it implicates policy concerns relating to the lawyer-client relationship. The work product privilege establishes a zone of privacy for an attorney's preparation to represent a client in anticipation of litigation. For the attorney to be subpoenaed to testify to the observations made in the course of that preparation in order to help the putative adversary prove the offense as to which the attorney was providing representation would do substantial injury to the values that justify the work product doctrine.

* * * [T]he Government's arguments about its demonstration of "substantial need" are not squarely on point. As noted above, the Government argued that it would have substantial need for Attorney's testimony in a trial of General Counsel on false statement charges. Without Attorney's testimony, the Government argues, the trial would come down to a swearing contest between the defendant General Counsel and the sole surviving IRS agent as to what General Counsel did or did not say in the interview. "[Attorney's] testimony has the potential to corroborate substantially the agent's testimony."

This argument, whatever its merit, relates to the Government's need for trial testimony, not to its need for grand jury testimony. The subpoena in question does not call for Attorney's testimony at trial. The subpoena seeks Attorney's testimony before the grand jury. The grand jury does not make a determination of guilt or innocence. It merely determines whether the Government has shown probable cause. Before the grand jury, the Government does not need to prevail in a swearing match. It can easily establish probable cause as to General Counsel's alleged false statements through the testimony of Agent Nass, regardless whether Nass's testimony is corroborated. Thus, the Government's arguments as to its substantial need for Attorney's testimony to resolve a swearing contest at trial are not directly pertinent to its need to compel Attorney's testimony before the grand jury.

Perhaps what the Government means is that, having a substantial need to call Attorney at trial to break the swearing match between the IRS agent and the defendant, it therefore has a substantial need to preview what Attorney's testimony will be by calling her first into the grand jury. We express no view on that question. We simply point out that the Government's argument of substantial need as presented to us relates to its need for Attorney's testimony at trial, while the subpoena in question calls for her testimony before the grand jury.

8. Work Product – Preexisting Documents

Many categories of documents are easily assigned the label "Work Product," such as drafts of memoranda, notes of meetings, and internal communications. Are documents obtained by an attorney in the course of legal representation that were not created for the purpose of the attorney-client relationship also work product?

In re GRAND JURY SUBPOENAS DATED MARCH 19, 2002 AND AUGUST 2, 2002 (THE MERCATOR CORPORATION)
318 F.3d 379 (2nd Cir. 2003),

RAGGI, Circuit Judge.

Appellants, The Mercator Corporation, its chairman James H. Giffen, and their attorneys, the law firm of Akin, Gump, Strauss, Hauer & Feld, L.L.P. ("Akin Gump"), appeal from the September 9, 2002 order of the District Court for the Southern District of New York (Denny Chin, Judge), granting the United States' motion to compel Akin Gump to produce bank records for thirty specific accounts at four Swiss banks called for in grand jury subpoenas. * * *

[The Department of of Justice was investigating possible violations of the Foreign Corrupt Pracitces Act, and filed a Mutual Legal Assistance Treaty ("MLAT") request with Swiss authorities seeking bank records relating to specific accounts held by a foreign country or its officials that were suspected of taking bribes from American corporations. The response received from Switzerland was incomplete or unsatisfactory in several respects.]

Throughout the relevant time, Akin Gump has represented Mercator and Giffen, and, on their behalf, has communicated with prosecutors on matters relating to the pending criminal investigation. Specifically, in the fall of 2000, Akin Gump offered to produce records from six of the Swiss bank accounts identified in the MLAT request with the understanding that production did not waive future privilege claims by Akin Gump's clients. Prosecutors declined to accept the documents on these terms. [Grand jury subpoenas were served on Akin Gump requiring the production of bank records for thirty accounts that were also sought in the MLAT request, and Akin Gump refused to compy by asserting the work product doctrine.]

* * * Carefully reviewing the law applicable to the attorney work product doctrine, Judge Chin concluded that the subpoenaed bank records did not in and of themselves constitute work product because they were "the pre-existing records of third parties, created and maintained in the ordinary course of business by those third parties without any reference to litigation whatsoever.". To the extent appellants argued that Akin Gump's selection and compilation of specific bank records transformed the documents into attorney work product, disclosure of which would reveal counsel's developing defense strategy, Judge Chin noted that in this circuit, "qualifying the 'selection' of records for [work product] protection 'depends upon the existence of a real, rather than speculative, concern that the thought processes of . . . counsel in relation to pending or anticipated litigation would be exposed.'" He expressly found that "Akin, Gump has failed to demonstrate such a genuine concern."

* * * [T]he principle underlying the work product doctrine–sheltering the mental processes of an attorney as reflected in documents prepared for litigation–is not generally promoted by shielding from discovery materials in an attorney's possession that were prepared neither by the attorney nor his agents. See In re Grand Jury Subpoenas (Paul Weiss), 959 F.2d 1158 (2d Cir. 1992) (rejecting work product claim with respect to telephone company records in possession of former attorneys of criminal target). Thus, the work product doctrine does not extend to documents in an attorney's possession that were prepared by a third party in the ordinary course of business and that would have been created in essentially similar form irrespective of any litigation anticipated by counsel. See *United States v. Adlman*.

Appellants submit that an exception to this third-party documents rule applies when an attorney has so specifically selected and compiled such documents in anticipation of litigation that production would necessarily reveal the attorney's developing strategy. This argument relies largely on decisions in two civil cases from outside this circuit: Sporck v. Peil, 759 F.2d 312 (3d Cir.1985); and Shelton v. American Motors Corp., 805 F.2d 1323 (8th Cir.1986). In both cases, the issue was not so much whether the work product doctrine shielded counsel from producing certain documents, for it appears they had been produced in the course of discovery; rather, the issue was whether counsel was obliged to identify from voluminous discovery materials those discrete documents that the attorney had selected for review with his client in advance of deposition, see *Sporck v. Peil*, or that an attorney specifically recalled as existing in her client's files, see *Shelton v. American Motors Corp.* The courts ruled that such narrowly focused inquiries constituted impermissible intrusions into attorneys' thought processes in preparing their clients' defenses.

Citing *Sporck*, we too have observed that "where a request is made for documents already in the possession of the requesting party, with the precise goal of learning what the opposing attorney's thinking or strategy may be, even third-party documents may be protected." *In re Grand Jury Subpoenas (Paul Weiss)* (distinguishing *Sporck* by noting, *inter alia*, that the subpoenaed telephone records appeared to be unavailable to the grand jury except from the law firm). That, however, is clearly not this case. The grand jury does not already possess the bank records subpoenaed from Akin Gump, at least not all of them. Further, the challenged subpoenas, in demanding any and all records for thirty specific Swiss bank accounts, are designed not to "glean what [bank records Akin Gump] deems relevant" but to mirror [Mutual Legal Assistance Treaty] requests that the government has pursued without success for more than two years. Indeed, at oral argument, prosecutors represented that they will not attempt to authenticate the subpoenaed bank records through a member of the Akin Gump firm.

Appellants submit that work product protection for an attorney's "selection and compilation" of third-party documents should not depend on the subjective intent of the prosecutors, but rather on an objective consideration of whether the disclosure of the documents will necessarily reveal the attorney's thought processes in anticipation of litigation. We agree that subjective intent is only one among many factors to be weighed in making an objective determination of whether documents constitute work product. But that conclusion hardly benefits appellants.

Not every selection and compilation of third-party documents by counsel transforms that material into attorney work product. To fit within what we have repeatedly characterized as a "narrow exception" to the general rule that third-party documents in the possession of an attorney do not merit work product protection, the party asserting the privilege must show "a real, rather than speculative, concern" that counsel's thought processes "in relation to pending or anticipated litigation" will be exposed through disclosure of the compiled documents. This burden of objective proof cannot be met through conclusory ex parte affidavits, such as those filed by appellants with the district court in this case, which simply assert that Akin Gump possesses only a subset of the materials subpoenaed and that this subset was created pursuant to a carefully orchestrated defense strategy. Akin Gump's failure to disclose that strategy ex parte to the district court made it impossible for Judge Chin to determine–and makes it impossible for us to review–whether the responsive subset indeed reflects Akin Gump's discriminating selection, or, instead, whether the subset is simply the product of document maintenance practices by the various banks, a lack of cooperation from some of the account holders, or some combination of these and other factors. Without such disclosure, no court can decide if Akin Gump's work product concern is real, or only speculative. Similarly troubling is the firm's failure to identify or submit the responsive documents for in camera review, a practice both long-standing and routine in cases involving claims of privilege. Without reviewing the documents, the district court could not ascertain whether Akin Gump's collection was missing only a few bank records out of a voluminous mass, or whether the subset consisted of so few records focused on such discrete transactions that counsel's strategic thinking was apparent, or something in between the two. Moreover, without the documents, the district court could not consider the possibility of issuing a protective order that disclosed some, if not all, of the account records in Akin Gump's possession to the grand jury, thereby confounding any conclusions that might be drawn about counsel's selection strategy.

B. WAIVER OF ATTORNEY-CLIENT PRIVILEGE AND WORK PRODUCT DOCTRINE

1. "Advice of Counsel" Defense

Does presentation of an attorney's testimony to show a "good faith" compliance with the law waive the attorney-client privilege as to other communications with the attorney? Consider the court's analysis in **United States v. Bilzerian**, 926 F.2d 1285 (2d Cir. 1991):

[Bilzerian] was convicted of nine counts of an indictment charging violations of securities fraud, making false statements to the Securities and Exchange Commission (SEC), and conspiracy to commit specific offenses, and to defraud the SEC and the Internal Revenue Service (IRS). * * *

At trial defendant argued that he did not intend to violate the securities laws, but believed the financing structure of the transactions, utilizing trusts to borrow funds, would allow him legally to avoid disclosure regarding other investors, and that describing the source of his funds as "personal" was lawful. A motion was made *in limine* seeking a ruling permitting him to testify regarding his belief in the lawfulness of describing the source of his funds as "personal" without being subjected to cross-examination on communications he had with his attorney on this subject, discussions ordinarily protected by the attorney-client privilege. * * *

Defendant contends the testimony he sought to introduce regarding his good faith attempt to comply with the securities laws would not have disclosed the content or even the existence of any privileged communications or asserted a reliance on counsel defense. As such, he continues, the attorney-client privilege would not be waived by his testimony and, therefore, the trial court committed reversible error when it denied his motion *in limine* seeking to protect the privilege. He alleges that this ruling, together with similar rulings made during the course of the trial, prevented him from refuting the charge that he acted with criminal intent—a central element of the government's case—and that his constitutional right to "the fullest opportunity to meet the accusation against him . . . [and] to deny all the elements of the case against him," was thereby encroached upon. * * *

[T]he attorney-client privilege cannot at once be used as a shield and a sword. * * * A defendant may not use the privilege to prejudice his opponent's case or to disclose some selected communications for self-serving purposes. Thus, the privilege may implicitly be waived when defendant asserts a claim that in fairness requires examination of protected communications. This waiver principle is applicable here for Bilzerian's testimony that he thought his actions were legal would have put his knowledge of the law and the basis for his understanding of what the law required in issue. His conversations with counsel regarding the legality of his schemes would have been directly relevant in determining the extent of his knowledge and, as a result, his intent.

* * * The district court took great pains to point out that application of the privilege would hinge on the testimony elicited on direct examination. In response to defense counsel's statement that "[t]he government presumably then would be able to call the attorney because the privilege is gone," the court stated:

> I am not going to go to that point. It may be that the government would be bound by the answer of the witness but I am not going to get to that point because I don't think I have to at this juncture. I don't know how this is going to play out. Until I do, I think it is inappropriate for me to give any advisory opinion.

In effect, defendant was seeking an advisory ruling in advance, assuring that the attorney-client privilege would not be waived regardless of what developed in his direct testimony. In order for the privilege to operate effectively defendants must be able to rely on its protection, but courts cannot sanction the use of the privilege to prevent effective cross-examination on matters reasonably related to those introduced in direct examination.

2. Waiver of the Corporation's Privilege

A client can waive the attorney-client privilege, while the protections afforded by the work product doctrine can be asserted in some cases even if the client is willing to waive the privilege. As demonstrated by *Upjohn*, a corporation can assert the privilege to the same extent as an individual, and given the resources of a large organization, the privilege will likely cover a much greater volume of communications than those by one person meeting with a lawyer. Who can waive the corporation's privilege? Usually, the issue is not difficult because the company's board of directors or chief executive has the authority to act on behalf of the corporation. In CFTC v. Weintraub, 471 U.S. 343 (1985), the Supreme Court held that a trustee in bankruptcy appointed to conduct the affairs of a bankrupt corporation had the authority to waive the attorney-client privilege. The corporation's waiver of its privilege can result in communications from senior officers to the company's attorney being used as proof of their knowledge or criminal intent. In a smaller corporation, the lines of authority are often less clear, and the authority to waive may depend on who has control of the entity at a particular time. Consider how the court resolved the issue in the following case.

In re: GRAND JURY PROCEEDINGS (Doe)
219 F.3d 175 (2d Cir. 2000)

FEINBERG, Circuit Judge.

This appeal raises significant questions of first impression in this court regarding application of the attorney-client and work-product privileges in the corporate context. The questions are (1) whether a corporate officer can impliedly waive the corporation's attorney-client and work-product privileges in his grand jury testimony, even though the corporation has explicitly refused such a waiver; and if the answer is yes, (2) what factors a district court should consider in deciding whether a waiver has occurred. We hold there can be such a waiver, and discuss below the relevant criteria in deciding its scope.

This case arises out of an ongoing grand jury investigation into allegedly illegal sales of firearms and other contraband by John Doe Corporation (Doe Corp.). Doe Corp. appeals from an order * * * directing it to produce documents subpoenaed by the grand jury for which Doe Corp. has claimed the attorney-client and work-product privileges. The district court found that statements made by a corporate officer and by in-house counsel to the grand jury waived the corporation's privileges because they unfairly, selectively and deliberately disclosed privileged communications for exculpatory purposes. On appeal, Doe Corp. argues that there was no waiver of either privilege as a result of the grand jury testimony. Further, Doe Corp. argues that even if some of the testimony could be construed as a waiver, the district court erred in failing to narrow the scope of discovery to cover only the disclosed subject matter. For the reasons set forth below, we vacate the order of the district court and remand for further proceedings consistent with this opinion.

Beginning in 1998, Doe Corp. learned that it was involved in facilitating transactions involving the sale of firearms and related items. Consequently, several representatives of Doe Corp. met with officials of the Bureau of Alcohol, Tobacco and Firearms (ATF) to discuss whether Doe Corp. should be concerned about any legal liabilities as a result of these sales. Doe Corp. claims that it was advised by the ATF officials that it need not be concerned about legal liability because of its limited role in the transactions.

Since approximately January 1999, a grand jury in the Southern District of New York has been investigating Doe Corp.'s firearms transactions. In

June 1999, the grand jury issued a subpoena in which it formally requested Doe Corp. to waive its attorney-client and its work-product privileges and produce "communications with attorneys regarding its policies and practices with regard to the sale . . . of firearms." The subpoena required Doe Corp. to produce a privilege log if it elected not to waive the privileges. After several discussions with the government regarding waiver, Doe Corp. decided not to waive its privileges and so notified the government. In July 1999, the government subpoenaed four Doe Corp. employees, including its chief in-house counsel, to testify before the grand jury. In response to the subpoenas, Doe Corp.'s outside counsel contacted the government to discuss the scope of witnesses' testimony in light of Doe Corp.'s refusal to waive its privileges and the likelihood that several areas of inquiry before the grand jury would implicate privileged communication. The government rebuffed Doe Corp.'s offer to engage in proffer sessions, and stated that the witnesses were free to assert the privileges in the grand jury. * * *

The government contends that Doe Corp. lost its attorney-client and work-product privileges primarily as a result of the grand jury testimony of two Doe Corp. witnesses: its in-house counsel (Counsel), and its founder, chairman and controlling shareholder (Witness). Counsel's testimony before the grand jury concerned the meeting with the ATF officials. The government argues that after recounting in detail what had transpired at that meeting, Counsel refused to turn over his notes of the meeting, improperly invoking the work-product privilege. Counsel claimed that the notes, although taken by his non-lawyer assistant, constitute work-product.

The government's claim of waiver, however, is principally based on Witness's day-long testimony before the grand jury. Witness, like Counsel, was subpoenaed to testify individually, as opposed to being proffered by the corporation as its representative. Witness's own counsel, as well as counsel for Doe Corp., were present outside the grand jury room during his testimony. According to both Doe Corp. and Witness, Witness knew that Doe Corp. had asserted the attorney-client and work-product privileges and that he was not authorized to divulge the contents of any privileged communications during his testimony. Doe Corp. had instructed Witness to invoke the privileges as necessary in the grand jury. Witness was also instructed that he could leave the grand jury room to consult with his attorney during questioning–an option he exercised at least once.

The government points to eight statements in Witness's testimony that, it argues, amount to a waiver of the attorney-client and work-product privileges of Doe Corp. Most of the statements can be characterized as generalized references to counsel's advice, such as "our approach was validated by counsel," "[our control of items for sale was validated] as a result of conversations with counsel," "everything I heard from counsel before the ATF meeting, everything afterwards . . . supports the fact that we are not legally responsible." A number of the statements, however, were more specific: one concerns counsel's recommendation about the use of credit cards as identification tools, another concerns counsel's advice about whether the company should monitor individual sales, and yet another refers to a report prepared by in-house counsel supporting the continuation of Doe Corp.'s current practices. Doe Corp. argues that the government is using at least some of these statements out of context, and that, in some instances, Witness had no choice but to refer to his counsel's advice in order to provide a complete answer. The government responds that its questions were not improper and were not calculated to "trick" Witness into disclosing privileged information. Indeed, one question by the government directed Witness to avoid discussing counsel's advice, yet he referred to counsel in his answer to that question. The parties agree that on several other occasions Witness did invoke the attorney-client privilege. * * *

Two months after Witness's grand jury testimony, the government moved to compel production of all of Doe Corp.'s withheld documents, to bar the company from asserting the attorney-client or work-product privileges as to any document that bears on the grand jury investigation, and to require Doe Corp. to respond to any questions previously unanswered on the ground of privilege. The government argued that because Witness repeatedly referred to advice of counsel in attempting to justify Doe Corp.'s actions to the grand jury, fairness demanded full disclosure of that advice. Additionally, the government submitted ex parte an affidavit setting forth its need for Doe Corp.'s work-product material.

Doe Corp. responded with a number of arguments. First, neither Witness nor Counsel could waive Doe Corp.'s privileges without its authorization. Second, there was no implied waiver of the attorney-client privilege because the corporation did not raise an advice-of-counsel defense, nor did it take any other affirmative steps that would support a finding of waiver. Third, even if some disclosure of privileged communications took place, the district court should limit the disclosure to cover only the narrow subject matter covered in the Witness's testimony. Finally, the work-product privilege was not waived and the government had not shown compelling need justifying disclosure of work-product.

Ruling from the bench, the district court held with regard to the corporation's attorney-client privilege that "[u]nder the facts of this case . . . there has been a selective disclosure of the substance of the attorney's advice by the chairman, founder and CEO of the company in his grand jury testimony in an exculpatory manner, and accordingly, . . . such action waive[d] the privilege." The court found that Witness had volunteered privileged information even when the question did not call for it. Further, the court rejected Doe Corp.'s argument that a more formal waiver was necessary. The judge noted that,

> the issue of privilege was known prior to this witness'[s] testimony. His personal counsel and counsel for the company were present outside the grand jury room if he wished to consult with them, and certainly the tenor of the testimony indicates that the waiver and the disclosure [were] intentional.

As a result of the exculpatory manner in which Witness referred to counsel's advice, the court, relying on United States v. Bilzerian, [p. 704], held that fairness required waiver of the privilege.

With regard to Doe Corp.'s work-product privilege, the court ruled that it too was waived "for reasons of fairness." The court also relied on the government's ex parte affirmation, which explained its need for "exceedingly relevant" material that it could not otherwise obtain. The judge also denied Doe Corp.'s request to limit the scope of the disclosure on the ground that Witness never saw or had access to many work-product items. Ruling on the scope of the work-product disclosure, the judge stated, "I do not think that [Witness's] access is the controlling fact in this instance. Given his reliance on counsel's advice in general, it seems to me that all of the communications on the topics at issue . . . must be disclosed. . . ." * * *

We turn first to the district court's ruling that Witness's testimony before the grand jury impliedly waived Doe Corp.'s attorney-client privilege. For purposes of this appeal, the parties do not dispute that the attorney-client privilege attaches to the communications that the government seeks to discover. The dispute centers only on the question of waiver. * * *

This court has recognized that implied waiver may be found where the privilege holder "asserts a claim that *in fairness* requires examination of protected communications." * * * In other words, a party cannot partially disclose privileged communications or affirmatively rely on privileged communications to support its claim or defense and then shield the underlying communications from scrutiny by the opposing party. "The quintessential example is the defendant who asserts an advice-of-counsel defense and is thereby deemed to have waived his privilege with respect to the advice that he received." * * *

Whether fairness requires disclosure has been decided by the courts on a case-by-case basis, and depends primarily on the specific context in which the privilege is asserted. Thus, in *Bilzerian*, we held that a defendant who intended to testify as to his "good faith" reliance on legal advice could not prevent the government from cross-examining him on advice received from counsel. Because the defendant raised the advice-of-counsel defense and sought to rely on privileged information in a judicial setting, the court found that if defendant so testified a broad waiver would be appropriate. By contrast, the D.C. Circuit declined to find a waiver when defendant testified at trial that he lacked the intent to commit the crime because, after meeting with his lawyers, he believed that his actions were lawful. United States v. White, 887 F.2d 267 (D.C. Cir.1989) (Ginsburg, J.). The *White* court * * * concluded that mere denial of mens rea through "[a]n averment that lawyers have looked into a matter does not imply an intent to reveal the substance of the lawyers' advice. Where a defendant neither reveals substantive information, nor prejudices the government's case, nor misleads a court by relying on an incomplete disclosure, fairness and consistency do not require the inference of waiver." * * *

We have also recognized that a more limited form of implied waiver may be appropriate where disclosure occurred in a context that did not greatly prejudice the other party in the litigation. * * * The scope of waiver has also been limited where "the disclosure occurred early in the proceedings, was made to opposing counsel rather than to the court, and was not demonstrably prejudicial to [the] other party." * * * Further, when waiver occurs as a result of inadvertent document disclosure, courts have limited the scope of that waiver based on the circumstances involved and overall fairness. * * *

The general rules governing waiver are more complicated when the issue arises in the context of corporate entities. The Supreme Court noted in Commodity Futures Trading Comm'n v. Weintraub, 471 U.S. 343 (1985), that the attorney-client privilege presents "special problems" in the corporate context:

> As an inanimate entity, a corporation must act through agents. A corporation cannot speak directly to its lawyers. Similarly, it cannot directly waive the privilege when disclosure is in its best interest. Each of these actions must necessarily be undertaken by individuals empowered to act on behalf of the corporation.

In *Weintraub*, the Court recognized that ordinarily the authority to assert and waive the corporation's privileges "rests with the corporation's management and is normally exercised by its officers and directors." Since *Weintraub,* courts have found that a corporate employee or officer could not assert the attorney-client privilege when the corporation has already waived the privilege. In *Teamsters,* we surveyed the law on this issue and concluded that employees or officers of the corporation "generally may not prevent a corporation from waiving the attorney-client privilege arising from ... communications [between the corporation's counsel and officers of the corporation]." * * *

Weintraub and *Teamsters* involved explicit waivers of the attorney-client privilege by the corporation. Neither one addressed the situation in this case, where the corporation has asserted its privilege in its communications to the government and the court and yet one of its officers arguably waived that privilege before a grand jury. * * *

In finding that Witness's testimony before the grand jury waived the corporation's privilege, the district court relied on the uncontroversial proposition that "a corporation must act through [its] agents."* * * While it is true, as *Weintraub* held, that when a corporation decides to waive the privilege its officers or counsel must communicate this decision, it does not necessarily follow that a corporate officer testifying in his *individual* capacity can waive the corporate privilege without that entity's consent. Indeed, in the reverse situation—that is, where a corporation waives its privilege but an officer wishes to assert that privilege as to his communications with corporate counsel–we have held that the privilege belongs to the corporation, not to the agent. * * *

Here, Witness was subpoenaed individually. Although Witness was called to the grand jury because he was a Doe Corp. officer, his testimony in the grand jury was not affirmatively offered by Doe Corp. on its own behalf. Doe Corp. is a publicly held corporation; it has a board of directors, numerous shareholders, and a large number of employees. It is far from being Witness's "alter-ego." It is true that Witness and Doe Corp. share many of the same interests: an indictment of Doe Corp. would likely harm Witness's financial prospects, not to mention his reputation. However, even if we accept the government's position that Witness's reference to advice-of-counsel was self-interested, it does not necessarily follow that, as a result, the corporation itself should be penalized. While it may be that Witness intended to abide by Doe Corp.'s decision not to waive its attorney-client privilege, the corporation had no direct means of controlling Witness's testimony while he was in the grand jury room. At oral argument, Doe Corp. made the significant suggestion that Witness's interest in exculpating his own conduct may override his fidelity to the corporation, including its interest in preserving the privilege. We believe the district court should consider this possibility. * * *

We recognize that other courts have attributed to the corporation an implied waiver of the attorney-client privilege as a result of testimony by a corporate officer. * * * While these cases can illustrate that, in some circumstances, a corporation may impliedly waive its privilege through the testimony of one of its officers, they hardly stand for the proposition that this must always be the case. Rather, as we have already noted, the district court should carefully weigh the circumstances surrounding Witness's testimony in deciding whether, in fairness, that testimony effected waiver of Doe Corp.'s privilege. * * *

In the situation before us, Witness was compelled to appear and to testify before the grand jury. Because the corporation does not enjoy the protection of the Fifth Amendment, Witness could not assert the Fifth Amendment on its behalf. Consequently, Witness's alleged waiver occurred in the context of purely compelled testimony.[8]

In that sense, the "shield and sword" analogy used by the government to justify waiver may be inappropriate. Unlike the defendant in *Bilzerian* who sought to testify at trial about advice-of-counsel and prevent the government from cross-examining him about it, * * * Doe Corp. did not *itself* take any

---

[8] Doe Corp. states that Witness is not the subject of the grand jury investigation and that there is no suggestion that he could be exposed to individual criminal liability. If that is so, as to which we express no opinion, then it is also likely that Witness could not assert his individual Fifth Amendment right against self-incrimination.

affirmative steps to inject privileged materials into the litigation or to otherwise explicitly raise the advice-of-counsel defense. * * *

On the other hand, it is true that Witness might have invoked Doe Corp.'s attorney-client privilege. As discussed below, * * *, the inquiry into whether Witness purposefully chose not to assert the privilege when it was appropriate to do so is relevant to the waiver analysis. An element of that inquiry is that Witness's testimony in the grand jury was unaided by counsel. We recognize that Witness was not entitled to counsel in the grand jury room. Yet, insofar as the waiver analysis is premised on fairness considerations, that the waiver took place in the context of uncounseled testimony in the grand jury room is relevant to the analysis. * * *

The government argues that Witness's disclosures in the grand jury were not inadvertent but rather a calculated and deliberate attempt to exculpate the corporation. Doe Corp. responds that the disclosures were inadvertent, that they were taken out of context, and that at most they would support a limited waiver. * * *

[O]n the basis of this limited record we are reluctant to evaluate the district court's conclusion that Witness's alleged waiver was purposeful rather than inadvertent.

* * * Because the waiver inquiry depends heavily on the factual context in which the privilege was allegedly waived, we leave it to the district court, on remand, to determine which—if any—of Witness's statements amount to waiver, and its appropriate scope. More importantly, the issue is not whether the reference to the attorney's advice was a deliberate attempt at exculpation, but rather whether it was a deliberate attempt *on the part of the corporation* to exculpate itself, as opposed to Witness's effort to exculpate himself personally. * * *

Finally, as the animating principle behind waiver is fairness to the parties, if the court finds that the privilege was waived, then the waiver should be tailored to remedy the prejudice to the government. The district court granted the government the full disclosure of Doe Corp.'s attorney-client communications and work-product material that it had requested: "all materials previously withheld on grounds of . . . privilege; . . . any document that bears on the Grand Jury's investigation; . . . and [answers to] questions previously unanswered on privilege grounds that implicates these subjects."

On this truncated record, we are not persuaded that the government has been prejudiced—especially to a degree that would justify the broad disclosure ordered by the court. First, as explained above, we do not believe that the "shield and sword" analogy neatly applies to the grand jury testimony. The grand jury is seldom portrayed as a "sword" for the defendant or the testifying witness. It is an accusatory body under the (almost) complete control of the prosecutor. Second, unlike exculpatory testimony at trial that could result in a permanent acquittal or have other res judicata effect, a no true bill from the grand jury might grant Doe Corp. only temporary relief. The government can usually choose to impanel another grand jury. It need not even recall witnesses; but can simply present selected transcripts to the second grand jury. Alternatively, the government could ask the district court to instruct the grand jury that Witness's mention of the advice of corporate counsel should not be considered on the issue of voting an indictment against Doe Corp. We agree that there can be unfairness to the government as a result of manipulative testimony before the grand jury; we note only that the gain to the subject of the investigation is limited. Third, as the government noted in its brief, the grand jury is separate from the courts, and is not restrained by many of the procedural and evidentiary rules that govern the conduct of criminal trials. * * * Without deciding whether limiting the scope of the waiver in this fashion is warranted, we note that it is an option open to the district court in assessing prejudice to the government. Finally, it is significant that this disclosure took place early in the grand jury proceedings. Witness was only the fourth to appear before the grand jury. It may well be that the government has other witnesses and other evidence to present.

In sum, we believe that sound judicial administration suggests that we remand this matter to the district court for reconsideration in view of the factors discussed above. * * *

We turn now to Doe Corp.'s contention that the district court erred in finding that the testimony of Witness and Counsel resulted in a broad waiver of Doe Corp.'s work-product privilege. As with the claim concerning waiver of the attorney-client privilege, the parties contest only the issue of waiver. As an initial matter, we note that the district court did not make any particularized findings in support of this part of its holding. The court simply concluded that fairness demanded full disclosure of *all* the work-product materials requested by the government, including "pure attorney opinion work-product." * * *

For largely the same reasons we outlined above, we believe that the district court on remand should consider further whether there was any waiver of Doe Corp.'s work-product privilege, and, if there was, the proper scope of the waiver. The fairness concerns that guide the waiver analysis above are equally compelling in this context.* * *

We vacate the order of the district court and remand so that it may consider further, in light of this opinion, the issues of waiver of Doe Corp.'s attorney-client and work-product privileges.

3. Demanding Waiver from Corporations

In 1999, the Department of Justice issued a memorandum called "Federal Prosecution of Corporations" – called the Holder Memo after then-Deputy Attorney General Eric Holder – that discussed the general policy of federal prosecutors in deciding whether th charge a corporation with a crime. One of the principles that informed the decision was a "corporation's timely and voluntary disclosure of wrongdoing and its willingness to cooperate in the investigation of its agents, including, if necessary, the waiver of the corporate attorney-client and work-product privileges." The policy has been refined several times since then, and in August 2008 the Department issued newly revised *Principles of Federal Prosecution of Business Organizations* that can be found in the United States Attorney's Manual. The current policy was adopted in response to significant criticism of earlier statements that encouraged prosecutors to seek waivers of the attorney-client privilege and work product protection by corporations being investigated, often at a very early stage before the company had even completed its internal investigation. The Department's policy now actively discourages federal prosecutors from seeking such waivers from a company under investigation, emphasizing instead the need for corporate disclosure of facts that are generated in an internal investigation:

> The attorney-client privilege and the attorney work product protection serve an extremely important function in the American legal system. The attorney-client privilege is one of the oldest and most sacrosanct privileges under the law. See *Upjohn v. United States*, 449 U.S. 383, 389 (1981). As the Supreme Court has stated, "[i]ts purpose is to encourage full and frank communication between attorneys and their clients and thereby promote broader public interests in the observance of law and administration of justice." Id. The value of promoting a corporation's ability to seek frank and comprehensive legal advice is particularly important in the contemporary global business environment, where corporations often face complex and dynamic legal and regulatory obligations imposed by the federal government and also by states and foreign governments. The work product doctrine serves similarly important goals.

> For these reasons, waiving the attorney-client and work product protections has never been a prerequisite under the Department's prosecution guidelines for a corporation to be viewed as cooperative. Nonetheless, a wide range of commentators and members of the American legal community and criminal justice system have asserted that the Department's policies have been used, either wittingly or unwittingly, to coerce business entities into waiving attorney-client privilege and work-product protection. Everyone agrees that a corporation may freely waive its own privileges if it chooses to do so; indeed, such waivers occur routinely when corporations are victimized by their employees or others, conduct an internal investigation, and then disclose the details of the investigation to law enforcement officials in an effort to seek prosecution of the offenders. However, the contention, from a broad array of voices, is that the Department's position on attorney-client

privilege and work product protection waivers has promoted an environment in which those protections are being unfairly eroded to the detriment of all.

The Department understands that the attorney-client privilege and attorney work product protection are essential and long- recognized components of the American legal system. What the government seeks and needs to advance its legitimate (indeed, essential) law enforcement mission is not waiver of those protections, but rather the facts known to the corporation about the putative criminal misconduct under review. In addition, while a corporation remains free to convey non-factual or "core" attorney-client communications or work product—if and only if the corporation voluntarily chooses to do so—prosecutors should not ask for such waivers and are directed not to do so. The critical factor is whether the corporation has provided the facts about the events, as explained further herein.

Eligibility for cooperation credit is not predicated upon the waiver of attorney-client privilege or work product protection. Instead, the sort of cooperation that is most valuable to resolving allegations of misconduct by a corporation and its officers, directors, employees, or agents is disclosure of the relevant facts concerning such misconduct. In this regard, the analysis parallels that for a non-corporate defendant, where cooperation typically requires disclosure of relevant factual knowledge and not of discussions between an individual and his attorneys.

Thus, when the government investigates potential corporate wrongdoing, it seeks the relevant facts. For example, how and when did the alleged misconduct occur? Who promoted or approved it? Who was responsible for committing it? In this respect, the investigation of a corporation differs little from the investigation of an individual. In both cases, the government needs to know the facts to achieve a just and fair outcome. The party under investigation may choose to cooperate by disclosing the facts, and the government may give credit for the party's disclosures. If a corporation wishes to receive credit for such cooperation, which then can be considered with all other cooperative efforts and circumstances in evaluating how fairly to proceed, then the corporation, like any person, must disclose the relevant facts of which it has knowledge.

U.S.A.M. § 9-28.710-720.

4. Coercing Employees

The Supreme Court has held that statements obtained by a governmental threat of serious economic consequences, such as the loss of government employment (Garrity v. New Jersey, 385 U.S. 493 (1967)), or state contracts (Lefkowitz v. Turley, 414 U.S. 70 (1973)), is "compelled" for Fifth Amendment purposes, so the statement may be suppressed and the prosecution cannot use it in the government's case-in-chief. The issue of governmental coercion becomes murkier when a corporation, seeking to show its cooperation, requires its employees to provide information to the government and threatening anyone who refuses with the loss of employment. In United States v. Stein, which is discussed more extensively in Chapter 16, the district court found a Fifth Amendment violation when the government coerced the accounting firm KPMG to require its employees to cooperate with the government under the threat of losing their position and any future payment of legal fees. The district court found that the firm had become an arm of the federal government's investigation, and therefore its conduct constituted state action that made the Fifth Amendment applicable. The Second Circuit did not address the Fifth Amendment issue in upholding the district court's dismissal of the charges for certain defendants because the government deprived them of their Sixth Amendment right to counsel.

If a corporation takes action to compel its employees to cooperate without a specific government request, is there sufficient *government* coercion to make an individual's statement subject to suppression under the Fifth Amendment? Consider Professor Garrett's analysis:

> [T]he state action doctrine does not support finding private employment decisions made during criminal investigations to be state action, absent a formal cooperation agreement with prosecutors or perhaps a change in corporation policy at the government's behest. Nor would coercion be easily shown, at least as to denial of attorneys fees. Further, sound practical reasons counsel against such a regime. For exclusion to apply to mere implicit encouragement to target entities to discipline potentially culpable employees would extend the penalty cases to any number of routine employment decisions made under the shadow of criminal investigations. The consequences could hamper corporate crime prosecutions and disrupt corporate governance.

Brandon L. Garrett, *Corporate Confessions*, 30 CARDOZO L. REV. 917 (2009).

5. Voluntary Disclosure

Will turning over documents to the government as part of an entity's effort to cooperate with a government investigation serve as a waiver of the work product doctrine? What effect will the disclosure of documents have on subsequent civil actions?

UNITED STATES v. MASSACHUSETTS INSTITUTE OF TECHNOLOGY
129 F.3d 681 (1st Cir. 1997)

BOUDIN, Circuit Judge.

This case concerns an attempt by the Massachusetts Institute of Technology to assert the attorney-client privilege and work-product doctrine in response to a document request by the Internal Revenue Service. The most important issue presented is whether MIT's disclosure of certain of the documents to another government agency caused it to lose the privilege. The background facts are essentially undisputed.

MIT is a famous university with tax-exempt status under 26 U.S.C. § 501(c)(3). In 1993, the IRS conducted an examination of MIT's records to determine whether MIT still qualified for exempt status and to determine whether it was complying with provisions relating to employment taxes and the reporting of unrelated business income. In aid of this examination, the IRS requested from MIT copies of the billing statements of law firms that had represented MIT and minutes of the MIT Corporation and its executive and auditing committees.

In response, MIT supplied the documents requested but redacted information claimed to be covered by the attorney-client privilege or the work-product doctrine or both. In mid-1994 the IRS requested that the redacted information be supplied, and MIT declined. At this point the IRS sought to obtain the same documents in unredacted form from the Defense Contract Audit Agency ("the audit agency"), the auditing arm of the Department of Defense.

It appears that the same billing statements and possibly some or all of the minutes sought by the IRS had earlier been provided to the audit agency pursuant to contracts between MIT and components of the Department of Defense. The audit agency helps entities in the Department of Defense review contract performance to be sure that the government is not overcharged for services. Not surprisingly, the audit agency often reviews the private contractor's books and records.

In November 1994, the audit agency advised the IRS that it would not turn over the documents provided to it by MIT without the latter's consent, which MIT declines to give. The audit agency had made no unconditional promise to keep the documents secret, but its regulations and practices offered MIT some reason to think that indiscriminate disclosure was unlikely. The IRS then served an administrative summons on MIT in December 1994 seeking specific unredacted minutes of nine meetings of the MIT Corporation and auditing and executive committees in 1990 and 1991, and attorneys' billing statements for almost all legal expenses paid or incurred by MIT from July 1, 1990, through June 30, 1991.

When MIT declined to comply, the IRS in early 1996 petitioned the district court to enforce the summons. * * * In January 1997, the district court issued a memorandum and order enforcing the IRS administrative summons as to the unredacted legal bills and the unredacted versions of most of the minutes sought by the IRS. * * *

We begin with the attorney-client privilege. That privilege has been familiarly summed up by Wigmore in a formula that federal courts have often repeated:

> (1) Where legal advice of any kind is sought (2) from a professional legal adviser in his capacity as such, (3) the communications relating to that purpose, (4) made in confidence (5) by the client, (6) are at his instance permanently protected (7) from disclosure by himself or by the legal adviser, (8) except the protection be waived.

8 J. Wigmore, Evidence § 2292, at 554 (McNaughton rev.1961). The government argues, and the district court agreed, that by its disclosure to the audit agency, MIT waived the privilege to whatever extent that it might otherwise have protected the billing statements and various of the minutes.

The attorney-client privilege is well-established and its present rationale straightforward: by safeguarding communications between lawyer and client, it encourages disclosures by client to lawyer that better enable the client to conform his conduct to the requirements of the law and to present legitimate claims or defenses when litigation arises. Waiver issues aside, the contours of the privilege are reasonably stable.

Quite a different scene presents itself when one turns to the problem of "waiver," a loose and misleading label for what is in fact a collection of different rules addressed to different problems. Cases under this "waiver" heading include situations as divergent as an express and voluntary surrender of the privilege, partial disclosure of a privileged document, selective disclosure to some outsiders but not all, and inadvertent overhearings or disclosures.

Even where the cases are limited to those involving a deliberate and voluntary disclosure of a privileged communication to someone other than the attorney or client, the case law is far from settled. But decisions do tend to mark out, although not with perfect consistency, a small circle of "others" with whom information may be shared without loss of the privilege (e.g., secretaries, interpreters, counsel for a cooperating co-defendant, a parent present when a child consults a lawyer).

Although the decisions often describe such situations as ones in which the client "intended" the disclosure to remain confidential, the underlying concern is functional: that the lawyer be able to consult with others needed in the representation and that the client be allowed to bring closely related persons who are appropriate, even if not vital, to a consultation. Cf.

Westinghouse Elec. Corp. v. Republic of the Philippines, 951 F.2d 1414 (3d Cir.1991). An intent to maintain confidentiality is ordinarily necessary to continued protection, but it is not sufficient.

On the contrary, where the client chooses to share communications outside this magic circle, the courts have usually refused to extend the privilege. The familiar platitude is that the privilege is narrowly confined because it hinders the courts in the search for truth. Fairness is also a concern where a client is permitted to choose to disclose materials to one outsider while withholding them from another.

Should this inclination not to protect a document disclosed outside the circle apply where, as here, the initial disclosure was to and at the request of a government agency? This problem has presented itself to six circuits. The most common cases have been disclosures of otherwise privileged attorney-client communications to the Securities and Exchange Commission by corporations during voluntary internal investigations or in response to SEC subpoenas. The Eighth Circuit, *en banc* but without more than a paragraph of analysis, treated this kind of disclosure as not comprising a total waiver of the privilege. *See* Diversified Indus., Inc. v. Meredith, 572 F.2d 596 (8th Cir.1978). Subsequently, the Second, Third, Fourth, Federal and D.C. Circuits took the opposite view and ruled that such limited disclosures do destroy the privilege.

The primary argument in favor of the Eighth Circuit position is that loss of the privilege may discourage the frank exchange between attorney and client in future cases, wherever the client anticipates making a disclosure to at least one government agency. We put to one side the interest of the government agency in obtaining voluntary disclosures; such agencies usually have means to secure the information they need and, if not, can seek legislation from Congress. By contrast, the safeguarding of the attorney-client relationship has largely been left to the courts, which have a comparative advantage in assessing consequences in this sphere.

But MIT, like any client, continues to control both the nature of its communications with counsel and the ultimate decision whether to disclose such communications to third parties. The only constraint imposed by the traditional rule here invoked by the government–that disclosure to a third party waives the privilege–is to limit *selective* disclosure, that is, the provision of otherwise privileged communications to one outsider while withholding them from another. MIT has provided no evidence that respecting this constraint will prevent it or anyone else from getting adequate legal advice.

Admittedly, the arguments on the other side are far from overwhelming. The IRS' search for truth will not be much advanced if MIT simply limits or recasts its disclosures to the audit agency. But the general principle that disclosure normally negates the privilege is worth maintaining. To maintain it here makes the law more predictable and certainly eases its administration. Following the Eighth Circuit's approach would require, at the very least, a new set of difficult line-drawing exercises that would consume time and increase uncertainty.

MIT says that even if we are not prepared to follow the Eighth Circuit onto new ground, MIT's disclosure to the audit agency should be regarded as akin to the disclosure by a client's lawyer to another lawyer representing another client engaged in a common defense. Invoking the concept of "common interest," MIT seeks to compare its situation to cases where disclosure has been allowed, without forfeiting the privilege, among separate parties similarly aligned in a case or consultation (e.g., codefendants, insurer and insured, patentee and licensee).

In a rather abstract sense, MIT and the audit agency do have a "common interest" in the proper performance of MIT's defense contracts and the proper auditing and payment of MIT's bills. But this is not the kind of common interest to which the cases refer in recognizing that allied lawyers and clients–who are working together in prosecuting or defending a lawsuit or in certain other legal transactions–can exchange information among themselves without loss of the privilege. To extend the notion to MIT's relationship with the audit agency, which on another level is easily characterized as adversarial, would be to dissolve the boundary almost entirely.

MIT further argues that the disclosure to the audit agency was not "voluntary" because of the practical pressures and the legal constraints to which it was subject as a government contractor. The extent of those pressures and constraints is far from clear, but assuming *arguendo* that they existed, MIT chose to place itself in this position by becoming a government contractor. In short, MIT's disclosure to the audit agency resulted from its own voluntary choice, even if that choice was made at the time it became a defense contractor and subjected itself to the alleged obligation of disclosure.

Anyone who chooses to disclose a privileged document to a third party, or does so pursuant to a prior agreement or understanding, has an incentive to do so, whether for gain or to avoid disadvantage. It would be perfectly possible to carve out some of those disclosures and say that, although the disclosure itself is not necessary to foster attorney-client communications, neither does it forfeit the privilege. With rare exceptions, courts have been unwilling to start down this path–which has no logical terminus–and we join in this reluctance.

We add, finally, a word about reliance and fair warning. MIT may have had some reason to think that the audit agency would not disclose the documents to the IRS (and the agency did not do so). But MIT had far less reason to think that it could disclose documents to the audit agency and still maintain the privilege when IRS then sought the same documents. The choice to disclose may have been reasonable but it was still a foreseeable gamble.

We turn now to the government's cross-appeal. Here, the IRS challenges the district court's refusal to require MIT to produce three specific minutes. The refusal reflected the district court's view that the documents contained privileged material, and that there was no waiver because MIT had not been shown to have disclosed those minutes to the audit agency. On the latter point, MIT effectively concedes error, and properly so.

Where privilege is claimed and the opponent alleges a specific disclosure, the burden of proof is upon the claimant to show nondisclosure wherever that is material to the disposition of the claim. Here, MIT concedes that it cannot prove that the minutes in question were withheld from the audit agency. Instead, it proffers alternative grounds for sustaining the district court's judgment as to these minutes, namely, that the minutes were protected under the attorney-client privilege and the work product doctrine and that these protections were not waived even though the minutes were turned over to the audit agency.

A party may defend a judgment in its favor on any legitimate ground without appealing from the judgment on that issue. Our discussion of the billing statements disposes of MIT's argument that the protection of the attorney-client privilege survived disclosure to the audit agency. We therefore turn to the work product doctrine. * * *

The district court assumed that work product protection did not apply because the minutes were not prepared "in anticipation of litigation," as required by Fed.R.Civ.P. 26(b)(3). MIT argues that the minutes contained substantive information that did represent attorney work product even if the minutes had a more general function. There is little law in this area—partly, one suspects, because work product usually remains embodied in documents unquestionably prepared for litigation or, if given to the client, in documents independently protected by the attorney client privilege.

The government has chosen in its brief to assume that, to the extent that the minutes contained "the mental impressions, conclusions, opinions, or legal theories" of MIT's attorneys, Fed.R.Civ.P. 26(b)(3), the district court erred in concluding that work product lost its protection when repeated in another confidential document not prepared in anticipation of litigation. A Third Circuit precedent supports this assumption, which MIT presses and the government does not resist. See In re Ford Motor Co., 110 F.3d 954 (3d Cir.1997). In view of the government's concession, we will take the point as settled for this case.

Nevertheless, the government claims that any such protection was lost when the minutes were turned over to the audit agency, MIT having conceded that it cannot prove that the minutes were not so disclosed. One might wonder why the standard of waiver for the attorney-client privilege—that any voluntary disclosure outside the magic circle constitutes waiver—would not also apply to the work product doctrine. Equivalent waiver standards would make easier the resolution of evidentiary disputes where, as often happens, the two objections are raised together.

Nonetheless, the cases approach uniformity in implying that work-product protection is not as easily waived as the attorney-client privilege. The privilege, it is said, is designed to protect confidentiality, so that any disclosure outside the magic circle is inconsistent with the privilege; by contrast, work product protection is provided against "adversaries," so only disclosing material in a way inconsistent with keeping it from an adversary waives work product protection. At least five circuits have adopted this rule in some form.

Perhaps such formulations simply beg the question. If one wanted to explain the discrepant outcomes, it might be more persuasive to say that the privilege is strictly confined because it is absolute; on the other hand, work product protection (with certain qualifications) can be overcome by a sufficient showing of need. In all events, it would take better reason than we have to depart from the prevailing rule that disclosure to an adversary, real or potential, forfeits work product protection.

MIT's disclosure to the audit agency was a disclosure to a potential adversary. The disclosures did not take place in the context of a joint litigation where the parties shared a common legal interest. The audit agency was reviewing MIT's expense submissions. MIT doubtless hoped that there would be no actual controversy between it and the Department of Defense, but the potential for dispute and even litigation was certainly there. The cases treat this situation as one in which the work product protection is deemed forfeit.

In closing, it may be helpful to stress that—with regard to both the attorney-client privilege and the work product doctrine—we are concerned only with loss of protection as to the very documents already disclosed to the audit agency. Nothing in this opinion is intended to be directed to the different and difficult question when disclosure of one document warrants forfeiture of protection for a different but related document.

Similarly, even where work product can be discovered, the governing rule directs that "the court shall protect against disclosure of the mental impressions, conclusions, opinions, or legal theories of an attorney or other representative of a party concerning the litigation." Fed.R.Civ.P. 26(b)(3). Conceivably, the strong policy underlying this reservation might serve to protect such materials, even if protection of ordinary work product materials were deemed waived because of selective disclosure. This possibility has not been briefed or argued to us; it may or may not be pertinent in this case; and we mention it only to stress that we are not deciding the issue.

Accordingly, on MIT's appeal, the judgment of the district court is affirmed. On the government's cross-appeal, the judgment of the district court refusing to order production of three specified minutes is vacated, and the matter is remanded to the district court for further proceedings consistent with this opinion.

6. Selective Waiver and Promises of Confidentiality

Does the voluntary disclosure of information to the government during an investigation waive the attorney-client privilege and work product protection when the government agrees to maintain its confidentiality? In **McKesson HBOC, Inc. v. Superior Court**, 9 Cal.Rptr.3d 812 (Cal.App. 2004), the California Court of Appeals found that disclosure waived confidentiality despite the government's agreement. The SEC and U.S. Attorney's Office launched civil and criminal investigations of McKesson HBOC related to possible improper recording of revenues. The company retained a law firm, Skadden, Arps, to represent it in shareholder suits and the to conduct an internal investigation. McKesson HBOC and the government entered into a confidentiality agreement stating that the company did not intend to waive the attorney-client privilege and work product protection by providing information from the internal investigation and an audit committee report, and "that McKesson believed it had a common interest with the government in obtaining information regarding the improperly recorded revenues." The government did not take any criminal or civil enforcement action against the company, but the plaintiff in a shareholder class action sought production of the materials produced to the government. In upholding a lower court decision requiring production of the documents, the Court of Appeals stated with regard to waiver of the privilege:

> We see no real alignment of interests between the government and persons or entities under investigation for securities law violations. Even if we credit McKesson's claim that it was interested in rooting out the source of the accounting improprieties, we still find the situation here is not qualitatively different than a defendant sharing privileged material with one plaintiff, but not another. Though McKesson and amicus curiae advance policy arguments for allowing sharing of privileged materials with the government , no one suggests that a defendant facing multiple plaintiffs should be able to disclose privileged materials to one plaintiff without waiving the attorney-client privilege as to the other plaintiffs.

Regarding waiver of the work product protection, the court found:

> McKesson's reliance on the agreements themselves to create a government interest in confidentiality seems to us to be bootstrapping. The government has no interest independent of the agreements to keep the information confidential. In simple terms, the SEC and United States Attorney agreed to keep the documents confidential if they did not need to disclose the document's contents to perform their duties. The agreements did not bind the government to maintain confidentiality under all circumstances.

More importantly, the SEC and the United States Attorney agreed to (conditional) confidentiality in order to obtain the documents. Their interest was not confidentiality, but instead to obtain the documents and thereby make their investigations and possible enforcement actions easier and more productive. In contrast, an interest in maintaining confidentiality exists when the parties are aligned on the same side in the litigation and have a similar stake in the outcome. Thus, there is an interest in confidentiality when the parties' individual cases might be damaged if work product were to be disclosed.

McKesson and the government are not aligned in any litigation, and they do not share the same stake or have the same goal. There is considerable debate in the briefing before us as to whether disclosure of work product will make future targets of government investigations reluctant to cooperate in the future. Ultimately, it is only this policy argument mounted by McKesson and amicus curiae that we find has some appeal. As the Legislature has not explicitly set out the parameters for waiver of work product protection, we are, perhaps, slightly less constrained in determining the bounds of the doctrine. Given the various incentives for cooperating with government investigations (see In re Steinhardt Partners, L.P., 9 F.3d 230 (2d Cir. 1993)), we are not sure if future investigative targets will be reluctant to share protected documents if we uphold the trial court's order. But an assurance of work product protection would certainly act as a carrot to encourage cooperation with the government. Also, the employment of outside counsel to investigate alleged corporate wrongdoing is a laudable practice, which presumably would be encouraged by an assurance of work product protection.

See also In re Columbia/HCA Healthcare Corp. Billing Practices Litigation 293 F.3d 289 (6th Cir. 2002) ("any form of selective waiver, even that which stems from a confidentiality agreement, transforms the attorney-client privilege into merely another brush on an attorney's palette, utilized and manipulated to gain tactical or strategic advantage.").

Not all courts take the position that any disclosure of privileged communications and work product is a waiver, at least when there is an agreement to maintain the confidentiality of the information. In In re Leslie Fay Companies, Inc. Securities Litigation, 161 F.R.D. 274 (S.D.N.Y. 1995), the district court refused to find a waiver in the disclosure of confidential information pursuant to a bankruptcy court order that included the agreement of the U.S. Attorney's Office "to hold all materials produced to it by the Company in confidence, disclosing the material to third parties only as necessary to further law enforcement objectives." If there is a confidentiality agreement in place, there is a stronger basis to argue for selective waiver.

7. Whose Privilege in Corporate Representation?

The client holds the attorney-client privilege and decides whether to waive it. When a corporation is the client, the communications by individual employees and officers to corporate counsel are privileged, but the corporation and not the individuals can decide to waive the protection for the communications. A lawyer representing a corporation represents the legal entity. See ABA Model Rule of Professional Conduct 1.13(a) (2006). Model Rule 1.13(d) provides: "In dealing with an organization's director's, officers, employees, members, shareholders or other constituents, a lawyer shall explain the identity of the client when the lawyer knows or reasonably should know that the organization's interests are adverse to those of the constituents with whom the lawyer is dealing." The Comment to Model Rule 1.13, ¶ 7, states:

> There are times when the organization's interest may be or become adverse to those of one or more of its constituents. In such circumstances the lawyer should advise any constituent, whose interest he finds adverse to that of the organization of the conflict or potential conflict of interest, that the lawyer cannot represent such constituent, and that such person may wish to obtain independent representation. Care must be taken to assure that the individual understands that, when there is such adversity of interest, the lawyer for the organization cannot provide legal representation for that constituent individual, and that discussions between the lawyer for the organization and the individual may not be privileged.

The Comment concludes with the following, which provides little if any real guidance to an attorney representing an organization: "Whether such a warning should be given by the lawyer for the organization to any constituent individual may turn on the facts of each case." If a lawyer represents both the corporation and an officer or director, is the lawyer then barred from representing either if a conflict of interest arises? Is the concern with keeping information confidential as great with an organization as it is with an individual? The problem of confused representation is especially acute in a closely-held corporation, in which a small group of managers—or even a single individual—owns a controlling interest in the corporation, so that the distinction between the organization and the individuals is often blurred.

When a corporation undertakes an internal investigation of possible wrongdoing by its employees, issues related to waiver of the attorney-client privilege and work product doctrine will arise as some point. A Report by the American College of Trial Lawyers states: "In a properly conducted investigation, the employees are informed at the outset that communications with counsel for the corporation are not privileged as to the employee; that is, the company lawyer is not the employee's lawyer, and the corporation is free to disclose such communications without the consent of the employee." The Report does note, however, that "[d]espite this caution, many employees as a practical matter consider the corporation's lawyers to be their lawyers and are otherwise hesitant for job security reasons not to answer their questions." *Report by the American College of Trial Lawyers: The Erosion of the Attorney-Client Privilege and the Work Product Doctrine in Federal Criminal Investigations* at 17 & n. 44 (2002).

8. Waiving Work Product Protection

Work product is treated somewhat differently from privileged communications because the doctrine protects the attorney's thought process and not just client communications. Courts are generally much less willing to find waiver of work product even when the work product is provided to a non-client, so long as the person receiving it is not viewed as an adversary or with interests inimical to the client. The prosecution of Martha Stewart for conspiracy, obstruction of justice, and making false statements raised this issue regarding whether the forwarding of an e-mail from Stewart to her daughter undermined the protection of the work product doctrine for the content of the e-mail. **United States v. Stewart**, 287 F.Supp.2d 461 (S.D.N.Y. 2003).

During the course of the government's investigation, and prior to her indictment, Stewart composed and sent an e-mail to one of her attorneys recounting her recollection regarding the sale of Imclone stock, the subject of the government's investigation. The following day, she forwarded the e-mail to her daughter, Alexis. Stewart prepared and sent the e-mail from her computer at Martha Stewart Living Omnimedia Inc. (MSLO), and a copy of it was retained on the company's computer server. During the investigation, the government subpoenaed MSLO for documents, including "[a]ll desktop and laptop computers used by Martha Stewart" and certain files located on the company's server. The company submitted the records, withholding the e-mail Stewart sent to her attorney on the ground that it was attorney work product but mistakenly submitted the forwarded e-mail sent the following day to Alexis. After the indictment, the government informed Stewart's attorneys that it had the e-mail and asked whether she asserted that it was protected by the work product doctrine, which she did. In response to the government's argument that forwarding the e-mail to her daughter waived any work product claim, the district court stated:

> By forwarding the e-mail to a family member, Stewart did not substantially increase the risk that the Government would gain access to materials prepared in anticipation of litigation. Martha Stewart stated in her affidavit that "Alexis is the closest person in the world to me. She is a valued confidante and counselor to me. In sharing the e-mail with her, I knew that she would keep its content strictly confidential." Martha Stewart Aff. ¶ 6. Alexis Stewart stated that while she did not recall receiving the June 24 e-mail, she "never would have disclosed its contents." Alexis Stewart Aff. ¶ 2. The

disclosure affected neither side's interests in this litigation: it did not evince an intent on Stewart's part to relinquish work product immunity for the document, and it did not prejudice the Government by offering Stewart some litigation-based advantage. Accordingly, I hold that Stewart did not waive work product protection over the June 23 and 24 e-mails.

9. Inadvertent Disclosure

With alarming regularity, otherwise privileged documents are accidently turned over to an opponent, in civil discovery, during an administrative investigation, or even in response to a grand jury subpoena. Disclosure usually takes place during production of a large volume of records, and it may include items protected by the attorney-client privilege or work product doctrine. Does inadvertent disclosure waive the confidentiality claim to prevent future use of the document? Hartford Fire Insurance Co. v. Garvey, 109 F.R.D. 323 (N.D. Cal. 1985), adopted a five-factor test for determining whether the privileged had been waived: "(1) the reasonableness of the precautions to prevent inadvertent disclosure; (2) the time taken to rectify the error, (3) the scope of the discovery; (4) the extent of the disclosure; and (5) the 'overriding issue of fairness.'" In **Harmony Gold U.S.A. v. Fasa Corp.**, 169 F.R.D. 113 (N.D. Ill. 1996), the Magistrate Judge rejected the five-factor test and opted to apply the "objective test" that asks whether the party claiming the privilege was responsible for the disclosure::

> [T]his court chooses to follow the objective approach since we believe it to be a more realistic, as well as practical, means to resolve the problem and issues inherent in the nature and circumstances of an inadvertent disclosure. Under the objective approach it would be an exercise in futility to examine the intentions of the disclosing party, or the adequacy of the discovery precautions, when in fact, once the documents had been disclosed their confidentiality was irretrievably lost. With the loss of confidentiality to the disclosed documents, there is little this court could offer the disclosing party to salvage its compromised position.

C. CRIME-FRAUD EXCEPTION

1. The Prima Facie Case

A frequently used means for prosecutors to avoid an assertion of the attorney-client privilege and work product doctrine is to argue that the communications were in furtherance of a current or future crime or fraud. The "crime-fraud exception" removes the confidentiality the normally attaches to attorney-client communications and attorney work product. To establish the exception, the traditional rule is that the party seeking to undermine the confidentiality the normally attaches to the communication or work product must establish a prima facie case that the client sought the assistance of the attorney for a present or future crime or fraud, but not a past crime. The attorney need not be a party to the misconduct, but the legal services must be related to the client's wrongdoing. The requirements for establishing a prima facie case that the consultation was in connection with a future crime or fraud are discussed in the following decision.

In re: GRAND JURY INVESTIGATION
445 F.3d 266 (3d Cir. 2006)

SLOVITER, Circuit Judge.

* * * In late 2003, a grand jury began investigating the financial arrangements and business dealings of the individual who we believe may be the Primary Target. Some of his business dealings have apparently been carried out by an entity we call, for want of a better designation, the Organization. The grand jury investigation led to inquiry of Jane Doe, the Executive Director of the Organization, who had, and has, intimate knowledge of and access to the papers and other material of both the Primary Target and the Organization. It appears that Jane Doe is also a target of the grand jury investigation. If she was not at the outset, she certainly has become a target in light of the events with which we are concerned. The Organization, through its counsel ("Attorney"), has entered into a joint-defense agreement with Jane Doe and her counsel in response to the investigation.

On April 27, 2004, the Government issued a grand jury subpoena to the Organization. It requested all documents, including email, from January 1, 1996 to the present, concerning, inter alia: the Organization's document retention and destruction policy; the payment of certain expenses, contributions, or donations to the Primary Target; and all grants, contributions, or donations to the Primary Target. * * *

The Government was unsatisfied with the document production, particularly with respect to what it perceived as the Organization's failure to search for and produce email stored on the Organization's computer hard drives. On January 18, 2005, the Government issued a second subpoena to the Organization, requesting essentially the same documents as in its previous subpoena. In a letter dated January 19, 2005, the Government notified Attorney that it wished to have FBI and IRS experts perform a scan of the Organization's computers to recover stored information, including deleted email files.

On February 10, 2005, pursuant to an agreement among the parties, an FBI computer technician went to the Organization's place of business and "imaged" the hard drive on Jane Doe's computer. The Government thus made an exact copy of the contents of the hard drive, including deleted email files. It uncovered numerous stored messages which could be construed to show a conscious effort by the Organization's staff to destroy emails.

Concerned about the potential obstruction of justice by Jane Doe and others at the Organization, the Government issued a subpoena duces tecum to Attorney on March 1, 2005. It sought to compel grand jury testimony regarding his discussions with Jane Doe as to her compliance (or apparent non-compliance) with the prior subpoenas for production of the Organization's email. The Government also sought production of Attorney's notes concerning his conversation with Jane Doe regarding the Organization's compliance with the two grand jury subpoenas and the January 19, 2005, letter. On March 10, 2005, the Government issued a separate subpoena for production of documents to the custodian of records at Attorney's law firm.

The Government, Attorney and Jane Doe then sought to reach an agreement that would limit the scope of Attorney's testimony before the grand jury. The Government proposed that Attorney testify on five subjects: (1) that he represents the Organization in connection with the April 27, 2004, and January 18, 2005, subpoenas; (2) that he received the January 18, 2005, subpoena and January 19 letter from the Government; (3) that he informed Jane Doe by telephone on January 20, 2005, of his receipt of the January 18 subpoena; (4) that he faxed a cover letter to Jane Doe enclosing the cover letter and subpoena from the Government; and (5) that he advised Jane Doe on January 20 regarding how to comply with the subpoena. Jane Doe voiced no objection to subjects (1)-(4), but she challenged number (5), claiming that Attorney's advice regarding compliance with the subpoena is privileged.

On January 4, 2006, the Government filed a motion to enforce the subpoena and to compel Attorney's testimony. Attorney and Jane Doe were permitted to intervene with regard to the motion, and they filed a motion to quash or to modify the subpoena to the extent that it required disclosure of privileged information.

On January 17, 2006, the District Court held a closed-court hearing on the motions. The Government argued that the crime-fraud exception should overcome the claim of privilege. In support of its position, it submitted an ex parte affidavit from an FBI agent with knowledge of the evidence gathered in the investigation. The District Court also heard testimony from Attorney and from Jane Doe's Attorney (hereinafter "Doe's Attorney"). With the Government absent from the courtroom, the two Attorneys testified essentially to their recollection of the conversations with Jane Doe on January 20, 2005, after receipt of the second subpoena and the Government's cover letter.

The dispute before the District Court was limited to whether Attorney should be compelled to reveal the substance of his January 20, 2005, telephone conversation with Jane Doe and to produce his handwritten notes concerning that conversation. On February 1, 2006, the District Court granted the Government's motion to enforce its subpoena. The Court concluded that although Attorney's advice regarding the subpoena is protected by the attorney-client privilege, and his notes are covered by the work-product doctrine, disclosure was appropriate in light of the crime-fraud exception. Based on its review of the Government's ex parte affidavit, the District Court found sufficient evidence that Jane Doe was in the process of committing obstruction of justice at the time of her January 20 conversation with Attorney, and used the information provided by Attorney in furtherance of the crime.

The Government promptly scheduled Attorney's appearance before the grand jury. The District Court denied a stay pending appeal. Jane Doe timely appealed, and this court also denied a stay. On February 7, 2006, Attorney provided the requested documents and testified before the grand jury.

* * * [Jane Doe] argues that the District Court's order enforcing and refusing to quash the subpoena to Attorney undermines the attorney-client privilege because the subpoena seeks to ascertain the contents of her conversation with Attorney on January 20, 2005. Although Jane Doe retained a personal lawyer, her lawyer and Attorney (who represents the Organization) entered into a joint defense agreement, and therefore the attorney-client privilege is applicable. In any event, the Supreme Court has held that communication between a corporation's counsel and the employees of the corporation are covered by the attorney-client privilege. Upjohn Co. v. United States, 449 U.S. 383 (1981).

The Court stated that the attorney-client privilege is the "oldest of the privileges for confidential communications known." "[C]ourts long have viewed [the privilege's] central concern as one 'to encourage full and frank communication between attorneys and their clients and thereby promote broader public interests in the observance of law and administration of justice.'" United States v. Zolin, 491 U.S. 554 (1989) (quoting *Upjohn*).

Despite the importance of the attorney-client privilege in the administration of justice, the Supreme Court in *Zolin* commented on the costs of the privilege in that it "has the effect of withholding relevant information from the factfinder." Therefore, the privilege can be overridden if the client used the lawyer's services to further a continuing or future crime or fraud.

Jane Doe argues that the crime-fraud exception is inapplicable in this case because she did not initiate the communication with Attorney or solicit any advice. She relies on the language in Doe, where this court stated, "[o]nly when a client knowingly seeks legal counsel to further a continuing or future crime does the crime-fraud exception apply." United States v. Doe, 429 F.3d 450 (3d Cir. 2005).

That sentence in the *Doe* opinion reflects the facts in that case, i.e., the client, a law enforcement officer, initiated the communication with the attorney and sought his advice as to how to circumvent the prohibition against investing in a witness's business. Nothing in that opinion, or in any opinion, suggests that the crime-fraud exception applies only if the client initiates the conversation.

To the contrary, the crime-fraud exception is equally applicable in situations where there has been a prior attorney-client relationship and the communication at issue was made in the context of that relationship. There would be no reason to limit the applicability of the crime-fraud exception to client-initiated contact, as the exception's purpose is to further frank and open exchanges between the client and his or her attorney, whether newly retained for purposes of the investigation or otherwise.

The burden to make the necessary showing for the crime-fraud exception falls on the party who seeks application of the exception. In criminal cases, it is the Government that seeks to invoke the crime-fraud exception to counter a defendant's effort to prevent disclosure of certain testimony or documents on the ground of the attorney-client privilege. Therefore, it is the Government that must bear the initial burden. We have described the showing that must be made as follows:

> [T]he government must make a prima facie showing that (1) the client was committing or intending to commit a fraud or crime, and (2) the attorney-client communications were in furtherance of that alleged crime or fraud. A "prima facie showing" requires presentation of "evidence which, if believed by the fact-finder, would be sufficient to support a finding that the elements of the crime-fraud exception were met."

In re Grand Jury Subpoena, 223 F.3d 213 (3d Cir. 2000).[a]

In Clark v. United States, 289 U.S. 1 (1933), the Supreme Court, in describing the evidentiary standard for the application of the crime-fraud exception, stated:

> There must be a showing of a prima facie case sufficient to satisfy the judge that the light should be let in . . To drive the

---

[a] Some circuits appear to apply a lower threshold for establishing the crime or fraud to vitiate the privilege. For example, the First Circuit stated that "it is enough to overcome the privilege that there is a reasonable basis to believe that the lawyer's services were used by the client to foster a crime or fraud." In re Grand Jury Proceedings, 417 F.3d 18 (1st Cir. 2005). The Ninth Circuit stated that a prima facie case is established when "[r]easonable cause existed to believe that the attorney was used in furtherance of an ongoing scheme." In re Grand Jury Proceedings, 87 F.3d 377 (9th Cir. 1996).

[attorney-client] privilege away, there must be "something to give colour to the charge"; there must be "prima facie evidence that it has some foundation in fact." When that evidence is supplied, the seal of secrecy is broken.

The burden is not a particularly heavy one. As the Court of Appeals for the Seventh Circuit stated, prima facie evidence cannot mean "enough to support a verdict in favor of the person making the claim." In re Feldberg, 862 F.2d 622 (7th Cir. 1988).

In this case, the District Court found that at the time of Jane Doe's January 20, 2005 conversation with Attorney, Jane Doe was committing the crime of obstruction of justice. The Court's finding that the Government met its burden of presenting evidence demonstrating a reasonable basis to suspect the perpetration of a crime, if based on adequate evidence, satisfies the first prong of the crime-fraud exception.

The District Court based its finding on the evidence before it, which included the ex parte affidavit provided by the Government. The Supreme Court has made clear that the district courts may use ex parte evidence supplied by the Government in order to make the required findings. *Zolin*

In *Zolin*, the IRS sought to use two tape recordings produced in an earlier case to make the required showing that the crime-fraud exception overcame the claimed attorney-client privilege. The Court of Appeals for the Ninth Circuit had opined that the determination of the applicability of the crime-fraud exception must be based on "sources independent of the attorney-client communications recorded on the tapes." In holding that was error, the Supreme Court stated that "a rigid independent evidence requirement does not comport with 'reason and experience,'... that in camera review may be used to determine whether allegedly privileged attorney-client communications fall within the crime-fraud exception," and that the party opposing the privilege "must present evidence sufficient to support a reasonable belief that in camera review may yield evidence that establishes the exception's applicability."

In accordance with *Zolin*, the District Court here used the affidavit of the FBI agent to support its finding that at the time of Jane Doe's January 20, 2005 conversation with Attorney, Jane Doe was committing the crime of obstruction of justice by participating in a scheme to delete emails on the computers of the Organization, its officers, and staff. That this was the crime on which the Government hinged its arguments with respect to the crime-fraud exception was made clear in the Assistant U.S. Attorney's arguments before this court.

In conducting our review of the District Court's finding, we too must base our decision on the evidence submitted to the District Court ex parte. We are hampered in articulating the basis for our conclusion by the need to keep the evidentiary support confidential because much of the relevant information

materials are protected by the work product doctrine. The question in that situation is whether the client's crime or fraud should vitiate the protections afforded to the attorney's work product, especially opinion work product. Consider the court's analysis in **In re Special September 1978 Grand Jury (II)**, 640 F.2d 49 (7th Cir. 1980), involving a subpoena to a law firm, Jenner & Block, that represented the Community Currency Exchange Association of Illinois. The grand jury investigated possible cash payments by the Association to the governor's reelection campaign, and Jenner & Block asserted both the attorney-client privilege and work product protection for communications and documents related to its representation of the Association in relation to tax and campaign filings. The court stated:

> In the face of ongoing client fraud, the policy underlying the attorney-client privilege does not apply because the benefit of obtaining complete legal advice is not deserved when the advice sought refers to ongoing or future rather than to prior wrongdoing. The attorney-client privilege, which may be asserted exclusively by the client and exists solely for his benefit, is therefore waived where there is ongoing client fraud.
>
> Because the work product doctrine may be asserted by both the client and the attorney, we bifurcate our analysis. We address the Association's situation first. A client may generally invoke the work product doctrine because, like the attorney-client privilege, it protects his interests by preventing disclosures about his case. When the case being prepared involves the client's ongoing fraud, however, we see no reason to afford the client the benefit of this doctrine. It is only the "rightful interests" of the client that the work product doctrine was designed to protect. We conclude that the client cannot assert the work product doctrine any more than he can assert the attorney-client privilege when there has been a showing of ongoing client fraud. Therefore, we hold that the Association cannot invoke the work product doctrine as to the subpoenaed documents because of its prima facie fraud in the filing of the reports.
>
> Where it is the attorney who asserts the work product doctrine, the fact of prima facie client fraud is not our only consideration. As we have noted one of the purposes of the work product doctrine is to protect the work of the attorney from disclosure for the benefit of the attorney. Jenner & Block argues that even if its client was engaging in fraud, the law firm should be able to claim the doctrine on its own behalf. As we perceive the problem, the policy in favor of insulating the attorney's work product for the sake of the attorney must be weighed against the policy which favors disclosure where the client has used his attorney to engage in fraud. We reach different conclusions depending on the type of information subpoenaed.

With respect to all information furnished to the attorney, whether transmitted in written form or communicated orally and recorded verbatim or in summary form, we conclude that the scale tips in favor of disclosure. We reach this result because we are persuaded that the strong policy disfavoring client fraud requires that the client relinquish the benefit he would gain from the work product doctrine, which benefit is just as real although it is his attorney, rather than he, who asserts the doctrine. We are persuaded, however, that the attorney's mental impressions, conclusions, opinions, and legal theories must still be protected in order to avoid an invasion of the attorney's necessary privacy in his work, an invasion not justified by the misfortune of representing a fraudulent client. We therefore hold that the work product doctrine is waived for client fraud even when asserted by the attorney except that it is assertable to protect the attorney's mental impressions, conclusions, opinions, and legal theories about the case.

The work product doctrine must yield to a showing of sufficient need by the party seeking to enforce the subpoena. However, we take note of Professor Moore's comment: "It has been a very rare case, indeed, in which inquiry has been permitted into the internal operation of the lawyer's office." 4 J. Moore, Federal Practice ¶ 26.03(8) at 394 (2d ed. 1979). The district judge failed to address the issue of the Grand Jury's need, and therefore we must remand for a determination of whether the Grand Jury has shown such extraordinary need as to justify production. * * *

The circuit courts have followed Seventh Circuit's lead in *September Special* in according greater protection to attorney opinion work product by requiring the party seeking production to show the attorney's involvement in the crime or fraud. In In re Green Grand Jury Proceedings, 492 F.3d 976 (8th Cir. 2007), the Eighth Circuit stated, "In keeping with the significant protection we accord opinion work product, we hold, as have our sister circuits, that an attorney who is not complicit in his client's wrongdoing may assert the work product privilege with respect to his opinion work product. In light of the lesser protection accorded ordinary work product, we conclude that an innocent attorney may be required to disclose ordinary work product."

3. Ex Parte and In Camera Submissions

In **Zolin v. United States**, 491 U.S. 554 (1989), the Supreme Court explained that a court considering a crime-fraud claim may review the purported communication to determine whether it was made in connection with an ongoing or future crime or fraud. Disclosure to the judge would not eviscerate the privilege because only the court reviews it, thus maintaining the confidentiality of the communication. The Court explained the standard under which a court can compel the ex parte and in camera submission of the privilege communication:

Before engaging in in camera review to determine the applicability of the crime-fraud exception, "the judge should require a showing of a factual basis adequate to support a good faith belief by a reasonable person," Caldwell v. District Court, 644 P.2d 26, 33 (Colo.1982), that in camera review of the materials may reveal evidence to establish the claim that the crime-fraud exception applies.

In criminal cases, the crime-fraud exception will often involve information gathered by a grand jury, which is subject to the secrecy requirement of Federal Rule of Criminal Procedure 6(e) that prohibits disclosure of matters occurring before the grand jury. Prosecutors often make their own ex parte and in camera submissions of such material to establish the prima facie case for the crime-fraud exception, or to show the factual basis to support a good faith belief under Zolin. Defendants object because they are not appraised of the information and so cannot respond to assertions about which they are kept in the dark. Courts do not require disclosure, however, as explained in **In re Vargas**, 723 F.2d 1461(C.A. 10th 1983):

> The petitioner claims that the trial court usurped its power by finding that the attorney-client privilege was not applicable. The privilege does not apply where the client consults an attorney to further a crime or fraud. Petitioner correctly argues that the government must do more than allege that an attorney is a target of a grand jury investigation to vitiate the privilege. Before the privilege is lost there must be prima facie evidence that the allegation of attorney participation in a crime or fraud has some foundation in fact. Petitioner, however, argues that certain procedures must be followed, including an opportunity for the attorney and client to rebut the prima facie evidence and to be present at any hearing which is intended to establish such a prima facie foundation. Petitioner misconstrues the law in this circuit. As this court held in its opinion In re September 1975 Grand Jury Term, 532 F.2d 734 (10th Cir.1976), "[t]he determination of whether the government shows a prima facie foundation in fact for the charge which results in the subpoena lies in the sound discretion of the trial court." In particular, that determination can be made ex-parte and a "preliminary minitrial" is not necessary. Furthermore, the prima facie foundation may be made by documentary evidence or good faith statements by the prosecutor as to testimony already received by the grand jury. * * * [I]t is clear that there was no abuse of discretion.

4. Rebutting the Prima Facie Case

As discussed in *In re Grand Jury Subpoenas*, a significant problem for defense counsel in rebutting a crime-fraud claim in a grand jury investigation is the secrecy rule of Federal Rule of Criminal Procedure 6(e). The government frequently invokes the Rule to limit the material disclosed to the subpoena recipient in its filings arguing that there is a prima facie case of a crime or fraud. Defense counsel may be in the dark as to exactly what crime or fraud is alleged to have occurred, and when it took place. Courts have been unwilling to require disclosure to the subpoena recipients of the government's information that relates to its grand jury investigation, as discussed in **In re Grand Jury Subpoena**, 223 F.3d 213 (3d Cir. 2000).

> The attorney who was subpoenaed has represented the target for more than a year in connection with the criminal investigation. The government subpoenaed the attorney "as a witness in the investigation" of his client. The attorney moved to quash the grand jury subpoena, asserting that testimony and production of documents concerning the subject matter specified in the subpoena would result in disclosure of privileged attorney-client communications and work product material * * *.

> Given the acknowledged need for secrecy in grand jury proceedings, we reject Appellant's argument that the 'unique facts and circumstances in this case,' including the length of time the investigation has been pending and the fact that the nature of the investigation has already been made public in several contexts, required the District Court to order disclosure of the government's ex parte affidavit. As we have stated, the ex parte affidavit includes excerpts of witness testimony and documents obtained during the investigation, which is ongoing. We conclude that the District Court did not abuse its discretion in denying Appellant and/or his attorney access to this information to protect grand jury secrecy.

> Our decision is in accord with those of the other federal courts of appeal that have already addressed this precise issue and rejected due process claims made under virtually identical facts. For example, in In re Grand Jury Subpoenas, 144 F.3d 653 (10th Cir.1998), the former president and chief executive officer of a hospital who was among various targets of a grand jury investigation appealed the order denying his motion to quash a grand jury subpoena directed to the hospital's counsel, with whom he had a personal attorney-client relationship. The Court of Appeals held there was no abuse of discretion or due process violation by the district court's refusal to disclose the ex parte government affidavit from which it determined that the crime-fraud exception applied.

> Similarly, when faced with the argument by grand jury targets that their due process rights were violated by their inability to inspect and rebut the ex parte affidavit submitted by the government in support of its invocation of the crime-fraud exception to the attorney-client privilege, the Second Circuit held that they were properly denied access. In re John Doe, Inc., 13 F.3d 633 (2d

Cir.1994). The court also stated that "[i]n light of the district court's legitimate concern that the secrecy of the grand jury be preserved, its in camera examination of the attorney was the most effective method of determining that the crime-fraud exception had been established." See also In re Grand Jury Subpoena as to C97-216, 187 F.3d 996 (8th Cir.1999) (court of appeals found no error and rejected argument that due process was violated by district court's reliance on ex parte affidavit to decide government made a threshold showing sufficient to justify an in camera hearing to determine whether the crime-fraud exception applied); In re Grand Jury Proceedings, Thursday Special Grand Jury September Term, 1991, 33 F.3d 342 (4th Cir.1994) (same general holding); In re Grand Jury Proceedings, 867 F.2d 539 (9th Cir.1989) (same); In re Special September 1978 Grand Jury (II), 640 F.2d 49, 57 (7th Cir.1980) (same).

We today join the ranks of our sister circuits in holding that it is within the district courts' discretion, and not violative of due process, to rely on an ex parte government affidavit to determine that the crime-fraud exception applies and thus compel a target-client's subpoenaed attorney to testify before the grand jury.

We do so confident that the district courts will vigorously test the factual and legal bases for any subpoena, and a court which questions the sufficiency of the affidavits has available various avenues of inquiry, among them discovery, in camera inspection, additional affidavits and a hearing. In the last analysis, however, we must rely on the district courts' discretion and appellate review of the exercise of that discretion to ensure that the power of the grand jury is not abused while preserving the secrecy that is a necessary element of the grand jury process.

5. Expanding the Crime-Fraud Exception

The crime-fraud exception is not limited to criminal cases, and it arises quite frequently in civil litigation. Moreover, the term "fraud" is much broader than "crime" so that is the more likely vehicle for seeking to vitiate the confidentiality accorded to attorney-client communications and work product. Does the breadth of white collar offenses enhance the government's position in claiming a crime-fraud exception? See Peter J. Henning, *Testing the Limits of Investigating and Prosecuting White Collar Crime: How Far Will the Courts Allow Prosecutors to Go?*, 54 U. PITT. L. REV. 405 (1993).:

The crime-fraud exception has expanded considerably due to the growth of government regulation of business activity that results in greater reporting requirements incorporating criminal penalties for failing to comply with the proper procedures or for supplying false information. Not only can more acts be labeled 'criminal' or 'fraudulent,' but lawyers play such a pervasive role in advising clients on complying with or avoiding regulatory schemes that the opportunity to use legal advice to commit an illegal act has increased correspondingly. The improper act does not have to be a violation of a specific criminal provision, and the act only has to be one objective of seeking the legal advice for the exception to apply. Therefore, the question of whether an alleged course of conduct qualifies as a crime or fraud is rarely at issue because the breadth of white collar criminal law encompasses most acts which are of questionable legality.

D. JOINT DEFENSE AGREEMENTS

In United States v. Moss, 9 F.3d 543 (6th Cir. 1993), the court noted that "[a] joint defense extension of the attorney client privilege has been applied to confidential communications shared between co-defendants which are part of an on-going and joint effort to set up a common defense strategy. The burden to establish the applicability of the privilege is upon the defendants." The court described the purpose of the application of the privilege in this context in John Morrell & Company v. Local Union 304A, 913 F.2d 544 (8th Cir. 1989):

[W]hen information is exchanged between various co-defendants and their attorneys [,] . . . this exchange is not made for the purpose of allowing unlimited publication and use, but rather, the exchange is made for the limited purpose of assisting in their common cause. It is fundamental that the joint defense privilege cannot be waived without the consent of all parties to the defense.

1. Establishing the Common Interest

The Joint Defense Privilege is an extension of the attorney-client privilege to a special situation where multiple parties can achieve significant benefits by pooling their resources, including the representation of counsel. Although the privilege claim is often based on a written agreement among the parties, that is not a necessary condition for a court to recognize that communications are privileged. A significant issue can be when the common interest among the parties arose.

In re: SANTA FE INTERNATIONAL CORPORATION
272 F.3d 705 (5th Cir. 2001)

DENNIS, Circuit Judge.

* * * Plaintiffs, who are present and former offshore drilling workers for Santa Fe and some twenty-one other offshore drilling corporations, filed this

action on August 14, 2000, naming those companies as defendants. The complaint alleges that the defendants secretly met over the past ten years to set, stabilize, maintain, or limit the wages and benefits paid to offshore drilling employees. The plaintiffs seek certification of a class of such employees, damages for defendants' alleged antitrust violations, and a permanent injunction to prevent such conduct in the future. * * *

Turning our attention directly to Santa Fe's claim for protection under the "common legal interest" extension of the attorney-client privilege ("CLI privilege"), we conclude that it has no merit. * * *

According to our circuit precedents, the two types of communications protected under the CLI privilege are: (1) communications between co-defendants in actual litigation and their counsel; and (2) communications between *potential* co-defendants and their counsel. With respect to the latter category, the term "potential" has not been clearly defined. However, because the privilege is "an obstacle to truthseeking," it must "be construed narrowly to effectuate necessary consultation between legal advisers and clients." In re LTV Sec. Litig., 89 F.R.D. 595 (N.D.Tex.1981).

Considering that caveat, and in looking at other cases discussing the CLI privilege in this circuit, it appears that there must be a palpable threat of litigation at the time of the communication, rather than a mere awareness that one's questionable conduct might some day result in litigation, before communications between one possible future co-defendant and another, such as the ones here made between one horizontal competitor and another, could qualify for protection. * * *

In the present case, Santa Fe admits in the motion for reconsideration it filed in the district court that the communications it claims are protected by the privilege were not made in anticipation of future litigation. Instead, the documents were "circulated for the purpose of ensuring compliance with the antitrust laws and minimizing any potential risk associated with the exchange of wage and benefit information." In sharing the communications, therefore, they sought to avoid conduct that might lead to litigation. They were not preparing for future litigation. Furthermore, Santa Fe denied, in its responses to the plaintiffs' requests for admissions, that it anticipated or perceived a threat of antitrust litigation against it in May of 1991, when Santa Fe's senior counsel prepared the memorandum that was distributed to the company's competitors. Considering that the original complaint in this case was not filed until August 14, 2000, we cannot say that the district court clearly erred in its implicit finding of fact that Santa Fe's disclosures to third persons of the 1991 memorandum were not made for the purpose of preparing a joint defense to lawsuits based on pre-1991 antitrust law violations. * * *

Here, the lack of any temporal connection to actual or threatened litigation is striking. Had these Defendants been jointly defending a suit, as opposed to merely discussing concerns, the long elapse of time would not bear so heavily on the Court's inquiry. But, when the threat of litigation is merely a thought rather than a palpable reality, the joint discussion is more properly characterized as a common business undertaking, which is unprivileged, and certainly not a common legal interest. There is no justification within the reasonable bounds of the attorney-client privilege for horizontal competitors to exchange legal information, which allegedly contains confidences, in the absence of an actual, or imminent, or at least directly foreseeable, lawsuit.

As the district court's reasons suggest, the record in this case is neither clear nor indisputable with respect to Santa Fe's motive for sending its in-house counsel's memorandum to its horizontal offshore drilling competitors. It is possible that the disclosures were made to facilitate future price fixing in violation of the antitrust laws, as the plaintiffs contend.[9] Alternatively, the disclosures were perhaps made in the sole interest of preventing future antitrust violations, as the defendants argue in their motion for reconsideration, in which case they hardly could be seen as the commencement of an allied litigation effort. Furthermore, it is difficult to find that the disclosures were made for the purpose of forming a common defense against alleged prior violations of the antitrust laws, in view of Santa Fe's stout denials that in 1991 it anticipated or perceived a threat of future antitrust litigation.

The ambiguity of the record and the cloudiness of the crucial legal concept involved strongly militate in favor of the conclusion that, if the district court erred at all, it certainly was not clearly and indisputably wrong in finding that Santa Fe's disclosures of its in-house counsel's memorandum to its horizontal competitors were not communications protected under any attorney-client privilege to which Santa Fe was entitled.

SMITH, Circuit Judge, dissenting.

[Judge Smith dissented on a number of grounds. On the issue of the Joint Defense Privilege, he stated:] As long as Santa Fe shows that the documents were given in confidence and that the communication regarded a common legal interest with respect to the subject matter of the communication—both assertions that Santa Fe says it can satisfy—the district court should not order production. * * *

Neither we nor the district court knows whether the documents are privileged. Neither the district court nor this court has viewed the documents. It may be that some are privileged and some are not. All that is recorded in the transcript of March 9 is Santa Fe's statement that they are privileged and the district court's decree that they are not.

---

[9] If so, they would fall outside the scope of any attorney-client privilege as communications made for criminal or fraudulent purposes.

More analysis is needed before any such documents should be ordered produced. Instead, however, the district court ordered all the documents, from all the defendants, to be turned over at once.

NOTES AND QUESTIONS

1. *Joint Knowledge.* One potential danger of using a joint defense agreement is that the government can try to defend its failure to produce Brady materials to all of the parties on the ground that since one of the participants was aware of the witness about whom the materials related, the entire defense team should be deemed to have been made aware, and by exercising due diligence been able to find the materials the Government failed to provide them individually.

2. *Pre-Agreement Communications.* In United States v. Weissman, 195 F.3d 96 (2nd Cir. 1999), a corporate officer made "damaging admissions regarding his own conduct" to corporate counsel, under the belief that the statements were protected by the privilege because there was a Joint Defense Agreement. The Second Circuit upheld the district court's finding that the statements were not protected because the parties had not yet entered into the Joint Defense Agreement, crediting the testimony of corporate counsel that they had not yet reached an agreement over the recollection of the witness' counsel that such an agreement had been reached.

The key issue in *Santa Fe Corporation* was the timing of the communication. As the litigation gets closer, does the attorney-client privilege extend to communications made to an attorney at a pre-representation meeting? What if individuals with common defenses approach the attorney together? In **In re Grand Jury Proceedings Jean Auclair**, 961 F.2d 65 (5th Cir. 1992), the court stated:

> * * * The Model Rules of Professional Conduct, which replaced the earlier Code of Professional Responsibility, require an attorney to evaluate the relevant facts, circumstances, and parties to determine the appropriateness and propriety of assent to representation. "A lawyer should not accept representation in a matter unless it can be performed . . . without improper conflict of interest." Of critical importance to a meaningful pre-representation interview is the availability of the attorney-client privilege from the initial salutation and greeting on. The existence of the privilege is an essential ingredient to a full and free exchange of information needed by the attorney for an intelligent assessment of the representation invitation. The early declining of representation is in the mutual best interests of both the attorney and the prospective client. For the attorney there is the obvious savings of time and the avoidance of possible future conflicts. For the prospective client the threshold declining of potentially problematic representation permits the

timely seeking of other counsel, thus minimizing the possible losses and difficulties experienced if the attorney must later withdraw from an improvidently undertaken representation.

It necessarily follows that when more than one person seeks consultation with an attorney on a matter of common interest, the parties and the attorney may reasonably presume that the parties are seeking representation of a common or joint matter. * * * Neither the fact that the joint representation ultimately proved impracticable nor the subsequent waiver by either or both * * * can effect a retroactive recharacterization of the attorney-client relationship as it existed during the pre-representation meeting so as to defeat the protection the privilege affords * * *.

3. *Disqualification.* By receiving confidential information from a member of the joint defense group, the attorney has a duty to maintain the confidentiality of those communications and not use them to the detriment of the person making the privilege communication. A significant problem can arise if a member of the joint defense group decides to cooperate with the government. Can defense counsel who may have received confidential information from the now-cooperating witness continue to represent other members of the group? This may be grounds for disqualifying counsel for the remaining members of the joint defense group because of the conflict, as discussed in Chapter 16.

4. *Waiver and the Joint Defense Agreement.* An important issue that arises with some regularity in joint defense situations is whether one party can withdraw from the agreement and provide the government with protected communications. While an individual can always choose to waive the privilege with regard to communications with his or her own attorney, it is less clear whether a member of a joint defense agreement can disclose communications with other members of the joint defense team. The agreement governs the issue, and defense counsel should be careful to address this issue at the inception of the joint undertaking rather than waiting until a problem arises. As with any contract, the parties can modify their agreement, as discussed in **United States v. LeCroy**, 348 F.Supp.2d 375 (E.D. Pa. 2004). The defendants, LeCroy and Snell, were employees of J.P. Morgan Chase Bank (JPMC), and entered into an oral joint defense agreement related to a grand jury investigation into their conduct on behalf of the bank that resulted in their indictment for wire fraud. During the investigation, JPMC informed counsel for the defendants that the bank planned to cooperate with the government and would turn over all materials from its internal investigation, including privileged information. Nevertheless, counsel allowed LeCroy and Snell to engage in further interviews with JPMC's counsel. The district court explained why JPMC did not violate the joint defense agreement by turning over notes of the interviews to prosecutors:

There were good and abundant reasons why LeCroy and Snell, with the advice of their counsel, rationally, intelligently and knowingly decided to allow JPMC and its counsel to interview them, knowing that the notes of the interviews may be turned over to the government, but also knowing the JDA would continue, as modified. Under the JDA, the parties could continue to share information, documents, and access to witnesses without fear that any party continuing with the JDA would divulge that information. The only change in the terms of the JDA was that the notes of the interviews of LeCroy and Snell by JPMC could be turned over to the government. Assuming LeCroy and Snell were telling JPMC counsel the truth, their counsel wisely advised them to proceed with the interview even though the notes may be turned over to the government. This may have been the best possible strategy to avoid indictment. This Court intends to uphold the JDA to the extent that it was not modified. However, it is clear that JPMC initiated a modification of the JDA, or a partial withdrawal from it, and that LeCroy and Snell, with their counsel's advice, by agreeing to be interviewed by JPMC's counsel, and knowing that the notes and memoranda of such interviews may be turned over to the government, knowingly and intelligently agreed to the modification and thus waived the protections of the JDA as to those notes and memoranda on a prospective basis.

The provisions in the prior 2000 written agreement between Recker and Dodds [counsel for LeCroy and Snell] regarding withdrawal were quoted above because it is clear to this Court that, notwithstanding and not necessarily inconsistent with the terms of the JDA – and the understanding of the lawyers who entered into it – there was indisputably, in January 2004, a partial withdrawal, or a modification, or a partial waiver by LeCroy and Snell, of the protections of the JDA to the extent that JPMC could turn over the notes of its counsel's interviews with LeCroy and Snell to the grand jury pursuant to the grand jury subpoena.

Modification took place by JPMC insisting that it would have to have the right to turn over the notes of its interviews of LeCroy and Snell to the government pursuant to the grand jury subpoena. By Dodds [counsel for JPMC] communicating this to counsel for LeCroy and Snell prior to the interviews, and counsel repeating this to their clients, and all parties proceeding with the interviews, there was an acknowledgment by all parties that the JDA had been modified to allow JPMC to produce the notes to the government. Notwithstanding Recker's and Suddath's dispute with Dodds as to whether JPMC had the right to do this, by the conduct of LeCroy and Snell (with their counsel's advice) of going to New York and submitting themselves to interviews with the knowledge that the notes of the interviews may be turned over to the government, the Court finds that this constituted a modification by their explicit conduct, done on a knowing and voluntary basis. LeCroy and Snell were not obliged to submit to the JPMC interviews. They could have refused to do so; what the consequences of their refusal may have been are undetermined but irrelevant.

5. *Payment of Legal Fees*. It is common in investigations of corporate misconduct that the company will provide representation to individual employees, officers, and directors who are called before the grand jury or who may be targets of the investigation. Many corporations have indemnification agreements–either in individual employment contracts or in the company's by-laws or charter–that require the corporation to pay for legal counsel in an investigation.   That arrangement can raise sensitive issues regarding conflicts of interest among the various defense counsel. ABA Model Rule of Professional Conduct 1.8(f) specifically deals with the issue of third-party payment of legal fees:

> A lawyer shall not accept compensation for representing a client from one other than the client unless:
>
> (1) the client gives informed consent;
>
> (2) there is no interference with the lawyer's independence of professional judgment or with the client-lawyer relationship; and
>
> (3) information relating to representation of a client is protected as required by Rule 1.6.

Corporations, particularly those whose shares are publicly-traded, often obligate themselves to pay the attorney's fees of employees, officers, and directors through individual employment agreements or in corporate by-laws.

Delaware law, which governs many larger corporations, provides:

> A corporation shall have power to indemnify any person who was or is a party or is threatened to be made a party to any threatened, pending or completed action, suit or proceeding, whether civil, criminal, administrative or investigative (other than an action by or in the right of the corporation) by reason of the fact that the person is or was a director, officer, employee or agent of the corporation, or is or was serving at the request of the corporation as a director, officer, employee or agent of another corporation, partnership, joint venture, trust or other enterprise, against expenses (including attorneys' fees), judgments, fines and amounts paid in settlement actually and reasonably incurred by the person in connection with such action, suit or proceeding if the person acted in good faith and in a manner the person reasonably believed to be in or not opposed to the best interests of the corporation, and, with respect to any criminal action or proceeding, had no reasonable cause to believe the person's conduct was unlawful.

8 Del. G.C.L. § 145(a).

In addition, state corporate codes authorize a company to agree to mandatory advancement of attorney's fees, often conditioned on the recipient's agreement to repay the fees if it turns out the person was not eligible to receive them. In **Westar Energy, Inc. v. Lake**, 552 F.3d 1215 (10th Cir. 2009), the Tenth Circuit considered a lower court's order directing a corporation to advance the legal fees of a former officer and director facing charges arising from his tenure at the company. The court explained the importance of advancement of attorney's fees:

> Lake's right to advancement is a contractual right originating in Westar's Articles of Incorporation. Advancement is a distinct right complementary to the right to indemnification. Indemnification and advancement work in tandem to encourage talented individuals to serve as corporate officers. Corporate service entails the risk of civil and criminal liability, and corporations may be willing to assume the expenses of defending such suits to attract talented employees. The right to indemnity, however, is often impossible to determine until the legal proceedings are finished. Absent advances, the officer himself must front the cost of defending the legal proceeding, significantly diminishing the attractiveness of indemnity. Advancement addresses this problem by providing timely relief in the midst of litigation. If a corporation withholds advances, the right will be irretrievably lost at the conclusion of the litigation, because at that point the officer will only be entitled to indemnity.

> In this case, Lake faces the possibility of a prison term if he is convicted in his third criminal trial. He is relying on advances to fund his legal defense. The district court's prospective remedy protects Lake's right to advances, and is thus crucial to Lake's defense of his liberty. Lake therefore meets the requirement of showing irreparable injury in the absence of the prospective relief granted by the district court.

2. Joint Representation of a Corporation and Its Officers

Counsel for an organization, will be in close contact with senior management, and when the corporation is closely-held the managers frequently are controlling shareholders. The distinction between representation of the entity and individual officers or shareholders will not be clear, and the lawyer may represent both at certain times. How does that type of representation affect the scope of the attorney-client privilege?

IN Re GRAND JURY SUBPOENA (CUSTODIAN OF RECORDS, NEWPARENT, INC.)
274 F.3d 563 (1st Cir. 2001)

SELYA, Circuit Judge.

[A company entered into a plea agreement and waived its attorney-client privilege with regard to communications with corporate counsel. A grand jury subpoena was sent to the law firm that represented the company, called "Oldco" by the court, and two former officers objected to disclosure of the documents because the communications were protected by the attorney-client privilege under a joint defense agreement between the officers and the corporation.]

At the time the subpoena was served, Oldco was a wholly-owned subsidiary of Newparent. Its records were in the possession of Newparent's counsel, a law firm that we shall call Smith & Jones. Newparent had acquired Oldco in June of 1998, but the grand jury investigation focused on conduct that occurred prior to the acquisition date. During that earlier period, Oldco had operated as a closely held corporation, owned by a number of members of a single family; one family member (Richard Roe) served as its board chairman and chief executive officer, and another (Morris Moe) served on the board and as executive vice-president for sales and marketing. A. Nameless Lawyer was Oldco's principal outside counsel. These three individuals—Roe, Moe, and Lawyer—intervened in the proceedings and filed a motion to quash the subpoena.

The factual premise for the motion to quash is derived largely from Lawyer's affidavit. He states that while representing Oldco he also represented Roe and Moe in various individual matters. Moreover, he claims to have conducted this simultaneous representation of corporate and individual clients under a longstanding joint defense agreement. According to Lawyer, this agreement, although never committed to writing, provided that communications among the three clients were jointly privileged and could not be released without unanimous consent. Despite the absence of any reference to this agreement in the corporate records—there was no resolution or other vote of the board of directors authorizing Oldco to participate in such an arrangement—the intervenors assert that Roe, as chief executive officer, had the authority to commit the corporation to it.

Pertinently, Lawyer claims to have represented Oldco and its officers in connection with the grand jury investigation from and after October 1997 (when the grand jury served Oldco with an earlier subpoena requesting the production of certain customer records). He says that the oral joint defense agreement applies to this multiple-party representation and that he told the government that he represented Oldco and "all of its executives." * * *

It is often difficult to determine whether a corporate officer or employee may claim an attorney-client privilege in communications with corporate counsel. The default assumption is that the attorney only represents the corporate entity, not the individuals within the corporate sphere, and it is the individuals' burden to dispel that presumption. This makes perfect sense because an employee has a duty to assist his employer's counsel in the investigation and defense of matters pertaining to the employer's business.

To determine when this presumption bursts, several courts have adopted the test explicated in In re Bevill, Bresler & Schulman Asset Mgmt. Corp., 805 F.2d 120 (3d Cir.1986). That test enumerates five benchmarks that corporate employees seeking to assert a personal claim of attorney-client privilege must meet:

> First, they must show they approached [counsel] for the purpose of seeking legal advice. Second, they must demonstrate that when they approached [counsel] they made it clear that they were seeking legal advice in their individual rather than in their representative capacities. Third, they must demonstrate that the [counsel] saw fit to communicate with them in their individual capacities, knowing that a possible conflict could arise. Fourth, they must prove that their conversations with [counsel] were confidential. And fifth, they must show that the substance of their conversations with [counsel] did not concern matters within the company or the general affairs of the company. * * *

[The court adopted Bevil, Bresler test and addressed whether the individual officers and corporate counsel could meet the fifth factor:] [T]heoretically, Lawyer could have represented Roe and Moe individually with respect to the grand jury investigation. Still, this attorney-client relationship would extend only to those communications which involved Roe's and Moe's individual rights and responsibilities arising out of their actions as officers of the corporation.

Having concluded that there are potentially some communications protected by the attorney-client privilege, we next consider the effect of Oldco's waiver of that privilege. The major difficulty—there are others, but we need not discuss them here—is that the individuals' allegedly protected communications with Lawyer do not appear to be distinguishable from discussions between the same parties in their capacities as corporate officers and corporate counsel, respectively, anent matters of corporate concern. The intervenors propose that such "dual" communications be treated as jointly privileged such that the consent of all parties would be required to waive the privilege. But they fail to cite authority supporting this position, and we ultimately decline to accept it: permitting a joint privilege of this type would unduly broaden the attorney-client privilege by allowing parties outside a given attorney-client relationship to prevent disclosure of statements made by the client.

The reference to an alleged joint defense agreement does little to advance the intervenors' argument on this point. "The joint defense privilege protects communications between an individual and an attorney for another when the communications are 'part of an ongoing and joint effort to set up a common defense strategy.'" Because the privilege sometimes may apply outside the context of actual litigation, what the parties call a "joint defense" privilege is more aptly termed the "common interest" rule. Even when that rule applies, however, a party always remains free to disclose his own communications. Thus, the existence of a joint defense agreement does not increase the number of parties whose consent is needed to waive the attorney-client privilege; it merely prevents disclosure of a communication made in the course of preparing a joint defense by the third party to whom it was made.

In the clamor over the existence *vel non* of a joint defense agreement, the parties tend to overlook case law dealing directly with the circumstances under which statements made in a joint conference remain privileged. Although these cases do not speak with one voice, they inform our resolution of the issue. They establish that joint communications with a single attorney are privileged with respect to the outside world because clients must be entitled to the full benefit of joint representation undiluted by fear of waiving the attorney-client privilege. Nevertheless, the privilege does not apply in subsequent litigation between the joint clients; in that sort of situation, one client's interest in the privilege is counterbalanced by the other's interest in being able to waive it.

The instance of a criminal investigation in which one former co-client is willing to aid in the prosecution of the other lies in the wasteland between these two doctrinal strands, and courts have split on whether the target of the prosecution may block disclosure in this context.

Although the instant case arises as a motion to quash a subpoena, rather than as an attempt to block a former co-client's testimony, the issue of privilege is entirely congruent. But there is another difference here–a significant one that cuts against the intervenors. In this iteration, the former co-clients were not independent actors, but, rather, corporate officers who owed a fiduciary duty to the corporation. Faced with an analogous assertion of privilege by corporate managers, the Fifth Circuit has held that the managers' interest must yield to the shareholders' interest in disclosure of the privileged materials. Garner v. Wolfinbarger, 430 F.2d 1093 (5th Cir.1970). Taking a similar tack, we hold that a corporation may unilaterally waive the attorney-client privilege with respect to any communications made by a corporate officer in his corporate capacity, notwithstanding the existence of an individual attorney-client relationship between him and the corporation's counsel.

* * * [I]t follows that Roe or Moe may only assert an individual privilege to the extent that communications regarding individual acts and liabilities are segregable from discussions about the corporation. When one bears in mind that a corporation is an incorporeal entity and must necessarily communicate with counsel through individuals, the necessity for such a rule becomes readily apparent. Holding otherwise would open the door to a claim

of jointly held privilege in virtually every corporate communication with counsel.

Here, neither Roe nor Moe have even attempted to make any showing of segrability. On the contrary, their main argument in the district court and on appeal appears to be that the documents at issue do not lend themselves to separation into individual and corporate categories. The intervenors' brief is replete with references to "joint privilege," but contains no allegation that any particular communication related solely to the representation of Roe or Moe. Given the absence of such an allegation and the allocation of the burden of proof (which, on this issue, rests with the intervenors), we perceive no error in the district court's explicit finding that "all communications in this case are corporate communications." That dooms the intervenors' claim of attorney-client privilege, and renders moot the question of whether Roe and Moe also possessed an attorney-client privilege in these documents.

The claim of work product privilege raises a similar set of issues anent joint privilege. The work product rule protects work done by an attorney in anticipation of, or during, litigation from disclosure to the opposing party. The rule facilitates zealous advocacy in the context of an adversarial system of justice by ensuring that the sweat of an attorney's brow is not appropriated by the opposing party. Hickman v. Taylor, 329 U.S. 495 (1947). Although the record does not include an index of allegedly privileged documents–a shortcoming to which we shall return–it appears that at least two categories of files contemplated by the subpoena might qualify as work product: Lawyer's interviews of employees during Oldco's internal investigation into the rebate program, and his notes and mental impressions of the investigation.

Roe, Moe, and Lawyer as their attorney may, at least in theory, invoke the work product privilege as to work done exclusively for Roe and Moe as individuals. Yet, their argument does not claim exclusivity,[2] but, rather, amounts to an insistence that they should have a veto over the disclosure of documents produced for the joint benefit of the individuals and the corporation. As in the case of the attorney-client privilege, however, the intervenors may not successfully assert the work product privilege with respect to such documents. Because they effectively conceded that the work was performed, at least in part, for the corporation, Oldco's waiver of all privileges negates their potential claim of privilege. In these circumstances, therefore, the work product privilege does not preclude disclosure of the documents sought by the subpoena.

Undaunted, the intervenors argue that the presence of the oral joint defense agreement demands a different result. We do not agree. Although a

---

[2] For example, with respect to the employee interviews conducted by Lawyer, the intervenors argued to the lower court that the work product privilege does not belong exclusively to Oldco because the work was performed on behalf of all three clients.

valid joint defense agreement may protect work product, one party to such an agreement may not preclude disclosure of work product by another party on whose behalf the work originally was performed. Nor can the parties, by agreement, broaden the scope of the privilege that the law allows. Such an agreement would contravene public policy (and, hence, would be unenforceable).

We add, moreover, that the type of joint defense agreement described in Lawyer's affidavit would be null and void. After all, a primary requirement of a joint defense agreement is that there be something against which to defend. In other words, a joint defense agreement may be formed only with respect to the subject of potential or actual litigation. Lawyer's affidavit avers that his three clients (Oldco, Roe, and Moe) entered into an oral joint defense agreement in 1990, at which time no particular litigation or investigation was in prospect. The agreement thereafter remained in effect, Lawyer says, attaching *ex proprio vigore* to all matters subsequently arising (including the current grand jury investigation). The law will not countenance a "rolling" joint defense agreement of this limitless breadth.

The rationale for recognizing joint defense agreements is that they permit parties to share information pertinent to each others' defenses. In an adversarial proceeding, a party's entitlement to this enhanced veil of confidentiality can be justified on policy grounds. But outside the context of actual or prospective litigation, there is more vice than virtue in such agreements. Indeed, were we to sanction the intervenors' view, we would create a judicially enforced code of silence, preventing attorneys from disclosing information obtained from other attorneys and other attorneys' clients. Common sense suggests that there can be no joint defense agreement when there is no joint defense to pursue. We so hold. * * *

E. OTHER PRIVILEGES

1. Tax Advice Privilege

In 1998, Congress adopted the Internal Revenue Service Restructuring and Reform Act of 1998, which, *inter alia*, created a limited privilege in federal actions involving tax advice. The privilege, codified at 26 U.S.C. § 7525(a)(1), provides: "With respect to tax advice, the same common law protections of confidentiality which apply to a communication between a taxpayer and an attorney shall also apply to a communication between a taxpayer and any federally authorized tax practitioner to the extent the communication would be considered a privileged communication if it were between a taxpayer and an attorney." A "federally authorized tax practitioner" includes certified public accountants and "enrolled agents" who are authorized to file tax returns with the IRS. The new privilege is not as extensive as the attorney-client privilege, covering only tax advice and subject to two important limitations: the privilege "may only be asserted in–(A) any noncriminal tax matter before the Internal Revenue Service; and (B) any noncriminal tax proceeding in Federal court brought by or against the United States." 26 U.S.C. § 7525(a)(2). In addition to the federal privilege under § 7525, some states recognize an accountant-client privilege. See Francis M. Dougherty, *Privileged Communications Between Accountant and Client*, 33 A.L.R. 4th 539. Section 7525 does not, however, extend the protection of the work product doctrine to tax advice provided by an accountant automatically, so that the usual requirements to qualify for the work product doctrine must be met. See Long-Term Capital Holdings v. United States, 2002 WL 31934139 (D. Conn. Oct. 30, 2002).

The scope of the accountant-client privilege under § 7525 is discussed the following case related to a broad IRS investigation of abusive tax shelters.

UNITED STATES v. BDO SEIDMAN
337 F.3d 802 (7th Cir. 2003)

RIPPLE, Circuit Judge.

Several unnamed clients of BDO Seidman, LLP ("BDO"), a public accounting and consulting firm, appeal from the district court's denial of their motions to intervene in an Internal Revenue Service ("IRS") enforcement action against BDO.

The IRS had issued twenty summonses to BDO as part of its investigation of BDO's compliance with Internal Revenue Code registration and list-keeping requirements for organizers and sellers of potentially abusive tax shelters. See 26 U.S.C. §§ 6111, 6112. The clients sought to intervene to assert a confidentiality privilege regarding certain documents that BDO intended to produce in response to those summonses. The clients argued that, because these documents reveal their identities as BDO clients who sought advice regarding tax shelters and who subsequently invested in those shelters, disclosure inevitably would violate the statutory privilege protecting confidential communications between a taxpayer and any federally authorized tax practitioner giving tax advice. See 26 U.S.C. § 7525. For the reasons that follow, we affirm the district court's denial of the clients' motions to intervene.

In September 2000, the IRS received information suggesting that BDO was promoting potentially abusive tax shelters without complying with the registration and listing requirements for organizers and sellers of tax shelters. Section 6111(a) of the Internal Revenue Code requires organizers of tax shelters to register the tax shelter with the IRS. Any tax shelter required to be registered under § 6111, as well as any "arrangement which is of a type which the Secretary determines by regulations as having a potential for tax avoidance or evasion," is considered to be "potentially abusive." 26 U.S.C. § 6112(b). Accordingly, the organizers and sellers of such tax shelters must keep a list identifying each person to whom an interest of the tax shelter was sold. See 26 U.S.C. § 6112(a). Failure to comply with the registration and listing requirements of § 6111 and § 6112 can lead to the imposition of penalties. Because the IRS suspected that BDO had violated these statutory provisions by organizing and selling interests in potentially abusive tax shelters without complying with the registration and list-keeping requirements, it issued a series of summonses to BDO, identifying twenty types of tax shelter transactions in which it suspected that BDO's clients had invested.

The summonses command production of documents and testimony relating to the identified transactions, as well as information about BDO clients who invested in the identified tax shelters. For example, the summonses demand documents identifying the investors in the transactions, the date on which those investors acquired an interest, and all tax shelter registrations filed and investor lists prepared with respect to the transactions.

In July 2002, when BDO failed to produce documents as required by the summonses, the IRS petitioned the district court for enforcement. BDO opposed enforcement. It argued that the investigation did not have a legitimate purpose, that the summonses were overbroad and issued in bad faith, and that the information sought was already in the possession of the IRS and was not relevant to the investigation. BDO also claimed that some of the summoned information was protected from disclosure by the attorney-client privilege, the work product doctrine, and the confidentiality privilege of § 7525 of the Internal Revenue Code. In October 2002, the district court ruled that the IRS had met its burden of showing that it issued the summonses in good faith, and that BDO had failed to show that enforcement of the summonses would constitute an abuse of process. * * *

Among the responsive documents not previously submitted for the court's in camera inspection were records that reveal the identities of the BDO clients who invested in at least one of the 20 types of tax shelters identified in the summonses. BDO informed its clients that it intended to produce these documents to the IRS. In response, two sets of unidentified taxpayers–the John and Jane Does and the Richard and Mary Roes (hereinafter referred to collectively as "the Does")–filed emergency motions to intervene in the enforcement proceedings pursuant to Federal Rule of Civil Procedure 24(a)(2). The Does, asserting that they are BDO clients who sought BDO's confidential advice regarding the potential tax effects of certain proposed financial transactions, argued that the documents revealing their identities are privileged under 26 U.S.C. § 7525, and that BDO was not adequately representing their interest in keeping that information confidential. The Does conceded that, aside from the fact that the documents reveal their identities as BDO clients who invested in at least one of the 20 types of tax shelters described in the summonses, the documents themselves do not contain any otherwise privileged communication. After a hearing, the district court denied the Does' emergency motions to intervene. * * *

The primary issue before us is whether the district court erred when it denied the Does' motions to intervene because it believed that they had failed to establish a colorable claim of privilege under § 7525. Unless the Does can establish that the § 7525 privilege can protect a taxpayer's identity from disclosure in the IRS enforcement action, the Does will not prevail on appeal. * * *

We first consider the regulatory context in which the Does' claim of privilege arises. The Does sought to intervene in proceedings involving the IRS investigation of BDO for potential violations of the tax code, including the provisions requiring organizers of tax shelters to register tax shelters with the IRS, 26 U.S.C. § 6111, and organizers and sellers of such shelters to keep lists of the investors, 26 U.S.C. § 6112. These provisions were enacted by Congress as part of the Deficit Reduction Act of 1984, for the purpose of providing the IRS with means to better monitor tax shelters, and, consequently, to deter abusive tax shelters that can adversely impact public revenues. Before 1984, no systematic information was available to assist the IRS in identifying the shelters that should be investigated. The IRS could audit individual taxpayers, but such a process only randomly identified participants in potentially abusive tax shelters. The statutory registration and list-keeping provisions allow the IRS to identify more easily those transactions that it deems to be abusive and "to identify quickly all of the participants in related tax-shelter investments." These provisions also enable the IRS to examine every purchaser of a given type of tax shelter investment and to treat those taxpayers in a more uniform manner. * * *

Having described the general framework of this regulatory authority, we now turn to the specific context of the Does' claim. The Does seek to intervene to prevent the disclosure, through IRS summonses, of documents that the Does contend are privileged. The Does' privilege claim rests entirely on § 7525, a statute enacted on July 22, 1998, to provide a confidentiality privilege for communications between a taxpayer and a tax practitioner. This limited privilege applies only to communications occurring after the date of the statute's enactment. Section 7525, provides in pertinent part:

With respect to tax advice, the same common law protections of confidentiality which apply to a communication between a taxpayer and an attorney shall also apply to a communication between a taxpayer and any federally authorized tax practitioner to the extent the communication would be considered a privileged communication if it were between a taxpayer and an attorney.

Thus the § 7525 privilege is no broader than that of the attorney-client privilege * * *. Because the scope of the tax practitioner-client privilege depends on the scope of the common law protections of confidential attorney-client communications, we must look to the body of common law interpreting the attorney-client privilege to interpret the § 7525 privilege.

The attorney-client privilege is "one of the oldest recognized privileges for confidential communications" known to the common law. Swidler & Berlin v. United States, 524 U.S. 399 (1998). The purpose of the privilege is to encourage full disclosure and to facilitate open communication between attorneys and their clients. However, because "the privilege has the effect of withholding relevant information," courts construe the privilege to apply only where necessary to achieve its purpose. Fisher v. United States, 425 U.S. 391 (1976). The mere assertion of a privilege is not enough; instead, a party that seeks to invoke the attorney- client privilege has the burden of establishing all of its essential elements.

A party that seeks to assert a § 7525 privilege bears the same burden. Among the essential elements of the attorney-client privilege are the requirements that the communication be made to the attorney in confidence, and that the confidences constitute information that is not intended to be disclosed by the attorney. Furthermore, the party asserting a privilege must show that the attorney-client communication was made for the purpose of obtaining legal advice, or, more precisely in the case of the § 7525 privilege, tax advice.

The attorney-client privilege protects confidential communications made by a client to his lawyer, and so ordinarily the identity of a client does not come within the scope of the privilege. However, over the years, a limited exception to this general rule has developed; the identity of a client may be privileged in the rare circumstance when so much of an actual confidential communication has been disclosed already that merely identifying the client will effectively disclose that communication.

In their discussion of this narrow exception, the parties primarily focus on two cases in which we held that attorney-client privilege could prevent the disclosure of a client's identity. In Tillotson [v. Boughner, 350 F.2d 663 (7th Cir. 1965)], an unidentified taxpayer had determined that he understated his tax liability on previously filed returns and retained an attorney to deliver a cashier's check in the amount of $215,499.95 to the IRS. The IRS sought to enforce a summons it had served on the attorney, demanding that he testify about his client. The attorney asserted the attorney-client privilege and refused to disclose his client's identity. We upheld the invocation of the privilege because "under the peculiar facts of this case, the attorney-client privilege includes, within its scope, the identity of the client." We reasoned that the IRS had become aware of the substantive content of the confidential communication between the unknown taxpayer and his attorney-namely, the taxpayer's tax liability–the moment the cashier's check was delivered. Because revealing the taxpayer's identity would also reveal the content of the confidential communication, the privilege attached. Similarly, in [In re Grand Jury Proceeding (Cherney), 898 F.2d 565 (7th Cir. 1990)], we held that the privilege encompasses the identity of a client when the Government knows that the unidentified client paid fees for a criminal defendant out of concern about his own involvement in the charged drug conspiracy. In that case, we explained, the client's identity was privileged "because its disclosure would be tantamount to revealing the premise of a confidential communication: the very substantive reason that the client sought legal advice in the first place." In other words, "the privilege protects an unknown client's identity where its disclosure would reveal a client's motive for seeking legal advice."

Relying on these cases, the Does submit that the IRS' summonses set forth such detailed descriptions about suspect types of tax shelters under investigation that any document produced in response that also reveals a client's identity will inevitably reveal that client's motivation for seeking tax advice from BDO. The Does define their "motive" for retaining BDO's services as the "desire to engage in financial transactions which the government might later decide to be questionable, or . . . 'potentially abusive.' " Because a client's "motive" for seeking legal advice is considered a confidential communication, the Does contend that the § 7525 privilege should protect against the disclosure of their motive for seeking tax advice, a motive that would be known if their identities are revealed.

The Does have not established that a confidential communication will be disclosed if their identities are revealed in response to the summonses. Disclosure of the identities of the Does will disclose to the IRS that the Does participated in one of the 20 types of tax shelters described in its summonses. It is less than clear, however, as to what motive, or other confidential communication of tax advice, can be inferred from that information alone. Compared to the situations in the Tillotson and Cherney cases, where the Government already knew much about the substance of the communications between the attorney and his unidentified client, in this case the IRS knows relatively little about the interactions between BDO and the Does, the nature of their relationship, or the substance of their conversations. Moreover, the Does concede that the documents that BDO intends to produce in response to the summonses are not subject to any other independent claim of privilege beyond the Does' assertion of privilege as to identity.

More fundamentally, the Does' participation in potentially abusive tax shelters is information ordinarily subject to full disclosure under the federal tax law. See 26 U.S.C §§ 6111, 6112. Congress has determined that tax shelters are subject to special scrutiny, and anyone who organizes or sells an interest in tax shelters is required, pursuant to I.R.C. § 6112, to maintain a list identifying each person to whom such an interest was sold. This list-keeping provision precludes the Does from establishing an expectation of confidentiality in their communications with BDO, an essential element of the attorney-client privilege and, by extension, the § 7525 privilege. At the time that the Does communicated their interest in participating in tax shelters that BDO organized or sold, the Does should have known that BDO was obligated to disclose the identity of clients engaging in such financial transactions. Because the Does cannot credibly argue that they expected that their participation in such transactions would not be disclosed, they cannot now establish that the documents responsive to the summonses, which do not contain any tax advice, reveal a confidential communication.

BDO's affirmative duty to disclose its clients' participation in potentially abusive tax shelters renders the Does' situation easily distinguishable from the limited circumstances in which we have determined that a client's identity was information subject to the attorney-client privilege. The district court committed no error when it concluded that the Does failed to establish a colorable claim of privilege under § 7525.

Because the Does cannot demonstrate a colorable claim of privilege, they have failed to establish a legally protectable interest in preventing the disclosure of the documents revealing their identities as individuals who participated in tax shelters promoted by BDO. For the reasons stated above, the district court's judgments denying the Does' motions for intervention are affirmed.

NOTE

In a subsequent decision in the same investigation of BDO, the Seventh Circuit determined that the burden of establishing the tax shelter exception to the accountant-client privilege rested with the party seeking to obtain the communication. The court stated, "Thus, based on the text, structure and purpose of subsection (b), it is clear that the tax shelter 'exception' is a true exception to the tax practitioner privilege. As with any other exception to a claimed privilege, the burden rests on the opponent of the privilege to prove preliminary facts that would support a finding that the claimed privilege falls within an exception. As with the crime-fraud exception, the opponent meets this burden by bringing forth enough evidence to show 'some foundation in fact' that the exception applies." U.S. v. BDO Seidman, LLP, 492 F.3d 806 (7th Cir. 2007).

2. Self Evaluation/Self-Criticism Privilege

Another privilege, thus far available with only very limited application, is the corporation "self-evaluation" or self-criticism privilege.

In general, the party asserting the privilege must demonstrate that the material to be protected satisfies at least three criteria: (1) the information must result from a critical self-analysis undertaken by the party seeking protection; (2) the public must have a strong interest in preserving the free flow of the type of information sought; and (3) the information must be of the type whose flow would be curtailed if discovery were allowed. In addition to these basic requirements, self-evaluative material must have been prepared with the expectation that it would be kept confidential and it must, in fact, have been confidential.

Thomas R. Mulroy & Eric J. Munoz, *The Internal Corporate Investigation*, 1 DEPAUL BUS. & COM. L.J. 49 (2002). In **Reichhold Chemicals v. Textron**, 157 F.R.D. 522 (N.D. Fla. 1994), the district court stated:

> The self-critical analysis privilege has been recognized as a qualified privilege which protects from discovery certain critical self-appraisals. It allows individuals or businesses to candidly assess their compliance with regulatory and legal requirements without creating evidence that may be used against them by their opponents in future litigation. The rationale for the doctrine is that such critical self-evaluation fosters the compelling public interest in observance of the law. See, e.g., Granger v. National R.R. Passenger Corp., 116 F.R.D. 507 (E.D. Pa. 1987) * * * The self-critical analysis privilege is analogous to, and based on the same public policy considerations as Rule 407, Federal Rules of Evidence, which excludes evidence of subsequent remedial measures.

Among the other types of communications that may be covered by this privilege are:

(a) communications with an organization's ombudsman. Kientzy v. McDonnell Douglas Corp., 133 F.R.D. 570 (E.D. Mo. 1991); *disagreed with by* Carman v. McDonnell Douglas Corp., 114 F.3d 790 (8th Cir. 1997) ("We do not find the reasoning of [*Kientzy*] convincing.").

(b) self-critical portions of affirmative action plans, O'Connor v. Chrysler Corp., 86 F.R.D. 211 (D. Mass. 1980); Banks v. Lockheed Georgia Co., 53 F.R.D. 283 (N.D. Ga. 1971). See Webb v. Westinghouse Elec., 81 F.R.D. 431 (E.D. Pa. 1978); Contra Martin v. Potomac Electric Power Co., CA # 86-0603 (D.D.C. 5-25-90); 58 Fair Empl. Prac. Cas. (BNA) 355.

(c) hospital's evaluation of its staff procedures concerning a patient's death, Bredice v. Doctor's Hospital, 50 F.R.D. 249 (D.D.C. 1970). Most courts have not recognized such a privilege, or reject its application in a particular context without rejecting it completely. See In re Kaiser Aluminum & Chemical Co., 214 F.3d 586 (5th Cir. 2000); In re Continental Illinois Securities Litigation, 732 F.2d 1302 (7th Cir. 1984); FTC v. TRW, 628 F.2d 207 (D.C. Cir. 1980); Wei v. Bodner, 127 F.R.D. 91 (D.N.J. 1989); Dowling v. American Hawaii Cruises, 971 F.2d 423 (9th Cir. 1992).

CHAPTER SIXTEEN
THE ROLE OF COUNSEL

A. PROTECTING CLIENT INFORMATION

1. Client Identity

Does the attorney-client privilege permit an attorney to withhold the name of a client or the fees paid for legal services? As the court noted in In re Grand Jury Subpoena, 204 F.3d 516 (4th Cir. 2000): "'[T]he identity of the client, the amount of the fee, the identification of payment by case file name, and the general purpose of the work performed are usually not protected from disclosure by the attorney-client privilege,' Chaudhry v. Gallerizzo, 174 F.3d 394 (4th Cir.1999) (quoting Clarke v. American Commerce Nat'l Bank, 974 F.2d 127(9th Cir.1992)), because 'such information ordinarily reveals no confidential professional communications between attorney and client . . . .' In re Grand Jury Matter, 926 F.2d 348 (4th Cir.1991) (quoting In re Osterhoudt, 722 F.2d 591 (9th Cir.1983)). " Nevertheless, occasionally an attorney can assert the privilege successfully for this type of information, as discussed in the following case.

In re: SUBPOENAED GRAND JURY WITNESS
171 F.3d 511 (7th Cir. 1999)

EVANS, Circuit Judge.

A federal grand jury sitting in Chicago issued a subpoena to an unnamed Illinois lawyer (we'll give him a fake name—Tom Hagen—in this opinion). The subpoena ordered Hagen to testify and produce documents and records identifying all "individuals, companies, corporations or any other entities (including, but not limited to, All Games Amusement, OK Amusement, Universal Amusement, Nicholas J. "Buddy" Ciotti, Rocco Circelli, and Robert Cechini and their agents or representatives) who paid legal fees, including the amounts and dates of payments," to him in connection with his representation of 21 specifically named defendants in various state court gambling cases. Hagen received a similar directive for fees paid by certain third parties to persons other than the 21 named state court defendants.

At a closed hearing in the district court to quash the subpoena Hagen argued that "any testimony concerning payment of fees will provide the government with the 'last link' and will identify a client and subject him to

762

prosecution for the very investigation for which the government intends to prosecute," and that "[a]s in the *Cherney* [Matter of Grand Jury Proceeding (Cherney), 898 F.2d 565 (7th Cir.1990)] case, [his] testimony . . . will give rise to an identification of an individual who has sought [Hagen's] legal advice and in disclosing these confidential communications and the fee arrangement structure, etc., [Hagen] will be compelled to testify against his own client as to attorney/client privileged communications." Hagen's "last link" comment referred to a theory embraced by two other circuit courts of appeals that could support withholding the requested information. See In re Grand Jury Proceedings 88-9(MIA) Newton, 899 F.2d 1039 (11th Cir.1990); In re Grand Jury Proceedings (Pavlick), 680 F.2d 1026 (5th Cir.1982). The district court concluded that the "last link" exception did not apply and that the subpoenaed material was not protected by the attorney-client privilege.* * *

But we backpedaled on this bright-line principle in *Cherney*, the case Hagen says is "directly on point" and compels reversal of the district court's ruling. In that case, Attorney David Cherney represented a chap named Hrvatin in a drug conspiracy trial. Hrvatin's legal fees were paid by an unknown person who was also, apparently, involved in the same conspiracy. That person, the government conceded, consulted Cherney for legal advice regarding the same conspiracy. Following Hrvatin's conviction, Cherney was served with a subpoena directing him to identify the person who paid Hrvatin's bill. Cherney's motion to quash the subpoena was granted by the district court, and we affirmed that decision on appeal.

Hagen argues that his situation is "strikingly similar" to that of the attorney in *Cherney*. In his case, Hagen represented 21 defendants (and perhaps others) in state gambling cases involving the use of video machines and other electronic devices. Hagen asserts that the 21 listed persons, all previously charged and tried in state gambling cases, are likely to be indicted or named as unindicted coconspirators arising out of the current federal grand jury proceeding to which he has been subpoenaed. The government has also set its sights on the third-party payor (or payors) of Hagen's bills, and Hagen says his testimony–linking the third-party fee payor(s) to the gamblers–will give the government the ammunition it needs to secure an indictment.

So our issue boils down to a simple proposition, i.e., whether Hagen can avoid the subpoena under the cover of *Cherney*. The answer to that simple question is, unfortunately, a bit elusive. Addressing a similar issue in Vingelli v. United States, 992 F.2d 449 (1993), the Second Circuit wrote:

> Recognizing that client identity and fee information are not presently sheltered under the privilege, defense counsel urges that the information sought falls into one of the special exceptions to that rule. What those "special circumstances" are that would protect this information has not been precisely defined. What they are remains as enigmatic as the smile that Leonardo Da Vinci left us on the face of the Mona Lisa.

We agree. While a bright-line rule would be easy to understand and enforce, *Cherney* requires that we read the nuance in Mona Lisa's smile. *Cherney* protects from disclosure certain, and limited, client identity and third-party fee payor information.

So, does Hagen's situation, as described in his four-page affidavit, sealed and a part of the record on this appeal, move him into one of the "special exceptions" that allows him to pass on the government's request for disclosure? We have examined the affidavit and, reviewing it *de novo* which we are required to do, we believe Hagen slides through the crack left open by *Cherney*. We think it is clear, based on Hagen's affidavit, that he would be forced to violate the attorney-client privilege if he were made to say who paid the fees in question. We will not go into detail as to why we make this finding—that would be showing the hand to the government—but we are sure that disclosure of this information would identify a client of Hagen's who is potentially involved in targeted criminal activity which, on this record, would lead to revealing that client's motive to pay the legal bills for some of Hagen's other clients. And motive, we think, is protected by the attorney-client privilege. For as we observed in *Cherney*, "A client's motive for seeking legal advice is undeniably a confidential communication. Accordingly, the privilege protects an unknown client's identity where its disclosure would reveal a client's motive for seeking legal advice." This case, as Hagen suggests, is in fact on all fours with *Cherney*, and the government can only prevail if we are prepared to walk away from that opinion. And that's a trip we decline to take. This conclusion also makes it unnecessary for us to consider Hagen's alternative argument regarding the "last link" exception. With that, the order denying the motion to quash the subpoena is REVERSED. The subpoena is quashed.

2. Providing Payment Information

UNITED STATES v. SINDEL
53 F.3d 874 (8th Cir. 1995)

MORRIS SHEPPARD ARNOLD, Circuit Judge.

Attorney Richard Sindel of Sindel & Sindel, P.C., appeals a district court order requiring him to disclose information about two clients, intervenors John Doe and Jane Doe, on Internal Revenue Service Form 8300. These forms, which are used to report cash transactions in excess of $10,000 pursuant to 26 U.S.C. § 6050I, request the name, address, tax identification number, and other information about each payor and each person on whose behalf payment is made. Sindel argues that completion of the forms would violate his own ethical duties and the First, Fifth, and Sixth Amendment rights of his clients. After considering the circumstances surrounding each client, we affirm the district court order with respect to John Doe and reverse it with respect to Jane Doe.

During 1990 and 1991, Sindel received a cash payment of $53,160 for John Doe and two cash payments of $10,000 each for Jane Doe for legal services rendered. Sindel reported each of these transactions using the August, 1988, version of IRS Form 8300, but omitted any identifying information regarding the payers or the persons on whose behalf payments were made. In an attachment to each form, Sindel claimed that disclosure would "violate ethical duties owed said client, and constitutional and/or attorney-client privileges that the reporting attorney is entitled or required to invoke," and that the client had not authorized release of the information. At the request of the IRS, Sindel later withdrew the two forms reporting payments on behalf of Jane Doe and consolidated them using the January, 1990, version of Form 8300, again omitting any identifying information. This later version of Form 8300 asks the reporting party to check a box if the payment is a "suspicious transaction." The instructions accompanying the January, 1990, version of Form 8300 define a suspicious transaction as "[a] transaction in which it appears that a person is attempting to cause this report not to be filed or a false or incomplete report to be filed; or where there is an indication of possible illegal activity." Sindel left the box blank.

After filing these forms, Sindel was served with an IRS summons requesting the missing information. The government then brought an enforcement action, and the district court ordered Sindel to show cause why the summons should not be enforced. The district court divided the ensuing proceedings into two parts, one held in open court and the other an ex-parte hearing held in camera. During the in-camera portion of the proceedings, Sindel presented evidence regarding his clients' special circumstances. The district court ordered enforcement of the summons, but stayed its order pending this appeal.

* * * Although the federal common law of attorney-client privilege protects confidential disclosures made by a client to an attorney in order to obtain legal representation, it ordinarily does not apply to client identity and fee information. The various Circuit Courts have, however, identified certain circumstances under which the privilege protects even client identity and fee information. One court has categorized these overlapping "special-circumstance" exceptions as the legal advice exception, the last link exception, and the confidential communications exception. [In re Grand Jury Subpoenas (Anderson), 906 F.2d 1485 (10th Cir. 1990)]. The legal advice exception protects client identity and fee information when "there is a strong probability that disclosure would implicate the client in the very criminal activity for which legal advice was sought." The last link exception, as its name implies, prevents disclosure of client identity and fee information when it would incriminate the client by providing the last link in an existing chain of evidence. The confidential communications exception, which we have recognized on another occasion, protects client identity and fee information "if, by revealing the information, the attorney would necessarily disclose confidential communications." * * * After examining Sindel's in-camera testimony about his clients' special circumstances, we conclude that he could not release information about the payments on behalf of Jane Doe without

revealing the substance of a confidential communication. We do not find any similar constraints upon the disclosure of information about the payments on behalf of John Doe.

[The court ruled that the Missouri Rules of Professional Conduct[a] did not "expand the scope of the exemption beyond what is established by the federal common law of attorney-client privilege."]

As we do not believe that the information regarding payments on behalf of John Doe is protected from disclosure to the IRS by the federal common law of attorney-client privilege or the Missouri Rules of Professional Conduct, we necessarily undertake a consideration of Sindel's constitutional claims.

Sindel first argues that application of 26 U.S.C. § 6050I to an attorney violates the client's Sixth Amendment right to counsel by inhibiting the ability to retain counsel, discouraging communication between attorney and client, forcing the attorney to act as an agent for the government, and disqualifying counsel of choice. As the Second Circuit accurately points out in United States v. Goldberger & Dubin, 935 F.2d 501 (2d Cir. 1991), the statutory reporting requirements do not prevent a would-be client from hiring counsel. Not only are cash payments not automatically forfeit, but a client is also free to pay counsel in some other manner to avoid being reported to the IRS. * * * Similarly, a client is not prevented from communicating with an attorney at will merely because the attorney must report large cash transactions. By contrast, we recognize the serious Sixth Amendment implications of Sindel's claim that an attorney becomes a de facto agent for the government when compelled to offer an opinion as to whether a particular cash payment was a "suspicious transaction," a question added to the January, 1990, version of Form 8300. Sindel used this later version of Form 8300 to consolidate his reporting of the payments made on behalf of Jane Doe. Because we have already determined that the federal common law of attorney-client privilege excuses Sindel from reporting any additional information regarding the Jane Doe payments, however, the constitutionality of the January, 1990, version of Form 8300 is not at issue in this case. Sindel's speculative claim that the reporting requirements of 26 U.S.C. § 6050I would disqualify counsel by allowing prosecutors to subpoena a reporting attorney to testify against a client is likewise not ripe for adjudication. There is thus no Sixth Amendment bar to enforcement of the IRS summons against Sindel.

Sindel next claims that requiring him to complete the Forms 8300 would violate his clients' Fifth Amendment privilege against self-incrimination. This guarantee, however, applies only to compulsion of the individual holding the privilege, not to other methods of obtaining potentially incriminating information. As compliance with the IRS summons would merely require

---

[a] Rule 1.6 of the Missouri Rules of Professional Conduct differed from the ABA Model Rules of Professional Conduct existing at the time of this case.

disclosure of information which Sindel's clients have already given to him, their Fifth Amendment privilege is not implicated. * * *

Sindel's final constitutional claim is that completion of Form 8300 constitutes "compelled speech" and thus violates both his own and his clients' First Amendment rights. * * * A First Amendment protection against compelled speech, however, has been found only in the context of governmental compulsion to disseminate a particular political or ideological message. * * * The IRS summons requires Sindel only to provide the government with information which his clients have given him voluntarily, not to disseminate publicly a message with which he disagrees. Therefore, the First Amendment protection against compelled speech does not prevent enforcement of the summons. * * * For the foregoing reasons, we vacate the district court's order with respect to Jane Doe and affirm the order with respect to John Doe.

NOTES AND QUESTIONS

1. *Special Circumstances.* Courts have held that "absent special circumstances" attorneys are required to provide the information requested by Form 8300. Does the court in *Sindel* provide a clear definition of what constitutes "special circumstances?" A failure to comply with the obligations of § 6050I can result in fines and criminal charges to the attorney. For example, in United States v. Lefcourt, 125 F.3d 79 (2d Cir. 1997), the attorney filed Form 8300 omitting the taxpayer's name. After paying the fine assessed against him, Lefcourt unsuccessfully sued the Internal Revenue Service for return of the funds. The court, in finding " no reasonable basis for failing to provide the information required by § 6050I, stated that "[a]lthough the contours of the special circumstance exception have not been exhaustively developed, no doubt due to the fact special circumstances are seldom found to exist, it is clear that there is no special circumstance in this circuit simply because the provision of client-identifying information could prejudice the client in the case for which legal fees are paid."

2. *Implications to Defense Counsel.* What effect does the government's proceeding against criminal defense attorneys have on the adversary process? Consider the following comments by Bennett L. Gershman, *The New Prosecutors*, 53 U. PITT. L. REV. 393, 401-03 (1992):

> Added to these new developments is an even more ominous threat to the adversary system: the unprecedented use by prosecutors of the grand jury and other means to attack and cripple the criminal defense bar. One of the most alarming events during the last decade has been the prosecutor's attempt to compel criminal defense attorneys to give testimony and produce documents that might incriminate their clients. The testimony is usually sought in connection with fees, a subject that most courts have held is not

covered by the attorney-client privilege. Recent statistics show that prosecutors in the United States issue subpoenas to defense attorneys at the rate of 645 per year. Further, most courts do not require any special evidentiary showing before a subpoena can be enforced against a lawyer. Attorneys have been jailed for refusing to cooperate with the prosecutor. As with grand jury subpoenas, prosecutors also have begun to use the statutory summoning power of the Internal Revenue Service to force criminal defense attorneys to disclose the identities of clients or third parties who pay fees in excess of $10,000 cash. * * *

3. SEC Disclosure Rules

In the wake of the various accounting problems that engulfed a number of large corporations, Congress enacted the Sarbanes-Oxley Act of 2002. "Section 307 of the * * * Act (15 U.S.C. § 7245) mandates that the [Securities & Exchange] Commission issue rules prescribing minimum standards of professional conduct for attorneys appearing and practicing before it in any way in the representation of issuers, including at a minimum a rule requiring an attorney to report evidence of a material violation of securities laws or breach of fiduciary duty or similar violation by the issuer or any agent thereof to appropriate officers within the issuer and, thereafter, to the highest authority within the issuer, if the initial report does not result in an appropriate response." *Implementation of Standards of Professional Conduct for Attorneys*, SEC Rel. No. 34-47276 (2003). In addition to the internal reporting requirements, the SEC rule permits disclosure to the Commission in the following circumstances:

(2) An attorney appearing and practicing before the Commission in the representation of an issuer may reveal to the Commission, without the issuer's consent, confidential information related to the representation to the extent the attorney reasonably believes necessary:

(i) To prevent the issuer from committing a material violation that is likely to cause substantial injury to the financial interest or property of the issuer or investors;

(ii) To prevent the issuer, in a Commission investigation or administrative proceeding from committing perjury, proscribed in 18 U.S.C. 1621; suborning perjury, proscribed in 18 U.S.C. 1622; or committing any act proscribed in 18 U.S.C. 1001 that is likely to perpetrate a fraud upon the Commission; or

(iii) To rectify the consequences of a material violation by the issuer that caused, or may cause, substantial injury to

the financial interest or property of the issuer or investors
in the furtherance of which the attorney's services were
used.

17 C.F.R. 205.3(d)(2) (2003). This rule is permissive, not mandatory, and the
ethics rules of the state in which an attorney is admitted to practice may
prohibit any disclosure of client wrongdoing except for a future crime of
violence. See ABA Model Rule of Professional Conduct 1.6(b) (lawyer may
reveal confidential client information "to prevent reasonably certain death or
substantial bodily harm" and "to prevent the client from committing a crime
or fraud that is reasonably certain to result in substantial injury to the
financial interests or property of another and in furtherance of which the
client has used or is using the lawyer's services).

B. SUBPOENA OF ATTORNEYS

The attorney for a target of a grand jury investigation may be able to
provide highly incriminating information about the client. The attorney-
client relationship is a cornerstone of the criminal justice system, and
attempts to interfere with that relationship are viewed with great suspicion.
Nevertheless, the government increasingly seeks to obtain information from
attorneys about their clients because it is so valuable, and is often reliable
evidence to evaluate the intent of a target. Put simply, clients trust their
attorneys and are as likely to be honest with them as with anyone else. The
Department of Justice permits federal prosecutors to subpoena attorneys for
information about their clients, but exercises "close control" over such
subpoenas by requiring prior approval of the Assistant Attorney General for
the Criminal Division. USAM 9-13.410 provides the following guidelines for
determining whether the subpoena is appropriate:

When determining whether to issue a subpoena to an attorney for
information relating to the attorney's representation of a client, the
Assistant United States Attorney must strike a balance between an
individual's right to the effective assistance of counsel and the
public's interest in the fair administration of justice and effective
law enforcement. To that end, all reasonable attempts shall be made
to obtain the information from alternative sources before issuing the
subpoena to the attorney, unless such efforts would compromise the
investigation or case. These attempts shall include reasonable efforts
to first obtain the information voluntarily from the attorney, unless
such efforts would compromise the investigation or case, or would
impair the ability to subpoena the information from the attorney in
the event that the attempt to obtain the information voluntarily
proves unsuccessful.

Chapter 15 reviewed issues related to the attorney-client privilege and work product doctrine, and exceptions to the privilege that permit the government to compel the attorney to provide information about a client. If an attorney is called before a grand jury, can the subpoena be challenged as unreasonable under Rule 17(c) if it infringes on the attorney-client relationship but does not seek otherwise privileged information? Should courts require a special showing of need when an attorney is the recipient of the subpoena that seeks information related to a client?

IMPOUNDED
241 F.3d 308 (3d Cir. 2001)

SCIRICA, Circuit Judge.

In this grand jury proceeding, the issue on appeal is whether, on the facts presented, the crime-fraud exception overrides the attorney-client privilege. In the proceedings below, the District Court declined to enforce a grand jury subpoena issued to an attorney. Citing the crime-fraud exception, the government has appealed.

Over four years ago in April 1996, a federal grand jury commenced investigating the target's business transactions and issued several subpoenas to the target's affiliated businesses. The target's attorney assumed responsibility in responding to the United States Attorney's office. The government's first subpoena sought,

> all records . . . relating to work performed [by the target]. . . . These records should include but are not limited to: All business checks, check registers, cash receipt and disbursement records. These records should also include contracts, invoices, billing documents, bid documents and correspondence specifically relating to [the target's activities] for the [relevant] period.

The attorney produced several documents. But believing them inadequate, the government requested fuller document production. The attorney responded that certain categories of requested documents did not exist.

In May 1996, the government again requested the documents under its initial subpoena and advised the attorney that "the grand jury will also request that the target appear before it with regard to the production of the documents in question." The attorney provided some additional documents including check ledgers and canceled checks. The target was not summoned to appear before the grand jury.

In September 1996, the government issued a second subpoena requesting additional documents including: general ledgers, cash disbursement journals, cash receipts, sales and accounts payable journals, as well as calendars, diaries and appointment books for all of the target's business officers and employees. The attorney again responded that most of the requested documents did not exist. On January 10, 1997 the government advised the attorney that it was subpoenaing "the custodian of records [of one of] the target business[es] to produce all responsive *original* records before the Grand Jury next Thursday [January 16]." The government also subpoenaed an officer of the target business to testify before the grand jury (also on January 16) about her knowledge of the existence of the subpoenaed documents. The government never enforced its subpoenas.

In April 1997, November 1998, and March 1999 the government subpoenaed more records from the target business. The attorney produced some of the requested documents but again represented that certain categories of documents did not exist. On March 8, 1999, the Federal Bureau of Investigation executed search warrants on the target's home and also on the target's business offices. The FBI uncovered and seized many records and documents the attorney had represented did not exist. On April 30, 1999, the government subpoenaed the attorney to testify before the grand jury about the "source[s] of information for [his] . . . factual assertions . . . and basis for failing to produces [sic] certain categories of records."

After the attorney invoked the attorney-client privilege, the government filed a motion to compel his testimony. Claiming the crime-fraud exception invalidated the attorney-client privilege, the government argued the target used the attorney to obstruct justice in violation of 18 U.S.C. § 1503 [Obstruction of Justice]. Holding it was "fundamentally unfair" to compel the attorney's testimony, the District Court declined to assess the applicability of the crime-fraud exception.

The government appeals contending the District Court erred in failing to decide whether the crime-fraud exception applied. It also contends the District Court exceeded its authority in quashing the subpoena because of "fundamental unfairness." * * *

Despite these broad investigatory powers, there are some limitations on the grand jury's authority to subpoena evidence. * * * The Supreme Court has stated, "grand juries are not licensed to engage in arbitrary fishing expeditions, nor may they select targets of investigation out of malice or an intent to harass." *R. Enterprises.* * * *

As a safeguard against potential abuse of the grand jury's broad investigative power, the Federal Rules of Evidence and the Federal Rules of Criminal Procedure grant limited authority for courts to review grand jury subpoenas. In this case, the two principal mechanisms for judicial review are Fed.R.Evid. 501, recognizing the attorney-client privilege which protects confidential communications between an attorney and his client from disclosure, and Fed.R.Crim.P. 17(c), providing that "[t]he court on motion made promptly may quash or modify the subpoena if compliance would be unreasonable or oppressive."

The District Court did not refer to Fed.R.Crim.P. 17(c) nor to the attorney-client privilege when it declined to compel the attorney's testimony. It stated,

> The Court will assume for purposes of its analysis that [the attorney] is innocent of any wrongdoing and has been used merely as a conduit for wrongdoing, i.e., the obstruction of justice. Nevertheless it is fundamentally unfair for the U.S. Attorney's Office to seek [the attorney's] testimony in this case.

Reasoning that to obtain the desired information, the government could have pursued avenues less harmful to the attorney-client privilege, including enforcing its subpoenas on the target and the records custodian, the District Court stated

> The award for neither appointing nor insisting upon a custodian of records cannot be securing the testimony of the subject's attorney. Instead the U.S. Attorney's Office should have acted upon the subpoenas it procured and not assume that it could fall back on the subject's attorney.

Compelling the lawyer's testimony, the court said, "goes against the core of the adversarial system and would unnecessarily 'drive a wedge' between a client and his attorney, thereby 'chilling' communications."[4]

Because the District Court relied on neither Fed.R.Crim.P. 17 nor an analysis of the crime-fraud exception, the government contends the Court exceeded its authority in quashing the subpoena. * * * It is well established that courts may not impose substantive limitations on the power of the grand jury to issue subpoenas nor place the initial burden on the government to prove the validity of its subpoenas. * * * The Supreme Court stated,

> Any power federal courts have to fashion, on their own initiative, rules of grand jury procedure is a very limited one, not remotely comparable to the power they maintain over their own proceedings. It certainly would not permit judicial reshaping of the grand jury institution, substantially altering the traditional relationships between the prosecution, the constituting court, and the grand jury itself. (citation omitted).

---

[4] In discussing the impact of this subpoena on criminal practice, the District Court stated it is common for criminal defense attorneys and the government to informally negotiate the production of materials for grand jury investigations. By forcing attorneys to testify against their clients, the court feared many criminal defense attorneys would be "unwilling to informally satisfy the subpoena for fear of the consequences."

* * * One form of restraint, however, may be found in Fed.R.Crim.P. 17(c). But as noted, the District Court never applied Fed.R.Crim.P. 17(c). Instead, it held that the government must demonstrate the evidence sought could not be obtained by other means. The District Court's prescribed course of action may be salutary and efficacious to safeguard the attorney-client privilege. Under appropriate circumstances, it may well constitute the better practice. But we see no authority for it in the rules or the case law. Generally, the government does not bear the initial burden to justify its grand jury subpoena.

The institutional independence and secrecy of the grand jury has been a hallmark of criminal indictments for over three centuries. Any deviation from the established practices governing court involvement should not be taken lightly. We recognize the District Court was concerned with the effect of this subpoena on the attorney-client relationship. But the proper course under Fed.R.Crim.P. 17(c) was to rule on whether the lawyer's testimony was protected under the attorney-client privilege. By employing "a different analysis" based on "fundamental fairness" the District Court deviated from the established procedures which ensure the institutional independence of the grand jury. Therefore, the District Court abused its discretion. * * *

The grand jury may not "itself violate a valid privilege, whether established by the Constitution, statutes, or the common Law." For this reason, courts may quash an otherwise valid grand jury subpoena for an attorney's testimony under the attorney-client privilege. When legal advice is sought in furtherance of a crime or fraud, however, the attorney-client privilege is waived and a grand jury may compel a lawyer's testimony.

* * * Here, the government asserts the target business obstructed justice by failing to disclose documents subpoenaed by the grand jury. * * * Challenging this assessment, the attorney contends the government presented insufficient evidence that the target and the target business corruptly intended to obstruct justice.

The District Court declined to decide whether the government submitted sufficient prima facie evidence of intent to obstruct justice. * * * We believe this was error. * * * The District Court must decide whether the government has submitted sufficient evidence of the intent to obstruct justice and determine whether this evidence supports a waiver of the attorney-client privilege. * * *

NYGAARD, Circuit Judge, dissenting.

Because I disagree with the Majority's conclusion that "the District Court never applied Fed.R.Crim.P. 17(c) [and instead] held that the government must demonstrate the evidence sought could not be obtained by other means," I respectfully dissent. I believe that the District Court validly exercised its discretion under Rule 17(c) and did *not* impose a broad "no-alternative-means" test. Therefore, I would affirm.

The Government claims that the District Court applied a broad-reaching "no-alternative-means test" to determine whether the attorney's subpoena was fair and therefore enforceable. Apparently, the Majority agrees. It holds that the court employed an analysis "based on 'fundamental fairness' [that] deviated from the established procedures which ensure the institutional independence of the grand jury." I agree that such a blanket rule, *if* it were imposed, would improperly place a substantive limitation upon the grand jury, is outside the District Court's supervisory powers, and has been implicitly rejected by this Court. * * *

However, I disagree with the Majority's characterization of the District Court's holding. The District Court did not impose a new substantive limitation upon the grand jury. * * * The Majority recognizes Rule 17(c) as a valid "form of restraint" upon the grand jury, but nonetheless holds that the District Court failed to apply it. I concede that the District Court never *explicitly* invoked Fed.R.Crim.P. 17(c), but such an omission is *not* fatal as long as what the court did is clear. * * *

The District Court in his case considered the specific facts and circumstances before it and found that it was "fundamentally unfair for the U.S. Attorney's Office to seek [the attorney's] testimony."[3] Rule 17(c) empowers a court to quash a subpoena if it is "unreasonable or oppressive." Presumably, the Majority believes that a finding of "fundamental unfairness" is insufficient to satisfy this standard. In contrast, I fail to see a difference. A subpoena described as "fundamentally unfair" could just as easily be described as "unreasonable and oppressive." Therefore, I believe that the District Court sufficiently invoked the authority of Rule 17(c). Unlike the Majority, I would not reverse based entirely upon an unimportant semantic distinction.[4]

* * * There is nothing in the record to suggest that the District Court's decision to quash the Government's subpoena *under these specific facts* constituted an abuse of discretion. The court was concerned that enforcing the Government's subpoena would put attorneys in a "very precarious position," subjecting them to grand jury subpoena any time they made representations pertaining to the existence of subpoenaed records. * * * This

---

[3] The court cited numerous avenues that the Government could have pursued to obtain the same information, "which are far less offensive [than] seeking to pierce the attorney-client privilege." These included subpoenas that the U.S. Attorney's Office choose not to enforce and the Government's failure to insist that a custodian of records confirm the attorney's assertions. The court also noted that compelling his testimony could "unnecessarily 'drive a wedge' between a client and his attorney, thereby 'chilling' communications."

[4] It is beyond dispute that "unfair," "unreasonable," and "oppressive" are often used synonymously. A Westlaw searched revealed 1710 federal decisions, 40 of which were Supreme Court decisions, where "unfair" appeared within five words of "unreasonable" or "oppressive." * * *

threat would certainly chill communication between attorney and client. Both the government and the Majority seem to believe, however, that the attorney-client privilege is the *only* means by which a district court can protect that relationship. I do not read a district court's discretion so narrowly. American jurisprudence has long recognized the central importance of the attorney-client relationship. The privilege is the most common means of protecting the relationship, but it is not the only one. In appropriate factual situations, such as the present case, a district court can, within its discretion, conclude that a subpoena is unreasonable and oppressive because it harms the attorney-client relationship, even if the privilege does not apply.

A constant threat of subpoena would also affect the ability of lawyers to cooperate with the government. The Government contends that "[t]he duty to safeguard 'the healthy relationship between the criminal defense bar and the U.S. Attorney's Office' lies squarely with the parties to that relationship itself, not the district court." It appears that the Government misunderstands the court's concern. If a court were to enforce a grand jury subpoena against an attorney in a case such as this, where there were numerous alternative avenues of gathering the desired information, it would impose the threat of subpoena over all representations made by counsel. It does not escape my attention that this would grant the U.S. Attorney's Office tremendous leverage—so much in fact that any competent counsel would produce a custodian rather than respond to inquires. This would severely hamper the efficient administration of justice, a matter of paramount concern to this Court.

These consequences might be acceptable (and reasonable) if the Government had no other means of obtaining the desired information. In this case, however, the U.S. Attorney's Office repeatedly served subpoenas that were never enforced, and it failed to insist upon authentication from a custodian of records. As a result, the District Court found that the burden upon the attorney was unreasonable, and I cannot disagree.

NOTE

Supervisory Power to Quash. While refusing to impose a special showing of need, several circuits have recognized a supervisory authority in the district court sufficiently broad to justify quashing a subpoena to an attorney in an exceptional case. The First Circuit upheld the quashing of subpoenas to attorneys who were currently serving as defense counsel in a state criminal prosecution where the district court concluded that the "forced disclosures would jeopardize the attorney-client relationship at a crucial point in the defense preparations" and constituted "harassment". In re Grand Jury Matters, 751 F.2d 131 (1st Cir. 1984) (also noting that the government had not shown an "urgent need" for obtaining at this time the information being sought from the attorney).

In **In re Grand Jury Subpoena for Attorney Representing Criminal Defendant (Reyes-Requena)**, 913 F.2d 1118 (5th Cir. 1990), the Fifth Circuit found that a district court correctly found a subpoena "oppressive" under Rule 17(c), discussed in Chapter 9, in quashing a subpoena to an attorney, DeGeurin, for fee information related to his current representation of Reyes-Requena. The government issued the subpoena to DeGeurin the same day that he represented Reyes-Requena at a bond hearing related to a cocaine possession charge. The grand jury subpoena required DeGeurin to testify about the identity of any party paying his fee for representing Reyes-Requena and the amount of the payment. The district court quashed the subpoena on various grounds, including a finding that the subpoena was oppressive because the "timing of the subpoena impinged upon the attorney-client relationship and severely hindered the effectiveness of DeGeurin's representation. The Fifth Circuit stated:

> In this case, the district court's exercise of its discretion to quash the subpoena because it created a serious interference with Reyes-Requena's relationship with his attorney is justified for several reasons. Reyes- Requena's Sixth Amendment rights had attached. The prosecution against him was moving swiftly–an indictment issued within three weeks of Reyes-Requena's detention hearing. DeGeurin's representation of Reyes-Requena was effectively stalled during the two-to-three-week interval that he contested the subpoena. The government made no effort to explain, even rhetorically, why it was necessary to subpoena DeGeurin during that critical juncture in his representation of the defendant. The government made not a single argument in the district court or before this court to suggest that a brief delay in the process, until a lull in the Reyes-Requena prosecution or until after his conviction, would have been imprudent.[15] Thus, when the district court quashed the subpoena to DeGeurin, solely because of its oppressive timing, we do not believe that the court abused its discretion. Alternatively, the court could have modified the subpoena, continuing it to a future date that would not have interfered so starkly with DeGeurin's representation of his client. As the government did not suggest a modification, the district court can be excused for not exercising its discretion to grant one.[a]

---

[15] We do not imply that the government was required to justify its subpoena of DeGeurin substantively beyond the usual minimum requirements of relevance, specificity, and timeliness. The government could, however, have furnished some factual basis, if one existed, for the exigency of enforcing a subpoena at this particularly onerous time.

[a] The Fifth Circuit ultimately reversed the district court because Reyes-Requena was convicted before the government's appeal could be decided, and the court found that the exigency supporting the finding of oppression had dissipated.

E. RIGHT TO COUNSEL

UNITED STATES v. STEIN
541 F.3d 130 (2d Cir. 2008)

DENNIS JACOBS, Chief Judge:

The United States appeals from an order of the United States District Court for the Southern District of New York (Kaplan, J.), dismissing an indictment against thirteen former partners and employees of the accounting firm KPMG, LLP. Judge Kaplan found that, absent pressure from the government, KPMG would have paid defendants' legal fees and expenses without regard to cost. Based on this and other findings of fact, Judge Kaplan ruled that the government deprived defendants of their right to counsel under the Sixth Amendment by causing KPMG to impose conditions on the advancement of legal fees to defendants, to cap the fees, and ultimately to end payment. See United States v. Stein, 435 F.Supp.2d 330, 367-73 (S.D.N.Y.2006) ("Stein I"). Judge Kaplan also ruled that the government deprived defendants of their right to substantive due process under the Fifth Amendment.

We hold that KPMG's adoption and enforcement of a policy under which it conditioned, capped and ultimately ceased advancing legal fees to defendants followed as a direct consequence of the government's overwhelming influence, and that KPMG's conduct therefore amounted to state action. We further hold that the government thus unjustifiably interfered with defendants' relationship with counsel and their ability to mount a defense, in violation of the Sixth Amendment, and that the government did not cure the violation. Because no other remedy will return defendants to the status quo ante, we affirm the dismissal of the indictment as to all thirteen defendants In light of this disposition, we do not reach the district court's Fifth Amendment ruling.

BACKGROUND

The Thompson Memorandum

In January 2003, then-United States Deputy Attorney General Larry D. Thompson promulgated a policy statement, Principles of Federal Prosecution of Business Organizations (the "Thompson Memorandum"), which articulated "principles" to govern the Department's discretion in bringing prosecutions against business organizations. [See Chapter 3] The Thompson Memorandum was closely based on a predecessor document issued in 1999 by then-U.S. Deputy Attorney General Eric Holder, Federal Prosecution of Corporations. Along with the familiar factors governing charging decisions, the Thompson Memorandum identifies nine additional considerations, including the company's "timely and voluntary disclosure of wrongdoing and its willingness to cooperate in the investigation of its agents." The Memorandum explains that prosecutors should inquire

> whether the corporation appears to be protecting its culpable employees and agents [and that] a corporation's promise of support to culpable employees and agents, either *through the advancing of attorneys fees*, through retaining the employees without sanction for their misconduct, or through providing information to the employees about the government's investigation pursuant to a joint defense agreement, may be considered by the prosecutor in weighing the extent and value of a corporation's cooperation.

A footnote appended to the highlighted phrase explains that because certain states require companies to advance legal fees for their officers, "a corporation's compliance with governing law should not be considered a failure to cooperate." In December 2006–after the events in this prosecution had transpired–the Department of Justice replaced the Thompson Memorandum with the McNulty Memorandum, under which prosecutors may consider a company's fee advancement policy only where the circumstances indicate that it is "intended to impede a criminal investigation," and even then only with the approval of the Deputy Attorney General.

Commencement of the Federal Investigation

After Senate subcommittee hearings in 2002 concerning KPMG's possible involvement in creating and marketing fraudulent tax shelters, KPMG retained Robert S. Bennett of the law firm Skadden, Arps, Slate, Meagher & Flom LLP ("Skadden") to formulate a "cooperative approach" for KPMG to use in dealing with federal authorities. Bennett's strategy included "a decision to 'clean house'–a determination to ask Jeffrey Stein, Richard Smith, and Jeffrey Eischeid, all senior KPMG partners who had testified before the Senate and all now [Defendants-Appellees] here–to leave their positions as deputy chair and chief operating officer of the firm, vice chair-tax services, and a partner in personal financial planning, respectively." Smith was transferred and Eischeid was put on administrative leave. Stein resigned with arrangements for a three-year $100,000-per-month consultancy, and an agreement that KPMG would pay for Stein's representation in any actions brought against Stein arising from his activities at the firm. KPMG negotiated a contract with Smith that included a similar clause; but that agreement was never executed.

In February 2004, KPMG officials learned that the firm and 20 to 30 of its top partners and employees were subjects of a grand jury investigation of fraudulent tax shelters. On February 18, 2004, KPMG's CEO announced to all partners that the firm was aware of the United States Attorney's Office's ("USAO") investigation and that "[a]ny present or former members of the firm asked to appear will be represented by competent coun[sel] at the firm's expense."

The February 25, 2004 Meeting

In preparation for a meeting with Skadden on February 25, 2004, the prosecutors–including Assistant United States Attorneys ("AUSAs") Shirah Neiman and Justin Weddle–decided to ask whether KPMG would advance legal fees to employees under investigation. Bennett started the meeting by announcing that KPMG had resolved to "clean house," that KPMG "would cooperate fully with the government's investigation," and that its goal was not to protect individual employees but rather to save the firm from being indicted. AUSA Weddle inquired about the firm's plans for advancing fees and about any legal obligation to do so. Later on, AUSA Neiman added that the government would "take into account" the firm's legal obligations to advance fees, but that "the Thompson Memorandum [w]as a point that had to be considered." Bennett then advised that although KPMG was still investigating its legal obligations to advance fees, its "common practice" was to do so. However, Bennett explained, KPMG would not pay legal fees for any partner who refused to cooperate or "took the Fifth," so long as KPMG had the legal authority to do so.

Later in the meeting, AUSA Weddle asked Bennett to ascertain KPMG's legal obligations to advance attorneys' fees. AUSA Neiman added that "misconduct" should not or cannot "be rewarded" under "federal guidelines." One Skadden attorney's notes attributed to AUSA Weddle the prediction that, if KPMG had discretion regarding fees, the government would "look at that under a microscope."

Skadden then reported back to KPMG. In notes of the meeting, a KPMG executive wrote the words "[p]aying legal fees" and "[s]everance" next to "not a sign of cooperation."

Communications Between the Prosecutors and KPMG

On March 2, 2004, Bennett told AUSA Weddle that although KPMG believed it had no legal obligation to advance fees, "it would be a big problem" for the firm not to do so given its partnership structure. But Bennett disclosed KPMG's tentative decision to limit the amount of fees and condition them on employees' cooperation with prosecutors.

Two days later, a Skadden lawyer advised counsel for Defendant-Appellee Carol G. Warley (a former KPMG tax partner) that KPMG would advance legal fees if Warley cooperated with the government and declined to invoke her Fifth Amendment privilege against self-incrimination.

On a March 11 conference call with Skadden, AUSA Weddle recommended that KPMG tell employees that they should be "totally open" with the USAO, "even if that [meant admitting] criminal wrongdoing," explaining that this would give him good material for cross-examination. That same day, Skadden wrote to counsel for the KPMG employees who had been identified as subjects of the investigation. The letter set forth KPMG's new fees policy ("Fees Policy"), pursuant to which advancement of fees and expenses would be

[i] capped at $400,000 per employee;

[ii] conditioned on the employee's cooperation with the government; and

[iii] terminated when an employee was indicted.

The government was copied on this correspondence.

On March 12, KPMG sent a memorandum to certain other employees who had not been identified as subjects, urging them to cooperate with the government, advising them that it might be advantageous for them to exercise their right to counsel, and advising that KPMG would cover employees' "reasonable fees."

The prosecutors expressed by letter their "disappoint[ment] with [the] tone" of this memorandum and its "one-sided presentation of potential issues," and "demanded that KPMG send out a supplemental memorandum in a form they proposed." The government's alternative language, premised on the "assum[ption] that KPMG truly is committed to fully cooperating with the Government's investigation," Letter of David N. Kelley, United States Attorney, Southern District of New York, March 17, 2004, advised employees that they could "meet with investigators without the assistance of counsel." KPMG complied, and circulated a memo advising that employees "may deal directly with government representatives without counsel."

At a meeting in late March, Skadden asked the prosecutors to notify Skadden in the event any KPMG employee refused to cooperate. Over the following year, the prosecutors regularly informed Skadden whenever a KPMG employee refused to cooperate fully, such as by refusing to proffer or by proffering incompletely (in the government's view). Skadden, in turn, informed the employees' lawyers that fee advancement would cease unless the employees cooperated. The employees either knuckled under and submitted to interviews, or they were fired and KPMG ceased advancing their fees. For example, Watson and Smith attended proffer sessions after receiving KPMG's March 11 letter announcing the Fees Policy, and after Skadden reiterated to them that fees would be terminated absent cooperation. They did so because (they said, and the district court found) they feared that KPMG would stop advancing attorneys fees–although Watson concedes he attended a first session voluntarily. As Bennett later assured AUSA Weddle: "Whenever your Office has notified us that individuals have not . . . cooperat[ed], KPMG has promptly and without question encouraged them to cooperate and threatened to cease payment of their attorney fees and

... to take personnel action, including termination." Letter of Robert Bennett to United States Attorney's Office, November 2, 2004.

KPMG Avoids Indictment

In an early-March 2005 meeting, then-U.S. Attorney David Kelley told Skadden and top KPMG executives that a non-prosecution agreement was unlikely and that he had reservations about KPMG's level of cooperation: "I've seen a lot better from big companies." Bennett reminded Kelley how KPMG had capped and conditioned its advancement of legal fees. Kelley remained unconvinced.

KPMG moved up the Justice Department's chain of command. At a June 13, 2005 meeting with U.S. Deputy Attorney General James Comey, Bennett stressed KPMG's pressure on employees to cooperate by conditioning legal fees on cooperation; it was, he said, "precedent[ ]setting." KPMG's entreaties were ultimately successful: on August 29, 2005, the firm entered into a deferred prosecution agreement (the "DPA") under which KPMG admitted extensive wrongdoing, paid a $456 million fine, and committed itself to cooperation in any future government investigation or prosecution.

Indictment of Individual Employees

On August 29, 2005–the same day KPMG executed the DPA–the government indicted six of the Defendants–Appellees (along with three other KPMG employees): Jeffrey Stein; Richard Smith; Jeffrey Eischeid; John Lanning, Vice Chairman of Tax Services; Philip Wiesner, a former tax partner; and Mark Watson, a tax partner. A superseding indictment filed on October 17, 2005 named ten additional employees, including seven of the Defendants-Appellees: Larry DeLap, a former tax partner in charge of professional practice; Steven Gremminger, a former partner and associate general counsel; former tax partners Gregg Ritchie, Randy Bickham and Carl Hasting; Carol G. Warley; and Richard Rosenthal, a former tax partner and Chief Financial Officer of KPMG. Pursuant to the Fees Policy, KPMG promptly stopped advancing legal fees to the indicted employees who were still receiving them.

Procedural History

On January 12, 2006, the thirteen defendants (among others) moved to dismiss the indictment based on the government's interference with KPMG's advancement of fees. In a submission to the district court, KPMG represented that

the Thompson memorandum in conjunction with the government's statements relating to payment of legal fees affected KPMG's determination(s) with respect to the advancement of legal fees and other defense costs to present or former partners and employees . .

. . In fact, KPMG is prepared to state that the Thompson memorandum substantially influenced KPMG's decisions with respect to legal fees . . . .

At a hearing on March 30, 2006, Judge Kaplan asked the government whether it was "prepared at this point to commit that [it] has no objection whatsoever to KPMG exercising its free and independent business judgment as to whether to advance defense costs to these defendants and that if it were to elect to do so the government would not in any way consider that in determining whether it had complied with the DPA?" The AUSA responded: "That's always been the case, your Honor. That's fine. We have no objection to that . . . . They can always exercise their business judgment. As you described it, your Honor, that's always been the case. It's the case today, your Honor." * * *

[After holding three days of hearings on the defendants' motion to dismiss the indictment,] Judge Kaplan arrived at the following ultimate findings of fact, all of which the government contests on appeal:

[1] "the Thompson Memorandum caused KPMG to consider departing from its long-standing policy of paying legal fees and expenses of its personnel in all cases and investigations even before it first met with the USAO" and induced KPMG to seek "an indication from the USAO that payment of fees in accordance with its settled practice would not be held against it";

[2] the government made repeated references to the Thompson Memo in an effort to "reinforce[ ] the threat inherent in the Thompson Memorandum";

[3] "the government conducted itself in a manner that evidenced a desire to minimize the involvement of defense attorneys"; and

[4] but for the Thompson Memorandum and the prosecutors' conduct, KPMG would have paid defendants' legal fees and expenses without consideration of cost.

Against that background, Judge Kaplan ruled that a defendant has a fundamental right under the Fifth Amendment to fairness in the criminal process, including the ability to get and deploy in defense all "resources lawfully available to him or her, free of knowing or reckless government interference," and that the government's reasons for infringing that right in this case could not withstand strict scrutiny. Judge Kaplan also ruled that the same conduct deprived each defendant of the Sixth Amendment right "to choose the lawyer or lawyers he or she desires and to use one's own funds to mount the defense that one wishes to present." He reasoned that "the government's law enforcement interests in taking the specific actions in question [do not] sufficiently outweigh the interests of the KPMG Defendants in having the resources needed to defend as they think proper against these charges." "[T]he fact that advancement of legal fees occasionally might be part of an obstruction scheme or indicate a lack of full cooperation by a prospective defendant is insufficient to justify the government's interference with the right of individual criminal defendants to obtain resources lawfully available to them in order to defend themselves . . . ." * * *

Judge Kaplan dismissed the indictment against the thirteen defendants on July 16, 2007. * * * Judge Kaplan concluded that no remedy other than dismissal of the indictment would put defendants in the position they would have occupied absent the government's misconduct. * * *

We review first [I] the government's challenges to the district court's factual findings, including its finding that but for the Thompson Memorandum and the prosecutors' conduct KPMG would have paid employees' legal fees-pre-indictment and post-indictment-without regard to cost. Next, because we are hesitant to resolve constitutional questions unnecessarily, [II] we inquire whether the government cured the purported Sixth Amendment violation by the AUSA's in-court statement on March 30, 2006 that KPMG was free to decide whether to advance fees. Since we conclude that this statement did not return defendants to the status quo ante, [III] we decide whether the promulgation and enforcement of KPMG's Fees Policy amounted to state action under the Constitution and [IV] whether the government deprived defendants of their Sixth Amendment right to counsel.

The government challenges certain factual findings of the district court. * * *

The government points out that the Thompson Memorandum lists "fees advancement" as just one of many considerations in a complex charging decision, and thus argues that Judge Kaplan overread the Thompson Memorandum as a threat that KPMG would be indicted unless it ceased advancing legal fees to its employees.

Judge Kaplan's finding withstands scrutiny. KPMG was faced with the fatal prospect of indictment; it could be expected to do all it could, assisted by sophisticated counsel, to placate and appease the government. As Judge Kaplan noted, KPMG's chief legal officer, Sven Erik Holmes, testified that he considered it crucial "to be able to say at the right time with the right audience, we're in full compliance with the Thompson Memorandum." Moreover, KPMG's management and counsel had reason to consider the impact of the firm's indictment on the interests of the firm's partners, employees, clients, creditors and retirees.

The government reads the Thompson Memorandum to say that fees advancement is to be considered as a negative factor only when it is part of a campaign to "circle the wagons," i.e., to protect culpable employees and obstruct investigators. And it is true that the Thompson Memorandum instructs a prosecutor to ask "whether the corporation appears to be protecting its culpable employees and agents." But even if the government's reading is plausible, the wording nevertheless empowers prosecutors to determine which employees will be deprived of company-sponsored counsel: prosecutors may reasonably foresee that employees they identify as "culpable" will be cut off from fees.

The government also takes issue with Judge Kaplan's finding that the prosecutors (acting under DOJ policy) deliberately reinforced the threat inherent in the Thompson Memorandum. It protests that KPMG considered conditioning legal fees on cooperation even before the February 25, 2004 meeting and that KPMG adopted its Fees Policy free from government influence. However, Judge Kaplan's interpretation of the meeting is supported by the following record evidence. Because withholding of fees would be problematic for a partnership like KPMG, Bennett began by attempting to "sound out" the government's position on the issue. The prosecutors declined to sign off on KPMG's prior arrangement. Instead they asked KPMG to ascertain whether it had a legal obligation to advance fees. KPMG responded with its fallback position: conditioning fees on cooperation. In Judge Kaplan's view, this was not an official policy announcement, but rather a proposal: Skadden lawyers repeatedly emphasized to the prosecutors that no final decision had been made. One available inference from all this is that the prosecutors' inquiry about KPMG's legal obligations was a routine check for conflicts of interest; but on this record, Judge Kaplan was entitled to see things differently.

Nor can we disturb Judge Kaplan's finding that "the government conducted itself in a manner that evidenced a desire to minimize the involvement of defense attorneys." During the March 11 phone call between the prosecutors and Skadden, AUSA Weddle demanded that KPMG tell its employees to be "totally open" with the USAO, "even if that [meant admitting] criminal wrongdoing," so that he could gather material for cross-examination. On March 12, the prosecutors prevailed upon KPMG to supplement its first advisory letter with another, which clarified that employees could meet with the government without counsel. In addition, prosecutors repeatedly used Skadden to threaten to withhold legal fees from employees who refused to proffer-even if defense counsel had recommended that an employee invoke the Fifth Amendment privilege. Judge Kaplan could reasonably reject the government's version of these events.

Finally, we cannot say that the district court's ultimate finding of fact–that absent the Thompson Memorandum and the prosecutors' conduct KPMG would have advanced fees without condition or cap–was clearly erroneous. The government itself stipulated in *Stein I* that KPMG had a "longstanding voluntary practice" of advancing and paying employees' legal fees "without regard to economic costs or considerations" and "without a preset cap or condition of cooperation with the government . . . in any civil, criminal or regulatory proceeding" arising from activities within the scope of employment. Although it "is far from certain" that KPMG is legally obligated to advance defendants' legal fees, a firm may have potent incentives to advance fees, such as the ability to recruit and retain skilled professionals in a profession fraught with legal risk. Also, there is evidence that, before the prosecutors' intervention, KPMG executed an agreement under which it would advance Stein's legal fees without cap or condition (and negotiated toward an identical agreement with Smith). And while the government maintains that the civil, criminal and regulatory investigations confronting KPMG constituted an unprecedented state of affairs that might have caused KPMG to adopt new and different policies, Judge Kaplan was not required to agree. Indeed, KPMG itself represented to the court that the Thompson Memorandum and the prosecutors' conduct "substantially influenced [its] determination(s) with respect to the advancement of legal fees."

For the foregoing reasons, we cannot disturb Judge Kaplan's factual findings, including his finding that, but for the Thompson Memorandum and the prosecutors' conduct, KPMG would have advanced legal fees without condition or cap. * * *

[The Second Circuit determined that the government had not cured any violation of the defendants' right to counsel by the later statement that KPMG was free to pay the attorney's fees. The court concluded:]

The appropriate remedy for a constitutional violation is one that as much as possible restores the defendant to the circumstances that would have existed had there been no constitutional error. Since it has been found that, absent governmental interference, KPMG would have advanced unlimited legal fees unconditionally, only the unconditional, unlimited advancement of legal fees would restore defendants to the status quo ante. The government's in-court statement and the ensuing 16-month delay were not enough. If there was a Sixth Amendment violation, dismissal of the indictment is required. * * *

Judge Kaplan found that "KPMG's decision to cut off all payments of legal fees and expenses to anyone who was indicted and to limit and to condition such payments prior to indictment upon cooperation with the government was the direct consequence of the pressure applied by the Thompson Memorandum and the USAO." The government protests that KPMG's adoption and enforcement of its Fees Policy was private action, outside the ambit of the Sixth Amendment. * * *

Actions of a private entity are attributable to the State if "there is a sufficiently close nexus between the State and the challenged action of the ... entity so that the action of the latter may be fairly treated as that of the State itself." Jackson v. Metro. Edison Co., 419 U.S. 345 (1974). The "close nexus" test is not satisfied when the state "[m]ere[ly] approv[es] of or acquiesce[s] in the initiatives" of the private entity, S.F. Arts & Athletics, Inc. v. U.S. Olympic Comm., 483 U.S. 522, 547 (1987), or when an entity is merely subject to governmental regulation, see Jackson. "The purpose of the [close-nexus requirement] is to assure that constitutional standards are invoked only when it can be said that the State is responsible for the specific conduct of which the plaintiff complains." Blum v. Yaretsky, 457 U.S. 991 (1982). Such responsibility is normally found when the State "has exercised coercive power or has provided such significant encouragement, either overt or covert, that the choice must in law be deemed to be that of the State." * * *

The government argues: KPMG simply took actions in the shadow of an internal DOJ advisory document (the Thompson Memorandum) containing multiple factors and caveats; the government's approval of KPMG's Fees Policy did not render the government responsible for KPMG's actions enforcing it; even if the government had specifically required KPMG to adopt a policy that penalized non-cooperation, state action would still have been lacking because KPMG would have retained the power to apply the policy; and although the prosecutors repeatedly informed KPMG when employees were not cooperating, they did so at KPMG's behest, without knowing how KPMG would react. We disagree.

KPMG's adoption and enforcement of the Fees Policy amounted to "state action" because KPMG "operate[d] as a willful participant in joint activity" with the government, and because the USAO "significant[ly] encourage[d]" KPMG to withhold legal fees from defendants upon indictment. The government brought home to KPMG that its survival depended on its role in a joint project with the government to advance government prosecutions. The government is therefore legally "responsible for the specific conduct of which the [criminal defendants] complain[ ]."

The government argues that "KPMG's decision to condition legal fee payments on cooperation, while undoubtedly influenced by the Thompson Memorandum, was not coerced or directed by the Government." But that argument runs up against the district court's factual finding (which we do not disturb) that the fees decision "was the direct consequence" of the Memorandum and the prosecutors' conduct. Nevertheless, it remains a question of law whether the facts as found by the district court establish state action.

State action is established here as a matter of law because the government forced KPMG to adopt its constricted Fees Policy. The Thompson Memorandum itself-which prosecutors stated would be considered in deciding whether to indict KPMG-emphasizes that cooperation will be assessed in part based upon whether, in advancing counsel fees, "the corporation appears to be protecting its culpable employees and agents." Since defense counsel's objective in a criminal investigation will virtually always be to protect the client, KPMG's risk was that fees for defense counsel would be advanced to someone the government considered culpable. So the only safe course was to allow the government to become (in effect) paymaster.

The prosecutors reinforced this message by inquiring into KPMG's fees obligations, referring to the Thompson Memorandum as "a point that had to be considered," and warning that "misconduct" should not or cannot "be rewarded" under "federal guidelines." The government had KPMG's full attention. It is hardly surprising, then, that KPMG decided to condition payment of fees on employees' cooperation with the government and to terminate fees upon indictment: only that policy would allow KPMG to continue advancing fees while minimizing the risk that prosecutors would view such advancement as obstructive.

To ensure that KPMG's new Fees Policy was enforced, prosecutors became "entwined in the . . . control" of KPMG. They intervened in KPMG's decisionmaking, expressing their "disappoint[ment] with [the] tone" of KPMG's first advisory memorandum, and declaring that "[t]hese problems must be remedied" by a proposed supplemental memorandum specifying that employees could meet with the government without being burdened by counsel. Prosecutors also "made plain" their "strong preference" as to what the firm should do, and their "desire to share the fruits of such intrusions." They did so by regularly "reporting to KPMG the identities of employees who refused to make statements in circumstances in which the USAO knew full well that KPMG would pressure them to talk to prosecutors." The government's argument that it could not have known how KPMG would react when informed that certain employees were not cooperating is at best plausible only vis-à-vis the first few employees. The prosecutors thus steered KPMG toward their preferred fee advancement policy and then supervised its application in individual cases. Such "overt" and "significant encouragement" supports the conclusion that KPMG's conduct is properly attributed to the State.

In *Blum* and *Albert*, it was decisive that [1] actions of the private entity were based on independent criteria (the medical standards; the college rules of conduct), and that [2] the government was not dictating the outcomes of particular cases. * * *

Here * * *, [1] KPMG was never "free to define" cooperation independently: AUSA Weddle told Bennett that he had "had a bad experience in the past with a company conditioning payments on a person's cooperation, where the company did not define cooperation as 'tell the truth' the[ ] way we [the prosecutors] define it." KPMG's fees advancement decisions in individual cases thus depended largely on state-influenced standards. In addition, [2] the prosecution designated particular employees for deprivation of fees (and, in some cases, termination of employment) by demanding that KPMG threaten and penalize those employees for non-cooperation. As Bennett later reported to the Deputy Attorney General, "[w]henever your Office has notified us that individuals have not . . . cooperat[ed], KPMG has promptly and without question encouraged them to cooperate and threatened to cease payment of their attorneys fees and . . . to take personnel action, including termination." Furthermore, by indicting the thirteen defendants after inspiring and shaping KPMG's Fees Policy and after exacting KPMG's compliance with it, prosecutors effectively selected which employees would be deprived of attorneys' fees. Having forced the constriction of KPMG's longstanding policy of advancing fees, the government then compelled KPMG to apply the Fees Policy to particular employees both pre- and post-indictment. This conduct finds no protection in *Blum* and *Albert*.

The government also directs us to another line of state action cases: D.L. Cromwell Investments, Inc. v. NASD Regulation, Inc., 279 F.3d 155 (2d Cir.2002), and United States v. Solomon, 509 F.2d 863 (2d Cir.1975). These cases involved parallel, cooperative investigations by private regulatory entities and government investigators. * * *

In both cases, we held that there was no state action because the private actors had independent regulatory interests and motives for making their inquiries and for cooperating with parallel investigations being conducted by the government. In *D.L. Cromwell*, the NASD had a preexisting "regulatory duty to investigate questionable securities transactions,"–that is, it would have requested interviews regardless of governmental pressure. And in *Solomon*, the NYSE's efforts were "in pursuance of its own interests and obligations, not as an agent of the [government],"–absent SEC involvement, the NYSE would have investigated anyway. Because the NASD and the NYSE had preexisting and independent investigatory missions, their cooperation with the government was not state action. By contrast (as the district court found), absent the prosecutors' involvement and the Thompson Memorandum, KPMG would not have changed its longstanding fee advancement policy or withheld legal fees from defendants upon indictment.

The government responds: Solomon declined to find state action even though it involved a private entity compelling interviews with one of its members, backed by the explicit threat of expulsion, in the context of continuous coordination between the NYSE and the SEC on the same side. So how can KPMG, an adversary of the government, also be its partner? See Brentwood Acad. v. Tenn. Secondary Sch. Athletic Ass'n, 531 U.S. 288 (2001) ("The state-action doctrine does not convert opponents into virtual agents.").

An adversarial relationship does not normally bespeak partnership. But KPMG faced ruin by indictment and reasonably believed it must do everything in its power to avoid it. The government's threat of indictment was easily sufficient to convert its adversary into its agent. KPMG was not in a position to consider coolly the risk of indictment, weigh the potential significance of the other enumerated factors in the Thompson Memorandum, and decide for itself how to proceed.

We therefore conclude that KPMG's adoption and enforcement of the Fees Policy (both before and upon defendants' indictment) amounted to state action. The government may properly be held "responsible for the specific conduct of which the [criminal defendants] complain[ ]," *Blum, i.e.,* the deprivation of their Sixth Amendment right to counsel, if the violation is established.

* * * Most of the state action relevant here–the promulgation of the Thompson Memorandum, the prosecutors' communications with KPMG

regarding the advancement of fees, KPMG's adoption of a Fees Policy with caps and conditions, and KPMG's repeated threats to employees identified by prosecutors as being uncooperative–pre-dated the indictments of August and October 2005. So we must determine how this pre-indictment conduct may bear on defendants' Sixth Amendment claim.

"The Sixth Amendment right of the 'accused' to assistance of counsel in 'all criminal prosecutions' is limited by its terms: it does not attach until a prosecution is commenced." Rothgery v. Gillespie County, 128 S.Ct. 2578 (2008). "Attachment" refers to "when the [Sixth Amendment] right may be asserted"; it does not concern the separate question of "what the right guarantees," i.e., "what the substantive guarantee of the Sixth Amendment" is at that stage of the prosecution. The Supreme Court has "pegged commencement [of a prosecution] to the initiation of adversary judicial criminal proceedings–whether by way of formal charge, preliminary hearing, indictment, information, or arraignment. The rule is not 'mere formalism,' but a recognition of the point at which the government has committed itself to prosecute, the adverse positions of government and defendant have solidified, and the accused finds himself faced with the prosecutorial forces of organized society, and immersed in the intricacies of substantive and procedural criminal law." * * *

[Judge Kaplan determined that the government's conduct before the indictment violated the Sixth Amendment for the following reasons:]

> * * * It is true, of course, that the Sixth Amendment right to counsel typically attaches at the initiation of adversarial proceedings–at an arraignment, indictment, preliminary hearing, and so on. But the analysis can not end there. The Thompson Memorandum on its face and the USAO's actions were parts of an effort to limit defendants' access to funds for their defense. Even if this was not among the conscious motives, the Memorandum was adopted and the USAO acted in circumstances in which that result was known to be exceptionally likely. The fact that events were set in motion prior to indictment with the object of having, or with knowledge that they were likely to have, an unconstitutional effect upon indictment cannot save the government. This conduct, unless justified, violated the Sixth Amendment.

In other words, the government's pre-indictment conduct was of a kind that would have post-indictment effects of Sixth Amendment significance, and did.

We endorse this analysis. Although defendants' Sixth Amendment rights attached only upon indictment, the district court properly considered pre-indictment state action that affected defendants post-indictment. When the government acts prior to indictment so as to impair the suspect's relationship with counsel post-indictment, the pre-indictment actions ripen into cognizable Sixth Amendment deprivations upon indictment. As Judge

Ellis explained in United States v. Rosen, 487 F.Supp.2d 721 (E.D.Va.2007), "it is entirely plausible that pernicious effects of the pre-indictment interference continued into the post-indictment period, effectively hobbling defendants' Sixth Amendment rights to retain counsel of choice with funds to which they had a right . . . . [I]f, as alleged, the government coerced [the employer] into halting fee advances on defendants' behalf and the government did so for the purpose of undermining defendants' relationship with counsel once the indictment issued, the government violated defendants' right to expend their own resources towards counsel once the right attached."

Since the government forced KPMG to adopt the constricted Fees Policy–including the provision for terminating fee advancement upon indictment–and then compelled KPMG to enforce it, it was virtually certain that KPMG would terminate defendants' fees upon indictment. We therefore reject the government's argument that its actions (virtually all pre-indictment) are immune from scrutiny under the Sixth Amendment.***

The Sixth Amendment ensures that "[i]n all criminal prosecutions, the accused shall enjoy the right . . . to have the Assistance of Counsel for his defence." U.S. Const. amend. VI. Thus "the Sixth Amendment guarantees the defendant the right to be represented by an otherwise qualified attorney whom that defendant can afford to hire, or who is willing to represent the defendant even though he is without funds." Caplin & Drysdale, Chartered v. United States, 491 U.S. 617, (1989). "[A]n element of this right is the right of a defendant who does not require appointed counsel to choose who will represent him." United States v. Gonzalez-Lopez, 548 U.S. 140 (2006).

The government must "honor" a defendant's Sixth Amendment right to counsel:

> This means more than simply that the State cannot prevent the accused from obtaining the assistance of counsel. The Sixth Amendment also imposes on the State an affirmative obligation to respect and preserve the accused's choice to seek this assistance . . . . [A]t the very least, the prosecutor and police have an affirmative obligation not to act in a manner that circumvents and thereby dilutes the protection afforded by the right to counsel.

Maine v. Moulton, 474 U.S. 159 (1985). This is intuitive: the right to counsel in an adversarial legal system would mean little if defense counsel could be controlled by the government or vetoed without good reason. * * *

It is axiomatic that if defendants had already received fee advances from KPMG, the government could not (absent justification) deliberately interfere with the use of that money to fuel their defenses. And the government concedes that it could not prevent a lawyer from furnishing a defense gratis. Presumably, such a lawyer could pay another lawyer to represent the defendant (subject, of course, to ethical rules governing third-party payments to counsel). And if the Sixth Amendment prohibits the government from interfering with such arrangements, then surely it also prohibits the government from interfering with financial donations by others, such as family members and neighbors-and employers. In a nutshell, the Sixth Amendment protects against unjustified governmental interference with the right to defend oneself using whatever assets one has or might reasonably and lawfully obtain.

* * * It is also urged that a company may pretend cooperation while "circling the wagons," that payment of legal fees can advance such a strategy, and that the government has a legitimate interest in being able to assess cooperation using the payment of fees as one factor. Even if that can be a legitimate justification, it would not be in play here: prosecutors testified before the district court that they were never concerned that KPMG was "circling the wagons." Moreover, it is unclear how the circling of wagons is much different from the legitimate melding of a joint defense.

The government conceded at oral argument that it is in the government's interest that every defendant receive the best possible representation he or she can obtain. A company that advances legal fees to employees may stymie prosecutors by affording culpable employees with high-quality representation. But if it is in the government's interest that every defendant receive the best possible representation, it cannot also be in the government's interest to leave defendants naked to their enemies.

* * *A defendant who is deprived of counsel of choice (without justification) need not show how his or her defense was impacted; such errors are structural and are not subject to harmless-error review. See *Gonzalez-Lopez* ("[T]he right at stake here is the right to counsel of choice, . . . and that right was violated because the deprivation of counsel was erroneous. No additional showing of prejudice is required to make the violation 'complete.'"). Of course, a completed constitutional violation may still be remediable. However, * * * the government has failed to cure this Sixth Amendment violation. Therefore, the government deprived defendants Gremminger, Hasting, Ritchie and Watson of their Sixth Amendment right to counsel of choice.

The remaining defendants–Bickham, DeLap, Eischeid, Lanning, Rosenthal, Smith, Stein, Warley, and Wiesner–do not claim they were deprived of their chosen counsel. Rather, they assert that the government unjustifiably interfered with their relationship with counsel and their ability to defend themselves. In the district court, the government conceded that these defendants are also entitled to dismissal of the indictment, assuming the correctness of *Stein I*. We agree: these defendants can easily demonstrate interference in their relationships with counsel and impairment of their ability to mount a defense based on Judge Kaplan's non-erroneous findings that the post-indictment termination of fees "caused them to restrict the activities of their counsel," and thus to limit the scope of their pre-trial investigation and preparation. Defendants were indicted based on a fairly novel theory of criminal liability; they faced substantial penalties; the relevant facts are scattered throughout over 22 million documents regarding the doings of scores of people; the subject matter is "extremely complex"; technical expertise is needed to figure out and explain what happened; and trial was expected to last between six and eight months. As Judge Kaplan found, these defendants "have been forced to limit their defenses . . . for economic reasons and . . . they would not have been so constrained if KPMG paid their expenses." We therefore hold that these defendants were also deprived of their right to counsel under the Sixth Amendment.[15]

NOTES AND QUESTIONS

1. **Principles of Federal Prosecution of Business Organizations**. *Stein* discussed the McNulty Memo that modified the Thompson Memo by limiting the Department of Justice's policy on considering payment of attorney's fees for employees suspected of being involved in wrongdoing. In August 2008, the Department issued the *Principles of Federal Prosecution of Business Organizations* [see Chapter 15] that rejects completely any consideration of the payment of attorney's fees in deciding whether a company has cooperated: "In evaluating cooperation, however, prosecutors should not take into account whether a corporation is advancing or reimbursing attorneys' fees or providing counsel to employees, officers, or directors under investigation or indictment. Likewise, prosecutors may not request that a corporation refrain from taking such action." *U.S. Attorney's Manual* § 9-28.730. Assuming federal prosecutors adhere to the *Principles* and do not take into consideration a company's payment of attorney's fees for its employees and officers, then the situation that arose in *Stein* is unlikely to occur again.

2. **What's Wrong with Attorney's Fees?** Unlike the Thompson Memo, which encouraged prosecutors to view the payment of attorney's fees as a sign of a lack of cooperation, the current policy does not view it as a negative sign. Why would the Department of Justice view the payment of attorney's fees as indicating a lack of cooperation? Consider the following:

> The payment of attorney's fees by a corporation is not a failure of cooperation unless one views the presence of a lawyer for a corporate officer as an impediment to an investigation. A lawyer is unlikely to recommend that a client, who is the target of an investigation,

---

[15]This case does not raise, and therefore we have no occasion to consider, the application of our holding to the following scenario: A defendant moves unsuccessfully in the district court to dismiss the indictment on the same Sixth Amendment theory. The defendant proceeds to trial with his or her chosen attorney, and the attorney is forced to limit the scope of his or her efforts due to the defendant's financial constraints. The defendant is convicted based on overwhelming evidence of his or her guilt.

cooperate with the government, or at least, not without the protection of an immunity agreement or plea bargain. This does not mean the lawyer's advice is wrongful or designed to obstruct justice.

Peter J. Henning, *Targeting Legal Advice*, 54 AM. U. L. REV. 669 (2005).

3. **State Action**. The key to the Second Circuit's application of the Sixth Amendment was the finding that KPMG was acting on behalf of the government in denying the attorney's fees. Companies often pledge their cooperation when a government investigation commences, and often interview employees as part of an internal investigation while keeping prosecutors informed of their progress. It is not unknown that prosecutors will ask that a certain employee be interviewed or that a specified set of questions be asked during the investigation. If the company agrees to follow the prosecutor's suggestions, is that state action so that various constitutional protections apply, such as *Miranda's* right to counsel in a custodial interrogation?

D. ETHICAL REGULATIONS

1. ABA Model Rule of Professional Conduct 3.8(e)

ABA Model Rule of Professional Conduct 3.8(e) (2002) provides:

The prosecutor in a criminal case shall: * * * (e) not subpoena a lawyer in a grand jury or other criminal proceeding to present evidence about a past or present client unless the prosecutor reasonably believes: (1) the information sought is not protected from disclosure by any applicable privilege; (2) the evidence sought is essential to the successful completion of an ongoing investigation or prosecution; and (3) there is no other feasible alternative to obtain the information; * * *

Most states follow Model Rule 3.8(e), and it appears to require a federal prosecutor to meet the same criteria for issuance of a subpoena to an attorney as the Department of Justice rules. An earlier version of Model Rule 3.8(e) also required prosecutors to seek prior judicial approval before issuing a subpoena to an attorney, but the ABA later dropped that requirement. The ethical rules do not create additional rights for an opposing litigant. Preamble ¶ 20 ("Violation of a Rule should not itself give rise to a cause of action against a lawyer nor should it create any presumption in such a case that a legal duty has been breached."). See United States v. Parker, 165 F.Supp.2d 431 (W.D.N.Y. 2001) ("even if the alleged misconduct, attributed by Defendants to the Government attorneys in this case, were deemed an ethical violation, and the relevant disciplinary rule were applicable to the instant facts, such does not warrant use of the exclusionary rule as a remedy for such violation.").

2. McDade Act (28 U.S.C. § 530B)

Ethical regulation of federal prosecutors has largely been through internal enforcement by the Department of Justice's Office of Professional Responsibility. In 1998, however, Congress adopted 28 U.S.C. § 530B, entitled "Ethical standards for attorneys for the government" that provides: "An attorney for the Government shall be subject to State laws and rules, and local Federal court rules, governing attorneys in each State where such attorney engages in that attorney's duties, to the same extent and in the same manner as other attorneys in that State."[1] The original bill called for the creation of a Misconduct Review Board and listed a number of actions that would subject a federal prosecutor to discipline. Those provisions were stripped out of the bill, and Congress ultimately passed it as part of a broader appropriations bill. The McDade Act was in part a reaction to efforts by the Department of Justice to exempt its attorneys from state ethics rules governing contacts with persons who were represented by attorneys. The McDade Act thwarted that effort by requiring federal prosecutors to adhere to state ethics codes. The McDade Act also requires the Department of Justice to adopt rules to implement the statute. The Department of Justice's interpretation of "State laws and rules" does not include "Any statute, rule, or regulation which does not govern ethical conduct, such as rules of procedure, evidence, or substantive law, whether or not such rule is included in a code of professional responsibility for attorneys." 28 C.F.R. § 77.2(h). For a discussion of the ethical regulation of federal prosecutors, see Bruce A. Green & Fred C. Zacharias, *Regulating Federal Prosecutors' Ethics*, 55 VAND. L. REV. 381 (2002).

Federal district courts commonly incorporate a state's rules of professional responsibility as the standards applicable in their courts. In Baylson v. Disciplinary Board of the Supreme Court, 975 F .2d 102 (3d Cir. 1992), the Third Circuit concluded that a district court could not incorporate a Pennsylvania disciplinary rule modeled after the earlier version of Model Rule 3.8(e), that required prosecutors to obtain prior judicial approval before issuing a grand jury subpoena to an attorney. The court held that the state rule was "not compatible with the Federal Rules of Criminal Procedure or well-settled grand jury practice" and therefore the local courts did not have the authority to adopt such a rule.

In United States v. Colorado Supreme Court, 189 F.3d 1281 (10th Cir. 1999), the Tenth Circuit found that a Colorado ethics rule almost identical to the Model Rule 3.8(e) could be enforced under the McDade Act to require

---

[1] The statute is named for former Representative Joseph McDade, who was acquitted of federal charges involving misuse of campaign funds. Although the statute was opposed by the Department of Justice, prior to taking the position of deputy attorney general, Larry Thompson wrote that the "McDade law is good for the profession." Larry D. Thompson, *The McDade Law: Necessary for Justice of Burden for Federal Attorneys?*, 48 Fed. Law. 20 (2001).

prior judicial approval of a subpoena to an attorney issued by federal prosecutors. The court stated:

> [A] prosecutor violating Rule 3.8 has violated the generally accepted principle that the attorney-client relationship should not be disturbed without cause. To do so would constitute essentially 'unethical' attorney conduct unbecoming any member of the bar, including prosecutors. Because of the characteristics of Rule 3.8, we conclude that the rule in its current incarnation is a rule of ethics applicable to federal prosecutors by the McDade Act.

In Whitehouse v. United States District, 53 F.3d 1349 (1st Cir. 1995), the court disagreed with *Baylson* and upheld a Rhode Island local district court rule, based on the earlier version of Model Rule 3.8(e) that was strikingly similar to the Pennsylvania rule. The First Circuit concluded that the rule in question was "not aimed at grand jury action," did not preclude "an *ex parte, in camera* [judicial] hearing," and operated "merely [to] change * * * the timing with respect to motions to quash in recognition of the fact that service itself of an attorney-subpoena seeking to compel evidence concerning a client may cause irreparable damage to the attorney-client relationship."

Five years later, in Stern v. United States District Court, 214 F.3d 4 (1st Cir. 2000), the same court *rejected* a new Massachusetts rule that was again modeled after the earlier version of Model Rule 3.8(e). The court distinguished *Whitehouse* on the ground that the Rhode Island rule only contained the three criteria listed in Rule 3.8(e) in the comments, and therefore those requirements were not mandatory but only precatory. The Massachusetts rule, on the other hand, "differs significantly in that it imposes new substantive requirements for judicial preapproval of grand jury subpoenas. In so doing, the rule alters the grand jury's historic role, place it under overly intrusive court supervision, curbs its broad investigative powers, reverses the presumption of validity accorded to its subpoenas, undermines the secrecy of its proceedings, and creates procedural detours and delays. It therefor impermissibly interferes with grand jury proceedings." Chief Judge Torruella, dissenting from a denial of rehearing en banc, argued that "it is difficult to conclude that the panel opinion in *Stern* is anything but a reversal of the panel opinion in *Whitehouse*. This outcome contravenes sound and well-established legal principles regarding the binding nature of panel opinions upon later panels considering the same or closely similar issues." *Stern* also rejected the argument that the McDade Act validated the local court rule by requiring federal prosecutors to adhere to all state ethics rules: "it simply cannot be said that Congress, by enacting section 530B, meant to empower states (or federal district courts, for that matter) to regulate federal attorneys in a manner inconsistent with federal law."

In United States v. Lowery, 166 F.3d 1119 (11th Cir. 1999), the Eleventh Circuit overturned a lower court decision suppressing evidence that the court determined had been obtained in violation of a state ethical rule, stating that the McDade Act does not alter the status of state ethics rules because such rules "cannot provide an adequate basis for a federal court to suppress evidence that is otherwise admissible. Federal law, not state law, determine the admissibility of evidence in federal court. * * * State rules of professional conduct, or state rules on any subject, cannot trump the Federal Rules of Evidence."

3. Lawyer Involvement in Client Misconduct

Counsel's representation of a client can trigger an accusation that the lawyer engaged in criminal conduct. Do the ethical rules of the profession provide guidance regarding whether a lawyer's conduct constituted a criminal act? In **United States v. Kellington**, 217 F.3d 1084 (9th Cir. 2000), the court considered whether the trial judge's limiting instruction to the jury on the role of the legal ethics rules in assessing the defendant's intent was proper in a prosecution for obstruction of justice (see supra Chapter 8).

> It is well settled that in the prosecution of a lawyer for conduct stemming from his or her representation of a client, expert testimony on the lawyer's ethical obligations is relevant to establish the lawyer's intent and state of mind. * * * [C]ounsel for Kellington was unable to frame and give content to the core of his defense–that Kellington was attempting (however imprudently in hindsight) to provide his client with bona fide legal representation, and that much of the conduct from which the government would have the jury infer criminal intent can be explained by his ethical obligations to McFarlane, his background and experience, and the nature of the attorney-client relationship. Combined with the court's instruction to the jury that the ethics testimony was merely background information, we can have no confidence that the jury gave due regard to the ethics evidence in assessing the government's largely circumstantial case against Kellington on the question of criminal intent. Accordingly, we affirm the district court's considered judgment that, "the evidence convicting Kellington of a violation of 18 U.S.C. § 1512(b)(2)(B) in conjunction with the court's restrictions on closing argument preponderates sufficiently heavily against the verdict that a serious miscarriage of justice may have occurred."

4. Regulatory Agency Representation

Does a lawyer representing a client before a governmental agency have a duty to disclose wrongdoing by the client? In **United States v. Cavin**, 39 F.3d 1299, 1308-09 (5th Cir. 1994), the court noted:

> Sometimes the interplay of conflicting duties is even more complex. Under what circumstances, for example, is a lawyer who represents a client in reporting to a regulatory agency, as here, obliged to

divulge potentially damaging facts? Under what circumstances is he obliged to maintain silence? The black-letter rule is that the lawyer must disclose a material fact when disclosure is necessary to avoid assisting a criminal or fraudulent act by a client, unless disclosure is prohibited by the rule against revealing client confidences. Because most such disclosures would consist of client confidences, it would seem that disclosure is prohibited, leaving the lawyer in the position of an accomplice. But that is not the rule; a lawyer may not commit a fraud. The parameters of his obligations, however, depend on the circumstances. How active a role does the lawyer play in the reporting process: is he a background advisor or the spokesperson? Is the context such that the agency likely would be misled without disclosure of the damaging fact? Would the omission mislead because of a statement by the lawyer or because of an oversight by the agency? Finally, what if the lawyer reasonably believes that the legal significance of the undisclosed information is such that the agency's reporting requirements do not call for disclosure, but the lawyer suspects that the agency would disagree? One authority holds that disclosure is not required. If disclosure is not required, arguably it is forbidden.

These are some of the complex considerations facing a lawyer whose client is using or has used his services to accomplish a fraud. To the extent that they guide his conduct, they are directly relevant to his intent. We therefore join our Eleventh Circuit colleagues in holding that a lawyer accused of participating in his client's fraud is entitled to present evidence of his professional, including ethical, responsibilities, and the manner in which they influenced him. Exclusion of such evidence prevents the lawyer from effectively presenting his defense.

The court in *Cavin* noted error in the trial court's failure to instruct the jury "concerning an attorney's duty of confidentiality": "The professional responsibilities of attorneys are relevant in instances as here presented, and a proper jury charge detailing those responsibilities should have been given." For a discussion of the use of ethical rules in criminal trials of lawyers, see Ellen S. Podgor, *Criminal Misconduct: Ethical Rule Usage Leads to Regulation of the Legal Profession*, 61 TEMPLE L. REV. 1323 (1988). How do the new SEC lawyer disclosure rules, discussed in Section A.2 supra, affect the analysis of whether a lawyer's decision not to disclose can be proof of the intent to obstruct justice? If the disclosure obligation is permissive rather than mandatory, is that proof that the lawyer acted in good faith?

E. CONTACT WITH REPRESENTED PERSONS

ABA Model Rule of Professional Conduct 4.2 (2002) states: "In representing a client, a lawyer shall not communicate about the subject of the representation with a person the lawyer knows to be represented by another lawyer in the matter, unless the lawyer has the consent of the other lawyer or is authorized by law to do so." The ABA amended the Rule in 1995 by substituting "person" for "party" so that the scope of the Rule was not limited to those who are adversaries in litigation. Even after the change, does the Rule limit the ability of the government to conduct undercover investigations that involve contact with individuals who the government knows has retained counsel?

In 1990, the Department of Justice issues a memorandum to its attorneys—known as the "Thornburgh Memorandum," named for then-Attorney General Dick Thornburgh—that purported to exempt federal prosecutors from state ethics rules, specifically Rule 4.2, that could interfere with federal criminal investigations. The Thornburgh Memorandum caused significant controversy and was one of the principal contributing factors to congressional adoption of the McDade Act, which now requires all federal attorneys to comply with applicable state ethics rules. Most courts read the state counterparts to Model Rule 4.2 in a limited way that does not restrict the government's ability to have contacts with the targets of its investigation, regardless of whether they are represented by counsel. Consider the district court's analysis of the issue in the following case.

UNITED STATES v. GRASS
239 F.Supp.2d 535 (M.D. Pa. 2003)

RAMBO, District Judge.

On June 21, 2002, a federal grand jury sitting in Harrisburg, Pennsylvania issued a thirty-seven count indictment against Defendants Grass and Brown, former officers and directors for the Rite Aid Corporation. The indictment alleges that Defendants engaged in a conspiracy intended to enrich themselves by defrauding Rite Aid and its stockholders, creditors, and vendors. This conspiracy allegedly lasted the duration of Defendant Grass's tenure as Rite Aid's Chief Executive Officer ("CEO"). The indictment also alleges that Defendants Grass and Brown engaged in a conspiracy to obstruct justice by impeding investigations by the United States Securities and Exchange Commission ("SEC"), the Federal Bureau of Investigation ("FBI"), the United States Attorney's Office for the Middle District of Pennsylvania, and the Grand Jury.

On September 4, 2002, Defendants Grass and Brown filed a motion to suppress tapes of conversations that they had with Timothy Noonan, Rite Aid's former President. Defendants contend that Assistant United States Attorney Kim Douglas Daniel obtained the recorded conversations in violation of Rules 4.2 and 8.4(a) of the Pennsylvania Rules of Professional Conduct. * * *

Most of the facts pertinent to this motion are not in dispute. Defendant Grass resigned as Rite Aid's CEO on October 18, 1999. * * * Around that same time, the FBI's field office in Harrisburg, Pennsylvania began an investigation in conjunction with the United States Attorney's Office for the Middle District of Pennsylvania. The Government assigned FBI Agent George Delaney and Assistant United States Attorney ("AUSA") Kim Douglas Daniel to lead its criminal investigation.

At the suppression hearing, Noonan testified that between October of 1999 and July of 2000 he met with Defendant Brown several times. During those meetings, the two men discussed what each would tell Rite Aid's internal investigators regarding the fraud allegations. Both men were aware, during this period, that both civil and criminal investigations were pending as well.

On February 12, 2001, AUSA Daniel phoned Defendant Brown's counsel at the time, Herbert Stern. During that conversation, the two agreed that the Government would interview Defendant Brown on April 4, 2001. Mister Stern, however, requested that the Government provide, in advance of the interview, an agenda listing the topics that would be discussed. On March 28, 2001, AUSA Daniel faxed Mr. Stern an agenda letter setting forth the topics that the parties would discuss during the interview. No later than March 30, 2001, Mr. Stern informed AUSA Daniel that Defendant Brown had changed his mind and would not consent to an interview.

Previously, on March 9, 2001, Noonan met with AUSA Daniel and Agent Delaney at the United States Attorney's Office in Philadelphia, Pennsylvania. During that meeting, the parties discussed the fraud allegations and any contact that Noonan may have had with Defendants Grass and Brown subsequent to Noonan's departure from Rite Aid in December of 1999. The following day, Defendant Brown called Noonan at his home requesting that the two meet. Noonan deferred the meeting until March 13, 2001. In the meantime–on either March 11 or March 12, 2001–Noonan contacted Agent Delaney and informed him of Brown's phone call. * * *

[Noonan agreed with Agent Delaney to wear a secret recording device to his meeting with Brown. At the meeting,] Defendant Brown informed Noonan that he would be meeting with the Government in early April. Defendant Brown also told Noonan that Defendant Grass had retained Attorney William Jeffress to represent him in any criminal proceedings that might occur. * * *

[Noonan agreed to cooperate in the government's investigation in March 2001, and arranged another meeting with Brown. Before the meeting,] Agent Delaney also gave Noonan a fake letter signed by AUSA Daniel and addressed to Attorney David Howard, Noonan's retained counsel. That document was similar in content to the agenda letter that AUSA Daniel had already sent to Mr. Stern regarding Defendant Brown's proposed interview. Agent Delaney instructed Noonan to use the letter as a prop to guide his conversation with Brown to the topics listed in the letter. However, Agent Delaney warned Noonan to avoid talking about Defendant Brown's conversations with his attorney. "[Agent Delaney] did say that if Franklin brought up or said he had this discussion with his attorney or that discussion or that these were topics that his attorney said, don't get into those conversations." [Noonan recorded his next meeting with Brown.]

* * * On either April 16 or April 18, 2001, Noonan, at Agent Delaney's behest, traveled to Defendant Grass's office in Lemoyne, Pennsylvania to attempt to record a conversation with Grass regarding the fraud allegations.[3] Defendant Grass, however, was not in his office.

Following this attempted meeting, Noonan met once again with Agent Delaney in Philadelphia. During this meeting, Delaney instructed Noonan to meet with Defendant Brown again to arrange for a meeting with both Defendants Brown and Grass. On April 27, 2001, Noonan and Defendant Brown met at the Hampden Center Shopping Mall in Mechanicsburg, Pennsylvania. As before, Noonan recorded the conversation. During the course of the meeting, Noonan, as instructed, requested an audience with Defendant Grass. Defendant Brown indicated that Defendant Grass would probably be amenable to such a meeting.

On May 1, 2001, Noonan met with Agent Delaney, another unidentified FBI agent, AUSA Daniel, and AUSA George Rocktashel at the Federal Building in Harrisburg. Although AUSA Daniel was aware of Noonan's cooperation, this marked the first time he and Noonan had spoken since Noonan's initial interview on March 9 in Philadelphia. Their conversation covered a wide variety of subjects relating to the Government's investigation of fraud at Rite Aid and what Noonan's conversations with Brown had unveiled. Noonan also informed AUSA Daniel that he would soon be meeting with both Defendants Grass and Brown. AUSA Daniel then delineated the topics that he wished to have Noonan raise during that meeting. Following his two to three hour meeting with the Government officials, Noonan jotted down on a sheet of paper notes regarding what topics AUSA Daniel wanted Noonan to discuss with Defendants Brown and Grass.

The following day, May 2, 2001, Noonan met with Defendants Grass and Brown at Grass's office. Once again, the Government recorded the conversations through a hidden microphone worn by Noonan. During the course of this meeting, Noonan removed his notes from his pocket and used them to guide the conversation. Noonan told Defendants Grass and Brown that the notes were taken during Noonan's meeting with the Government in Philadelphia in March of 2001. Following the meeting with Grass and Brown, Noonan met with AUSA Daniel. Noonan subsequently threw the notes away.

---

[3] As he did before Noonan's meeting with Defendant Brown, Agent Delaney instructed Noonan to stay clear of the substance of Defendant Grass's conversations with his attorney. "[Agent Delaney] said if they start talking about their lawyers or conversations with their lawyers, I don't want you to get into any conversation. He said that to me."

After the May 2, 2001 meeting, Defendant Brown called Noonan and stated: "That he would like to get together." Noonan and Brown met for the last time on May 21, 2001. As with the other conversations, the Government surreptitiously recorded this conversation through a wire that Noonan was wearing.

Although AUSA Daniel only met with Noonan twice, he approved the recording of each conversation. It is undisputed that at the times he authorized these recordings, AUSA Daniel knew that Defendants Grass and Brown were both represented by counsel. Additionally, it is likewise beyond dispute that, at least with respect to five of the six conversations, AUSA Daniel knew that Defendant Brown had refused to consent to an interview with the Government. Finally, it is also undisputed that neither Defendant was under indictment at the time Noonan recorded their conversations. As stated at the outset of this memorandum, the indictment in this case did not issue until June 21, 2002.

In the instant motion, Defendants argue that AUSA Daniel violated Rules 4.2 and 8.4(a) of the Pennsylvania Rules of Professional Conduct by using a surrogate to communicate with parties whom he knew to be represented by counsel. Thus, according to Defendants, the tapes of these conversations should be suppressed pursuant to the court's inherent supervisory power. For the following reasons, the court will deny Defendants' motion: (1) AUSA Daniel did not violate the Rules of Professional Conduct; and (2) even if he did violate those rules, suppression of the evidence is not an appropriate remedy under the facts in this case.

Rule 4.2 of the Pennsylvania Rules of Professional Conduct, also known as the "no-contact rule," prohibits an attorney from communicating "about the subject of the representation with a party the lawyer knows to be represented by another lawyer in the matter, unless the lawyer has the consent of the other lawyer or is authorized by law to do so." Rule 8.4(a) states that it is professional misconduct for an attorney to knowingly assist another in violating the rules of professional conduct. Defendants argue that the tapes of the conversations between Noonan and Defendants must be suppressed because AUSA Daniel violated Rule 4.2. According to Defendants, AUSA Daniel employed Noonan as his surrogate to communicate with Defendants after AUSA Daniel knew that Defendants had retained counsel; thus, violating Rule 8.4(a).

In order to prevail on this motion, Defendants must demonstrate the following. First, AUSA Daniel violated Rule 4.2. Second, Defendants were represented by counsel at the time the statements were elicited. Third, suppression is an appropriate remedy for violation of the Rule.

In the past, significant debate surrounded the issue of whether state rules of professional responsibility apply at all to federal prosecutors. However, in 1998, Congress eliminated all doubt regarding this issue by enacting what is commonly referred to as the McDade Amendment. The

McDade Amendment states, in relevant part: "An attorney for the [Federal] Government shall be subject to State laws and rules . . . governing attorneys in each State where such attorney engages in that attorney's duties, to the extent and in the same manner as other attorneys in that State." [28 U.S.C.] § 530B(a).

Therefore, it is beyond doubt that AUSA Daniel was bound by the Pennsylvania Rules of Professional Conduct at all times relevant to the instant motion. Furthermore, based on Rule 8.4(a) of the Rules of Professional Conduct, AUSA Daniel could not avoid the dictates of Rule 4.2 by employing Noonan as his surrogate to accomplish what he himself could not do without violating the Rules of Professional Conduct. However, it remains to be seen whether AUSA Daniel's conduct in this case violated Rule 4.2. Although the McDade Amendment makes clear that state rules of professional conduct apply to Government attorneys, that legislation does not define what those standards are, when they attach, or what is an appropriate remedy to impose if Government lawyers breach those rules. Instead, it is completely silent as to these matters.

The Government argues that AUSA Daniel did not violate Rule 4.2 because (1) neither Defendants Grass, nor Brown, were a "party," as no indictment had issued at the time Noonan recorded the conversations, and (2) even if either Defendant Grass or Brown were a "party," the communications were "authorized by law," as that term is used in the no-contact rule. Pa. R. Prof'l Conduct 4.2. In support, the Government cites the Third Circuit's decision in United States v. Balter, 91 F.3d 427 (3d Cir.1996). In this pre-McDade Amendment case, the Third Circuit affirmed the District Court's refusal to suppress recordings of non-custodial conversations between a Government agent and the defendant made after the Government learned that the defendant was represented by counsel.

The Circuit Court's holding in that case was based on the identical two-prong argument that the Government proffers in opposition to the instant motion. That is, first, the court held that the Government did not violate the no-contact rule because the agent recorded the conversations prior to the defendant's indictment. Therefore, at that time, the defendant was not a party. Second, even if the defendant were a party, the court held that the communications fell within Rule 4.2's "authorized by law" exception.

It is important to note that, in *Balter,* the court addressed whether the Government violated the no-contact rule as that rule appears in the New Jersey Rules of Professional Conduct. Crucial to the court's holding that the defendant was not a "party," as that term is used in the rule, was the fact that courts interpreting the New Jersey no-contact rule had concluded that it does not attach until after initiation of formal legal or adversarial proceedings. This portion of the *Balter* holding is, therefore, inapplicable to the instant case. Although the Pennsylvania and New Jersey no-contact rules employ virtually identical language, there is no caselaw limiting application of the Pennsylvania no-contact rule to post-indictment contacts. In fact, the commentary to Pennsylvania Rule 4.2 states the contrary: "This Rule covers any person, whether or not a party to a formal proceeding, who is represented by counsel concerning the matter in question." Therefore, it is clear that, at the time of the recorded conversations, Defendants Grass and Brown were parties as that term is contemplated in Rule 4.2 of the Pennsylvania Rules of Professional Responsibility.

However, this does not, as Defendants contend, automatically lead to the conclusion that AUSA Daniel violated the no-contact rule by employing Noonan as his alter ego to communicate with Defendants. Rule 4.2 does not prohibit all contact between attorneys and parties represented by counsel. Rather, that rule specifically makes an exception for those contacts which are "authorized by law." In fact, the *Balter* court specifically held that the person-party distinction under the New Jersey no-contact rule was irrelevant to its holding that the Government did not violate the rule because "even if a criminal suspect were a 'party' within the meaning of the rule, pre-indictment investigation by prosecutors is precisely the type of contact exempted from the Rule as 'authorized by law.' " Therefore, *Balter* makes clear that pre-indictment non-custodial interrogations by Government agents do not violate the no-contact rule because such contacts are authorized by law.

With the exception of the Second Circuit, every other court of appeals that has considered the issue has similarly held that the no-contact rule does not prevent non-custodial pre-indictment communications by undercover agents with represented parties which occur in the course of legitimate criminal investigations. * * *

Moreover, such a reading is consistent with the intentions of the authors of the original no-contact rule. The commentary to American Bar Association Model Rule of Professional [Conduct] 4.2 states the following:

Communications authorized by law also include constitutionally permissible investigative activities of lawyers representing governmental entities, directly or through investigative agents, prior to the commencement of criminal or civil enforcement proceedings, when there is an applicable judicial precedent that either has found the activity permissible under this Rule or has found this Rule inapplicable. However, the Rule imposes ethical restrictions that go beyond those imposed by constitutional provisions.

Because there is caselaw indicating that AUSA Daniel's pre-indictment investigation was permitted pursuant to the no-contact rule, according to the commentary to the Model Rule, his conduct was "authorized by law" so long as it was constitutionally permissible. Defendants do not contend that the Government's actions here violated their Fifth or Sixth Amendment rights to have counsel present. Nor could they present a credible argument regarding either. Noonan's interrogation, if any, did not take place in a custodial setting nor were Defendants compelled to speak to Noonan. Thus, Defendants' Fifth Amendment right to counsel was not implicated. Additionally, Noonan recorded the conversations with Defendants before the initiation of adversarial proceedings; placing those contacts outside the scope of the Sixth Amendment right to counsel. Nor is there any allegation that AUSA Daniel authorized Noonan to engage in more egregious conduct which might constitute a due process violation. Thus, because AUSA Daniel's conduct did not violate Defendants' constitutional rights, in addition to the fact that there is a significant body of caselaw indicating that such conduct is not prohibited by the no-contact rule, it must be that his conduct was "authorized by law."

In support of their contention that AUSA Daniel violated Rule 4.2, Defendants rely primarily on the Second Circuit's decision in United States v. Hammad, 858 F.2d 834 (2d Cir.1988). In that case–on facts somewhat similar to those in the instant matter–the court initially rejected the Government's contention that the no-contact rule only applied to the same extent as the Sixth Amendment right to counsel; *i.e.* only upon the initiation of formal legal proceedings. * * * Having determined that the no-contact rule applied to the Government attorney's pre-indictment conduct, the court went on to hold that, normally, the no-contact rule would not serve to prevent the Government from using confidential informants to elicit incriminating statements from parties that the Government knows to be represented by counsel. The court, however, went on to state the following:

> Notwithstanding this holding, however, we recognized that in some instances a government prosecutor may overstep the already broad powers of his office, and in doing so, violate the ethical precepts of [the no-contact rule]. In the present case, for example, the prosecutor's use of a counterfeit grand jury subpoena, bearing the purported seal of the district court and the false signature of the Clerk, was an improper and illegitimate stratagem. We will not countenance such a misuse of the name and power of the court. The employment of a specious and contrived subpoena is the sort of egregious misconduct that, even before the 6th amendment protections attach, violates [the no-contact rule] . . . .

> Notwithstanding requests for a bright-line rule, we decline to list all possible situations that may violate [the no-contact rule] . . . . As our holding above makes clear, however, use of informants by government prosecutors in a pre-indictment, non-custodial situation, *absent the type of egregious misconduct that occurred in this case,* will generally fall within the "authorized by law" exception to [the no-contact rule] and therefore will not be subject to sanctions. (emphasis added)

Thus, it appears that the court, in *Hammad,* was more concerned with curbing prosecutorial skullduggeries than it was with preventing the use of government informants to obtain incriminating statements from parties represented by counsel in the pre-indictment non-custodial setting.

Defendants, however, argue that the no-contact rule bars the introduction of the Noonan tapes because "[t]he facts in *Hammad* almost precisely parallel the facts of this case." Like the Government attorney in *Hammad*, AUSA Daniel used fake documents and had his informant falsely indicate to the targets of the investigation that the informant himself was still under investigation. Thus, according to Defendants, "Daniel's actions are clear cut violations of Rules 4.2 and 8.4(a)."

The court disagrees both with Defendants' interpretation of the facts in this case and the weight it gives to the *Hammad* decision. Although the Second Circuit, in *Hammad*, held that the use of fake documents places a prosecutor's conduct outside of the authorized by law exception to the no-contact rule, that portion of the *Hammad* decision is inapplicable in the instant matter. First, AUSA Daniel did not employ a counterfeit grand jury subpoena bearing the forged signature of the Clerk of Court as the Government prosecutor in *Hammad* did. Instead, AUSA Daniel simply drew up a fake agenda letter addressed to Noonan's attorney and signed by AUSA Daniel himself. This document was fake only insofar as there was no pending interview between the Government and Noonan scheduled for April of 2001, as indicated in the letter. By the time AUSA Daniel had written this letter, Noonan was already cooperating with the Government. At the hearing, Noonan testified that the Government fabricated the letter for Noonan to use during his meeting with Defendant Brown. Although preparing and presenting such a letter to an unwitting criminal suspect involves a certain level of dishonesty, it certainly does not rise to the level of employing a sham grand jury subpoena. Second, even if the court were to find that this practice was equivalent to the prosecutor's actions in *Hammad*, the Third Circuit has long held that the use of a fabricated grand jury subpoena "to protect a cover in an ongoing undercover investigation" does not constitute prosecutorial misconduct. United States v. Martino, 825 F.2d 754 (3d Cir.1987). Given that the holding in *Hammad* explicitly relied on the finding of prosecutorial misconduct, the court finds its applicability to the instant matter limited based on the fact that no prosecutorial misconduct occurred here.

Defendants also argue that a finding that AUSA Daniel's conduct in this case is "authorized by law" would allow the exception to swallow Rule 4.2's prohibition against contact with represented parties. Moreover, according to Defendants, such a ruling would eviscerate the purpose of the McDade amendments; that is, making the no-contact rule explicitly applicable to the conduct of Government attorneys. In support of their position, Defendants cite the following passage from United States v. Lopez, 765 F.Supp. 1433 (N.D.Cal.1991):

> Were this court to accept the Department's argument in this regard, it is not clear that there would *any* conduct the prosecutor could not undertake, as long as it was pursuant to his or her responsibility to investigate and prosecute crimes. [Department of Justice] attorneys would be exempt from rules adopted by federal courts to govern

ethical conduct of attorneys practicing before them. This, quite simply, is an unacceptable result.

Lopez, however, is readily distinguishable from the facts in this case. That case involved multiple defendants who had already been indicted on various drug charges. Apparently, an attorney for one of Lopez's co-defendants contacted Lopez and encouraged him to engage in plea negotiations with the Government without having his attorney present. Once these protracted negotiations broke down and the Government's conduct came to light, Lopez's attorney withdrew from the case. Lopez subsequently moved to have the indictment dismissed because, he alleged, the Government attorney violated the no-contact rule. The District Court agreed and granted the motion. In doing so, it made two specific holdings. First, attorneys representing the Federal Government are not exempt from state rules of professional responsibility. Second, post-indictment contacts by Government attorneys are not "authorized by law." The first of these holdings is unexceptional after the enactment of the McDade Amendment. The second is irrelevant to the instant matter because it is beyond dispute that Defendants were not indicted until well over a year after Noonan's last recording took place. Therefore, to the extent Defendants rely on *Lopez* for the proposition that it would impermissibly stretch the no-contact rule to hold that the Government's conduct in this case was authorized by law, the court finds that *Lopez* is neither instructive, nor relevant to that point.

The McDade Amendment's lone function was to make state rules of professional responsibility applicable to the conduct of Government attorneys. That legislation did not state what those rules were, nor did it amend the well-established contours of those rules. Therefore, as it applies in this case, the McDade Amendment makes it clear only that Rules 4.2 and 8.4(a) applied to AUSA Daniel's conduct. Those rules prohibit attorneys, or their agents, from contacting parties that are represented by counsel unless such contact is authorized by law. As previously stated, AUSA Daniel's conduct was authorized by law and, thus, did not violate the Pennsylvania Rules of Professional Conduct. Defendants, however, contend that such a reading would allow the exception to swallow the rule, thus weakening the purpose behind the McDade Amendment. However, Defendants fail to recognize that the exception is part and parcel of Rule 4.2. Therefore, the McDade Amendment made the entire Rule 4.2, including the authorized by law exception, applicable to the conduct of Government attorneys. To adopt Defendants' argument would be tantamount to reading the McDade Amendment as amending all fifty states' rules of professional responsibility as they apply to Government attorneys. Absent a clear indication from Congress that it intended to do so, the court will not read such an awesome power into the McDade Amendment's humble command that attorneys for the Government "shall be subject to State laws and rules ... governing attorneys in each State . . . to the extent and in the same manner as other attorneys in that State." 28 U.S.C. § 530B(a).

Moreover, reading the McDade Amendment according to Defendants' interpretation raises serious public policy concerns regarding the fairness of the judicial system. It is axiomatic that criminal defendants' trial rights should not depend on the extent of their financial resources. Yet, adopting a rule that the McDade Amendment prohibits the Government from contacting any person known to be represented by counsel in any way whatsoever, will insulate from undercover investigation any defendant with enough financial resources to permanently obtain private counsel. Such a rule would dramatically impugn the integrity of the judiciary; not to mention the crippling effect it would have on the Government's ability to investigate on-going criminal activity. Although Defendants argue that such a contention is irrelevant, it would ignore reality to deny the very real consequences that Defendants' interpretation would have on the day-to-day administration of justice.

[The District Court concluded that "[e]ven assuming that the court were to find that AUSA Daniel violated Rule 4.2 of the Pennsylvania Rules of Professional Conduct, the court doubts that suppression of the Noonan tapes is a proper remedy for such a violation."]

NOTE

When a corporation is the target of an investigation, can its counsel represent both the organization and the individual employees, at least during the investigation? While there may be a conflict of interest in a joint representation after an indictment, discussed in the next section, the company has a strong interest in having its counsel present for any contacts with the government because the employees' statements can be used to establish the company's criminal liability. In In re Criminal Investigation of John Doe, Inc., 194 F.R.D. 375 (D. Mass. 2000), the district court granted the government's ex parte motion for an order permitting it to contact three employees of a corporation that was represented by counsel. The court noted that "[i]n such an unsettled legal wilderness, government counsel should not be placed in a position of being handcuffed in pursuing a valid criminal investigation for fear of being personally at risk." The court did require the prosecutor to avoid speaking with the employees about privileged information and to inform them that they can elect to have a personal attorney or the corporation's counsel present during an interview.

In **United States v. Taleo**, 222 F.3d 1133 (9th Cir. 2000), the government subpoenaed a corporation's bookkeeper, Ferrer, to testify about wrongdoing by the corporation and its controlling shareholders. The corporation's attorney informed the government that he represented the corporation and all of its employees, and met with Ferrer prior to her testimony. In addition, the controlling shareholders allegedly told Ferrer to "stick with the story" in her grand jury testimony. On the date of her grand jury testimony, Ferrer initiated contact with the Assistant U.S. Attorney and said that she did not want the corporation's attorney to represent her and that "she did not believe she could" tell the truth if the attorney were present. After being interviewed by the prosecutor, she testified before the grand jury. After the indictment of the corporation and its controlling shareholders, the district court refused to dismiss the indictment because of the prosecutor's conduct, but did find that prosecutor violated the California Rule 2-100, which is the counterpart of Rule 4.2. On the issue of the district court's finding that the prosecutor acted unethically in meeting with a "represented party," the Ninth Circuit stated:

> Under the circumstances of this case, we conclude that Rule 2- 100 did not prohibit Harris's conduct. Despite the apparent conundrum created by Ferrer's dual role as employee/party and witness, the interests in the internal integrity of and public confidence in the judicial system weigh heavily in favor of the conclusion that Harris' conduct was at all times ethical. We deem manifest that when an employee/party of a defendant corporation initiates communications with an attorney for the government for the purpose of disclosing that corporate officers are attempting to suborn perjury and obstruct justice, Rule 2-100 does not bar discussions between the employee and the attorney. Indeed, under these circumstances, an automatic, uncritical application of Rule 2-100 would effectively defeat its goal of protecting the administration of justice. It decidedly would not add meaningfully to the protection of the attorney-client relationship if subornation of perjury, or the attempt thereof, is imminent or probable.
>
> Few, if any, unethical acts by counsel are more heinous than subornation of perjury. It would be an anomaly to allow the subornation of perjury to be cloaked by an ethical rule, particularly one manifestly concerned with the administration of justice. As commentators have noted with regard to the crime-fraud exception to the attorney-client privilege, "[s]ince the policy of the privilege is that of promoting the administration of justice, it would be a perversion of the privilege to extend it to the client who seeks advice to aid him in carrying out the illegal or fraudulent scheme." In a similar vein, it would be a perversion of the rule against ex parte contacts to extend it to protect corporate officers who would suborn perjury by their employees.
>
> Appellees maintain that application of Rule 2-100 is necessary here in order to protect the attorney-client relationship between the corporation and its counsel. We are keenly aware that assuring the proper functioning of the attorney-client relationship is an important rationale behind the rule. Again, however, like the attorney-client privilege, the prohibition against ex parte contacts protects that relationship at the expense of "the full and free discovery of the truth." For that reason, the attorney-client privilege "applies only where necessary to achieve its purpose." When a

corporate employee/witness comes forward to disclose attempts by the corporation's officers to coerce her to give false testimony, the prohibition against ex parte contacts does little to support an appropriate attorney-client relationship. Once the employee makes known her desire to give truthful information about potential criminal activity she has witnessed, a clear conflict of interest exists between the employee and the corporation. Under these circumstances, corporate counsel cannot continue to represent both the employee and the corporation.

F. CONFLICTS OF INTEREST

1. Concurrent Representation

Federal Rule of Criminal Procedure 44(c) requires a court to promptly inquire about the propriety of joint representation of defendants in the same criminal case to insure each defendant's right to effective assistance of counsel is protected. The Rule presumes the likelihood of a conflict of interest arising from a joint representation by providing that "[u]nless there is good cause to believe that no conflict of interest is likely to arise, the court must take appropriate measures to protect each defendant's right to counsel." In **Mickens v. Taylor**, 122 S.Ct. 1237 (2002), the Supreme Court noted the distinction between Rule 44's application to conflicts arising from concurrent and prior representation:

> Thus, the Federal Rules of Criminal Procedure treat concurrent representation and prior representation differently, requiring a trial court to inquire into the likelihood of conflict whenever jointly charged defendants are represented by a single attorney (Rule 44(c)), but not when counsel previously represented another defendant in a substantially related matter, even where the trial court is aware of the prior representation.

2. Waiver

To what extent is a court required to accept a defendant's waiver of a conflict of interest, especially a concurrent conflict? In **Wheat v. United States**, 486 U.S. 153 (1988), the defendant selected counsel who also represented two other members of a large drug importation conspiracy. The government sought to disqualify counsel–who happened to have won an acquittal of the alleged kingpin in an earlier trial–on the ground that there was a potentially serious conflict of interest because the government planned to call one of the other clients to testify against the defendant. Although all three clients of the attorney were willing to waive any conflict of interest, the Supreme Court held even an apparently intelligent and knowing waiver does not preclude ordering disqualification where a serious potential for conflict exists. The Supreme Court noted that while a defendant usually has a right to the counsel of choice, that right does not overcome the government's interest in the trial untainted by a conflict of interest. The Court stated:

> Petitioner insists that the provision of waivers by all affected defendants cures any problems created by the multiple representation. But no such flat rule can be deduced from the Sixth Amendment presumption in favor of counsel of choice. Federal courts have an independent interest in ensuring that criminal trials are conducted within the ethical standards of the profession and that legal proceedings appear fair to all who observe them.

The *Wheat* Court also cited the difficulties presented in obtaining a truly knowledgeable waiver at a pretrial stage. The Court then concluded:

> For these reasons we think the District Court must be allowed substantial latitude in refusing waivers of conflicts of interest not only in those rare cases where an actual conflict may be demonstrated before trial, but in the more common cases where a potential for conflict exists which may or may not burgeon into an actual conflict as the trial progresses.

Wheat, of course, was dealing with waivers by persons already charged. Should a waiver be given more, less, or the same weight where the persons seeking to waive simply are grand jury witnesses or targets?

UNITED STATES v. MALPIEDI
62 F.3d 465 (2nd Cir. 1995)

WINTER, Circuit Judge.

Stephen Delli Bovi appeals from his convictions by a jury * * * for fraud and obstruction of justice. He argues that his trial counsel rendered constitutionally ineffective assistance due to a conflict of interest arising from counsel's previous representation of an important government witness.

Delli Bovi was convicted of two counts of wire fraud in violation of 18 U.S.C. § 1343, five counts of interstate transportation of checks taken by fraud in violation of 18 U.S.C. § 2314, and one count of obstruction of justice in violation of 18 U.S.C. § 1503. The fraud charges arose out of an alleged kickback scheme in which Delli Bovi, an outside contractor, submitted inflated invoices to the Twenty-First Century Corporation and shared the illicit profits with certain executives of that company. The obstruction of justice charge concerned certain checking records that had been subpoenaed by a grand jury from one of Delli Bovi's companies. A number of cancelled checks did not match copies retained by the bank when the checks were cashed, allegedly because they had been altered before being turned over to the grand jury.

At trial, Susan Goldfine, Delli Bovi's sister-in-law and part-time secretary and the daughter of two co-defendants, was an important government witness. Goldfine testified that she saw Delli Bovi alter check stubs when she assisted him in gathering documents in response to the grand jury subpoena. This testimony was direct evidence of Delli Bovi's obstruction of justice and of his consciousness of guilt of the other charges.

In an appearance before the grand jury, Goldfine had testified as a custodian of records to authenticate the subpoenaed documents, including the altered checking records. Prior to testifying, Goldfine had reviewed copies of the documents in the office of Delli Bovi's attorney, John Kelly. Kelly then accompanied Goldfine to the grand jury, waiting outside the grand jury room until her appearance had been completed. Goldfine considered Kelly to be her lawyer. She later stated that she had asked Kelly questions about the grand jury proceedings and that he answered those questions.

In her testimony before the grand jury, Goldfine falsely claimed not to recognize Delli Bovi's handwriting. She also gave testimony regarding the collection of documents in response to the grand jury subpoena. This testimony failed to disclose any tampering with the documents by Delli Bovi.

More than a year later and after being granted immunity, Goldfine made a second grand jury appearance in which Kelly did not represent her. On this occasion, she testified that she did not know what the initials "BG" stood for when they were in fact a reference to her father, who was then under indictment in connection with the kickback scheme. She again failed to mention Delli Bovi's tampering with the documents, although a direct question on that subject was not asked.

The government decided to call Goldfine as a witness in Delli Bovi's trial to testify as to routine custodial matters. After this decision was made and some weeks before trial, Goldfine disclosed to the government that she had seen Delli Bovi alter the documents. Her importance as a government witness was thus greatly enhanced. Nevertheless, the government failed to alert the district judge to Kelly's role in Goldfine's first grand jury appearance until the morning that Goldfine was to testify. At that point, the government informed the court that Goldfine would give "some fairly powerful testimony against [Delli Bovi]" and that "Mr. Kelly had represented her in the past." The delay in informing Judge Raggi appears not to have been an oversight but the result of the government's desire to use Kelly's prior representation of Goldfine to its advantage.[1] The government thus informed the district

---

[1] At oral argument, the government took the position that it delayed bringing Kelly's conflict to Judge Raggi's attention because it believed Kelly's assertion that he had not represented Goldfine. However, the prosecutor's statement to Judge Raggi indicated in the clearest fashion the government's understanding that Kelly had

court that it would elicit from Goldfine testimony that Kelly had represented her at the first grand jury appearance. It hoped that evidence of her close association with Kelly and Delli Bovi would "bolster her testimony and lend credence to it."

Kelly claimed he did not raise the matter earlier because he believed that he had no attorney-client relationship with Goldfine and that she was therefore "fair game" for cross-examination. Judge Raggi was understandably displeased that she had not been informed of this problem earlier.

Before Goldfine testified, the government and the defense agreed that Kelly would question Goldfine only about whether she was alone with the documents in a conference room while preparing for the first grand jury appearance and that the government would elicit from her only that Kelly had accompanied her to that proceeding. Nevertheless, Kelly's cross-examination of Goldfine strayed into detailed questions concerning the first grand jury appearance. Judge Raggi interrupted Kelly's cross-examination and, outside the presence of the jury, conducted an inquiry into the nature of Kelly's representation of Goldfine. Kelly stated that "in [his] mind," he was never Goldfine's lawyer. However, Goldfine stated that Kelly had answered her questions about the grand jury proceeding and that she had believed that Kelly was her lawyer.

Judge Raggi then chastised Kelly for not recognizing that he had "an ethical problem." In response, Kelly stated, "Judge, I will certainly move away from that at this point," apparently a reference to the line of questioning about Goldfine's first grand jury appearance.

Goldfine, through another lawyer, thereafter invoked the attorney-client privilege. Judge Raggi prohibited Kelly from making arguments about Goldfine's testimony in the first grand jury proceeding, forbidding him from using "any of the evidence that was developed because Mr. Kelly represented Ms. Goldfine in any way to suggest wrongdoing on her part. He owes her . . . the loyalty of an attorney representing a client during that period of time." Kelly agreed to limit his argument, but stated:

> But there—the one thing I'd—I keep getting into hot water—that I wanted to touch upon now is, I was intending, and I guess I'm asking for guidance on this, to use her first grand jury testimony for impeachment purposes in terms of her being asked about—there were a couple of questions about her collecting the records and her being with Stephen Delli Bovi and what they did at that time. There is no mention certainly of records being changed or her observing anything Mr. Delli Bovi did.

---

represented Goldfine.

After further discussion with the court and Goldfine's counsel, Kelly agreed not to cross-examine Goldfine about her first grand jury appearance and stated that cross-examination about the second grand jury appearance would suffice.

During the proceedings described above, the district court and the parties focused exclusively on Goldfine's attorney-client privilege. Delli Bovi's right to conflict-free counsel was not raised until the end of the trial day when Judge Raggi inquired whether Delli Bovi was satisfied with Kelly's cross-examination of Goldfine. Although Delli Bovi responded that he was satisfied, it is undisputed that this was not a valid waiver under United States v. Curcio, 680 F.2d 881 (2d Cir.1982).[2]

After his conviction, Delli Bovi, represented by new counsel, informed the district court that he would appeal on the ground that Kelly's conflict of interest deprived Delli Bovi of effective assistance of counsel. Judge Raggi suggested that Delli Bovi pursue this claim first as a motion for a new trial, so that a record could be developed in the district court. The parties agreed to this suggestion, and the district court conducted an evidentiary hearing at which Kelly testified.

After the hearing, Judge Raggi read her findings into the record. The district court found Kelly to be a "totally credible" witness at the hearing and credited his testimony that he had made a strategic decision not to cross-examine Goldfine about the first grand jury appearance. The district court determined that Kelly's representation of Delli Bovi was not adversely affected by the conflict because (i) Kelly's cross-examination of Goldfine was, over all, very effective, (ii) Kelly was able to "indirectly" establish that Goldfine's grand jury testimony was inconsistent with her testimony at trial, (iii) Kelly effectively impeached Goldfine with other evidence that was stronger than the grand jury testimony, and (iv) Kelly established that Goldfine had lied in the second grand jury proceeding, rendering her lies in the first proceeding cumulative for the purposes of impeaching her

---

[2] In United States v. Levy, 25 F.3d 146 (2nd Cir.1994), we stated that once a district court is apprised of even a possible conflict of interest, it is obligated to investigate the conflict. If the court determines that an actual or potential conflict exists, it must either (i) disqualify the defense attorney if the conflict is so severe that no rational defendant could knowingly and intelligently desire that lawyer's representation, or (ii) secure a valid waiver under Curcio. Here, the district court fulfilled its inquiry obligation by questioning Kelly and Goldfine about the nature of their previous relationship. However, there was no Curcio hearing. In United States v. Iorizzo, 786 F.2d 52 (2nd Cir.1986), we summarized the requirements of Curcio as applicable in the context of the present case. Curcio requires the district court to (i) advise the defendant of the dangers arising from the particular conflict and ascertain that he or she understands the risks involved, (ii) encourage the defendant to seek advice from independent counsel and provide time to digest and contemplate the risks, and (iii) secure a knowing waiver of the right to conflict-free counsel before proceeding.

credibility. Accordingly, the district court denied Delli Bovi's motion for a new trial. This appeal followed.

The principles to be applied are familiar ones. Every defendant is entitled to "representation that is free from conflicts of interest." Wood v. Georgia, 450 U.S. 261 (1981). An actual, as opposed to a potential, conflict of interest exists "when, during the course of the representation, the attorney's and defendant's interests 'diverge with respect to a material factual or legal issue or to a course of action.'" Winkler v. Keane, 7 F.3d 304 (2d Cir.1993) (*quoting* Cuyler v. Sullivan, 446 U.S. 335 (1980)).

In the instant matter, Kelly had an actual conflict of interest because his duty to Goldfine conflicted with Delli Bovi's interest in a full and effective cross-examination of Goldfine. Goldfine was a key government witness. Her testimony as to document tampering was direct evidence of obstruction of justice and also demonstrated Delli Bovi's consciousness of guilt of the other charges. It was therefore in Delli Bovi's interest to have his attorney conduct a thorough, no-holds-barred cross-examination of Goldfine. Kelly was unable to cross-examine Goldfine on her testimony during her first grand jury appearance because of his obligations as her prior attorney and her invocation of the attorney-client privilege.

Although a defendant generally is required to demonstrate prejudice to prevail on a claim of ineffective assistance of counsel, prejudice is presumed when counsel is burdened by an actual conflict of interest.[c] This presumption is "fairly rigid." Moreover, "once the defendant establishes that there was an actual conflict, he need not prove prejudice, but simply that a 'lapse in representation' resulted from the conflict." *Iorizzo*. To prove a lapse in representation, a defendant must "demonstrate that some 'plausible alternative defense strategy or tactic might have been pursued,' and that the 'alternative defense was inherently in conflict with or not undertaken due to the attorney's other loyalties or interests.'" *Levy*.

This is not a test that requires a defendant to show that the alternative strategy or tactic not adopted by a conflicted counsel was reasonable, that the lapse in representation affected the outcome of the trial, or even that, but for the conflict, counsel's conduct of the trial would have been different. Rather, it is enough to show that a conflict existed that "was inherently in conflict with" a plausible line of defense or attack on the prosecution's case. *Levy*. Once such a showing is made, [the] "fairly rigid" presumption of prejudice applies.

---

[c] In Mickens v. Taylor, 535 U.S. 162 (2002), the Supreme Court noted that the presumption of prejudice may not apply to a successive conflict of interest rather than an actual, concurrent conflict of the type that occurred in *Malpiedi*. See WAYNE R. LAFAVE, JEROLD H. ISRAEL, NANCY J. KING, & ORIN S. KERR, CRIMINAL PROCEDURE 3D § 11.9(d)(2007).

The test is a strict one because a defendant has a right to an attorney who can make strategic and tactical choices free from any conflict of interest. An attorney who is prevented from pursuing a strategy or tactic because of the canons of ethics is hardly an objective judge of whether that strategy or tactic is sound trial practice. Counsel's inability to make such a conflict-free decision is itself a lapse in representation.

We do not exclude, of course, the possibility that a foregone strategy or tactic may be so insubstantial that even the most ardent and talented, conflict-free advocate would likely have avoided it. Nor do we exclude the possibility that the foregone strategy or tactic might be so clearly against the defendant's interest that unconflicted counsel would never pursue it. Under such circumstances, we would conclude that no lapse of representation occurred.

Moreover, we emphasize that the government can protect itself by informing the district judge of potential conflicts at the earliest possible moment. The court can then secure a waiver under *Curcio* or disqualify defense counsel under *Levy*. The government can itself seek to disqualify defense counsel because of a conflict. Indeed, it frequently does so.

Cross-examination of Goldfine about testimony at her first grand jury appearance was a tactic that was entirely plausible but barred by Kelly's conflict of interest. The record clearly shows that Kelly began this line of cross-examination, and the district court quite properly interrupted him. Kelly stated that he wished to impeach Goldfine's testimony with her testimony before the first grand jury but needed guidance from the court. When the court's reaction was decidedly negative, Kelly retreated. The foregone opportunity involved cross-examination regarding not only Goldfine's failure to give the grand jury the damaging testimony she offered at trial, but also her perjury regarding Delli Bovi's handwriting.

Even if we accept Kelly's testimony that he had strategic reasons for not cross-examining Goldfine about her first grand jury appearance–an assertion not entirely reconcilable with his seeking a ruling from the court on the matter–Delli Bovi had a right to a lawyer who could make strategic and tactical decisions free from any conflict of interest. Kelly was clearly in no position to make an objective, professional decision regarding cross-examination as to Goldfine's first grand jury testimony. Indeed, that option was not his to exercise.[d]

---

[d] The events here were largely a replay of *Iorizzo* by both the defense and the government. We trust that it will not take yet another decision of this court to induce counsel for a potential defendant to refrain from assisting or accompanying a witness who testifies before an investigatory tribunal looking into the client's conduct. We also trust that it will not take another decision to induce the government to bring any conflict of interest to the district court's attention, rather than remaining silent in order to gain a tactical advantage from that conflict.

We give no weight to the post-trial hearing or findings regarding the need for cross-examination on Goldfine's first grand jury appearance or Kelly's thought processes in that regard. First, the applicable standard requires only the demonstration of a conflict inconsistent with a plausible trial strategy or tactic. Cross-examination regarding Goldfine's failure to mention document tampering and her perjury as to Delli Bovi's handwriting, even if not mandatory, was certainly a plausible strategy. Second, after-the-fact testimony by a lawyer who was precluded by a conflict of interest from pursuing a strategy or tactic is not helpful. Even the most candid persons may be able to convince themselves that they actually would not have used that strategy or tactic anyway, when the alternative is a confession of ineffective assistance resulting from ethical limitations. * * * We therefore vacate the judgment of conviction and remand for further proceedings.

3. Strategic Removal of Defense Counsel

In *Wheat,* the Supreme Court took note of the possibility that the government "may seek to 'manufacture' a conflict in order to prevent a defendant from having a particularly able defense counsel", stating that this was a factor "to be taken into consideration along with all other factors which inform this sort of decision." Should the government be seen as "manufacturing" a conflict when counsel is representing two targets and the government offers one leniency if that person will testify against the other? Can such a situation be handled without full disqualification, by having the witness seek the advice of a different attorney as to acceptance of the offer, and then allowing the original counsel to resume representation if the offer is rejected?

On occasion, prosecutors have maintained that courts may bar multiple representation where counsel has represented a large group of grand jury witnesses and has led them to take a united position of refusing to testify on self-incrimination grounds. See, e.g., Pirillo v. Takiff, 341 A.2d 896 (Pa. 1975) (disqualifying an attorney, paid by the policeman's fraternal order, who represented all 12 police officers subpoenaed to testify before grand jury investigating police corruption, where all 12 relied upon the privilege). The argument here is that though witnesses are free to choose independently to subscribe to a joint "stonewalling" strategy, that strategy, because it threatens the effectiveness of the grand jury's investigation, should not be facilitated by multiple representation, which naturally leads the lawyer to treat the clients as a group and to insist upon a group strategy. The few federal courts that have considered disqualification motions in such "stonewalling cases" have frowned upon this argument, and have refused to disqualify in the absence of a specific showing of conflicting interests among the clients. See, e.g., In re Investigation Before April 1975 Grand Jury, 531 F.2d 600 (D.C.Cir. 1976); Matter of Abrams, 465 N.E.2d 1 (N.Y. 1984) ("disqualification of an attorney representing multiple witnesses * * * may never be ordered if the sole reason for the request is to allow the prosecutor * * * to pit the witnesses against each other so the maximum amount of testimony can be obtained while granting the least amount of immunity"). In In re Grand Jury Investigation, 182 F.3d 668 (9th Cir. 1999), the district court disqualified an attorney who represented multiple witnesses in a grand jury investigation after the government designated certain of them as "targets." The Ninth Circuit refused to consider the appeal of the disqualification order because it was a "collateral order" and therefore unappealable until there was a final judgment in the case.

There is a danger in seeking to disqualify defense counsel if an appellate court determines that the removal violated the defendant's counsel of choice. The Supreme Court explained in **United States v. Gonzalez-Lopez**, 548 U.S. 140 (2006), that the Sixth Amendment's guarantee of the right to counsel of choice is not simply to ensure that a defendant receives a fair trial. In *Gonzalez-Lopez*, the district court erroneously refused to permit defendant's retained counsel to appear at trial pro hac vice, thus requiring him to retain a local attorney. Although new counsel was not found to be ineffective at the trial, the defendant asserted that the judge's improper refusal to permit his chosen attorney to represent him was a constitutional violation regardless of whether he was prejudiced by the decision. The Court stated:

> [The Sixth Amendment] commands, not that a trial be fair, but that a particular guarantee of fairness be provided-to wit, that the accused be defended by the counsel he believes to be best. "The Constitution guarantees a fair trial through the Due Process Clauses, but it defines the basic elements of a fair trial largely through the several provisions of the Sixth Amendment, including the Counsel Clause." Strickland [v. Washington, 466 U.S. 668 (1984)]. In sum, the right at stake here is the right to counsel of choice, not the right to a fair trial; and that right was violated because the deprivation of counsel was erroneous. No additional showing of prejudice is required to make the violation "complete." * * *

> The right to select counsel of one's choice, by contrast, has never been derived from the Sixth Amendment's purpose of ensuring a fair trial. It has been regarded as the root meaning of the constitutional guarantee. See Wheat. Where the right to be assisted by counsel of one's choice is wrongly denied, therefore, it is unnecessary to conduct an ineffectiveness or prejudice inquiry to establish a Sixth Amendment violation. Deprivation of the right is "complete" when the defendant is erroneously prevented from being represented by the lawyer he wants, regardless of the quality of the representation he received. To argue otherwise is to confuse the right to counsel of choice–which is the right to a particular lawyer regardless of comparative effectiveness–with the right to effective counsel–which imposes a baseline requirement of competence on whatever lawyer is chosen or appointed.

The remedy for a violation of the right to counsel is automatic reversal of the conviction, and the defendant need not show prejudice from the removal of the counsel of choice. At the same time, the majority noted that the decision did not limit "previous holdings that limit the right to counsel of choice and recognize the authority of trial courts to establish criteria for admitting lawyers to argue before the." The right to counsel of choice does not extend to defendants who require appointed counsel, and a defendant cannot "insist on representation by a person who is not a member of the bar, or demand that a counsel honor his waiver of conflict free representation." *Gonzalez-Lopez* was not "about a court's powers to enforce rules or adhere to practices that determine which attorneys may appear before it, or to make schedule and other decisions that effectively exclude a defendant's first choice of counsel."

4. Attorney Participation in the Conduct

If there is a possibility that the attorney participated in the misconduct under investigation or the subject of an indictment, then counsel likely has a conflict of interest because the range of defenses that can be raised at trial would be limited if any of them implicated the attorney. See United States v. Hanna, 207 F.Supp.2d 45 (E.D.N.Y. 2002) (disqualifying counsel in a securities fraud prosecution when the law firm had advised the brokerage firm controlled by the defendants on their compliance with the securities laws, and the lawyer had "a strong personal interest in avoiding criminal prosecution, civil lawsuits, professional sanctions and harm to reputation arising from" his representation of the broker). In United States v. Matta-Timmins, 81 F.Supp.2d 193 (D. Mass. 2000), the district court denied the government's motion to disqualify counsel because the potential conflict was "too remote" when counsel received funds from the defendant that might be subject to forfeiture if the defendant were convicted. The court also found that the defendant's waiver of any conflict was effective at the pre-trial stage, but noted that an actual conflict "might arise if Matta-Timmins decided to plead guilty to money laundering counts, thereby subjecting [attorney] Thornton's attorney's fee to civil or criminal forfeiture."

5. Conflicts From Joint Defense Agreements

As discussed in Chapter 15, a group of defendants in an investigation may enter into a joint defense agreement under which the communications by any one member with any attorney will be privileged. The issue raises significant conflict of interest questions, especially if the attorney must maintain the confidentiality of the information and cannot use it to cross-examine the cooperating witness. ABA Model Rule of Professional Conduct 1.9(a) provides, "A lawyer who has formerly represented a client in a matter shall not thereafter represent another person in the same or a substantially related matter in which that person's interests are materially adverse to the interests of the former client unless the former client gives informed consent, confirmed in writing." Could the government make it a condition of a cooperation agreement that the former member of the joint defense refuse to give the consent required by Rule 1.9(a)? Would that constitute the type of strategic conduct manufacturing a conflict that the Supreme Court said in *Wheat* that a court should consider in disqualifying an attorney? Would the agreement show that the government acted in bad faith?

For a detailed discussion of the prosecution and defense views on conflicts created by joint defense agreements see Ronald J. Nessim & Paul L. Seave, *Conflicts and Confidences: Does Conflict of Interest Kill the Joint Defense Privilege?* 7 Crim. Justice 6 (1992). Ronald J. Nessim, representing the defense view, states, "[e]ven if there is a conflict when a defendant's attorney examines a witness from whom he or she received confidential joint defense communications, withdrawal or disqualification of the attorney should never be the remedy." In contrast, Paul L. Seave, taking the prosecution view, argues for use of conflict of interest rules concerning confidential information. He states that when inconsistent theories develop between the parties to a joint defense agreement, "[t]he conflict of interest rules * * * require that the attorneys for defendants demonstrate that they were not privy to the confidences (if any) previously communicated by the parties who now stand ready to testify for the government." Consider the court's resolution of the issue in the following.

UNITED STATES v. HENKE
222 F.3d 633 (9th Cir. 2000)

PER CURIAM.

Chan Desaigoudar and Steven Henke, former executives of California Micro Devices, Inc. ("Cal Micro"), appeal their convictions for conspiracy to make false statements to the Securities Exchange Commission, making false statements, securities fraud, and insider trading. * * *

The defendants claim that their convictions must be set aside because a conflict of interest prevented their counsel from cross-examining a key government witness and because there was insufficient evidence to support their insider trading convictions. * * * We agree with the defendants that a new trial is necessary because their lawyers' ability to conduct their defense was impaired by a conflict of interest.

This case arises from a false revenue reporting conspiracy carried out by Cal Micro executives in order to preserve the appearance that the company was a good investment option when in fact it was struggling financially. Cal Micro designs, manufactures, and markets electronic components and semiconductor products for the defense and electronics industries. The company was purchased in 1980 by Desaigoudar, who turned it into a multi-million dollar company during the 1980s. In addition to being Cal Micro's largest shareholder, Desaigoudar served as its Chief Executive Officer and Chairman of the Board until he was removed in 1994. * * *

Unable to close the widening gap between revenue targets and actual sales, some Cal Micro executives devised a plan to make it appear on paper that the company was meeting its financial goals. Under Cal Micro's stated revenue recognition policy, revenue was recognized when an order was shipped. These Cal Micro executives began to deviate from this practice in several ways. They started: (1) recognizing revenue when some orders were received, rather than when shipped; (2) shipping orders earlier than requested in order to recognize the revenue during a certain fiscal period; (3) sending unwanted shipments; (4) creating false orders; and (5) executing "title transfers" falsely reflecting that products stored at Cal Micro had been purchased by a client. * * *

Things then took a turn for the worse. Those involved began to worry about the implications of the revenue scheme. Moreover, the company's plan to write off several million dollars in "bad debts" caused Cal Micro's investment bankers to balk at a second public offering. The Board eventually instituted an investigation and ultimately ousted Desaigoudar.

Desaigoudar and Henke, a former Chief Financial Officer, Vice President, and Treasurer of Cal Micro, were indicted on charges of conspiracy, making false statements, securities fraud, and insider trading. Surendra Gupta, Cal Micro's President during the revenue reporting scheme, was also indicted, but reached a plea agreement with the government shortly before trial was to begin. The central issue at trial was whether the defendants had early knowledge of the false revenue reporting scheme and whether they traded their stock because of this inside information. Several of Cal Micro's executive officers, including former co-defendant Gupta, testified that the defendants did have such early knowledge. The jury believed the government's witnesses and convicted the defendants.

The defendants' principal claim is that they are entitled to a new trial because their attorneys worked under an actual conflict of interest that prohibited them from cross-examining one of the government's key witnesses, Gupta.

Before trial, Desaigoudar, Henke, and Gupta participated in joint defense meetings during which confidential information was discussed. Communications made during these pre-trial meetings were protected by the lawyers' duty of confidentiality imposed by a joint defense privilege agreement. Before trial was to begin, Gupta accepted a plea agreement and promised to testify for the government.

Desaigoudar's attorney then moved for a mistrial and to withdraw because his duty of confidentiality to Gupta under the joint defense agreement prevented him from cross-examining Gupta on matters involving information he learned as a result of the privileged pre-trial meetings. Henke's lawyer was also present at the joint defense meetings and felt that his duty to Gupta impaired his ability to adequately represent Henke.

The district court denied the motion to withdraw. It reasoned that any privileged impeaching information counsel learned about Gupta would not be known to new counsel and the defendants were therefore no worse off for being represented by their original attorneys. The court granted the motion for a mistrial to allow defense counsel to regroup after Gupta's plea.

Once the new trial began, Gupta testified for the government. Defense counsel conducted no cross-examination for fear that the examination would lead to inquiries into material covered by the joint defense privilege.

The issue for our decision is whether the government's use of a former defendant, with whom both Henke's and Desaigoudar's attorneys had an attorney-client relationship arising from a joint defense agreement, as a key witness at trial created a conflict of interest that impaired defense counsel's ability to defend their clients.

The joint defense privilege is an extension of the attorney-client privilege. It has been recognized by this Circuit since at least 1964. A joint defense agreement establishes an implied attorney-client relationship with the co-defendant, here between Henke's and Desaigoudar's attorneys and Gupta. *See* Wilson P. Abraham Constr. Corp. v. Armco Steel Corp., 559 F.2d 250 (5th Cir.1977). The government concedes in its brief the existence of this privilege in this case.

This privilege can also create a disqualifying conflict where information gained in confidence by an attorney becomes an issue, as it did in this case. As the court said in *Abraham Construction,*

> Just as an attorney would not be allowed to proceed against his former client in a cause of action substantially related to the matters in which he previously represented that client, an attorney should also not be allowed to proceed against a co-defendant of a former client wherein the subject matter of the present controversy is substantially related to the matters in which the attorney was previously involved, and wherein confidential exchanges of information took place between the various co-defendants in preparation of a joint defense.

Here, what Gupta allegedly said in confidence during pre-trial joint defense meetings about the defendants' presence at a critical meeting of Cal Micro executives was claimed to be at odds with his trial testimony for the government. This evidence put the two defense attorneys in a difficult position. Had they pursued the material discrepancy in some other way, a discrepancy they learned about in confidence, they could have been charged with using it against their one-time client Gupta. In fact, Gupta's lawyers had threatened Henke's and Desaigoudar's attorneys with legal action if they failed to protect Gupta's confidences. Here is the text of the letter received by defense counsel:

June 26, 1998

Re: U.S. v. Desaigoudar and Henke

Dear [attorneys for defendants Desaigoudar and Henke]:
It has come to our attention you may be contemplating filing an ex parte in camera submission to Judge Walker outlining what you contend are the contradictory statements made by Mr. Gupta in what you have conceded was a joint defense privileged meeting.

Please be advised that we do not, waive, and at no point ever have waived the joint defense privilege. Please be further advised that we are aware of no legal basis upon which you have any right to breach the privilege and that we reserve Mr. Gupta's right to pursue any and all appropriate legal remedies for any unauthorized breach of the privilege.

Please consider this letter as a formal objection to any ex parte in camera submissions to Judge Walker of any joint defense privileged information.

Yours very truly,
[Signed]
Attorneys for Suren Gupta

Under these circumstances, the district court erred in not fully acknowledging the conflict and then acting on its implications.

Nothing in our holding today is intended to suggest, however, that joint defense meetings are in and of themselves disqualifying. We stress that it was defense counsel in this case that timely moved for disqualification. As the Supreme Court said in Holloway v. Arkansas, the attorney "is in the best position professionally and ethically to determine when a conflict of interest exists or will probably develop in the course of a trial." 435 U.S. 475 (1978). There may be cases in which defense counsel's possession of information about a former co-defendant/government witness learned through joint defense meetings will not impair defense counsel's ability to represent the defendant or breach the duty of confidentiality to the former co-defendant. Here, however, counsel told the district court that this was not a situation where they could avoid reliance on the privileged information and still fully uphold their ethical duty to represent their clients. There is nothing in this record to suggest that the attorneys were doing anything other than attempting to adhere to their ethical duties as lawyers.

Few aspects of our criminal justice system are more vital to the assurance of fairness than the right to be defended by counsel, and this means counsel not burdened by a conflict of interest. Here, because of that conflict, the appellants' lawyers were constrained to impair yet another primary right of their clients: the right to cross-examine a witness who testified against them. By choosing to convert Gupta into a prospective witness shortly before the trial was scheduled to start, the government—which may not have anticipated this complication when it made a deal with Gupta—caused this problem, and should not now be heard to complain.

6. Limiting Joint Defense Agreement Conflicts

If a joint defense agreement creates a confidential relationship among the various defendants and their defense counsel, then there is a risk in every case that involves such an agreement that a large number of defense counsel will be disqualified if one member cooperates with the government. Can a court limit the scope of such agreements by requiring that a defendant participating in such agreements prospectively waive the right to confidentiality from counsel for other defendants? In **United States v. Stepney**, 246 F.Supp.2d 1069 (N.D. Cal. 2003), the district court required such a waiver as a condition to permitting them to participate in a joint defense agreement in a complex, multi-defendant case. The court relied on its supervisory power and the requirement of Federal Rule of Criminal Procedure 44(c) that a court protect against conflicts of interest arising from concurrent representation, to require defendants to prospectively waive any confidentiality claim against an attorney other than their own, explaining:

> The conditional waiver of confidentiality also provides notice to defendants that their confidences may be used in cross-examination, so that each defendant can choose with suitable caution what to reveal to the joint defense group. Although a limitation on confidentiality between a defendant and his own attorney would pose a severe threat to the true attorney-client relationship, making each defendant somewhat more guarded about the disclosures he makes to the joint defense effort does not significantly intrude on the function of joint defense agreements. The attorney-client privilege protects "full and frank" communication because the attorney serves as the client's liaison to the legal system. Without a skilled attorney, fully apprised of her client's situation, our adversarial system could not function. Any secret a client keeps from his own counsel compromises his counsel's ability to represent him effectively and undermines the purpose of the attorney-client privilege.
>
> Joint defense agreements, however, serve a different purpose. Each defendant entering a joint defense agreement already has a representative, fully and confidentially informed of the client's situation. The joint defense privilege allows defendants to share information so as to avoid unnecessarily inconsistent defenses that

undermine the credibility of the defense as a whole. In criminal cases where discovery is limited, such collaboration is necessary to assure a fair trial in the face of the prosecution's informational advantage gained through the power to gather evidence by searches and seizures. Co-defendants may eliminate inconsistent defenses without the same degree of disclosure that would be required for an attorney to adequately represent her client. The legitimate value of joint defense agreements will not be significantly diminished by including a limited waiver of confidentiality by testifying defendants for purposes of cross-examination only.

For the foregoing reasons, the Court rules as follows:

(1) Any joint defense agreement entered into by defendants must be committed to writing, signed by defendants and their attorneys, and submitted in camera to the court for review prior to going into effect.

(2) Each joint defense agreement submitted must explicitly state that it does not create an attorney-client relationship between an attorney and any defendant other than the client of that attorney. No joint defense agreement may purport to create a duty of loyalty.

(3) Each joint defense agreement must contain provisions conditionally waiving confidentiality by providing that a signatory attorney cross-examining any defendant who testifies at any proceeding, whether under a grant of immunity or otherwise, may use any material or other information contributed by such client during the joint defense.

(4) Each joint defense agreement must explicitly allow withdrawal upon notice to the other defendants.

The Eleventh Circuit adopted a waiver approach to the question of whether a joint defense agreement prevents a counsel for a defendant from cross-examining a former member of the joint defense team about otherwise confidential communications. In **United States v. Almeida**, 341 F.3d 1318 (11th Cir. 2003), the district court precluded counsel for the defendant from utilizing statements made by a cooperating witness when the witness was a participant in a joint defense agreement. The Eleventh Circuit reversed the conviction and found that the cooperating witness's decision to leave the joint defense agreement operated as an implied waiver of any privilege with counsel for other defendants:

While the privilege may be waived by the client, it is generally held that he does not do so merely by becoming a witness and testifying in his own behalf. But when one jointly indicted with others turns state's evidence, and attempts to convict others by testimony which also convicts himself, the rule must be different, and he has no right to claim any privilege concerning any of the facts pertinent to the issue, nor any exemption from the broadest latitude of cross-examination. He thereby waives all privilege against criminating himself, and against disclosing communications between himself and his counsel touching the offense charged. Both client and counsel may, in such case, be compelled to disclose such communications.

Both exceptions to the attorney-client privilege are open to criticism. By finding implied waivers, courts risk eroding the public's confidence that their communications will remain confidential so long as communicated to a lawyer. For this reason, we do not hold that accomplices always waive the privilege when they testify on behalf of the government; nor do we hold that persons represented by the same attorney always waive the privilege in the event that one of them becomes a government witness against the other. In the joint defense agreement context, however, the policy rationales behind the two exceptions outweigh the minimal benefit of the attorney-client privilege. As one court recently explained:

Although a limitation on confidentiality between a defendant and his own attorney would pose a severe threat to the true attorney-client relationship, making each defendant somewhat more guarded about the disclosures he makes to the joint defense effort does not significantly intrude on the function of joint defense agreements . . . .

"Co-defendants may eliminate inconsistent defenses without the same degree of disclosure that would be required for an attorney to adequately represent her client. The legitimate value of joint defense agreements will not be significantly diminished by including a limited waiver of confidentiality by testifying defendants for purposes of cross-examination only." United States v. Stepney, 246 F.Supp.2d 1069 (N.D.Cal.2003).

We hold that when each party to a joint defense agreement is represented by his own attorney, and when communications by one co-defendant are made to the attorneys of other co-defendants, such communications do not get the benefit of the attorney-client privilege in the event that the co-defendant decides to testify on behalf of the government in exchange for a reduced sentence.

7. Conflicts with the Trial Judge

In addition to conflicts an attorney may have with different clients, counsel can have a relationship with the trial judge that would affect the judge's ability to hear the case. Can a defendant attempt to disqualify a judge by hiring a lawyer whose relationship with the judge would trigger a successful request for recusal? In United States v. Casey, 480 F.2d 151 (5th Cir. 1973), the Fifth Circuit pointed out that "[t]he freedom to choose one's counsel may not be sued as a device to manipulate or subvert the orderly procedure of the courts or the fair administration of justice." In **McCuin v. Texas Power & Light Co.**, 714 F.2d 1255 (5th Cir. 1983), the Fifth Circuit held that counsel can be disqualified if the party employs the lawyer for the purpose of seeking recusal of the judge to whom the case is assigned:

> A lawyer's acceptance of employment solely or primarily for the purpose of disqualifying a judge creates the impression that, for a fee, the lawyer is available for sheer manipulation of the judicial system. It thus creates the appearance of professional impropriety. Moreover, sanctioning such conduct brings the judicial system itself into disrepute. To tolerate such gamesmanship would tarnish the concept of impartial justice. To permit a litigant to blackball a judge merely by invoking a talismanic "right to counsel of my choice" would contribute to skepticism about and mistrust of our judicial system.

CHAPTER SEVENTEEN
SENTENCING

A. INTRODUCTION

1. The United States Sentencing Commission

Federal Guideline Sentencing was established by the Sentencing Reform Act of 1984. The Act, which became effective in 1987, created determinate sentencing, eliminated parole, and limited "good time" reductions to fifty-four days a year after the first year of incarceration. Congress' intention in enacting the Guidelines was to ensure truth in sentencing: that a defendant would serve close to the total sentence imposed.

Congress established the United States Sentencing Commission as an independent entity in the judicial branch (28 U.S.C. § 991(a)). The Commission is composed of seven voting members–including no more than three federal judges–appointed by the President with the advice and consent of the Senate, and two non-voting ex-officio members – the Attorney General and the Chief of the Parole Commission. The Sentencing Commission drafted the original Guidelines, and after referral to Congress, they became law when Congress did not chose to exercise its authority to veto or change them. This same procedure applies to subsequent amendments to the Guidelines proposed by the Commission. Congress, of course, is free to legislate amendments sua sponte to the Guidelines, as it did in the Prosecutorial Remedies and Tools Against the Exploitation of Children Today [PROTECT] Act of 2003. See infra p. 843.

A major impetus for guideline sentencing was to level the playing field between white collar offenders and street offenders. Senator Edward M. Kennedy, co-sponsor of the Act with Senator Strom Thurmond, stated: "One important goal of the 1984 Act was to eliminate the two-tier system of justice in which white collar criminals received lenient treatment for acts of theft and fraud that would merit lengthy prison terms if committed on the street." *Address of Senator Kennedy before the U.S. Sentencing Commission Symposium on Corporate Crime*, September 12, 1995.

2. Basic Statutory Structure

An Introduction to Guideline Sentencing, by the Federal Public and Community Defender, Henry J. Bemporad, provides an explanation of the

Act's original requirements and how Supreme Court precedent has changed the Federal guideline sentencing:

> As originally written, the Sentencing Reform Act directed the sentencing court to consider a broad variety of purposes and factors, including "guidelines" and "policy statements" promulgated by the Commission. * * * But while it provided for a broad range of sentencing considerations, the Act did not allow an equally broad range of sentencing discretion. Instead, the Act cabined the court's discretion within a grid of sentencing ranges specified by the guidelines, absent a valid ground for departure. § 3553(b)(1), (b)(2). A departure from the applicable range was authorized only when the court found "an aggravating or mitigating circumstance of a kind, or to a degree, not adequately taken into consideration by the Sentencing Commission in formulating the guidelines that should result in a sentence different from that described."* * * In determining whether a circumstance was adequately considered, the court's review was restricted to the Commission's guidelines, policy statements, and official commentary. § 3553(b)(1). * * *

> The Supreme Court's decision in *Booker* fundamentally changed § 3553. Applying a line of recent constitutional decisions, *Booker* held that the mandatory system created by § 3553(b)(1) triggered the Sixth Amendment right to jury trial with respect to guideline determinations. * * * Rather than require jury findings, however, the Court removed the provisions that made the guidelines mandatory. The result was a truly advisory guidelines system. * * *

> After *Booker*, the sentencing court must consider the Commission's guidelines and policy statements, but it need not follow them. * * * They are just one of the many sentencing factors to be considered under § 3553(a), along with the nature and circumstances of the offense, the history and characteristics of the defendant, the kinds of sentences available, the need to avoid unwarranted sentencing disparities and provide restitution, and others. * * * The only restriction § 3553(a) places on the sentencing court is the "parsimony" provision, which requires the court to "impose a sentence sufficient, but not greater than necessary," to achieve a specific set of sentencing purposes:

> > • to reflect the seriousness of the offense, to promote respect for the law, and to provide just punishment for the offense;

> > • to afford adequate deterrence to criminal conduct;

> > • to protect the public from further crimes of the defendant; and

• to provide the defendant with needed education or vocational training, medical care, or other correctional treatment in the most effective manner.

§ 3553(a)(2). Beyond this parsimony requirement, and the procedural requirement that the court give reasons for the sentence it selects, § 3553(c), the Sentencing Reform Act as modified by *Booker* places no restriction on the sentence the court may impose within the limits of the statute of conviction. And the sentence the court chooses is subject to appellate review only for "unreasonableness."

* * * Under *Booker*, it is the essential starting point for federal sentencing today. But *Booker* and the statute are only the beginning. The Supreme Court has subsequently issued a series of decisions that begin to map out the advisory guideline system *Booker* created: Rita v. United States, 127 S. Ct. 2456 (2007); Kimbrough v. United States, 128 S. Ct. 558 (2007); Gall v. United States, 128 S. Ct. 586 (2007); Irizarry v. United States, 128 S. Ct. 2198 (2008). * * *

Henry J. Bemporad, *An Introduction to Guideline Sentencing* 4 (11th ed. 2009).

B. THE GUIDELINES

1. Computing the Sentence

The *Guidelines Manual* comprises eight chapters and three appendices. It contains the guidelines, policy statements, and commentary promulgated by the Sentencing Commission for consideration when a court imposes sentence in a federal case. *See* 18 U.S.C. § 3553(a)(4)(A) (court must consider guidelines); § 3553(a)(5) (court must consider policy statements). The *Manual* establishes two numerical values for each guidelines case: an offense level and a criminal history category. The two values correspond to the axes of a grid, called the sentencing table; together, they specify a sentencing range for each case. * * * Although the guidelines are advisory only, counsel should expect that the guideline range suggested by the *Manual* will receive full consideration by the sentencing court. While *Booker* returned a large measure of sentencing discretion to the court, it did not diminish the importance of understanding the guidelines' application in a particular case. This is not just because the guidelines remain the "starting point and the initial benchmark" for the sentencing decision. *Gall*, 128 S. Ct. at 596. Statistics show that, even after *Booker*, courts still follow the guidelines' sentencing recommendation more often than not.

Id. at 7-8.

The offense level is determined by establishing the base offense level for the crime(s) of conviction and, as applicable, the specific offense characteristics and adjustments. In addition to setting a "base level," each offense-conduct category lists specific offense characteristics which may or may not be applicable, depending on the circumstances of the particular case. Where specific offense characteristics are applicable, they generally increase the offense level and, accordingly, the sentence. Specific offense characteristics include: (1) more than minimal planning; (2) amount of loss involved; and, (3) infliction of bodily injury.

In applying the specific offense characteristics, the court looks to both the crime of conviction and any other conduct deemed "relevant" under U.S.S.G. § 1B1.3. Relevant conduct includes a wide range of conduct beyond the specific crime of conviction. Relevant conduct includes "all acts and omissions" of the defendant (and of accomplices for which the defendant is legally accountable) which occurred "during the commission of the offense of conviction, in preparation for that offense, or in the course of attempting to avoid detection or responsibility for that offense." Section 1B1.3(a)(1) . These acts or omissions need not have been charged in the offense of commission. Indeed, they can constitute separate offenses that were (1) uncharged, (2) charged and dismissed, or (3) charged and resulted in acquittal. For sentencing purposes, proof beyond a reasonable doubt is not needed to hold defendant responsible for an act that increases the base offense level as a specific offense characteristic; a preponderance proof level is sufficient. Illustrative is an obstruction of justice by the defendant in an attempt to avoid detection on the charged crime. The prosecution need not charge obstruction as a separate offense to increase a sentence based on the conduct.

Section 1B1.3(a)(2) adds still more relevant conduct that is not part of the offense of conviction. It includes, with respect to separate offenses of "a character for which §3D1.2(d) would require grouping of multiple counts," all acts and omissions "that were part of the same course of conduct or common scheme or plan as the offense of conviction." Here too, the provision adds offenses that were uncharged, charged and dismissed, or charged and producing an acquittal. In one sense, the range is broader than under §1B1.3(a)(1), as it extends to all offenses that were part of "a common scheme," even though they did not occur during the commission, preparation, or detection-avoidance phases of the offense of conviction. However, to be included, the offenses must be of a character that would have required their grouping for a single sentence if they had been charged and had produced multiple counts of conviction.

Consider, as an illustration, a case in which a defendant used a common scheme to swindle a series of victims, but is prosecuted and convicted for the fraud as to one victim (A). The additional criminal conduct as to the other victims will be used in calculating the specific offense characteristics of the single count of conviction. This means that all harm flowing from the additional uncharged conduct and all the specific offense characteristics of that conduct will be added to the offense of conviction. Thus, the harm would be measured by reference to the total loss caused by all of the frauds and consideration would be given to aggravating factors – e.g., the use of foreign bank accounts to conceal transactions – involved in the uncharged fraud, as well as in the fraud against A.

Chapter Three of the Sentencing Guidelines contains five major groups of adjustments: (1) victim-related; (2) defendant's role in the offense; (3) obstructing the administration of justice; (4) multiple count convictions; and, (5) defendant's acceptance of responsibility. Application of adjustments, even in a single count conviction, can result in multiple level increases or decreases.

The Guidelines for determining the offense level where conviction is on multiple counts are found at U.S.S.G. §§ 3D1.1-3D1.5. The basic rules are as follows: (1) counts having a specified relationship to each other must be placed into "groups of closely related counts;" (2) the offense level for each group of closely related counts is then determined; and (3) the combined offense level for all of the different groups is then determined. After the offense level for each count of conviction is individually determined, all counts involving substantially the "same harm" are grouped together as "closely related counts."

The guidelines utilize the combined offense level as an alternative to consecutive sentences. Multiple convictions for offenses falling in separate groups result in the "reasonable incremental punishment" of § 3D1.4, rather than the much longer increase of consecutive sentences. However, sentences will be made consecutive where that is needed to achieve the applicable guideline total. Thus, if the guideline total for the various counts of conviction exceeds the statutory maximum for the most serious count of conviction, the guidelines suggest the use of consecutive sentencing to reach the guideline range. § 5G1.2(c)-(d).

Under the guidelines, the prosecution will not gain in sentence length by separate prosecutions. The guidelines express a presumption in favor of concurrent sentences when the court sentences a defendant already subject to an undischarged term. If the second prosecution presents a charge already given weight as relevant conduct in the sentence in the first count, the guidelines will not add to the length of sentence served. If the offense was unrelated, the incremental punishment will be no greater than that which would have been provided under § 3D1.4. The object is to achieve a sentence that will achieve a total punishment equal to what would have been imposed had the sentence covered all the offenses in a single proceeding. See § 5G1.3. The exception is an offense for which the statute mandates a consecutive offense when committed while incarcerated or on probation.

2. Relevant Conduct

Establishing the nature and extent of a defendant's involvement in the offense can be important for determining the sentence because the Guidelines use what is termed a "modified real offense" system that considers the circumstances of the crime in imposing the sentence. The first step in the Guidelines sentencing process is ascertaining the defendant's "relevant conduct" for purposes of applying the offense level.

In **United States v. Williams**, 216 F.3d 1099 (D.C. Cir. 1999), the court remanded to the trial court for more complete development of the record concerning the scope of one defendant's involvement in a scheme to accept bribes in exchange for automobile inspection stickers issued by the District of Columbia government. The court stated:

> Defendants Ellis Williams and Leon Depp challenge the district court's calculation of the relevant conduct attributable to them for their roles in the bribery scheme. They complain that the court failed to make specific findings concerning when they joined the conspiracy and attributed bribe amounts to them that were not reasonably foreseeable in furtherance of jointly undertaken criminal activity. The district court held, and the government now argues, that Depp and Williams are responsible for all bribes taken after they began working at the inspection station, in 1991 and 1992 respectively.

> Under the Sentencing Guidelines [§2C1.1], bribery of a public official carries a base offense level of ten, which is increased when the offense involves multiple bribes or amounts more than $2,000. When calculating the number and amount of bribes involved, the sentencing court may consider all relevant conduct attributable to the defendant. In the case of a jointly undertaken criminal activity, this includes any acts and omissions of others in furtherance of the jointly undertaken criminal activity that were reasonably foreseeable to the defendant. Applying this standard, the district court held that Depp and Williams were accountable for the bribes taken by the other inspectors because those actions were both in furtherance of jointly undertaken activity and reasonably foreseeable to them. Accordingly, the court held Williams responsible for payments totaling between $40,000 to $70,000 and Depp for payments between $70,000 to $120,000.

> The court based its determination * * * on the assumption that Depp and Williams began participating in the bribery scheme as soon as they began working at the inspection station. Instead of identifying specific facts to establish that their involvement began at that time, the court relied on the fact that the "conspiracy . . . started back in the '80s" and required the cooperation of other inspectors to make it

work. With respect to Depp, the court found it significant that "there was never any indication that he was not involved from the beginning." From this, the court inferred—unreasonably, we think—that both must have joined the scheme quite soon after starting work at the station. That inference is without an evidentiary basis. For one thing, the record shows that not all of the inspectors at the inspection station were involved in the conspiracy. It is possible that Williams and Depp waited some time before opting to join in. The district court's conclusion was thus improper in the absence of particularized findings demonstrating that Williams and Depp joined the conspiracy soon after their employment began.

Nevertheless, as applied to Williams, the district court's erroneous determination is harmless. The court held Williams responsible for bribes taken as of 1992. Williams maintains the evidence established his involvement began no earlier than 1994. Even if Williams is correct, and we subtract the bribe amounts from 1992 to 1994, Williams is still accountable for more than $40,000. The district court relied on figures submitted by the probation officer and the government, both of whom put the total amount at more than $49,000. Eliminating bribes taken before 1994 only reduces the total amount by about $4,700. Had the district court included only bribes taken after Williams is known to have joined the scheme, the total would still have been more than $44,000. Because the district court's error made no difference to its relevant conduct determination, resentencing of Williams is unwarranted.

As to Depp, the error is not inconsequential. The district court used a conspiracy period from 1991 through the indictment in 1998. At the sentencing hearing, Depp disputed the length of this period, contending the evidence establishes his involvement only as of February 1996. Refusing to shorten the conspiracy period, the court held Depp responsible for bribes valued at the low end of the $70,000 to $120,000 range—calculating the total as $70,065 but conceding that the government's figure of $86,325 was largely credible. If we recalculate the amount without bribes taken from 1991 through 1995 the total figure is significantly reduced. The reduction for bribes provided by just one individual (Otoo) to Johnson alone, even crediting Depp's objections, amounts to at least $24,500. Given the potential for such a substantial reduction, a remand for a new assessment of Depp's relative conduct is necessary. In making that reassessment, the district court may rely on either of the two methods the government presented for calculating relevant conduct—the testimony of the inspectors' customers or the extrapolation from a sampling of illegal stickers. It may not, however, decide that Depp's participation in the scheme began at the same time as his employment without the support of particularized findings.

NOTE

Statutory Minimums. *Booker* does not change the court's inability to sentence below a statutory minimum. "Even if the guidelines or other § 3553(a) factors appear to warrant a sentence below the statutory minimum, or above the statutory maximum, the statutory limit controls. *Edwards v. United States*, 523 U.S. 511, 515 (1998); *see also* USSG §5G1.1. Numerous federal statutes include minimum prison sentences; some, like the federal "three strikes" law, 18 U.S.C. § 3559(c), mandate life imprisonment. Defendants most commonly face statutory minimum sentences in three types of federal prosecutions: drugs, firearms, and child-sex offenses." Henry J. Bemporad, *An Introduction to Guideline Sentencing* 4 (11th ed. 2009). A court, however, can depart below a statutory minimum when the government files a motion asking the court to depart below the guidelines. See p. 851.

3. Sentencing the White Collar Offender

UNITED STATES v. PARRIS
573 F.Supp.2d 744 (E.D. N.Y. 2008)

MEMORANDUM AND STATEMENT OF REASONS

BLOCK, Senior District Judge:

I have sentenced Lennox and Lester Parris today to a term of incarceration of 60 months in the face of an advisory guidelines range of 360 to life. This case represents another example where the guidelines in a securities-fraud prosecution "have so run amok that they are patently absurd on their face," United States v. Adelson, 441 F.Supp.2d 506, 515 (S.D.N.Y.2006), due to the "kind of 'piling-on' of points for which the guidelines have frequently been criticized." * * *

Although I do not consider my sentence to be unusually lenient, I am nonetheless mindful that a departure of 300 months from the low end of the advisory guidelines range is a major one and "should be supported by a more significant justification than a minor one," Gall v. United States, ---U.S. ----, 128 S.Ct. 586, 597, 169 L.Ed.2d 445 (2007); moreover, since I am of the view that the guidelines range "fails properly to reflect § 3553(a) considerations," Kimbrough v. United States, --- U.S. ----, 128 S.Ct. 558, 575, 169 L.Ed.2d 481 (2007) (quoting Rita v. United States, ---U.S. ----, 127 S.Ct. 2456, 2465, 168 L.Ed.2d 203 (2007)), "a closer review may be in order" in the event of an appeal by the government. United States v. Cutler, 520 F.3d 136, 156 (2d Cir.2008) (quoting Kimbrough, 128 S.Ct. at 575). For these two reasons, I believe a fuller exposition of how I arrived at my sentence is warranted than normally would be set forth in the space provided in the Statement of Reasons section of the judgment; hence, I am attaching this document to the judgment as the requisite written statement of reasons for the sentences I have imposed. *See*18 U.S.C. § 3553(c)(2). As the Second Circuit has made clear, § 3553(c)(2) remains obligatory despite the now-advisory nature of the Guidelines. *See* United States v. Rattoballi, 452 F.3d 127, 138 (2d Cir.2006). * * *

Although the jury found each defendant guilty of conspiracy to commit securities fraud, six counts of securities fraud, one count of conspiracy to commit witness tampering and one count of witness tampering, the nature of their crimes-while clearly deserving of the punishment which I have meted out-is simply not of the same character and magnitude as the securities-fraud prosecutions of those who have been responsible for wreaking unimaginable losses on major corporations and, in particular, on their companies' employees and stockholders, many of whom lost their pensions and were financially ruined. Yet the sentences entailed in those cases, such as Enron, WorldCom and Computer Associates, were each less, and in some cases markedly less, than the lowest end of the guidelines range in this case.

Here, the Parris brothers were engaged in a rather typical "pump and dump" scheme in the world of the high-risk penny-stock investor. At trial, the Government established that, in January and February of 2004, they issued several press releases falsely representing the business prospects and financial condition of Queénch, Inc. ("Queénch"), a fledgling publicly traded company based in Jericho, New York. As a result, shares of Queénch-which had traded at around $0.18/share immediately before the first press release was issued-began trading at artificially inflated prices; the share price peaked at $0.32 on January 29th, following the issuance of the third press release. The increased demand was also reflected in a dramatic surge in Queénch's trading volume, which had hovered at around 30,000 shares per day; during the period of the fraud, the volume of shares traded regularly reached into the millions.

"Queénch" was also the name the Parrises gave their company's product, a new breed of bottled water which they wanted to pitch to minorities. They were the sole directors and their criminal misdeeds centered around their efforts to establish a market for their new product; by and large, their press releases contained some degree of truthfulness about Queénch's business prospects, but they clearly went beyond mere puffing and the jury was entitled to view them as material misrepresentations.

More telling, perhaps, was the means by which the Parrises personally capitalized on these misrepresentations. Between January and March of 2004, Queénch issued a total of 28.6 million new, unregistered shares to two Florida stock-promotion companies, Sprout Investments LLC and Alpine Equity LLC; the corporate resolutions authorizing Queénch's transfer agent to execute the issues were signed by both defendants as principals for the company.

In late February, Queénch's transfer agent, Richard Day of American Registrar, began questioning the issues of stock to Sprout and Alpine. The defendants provided a legal opinion supporting the transfers, but Day rejected it as inadequate. The defendants thereupon switched to a different transfer agent.

Sprout and Alpine sold the newly issued Queénch shares to the investing public for a total of approximately $4.9 million. At the same time, the companies made wire transfers totaling $2.56 million to Parris Global Sports Network, LLC, whose bank account was controlled by Lester Parris. The money ultimately made its way to both defendants.

The Securities Exchange Commission ("SEC") launched an investigation. During the investigation, Lennox asked his then-girlfriend, Terry Dussek ("Dussek"), to sign a back-dated statement that she had sold 4 million Queénch shares to Sprout and lent Parris Global Sports Network $300,000. Although Dussek refused, Lester nevertheless submitted the statement to the SEC with her forged signature. Both defendants later told Dussek to tell investigators that she had authorized them to sign her name.

The investigation was made public on March 19, 2004, when the SEC suspended trading of Queénch's stock, which was then trading at $0.13/share. When trading resumed on April 2nd, the share price was $0.12; it steadily fell to between $0.01 and $0.02 by the beginning of 2005. As of September 2005, Queénch shares traded at $0.0005-1/20th of a cent-per share. * * *

As explained during the sentencing, under the strictures of the Guidelines, the Presentence Report ("PSR") correctly added up the applicable guidelines points to be 42 for each defendant because, pursuant to Guidelines § 2B1.1(a)(1), the base offense levels were 7 and the following upward adjustments were applicable:

(1) 18 levels because the securities frauds caused more than $2,500,000 in loss, *see* Guidelines § 2B1.1(b)(1);

(2) 6 levels because the securities frauds involved 250 or more victims, *see id.*§ 2B1.1(b)(2)(C);

(3) 2 levels because the securities frauds involved "sophisticated means," *id.*§ 2B1.1(b)(9)(C);

(4) 4 levels because the defendants were officers or directors of a publicly traded company, *see id.*§ 2B1.1(b)(15)(A);

(5) 3 levels because the defendants were managers or supervisors of criminal activity involving 5 or more participants, *see id.*§ 3B1.1(b); and

(6) 2 levels because the defendants obstructed justice by tampering with a witness and providing forged documents and false testimony to the SEC, *see id.*§ 3C1.1.

1. Amount of Loss

The Government and the PSRs relied on Application Note 3 of Guidelines § 2B1.1, permitting the court to "use the gain that resulted from the offense as an alternative measure of loss" if actual loss "reasonably cannot be determined," and I agreed that the difficulties inherent in calculating loss to the market in this case made its use appropriate. * * * There were two potential bases for calculating the gain: the $4.9 million that Sprout and Alpine received from the sale of Queénch shares, and the $2.56 million that found its way back to the defendants. The issue was academic insofar as both equated to an 18-level enhancement under § 2B1.1(b)(1).

I also determined that the gain was traceable to the defendants' frauds. Although Queénch's stock had pre-fraud value, injecting a total of 28.6 million new shares into the market over a period of only two months would have exerted an immense downward pressure on Queénch's share price, as the value of each share became increasingly diluted. I concluded, therefore, that there would have been no significant market for the new shares-and little to be gained from their sale-without the artificially inflated demand created by the false press releases. Although it was impossible to determine with precision, I was satisfied that the frauds generated enough of the $4.9 million realized by Sprout and Alpine to account for the $2.56 million that was kicked back to the Parrises. * * *

2. Number of Victims

An analysis of the trading data for Queénch shares proffered by the Government, without objection from the defendants, revealed "over 500 individuals who purchased Queénch stock after January 15, the date of the first false press release, and before February 5, 2004 (the date of the final charged press release), and who had not yet sold the stock by March 19, 2004, the date the SEC halted trading in Queénch stock and the fraud was revealed." Letter from Taryn A. Merkl & Jonathan E. Green (Jan. 8, 2008), at 6. Because the number of identifiable victims exceeded 250, a 6-level enhancement was required under Guidelines § 2B1.1(b)(2)(C).

3. "Sophisticated Means "

On a prior occasion, I had stated that I was not inclined to impose a 2-level enhancement for sophisticated means because there was nothing particularly complex about issuing false press releases. * * * In response, the Government persuasively argued that the defendants' fraudulent scheme also involved concealing their involvement by issuing the press releases under a pseudonym, by using Sprout and Alpine to sell the newly-issued shares (which defendants would have been unable to do directly), and by channeling the "kickbacks" from Sprout and Alpine through Parris Global Sports Network. I was satisfied, therefore, that defendants' conduct, taken as a whole, was sufficiently sophisticated to warrant this enhancement.

4. Officers/Directors

There was no dispute that Lennox was a director of Queénch during the period of the fraud. Lester, on the other hand, argued that he had resigned from the board of directors before the press releases were issued; however, he did not offer any corporate minutes or other evidence attesting to this claimed resignation. Tellingly, both Lester and Lennox continued to sign documents as directors as late as March 5, 2004, when the company entered into a memorandum of understanding to promote its product in the Caribbean and Europe. Based on this evidence, the 4-level enhancement under Guidelines § 2B1.1(b)(15)(A) was required.

5. Role in the Offense

The evidence at trial established that the defendants directed Dussek to proofread the fraudulent press releases and directed Jonathan Sinclair and Herbert Haft to disseminate them on the Internet and elsewhere. In addition, the defendants directed two transfer agents to issue Queénch stock to Sprout and Alpine. Thus, the defendants satisfied the criteria for a 3-level "manager or supervisor" enhancement under Guidelines § 3B1.3.

6. Obstruction of Justice

The defendants' conduct during the SEC investigation fell squarely within the ambit of Guidelines § 3C1.1. *See* Application Note 4(a) ("threatening, intimidating, or otherwise unlawfully influencing a co-defendant, witness, or juror, directly or indirectly, or attempting to do so"), 4(c) ("producing or attempting to produce a false, altered, or counterfeit document or record during an official investigation or judicial proceeding"). The two-level enhancement for obstruction of justice was, therefore, justified. * * *

The defendants have no prior criminal record; therefore, with a Criminal History Category of I and total offense levels of 42, I could not have sentenced them to less than 30 years if not for *Booker* and its progeny because there was no basis that I could perceive, and none advanced by the defendants, for any downward departure. Indeed, neither defendant presented any particular health concerns or unique family responsibilities. * * *

In sum, if not for the wisdom of the Supreme Court in recognizing the need to free district courts from the shackles of the mandatory guidelines regime, I would have been confronted with the prospect of having to impose what I believe any rational jurist would consider to be a draconian sentence. * * *

Although I began the sentencing proceeding "by correctly calculating the applicable Guidelines range,"*Gall,* * * *, and recognized that "the Guidelines should be the starting point and the initial benchmark,"id., it is difficult for a sentencing judge to place much stock in a guidelines range that does not provide realistic guidance. My search for more relevant guidance, therefore, had to proceed in other directions, although I would have much preferred a sensible guidelines range to give me some semblance of real guidance. Accordingly, I reached out to the parties for their thoughts.

To its credit, the Government shared my angst, recognizing that "your Honor is in a difficult position where you have an enormous guideline range," and conceding that "many reasonable sentences would fall outside that range." * * * In the admirable discharge of the higher duty of Government lawyers "to seek justice, and not merely to convict," * * *, AUSA Green commendably stated that "the Government is not advocating for a sentence under the Guidelines," and understood that a reasonable sentence "may well be one less, perhaps significantly less, than the guidelines range." * * * Consequently, the Government joined me and defense counsel in a collaborative effort to search for an effective means to avoid what Judge Rakoff has appropriately described as "the utter travesty of justice that sometimes results from the guidelines' fetish with absolute arithmetic, as well as the harm that guideline calculations can visit on human beings if not cabined by common sense." *Adelson,* 441 F.Supp.2d at 512.

We first explored whether the Second Circuit's recent decision in *United States v. Wills,* 476 F.3d 103 (2007), might have some relevance. There, the circuit court recognized that the "primary purpose" of § 3553(a)(6)-calling for "the need to avoid unwarranted sentence disparities among defendants with similar records who have been found guilty of similar crimes"-was "to reduce unwarranted sentence disparities *nationwide.*" * * *

In light of *Wills,* I asked counsel to search for nationwide similarities in securities-fraud cases. * * * It shows, in contrast to the 360-to-life guidelines range for the Parrises' crimes, the mean terms of imprisonment, in months, imposed by district courts nationwide for just about all crimes other than securities fraud, including murder (253.1), manslaughter (46.7), sexual abuse (103.5), robbery (91.5), drug trafficking (84.4), firearms (82.1), racketeering/extortion (95.6), pornography/prostitution (98.6), and general fraud (26.2).

After reviewing all of these data, I concluded that the holding in *Wills* was essentially conceptual since the data showed, as one might suspect, marked dissimilarities from case to case, causing me to surmise that it was realistically impossible "to line up similarly situated defendants on a national scale." * * *

The Government and I were in agreement, therefore, that even if there were dissimilarities in the array of national securities-fraud sentences precluding the applicability of § 3553(a)(6) under *Wills,* they nonetheless bore upon the relative seriousness of the nature of the defendants' crimes under § 3553(a)(1). Thus, although the sentences in the Government's compendium obviously were impacted by many variables, such as whether they were imposed before or after the passage of the Sarbanes-Oxley Act, or whether the defendant pleaded guilty or was a cooperator, it was perfectly clear that there was a correlation between the losses in those cases and the periods of incarceration: Those who were not cooperators and were responsible for enormous losses were sentenced to double-digit terms of imprisonment (in years); those whose losses were less than $100 million were generally sentenced to single-digit terms.

Thus, on the double-digit side, amongst the non-cooperators, there are, as representative, the following:

Name	Amount of Loss	Sentence
Bennett	$100 million	14 years
Ebbers	over $100 million[8]	25 years
Rigas (John)	over $200 million	15 years
Rigas (Timothy)	over $200 million	20 years
Skilling	over $1 billion	24 years
Forbes	approx. $14 billion	10 years
Kumar	$2.2 billion	12 years
Ferrarini	$25 million	145 months

And on the single-digit, non-cooperator side of the Government's compendium, there are:

Name	Amount of Loss	Sentence
Hotte	$67 million	108 months
Formisano	$9.8 million	78 months
Smirlock	$12.6 million	48 months
Adelson	$50-$100 million (intended)	42 months
Betts	$1.3 million	366 days
Chavrat	$1.1 million	6 months
Tursi	$1.1 million	41 months
Scuteri	$2.5 million	21 months
Kearney	$1.3 million	51 months
Rutkoske	$12 million	108 months
Cushing	$24 million	97 months

* * * To be sure, there were undoubtedly a host of factors that entered into these sentences, and there were others that seem on the surface to defy this pattern- * * * but I simply could not dismiss, in assessing the nature and

---

[8] Although Appendix A simply states the loss as over $100 million, presumably because any loss over this sum represented the outer limit for the loss enhancement under the applicable guidelines at that time, the loss occasioned by Ebbers, as CEO of WorldCom, with 2.9 billion shares of stock outstanding, was $2.2 billion. *See* United States v. Ebbers, 458 F.3d 110, 128 (2d Cir.2006).

seriousness of the Parrises' crimes under § 3553(a)(1), the overall relationship of the amount of losses in those cases to the sentences imposed; fairness in sentencing required that I recognize that, although the Parrises' criminal conduct was reprehensible, they were simply not in the same league as the likes of the Enron, WorldCom and Computer Associates defendants. * * *

There were other concerns that I had in evaluating the nature and seriousness of the Parrises' crimes under § 3553(a)(1). Initially, I was cognizant of how the changes in the Sentencing Guidelines over the past several years reflected Congress' appropriate disdain for the current crop of corporate predators: If the Parrises had been sentenced under the pre-November 1, 2001 guidelines, their sentencing ranges would have been 78 to 97 months. Between then and January 25, 2003-when the Guidelines were amended pursuant to the directives of Sarbanes-Oxley, seeU.S.S.G., app. C, amend. 647-the ranges would have risen to 168 to 210 months; the differences were occasioned by an increase in the loss calculation from 13 to 18 points and an additional two points for more than 250 victims. The spike in the current, post-Sarbanes-Oxley Guidelines applicable to the Parrises reflects an increase of one point to the base offense level, two more points for 250 or more victims, and the advent of a four-point uptick for the previously unaccounted-for category covering officers or directors of publicly traded companies.

As a consequence, we now have an advisory guidelines regime where, as reflected by this case, any officer or director of virtually any public corporation who has committed securities fraud will be confronted with a guidelines calculation either calling for or approaching lifetime imprisonment. Indeed, in *Ebbers,* the circuit court recognized that "[u]nder the Guidelines, it may well be that all but the most trivial frauds in publicly traded companies may trigger sentences amounting to life imprisonment." * * * While I acknowledge that the Guidelines "reflect Congress' judgment as to the appropriate national policy for such crimes," * * * this does not mean that the Sentencing Guidelines for white-collar crimes should be a black stain on common sense.

Fortunately, thanks to the Supreme Court, district courts are now "allowed to impose a sentence that varies from the Guidelines based solely on ... disagreements with the Guidelines," as long as they "state the basis for [their] disagreement along with 'sufficient justifications' for 'the extent of any departure.'" * * * While it may well be that the 25-year sentence for someone like Ebbers-who, as CEO of a major multinational corporation with 2.9 billion shares of outstanding stock, was responsible for a $2.2 billion loss to hundreds of thousands of investors-was "harsh but not unreasonable," * * * , any comparable sentence meted out to the Parrises, would, in contrast, be unreasonable as a matter of law.

My disagreement with the advisory guidelines range was not only driven by the double-digit/single-digit sentencing comparators * * * , but also by the guidelines' "one-shoe-fits-all" approach for its number of victims, officer/director and manager/supervisor enhancements. Thus, in all securities-fraud cases, once the threshold of 250 victims is met, the same 6 points applies for the victim enhancement, whether the number of victims be in the neighborhood of 500, as apparently in this case, or in the hundreds of thousands, as in WorldCom. The three-point leadership role enhancement attaches regardless, for example, of whether the requisite minimum of five, as here, were supervised, or 500. As for the four-level enhancement for officers and directors, there is simply no accounting for the differences their decisions may have had on destroying a major corporation affecting the lives of hundreds of thousands, compared to decisions-although inexcusable-of those jeopardizing the investments of several hundred investors in speculative penny stocks.

All of these thoughts impacted my assessment of the nature of the defendants' securities-fraud convictions under the first subparagraph of § 3553(a). I also considered, of course, the fact that the defendants were also convicted of obstructing justice; if not for that, their guidelines ranges would have been between 292 and 365 months, and the sentences somewhat lower. I also assessed each defendant's personal history and characteristics, as put forth in their attorneys' submissions, as also required under § 3553(a)(1), as well as all the other § 3553(a) factors. * * *

NOTES AND QUESTIONS

1. *Loss.* Should "loss" be a significant and controlling factor in determining a white-collar sentence? The main Guideline provision for fraud and theft offenses is § 2B1.1, which increases the base offense level depending on the amount of the loss caused by the defendant's conduct. The Sentencing Commission substantially revised the Guideline's definition of loss to clarify that crucial determination. The Guideline now defines loss to include both "actual loss" and "intended loss." Actual loss is "the reasonably foreseeable pecuniary harm that resulted from the offense," while intended loss is "the pecuniary harm that was intended to result from the offense; and * * * includes intended pecuniary harm that would have been impossible or unlikely to occur (e.g., as in a government sting operation, or an insurance fraud in which the claim exceeded the insured value)." The Guideline in turn defines "pecuniary harm" as "harm that is monetary or that otherwise is readily measurable in money. Accordingly, pecuniary harm does not include emotional distress, harm to reputation, or other non-economic harm," and "reasonably foreseeable pecuniary harm" as "pecuniary harm that the defendant knew or, under the circumstances, reasonably should have known, was a potential result of the offense." The Guideline further notes that "[t]he court need only make a reasonable estimate of the loss. The sentencing judge is in a unique position to assess the evidence and estimate the loss based upon that evidence. For this reason, the court's loss determination is entitled to appropriate deference." Not all fraudulent schemes result in a direct loss by the victims, even though the defendant realizes a gain from the offense

conduct. Therefore, the Guideline also provides that a "court shall use the gain that resulted from the offense as an alternative measure of loss only if there is a loss only if there is a loss but it reasonably cannot be determined."

2. *Acceptance of Responsibility.* A defendant who manifests acceptance of responsibility for the crime can receive a two- or three-level reduction in the offense level. The judge determines whether to grant the two-level reduction. Under the PROTECT Act, effective April 30, 2003, for a defendant to be eligible for an additional one-level reduction, the government must make a motion indicating that the defendant has "timely notif[ied] authorities of his intention to enter a plea of guilty, thereby permitting the government to avoid preparing for trial and permitting the government and the court to allocate their resources efficiently . . . ." U.S.S.G. § 3E1.1(b). Often, the two- or three-level reduction can have a significant impact on the length of the sentence or even the possibility of home confinement as a substitute for incarceration. Can a defendant go to trial and still receive the two-level acceptance of responsibility reduction at sentencing? Consider the Seventh Circuit's analysis of the trial court's grant of the acceptance of responsibility reduction in **United States v. Szarwark**, 168 F.3d 993 (7th Cir. 1999):

> The Sentencing Guidelines provide that a defendant who "clearly demonstrates acceptance of responsibility for his offense," is entitled to a two level reduction. U.S.S.G. § 3E1.1(a). In order to receive this reduction, it is normally necessary, (although not sufficient) for the defendant to plead guilty. This bias in favor of guilty pleas arises from the Guidelines' admonition that an acceptance of responsibility reduction "is not intended to apply to a defendant who puts the government to its burden of proof at trial by denying the essential factual elements of guilt." Consistent with this policy, however, a defendant may, in 'rare situations,' clearly demonstrate acceptance of responsibility even after going to trial if the defendant does so only to "assert and preserve issues that do not relate to factual guilt." U.S.S.G. § 3E1.1, Application Note 2. Unfortunately for Szarwark, this is not one of those "rare situations." Although Szarwark admitted that he embezzled money from his law firm, he put the government to its burden of proof (at a three day trial involving live testimony) by denying that the mailings were in furtherance of his scheme to defraud and by challenging the government's evidence that the mailings actually occurred. While Szarwark was certainly within his rights in contesting these issues, his election to do so forced the government to expend its resources to prove his guilt. Therefore, Szarwark acted in a manner that was inconsistent with acceptance of responsibility.
>
> We could, nevertheless, affirm the sentence reduction if we were to find, as the district judge did, that Szarwark made a "voluntary payment of restitution prior to adjudication of guilt." * * * Szarwark did not repay the entire amount owed (in fact he repaid only $87,346.29 out of $465,998.33). More importantly, his restitution (if

you could call it that) was far from voluntary. Szarwark left Barnes & Thornburg on April 15, 1997, before his fraudulent scheme was discovered. Under the firm's partnership agreement, Szarwark was entitled to be paid the balance of his capital account sixty days after his departure. However, Barnes & Thornburg discovered Szarwark's fraud before the sixty days were up and exercised its right to offset the $78,185.82 in Szarwark's capital account against the firm's losses from the fraud. The firm also retained $9,160.47 of income which Szarwark had not received prior to his departure. In this way, Barnes & Thornburg was able to recover the $87,346.29 that the district judge subsequently ordered as restitution. This is clearly not what the framers of the Sentencing Guidelines meant by voluntary payment of restitution. Because Szarwark both put the government to its burden of proof and failed to make any voluntary payment of restitution, it was clear error for the district judge to reduce Szarwark's sentence for acceptance of responsibility.

3. *Sophisticated Means.* The Guidelines provide a two-level enhancement for using "sophisticated means" to accomplish fraud and tax offenses that involve "especially complex or especially intricate offense conduct pertaining to the execution or concealment of an offense.   In **United States v. Kontny**, 238 F.3d 815 (7th Cir. 2001), in which the defendants were convicted for failing to pay federal payroll withholding taxes, Circuit Judge Posner described the type of "sophisticated" conduct that the Guidelines recognize as the basis for increased punishment:

> Moving to the sentencing issue, we confront the argument that the efforts the Kontnys made to conceal their scheme of tax evasion did not amount to the "sophisticated concealment"[i] that requires a two-level sentencing bonus under U.S.S.G. § 2T1.4(b)(2). That they did make such efforts is not in question. They wrote separate checks to the employees, one for regular wages and one for overtime, and sometimes the overtime checks would include reimbursement for expense items to disguise the fact that the checks were for wages. The Kontnys programmed their computer so that the amount of the overtime checks was classified in nonwage expense categories. The stubs for the overtime checks, which they gave their accountant, likewise placed the expense in nonwage categories.

> But did these efforts amount to "sophisticated concealment"? They were not very sophisticated in the lay sense of the word, especially in context. By creating a fraud that involved the knowing participation of more than two dozen employees, they not only armed the employees to blackmail them but greatly increased the

---

[i] The Guidelines were amended in November, 2001, by changing "sophisticated concealment" to "sophisticated means" for the tax-related provisions. There was no substantive change in the scope of the enhancement.

risk of eventual detection, though it is true that the fraud persisted for at least a decade before the inevitable occurred. The Kontnys' efforts at concealment were sophisticated in relation to a case in which the owner of a shop evades taxes by emptying the drawer of the cash register before counting the day's cash receipts and puts the cash thus skimmed into a shoebox and slides it under his bed, but unsophisticated in relation to a scheme of evasion that does not depend on the continuing goodwill of one's entire workforce and that creates a paper trail that is more difficult to follow to its guilty conclusion than the one the Kontnys created. * * *

The more sophisticated the efforts that an offender employs to conceal his offense, the less likely he is to be detected, and so he should be given a heavier sentence to maintain the same expected punishment, and hence the same deterrence, that confronts the average offender. Implementation of this rule requires both determining how much the average offense is concealed and relating the guideline concept of "sophistication" to deterrent needs. The complication in the first half of this inquiry is that fraud is by nature self- concealing–its success depends on its being hidden from the victim. The average criminal tax fraud thus involves some concealment; "sophisticated" tax fraud must require more. A parallel distinction has arisen in determining when statutes of limitations in fraud cases are tolled. If concealment were enough to toll such a statute of limitations, the statute would be tolled in almost every case, because fraud is inherently covert. So the courts distinguish between the initial fraud and any distinct efforts at cover up ("fraudulent concealment") and toll the statute only when the defendant has resorted to such efforts. Likewise the concealment that is inherent in criminal tax fraud, as in our shoebox example, must be distinguished from efforts over and above that concealment to prevent detection. Only the latter permit the sentencing enhancement.

In light of its purpose and context, we think "sophistication" must refer not to the elegance, the "class," the "style" of the defrauder–the degree to which he approximates Cary Grant–but to the presence of efforts at concealment that go beyond (not necessarily far beyond, for it is only a two-level enhancement that is at issue, which in this case added roughly six months to the defendants' sentences) the concealment inherent in tax fraud. It is true that the guideline commentary illustrates with examples suggesting a higher level of financial sophistication: "'sophisticated concealment' means especially complex or especially intricate offense conduct in which deliberate steps are taken to make the offense, or its extent, difficult to detect. Conduct such as hiding assets or transactions, or both, through the use of fictitious entities, corporate shells, or offshore bank accounts ordinarily indicates sophisticated concealment." U.S.S.G. § 2T1.4, Application Note 3. But these are offered as examples * * * the essence of the definition is merely "deliberate steps taken to make the offense ... difficult to detect." When the term "sophisticated" is defined so, it becomes apparent that the district judge did not commit a clear error in enhancing the defendants' sentences.

4. *Abuse of Position of Trust.* Individuals in white collar cases may sometimes be subject to a sentence enhancement for occupying a "position of trust." What constitutes a "position of trust" for purposes of sentencing? In **United States v. Brogan**, 238 F.3d 780, 783-84 (6th Cir. 2001), the court noted that one looks at "the inherent nature of the work" as opposed to what "in fact happened" in the case:

> A position of trust under the guidelines is one "characterized by professional or managerial discretion." USSG § 3B1.3, comment. (n. 1). The guidelines continue by explaining that "[p]ersons holding such positions ordinarily are subject to significantly less supervision than employees whose responsibilities are primarily non-discretionary in nature." Although a number of cases on this issue look to how well the individual in fact was supervised, we have recently reaffirmed that "the level of discretion accorded an employee is to be the decisive factor in determining whether his position was one that can be characterized as a trust position." * * * The "position" must be one "characterized by substantial discretionary judgment that is ordinarily given considerable deference."

> * * *The trust relationship arises when a person or organization intentionally makes himself or itself vulnerable to someone in a particular position, ceding to the other's presumed better judgment some control over their affairs. Indeed, the guideline examples of where the enhancement is appropriate correspond to the types of relationships where fiduciary duties are often implied: physician-patient, lawyer-client, officer- organization. By contrast, basic employment positions such as an "ordinary bank teller" or "hotel clerk" are mentioned as inappropriate. * * *

5. **Departures.** Consider the departure in the *Parris* case above. Congress authorized judges to depart upward or downward if "there exists an aggravating or mitigating circumstance of a kind, or to a degree, not adequately taken into consideration by the Sentencing Commission in formulating the guidelines that should result in a sentence different from that described." 18 U.S.C. § 3553(b). When is a departure appropriate in a post-*Booker* world?

> Before *Booker* excised § 3553(b)(1) from the Sentencing Reform Act, these parts strictly limited the district court's authority to sentence outside the guideline range; departures were available only when a case presented an aggravating or mitigating circumstance "of a kind,

or to a degree, not adequately taken into consideration by the Sentencing Commission in formulating the guidelines." *See* §5K2.0(a), (b), p.s. Now, with the exception of special government-sponsored downward departures, courts more often sentence below the guideline range based on § 3553(a) factors than on the departure grounds listed in Chapter Five. Despite the increase in non-guideline sentences, however, the Commission's Chapter Five policy statements on departures can have a profound effect on the sentence in an individual case.

Part H states the Commission's policy that many important offender characteristics, including age, education and vocational skills, employment record, family ties and responsibilities, and community ties, are "not ordinarily relevant" in determining the propriety of a departure. USSG Ch.5, Pt.H, intro. comment. The operative word is "ordinarily"—in exceptional cases, one or more of those characteristics may support a departure. Even in the ordinary case, those characteristics may be relevant for courts deciding where to sentence within the guideline range, or whether to impose a sentence outside the range under *Booker* and § 3553(a). * * *

Henry J. Bemporad, *An Introduction to Guideline Sentencing* 16 (11th ed. 2009).

6. *Cooperation.* In *Parris*, the court compares sentences of non-cooperators. Should the sentences of those who cooperate with the government also be considered? For example, Andrew Fastow, former Chief Financial Officer (CFO) of Enron, received a sentence of six years after a guilty plea and cooperation with the government. His plea agreement had called for a maximum sentence of ten years. In contrast, CEO of Enron Corporation, Jeffrey Skilling, received an initial sentence of twenty-four years after a trial by jury. His sentence will likely be reduced because of the appellate decision issued in his case. See p. 170. Should a defendant receive a substantial benefit for his or her cooperation with the government? If so, how much should that benefit be in terms of time to be served in prison? Should the amount of cooperation provided make a difference in the sentence received? See Ellen S. Podgor, *Fastow Receives a Six Year Sentence*, White Collar Crime Prof Blog, Sept. 26, 2006 available at http://lawprofessors.typepad.com/white collarcrime_blog /2006/09/fastow_receives.html. See also p. 852. What if a defendant has nothing to offer in cooperation?

7. *Collateral Consequences.* White collar offenders often have collateral consequences as a result of a conviction. Although all offenders face the collateral consequences of a felony conviction, such as the right to vote, unique to the white collar offender can be consequences such as a loss of a license to practice law, or to practice before the Securities Exchange Commission. See p. 670. See also *Internal Exile: Collateral Consequences of Conviction in Federal Law and Regulations*, available at http://www.abanet.org/cecs/internalexile.pdf.

8. *Special Skills.* A sentencing issue that can arise in a white collar crime case is whether the defendant should have his or her sentence increased because of a "special skill." Being an attorney or accountant can be considered a special skill when the defendant's crime related to those skills. But how far should a court go in determining whether something is a "special skill?" The court considered this question in the following case:

UNITED STATES v. LIANG
362 F.3d 1200 (9th Cir. 2004)

O'SCANNLAIN, Circuit Judge.

We must decide whether extraordinary eyesight may be considered a "special skill" supporting an enhanced sentence in a casino card cheating scheme.

Jing Bing Liang had long gambled at cards when he met a group of players sharing a mutual dissatisfaction with the odds imposed upon them by casinos. They decided to get together and remedy the situation, so they began to cheat. It started with the game of baccarat, and the revelation that by turning the shoe[1] in a particular way, they could see the next card to be dealt. Although this could not guarantee a win, it significantly increased the chances of a payout and, when employed over the course of an evening, apparently proved quite remunerative. For example, in November 1994 at a casino in Las Vegas, Liang and four others won $1,500,000 by peeking at the shoe.

This proved enticing, so the scale and sophistication of the group steadily increased. Members began to differentiate their roles: aside from the overall ringleaders, there were those who organized particular cheats at varying casinos and those that were lookouts; some would distract the dealers, while still others did the actual cheating. Liang's expertise was as a cheater. He perfected his ability not only to peek, but to mark cards by "crimping" or "daubing" them,[2] and then utilized these methods in baccarat, its mini- and midi-variations, and blackjack. All told, Liang participated in at least six cheats from 1994 through 1999 at casinos in Las Vegas, Lake Tahoe, and Atlantic City.

---

[1] A "shoe" is a device casinos use to dispense playing cards from a reservoir containing a large number of shuffled decks.

[2] Certain cards can be marked for future detection either by slightly folding them ("crimping") or by smearing on a small bit of petroleum jelly or similar substance that subtly can be identified by touch ("daubing"). These cards later can be identified without seeing their faces, which can thereby substantially increase the odds of winning a particular hand.

Federal authorities eventually caught wind of the scheme, and on October 17, 2000, Liang and his co-conspirators were indicted on charges of conspiracy to participate in an enterprise through a pattern of racketeering by cheating. See 18 U.S.C. § 1962(d). Liang pleaded guilty on May 9, 2002.

After some wrangling at his sentencing hearing, all parties eventually agreed that at least a guideline offense level of 16 applied which, in conjunction with criminal history category I, specified a 21 to 27-month term of incarceration. The government then orally moved for a two-level sentence enhancement for the use of "special skills," pursuant to United States Sentencing Guidelines Manual § 3B1.3 (2001) ("U.S.S.G."). It argued that Liang had "extraordinary eyesight" allowing him to peek at the cards in the shoe, and that he had become specially trained in the art of cheating at cards. Liang objected, but the district court agreed with the government:

> The fact that very few members of the public have the skill [of card cheating and extraordinary eyesight] suggests that it is not quite that easy to become proficient and successful at it. [A special skills enhancement] usually requires substantial education, training, or licensing. It's the core the Court takes note of. Obviously there are a lot of special skills that are not licensed. There are a lot of special skills that are not formally obtained by formal education. It says substantial education. I don't think it's formal education, and obviously there was some training done to do this as efficiently and successfully as they have done it. Accordingly, the Court will [grant] the motion . . . .

As a result, Liang's offense level increased to 18 (27 to 33 months), and the district court entered a judgment sentencing him to 27 months imprisonment on October 24, 2002. * * *

Section 3B1.3 provides for a two-level sentence enhancement "if the defendant abused a position of public or private trust, or used a special skill, in a manner that significantly facilitated the commission or concealment of the offense." The application note defines a "special skill" as "a skill not possessed by members of the general public and usually requiring substantial education, training or licensing. Examples would include pilots, lawyers, doctors, accountants, chemists, and demolition experts." * * * When read in conjunction with the abuse of a "position of public or private trust" provision, it is clear that a § 3B1.3 "special skill" involves legitimate, socially valuable expertise that a criminal has perverted to uncivilized and illegal ends.

Indeed, each of the guidelines's own illustrating examples—"pilots, lawyers, doctors, accountants, chemists, and demolitions experts"—involve legitimate and important skills that only have the potential to be abused. Conversely, the ability to kidnap, to rob, or to smuggle is inherently illegitimate, creating little or no potential for gainful employment, and thus would not belong in this class even if arguably classified as a "skill." * * *

Liang's ability to cheat at cards cannot be understood as legitimate: It was basically useless outside the criminal context, no matter how good he got. And unlike a doctor or lawyer gone bad, Liang abused no societal trust by appropriating an otherwise positive educational investment for illegal personal gain. * * * Rather, he only developed his criminal expertise, a course of conduct we do not condone, but which cannot form the legal basis for a § 3B1.3 enhancement.

Moreover, a skill is only "special" for purposes of § 3B1.3 if a district court determines "not just whether the skill is 'not possessed by members of the general public,' but also, as a sine qua non, whether it is a skill 'usually requiring substantial education, training, or licensing.'" United States v. Lee, 296 F.3d 792 (9th Cir.2002). Perhaps most of us are unable to mark or to peek at cards. Nevertheless, the district court made no findings with respect to the extent of Liang's training or sophistication at card cheating, and whether it required "substantial" effort to obtain.

Liang suggests that peeking, crimping, or daubing is relatively simple, and that anyone could learn to do it in a short amount of time. In any event, without additional findings by the district court, it certainly seems no more sophisticated than many skills that have been insufficient to trigger § 3B1.3. In light of the district court's limited findings on the matter, the enhancement cannot stand.

For these reasons, the district court erred by applying a "special skills" enhancement based on Liang's ability to cheat at cards.

The government also argues that the district court correctly based the application of § 3B1.3 on Liang's "extraordinary eyesight." Whether an underlying physical characteristic may form the basis for a "special skills" enhancement appears to be a question of first impression. It is not unusual to describe certain well-developed physical capabilities as "skills." Indeed, in some instances, formalized physical training might result in "special skills" that could be abused for illegal gain. For example, an ex-soldier theoretically might apply armed combat skills, acquired in the military, in order to facilitate a murder or a bank robbery.

Still, the fact that a skill can involve physical ability does not mean that a physical characteristic, standing alone, can also be described as a skill. While the ability to use one's hands in a certain way might be deemed a skill, the power to use them in the first place cannot. Intrinsic physical attributes are not skills—no matter how impressive they may be—because skills involve proficiency with respect to a discrete task or set of tasks. See Webster's New International Dictionary Unabridged 2133 (3d ed.1986) (defining "skill" as "knowledge of the means or methods of accomplishing a task"). Physical characteristics, on the other hand, are not knowledge nor acquired know-how: one cannot be skilled at "stamina" no matter how much he or she jogs. Likewise, it makes little sense to describe Liang as possessing the "skill of good eyesight." No matter how much it contributed to his ability to peek at cards, Liang's extraordinarily acute vision cannot be described as a skill. And because substantial training or education is what makes a skill "special" for purposes of § 3B1.3, Liang's visual acuity is simply irrelevant to the question of whether he should be subject to the enhancement.

Accordingly, the district court also erred by considering this factor.

C. PLEA AGREEMENTS

1. Substantial Assistance

The Sentencing Guidelines authorize the government to file a motion requesting that the sentencing judge depart downward from the sentence range prescribed by the Guidelines if the defendant provides "substantial assistance" to the prosecutor. The Guidelines provide in § 5K1.1:

Upon motion of the government stating that the defendant has provided substantial assistance in the investigation or prosecution of another person who has committed an offense, the court may depart from the guidelines.

(a) The appropriate reduction shall be determined by the court for reasons stated that may include, but are not limited to, consideration of the following:

(1) the court's evaluation of the significance and usefulness of the defendant's assistance, taking into consideration the government's evaluation of the assistance rendered;

(2) the truthfulness, completeness, and reliability of any information or testimony provided by the defendant;

(3) the nature and extent of the defendant's assistance;

(4) any injury suffered, or any danger or risk of injury to the defendant or his family resulting from his assistance;

(5) the timeliness of the defendant's assistance.

NOTES AND QUESTIONS

1. *Mandatory Minimums.* In **Wade v. United States**, 504 U.S. 181 (1992), the Court found that § 5K1.1 gives "the Government a power, not a duty, to file a motion when a defendant has substantially assisted," and therefore a defendant cannot challenge the government's refusal to file by claiming that the defendant did, in fact, provide substantial assistance. The Court noted,

however, that "a defendant would be entitled to relief if a prosecutor refused to file a substantial-assistance motion, say, because of the defendant's race or religion." The Court left open the question whether a downward departure can go below the mandatory minimum prescribed by statute for an offense if the government does not request such a departure. In **Melendez v. United States**, 518 U.S. 120 (1996), the Court reached the question "whether a Government motion attesting to the defendant's substantial assistance and requesting that the district court depart below the minimum of the applicable sentencing range under the Guidelines also permits the district court to depart below any statutory minimum. * * * We now hold that such a motion does not authorize a departure below a lower statutory minimum." In a footnote, the Court stated that "the Government must in some way indicate its desire or consent that the court depart below the statutory minimum before the court may do so." Thus, even in a post-*Booker* world, judges cannot depart below a statutory minimum absent a government motion for such a departure.

2. *Prosecutorial Discretion.* In United States v. Jones, 58 F.3d 688 (D.C. Cir. 1995), the court, although affirming a judgment of the district court denying defendant's motion to compel the government to file a § 5K1.1 motion, expressed concern "that prosecutors might dangle the suggestion of a § 5K1.1 motion in front of defendants to lure them into plea agreements, all the while knowing that the defendant's cooperation could not possibly constitute assistance valuable enough for the * * * [government] to find it 'substantial.' " In **United States v. Moore**, 225 F.3d 637 (6th Cir. 2000), however, the Sixth Circuit stated:

> [T]his Circuit has expressly ruled that when a plea agreement allocates complete discretion to the government to consider whether a substantial assistance motion should be filed, we may only review the government's decision for unconstitutional motives. On the other hand, when the government bargains away its discretion and agrees to a plea agreement in which it promises to file a substantial assistance motion, we may ascertain whether the government complied with the terms of the agreement.

2. Plea Bargaining Under the Guidelines

Most federal prosecutions end with a plea bargain rather than proceeding to trial. What is the effect of the Sentencing Guidelines on the plea bargaining process? Consider the following excerpt from *An Introduction to Federal Guideline Sentencing* (11th ed. 2009), by the Federal Public and Community Defender, Henry J. Bemporad:

> Federal Rule of Criminal Procedure 11(c)(1) and policy statement §6B1.2 describe three forms of plea agreement: charge bargain, sentence recommendation, and specific, agreed sentence. While other forms of plea agreement are possible, these are the most

common, and each has important consequences for sentencing under the advisory guidelines. A charge bargain must be carefully analyzed to determine whether its supposed guideline benefit is real or illusory, once the effects of relevant conduct and multiplecount grouping have been considered. Other, equally important considerations affect the possible benefits of sentence-recommendation and sentence-agreement bargains. In all cases, the potential value of an acceptanceof-responsibility adjustment must be carefully considered. And because cooperation by the defendant is a common element of plea bargains, the statutory and guideline provisions that affect cooperating defendants can be of central importance. * * *

Charge Bargaining. Policy statement §6B1.2(a) authorizes the court to accept a defendant's plea to one or more charges under Rule 11(c)(1)(A), in exchange for the dismissal of others, if "the remaining charges adequately reflect the seriousness of the actual offense behavior" and "accepting the agreement will not undermine the statutory purposes of sentencing or the sentencing guidelines." Federal plea bargaining has typically involved this form of agreement, under which a defendant has the right to withdraw his plea to the bargained charges if the other charges are not dismissed. Charge bargains, however, will often have little effect on the guideline range. This is because of the dramatic impact of two related guideline concepts: relevant conduct and multiple-count grouping.

Relevant conduct.A plea agreement calling for dismissal of counts will not reduce the offense level if the subject matter of the dismissed counts is deemed "relevant conduct" for purposes of determining the guideline range. *See* USSG §1B1.3. Thus, for example, if a defendant pleads guilty to one drug count in exchange for the dismissal of others, the base offense level will usually be determined from the total amount of drugs involved in all counts, even the dismissed ones. Despite the effect of relevant conduct, however, charge bargaining can still confer important sentencing benefits. When one of the counts is governed by a Chapter Two guideline with a lower offense level, a plea to that count may produce a lower guideline range. Even if a count does not have a lower guideline range, it may carry a lower statutory maximum. Because statutes trump guidelines, a charge bargain may have the effect of capping the maximum sentence below the probable guideline range, *see* §5G1.1(a), or avoiding a statutory minimum that would raise the guideline range, *see* §5G1.1(b). * * *

D. APPELLATE REVIEW

UNITED STATES v. TOMKO
562 F.3d 558 (3rd Cir. 2009)

SMITH, Circuit Judge, with whom McKEE, BARRY, AMBRO, FUENTES, CHAGARES, JORDAN, and HARDIMAN, Circuit Judges, join.

The Government appeals the reasonableness of William Tomko's below-Guidelines sentence of probation, community service, restitution, and fine for his tax evasion conviction. If any one of a significant number of the members of this Court-including some in today's majority-had been sitting as the District Judge, Tomko would have been sentenced to some time in prison. But "[t]he fact that the appellate court might reasonably have concluded that a different sentence was appropriate is insufficient to justify reversal of the district court." Gall v. United States, 128 S.Ct. 586 (2007). *Gall* reminds us that "[t]he sentencing judge is in a superior position to find facts and judge their import under § 3553(a) in the individual case. The judge sees and hears the evidence, makes credibility determinations, has full knowledge of the facts and gains insights not conveyed by the record." This reality is why, post-*Booker*, "the familiar abuse-of-discretion standard of review now applies to appellate review of sentencing decisions." Where, as here, a district court decides to vary from the Guidelines' recommendations, we "must give due deference to the district court's decision that the § 3553(a) factors, on a whole, justify the extent of the variance." These principles require us to affirm Tomko's sentence.

On May 11, 2004, Tomko pleaded guilty to a one-count information charging him with tax evasion in violation of 26 U.S.C. § 7201. Tomko was the owner and Chief Executive Officer of W.G. Tomko & Son, Inc. ("Tomko, Inc."), a plumbing contractor. From 1995 to 1998, Tomko directed numerous subcontractors, who were building his multimillion dollar home in Washington County, Pennsylvania, to falsify information on billing invoices so that the invoices would show work being done at one of Tomko, Inc.'s many job sites instead of at Tomko's home. As a result, Tomko, Inc. paid for the construction of Tomko's home and illegally deducted those payments as business expenses. Tomko also did not properly report those payments as income on his personal tax return. All told, Tomko's tax evasion scheme involved twelve different subcontractors and his general contractor, and resulted in a tax deficiency of $228,557.

The United States District Court for the Western District of Pennsylvania conducted Tomko's sentencing hearing on September 30, 2005. Using the 1997 edition of the United States Sentencing Guidelines Manual, the District Court calculated Tomko's total offense level to be thirteen and his criminal history category to be I. Based on these calculations, the Guidelines recommended a range of imprisonment between twelve and eighteen months and a fine between $3,000 and $30,000.

Tomko, however, proposed that in light of the then-recent Hurricane Katrina catastrophe and his construction expertise, the Court should sentence him to probation and home detention, and require him to work for Habitat for Humanity. The Executive Director for Habitat for Humanity's Pittsburgh affiliate testified that the organization would appreciate Tomko's help in its efforts to rebuild the Gulf Coast and that Tomko had performed well in past projects, including providing onsite assistance and advice.

Tomko also proffered testimony from Tomko, Inc.'s Chief Financial Officer that the company was in danger of losing its line of credit if he were imprisoned. If this happened, Tomko, Inc. would be in dire straits financially and the jobs of its 300-plus employees would be threatened.

Finally, Tomko submitted a Motion for Downward Departure. The motion argued that Tomko should be sentenced below his Guidelines range because 1) his incarceration could cause Tomko, Inc.'s innocent employees to lose their jobs; 2) he has performed exceptional charitable acts and good works; 3) he has demonstrated an extraordinary degree of acceptance of responsibility; and 4) a combination of these three factors. As exhibits, Tomko attached over fifty letters from family, friends, community leaders, and others attesting to his pre-indictment charitable activities and other good works.

After hearing these arguments and stating that it had reviewed all the motions and briefs that the parties submitted, the District Court stated its Guidelines calculations for the record and considered the sentencing factors listed in 18 U.S.C. § 3553(a): * * *

> I am to consider first the nature and circumstances of the offense, which are as follows.
>
> The offense was not violent in nature.
>
> The offense was not ongoing in nature.
>
> The offense was not part of a larger pattern of criminal activity.
>
> There are also no identifiable victims of the offense.
>
> I am also to consider the history and characteristics of the Defendant. [The District Court here discussed Tomko's childhood, family, education, drinking problem, and prior criminal conviction for operating a boat while intoxicated.]
>
> I am also going to consider the need for the sentence imposed to reflect the seriousness of the offense, promote respect for the rule of law, and provide just punishment for the offense. Here, the Defendant has pled guilty to tax evasion, which is a serious offense.

I am to afford adequate deterrence to the Defendant's criminal conduct. Here, the Defendant has one prior criminal incident which is alcohol-related, but has otherwise led a crime-free life.

I am to protect the public from further crimes of this Defendant. Here, the Defendant has not been involved in other crimes even though this is a serious offense here. The likelihood of recidivism in this case I find is very little.

And to provide Defendant with needed educational/vocational training, medical care, or other correctional treatment in the most effective manner possible.

I am also to consider the kind of sentences available, including federal prison, house arrest, probation, and fines, which I am going to do.

I am to consider the need [to avoid] unwarranted sentence disparities among Defendants with similar records who have been found guilty of similar conduct. These considerations generally weigh in favor of sentencing a Defendant within the guideline range. * * * I recognize the need for consistent sentencing; however, in this case, given the Defendant's lack of any significant criminal history, his involvement in exceptional charitable work and community activity, and his acceptance of responsibility, we find that a sentence that is mitigated by the factors of 3553[is] warranted.

In response, the Government insisted that the Court impose a sentence that included a term of imprisonment. The Government did not challenge Tomko's factual assertions or submissions. Instead, it juxtaposed his criminal conduct with the patriotism of American soldiers fighting wars abroad and argued that greed, not community service and philanthropy, defined Tomko's character. It focused on the fact that Tomko coerced his subcontractors to file false documentation, and highlighted the "gilded cage" nature of a sentence of home detention. The Government claimed that it would be "absurd" to sentence Tomko to live in the same multimillion dollar mansion that the illegally obtained tax monies helped fund. * * *

Despite the Government's arguments, the District Court did not sentence Tomko to a term of imprisonment. Instead, the Court sentenced Tomko to three years of probation (the first of which would be served as home detention), participation in an alcohol treatment program, 250 hours of community service, full restitution, and the statutory maximum fine of $250,000. * * *

Two basic principles underlie the application of the abuse-of-discretion standard. First, "deferential review is used when the matter under review was decided by someone who is thought to have a better vantage point than we on the Court of Appeals to assess the matter." * * * Accordingly, the Supreme Court has applied the abuse-of-discretion standard where it "noted that deference was owed to the 'judicial actor . . . better positioned than another to decide the issue in question.'" Koon v. United States, 518 U.S. 81 (1996) (quoting Pierce v. Underwood, 487 U.S. 552 (1988)). As one leading commentator has put it, "[i]n the dialogue between the appellate judges and the trial judge, the former often would seem to be saying: 'You were there. We do not think we would have done what you did, but we were not present and we may be unaware of significant matters, for the record does not adequately convey to us all that went on at the trial. Therefore, we defer to you.'" * * *

Second, courts of appeals apply the abuse-of-discretion standard to fact-bound issues that are ill-suited for appellate rule-making. As the Supreme Court explained in *Pierce*:

> One of the "good" reasons for conferring discretion on the trial judge is the sheer impracticability of formulating a rule of decision for the matter in issue. Many questions that arise in litigation are not amenable to regulation by rule because they involve multifarious, fleeting, special, narrow facts that utterly resist generalization-at least, for the time being.

Pre-*Booker*, these two basic principles motivated the Supreme Court to hold that the abuse-of-discretion standard should be used to evaluate sentencing departures under the mandatory Guidelines system. In *Koon*, the Supreme Court noted that "[a] district court's decision to depart from the [mandatory] Guidelines . . . will in most cases be due substantial deference, for it embodies the traditional exercise of discretion by a sentencing court." The Court pointed out that determining whether a departure was permitted required "the district court [to] make a refined assessment of the many facts bearing on the outcome, informed by its vantage point and day-to-day experience in criminal sentencing." Additionally, "a district court's departure decision involves the consideration of unique factors that are little susceptible . . . of useful generalization, and as a consequence, de novo review is unlikely to establish clear guidelines for lower courts." As a result, the Court concluded that "[t]he appellate court should not review the departure decision de novo, but instead should ask whether the sentencing court abused its discretion."

Post-*Booker*, the sentencing court's superior vantage point has been the oft-cited reason for applying the abuse-of-discretion standard to sentencing review. In *Gall*, the Court emphasized that "[t]he sentencing judge is in a superior position to find facts and judge their import under § 3553(a) in the individual case. The judge sees and hears the evidence, makes credibility determinations, has full knowledge of the facts and gains insights not conveyed by the record." This means that "[t]he sentencing judge has access to, and greater familiarity with, the individual case and the individual defendant before him than the [Sentencing] Commission or the appeals court." Id. at 597-98 (quoting Rita v. United States, 551 U.S. 338 (2007)).

Additionally, "district courts have an institutional advantage over appellate courts in making these sorts of determinations, especially as they see so many more Guidelines sentences than appellate courts do." * * *

In the wake of *Booker*, it is essential that district courts make an "individualized assessment based on the facts presented." *Gall.* In doing so, it is equally important that district courts provide courts of appeals with an explanation "sufficient for us to see that the particular circumstances of the case have been given meaningful consideration within the parameters of § 3553(a)." We also must have "sufficient justifications on the record to support the sentencing conclusions." Although we can articulate no uniform threshold for sufficiency because of the fact-bound nature of each sentencing decision, we certainly always demand more than a rote recitation of the § 3553(a) factors if "at sentencing either defendant or the prosecution properly raises a ground of recognized legal merit (provided it has a factual basis) and the court fails to address it." United States v. Cooper, 437 F.3d 324 (3d Cir.2006). Only then will we have enough to conduct our "limited yet important" review.

District courts must provide their explanations and justifications while going through three steps at sentencing. As we outlined in *Levinson*:

> A district court must begin the process by first calculating the applicable Guidelines range. After that initial calculation, the court must then rule on any motions for departure and, if a motion is granted, state how the departure affects the Guidelines calculation. Finally, after allowing the parties an opportunity for argument, the court must consider all of the § 3553(a) factors and determine the appropriate sentence to impose, which may vary from the sentencing range called for by the Guidelines. * * *

Our appellate review proceeds in two stages. It begins by "ensur[ing] that the district court committed no significant procedural error, such as failing to calculate (or improperly calculating) the Guidelines range, treating the Guidelines as mandatory, failing to consider the § 3553(a) factors, selecting a sentence based on clearly erroneous facts, or failing to adequately explain the chosen sentence-including an explanation for any deviation from the Guidelines range." *Gall.* We do not presume that a district court considered the factors solely because the sentence falls within the Guidelines range. If a district court's procedure passes muster, "we then, at stage two, consider its substantive reasonableness." *Levinson.* Our substantive review requires us not to focus on one or two factors, but on the totality of the circumstances. Indeed, we cannot presume that a sentence is unreasonable simply because it falls outside the advisory Guidelines range. At both stages of our review, the party challenging the sentence has the burden of demonstrating unreasonableness.

The abuse-of-discretion standard applies to both our procedural and substantive reasonableness inquiries. For example, an abuse of discretion has occurred if a district court based its decision on a clearly erroneous factual conclusion or an erroneous legal conclusion. This also means that, absent any significant procedural error, we must "give due deference to the district court's determination that the § 3553(a) factors, on a whole," justify the sentence. *Gall.* In other words, if the district court's sentence is procedurally sound, we will affirm it unless no reasonable sentencing court would have imposed the same sentence on that particular defendant for the reasons the district court provided.

Ultimately, "[t]he touchstone of 'reasonableness' is whether the record as a whole reflects rational and meaningful consideration of the factors enumerated in 18 U.S.C. § 3553(a)." United States v. Grier, 475 F.3d 556 (3d Cir.2007) (en banc). "An estimation of the outer bounds of what is 'reasonable' under a given set of circumstances may not always be beyond debate, but the abuse-of-discretion standard by which that estimation must be judged limits the debate and gives district courts broad latitude in sentencing."

The Government makes only one claim of procedural error: it argues that the District Court failed to meaningfully consider general deterrence. Based on our review of the record, we cannot agree. A sentencing court does not have to "discuss and make findings as to each of the § 3553(a) factors if the record makes clear the court took the factors into account in sentencing." Here, "[t]he record makes clear that the sentencing judge listened to each argument," *Rita*, and rejected the ones the Government made concerning general deterrence. * * *

* * * The District Judge noted that he viewed Tomko's sentence as "address[ing] the sentencing goals of punishment, *deterrence* and rehabilitation." (Emphasis added.) This demonstrates that the District Court heard the Government's impassioned plea, considered general deterrence, and handed down Tomko's sentence. Therefore, we conclude that the District Court did not commit any procedural error at Tomko's sentencing.

The crux of the Government's appeal is its claim that Tomko's sentence is substantively unreasonable. * * * In essence, the Government is asking this Court to apply the already-rejected "proportionality test" by a different name. The Government's appeal boils down to a claim that Tomko's criminal history, employment record, community ties, and charitable works do not differentiate him enough from the "mine-run" tax evasion case to justify his below-Guidelines sentence. Similarly, a "proportionality test" rests on "the proposition that the strength of the justification needed to sustain an outside-Guidelines sentence varies in proportion to the degree of the variance." *Rita.* As applied by some courts of appeals, this meant that "a sentence that constitute [d] a substantial variance from the Guidelines [had to] be justified by extraordinary circumstances." *Gall.* In *Gall*, the Supreme Court explicitly barred the application of such an approach because it necessarily applies a "heightened standard of review to sentences outside the Guidelines range." That, of course, is "inconsistent with the rule that the abuse-of-discretion standard of review applies to appellate review of all sentencing decisions-whether inside or outside the Guidelines range." * * *

Based on our review of the record, we conclude that the District Court did not abuse its discretion here. At Tomko's sentencing hearing, the District Court explicitly examined subsections (a)(1), (a)(2)(A), (a)(2)(B), (a)(2)(C), (a)(2)(D), (a)(3), (a)(4), and (a)(6) of § 3553. The District Court also ordered full restitution. After hearing argument from the Government concerning the need for a term of imprisonment, the Court reiterated its reasons for imposing a sentence without one. The District Court gave specific reasons for why Tomko's sentence varies from the Guidelines range. This variance took into account his negligible criminal history, his employment record, his community ties, and his extensive charitable works as reasons for not incarcerating Tomko, while also factoring in his substantial wealth as a reason for imposing a fine far above the Guidelines range. Indeed, the District Court provided more than just a boilerplate recitation of the § 3553(a) factors; it detailed, step-by-step, its individualized assessment of the sentence that it believed appropriate in this particular case. * * *

It bears mentioning that the District Court's variance here was not substantial. The difference between Tomko's actual sentence and the lower end of his Guidelines range is twelve months. * * * We cannot say that, in absolute terms, the variance here was so large that it was per se unreasonable. In *Gall*, the Supreme Court affirmed a district court's probationary sentence where the advisory Guidelines range was thirty to thirty-seven months of imprisonment. Similarly, post-*Gall*, a number of courts of appeals, including our own, have affirmed sentences that involved greater variances or departures than the one here. "It will be a rare case when it is clear that no acceptable reasoning can justify a given sentence." * * * This is not one of them.

The Government claims that affirming Tomko's sentence promotes sentencing disparities and, in turn, undermines general deterrence. Whatever the merits of this possibility, it does nothing to change our disposition. The Government's concern is not new; it has been a point of constant focus throughout sentencing review's evolution. * * * When the Supreme Court rendered the Guidelines advisory, it was fully aware that sentencing disparities would likely increase.

Despite that awareness, the *Booker* Court was confident that the advisory Guidelines system would "continue to move sentencing in Congress' preferred direction, helping to avoid excessive sentencing disparities while maintaining flexibility sufficient to individualize sentences where necessary." In *Gall*, the Court reaffirmed that "a more deferential abuse-of-discretion standard could successfully balance the need to 'reduce unjustified disparities' across the Nation and 'consider every convicted person as an individual'" *Koon*.

If abuse-of-discretion review cannot strike such a balance, it is not our role as appellate judges to adjust the scales. * * * The risk of affirming an unwarranted sentencing disparity in this case is one we must accept while following the Supreme Court's "pellucidly clear" command that we apply the abuse-of-discretion standard of review. *Gall.*

Our decision today should not suggest that variances of the size and character of Tomko's will always be substantively reasonable. District courts must make sentencing determinations on an individualized basis. Accordingly, the substantive reasonableness of each sentence must be evaluated on its own terms, based on the reasons that the district court provided, in light of the particular facts and circumstances of that case.* * *

Our holding in this case is not an exercise in self-abnegation. Courts of appeals unquestionably have an important role to play in reviewing district courts' sentencing decisions. But it is a limited role. Neither *Gall* nor *Rita* suggests that courts of appeals should do anything more than ensure the reasonableness of federal sentences. * * * Simply put, reasonableness review requires us to do nothing more and nothing less than to apply the deferential abuse-of-discretion standard, a role quite familiar to us. "We do not seek to second guess. Given the widely recognized institutional advantages that district courts have in access to and consideration of evidence, we would be foolish to try."

* * * Here, the record demonstrates the District Court's thoughtful attempt to tailor the off-the-rack Guidelines recommendations into a sentence that fits Tomko personally. Where it believed the Guidelines recommendations too large or too small-for example, in the advisory ranges for imprisonment and fine-the Court took care to explain why this was the case before making the adjustments it felt necessary. This is precisely the type of individualized assessment that *Gall* demands, and to which we must defer. Accordingly, we will affirm the sentence that the District Court imposed.

FISHER, Circuit Judge, dissenting, with whom Chief Judge SCIRICA, Judge SLOVITER, Judge RENDELL and Judge COWEN join.

As the procedural history of this appeal clearly shows, this Court has wrestled with the decision in this case for close to two and one half years, during which time the judges on this Court have tried to determine whether the sentence given for this crime was substantively reasonable. The offense we encounter in this case is no garden variety tax evasion. The conduct underlying the offense involved an intricate scheme spanning several years and involved the coercion and coordination of numerous other individuals, all for the personal gain of one man, William G. Tomko, Jr., a successful business owner with the means to easily pay the taxes he owed to the Government.

* * * This case presents the opportunity for us to examine the implications of the Supreme Court's directive in *Gall* that in reviewing for reasonableness, appellate courts are to conduct a substantive inquiry as well as a procedural one.

* * * If the substance of a sentence is not "logical and consistent" with the § 3553(a) factors or fails to "reasonably appl[y]" them to "the circumstances of the case," United States v. Cooper, 437 F.3d 324 (3d Cir.2006), the sentence is not substantively reasonable and does not survive abuse-of-discretion review. * * *

[The dissenting judges agreed with the majority that the district judge properly addressed the question of general deterrence in the sentencing.]

Viewed cumulatively, out of the three reasons offered by the District Court for mitigating Tomko's sentence, only one – community support based on charitable work – even begins to justify a downward variance in this case. Thus, these considerations fall short of placing the sentence imposed within the albeit broad range of permissible choices, even when we add them together. Moreover, the "mitigating" circumstances relied upon by the District Court only address one of the § 3553(a) factors, namely "the history and characteristics of the defendant" under § 3553(a)(1), and therefore do not reflect the "totality of the circumstances" and the "§ 3553(a) factors, on a whole." *Gall*, 128 S.Ct. at 597. As a number of our sister courts of appeals have recognized, excessive reliance on a single § 3553(a) factor is indicative of an unreasonable sentence. As the remainder of our analysis reveals, the District Court's over-reliance on § 3553(a)(1) as justification for the significant qualitative and quantitative variance it granted pales in comparison to the numerous § 3553(a) factors which suggest that a term of imprisonment is warranted in a case of tax evasion as willful and brazen as Tomko's.

Viewed cumulatively, we conclude that the relevant § 3553(a) factors advocate in the strongest possible terms for a sentence including a term of imprisonment. Beginning with § 3553(a)(1), district courts are instructed to consider not only a defendant's "history and characteristics," but also "the nature and circumstances of the offense," which the District Court did not emphasize. In this respect, Tomko did much more than fail to report income on a form; he conceived of a sophisticated plan to evade taxation and compelled multiple individuals to aid him in the scheme. This scheme spanned several years, involved the planning, coordination, and coercion of numerous subcontractors, required a complicated system of concealment through fraudulent billing, and resulted in a stipulated tax loss of over $225,000. Thus, while the District Court's stated justifications for mitigating Tomko's sentence fail to differentiate him from other tax evaders, the severity of his offense and the extent of his culpability, as evidenced by the willful and brazen nature of his conduct, remove Tomko's tax evasion from the garden variety type. As such, even assuming "the history and characteristics of the defendant" point in the direction of a lenient sentence, "the nature and circumstances of the offense" certainly do not. * * *

NOTE AND QUESTION

Reasonableness. What is the effect of prior good works of the defendant in deciding whether a sentence was unreasonable? See Peter J. Henning, *Prior Good Works in the Age of Reasonableness*, 20 Fed Sent. Rept. 187 (2008).

E. SENTENCING CORPORATIONS

1. Development of the Organizational Guidelines

Like an individual, an organization–such as Arthur Andersen–can be charged and convicted for violating the law. See supra Chapter 3. Chapter 8 of the Guidelines, effective November 1, 1991, covers Sentencing of Organizations. This Chapter reflects the view that organizations must be dealt with, in addition to their agents who can be prosecuted separately, to reach the goal of "just punishment, adequate deterrence, and incentives for organizations to maintain internal mechanisms for preventing, detecting, and reporting criminal conduct." Ch. 8, Introductory Commentary.

The Commission endorsed the following principles in establishing the Guidelines for organizational punishment:

a. Remedy any harm caused by the offense.

b. "If the organization operated primarily for a criminal purpose or primarily by criminal means, the fine should be set sufficiently high to divest the organization of all its assets."

c. Base the fine on the seriousness of the offense and the culpability of the organization. In determining organizational culpability, the Commission emphasized the importance of preventive steps taken by the organization to prevent misconduct: "Culpability generally will be determined by the steps taken by the organization prior to the offense to prevent and detect criminal conduct, the level and extent of involvement in or tolerance of the offense by certain personal, and the organization's actions after an offense has been committed."

d. Impose a probationary sentence on the organizational defendant when necessary to "ensure that another sanction will be fully implemented, or to ensure that steps will be taken within the organization to reduce the likelihood of future criminal conduct."

These principles lay out a very clear roadmap for an organization to follow *before* any criminal charges are even brought, to wit, implement a plan to prevent and detect criminal conduct.

Chapter 8 applies to felony and Class A misdemeanor offenses. The Commission sets forth General Application Principles and Remedies. The latter include restitution, remedial orders, community service, and notice to victims. The organizational Guidelines also provide directions for the sentencing judge to utilize in determining an appropriate fine. Significant factors for the court's utilization include the organization's culpability, prior history, violation of an order, obstruction of justice, whether it had an effective program to prevent and detect violations of law, and whether it engaged in self-reporting, cooperation, and acceptance of responsibility. Further, the Guidelines in §8C2.6 provide for "multipliers" to be applied to fines based on the organization's culpability.

As with the Guidelines applicable to individual defendants, Chapter 8 provides for "Departures [upward and downward] from the Guideline Fine Range" for:

a. Substantial assistance

b. Creating a Risk of Death or Bodily Injury

c. Threat to National Security

d. Threat to the Environment

e. Threat to a Market

f. Official corruption–payment to a public official

g. Whether or not the organization is a public entity

h. If members or beneficiaries of the organization, other than shareholders, are direct victims of the offense

i. If the remedial costs paid by the organization greatly exceed the organization's gain

j. If there is Exceptional Organizational Culpability

Finally, Chapter 8 deals with the circumstances under which a probationary sentence is required. A probationary sentence can include:

a. Making periodic submissions to the court;

b. Submitting to regular unannounced examinations of books or interrogations of individuals; and

c. Developing a program to prevent and detect further violations of law.

If probation is violated, the corporation could have more restrictive conditions imposed, or even have probation revoked and be resentenced.

2. "Encouraging" Cooperation

Can a corporation resist cooperating with the government when the guidelines provide concrete benefits by lowering the fines that will be imposed? Recall the Department of Justice's policy regarding charging corporations discussed in Chapter 3, supra, and the premium placed on cooperation in deciding whether to even charge a corporation with a criminal offense. Also consider the role of the corporate directors in deciding whether corporation would be in the best interests of the corporation. See p. 85. In **In re Caremark International Inc. Derivative Litigation**, 698 A.2d 959 (Del. Ch. 1996), a Delaware Chancery Court Judge considered whether a corporations board of directors could fulfill their fiduciary duty to the corporation by not informing themselves about actual or potential corporate wrongdoing and then cooperate with the government if such misconduct occurred. The court stated:

> Can it be said today that, absent some ground giving rise to suspicion of violation of law, that corporate directors have no duty to assure that a corporate information gathering and reporting systems exists which represents a good faith attempt to provide senior management and the Board with information respecting material acts, events or conditions within the corporation, including compliance with applicable statutes and regulations? I certainly do not believe so. I doubt that such a broad generalization of the *Graham* [*v. Allis-Chalmers*] holding would have been accepted by the Supreme Court in 1963. The case can be more narrowly interpreted as standing for the proposition that, absent grounds to suspect deception, neither corporate boards nor senior officers can be charged with wrongdoing simply for assuming the integrity of employees and the honesty of their dealings on the company's behalf. A broader interpretation of Graham v. Allis-Chalmers—that it means that a corporate board has no responsibility to assure that appropriate information and reporting systems are established by management—would not, in any event, be accepted by the Delaware Supreme Court in 1996, in my opinion. In stating the basis for this view, I start with the recognition that in recent years the Delaware Supreme Court has made it clear—especially in its jurisprudence concerning takeovers* * *. Secondly, I note the elementary fact that relevant and timely information is an essential predicate for satisfaction of the board's supervisory and monitoring role under Section 141 of the Delaware General Corporation Law. Thirdly, I note the potential impact of the federal organizational sentencing guidelines on any business organization. Any rational person attempting in good faith to meet an organizational governance responsibility would be bound to take into account this development

and the enhanced penalties and the opportunities for reduced sanctions that it offers.

Consider Professor William S. Laufer's analysis of the pressure on corporations to cooperate with the government's investigation in his article *Corporate Prosecution, Cooperation, and the Trading of Favors*, 87 Iowa L. Rev. 643 (2002):

> Congress approved the Sentencing Guidelines at a time of increasing dissatisfaction with the command and control strategies of corporate regulation. Theories of cooperative regulation, co-regulation, enforced self-regulation, and negotiated compliance had developed, and the Commission and regulators were ready to implement mixed regulatory strategies. Drafters of the Sentencing Guidelines wanted corporations to face the threat of significant punishment and, at the same time, the possibility of mitigation, leniency, and amnesty. In the ideal, the objective was to construct regulatory strategy at once both provokable and forgiving.

> The Sentencing Guidelines became * * * the centerpiece of a dynamic enforcement game backed by a "tall enforcement pyramid." Voluntary corporate compliance under the Sentencing Guidelines is achieved through the old carrot and stick trope. Understandably, this approach earned praise for encouraging businesses to join the government in the battle against corporate crime. Good corporate citizenship that institutionalizes ethics and sound compliance practices minimizes corporate deviance. When wayward employees are identified, the Sentencing Guidelines reward post-offense corporate cooperation, strong internal disciplinary action, and the organization's acceptance of responsibility. Recently released prosecutorial guidelines for corporations ("Prosecutorial Guidelines") extend this valuable partnership to charging decisions and plea negotiations and address concerns that the Sentencing Guidelines shift discretion from judges to prosecutors.

> Both Guidelines translate into reciprocal promises—organizational cooperation and acceptance of responsibility in exchange for mitigation, exculpation, or absolution. This bargained-for exchange, or trading of favors, with an arsenal of sanctions in the background, is a decision template for prosecutors and judges in cases of corporate crime. With the threat of significant Guideline-prescribed fines, corporations have little choice but to trade favors with authorities. The importance of and need for these reciprocal promises is rarely challenged. Given extremely limited resources, the complex nature of the corporate form, and the accompanying evidentiary challenges facing prosecutors, it is little wonder that the government often exchanges leniency for conciliatory post-offense behavior. Strict enforcement, sanctioning, or deterrent styles of regulation focusing on criminalization and prosecution have long

been recognized as significantly inhibiting corporate cooperation by keeping control of information and incriminating evidence in the hands of the regulated rather than the regulator. If anything, this promotes gaming by organizations and, according to some commentators, encourages law evasion and deviance.

To free the hand of regulators and prosecutors and minimize the costs of compliance, reciprocity and negotiated forbearance are now preferred strategies. Substantial assistance departures and mitigation credits, as well as voluntary disclosure, leniency, and amnesty programs, dot the enforcement and regulatory landscape. In theory, the substantive corporate criminal law is ruled by principles of vicarious liability that stretch back to rules articulated in *New York Central & Hudson River Railroad Co. v. United States*. [p. 50]. In practice, cases of corporate crime are adjudicated by a brand of negotiated compliance. Corporate cooperation that facilitates the flow of evidence to authorities is the critical feature of this regulatory strategy.

3. Voluntary Disclosure

Is it always advantageous for a corporation to voluntarily disclose information to the government? Consider the following excerpt from Richard S. Gruner, *Towards an Organizational Jurisprudence: Transforming Corporate Criminal Law Through Federal Sentencing Reform*, 36 ARIZ. L. REV. 407 (1994):

* * * Given that managerial cooperation concerning such offenses may result in increased corporate costs if following by corporate changes and liability, managers may tend to refuse to cooperate unless they are confident that prosecutors will reciprocate in kind. Put into economic terms, corporate managers possessing information about a corporate offense and considering cooperation with prosecutors are placed in a form of prisoner's dilemma. Their optimal result would be achieved by cooperating with prosecutors and having prosecutors cooperate with them through favorable prosecutorial treatment producing no corporate penalty. However, if corporate managers perceive that disclosures to prosecutors may hurt their firm by triggering new corporate charges and liability, they may conclude that their optimal strategy is to withhold cooperation with prosecutors. That is -- in the absence of certainty about prosecutors' responses -- corporate managers may believe, perhaps correctly, that the interests of their firms are best served by avoiding disclosures and hoping that, absent the information the managers hold, prosecutors will not detect the crime involved or will be unable to prove it. * * *

4. Determining the Fine

Organizations convicted of an offense are subject to a fine and probation, but cannot be sentenced to a term of imprisonment. The Sentencing Guidelines adopted a system for determining the applicable range for a fine that may be imposed on an organization that is similar to the sentencing for an individual. The starting point is the determination of the base offense level, and then consideration of the size of the organization, the level of involvement of senior officers, and the cooperation of the organization in the government's investigation. The results in a "Culpability Score," which provides a multiplier for the fine that may be imposed. The multiplier ranges from .05 to 2.0, depending on the Culpability Score, as explained by Professor Michael A. Simons in his article, *Vicarious Snitching: Crime, Cooperation, and "Good Corporate Citizenship,"* 76 St. John's L. Rev. 979 (2002):

> Under the Organizational Sentencing Guidelines, a corporation's sentence—like an individual's sentence—is "based on the seriousness of the offense and the culpability of the organization." The seriousness of the offense is typically determined either by the economic impact of the crime (i.e., the loss to the victim or the gain to the offender) or by reference to the "offense levels" in the individual sentencing guidelines.
>
> This calculation will yield the corporation's "base fine," which is then adjusted up or down based upon the corporation's "culpability score." The culpability score is determined by a mathematical calculation based on the following factors: (1) whether the organization's top management "participated in, condoned, or was willfully ignorant of the offense"; (2) whether "tolerance" of the offense by middle management was "pervasive throughout the organization"; (3) whether the organization has a history of criminal convictions or regulatory violations; (4) whether the organization obstructed justice or violated specific court orders; (5) whether the organization had in place "an effective program to prevent and detect violations of law"; (6) whether the organization reported the offense prior to any imminent threat of disclosure or government investigation; (7) whether the organization "fully cooperated in the investigation"; and (8) whether the organization "demonstrated recognition and affirmative acceptance of responsibility for its criminal conduct." A corporation with a high culpability score could see its fine increased by up to 400%, while a corporation with a low culpability score could see its fine cut by up to 95%.

NOTE

Ability to Pay Fine. Issues regarding the ability to pay the fine, and the terms of its payment, can be contested in the sentencing of a corporation. In **United States v. Electrodyne Systems Corp.**, 147 F.3d 250 (3d Cir. 1998), the court considered a company's ability to pay a fine and vacated and remanded the district court's ruling "with instructions to make factual findings on both the ability to pay a fine and the time within which the fine can be paid." Senior District Judge Schwartz stated:

> We do not believe the district judge must be a puppet dancing to whatever financial disclosure strings a defendant corporation wishes to pull. We can think of no reason why the district judge does not have the power to require production of necessary financial documents so as to have a basis in fact for any fine which is to be imposed. Should the defendant corporation fail to produce financial documentation requested by the probation office and/or the court, the necessity for the district judge to have a basis in fact for establishing the amount of fine is reduced. Similarly, the sentencing judge is not controlled by, but may accept, a fine amount negotiated by the corporate defendant and the government. If the judge accepts the negotiated fine, no detailed finding of ability to pay is necessary because the defendant has implicitly acknowledged its ability by virtue of the agreement.

> Section 3572(a)(1) of Title 18 of the United States Code mandates that when a court imposes a fine and determines "the amount, time for payment and method of payment," the court must consider, inter alia, "the defendant's income, ensuring capacity and financial resources." Further, it is well settled in this circuit that "[t]he district court must make findings regarding a defendant's ability to pay a fine." United States v. Seale, 20 F.3d 1279 (3d Cir.1994). "Where the court has created enough of a factual record that it is clear that it considered a defendant's ability to pay, its findings may be deemed adequate." Here the district judge failed to make any findings pertaining to imposition of a fine Without factual findings there can be no meaningful appellate review. * * *

Criminal fines may still be required even if the company goes into bankruptcy, dissolves, or transfers the company to new owners. See p. 66.

5. Corporate Versus Individual Liability

To what extent should the potential liability of individual agents and officers affect the court's decision to accept a plea bargain by the organization? Should corporate liability be a substitute for prosecuting individuals? Consider the district court's analysis in the following case.

UNITED STATES v. C. R. BARD, INC.
848 F.Supp. 287 (D. Mass. 1994)

WOLF, District Judge.

There is in this case a binding plea agreement pursuant to Federal Rule of Criminal Procedure 11(e)(1)(C). The court is called upon to accept it, or reject it and give the defendant the opportunity to withdraw the plea. I have decided to accept the plea agreement, and I will impose the sentence which it provides.

The essential facts of this case are as follows. C.R. Bard, Inc. has pled guilty to 391 felonies. These are one count of conspiracy, in violation of 18 U.S.C. § 371; 17 counts of mail fraud involving submissions to the Food and Drug Administration ("FDA)", in violation of 18 U.S.C. § 1341; eight counts of submitting false statements to the FDA, in violation of 18 U.S.C. § 1001; 363 counts of shipping adulterated medical devices, in violation of 21 U.S.C. § 333(a)(2), including 75 counts of shipping medical devices from an unapproved facility, 108 counts of shipping products that had been changed without the required FDA approval of that change, and 98 counts of shipping devices for human testing where such testing had not been approved; and two counts of failing to submit required reports to the FDA, in violation of 21 U.S.C. § 333(a)(2).

These are serious criminal violations. In essence, Bard knowingly and willfully kept adverse information from the FDA, made product changes that affected the safety or effectiveness of angioplasty catheters produced by its USCI Division without the required FDA approval, and illegally did testing on human beings without the required exemption from the FDA.

There were reports of product malfunction, injuries, and deaths associated with the catheters identified in the Information. Two patients died during or shortly after a medical procedure involving a Mini Profile angioplasty catheter during the time period charged in the Information; 50 patients had the tip of the Probe B catheter break off inside them during a catheterization procedure; and at least 17 patients had coronary bypass surgery following a Probe B tip break.

The court need not and will not make findings as to whether or not these deaths, or any injuries resulting from the tip breaks, were proximately caused by Bard's criminal violations. It is sufficient to recognize that these are the kinds of foreseeable consequences that violations of laws designed to protect the public health and safety may have. The people at Bard who had responsibility for making products important to the care of seriously ill patients failed in their responsibility to comply with these laws.

It appears to this court that as a result of the subversion of the FDA process designed to assure that medical products are safe and effective, Bard made inherently risky procedures more dangerous. As Mrs. Linda Talbott eloquently explained, patients must rely primarily on their doctors to decide if procedures are sufficiently safe to be warranted. Doctors, in turn, must rely on the FDA and the company for the information necessary to make such decisions on a properly informed basis. Bard's crimes deprived the FDA, doctors, and their patients of the benefit of crucial information. In doing so, Bard betrayed an important trust.

Each of the 391 criminal violations was committed intentionally. The false statement violations were committed knowingly and willfully. The mail fraud violations, the shipping violations, and the failure to submit required reports were done with the intent to defraud or mislead.

These were not isolated violations. They involved several Bard products, and extended over more than two years.

The sentence to be imposed as a result of the plea agreement is $30,500,000 payable within 30 days as part of the civil settlement; $15,250,000 payable in one year as part of the criminal fine; $15,250,000 payable within two years as the remainder of the criminal fine; and a $78,200 mandatory special assessment.

The plea agreement also provides, although it is not part of the sentence, that Bard will implement specified corporate remedial measures and keep them in effect for four years. Bard is also obliged to cooperate fully and truthfully in the investigation and prosecution of its present and former officers and employees. Six have been indicted, including the former Chairman of the Board and Chief Executive Officer, who has been removed from his position, but continues to be paid by Bard.

There are a number of factors which together influence the court to conclude that the plea agreement is reasonable. First among these is the fact that the six individuals who allegedly acted for the defendant in conspiring to subvert the FDA process intended to assure the safety and effectiveness of inherently risky medical instruments are being prosecuted. I would not have accepted this plea without this provision.

Often, in my experience, companies will offer to plead guilty if the investigation or prosecution of its individual employees is dropped. I would have found that particularly inappropriate in this case. A corporation is a legal fiction. Individuals act for a corporation. Individuals commit crimes on behalf of a corporation. In this case, Bard's crimes have heightened risk to human life.

It is essential, in my view, that the law seek to hold individuals responsible for those crimes. They are properly presumed innocent. An individual's guilt will have to be proven beyond a reasonable doubt in a criminal case. It is, however, essential in a case like this, that individuals as well as corporations be the targets of criminal prosecution.

For, in a case like this, it is inadequate, and indeed somewhat frustrating, to seek to punish only a corporation. Sentences are, among other things, intended to address the defendant's conscience and influence future behavior. It is difficult to deal with what is essentially a legal abstraction in seeking to do that.

This is a fundamental and enduring problem. As my learned colleague, Judge Douglas Woodlock, had occasion to note in an opinion several years ago, when the Lord Chancellor of England sentenced a corporation centuries ago, he remarked: "Did you ever expect a corporation to have a conscience when it has no soul to be damned and no body to be kicked?" * * *[4]

There is a poignant echo of Baron Thurlow's observation in the Presentence Report. Another of Mrs. Beavers' relatives, one of her adult granddaughters, wrote about her love for her grandmother and what she feels she and her family have been cheated of because of Mrs. Beavers' death. She ended her submission to the Probation Department by saying:

> I know this probably won't mean anything to you, but while I have a chance to put in my two cents worth, just call it a healing thing, I would like to see those S.O.B.'s tried for murder. And I'm sure if the word was out, there are many, many more. But I know this is not possible, and their pocketbook is why this was done in the first place and that is the only thing that will hurt them. I hope you can kick their ass. Thank you for your time. I feel much better now.

In this case, the individuals allegedly responsible for Bard's crimes are being tried, not for murder, but for serious federal crimes, which could result in serious terms of imprisonment. Criminal prosecution of individuals in this case has the potential to provide a better sense of just punishment for the crimes committed. It also has the potential to send a message to corporate officials everywhere that crimes can have serious personal consequences and, therefore, to deter future criminal conduct.

This case shows that it is not appropriate to rely exclusively on corporations alone to send this message. In my view, various individual employees allegedly involved in these crimes have been treated generously by Bard. They have received substantial severance pay. The corporation's former Chief Executive Officer is still getting full pay. All are having their legal fees paid by Bard, with an undertaking to repay them if convicted, but it is doubtful if that will be possible.

---

[4] Indeed, as Professor Coffee has noted, the dilemma presented in seeking to sentence a corporation was recognized well before Baron Thurlow's time. "In the thirteenth century Pope Innocent IV forbade the practice of excommunicating corporations on the unassailable logic that, since the corporation had no soul, it could not lose one. He thus became the first legal realist." 79 MICH.L.REV. at 386 n. 2.

I also note, however, that Bard is cooperating with the Government to the Government's full satisfaction in the prosecution of those individuals. That is a benefit of the plea agreement, as it increases the possibility that the individuals responsible for Bard's crimes will be held responsible for them.

The agreed sentence is also reasonable because Bard is paying a substantial penalty in the form of fines and suspension by the Defense Logistics Agency. While it is essential to the reasonableness of the plea agreement that individuals not be relieved of potential criminal responsibility, it would also in my view be unreasonable if only the individual employees had been charged and were subject to possible punishment. This would be especially true with regard to lower-level managers.

This is a case in which a pervasive and powerful corporate culture exalted the value of profit above the value of human life. The Presentence Report quoted one Bard engineer who wrote a memorandum during the time of these crimes. He apparently had qualms about them. He said in his memorandum to his colleagues:

> We never give our people enough time to accomplish their jobs but rather rush the program to the next step before it is ready. We feel enormous pressure from upper management and marketing to continue despite the unsolved technical issue . . . . We chose not to address these design flaws, but rather to begin production and fix these things on the way. We now find ourselves in the most uncomfortable position of trying to decide what to sell without adequate tests in place to identify the quality of our results . . . Test protocol: how was this missed? Were we so with the program that we failed to anticipate that something could be wrong? Does asking tough questions or making waves put one in the political shithouse?

One would hope that there were human beings at Bard who had these qualms. Remarkably to me, and disturbingly, in this case there was no public whistle-blower. Evidently no one in the company felt he or she could go to anybody at Bard to attempt to stop the deliberate scheme to subvert the FDA process intended to assure the safety and effectiveness of its catheters. Indeed, when people raised these reservations, they were urged to abandon them, or at least to stop expressing them, with implicit threats that their jobs and the jobs of others could be jeopardized. It also appears that there was a corporate culture in which nobody felt that he or she could publicly go to the FDA without a well-founded fear of retribution by Bard.

The trial of the individual defendants should determine which, if any, people are criminally responsible for the crimes which Bard admits were committed.[5] In the view of this court, however, the officers and directors of Bard during the relevant period are morally responsible for a corporate culture which placed potential profit above the value of human life.

This is particularly disturbing in this case, where the corporation made instruments to be used by doctors. Doctors in this country, acting in the Hippocratic tradition, have as a first principle of medical ethics, "Do no harm." Ideally, a company which makes medical instruments should be the institutional embodiment of a reverence for life. In this case, Bard exhibited an institutional ethic of greed and indifference to life.

Since it was greed that was the obvious motive for this culture, it is appropriate that Bard pay a substantial financial penalty. $61,000,000 in criminal fines and civil settlement is a substantial and reasonable penalty. The Government estimates that Bard derived gross sales (total revenues from all relevant catheters net of returns and recalls) of $61,000,000 from its unlawful activities. The plea agreement provides for a criminal fine and civil settlement equal to the estimated gross sales.

I am satisfied that Bard's net profit from these illegal activities, although difficult to determine with precision, was well below that figure. As a result, this plea agreement does not merely require Bard to pay back the profit obtained from its misconduct, it requires Bard to pay the Government all of the estimated revenues it obtained from illegally marketed products, and it ensures that Bard will have lost far more from its conduct than it gained.

The $30,500,000 criminal fine appears to be within the fine range which would have been required if the Sentencing Guidelines were applicable. This fine is more than three times higher than the next highest fine ever imposed in an FDA case. In addition, Bard has been suspended by the Defense Logistic Agency, which should cost it income in the future.

At the change of plea hearing, I expressed concern about whether the defendant could and would pay the $61,000,000 fine and civil settlement. Subsequent submissions and representations indicate that Bard has the capacity to pay the fine. I am satisfied that this is a real penalty, which the defendant can and will pay.

In assessing reasonableness, I have also been influenced by the fact that the plea agreement contains provisions for minimizing the risk that Bard will

---

[5] Bard has admitted there was a conspiracy of members of its corporate management to commit many federal felonies. The six individual defendants are, of course, each presumed innocent. It is possible that in their case the conspiracy to which Bard pled guilty, or each individual's membership in it, will not be proved beyond a reasonable doubt. There remains, therefore, the possibility that only the corporation will be held liable and punished for crimes it acknowledges some of its employees committed.

commit similar offenses in the future. The fine should discourage repetition of criminal conduct, but the plea agreement does not rely on the fine alone.

As contemplated by the Sentencing Guidelines, Bard is required by the plea agreement to reorganize in many ways to minimize the risk that its crimes will recur. Indeed, while I condemn Bard for its criminal conduct, I do credit it with having accepted responsibility for its past behavior, while not attempting to diminish, excuse or justify it, and with taking steps designed to prevent it from recurring. Among those steps are the implementation of a new corporate compliance program, the hiring of a new Vice President for Scientific Affairs with responsibility for medical and regulatory affairs company wide, the creation of a Regulatory Compliance Committee of the Board of Directors, the retention of an outside regulatory compliance consultant to inspect Bard each year and report his or her findings and suggestions to both Bard and the FDA, and the adoption of additional reporting obligations to the FDA.

In addition, the FDA will subject Bard products to especially intensive scrutiny under its Applications Integrity Policy. This means, among other things, that all time limits for the FDA to act on Bard's applications to test or market medical devices are suspended. This should assure that the FDA has the time to perform its functions properly, and does so.

As I discussed previously with counsel, the agreed sentence does not provide for restitution for victims. Although this is not the case in which to determine who has been victimized by Bard's conduct, it does appear that there are real human victims. The pleas of these perceived victims are eloquently expressed in their statements to the Probation Department. * * *

The criminal sentence provided by the plea agreement does not provide restitution for the possible victims of Bard's crimes. In this case, however, that does not render the agreed-upon sentence unreasonable. Orders of restitution are discretionary. The court may decline to order restitution if the complication and prolongation of the sentencing process outweighs the need to provide restitution. This is such a case.

It would be very time-consuming and complicated to litigate in this criminal case whether catheters involved in Bard's crimes proximately caused injuries to numerous individuals. Much more importantly, at the end of that process, the court could only award victims compensation for their medical expenses and lost earnings. The court could not award damages for pain and suffering or punitive damages, which may be available in civil suits. Accordingly, individual civil suits are a much more appropriate means of addressing restitution, if the possible victims have notice of their possible claims.

Since the plea hearing I have been concerned that the plea agreement did not provide for notice to possible victims. There had been publicity and Bard had written to cardiologists, but I questioned whether this was sufficient to get essential information to people who may have been victimized by Bard's crimes. These concerns were heightened when the submissions revealed that the Beavers family was first informed by a newspaper report that a Bard catheter was used in the procedure during which Mrs. Beavers died.

However, since the plea there has been massive publicity which led to many calls to the United States Attorney's Office. In addition, the parties have assisted the Probation Department in an effort to notify possible victims of Bard's crimes, and the Beavers family would have been informed by that process had it not learned earlier of Bard's involvement.

Many possible victims have responded to the Probation Department. None have objected to the acceptance of the plea agreement or sentence.

In addition, Bard has agreed to the court's suggestion that a letter satisfactory to the court and the FDA, which has already been drafted and reviewed, be sent to cardiologists, explicitly explaining the crimes and the products involved.[6] The letter will ask doctors to send a copy to patients injured during angioplasty using a relevant Bard catheter, or to give Bard the information necessary to send the letter to the patients directly. If Bard gets that information, it will be shared with the United States Attorney's Office and the Probation Department.

This procedure should assure that possible victims receive adequate notice to decide if they have a claim they wish to assert in civil litigation. As I said, individual civil cases are much better than this criminal sentencing for the resolution of such claims.

For the foregoing reasons, the court finds that the agreed sentence provides just punishment for Bard. It should prevent Bard from committing comparable crimes in the future. It should also send a message to corporate officials and the companies they personify that to subvert the Food and Drug Administration process intended to assure the safety and effectiveness of medical products is not just wrong, it is dumb.

If they violate the law, they will be caught. Most of them will lose their jobs. They will be prosecuted personally and face the prospect of imprisonment. In addition, the companies that employ them will pay substantial financial penalties and, in the process, their crimes will receive widespread publicity.

---

[6] As this case involves a binding Rule 11(e)(1)(C) plea agreement, the court could not order Bard to send this letter. However, recognizing the risk that the court would reject the plea agreement because of its reservations concerning the adequacy of notice to possible victims, Bard commendably undertook to send the letter.

If this message is received and taken seriously by other companies and those who personify them, perhaps this disturbing case will ultimately have some redeeming value.

In connection with the 391 felonies to which Bard has pled guilty, I hereby impose the following sentence

Bard shall pay criminal fines in the amount of $30,500,000, to be paid as follows. $15,250,000 shall be paid on or before April 5, 1995, and a second and final installment of $15,250,000 shall be paid on or before April 5, 1996. In accordance with the plea agreement, the specific sum of $30,500,000 includes interest.

In addition, Bard shall pay the Clerk of this Court a mandatory special assessment of $78,200, $200 for each of the 391 counts, not later than April 19, 1994.

Bard shall also pay the sum of $30,500,000 to the United States on or before May 5, 1994, in accordance with the terms of the civil settlement agreement.

NOTE

Deferred Prosecution Agreements. Corporations routinely enter into deferred prosecution agreements with the government that allow for the corporation to continue its business. Many of these agreements require the corporation to provide information to the government concerning culpable individuals in the company. Deferred and non-prosecution agreements frequently include a provision on fines, civil penalties, and restitution, which effectively shifts the decision from the court to the Department of Justice to determine the appropriate punishment. See Chapter 3, part 5; Chapter 16.

INDEX

References are to Pages